SAVING THE WORLD

Saving the World

Chen Hongmou and Elite Consciousness
in Eighteenth-Century China

WILLIAM T. ROWE

Stanford University Press
Stanford, California

Published with the support of the
Leon E. Seltzer Memorial Book Fund
Frontispiece: Chen Hongmou, 1696–1771. From
Chen Rongmen xiansheng yishu.

Stanford University Press
Stanford, California

Printed in the United States of America
on acid-free, archival-quality paper

Library of Congress Cataloging-in-Publication Data
Rowe, William T.
    Saving the world : Chen Hongmou and elite
consciousness in eighteenth-century China /
William T. Rowe.
        p. cm.
    Includes bibliographic references and index.
    ISBN 0-8047-3735-5 (alk. paper)
    ISBN 0-8047-4818-7 (pbk., alk. paper)
    1. Ch'en, Hung-mou, 1696–1771. 2. China—
Politics and government—18th century. I. Title:
Chen Hongmou and elite consciousness in
eighteenth-century China. II. Title.
DS754.84.C45 R68   2001
951'.032—dc21   00-061248

Original printing 2001

Last figure below indicates year of this printing:
10 09 08 07 07 06 05 04 03 02

Typeset by BookMatters in 10/13 New Baskerville

This is for Jill

CONTENTS

ILLUSTRATIONS

PREFACE

This study was in part financed by research grants from the John Simon Guggenheim Foundation, the Committee on Scholarly Communication with China, and the Committee on Scientific and Scholarly Communication with the United States (Taiwan). I am deeply grateful for the compassionate concern of my host units in China: the Institute of Qing History of Chinese People's University, the Institute of Modern History of the Chinese Academy of Social Sciences, and Guangxi Normal University. I wish also to thank the staffs of the many collections that allowed me access to their rich historical materials, including the National Palace Museum (Taiwan), the Fu Ssu-nien Library of the Academia Sinica, the Number One Historical Archives (Beijing), the Beijing Library, the Beijing University Library, the Guilin Library, the Guilin Museum, and the Guangxi Normal University Library.

Earlier versions of some material presented here have been published in the journals *Late Imperial China, Modern China, Études chinoises*, and *Qingshi yanjiu*, and in the volumes *Education and Society in Late Imperial China* (Berkeley: University of California Press, 1994), edited by Benjamin Elman and Alexander Woodside, and *Constructing China: The Interaction of Culture and Economics* (Ann Arbor: Center for Chinese Studies, 1997), edited by Kenneth G. Lieberthal, Shuen-fu Lin, and Ernest P. Young. I am grateful for the permission of the editors and publishers to reuse that material here.

Without the generous assistance of many good friends and colleagues, this work would clearly be a lesser one. The manuscript was read and critiqued, in whole or in part, by Mary Backus Rankin, Susan Mann, Wm. Theodore de Bary, Susan Naquin, Philip Kuhn, Benjamin Elman, Pamela Crossley, Paola Paderni, Kwang-Ching Liu, Ernest Young, Philip Huang, and Joseph Esherick. In the course of its preparation I received scholarly and other help from Kent Guy, Kai-wing Chow, Joshua Fogel, Anne Birdwhistell, Robert Marks, Kerrie MacPherson, Peter Bol, Donald Sutton, Timothy Brook, Michael Szonyi, R. Bin Wong, Helen Dunstan, Ning Chia, Wang Fuming, Ma Zhao, Di Wang, Weikun Cheng, Grant Alger, Pamela Crossley, Noriko Kamachi, Ellen Widmer, James Hevia, Pierre-Henri Durand, Elizabeth Cropper, Paolo Santangelo,

Marie-Claire Bergère, Gareth Stedman Jones, James Millward, Steven Shutt, Richard Belsky, and Keith Clemenger. My field research was made infinitely more fruitful and pleasurable by (in Taibei) Liang Qizi, Su Yunfeng, Zhang Pengyuan, Xiong Bingzhen, Pu Muzhou, Lin Manhong, Huang Kewu, and Liu Shiji; (in Beijing) Wang Qingcheng, Zhang Zhilian, Wang Sizhi, Qin Guojing, Gao Xiang, Yang Nianqun, Gao Wangling, Zhao Shiyu, Wu Jianyong, Peng Zeyi, and Cheng Chongde; (in Guilin) Zhang Jiafan, Hou Xiaonan, Zhou Liangren, and Guo Zhigao.

Several persons must be singled out for their special contributions to this project. First among these would be my good friend Pierre-Étienne Will, who shares with me a deep fascination with the subject of this book. No scholar could be more generous to a fellow researcher than Pierre-Étienne has been to me, sharing source materials, insights, and comradery with an admitted poacher upon his own long-established scholarly turf.

To Chen Naiguang, current head of Chen Hongmou's lineage and chief custodian of his legacy, I will be forever grateful for the opportunity to visit the Chen homestead in Hengshan and share impressions of the illustrious ancestor.

My longtime friend and editor, Muriel Bell of Stanford University Press, has been patient beyond all reason in waiting for this work and supportive of its author in any number of ways.

John Russell-Wood, erstwhile chair of the History Department of Johns Hopkins University, has always come to my aid, materially and otherwise, during the long gestation of this work. My departmental colleagues, likewise, have been unfailingly generous with their time and forthright with their criticisms as I presented portions of this work to a succession of seminars over the past ten years. Every scholar should be so blessed as to work in an environment as personally and intellectually nurturing as this department.

Finally, words cannot express the sense of gratitude and affection I hold for my wife, Jill, and my children, Josh and Sara. Without them my work would have little meaning.

救世

Principle continually evolves and never reaches equilibrium.
Scholarship must likewise continually develop and never come to rest.
If I, a scholar, don't leave my study to circulate through the
world around me, how can my knowledge possibly serve my times,
or my writings save the world?

—Chen Hongmou, 1750

Introduction

FEW WOULD DISPUTE the pivotal position of the middle eighteenth century—roughly 1725 to 1775, or the Yongzheng and early Qianlong reigns—in the long-term history of China. Epitomizing the era that Western scholars have admiringly viewed as "high Qing" and historians in China itself have characterized as "the prosperous age" (*sheng-shi*),[1] these years saw the empire's highest attainment of material and political success prior to its crisis of confrontation with the West and inundation by Western cultural influences. If preceding generations had suffered the devastations of dynastic decline, conquest and repression by an alien regime, and the reputed "general crisis" of the seventeenth century,[2] and if the later Qianlong reign saw renewed problems of bureaucratic degeneration, ecological and hydraulic decay, and growing security threats from both within and without, the mid-1700s were the standard by which other, less happy eras were gauged. They were the years when things went right.

It was a time of relative peace and prosperity but also of vigorous growth and change. Domestic unrest was largely absent. The population grew dramatically, due in large part to a declining mortality rate, as disease and malnutrition were better controlled than in the past. The geographic scale of empire grew enormously as borderlands on all sides were effectively incorporated. Internal expansion was also impressive, with China's traditional lowland civilization moving uphill—clearing and settling highlands—and with the reclamation of massive stretches of seacoast, lakeshore, and riverbank. Agricultural output expanded greatly in aggregate, and productivity intensified, certainly per unit of land and possibly per capita as well. Commerce and industry likewise intensified, and regional patterns of exchange began to coalesce into a vast national market. Overseas trade with both Southeast Asia and the West recovered from its seventeenth-century depression and underwent a steady growth unaccompanied by serious diplomatic tensions. The mid-eighteenth century also saw a continuing rise in literacy and popular education, a further expansion of publishing and the print culture, and a flourishing of the arts, perhaps most notably in theater and the novel.

There were many causes for all of this, but political factors certainly played a part.

1

The era saw a remarkably high level of bureaucratic discipline and morale, spawned in good measure by unusually capable and energetic occupants of the throne itself. Potentially devastating ethnic tensions within both the ruling elite and the overall society were kept in check. A complex currency system was managed with great success. Fiscal stability was brilliantly achieved, with the burgeoning economy tapped to provide a comfortable level of government finance without increasing, and probably even reducing, the popular tax burden. The empire's hydraulic infrastructure, all-important for purposes of flood control, irrigation, and (increasingly) commercial transport, was effectively maintained, indeed greatly expanded, despite population growth. The bureaucracy of "high Qing" enjoyed nearly unprecedented success in managing the massive problems of food supply and food prices and in controlling instances of local or regionalized dearth. Not least, it demonstrated satisfactory responsiveness to the accelerating rate of civil litigation and provided facilities for popular conflict resolution. It was not without reason that later generations of Qing literati wistfully remembered these years as a classic era of good governance.

There is perhaps no better single window on this era, and most especially on the mentality of its ruling elite, than the figure of Chen Hongmou (1696–1771). Chen was arguably the eighteenth-century Qing empire's most influential Chinese official; certainly, he was its most celebrated field administrator. Between 1733 and 1763 Chen served as governor-general, governor, or in lesser provincial posts in more than a dozen provinces. He served longer as a provincial governor, and received more separate gubernatorial appointments, than any other man in Qing history.[3] In each of these posts, covering the span of the empire from Yunnan to Jiangnan, Gansu to Guangdong, Chen was both famously attentive to local societal conditions and profoundly ambitious in crafting administrative responses to them. Widely heralded in his time—the eminent Fang Bao (1668–1749) pronounced him "the only official today who devotes himself wholeheartedly to the people, like the great statesmen of antiquity"[4]—he increasingly over his career came to be used by the throne as a regional crisis manager. Chen was hardly an original thinker, nor did his style of administration differ substantially from that of his most capable colleagues, but his energy level and his thoroughness in addressing the needs of his various jurisdictions was nothing short of astounding. In the last years of his life Chen rose to the exalted posts of grand secretary (the first man from his native Guangxi to achieve this honor in the Qing, and the third in imperial history) and senior guardian of the heir apparent.[5] After twice rejecting his terminally ill minister's request for retirement, the Qianlong emperor in 1771 wrote him this poem:

> You've trod the Empire's breadth in diligent service
> And guided and instructed Me here in the palace.
> None can match your administrative experience and skill. . . .
> How grievous that I must at last let you leave![6]

Chen Hongmou's importance, however, derives less from his durability or his bureaucratic accomplishments than from his stature as a model official, specifically as an exemplar of the style of governance known as "*jingshi*"—usually translated "statecraft" but (because the notion of "state" is not explicitly invoked in the Chinese) more appropriately rendered as "social management" or, better yet, "ordering the world."[7]

Chen was the official most closely associated by later scholars with the reputed "state-craft revival" of the mid-Qing. In the *Huangchao jingshi wenbian* (Statecraft compendium), the bible of *jingshi* thought compiled in the 1820s by Wei Yuan, no fewer than fifty-three of Chen's writings were reprinted, making him the second most represented individual, after Gu Yanwu, in this incomparably influential collection. Statecraft as a political creed has attracted a great deal of attention in recent years, from both Chinese and Western scholars,[8] but there remains considerable ambiguity about what it did and did not mean. One of the goals of the present study is to contribute to sorting this out. In the view of one well-informed scholar the essence of *jingshi* was a turning away by officials from a normative Confucian style of administration (based on moral exhortation and personal example), a renewed preference for practical manipulation of institutions and organizations (a style of governance tainted in the more orthodox view by association with amoral Legalist agendas), and an unabashed acceptance of pursuing wealth and power as proper political goals.[9] Accordingly, Chen Hongmou was revered by subsequent generations of Chinese scholar-officials as a pioneer of a pragmatic, technocratic, "hands-on" approach to governance—the opposite of what Joseph Levenson termed the "amateur ideal" of the late imperial Confucian elite[10]—and was praised for his demonstrated expertise in such diverse technical areas as hydraulic engineering, agronomy, fiscal administration, and military logistics.

Yet herein lies one of the seeming paradoxes that make Chen such an intriguing subject of study. This man, who epitomized a hardheaded, "learn truth from facts" style of technocratic social management, can also be seen, and routinely *has* been seen, as the sincere and zealous promoter of a rather stern and at times almost simpleminded moralism as the basis of benevolent government (*renzheng*) and the good society. Chen's activities in the development of educational curricula stressing indoctrination in cultural values served as models for later officials, and the moral treatises he compiled on proper child rearing, proper behavior for women, proper community values, and integrity in public life have served as texts for Chinese educators, both private and governmental, down to the present day. In his own conduct of office Chen laid heavy stress on inducing popular participation in rituals of moral reaffirmation. One of my goals here will be to attempt a resolution of this apparent tension—the juxtaposition of pragmatism and moralism—which often appears to lie at the heart of late imperial political style.

A related tension involves the balance of power between the central imperial state and its local agents, on the one hand, and local societal self-management on the other. Landmark studies by Philip Kuhn and by Min Tu-ki have highlighted a strand of alternative political discourse in the Qing (and earlier) that systematically critiqued bureaucratic rule and called for governance as much as possible through the agency of indigenously generated economic and cultural elites.[11] Usually termed *"fengjian"* (very loosely, "feudal"), this political persuasion intertwined with *jingshi*, or statecraft, through the discernable association of such key thinkers as Gu Yanwu (1613–82), Wei Yuan (1794–1856), and Feng Guifen (1809–74) with the histories of both discourses. The actual degree of linkage between the two, however, remains less clear. Because of Chen Hongmou's own association with these figures (to be discussed below), it is tempting to see him as falling into this lively countertradition of political thought. And, indeed, there is no shortage of evidence of his interest in empowering indigenous elites and cultivating the mechanisms of local community self-governance, as well as his consistent attack on what he and others saw as the predations of the central state, fiscal and otherwise. On the other hand, the conclusion is inescapable that in practice Chen was a state-maker of the highest order, continually devising techniques for making state control more efficient and its penetration of the society ever more thorough. How can these seemingly contrary directions of his thought and policy be reconciled?

Yet a third apparent paradox in Chen Hongmou's thought and policy will also prompt our concern. That is the juxtaposition in Chen of a very deeply felt sense of the value and autonomy of all human beings, regardless of gender, ethnicity, cultural status, or economic class—an urge that in some contexts seems to warrant description by such terms as *populist, egalitarian,* or even *democratic*—with his also very committed hierarchical and authoritarian view of properly functioning human society. Put another way, we can see in Chen both an emergent valuation of the individual, and his or her needs, desires, and even perhaps "rights," and a simultaneous assertion of the primacy of the group (family, lineage, local community, state) and the need for the individual to subordinate self to the dictates of his or her predetermined functional role (*fen*) within such groups. This complex, and to our eyes at times contradictory, view of human nature and the human condition provided the foundation for Chen's practical social and economic policy formation.

To the extent that these juxtaposed strands of thought appear paradoxical, they do so in terms of categories we impose based on our modernist experience. Were they so in terms of the universe of attitudes and assumptions in which Chen Hongmou himself functioned? Perhaps not. They may, in fact, have been fundamental to the Confucian worldview itself, of which Chen was a remarkable but not altogether unrepresentative exemplar. Using Western categories of analysis (such as "individualism" or economic "liberalism") and sociohistorical models (such as "early modern") is useful up to a point, and in this study we will not shy away from drawing parallels and contrasts with the early modern European experience when and where that seems instructive. To avoid doing so would be to cavalierly discard one of the most potent frameworks of reference and analysis available to the contemporary Western historian, as well as to ignore the fact that by the eighteenth century China and the West were already operating in a global setting of significant mutual contact and influence. But ultimately our goal in this book is to comprehend, as fully as possible and on its own terms, the ground of consciousness occupied by Chen Hongmou and his colleagues in the late imperial official elite.

Chen Hongmou as Model and Informant

Chen Hongmou's iconic status as a model official was essentially a nineteenth-century product. Interest in him as a man, a moralist, and a pragmatic administrator seems to have arisen rather suddenly, from many diverse quarters, in the Daoguang era of the 1820s and 1830s. It coincided with the gathering sense of crisis of these years, sparked variously by hydraulic breakdown, economic depression, and awareness of the gathering foreign threat. Attention to Chen increased progressively after that time, but it did so in spurts, the timing of which seem again not accidental. He proved especially interesting during the frenetic years of post-Taiping reconstruction in the 1860s and early 1870s, the desperate reformist era of the late 1890s and early 1900s, and once again in the war-torn 1930s and 1940s. When scholars and policy makers troubled by their times sought a guide for intensifying their personal resolve and a blueprint for social action, they turned repeatedly to Chen.

Other than a few recollections by younger acquaintances, such as Peng Qifeng (1701–84) and Yuan Mei (1716–96), I have found few appreciative notices of Chen by scholars or officials in the half century following his death. He seems to have faded from the cultural memory or, more precisely, to have not yet developed his cult. After the energetic publication project undertaken by his descendents in the 1760s and 1770s, virtually none of his many works were reprinted until the 1820s.[12] The colossal Imperial Library bibliographic project (*Siku quanshu*) brought to completion in 1782, barely a decade after Chen's death, turned up (or found worthy of notice) just four books attributable to him, only one of which—the *Sourcebook on Reform of Social Practice* (*Xunsu yigui*)—would be among those for which he would subsequently be known and admired.[13] The *Qiewenzhai wenchao* (Writings compiled in the Qiewen studio), a 1775 anthology by Lu Yao often cited as predecessor of Wei Yuan's half-century-later *Statecraft Compendium*, included but a single essay by Chen Hongmou, his popular but highly uncharacteristic treatise on exorcizing a flood dragon.[14] Chen did only slightly better in Wang Chang's massive compendium of Qing-dynasty nonfiction prose, the *Huhai wenchuan* of ca. 1800, being limited to five fairly innocuous entries.[15]

The great wave of republication of Chen's works began rather abruptly with the new edition of his *Sourcebook on Bureaucratic Discipline* (*Zaiguan fajie lu*) by Chen Xi in 1821 and of his personal correspondence by Fei Bingchang two years later. Both men's prefatory comments are revealing. Chen Xi (no relation to Hongmou) tells us that Chen's various sourcebooks on personal, communal, and official conduct had long been required reading in his lineage school in Yaojiang (Zhejiang), where they were prized for the honest and unpretentious (*shixin*) guide they provided to the motivation of both self and others. Because of the critical relevance of the text at hand to pressing issues of popular livelihood and effective governance, Chen Xi was reprinting it for circulation among his "fellow bureaucrats" (*tongliao*). Fei Bingchang notes that he came across Chen's collected correspondence through word of mouth of his colleagues while serving as Guangxi provincial judge and was astonished at the eloquent way they spoke to current problems of economics and government finance, so unlike the self-aggrandizing drivel served up in the published letters of other officials.[16] The pattern was set. Numerous new editions of Chen's works throughout the succeeding decades would come at the hands of reform-minded serving officials—typically provincial-level officials like Chen himself—who felt the need to bring to their colleagues' attention the model of this newly discovered, like-thinking predecessor. (Indeed, between 1829 and 1854 twenty-nine such officials produced written testimonials on Chen's exemplary status, which were collected and published by Hongmou's sixth-generation descendent Chen

Qinghong.)[17] Chen Hongmou had clearly become something of a vogue, at the center of which were his letters, by turns preachy and self-critical but always imbued with a depth of seriousness his devotees found refreshing in their own day.

The major political anthologies of the Daoguang era show how deeply Chen had caught the imagination of the scholar-official class. Chen's fifty-three selections in Wei Yuan's 1826 *Statecraft Compendium* have already been mentioned and were a far cry from his single entry in that work's 1776 antecedent, the *Qiewenzhai wenchao*. In Wei's work Chen is cited authoritatively on a broad spectrum of topics, both technological (water conservancy, agricultural improvement, fiscal administration) and cultural (personal morality, ritual propriety, educational reform). We have noted that Gu Yanwu was the figure most represented in Wei's landmark compilation, with ninety-seven entries, but no other individual comes remotely close to Chen—the next most represented by my count are Lu Shiyi, with a mere twenty-three entries, and Fang Bao, with nineteen. In Xu Dong's influential handbook for local officials, the *Muling shu* of 1838, there were forty-seven selections from Chen (more than 7 percent of the total of 667), ranking him behind only Wang Huizu and Wang Fengsheng.[18] Even in Li Zutao's less politically focused 1839 compendium *Guochao wenlu* (Prose writings of the present dynasty), the fashionable Chen Hongmou could not escape notice and was represented by some eleven miscellaneous works.[19] As the Cantonese scholar-official Zhang Weiping wrote around 1825, "Nowadays, a great many readers receive the benefit of Mr. Chen's instruction."[20]

Chen Hongmou's collected moral treatises, the *Five Sourcebooks* (*Wuzhong yigui*), also first captured a national audience in these years. Li Fuyuan, headmaster of the Doushan Academy of Hanzhong (Shaanxi), noted in 1828 that he had been featuring these works in his curriculum for some time, prior to bringing out his own new edition in that year.[21] After a lull of some decades and the chance discovery of a copy in a Liulichang (Beijing) bookshop around 1850, Li's version became the basis for a number of new editions in the post-Taiping decades, produced by quasi-official provincial presses in Nanjing, Wuchang, Nanchang, and Hangzhou. Chen's official papers, known today as the *Peiyuan tang oucun gao* (Draft writings from the Peiyuan studio) and probably now the most valued of his works, were the last to gain wide circulation. Compiled initially by his dutiful son while the author was still serving as a metropolitan official in 1765, the work was expanded and republished by his descendents during Chen's Daoguang revival in 1837 (interest had been sparked no doubt by inclusion of some of its contents in Wei Yuan's *Statecraft Compendium* a decade earlier). The version that has become standard today, however, is an official edition published by Hubei provincial treasurer Zhang Jiamou in 1896. The coincidence of this major publication with reformist Viceroy Zhang Zhidong's tenure in Huguang and the still more ambitious Hunan reform movement of 1895 could not have been accidental. In his preface Zhang Jiamou laments that this blueprint for "vigorous action" (*lixing*), of so much utility for building a healthy economy and a financially sound state, has for over a century been in circulation almost exclusively in Guangxi, where few officials ever get posted. Now through the agency of his *yamen* he is making it available to all.[22]

It was in this light, as a hero to be emulated by like-minded colleagues (*tongzhi*) who would reform the degenerate ways of the times (*shidao*) and regenerate the human spirit (*renxin*), that Chen came to be venerated by his nineteenth-century partisans. He was acclaimed for his personal conduct (*weiren*), his simple genuineness and freedom from pretense (*pushi*), and his avoidance of convention and routine in assessing the tasks he confronted (*shixin ticha*). His writings served as a textbook for penetrating the complex workings of the economy (*jingji*) and the demands of popular livelihood (*minsheng*). They also pointed the way to resolving the problem that increasingly perplexed nineteenth-century thinkers: how to bridge the gap between state and society, to "serve as an official while remaining close to the people" (*juguan linmin*). Chen did all of this, his nineteenth-century admirers noted, while proceeding from a thoroughly Song neo-Confucian moral-rational construction of the universe. His life and work exemplified the way that ethical substance (*ti*) and technological function (*yong*) might be seamlessly combined.[23]

Although Chen found professed latter-day disciples (*houxue*) in many regions of the empire, nowhere was his influence more pronounced than in the Xiang River valley of Hunan—Chen's presumed ancestral home, the empire's self-proclaimed heartland, and the spawning ground of a succession of deeply reflective yet highly activist scholar-officials who, following their fellow provincial Wei Yuan, saw themselves as keeping alive the statecraft (*jingshi*) tradition in radically changing times.[24] Chief among these was the great soldier-statesman Zeng Guofan (1811–72), who saw Chen's works as something that "constantly must be read and reread." Writing home in 1847 to his younger brother Guohuang, the delegated household manager, Zeng instructed him as follows: "You must read the *Five Sourcebooks* on a daily basis, and ruminate on them line by line. What I expect of you, my brother, is this above all else."[25] Four years later he wrote to another brother, Guobao, that in order to become a sage it was necessary to read just two works, Chen's *Sourcebooks* and Zhu Xi's *Elementary Learning* (*Xiaoxue*). "There will be no immediate loss if you do not read other books," he wrote. "What is important is to abide by [the teachings of these two], and put them into practice as much as possible."[26]

Jiang Yili (1832–74), Zeng Guofan's landsman from Xiangxiang County, and like him an anti-Taiping general and Restoration-era governor (Guangdong), perhaps typified the kind of activist autodidact to whom Chen Hongmou most appealed. In a preface to his 1865 edition of Chen's *Sourcebook on Proper Official Conduct* (*Congzheng yigui*), Jiang wrote:

> When I was young, I gave up my studies and joined the army. Through Imperial grace I received promotions into important [civil] posts. Since I long ago had put aside my pen, I was ashamed and fearful lest I prove ignorant of the proper way to lead my subordinates and govern the people. Last year, when the war was concluded, I returned to reading and discovered this book. It is both substantive and practical [*you ti you yong*], and warrants emulation and passing on to others. Whoever bears responsibility for overseeing the people's affairs ought to get this book, learn from it, and keep it close at hand. I myself have had little time for serious study of the classical canon, and yet whenever I open this anthology I feel as if I had deep learning. Consequently, I am reprinting this book . . . and distributing it to my fellow officials. It is a small one-volume work, which they can easily carry around on their person and use as a guide for action.[27]

In the course of China's turbulent twentieth century, Chen Hongmou remained a potent cultural icon, even as his significance was gradually redefined. Leading scholars and politicians who venerated him still respected his technological prowess, to be sure, but his reputation rested not so much on his practical know-how as on his sagacious moral advice. In the process Chen became less a model for a self-conscious elite of reformist scholar-officials (although he did to an extent remain this) than a guide to good behavior for the masses. The process began as early as the "new policies" (*xinzheng*) reforms of the late Qing. Between 1899 and 1908 the fledgling Ministry of Education brought out its own official editions of Chen's moral treatises, in cheap pocket-sized editions (one copy I have examined was priced at twenty-two cents) stripped of all scholarly apparatus, as a component of its new national elementary school curriculum.[28] Chen's books indeed became so central to the educational practice of this era that the missionary Evan Morgan opted in 1912 to prepare a sixty-page bilingual selection from the first of them, the *Yangzheng yigui* (Sourcebook on childhood education), to serve simultaneously as a primer for Westerners in classical Chinese and a handy guide to Chinese moral norms.[29]

In this incarnation Chen became a darling of the Nationalist Party, with its sometimes awkward combination of moral traditionalism and self-conscious modernism. Li Zongren (1891–1961), for instance, Chen's fellow provincial and erstwhile president of the Republic of China, extolled him as both an exemplar of the revivalist "Guangxi spirit" and a behavioral model for all contemporary Chinese.[30] Xie Kang, a longtime Guomindang establishment intellectual and legislator, wrote of him in maudlin tones:

> My grandfather loved best of all to read Chen Hongmou's letters. He kept them always beside his chair, to serve as a constant remonstrance to his conduct. When I was young, he frequently read them to me, and they have had a deep and lasting influence on my development. Ten years ago, when I was assigned to serve in Guilin, I rode the Hunan-Guilin train. When we passed by Chen's native village of Hengshan, my thoughts inevitably turned to this lofty man. This region of entrancingly beautiful mountains and streams, and luxuriant growth of cassia forests, reminded one of the deep spiritual power of nature. Mr. Chen's conduct was similarly incomparable, and serves as a beacon to subsequent generations.[31]

Chen's works were republished in large editions by Shanghai's Commercial Press in the 1930s and in various dramatically abridged popularizations in Chiang Kai-shek's Taiwan (including, for example, a slender volume of selections from the *Five Sourcebooks* published by the "Moral Commitment Press" in 1961).[32] The high point of this proselytizing may have come in March 1987, when Taiwan Television ran a three-minute nightly spot over the course of several weeks, introducing homilies drawn from Chen Hongmou's moral treatises, explicated by a narrator as a guide to good citizenship.[33] It should be added here that this popularization of Chen's work, crude as some of it may have been, was by no means totally out of step with his own intentions, as we shall see in chapters to follow.

Chen Hongmou has assumed a pivotal importance for our own contemporary understanding of late imperial China in yet another way: as an informant. His *Peiyuan tang oucun gao,* a record of the downward bureaucratic correspondence of a field official probably unique in its scale and scope, was one of the major sources for Hsiao Kung-ch'uan's epochal 1960 work *Rural China: Imperial Control in the Nineteenth Century* and was also used extensively in Ch'u T'ung-tsu's *Local Government in China Under the Ch'ing* (1962), still the standard work in English on that subject.[34] These works—which seem to me to occupy a liminal position between contemporary Western historical scholarship and China's own indigenous tradition of *jingshi*-style political criticism—do not attempt in any significant way to individualize Chen, as much as they rely on him, but instead employ him as a faceless (albeit eminent) reporter of the conditions of his day. What Chen sees is what we see as well.

More recently, Chen's written testament has been drawn on by a number of historians interested in more specific elements of Qing administration and of late imperial culture. Examples would include studies of penal law by Fu-mei Chen, of subsistence crisis management by R. Bin Wong, of hydraulic planning by Peter C. Perdue, of economic policy by Gao Wangling and Helen Dunstan, of educational policy by Alexander Woodside, and of women's history by Susan Mann and Tani Barlow.[35] In these studies Chen is somewhat more individuated than in the earlier works of Hsiao and Ch'u in the sense that he is typically seen as articulating a particular position that may or may not be assumed to be representative of his times. Yet even here there is little effort to understand where Chen is coming from culturally or politically or to view the positions he takes on the issue at hand as part of a fully developed approach to the world. (None, for example, reveal that he hailed from the highly distinctive Guangxi Province.) One could argue, of course, that there is no reason these authors ought to do so, given the topics of inquiry they have selected. Nevertheless, given the increasing salience that Chen has come to assume in formulating what we know of so many aspects of the Qing era, it seems ever more critical to try to comprehend just who he was and why he spoke and acted as he did.

And although Chen has been much utilized by historians, he has not been very much studied by them. There exists but one full-length biography (excepting the *nianpu,* or chronological record of his life, compiled after his death by Chen's son), and that is essentially a work of homage to a local hero by the Guilin scholar Gao Jiren in 1945. Beyond this, my research has turned up only four very brief articles done in the People's Republic (two of these, like Gao's book, the work of Guilin local historians), one short chapter in a collection of exemplary biographies produced in Taiwan, two entries in Japanese historical dictionaries (one by the great Marxist historian Shigeta Atsushi), an entry in the Qing biographical dictionary compiled by Cai Guanluo, and another by Rufus O. Suter in Arthur Hummel's *Eminent Chinese of the Ch'ing Period.*[36] For a figure who was at the center of so many of the major developments of mid-Qing history, for so long, this is a remarkably meager corpus of work.

There is one exception to all of this: the work of Pierre-Étienne Will. In Will's various published and unpublished studies of mid-Qing governance—dealing with famine administration, agricultural improvement, bureaucratic corruption, public opinion, and so on—Chen Hongmou appears regularly as a central actor.[37] Although Will has not to date addressed Chen's position either directly or holistically, and although his geographic focus is usually restricted to the single province of Shaanxi (where Chen served as governor four times in the decades from 1740 to 1760), the volume and range of Will's work on this individual comes as close as anything we have to a comprehensive effort to come to grips with who and what he was. The present study has been accomplished as part of a cooperative effort with Professor Will, which I hope we would both agree has been mutually beneficial.

Some Considerations of Method

Academic fashions change. I began thinking about writing this book in the heady atmosphere of the "social history revolution," pioneered by scholars of the *Annales* school, in which the biographies of "great men" seemed an anachronistic way of doing history. Sympathetic as I was to this movement (and having myself written two books in which dominant individual actors were appropriately absent), I took solace in such things as Lawrence Stone's pronouncement that narrative history not only seemed on the point of revival but also perhaps deserved that revival as well, and Jack Hexter's somewhat cautious suggestion, in a judicious review article on the work of *Annales* demigod Fernand Braudel, that there might yet be a place in historiography for studies of critically situated individual lives.[38] If, as Hexter reminded me, social historians of no less stature than E. P. Thompson and C. Vann Woodward could write biographies, so then could I.[39]

Then came another revolution, that of "the new cultural history." This brought me both consolation and yet another cause for worry. Narrative writing and the intensive study of historical texts now seemed fully legitimate, and the new emphasis on "microhistory" even gave the detailed investigation of past individual lives (à la Carlo Ginzburg's *The Cheese and the Worms*) a place of honor in the project of historical scholarship. But once again I was given to question whether the study of an elite male, and an important political figure at that, was really the most effective way the scholar, in this day and age, could spend his or her time. And again, one of the current genre's most vaunted practitioners, Giovanni Levi (writing in, of all places, the *Annales*), came to my aid, arguing with eloquence that, properly handled, biographies of the great and powerful, as much as of the common man or woman, can have a certain utility in our efforts to come to grips with the past.[40]

Through all of this I emerge convinced that study of a well-situated, well-documented individual can indeed assist more than distort our understanding of that person's milieu. It can offer, I believe, a kind of personal testimony to history of the sort that I found naggingly absent in my own previous work. I hope at the same time that my reasonably extensive exposure to the concerns, innovations, and insights brought to the fore by both social and cultural history allow me to produce that study in a way that would have been difficult if not impossible before those two historiographic revolutions took place. One of the virtues of the biographical genre that I most welcome, for example, is the opportunity it offers for deep immersion into the textual output of a single historical person and, through that immersion, for an unusual appreciation both of rhetorical strategies and of habits of mind, which can tell us much about the social and cultural context in which that individual operated.

Of course this book is not a biography at all in the conventional sense, that is, a chronological narrative of an individual life. Only the first two chapters are chronologically arranged—offering information, respectively, on Chen's life before and after his entry into official service—and even here the chronology is often subordinated to other, topical concerns. The bulk of the chapters are strictly topical. There are problems involved in this presentational strategy, to be sure, such as the relative neglect of Chen's personal development over time. And in fact, although there are certain moments, such as Chen's effective discovery of the "Guanxue" school of neo-Confucian thought in the 1740s, that may be seen as markers of change in his approach, for the most part I do see his entire adult life and career as representing a consistent outlook to which Chen had already come by the time he became interesting historically. His administrative policies in the field responded to some extent to changes in the macropolitical environment (most notably the Qianlong succession) and to differences in the specific provinces he was charged with governing, but to an even greater degree he tended to repeat himself from one jurisdiction to another and did so ever less creatively over time. My relative deemphasis on personal development, moreover, is expressive of the fact that this is less a book about Chen himself than about the eighteenth-century official elite of which he was a part.

By "official elite" I mean to refer to classically educated adult males whose intellectual orientation was significantly directed toward problems of governance, whether or not they were currently—or indeed ever had been—in actual official service. Thus I would include not only career civil servants such as Chen himself but also figures such as Gu Yanwu and Li Yong, who actively abjured government office and/or sitting for the civil service examinations, and Yuan Mei, who, although primarily a poet, had briefly held minor office and continued to reflect on political matters in private life. As we shall see, Chen Hongmou had a sense of common identity with such an official-elite cohort, which he sometimes referred to in his personal correspondence as *wubei* (people like us).

One of the highest items on my agenda here is to bridge the rather enormous gap between intellectual history and social history that has characterized the field of Chinese studies (with but a few recent exceptions)[41] over the past decades. I hope to do this in part by developing a middle ground, which an *Annaliste* historian might call "the history of *mentalité*" or a cultural historian "the history of consciousness." It will be seen readily enough that I do this with no great concern for theory. Put simply, what I want to do above all is to root Chen Hongmou's practical administrative policies, those things for which he is best known, firmly in the way he—and others among the official elite—understood the nature of the cosmos, the human condition, and the bases of social relations. "Consciousness," here, would include both articulated thought and unarticulated mental sets or attitudes. What, for example, does Chen assume to be the feasible parameters of human action? How are males and females alike or different? How does society function? What would the ideal society look like? What does it mean to be "civilized"? What is wealth and where does it come from? It works to my advantage here that Chen was not a very profound or original thinker; he was rather, as J. G. A. Pocock described Sir John Fortescue, "the kind of amateur of philosophy who helps us to understand the ideas of an age by coarsening them slightly."[42]

I proceed on the assumption that a fruitful way to get at this history of consciousness is by paying close attention to language and discourse. Again, I must stress at the outset that I harbor no ambitions to make any contribution to the highly sophisticated body of theory that has developed on this issue in recent decades. What I have found most useful for my purposes within this (perhaps overly fertile) field have been the reflections on how language functions by historians of political thought such as John Pocock and Quentin Skinner and by intellectual historians such as William Bouwsma.[43] I understand language to be a vital and relatively autonomous thing, which grows and mutates, and which constrains as well as enables. As Skinner explains it:

> Consider the position of a political actor who is anxious to engage in a particular course of action which he is also anxious to exhibit as legitimate. Such an agent may be said to have a strong motive for seeking to ensure that his behaviour can plausibly be described in terms of a vocabulary already normative within his society, a vocabulary which is capable of legitimating at the same time as describing what he has done. . . . The problem facing [such] an agent . . . cannot simply be the instrumental problem of tailoring his normative language in order to fit his projects. It must be in part the problem of tailoring his projects to fit the available normative language.[44]

At the same time, as Pocock in particular has stressed, this "available normative language" is neither stable nor uniform. Idioms in the common political discourse are continually appropriated by certain parties within the discourse community, contested by others, and stretched and applied, often with deliberate ambiguity, to actions those parties seek to validate. Furthermore, a speaker may frequently through language choice reveal much that is unintended of the underlying assumptions about how his or her universe of meaning is ordered. Chen Hongmou was, as we shall see, both a member of a community sharing an extraordinarily fecund and fluid discourse—that of neo-Confucian literati and the imperial bureaucracy—and a vigorous independent actor capable of creatively turning this shared language to the promotion of his own sociopolitical vision.

Finally, the reader will already have noticed, quite likely with alarm, that this is a large book. I would apologize for this but at the same time insist that a certain exhaustiveness is key to what I hope to accomplish. It is precisely its attempt to explore how Chen Hongmou's notions regarding such things as gender roles and funerary ritual related to his economic thought, or the way his experience negotiating the perilous Qing bureaucratic culture conditioned his approach to social policy, that I hope will make this work a useful step toward illuminating the consciousness of late imperial China's official elite.

PART ONE

Being a Man

CHAPTER 1

Home

WHERE HE CAME FROM was deeply important to Chen Hongmou. For most of his professional career he was the highest-ranking official in the empire of Guangxi birth, and, indeed, the case could be made that he was the most influential native son that province produced in all of Chinese history. Every locality of China is distinctive, but in the world of Qing officialdom Guangxi was more distinctive than most. It was the frontier. Liang Qichao reflected this view when he wrote, as late as 1924, that "Guangxi is all craggy mountains, far removed from any centers of culture, and has produced no scholars worthy of mention."[1] Chen Hongmou carried the stamp of this frontier upbringing, sometimes intentionally and sometimes not, throughout his life.[2] He clearly appeared to the most esteemed statesmen and intellectuals of his day as a country bumpkin, formally correct but unrefined in manner, shockingly ignorant (indeed, disdainful) of the latest aesthetic trends and scholarly debates, and imbued with backwoods fundamentalist values that, to most mid-Qing literati, must have seemed anachronistic. At the same time, however, he was possessed of a practical savvy in worldly affairs that was in line with certain emerging intellectual trends—what would become known as "statecraft" (*jingshi*)—that eventually earned him admirers in various and unexpected quarters.

However defensive Chen might have been about his personal background (and, as we shall see, he fought a continuous battle against the kind of prejudice to which persons such as he were subjected in Qing society), he chose adamantly to present himself in public as reveling in his frontier upbringing. At the age of sixty he declared himself to his emperor as "a man of middling abilities and humble origins, who has been favored by being lifted up and granted important posts by Your Sagacity."[3] More often, though, and especially in private, he was inclined to picture himself as a rough-hewn, impoverished scholar who had succeeded on his own merits, despite enduring the contempt of privileged and effete literati.[4]

15

Ancestors

Hongmou was the ninth-generation descendent of Chen Baoju, a man who had migrated to Guangxi's Lingui County in the sixteenth century.[5] The details of the move are unclear. On his arrival in Lingui Chen Baoju was a registered native of Chenzhou Prefecture in southern Hunan, where his family had apparently lived for some generations. However, he carried with him an image of the family's patron deity, known as "Dongting shen" (Lord of the Dongting Lake), which suggests an earlier origin for the Chen line in north-central Hunan, perhaps, as one source suggests, in Yingchuan County. Chen Baoju was part of the broader southerly and westerly migration of pioneering settlers into Guangxi that characterized the late imperial era,[6] but Chen family sources insist that the major impetus for his move was flight from the devastations of warfare; precisely which military incidents, like the precise date of his move, are unrecorded.

Chen Baoju settled in what is now Hengshan village, some forty *li* west of the provincial capital, Guilin, in Lingui's West Township.[7] He was likely among the village's first settlers, for he secured a prime site for his farm, and even today the Chens make up more than half of the village's households (the remaining households are split among seven other surnames).[8] The family remained subsistence farmers, gradually accumulating more property, for its first several generations in Hengshan. A somewhat cryptic account by Chen Hongmou himself, characteristically celebrating the family's rustic virtue, offers the hint that what modest wealth the family might have built up by then was wiped out during the time of his grandfather, Chen Shiyao. The reference is almost surely to the turbulent politics that gripped Guangxi during the Sanfan Rebellion of the 1670s:

> My paternal grandfather was honest, generous, and unpretentious, a filial son and a pillar of his community. Neither he nor any of his ancestors had ever held bureaucratic office, nor enjoyed the luxurious lifestyle that that may bring. In his middle years, military devastation turned the world upside down, causing great suffering to the people. In such circumstances, he was unwilling to go against conscience and turn his back on others, and in the end suffered betrayal himself. He lost all his property, but maintained his integrity, secure in the faith that his conduct would be rewarded with blessings to come in the future.[9]

Chen Shiyao may well have remained illiterate all his life. He was certainly a working farmer, as was his son, Hongmou's father, Chen Jiyu (1654–1731). The Chens were stable, struggling property owners. Both Shiyao and Jiyu married only once, to women of neighboring villages.[10] Chen Hongmou reflects that his father "worked ceaselessly to extract the family from the difficulties in which it [had] been placed during grandfather's time, and to provide for the future." But Chen Jiyu was also evidently literate and an avid reader.

Chen Jiyu embodied a rigid, almost stifling peasant ideology that deeply marked his children throughout their lives. Hongmou writes: "What my father detested above all else was the reckless dissipation of material goods. He was extremely clean, and all utensils were immediately washed upon being used. We were diligently frugal with even

FIGURE 1. The Chen homestead in Hengshan, Guangxi, with Mount Heng in the background. Photograph by the author, January 1994.

the smallest item, and not a grain of rice ever went to waste. These habits were maintained out of respect for our ancestors, and were assiduously inculcated in the younger generation."[11] This obsessive frugality was combined with an imperative to hard work and a deep respect for the dignity of human labor:

> Our father, even into his seventies, regularly went out into the fields to oversee the work of agriculture, walking with his cane amidst the ditches and paddies. We children were always afraid he would fall, but he brushed away our concerns, telling us we must never forget the exhaustive toil that farming represents. I have never forgotten this lesson. Men of our family have always known that literary pursuits are only possible for us because of agricultural labor, and it is for this reason that we have continually sought to improve the life and relieve the burden of the rural population.[12]

Wealth granted by Heaven's bounty and painstakingly accumulated through human industry must not be turned to personal indulgence but must continually be reinvested. One of the most appropriate outlets for this investment was education. Chen Jiyu used all his spare resources to bring the best available teachers into his family's home to train his sons, banking heavily on their examination success. His own moods followed closely on their ups and downs in this enterprise, and he coaxed them unceasingly to fulfill his expectations and to repay his own labors.[13] The message took: "My father told us, 'Generations succeed one another, and are mutually responsible for each other. Never forget this!' Indeed, I believe that all the Imperial favor I have received, and the official appointments I have been granted, have come only as recompense for the accumulated virtue of my ancestors."[14] Imperial ideology of course agreed. In 1752, in honor of the sixtieth birthday of his own mother, the Qianlong emperor conferred posthumous honors on the forebears of certain of his long-serving officials. Chen Hongmou's great-grandfather, grandfather, father, and their wives were all granted noble titles, and Chen Jiyu was posthumously appointed governor of Henan.[15]

Guilin

The Guilin area of Chen Hongmou's youth was a frontier, but a frontier of a special sort. It has long been a locus of very intense local pride, a pride that Chen most definitely shared. Although there are remains in the area of prehistoric and classical-era cultures, it was effectively made part of "China" by Qin Shihuang, who in the late third century B.C. constructed the famous Ling Canal, linking the Li River with the Xiang and thereby connecting Guilin directly by water with the Yangzi Valley. Qin established an administrative seat in what is now Xing'an County, slightly north of today's Guilin city. Guilin itself remained essentially the domain of non-Han peoples until the Tang made it, too, an administrative center in the seventh century A.D. A succession of cities followed on the site, but Guilin's current form is largely the legacy of the Ming founder Zhu Yuanzhang. Zhu enfeoffed some twenty-two of his offspring at key locations throughout China, one of whom, the so-called Jingjiang King, was ensconced at Guilin. During the 1370s and 1380s a stately palace complex was constructed at what is now the heart of the city's downtown (its walls and gates still stand), replicating on a smaller scale the main imperial palace at Nanjing. Zhu also declared the city the capital of his newly carved-out Guangxi Province and Guilin Prefecture and began the process of extending formal bureaucratic administration progressively beyond the capital area.[16]

Despite being the site of continued large-scale violence—wars of resistance to Han domination by indigenous peoples, Ming loyalist activity, the Sanfan Rebellion—Guilin and Guangxi as a whole experienced a remarkable economic boom between the sixteenth and eighteenth centuries. The region received a steady flow of immigrants, primarily from Hunan, Guangdong, and Guizhou.[17] A complex and sprawling hydraulic system, serving both irrigation and transportation needs, was gradually pieced together in the prefecture, including a major reconstruction of the two-millennia-old Ling Canal itself. Vast stretches of newly irrigated land were brought under cultivation; in Chen Hongmou's native Lingui County, for example, registered farmland more than doubled between ca. 1550 and 1750.[18] This was very largely commercialized farming, and by the beginning of the nineteenth century there were some thirty permanent market towns within a twenty-five-mile radius of Guilin city, bringing in rural produce for both the urban and the extraregional market. Cash crops included sugarcane, peanuts, tea, Lingui's nationally famous water chestnuts, and a wide array of fruits. Mining of copper, tin, and silver was underway in Guangxi by the 1720s, and Guilin's salt trade was flourishing. The city, which was rapidly becoming a major center of interregional exchange, hosted by the mid-Qing more than forty guilds of extraprovincial merchants, some of which, like the Hunan *huiguan*, were themselves complex amalgams of thirty or more component groups, specialized by county of origin or by line of business. Guilin manufactured rice wine, hemp cloth, and umbrellas for extraprovincial markets.

Nevertheless, Guangxi's economy in these years was based even more on paddy rice production, and the most dramatic aspect of the region's early modern economic boom was the emergence of the export rice trade to Guangdong.[19] The increasingly adverse population: food supply ratio in Guangdong—the growing percentage of the population engaged in occupations other than food production—combined with Guangxi's own enhanced ability to produce a local surplus to create wide differentials in grain prices in the two provinces, a fact of which both merchants and the state took notice. The trade was privately managed, but stimulated repeatedly by actions of concerned officials (including, in the 1750s, Liang-Guang viceroy Chen Hongmou himself).[20] More than three million *shi* per year of rice was collected via Guangxi waterways and shipped, via the border town of Wuzhou, to various parts of Guangdong.

The prosperity brought by this extraprovincial demand for its chief product, especially during the first half of the eighteenth century, affected all parts of Guangxi and underwrote in no small measure the cultural florescence of the provincial capital, the city in which Chen Hongmou spent his youth. He was thus predisposed to like it. It seems beyond doubt that several key elements of Chen's later economic thought and policy—his promotion of agricultural surplus production specifically linked to market sale, his abhorrence of administrative restrictions on interjurisdictional commodity flows, and so on—reflected in large part his cultural origins in a milieu of highly successful, market-driven rice planters. But how immediately Guangxi's experience of the early Qing rice export boom affected his own family's fortunes is less clear.

Despite their status as major rice producers, Lingui County and Guilin Prefecture were not as directly linked by transport routes to Guangdong as were other parts of Guangxi. Indeed, a leading student of the Guangxi-Guangdong trade, Robert Marks, has concluded that, given the growing rice consumption of Guilin city itself, the prefecture as a whole may even have been modestly grain-deficient in this era.[21] The major reconstruction and extension of the Tang-dynasty Tihe Canal undertaken in Lingui in the early 1730s, a project in which the county's fast-rising native son Chen Hongmou seems to have taken an active part, was explicitly designed to plug the county more effectively into nonlocal markets. But the markets, in this case, were not Guangdong but southwestern Guizhou and Yunnan, whose swelling immigrant populations were heavily composed of non-food-producing miners and soldiers.[22]

The area around Chen Hongmou's native village of Hengshan, in the extreme western part of Lingui County, was especially poorly placed to profit from the rice export boom. Its principal transport orientation was neither to Guangdong nor to the southwest but instead north to Hunan. The age-old route by which Chen's own ancestors had initially entered Guangxi from Hunan, and that today is occupied by an important interprovincial railroad line, in fact runs directly through Hengshan. Unfortunately for the village's eighteenth-century residents, however, Hunan's Xiang River valley, famous for its grain surplus, was hardly likely to provide a market for Hengshan rice. The most likely demand would come from Guilin city, and certainly the provincial capital did take (then as now) a modest amount of Hengshan's grain surplus, as well as its other major products: sweet potatoes, hemp root, peanuts, yellow beans, sugarcane, and dates.[23] But Hengshan lay on the remote fringe of Guilin's greenbelt and was far less well served by collection routes than were many of the city's other food suppliers. In general, the village and its surroundings constituted a highly fertile and productive agricultural area, too inadequately endowed with market links to be able to exploit effectively its profit-making potential. Thus when, throughout his official career, Chen Hongmou repeatedly complained about and sought to redress the competitive disadvantages—cultural as well as economic—suffered by remotely located populations, he clearly had in mind the experience of his own native place.

As best as can be reconstructed, it would appear that the Chens at the time of Hongmou's birth were the most prosperous family in a not very prosperous village. They grew primarily rice, and primarily for subsistence, although they marketed a modest surplus. They probably owned in the vicinity of fifty *mu* (seven to eight acres) of land, most or all of which they farmed themselves, with the assistance of hired labor.[24] They enjoyed a level of comfort sufficient to free their sons' labor for educational pursuits—Hongmou himself grew up intimately familiar with agricultural practice but was rarely if ever called on personally to work in the fields—but, as we shall see, hardly sufficient to absorb the costs of Hongmou's trip to Beijing to sit for the metropolitan examination.

Culturally, early Qing Guilin both reflected and transcended its status as a booming frontier town. It was home to a distinctive scholarly tradition, which combined a self-conscious pioneer hardihood with intensive study of a narrow range of classical texts. Practicality and know-how were highly valued in this culture. So too were a stubborn perseverance and an indomitable intellectual autonomy that came to be ideologized two centuries later during the anti-Japanese war as "the Guangxi spirit." As one enthusiast put it: "The craggy peaks of Guilin are upright and unyielding, pillars against the southern sky. From this place, ever since the Qin, have emerged scholars of independent spirit. Chen Hongmou was one of these."[25]

This frontier-bred "independent spirit," however, although compatible with a broad critique of the corruptions of contemporary life and scholarship, by no means sanctioned intellectual originality or an equally critical appraisal of received wisdom. It was profoundly traditionalist, even fundamentalist. The Four Books of the Cheng-Zhu tradition, at once the most accessible and the most explicitly didactic components of the classical canon, held the status of revealed truth.[26] We will return in later chapters to Chen Hongmou's precise relationship to the emerging current of "Song learning," or Cheng-Zhu partisanship, but here let us simply consider the way it fit into the broader intellectual milieu of Guilin. The key element, it seems to me, was Guilin's relative isolation from major scholarly trends of the times. As Kai-wing Chow and Kent Guy have pointed out, to be an adept practitioner of the newfangled philological scholarship (*kaozheng xue*), which under the rubric of "Han learning" was rapidly becoming the sine qua non for intellectual worthiness, a person required access from early childhood to enormously well-stocked libraries, such as existed throughout Jiangnan. "Han learning" experts, Chow convincingly argues, intuited this and used their privileged access to such collections to assert an effectively class-based dominance over aspirants to intellectual-political status from less favored regions of the empire.[27] Guangxi, needless to say, was one such region. The paucity of books in the area was nowhere more dramatically underlined than in the collection process that yielded the *Siku quanshu* imperial library of the 1770s and 1780s. Of the 4,831 books submitted by provincial officials and eventually included in the *Siku* corpus, a full four thousand (83 percent) came from the lower Yangzi provinces; not a single title came from Guangxi.[28] Like others of his compatriots, Chen Hongmou grew up poignantly aware of this deficiency, and the awareness stayed with him throughout his life. It prompted him, for example, to complain as Fujian governor in the 1750s that the provincial capital's famous Aofeng Academy hogged all the province's books—"more copies of each book than the entire student body can read at once!"—and to redress this imbalance by redistributing Aofeng's surplus editions to schools in more remote parts of the province.[29] It also underlay Chen's continued emphasis throughout his career on *primary* education, an issue to which we shall return. He saw the very act of learning to read as more difficult on the frontier. In issuing his own condensations of Zhen Dexiu's *Daxue yanyi* and Qiu Jun's sequel, the *Daxue yanyi bu*, Chen attached as an envoi a seemingly autobiographical statement: "Mr. Zhen's book is in 43 chapters, and Mr. Qiu's in 160. They are long and complex. Scholars cannot but sigh as they look over this vast ocean of verbiage. In particular, students in far-off regions [*yuanfang xuezhe*] not only find these works unusually difficult to read, but they are difficult for them even to afford."[30] Likewise, he compiled his handbook to the allusions and personal and place names in the Four Books, the *Sishu kaojiyao*, to aid those students, especially from his native province, who lacked the library resources to track down all these references on their own.[31]

Yet, like other Guilin literati, Chen Hongmou tended to turn what was in fact a practical educational debility into a self-professed intellectual strength. Consider the following. In 1729 Chen captured the attention and approval of the Yongzheng emperor by his surprising endorsement of Guangxi education commissioner Wei Changji's request that a special official be appointed to clean up the disgraceful customs of Chen's native province. Guangxi people, Wei had complained, lusted indecorously after material advantage, valued human life lightly, and were overly litigious; local elites were wantonly domineering. Chen Hongmou, already (as a lowly assistant in the Board of Civil Office) the ranking bureaucrat in the empire of Guangxi birth, announced his concurrence in this assessment, which was little more than a stereotypical condemnation of a peripheral society by a scholar-official of smugly superior refinement. He seconded Wei's call for an intensified provincial campaign of indoctrination in ritual propriety as the proper course of action.[32] That Chen was sincere about this is suggested by his own call to Guangxi governor Yang Xifu to do something simi-

lar several years later. But, although like Wei he couched his appeal in terms of a lament
for the impropriety of Guangxi's commoners and elites, he did so in strikingly different language. He began: "The people of Guangxi are poor [*qiong*] and ignorant [*yu*];
even the literati there are rustic [*pu*] and vulgar [*lou*]."[33] In this passage the term "*lou*"
is unambiguously condemnatory; other terms, however, may be read in different
senses. Let us concentrate for a moment on the notion of "rusticity."

The term "*pu*" emerges in Chen Hongmou's discourse, and in the writing of others about him, as a code word for all that is distinctive about his Guangxi roots. It can
be used in a negative sense—a sense it clearly conveys in part in the passage just
quoted—to suggest a coarse bumpkin quality. But far more frequently Chen gives the
word an ironic, approving twist, especially when using it in compounds such as "*zhipu*"
(unpretentiousness, guilelessness) or "*puhou*" (unaffected and generous of spirit). In a
letter to an unnamed Sichuan governor, he distinguishes between the customs of that
frontier province, which are "wild and barbarous" (*hanye*), and those of his equally peripheral native place, which are "honest and simple" (*chunpu*).[34] Writing to his nephew
Chen Zhongcan in 1733, he complains of the "dissolute extravagance" (*fuhua*) of
Beijing, so different from the "straightforward simplicity" (*chengpu*) of home.[35] And late
in life he recalls the advice of his father: "After I became an official, each time I saw my
father he would look me in the eye and say, 'Don't abandon the forthright honesty
[*chengpu*] you displayed as a beginning student.' I took this to heart, and have never
dared for a single day to neglect it."[36] Consequently, even Chen's most negative depictions of Guangxi's untutored rusticity were tinged with an admiring recognition of its
developmental potential, both economic and spiritual, based on its culture of yeoman-
like industry and integrity.

Accompanying this image of his native place as the epitome of genuineness and
substantiality was an undertone of resentment of the domination of Jiangnan in late imperial culture and politics. "The Way," Chen notes, "pervades everywhere under
Heaven. It is not the exclusive property of any particular region."[37] In a 1746 letter to
his longtime friend and administrative superior Yinjishan, a letter with strong autobiographical implications, he again hinted at his bitterness: "Poor and isolated scholars on
the frontiers [*bianfang hanshi*] over many years and through many official tenures, one
by one in a mere trickle, have only very slowly gained the recognition of Heaven and of
the Imperial house. Yet they remain solid in their personal conduct and unusually
steadfast in their moral commitment."[38]

But however much Chen may have felt the sting of prejudice for his peripheral
place of origin, and however much he may have shrouded himself in the myth of its
stalwart pioneer spirit, the fact remains that the Guilin area was not simply a frontier
like any other. It had enjoyed a formidable record of academic success. Over the course
of the Ming-Qing era Guilin Prefecture produced nearly five thousand holders of the
second examination degree (*juren*); Lingui County itself produced some 53 metropolitan degree holders (*jinshi*) in the Ming and no fewer than 190 in the Qing, four of
whom placed first in that exam.[39] Chen, then, was hardly the "isolated scholar" he
sometimes presented himself as but instead was the product of an area that had developed its own rich and distinctive literary culture over the course of centuries. The fact

that such a culture could emerge in an area so marginally tied into the economy and society of the heartland was in no small measure the product of Guilin's most significant capital asset, its fabled natural beauty, lauded throughout the imperial era as "foremost under Heaven" (*jia yu Tianxia*). At least since the Tang, Guilin's mountains, rivers, and caves had induced the empire's most famous literary figures to make the pilgrimage. Han Yu, Li Bo, Liu Zongyuan, and countless others had celebrated it in poems and essays, which in turn were recited with pride by local citizens. The city had also long been a center of neo-Confucian studies, in a tradition established by the eminent Song *lixue* scholars Zhang Shi (a Hunanese sojourner) and Lü Zuqian (a local native).[40] In the Ming the philosopher-statesman Wang Yangming had likewise spent time in the area, leaving, as he so often did, a lasting influence on local culture and society.

The embodiment of Guilin's scholarly heritage was its remarkably highly developed school system, which had a venerable history but was considerably revitalized and expanded in the course of the early Qing economic boom. Backed by merchant capital, Guangxi governor Chen Yuanlong in the 1710s undertook a major reconstruction of the prefectural school (where the young Chen Hongmou matriculated) and led a drive to establish some eighteen public elementary schools (*yixue*) "both in and outside the city."[41] Apparently these schools did not extend to Chen Hongmou's own relatively remote West Township, however, for in 1731 we find him returning home from office to help in then-governor Jin Hong's campaign to further extend the *yixue* network, primarily into areas, such as Chen's hometown, that had been neglected in the earlier expansion. As we shall see in Chapter 12, both the virtues of the *yixue* institution and the need for care not to exclude more outlying districts from their benefits were lessons that Chen applied from Guilin's experience to his own educational policies elsewhere.[42]

But the centerpieces of Guilin's cultural establishment were its three nationally known private schools (*shuyuan*)—the Xuancheng, Xiufeng, and Fucheng Academies—and the several supplementary prep schools they ran for younger students.[43] Xuancheng (known also as the Huazhang Academy) was the most ancient of these, tracing its origins to the Northern Song. The premier training ground for all of the province's best students, it was repeatedly refurbished in the Yuan and Ming, and, again with merchant underwriting, in 1682 and 1724.[44] Jointly with the likewise venerable Xiufeng Academy, Xuancheng was endowed with large tracts of rural rental land that were repeatedly augmented in the early Qing.[45] The Fucheng Academy, in Guilin's eastern suburb, was a later institution, founded in 1713 by Governor Chen Yuanlong as part of the same early-eighteenth-century drive to push education at the cultural margins to which Chen Hongmou himself would also contribute in the southwest. Using rhetoric that Hongmou would subsequently echo in Yunnan, Chen Yuanlong wrote: "Although Guangxi lies on the frontier and is remote and isolated, its leading citizens are well off and highly civilized (*huacheng*). They can certainly support an additional academy, which will aid in extending this civility to the broader population."[46]

Beginning at roughly the time of Chen Hongmou's adolescence, Guilin's academies became the center of a self-conscious movement to break away from the intellectual straitjacket represented by the civil service examination system. This of course was a common trend of the time, but in Guilin the movement sought to substitute for the examination curriculum a particular and distinctive "quest for substance and practicality" (*qiushi*). Representative of this movement was Liu Lingxi, a native of Guilin's Wuyuan County, a *jinshi* of 1748, and a Hanlin academician. Liu became headmaster of the Xiufeng Academy around 1750 and used that pulpit to proclaim his own version of "substantive learning" (*shixue*), a doctrine also associated with Guilin's by then famous native son, Chen Hongmou. The rallying cry of the entire early-eighteenth-century intellectual movement in Guilin, which clearly influenced Chen deeply, was "Study of history is of equal importance to study of the classics" (*jingshi bing zhong*).[47]

To sum up our discussion of the milieu into which Chen Hongmou was born, then, let me propose an idea to which we must return later, that of the "semiperiphery." I use this term less in a Skinnerian or Wallersteinian political-economic sense than in a cultural one, although I see the two as, at least loosely, interconnected. Chen was the product of an environment that was on the frontier yet was far from primitive. It was fairly prosperous but also fairly recently so; it was wealthy enough to support a flourishing educational establishment but not wealthy enough (or wealthy *long* enough) to have supported the great accumulations of texts that graced libraries of Jiangnan and Beijing. Nor was its wealth secure enough to foster an indigenous literary scene of graceful belles lettres, of profound philosophizing, or of deep textual erudition. It prized what it fondly presumed to be grassroots agrarian values, but these were values with a decidedly commercial bent. It combined, moreover, a self-conscious pioneer practicality with a rigid and relatively unsophisticated moral fundamentalism. This was an environment in which an ideology of *shixue*—of "substantive learning"—could readily take hold.

Youth

Chen Hongmou was born in 1696, the fifth surviving child, and second son, of a family of six children. It is not surprising, given the recording biases of the day, that next to nothing is known of the lives of his three elder sisters. His younger brother, Chen Hongyi (born 1700), was close to Hongmou but otherwise led an uneventful, family-oriented life.[48] The eldest Chen sibling, on the other hand, was a pivotal figure for Hongmou in many ways. Chen Hongxian (1674–1763) was more than twenty years older than Hongmou. The initial focus of his father's ambitions for the family, he passed the prefectural-level examination in the year of Hongmou's birth but repeatedly failed to progress higher through the system. He turned, then, to the customary alternative, becoming a village schoolteacher and local community leader. Hongxian devoted his energies to the finance and management of township irrigation projects, granaries, and relief agencies. He was also Chen Hongmou's earliest tutor, role model, and lifetime confidante.[49] Hongmou credited his brother-cum-teacher in large part for his own populism, frequently citing his admonition, "Exert yourself for the common people, rather than promoting yourself at their expense."[50]

It was clearly a source of great discomfort for both brothers, and for the family as a whole, that Hongmou so greatly eclipsed his elder sibling in academic and political success. Throughout his official career Hongmou repeatedly recommended his brother for an honorary *juren* degree, but the nomination was never accepted. The two gradually developed an elaborate apologia for Hongxian's consistent failure to be recognized by the examination establishment: his unfashionable concentration on scholarly issues of "substantive utility" (*shiyong*). In his 1763 obituary for his brother, written at a time when the Han Learning movement was approaching its apogee of dominance, Hongmou complained that "to achieve examination success today, you must know how to discuss antiquity by the manipulation of texts"; in contrast to this, "our own family has always held that the proper role of study is as an aid in ordering the world [*jingshi*], and we have valued literary pursuits only to this end."[51] The brothers' resentment at Hongxian's academic failures throws into sharper perspective, it seems to me, the relationship between the pragmatic bent of Hongmou's intellectual agenda—what would become known as statecraft—and his ingrained defensiveness in a political world controlled by more self-consciously refined literati from more favored regions of the empire.

Chen Hongmou's eventual achievement of the *jinshi*, coming as he did from an obscure and remote family with almost no past history of examination success, may not have been unheard of in Qing society, but it was certainly unusual. It was the stuff of myth and seems to have been made possible in roughly equal measure by his natural gifts, a deeply entrenched will to succeed, and the surprising degree of political acumen he and his family displayed in the cultivation of patrons. Chen's many contemporary hagiographers all stress the remarkable diligence he demonstrated in his studies as a youth, and there is no reason to doubt them.[52] Tellingly, perhaps, there are none of the colorful accounts of childhood precocity conventional to the genre; he was not viewed by himself or by others as an exceptionally brilliant man. Perseverance through poverty is a major theme, as it later became in Chen's own exhortative writings.[53] Coming from the family he did, it is of little surprise that the young man proved self-motivating. At school he was seen as possessed by ambition; as an adult he conceded that this may have alienated him from his classmates.[54]

Studying on his own and under his brother's tutelage, Chen first took and failed the prefectural examination in 1711, when he was sixteen. After a period of redoubled effort at home he managed to pass on his next try, in 1714, but failed the provincial examination later that same year. He became a stipended student of the Lingui County school and a few years later was selected for admission to the exclusive Xuancheng Academy at the provincial capital. In 1720 he again failed the provincial exam. As had his brother before him, Hongmou turned to the fallback vocation of schoolteacher, in the village of Luxi near his home.[55] Deeply depressed about failing to fulfill his family's hopes, however, he ultimately withdrew to the precincts of the Xishan Temple, in the hills outside Guilin, where he engaged in a period of further self-study, psychological counseling offered by a kindly monk, and prayers for assistance by the Buddhist deity Vedas (Weituo). The following year he extended his devotions to the Daoist spirit Tongyan shen, who was locally reputed to be efficacious in aiding examination success. Tongyan shen appeared to Chen in a dream, predicting triumph on his next attempt. The god proved faithful to his word: Chen passed the provincial examination, placing first in the middle rank, in 1723, at the age of twenty-eight *sui*. Later that year he journeyed to Beijing for the metropolitan examination and passed it in 108th place. He was appointed a scholar of the Hanlin Academy.[56]

Whatever role divine intervention may have played in Hongmou's ultimate examination success, however, there was no shortage of human patronage along the way as well. Each stage of Chen's early progress toward imperial recognition was accomplished with a boost from a well-placed sponsor with whom Hongmou and his family had assiduously cultivated ties. Earliest and most important of these were the Yangs of Diantou village, the wealthiest and most prominent family in Lingui's West Township. As early as 1707, when Hongmou was just eleven years old, his father dragged him along to pay a call on Yang Jiaying, poet, intellectual, and renowned patron of local scholarship. Yang prided himself on his acumen in picking out local boys of promise, helping them finance their studies, and in some cases offering them marriage to one of his several daughters. He liked the look of young Hongmou and in 1709 betrothed him to his eldest girl; they were formally married eight years later. Jiaying's brother, Yang Jiaxiu, a *juren* of 1713 and later magistrate of Henan's Baofeng County, became Hongmou's tutor after 1715.[57] In his subsequent official career Chen remained close to his affinal relatives, relying on them to keep him apprised of developments in his home township that might demand intervention of one sort or another.[58]

In 1719 the former deputy magistrate and low-level metropolitan official Zhu Ti'an returned to his home in Guilin to take up the headmastership of the Xuancheng Academy. Because Zhu was also a native of West Township, immediately on his arrival Chen Jiyu ordered his son Hongmou to pay a call on him and request his assistance in promoting his career. Zhu gave the young man his calling card and a writing brush and bestowed on him the courtesy name Ruzi (which he continued to bear all his life), effectively accepting him as his protégé. The following year the "rustic" farm boy was accepted into the prestigious academy, formally by dint of a special provincial-wide examination but doubtless with some influence on the part of the academy's new headmaster.[59]

Next in line was Xu Shumin (*hao*: Xu Shengyan), a Jiangsu native, *jinshi* of 1703, and after 1720 educational commissioner of Guangxi. A frequent lecturer at the Xuancheng Academy, Xu identified Hongmou as the brightest of the school's current crop of students and in the prefectural requalifying exam of 1720 ranked him first. Xu actively talked up Chen's abilities, making him for the first time visible to a wider circle of potential patrons. He also introduced him to his own nephew, Ge Zhenghu, a brilliant young man whom he had brought along on his tour of duty in Guilin. Ostensibly too frail to withstand the physical rigors of the examination process, Ge nevertheless became a nationally respected scholar and bibliophile. He and Hongmou became fast friends, and after they reacquainted themselves in Beijing during Hongmou's Hanlin apprenticeship of the mid-1720s, Ge became Chen's private secretary and counselor on scholarly matters. One modern writer, indeed, has suggested that it was Ge Zhenghu who actually did the compilation work for Chen Hongmou's most famous publications, his *Five Sourcebooks* (*Wuzhong yigui*).[60] Ge was probably Chen's closest confidante throughout his long provincial career.

Hongmou added yet more prominent names to his roster of patrons when he sat successfully for the provincial examination in 1723. The chief examiner was the well-known Sichuan *lixue* scholar and current Zhejiang governor Zhu Jingxian. Hongmou cultivated a long-term relationship with Zhu, eventually contributing a preface to the older man's collected works (*wenji*). The associate examiner was Deling (De Songru), who became the first of Hongmou's many Manchu friends. When Chen traveled to Beijing that autumn to sit for the metropolitan exam, Deling arranged for him to lodge at the townhouse of his mother. Chen was treated extremely well, and a lasting bond was formed. Many years later he would write a ninetieth-birthday elegy for the mother and a funerary address for Deling himself.[61] Chen's immediate examiner at the provincial exam was one Lin Yuchun, who had also been his teacher at the Xuancheng Academy; Lin arranged for his wealthy friend Liu Xinhan to pay the cost of Hongmou's travel to Beijing for the *jinshi* examination that fall.[62]

This record of attachment to patrons seems remarkable but probably should not be viewed with undue cynicism. Chen's success was the Qing version of "the American Dream," and the fact was that there was no other way it could have been achieved. Without great wealth or a family history of examination success, a young man of obscure origins could achieve recognition only through the cultivation of patrons. There is no reason to doubt that powerful persons genuinely perceived in Chen an unusually talented young man and sought to help him for this reason (in addition, perhaps, to other reasons of their own). What does seem remarkable, however, is that Chen Hongmou, coming from the background he did, was able to play the patronage game with such adeptness and finesse. No one ever seems to have seen in him or his family crude social climbers. Hongmou was able to cultivate the most diverse range of patrons without any apparent loss to his integrity—indeed, his reputation for integrity became an evident asset in his quest for ever more influential patrons. This instinctive grace in handling those who would benefit him was a gift Chen retained throughout his political career.

Throughout Chen's many years of preparation for official service, the content of his education had a consistent, distinctive bent. From his earliest days of study with his brother, his curriculum had centered on the Four Books, the canonical texts of the Song *lixue* movement. The neo-Confucian emphasis on self-cultivation (*xiushen*) attracted Hongmou early and stayed with him all his life. His period at the Xuancheng Academy only strengthened this commitment—the Xuancheng from its founding had envisioned itself as a bastion of neo-Confucian learning on the cultural pale—but it also deepened the practical orientation that family and locality had bequeathed him. Elitist it may have been, but there was no ivory-tower quality about the Xuancheng in Chen's day. His headmaster and patron Zhu Ti'an was an outspoken advocate of "substantive learning" (*shixue*) and of "ordering the world" (*jingshi*). Even while basing his curriculum on the "Eastern Zhejiang" (Zhedong) school of *lixue* thought, Zhu taught his students to abjure the "empty" metaphysical speculation (*kongtan*) in which many members of that school engaged. The Xuancheng style of inquiry stressed instead *shijian* (practice) and *gongfu* (strenuous moral or intellectual effort) as the necessary means to perfect that "practice." Students were trained in reading not only the dynastic histories but also raw historical documents. Most distinctively, the academy retained a subscription to the *Beijing Gazette* (*Dibao*) and encouraged its students to pay close heed to the factors influencing contemporary government policies, both in the capital and in the provinces. Chen Hongmou ate it up. Mocked by classmates for the unseemly passion with which he threw himself into debates on current affairs, Hongmou announced that he, for one, would never settle for the life of a *ziliao han*, an aloof hermetic scholar (the ironic nickname *ziliao han* stuck, applied by his old intimates to Chen throughout his life).[63] If he had ever lacked for a sense of personal mission, he discovered it now. He inscribed a plaque to hang over the door of his room, announcing, "If you want to be an indispensable man for your generation, you must do what others of your generation cannot."[64]

Family

Other than her origin in one of Lingui's leading families, little is known of Chen Hongmou's wife (nee Yang).[65] Few of Hongmou's surviving writings discuss her, and none are addressed to her. We know, however, that the marriage was long, amiable, and extremely successful. Madame Yang accompanied her husband from one provincial post to another until her death at his Changsha governor's residence in 1763. She is described as gentle and magnanimous and as an extraordinarily competent manager. She particularly loved devoting her talents and wealth to the people of her native place and on several occasions returned home to undertake management of relief or capital improvement projects in her husband's stead.[66] As he rose in official life, however, Chen also formed affinal alliances by taking concubines. The pattern is an almost perfect reflection of the country boy's gradual odyssey of "making it," breaking free of his frontier roots and approaching the empire's cultural center. His first concubine (nee Long) came from a nearby village in Lingui; his second (nee Dong) from adjacent Yongfu County; the third (nee Xia) from Wuchang, in central China; and the fourth (nee Zhang) from Xuzhou Prefecture, in the heart of Jiangnan.[67]

Chen and his wife were extremely unfortunate in the fate of their children. None of their sons lived beyond early childhood, and none of their daughters survived early adulthood. The first child, a daughter born in 1719, lived longest, dying at age thirty-one, and the second, also a daughter, died at twenty-five. Then came two boys, both of whom died at five or six. The next child, a daughter, lived only into her early twenties, and the next child died in infancy. The only child to survive her father was the youngest daughter, and she too died young, at the age of twenty-seven.[68] Again, little remains in the historical record of the daughters beyond information on their births, marriages, and deaths. They married well. The eldest daughter married Xie Rongsheng, a future president of the Board of Rites and friend of such eminent late-eighteenth-century literati as Yuan Mei and Ruan Yuan.[69] The second married Dingzhou (Fujian) prefect Jiang Zhixiu; her son, Jiang Benlian, was a favorite of Hongmou and became a celebrated academician. The family had come far, by this time, from its obscure roots.[70] But even while contracting these marital alliances on a national political scale, home (and what Robert Hymes has called the "localist strategy") was never too far from Hongmou's mind; he thus betrothed one of his daughters to a promising young scholar from Lingui named Tang Yin, and his adopted son to a gentry family of adjacent Yongfu County.[71]

The most intriguing of the Chen daughters in her own right must have been the youngest, Chen Duanwen, who became (perhaps posthumously) a published poet. At some point in the 1770s or 1780s Duanwen's male cousin Chen Zhongcan collected some hundred of her poems and published them under the title *Hanzhen xianshi* (Poems from the Pavilion of Blushing Modesty). As recent scholarship has shown, the publication of works by female poets, usually with male sponsorship, was increasingly fashionable in the early modern era. That one of Chen Hongmou's daughters should be included in this company is probably not surprising, but it is noteworthy. Chen himself was a renowned champion of female literacy (see Chapter 12), but he disparaged poetry as a socially useful outlet for literary energies. At least, he did so for males. For a female, deprived of the opportunity for bureaucratic service, he may have tolerated it, especially if (as the title of Duanwen's collection suggests) it was properly "modest" and moralistic in its sentiments.[72]

After Chen Jiyu arranged the betrothal of his thirteen-year-old son, Hongmou, in 1709, the patriarch stated that his principal reason for doing so had been to secure a grandson in Hongmou's line. Probably he had already concluded (as had the father of the bride, Yang Jiaying) that it was Hongmou, not his elder brother, who was most likely to fulfill the family's upward mobility aspirations. When, nearly two decades later, Hongmou had already been appointed an official of the Board of Civil Office but had yet to produce a surviving male heir, Jiyu once again was moved to action. Invoking his authority as paterfamilias, he ordered in 1727 the donation of an heir (*chusi*) by Chen Hongxian to his eminent younger brother. Hongxian's third son, Chen Zhongke (1710–ca. 1785), was transferred out of his natural father's line into that of Chen Hongmou. Hongxian and Zhongke were immediately packed off to Beijing, where the latter could presumably bond with his newly adoptive father. Chen Hongmou later recalled this period of reunion with great emotion; he had been away from home now for several years (his first such experience) and, despite his great career expectations, was living on the margins of poverty. The arrival of the brother he idolized and of the son he longed for cheered him up immensely.[73]

There is plenty of evidence of the psychological tension this ambivalent paternity caused in Chen Zhongke; mentions of his natural parents in Zhongke's own writings are couched in evident deep affection.[74] He nevertheless became the most filial of sons to his adoptive parents as well. Formal biographies of Zhongke all stress the unusual attentiveness he and his wife showed to his adoptive mother, Ms. Yang, during her final illness.[75] And, abandoning any official aspirations of his own after achieving the *juren* degree in 1741,[76] Zhongke instead trailed Chen Hongmou around the empire, serving as his Boswell and, eventually, his literary executor. Chen Zhongke was the chief compiler of the massive forty-eight *juan* edition of Hongmou's official directives (a surviving archive matched perhaps by that of no other official in imperial history) and of other posthumous collections of Hongmou's works. He also wrote his adoptive father's biography (*nianpu*) in twelve *juan*. It is no exaggeration to say that Chen Hongmou's subsequent reputation as a model late imperial official has been a direct result of the labor put into the detailed recording of his career by his adoptive son.

It was Chen Zhongke's generation, the combined eight male offspring of Hongmou's two brothers, that effectively consolidated the prominence that the family had achieved with Hongmou's breakthrough success. Chen Hongxian's eldest son, Zhongfan, became a student of the Imperial College (*guoxuesheng*) but died young. The second, Zhongyao, was designated the recipient of Hongmou's *yin* (inherited office) privilege when this was awarded in 1735; his long official career included many county magistracies and subprefectural posts in north China, as well as special imperial commissions in his area of expertise, hydraulic maintenance.[77] The fifth son, Zhongli, a *juren* of 1741, had an even longer career as a magistrate, primarily in Hunan.[78] Chen Zhongcan, the eldest son of Hongyi, rose to become acting governor of Shandong; he assisted in the editing of Hongmou's posthumous works and, as we have seen, of Hongmou's daughter's poetry. His brothers Zhongxuan and Zhongqiu became, respectively, a county magistrate and a county director of education. Although protesting piously (as president of the Board of Civil Office in the 1760s) that honor forbade him from using his position to advance his progeny's careers, Hongmou nevertheless drew quietly on his hard-earned intimacy with the Qianlong emperor to do just that.[79] He took enormous satisfaction in their success.

Without question, however, the descendent sentimentally closest to Chen Hongmou was his grandson, Zhongke's son, Chen Lansen. Having tried unsuccessfully for years to produce a surviving natural son of his own, and having adopted Zhongke when the latter was already sixteen years old, the opportunity to enjoy the boyhood of his own male heir was one Hongmou, a thirty-nine-year-old provincial official at the time of Lansen's birth in 1734, would exploit to the fullest. It was also a chance to put into personal practice the childhood educational theories he had been developing for years. Given that his father had by then become his grandfather's most trusted administrative aide, Lansen spent his youth following Hongmou from one provincial post to another, serving, in his words, as "attendant in grandfather's official study" and performing research assignments of increasing complexity, contributing both to his own education and to Hongmou's various compilation projects. He returned to Guilin in 1751 to sit successfully for the prefectural examination and to enroll in the prefectural school. He achieved his *juren* five years later and his *jinshi* the following spring, like his grandfather being assigned to the Hanlin Academy. When Chen Hongmou was serving in the capital as grand secretary, Lansen was serving in the Board of Punishments, and when in 1771 the emperor granted Hongmou's request to retire to his native place, he relieved Lansen of his duties and instructed him to see to his father's safe return home. Thereafter, Lansen devoted his life to preparing Hongmou's many draft manuscripts for publication. Continuing the family practice of building ties to other official families, he betrothed his daughter to Guizhou governor Wei Jianheng.[80]

One final Chen descendent must be mentioned, however briefly. Hongmou's great-great-grandson Chen Jichang took his *jinshi* in 1820 and went on to serve as a prefect and as Jiangxi provincial treasurer. Above the front gate to the Ming walled city, which today constitutes downtown Guilin, stands an enormous stele erected by Liang-

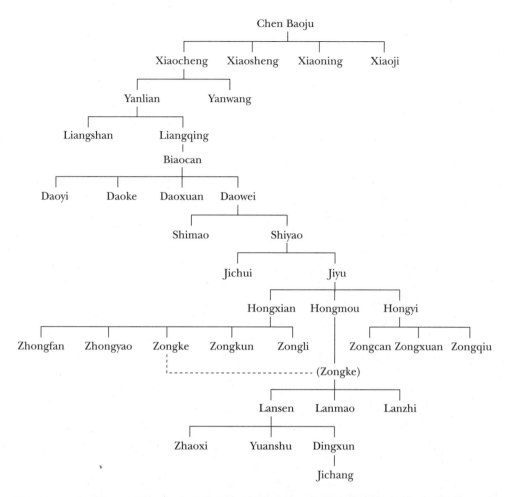

FIGURE 2. A segment of the Lingui Chen patriline, showing individuals mentioned in the text. Sources: *Zongpu liuzhuan; Chen Rongmen xiansheng yishu, ce* 14; *Lingui xianzhi* 29:11.

Guang viceroy Ruan Yuan in Jichang's honor. It reads "Sanyuan jidi" (three firsts). Chen Jichang had the honor of placing first in the provincial examination, the metropolitan examination, and the palace examination—one of only two men in Qing history to achieve such a feat and an immense source of pride to the people of Guilin, further testimony, if they needed such, to the superiority of their local scholarly tradition.[81]

The efflorescence of the Chen line in mid-Qing scholar-official circles was obviously not by happenstance. Nor would it seem to result primarily from string pulling by Chen Hongmou (although he was not loathe to put in a good word for his progeny when necessary).[82] More basically, it was a late fruition of the same familial and cultural pressures that had produced the hard-driven Hongmou himself, forces that he in turn reproduced among his descendents.

Some of the relatively rare displays of emotion Chen allowed himself in his letters concern his pain at separation from home and family. He wrote from his post as Jiangxi governor in 1742:

> As soon as the formal transfer of duties is completed, I will set sail for home. The days and months in Nanchang have been interminable, and I long for my children morning and night. The fact that they are healthy and developing nicely fills my heart with joy; it is a poor man's delight. Even more wonderful is the prospect of a stroll through the woods with my son, in the year that he reaches young manhood, and of observing his progress in his studies. There is no greater joy that we literati can attain.[83]

Again, four years later, he wrote to a colleague: "I have been in active official service now for twenty years, during which time I have hardly ever enjoyed the warm affection of home and family. This is, unfortunately, the way it must be; those like us who are determined to make something of themselves inevitably face such a situation."[84]

Beyond genuine affection, ideological reasons also underlay Chen's longing for family togetherness. Being with one's family was, for him, a political act. Chen shared the widespread belief in the homology of family (*jia*) and polity (*guo*); living one's family life in accord with the dictates of the classics was an active step in reproducing the proper political order. As he wrote to his longtime friend Jia Yuquan:

> Serving one's senior relatives, studying, and running one's own family are the three most important things one does in life, and they are also the most difficult to do well. Over the years, I have learned that it is necessary to take time out for strenuous reflection on one's performance in these areas. This benefits both oneself and others, both the family and the polity. This is even more critical when one is in a position of official service.[85]

In the eyes of his contemporaries Chen was singularly successful in keeping his family life in order.[86] And the "family" in question was a large one, far transcending the nuclear household:

> The ideal is for brothers, on the death of their father, to continue to dwell together, continuing to show filiality and to share in their mother's love. Because of the pressures of career and such, it is very difficult to do this. Sometimes there is no choice but to live apart. . . . But in that case it should be possible to divide material possessions, such as land and house, without rending the emotional bond of love that is proper among brothers. That should remain intact to the end of their days. There is no family under Heaven that can stay undivided for a hundred years. And yet fraternal affection should never be sundered, for it is a dictate of our heavenly natures [*tianxing*].[87]

Throughout his career, whenever circumstances allowed, Chen brought together under his roof as many as possible of the growing number of his father's progeny. His parents themselves joined him in his first provincial post, in Jiangsu in 1730, and remained with him until their deaths four years later. Both older and younger brothers, with their wives and families, spent time with him in Yunnan in the mid-1730s, and frequently resided at his yamens in Nanchang and Xi'an. So, too, once he became established, did his own wife and children, including his daughters' families. The greatest period of blissful family togetherness, we are told, came in the winter of 1755, when for three months following Hongmou's appointment to the family's ancestral home of Hunan nearly two dozen Chens of three generations realized the ideal of kinship co-

FIGURE 3. Stele erected by Liang-Guang viceroy Ruan Yuan in honor of Chen Jichang's "Three Firsts," Guilin. Photograph by the author, January 1994.

habitation at the Changsha governor's mansion. At periods such as these Chen de-ferred to the genealogical seniority of his older brother (eighty years old at the time of the Changsha experience), but it is clear that it was he himself—the Chen with the highest official rank—who effectively exercised the role of paterfamilias.[88]

It was a role he relished, especially in its aspect as dispenser of moral and literary training. He wrote to a friend that the most fitting recreation for an official, in the time away from his government duties, was "to draw family members around him each day, and lecture them on the words and deeds of the worthies of antiquity and of today." As Chen Lansen later recalled, "We lived within an itinerant family school" (*jiashu*), whose location shifted along with Hongmou's many and scattered official postings. The prize pupil was Lansen himself, but others periodically included his uncles and cousins, affinal kinsmen, and, conspicuously, his female relatives as well. Chen Hongmou was, as we shall see, a celebrated advocate of literary education for women, and he practiced what he preached. Chen regularly invited famous teachers to live with them and to share instructional duties—Wang Jishan and Fan Huanpu from Hangzhou, Zhang Wugang from Suzhou, and the ubiquitous Ge Zhenghu—but the governor was also very actively involved himself.[89]

The basic curriculum was the Four Books and other works of the Cheng-Zhu tradition. "It was not," recalled Ge, "a matter of proceeding randomly from book to book,
arbitrarily deriving one's own meanings from them." Rather, Chen's lecture style was to
select a single passage from the Four Books and patiently draw out its significance.
Lansen noted, "His method of explicating a passage was to assemble a range of modern annotations and commentaries on it and to systematically compare the 'flavor' of
these readings, discarding those that were too trivial or vulgar, and seizing upon those
which best distilled the essence of the text, so as to provide models of interpretation for
our group of students." In teaching his charges how to compose a proper essay Chen
similarly stressed the purpose of arriving at the most "direct and penetrating" (*zhijie*)
understanding of a text, avoiding the flights of discursive fancy that he saw as plaguing
contemporary scholarship. An essential means of achieving this faithful textual reading
was to subject one's own interpretations to collective criticism and cross-examination
(*gongxiang zhizheng*) by friends and colleagues, such as the brain trust he had assembled
in his own studio or the circle of correspondents—the brothers Jia Shengquan and Jia
Yuquan; the poet Gong Yiyun; and fellow officials Yinjishan, Depei, and Zhou Renjue—
with whom he routinely discussed such matters. It was this collegial enterprise that produced Chen's various pedagogical works, as well as his more famous *Wuzhong yigui* (Five
sourcebooks) of exemplary texts. These sourcebooks served, as Lansen noted, not only
as teaching materials for the younger Chens but also as, in effect, "our family rules."[90]

Like many another scion of a proud but obscure family who suddenly made it big,
Chen Hongmou took it on himself to perform the various tasks that would formalize
the family's status as a recognized, semicorporate lineage (*zong*). Around 1739 he began
to mythologize the story of the family's origins in Hunan and to draw up a printed genealogy (*zongpu*)—a document that has continued to the present day to be revised and
updated, although it has never been published.[91] The decision was made to date the origins of the lineage from the first ancestor to settle in Hengshan, although something of
a diplomatic compromise apparently granted collateral or cadet status to descendents
of Baoju's younger brothers Baozhao and Baojian, who subsequently followed him into
the area (Baozhao's and Baojian's descendents are recorded only very sketchily in the
surviving genealogy). The membership group was further shaped by restricting it to
male descendents who retained their legal residence in Hengshan. Hongmou's nephew
Chen Zhongcan was assigned the task of investigating grave inscriptions and other available local documents to aid in delineation of the family tree. Hongmou's immediate
forebears were likely thinking in lineage terms when they began, in his great-grandfather's generation, to adopt standardized generational characters (*pai*) for all male children. Still, it was Hongmou himself who decreed adherence to this with the generation
of his son and nephews and he who determined in advance what the particular generational characters were to be for ten generations to come.[92] Chen also dictated a set of
lineage rules (*jiaxun*) to govern lineage members for posterity. As in his management
of office, so in family matters Chen Hongmou labored to plan for the long term and to
make his own innovations as permanently binding as possible.

The Chen lineage had always had a ritual focus in the small shrine they had built
to their image of Dongting shen. But now Hongmou cleared a piece of land on the

commanding high ground at the front of Hengshan Mountain, constructed a spacious ancestral temple and meeting hall (Chenshi zongsi), and purchased for it vessels and implements for ancestral sacrifice. He established procedures whereby the headship of the lineage temple (*sizheng*) would rotate among members of the senior generation but delegated his fourth-eldest nephew, Zhongkun—the one nephew with little in the way of official aspirations—as manager of lineage property. This property, a lineage estate (*yitian*) that Hongmou purchased and donated to the group, was apparently not very great, and its modest revenue was restricted for use in underwriting collective sacrifice.[93] From 1764 to 1766, while serving at Beijing, Chen financed and directed in detail the construction of a lineage school and library (*shulou*) adjacent to the temple.[94]

Hongmou's return to his native place in 1742, when this spurt of lineage building was undertaken, was his third since his initial departure to sit for the metropolitan examinations in 1723. He had returned very briefly en route to his first provincial post in 1729, then again for nearly six months, to bury his parents, in 1732. Between 1742 and his death in 1771, although briefly in the 1760s holding the extraordinary honor of serving as governor-general of his native province, he never again saw home. In 1769, serving in the capital as grand secretary and beginning to feel the onset of his final illness, he requested sick leave to return to his native place. Three times his request was denied. Finally in mid-1771 he was relieved of his duties, and with the full trappings of imperial favor accompanying his passage, he began the homeward journey toward his longed-for retirement. He died en route.

Although rarely at home, Chen continued to identify strongly with his native place and to be identified with it by others. (While in Beijing at the close of his career he was known to associates as "the Grand Secretary from Guilin.")[95] He sought as much as possible to remain a presence in local affairs. For example, he kept an eye on food supply matters, extending or arranging loans for kinsmen and fellow villagers in times of dearth and taking a personal interest in the stocking levels and management of local granaries.[96] He financed and managed the construction of a number of large-scale water conservancy projects serving the drainage and irrigation needs of his native West Township.[97] Anxious over the commercial and cultural isolation of his hometown, he built in 1742 the major access road that still today links Hengshan to the county seat and donated endowment land (*gongchan*) to underwrite the operation of a public ferry; in 1764 he reconstructed the much-traversed Fengshan Bridge.[98] We have already spoken of his efforts to extend to West Township the county's system of public elementary schools (*yixue*). In 1762 he made a bequest to the county schools of Lingui and adjacent Yongfu of over five hundred *mu* of endowment land and seven years later made a substantial grant of books to each of Guangxi's seventy-two county schools and eight academies, explicitly to overcome the deficiencies of the province's library resources.[99] In all of these matters—provisioning, water conservancy, communications, education— Chen's developmental programs at home mirror those he undertook in his provincial tenures throughout the empire.

In his political career as well Chen continued to be discreetly solicitous of hometown interests, even while maintaining a high-profile public posture of prohibiting efforts to touch him for favors (*guanfang*). Emblematic of this was his refounding of the

Guangxi Native Place Association (*huiguan*) in Beijing, an organization dating originally from the early Ming that had been decimated during the dynastic transition and
that served as lobby for provincial interests in court politics.[100] Chen's most famous effort at pork-barrel politicking concerned land reclamation efforts in his native province
and will be discussed at length in the chapter to follow. A more subtle episode, perhaps
apocryphal and recounted with glee by a hostile writer, involved a variety of taro held
to be extremely tasty and native to Guangxi's Lipu County. An unnamed Manchu
prince asked Chen to arrange a shipment to him of a sample, with the intention of imposing a tax on the product. Chen managed to have him sent a sample of unusually
poor quality, and the product remained untaxed.[101]

Chen's intervention in Guangxi affairs could also be more programmatic, as he
sought to have applied to his native province the same broad sorts of developmental
policies that characterized his own regional administrations, particularly in provinces
suffering the same disadvantages of peripherality. In a celebrated letter to an unnamed
Guangxi governor—probably Chen's like-minded associate Yang Xifu—he laid out
these views:

> The people of Guangxi are poor and backward. . . . In the past, political authorities
> there have concentrated on suppression and pacification of the savage population, and
> shown little effort in more compassionate [*tixue*] programs of relief and development.
> My own belief is that, wherever a population exists, we cannot but attempt to improve
> it by means of incentives and sanctions; wherever a territory exists, we cannot but at-
> tempt to develop its agricultural potential. In each and every province there are op-
> portunities for benefit [*li*] which can be exploited, and dysfunctions which can be re-
> dressed.

Chen goes on to offer a line of reasoning that guides his own policies empire-wide and
that we will encounter repeatedly throughout this book. Population growth dictates that
officials pay strenuous attention to developing new means of productivity; this must
involve long-term planning and ignore the individual official's short-term career interests; the only effective way to increase productivity is through enhancing the population's capacity for self-reliance and its entrepreneurial spirit; this is a task that has moral-
cultural, as well as economic, aspects. In all of this Guangxi can serve as a model—as it
did two centuries later for Li Zongren and his associates of the "Guangxi clique"—
because of the unusual "spirit" (*xin*) and developmental potential of its people.[102]

The Man

Chen Hongmou believed in the determinative importance of childhood socialization.
He complained of the excessive leniency of contemporary parents who, during their
son's first years, "continually spoil him, smiling at his behavior when they ought to be
scolding him. By the time he is grown, he has been socialized to become willful and arrogant. No matter how much one might wish to correct it, at this point there is nothing
that can be done."[103] When writing this, Chen was clearly using as a standard his own severe upbringing and the formative influence it had on his adult personality. The mature
Qing bureaucrat who emerged from this socialization process was a straitlaced neo-

Confucian but one with his own pronounced eccentricities. Although, as we shall see, he worked hard to maintain friendships, he cannot have been very pleasant company.

As far as can be determined from the enormous corpus of writings by and about him, Chen was utterly humorless. Even the wry irony often employed by other serious-minded scholar-officials is nearly absent from his prose. The poet and bon vivant Yuan Mei, who admired Chen and wrote a revealing biographical sketch of him, contrasted him with their mutual friend, the Manchu official Yinjishan:

> Chen and Yinjishan, though they passed the examinations together and regularly served side-by-side, were vastly different in temperament. Yinjishan was brilliantly gifted, yet kindly, easygoing, and genial [*kuanhe*]. He accomplished anything he wanted to in a relaxed and natural manner. Chen, on the other hand, was obsessive and uptight [*keli*] both day and night, never allowing himself any time for amusement or relaxation. Yet the two of them were perfectly suited to complement one another.[104]

Following his father's example, Chen Hongmou imbued the imperative to personal frugality with a religious intensity. Valorizing frugality (*jiesheng*) was, to be sure, part of the cant of Cheng-Zhu ideology and likewise of calculated Qing economic policy.[105] But it is equally clear that in Hongmou's case deep-seated psychological needs were even more determinative of his behavior. Chen's letters home from the capital at the close of his career, for example, are amusingly shot through with gripes about the cost of food, transportation, repairs to his Beijing townhouse, and so on.[106] His compulsive parsimony could even invite the ridicule of fellow officials. While he was serving as president of the Board of Civil Office late in his career, for example, the story circulated that he routinely saved any unwritten-upon pieces of paper from documents sent to him and reused them himself, even going so far as to clip off the originating office's name and replacing it with his own.[107]

The economizing dictated by Chen's alarmed concern for the empire's resource base was grounded in a religious faith that was, I am convinced, quite devout and sincere. Natural resources were the bounty bestowed by Heaven (*tianliang* or *tianwu*), and waste or extravagance was an act of defiance of Heaven's will. It was, quite literally, sinful.[108] So too was any dissipation through personal indulgence of the human body, which was also "born of Heaven" (*sheng yu tianran*).[109] The moral obligation to frugality was also familial, a duty to the patriline, which, like one's body and the bounty of nature, was Heaven's creation. Chen insists repeatedly that "what is heedlessly used up today cannot be bequeathed to one's heirs."[110]

For those in an official capacity these dictates to frugality, which were shared by all human beings, were intensified by the demand to act in an exemplary fashion. Chen wrote to a colleague, "If you want to influence popular practice in the direction of thrift and frugality, you must provide a model by avoiding any waste or extravagance in your conduct of office."[111] He was notorious for shunning anything beyond the demands of minimal courtesy in entertaining official guests (*yingchou*).[112] As an official, Chen took deeply to heart the compulsion—clearly verging on a sense of guilt—not to abuse the products of others' physical labors. Never forget, he told his audience at Yangzhou's hyperelite Ziyang Academy, that in enjoying the luxury of study you are consuming the surplus generated by, and properly belonging to, the "people" (*minfei mingao*).[113] For

Chen Hongmou the imperative to "cherish the people and be sparing of their wealth" (*aimin xicai*) could not have been more personal.

There was also in Chen a very marked streak of asceticism. Deriving from the Song *lixue* emphasis on repression of human appetites, it partook as well of the broad reaction to the "almost cultural revolution" of the late Ming on the part of Qing elites, a reaction well described by Keith McMahon as the imperative to "containment."[114] But in Chen's case a deeper, more personal set of compulsions was also at work.

Good fortune or "blessings" exist in the world in finite measure; it is each person's duty to husband these blessings (*xifu*) by minimizing consumption. Put another way, one demonstrates one's basic respect for life (*zunsheng*) by using prudence in matters of food and drink (*jie yinshi*).[115] Alcohol is especially anathema. Chen's regular crusades against wine and tobacco production throughout his career seem to have been prompted no less by a distrust of the relaxed enjoyment they might bring the consumer than by more strictly economic concerns. His equally frequent campaigns against social events conducive to sexual mingling were also motivated both by practical concerns (avoidance of incidents that might spawn litigation, for example) and by personal prudery. Chen Hongmou dreaded the idea of recreational sex. He stated categorically that "there is no greater evil than sexual debauchery,"[116] and when as Jiangxi governor he sought to influence Heaven to end a drought by releasing prisoners from provincial jails, he specifically exempted adulterers.[117] Sexual activity, for Chen, was morally justifiable only with the goal of procreation, spilling one's seed in nonprocreative sex being an affront to Heaven, the creator. This gives a literal, physical reading to the notion of "self-cultivation" (*xiushen*) as the preservation of one's heavenly endowed corporality; Chen cites Lu Shiyi to the effect that, if one has proper respect for the sanctity of one's own body (*shen zhi zhonggui*), one will avoid "weakening" it (*ruo*) by sexual licentiousness (*bu yin yu se*).[118]

Again, this applies to gastronomic as well as sexual appetites. Although there is no evidence that Chen followed Lu's counsel to adhere to a vegetarian regime (perhaps the association of vegetarianism with Buddhist sectarianism was strong enough in Chen's day to discourage such a choice), by all accounts he kept to a severely abstemious diet.[119] And here too the compulsion is redoubled for those serving in official posts. In his sourcebook on proper official deportment Chen cites an inscription he encountered as a youth in Guilin's famous Longyin Cave. Left there by a Guilin magistrate of the Song era, it associates visitation of epidemic disease on a locality with sexual dalliance on the part of the incumbent official.[120]

Such a repressive ethic is unmistakably religious in the sense both that it is grounded ultimately in the relationship between the subject and an ontological "First Principle" (Heaven) and that it involves a set of mental constructs nearing those of guilt and sin. Hellmut Wilhelm's intriguing studies of Qing thought identify a distinctive stream of highly emotional, angst-ridden Confucianism, running from Lu Shiyi and Lu Longqi in the seventeenth century to Tang Jian and Zeng Guofan in the nineteenth—a line of highly activist thinkers into which Chen Hongmou very explicitly fell.[121] Similarly, Pei-yi Wu has found an unprecedented sense of guilt (as opposed to the more orthodox Confucian sense of shame) in the writings of Confucian scholars after the mid-sixteenth century, seen above all in their compulsive urge to confess "anguish and remorse" over their own shortcomings. Wu cites especially Lü Kun, by all odds one of Chen's most profound intellectual influences: "My mind is responsible for all the sins [*zuiguo*] of my person; my limbs and organs are guiltless. My person is responsible for all the sins in the universe; heaven and earth and the myriad things are guiltless."[122] Both Wilhelm and Wu draw out the elements of personal religiosity in this line of thought. For Wilhelm the highly disciplined struggle of all the figures in this tradition to "overcome individuality" ("*keji*"—a key word in the writings of Chen himself) amounts to "a rediscovery of the human mind along psychological rather than philosophical lines" and is a quest for moral rectitude based on "alienation," "insecurity," and (a notion made explicit by one of Chen's most devoted admirers, Tang Jian) "fear." The deeply felt psychological need for constant self-reproach—clearly evident in Chen Hongmou's letters—has for Wilhelm "a strangely modern ring," encompassing as it does a "dissolution into the irrational of the very root of their thinking and being."[123]

Although I am less comfortable with this sort of psychoanalytic approach than were Wilhelm and other scholars of his day, I cannot help but feel that he has gotten at some valid aspects of the personality of a man such as Chen Hongmou. Moreover, where Wilhelm suggests "Xavarian" parallels for this mental outlook, I myself am reminded more of Anglo-American Puritanism. Certain elements are obviously lacking, notably the focus on an afterlife and the doctrine of salvation by faith. But the religious and psychological abhorrence of human desire (especially but not exclusively sexual), the explicit linkage of this with the economic ethic of frugality (highlighted in the Chinese case by the use of the same term, "*jie*," to denote both sexual and economic restraint), and the anguished feeling of guilt associated with the satisfaction of human desires—combined with a stern patriarchal ideology, a valorization of gradual economic accumulation, and, as we shall see, an evangelical sense of mission—all sound very familiar to an American ear.[124] In Chapter 3 we will look at the way Chen and some of his contemporaries sought to rescue human emotional response (*renqing*) from the utter disrepute to which this mental set threatened to banish it; it is clear enough, however, that for Chen this process took place against the background of a consciousness severely distrustful of satiation. "Fending off desires is like pulling a boat against the current," he wrote late in life. "If you relax your efforts for a moment, you will surely drift downstream."[125]

Closely related to this puritanical approach to life is what we might term Chen's anti-aestheticism. Dismissal of the value of connoisseurship and of aesthetic indulgence was an intellectual position associated with this same line of activist scholars, from Lü Kun to Tang Jian.[126] But Chen's own antipathy to the literary and visual arts was evidently more visceral. He genuinely believed himself immune to the sensory experience of beauty and flouted this immunity almost pugnaciously. For example, in the detailed letter of instructions he wrote to the editorial board of a Hunan provincial gazetteer under his general editorship, he imposed a strict utilitarian standard on inclusion of literary contributions by local worthies: "All poetry and belles lettres on the beauties of nature, and so on, however elegant they may seem to you, you may certainly leave out!"[127]

He followed this advice in his own writing. Indeed, probably the most striking feature of Chen's truly enormous surviving oeuvre is the virtual absence within it of poetry, no less than shocking in an eminent literatus of his era. By my count there are but twelve poems in all his prodigious publications, nearly all of which are occasional pieces that he was clearly called on reluctantly to produce out of social or political obligation. The only verse of any length is a clumsy celebratory ode on the Qianlong emperor's military victories in Xinjiang (adventures that, as we shall see, Chen had personally sought to discourage); two others are birthday greetings addressed to Gaozong himself and to the empress dowager.[128] Only one poem may be construed as purely aesthetic, a quatrain seemingly written at a colleague's request for inscription on that colleague's painting.[129] Chen's corpus likewise contains almost no prose writing of an essentially literary nature. The one exception is a brief commemorative essay in pure classical style on the meaning of the name of a local landmark, composed during his mid-1730s tenure in Yunnan. Even this is not without its utilitarian overtones, however: the landmark's name is the "Pavilion of Sobriety."[130]

Chen's objection to literary pursuits stemmed above all from his sense of outrage that individuals so obviously gifted, and capable of doing so much good for the world, would instead dissipate their energies and talents on the vain and frivolous. His experience in Beijing's Hanlin Academy, home of the empire's best and brightest, coming as it did on the heels of his years in Guilin's own infinitely more humble and workmanlike academies, shocked his sensitivities and heightened his view of the misdirection of contemporary scholarship. For years thereafter he complained in letters to friends that Hanlin students, blessed with unparalleled access to sources on political and economic affairs, wasted their time composing "essays on the wind, clouds, and mist, refined courtly verses which are superfluous trinkets of no use to the management of worldly affairs."[131] And again:

> The Hanlin is where the brightest talents in the country are assembled. . . . Yet in the essays they compose, punctiliously correct as they are in literary style, they all too often forget that writing must have substance. The proper substance is, internally, the cultivation of the moral mind [*xiuxin*], and, externally, the study of economic matters [*jingji*]. . . . How can these fellows waste so much time waxing lyrical about the moon and clouds?[132]

To describe his own aesthetic of nature, Chen cited approvingly the line of Wei Xiangshu: "In admiring a beautiful landscape, I prefer above all the one with altars, graves, productively cultivated fields, and farmers' cottages."[133] Rusticity, yes; pastoralism, not at all.

Beyond wasting the time of otherwise useful public servants, aesthetic pursuits had come, in Chen's view, to subvert the integrity and effectiveness of the bureaucratic corps, as literary elegance increasingly eclipsed administrative skill as a criterion for promotion. Furthermore, if most nature poetry and ornate prose stylings were innocuous wastes of time, at least some literature—that dealing with romantic or erotic subjects—was an active agent of moral corruption, "like the yeast which ferments liquor," and must be shunned with all of one's resolve.[134]

A central theme with which we will be concerned throughout this study is the tension in Chen Hongmou's thought and policies between his support for the hierarchical social order and his quasi-egalitarian populism. At this point we can consider one element in this complex equation, one that was deeply rooted in his psychological makeup and was related to his aversion to artistic pursuits. That would be his frontier-bred, almost knee-jerk antipathy to any form of exclusionary elitist pretense. One cardinal article of faith for Chen was that moral worth transcends social class: "The common people [*xiaomin*] all have within them the goodness of Heaven [*tianliang*]."[135] Moral conduct and even ritual propriety were open to all, and there was no reason to suspect that the rich or well-placed would better fulfill the ethical urges common to all men. Indeed, Chen often voiced his impression that the reverse is true. Decrying the apparent coincidence between idle wealth and deviant behavior, he wrote, "If the night is long, there will be many dreams," and he quoted with approval the dictum "In recognizing good men, look first to the poor, humble, and unlettered."[136] Chen's unusually ready recourse as provincial governor to the sale of civil service degrees for practical administrative needs (see Chapter 8) is indicative of how little sanctity he invested in the Qing empire's preeminent badge of social distinction.

Elegance in personal appearance, like elegance in literary style, was of no value in itself and might indeed cloud honest appraisals of personal worth. Thus, in overseeing provincial examinations, Chen enjoined his subordinates not to be guided by refined dress and manners but to treat candidates with equal respect.[137] Refinement, he insists, is part of the problem, not part of the solution. In a highly revealing passage in his *Sourcebook on Childhood Education* Chen extols the virtue of rustic simplicity, which, as we have seen, he routinely identified as the central distinguishing feature of his own family and local cultural background: "The problem in ancient times was too much rusticity [*pu*]; nowadays, however, it is overmuch refinement [*wen*]. In the past it was necessary to cultivate greater refinement in the people, whereas today it is necessary to reintroduce a dose of rusticity [*fan yifen pu*]. Moreover, this process of rustication [*fanpu*], should start in early childhood. Excesses of refinement [*shiwen*] must be rooted out as soon as possible."[138]

As we have seen, Chen tended to impose a spatial dimension on this problem: core areas of the empire were more *wen*, peripheral areas more *pu*. A basic thrust of his administrative career was to counter elite prejudice against the latter and, to a certain extent, to redress the imbalance. The sharpness of his sensitivity to the unequal distribution of cultural resources, as well as to economic ones, led Chen to a rather unstatesmanlike readiness to stereotype the populations of provinces in which he served. Again, it was his first experience in Beijing, following his passing of the metropolitan examination, that acutely brought home for Chen just how different were the cultural styles of other places from that of his native Guangxi. Beijing society was "gay and dissolute." That of Yangzhou was "consumed by trivialities"—he cited with relish the diatribes on this theme of a disgruntled local native, Shi Dian. Jiangsu people, and especially those of Suzhou, were crafty, disingenuous, and contentious; their competitiveness in consumption and gifting disgusted him. He saw a clear contrast to the "diligent and frugal" (*qinjian*), "rustic and genuine" (*pushi*) population of neighboring Jiangxi and still more to the province that became effectively his second home, Shaanxi. Shaanxi folk were "plain and simple" (*jianpu*), neither devious, litigious, nor corrupt.[139]

It must be stressed that the moral superiority of Shaanxi culture over that of Jiangsu was not, for Chen, a function of its relative freedom from the corruptions of the marketplace; people there are as commercially oriented as those anywhere else—they are simply more honest. Although a trace of antiurbanism may underlie Chen's cultural prejudices, he sees no simple link between population density and the moral character of a regional population; both Shaanxi and Jiangsu are relatively crowded places, Chen claims. Similarly, there is no necessary connection between geographic peripherality and cultural propriety. The Fujianese, the regional group Chen loathes above all others, are so "deceitful and cunning" precisely because of their spatial isolation, whereas peripherality has had largely positive moral effects in his native Guangxi.[140]

To a considerable degree, of course, Chen is simply repeating broadly shared cultural stereotypes, but it is clear that he does so because they resonate so well with his own visceral reactions. When they do not, he tells us so: Hubei people, for example, do not deserve the reputation for stubbornness and querulousness that contemporaries ascribe to them.[141] For an official who sees the role of government as centrally concerned with the moral enlightenment of its population, this willingness to generalize about the cultural styles of the regions in which he serves, and effectively to measure them against the standard of his own place of origin, acts as a crucial springboard for the formation of policy.

Chen Hongmou was a man with an intense sense of mission to put the world in order and to ameliorate the human condition—literally, to "save the world" (*jiushi*).[142] His statements to this effect are often couched in commonplaces of Qing official rhetoric—for example, the duty to repay the trust placed in him by imperial grace (*bao'en*)—but they are often more idiosyncratic. All who knew him recognized that his messianic drive far exceeded that of other bureaucrats. When he wrote that he "accepted the fate of the world as his own responsibility" (*yi tianxia wei jiren*), or that "if any man is denied succor, it is my fault" (*woze*), he was giving voice to the strongly personal nature of his commitment to the public good.[143] This often crushing responsibility was shared by all those of official-literati status—the "men like us" (*wubei*) who figure so frequently in Chen's discourse—but Chen experienced it as a very individual burden. He wrote often of the trust people of his jurisdictions put in his personal ability to care for them, and although he generally avoided invidious comparisons with fellow bureaucrats, he clearly held faith in the uniqueness of his own capacity for governance. This appears, for instance, in his intense concern that reforms or innovations he institutes in a given post survive his own tenure there and in his attention to developing safeguards against their erosion under the anticipated neglect of subsequent incumbents.[144] For a man like Chen Hongmou this was no less than a quest for bureaucratic immortality.

This sense of vocation, of calling, was personal not only in the duty he felt toward others but also in terms of personal self-fulfillment. Already as a teenager Chen had written that failure to distinguish himself from others in terms of his accomplishments would amount to living an "empty life" (*xusheng*).[145] Throughout his career he papered the walls of his office with stories of the great deeds of past officials, constantly exhorting himself to emulate or exceed them.[146] Yet along with this commitment went a poignant acknowledgment of the ultimate impossibility of this self-assigned task of world salvation, the sense of inevitable failure that Thomas Metzger has identified as the "predicament" of the late imperial scholar-official.[147] There are any number of signs, even frank discussions, of this personal angst in Chen's writings. One form this takes is the nagging obsession with the philosophical problem of self (*ji*): How can one have faith in one's own superiority, and strenuously pursue self-fulfillment, recognizing at the same time that the key to this success is precisely the overcoming of self (*keji*)? Another is Chen's running discourse on "tribulation" (*fannan*), his sense of struggle for moral self-improvement (*gongfu*), which clearly borders on the compulsive. Yet a third is the more practical one of how to deal with the career frustrations and vicissitudes of bureaucratic life (*shitu*). We will look in some detail at each of these at later points in this study.

More at issue here is one particular aspect of this generalized anxiety that plagued Chen in midcareer, that is, worry over the inadequacy of his own official performance. Such nagging fears must have been fairly widespread among the more sensitive officials of the day, but in Chen's case they bore a heightened sense both of urgency of situation and of personal obligation. Cumulatively, Chen's letters paint a harrowing picture of the world of official service (*guanchang*) as a world of fear (*kong*): fear of the temptation to relax, fear that one's duties will outrun one's energies, fear that one has overlooked or neglected something critical, the potentially paralyzing fear of the unforeseen consequences of one's initiatives, fear that one's very success in past assignments has bred a complacency that will impede one's current performance.[148] These fears are coupled with the deadening frustration of repeatedly seeing one's best plans turn out differently than one had envisioned.[149] Underlying this complex of attitudes is the intensely painful recognition of an actual expansion in recent times of the range of duties of a given post, a growing complexity of the task that ever more clearly outruns the physical capacities of even the most dedicated and gifted official.[150] Under such conditions Chen's espoused recourse to faith in oneself (*xinwo*), however genuine, is increasingly couched in a rhetoric of desperation.

The consensus of contemporary officialdom seems to have viewed Chen as honest, courageous, and rather disconcertingly energetic but also as stubborn and not a little arrogant. One detractor wrote, "He disposes of official matters, large and small alike, however he sees fit, trusting only to his own presumed superior judgement."[151] For his own part, and despite his network of friends and correspondents, Chen had a tendency to view himself as isolated within the bureaucracy as a result of his own uncompromising integrity. Partly this isolation was a self-imposed administrative expedient: As a self-consciously upright official, Chen moved ostentatiously to seal himself off from access by any acquaintance whose familiarity might give rise to suspicions of influence peddling.[152] To an extent as well, Chen welcomed the solitude such isolation brought him. Claiming in a letter that he preferred to spend his personal time in private study, he boasted, "Compared to frittering away this time each day in meeting with irrelevant people, chitchatting about idle trivialities, this is far more productive!"[153] But even such self-satisfied protestations at times have a hollow ring. As he lamented to a colleague, in midcareer: "The common people, who think of officialdom as so grand a thing, can never understand [our loneliness]. All we can do is be stoic in the face of whatever comes our way, and bear with the chilly isolation that our chosen path of life brings with it."[154]

Neither Chen Hongmou's general consciousness as a member of the mid-Qing bureaucratic elite nor the celebrated array of policy choices to which, in his case, that consciousness gave rise can be fully understood without considering the rather unique individuality he had come to develop by his adult years. The product of a remote, semiperipheral area with a highly self-conscious frontier ethos, and of a compulsively parsimonious and success-driven family that had placed its hopes in him alone, Chen emerged as an unusually severe personality—puritanical, prosaic, obsessed by a sense of calling, and more than a little self-righteous. Other elements of Chen's bureaucratic style that we will observe in what follows—his compulsive thoroughness, for instance, and his passionate attachment to regularity and routine—also unquestionably had deep personal roots. What softened this extreme severity in Chen, even his critics agreed, was a genuine and heartfelt compassion for the common people, as well as a flexible pragmatism about administrative means. It was, I would suggest, this distinctive combination of administrative pragmatism and moral rigidity that located Chen so centrally within the late imperial statecraft tradition.

CHAPTER 2

Politics

CHEN HONGMOU IS OF HISTORICAL INTEREST primarily because of the policy positions he took and because of a style of political action that he came to epitomize. These policies were not generated in a vacuum, however. They were neither unmediated responses to natural or social conditions nor simple outgrowths of a tradition of literati statecraft nor products of Chen's own original genius. They were in part all of these things, of course. But they were also the result of a particular personality with a highly distinctive social background, as we saw in the previous chapter. And they were embedded in a complex web of practical politics. The Qing political system was an enormously sophisticated one, and virtually all political action within it of necessity responded to the system's own demands, and to those of personal and factional alliances, often as much as it did to the needs of the society at large. Chen not surprisingly claimed to be aloof from such partisan concerns, and it may in fact be that he was more free from them than were many of his colleagues. But he was, as we shall see, an astute politician—indeed, had he not been, he could never have lasted as long in Qing politics as he did. In this chapter, then, we will explore Chen's ongoing struggle for positioning within the political system of the mid-Qing empire.

From Yongzheng to Qianlong

We begin with a look at imperial politics. Chen Hongmou, as a high provincial official, was an unmistakable product of the Yongzheng reign who, as it turned out, spent most of his career under another, very different sort of imperial master. This was important not merely because lines of patronage shifted but also because the Yongzheng and Qianlong emperors had different notions of what kind of men their bureaucratic subordinates should be and what kind of relationship emperor and official ought to enjoy. Moreover, as much recent (and not so recent) scholarship has shown, during the first fifteen or so years of his reign the Qianlong emperor systematically reversed the course of policy that had been set by his father and imperial predecessor, in a direction that

Gaozong himself characterized as *kuan* (liberal, magnanimous) rather than *yan* (strict, severe).[1] This period coincided with the most fruitful years of Chen Hongmou's own provincial career. Consequently, in both personality and policy preference, there remained throughout these years an awkward tension between one of the Qing imperium's most able rulers and the man who was arguably that ruler's most able field administrator.

The economic historian Gao Wangling has characterized this policy shift from Yongzheng to Qianlong as an "unfinished experiment" in big government, a Qianlong retreat from the large, well-financed, and highly interventionist state that the Yongzheng emperor had labored aggressively to create.[2] In fact the reorientation was both less simple and more broad-ranging than this—it involved a set of cultural preferences as well as political-economic strategies—but, at least in very general terms, Gao's formulation rings true. That is to say, the relatively weak state that the Qing found itself with when it came to face an expansive and predatory West in the mid-nineteenth century was a deliberate product of the early Qianlong reign and ran counter to what the Yongzheng emperor would have envisioned. Chen Hongmou's own vision of the state, as the remainder of this study will show, was a complex one and probably less interventionist than that of his first imperial patron. But there is no shortage of evidence that his view of benevolent government was considerably more activist than that of the man under whom he ended up serving for most of his career and that, in a variety of ways, Chen offered resistance to the state downsizing that characterized the early Qianlong reign. This was one factor, among others, in the ambivalent and sometimes awkward personal relationship these two very strong-willed men enjoyed.

Two of the most obvious issue areas in which the contrast between Yongzheng and early Qianlong political-economic agendas were played out were those of land reclamation, which we will shortly examine in detail, and of state granaries, which will be the focus of Chapter 8. Both of these witnessed a very deliberate pullback in the level of central government activism in the years from 1736 to 1749. In what follows here we will more briefly survey a variety of other policy areas—economic, cultural, personnel—in which this virtual sea change from Yongzheng to Qianlong was reflected.

Foremost among these was that of local government finance, studied in a landmark 1984 book by Madeleine Zelin.[3] As Zelin shows in detail, Yongzheng was committed to "rationalizing" (her word) such finances, by establishing a budgetary line (*gongxiang*) for local government operations and capital expenses, funded primarily by a newly regularized surtax (*haoxian*) on the land tax. The reform was based on an unprecedentedly frank acknowledgment of the *need* for an expanded state apparatus on the local level; it was intended to provide adequate funding on a routine basis for local administration, while simultaneously allowing, through codification and routine reporting, a greater measure of central oversight of such activities. Zelin concludes, convincingly to my mind, that the Yongzheng reforms were both necessary and workable; in her words, "This marked an important step in the development of a *modern state* [italics mine] in which the concept of government responsibility goes beyond the collection of taxes and the maintenance of public order."[4] But within months of Yongzheng's death his successor was deluged with memorials urging a return to "a nonactivist conception of the role of local administration," reiterating the notion of a fixed economic pie and advocating "storing wealth among the people" (*cangfu yu min*) by a policy of light taxation.[5] It was this advice that Qianlong effectively followed, not by decisively annulling his father's reforms but by steadfastly refusing to allow local administrative budgets to grow so as to keep pace with continuing inflation and population growth.

Although Qianlong must certainly have appreciated the benefits of his father's major tax reforms, the *haoxian guigong* (control of surtaxes and application of them to centrally approved public purposes) and the *tanding rudi* (merger of the head tax and land tax),[6] he chose instead to emphasize their dysfunctional side effects. He portrayed both of these innovations as prompted, at least in part, by an unseemly greed for tax revenues. This ran counter to his grandfather Kangxi's 1713 pledge never to raise tax assessments (*yongbu jiafu*) and his own rather minimalist conception of "benevolent government" (*renzheng*).

A lessened demand for tax revenues was indeed a pervasive theme of the early Qianlong reign. In his first year on the throne the new emperor moved to eliminate hereditary service obligations in certain provinces, which had in the Yongzheng era been commuted to cash and merged into general county tax assessments. That same year he reduced county tax quotas in a number of provinces, in cases where they had been swollen by those counties' recent administrative absorption of *tuntian* (military colonies) and their attendant fiscal liabilities. (In effect the court abrogated its claim to the product of those colonies.) He worked assiduously to eliminate a variety of "contributions" and irregular fees still being levied in many localities, as well as the empire-wide assessment that his father had declared in support of military initiatives on the northwest and southwest frontiers. He rescinded a Yongzheng-era deed and transfer tax on urban real estate and halted a campaign started by his father to enforce the state's salt monopoly against competition by smugglers on the grounds that consumers needed the salt being supplied by the illicit private market. In 1745 he declared an empire-wide tax holiday to celebrate his first decade on the throne, remitting nearly twenty-eight million taels in land taxes. And in the next few years he ordered a series of more localized remissions in the grain tribute.[7]

Many of these moves were in the direction of greater fiscal equitability, but this equitability was in each case achieved at the sacrifice of tax revenues. Indeed, for the most part the Qianlong emperor was loathe to challenge the fiscal advantages enjoyed in practice by entrenched local elites. Yongzheng drives to clear up (*qingcha*) accumulated tax arrears, such as that undertaken in the economically favored Jiangnan from 1729 to 1731, were quietly abandoned in the first years of his successor's reign, and whereas Yongzheng had abolished the legal categories of *ruhu* (Confucian scholar) and *huanhu* (official) households, which carried tax privileges, Qianlong in 1736 immediately ordered reinstatement of gentry exemptions from several categories of taxation.[8] Following the observations of contemporaries, some modern scholars have attributed to such policies a marked concentration of landed wealth in the middle decades of the eighteenth century.[9]

This programmatic shift in political-economic policy can be linked with, indeed better understood in the context of, policy changes in the sociocultural spheres that had little direct economic content. A major example would be racial or ethnic policy. Pamela Crossley has drawn our attention to a major shift from Yongzheng to Qianlong in the way the throne legitimated itself culturally.[10] The Yongzheng emperor held that ethnic particularities were malleable or even illusory characteristics that could be transcended by a homogenizing process of civilization (*hua*), such as that which he and his people had undergone. In his central manifesto on this subject, the 1730 *Dayi juemi lu*, he sought to portray the population under his rule as an undifferentiated whole (*tianxia yijia, wanwu yiti*); geographic locators such as *nei* and *wai* might reasonably be employed to describe distinctions between social groups, in his view, but ethnic or racial typings were merely historically introduced linguistic distortions.[11] One of the very first acts of the Qianlong emperor on his accession, however, was to recall and destroy all known copies of this heretical tract and execute the man (Zeng Jing) whose anti-Manchu activities had called it forth—a man whom his father, to underline his own ethnic cosmopolitanism, had pardoned.[12] By around 1743 Qianlong had firmly reconstructed his identity as a non-Chinese "Manchu," ruler over what Crossley describes as a federated, universal empire comprising distinct and semicorporate national groups.[13] At the other end of the empire, an energetic Yongzheng drive to bring non-Han, indigenous peoples of the southwest into the mainstream of a homogeneous Qing culture, through universal Confucian education and affirmative action quotas in the civil service examinations, was largely reversed under Qianlong on the grounds that these people were incapable of civilization and ought prudently to be left in their hereditary savage state.[14] And within Han China itself, Yongzheng's efforts to achieve linguistic unification by requiring degree holders from non-Mandarin-speaking provinces to pass an examination in "standard pronunciation" (*zhenin*) were quickly rescinded on Qianlong's succession.[15]

Just as the Qianlong emperor was willing to admit far greater cultural diversity within his realm than was his predecessor, so too was he more tolerant of—indeed, *supportive* of—social stratification. The Yongzheng emperor's celebrated initiatives to emancipate various debased social groups were not followed up in the reign of his successor, who, on the contrary, enacted legislation to blunt their impact.[16] Qianlong also made it clear from the outset that he supported literati privilege, not only through the fiscal exemptions already noted but also in the gentry exemption from routine criminal prosecution that he reinstated at the start of his first full year on the throne.[17] Whereas Yongzheng had tended to view extrabureaucratic local elites as competitors in his quest for a more activist centralized state, Qianlong quickly made it clear that he saw them instead as partners in the maintenance of social control. Overall, as one Chinese scholar has recently concluded, the Qianlong emperor had a much more rigidly hierarchical view of the proper social order than had his predecessor, and his early policies worked consistently to strengthen such an order wherever he saw it as having come under threat.[18]

There was also a more ingrained cultural elitism at work. As R. Kent Guy and others have shown, the content of the civil service examinations was reshaped between Yongzheng and Qianlong to accord far greater emphasis to refined prose and poetic style, as well as to esoteric philological questions that required candidates to have en-

joyed access since childhood to the sorts of well-endowed libraries found disproportionately in the empire's wealthiest regions. Through this and other means, the composition of the bureaucracy shifted rather markedly in the early Qianlong reign toward
men of greater wealth and cultural refinement.[19]

Running through selected policy decisions of the Yongzheng and early Qianlong
reigns, as I have just done, admittedly presents an overdrawn sense of contrast. There
were many continuities. There were changing external factors that dictated ad hoc policy adjustments of an unprogrammatic nature. And there were clearly also specific dysfunctions generated by the ambitious and often reckless Yongzheng initiatives that demanded redress by his successor, no matter whom that successor might have been.
Nevertheless, the evidence presented here does to my mind support the view that the
two rulers had systematically differing visions about the nature of the polity they wished
to govern.

The Yongzheng emperor sought a polity within which both ethnic and status distinctions were of diminished significance; the population was to be a relatively uniform
mass of free subjects of the state, which would govern them directly rather than
through elite mediators. The state itself would be unprecedentedly centralized, bureaucratized, and efficient. It would closely monitor the routine processes of the society and economy and would intervene by an unprecedented activism in such areas as
provisioning, education, and public works. This activist state would be financed by a
progressively expanding tax base and a fiscal system that was regularized, standardized,
and centrally controlled. By contrast, the Qianlong emperor moved (or returned) over
the first decades of his reign to a vision of society that was divided into semicorporate
ethnic groups, internally stratified into a hierarchy of privilege, and to a great extent
self-nurturing. His rule was to be universal in scale but far less direct and managerial
than that of his predecessor. His state offered less to, and demanded less of, its subjects.
He was content to see government revenues progressively shrink as a percentage of
total economic output and even, as we shall see in a moment, to let a growing percentage of the empire's wealth simply go unrecorded by the state.

These divergent imperial visions had a direct bearing on the very different sorts of personal relations Chen Hongmou enjoyed with the two monarchs he served. From the
outset of his provincial career Chen was explicitly identified by the Yongzheng emperor
as his own protégé, a hand-picked (albeit junior) member of the corps of "new men"
with which he sought to reconstitute officialdom in the wake of his highly controversial
ascent to the throne. To provide a counterweight to the inherited late Kangxi-era bureaucracy, and because of an active preference on his part, the new ruler sought to promote men from outside established recruitment pools—Manchus from outside the imperial clan, Chinese from outside Jiangnan and other core cultural areas. He wanted
his men to be talented and loyal but not necessarily of high family pedigree. They
should be doers. He was skeptical of profound scholarly achievement (one of his most
trusted Han officials, Tian Wenjing, held only the lowest civil service degree and was all
but boastful of that fact). Yongzheng was a partisan of the non-fussy, moralistic
Confucianism of the Four Books variety and thought his officials should be as well. His

own term for the kind of men he wanted was "*shi*" (substantive)—a term with great resonance for Chen Hongmou and the movement he represented, as we shall see. To
Yongzheng this meant a man with both concrete expertise (he liked men with technical specialties, whom he sought to assign to specialist jobs) and the thick-skinned personal fortitude he believed requisite for bureaucratic effectiveness. A blunt and
brusque man himself, Yongzheng preferred his officials to be the same way. He had an
unusually high tolerance for those who disagreed with him and liked officials who were
not afraid to speak up. He also encouraged disagreement among his officials, provided
they proved capable of working smoothly with each other despite differences over policy. By all of these standards Chen Hongmou was a near perfect specimen of the kind
of man Yongzheng sought.[20]

After passing the palace examination in 1723 Chen had been appointed a bache-
lor (*shujishi*) of the Hanlin Academy. He remained there for three years, with temporary assignments as an editorial assistant on the *Consolidated Qing Gazetteer* (*Qing yitong
zhi*) project and as associate examiner for the Shuntian prefectural examination.[21]
Unquestionably his most significant achievement of these years, however, was his success in cultivating the patronage of the most powerful Chinese official in the realm,
Grand Secretary Zhang Tingyu. Zhang (1672–1755) hailed from a great literati family of Tongcheng, Anhui, but from young adulthood had abjured private scholarship
(such as the *guwen* movement, in which many of his compatriots were beginning to take
leading roles) in favor of government service and a self-conscious focus on practical administration. He had learned the Manchu language and become a trusted advisor in
the so-called inner court (*neiting*), first as a member of the Kangxi emperor's "Southern
Study" and subsequently in the Grand Council (*junjichu*) as it became institutionalized
under Yongzheng; he is said to have drafted many of the latter emperor's key policy
documents.[22] Zhang served as chief examiner for the metropolitan examination of
1723, at which Chen Hongmou received his *jinshi*, and after the exam Chen found the
temerity to pay a personal call on the great man. He invited Zhang to bestow on him a
studio name, and Zhang's choice, "Peiyuan tang," became associated with Hongmou all
his life. While at the Hanlin Academy, Chen's chief duties involved sifting through
archives in the preparation of the *Ming shi* (Ming dynastic history), of which Zhang
Tingyu was editor-in-chief. Chen continued to correspond with Zhang throughout his
subsequent provincial career and wrote a glowing eulogy for him on Zhang's death.[23]

Another eminent official cultivated by Chen during his sojourn at the capital was
Gan Rulai, president of both the Board of Civil Office and the Board of War. Gan had
formerly been governor of Guangxi, and Chen, visiting him in 1723, complimented
him on the great work he had done in patronizing Guizhou's private academies, in raising popular literacy, and in easing tensions between Han and non-Han populations during his tenure there. Again, the junior and senior men remained in communication,
and Chen eventually contributed a preface to Gan's posthumous collected works.[24]

Then in early 1726 Chen received his first big break. Seeking fresh talent, the
Yongzheng emperor announced a program of selecting promising candidates from the
Hanlin, giving them probationary appointments in one of the Six Boards and then
posting the most successful of these directly to high provincial office. Despite the fact

that many of his Hanlin superiors thought poorly of Chen because of his unrefined demeanor, he was one of those selected. Evidently Zhang Tingyu had a hand in this; he is reported to have exclaimed on hearing of Chen's selection, "Young Chen's abilities are so suited for high office that I hated to see him lost in the paperwork of the Hanlin!" Zhang secured Chen's appointment at the relatively high rank of senior secretary (*langzhong*) in the Board of Civil Office, of which Zhang and Gan Rulai were presidents, and put him in charge of screening candidates for provincial treasurer and provincial judge positions.[25]

Chen's next breakthrough came just after the New Year's holiday of 1729. Presidents of each of the boards were ordered by Yongzheng to nominate one of their younger subordinates for an imperial audience so that the throne could determine for itself what the best and the brightest looked like. Zhang Tingyu nominated Chen, and the emperor was delighted with what he saw. Audience notes survive, in Yongzheng's own hand, and include the following comments: "This man is outstanding, to a degree that Zhang Tingyu himself fails to appreciate. . . . In the future we can expect great things from him. . . . He is earnest and fundamentally sound, and has a penetrating understanding of things. It is hard to believe that he is from Guangxi!"[26] Yongzheng cited the fact that Chen had brought his aged parents to live with him in Beijing as testimony to his strong family values and added, "He is said to be good at the horsemanship and archery competitions as well!" At the suggestion of Zhang and of Zhu Shi (on whom more below), the emperor directed that he be granted the rank of prefect and appointed censor for the Zhejiang Circuit.

In this post an incident occurred that, in the view of many contemporaries, effectively made Chen's reputation. Over the course of the early eighteenth century it had become routine for lower-degree holders (*jiansheng*) to hire professional proxies to sit for them in their annual requalifying examinations. On coming to the throne the Yongzheng emperor determined to put an end to this practice. He ordered all the guilty parties to publicly confess, promising imperial pardon for those who complied. Although this decision caused widespread consternation within the bureaucracy, only the novice Zhejiang censor dared speak up. Chen memorialized that Yongzheng's announced solution would be worse than the problem; the spectacle of so many local elites demeaning themselves in public would seriously undermine social order. A better course of action would be to concede that the practice had been nearly universal, issue a blanket pardon for past misdeeds, and simultaneously tighten controls so as to prevent recurrence. The emperor, aghast, summoned Chen back to Beijing for a series of three audiences, during which Chen defended his position and refused to back down. In the end Yongzheng adopted Chen's proposal, praising his "straightforward way of addressing a superior" in defense of the public interest (*yungong*). Bypassing normal procedures, he dispatched Chen to oversee the upcoming Shanxi provincial examination ("If he has such a grasp of the essentials of governance, he can certainly judge an examination essay!") and on his return installed him as Yangzhou prefect, with the continuing—and extraordinary—right to memorialize on any issue he saw fit.[27]

During the next four years, 1729–32, Chen held a number of middle-level posts in the Jiangsu area, culminating with a stint as acting provincial treasurer. This period of service coincided with Yongzheng's prosecution of a major tax clearance campaign in the region, the complex details of which need not concern us here.[28] Chen played a key subsidiary role in this delicate affair, performing so ably that when he ran briefly afoul of a superior in an examination cheating scandal in his jurisdiction, Yongzheng conspicuously dismissed all charges against him. Communications between the two men became quite personal and familiar; clearly, Chen had been singled out as an imperial favorite.[29]

Of even greater long-term importance for Chen, his effective work in Jiangsu won him the patronage of the provincial governor, a young Manchu named Yinjishan, who had been sent to the province with specific instructions to clear up tax arrears and with the explicit understanding that his subsequent career would hinge on his success. Like Chen Hongmou, Yinjishan was a quintessential Yongzheng "new man." Hailing from the relatively obscure Janggiya clan, he had come to Yongzheng's attention initially in storybook fashion—in the course of an assignment from his father, the Kangxi emperor, the then prince Yinzhen had been caught in a rainstorm, taken shelter in Yinjishan's father's house, and been struck by the young man's evident intelligence. Selected by Yongzheng for a fast-track career, Yinjishan had the further good fortune to be affianced to the niece of Ortai, Yongzheng's confidante and, like himself, a highly sinified Manchu of minor noble origin.[30] An exact contemporary of Chen Hongmou (1696–1771), and fellow metropolitan graduate (*tongnian*) of 1723, the two men's careers tracked each other around the empire—the lower Yangzi in the early 1730s, the southwest in the mid-1730s, the northwest in the 1740s, the lower Yangzi again in the 1750s, Beijing as grand secretaries in the 1760s. On countless occasions, as superior and subordinate, as immediate successors in the same region, or as simultaneous incumbents in adjacent jurisdictions, the two worked closely together in support of each other's wide-ranging, highly activist policies.[31]

Yinjishan and Chen Hongmou were routinely spoken of by contemporaries as a pair. According to Chen's biography in the Qing dynastic history, they were held to be the two greatest field officials of the eighteenth century.[32] But they were also seen (by, among others, the Qianlong emperor) as contrasting personality types—the dour, repressed, and prosaic Chen versus the relaxed, outgoing, and urbane Yinjishan, an enthusiastic poet who over many years engaged in a linked-verse correspondence with the Nanjing aesthete Yuan Mei.[33] Chen Hongmou's own regular correspondence with Yinjishan concerned other matters: meditations on scholarly practice, on issues of personal morality, and on the frustrations of a bureaucratic career, as well as discussions of policy questions.[34] They shared an interest in the so-called Shaanxi school of neo-Confucianism (see Chapter 4) and debated the Manchu's efforts at reforming literati prose style.[35] Despite their differences in seniority (Chen always in his letters addressed Yinjishan deferentially), they were clearly close friends. Yinjishan also saw Chen as an indispensable subordinate. When Chen's father died in late winter of 1731, during Chen's Yangzhou tenure, Yinjishan as Jiangsu governor petitioned the throne to allow him to observe mourning while remaining at his post; he did the same again when Chen's mother died the following year.[36] On several subsequent occasions, as we shall see, Yinjishan would be called on to intervene in defense of Chen's threatened political career.

From Jiangnan Chen was reposted in 1733 to Yunnan, as provincial treasurer. It is impossible to overestimate, in my opinion, the importance of the southwest during the Yongzheng years as a testing ground for the "new men" and a crucible for the formation of a bureaucratic cadre that would be in place for decades to come. As Kent Smith and others have shown, Ortai was the spearhead of this empire-building task force, leading the wars of incorporation of aboriginal peoples and beginning the process of wholesale conversion to centralized bureaucratic administration (*gaitu guiliu*) that had only been experimented with in the past.[37] It fell to the next wave of more civilian-minded administrators, however, to establish a viable economic, social, and cultural order that would both facilitate pacification and reduce the region's economic drain on the empire's core provinces. These men included Yinjishan, granted the Yun-Gui governor-generalship in 1733, and others such as Zhang Yunsui, Emida, Huang Tinggui, Zhang Guangsi, Yan Sisheng, and Chen Hongmou. Many of Chen's truly remarkable accomplishments during his four-plus years in Yunnan will be discussed at later points in this study: his establishment of a massive public school system, his extensions of agricultural cultivation and of the hydraulic infrastructure, his establishment of a stage-transport system for military logistics and food supply purposes, his development of the region's rich mineral deposits, and so on. What matters here is the fact that these achievements hardly went unnoticed; they all but guaranteed for him a long and prominent career.

Apart from Yinjishan, the most important champion whom Chen won for himself during these years was Zhang Yunsui, governor of Yunnan. A Han bannerman who held no examination degree, Zhang came to specialize in the affairs of the southwest, where he remained for over thirty years, rising eventually to the rank of grand secretary. He and Chen seem to have been a perfect fit. The junior man acknowledged the influence Zhang exerted on him in defining a provincial administrator's proper range of concerns, and the two continued to correspond about such matters long after Chen had left the southwest. When Zhang died in the early 1750s, Chen wrote an obviously heartfelt epitaph for him, praising his devotion to popular livelihoods (*minsheng*) and his grasp of economics and detailing how these had been applied in practice. For his part Zhang became a vocal and persistent advocate of Chen's abilities. In early 1735 he talked the Yongzheng emperor into issuing Chen a special commendation for his development work in Yunnan, and on being rotated out of the governorship he (unsuccessfully) nominated Chen to succeed him. He continued to pepper the court with "unsolicited" (*zidai*) recommendations for Chen throughout the remainder of his life.[38]

When the Yongzheng emperor suddenly died in October of that year and his newly enthroned successor issued an edict calling for senior officials to suggest suitable persons for promotion, Zhang Yunsui once again singled out above all others the Yunnan provincial treasurer.[39] In accordance with standard practice, Chen submitted his resignation to the new emperor, formulaically requesting to "retire to his native place and care for his aged parents" (they had, of course, already died); unsurprisingly, given the endorsements of Zhang and other high officials, the new ruler chose to retain Chen in place.[40] As it turned out, however, Chen's dealings with the Qianlong emperor were never to be as warm and untroubled as they had been with Yongzheng. Qianlong had strained relations with many Yongzheng holdovers, of course, identified as they were with a personality and a style of governance he found basically uncongenial. But Chen—fifteen years older than Gaozong and a forty-year-old veteran bureaucrat when the young adult prince assumed the throne—proved more tricky to deal with than many other inherited officials, who could either be discarded or remade along lines Qianlong preferred. Chen Hongmou was so spectacularly successful in the field that Qianlong quickly discovered he could not do without him yet so self-righteously devoted to his own ways of doing things that Gaozong could never feel he had made him his own. The new emperor, as one scholar has concluded, came rather quickly to develop a "complex" about his star provincial official.[41]

This ambivalence is most tellingly revealed in the imperial audience question. Fairly shortly after Qianlong's succession, he came to utilize the multitalented Chen as a provincial troubleshooter. Chen's gubernatorial transfers usually came quite suddenly, as he was needed to deal with food supply emergencies, or revive collapsing hydraulic structures, or handle urgent minority relations problems, or manage logistics for impending military campaigns, or clear up critical litigation gluts, or simply rescue a province mired in maladministration. Often he would be diverted to one hot spot while just en route to another. At such times Qianlong expressed great faith in Chen, imploring him to "carry out this task with your best efforts, and don't bother to await specific instructions from Me."[42] But there was another side to this imperial haste. Although it was customary for an official of Chen's rank to be granted an imperial audience in transit from one post to another, over a course of nearly thirteen years and more than a dozen provincial transfers, between 1744 and 1757, Chen saw his emperor but once. Gaozong would either deny him an audience outright, on grounds that he was needed in his new post, or tantalize him by initially granting an audience and then redirecting him elsewhere just as he approached Beijing. Chen repeatedly whined and pleaded to be received during this long interval, and the whole matter took on a distinct comic opera quality. Reading the correspondence involved, one cannot escape the conclusion that the emperor, much as he valued Chen's service in the field, just did not want to be troubled in person by this difficult man.[43]

And Chen could indeed be obstinate. Like many another eighteenth-century provincial official, concerned over the livelihoods of his constituents and relatively development-minded, he frequently found himself at loggerheads with more conservative officials at the Board of Revenue over issues of mine openings, expanded foreign trade, and so on. Chen was hardly averse to pulling end runs around the board, presenting his case directly to the throne and, on occasion, having a board ruling overturned by imperial fiat (as happened, for example, in the matter of selling civil service degrees for grain in Jiangxi in 1742).[44] He was also willing, when his basic policy premises were challenged, to tell the throne itself what he well knew it did not want to hear; we will later see instances of this in the matters of granary quota reductions and of military campaigns in the northwest. Chen did not back off from hardheaded negotiations with his sovereign over policy implementation. We have already seen him rather precociously doing so with Yongzheng in the student requalification scandal of 1729. Qianlong, who was less receptive to challenges from his officials, required more tact. Yet by the latter years of Chen's career we not infrequently find him engaging in scrappy back-and-forth policy debate with Gaozong as well, at least sometimes bringing the emperor around to a position he had initially dismissed.[45] What we do *not* find in Chen, of course, is even the slightest hint of a more fundamental critique of imperial autocracy; if he ever felt uncomfortable with this in private, he was far too loyal and career-minded a public servant to let it on.

Gaozong's correspondence with Chen perfectly epitomizes the wheedling style that Philip Kuhn has found in his relations with all his provincial officialdom: alternately admonishing, cajoling, and exhorting, all in the most personal and familiar of tones.[46] Kuhn cites one instance from 1762 in which Qianlong tweaked Chen and Yinjishan, publicly lambasting them for favoritism, do-nothingness, and a slovenly work style in Jiangnan—attributes he well knew to be uncharacteristic of either man.[47] In another representative case (more will be encountered later), in 1753, Fujian governor Chen and his superior, Viceroy Karjishan, memorialized regarding their failure to capture a local bandit and were greeted with an acid vermilion rescript accusing them of covering up inaction with slickly phrased excuses (*wuwen zhi pi*). When they memorialized once more to apologize, Gaozong exploded that the imbecilic Karjishan would only do so because he was being hoodwinked by his subordinate, Chen, who was too "guileful" (*yongqiao*) for anyone's good.[48]

At other times, however, Qianlong was full of praise. Rescripts on Chen's memorials include phrases such as "this is extremely satisfying to me" (*shen shu tuoxie*), a comment Gaozong used only at his most enthusiastic, and "sincere without the slightest duplicity" (*cheng yi buqi*), an imperial observation that became associated with Chen ever after in bureaucratic folklore. Or the following: "If only all My officials were like you [the intimate "*ru*" form of address], and oversaw things with such genuine diligence!" Or again: "Chen Hongmou in this matter does not fret about trivialities, like an old woman. This is precisely how field administration *ought* to be conducted!"[49] As Hongmou's career progressed, he ever more frequently received the sorts of gifts Gaozong employed to show favor to his most trusted officials—samples of his calligraphy, deer meat from the imperial hunt, ointments and medications demonstrating concern for their health, birthday greetings to the official's senior relatives, and, on at least three occasions, samples of imperial verse penned especially to celebrate Chen's achievements.[50] Chen's correspondence home during his Beijing tenure of the late 1760s finds the two venerable statesmen chatting intimately about the health of family members and Chen presenting both his nephew and grandson to the monarch.[51] The most telling mark of imperial favor, though, came in early 1758, when Gaozong took the extraordinary step of suspending the law of avoidance, allowing Chen to serve as governor-general of his own native province, Guangxi. "In his long tenure in provincial service," wrote the emperor, "Chen has earned My deepest trust."[52]

Crisis: The Guangxi Land Scam of 1733–1737

During the course of his bureaucratic career, Chen Hongmou suffered a number of reversals of fortune—impeachments, demotions in grade, removals from office—of the sort that must have been well nigh inevitable for one whose term of service was so lengthy. The first of these was by far the most dramatic and very nearly ended his career as it was just getting underway. Because of the complex way this affair combined the factors of personal politics and basic imperial policy, it will repay our study in some detail. The issue in question was the clearing for productive (and taxable) use of new farmland, a process known in the Qing administrative lexicon as "reclamation," or "*kaiken*."[53]

Kaiken had been a central thrust in Qing economic policy making since the dynasty's founding in 1644, initially to achieve economic recovery from the military devastations of the dynastic transition and to reestablish the central government's fiscal base. A wide variety of programs—including the establishment of military colonies (*tuntian*); granting of loans of seed, tools, and livestock; and declaring tax holidays for several years on new or resettled farmland—marked the dynasty's first eighty years.[54] Throughout this era government policy was fixed on the goal of recovering both the productive acreage and the fiscal yield recorded in the last complete Ming cadastral survey prior to the dynastic collapse, the *Fuyi quanshu* of 1581. Indeed, by assigning its local officials tax quotas based on these figures, well in advance of their achievement in fact, the Qing provided strong material incentive to these officials to promote reclamation. And in his famous 1713 edict pledging never to raise tax assessments (*yongbu jiafu*), the Kangxi emperor stood by this goal.[55] Announcing that the 1581 levels had finally been reachieved, he expressed his doubt that much further acreage remained to be exploited. In any case this now-recovered fiscal base was fully adequate to his dynasty's needs. Should new lands fortuitously be reclaimed, they ought to be reported, but local officials need no longer trouble themselves with deliberate initiatives to uncover or develop new taxable acreage.

This attitude changed dramatically with the accession of the ambitious Yongzheng. Yongzheng came to the throne in 1722 as a mature adult who had for some years watched with alarm the growth of what might be termed the Qing's dilemmas of prosperity. Political stability and economic development over the course of the dynasty had been so successful, in his view, that population had grown to historically unprecedented levels, necessitating a frantic search for new sources of food. Accordingly, in a pivotal edict of 1723 Yongzheng reopened with even greater intensity the central government's *kaiken* campaign, ordering provincial and local officials to step up their efforts to promote private land reclamation.[56] He stressed that no official compulsions on developers or settlers would be tolerated; reclamation was to be wholly voluntary, and decisions over which new lands might be productively cultivated were best left to the cultivators themselves. On the other hand, he demanded that officials remove any active disincentives to potential developers, such as the local government "reclamation fees" then in effect in many areas. I think it is fairly clear that food supply was genuinely Yongzheng's foremost concern, but he was also a state-maker of the highest order, and

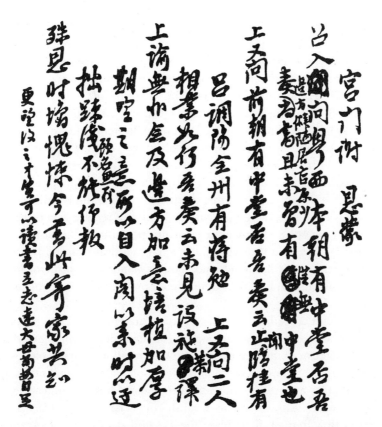

FIGURE 4. A sample of Chen Hongmou's casual calligraphy, drawn from a letter home to Guilin dated QL 29/9/11. Chen reports a bit of dialogue from an imperial audience on the occasion of his appointment as grand secretary. The Qianlong emperor inquires whether there has ever before been a grand secretary from Guangxi; Chen responds that during the present dynasty there has not but that during previous dynasties there had been two. Source: *JS* 45.

he had no intention of letting new productive farmland go untaxed. The tax holidays he decreed for new lands in 1723—six years for paddy and ten for dry fields—were somewhat more liberal than those formerly on the books. Yet, contrary to the evident spirit of Kangxi's 1713 edict, Yongzheng made it clear that registration of new farmland and payment of taxes at the expiration of the period of exemption was to be strictly enforced. He underlined this message in a subsequent edict of 1727, in which he pronounced himself satisfied with the pace of new reclamation but suspicious of the growing incidence of nonreporting of new lands on the parts of both cultivators and local officials reluctant to increase their jurisdiction's annual tax quota. He accordingly resurrected a policy of 1689 under which "secretly reclaimed" (*yinni*) farmland might be voluntarily reported (*shoubao*) in return for an amnesty on past taxes due during its period of concealment.[57]

According to calculations derived by Peng Yuxin from Board of Revenue archives, reports of newly reclaimed land rose in direct response to imperial initiatives as Yongzheng's provincial subordinates began to comprehend his shifting concerns.[58] None was more sensitive in this regard than Ortai, governor general of southwestern Yunnan and Guizhou, and Yongzheng's favorite field official. In a sequence of correspondence exchanged during 1726 and 1727, Ortai and his emperor worked out what became known as the "Yunnan model" of land development.[59] Although many details of this system remain unclear, in essence it involved the contracting out of large tracts of land to lower gentry (*guansheng*), special political appointees (*weiyuan*), or local officials. These contractors would make "contributions" to the provincial administration in exchange for development rights, subdivide their holdings, and recruit tenant cultivators, usually from outside the province, who would receive government loans of "working capital" (*gongben*) to finance the clearing and initial cultivation of their plots. When and if the land proved productive, the tenant cultivator would be granted title (in return for acceptance of immediate tax liability), and the contractor would be rewarded with an honorific rank or title, determined on the basis of acreage successfully reclaimed.

There were rough precedents for this sort of arrangement in Qing history, and the results had never been good.[60] But the imperial state was just then engaged in a strenuous effort to displace or domesticate the southwestern aboriginal peoples, with several of whom it was actively at war, and there were clear political advantages to be gained by introducing sedentary agriculture and extraprovincial Chinese homesteaders. (Note that the Chinese term "*kaiken,*" like its English counterpart *reclamation*, linguistically masks a process that frequently involves the forceful displacement of one land-use regime—and often, correspondingly, one people—by another.) At the same time, government efforts to exploit the mineral resources of the southwest had introduced waves of nonagricultural migrants, making it imperative to step up food production in this chronically grain-deficient region. This combination of political and economic concerns made Ortai's unorthodox scheme appear worth the risk.

Chen Hongmou became involved in this issue when Ortai's programs for Yunnan and Guizhou began to be expanded to his native province of Guangxi. Guangxi lies just east of this Yunnan-Guizhou region, along the Sino-Vietnamese border. It shared with the southwest a large aboriginal highland population and had periodically witnessed spillovers of the military campaigns from adjacent Guizhou. It too was a frontier area of recent and continuing Han Chinese immigration. There was one key difference, however. Whereas Yunnan and Guizhou always depended largely on imports of food, Guangxi as we have seen had already by this time developed into a major grain export area, principally feeding the commercially cropped Canton delta.[61] Along with this there had emerged in the province a class of moderately wealthy, capitalist-style grain farmers.

Yongzheng's initial promotion of *kaiken* empire-wide had not gone unnoticed in Guangxi.[62] Li Fu, a celebrated and controversial writer whose volatile political career included a brief tenure as Guangxi governor, had memorialized in 1724 that despite waves of immigration and agricultural development in recent decades, much good land remained unreclaimed. Li systematically outlined a variety of factors that had impeded an even more rapid extension of cultivation, including ignorance of the techniques of upland farming, the fear of expropriation of newly reclaimed land by local magnates, and anxiety over resulting tax liabilities. He proposed an equally impressive program of provincial government initiatives to overcome these impediments.[63] But, perhaps because of Li's administrative ineptness or his rapid transfer out of the province, little came of his proposals, and Guangxi remained in the rear of the empire-wide *kaiken* campaign.[64]

This began to change in 1729, in the wake of an attempt by Yongzheng to jump-start his faltering program. In an edict of that summer the emperor ordered each province to draw up comprehensive proposals for bringing all possible land under cultivation. Officials were to identify local people who were willing and able to reclaim land, but lacked financial resources, and offer them the necessary loans of cash, grain, and livestock out of local public funds (*cunyong yingu*). These loans were to be repaid on a three-year schedule, and the six-year tax exemption rule would apply.[65]

For Guangxi Yongzheng now had special plans. Late that year he incorporated that province into the governor-generalship of Yunnan and Guizhou, held by Ortai. Just after New Year's day of 1730, that earnest official submitted a lengthy report describing impressions gleaned during a tour of his new jurisdiction, writing in glowing terms of its potential for economic development. About reclamation he had this to say:

> The land of Guangxi is fertile, broad, and level. It takes second place to none of the interior provinces. Previous claims that it was all steep and dangerous terrain were nothing but bunk. In passing through Liuzhou and Binzhou departments I saw no fewer than hundreds of thousands of *mu* of potentially cultivable land, and local official Zhang Pu tells me the actual amount is several times this. Such a waste of the land's potential is truly deplorable! Last year, Governor Jin Hong visited me in Canton and suggested a plan to develop this land along the military colony [*tuntian*] model. I responded that a better idea might be to open it for civilian *kaiken*. . . . Now that I have seen the land myself, I realize how feeble are the results that have been achieved so far. It is absolutely essential that a serious reclamation program be implemented at once.[66]

Ortai went on to suggest that there had been considerable unreported reclamation by wealthy Guangxi farmers in the past, and in order to put this on the tax rolls he ordered a detailed investigation of all land titles and contracts in county archives. He further directed a systematic survey of all fallow land, grading it in terms of potential cultivability, and ordered active solicitation of developers.

As the passage just quoted implies, Guangxi governor Jin Hong was Ortai's candidate to head up this reclamation program, and, if he was less than satisfied with Jin's progress to date, he had general confidence in his abilities. A Han bannerman of the Bordered Red Banner and possessor of only the lowest civil service degree (and that very likely by purchase), Jin Hong was a quintessential Yongzheng "new man." He had risen rapidly in the bureaucracy under the personal patronage of the emperor, who had groomed him as a specialist in the problems of frontier areas. In the first year of his governorship Jin had scored considerable success in bringing to Guangxi the copper-mining boom first begun in Yunnan.[67] In late 1729, however, he had aroused the pique of his imperial patron, who, although continuing to profess admiration for Jin's initiative and local expertise, was growing increasingly exasperated by his lack of decorum in correspondence (even by relatively rough-hewn Yongzheng standards) and his slovenly style of record keeping. At this critical juncture it was Ortai who had interceded in Jin Hong's behalf, insisting that, although Jin's educational level left something to be desired, there was no man better suited to the task of developing Guangxi's agrarian economy.[68]

Jin Hong thus clearly had something to prove to his disgruntled emperor and his newfound champion, Ortai. He sought to do this by turning his attention to *kaiken* with a vengeance. On receipt of imperial approval he set out to apply to his province the "Yunnan model," under which gentry degree-holders would contribute funds in exchange for grants of land to be developed by individual settler-households whom they would recruit.[69] When the initial response proved only modest, Jin secured imperial permission to kick in the other half of the Yunnan program, the dispensation of start-up capital (*gongben*) from local government accounts. But when even this failed to generate sufficient action, Jin added a new twist of his own.

The new scheme was originally the brainchild of Jin's subordinate, Provincial Treasurer Zhang Yue. In early 1732, just as the scheduled auction of land development rights was winding down, Zhang informed Jin that he had struck a deal with one Pan Zhi for the reclamation of some three thousand *mu* of "wasteland" in Lingui County, just outside the provincial capital. Pan was a former magistrate of Guangxi's Lipu County (and hence necessarily of non-Guangxi origin) who had been relieved and degraded for a succession of offenses, including promotion of corrupt subordinates and racketeering by his relatives. As a reward for undertaking *kaiken* responsibility, Zhang recommended that Pan be restored to his official rank, under an old statutory provision known as *yingtian kaifu* (restoration of rank in exchange for donations of land to the needy). This provision had been invoked periodically in Guangxi but never in conjunction with a land reclamation campaign. Jin Hong thus requested, and received, imperial approval for restoration of Pan to his former rank of county magistrate. The case became a model for Guangxi *kaiken* thereafter, with dozens of degraded officials and gentry of extraprovincial origin invited in to develop new land.

The scheme must have appeared virtually ideal. Elites of tarnished reputation would be granted the opportunity to achieve rehabilitation through an act of manifest public service; hard-working cultivators would be granted titles to land that they otherwise could not afford; and the state would receive both cash contributions and an almost immediate rise in tax revenues. (Recall that under the Yunnan system reclaimed land would immediately go on the tax rolls rather than enjoying a protracted tax holiday, this being the price paid by settler households in return for their receipt of land title.) Even better, the scheme appeared to work in practice. Jin Hong reported in 1735 that whereas only 20,880 *mu* of land had been reclaimed under the first year of the Yunnan system's operation in Guangxi, once the *kaifu* (restoration of rank) provision had been incorporated, more than three times this amount of new acreage had been added. As a bonus, nearly half a million taels of silver had been received in the form of contributions by his provincial treasury.[70]

But if all three of these parties—the administration, the degraded extraprovincial gentry, and the settler households—appeared to benefit from this system, one other group felt itself the object of plunder: the existing landed elite of Guangxi. This group rapidly came to mobilize itself in an effort to expose what it saw as the massive fraud underlying the governor's scheme, and by early 1733 it had found a champion in the highest-ranking official in the empire of Guangxi birth, Yunnan provincial treasurer Chen Hongmou.

The thirty-eight-year-old Chen proved a devastating adversary for Jin Hong. As we have already seen, Chen was a man of immense energy, self-confidence, and political will. Like Jin himself, he was a not overly refined product of the cultural periphery who had been personally spotted by the Yongzheng emperor and groomed for service in key positions of trust; like Jin, as well, he was seen by his monarch as best suited for a specialization in frontier affairs. Even more than Jin, he had scored celebrated successes in his first few official tenures, and, most critically, he had done a far better job of developing a network of powerful political patrons and allies. Not least among these were Grand Secretary Zhu Shi and Ortai's own affinal nephew, Yinjishan.

Chen Hongmou's distaste for Jin Hong's heavy-handed administration of his native province had clearly been growing for some time. As early as 1730 he had memorialized from his post in Jiangsu, protesting what he saw as the exploitative and economically irrational way Jin had handled the opening of copper mines in Guangxi.[71] When Chen was finally released from his duties to return home and oversee his parents' burial, in the winter and spring of 1732–33, he immediately assumed a leadership role in the local community by spearheading reconstruction of an irrigation system in his native district.[72] As a resident and major landholder in Lingui County, site of Provincial Treasurer Zhang's first experiment with the *yingtian kaifu* incentive program, Chen had direct opportunity to observe its baleful results. As he wrote to a neighbor, Yang Xingting: "Land falsely reported as 'reclaimed' in our township alone totals no less than several hundred thousand *mu*. I am now at the point of launching an exposé of this activity, in the hopes of reversing the process. I cannot bear to permit such an outrage to occur in this small piece of barren land, which cannot support so many livelihoods."[73] When he received his appointment as Yunnan provincial treasurer, and with it the right once again to memorialize the throne, Chen had his chance. He fired off his first attack on Jin Hong's policies even before leaving to take up his duties in the southwest.

Strictly speaking, of course, it was thought improper for officials to presume on their privilege of memorializing to pursue the parochial interests of their home area. But there was also a sense in which the throne relied on just such information to monitor the performance of its field administrators. In 1729, for example, Yongzheng had gone so far as to systematically canvass Chen and other officials of Guangxi origin on their reaction to a piece of moral legislation instituted in their native province by a newly appointed education commissioner.[74] And there were also known instances of officials being cashiered for failing to report on irregularities back home, on the presumption that if they failed to blow the whistle on widespread corruption in their native province, they must be in on the take.[75] So Chen must have felt on fairly secure ground in this instance.

Chen's memorial of April 1733 was a sweeping indictment of Jin Hong's land reclamation program in Guangxi, but it was couched in cautious language that avoided any
direct allegation of gubernatorial malfeasance.[76] Beginning with an expression of
thanks to the emperor and to Ortai for their concern with the livelihoods of "border
people" such as his fellow provincials, he went on to identify five specific areas of the
kaiken drive that required intensified scrutiny. First, under the Yunnan system, when
working capital was issued to new cultivators, a time limit was imposed for their making
the land productive; if the deadline was not met, the land was not placed on the tax
rolls and might be reassigned to another prospective cultivator. This provision was not
being followed in Guangxi. Second, when land for reclamation was appraised for future tax assessments, site inspections should be undertaken to determine its actual productivity, rather than relying on outdated and arbitrary classification schedules. Third,
when the developer claimed that reclamation had been accomplished, this should be
independently verified. Fourth, it was necessary to ensure that extraprovincial degraded officials and gentry actually involved themselves in the reclamation projects for
which they had contracted. One means of encouraging this would be to demand that
their "contribution" to provincial accounts be made in grain rather than silver, as in
current Guangxi practice. Finally, Chen suggested that land accepted by the government as "reclaimed" be limited to that in bona fide grain production; excuses for the
manifest failure to cultivate, such as that the land was being used for pasturage or gathering of ramie and other grasses, should be considered unacceptable.

Chen did not spell out in his memorial what he clearly believed to be the case: that
Guangxi was the site of a major racket in the *kaiken* business. Certificates of restoration
of rank were simply being sold for cash, by reclamation bureau managers, to extraprovincial miscreants who had no intention of reclaiming any land whatsoever.
Cultivation rights to patently uncultivable land would then be issued to supposed settler households, along with grants of "working capital," with which, presumably, they
would simply abscond. But the district's, and ultimately the province's, aggregate land
tax assessment would rise in direct proportion to the amount of "contributions" taken
in by the treasury.

The liability for Jin Hong and his cronies would of course be that in future years
they would be required to produce artificially inflated tax quotas, but they knew just
where to come up with the needed additional revenue. Simultaneously with their auction of rank-restoration certificates, they undertook a search for "hidden land," paddy
actually developed over the years by landholders participating in Guangxi's rice-export
boom but allegedly never reported for tax purposes. This land was then labeled as
newly reclaimed, and its owners' tax assessments increased accordingly. It was therefore
this established landed elite—those persons whom Chen Hongmou described as "the
people" (*minjian*)—who were made to bear the cost of the entire reclamation scheme,
from which they alone received nothing.

Chen must have been highly gratified by the response his memorial received from
the throne. In a terse rescript the Yongzheng emperor ordered a thorough investigation of the Guangxi case by the incoming governor-general—that is, Chen's patron
and friend Yinjishan. Now suddenly put on the defensive, Jin Hong used the occasion

of his year-end *kaiken* report for 1734 to construct a systematic apologia, in anticipation of Yinjishan's forthcoming report.[77] Although never explicitly acknowledging that his conduct was under investigation, he made sure in narrating the history of his policies to specify that at every stage he had acted only under Ortai's orders and with prior written approval from the throne.[78] He reiterated that he had been pushed to each new stage of policy innovation by the slow progress of the preceding one and attributed this slow progress to a variety of factors. First, there was the resistance of local custom to new modes of upland cultivation, the factor identified a decade earlier by Governor Li Fu. Second, he conceded that there really was rather little good new land to be reclaimed in the province; in so doing he for the first time threw in doubt the rosy depiction of expanses of rich virgin land presented by Ortai, and eagerly accepted by the Yongzheng emperor, and edged a bit closer to Chen Hongmou's own position. But whereas Chen would have preferred to attribute all of Jin Hong's problems to his attempt to curry political favor by squeezing blood out of a stone, Jin went on to elaborate yet a third, and in his view most critical, obstacle to his land development program: the devious and self-serving behavior of Guangxi landed elites, including certain "illustrious officials" (*xianhuan*) like the unnamed Chen Hongmou himself.

Jin pointed out that the very smallness of the numbers of gentry in this remote province disproportionately increased their grip on local society. For years these local big shots had engaged in a pattern of bullying and deception at the expense of both the *real* common people (*baixing*) and the state, including widespread tax fraud and outright expropriation of the land of the defenseless poor (this too had been hinted at earlier by Li Fu). No wonder the gentry were so up in arms about his reclamation projects! It was precisely at such times of unusual government oversight (and Jin pointed out here that his own intelligence on local land conditions had been gathered by extensive interviews with tenant farmers, not elites) that such patterns of past misconduct came to light.

But whatever impact Jin Hong's countercharges might have had was negated when Yinjishan's investigative report came in the following month. The report was extraordinarily thorough, and it was all bad news for Jin.[79] Yinjishan agreed with Chen Hongmou's indictment point by point; although he claimed to have interviewed Provincial Treasurer Zhang Yue and other officials, the text of the report strongly suggests that Chen and his network of fellow landholders must have been its major source. The level of detail provided is highly convincing and the details themselves quite fascinating, but we cannot linger on them here. In essence Yinjishan found massive false reporting of "reclaimed" land, labeled the *kaifu* incentive scheme a "hoax," and identified a number of specific rackets not hinted at in previous correspondence. He gently suggested that Ortai's methods of appraising the potential for reclamation of Guangxi land, and of assessing taxes on grades of marginal land, were naive; he supported instead those methods outlined by Chen. The entire provincial administration was found guilty of gross negligence in providing oversight for the local-level reclamation bureau managers, whom Yinjishan characterized as "thugs" (*tugun*). He concluded that the whole idea of relying on extraprovincial carpetbaggers with a demonstrated lack of integrity was simply foolhardy, and he recommended a blanket removal from the tax rolls of land reclaimed under this program, pending independent verification of its genuine productive cultivation. The emperor turned Yinjishan's report over to the Board of Revenue for deliberation, without comment.

On October 18, 1735, the progress of the investigation was thrown into new uncertainty when the Yongzheng emperor unexpectedly died. Before the year was out his successor, Qianlong, had acted decisively to declare his own position on the empire-wide *kaiken* drive, a position that, as we shall see, was far from optimistic. For the moment, however, let us keep our sights trained on developments in Guangxi.

In early summer of 1736 the Board of Revenue announced its concurrence with Yinjishan's finding that there were vast amounts of land in that province falsely reported as reclaimed, and commanded newly installed Governor-general Emida, along with Jin Hong, to work out the best means to rectify the situation.[80] This was not satisfactory to Chen Hongmou, who was no doubt both anxious, lest the imperial transition diminish the triumph he had already achieved, and hopeful of capitalizing on the new emperor's expressed reservations about *kaiken* in general. He submitted a second memorial on what he now felt confident in terming the "great corruption" (*dabi*) in Guangxi and explicitly impeached Jin Hong for his part in it.[81] Making special reference to his home county of Lingui, Chen sought to emphasize just how much land ought to be stricken from the tax rolls. He knew of one tract of two hundred thousand *mu* reported as reclaimed, of which not a single *mu* was actually in cultivation. Moreover, most of the new land that had actually yielded a harvest was so marginal that within a year or two he could confidently predict a decline in productivity almost to nil. This too should not be taxed. Most urgently, Chen wished to point out that Jin Hong, with characteristic laxity, had simply turned the job of investigating falsely reported land over to *lijia* tax farmers and other local miscreants. (As throughout the course of the dispute, Chen as native elite and Jin as non-native bureaucrat revealed deep divisions on the issue of just who in local society could be trusted to serve the public interest.) "How," Chen complained, "can the investigation of past misdeeds be accomplished in such a way?"

For his part Jin Hong took the path of many another beleaguered politician: He found a scapegoat. He memorialized that Provincial Treasurer Zhang Yue, who had concocted the *kaifu* scheme in the first place, wished to retire because of age and infirmity. In early fall the throne allowed Zhang to do so, replacing him with Yang Xifu.[82] (More bad news for Jin: Yang and Chen Hongmou were like-minded officials who had already begun to develop a great mutual respect for one another.)[83] Two weeks later the news was even worse. Jin was summoned to the capital for an imperial audience, with his gubernatorial records subpoenaed for audit by the Board of Punishments. A midlevel metropolitan official, Yang Chaozeng, was ordered to proceed to Guangxi to assume the acting governorship, with Yang Xifu fulfilling those duties pending his arrival.[84] It was all downhill from there. Shortly after New Year's in 1737, newly arrived governor Yang Chaozeng impeached Jin for a variety of fiscal offenses unrelated to the land scam, and when the Board of Punishments at first recommended leniency for Jin on the grounds that his crime was more incompetence than venality, the Qianlong emperor angrily disagreed. He personally ordered Jin put in the cangue and publicly beaten. Then, when the final report on Guangxi *kaiken* came in, submitted in late 1737 by Viceroy Emida and Governor Yang Chaozeng, it found Jin culpable for all the irregularities Chen Hongmou had alleged.[85] It was only in 1740 that Qianlong's wrath abated enough to order Jin Hong granted a probationary appointment to the lower post of Henan provincial treasurer, but unfortunately it was discovered that Jin had already died.[86]

The Guangxi experience was replicated in much of the empire during the 1720s and 1730s. The Yongzheng emperor's urgent emphasis on land reclamation, out of concerns both for his population's food supply and his imperial tax coffers (the formulaic paired goals of *guoji minsheng*), in practice put unrealistic pressure on field administrators to produce reports of new taxable farmland. Provincial governors in turn put pressure on county-level subordinates, who devised a variety of stratagems to further pass this pressure along to the local population. The results certainly included an appreciable increase in the empire's genuine total arable land and grain production but also an epidemic of false reporting and a crippling pattern of mutual deception and recrimination between administration and society, as well as among levels of administration. Many provinces witnessed a variant of the particular dysfunctions seen in Guangxi: a flurry of bogus reporting of new land, coupled with an equally frenetic search to "uncover" for tax purposes land previously developed by local landholders, with the intent of making these landholders bear the burden (*baopei*) of a rapidly rising aggregate tax quota. Because it had adopted the Yunnan model, under the terms of which the normal six-to-ten-year tax holiday was reduced to one, Guangxi experienced societal resistance more suddenly and dramatically than elsewhere. But in other provinces, whose compliance with Yongzheng's directives had been more prompt, the approaching end of the exemption period brought similar choruses of local elite protest.[87]

Already by the last years of the Yongzheng reign these protests had begun to be heeded by the throne, as the imperial commissioning of Yinjishan's investigation in Guangxi suggests. A 1734 directive of the Board of Revenue reflected this newfound sensitivity, identifying the problem of "overreporting" of reclaimed land (*baoduo kenshao*) as perhaps as serious a problem as the "underreporting" (*kenduo baoshao*) it had been decrying for years.[88] One Chinese scholar has suggested that the Yongzheng emperor himself might have taken dramatic action to clean up the mess in the last years of his life had not the interests of so many of his most loyal supporters been at stake.[89] The imperial succession removed all such obstacles to reform.

The young Qianlong emperor came to the throne already committed to a broad-ranging policy shift that would "relax" (*kuan*) many of the excessively "rigorous" (*yan*) initiatives that had marked his father's reign, *kaiken* policies foremost among them. But his immediate initiative to act in this case came in the form of a memorial from the septuagenarian Grand Secretary Zhu Shi (1665–1736), submitted within a month of Qianlong's accession to the throne.[90] Zhu's critique of *kaiken* policy empire-wide was so comprehensive and well informed that it seems certain he was acting as spokesman for broadly shared literati opinion; his uniquely personal relationship to the new ruler (Zhu had been Qianlong's childhood tutor and was expressly recalled from retirement to serve as his personal advisor during the transition) suggests that his memorial came at imperial initiative itself. Zhu Shi was also, it should be added, one of those high metropolitan officials whom Chen Hongmou had assiduously cultivated during his years in Beijing in the 1720s. Zhu had been chief examiner jointly with Zhang Tingyu on the metropolitan examination where Chen received his *jinshi* (Chen thereafter referred to him as "my teacher" [*wushi*]) and had been Chen's direct supervisor on the *Ming History* project at the Hanlin. As we shall see later, he had come to exert a formative influence on Chen, both in selecting intellectual models (Sima Guang, Lü Kun, Wang Fengchuan, and the "Shaanxi school") and in seeking out inviting areas of policy innovation. In the preface Chen wrote for Zhu's posthumous collected works, he extolled the "genuineness" of his character, of his scholarly practice (*shixue*—see Chapter 4), and of his economic policies (*jingji*).[91]

Citing reports of massive fraud in many provinces (and noting Jin Hong's Guangxi as a major example), Zhu Shi's memorial reiterated the late Kangxi position that there really was no longer significant virgin land left in the empire awaiting cultivation. The throne should not harbor unrealistic plans for acreage that was in effect uncultivable and ought really to be left as waste. Indeed, there was little reason to have confidence even in the verified figures for total existing arable land because much of this land could not sustain continuous cultivation. Zhu cautioned his former pupil that excessive greed for tax revenues (à la Yongzheng) was counterproductive, and he recommended against putting pressure on the population to report new land. On the contrary, provincial officials should be ordered to conduct audits of all recent *kaiken* accounts, with a view to striking all falsely reported or insufficiently productive land from the tax ledgers.

The immediacy of Qianlong's response offers further evidence that Zhu Shi's memorial and the edict in reply had been jointly prepared. With appropriate filiality Qianlong applauded his father's goal of promoting agricultural production to better feed his people and blamed the current crisis on the failure of provincial officials to effectively monitor their subordinates' activities in pursuit of this benevolent goal. Citing his awareness of widespread fraud, he deftly presented his own intended policy shifts as continuities: "From now on, provincial governors must show respect for my dead father by taking his love for the people as their guiding concern, and carry out his program as he actually intended." But the edict made absolutely clear that, contrary to Yongzheng's paired concern for popular livelihoods and state finances, in Qianlong's own reign the latter would be decidedly subordinated to the former.[92]

In the wake of this landmark edict, audits of *kaiken* land were conducted in every province. By one conservative calculation more than 3,800,000 *mu* were removed from the tax rolls in the first few years of the Qianlong reign.[93] Several officials lost their jobs, including not only our friend Jin Hong but also Henan-Shandong governor-general Wang Shijun.[94] As Zhu Shi had recommended, an empire-wide cadastral survey in the planning stages under Yongzheng was called off under his successor. And the central government openly hinted at a new policy of tolerance for unreported new cultivation. In 1740 this policy was formalized in a series of schedules, determined at the provincial level, under which new reclamation of "odd-lots" (*lingxing*) of land below specified dimensions were legally unreportable and permanently tax-exempt.[95] The clear intent was that any new expansion of the pale of cultivation be undertaken by household-scale peasant proprietors for their own subsistence rather than by large-scale land development entrepreneurs.

As for Chen Hongmou, it would appear that he had emerged triumphant. His adversary Jin Hong had been cashiered, and he had effected a dramatic reduction in his home province's land tax burden (an achievement for which he, unsurprisingly, became a major local hero).[96] Only adding to his delight, given his persistent championing of the institution of community granary (*shecang*) both at home and in his various posts throughout his career (see Chapter 8), was the fact that Jin Hong's successor Yang Xifu opted to use the leftover pool of "working capital" (*gongben*) collected from extraprovincial would-be land developers to endow a network of such granaries throughout rural Guangxi, the funds "to be placed in [local] people's hands and retained for popular use."[97] In the hour of his victory, however, Chen had unwisely refused to let matters take their course. He had memorialized yet a third time from Yunnan in late 1737, detailing instances of land that ought to be stricken from the Guangxi tax rolls and complaining that many of the extraprovincial carpetbaggers most guilty of complicity in the fraud there had ironically become ensconced as county magistrates or executive secretaries (*muyou*) to local officials.[98] How were they, of all people, expected to pursue investigation of a cover-up? But by now the Qianlong emperor had heard enough. Acidly reminding Chen that, as a Guangxi native he technically had no business meddling in this affair, the emperor expressed his suspicion that Chen was acting merely "as a vehicle for local gentry to manipulate the court." Turning Chen's conduct over to the board for deliberation of punishment, he voiced his annoyance:

> When Chen's first memorial on this subject was received, [the Yongzheng emperor] accepted it as an honest report of what he felt to be true, and on that basis selected other, independent parties to investigate the situation. Chen thereupon ought to have stuck to his own jurisdiction [of Yunnan], and quietly awaited their findings. There was no reason for him to say any more. Yet he is unwilling to wait for the governor-general and governor's report, but once again badgers us with this nagging memorial. It seems as if he is anxious lest their findings not tally with his own wishes. Just who does he think he is?[99]

Chen was demoted two grades and reassigned to the lesser post of Tianjin *daotai.*

He learned his lesson. Although he certainly continued to work behind the scenes to promote the interests of his native place, as all officials did, Chen never again quite so transparently took on the role of advocate for Guangxi provincial causes. Nor did he ever again so openly and aggressively attack the policies of a fellow administrator. Indeed, very nearly as interesting as the behavior that got Chen into trouble in this case was the adept way he moved to restore himself to imperial favor and get his stalled career back on track. He was helped, of course, by the fact that the two investigative reports issued by his two colleagues in the Yongzheng-era Yun-Gui task force, Yinjishan and Emida, so explicitly supported his allegations to the letter. At roughly the same time, moreover, Yinjishan and his other Yunnan superior, Governor Zhang Yunsui, arranged the publication of the *Quan Dian yixue huiji* (Guide to the public schools of Yunnan), an extremely detailed record of Chen's most impressive achievement in the southwest (see Chapter 12), with laudatory introductions by themselves. Although this work undoubtedly had some continuing practical utility for administrative purposes in Yunnan, the timing of its publication (directly after Chen's departure from the province in disgrace) and the large numbers in which it was apparently produced (allowing its survival in the U.S. Library of Congress) suggest the political motive on the part of Chen's grateful patrons of resurrecting his career from the limbo into which it had fallen.[100] Thus, when he was summoned for an audience by Gaozong in the spring of 1738, Chen was relieved that he "was not severely scolded" by his sovereign but merely admonished to keep his nose clean in his new post.[101]

Even more interesting is the fact that Chen availed himself of the opportunity offered by his presence in the capital to pay a call on Ortai (1680–1745), grand councilor and one of the empire's most powerful officials.[102] This was both politic and a bit courageous on his part. After all, Chen had just single-handedly effected the dismantling of the Guangxi land reclamation project, which had been Ortai's brainchild, in which he must have invested much hope, and in the process completely ruined the career of Jin Hong, Ortai's protégé whom he had gone to the wall to defend before the throne. But Chen's gamble paid off handsomely. By his own account the meeting went something like this:

> I had never met Ortai before, and expressed my regret at having waited so long to do so. His eminence congratulated me on the good work I had been doing in my post in Tianjin, which had succeeded in opening up the river channel. He consoled me in my present distress. And he [rather pointedly, it would seem] exhorted me in the future to keep the distinction between public and private interest very clear. I regretted that I could never thank him enough.[103]

Not only had Chen gotten himself out of disfavor with the eminent Manchu grand councilor, but he had gained a new patron. He had indirectly served Ortai in the past as a member of the southwest task force, particularly in his educational work there, in which Chen quite correctly acknowledged Ortai's formative influence.[104] For such service Chen had been prominently included on Ortai's list of nominees for promotion, submitted on the Qianlong emperor's succession.[105] Nevertheless, up until this moment Chen had been far more visibly identified as a protégé of Zhang Tingfu, the Chinese grand councilor with whom Ortai was increasingly in rivalry for the new emperor's ear. Chen's overture to Ortai at this point thus not only represented an atonement for recent affronts but was a brilliant stroke of personal politicking. Chen continued to pay homage to Ortai—corresponding with him occasionally about the proper duties of an official, complimenting him on his editorship of the imperially sponsored agricultural handbook *Shoushi tongkao*, and writing a glowing eulogy for him on his death in 1745 (just as he would do for Zhang Tingyu a decade later).[106] But as the Qianlong emperor showed himself increasingly hostile to the struggles between the two grand councilors' factions in the 1740s—board president Sun Jiagan had impeached both men for faction building as early as 1738—Chen remained on cordial terms with partisans of both camps (and with Sun Jiagan as well).[107] Nothing more clearly reveals his remarkable ability to cultivate patronage ties with powerful men while at the same time avoiding the potentially embarrassing factional entanglements to which this might give rise.

More Adversity

Chen Hongmou's second major career crisis came just after the New Year's festival of 1747. Returning from a nearly four-year tour of duty in Shaanxi en route to his new assignment as governor of Hubei, he stopped by the capital for an imperial audience and found himself greeted with a devastating twelve-point impeachment from his former superior, Sichuan-Shaanxi viceroy Qingfu. Having himself been recalled from his post for an audience late the previous year, Qingfu had prior to his arrival at court fired off a memorial condemning in general terms the poor state of administration in Chen's Shaanxi. Qianlong had rescripted this memorial with the comment: "Public opinion (*gonglun*) sometimes holds that Chen is outwardly correct but inwardly conniving (*wai si zheng er nei yuanyong*), yet I have never had reason to doubt his integrity." He called on Qingfu to spell out his allegations. In his audience, in the first lunar month of 1747, Qingfu did just that. He conceded that Chen was financially incorrupt (rather cattily noting that the *yanglian* stipend attached to the Shaanxi governor's office was so handsome that there was no need to steal) but then went on to present a long list of defects in Chen's work style.

The most telling of these complaints might be classified into three groups. First, Chen was a loose administrator, the implication being that he courted popularity by a relaxed pursuit of the state's interests in society. In Qingfu's words he was "slack in handling public affairs" (*feishi gongshi*) and "lenient in his prosecution of criminality" (*kuanzong taoan*). Second, Chen exhibited favoritism in his selection of subordinates and shielded these favorites from outside criticism (*xunbi shuyuan*). Finally, he was stubborn and arrogant. Qingfu found Chen to be "excessively fond of his own cleverness in getting things done" (*hao zizuo zongming*), "arbitrary in his decision making" (*aizeng renqing*), and "unwilling to do things by the book" (*buchi zhengti*). Altogether these were very serious charges.[108]

Why did Qingfu bring them? Chen Hongmou himself professed to be startled by the allegations and probably genuinely was so; never again in his career would he be quite so trusting of fellow officials. His immediate reaction when presented with this list of particulars was to recall how smoothly his relationship with Qingfu had gone in the several years they had worked together in the northwest and to question why he had never been informed personally of his superior's dissatisfaction with his performance.[109] In fact, the archival record is rich in evidence of the two officials collaborating effectively over the mid-1740s in such projects as adjusting local tax schedules, opening new mines, managing currency exchange rates, administering famine relief, and so on.[110] But there may have been a tension gradually building of which Chen was insufficiently aware. In his impeachment Qingfu noted (a bit self-servingly, of course) how he had patiently and continually tried to "guide" Chen along the path to better work habits, but Chen had been impervious to such hints. Chen's sense of his own mission and superior ability almost certainly grated on the viceroy; the contemporary Yuan Mei, who is generally sympathetic to Chen but not naive about his weaknesses, suggests that he had been somewhat dismissive of his superior's opinions in the time leading up to the impeachment, and the senior man had naturally resented this.[111]

By most accounts, Qingfu's impeachment of Chen was a defensive move prompted
by his own rapidly deteriorating political position. Born into a family of Han banner-
men surnamed Tong, who had managed to have their ethnicity redefined by promotion into the Manchu Bordered Yellow Banner, Qingfu was distantly related on his
grandmother's side to the imperial line and had inherited from his father, Tong
Guowei, the title "Duke of the First Class." He had been appointed Chuan-Shaan
viceroy in 1743, with the principal task of suppressing minority peoples in western
Sichuan. But by 1746 things were not going well in the campaigns, and his recall for an
imperial audience at the end of that year was to force an explanation of his failures in
the field. Several of Chen Hongmou's Qing-era biographers see Qingfu's unexpected
attack on Chen as a preemptive strike, designed to discredit him in advance should
Chen during his own impending audience offer further testimony regarding the military failures. One writer, Peng Qifeng, suggests that what Qingfu feared most was that
Chen would spill the beans about extraordinary taxes levied in Shaanxi to finance the
campaigns, exactions that Qingfu had consistently underreported to the throne. That
Qingfu was a dissembler was ultimately borne out by the revelation that minority leaders whom he claimed to have defeated and executed turned up in revolt again in 1749,
a setback in recompense for which the throne allowed him to commit suicide.[112]

Nevertheless, there was just enough plausibility in Qingfu's charges against Chen
to warrant the court's conducting a thorough investigation. The case came to center on
a single local official—the one to whom Chen had allegedly shown the greatest degree
of favoritism. That official was Dong Sanxi, who, during Chen's tenure as governor, had
held a succession of key county magistracies and, on Chen's recommendation, had
been promoted into the important post of Fenzhou prefect. There is no doubt that
Dong was indeed a favorite of Chen, for Dong had played a pivotal role in implementing at the local level various of the governor's pet reform projects in Shaanxi. He had
achieved results in Chen's drive to improve agriculture and promote sericulture. He
had intervened as prefect to clear up backlogs of judicial cases accumulated by his
county-level subordinates. And in the project to rehabilitate the city walls of Shaanxi's
many county seats, Dong had been a point man in Chen's shifts from conscript to hired
labor and from financing by assessed subscription to that by direct government allocation—that is, away from the systems of "harassing the people by compulsory quotas"
(*jiangpai leimin*), which Chen worked so consistently throughout his career to replace
with market-based strategies. It was in this last activity that Dong had opened himself up
to charges by local project managers of extortion and embezzlement. In the case of
Dong Sanxi, then, policy and politics were inextricably intertwined. Dong was an exemplary practitioner of the kinds of policies Chen advocated, so Chen had to stick with
him when he came under attack, even though he proved a political liability in Chen's
clash with Qingfu.[113]

After hearing the case, the Board of Civil Office recommended that Chen Hongmou
be stripped of his rank and dismissed from office, but the emperor disagreed. He instead
ordered Chen (and Dong Sanxi as well) demoted in rank but retained in post on a probationary basis.[114] Within the next few years Chen was not only restored to his former
rank, but he was also returned to the Shaanxi governorship and awarded a presidency

of the Board of War, all indications that he had hardly lost Gaozong's favor. Nevertheless, although the emperor clearly never put much credence in Qingfu's impeachment, knowing as he did the relative merits of accuser and accused, Qianlong used the opportunity of resolving the case to subject Chen to one of the alternately chastising and cajoling lectures he was wont periodically to deliver:

> Although this time I have ordered your retention in office, you really should not be so over-confident in your handling of affairs. This is a chance for you to grab hold of the reins and put yourself on the right path. You must firmly cleave to the public interest and get your priorities straight. Do not assume yourself to be above the system. Do not make a show of yourself to win popular favor [*guming*]. Purge yourself of the bad habits you have picked up, be sincere and straightforward, and you can really achieve great things![115]

The comment about currying popular favor, echoing as it does Qingfu's allegations along the same line, is especially interesting and probably on target. Chen Hongmou was known, both in his own lifetime and after, as virtually the most "popular" provincial official of the mid-Qing. This fact was touted by his literary executors such as Shen Deqian and by contemporary biographers such as Peng Qifeng. His unusual empathy or identification with the people (*min'gan zhi zetong*) was even officially recorded in the summary judgment (*lunyue*) section of his biography compiled by the Qing History Office.[116] It has been duly repeated in recent scholarship, even that produced in the People's Republic, where it is cited in amelioration of the charge that Chen was also a dutiful agent of elite class interests and of the Manchu "ruling clique."[117] The question of just who were the "people" with whom Chen was so wildly popular is of course a complex one; he was known, for example, to be the darling of merchants and also clearly found favor with such elite groups as the lower Yangzi literati represented by Peng Qifeng himself, by Yuan Mei, and by Fang Bao. The related question of Chen's own putative "populism" will be discussed in a later chapter. Here, however, we should simply note the contemporary perception that both Chen's populist orientation and his popular constituency extended well beyond the elite. Early in Chen's career Zhang Yunsui singled out as the defining feature of his administrative style that "he has the knack of making the people's feelings his own" (*yi minxin wei jixin*), and this characterization stuck with him throughout his career.[118]

Pierre-Étienne Will has explored the surprising degree of similarity between many mid-Qing field officials and more recent "politicians" in their emphasis on getting out among the grassroots populace and "pressing the flesh," being seen, being heard, and being perceived as listening and approachable.[119] Chen Hongmou (who serves as one of Will's prime examples) stressed the need to do just this in his own voluminous writings on proper official conduct.[120] Both Chen and Will link this style with a strategy for good governance based on direct contact with the masses, establishing clear and open lines of communication, and eliminating the potential for self-serving middlemen (either government clerks or community leaders) to divert administrative policy to their own private ends. This was certainly the case, but it was also true (as Will notes only in passing and Chen discreetly neglects to mention at all) that it was also a strategy for political self-preservation: In a universe of back-biting bureaucrats a reputation for populist appeal provided invaluable insulation against attacks from one's flank. It is beyond any question that Chen Hongmou understood this well and used his popularity masterfully as a source of political capital.

The downside of this was that others in the system saw him doing it and used it against him. Qingfu was but one in a long list of official detractors who portrayed Chen to the throne as shamelessly self-aggrandizing and scurrying after public approval.[121] Worse yet, the Qianlong emperor picked up on this perception and used it in his own baiting harangues of his prize provincial official. (He did the same, apparently with similar justification, with Chen's Manchu alter ego, Yinjishan.)[122] For instance, when Chen reported in 1759 on his reconstruction of a system of charity halls in Suzhou, Gaozong's rescript applauded the contribution of this act to the public interest, adding mischievously that "it also does much to further your own reputation" (*er ru yi yinzi deming*).[123] At other times he was less good-humored, as in his oft-repeated admonition of Chen for "pandering in the marketplace to enhance your popularity" (*shisi guming*). "How can it be," the emperor added in 1752, on reading Chen's list of notorious criminals recommended for clemency, "that after so many years of service you have still not reformed your [overly lenient] conduct?"[124]

In practice, however, Gaozong came routinely to shield Chen Hongmou from the consequences of enmities his aggressive style of governance stirred up. Especially after midcentury Chen was nearly always under impeachment from one corner or another. The results were usually minimal—either outright imperial exoneration or a fairly limp imposition of probation, to be lifted soon thereafter. The very routineness of the impeachment process surely served in most cases, for a veteran official such as Chen, to blunt its effectiveness.[125] Still, there were moments of real danger to be faced, and for Chen, as for many others, such a moment came in 1755.

The twentieth year of the Qianlong reign was one of those relatively rare times in the eighteenth century when racist fears came to dominate the Qing political scene—or at least one of the relatively rare times when the surviving sources allow us to glimpse such fears. In 1755, just as Gaozong was preparing to launch major campaigns of subjugation of non-Han peoples in the northwest, he ordered the execution of former Guangxi and Hunan education commissioner Hu Zhongzao for having written examination questions allegedly satirical of his Imperial Person. Also to be executed was Hu's friend, former Gansu governor Ochang, for anti-Mongol (and implicitly by extension anti-Manchu) slurs. Several of the two culprits' associates were implicated and received lesser sentences. Both Hu and Ochang were political clients of the deceased grand councilor Ortai (Ochang was his nephew), and the case has often been seen as a final effort on the part of Qianlong to purge himself of the last remnants of the factions of both Ortai and Zhang Tingyu, the two chief ministers he had inherited from his father's reign two decades before. Given that Zhang's party was sometimes dubbed the "Chinese faction" (*Handang*) and Ortai's the "Manchu faction" (*Mandang*), it might seem odd that it was followers of Ortai and not of Zhang who fell victim to charges of anti-Manchuism. But when one observes that Ortai's clique was composed of such sinicized, poetry-loving Manchus as Ortai himself, Yinjishan, and Ochang, along with

Chinese of the likes of Hu Zhongzao and Yuan Mei, it is less surprising that a highly race-conscious emperor might find them the greater threat.[126]

Chen Hongmou's position in all this was ambiguous, but there were certainly reasons for him to feel vulnerable. He seems not to have been acquainted with Hu Zhongzao, but he had been at least periodically Ortai's protégé. Chen had a number of Manchu friends (Deling and Depei, as well as Yinjishan), had worked amicably alongside many more (Emida, Karjishan), and in 1747 had been rewarded for years of loyal service with an imperially ordered entry into the registry of Manchu clans (*Manzhou shizu tongpu quanbu*).[127] Yet at the start of 1755 Chen had survived his own brush with charges of treason. Fujian governor Zhongyin (a long-serving Manchu provincial official whose policy views often clashed with those of Chen) reported that he had been stopped while touring Xianyu County and handed a petition by a local *shengyuan* named Li Guanchun. He had interpreted the contents as seditious and anti-Manchu and in consequence obtained permission to impose on Li a summary death penalty. In his defense, however, Li contended that he had presented a similar petition to former governor Chen Hongmou years before and received no punishment for doing so. Zhongyin and his superior, Chen's old colleague Karjishan, thereupon searched the provincial archives. They turned up the document, sure enough, but found its contents more innocuous than the one that had sealed Li's fate (can we surmise that Karjishan's reading of the text prevailed?). Just the same, they reported the matter to the throne. Qianlong chose to exonerate Chen of any complicity in sedition, although he censured him for having let such an unwarranted act by a *shengyuan* go completely unpunished. The verdict was the usual one—Chen was habitually too lenient—and he replied with abject apologies. But even though cleared of any hint of treason in this instance, Chen could not have but felt especially nervous as he watched the Hu Zhongzao case unfold just a few months later.[128]

Chen observed the case from the northwest, where the campaign against the Dzungar leader Amursana was not going well, and those in charge—Manchu, Mongol, and Han—were feverishly trying to deflect the ire of their increasingly frustrated monarch from themselves onto their colleagues. Chen emerged as a conciliatory voice and a one-man cleanup crew. In February the Mongol general Salar had passed through Shaanxi and memorialized that the military packhorse system there had been hopelessly mismanaged by the Manchu former Shaan-Gan viceroy Yongchang, who as it happened was now Salar's field commander in the suppression campaign. Ordered by Gaozong to investigate and allocate proper blame, new Shaanxi governor Chen hastened to defend the reputations of both men but stressed his view that Yongchang had not been as poor an administrator as alleged. On subsequent inspection he did find incompetent management at a lower level, impeaching Jiazhou magistrate Wu Bing and, as was de rigueur in such cases, inviting investigation of his own culpability in offering inadequate supervision.[129] Then in April Chen was suddenly transferred to the Gansu governorship, replacing Ochang, who had been precipitously recalled to Beijing to stand trial for both his alleged racial slurs and his botched handling of military finances. Auditing provincial accounts in conjunction with incoming Shaan-Gan viceroy Liu Tongxun,[130] Chen found little evidence that Ochang had been corrupt but ample testimony that he had been truly incompetent. Budgetary transactions had been mishandled, litigation backlogs were astounding, and provincial record keeping as a whole was in such disarray that it was difficult to figure out what was what.[131] Then, in the summer, the military campaigns fell apart altogether, and Yongchang and Liu Tongxun were forced to memorialize that they had abandoned all the territory west of Hami to the rebels.[132]

With all of this, it was effectively Chen alone who emerged unscathed. Ochang was executed. Yongchang, recalled to the capital to face a wrathful emperor, died the same year (I have not been able to determine whether he too was executed). Liu Tongxun was likewise cashiered and interrogated by Qianlong but succeeded in deflecting blame to Yongchang. (Ultimately rehabilitated, he spent most of the 1760s serving alongside Chen Hongmou as a grand secretary in Beijing.) Chen himself was exonerated in June by imperial writ of any liability in the packhorse affair and in August was in fact granted promotion in grade in recognition of his exemplary service to the war effort (*jun-gong*).[133] There could no longer be any doubt of the special confidence and favor the Qianlong emperor now placed in this man, his father's protégé.

This pattern carried over into Chen's next tenure, in Jiangsu. The local observer Peng Qifeng accorded Chen an honored place in the tradition of reformist governors the region had seen in the Qing, a tradition including the revered Tang Bin and Zhang Boxing, but allowed that Chen had achieved even greater successes than his predecessors because he had been more staunchly supported by his emperor against the recriminations of entrenched interests.[134] During his two terms as Jiangsu governor in the late fifties and early sixties, Chen took action against the province's notoriously corrupt grain tribute administration and against the powerful Buddhist and Daoist clergy, and (in a move sure to win him enemies throughout the establishment) he also introduced sumptuary legislation to combat "waste and extravagance" by wealthy families. His ambitious hydraulic works innovations, too, ran him afoul of the local river control bureaucracy.[135] When the inevitable impeachments came, they came (as was often the case in late imperial politics) on charges of convenience, which disguised the true nature of the conflict. In 1759 Chen was impeached by an unnamed Shandong official for having provided insufficiently energetic leadership in combating an infestation of locusts; he was stripped of his brevet governor-general's rank but retained in his post.[136] Two years later a scandal broke out in the Xuye Customs, sparked by Provincial Treasurer Hu Wenbo's impeachment of recently deceased superintendent An Ning. Chen rallied to defend An Ning's reputation, but when an independent investigation by Suzhou silk factory superintendent Sazai confirmed the charges (the honorable but obtuse An Ning had for years failed to catch on to the extent of corruption practiced by his two chief clerks), the governor himself was caught in the web. Chen was reprimanded yet again for laxness of discipline.

Chen was beginning to lose his touch as a provincial official, and he knew it. In two successive memorials submitted during the winter of 1760–61, the sixty-five-year-old governor confessed, "Your servant's energies are diminishing, while the tasks remain great. I am making more frequent mistakes every day." He asked to be temporarily relieved while proceeding to Beijing for direct imperial "guidance," but, as Gaozong surely perceived, he was really asking for promotion into a less arduous position at the capital. At this point the emperor merely chided him for false modesty and ordered him to remain in his post, but he too began to suspect that the aging governor had outlived his usefulness in the field.[137] The next year he transferred Chen from Jiangsu to the more congenial Hunan and in fact showed his continued favor by promoting him to acting Huguang viceroy and president of the Board of War.[138] But by the end of 1763 Chen had indeed been kicked upstairs to Beijing.

Before leaving the subject of Chen's political difficulties altogether, we should examine one final case. I have saved this case for last because of the special way it bears on the interplay between politics and policy. The year was 1758 and the place Liang-Guang, where Chen had been granted his one full appointment as a governor-general, the highest field appointment he was ever to receive. It was also in this post that Chen had received the extreme honor of being allowed to administer his home province of Guangxi, as we have already noted, but as it turned out the affair that undid him concerned not Guangxi but the other Liang-Guang province, Guangdong. The subject of the incident was salt administration. The twenty-eight saltworks (*yanchang*) located in Guangdong's Huizhou Prefecture produced each year enough salt to supply the consumption needs of six southeastern provinces. The salt was distributed by government-franchised merchants who were allocated loans (*guopi*) at the start of each spring season by the Guangdong provincial administration. The merchants used these loans to purchase their stocks at the saltworks. They then transported the salt in quotas allotted to each point within their assigned district, sold it at a prescribed markup, collected and paid government duty (*ke*) at the point of resale, repaid their loans, and pocketed the profits. This was all long-established procedure.

At the start of his Liang-Guang tenure Chen investigated the health of the system in both of his provinces.[139] Guangxi, he determined, was doing fine: The market was booming, and profits to both the government and the merchants had been usefully applied to local construction projects. In Guangdong, however, there were serious problems, which Chen tellingly chose to subsume under the rubric "shortage of merchant capital" (*shangben*). The past several years had seen a boom in production at the saltworks, spurred by unusually favorable weather, and the upcoming year promised a continuation of the same. Chen argued that this overproduction spelled danger as well as opportunity; if the franchised merchants (*guanshang*) could not afford to buy it up, the saltworks would "inevitably" sell it to private smugglers (*sixiao*). The solution he proposed was to raise the level of loans authorized to merchants from provincial sources and likewise their sales quotas in the consumer localities. If it turned out that some merchants ended up with unsalable surpluses that year, this would not be a problem because there was little risk of spoilage and they could simply keep this unsold inventory on hand for sale in the future.

Both Chen's analysis of the problem and his proposed remedy clearly reveal the market-oriented, entrepreneurial approach that, as we shall see in detail in later chapters, were hallmarks of his style of governance. He presented his appeal for increasing merchant capital in terms of an *investment* the state ought to make in the development of Guangdong's salt industry. His preferred method for combating smugglers was a market one: Rather than beefing up security patrols or clamping down on the saltworks for illegal sales, he suggested driving smugglers out of the market by underselling them with expanded supplies of government-franchised salt. And, although he defended his proposals by reference to their benefit to the principles of *guoji* (state finances— that is, the increasing salt duty that would be collected) and *minsheng* (popular liveli- hoods—in this case, the expanded supply of a necessary foodstuff to consumers), there was a third potential benefit that Chen left unstated, but others would not. That was *shangli* (merchant profits—the increased earnings salt merchants would make on their expanded business). For a person of Chen's persuasion these profits were both legiti- mate and in themselves an important contributor to the development of a robust re- gional economy. The Qianlong emperor turned Chen's proposal over for discussion by the Board of Revenue, where it was ultimately rejected.[140]

Two months after submitting his proposal, indeed, Chen himself began to suspect that there was more to the case than he had first understood. Although he still held faith in the merchants, his suspicions regarding the ethical practices of the saltworks had been raised. There were many opportunities for corruption available to saltworks operators—manipulating the price of sales to merchants, adulterating the product, selling to unauthorized distributors—and in the past they had not been adequately po- liced by the overburdened administration. Chen suggested assigning oversight duties to the underemployed Huizhou maritime defense subprefect, who was conveniently stationed close by the saltworks in the market town of Changshi. The court con- curred.[141] But within another two weeks a specially appointed imperial envoy (*qincha*) had arrived in Guangdong to clear up (*qingli*) the entire provincial salt administration, and Chen himself had been precipitously transferred to the governorship of Jiangsu, after a tenure in Liang-Guang of less than three months.[142] Gaozong had clearly devel- oped second thoughts about Chen's suitability for this post, and, equally clearly, Chen's handling of salt affairs had been a significant contributor to those doubts.

The imperial envoy sent to Guangdong was Board of Revenue senior secretary Jiqing, a young but experienced imperial clansman who had served several years as Liang-Huai salt commissioner. His report, based on an extensive audit of salt adminis- tration accounts, was both contrary to Chen's and (from Chen's perspective) damn- ingly thorough. Jiqing found that Guangdong salt merchants had no shortage of capi- tal, as they had claimed to Chen. In fact, their collective treasury contained well over one hundred thousand taels, and merchants had in their own warehouses salt enough to supply their entire district's consumer needs for a full year, even if they were to sus- pend all further purchases from the saltworks. Why then had they petitioned for greater loans of capital? Jiqing found that the merchants were collectively in arrears on repayments of past loans to the government to the tune of over fifty thousand taels, a fact unreported in Chen's own memorials, and moreover that there were outstanding deficits in payment at every point in the complex salt distribution hierarchy. He de- duced from this that the merchants had for years simply been siphoning off proceeds from the salt business into their pockets or into other lines of trade and that their request for larger government loans, which Chen had blithely endorsed, was simply for the purpose of increasing their illicit gains.[143]

It is worth noting that although Jiqing strongly condemned Chen's proposal to increase loans to merchants, he did not disagree with all aspects of his analysis of the situation. In particular, he agreed that one of the major problems in the Guangdong salt administration was smuggling and that this resulted largely from the fact that official distribution quotas were too low to meet the needs of the growing population. Thus, in the revised regulatory code that he drew up for the salt district, he raised the quotas of purchase at the saltworks and resale in local markets allowed the franchised merchants.[144] Like Chen, then, he sought to drive out smugglers through market-competitive means. He differed primarily in his view that the merchants could afford these increased purchases using capital they already possessed.

The Qianlong emperor read Jiqing's report and found his worst fears about Chen confirmed. He turned the case over to the Board of Civil Office for deliberation regarding Chen's punishment, attaching to it the following remarks:

> Who is there who doesn't occasionally make a mistake? And yet, Chen Hongmou is a man of such long-established managerial expertise that he has become complacent in his abilities. When he arrived in Guangdong he had no specific program in mind, but instead acted unthinkingly in forwarding the self-serving requests of local salt merchants for more funds, simply as a means to curry favor with his administrative subordinates [the reference is to Guangdong salt commissioner Fan Shiji, who had passed along the merchants' petition to Chen] and the mercantile community. He could not have acted this way if he had first troubled to make the sort of detailed audit that Jiqing has made. This is yet one more instance of Chen's habit of fishing for reputation in the marketplace. Not only has he not reformed this habit, as I previously ordered, it has only gotten worse with his promotion!

Confronted with this diatribe, the board had little choice but to condemn Chen's "gross negligence" in his conduct of office and recommend that he be cashiered from his current post in Jiangsu. Gaozong demoted him in grade but "magnanimously" (*zongkuan*) retained him in office.[145]

We see in this case an unusually clear instance of Chen's policy viewpoints getting him into political hot water. There is no doubt but that Chen had indeed been sloppy, as his accusers alleged, and that quite likely this was related to the increasingly routinized way he had come to approach each new provincial assignment. But there were also philosophical differences at play. Chen's readiness to accept the merchants' story reflected the unusual degree of faith he placed in their overall contribution to the economy and society.[146] Moreover, it seems probable that the "commercial deficits" (*shangkui*) throughout the chain of distribution, which so alarmed Jiqing, failed to similarly alarm Chen because he viewed them as normal extensions of credit within a sophisticated merchant network. Jiqing was hardly an incompetent; nor is there any particular reason to believe that, like others who impeached Chen during the course of his long career, he was indulging in factional animosities or acting in defense of hidden interests. Like the Qianlong emperor himself[147] he shared several of Chen's policy goals and differed with him on others, and these differences had consequences in the arena of careerist personal politics.

Negotiating Qing Bureaucratic Culture

Over the course of his long career Chen proved himself a master operator within the distinctive political culture of Qing China and more especially in the special niche within that culture made up of career provincial bureaucrats. Philip Kuhn has nicely described this coterie of provincial officials as an "exclusive club," comprising at any given time a few more than three-score individuals who had come to develop habituated ways of perceiving and of managing not only policy issues but also their central government superiors and local-level subordinates. Chen Hongmou in his correspondence uses the term "*wubei*" (men like us) at times in a broader sense to refer to all literati but not infrequently to refer to just this "club," with other members of which experience has taught him to identify.[148] Like others, but perhaps more religiously than most, Chen scoured the pages of the club's internal publication, the *Beijing Gazette* (*Dibao*), for news of policies adopted by provincial administrators elsewhere, as well as for political gossip. Keeping advised through this medium of which way the political wind was blowing was an indispensable survival technique for any Qing bureaucrat. The *Dibao* also served as primer in fashionable bureaucratic discourse; in its pages an activist official such as Chen could discover the legitimating phrases—"*jin dili*" (fully exploit local resources), for example, or "*cangfu yumin*" (store wealth among the people)— that, given the current mood of the court, were most likely to get his policy proposals approved.[149]

Despite his persistent susceptibility to charges of fishing for praise among local populations, within the officialdom itself Chen seems genuinely to have strained to avoid self-promotion and to have seen popular praise as a means both of career survival and of getting things done. Fujian, during 1752 and 1753, provides an excellent case of how Chen moves into a new province, one that enjoys a reputation for ungovernability among both the bureaucracy and the court, and moves to reassert proper governance (*lizhi*). Significantly, his strategy is to make this as much as possible a team effort, avoiding the impression of single-handedly bucking the establishment (what might be called the "Hai Rui syndrome"). First, Chen tries as much as possible to work closely with Governor-general Karjishan, and the two men end up cosigning many memorials to introduce new policies. Chen makes a show of respect for Karjishan's administrative skill; he often cites approvingly innovations that the senior man has introduced prior to his arrival. Yet Karjishan has been in his particular post a long time and has apparently lacked the initiative or the strength of will to clean things up on his own. He is willing to share with Chen some political risks (for example, advocating increased overseas trade) but needs Chen to supply the vision and the momentum.

For help in implementing his activist agenda, then, Chen enlists a few selected subordinates, notably current provincial treasurer Deshu and *former* provincial treasurer Gu Jimei. Chen clearly respects these men's abilities but believes they need his special brand of pushing to perform as he wishes. The tax system in Fujian has been notoriously corrupt, a captive of the provincial-level clerical sub-bureaucracy in league with local private interests. During his tenure Gu has identified the problem and moved to clear it up but without much success. After the arrival first of Chen and then of Deshu, things improve. Chen pulls a brilliant maneuver: He gets imperial permission to retain the since-relieved Gu in Fujian, who is appointed simultaneously provincial judge, provincial grain intendant, and provincial postal intendant. Chen charges him with the special task of following up his earlier charges of corruption in the province's fiscal apparatus. Gu and Deshu both know that Chen is watching them, and he expects the two to spur each other on to greater activism, which, evidence suggests, they do. Finally, there is Provincial Education Commissioner Feng Jin, whom Chen and Karjishan take into their special confidence. Chen quite clearly sees this man as a bold and noncomplacent official, in contrast to his predecessors in his post, and he gives him the green light to seek out corruption wherever he may find it. With this new provincial task force now in place, Chen at last is able to turn his energies to cleaning up maladministration at the local level.[150]

When the occasion arose, as we shall see in subsequent chapters, Chen could be tough and forthright in dealing with the court. With his provincial superiors, such as Karjishan, he had a more diplomatic touch. The following anecdote (from an early-nineteenth-century source) may well be apocryphal, but it illustrates how Chen was perceived as working by his fellow bureaucrats:

> Once when Chen Hongmou was serving as Circuit Intendant [of Tianjin], he was discussing with his superior a policy issue upon which they disagreed. The approach favored by the superior was naively vague and high-flown. Chen backed off from his own position, unwilling to challenge the man too directly. Instead, he commended the superior's plan as "long-range thinking," and its high-flown aspects in particular as "grand." He did so in such a way, however, as to make the superior realize the impracticability of his ideas, and come around to Chen's own views.[151]

In his relations with colleagues more generally, Chen's reputation for "leniency" takes on a new significance. Being magnanimous about the failings of others in the system was politic, of course, and it clearly contributed to Chen's longevity in the often vicious world of Qing officialdom. But Chen's behavior in this regard also reflected the same basic generosity of spirit that, coexisting improbably with his puritanism, humorlessness, and compulsive sense of mission, we will later see revealed in his policies toward yamen clerks, convicted criminals, non-Han peoples, and other disenfranchised types. Chen could not have been wildly popular with his local-level subordinates; he rode herd on them mercilessly and had the unpleasant habit of spending his own *yanglian* stipend on public projects and expecting his prefects and magistrates to do the same.[152] Yet, as was noted by Chen's Qing-era biographer Li Yuandu, he was remarkably slow to impeach those who laggardly or ineffectually carried out his bidding.[153] Even suspicions of venality brought administrative sanctions from the governor only in the most egregious of cases—the record shows fewer than a half dozen impeachments of subordinates in his more than three decades in the provinces.[154] We have already seen Chen getting himself in trouble for viewing too charitably the offenses of underlings impeached by others, and in at least one instance he rushed unsolicited to defend a former subordinate whom a subsequent governor had impeached (he read about the case in the *Beijing Gazette*). He was also known to plead for reinstatement of cashiered officials residing in his jurisdiction.[155]

With regard to collateral officials—"men like us"—Chen counseled an acquaintance to "give credit to others and accept blame for oneself."[156] A sentiment both pious and politic, it was advice Chen at least in some measure lived up to. How many times in his career must he have come into a province and sighed at the inferior job his predecessor had done, and yet, with the single exception of the Ochang case (where the man's incompetence had already been amply attested to by others), he kept his mouth shut. Indeed, as he wrote to a colleague, whistle-blowing in most cases serves no useful purpose: "When one succeeds another official in a given post [*jiaodai*], and the two jointly go over the post's accounts, treat these accounts as matters of mutual responsibility and good faith. It is just as in the popular saying, 'The bones and the flesh are intimate relatives.' . . . In other words, [one must] treat others with the same toleration and forgiveness one hopes to receive oneself."[157] Chen's deeply held sense of personal superiority, it would seem, was tempered by his sense of bureaucratic esprit de corps regularly enough in practice to allow his survival.

Chen Hongmou, as we have seen, both advertised himself as a man who abhorred factions and proved himself adept at avoiding the partisan entanglements his energetic pursuit of patrons might entail. Neither does he seem to have been a faction builder himself. Like most Qing officials, no doubt, he fancied himself an astute judge of talent, and he dispensed his own patronage to those subordinates he deemed to have served him well or those whose approach to scholarship seemed congenial to him. However, although the names of dozens of men whom Chen recommended throughout his career survive in the sources, I have found no evidence that these men constituted a bloc of loyal disciples and only rare indications that Chen himself troubled to follow their subsequent careers. In only one instance did one of Chen's protégés achieve real distinction; this was the famous—and famously anomalous—Wang Jie (1725–1805).

A native of the remote but commercially prosperous Shaanxi county of Hancheng, a product of Xian's Guanzhong Academy (center of the "Shaanxi school" [*Guanxue*] of neo-Confucian studies), and a calligrapher of note, Wang went to work in 1756 as correspondence secretary for Shaan-Gan viceroy Yinjishan and then, when Yinjishan was rotated out of the region shortly thereafter, for Governor Chen Hongmou. He remained with Chen for nearly three years, becoming the governor's great favorite. He passed the provincial examination in 1760 and the metropolitan exam the following year, beginning his meteoric ascent to grand secretary. Apart from his gorgeous handwriting, however, what Wang Jie was most celebrated for was his part in an unusual bit of politicking by the Qianlong emperor in the palace examination of 1761. In that examination the judges placed the famous Jiangnan scholar Zhao Yi first and Wang third, but Gaozong, observing that Shaanxi had perennially been denied the honor of a first-place finisher, ordered the rankings reversed. Qianlong's intervention has been seen as an attempt to curb the disproportionate examination dominance of Jiangnan and an effort to rein in the alarming autonomous power of the Grand Council, whose protégé Zhao Yi turned out, upon investigation, to be.[158] Less noticed, however, probably because more discreetly displayed, was the fact that the beneficiary of Zhao's demotion, Wang Jie, was himself the client of a certain venerable provincial official from Guilin.

Friendship

If in most instances Chen kept himself aloof from obvious factional allegiances, he did nevertheless develop through private letter-writing a diffuse but wide-ranging network of familiar correspondents. Some of these men were the diverse but well-placed patrons whose role in the progress of Chen's career we have already noted: Zhang Tingyu, Ortai, Zhang Yunsui, Sun Jiagan, Huang Tinggui, and Deling. More surprising and suggestive, perhaps, is Chen's correspondence with the eminent Fang Bao (1668–1749). An affinal kinsman of Zhang Tingyu, hailing like Zhang from Anhui's Tongcheng County, and nearly three decades older than Chen Hongmou, the two would seem unlikely associates. Fang was unabashedly elitist and a champion of the refined "ancient prose" (*guwen*) literary style, mastery of which he felt to be the true test of a person's superiority. Basically a private scholar residing in Nanjing, he had never served in the field administration, for which he was clearly ill suited by temperament. He abhorred technocratic rule and any emphasis on "practice" over scholarship. Yet his scholarly reputation was such that he was asked to serve in a number of high cultural posts at Beijing (one being as a director of the Hanlin Academy, where he encountered the young Chen in the 1720s) and periodically enjoyed considerable influence with the throne. Identified as a late-Kangxi-era official, Fang unsurprisingly fell out of favor in the Yongzheng reign (he was a highly vocal critic of Yongzheng's statist policy innovations) but enjoyed a comeback under Qianlong, rising to the post of grand secretary. This period of resurgence coincided with Chen's own period in the wilderness—Chen being a quintessential Yongzheng "new man," closely identified with the very sorts of policies detested by both Fang and Gaozong. For this very reason, of course, Fang Bao would be an unusually useful patron for Chen to recruit, if their personal and ideological differences could be overcome.[159]

And indeed there were grounds for conciliation. For all his elitism and cultivated tastes, Fang was, like Chen, a strong critic of indecorous elite extravagance. Both men preferred "Song learning" over "Han learning," admired such early Qing Cheng-Zhu partisans as Li Guangdi (1642–1718), saw a crucial role for ritual practice in the maintenance of local social order, and distrusted commandist economic policies. Chen seems genuinely to have respected Fang's scholarship (in an inventory of a portion of his library from 1754, at least ten of the 170 books are by Fang, the largest number by any single individual).[160] For his part, like such other lower Yangzi literati as Yuan Mei and Peng Qifeng, Fang grew to appreciate the humane yet principled way Chen as field official administered his home region.[161] By the mid-1740s we find Chen and Fang debating in correspondence such matters as the meaning of the *Zhouli* (see Chapter 4) and the proper definition of *talent*—Chen respectfully offering his view that moral substance is more critical than the breeding and refinement insisted upon by Fang.[162]

Two other senior officials with whom we find Chen in regular correspondence were Depei and Yin Huiyi. Both were very interesting men. Depei (1688–1752), an imperial prince who took as his Chinese courtesy name "De Jingji" (the Economist), had been coaxed out of quiet retirement by the Yongzheng emperor in 1735 and thereafter served in a number of key provincial posts. He was Liang-Jiang viceroy in 1742 and

1743, during Chen Hongmou's tenure in Jiangxi, and worked with the first-time governor in dealing with the terrible famine of those years.[163] But it was Depei's intellectual stance more than his policy positions that Chen found so fascinating. The prince had worked out an idiosyncratic accommodation among his various items of faith: Cheng-Zhu neo-Confucian ethics, the transcendental mysticism of the *Yi jing*, Christianity (he appears to have been baptized in 1718), Western science, and the contemporary intellectual stress on "practice" or "practicality" (*shijian*). He published his views on these questions in the 1736 *Shijian lu* (On practice), a lyrical paean to the universal numinous power (*lingxing*) and the human soul (*ren zhi lingxing*), which Chen claimed to have affected him deeply.[164] Yin Huiyi (1691–1748) was an activist scholar-official in the mold of Lü Kun and Tang Bin, both of whose works Yin edited and republished. His profound and wide-ranging intellectual influence on Chen will be discussed in Chapter 4, but he was a patron and administrative model for the young official as well, dating from Chen's days as Tianjin circuit intendant in 1739.[165]

Most important among Chen's network of correspondents were a handful of men—Zhou Renji, Gong Erquan, Lei Hong, Zhu Xiaoyuan, Zhu Nanhu, and the brothers Jia Shengquan and Jia Yuquan—who were clearly close confidantes. Chen's many surviving letters to these individuals have a far more personal tone than does his other correspondence. Most of them were relatively obscure minor officials whom Chen had encountered at some point early in his official career and with whom he chose to remain in contact. Zhou and Gong he seems to have met during his formative years in the southwest; both men remained in that region throughout their careers, Zhou rising by the 1760s to become Guizhou governor and Gong (a minor poet) to be provincial treasurer of Yunnan.[166] Lei Hong (Lei Cuiting) was a Fujianese Cheng-Zhu scholar of modest renown. Chen was one of his examiners on the metropolitan examination in the early 1730s, and Lei visited him periodically thereafter to discourse on *lixue* thought. After serving briefly as a censor, Lei retired from officialdom, and during his Fujian tenure in the 1750s Governor Chen invited him to take over management of Fuzhou's prestigious Aofeng Academy.[167] About the others in this coterie little is known.[168]

Chen's relationship with these individuals quite clearly drew on a cultural model of "friendship" (*you* or *jiaoyou*) that had become charged with intense meaning in the early seventeenth century and remained so at least through the early nineteenth. Friendship in this special sense involved a dramatic revaluation of the fifth of the classic Confucian "five relationships" (*wulun*)—the only one of the five, in most interpretations, that was explicitly between status equals—from the calculated indifference with which it had been treated in the orthodox Cheng-Zhu tradition.[169] Its resurgence in China at this time was a decidedly early modern cultural trend; it was clearly related to notions of "sociability" and "civility" that had preoccupied the European elite since the time of Castiglione and Erasmus. Indeed, as Joseph McDermott has demonstrated, one specific trigger for its popularity in the late Ming was Matteo Ricci's marshaling of Western thinking on the subject in his influential 1595 tract *Jiaoyou lun* (On friendship).[170] In early modern China, friendship's renewed appeal transcended the sharpest of political-intellectual boundaries, the notion figuring importantly in the social thought of such diverse figures as the egalitarian iconoclast Li Zhi, the Cheng-Zhu revivalist Lu Shiyi, the Han-learning philologist Zhu Yun, and the statecraft reformer Wei Yuan.[171] Friendship as a cultural construct could be invoked in the cause of collective political action—it seems to have been so by the Donglin party in the late Ming and the Xuannan "poetry club" of the early nineteenth century, among others—but it was far more than this, and collective action certainly played no role in Chen Hongmou's own use of the idea. As Zhu Yun wrote, there were essentially three kinds of friendships: (1) those formed out of concerns of reciprocal self-interest, especially political self-interest, (2) those formed simply for recreation, as with wine drinking or poetry clubs, and (3) those formed between Confucian gentlemen (*junzi*) as an aid to mutual progress in self-cultivation.[172] It was with the last of these forms that the new early modern fascination with friendship was chiefly concerned.

Chen Hongmou found this construction of friendship of consuming personal importance. In his *Sourcebook on Reform of Customary Practice* (*Xunsu yigui*), he cited at length such early Qing luminaries as Lu Shiyi and Wei Xi on the responsibility of true friends to upbraid and correct each other's conduct, and in a comment on the Yangzhou scholar Shi Dian he wrote, "The only proper basis of friendship is common moral purpose" (*tongzhi*).[173] In a model examination essay he wrote to explicate the classical phrase "friends arrive from afar," he described the process of building up an expanding network of confidantes as the only sure way to come to truly know oneself. "The vocation of the scholar," he concluded, "is pursued through the instruction and admonition of friends [*pengyou jiangxi*], and through mutual assistance."[174] It was just this set of relationships that Chen labored to build up among his closest correspondents—"men like us" (*wubei*) in its narrowest sense, as contrasted to the bulk of "vulgar officialdom" (*suli*).[175]

Among this circle of friends Chen unburdened himself about his self-doubts, both professional and moral. A remarkably persistent theme in this correspondence, however, is frustration with the vicissitudes of an official career (*shitu*) and the constant battle for survival in the dog-eat-dog world of bureaucratic politics. "The seas of officialdom," Chen laments, "do not run smooth" (*huanhai wuding*). One must patiently ride the waves. Disappointments are inevitable and their severity proportionate to one's ambition; fatigue and depression (*laocui*) will set in periodically. Chen paints a poignant portrait of the field official, quietly doing his job, waiting for his good work to catch the eye of a superior, eagerly reading the official posting reports in hopes of seeing his name listed with a promotion, and watching in pained silence as others less capable than he "soar like eagles" (*pengfei*) into more exalted posts. The sad result, for many, is a retreat into inertia and bureaucratic time-serving.

For those who persist in their initiative to serve the people (*weimin*), there will always be the carping of "bystanders" (*bianguanzhe*) to be withstood. And then there are more overt political attacks. One must be patient and tranquil in the face of charges brought by others, Chen concludes, and quietly attempt to "deflect slander" from oneself. It is counterproductive to attempt active resistance or revenge. In 1741 he warns Zhu Nanhu of the treachery of backstabbing fellow officials: "Men like us, no matter how high our rank, must always be alert for those scheming against us. It is necessary to keep a secure footing and be very circumspect about each move one makes. Always cover yourself. Men's hearts are not always the same as their faces, and it is crucial to remain aware at all times of with whom you are dealing."[176] Chen's confidence in his abilities and his vocation, his optimism about human nature, and his faith in the positive role government could play in improving the lives of the people—all deeply and persistently held—appear all the more striking against the background of this jaundiced view of the bureaucratic life.

Politics and policy were linked in subtle ways. It would be convenient if we could trace a hard-and-fast body of policy positions pursued by Chen throughout his career to a distinct factional alignment with which he was associated, but the evidence suggests that no such alignment existed. Even with the two emperors he served, and who showed him great favor, Chen's ideological fit was problematic. Although in style he was clearly a Yongzheng "new man," his commitment to big government was less thoroughgoing than that of Shizong, and on many issues he was more closely in line with that of his successor. He was not loathe to oppose either of his imperial masters where he saw fit. As we shall see, for example, he was a much more vigorous proponent of mineral development than Yongzheng and of high granary reserves than the mature Qianlong.

Among the many senior officials whom Chen cultivated and who intermittently worked to advance his career, a few stand out as significant influences on the themes he would pursue in his provincial tenures and the specific institutions whose development he would champion. Perhaps surprisingly, the two great bureaucratic powers of mid-century politics, Zhang Tingyu and Ortai, do not seem to have played much of a role as Chen's policy mentors, although each in his own way greatly facilitated Chen's rise. Instead it was the éminence grise of Yongzheng and early Qianlong politics and Chen's acknowledged "teacher," Zhu Shi, whose policy agenda seems most closely to parallel that of his protégé. Perusing Zhu's collected writings, which Chen extolled for their "genuineness" and "substantiality" (shi), we continually encounter a range of concerns—such as opposition to state procurement quotas of goods and labor; energetic development of the hydraulic infrastructure; and promotion of such specific institutions as yixue (public elementary schools), shecang (community granaries), and the xiangyin jiuli (community libationer ritual)—that would become distinctive hallmarks of Chen's own policy agenda.[177] But Zhu was not alone. Chen himself stressed the influence on his economic development ideas of his early Yunnan superior, Zhang Yunsui. He learned the practical value of mass education and the techniques of ethnic conflict resolution from Gan Rulai. He was prompted in his vigorous pursuit of light taxation policies and promotion of staple grain production by Fang Bao. From Gao Qizhuo (1676–1738)—Chen's patron as Guangxi governor in 1721, his superior in Jiangsu during 1730 and 1731, and his predecessor in Fujian—he picked up an advocacy of opening maritime borders to migration and trade.[178] And from Yin Huiyi, his longtime intellectual guide and confidante, Chen found reinforcement, at least, for his pursuit of institutional means for the moral enlightenment (jiaohua) and cultural reform (xunsu) of the populations he administered.[179]

But if Chen's social, economic, and cultural policies were not produced ex nihilo, independent of the real world of Qing bureaucratic politics, neither were they simply the sum of the influences of his patrons, mentors, and friends. As subsequent chapters will show, Chen took a number of policy positions—for example, his hostility to military solutions to frontier issues, his insistence on treating marginalized social groups with a respect due their common humanity, his support of major state investment in economic development projects and of high state grain reserves, and his nearly unqualified enthusiasm for commercial exchange—that could be contentious even among his closest circle of associates, and he pursued certain of his policy initiatives with a highly idiosyncratic zeal.

Politics and policy, again, interacted in complex ways. If there seems to have been nothing like a single, ideologically based faction—say, a "statecraft clique"—to which Chen Hongmou belonged, we might nevertheless offer two more modest conclusions on this point. First, there was an established repertoire of initiatives and institutions in the eighteenth century that activist scholar-officials might choose to promote, even though there was lively disagreement over the efficacy and even desirability of some of these. And second, despite disparate personal backgrounds and disagreements on specific policies, those officials who shared a commitment to this broad and loosely defined activism (which we might for the moment term a statecraft agenda) at least sensed who each other were and sought to further each other's careers.

CHAPTER 3

First Things

IT IS A COMMONPLACE that metaphysical speculation, a staple of intellectual activity in the Song and Ming, receded from the agenda of reflective thought in the early Qing. Chen Hongmou not only conforms to this perception, but he was notably more vehement than many of his contemporaries in his uncompromising dismissal of speculative thinking as "of no utility" (*wuyong*) for human life.[1] This cannot, however, be taken to mean that Chen or his contemporaries had become fully "secularized," that they did not hold basic cosmological beliefs, or even that such beliefs were relatively unimportant in their approach to life. In Chen's case, at least, precisely the contrary is true. The relegation of such ideas to a realm of faith, beyond critical analysis, testified not to their irrelevance but rather to the depth of their hold on his mind.

In general, Chen's views of first things can be described as orthodox and ordinary; they might therefore seem uninteresting as well. Yet, as with all human beings, he accepted received wisdom on his own terms, according it subtle variations and shifts of emphasis. Precisely *because*, in the Qing, metaphysical doctrines were so rarely discussed out in the open but were instead presumed to be common assumptions there was more latitude than there otherwise might have been for idiosyncratic tailoring of these beliefs, if only in small ways, to fit one's own predispositions. And Chen Hongmou, although far from an innovative thinker, was certainly stubbornly independent in the formation of his opinions.

In this chapter we will try to piece together what we can about Chen's most basic assumptions on ontological matters, drawing on scattered comments and language use in his various writings. In the chapter to follow we will look more specifically at the way these beliefs situated him in a more self-conscious historical tradition of Chinese reflective thought. Despite Chen's lack of intellectual originality and his evident reluctance to dwell on such issues, it will become clear in the remainder of this book, I hope, how important his basic assumptions about the nature of man and the cosmos were to his social and economic thought and to the formation of his administrative policies.

Heaven

One of the most immediately striking aspects of Chen's discourse as a whole is the virtual absence of fundamentalist reasoning, in the sense of a belief in the revealed truth of ancient texts or the inherent correctness of the practices of a golden age.[2] To be sure, Chen regularly contrasts the behavior of the ancients (*xiren, guren*) favorably with the debased practices of his contemporaries (*shiren*), and this nostalgia forms a very basic trope in his rhetoric. But he never, or nearly never, seeks to legitimate any action or policy simply because it conforms to the practices or the prescriptions of the classical age. This peculiarity marked Chen off as distinct from many of his contemporaries. For example, recent scholarship on eighteenth-century Chinese thinkers, and in particular those of the "empirical research" (*kaozheng*) style, has pointed out the importance to this project of the belief that if one could only strip surviving descriptions of ancient practices of subsequent corruptions—copyists' errors, interpolations, and the like—one could recover the precisely correct way to do things, even in the contemporary world.[3] Chen Hongmou harbors no such ambition. Indeed, in a remarkable essay (to which we must return later) he argues that Confucius himself chose to valorize the ritual practices of the early Zhou, as opposed to some other past era, not out of his conviction of their absolute correctness but rather out of political expedience and his positive assessment of their practicability.[4]

It is this relativist and pragmatic bent that, at least in part, underlay Chen's preference for the humanistic ethics of Zhu Xi's Four Books over the Five Classics, with their claims to mythic authority, and his arguably even greater preference for the study of history. Chen is what Robert Hartwell would have called an "historical analogist." He routinely cites historical sources and uses the evidence of the past, including the classical past; but he is no uncritical classicist. Rather, he uses history selectively: at some point long ago, someone hit on such-and-such a way of doing something, and by golly it worked! The Four Books, even when they purport to convey the words of the Sage himself, are valid not because they contain revealed truth but because their message is sensible, substantive, and workable, unlike the "empty and useless chatter" of later philosophers.[5] The Four Books and the classical tradition are worthy of great veneration and study but are not in themselves the source of normative values or the fount of legitimation for the social, political, and ethical system Chen strives to establish and uphold.

Ultimately, that source is Heaven.[6] "Heaven" (*tian*) is a term that appears with great frequency in Chen's discourse. Most often it appears in compound lexical forms—*tianli* (heavenly principle), *tianlun* (heavenly regularities), *tianliang* (heavenly goodness or bounty)—that have significance independent of the notion of "Heaven" per se but that, I would insist, never completely suppress the literal notion of Heaven as an active prime mover. Only sporadically and highly unsystematically does Chen offer us his views on the nature of Heaven as an entity apart from its various functional derivatives. Yet these passing references are sufficient to convince me of his unquestioning acceptance of Heaven as something actually "out there" rather than as merely a convenient abstraction to express in shorthand form why he believes certain natural and social arrangements exhibit and demand continual reproduction.

For Chen's younger contemporary Zhang Xuecheng (as depicted by David Nivison), Heaven was little more than "nature." Nivison writes: "The *dao* 'comes from Heaven.' But 'Heaven' for Zhang is really the order of nature, regarded with reverence. His *dao* therefore commands all the respect of a religious absolute, even though it is not supernatural." Inasmuch as, for Zhang, Heaven is reducible to "the sum total of the forces operating in history and human life," he therefore "has an essentially religious reverence for the human moral order, yet at the same time he sees it as completely evolutionary and naturalistic."[7]

For Chen Hongmou Heaven was this but also more. As humanistic as Chen genuinely was in many ways, the religiosity with which he viewed his Heaven went beyond the naturalistic anthropocentrism of Zhang Xuecheng. Chen's Heaven, like Zhang's, is good, rational, and knowable. It is the rule maker, the source of all perceived regularities in human experience. Politically, it legitimates the authority of the ruler, whose "sagacity and *virtú* reflect that of Heaven."[8] Particularly when employing the compound *tiandi* (Heaven-and-earth), Chen sometimes seems to be expressing belief in what might be called an "organismic universe," uniting the numinous and the natural in an undifferentiated whole. For example: "Human beings are a microcosm of Heaven-and-earth," and "Human beings exist to serve Heaven-and-earth as a child does its parents."[9] But frequently enough he is explicit about the agency of Heaven, independent of and (apparently) external to the world of daily human experience. It creates order and predictability out of chaos. It judges and rewards human conduct.[10] It is invoked by the ruler or his proxies to influence the weather.[11] Following a line of Confucian thinking at least as old as the Han, Chen further imparts to his Heaven some of the aspects of a Creator: "All things are granted their essences by Heaven, and assume their characteristic forms on earth" (*wanwu bingqi yu tian, chengxing yu di*).[12]

Heaven is also, among other things, the celestial sphere. In the gazetteer of Hunan that Chen produced in 1757 while serving as that province's governor, in which he declared his emphatic intent to abjure the literary frivolities often associated with that genre in favor of those items of direct import to effective governance and popular well-being (*lizhi minsheng*), he took the unusual step of devoting the work's long first chapter to the "starry firmament" (*xingye*) that governed the province's destiny. Following the *Lingxian* (Spiritual constitution of the universe) of the great Han astronomer Zhang Heng (78–139), Chen laid out a model of cosmic ordering (*fenye*) in which "Heaven has nine positions and the earth nine corresponding regions" and proceeded to reprint the detailed star maps revealing the natural capacities and secrets of good governance specific to Hunan. Charting and measuring both the heavenly and terrestrial spheres, which are "spontaneously and reciprocally generated" (*ziran xiangsheng*), is thus for Chen clearly a religious obligation; observing sudden alterations in his provincial jurisdiction's governing constellations is key to anticipating the vicissitudes of change that Heaven has in store for it.[13]

But if the vital presence of Heaven in worldly affairs may be felt, for Chen Hongmou, in extraordinary and almost personal acts of intervention, there is no question that its more significant role is that of passive guarantor of the principles (*li*), regularities (*chang*), and constant relationships (*lun*) that govern the universe. As a self-professed adherent of *lixue*—Cheng-Zhu neo-Confucianism (see Chapter 4)—Chen saturates his prose with the language of *li*.[14] *Li* is the basic law of the universe. It is inviolable, moral, rational, and accessible to human understanding. Chen attests to his basic faith that "every affair and object under Heaven, ancient and modern, has *li*. If one comprehends this *li*, then one can master oneself internally and extend this control externally to deal with human affairs."[15] And again: "Human beings have their natural disposition [*benxin*], and events have their predetermined principles [*dingli*]. When the time is ripe, an event cannot be avoided, and discussions after the fact are simply wasted."[16] And yet, like others of his time, but somewhat more emphatically than most, Chen interprets *li* in a highly empirical and pragmatic way. "The realization of principle," he writes, "cannot be divorced from daily use and practice" (*riyong*).[17] In other words, Chen subjects his *li* to a sort of utilitarian test: what is right and moral will work in practice, and what truly works in practice must do so because it conforms to principle.

The operation of heavenly principle (*tianli*) ensures that there are rational and constant laws of nature and of human behavior (*chang*), which, if properly understood, can be accommodated by personal conduct and by government policy to achieve the maximum productive benefit for all.[18] It is significant that this same term, "*chang*," is also used by Chen to speak of constant regularities of economic behavior, suggesting that these observed laws, too, are part of an overarching divine plan—they are created and enforced by Heaven, and attempting to breach them is in this sense an immoral act.[19] Thus, for example, he condemns the theft of grain, which properly belongs to those who have labored in its production, as a violation of *tianli* (see Chapter 6). In postulating constant regularities and "predetermined principles" (*dingli*) that are simultaneously part of the natural order of things and mandates for human conduct, Chen clearly expresses his faith in a sort of "natural law." He manages this, however, without sacrificing much of his cherished pragmatism and situational relativism: However transcendent these natural laws, the fact that they are rationally knowable allows a highly creative role for human agency not only to act on the laws but to interpret them.[20]

Chen routinely uses the term for proper human relationships, "*lun*," in compound form with "*chang*" (regularity or law) or "*li*" (principle) to emphasize their grounding in the natural order of things. Like *li* and *chang*, the relationships are the work of Heaven—they are *tianlun*.[21] Although rooted in the particularized relationships of the orthodox Chinese family system, Chen's use of terms such as "*lunchang*" and "*lunli*" naturalizes them as self-evident rules of human cultural behavior. It is in their rational recognition and observance of the *lunli*, in fact, that human beings are essentially distinguished from beasts.[22] By a seamless process of universalizing the local, Chen makes the socioethics of the Chinese elite—of Confucian "civilization"—into a priori categorical imperatives. Thus, cultural practices of non-Han peoples, even (perhaps especially) Chinese Muslims, are seen as violations of heavenly principle, of *tianli*.[23] But so too are many practices of Han Chinese, especially but not exclusively the unlettered masses (*yumin*).

There is, then, a classic "is/ought problem"—a conflation of the ideal and the actual—in Chen's vision of natural law. For, as strongly as he holds that the mainsprings of human conduct are rooted in the will of an omnipotent Heaven, he must admit that they are routinely breached in practice. Heaven does, it is true, provide occasional guidance in bringing human practice into realignment with its will, through omens and portents. For example, Shaanxi province in 1745 is suffering a drought, which Governor Chen interprets (at least in part) as an indication of Heaven's displeasure; he responds by releasing prisoners from government jails (signaling a recommitment to benevolent governance) but exempts from his amnesty those whose crime constitutes a breach of the *lunchang*, the laws and relationships governing human conduct that Heaven has decreed and that, Chen believes, it demands to see vigorously enforced.[24] Despite his own official efforts, however, Chen must concede that human violations of Heaven's will are routine.

It is in his epistemological views, above all, that Chen seeks to resolve the is/ought problem of his ethics. Although it had been a cardinal doctrine of *lixue* thought since the Song, Chen in his own day feels a special need to reiterate, constantly and emphatically, the virtual identity of *li* and *lun* with human consciousness (*renxin*) and human emotional response (*renqing*).[25] We shall return to the particular saliency of *renqing* in Chen's thought shortly, but here we must stress merely that it is a deep article of faith for Chen Hongmou that heavenly principle fully accords with human sensibilities; it is therefore not only rationally knowable (*kezhi*)[26] but also instinctive. The remarkable thing is that so few among the general population seem to abide by it.

It is the function of the scholar-elite, a group Chen often refers to as "people like us" (*wubei*), to put the general population in better touch with their own true selves, so as to *mingli* and *minglun*, to "realize" (in the senses both of "to become aware" and "to actualize") their own instinctive cognizance of *li* and *lun*.[27] It is the task also of the state, which is charged with "implementing principle through administration" (*zhili*). As often as Chen's rhetoric pairs "heavenly principle" (*tianli*) with "human consciousness" (*renxin*) or "human sensibility" (*renqing*), it does so also with "the law of the sovereign" (*wangfa*).[28] It is the mandate of the true ruler, such as the one Chen himself serves, to transform, especially through the judicial process, the unprincipled (*wuli*) into the principled (*youli*).[29] If the *tianlun* have not fully "saturated" popular consciousness (*renxin*), even though by definition the two are nearly identical, the blame must lie with faulty administration.[30] This dynasty, Chen repeatedly asserts, has continually demonstrated its sincere commitment to upholding and extending the heavenly generated regularities and relationships[31] and so, presumably, has manifested its own legitimacy.

It would appear that for Chen Hongmou all of the above, as self-serving and logically flimsy as it might seem to an outside critic, was serenely unproblematic. Two other questions regarding the operation of heavenly principle do, however, clearly bedevil him: that of change and that of fate. Chen continually emphasized his recognition of human affairs as an ever-changing process. In one of his posthumously collected "Maxims" (*Yulu*), he spoke of his comfort with accepting this fact: "The common expression 'peaceful stability' [*pingwen*] [implying the essential identity of the two concepts] is really amusing. Now, when worldly affairs are at peace, they may indeed sometimes appear 'stable.' And yet, it is often the most perilous undertakings which yield the most significant results, and these may be very far from 'stable.' Accordingly, the superior man is most at peace with the reality of change."[32] He wrote to similar effect in a letter to a friend, discussing the passage from the *Appended Remarks* (*xici*) to the *Book of Changes*, which states that, no matter how complex worldly affairs may get, they can always be resolved by the application of *yi* and *jian*. Chen concurs but disputes the common reading of these two terms as "ease" and "simplicity." Rather, they mean "change" and "the essential." In other words, the passage by no means suggests that confronting human problems is natural or effortless; on the contrary, dealing with such difficult matters requires constant effort, precisely because no solutions can be timeless and immune from changing circumstances.[33]

For Chen the world around him changes not in spite of principle but rather because the essence of principle itself is process. He is not rigorous in his thinking about this issue and seems to leave some questions open-ended. For example, in reprinting a work by Li Tingji recounting the words and deeds of great statesmen of the Song, he argues that their exploits remain exemplary because "although the times and circumstances have changed, human consciousness and principle remain the same."[34] Other writings make clear, however, that this sameness is not one of stasis but of dynamism. "Principle continually evolves," Chen tells us, "and never reaches equilibrium" (*bianhua er wuqiong*).[35] For this reason one needs an approach to study that likewise "continually develops and never comes to rest" (*jingjin er buji*) and that emphasizes getting out into the contemporary world (*tong dangshi*) to observe the changing scene. Indeed, it is precisely this dynamic nature of *li* that recommends it to Chen as an ultimate legitimation for human action. Grounding his scheme of values in an evolving rather than a static first principle frees him to transcend the fundamentalist authority of the classics or the golden age of antiquity and to seek more pragmatic and relativist solutions for contemporary problems.

The second problem, fate, was far more troubling for Chen Hongmou; rather than an intellectual puzzle, with which he could confidently, if slowly, come to grips, the question of why bad things happen to good people in this essentially moral universe clearly confronted Chen with cause for doubt. Chen's reflections on this issue were intimately tied up with his belief in the reality of Heaven-sent rewards and retribution (*bao, baoying*) for moral and immoral conduct. As a number of scholars have recently emphasized, this hoary notion had assumed a particular salience in the expanding popular-print culture of China's early modern era, and Chen Hongmou was not immune to it.[36] We have already seen how, in his personal life, Chen was inclined to credit his eventual examination success to his distributions of grain to the needy in a local subsistence crisis.[37] There was no question for him but that such "accumulations of personal virtue" (*jide yu ji*) would be rewarded or that ill-gotten gains would necessarily out in the end or that personal cruelty, say, to household servants would bring calamity on one's house.[38] The question, rather, was how to justify this belief in terms of his *lixue* intellectual underpinnings and at the same time divorce it from the taint of either Buddhism or occultism.

He seems to have tried several approaches to this dilemma. Probably his most orthodox attempt, derived from his reading of Lü Kun, came with his theory of heavenly portents. Such portents, he argued, are not the manifestation of some darker forces in the universe but rather have a logic that is fully consonant with principle (*you dangjin zhi li*), and such portents demand a moralistic human response. The calamities that they portend can be averted, and the good consequences of favorable omens can be claimed, only if one heeds the prompting to "rectify one's virtue" (*xiude*). He goes on to put this insistence on human agency into a broader ethical context in an attempt to reconcile faith and reason:

> Human beings exist to serve [*shi*] Heaven-and-earth, as a child serves his parents. If the parents treat him poorly, he must then redouble his efforts at filiality and respect. If they treat him with favor, he yet cannot shirk his filial duties. If one responds to a good omen by not rectifying his virtue, it is like arrogantly taking that favor for granted. If one responds to bad portents by not anxiously repenting, it is showing contempt for Heaven's powers of agency [*tianbian*].[39]

Chen employs not only metaphysical but also psychological arguments to explain the regularity of retribution for misconduct. Such actions will certainly weigh on one's conscience, he maintains, and thus inevitably be revealed in one's speech and demeanor. If, for instance, the offender is an official like himself, his personal sense of guilt will be manifested in the overcrafty and perverse way he decides legal cases, and this cannot escape popular notice.[40] Fancying himself an astute judge of human character, Chen acknowledges the genuineness of the physiognomist's craft: A man's mind or spirit is inevitably reflected in his physical appearance (*yixin weixiang*). He hastens to add, however, that there is no occult art implied in this because the reflection of conscience in countenance simply conforms to the laws of nature, which constitute principle itself.[41]

Yet a third manifestation of *bao* is social; it appears in the reputation (*ming*) one garners among one's peers. This is not only the most significant index of moral worth for Chen, as for any Confucian, but it is also the surest one, the ultimate proof of the existence of a moral universe: "It often happens that a person acts morally and yet suffers a calamity, or that a person acts immorally and yet is blessed with good fortune. But it absolutely never happens that a moral person receives a bad reputation, or an immoral person a good one. Consequently, the superior man is judged not by short-term failures or misfortunes, but rather by his enduring reputation for propriety."[42] Social reputation is, then, the ultimate consolation in instances where bad things happen to good people. It shows the workings of Heaven through society in dispensing appropriate recompense. But it does not explain why such bad things happen to begin with, and this problem troubles Chen above all others.

His resolution—a classic neo-Confucian one but one with special personal meaning for Chen—is the distinction between the workings of principle and those of fate (*shu*).[43] Like principle, fate is predetermined (*ding*) and expresses the will of Heaven, but unlike principle it cannot be intuited through human reason: "Situations and events which we encounter in our lifetimes include those which can be known, which are the domain of principle, and those which cannot be known, which are the domain of fate."[44] Heaven provides portents (in effect, the evidence from which logical inference may be drawn) of the working of principle but not for the workings of fate, which to human beings appears serendipitous (*eran*).[45] Beyond this, Chen feels little inclined to speculate about the nature of fate. Indeed, any such speculation, as in divination and other popular occult arts, is an attempt to know what is by definition unknowable and is thus a waste of human energies.

Yet fate, far more than principle, determines one's life chances: one's economic status and (clearly of utmost concern to Chen and his circle) the trajectory of one's official career. It seems revealing that Chen's discussions of principle come largely (although hardly exclusively) in his public papers, whereas his ruminations about fate appear primarily in his private correspondence with a cohort of fellow officials who share with him a daily burden of frustrated ambition. Fate also determines the outcome of one's administrative policies, another source of nagging anxiety. He consoles himself as follows:

> The basic principle underlying a situation or event can never change. The concrete results of policy, however, are a matter of fate. Although one cannot know what that fate will be, one can have faith that, in the end, principle will prevail. Thus, a serving official must accept the fact that what is fated to be lies in the hands of Heaven, yet must still adhere to the faith that principle is in his own power to grasp. This is what is known as "having a secure foothold for one's actions."[46]

Success in life is hardly out of one's control altogether. The key is to concentrate one's energies on matters that are genuinely under one's control (*weiwo* or *zaiwo*) and leave to fate those that are not.[47] Coping effectively with one's existence requires simultaneously accepting personal responsibility (*zeji*) in those matters that are controllable and "resting content with one's fate" (*anshu, anming*) in matters that are not.[48] There is no question that for Chen Hongmou the latter requires the greater effort.

Beyond Rationalism

The empirical and practical cast of Chen Hongmou's mind presents us with the danger of seeing him simply as a rational humanist, with deistic underpinnings, very much on the model of the Western Enlightenment. To do so would be an error. In fact, for Chen there were many more things in Heaven and earth than were dreamt of in rational philosophy. I have tried thus far to emphasize the religious character of Chen's faith—his adherence to what Romeyn Taylor has aptly termed the "official religion" of late imperial China, distinguishable from popular religious traditions but sharing many elements in common with them.[49] The core of the official religion was the cult of Heaven, but it did not end there. It extended as well to Arthur Wolf's famous trinity of "gods, ghosts, and ancestors."[50]

First come the gods. In Chen's rigorously orthodox pantheon, overwhelmingly preeminent among these is the god of literature, Wenchang. Chen says nothing about the person of this highly abstracted divinity, but he is at great pains in each of his provincial posts to establish or refurbish the Temple of Literature (*wenmiao*), or School-temple (*xuegong*), which is the locus of his worship.[51] For Chen, as of course for many others, this institution is the key element in the cultivation of orthodox religious practices, of the process of "civilization" or "redemptive transformation" (*hua*) of deviant local cultures. The policy implications of Chen's patronage of the *wenmiao* are so apparent that it is tempting to see his faith in it as instrumental rather than personal. Yet the obsessive attention he lavished on the proprieties of temple construction, care of ritual implements, and liturgical details (see Chapter 12) do seem to convey a perception on his part of their relevance to his own spiritual life. Chen was, after all, a public man and would have vehemently denied any divorce between his personal and public religious beliefs.

He is noticeably less enthusiastic in his support for other deities proper to the "official religion," city gods (*chenghuang*) and local tutelary gods (*tudigong*). Chen acknowledges that these are orthodox deities (*zhengshen*), whose worship has an imperially prescribed liturgy, and so he tolerates them. But it is evident that they have no personal meaning for him. Although, as we shall see, Chen Hongmou's views on social class are highly complex and tension filled, in this instance his religious views seem to reflect his own class consciousness. Tutelary gods are for the common people (*xiaomin*); indeed, they are the appropriate vehicle through which the general population communicates with Heaven.[52] They have little relevance for a member of the official elite such as Chen himself.

What of the spirits of the dead? Ancestors, at least, seem for Chen a genuine numinous force. They are properly attended through the medium of the patriline, at semiprivate ancestral shrines such as that Chen himself has constructed for his own lineage.[53] But Chen is in fact highly ambiguous, perhaps by choice, in expressing his understanding of what happens after death. He argues in favor of prompt execution of convicted murderers on the grounds that the dead, their victims, can "cherish a grievance," which must be redressed; the context of this statement makes clear, however, that the agency of redress Chen most foresees (and hopes to forestall) is the very terrestrial one of vendettas by kinsmen.[54] He struggles, with the urgency of personal conviction, to enforce orthodox funerary and burial practices but justifies this with ambivalent passages such as this one: "After death, all that is left is a corpse; regardless of a person's wealth in life, he can only rest at peace when his corpse is put into the earth."[55] He deprecates the contemporary fashion for concern for the afterlife, associated with sectarian Buddhism and other heresies, and characteristically urges that persons instead accumulate merit through socially useful (*weigong youshi*) philanthropic acts.[56] Most intriguing is the statement attributed to Chen by his Qing-era biographer Li Yuandu: "There is nothing beyond daily life to which one can aspire" (*shengping wu ta shihao*). The context of this passage is a familiar injunction by Chen to devote all of one's effort unstintingly to the task immediately at hand, but the radically humanist implications of his statement still seem striking.[57]

Even if Chen Hongmou held an essentially instrumental view of the official pantheon, and was as skeptical of the afterlife as the above might suggest, he clearly accepted certain beliefs common to Chinese folk religious traditions. In the spring of 1746, while serving as Shaanxi governor, Chen ordered the reconstruction of the temple at Xi'an to the "three spirits"—Mawang (the horse god), Yaowang (the medicine god), and Longwang (the dragon god)—so as "to acknowledge their divine power" (*yi*

FIGURE 5. The youthful Guandi takes leave of his parents. The caption reads in part: "The Sagely Lord was wondrously brave from birth, [but also] naturally loyal and filial, and devoted to reading. He was especially fond of the *Spring and Autumn Annals* and the *Zuo Commentary*, and took as his personal mission understanding the past in order to manage the present." Source: *Guandi shengji tuzhi quanji,* 1838 edition, *juan* 1.

tao shenling) and "to reveal their majesty" (*yi zhao mingsu*). He explained his actions in this way:

> The role of the official is to receive the orders of the Son of Heaven, to bring order and peace to his assigned jurisdiction, and to represent and pray to the spirits which govern that place. By so doing he ensures the timely arrival of rain and the ripening of the hundred grains. . . . It is the spirits who, year after year, bring these blessings to you, my people of Shaanxi. . . . Do not neglect proper priorities![58]

Accordingly, in many of his duty stations Chen made a point of seeking out sacred sites and the spirits who inhabited them, spirits that possessed unusual charisma and magical power (*ling*).[59] Characteristically, however, in ceding to the spirits power over meteorological phenomena, Chen continued to insist that human beings held the power in turn to control the spirits through the sincerity (*cheng*) of their worship. More specifically still, it was the moral quality of the government, and of the individual official, that held the key to this power.[60]

In a similar fashion, as grand secretary in 1768 Chen oversaw republication of Lu Zhan's 1693 *Guandi shengji tuzhi quanji*, a lavishly illustrated, mass-audience edition of tales of the "sagely deeds" of the popular Three Kingdoms folk hero Guandi. Guandi's divine powers (*ling*) are in no way questioned, but it is rather his very human moral conduct—his exemplary filiality and loyalty—that is the work's main point; his military prowess is appreciated, but it is his distinctly *civil* virtues—his sense of justice and his mastery of the classical literary curriculum—that receive greatest emphasis. As one scholar has noted, the *Shengji tuzhi* is "a massive effort to Confucianize Guandi," a divinity capable of multiple popular readings, some of them potentially subversive.[61]

Chen Hongmou's patronage of the spirits was thus a carefully managed public posture, but there is no reason to conclude from this that it was not also an item of personal faith. Frequently enough, it is true, his official statements of tolerance for popular spirit-worship come only in conjunction with prohibitions on its abuse: worship that is overly enthusiastic, that involves large public assemblies, that threatens familial authority, or that is financially extravagant. The spirits, he insists, do not respond favorably to invocations of their power that do not adhere to orthodox ritual practice nor to supplications that involve evident wastefulness of Heaven's bounty.[62] As we shall see later in some detail, Chen was very vigorous throughout his career in "reforming" any type of ritual observance that in his view jeopardized either social mores or economic productivity. But as often as he takes this tack, he also insists that it is a basic duty of the local official to represent his people properly before the spirits—to observe his ritual duties scrupulously and above all to demonstrate sincerity and respect (*chengjing*).[63] The public character of sacrificial performance is paramount; its major purpose is to ensure climatic regularity for the benefit of all. Chen cautions that prayers that lay excessive private demands before the spirits are not only fruitless but blasphemous, although he acknowledges certain exceptions. It is filially proper, for instance, to invoke divine aid to cure the illnesses of parents and even to make vows of service to the spirits for this purpose.[64] And we have already seen that Chen himself did not shrink from seeking spiritual aid in his quest for success in the examinations.

Ironically, for a man best known to posterity as a pragmatic technocrat and a strict *lixue* rationalist, Chen Hongmou seems to have been widely appreciated in his own day for his efficacy at what Donald Sutton has termed "Confucian magic."[65] The compiler of his collected works (published in Suzhou in 1769, while Chen himself was still in office) went to the trouble of including the full texts of eight of Chen's prayers for rain in his various jurisdictions.[66] A large encyclopedia of Daoist spirits and immortals, the *Shenxian tongjian*, published after Chen's death in 1787, was also popularly attributed to him, although I am persuaded the attribution is false.[67] Most interesting of all is the case of the "Essay on Taming the Flood-Dragon" (*Fajiao shuo*), which unquestionably was authored by Chen and became in the Qing probably his single most famous work. The essay describes the history of a giant beast that haunts Mt. Ying in Jiangxi. This dragon has emerged periodically since the Yuan to bring about devastating floods, and Chen reports on how officials of the past have successfully driven it back into its lair. The work was reprinted numerous times: by Lu Yao in his 1775 *Qiewenzhai wenchao* (the only work by Chen included in this large anthology of contemporary prose), by Wang Chang in his *Huhai wenchuan* (compiled ca. 1800), by He Changling and Wei Yuan in the *Huangchao jingshi wenbian* (1826), by Xu Dong in his *Muling shu* (1838), and in various local gazetteers.[68]

In his provincial career Chen regularly prayed for timely rains in his jurisdiction, not merely worshiping at the standard altars for such purposes in the provincial capital but traveling in person to severely drought-stricken localities to conduct services on the spot and making pilgrimages to remote mountain temples to seek out particularly efficacious spirits.[69] In customary fashion, but with a thoroughness that appalled many of his colleagues, he accompanied such prayers with demonstrations to cosmic forces of the benevolence of his administration, by auditing prison records and releasing inmates convicted of lesser offenses.[70] Chen saw his prayers for rain as but one part of an integrated strategy for dealing with drought that included provisions for dispensing relief and elaborate preparations for getting planting underway at the first sign of rain or shifting to alternative drought-resistant crops as soon as that decision became necessary. There is no suggestion, however, that Chen saw his invocation of spiritual aid as mere window dressing to accompany more concrete planning nor indeed that he saw prayer as any less "pragmatic" a response to the crisis; it was part of an overall package of appropriate responses. He was justly proud of those instances when his prayers were promptly answered.[71] Because of his growing reputation for success in facing drought—a success that surely was seen as including the power of his prayers—he became something of an imperial troubleshooter, specifically posted to provinces in which drought was imminent.

At the same time that Chen Hongmou cultivated his reputation for "Confucian magic" he remained exceedingly anxious to deny that his practices deviated in any way from *lixue* orthodoxy. To the extent that his religious world included elements of popular tradition, he *standardized* such traditions (to use James Watson's term)[72] by scrupulously accommodating them to approved views. We have seen, for example, how he insisted that his faith in the revelatory powers of physiognomy did not stem from any occult art but reflected merely the manifestation of heavenly principle. In reprinting a text on how to cultivate long life through proper diet, he noted that this particular set of prescriptions was refreshing because it omitted the "Daoist babble about the void" commonly found in such texts.[73]

Chen periodically relied on various kinds of diviners to reach decisions in his personal life.[74] Nevertheless, even when acknowledging the utility of divination, he sought to impose on it a commonsense interpretation and to deride its claims to occult powers. This was especially the case with regard to geomancy (*fengshui*). Citing the early Qing scholar Wei Xiangshu, for example, Chen lists several injunctions on where to situate a grave—not in a swamp, not within city walls, not alongside a major thoroughfare—and concludes with Wei's own disclaimer: "You can see that these rules are all derived from common logic. They have nothing whatsoever to do with *fengshui*!" He follows this up with a lengthy diatribe by another early Qing figure, Wang Zhifu, lambasting the delay of timely burials caused by excessive concern for geomantic niceties, in Chen's view "a decadent modern trend."[75]

Similarly, in distinguishing his own vaunted rainmaking prowess from that of less orthodox practitioners, Chen cites a passage from Wang Yangming:

> When the ancients experienced a year of drought, the political authorities would reduce their personal food consumption, curtail musical entertainments, release prisoners, lighten taxes, ensure that sacrificial rites were properly performed, inquire whether any among the population was suffering under oppressive local officials, and accept personal blame for any climatic irregularities, all on behalf of the people. They would beseech the aid of the spirits of mountains, rivers, the earth, and the grains. . . . All of this is documented in the *Spring and Autumn Annals*. But there is absolutely no mention of anything like writing magic charms [*shufu*] or divination, of the sort practiced by the necromancers who abound these days.[76]

Chen Hongmou's measured and stately Confucian magic, as Sutton suggests, was distinguished by its "moral message" from that of its popular competitors, which sought to manipulate the supernatural in a manner that was "crudely direct."

Chen's antagonism to popular occultism, and, as we will see, to organized communal faiths such as messianic Buddhism, Islam, and Christianity, derived from a variety of urges. These included the pragmatic concern to uphold social order and economic productivity, the more visceral defense of a hegemonic and uniform elite culture, and, certainly not least, his own deeply held system of personal belief, which conditioned his perception of the world and underlay his choices in policy.

Tianliang: *The Moral Essence of Human Nature*

In both his public and private writings Chen Hongmou constantly returned to the theme of a generalized "human nature," and his views on this subject very clearly conditioned his overall approach to life and politics. This emphasis in Chen's thought set him apart from many of his contemporaries. As Kai-wing Chow has recently reminded us, discussion of any generalized "essence" of the human mind had become extremely unfashionable in the early and mid-Qing, largely in reaction to the populist extremes to which such ideas seemed to have been taken in late Ming thought.[77] Those, such as Lu Shiyi, Li Guangdi, and Li Yong, who still sought to generalize about human character did so in terms not of mind (*xin*) but of a more encompassing "nature" (*xing*), which deliberately transcended the mind/body dualism of high neo-Confucian theology.[78] Although he himself was not reluctant to refer at times to "mind" (*xin*), it was the thinking of these men on this issue that Chen seems to have followed.

Setting Chen Hongmou even further apart from the mainstream thought of his day (but again in line with Lu Shiyi and Li Yong) was his emphatic insistence that human nature was basically good. The regularity with which he felt compelled to drive this point home, both in official pronouncements and in personal correspondence, and the special vigor with which he defended the sometimes radical policy choices he derived from it (see below) make clear beyond any doubt that he perceived himself to be championing a hallowed philosophical position that had lost favor among his contemporaries.

Chen's reflections on human nature center on two related idioms, widely employed within the discourse community of which he was part: those of *tianliang* (the goodness of Heaven) and *renqing* (human feelings). In both cases the meaning of these idioms was being contested within the community, and Chen worked doggedly, if not always self-consciously, to claim for them the interpretations he thought most socially useful.

Chen employs a variety of terms, nearly interchangeably, to refer to the essential nature of human beings. These include "*benxin*" (original mind), "*liangxin*" (moral mind), "*dexing*" (virtuous nature), "*tianxing*" (heavenly nature), and, most commonly, "*tianliang*." The phrase "All human beings have within them *tianliang*" is a recurring litany in his prose. As we shall explore more fully in Chapter 9, Chen is particularly fond of invoking this idea in reference to social categories that, he suspects, his elite audience considers outside the pale of civilized humanity: illiterate peasants, yamen clerks, non-Han indigenous peoples, Muslims.[79] In dealing with such groups one must constantly keep in mind that their nature is common to our own and that, like us, they have an ingrained propensity to moral behavior. He addresses these groups themselves in the same terms, appealing to their innate *tianliang*, to act as principle demands. We know that the behavioral impulses most prized by Qing elite society—ties of familial affection, deference to elders, neighborliness, sympathy for those in plight—are both universal and inviolable precisely because they are natural rather than cultural; they are "rooted in [human beings'] most basic nature" (*gen yu zhixing*).[80]

Stressing so emphatically the goodness and inherent rationality of human beings, in an intellectual and bureaucratic environment in which such cardinal elements of Mencian optimism were no longer broadly assumed, put Chen Hongmou on the defensive in one particular way. In the early and mid-Qing such a position could not fail to be associated with Wang Yangming's (1472–1529) doctrine of *liangzhi* (innate moral wisdom), which was held by most to have been responsible for the radical iconoclasm of late Ming thought and, thus, the social and cultural turmoil precipitating that dynasty's collapse.[81] And indeed, although Chen most often used "*tianliang*" or some other term to refer to his own conception of the goodness of human nature, he did not shrink from sometimes employing Wang's term "*liangzhi*," and at times he explicitly defended his position by comparing it directly with Wang's. (We shall see in the

next chapter how Chen positioned himself with regard to Wang's legacy more generally.) Chen expressed his complete agreement with the Ming scholar's positions that
human nature is never devoid of goodness (*renxing wu you bushan*), that this innate
goodness or conscience (*liangxin*) can never fully be obscured, and that official policy
formation ought at all times to be based primarily on appeals to this innate moral
sense. He wrote, for example, of the approach to governance proper for a local official:
"The moral mind [*liangxin*] which causes one to be attracted to good and to shun evil
is instinctive and automatic. It follows that if you treat the people according to the gen-
tlemanly way, they will respond by likewise conducting themselves as gentlemen. To do
otherwise would be contrary to basic human feelings [*renqing*]."[82]

Every so often in his writings Chen suggests his awareness of a dichotomy between
mind (*xin*) and body (*shen*). In his *Sourcebook on Childhood Education*, for instance, he
cites Fang Xiaoru's (1357–1402) observation that inasmuch as our nature is that of
Heaven and our physical form that of mere men, we must be vigilant not to allow our
heavenly nature to degenerate into the beastly.[83] Again, he notes a passage from Lü
Kun (with whom he claims to nearly always agree): "All sentient beings receive their
essence from Heaven and their physical forms on earth." Chen hastens to add to Lü's
text, however, that just as Heaven and earth form an organic whole, so too do mind and
body.[84]

Just as Chen was fully in line with the early modern trend of rejection of the classical neo-Confucian dualism between mind and body, he seems completely to have ignored the homologous dualism between principle (*li*) and material force (*qi*), likewise
widely repudiated in his day. (The term "*qi*" only rarely appears in his writings and even
then with little or no metaphysical import; most commonly it figures in the compounds
"*yunqi*," meaning simply "fate," and "*yuanqi*," referring to the economically productive
energies of an individual or society.)[85] On this score Chen was probably most influenced by Lu Shiyi, the early Qing Cheng-Zhu revivalist who put a radically monist and
materialist spin on the doctrines of the masters. It was Lu Shiyi whom Chen invoked to
insist that even the corporeal human body is, after all, ultimately the creation of
Heaven (*sheng yu tianran*).[86] Acceptance of a *li/qi* or mind/body dualism would have
compromised Chen's attempts to rehabilitate the validity of human emotional response
(*renqing*), which, as we will see shortly, was high on his intellectual agenda.

However, rejection of the notion of competition between a moral mind and a car-
nal body did seriously complicate the potential contradiction between Chen's sanguine
view of human nature and the observed fact of routine human deviation from moral
norms. Chen, as I understand him, never sought to resolve this philosophical problem
in any systematic way. Rather, his copious but fragmentary references to human nature
convey an ambiguous message about the determinative effect of this on actual behavior. The moral mind is equated by Chen with principle: it is constant, universal, and
predetermined.[87] Yet it is not binding on human conduct. As with the Western notion
of conscience, *tianliang* may be easily obscured (*meiliang*).[88] The role of the teacher or
official or social superior is to put people in touch with this, their better nature, to appeal to it via reason, to cultivate it, and to "awaken" (*tixing*) and draw it out.[89]

Chen is drawn, rather uneasily it seems to me, to a conception of the natural innocence (*tianzhen*) of the child. He describes the task of the educator, for example, as that of harnessing or developing this original simplicity and unaffectedness before it dissipates or becomes corrupted. Chen adopts Zhu Xi's famous image of the stream— perfectly clear at its source but increasingly sullied by turbulence and pollution as it gradually flows onward.[90] Yet Chen cannot have been fully comfortable with a doctrine that places so low a premium on the continuous effort (*gongfu*) involved in self-cultivation. Later in life he writes to a friend in terms that emphasize not the purity but rather the precarious vulnerability of childhood virtue: "One's natural powers [*fuxing*] are initially in a feeble state. As one grows out of infancy and begins to read, one becomes ever more resolute of spirit, and no longer so clinging and dependent." True achievement of the supposedly "natural" goodness, then, is really only the product of a long and complex process of self-examination that involves many factors, not least of which is the prolonged exposure to "tribulation" (*jiannan*—increasingly as he ages a key word in Chen's discourse) that only comes with mature experience.[91] The innate goodness of human beings was for Chen Hongmou an incontestable fact, but he was not similarly unequivocal in linking this with a pristine state of infancy.

Far more strongly than many others in the *lixue* tradition, it seems to me, Chen identifies the innate goodness of human beings with their powers of practical reason, in the sense of the close calculation of means to ends. This association is in line with Chen's oft-repeated assertion that moral behavior and political economy are but two sides of the same coin and provides an ethical underpinning for his comprehensive regional development schemes. Arriving in Shaanxi Province in 1745, for example, he compiles a long list of deplorable behaviors on the part of the local rural population, including especially those that run counter to the dictates of proper human relations and those that represent less than maximum productive use of the environment. He then asks how these behaviors came about and responds in a way that seems uncannily reminiscent of Max Weber's famous typology of social action: they derive either from the people's responding to immediate sense perceptions only (Weber's "affective" behavior) or from their being "infected by customary practice" (*ran yu xisu*) (Weber's "traditional" behavior). Chen's own proposed courses of action, by contrast, are "rational" in Weberian terms; they accord with both rational principle (*li*) and the innate virtue of human nature, as well as with the dictates of long-term economic planning.[92]

Although in this instance Chen holds spontaneous affective responses (or economic shortsightedness) in part responsible for immoral-cum-dysfunctional human behavior, overall he is rarely inclined to see human appetites or desires as a significant force obscuring the innate goodness of human beings. (Indeed, the technical terms for "desire," "*yu*" or "*renyu*," so significant in Confucian moral discourse from Mencius through Dai Zhen, seldom appear in Chen's writing at all.) We shall see shortly that Chen was fully in line with the tendency of his day to rehabilitate human emotional response, seeing it as reinforcing rather than opposing moral conduct. It is rather the second of the two deviations he has observed in Shaanxi society, the unthinking adherence to habitual practice, that is the major force for ill in Chen's moral universe.

Both individuals and social groups become constrained by unthinking repetition of patterned actions, instead of confronting each new situation with an unobscured moral mind. Bad habits become ingrained. He warns, for example, that spoiling young children systematically cultivates in them an unhealthy willfulness and pride.[93] In childhood education too much drilling to achieve stylistic elegance or the memorization of obscure texts systematically erodes the student's moral judgment (*liangxin*).[94] Within groups of people there is a contagion effect to be feared. Among agricultural populations, for instance, collectively reinforced habitual practice can give rise to laziness in responding creatively to the environment.[95] Popular litigiousness—the bête noir of Chen and many another mid-Qing bureaucrat—is described in effect as a social disease, imitated and habituated within broad regional populations.[96] Widow chastity, an impulse that springs from the goodness of the woman's own nature, is scoffed at by populations that have become so jaundiced by social practice that they fail to recognize the virtuous widow as a symbol of the goodness that resides within their own selves.[97]

Like many other *lixue* adherents, Chen is silent on the key question of precisely *how* accumulated practice can despoil innate virtue. He comes closest to addressing this issue, perhaps, when reprinting and discussing the famous community covenant (*xiangyue*) drawn up by Wang Yangming during his mid-Ming tenure at Nanchang. Wang argues that the quality of "popular customs" (*minsu*) is the product of accumulated practice. As defects are successively introduced into this practice, local behavior comes to diverge ever more dramatically from what each individual's innate moral sense, acting independently, would dictate. Wang identifies two specific origins for these defects, both the product of human sensitivity to popular opinion. The first arises when local elites, whose duty it is to oversee popular mores, inadvertently commit improprieties themselves and are then led to legitimate their misconduct before the public forum. The second occurs when rumor falsely imputes immoral behavior to a member of the community, and the individual's conduct is so altered by peer-group ostracism as to make the rumor effectively a self-fulfilling prophecy.[98]

These explanations by Wang Yangming, sketchy as they are, are just about all Chen Hongmou has to say on this subject. Clearly, he was not really interested in working out an answer to this logical problem. That practice corrupted innate goodness was something he accepted on faith; the mechanisms of just how it did so constituted a question that, for him, did not repay the effort of reflection.

Although a term such as *shisu* (contemporary practice)—constructed rhetorically as the converse of the ritually correct practice of the imagined past—nearly always bears a pejorative connotation, it is worth noting that in Chen's discourse neither "practice" itself (*xi*) nor "custom" (*fengsu*) are necessarily negative. Indeed, it would be odd if so practical-minded a man, with such a deep respect for empirically observed situational variation, were to think this way. For Chen Hongmou, as for Lu Shiyi and many other early Qing literati, "practice" is indeed the proper way to nurture one's inherent goodness, provided it is regularly measured against appropriate corrective models.[99] "Customs," for Chen, include not only those that are dysfunctional (*bi*) and call for correction but also those that are advantageous (*li*) and ought to be further encouraged.[100] As we shall see, correcting the dysfunctional and encouraging the advantageous formed a central goal of Chen's administrative policies. In the preface to his *Sourcebook on the Reform of Social Practice* he summarized his position this way:

The task of governance and moral regeneration [*zhihua*] must always focus above all on local social practice. Such practice everywhere is symptomatic of popular consciousness [*renxin*]. When popular consciousness is magnanimous and broad-minded, then courtesy and ritual propriety will abound. . . . Only by educating the people on a routine basis can we officials avoid having to subject them to criminal punishments when they err. Is this not why we are called "the fathers and mothers" of the people?[101]

Renqing: *The Power and Propriety of Human Emotional Response*

If Chen Hongmou's verbal maneuvering with regard to *tianliang* can be seen as an effort to reclaim and refurbish a cherished ancient doctrine that he feared had lost its appeal, his preoccupation with the idiom of "*renqing*" (human feelings) involved more nearly the reverse. Interest in *qing* or *renqing* had never been higher than in Chen's own day, and his concern with the notion was in large part directed toward narrowing the breadth of interpretations to which the idiom was being subjected, at once championing the notion and claiming it for his own moral and political purposes. This contest over the meanings of *qing* and *renqing* was a distinctively early modern phenomenon, and as an active participant in this contest, Chen Hongmou revealed himself as a thoroughly early modern individual.

"*Qing*" is an ancient Chinese term, meaning variously "circumstances," "genuineness," "reality," "affection," and "desire," a set of meanings it conveyed as early as the *Yi jing*. In classical texts it was frequently used as an abbreviation for *qiqing*, the "seven emotions" of love, fear, anger, and so on. "*Renqing*," which in some (but not all) usages was synonymous with or abbreviated by "*qing*," was used as early as the Han-dynasty *Book of Rites* (*Li ji*) to refer to ties of filial and familial affection. Its most generalized late imperial meaning of "human emotions" could be stretched to refer to notions as divergent as "empathy," "reciprocal obligation," "romantic attachment," "common sense," "popular attitudes," and even (as we shall see in Chapter 11) "public opinion."[102]

The two idioms together underwent a dramatic flush of empowerment, expansion of meaning, and contestation in the late Ming through mid-Qing period. Let me cite here but a few examples:

1. The Qing Code (*Da Qing lüli*), following Ming precedent, used the term "*qing*," alone or in the compound "*shenqing*" (expressing or acting on human feelings), to justify statutory distinctions in punishment according to degrees of kinship between the offender and the injured party.[103]

2. In his preface to the 1740 revision of the Code, the Qianlong emperor, again following precedent, noted that its provisions were simultaneously grounded in heavenly principle (*tianli*) and "weighed against the standard of *renqing*." Studying citations of the Code in local-level civil judgments, Philip Huang concludes that this criterion of *renqing* meant in practice that magistrates should try to achieve a face-saving compromise between litigants, who would, after all, have to live in close proximity to one another in the future.[104]

3. In *Honglou meng* (Dream of the red chamber) and other Ming and Qing fiction,

renqing was regularly used to mean worldliness, social polish, or savvy in the ways of the world.[105]

4. The burgeoning Qing literary genre of merchant guidebooks used the term "*renqing*" to refer to the warm personal relationships the books' readers were advised to cultivate with business partners, employees, and customers.[106]

5. The late Ming official and social critic Lü Kun used the terms "*renqing*" and "*minqing*" to refer to "the feelings of the people," with which local administrators were enjoined to keep in touch.[107]

6. The action of Tang Xianzu's extraordinarily popular 1598 romantic melodrama *Mudan ting* (The peony pavilion) hinged on the powerful effect of *qing*, in a usage Cyril Birch translates simply as "passion."[108]

7. Finally, in frank acknowledgment of the contestation to which the meaning of "*qing*" was subject in his day, the great short story writer Feng Menglong (1574–1646) produced his *Qingshi leilue* (The anatomy of *qing*), in which he illustrated by tales or anecdotes no fewer than twenty-seven differing usages of the term in popular parlance.[109]

Juxtaposed to all this linguistic activity celebrating *qing* (although in widely varying guises) was the Song *lixue* tradition, which, although not condemning human emotion outright, tended, through a variety of ontological schemes, to segregate *qing* from principle and from human nature and to assign it a pernicious and corrupting role in human life. Cheng Yi, for example, wrote, "The mind [*xin*] is originally good. As it is aroused and expresses itself in thoughts and ideas, there is both good and evil. When the mind has been aroused, it should be described in terms of feelings [*qing*], and no longer as the mind itself. . . . When [feelings] become vigorous and increase their immoderateness, human nature [*xing*] is weakened." According to Zhu Xi, human nature (*xing*) is common to all persons and corresponds to universal principle (*li*), whereas feelings (*qing*) are a function of individual personality (*zhi*), which is quite distinct from the shared human nature. Zhu adds as an illustration: "Love and hate are feelings [*qing*], whereas love of good and hatred of evil are part of human nature [*xing*]."[110]

This dualism between human feelings and human nature (or human feelings and principle), and the deep moral distrust of emotions, was held in subsequent centuries to be a key component of the Song neo-Confucian legacy, more often than not in a manner that failed to acknowledge the subtlety and ambiguity in the original Song masters' analyses. And it was this dualism and negative view of *qing* that was roundly challenged in the early modern era. The reader will have noted that every one of the widely divergent late Ming–early Qing usages of "*qing*" in the samples cited above bears a positive connotation, including the radical usage in *Mudan ting*, in which *qing* is seen as opposing and conquering the contrasting claims of principle (*li*), construed as conventional morality.[111] A wide range of latter-day neo-Confucian thinkers, ranging from relative iconoclasts like He Xinyin and Li Zhi to more orthodox (although each in his own way innovative) figures such as Lü Kun, Yan Yuan, Qian Daxin, and Dai Zhen, explicitly participated in a collective cultural project of rehabilitating human emotions.[112] Meanwhile, in the burgeoning world of middlebrow print culture, *qing* experienced a remarkable and widespread vogue, perhaps even a cult. In the romantic and erotic mass-market fiction of the era, and in fashionable poetry collections (in which female

poets were increasingly represented), *qing* as romantic attachment and as passion became central themes. As one late Ming literatus declared, "*Qing* is what life is all
about!"[113] One of the fullest developments of the revaluation of emotions came in the
writing of the celebrated late Ming poet and social activist Chen Zilong, who linked *qing*
as an idealized romantic love to *qing* as heroic dynastic loyalism; he saw in both a virtue
and an ardor that cut through the dross of routinized daily experience. Far from corrupting an innate human goodness, *qing* was now seen as epitomizing a transcendent
moral purity.[114]

In this tumultuous context the idioms of "*qing*" and "*renqing*" came to occupy a
central position in Chen Hongmou's thought and discourse. He is highly emphatic and
absolutely consistent on one point above all: There is no dichotomous distinction, either ontological or ethical, to be drawn between human feelings and principle. The
two are but differing aspects of a single entity. Chen's rhetoric is strewn with paral-
lelisms identifying such-and-such a sentiment or policy as reflecting both *renqing* and
tianli; he links *qing* and *li* in four-character idioms such as "dear to human feelings and
according with principle" (*jinqing dangli*) or "demonstrating genuine feelings and principle" (*shiqing shili*). Frequently, he simply collapses the two terms into a single compound, "*qingli*."[115]

To the extent that this is an early modern reading of *qing*, in contradiction of the
teachings of the Cheng-Zhu masters, Chen refuses to acknowledge it as such. He never
cites Song writers themselves on this subject but instead, by routinely presenting himself as an orthodox spokesman for the Cheng-Zhu *lixue* tradition, makes clear that he
sees his own views as reflecting their general message as well. Chen does, however, suggest on at least one occasion that the dualism of *renqing* and *tianli* is a latter-day corruption of the intent of the classics. He cites approvingly the late Ming scholar Gao
Suqing:

> It used to be accepted that *tianli* is nothing other than *renqing*, and that therefore the
> sage takes understanding *renqing* as the means to know what heavenly principle is. And
> yet, later generations of Confucians moved far away from this position, denying that *ren-
> qing* and *tianli* were the same. It was because of this that the teachings of the sages be-
> came far less sagely, and instead ever more repressive.[116]

But if the Song moral philosophers had tended to oppose principle and human emotions, so too did the popular literature of Chen's own day. The difference was that the
philosophers had privileged principle, whereas in the literature it was emotion that
conquered all. Chen Hongmou's own rehabilitation of *renqing*, which doggedly
identified it with *tianli*, can be seen as directed equally against both positions, the
moral idealist and the romanticist.[117]

Especially inasmuch as it cannot be distinguished from heavenly principle, *renqing*
becomes for Chen the basis both of personal conduct and public policy. For example,
he details a variety of common forms of mistreatment of others, asking his reader in
each case, "Does this behavior truly conform to *renqing*?" He argues that what is generally accepted as proper conduct is so precisely because it "meets the standard of human
feelings" (*zhun yu renqing*). It is *renqing* that provides the basis for reciprocity (*shu*) in
human relations and for an individual's capacity to empathize with others (*tiren*), as-

sume responsibility for others (*zeren*), and educate others (*jiaoren*).[118] The same holds true in the sphere of governance. The proper means to order and pacify the empire is only a logical extension of the principle of respect for human feelings. The scholar-official's mandate to "investigate the past" in order to "plan for the present" must be accomplished "in accord with human feelings." "The Kingly Way," Chen concludes, "is rooted in *renqing*."[119]

But what precisely does "*renqing*" mean in Chen's usage? It is clear, first of all, that he uses the term in more than one sense. When he describes the *renqing* of Hunan as being "deceitful," for instance, he is referring to a particular set of localized popular mores, not any transcendent phenomenon.[120] Chen also uses "*renqing*" extensively to denote something we might translate as "public opinion," a concept to which we will return. Suggestive as this terminological overlap may be (using the same idiom for "public opinion" that he does for human feelings and reason more generally certainly imputes to the former an aura of power that it otherwise might not enjoy), it is not our immediate concern here. What is of concern is the manner in which Chen takes an idiom of great currency in his day and stakes a claim on it, narrowing its meaning and reinfusing it with moral content.

Renqing for Chen Hongmou embraces both human reason and human affections, both of which are morally positive. They are powerful forces but hardly hotheaded or passionate (Tang Xianzu's *qing* as passion is decidedly foreign to Chen's usage). *Renqing*, every bit as much as heavenly principle, is "natural" (*ziran*). In tandem with principle it exhibits "regularities," or fixed and predictable laws of operation (*qingli zhi chang*). Like principle it is "inviolable" (*bukefei*).[121] It cannot be ignored or suppressed by an individual considering a course of action or by a government in the making of policy.[122] Thus it places effective limits on political action: A policy, for instance, that placed undue demands on the population would be contrary to *renqing* and hence both unworkable and immoral.[123] Chen is of course aware that the state in practice does not perfectly craft its policies in conformity to *renqing*. He cites, for example, cases of exploitative behavior by members of the elite that clearly run counter to *renqing* and yet have not been prohibited by law; nevertheless, he believes it is his duty to combat them.[124]

Qing/renqing as an irrepressible force is nowhere more clearly seen than in market behavior, and the policy implications here are quite significant. The stimuli for economic actors to buy or sell at a favorable price is nothing other than the response of their innate reason to conditions of supply and demand; behavior so determined conforms to both *qing* and *li*, and state policy must be tailored to permit it full play.[125]

But *renqing* is not merely rational calculation; it is simultaneously affection or empathy (*tixu*).[126] The clearest example is the pattern of human beings living in Chinese-style family situations, an impulse (which Chen assumes to be universally correct) that is *renqing* because it displays a natural and reasonable affection for kin.[127] *Renqing* as empathy imposes constraints on what one may expect of popular behavior, just as does *renqing* as market calculation. We shall see, for example, that Chen considers demands for formalistic adherence to ritual propriety that fly in the face of commonsense understandings of humane behavior to constitute "excessive ritualization" (*guoli*) and violations of *renqing*. Because we all share this *renqing*, when ritual demands seem inappropriate, we can determine the sensible course of action simply by self-examination, by reflection on our own accumulated experience of hardship and tribulation.[128]

In his running commentary on Lü Kun, the late Ming activist thinker whose views on *renqing* were most influential on his own, Chen Hongmou poses for consideration a new problem, one that he finds inadequately addressed in the master's works but that he himself believes critical to any true comprehension of human feelings. That question is, What is the relationship of *renqing* to self-interest?[129] To claim that *renqing* equates neatly with the public interest (*gong*), Chen asserts, is naive; it tells but part of the story. In actuality human emotions contain elements both of public-mindedness and of self-interest (*renqing you gong, yi you si*). Self-interested emotions (*siqing*) are both legitimate and intrinsic to *renqing* as a whole; as such they cannot and should not be altogether suppressed or ignored. Chen essays various strategies for working out precisely how *siqing* fit within his overall conception of human feelings. He states at one point that, although *renqing* as a generalizable phenomenon are public-spirited, when reduced to the level of individual behavior (*gezuo*) they become self-interested. Elsewhere he divides feelings (*qing*) into two types: those that express heavenly principle and those that reflect personal interests; both, he hastens to insist, are equally "natural." Yet again he suggests a rather clumsy tripartite division of *renqing*: that which is natural or intuitive (*ziran*), that which expresses one's sense of what one ought to do (*dangran*), and that which one cannot escape doing (*budeburan*).

The question then becomes how to acknowledge sentiments favoring self, or those close to oneself, as rational and legitimate and yet prevent them from being overindulged. Chen's answer to this question appears groping, a reflection of genuine thought-in-progress, with no pat solution emerging with which he can be fully comfortable. One must be guided by the standard of one's own internalized principles (*zhun zhi yu li*). It is critical to maintain a sense of empathy, to be able consistently to put oneself in the position of others (*tita*). In general, Chen has faith in the social process; the balance of self-interest and obligation to others is in practice worked out through the continuing negotiation of social interaction.

Chen also returns, ultimately, to his faith in human regard for order and precedence. He cites Lü Kun's oddly optimistic metaphor of urban traffic flow: "When people pass along the streets, males give way to females, those on horseback give way to those on foot, the more maneuverable give way to those less maneuverable, and youth respectfully give way to elders." Note especially how, in Lü's idealized street scene, he juxtaposes instances of proper Confucian deference (youth yields to age) with a decidedly un-Confucian courtliness (males yield to females), and instances of the strong yielding to the weak with those of its opposite. Chen picks up on this in his commentary:

> In the open marketplaces of the great cities, one sees carts and horses in great clamor and commotion. They come and go chaotically, without conceding an inch to one another. And yet, when they pass each other along a narrow road, pedestrians give way to sedan-chairs, and horses do likewise. Small carts give way to larger ones, and lighter carts to heavier ones. Even those who are strong and overbearing by disposition do not find it inappropriate to give way; even the normally timid and pliant are unwilling to concede their rightful place. . . . This intuition, that there is a prescribed order of precedence [*yiding zhi xu*], is none other than *renqing*.

Renqing in this sense simply manifests the *wuli*, the principles governing material life, to which "people naturally conform without any laws to enforce their doing so." The state, Chen concludes, can do no better in formulating its policies than to take this ingrained and natural sense of order as its guide.[130]

Chen's various solutions to the philosophical problem of self-interest (except perhaps this last one) are conventional and unimpressive, but his focus on the problem is itself significant. In part, of course, Chen was simply participating in what Anthony Yu has termed "the quarrel between philosophy and poetry" over the issue of personal desire, with the "philosophers" insisting that *qing*, to be morally and socially acceptable, must be subjected to the restraints (*jie*) of reasoned moderation and ritual practice; this, quarrel, as Yu points out, had a history stretching back at least as far as the *Xunzi*.[131] More specifically, however, in his repeated insistence on the legitimacy and compulsion of human appetites, Chen Hongmou was participating in a distinctively early modern rehabilitation of the notions of self-interest (*si*) and personal advantage (*li*) among Chinese thinkers, rescuing these notions from what was widely perceived as the naive, knee-jerk condemnation they had suffered in the Song *lixue* tradition.[132] As I shall argue in the chapters to follow, Chen and his contemporaries were in the process moving toward a newly heightened sense of the importance of the individual, versus the collectivity, that had wide implications in many areas of thought and policy.

CHAPTER 4

Study

IF CHEN HONGMOU'S REPUTATION were to rest primarily on his contribution to the Chinese intellectual tradition, he would remain deservedly unknown today. He was not an original thinker, and he did not reflect deeply on philosophical issues. Neither was he a textual scholar of any significant distinction; his modestly respectable output of publications was limited largely to anthologizing the works of others for purposes essentially of popularization and a rather uninspired moral didacticism. As Liang Qichao remarked, the fact that Chen wrote books at all made him look impressive by Guangxi standards, but "other provinces produce scholars like him by the cartload!"[1] Chen was first and foremost a political actor and one, at that, whose views most often fell well within the confines of conventionality.

Yet scholarship as an ideal was crucial to his vision of the life worth living. Chen heartily despised, as we shall see, any form of pedantry or ivory-tower learning for learning's sake, insisting instead on an activist public service as the sine qua non of anyone who would presume to call himself a "scholar." But at the same time he insisted that a career of sociopolitical activism pursued in the absence of continued painstaking study of the classical curriculum and of history was neither morally justifiable nor likely to yield worthwhile substantive achievements. The unity of knowledge and action (*zhixing heyi*), the imperative to take as one's vocation parallel and interrelated processes of textual study and practical implementation (*jizhi jixing*), was the central theme of the last of Chen's didactic anthologies, his 1769 *Sourcebook on Proper Scholarship* (*Xueshi yigui*), where he put his views this way: "The purpose of study is to seek to implement the Way. True knowledge of the Way involves understanding both of external things and of oneself, and the goal of study is both knowledge and action. One seeks to perfect oneself [*chengji*], and thereby to perfect the external world [*chengwu*]."[2] This in fact was a view Chen held and reiterated frequently throughout his adult life. As he wrote to the director of Suzhou's prestigious Ziyang Academy around 1758, "The distinction between knowledge and action is one made only by vulgar scholars."[3]

Chen read the works of former scholars assiduously throughout his life and, as with any reader, read them in his own individual manner. He read broadly and appreciated the contributions of many schools of thought (including at times even classical works outside the canons of Confucian orthodoxy).[4] Although his pattern of intellectual influences was not startlingly unique, the specific way in which he put together what he learned formed the basis of his approach to public policy. It also, as this chapter will show, contributed to the peculiar mix of notions that, in Chen's own day and later, came to be seen as the basis of "substantive" or "practical" learning (*shixue*) and of Qing statecraft (*jingshi*) thought.

Intellectual Alienation

Chen was very self-consciously at odds with what he took to constitute the intellectual world of his day. His personal letters, in particular, are full of bitter attacks on the glibness, aestheticism, and pedantry of contemporary scholarly fashion. Indeed, such critiques, infused with reformist zeal, a sense of personal moral superiority, and perhaps not a little defensiveness, are among his letters' most compelling themes. Unsurprisingly, criticisms of the examination system and exam-directed study figure prominently in these grumblings; as David Nivison long ago observed, by the eighteenth century such complaints had become nearly as conventional as the form of scholarship they decried. Chen lambasted "scholars" who rarely opened a book in normal times but feverishly crammed, usually via rote memorization with little comprehension of meaning, as the exams approached. The entire educational system had become oriented toward mercenary (*houli*) self-advancement rather than the system's proper focus, elevation of the cultural level of the society as a whole (*jiaohua*). Study so conceived could not but take on a bad odor even for the students themselves, and Chen with equal fervor condemned the fact that successful examination candidates thereafter were so turned off from study that they pursued their official careers without ever again consulting the great works of the tradition. The fault lay in great measure with the examinations and the examiners, who tended to judge essays on the quality of their prose alone, selecting for a pass "those which sound beautiful when intoned aloud," with little or no concern for the soundness of the ideas expressed. The result of such routinization at the lower tiers of the examination system was that candidates tended to rise to the level of their demonstrated incompetence (the well known "Peter Principle"), with the state ending up poorly served.[5]

Chen in fact valued the examinations as a vehicle for the state's recruitment of talent and so worked diligently in practice to ensure the system's integrity from fraud.[6] At the same time, he viewed the examinations as a means rather than an end. He hardly fetishized examination degrees and as we shall see was far more eager than many of his official colleagues to offer them for sale (through the *juanjian* system) in order to stock granaries or finance other socially useful projects. Nor did he confuse examination preparation with genuine study. Even so, he believed the examinations might be made more useful than they were by improving the quality of their questions, and in 1769 he published as his final work his own examination study guide, the *Keshi zhijie*, to illustrate the kinds of "substantive" questions and answers he had in mind—questions dealing with local public security organization, the textual bases of ritual propriety, and a range of other ethical and administrative concerns.[7]

The examination culture contributed to the formation of a broader intellectual and moral climate that Chen found deeply distressing. Most frequently he summed up this malaise in the term "*chuaimo*" (literally, "rubbing and polishing"). In common usage the term meant "to feel for" or "to guess," but in Confucian ethical theory "*chuaimo*" sometimes carried a positive connotation: by repeatedly "brushing up against" exemplary texts or persons, an individual might seek to refine his or her own conduct. Chen instead used the term ironically, to refer to any action done for the sake of appearances, as when a bureaucrat arrived at a policy or judicial decision simply to "feel for" the favor of superiors.[8] In terms of scholarly practice he used it to refer to a form of literary plagiarism, the mindless repetition or imitation of passages from previous texts (usually found in commercially available crib books) that were calculated to sound good and impress one's readers.[9] *Chuaimo* substituted finesse for substance and was in Chen's view the order of the day.

Beyond his complaints about examination cramming, probably Chen's most persistent target was what he saw as a pervasive fixation with literary refinement or style (*wen*). Peter Bol has shown how for besieged Southern Song intellectuals *wen* epitomized Chinese culture, forming part of an indivisible trinity of civilized literary values along with substance (*ti*) and practical utility (*yong*).[10] If pushed on this question Chen Hongmou would likely not have disagreed. He conceded that a scholar's *wen*, or literary output, was essential to his presentation of self and his contribution to society; there was no better gauge of the mature perspective on the world that he had deliberately cultivated through a lifetime of study.[11] In his later years Chen went yet a step further, seeming to acknowledge that contemplation of a well-crafted cultural artifact could in fact contribute to the "implementation of the Way and the refinement of social practice" (*daocun fengya*). Setting aside his own lifelong antipathy to poetry, he counseled the throne in 1760 to reprint for wide distribution an imperial compilation of Tang-Song verse to humanize and broaden the coldly mechanical examination cramming that passed for education among younger scholars. Even here, though, aesthetic appreciation for its own sake plays little or no role in Chen's scheme of values; rather, his primary concern is an instrumental "cultural training" (*wenjiao*) in selected examples of the common literary heritage.[12] Far more representative were Chen's blanket condemnations of scholars who "know only literary style" (*zhiwen*), who esteem poetics over principle, and whose writing is nothing but "empty verbiage" (*kongyan*). In a typical diatribe he wrote one Zhu Ling in 1744:

> These days, there is no shortage of men who are highly adept at writing polished belles-lettres, and yet no longer engage in reading substantive works. They are interested only in churning out their own drivel, for their own self-gratification. When I look at them, I see no difference between them and others who have never opened a book at all. Having once read the canonical works, they are no different than they were before reading them; having been exposed to the glories of substantive scholarship, they instead push their pens to produce the pretentious and superficial [*qianshuai*]. What pains me most is that this is true of the majority of contemporary scholars![13]

This majority, for Chen, lives out a fundamentally false division between literary pursuits and real life (*shu zi shu, er wo zi wo*); their writing looks good, but their personal conduct shows no comparable degree of cultivation (*wen ze shi, er ren ze fei*).[14]

Properly understood, *wen* is indivisible not only from personal deportment but also from the educated elite's mission of governance. "I'm sick and tired," Chen complains, "of hearing that so-and-so is good at writing, while so-and-so is good at political administration. It's as if the two were separate vocations!"[15] By the same token, literary skills are more appropriately applied to certain subjects than others. He decries individuals who make their living composing effete verses for idle aesthetes or, in the new world of commercial publishing, cranking out "trinkets" (*fenshi*) to satisfy popular taste: "These men, who claim to be 'literati' [*dushuren*] by profession, in fact haven't the slightest idea what 'literature' really is! They themselves are of no use at all to society, and on the contrary do positive harm, discouraging others from genuine scholarship by their negative example." Railing against "the glibness of contemporary letters" (*shiwen zhi tuibi*), Chen derides the "vacuousness" (*kongqu*) of all this "superfluous noise" (*fuxiang*).[16] He insists that the proper subject of writing is the explication of the Way and, of at least equal importance, that this Way is something "of daily use in the management of things" (*riyong shiwu*). "To view it as a subject for empty metaphysical chatter (*tanyuan zuokong*) is to miss the boat entirely!"[17]

The style of writing used to address such weighty matters should be similarly uncluttered and unadorned. At one point Chen seems to criticize the stylistic fetishism even of the *guwen* (ancient prose) movement of the Tongcheng school (Fang Bao et al.), which itself sought to combat literary pretense and with which, as we shall see, he was otherwise much in sympathy. Imitating such "archaic and abstruse" (*gu'ao*) forms of writing only gets in the way of effective communication. "The real purpose of writing," Chen notes, "is to get to the heart of what one has to say, and to express oneself as directly as possible."[18] As we have seen, he was fully comfortable using the vernacular when doing so facilitated reaching the intended audience.

Chen Hongmou's attacks on the examination culture, frivolous subject matter, and self-indulgent stylistic refinement would not necessarily have put him much out of the mainstream of dedicated scholar-officials of his day had not his antipathy extended as well to what he saw as the dry, unengaged pedantry of what was fast becoming the dominant intellectual movement of his day, the style of philological investigation that we know as "evidential research" (*kaozheng* or *kaoju*). *Kaozheng*, the origins of which were frequently traced to the great seventeenth-century scholar Gu Yanwu, represented a conscious rejection of Song-Ming neo-Confucianism both as a philosophic system— *lixue* came under attack, for example, for its metaphysical speculation, its ontological dualism between moral mind and corrupt material force, its selfish goal of achieving personal sagehood, and its insistence that moral principle was intuitable in the mind rather than revealed in the classical canon—and also as a sterile pedagogical tool serving a state examination system and inhibiting the scholar's intellectual, moral, and political autonomy. Practitioners of *kaozheng* gradually developed an impressive arsenal of techniques of linguistic analysis in their quest to purge forgeries, interpolations, and copyists' errors from the corpus of ancient texts and engaged in a dizzying series of debates over authenticity of various works and editions.[19] On the basis of this philological sophistication and the movement's avowed antimetaphysical bent, patriotic scholars ever since Liang Qichao and Hu Shi have tended to valorize it over competing intellectual trends as an indigenously Chinese strand of detached protoscientific inquiry. As Kai-wing Chow has convincingly demonstrated, however, there was also a powerful streak of authoritarian fundamentalism motivating many *kaozheng* scholars, who sought to recover the moral perfection of the classical age by implementing in the present the actual social and ritual institutions of the classics, purged by scholarship of profane latter-day corruptions.[20]

Because of many philologists' distaste for Song dynasty neo-Confucianism, they gradually became identified as partisans of "Hanxue" (Han studies), and their opponents, those who refused to break with the Cheng-Zhu tradition, came to be identified as adherents to "Songxue" (Song studies). Beginning at least with the classical scholar Hui Dong in the 1730s and 1740s,[21] self-proclaimed Hanxue partisans insisted on the authority of the Five Classics over the Four Books (the *Analects, Mencius, Great Learning,* and *Doctrine of the Mean*) privileged by Zhu Xi and, following him, made the core of the examination curriculum. They also criticized Zhu's commentaries on the Classics themselves as overly original efforts to update their message so as to conform to the more complex imperial society in which Zhu lived. As Benjamin Elman has shown, *kaozheng* in general and Hanxue in particular was very much a regional phenomenon, overwhelmingly concentrated in the empire's hyperdeveloped Lower Yangzi economic core. The detailed textual comparisons on which the new philology was based were possible only because of the impressive book collections spawned by the region's unparalleled wealth. *Kaozheng*'s institutional home lay in the area's prestigious and well-endowed private academies (*shuyuan*), and the scholarly debates that drove the movement took place largely in the mutual correspondence of an increasingly self-conscious and tight-knit intellectual community of Jiangnan and Yangzhou.[22] And as R. Kent Guy has demonstrated, this regionalized scholarly community and its intellectual agenda gradually became a political movement as well. Through their growing control over the kinds of scholarship rewarded with passes on the civil service examinations, and through an ever more systematic influence over official appointments, Hanxue devotees managed to achieve a significant interest-group hegemony within the imperial bureaucracy. This hegemony was becoming increasingly apparent during the last several decades of Chen Hongmou's own career and, according to Guy, reached its pinnacle during the politically charged Imperial Library (Siku quanshu) project of the 1770s and early 1780s—nearly totally a Hanxue affair.[23]

For its part, Cheng-Zhu *lixue* scholarship had its own intellectual champions in the early and mid-Qing, to whom we shall turn in a moment. In the last years of the Kangxi reign it had also received a number of signs of special imperial patronage—the installation of Zhu Xi's tablet in the main hall of the Confucian Temple at Beijing in 1712, the imperially sponsored promulgation of the *Zhuzi quanshu* (Complete works of Zhu Xi) and the *Xingli jingyi* (Essential Cheng-Zhu scholarship on human nature and principle) as examination textbooks in 1714 and 1715—all of which only served to further taint it among the era's *kaozheng* intellectuals as politically compromised. As Elman suggests, Cheng-Zhu scholarship during the heyday of Hanxue also had its regional bases, outside the Lower Yangzi (Elman particularly identifies Hunan, Guangdong, and Fujian, but as we shall see, there were others as well).[24] Overall, however, *lixue* adherents were increasingly put on the defensive by Hanxue's intellectual and political hegemony in the mid-eighteenth century, leading ultimately to the formal articulation of a "Songxue" countermovement by the Tongcheng scholar and disgruntled Imperial Library compiler Yao Nai in the 1780s.[25] This countermovement would reach its height with the devastating attacks on Hanxue by Fang Dongshu and others in the second quarter of the nineteenth century—not coincidentally, when Chen Hongmou himself was beginning to achieve his own revival of scholarly acclaim.

How did Chen fit into the intellectual debates of his own day? As he did in politics, in scholarly matters Chen condemned partisanship and sought to present himself as above the fray. For him intellectual factionalism was simply a manifestation of an unseemly trendiness. He wrote to a frequent confidante, Jing Guoyuan: "There is no legitimate reason to break down into schools, or to set oneself up as the doyen of some new literary cult."[26] One of Chen's Qing-era biographers, Tang Jian (himself a vigorous nineteenth-century Songxue adherent, as we shall see), agreed that Chen remained throughout his life aloof from partisan intellectual debates (*bianlun*).[27] The fact that during Chen's most active years the battle lines between Hanxue and Songxue had not yet been firmly drawn certainly helped him maintain this posture, as, apparently, did his personal relations skills. A poignant example involved the poet and literary critic Shen Deqian (1673–1769) and Suzhou's prestigious Ziyang Academy. The academy had been founded by the famous early Qing scholar-official Zhang Boxing (1652–1725) as a center of Cheng-Zhu learning, but with the installation of Shen as headmaster in 1751 its curriculum began to shift toward the increasingly fashionable Hanxue philology. Among the young *kaozheng* luminaries whom Shen hired as faculty were Qian Daxin (1728–1804) and Wang Chang (1725–1807).[28] Chen Hongmou, as Jiangsu governor for much of the middle 1750s, also frequently lectured at the academy, expounding on such moral themes as the overcoming of self (*keji*) and the responsibility of scholars to engage in official service. Headmaster Shen was so impressed that in 1769 he contributed a preface to Chen's collected works, where, despite being Chen's senior by more than twenty years, he signed himself his "pupil" (*wansheng*).[29]

Nevertheless, the fact was that all the while Chen decried the ivory-tower scholarship that *kaozheng* epitomized, and he even wrote to complain about trends in that direction to members of the Ziyang faculty itself.[30] He especially hated antiquarianism. In a famous letter, selected for reprinting by Wei Yuan in the *Huangchao jingshi wenbian*, Chen claimed that classical scholars of his day were "mired in the past" (*ni yu gu*) and thus "sinned against the present" (*li yu jin*); they knew only how to study the ancient, not how to connect their scholarship with the world in which they lived (*weizhi xuegu, buzhi jujin*).[31] He pointed out that the true derivation of the term "*kaozheng*" was "*kaogu zhengjin*"—investigate antiquity so as to compare it with the present—a mandate that was lost on current practitioners of the art.[32] Chen likewise had no patience for displays of philological expertise. He complained, "Scholars today ask questions like: 'This particular passage was transmitted from which text to which text?' Or: 'This particular usage belongs to which philosophical school?' They merely fasten upon the particular phraseology and expound upon its relative antiquity, never dwelling upon the genuineness of its message in terms of human relations or the ways of the world."[33] Most of all Chen demanded of any worthwhile scholarship that it concentrate on practical application in the moral and political realms. Around 1747 he wrote to Sun Jiagan, one of the *kaozheng* movement's leading lights but, unlike many philologists, also an eminent statesman (and an early patron of Chen himself), that what he lamented among current intellectuals was their settling for "passive reading" (*zuokan*). If one doesn't make effective use of the Classics in practice, Chen insisted, one can't really claim to have "thoroughly investigated" them at all.[34]

Chen neither wrote nor, apparently, read much *kaozheng* scholarship. In the massive compilation *Huang Qing jingjie* (Classical scholarship of the Qing dynasty) produced in 1829 by Ruan Yuan, a work intended as an encyclopedic summation of the *kaozheng* legacy (and often seen as a contrasting counterpart to Wei Yuan's near contemporaneous *Statecraft Compendium*), Chen did not merit a single entry—despite the fact that we know Ruan to have deeply respected Chen's achievements as an administrator.[35] And in a bequest of some 170 books that Chen made from his personal library to Fujian's Aofeng Academy in 1754, an inventory brimming with works of *lixue* adherents both old and new, not a single one of the many important products of Hanxue scholarship in print by that date can be found.[36] Chen was, in fact, a staunch Cheng-Zhu loyalist in an era when that stance was both intellectually unfashionable and, increasingly, politically incorrect.

The Lixue *Tradition*

As we have seen, Chen Hongmou identified himself as a scholar of the *lixue* (school of principle, or more loosely "neo-Confucian") persuasion. He was viewed as such by his contemporaries and has consistently been so presented by his biographers, in the Qing era and beyond. Although he would not have described himself as a narrow partisan either of Zhu Xi in particular or Song philosophy in general, he has also been routinely depicted as a Songxue enthusiast by later writers.[37] Throughout his field career he sought to confer special honor on historical sites associated with Zhu and his teachings, such as the White Deer Grotto Academy in Jiangxi and the Ziyang Academy in Jiangsu.[38] Holding Zhu's pedagogical writings in especially high esteem, Chen reprinted several of his and his immediate disciples' works at the outset of his own *Yangzheng yigui* (Sourcebook on childhood education), and in various provinces he mandated the study of Zhu's *Xiaoxue* (Elementary learning), *Jinsi lu* (Reflections on things at hand), and *Zhuzi quanshu* (Complete works), as well as the imperially authorized anthology of Cheng-Zhu selections, *Xingli jingyi*, as the basic curriculum of elementary education in state-supported schools.[39] In the midst of a vexing tax clearance campaign in Jiangsu in 1740 he wrote his confidante Jia Shengquan: "Lately I have found my energy level flagging from what it once was, and here, in the most difficult of jurisdictions, I find each matter I confront bitterly frustrating to manage. . . . But when I read Zhu Xi, I always feel at once refreshed. It is like being given rice to appease my hunger and clothing to warm my chill."[40]

As would be true for any person attaching him- or herself to the writings of another, however, the Zhu Xi whom Chen read reflected Chen's own subjectivity. It was a Zhu Xi filtered through the readings of six centuries of intermediaries, as we shall see in a moment. It was also a Zhu Xi read selectively. We have seen in the preceding chapter, for example, that Chen denied or ignored the ideal-material dualism and the condemnation of human emotional response that he, like most eighteenth-century scholars, found uncongenial; we have also seen that his notion of principle made ample allowance for the recognition of historical change. We will see in later chapters how he was capable of glossing over nearly completely the harshest dictates on female propriety attributed by mid-Qing contemporaries to Cheng-Zhu teachings. Above all, Chen Hongmou's Zhu Xi was an eminently practical thinker, far from the speculative metaphysician dismissed as a self-indulgent scholastic by his early modern critics. As Chen wrote, "If it is genuine *lixue*, it will produce genuine practical results. *Lixue* properly understood is rooted in what may be put into practice [*you yu suo xi*], and concrete results are its test. If there are no achievements, then it is not genuine *lixue*."[41] In Chen's rhetoric, even more specifically, "*lixue*"—the study of rational and moral principle—routinely appears coupled with "*jingji*"—the study and practice of political economy.[42] They were an inseparable pair, each necessarily complementing the other.

Where Chen was probably most partisan a Zhu Xi disciple was in his championing of the Four Books as more relevant to contemporary life than the Five Classics. Most *kaozheng* scholars dismissed the Books as Song-era concoctions that only imperfectly reflected the revealed truth of the Classics, when they did not distort it outright. For many they were only further compromised by the decision of the Yongzheng emperor to make essays on these works (*sishu wen*) the basis of his civil service examinations.[43] Not so for Chen Hongmou. Chen prized the Books' straightforwardness, accessibility, and concentration on questions of personal deportment. Following Zhu Xi, he claimed them to be the "fountainhead" of the Classics, and the "ladder" by which the far more abstruse Classics could be approached.[44] In fact, however, it is clear that his preferences went still further. What Chen almost surely believed, but was too prudent to say outright, was that if the Books were thoroughly mastered (not simply memorized for examination purposes), the Classics might be placed on the shelf altogether, as a cultural relic of little use to the present. He argued that the Books had formerly, and properly, been considered "classics" themselves and that their relegation to secondary status vis-à-vis selected other ancient works was a modern and wholly arbitrary judgment. Whereas in his own scholarship, his struggles for personal moral improvement, and his educational policies the Five Classics were nearly invisible, he regularly printed up copies of the Books for distribution to schools in the provinces where he served, discussed interpretations of passages in the Books with his familiar correspondents, and routinely debated their significance with headmasters of the most renowned academies in his jurisdictions.[45] He reinforced his claim to expertise on the subject by compiling (with his grandson Chen Lansen) an updated handbook to personal and place names in the Four Books, the *Sishu kao jiyao*. As Chen would have hoped, this novice-level study aid seems to have achieved wide popular circulation in the Qing—and indeed remains in print today for just such purposes.[46]

Among the Four Books, far and away most central was the *Daxue* (Great learning), that incomparably elegant and powerful text setting out the homologous unity of moral self-cultivation, family management, and political order. Chen surely found the *Daxue*'s themes of regularity, symmetry, precedence, and correspondence in line with his own temper, as he did its optimistic view of a rational, predictable, and moral universe and the contagiousness of personal virtue within a community of human beings who were basically good; he described this text as the key to understanding all other works in the classical canon.[47] Chang Hao has argued for the fundamental importance of the *Daxue* to the late imperial Confucian tradition but notes as well that its appeal was episodic. It proved especially attractive in eras (and to individuals) disposed toward, on the one hand, a conservative rejection of the critical spirit (manifested quite differently, for example, in the egalitarian individualism of late Ming thought and the skeptical philology of the mid-Qing) and, on the other hand, a vigorous and pragmatic engagement in sociopolitical action.[48] The latter of these characterizations certainly fit Chen Hongmou, and to an extent the former did as well. Chen himself stressed the *Daxue*'s centrality to the understanding of cosmology and of moral obligation he shared with his contemporaries, but he lamented that others failed to draw from it the clear implications he saw for political economy. In one of his relatively rare usages of the term we translate "statecraft," Chen argued that if the *Daxue* were not seen as a practical guide for "ordering the world" (*jingshi*) and serving the material needs of society, it was reduced to a collection of meaningless homilies.[49]

Over the course of the late imperial era, the *Daxue* had been employed as the framework for a variety of prescriptive texts on morality and governance, the most famous of which were Zhen Dexiu's 1229 *Daxue yanyi* (Extended meaning of the Great Learning) and Qiu Jun's 1488 *Daxue yanyi bu* (Continuation of the extended meaning of the Great Learning). Zhen's work was structured around the first six of the *Daxue*'s eight stages (*ba tiaomu*) toward the achievement of universal order and was essentially a moral blueprint for the ruler's cultivation of self and management of his personal household. Qiu's enormous 160-*juan* sequel covered the two stages omitted by Zhen, "governing the state" and "bringing peace to the world." Both works marshaled extensive examples from history, as well as from the Classics and ancient philosophers, to illustrate their themes, and the two together had come to be accepted by Qing times as the normative authority on the art of benevolent rulership.[50]

Chen Hongmou was greatly affected by these works and viewed them as required reading for even the most beginning students, especially but not exclusively those on the cultural frontiers. For this purpose in 1736 he assembled a radical abridgment of the combined texts—their original 203 *juan* boiled down to a mere eighteen and devoid of commentary save his preface. He printed up and distributed copies of this abridgment that year to all Yunnan elementary schools and again in 1744 throughout Shaanxi. Chen's popularization of Zhen's and Qiu's books indeed became one of his most widely circulated publications; it was submitted by an unnamed Jiangsu governor for inclusion in the 1782 Imperial Library (Siku quanshu) project, and was frequently reprinted throughout the later Qing era.[51]

It is not hard to see what Chen found so attractive about the *Daxue yanyi* and its sequel. In method they relied on appeals to concrete historical example (Chen particularly liked Zhen Dexiu's injunction to "keep the histories by one hand and maps by the other") rather than to the normative conditions of a presumed golden age. In content they insisted that the basis of rule and of the state's very existence was to serve the needs of the people. This should be done by keeping taxes low, avoiding "harassing" procurement quotas, shunning dirigiste policies, establishing granaries to promote accumulation of surplus, opening the empire's borders to maritime trade, and encouraging the commercial market to do what it did best: stimulate productivity and efficiently allocate the goods of the society.[52] Most important, Zhen's and Qiu's books together were the most eloquent possible testimony to "the unity of substance and function" (*tiyong yiyuan*). Too many contemporary scholars, in Chen's judgment, proceeded as if the principles of moral self-cultivation (*ti*) and the practical application of techniques of political and economic administration (*yong*) were discrete. The separation of these two bulky works in the past had only perpetuated this fallacy; his own integration of the two—accessible, portable, and, not least, affordable—was designed to underscore their indivisibility.[53]

Many of these same qualities underlay Chen's special attachment to Sima Guang (1019–86), the great Northern Song scholar-official whom he admired perhaps more than any other figure in the lixue pantheon. Chen compiled his own eighty-two-*juan* edition of Sima's works, appending his own biography of the great man, and submitted it to the throne for ready reference.[54] Chen admired especially Sima's personal character, the directness of his prose, and the consistent way he worked for the material benefit of the populace. He found Sima's somewhat more tolerant stance on female propriety and on family management—recognizing in both cases the reality of personal and material considerations as complements to ritual correctness—more congenial than that of the Cheng brothers and Zhu Xi, and he accordingly gave Sima's "Jujia zayi" (Miscellaneous rules for dwelling in a household) rather than Zhu's better-known competing works pride of place in his own *Sourcebook on Reform of Social Practice*.[55] He shared with Sima a belief in the indispensable role of ritual in cultivating normative behavior among the people, while avoiding any fetishism about the minutiae of ritual practice. He may also have identified with Sima's attacks on the vacuousness of narrow examination-directed study and on the monopolization of examination success by students from the empire's most-favored economic areas.[56] Most of all, Chen liked the fact that Sima had been among the most dedicated statesmen, and the least given to metaphysical speculation, of all major Song Confucians, extolling his life and work as a near-perfect exemplar of "the unity of substance and function" (*tiyong yiyuan*).

Two particular aspects of Sima Guang's thought are of special relevance for Chen's appropriation of him. The first is a faith in the unequaled instructive power of history. Chen edited and reprinted Gu Xichou's *Gangjian zhengshi yue*, a Ming-era abridgment of Sima's monumental historical work *Zizhi tongjian* (Comprehensive mirror for aid in governance), by way of Zhu Xi's redaction, the *Tongjian gangmu* (Outline of the Comprehensive Mirror), distributing his edition to all elementary schools in Yunnan in 1737 and those in Shaanxi in 1745. He also apparently played some role in the compilation of the *Zizhi tongjian gangmu sanbian* (Third continuation of the Outline to the Comprehensive Mirror), an imperially authorized sequel to Sima's work covering the history of the Ming, edited under Zhang Tingyu's direction in 1746.[57] In promulgating his own *Gangjian zhengshi yue* in Yunnan, Chen wrote that even the most novice of students on the frontiers ought to become familiar with its subject matter, inasmuch as one can "only comprehend the Way through observation of practical affairs, and only understand the general truths of the Classics through observing their working out in history."[58] Chen was, as Robert Hartwell described Sima Guang himself, a "historical analogist," believing "that the comparative study of similar historical phenomena could provide an accurate guide to evaluating contemporary policy." As such both men were, as Hartwell suggests, outside the mainstream of late imperial thought, for which the transcendent authority of the Classics and of neo-Confucian moral imperatives were more compelling legitimations in policy making than was historical practice.[59]

The second key aspect of Sima's legacy for Chen was his celebrated opposition to the New Policies (*xinfa*) of Wang Anshi (1021–86).[60] The highly articulated debate between Sima and Wang in the eleventh century was one of the defining moments in the political history of the empire; in the words of Peter Bol, for centuries thereafter the contrasting views of the two great Confucian scholar-statesmen "presented the literati with a classic choice between an activist government, which sought to manage economic developments in the interests of all, and a more limited government, which sought to maintain necessary public institutions at minimum expense to private interests."[61] To my knowledge Chen Hongmou never so much as mentioned Wang Anshi's name in print. This curious fact can only be explained by the extraordinary vilification Wang had come to receive in the late imperial historical record, most especially within the discourse of *fengjian* or "local autonomy" to which Chen is sometimes seen as belonging.[62] Explicitly invoking Wang, even to disagree with him, must have appeared a highly iconoclastic act. Nevertheless, that Wang Anshi was a decided presence in Chen's political consciousness cannot be doubted, not only as an implied adversary to the Sima Guang he idolized but also as an advocate of a line of political action with which Chen himself at times dangerously flirted. In many respects, then, attempting to position Chen in relation to the opposed agendas of Wang and Sima is an unusually useful way to bring into focus his own sociopolitical values and goals.

Wang Anshi's New Policies, typically described as "radical" or "utopian," have a curiously modern ring. Inspired by his reading of the Confucian classics (especially the *Rites of Zhou*), his idea was to mobilize as vigorously as possible all existing and potential powers of the central state to achieve two simultaneous goals: to enhance the wealth and power of both state and society by a process of consciously growth-oriented central planning, and to direct a course of basic social change leading to greater socioeconomic equality. He tended to view private interests and private wealth, in the hands of both aristocratic landholders and monopolist commercial-industrial guilds, as the chief obstacles to be overcome in the achievement of his project. The major compo-

nents of his policies included the following: (1) a central Financial Planning Commission to minutely direct the empire's economy; (2) equalization of the land tax burden; (3) a so-called Green Sprouts administration to make annual loans of seed grain
to farmers; (4) a Tribute Transport and Distribution Administration to manage state
procurement of agricultural and other produce and to achieve empire-wide price stabilization; (5) a State Trade System to purchase goods from small-scale merchants and
manage their distribution, bypassing private middlemen and guilds; (6) large-scale government enterprises in selected sectors of production, such as tea and horses; (7) a
Hired Service System designed to shift manpower needs for local-government capital
construction and maintenance programs from corvée to hired labor; (8) salaries
rather than gratuity remunerations for low-level government clerks; (9) an enhanced
baojia public security apparatus, feeding into a military reserve system manned by universal male conscription; (10) a heightened importance of the state civil service examination as the avenue of official recruitment, and a reform of its curriculum, giving
greater weight to technical subjects; and (11) a greatly expanded system of state schools
to facilitate recruitment of talent from all classes of society.

Wang's attacks on private interest, and the qualitatively greater claims his expanded state made on the resources of the society, provoked a variety of angry responses that ultimately brought his program down. The response of Sima Guang was
the most sophisticated and probably the most decisive. Sima came from an aristocratic
northern family and was a pioneer of Song neo-Confucianism. An eloquent writer on
self-cultivation (what Chen Hongmou would term "*ti*" [moral substance]), he was uneasy about the dehumanized and mechanically instrumental (*yong*) character of Wang's
state programs. Less optimistic about human nature than was Wang—Sima was skeptical about the *Mencius* and more comfortable with the darker interpretations of the
Xunzi—he was concerned first and foremost with maintenance of social order and discipline. Society was properly ordered in terms of social roles (*fen*); individuals should
be taught and habituated through practice to respect social distinctions (*bian*), to engage in self-restraint (*jie*), and to fulfill contentedly the duties proper to their role
(*anfen*). This was certainly a conservative and hierarchical social vision and very likely
a classist one as well.

Sima did not deny the necessity for a strong central state or for laws and institutions
per se, but he saw the state's role as largely limited to maintaining order rather than
pursuing a proactive socioeconomic agenda. Although he wrote with fervor about the
public-mindedness (*gong*) that officials ought to bring to their task, Sima was influenced by Daoist natural fatalism and was skeptical of the efficacy of any aggressive state
activism. He saw the results of Wang's efforts at centralized planning as having created
a bloated, wasteful bureaucracy (an interest group in itself) and officials who were
more concerned with meeting arbitrary output quotas than with sensitively responding
to the needs of the people. Certainly, Sima felt that the deliberate cultivation of social
change, egalitarian or otherwise, had no part in state agendas. He tended to dismiss the
value of state-sponsored schools and of the civil service examination as a facilitator of
upward mobility, preferring instead to rely for bureaucratic recruitment on the recommendations of serving officials. He also patently dismissed the possibility of gener-

ating economic growth (his arguments on this score were repeated often in later eras), and any state programs designed for this purpose were counterproductive in practice, as well as unseemly graspings after "profit" (*li*). Private wealth was properly left in private hands, where it was in any case most socially useful, and allocation of economic resources best left to the private market. At the same time, Sima also decried contemporary trends toward commercialization and monetization of the economy and saw the duty of the elite as one of leading the people back into productive agricultural work.

As subsequent chapters will make clear, there were quite a few major areas in which Chen Hongmou's own views and policy approaches were closer to those of Wang Anshi than to those of Sima Guang. Like Wang, and very unlike Sima, he held passionately to an optimistic, Mencian view of the basic goodness and rationality of all human beings. He held a dramatically more positive view than did Sima of profit seeking, of the beneficial role of commerce, and of the stimulative effect of monetization (Chen was a persistent advocate of minting new currency throughout his provincial career). Like Wang Anshi, Chen believed in the possibility of generating new wealth, of economic growth even (it appears) on a per capita basis, and of the positive role state economic development programs might play in this regard. In terms of specific policies Chen was as strongly identified in his time as Wang was in his with the transformation of labor recruitment for state construction and maintenance projects from corvée to hired labor (with the entailed increase in local administrative budgets)[63] and with substantial extension of the system of state-run local schools. As the latter implies, he was far more comfortable with the possibility of social mobility than was Sima and, like Wang Anshi, with the role of the state in positively facilitating this process. Although he was in fundamental agreement with Sima Guang's notion of social roles (*fen*), Chen's view of the social order was in fact considerably less hierarchical than that of the aristocratic Sima; the dictate of *anfen* (contentment with one's role or lot) never meant for Chen, as it seems to have meant for Sima, denial of the propriety of actively seeking social or material self-betterment.

In spite of all this Chen not only came down more closely on the side of Sima than that of the disreputable Wang Anshi, but he actively singled out Sima as one of his most cherished individuals in the entire historical pantheon. On what basis could he do so? In terms of political-economic thought he fully endorsed Sima's cardinal belief in the sanctity of private property and private interest versus public need; even in dire food crises, as we shall see, Chen refrained from confiscation of private wealth as a course of action both immoral and self-defeating. He was wholeheartedly in line with Sima's attack on all forms of economic dirigisme—price setting, government monopolies, and so on. Both men believed in low taxation as a virtue in itself, although Chen was probably more willing to qualify this to meet practical needs. Although Chen's ideal state was considerably more active as an agent of economic, social, and cultural development than one Sima would have imagined or perhaps condoned, there was ample room in Sima's written testament—most notably in the *Comprehensive Mirror* itself—in which to find legitimation for state activism of one sort or another. Sima's flexible historicism was immeasurably more congenial to Chen, confronted as he was with a rising tide of Hanxue fundamentalism, than was the "golden age" idealism of Wang Anshi.[64] Not

least, Sima represented a perfect balance between *ti* and *yong*; whereas Wang, despite
his idealism, flirted dangerously with a love of technological skill and institutional sophistication for its own sake, Sima consistently demanded of all public servants not a
mere technical prowess but also a persistent concern for personal moral self-cultivation
and a thoroughly humanistic approach to the tasks of governance. All things considered, I am inclined to see the groundings of Chen's consciousness as essentially in accord with those of Sima and his divergences from the Song master, profound as they
were, as adaptations of these to the changed material and cultural milieu of the early
modern Qing world.

It is clear that Chen's reading of Song-era *lixue* texts as a whole was significantly filtered
through the readings given them by other, more recent Cheng-Zhu devotees. The impressive cohort of seventeenth- and early-eighteenth-century Cheng-Zhu scholar-
officials—figures such as Lu Shiyi (1611–72), Zhang Luxiang (1611–74), Wei
Xiangshu (1617–87), Lu Longqi (1630–93), Li Guangdi (1642–1718), and Zhang
Boxing (1652–1725)—was long dismissed as anachronistic and politically opportunist
by early-twentieth-century nationalist Chinese scholars and those they influenced.
Liang Qichao, for example, in his pioneering *Intellectual Trends of the Qing Period,*
justified his neglect of them as scholars "who stubbornly clung to the broken fortress of
the older views . . . and would not leave in the face of destruction"; they were likewise
omitted in Qian Mu's widely influential 1937 history of Qing thought, and they go entirely unmentioned in the standard English-language sourcebooks of Chinese intellectual history edited in the 1960s by Wm. Theodore de Bary and by Wing-tsit Chan.[65]
More recently, however, largely through the subsequent work of Chan and de Bary
themselves, we have come to recognize not only their importance within the world of
Qing thought but also the subtle yet powerful shifts of interpretation they put on the
Song *lixue* tradition.[66]
     For Chen Hongmou they were major influences both intellectually and politically.
All of these individuals were amply represented in Chen's various sourcebooks on personal, social, and political reform, and he referred to them with great reverence in his
correspondence. On the few occasions where he followed them in an administrative
post (as he did Zhang Boxing as Fujian and Jiangsu governor) he took their policies as
cues for his own.[67] The *Xingli jingyi*, the anthology of Cheng-Zhu texts compiled at imperial direction by Li Guangdi in 1715, and which, as Chan shows, reflected the distinctively activist reading put on these texts by Li and his cohort, was consistently promoted by Chen Hongmou as a basic primer in elementary schools in whichever
province he served. Chen explicitly identified what he so liked about these men as their
faithful attachment to the Cheng-Zhu tradition and the insistent ethical focus of their
thought, as contrasted to the detached scholarship-for-scholarship's-sake style of inquiry he found to dominate the intellectual world of his day.[68]
     It was from these early Qing Cheng-Zhu masters that Chen most directly absorbed
his passion for intensive, wrenching moral self-criticism that we discussed in Chapter 3.
In his eyes this group of scholars, perhaps most especially Lu Shiyi in his *Sibian lu*
(Record of discriminating thought), had kept alive the imperative to seek personal

moral perfection in an age when other more careerist, literary, or academic concerns had become for the majority the focus of study. As Hellmut Wilhelm and Pei-yi Wu have stressed, there was in the self-cultivation techniques of these men an element of guilt-ridden religiosity that was unusually pronounced even within the *lixue* tradition; this compulsion and angst was clearly evident in the quest of Chen Hongmou to "overcome self" (*keji*) and was passed on, in part through his influence, to nineteenth-century Songxue partisans such as Tang Jian.[69] Chen also picked up from Lu Shiyi, or at least found reinforced there, his sense of the importance of ritual practice as a practical instrument of social ordering, rather than an object of fetishistic philological study.[70]

But as Wing-tsit Chan has demonstrated, by far the signal importance of this cohort of scholars within the *lixue* tradition was to dramatically shift the emphasis of Cheng-Zhu thought toward practical worldly concerns. As a group they differed little from their philologist contemporaries in their distaste for metaphysics, held by others to be the essential focus of Song learning. In particular they denied the scholastic dualism of principle and material force (*qi*), which tainted Zhu Xi's philosophy in the eyes of many, and with it the disparagement of material concerns. For these men Zhu's call to *qiongli* (exhaustively investigate principle) was a call to empirical inquiry. Zhu's masterpiece, the *Jinsi lu* (Reflections on things at hand), underwent a renewed vogue of appeal—emphatically shared in by Chen Hongmou—and was read in a far more empirical light than in the past. The early Qing Cheng-Zhu devotees were students of economics and, in their official careers, were instrumental in effecting the empire's economic recovery from the depression of the dynastic transition era. They were also intrigued by the possibilities of Western science. As Lu Shiyi wrote, "The Six Classics are not the only thing people of today should study. They must study astronomy, geography, river work and irrigation, military craft, and so forth, which are of practical use. Vulgar scholars who talk about nature and destiny with an air of superiority are of no help to the world."[71] Chen Hongmou, of course, relished this reemphasis on the practical implications of *lixue* thought. In his *Sourcebook on Proper Scholarship* he praised Lu Longqi for showing, in both his writings and his life, that "those who do research on the Classics and the Four Books must also know how to implement their message in the day-to-day world."[72] But just as important was the stress on personal ethics in the work of Lu and his cohort, the careful balance they struck between *ti* (moral substance) and *yong* (practical application).

In Chen Hongmou's own day Cheng-Zhu scholarship was kept alive perhaps most contentiously by the group of scholar-officials from Anhui whose intellectual posture was in the process of hardening into an acknowledged "Tongcheng school." We have already seen that the doyen of this group, Zhang Tingyu, had been Chen's most prominent early patron and that Chen admired and regularly corresponded with another Tongcheng luminary, Fang Bao. Their policy positions, especially on issues of political economy, were quite close. Chen could not be called a Tongcheng partisan per se; there was an element of cultural elitism in that camp that seems to have put Chen off, and he did not sympathize greatly with the emphasis on literary purity that came to be known as the *guwen* (ancient prose) movement, spearheaded by Fang and his student

Yao Nai. Nevertheless, Chen was fully in accord with the devotion to Song *lixue* and to the Four Books preached by the Tongcheng group, and his reading of that tradition was clearly influenced by them, especially by Fang Bao. We know Chen to have owned and read copies of more than ten of Fang's works, including his studies of the *Book of Rites* and the *Spring and Autumn Annals,* and to have particularly recognized Fang's scholarly authority on questions of ritual.[73]

Probably the most contentious and politically sensitive ritual controversy in which Chen deferred to Fang was that involving the *Rites of Zhou* (*Zhouli* or *Zhouguan*). The *Zhouli* was an enigmatic text in which diverse individuals could find nearly whatever they sought. Whereas Wang Anshi had invoked it to legitimate his dirigiste economic planning in the Song, other economic thinkers from Li Gou (1009–59) on read it as counseling laissez-faire respect for private wealth (*baofu*). Gu Yanwu found in it a prescription for elite-led local autonomy and critique of big government of any kind. Yet Ming founder Zhu Yuanzhang had cited its authority for instituting a government-mandated hereditary occupational order, and the Qianlong emperor appealed to it in launching his agricultural improvement drives of the 1730s and 1740s. The iconoclastic early Qing scholars Yan Yuan and Li Gong also claimed it as the basis for their severe regimen of ritual practice. Clearly, the *Zhouli* could be all things to all people. The problem was that, since the early Qing, philologists had increasingly come to view the *Zhouli* as wholly or partly a falsification of the first century A.D., representing itself as more than a millennium older.

Fang Bao occupied a centrist (although shifting) position in this debate, gradually coming to accept portions of the text as genuinely Zhou dynasty and others as later interpolations. In the 1740s, under the joint supervision of Zhu Shi, Zhang Tingyu, and Ortai, Fang compiled an imperially sponsored variorum edition, the *Qinding Zhouguan yishu,* in which arguments on differing sides of the debate were laid out. The net result of Fang's scholarship has been read variously by historians, with Benjamin Elman, for example, stressing Fang's efforts as an "Old Text" partisan to rehabilitate the *Zhouli,* and Kai-wing Chow tending instead to emphasize Fang's skepticism. For his own part, Chen Hongmou seems to have taken the former view. On several occasions he applauded his patron Fang Bao's success in restoring the canonical status of a work he prized, not as an inscribed record of the "golden age" but rather as a practical guide to contemporary statecraft (*jingshi*), especially—in a reading contrary to that of Wang Anshi—as a prescription for low taxation and frugality in government spending.[74]

One of the things that kept Chen aloof from the aggressive "Songxue" position articulated by the Tongcheng camp and others was his receptiveness to the message of the great Ming-dynasty philosopher-statesman Wang Yangming. When he boasted of his lack of intellectual partisanship, indeed, it was clearly this factor that Chen had foremost in mind. We have seen earlier that Wang Yangming was a pervasive historical presence in many of the regions in which Chen came to maturity—in his native Guangxi; in the southwest, where he made his most striking early mark; and in Jiangxi, where he held his first governorship—and Chen could not but emerge with a deep admiration for the man and his practical achievements in the sphere of sociocultural reform (*jiao-*

hua) and institution building. But he was also strongly attracted to Wang's ethical and epistemological views. In the wake of their appropriation by the radically individualist and egalitarian Taizhou school of the late Ming, these views had become anathema to a wide spectrum of Qing literati, who felt obliged to rescue the cultural tradition from the harm Wang's reckless notions had done.[75] There were some among the late Ming–early Qing *lixue* scholars whom Chen most admired—Lu Shiyi, for example, and (as we will see below) Lü Kun, Li Yong, and Tang Bin as well—who clung to a defense of Wang's essential orthodoxy, but there were many more, including Gu Yanwu, Lu Longqi, Li Guangdi, Zhang Luxiang, and Fang Bao, who could not forgive him for having, in their view, effectively precipitated the fall of the Ming.[76]

Chen Hongmou himself felt sufficiently confident of Wang's correctness to include substantial selections from his writings in various of his own moral tracts. He was influenced by Wang's ideas on the social utility of ritual practice, by his institutional innovations in local community and public security organization (in the *xiangyue* and *baojia* systems), and by his pedagogical techniques (the specific form of ethical debate known as *jiangxue*).[77] Wang's emphasis on meditation as a technique of self-cultivation, by contrast, had little appeal for him.[78] Where Chen found Wang Yangming's thought most attractive, however, was in the two doctrines for which he is probably best known today, that of "innate wisdom" (*liangzhi*) and of the unity of knowledge and action.

The first of these was highly problematic, for it was precisely the aspect of Wang's thought that was most condemned by Qing literati, who feared its radically individualist implications. For Chen, as we have discussed in Chapter 3, Wang's message that all human beings have equally within them the essence of Heaven, the inherent rational faculty to distinguish right from wrong, and the inclination to pursue the right was the very core of civilized thought. It was what assigned to human beings their intrinsic dignity and was the first assumption on which benevolent governance ought to proceed. The more pessimistic view of human nature that he sensed in many of his fellow officials spawned elitist and commandist policies that in the end must prove counterproductive. Chen insisted, to the contrary, that the presumption of universal reason and goodness was the foundation of more enlightened policies to encourage popular fulfillment of productive vocations and social roles.[79] The danger in the doctrine of *liangzhi* that so alarmed Chen's contemporaries, and that he himself admitted had produced dire consequences in the late Ming, was that the belief in innate moral knowledge might obscure recognition of the need for an ongoing effort (*gongfu*) at moral self-improvement. Whereas Wang Yangming had consistently stressed that *liangzhi* can only be brought to its proper fulfillment by intensive cultivation through textual learning (*xuewen*), this key caveat had been ignored by Wang's later followers in introducing their own "unfounded corruptions" (*daokong zhi bi*) into his thought. By purging Wang's thought of these subsequent interpolations, Chen sought to rehabilitate the idioms of *liangzhi/liangxin* and lay claim to the body of sociopolitical thought behind them.[80]

Wang's epistemological doctrine of the unity of knowledge and action (*zhixing heyi*) necessitated for Chen no similar apology. It had after all been accepted by all early Qing Cheng-Zhu partisans, regardless of their stance on Wang's other teachings,[81] and was, as we have seen, the touchstone of Chen's own thought. Chen pointed out on one occasion the irony that many of Wang's followers who most trumpeted his theory of "innate wisdom" found in this the legitimation for a life of detached contemplation, whereas Wang himself could not have been more clear on the point that wisdom is only actualized in committed daily practice.[82] Wang Yangming's own career as an eminent public servant, perhaps along with that of Sima Guang, provided for Chen Hongmou the very model of how moral reflection, study, and sociopolitical activism ought to be combined in an individual life.

Northern Neo-Confucianism: Lü Kun and Guanxue

Chen Hongmou was a man from the deep south who nevertheless felt more comfortable in the social and intellectual world of the north. There was something in the "simple and direct rusticity" (*zhipu*) of northern Chinese culture with which Chen deeply identified and that he preferred to the polish and sophistication of Jiangnan and the southeast coast. The *lixue* tradition had of course for centuries been the subject of hegemonizing claims by the great academies and scholarly communities of the lower Yangzi. As early as the Southern Song, however, and even more dramatically in the wake of the wrenching Ming-Qing transition, self-consciously regionalized schools of Confucian elites outside this Zhejiang-Jiangsu core came to pursue diverging and distinctive scholarly agendas of their own—schools such as the "Minxue" of Fujian, the "Lianxue" (or "Xiangxue") of Hunan, the "Luoxue" of Henan, and the "Guanxue" of Shaanxi, to name but a few.[83] Their affiliation with specifically northern regional schools was likely a significant factor in the consciousness of many of Chen's scholarly influences discussed so far—Sima Guang in the Song, for example, and Wei Xiangshu, Lu Longqi, and Zhang Boxing in the early Qing—but it was not nearly so deliberate a part of their scholarly identity as it was for several other figures who would come to constitute the most direct and proximate influences on Chen Hongmou's intellectual development.

Foremost among these was Lü Kun (Lü Xinwu, 1536–1618), almost surely the historical figure who had the single greatest influence on Chen Hongmou's life and thought. A native of Ningling, Henan, Lü had achieved his *jinshi* in 1574 and served in local and provincial posts throughout north and northwest China, producing in the process a number of didactic texts to uplift the moral conduct of the populations he governed. As a board official in 1597 he submitted a memorial warning of the restless mood of the people in the face of the state's increasing fiscal demands. When the Ming court ignored his remonstrance, he retired from public office and returned to his home county, where he turned his energies to a wide variety of local institutional reforms, including the establishment of elementary schools and charitable granaries.[84] Although he vigorously denied affiliation with any particular school of scholarship, in the Qing period Lü's activities and writings exerted a very broad appeal, achieving virtual cult status among figures in the tradition of self-consciously activist, *lixue*-oriented officials to which Chen Hongmou belonged. Lü's works were regularly cited and reprinted by Li Yong and Lu Longqi, by Chen's patron and teacher Zhu Shi, by his colleague and friend Yin Huiyi, and by Wei Yuan, Lin Zexu, and Zeng Guofan in the nineteenth century. Chen himself was among the most vigorous proselytizers of Lü's cult. In Chen's various sourcebooks on education, social reform, and official conduct the writings of Lü Kun and his father, Lü Desheng (Lü Jinxi), occupy more pages than those of anyone else, including Zhu Xi, and Chen's 1736 redaction with commentary of Lü's *Shenyin yu* (Groaning words), under the title *Lüzi jielu* (Quotations from Master Lü), was picked up for inclusion in the Imperial Library and was widely read in Chen's day and after.[85]

Lü's influence on Chen was extremely wide-ranging, affecting nearly every aspect of his thinking. Many of these elements have already been dealt with in passing; it remains here to attempt an encapsulation of Lü Kun's overall vision as it was understood by Chen and, I believe, by other activist officials over the course of the Qing. Lü proceeded from a highly ordered view of the universe and human society as structured and driven by a kind of natural law he preferred to call the *dao* (Way), rather than the more scholastic-sounding *li* (principle). His reading of the Confucian textual tradition strongly emphasized its naturalistic and humanistic strains and downplayed or even rejected its formalist and idealist ones.[86] But this reading was also an uncompromisingly normative one, attaching great priority to the scholar's mission to achieve both personal moral perfection or "self-mastery" (*zhishen*) and the moral and material betterment of society. He called this linkage of scholarship and social activism "*shixue*" (substantive learning, on which more below) and stressed its practical content. As Chen wrote to Yin Huiyi, "Mr. Lü's learning on political economy and such matters is truly estimable and genuinely efficacious. . . . Compared to his, the writings of others [which lack this practical dimension] are one-sided and pretentious."[87]

Lü Kun's ordered view of the universe translated into a vision of society that was hierarchical and somewhat elitist; he was a thoroughly unsympathetic reformer of many forms of popular culture, which he held to be "indecent."[88] Chen Hongmou appears to have softened Lü's elitism considerably and was evidently far more comfortable than Lü with the reality of social mobility but otherwise generally accepted Lü's social and cultural vision. He was impressed by, and adapted in modified forms, the institutional means Lü had worked out in support of a stable, well-ordered local society: community rituals, the *xiangyue* community compact, and (to a lesser extent) *baojia* household regimentation. On the other hand, Lü (and Chen following him) was fundamentally committed to the principle of the educability of all human beings; consequently, in the cultivation of individual moral autonomy he favored moral suasion and didacticism over coercion and disciplinary sanctions. This was the basis of his efforts at school building and of his passion for producing and distributing moralistic tracts. As with Chen, Lü held faith in the elite's ability to "reach" (*tong*) the common people and believed this goal justified radical compromises with popular capacities and tastes—use of vernacular language, of doggerel verse, and (in Lü's case but not Chen's) of ample pictorial illustration.[89]

Also softening Lü's defense of social hierarchy was his pervasive humanism, his very deep-seated belief in human emotional response (*renqing*), and a commonsense recognition of each person's emotional and material needs as the only true basis of morality and the viable society. He opposed any arbitrary and inhumane dictates of ritual propriety as excessive (*guoli*) and thus, among other things, rejected the harsher prescriptions for female conduct of the Song *lixue* tradition. Lü's belief in the primacy of *renqing* was not a matter of accommodation of higher principle to empirical practicability but rather was firmly embedded in his naturalistic view of the universe. *Renqing*, like the parallel nature of material forces (*wuqing*), was an ontological reality, and not complying with it was simultaneously immoral and fruitless. Inasmuch as human beings were a microcosm of the moral, ordered universe (*renshen yi xiao tiandi ye*), human instincts, once purified of accumulated bad habits, formed a sure guide to moral conduct. Chen Hongmou took deeply to heart this aspect of Lü's thought. "Every single sentence that Lü wrote," he gushed, "is valuable for understanding the actual way of the world and the workings of the human heart."[90]

This view had political implications as well. The responsibility of the benevolent official was not to proceed along any arbitrary or predetermined course of policy but rather to pay close heed to the collective attitudes and material needs of the people (*minqing*) and to respond accordingly. The harsher compulsions of laws and punishments were inferior to an open but morally informed dialogue. And, analogously, commandist economic policies were inferior to a sensitive appreciation of popular needs and desires, as reflected in the behavior of the market and the rational search for private profit. In his series of handbooks known collectively as the *Shizheng lu* (Notes on substantive governance), Lü laid out in considerable detail the practical ways each official might carry out his comprehensive duties on a basis of love and empathy (*aixi*) for the people. These handbooks were heavily cited in Chen Hongmou's own administrative guides.[91]

Chen was already aware of and influenced by Lü Kun from the start of his bureaucratic career, likely a result of his education in Guilin's statecraft-oriented academies. His appreciation of related, but more localized, strains of northern neo-Confucianism seems to have been a later acquisition. In the year 1739 Chen, having been dismissed and degraded from his post as Yunnan provincial treasurer, was serving as Tianjin circuit intendant and engaged in a massive overhaul of the Yellow River drainage system. This project necessitated detailed coordination with Henan governor Yin Huiyi, and the two men became regular correspondents.[92] Yin (1691–1748) was only a few years older than Chen and like him a Yongzheng protégé. As it turned out, the two had a great deal more in common: they both had a passion for re-editing and distributing for novice students throughout their jurisdictions their favorite texts from the Confucian tradition, and their tastes ran rather remarkably to the same works. Just a year earlier, Yin had published his own redaction of Lü Kun, the *Lü Yu zecui* (1738), and before that had brought out new editions of Zhu Xi's *Jinsi lu* and Zhen Dexiu's *Daxue yanyi*. Yin's own *Sijian lu* (Four mirrors) was a set of moral lessons drawn from Sima Guang's *Comprehensive Mirror for Aid in Governance,* arranged respectively for the target groups of the ruler, the minister, the gentleman, and the good woman—the parallel with Chen's own *Five Sourcebooks* is notable. In their correspondence the two officials routinely discussed their mutual enthusiasm for this particular constellation of past scholars and their goals in seeing to their republication.[93]

But Yin Huiyi, hailing from Zhili's Boye County, was also heir to a specifically northern line of neo-Confucian thought that up to that time seems to have been relatively foreign to Chen Hongmou. In the late 1730s Yin updated and republished two parallel works that had first been compiled roughly half a century earlier by two students of the great seventeenth-century scholar-official Sun Qifeng (1585–1675). These were Wei Yi'ao's 1646 *Beixue bian* (Anthology of the Hebei school) and Tang Bin's 1673 *Luoxue bian* (Anthology of the Henan school).[94] Both works reflected Sun Qifeng's determination to reconcile the messages of Zhu Xi and Wang Yangming, as well as his strong orientation toward practical administrative and social reform, and Chen Hongmou found them to his liking on both scores. He wrote to Yin Huiyi of his appreciation of Wei Yi'ao and his work,[95] but, as it was for Yin, it was the activist Henanese official Tang Bin (1627–87) and the curriculum of Luoxue he had constructed at Kaifeng's Daliang Academy that was closer to his heart.

Tang had been an illustrious predecessor of Chen in his governorships of Jiangxi, Shaanxi, and Jiangsu, and Chen explicitly cited his administration of these provinces as models for his own. Celebrated for the puritanical style of his personal life, in office Tang was known for his dogged opposition to gentry extravagance and also to the morally suspect tendencies of most of popular culture. Chen particularly admired the way he had worked to ameliorate the hostilities to which blatant distinctions of wealth and poverty gave rise, especially in the lower Yangzi region.[96] Tang's *Luoxue bian* prominently included selections from the great Song-era Henanese *lixue* masters Cheng Yi, Cheng Hao, and Shao Yong, but even more prominent were selections from another, more recent Henanese—and erstwhile critic of the Chengs' metaphysical preoccupations—Lü Kun. Tang prefaced his selections from Lü by lauding his stress on the "mutual interdependence of moral substance and practical application" (*tiyong jianbei*), which, to the contemporary reader, was as stimulating as "having ice-water poured down one's back." He added:

> My home is near to Mr. Lü's native place. When I look at the walls of the county seat, the local irrigation and tax-collection systems, and the proper way in which the rites of capping, marriage, funerals, and ancestral sacrifice are carried out there, I see in all of this Mr. Lü's handiwork. Although it has been many decades since his death, the local people still dare not alter anything he instituted. . . . His prescriptions for community covenants [*xiangyue*], for *baojia*, for charitable granaries [*yicang*], for community schools [*shexue*], for adjudication of local disputes, and for nurturance of the aged and the young, all expounded in his *Shizheng lu*, provide the very model for the way these matters ought to be handled. Throughout my own official career, I have always considered Mr. Lü my teacher.[97]

What we see here, then, is one lineage of a highly particular agenda of activist local administration, passing from Lü Kun, to Tang Bin, to Yin Huiyi and Chen Hongmou (and likely a significant number of others) in the Yongzheng and Qianlong reigns.

Even more important for the development of Chen Hongmou's own social and political thought, though, was the third of the northern schools, with which, as Yin Huiyi

insisted, Beixue and Luoxue shared a common orientation. This was the so-called
Shaanxi school, or Guanxue. It is hardly an exaggeration to say that when Chen discovered Guanxue, in the early and mid-1740s, he found his true intellectual home.
Guanxue's near-complete shunning of metaphysics, aesthetics, and classical philology
in favor of personal ethics and political economy, and its insistence on the equal importance of the latter two (*tiyong chuanxue* [study of both substance and function si-
multaneously]), was perfectly suited to Chen's own scheme of scholarly priorities.

Guanxue in the late imperial era was centered in Xi'an's venerable Guanzhong
Academy, where most of its major exponents had in their day taught.[98] It identified it-
self as direct heir of the ancient sage-kings, whose domains had presumably been
Shaanxi-based, but it traced its teachings more directly to the great Northern Song *lixue*
scholar and Shaanxi native Zhang Zai (1020–77). It also claimed as its own several mid-
Ming neo-Confucian revivalists: Xue Xuan (1389–1464) (also claimed by Luoxue),
Xue Jingzhi (1434–1508), and the high metropolitan official Lü Nan (1479–1542).
All three had been ardent Cheng-Zhu partisans (with a special affection for Sima
Guang), and Lü had actually disputed the teachings of Wang Yangming in public debate.[99] But it was the late Ming scholar Feng Congwu's (1556–1627) anthology of past
Shaanxi writers, the *Guanxue bian*, that gave Guanxue its name and identified it as a coherent, self-conscious tradition.[100] Alarmed by his home region's growing social and
ecological crisis, Feng preached a message of overcoming self and of "doctoring" to the
ills of society. He was also deliberately more eclectic in drawing on the neo-Confucian
tradition. At his renovated Guanzhong Academy he practiced the pedagogical technique of "discussing learning" (*jiangxue*) advocated by Wang Yangming[101] and selectively
distinguished between what he believed useful in Wang's thought (the notion of innate
goodness, *liangzhi*) and what he found dangerous (Wang's *xinxue* intuitionism). And indeed, despite its Cheng-Zhu roots and its commitment to local practical activism,
Guanxue in the hands of Feng Congwu shared many common elements with other contemporaneous evangelical movements in the Wang Yangming tradition, including the
much-disparaged Taizhou school. The academy hosted weekly meetings of a "study society" (*xuehui*) for collective discussion of works in Feng's idiosyncratic curriculum. The
several hundred members of this congregation—democratically open, at Feng's insistence, to "any farmer, artisan, or merchant of genuine moral commitment"—pledged
to abjure smoking, drinking, litigating against one another, and involving themselves in
the increasingly sordid late Ming politics.[102]

In the early and mid-Qing Guanxue was carried on by a line of prominent scholars
including Li Yong (1627–1705), Wang Xinjing (courtesy name Fengchuan, 1656–
1738), and Yang Shen (1699–1794). Li Yong was nationally known for his passive resistance to Qing rule, including engaging in hunger strikes. Although poor and almost
entirely self-educated, Li was so renowned for his scholarship that he was offered a high
official post by the Kangxi emperor, which he courageously declined.[103] Instead, Li
turned very self-consciously to the vocation of teaching. He renovated the Guanzhong
Academy and used it as a base to formulate practical programs for the social and agrarian reconstruction of Shaanxi from the havoc wreaked by the late Ming rebellion of Li
Zicheng.[104] He spread his message empire-wide in the course of celebrated lecture

tours of Jiangnan and other parts of eastern China. Li epitomized the same distinctive blend of intellectual influences that later animated Chen Hongmou: a balanced appreciation of Zhu Xi and of Wang Yangming, attraction to Zhen Dexiu's *Daxue yanyi* and Qiu Jun's *Daxue yanyi bu*, and a special fondness for the prescriptions for social activism advanced by Lü Kun. Wang Xinjing, who became a great favorite of Chen, devoted himself to further disseminating Li Yong's teachings; his major work, *Fengchuan zashu*, contains three sections, on agricultural technology, famine relief, and family and community ritual. Wang's student Yang Shen we shall meet in Chapter 7; author of the *Binfeng guangyi* (Explication of the customs of Bin), which discourses on agricultural techniques in the context of a ritual calendar for the morally correct farm household, Yang served as Chen Hongmou's longtime personal advisor and the head of his sericulture bureau in Shaanxi.

Chen recalled that his initial awareness of Guanxue came in the mid-1720s, when he was a Hanlin academician assigned to work on the *Ming History* under Zhang Tingyu and Zhu Shi. Zhu, whom Chen called "my teacher," had once taught at the Guanzhong Academy and had edited a collection of Zhang Zai's works. A fervent admirer of Wang Xinjing, Zhu invited him to come to Beijing to serve as consultant on the *History* project, but Wang declined on grounds of illness, sending in instead several comments by mail.[105] Chen's interest lay effectively dormant from this time until his acquaintance with Yin Huiyi in 1739 sparked greater attention to all the northern schools, and on his first posting as Shaanxi governor in 1744 he became a full-fledged convert to the Guanxue message, which he described on several occasions as "right on the money" (*qieshi*).[106] A brief term as Hubei governor in 1747, sandwiched between two tenures in Shaanxi, brought Chen into contact with Huanggang County native Jing Guoyuan, who had been a student of Wang Xinjing at Xi'an, and the two men conversed enthusiastically about the recently deceased Guanxue master.[107] Back in Shaanxi Chen made a pilgrimage to Wang's native village, where he visited his study and admired his book collection. He contributed prefaces to a collection of Wang's later writings, *Wang Fengchuan xiansheng xuji*, and to a new reprinting of Wang's expanded edition of Feng Congwu's *Guanxue bian*. He also memorialized successfully to have Wang's tablet installed in the Confucian temple at Beijing.[108] Whereas Chen Hongmou's first five moral sourcebooks, the *Wuzhong yigui*, were all compiled prior to his first Shaanxi tenure and betray no Guanxue influence, his final work in this genre, the 1769 *Xueshi yigui*, takes Guanxue as its centerpiece, with no fewer than five Shaanxi scholars represented among the work's total of twenty-two.[109]

Throughout his four tenures as Shaanxi governor, Chen never lost an opportunity to publicly laud the province's special scholarly legacy. He showered his patronage on the Guanzhong Academy and intervened directly in its management. He ordered province-wide special examinations to recruit for Guanzhong the best students, specifying that this did *not* mean individuals who were simply elegant writers (*nengwen*); one of those selected, Wang Jie, would turn out to be Chen's protégé and eventual grand secretary. He canvassed the province for scattered works of Guanxue scholars, deposited these in the academy's collection, and in 1751 submitted a range of them to the Qianlong emperor as part of that ruler's initial attempt to constitute an Imperial

Library.[110] When serving as Fujian governor in 1754, Chen also donated to Fuzhou's Aofeng Academy a selection of Guanxue works and ordered that these be scrutinized by the academy's scholars in order to derive ideas on how to conduct an agricultural improvement campaign in their own province.[111]

In his administration of Shaanxi itself, many of Chen Hongmou's most highly touted activist policies were influenced quite directly by Guanxue prescriptions. His ambitious extension of the province's irrigation infrastructure was based, Chen acknowledged, on models formerly proposed by Wang Xinjing. His attempt at revival of the regional sericulture industry was both inspired and led by Yang Shen. Even Chen's remarkable 1745 campaign to have each magistrate survey a broad range of infrastructural features and local cultural practices in his county and to systematically determine "factors which should be promoted or should be expunged" (*xingchu shiyi*) drew on the recommendations and language of Wang Xinjing several decades earlier.[112]

The core of Guanxue, as Chen Hongmou understood it, might be reduced to two fundamental recognitions. First was a kind of transcendental holism, expressed in the oft-repeated Guanxue dictum, "Heaven-and-earth and the ten-thousand things are essentially one" (*tiandi wanwu yiti*). In the enigmatic text that served as Guanxue's point of departure, Zhang Zai's "Western Inscription" (*Ximing*), this holism was couched in terms at once subjective, material, and warmly familial:

> Heaven is my father and Earth is my mother, and even such a small creature as I finds an intimate place in their midst. Therefore that which fills the universe I regard as my body and that which directs the universe I consider as my nature. All people are my brothers and sisters, and all things my companions. . . . Even those who are tired, infirm, crippled, or sick; those who have no brothers or children, wives or husbands, are all my brothers who are in distress and have no one to turn to.[113]

Chen wrote to Ortai on his arrival as governor in Shaanxi in 1744 that the profundity of this text now struck him in ways it had never done before. It presented him, as an individual, with the obligation to care for all his siblings and companions, to accept "all things as my personal responsibility."[114] With Zhu Xi's scholastic veneer of the differentiation of the unity into ideal forms pared away from it, and read in the context of Wang Yangming's doctrine of the coequal innate goodness of all persons (*liangzhi*) and of the macrocosmic-microcosmic correspondences of the *Daxue*, Zhang Zai's ethical transcendentalism became a straightforward call to (as the 1990s activist slogan had it) "Think globally, act locally."

Guanxue's second key recognition was of the reality of change. In his preface to Wang Xinjing's updated *Guanxue bian*, Chen writes that the most important of the Six Classics is the *Yijing* (Book of changes) and that it is the Way first identified in that work that has continued to be worked out in the subsequent scholarly tradition. To think in terms of a past "golden age," that of the Duke of Zhou or of Confucius, when this Way was statically fixed for all time, misses the essential point that the Way or, if you choose to call it that, principle is constantly in flux. To properly comprehend its workings, one must both study history—a cardinal dictate of Guanxue-tradition scholars, as well as of Chen—and also carefully observe the conditions of one's own day. It is precisely because of its basic acceptance of change, Chen notes, that Guanxue offers such a useful guide to formulation of contemporary policy. It is this recognition that enables the committed individual to "save the world" (*jiushi*).[115]

Activism begins with self-cultivation. One of the things Chen so admired about Li Yong was the fact that, among the great figures whose scholarly careers began in the late Ming and who refused service under the Qing—Gu Yanwu, Huang Zongxi, Wang Fuzhi—Li alone drew as a lesson from the Ming debacle that an intensified effort at personal moral improvement was a necessary focus of study, and he thereby put the *ti* on an equal footing with the *yong*. As Chen himself had long done, Li and his pupils placed zealous emphasis on a continual process of "self-criticism" (*ziwo pipan*), "self-renewal" (*zixin*), and what Li termed "*fanshen*" (self-reflection or turning over a new leaf). Li's work *Fanshen lu* (Record of self-reflection), heavily excerpted by Chen in his *Sourcebook on Proper Scholarship*, stood in sharp contrast to Gu Yanwu's philologically and politically oriented *Rizhi lu* (Record of knowledge acquired daily). Invoking Wang Yangming, Li argued that self-criticism and self-renewal were the true way to achieve what Wang had called the realization or perfection of innate goodness (*zhi liangzhi*).[116]

Education, both of oneself and of the public, played a central role in Guanxue's prescriptions for social improvement. From the mid-Ming Lü Nan (himself a *zhuangyuan*, or first-place finisher on the metropolitan examination) to Chen's own friend and contemporary Yang Shen, Guanxue scholars consistently decried the lack of substance in the examination curriculum of their day. They railed against the selfish emphases of contemporary scholarship, either the morally vacuous pursuit of social advancement through examination success or the preening display of sophisticated philological methods. Both personal study and education of the populace, via schools and *jiangxue*-style public lecturing, must above all be socially useful (*youyong zhi xue*). It should be based on the Four Books of the Cheng-Zhu tradition but also pointedly emphasize "broad" or eclectic learning (*boxue*), crossing partisan lines and including historical and practical materials as well. Public education, as Li Yong and Wang Xinjing stressed, should include the "civilizing" (*jiaohua*) of popular lifestyles and the elevation of popular cultural practice (*hou fengsu*) but should concentrate equally on the improvement of the people's material life through the study and explication of economic laws. Chen repeatedly marveled of Wang Xinjing, for example, that such a private scholar who never served in office a day in his life could have achieved such an evident practical mastery of the principles of political economy (*jingji*).[117] As an intellectual package, then, the Guanxue that Chen came gradually to discover in the 1740s offered him a coherently articulated scholarly grounding for the very agenda of thought and action he had been working out for himself since childhood, and he embraced it wholeheartedly.

Substantive Learning (shixue)

The term regularly invoked by Chen Hongmou to denote the only kind of study he believed worthwhile was *shixue*. Usually translated as "practical learning" and associated with the newly valorized "practice" or "practicality" (*shijian*), "*shixue*," as a rallying cry of late-seventeenth- and eighteenth-century scholars, was a transcultural movement in East Asia, linked directly with the espousal of *sirhak* in Korea and of *jitsugaku* in Tokugawa Japan.[118] Ever since Liang Qichao, the term in its Chinese incarnation has been conventionally identified with the particular teachings and behavioral regimen of the Hebei scholar Yan Yuan (1635–1704) and his student Li Gong (1659–1733).[119] It is worth remarking, however, that the professed *shixue* devotee Chen Hongmou never so much as mentioned Yan or Li in his countless references to the doctrine (in spite of the fact that his intellectual confidante Yin Huiyi was a younger neighbor of Yan from Hebei's Boye County). In fact, as recent scholarship has underlined, there were many different histories of *shixue* in the late imperial era, and these coalesced into a more general enthusiasm for the concept in the early and mid-eighteenth century.

The locus classicus for the term was Zhu Xi's commentary on the *Zhongyong* (Doctrine of the mean), in which he identifies that notion as the work's central message.[120] In the Ming *shixue* enjoyed a highly ambivalent identification with the school of Wang Yangming. Wang used the term himself, and his doctrine of the unity of knowledge and action (*zhixing heyi*) came close to defining the essence of *shixue*, but in fact in the sixteenth and seventeenth centuries the slogan was often most pointedly brandished by scholars who were repelled by the seemingly antiacademic and antiempirical implications of Wang's subjectivism (*xinxue*). This encompassed a very disparate group, from the Changzhou classicist and "ancient prose" master Tang Shunzhi (1507–60), to the great Shanghai statesman, agronomist, and Christian convert Xu Guangqi (1562–1633), to the Song revivalists of Suzhou's Donglin Academy, to the Henan social activist Lü Kun. Into the early Qing the *shixue* banner was waved especially by scholars who saw themselves as Ming "remnants" (*yilao*), including the brilliant Hunanese recluse Wang Fuzhi (1619–92) and, more influentially, by the venerable Sun Qifeng (1584–1675). As discussed above, Sun was a major inspiration for the various provincially defined schools of northern neo-Confucianism to which Chen Hongmou became attracted in the 1740s, and a number of Sun's disciples, notably Diao Bao (1603–69), Wei Xiangshu, and Tang Bin, were articulate champions of *shixue*, as well as special favorites of Chen himself.[121] The term was also employed by early Qing Cheng-Zhu loyalists such as Li Guangdi and Lu Longqi, with Li even working out a metaphysical grounding for it in his doctrine of "nature" (*xing*).[122] But Chen came to his *shixue* advocacy through other paths as well, as we shall see.

Was "*shixue*" anything more than simply a fashionable buzzword, and if so what did it mean? For many it was defined as much by what it opposed as by what it promoted. In the sixteenth and seventeenth centuries *shixue* proponents staked out positions against examination-oriented memorization and "empty" literary production, gradually adding metaphysical speculation to their list of targets. By the latter years of Chen Hongmou's own lifetime, and continuing into the nineteenth century, Hanxue-style philology came to replace these as the principal bête noir.[123] But there were considerable internal disagreements among those who invoked this idiom; some, for example, saw their advocacy of *shixue* as basically a defense of the good old-fashioned ethical and ritual values of Zhu Xi, whereas others (such as Yan Yuan) invoked the term in a frontal attack on Zhu.

In terms of its positive content, *shixue* encompassed at least two disparate strains. For Zhu Xi himself and for Song revivalists such as the Donglin scholars, the central element was moral initiative and cultivation of the ethical self. But for others, notably Xu Guangqi, it meant rather the pragmatic pursuit of worldly ends, especially economic prosperity and political-military strength. The history of the idiom over the late Ming to mid-Qing period was one of the (sometimes uneasy) blending of these two originally disparate strains. As "*shixue*" gradually became "*shixue zhiyong*" (substantive learning to achieve maximum applicability), the materialist and utilitarian element was increasingly highlighted; David Reynolds has pointed out that in mid-Qing casual usage "*shixue*" was the common term of reference for Western *science*.[124] But for many proponents the moral element was not lost; it was simply reconfigured to specify the study of moral action that took sincere account of human emotional needs and of actual social and political conditions and was thus in this sense likewise "practical."[125]

We see this blending of meanings especially clearly when we examine Chen Hongmou's own emphatic usage of this idiom. The term "*shi*" itself may well have been his favorite adjective, employed it seems as an all-purpose modifier to characterize anything of which he strongly approved. In this he was hardly alone. The word turned up as a litany in the titles of works Chen cited and admired—works such as Lü Kun's *Shizheng lu* (1598), Huang Shi'e's *Shixue lu* (ca. 1730), and Depei's *Shijian lu* (1736)—and one Japanese scholar has seen China's entire early modern literati culture as preoccupied by a "discourse of *shi* vs. *ming*" (*shiming lun*).[126] Like most of his contemporaries, Chen used "*shi*" in opposition to terms such as "*ming*" (representation), "*kong*" (empty), "*xu*" (vacuous or fabricated), and "*fou*" (frivolous or superfluous) rather than to any term that we might translate as literally "false" or "heterodox." "*Shi*" meant, in other words, "real" or "genuine" or "solid" or "substantive" but rarely "correct." In regard to personal character Chen used "*shi*" much like he used "*pu*" (rustic or stolid, as discussed in Chapter 1), to refer to a positive personality trait embodying honesty, straightforwardness, frugality, and lack of pretense. This quality is cultivable through education—an education, ideally, that incorporates personal experience of agricultural labor—and it is empowering. "If one's mental makeup [*xin*] is vacuous [*xu*]," he writes, "one cannot achieve anything. If it is genuine [*shi*], all things are possible."[127]

In Chen's bureaucratic discourse "*shi*" referred to anything that was what it claimed to be—granaries that were genuinely filled (not merely reported as such), government workers who were actually on the job (not merely on the payroll), legal plaints that were true and just (not merely trumped up), processes of judicial review by superiors that were actually being carried out. The opposites in each case "existed in name only" (*youming wushi*). Policies that were *shiyong* (truly workable rather than hopelessly idealistic) and were carried out with *shili* (genuine effort) would yield *shixiao* (concrete results). Conditions that were truly current in an official's jurisdiction rather than simply inferred from out-of-date documents were "*shizai*" (actually there), a phrase Chen frequently coupled with "*jimin*" (close to the people) to refer to a style of administration genuinely in touch with the locality. Subordinates should be less concerned to follow the letter (*ming*) of an instruction than its spirit or intent (*shi*). Too much paperwork or too much minute regulation, indeed, nearly guaranteed that an administration be *ming* rather than *shi*. Efficiency, workability, diligence, and integrity were essential to what Chen, following Lü Kun, called "*shizheng*" (genuine governance), a regime in which "facts and representations truly correspond" (*xunming ceshi*).[128]

Chen also on occasion used the voguish term "*shijian*" (practice) in a technical sense but not in the doctrinaire way it was read by those whom Yamanoi Yū calls the "*shijian pai*" (faction of practice). Chen's "practice" was far from utilitarian pragmatism; it affirmed rather than sidestepped the need for moral self-cultivation. Following his Guanxue models, he lectured his student audiences on the need to pursue *fanshen shi-jian*, the "practice of self-renewal."[129] Neither did "practice" for Chen negate the imperative for textual study of the neo-Confucian canon, as it did for Yan Yuan, although he insisted that this study be paired with empirical observation of the material and social worlds. The key was to apply what one learned from textual study in one's daily life (*gongxing shijian*), to "implement its substance" (*jian qi shi*), and conversely to focus one's own scholarship on the genuinely realizable. Scholarship worthy of the name, in Chen's view, "exhausts Principle and puts it into practice" (*qiongli shijian*).[130]

This was precisely *shixue*: not "practical learning" per se but rather a "substantive learning" that focused simultaneously on a workable personal ethics and on the techniques of social and economic management. Chen Hongmou invoked this fashionable term in a way he professed to be nonpartisan yet pointedly self-conscious; it called to mind a deliberate movement, a fact of which he was well aware. "Substantive learning" had indeed been a rallying cry in the Guilin scholarly communities of Chen's youth— the Xuancheng and Xiufeng Academies—and he trumpeted it provocatively at his first official opportunities in the field. In 1729, as an examiner in the Shanxi provincial examinations, we find him insisting that what candidates must display in order to pass is "substantive learning"; six years later, in Yunnan, he sets down regulations for his hundreds of new and revived elementary schools, ordering that the instruction imparted therein be *shixue* and nothing else.[131]

In 1736, at the New Year's festival marking the start of Qianlong's first year on the throne, Yunnan provincial treasurer Chen submitted a bold memorial setting out his proposals for a reform of the examination system that would "encourage *shixue*." The timing of Chen's memorial makes it likely that part of his intention was to encourage the new emperor to continue in general the hardheaded, unpretentious style of administration favored by his predecessor, to which Chen, like other Yongzheng protégés, was himself strongly inclined. Arguing on the basis of the dynasty/nation's (*guojia*) manifest need for scholars who were "of use" (*youyong*), rather than mere pedantic bibliophiles or masters of stylistic elegance, Chen called for systematically greater weight to be placed on the third session of the examination, that on "policy" (*ce*), and for greater emphasis within that part on issues of political economy (*jingji*). He noted that there had been several initiatives from the throne on this matter in the recent past but that lazy examination officials still persisted in looking closely only at the first session of the examination, which dealt with textual exegesis, and glossing over the others. This fact did not go unnoticed by candidates, who thus concentrated all their efforts in this area.[132]

Chen went on to describe to the throne his own attempt to counter the prevailing dysfunctions by instituting a monthly examination at the Yunnan Academy reflecting his conception of "substantive learning." In the second session of the examination the *lun* or "discourse essay" section would give more weight to the Four Books than to the Five Classics and would concentrate on basic issues of personal ethics. Both the "legal judgment" (*pan*) portion of the second session and the "policy" portion of the third session would demand discussion of "current issues" (*shishi*) on either the national or local administrative agenda. In all cases questions would be simply and straightforwardly phrased, and answers judged successful must be unadorned, direct responses, rather than predigested conventionalisms.[133]

Chen most frequently identified as exemplars of *shixue* members of the Guanxue school, although he paid the compliment as well to such venerable figures as Zhen Dexiu and Fan Zhongyan and to other relatively contemporary scholars such as Diao Bao. These he distinguished from more run-of-the-mill "pseudoscholars" (*weishi*) who specialized in rote memorization and other forms of pedantry. *Shixue* was not something so mechanically acquired; it must be continually refined through study and lived on a daily basis. In a letter written around 1755 to a Manchu acquaintance, Chengde, he links *shixue* to the discourse of personal tribulation (*fannan*), which figures largely in his notion of personal and professional development: "Each time one goes through a little tribulation, one gains a slightly greater sense of perspective. Each time one undergoes a little hardship, one finds within oneself a little more fortitude. This is the only way we in official life can find peace within ourselves, and make sense of our fate. Substantive learning, understood this way, is nothing but laborious effort."[134]

Substantive learning that was truly "useful" (*youyong zhi shixue*, a formulation Chen invoked with regularity) encompassed both personal moral commitment—the overcoming of self (*keji*) and an intense acceptance of social responsibility—and a technical sophistication in what today would be called the social sciences. He explicitly identified as *shixue*, for instance, the solicitous economic policies of the famous Tang minister Liu Yan (715–80) and also the actions of contemporary colleagues in reducing dysfunctional and onerous tax burdens. "Substantive learning" is more likely to be pursued in the Four Books than the Five Classics, but it demands as well the mastery of space and time acquired through routine consultation of maps and histories.[135] And inasmuch as classical and historical knowledge is useful only insofar as it serves the present, these studies must be supplemented, for any learning that would claim *shixue* status, by a conscientious and detailed acquaintance with current affairs derived from journalism, from the *Beijing Gazette*. Only learning that is in this way "substantive" and "useful" can aid in one's mission to "order the world."[136]

Ordering the World (jingshi)

Even more than *shixue*, the intellectual agenda subsumed under the indigenous category *jingshi* (appropriately translated by Hymes and Schirokauer as "ordering the world") has piqued the curiosity of historians of late imperial China—most especially those writing in the West but also those in East Asia. In large part this is because it has seemed to provide a baseline for understanding the preconceptions and constraints under which the Qing official elite operated in their herculean task of coping with an aggressively expanding nineteenth-century West. But, even for those most concerned with the question, *jingshi* has proven a maddeningly frustrating notion to define because it was at once part of the basic credo to which all neo-Confucians subscribed and a specific and controversial style of public action and (at least *seemingly* to some) a particular political program; it was simultaneously a timeless value and a special concern (perhaps even a "movement") of discrete historical eras.

One of our most accomplished analysts of late imperial thought, Yu Yingshi, opts for a broad definition. He sees *jingshi* as the simple commitment to activist public service, to "setting the world right," in accord with the dictates of the *Great Learning* (*Daxue*) and encompassing that tradition's assumptions about cosmology and personal ethics. It was integral to the Confucian gentleman's general approach to life.[137] Other scholars, however, such as Benjamin Elman, have insisted that a more analytically useful definition must include the particular emphasis on technical competence—in such areas as hydrology, cartography, and calendrical studies—championed by certain self-conscious *jingshi* practitioners in the face of perceived indifference or opposition by other literati.[138] Still others have advanced yet more distinctive readings, highlighting a more focused political agenda. Peter Perdue, for example, sees as the hallmark of Qing *jingshi* a dedication to the comprehensive improvement of the localities through the creative agency of formal governmental institutions (a reading essentially in accord with the conventional English rendering of *jingshi* as "statecraft").[139] Yet Joshua Fogel, following the early-twentieth-century Japanese sinologist and *jingshi* aficionado Naitō Konan, argues on the contrary that the essential *jingshi* vision called for a heightened degree of local autonomy and freedom from bureaucratic meddling and that this was intrinsic to the understanding of the term itself.[140]

Chang Hao, perhaps the scholar who has thought longest and hardest on the issue, argues that two novel considerations distinguished the particular form of *jingshi* commitment on which the historical literature has concentrated. First was a rather bold and explicit prizing of utility as a criterion for social-political action. All participants in the neo-Confucian cultural system, Chang concedes, acknowledged the "cosmological myth" and the dictates to normative conduct embodied in the *Daxue* and related texts, but adherents to a *jingshi* orientation were rather more willing to "differentiate" practical from normative criteria for action and to act on the former when appropriate. Second, Chang perceives in late imperial *jingshi* ideology a frank acceptance of the achievement of "wealth and power" as legitimate goals of action and, accordingly, of economic and military techniques as legitimate subjects of study for their own sakes. Chang is careful to point out, however, that this reading applied only to a specialized style of *jingshi* scholarship, which he dubs alternately "practical statesmanship" or "bureaucratic statesmanship" (*guanliao jingshi*), and that it coexisted with a view of "moral statesmanship" that, although not unconcerned with political economy, adhered more closely to an orthodox reading of the tradition's normative texts. Kwang-Ching Liu, who basically accepts Chang's analysis, argues further that this "practical statesmanship" reading of *jingshi* was effectively an early-nineteenth-century phenomenon and that it constituted a fundamental and uniquely "modern" reorientation of literati thought in the late Qing.[141]

Indeed, it has been this so-called statecraft movement of the 1820s and after that has drawn the bulk of scholarly attention and has to a considerable degree retrospectively conditioned our understanding of *jingshi* in earlier eras.[142] In these years a number of prominent literati both in and out of government—among them Bao Shichen (1775–1855), Gong Zizhen (1792–1841), He Changling (1785–1848), Wei Yuan (1794–1856), Tao Zhu (1779–1839), and Lin Zexu (1785–1850)—conspicuously turned away from classical scholarship toward a renewed commitment to political action and the detailed study of techniques of institutional reform. They were stimulated to do so by a sense of crisis growing out of the compounding policy debacles of their own and the immediately preceding years: the Heshen corruption scandal and the celebrated protest of Hong Liangji to its incomplete resolution, the devastating and costly White Lotus Rebellion, mounting problems of defense along the northwest frontier, the gradual collapse of the Grand Canal as a usable transport artery, and the problems of opium imports and silver outflow, which led to the alarming economic depression of the early Daoguang reign.[143] As Feng Tianyu in particular has demonstrated, these literati and their followers engaged in an increasingly self-conscious movement that involved not only an orchestrated intellectual attack on Hanxue philology but also coordinated bureaucratic factional self-promotion.[144] Their disciples in succeeding generations included some of the empire's most powerful statesmen, including Zeng Guofan and Zuo Zongtang (on which more below). The textual product that most epitomized this movement, the *Huangchao jingshi wenbian* (Compendium of statecraft writings from the present dynasty), produced by Wei under He's patronage in 1826, was a work of watershed influence, spawning several sequels and quickly becoming a standard reference for policy guidance by field officials throughout the realm.

The contents of this massive work were eclectic and its coverage of subjects comprehensive. As Kwang-Ching Liu points out, the novel decision to arrange its contents topically rather than chronologically, as had been done in Chen Zilong's late Ming precursor, demonstrated in itself a commitment to practical utility rather than pedantic archivalism.[145] The central thrust was clearly on technical expertise and what Chang Hao calls "piecemeal renovation" of institutions. Within this textual arrangement, considerable attention was paid to policies that might promote economic development, and, as Liu argues, both the book itself and the larger movement it represented took a very sympathetic attitude toward merchants and commercial activity.[146] But the *Jingshi wenbian* was by no means simply materialist and utilitarian. Ritual propriety was taken seriously, as was scholarly practice. In keeping with its emphasis on striking an appropriate balance between *ti* and *yong*, substance and function, the anthology devoted considerable space to writings on moral self-improvement of the sort long promoted by Qing-era Songxue scholarship.[147] Even literary studies—the domain of *wen*—received some treatment. What were strikingly, if unsurprisingly, absent were writings about issues of metaphysics and of classical philology. The unifying tone, as Frederic Wakeman long ago pointed out, was one of historicism rather than golden-age classicism, an acceptance of historical change and the corresponding need to "accord with the times" (*heshi*).[148]

Jingshi was hardly a new idea in the nineteenth century, however. The term itself had been used in the late Zhou-dynasty Daoist classic *Zhuang zi*, in an apparently unrelated usage ("passing through the ages"), and in the *Later Han History* in a usage approximating its subsequent one of sociopolitical ordering. The term's late imperial currency, though, was essentially an outgrowth of its widespread use by Confucian revivalists of the Song, when it was invoked in deliberate opposition to the *chushi* (withdrawal from the world) ideal associated with Buddhism. Neo-Confucian scholars of all shades of belief were fond of the term: from the radical state-maker Wang Anshi, to the *lixue* numerologist Shao Yong (1011–77), to the *xinxue* (school of the mind) forerunner Lu Xiangshan (1139–93), to the Zhedong (Eastern Zhejiang) pragmatists Chen Liang (1143–94) and Ye Shi (1150–1223), whose utilitarian philosophy earned Zhu Xi's punning sobriquet "*lixue*" (school of profit). With Chen and Ye we see as well what would be a recurring pattern, the impassioned interest in institutional study, or *jingshi*, growing out of a perceived need to rescue the world from sociopolitical crisis—in the case of the Zhedong group the quest to recapture north China from the heathen Jin. Again in the fifteenth century the term and its agenda gained fevered attention in response to the Tumu debacle of 1449, culminating in Qiu Jun's statecraft masterpiece, the *Daxue yanyi bu* of 1488.[149]

But as a matter of conscious influence the "statecraft movement" of the nineteenth century related most directly to the renewed vogue of self-described *jingshi* scholarship that began in the later sixteenth century and continued through the first decades of the Qing. According to its foremost student, Yamanoi Yū, *jingshi* in this era constituted the pervasively dominant intellectual trend, bridging the periods of dominance of Wang Yangming's *xinxue* in the earlier sixteenth century and *kaozheng* classical philology in the eighteenth. Yamanoi sees the late Ming turn away from pursuit of individual sagehood toward social activism as a response to increasingly obvious signs of sociopolitical collapse. It also reflected the deep impact on intellectual life of the monetization of the economy epitomized by the Single Whip tax reforms, spurring scholars to turn, first, toward more pragmatic, mundane foci of study and, second, to a revived stress on social obligations (versus marketized social relations) of the sort found in the Cheng-Zhu school. Yamanoi sees the genesis of this statecraft revival most directly in the activity of the Donglin Academy group, but he also notes the influence of Christianity and other elements of Western learning.[150]

As Yu Yingshi points out, "*jingshi*" was such a broadly shared rallying cry among neo-Confucian activist literati of this late Ming–early Qing era that it is probably a mistake to see it as an isolated "movement" at all.[151] Nonetheless, I am tempted to identify three fairly distinct lines of scholarship within which this shared discourse was appropriated in rather diverse ways; this scholarship left a complex legacy that mid- and late Qing statecraft literati could select from as they chose. The first was that of Lü Kun and the northern regional schools of Cheng-Zhu neo-Confucianism, notably Guanxue. This line has been by far the least identified by historians as part of the late Ming–early Qing *jingshi* tradition, even though that term figured very prominently in their rhetoric, and as I will argue below, its influence in shaping later statecraft thought was far from inconsiderable.[152] The other two lines, more conventionally associated with seventeenth-century *jingshi* thought, both originated in the Jiangnan region and are linked most prominently with the names of Chen Zilong and Gu Yanwu.

Chen Zilong (1608–47), a native of Songjiang, was chief editor of the *Huang Ming jingshi wenbian* (Compendium of statecraft writings from the Great Ming dynasty), a 1638 anthology that probably did more than any previous work to enshrine the term "*jingshi*" in the empire's enduring political vocabulary. Chen was a youthful leader of the political action groups the Fushe (Restoration society) and Jishe (Immanent change society), which owed some of their ideas to the Cheng-Zhu revivalist Donglin party but even more, perhaps, to the Shanghai agronomist, Christian convert, and statesman Xu Guangqi, whose work Chen Zilong also republished.[153] Gu Yanwu, of course, was the seventeenth century's most famous polymath—geographer, political theorist, and pioneer of *kaozheng*-style classical philology. Chen and Gu shared many things: an aversion to metaphysics and literary aestheticism, hostility to Wang Yangming's school in particular and to excessive concern for personal self-cultivation in general (factors that clearly differentiated them from Lü Kun and the Guanxue scholars), a faith in the positive social role of ritual and of appropriately transformed (*hua*) local customary practice, and a devotion to the foundering Ming cause that prompted their impassioned search for sociopolitical solutions. But they diverged on the character of the solutions they sought. As Thomas Metzger has argued, Chen represented an "accommodative" or "realistic" approach to reform, stressing piecemeal change and "administrative flexibility," whereas Gu (and others such as Huang Zongxi) inclined more to a "basic change" or "radical" approach, advocating fundamental transformation of the empire's institutional structure.[154] We will return in a moment to the content of Gu's politics, but we should note here that it was informed in part by a fundamentalist belief in the literal truth of the classics (that is, those portions of the classics that could be verified as genuinely ancient), a belief he bequeathed to the Qing philological movement as a whole.[155]

This survey of recent scholarly attempts to map the terrain of Ming-Qing *jingshi* at last leads us into our major questions in this section: Precisely where did Chen Hongmou fit into the notion's history, and what does a better appreciation of his role contribute to our understanding of that history overall? In most discussions the "prosperous" and "stable" eighteenth century is identified, either implicitly or explicitly, with the nearly total eclipse of *jingshi* thought by philology and other intellectual agendas; it is the black hole between the empire-wide fixation with statecraft reform of the century surrounding the Ming-Qing transition and the first stirrings of literati concern about Qing dynastic decline, and a resulting statecraft movement, in the nineteenth century.[156] The latter is customarily seen as in some fashion a rediscovery of the former, and few scholars have even cared to speculate about how the complex and at times contested package of ideas that constituted the *jingshi* tradition negotiated the passage between the Kangxi and Daoguang reigns. One exception is Benjamin Elman, who has—somewhat too narrowly in my view—identified the school of New Text classical scholarship based in Changzhou (Jiangsu) as "unique" in keeping statecraft concerns alive during the otherwise complacent mid-Qing era.[157] Others have pointed to the late-eighteenth-century historian and cultural critic Zhang Xuecheng as one who explicitly advocated *jingshi* scholarship several decades before its more celebrated Daoguang revival.[158] Yet a third trace of continuity has been found in Lu Yao's 1776 anthology of political essays *Qiewenzhai wenchao* (which, significantly, was republished in the Daoguang era with the newly marketable term "*jingshi*" inserted in its title).[159] But there were other, even more persistent scholarly conduits, in relatively neglected places such as Shaanxi and Hunan, to which we will turn in a moment.

Does Chen himself provide a conscious link? The claim that Chen Hongmou's thought and writings typified a *jingshi* intellectual orientation began very early, at least with his grandson and editor Chen Lansen in Hongmou's own lifetime and with his sometime colleague and biographer Peng Qifeng in 1785. Following his anointment as a statecraft exemplar by Wei Yuan—who represented him by some fifty-two entries in the 1826 *Huangchao jingshi wenbian* (second most, as I have said, after Gu Yanwu)— Chen's mid-nineteenth-century editors and biographers such as Jiang Fangzheng (writing in 1837), Xu Zeshun (1846), Wang Zhichun (1868), and Li Yuandu (1869) characterized him ever more emphatically by invoking this idiom.[160] So too have scholars and historians today.[161]

And yet Chen himself seems never to have made this claim. In contrast to the term "*shixue*" (substantive learning), which as we've seen was for Chen Hongmou a regularly brandished emblem of his scholarly identity, "*jingshi*" surfaces in his discourse only rarely and even then, it seems, with few claims of appropriation. The related term "*jingji*" (political economy) he uses more frequently and more pointedly, at times eliding it with "*shixue*" (*jingji shixue*) and at others declaring it the necessary counterpart of "*lixue*" in any worthy scholar's curriculum of study. Inasmuch as the term "*jingji*" emerged as a shorthand form for "*jingshi jimin*" (ordering the world and relieving the people), it may be that Chen saw the two terms as essentially interchangeable.[162] Still, the relative absence from his rhetoric of "*jingshi*" itself, an idiom of recognizable power in his day, remains striking. At the very least it argues that he did not identify himself as part of any contemporary, self-conscious statecraft movement.

I have counted less than half a dozen uses of the term "*jingshi*" in all of Chen's enormous surviving literary output prior to 1769—by which time he was well into his seventies and his active official career was essentially behind him. Before this date he applies the term to the teachings of the classical works the *Great Learning* and the *Rites of Zhou*, links it with the parallel tasks of "overcoming self" (*keji*) and "taking responsibility upon oneself" (*zeji*), calls for a greater inclusion of *jingshi*-related subjects in the examination curriculum, and speaks of "*jingshi fuwu*" (ordering the world and serving material needs") as the proper goal of study.[163] But all these mentions are isolated and fleeting. In 1769, by contrast, in his last major publication, the *Xueshi yigui* (Sourcebook on proper scholarship), Chen quite liberally applies the term "*jingshi*" to a number of diverse writers—Feng Congwu, Xin Quan, Ge Duantiao, Diao Bao, Wei Xi— whose works he chose to include in his compendium.[164] All of these writers, it should be noted, were part of the broad seventeenth-century wave of self-conscious interest in *jingshi* matters, and most if not all of them had featured the term in their own rhetoric. Thus, what may appear a noticeably stronger attraction to this term on Chen's part during the final years of his life was to a large extent a function of his sources. Yet those sources, of course, were not arbitrarily selected; they reflected a consistent pattern of reading over Chen's mature years.

The decisive influence, it seems clear, was the salient position the Guanxue school of northern neo-Confucianism had come to assume for Chen by this time. We have noted that Guanxue provided the dominant ordering motif of the *Xueshi yigui* as a whole. Every one of the leading Guanxue scholars, from Lü Nan in the mid-Ming, through Feng Congwu, Li Yong, and Wang Xinjing, to Chen's own contemporary and friend Yang Shen, had accorded the term "*jingshi*" a central, indeed a defiant, role in their discourse. It was featured prominently in the texts by these men that Chen chose to reprint in the *Xueshi yigui* and was further highlighted in the prefaces Chen supplied to these, as well as in others of his writings on them.[165] In other words, although Chen Hongmou seems not to have defined *himself* as a participant in a deliberate statecraft movement, he gradually came to understand himself as at least the indirect heir of a regional school, Guanxue, for which a *jingshi* orientation was a cardinal element of self-definition.

By contrast, Chen's *jingshi* inheritance from Chen Zilong and from Gu Yanwu appears to have been slight. Thomas Metzger places Chen Hongmou within the less radical "administrative flexibility" branch of *jingshi* advocacy, implying for him a role as historical intermediary between other key figures in that branch, Chen Zilong in the seventeenth century and Wei Yuan in the nineteenth.[166] But although there may be cause for this based on the rough similarity of approaches, it would be difficult to argue for a direct influence at work. The simple fact is that Chen Hongmou never once refers, in any of his writings that I have seen, either to Chen Zilong or to his *Huang Ming jingshi wenbian*, the most celebrated and sustained repository of *jingshi* scholarship to have appeared by Hongmou's day. This was probably because Chen Zilong's work had been proscribed by the Qing court for its anti-Manchu tone,[167] and Hongmou, as we have seen, was not a man to court political danger of this sort. But memory of the work was certainly strong enough a half century later to invite Wei Yuan's reference to it in the title of his own *Huangchao jingshi wenbian*, so I am inclined to conclude that for Chen Hongmou the line of statecraft thought that Chen Zilong and his Fu She associates represented was simply not one with which he significantly identified. Other lines of transmission were much more compelling.

The influence of Gu Yanwu is at once more problematic and of greater potential importance for our understanding of Chen's sociopolitical thought. Despite some affinities and areas of shared views, I find it difficult to discern any significant degree of direct influence of Gu, *jingshi*'s most celebrated seventeenth-century exemplar, on Chen, arguably its best eighteenth-century representative. Gu was not one of those historical model thinkers, such as Sima Guang, Zhen Dexiu, Qiu Jun, Lü Kun, or Wang Xinjing, whom Chen edited, republished, and actively promoted in his provincial jurisdictions. I have found not a single reference to Gu in Chen's letters, the venue in which he most frequently extols past and present writers he deems of central importance. Chen does extract brief passages from Gu's most celebrated work, the *Rizhi lu* (Record of knowledge acquired day-by-day), in three of his six sourcebooks, the *Xunsu yigui, Congzheng yigui,* and *Zaiguan fajie lu.* These selections deal, respectively, with Gu's views on funerals, on lineage organization, and on yamen clerks. In at least one of these instances, though, he cites Gu only to turn his argument on its head. (Gu offers a diatribe on the evils of yamen clerks, whereas Chen in his commentary takes off from this to a discussion of how clerks might be rehabilitated by more humane treatment.) And although Chen in his prefatory notes to Gu's writings is profuse in his praise (as he is for virtually all figures he excerpts), he also points out that he has had to be unusually selective in his citations from Gu because so much of what the great man wrote seems today "hollow sounding" and impracticable.[168]

Chen admired Gu's consistent stress on the unity of thought and action, his broad learning, his doggedly empirical scholarly style (he especially praised the use Gu made of field observation), and his historicism and detailed knowledge of the past.[169] As his choice of extracts from the *Rizhi lu* suggests, Chen shared Gu's view of the sociopolitical utility of ritual and of the importance of reforming local customary practice. On the other hand, as Thomas Bartlett has shown, by Chen's time Gu's public image had come to focus less on his statecraft writings and more on his pioneering contributions to *kaozheng*-style classical philology, a mode of inquiry Chen found uninteresting, if not actively degenerate.[170] Moreover, Chen almost certainly found Gu's scholarship wanting in the area of personal moral cultivation—a Song-Ming *lixue* preoccupation on which Gu rather consciously turned his back. For Chen Hongmou, Gu would appear (like the Wang Anshi whom Gu professed to despise) all *yong* and no *ti*.

But the central question we need to ask—for this, I think, bears critically on our understanding of just what *jingshi* actually was—is how Chen responded to Gu Yanwu's sometimes rather startling political ideas. In separate landmark articles Philip Kuhn and Min Tu-ki have identified a persistent tradition of alternative political thought in the Qing dynasty that cohered around a critique of centralized bureaucratic administration (*junxian*), advocating instead some form of local autonomy and political empowerment of local-level sociocultural elites.[171] Often subsumed under the rubric *fengjian* (loosely, "feudal") thought, this tradition is seen as finding its most important early Qing spokesman in Gu Yanwu. In a famous essay written around 1660 entitled "Junxian lun" (On centralized bureaucracy), Gu called for the implementation of a hereditary local magistracy, the incumbents to be selected from among the leading gentry-landlord families of the locality itself, and for the removal of various levels of higher oversight personnel (such as provincial governors) who might constrain the freedom of this magistrate to act in the interests of his district.[172] After something of a hiatus in the eighteenth-century heyday of bureaucratic efficacy (although social critics such as the poet Yuan Mei provided some continuity), the tradition, according to Kuhn and to Min, revived in the nineteenth century with Wei Yuan and Feng Guifen, culminating in the prescriptions for local-level representative government of Kang Youwei and other fin de siècle reformers. Because Gu, Wei, and others within this tradition also conspicuously invoked the term "*jingshi*" to describe what they were about, this *fengjian* idea has frequently been conflated by historians with a larger late imperial statecraft tradition.[173] And because scholars such as Wei and Feng were highly attracted to the activities of the exemplary eighteenth-century official Chen Hongmou, implicitly claiming him as one of their own, there is cause for considering Chen as falling within the *fengjian*, that is, the antibureaucratic and local-empowerment camp.

But how well does Chen fit into this tradition? As will become clear in our discussions of Chen's views of the economy, kinship, community, and the state in the chapters to follow, the fit is highly uncomfortable. To be sure, in his conduct of office Chen routinely displayed sympathies in favor of market autonomy and local empowerment and pioneered a variety of practical methods of sharing authority with local elites (even commercial ones), but he perhaps equally often recoiled at such strategies. As Chapter 10 will show, no one could have worked harder in practice to build up the powers of the field bureaucracy for intelligence and control over society than did Chen Hongmou. And the extraordinary activism he brought to his exercise of the provincial governor's powers of oversight, of policy innovation, and of redistribution of resources among localities could not have run more counter to Gu Yanwu's desire to abolish that post altogether.

Although they each inevitably carry some of the flavor of Gu's deep-seated antistatist views, none of the passages Chen excerpted from Gu in his sourcebooks deal directly with the latter's proposals for basic constitutional reform. My suspicion, indeed, is that it was to these Chen was referring when he somewhat cryptically dismissed certain of Gu's writings as "hollow sounding." It may be that Gu Yanwu indeed belonged to a "radical" or "basic change" wing of *jingshi* thought (he of course had much to say in areas of more modest institutional reform) and Chen Hongmou to the "realist" or "administrative flexibility" wing,[174] that Gu inclined more to the *fengjian* side of the local autonomy/bureaucratic centralism equation and Chen perhaps a bit more to the *junxian* side. Both men, however, and no one more creatively than Chen, worked to open up that middle area between direct state proprietorship and private interest that we shall explore in Chapter 11—that arena of communal responsibility, activism, and opinion known intermittently as "public" (*gong*). And both Gu and Chen found a home in the Qing statecraft tradition as retrospectively constructed by Wei Yuan in the nineteenth century. It was a broad net that Wei cast.

The Hunan Connection

As seen in my introduction, Chen Hongmou became in the nineteenth century a favorite authority and model for political action for reformist scholar-officials from a wide range of backgrounds. For none, though, was he more central than for the self-conscious *jingshi* theorists and practitioners of the 1820s generation (the era of the perceived Daoguang crisis) and their successors in the 1850s and 1860s (the years of anti-Taiping mobilization and of the Tongzhi "Restoration"). It has often been noted that a disproportionate number of these figures hailed from Hunan (more precisely Hunan's Xiang River valley and Dongting Lake regions)—men such as Wei Yuan, He Changling, Tao Zhu, Tang Jian (1778–1861), Luo Zenan (1808–56), Hu Linyi (1812–61), Zeng Guofan (1811–72) and his brother Guoquan (1824–90), Zuo Zongtang

(1812–85), Liu Rong (1816–73), Guo Songdao (1818–91), Li Yuandu (1821–87), and Jiang Yili (1832–74). We have also observed throughout this study how many individuals within this so-called Hunan clique—as well as others, such as Feng Guifen, who, although not themselves Hunanese, were closely affiliated with the Hunanese group—cited Chen Hongmou as a critical influence on their sociopolitical views.[175] Tang Jian, in many ways the central linkage in this group, authored a hagiography of Chen, the model *jingshi* official, in which he wrote:

> As a scholar, Chen exemplified sincerity and lack of guile. He did not indulge in speculative idle chatter [*kongtan*], nor stoop to partisan debates [*bianlun*]. His purpose in investigating the words and deeds of the famous sages, statesmen, and Confucian scholars of antiquity was merely to respectfully learn what they had to say and put it into practice in his own day [rather than for academic pedantry]. In intellectual life he engaged the ancient texts, but in action he responded to contemporary conditions.[176]

It is the task of this section to explore the roots and the quality of this special attraction of the Hunanese reformers of these generations—men often seen as the critical shapers of mid- to late-nineteenth-century Chinese history—for this century-earlier provincial governor from Guilin. In so doing I hope to contribute to the archaeology of Qing statecraft thought.

We have seen that Chen traced his own family origins to Hunan's Xiang Valley, but if Hunanese of later eras knew this, they did not make much of it (it is not mentioned, for instance, in Tang Jian's biography). A more important personal link (to be discussed below) was the fact that Chen had twice served as Hunan governor in the 1750s and 1760s and was actively remembered a century later as a special benefactor of the province.[177] Two of Chen's nephews, Zhongli and Zhonglu, had also served lengthy tenures as Xiang Valley magistrates. And, as we shall see in Chapter 6, Hongmou had acquired and bequeathed to his heirs a substantial landholding in rural Changsha, granting him membership, at least by extension, in the same social network as the Zengs and their cohort.[178] But more relevant still, I would argue—and here I readily confess I am dangerously speculative—were the ecological similarities of the regions in which Chen and his subsequent Hunanese admirers grew up.[179]

Both the Li River valley of Guangxi and the Xiang River valley of Hunan were, in the mid-Qing era, what I would term "semiperipheries." They enjoyed relatively little foreign contact, either coastal or Inner Asian, leaving them with perhaps a somewhat nativist cultural tone; at the same time they were in routine contact—within the same province—with significant populations of non-Han aboriginal peoples, giving rise to a self-conscious sense of cultural frontier. This frontier sensibility was certainly heightened by the fact that so much of the Han population itself was immigrant, taking advantage of recent and ongoing land reclamation. The pioneering settler mentality among these new arrivals, as well as among those whose memory of arrival was still vivid, emphasized a combination of practical activism and basic, grassroots moral values. Both regions hosted with great pride an indigenous intellectual tradition, embodied institutionally in a handful of prominent academies (*shuyuan*), which, however, remained relatively isolated from intellectual movements in more cosmopolitan regions of the empire.

Both river valleys had experienced relatively recent booms in export grain production, to serve the needs of the increasingly food-deficient regions of Jiangnan (fed by Hunan) and Guangdong (fed by Guangxi). The modest but impressive wealth thus created allowed the conditions for an accompanying boom in education and examination success[180] and even for elevation of some of the regions' native sons into positions of national political prominence. The fact that the actual management of this export rice trade remained largely in the hands of extraregional merchants (those from Jiangxi in the Xiang Valley case and from Guangdong in the Li Valley) who dominated the regions' only modestly developed urban areas[181] meant that the indigenous economic and cultural elite constituted primarily a class of rural planters whose values were firmly agrarian but whose market-derived wealth inclined them at the same time to a largely favorable view of commercial activity. Finally, this new wealth had not yet been translated into large private libraries whose extensive collections could facilitate the needs of scholars engaged in detailed textual and philological studies.[182]

Like Chen's native Guilin, the Xiang Valley had its own distinct intellectual tradition, dating from the Song, which reflected its particular ecological and social setting. The progenitor of this tradition was the great neo-Confucian pioneer Zhou Dunyi (1017–73), who bequeathed to later generations of Hunanese scholars not only their collective sobriquet (the "Lian" of Lianxue, the "Hunanese school," derived from Zhou's personal style, "Lianxi") but also a conception of rational principle that was more embedded in a materialist, natural mysticism than the *li* espoused by other neo-Confucians writing in his wake.[183] Of probably greater personal influence on Lianxue than its namesake, however, was the Sichuanese Zhang Shi (Zhang Nanxian, 1133–80), longtime director of Shanhua County's eminent Yuelu Academy. An authority on the *Book of Changes* and the *Mencius*, Zhang conducted a famous debate with his friend Zhu Xi at the Yuelu in 1167 in which he accepted the basic understanding of *lixue* espoused by Zhu, but he pushed, within this framework, for a stronger emphasis on the unity of knowledge and practice and for a more focused study of *jingshi*, the techniques of political administration. Proceeding from his faith in the moral nature of the human mind, Zhang argued that human appetites, self-interest, and the profit motive were natural and by no means necessarily in conflict with principle. Zhang's arguments in the course of this debate set the curriculum of the Yuelu, and of other academies in Hunan, from that day on.[184] It is probably not coincidental that, as we saw in Chapter 1, Zhang Shi's long sojourn in Guilin also proved the decisive influence on the development of that area's academic culture as well, within which Chen Hongmou himself grew up.

As Yang Nianqun has argued, in the wake of the tumultuous late Ming sociocultural changes and of the Manchu conquest the intellectual agenda pursued in the Yuelu and Hunan's other major *shuyuan*—Changsha's Chengnan Academy, Xiangtan's Longtan Academy, Liuyang's Nantai Academy, and others—took on an even more distinctive provincial coloration. The challenge of the late Ming Taizhou school, with its perceived deviations toward mysticism and mass popularization, which threatened properly constituted authority, led differing provincial schools to espouse differing corrective strategies. Scholars in the lower Yangzi, Yang suggests, characteristically chose to turn to classical textual study (demeaned by the Taizhou group) in order to recover the timeless principles of the ancients (*fugu*) from their corruption by recent, populist trends; scholars in the Hunanese academies, by contrast, rededicated themselves yet more fully to study of the practical techniques of social ordering (*zhishu*) for essentially the same reason. What emerged in Hunan was a scholarly discourse, grounded deeply in historical experience, and a curriculum designed forthrightly to train prospective statesmen, who would scour the historical record in search of viable solutions to contemporary problems of governance.[185]

Especially during his second tenure as Hunan governor in 1763, Chen Hongmou played a remarkable personal role in reinventing this Xiang Valley cultural tradition, providing the key mid-Qing bridge to the tradition's self-conscious revival under Wei Yuan and Tang Jian in the 1820s. Chen reestablished the temple at Changsha to past local worthies and eminent officials, orienting sacrificial performance within it above all to former governor and Song-era *jingshi* master Zhen Dexiu.[186] He undertook the compilation of the first-ever *Hunan Provincial Gazetteer* (*Hunan tongzhi*), noting that previous volumes had always taken Huguang (Hubei and Hunan) as their jurisdiction and, being compiled at Wuchang (in Hubei), had relegated Hunanese conditions and Hunanese authors to secondary status; in Chen's new volume they would achieve the centrality they deserved.[187] Similarly, he ordered that works by great Hunanese scholars of the past—those with a consistent focus on "useful and substantive learning" (*youyong zhi shixue*)—be collected as the core holdings of the new library he endowed at the Yuelu Academy.[188]

It would be fascinating to know if Chen privately included among these past Hunanese luminaries Wang Fuzhi (1619–92), the great seventeenth-century philosopher whose anti-Manchu diatribes had brought about banning public discussion of his works for much of the Qing. Although He Changling, Zeng Guofan, and Guo Songdao at the height of their prestige in the mid-nineteenth century were able to effect the republication of this Hunanese culture-hero,[189] Chen Hongmou a century earlier was necessarily more circumspect. Chen, in any case, would probably have recoiled at Wang's anti-Manchuism and his more general racial theories. But he would equally likely have applauded (had he been free to do so) Wang's famous dictum "Principle and material circumstance are one and the same" (*lishi heyi*), a materialist and historical relativist redefinition of Song *lixue* that gave unspoken direction to the Hunanese brand of neo-Confucianism from Wang's day on.[190] What is more certain is that Chen included prominently among his Hunanese pantheon Wang Zhifu (Xiangyin County native, Kangxi-era *shengyuan*), a locally beloved Songxue teacher whose strikingly vernacularized moral tracts on such matters as household management, wifely conduct, and the dos and don'ts of wedding and funeral ritual Chen compared to those of Lü Kun, liberally excerpting them in four of his own didactic sourcebooks.[191]

Chen Hongmou's most lasting contribution to the development of the Xiang Valley cultural tradition came in connection with its academies. After languishing in the late Ming and apparently suffering significant destruction during the dynastic transition, the Yuelu Academy had begun to be restored by a series of provincial and local officials in the late seventeenth century.[192] In 1756, however, Chen undertook its transformation into a considerably more vital and public institution of higher education. He

FIGURE 6. The Yuelu Academy, ca. 1687. Source: *Xinxiu Yuelu shuyuan zhishu.*

conducted special examinations in localities throughout Hunan in order to select an entering class that would genuinely represent the brightest students the province had to offer, providing scholarships and travel stipends for those who needed them.[193] Seven years later, on his return to the governorship, he completely refounded the institution, raising its student body from the fourteen he had decreed in 1756 to a total of seventy (fifty regular students and twenty part-time associates). Although Chen himself prized Yuelu's mountainous seclusion in Shanhua County as an atmosphere conducive to study (imposing strict limitations on visitors and on student travel away from school), he acknowledged that its location "away from the river" made it inconvenient for some prospective students to attend and so incorporated the Chengnan Academy in suburban Changsha city to serve as a branch campus. He provided for the two academies an impressive endowment of altogether eighty-seven hundred taels, invested with Hankou's salt merchants and Xiangtan's pawnbrokers so as to yield the handsome return of 1,938 taels per year. This money was used to provide stipends for the students and to finance the hiring of the best teachers money could buy—the chief instructor of the Yuelu was paid 360 taels per year *plus* his entire living expenses. The schools also shared an endowment of rice land yielding over five hundred *shi* of grain per year for their direct consumption.[194]

Chen Hongmou also personally dictated the curriculum to be followed in the two academies, specifying from the outset that their orientation was to be toward no-nonsense
"substantive learning" (*shixue*). In large measure this meant an examination-directed
course of study, the aim of the schools being above all to recruit and train the best and
brightest for a career of public service. The student bodies of both schools were to be
augmented by nearly 50 percent in the years of the triennial provincial examination;
teaching materials focused on government-issue examination textbooks such as *Yuzuan
zhujing* (Imperial selections from the Classics), *Qinding shijian* (Imperially commissioned edition of the Mirror of History), and *Qinxuan guwen yuanlan* (Imperially commissioned anthology of "ancient prose" texts); and the students were required to sit
twice monthly for a practice examination, prepared alternately by their instructor and
by a high provincial official, including, according to a rotating schedule, the governor
himself. Still, within this framework of imperial orthodoxy Chen made it clear what his
particular reading of *shixue* entailed: the practice examinations were to lay special stress
on questions involving contemporary policy issues, and the curriculum beyond simple
examination preparation was to remain rather narrowly a Song-learning one, with the
addition of key statecraft texts such as Zhen Dexiu's *Daxue yanyi*. The academy libraries
were to encourage students to read more widely in local archival documentary collections and, as we have seen, in the works of upright home-province authors.

At roughly the same time Chen also turned his attention to one other educational
institution. In the heart of Hunan's export rice belt in Xiangxiang County, gentry members sought to enhance local educational opportunities and at the same time to wrest
control of studies away from the local bureaucracy by founding their own *shuyuan*, the
Lianbin Academy. They went directly to Governor Chen for his support, and he responded by inscribing for them a dedicatory stele, offering his office's protection for
the school's endowment, ordering the local tablets for former sages and worthies relo-
cated there from county offices, and even declaring the academy the site for future prefectural examinations. A less governmental institution than the provincial Yuelu
Academy, the Lianbin seems to have catered to younger students—selected by special
examination from among those at the county school (*xianxue*)—and to have had a
broader, more policy-oriented curriculum in "useful and substantive learning" (*youyong
zhi shixue*); Chen expressed his expectation that, like Jiangxi's nationally famous White
Deer Grotto Academy, the Lianbin would turn out scholars of great expertise in political economy (*jingji*) and public servants who would concentrate on the "genuine tasks
of relieving the people" (*jimin zhi shishi*).[195] I have not been able to determine which
(if any) of Xiangxiang's celebrated nineteenth-century native sons—Luo Zenan, the
Zeng brothers, Liu Rong, Jiang Yili—actually enrolled at the Lianbin in their youth,
but its influence on their personal development in any case seems likely to have been
significant.

This entire nexus of educational institutions, in large part the reconstructed project of Chen Hongmou, became in the early nineteenth century the center of a powerful intellectual movement involving men who would become leading soldier-statesmen
of the Xianfeng and Tongzhi reigns.[196] He Changling, Wei Yuan, and Tang Jian all studied at the Yuelu Academy in the first decades of the century.[197] Tang became the prin-

cipal instructor at Yuelu in the 1830s and 1840s, his students including Zeng Guofan, Liu Rong, Guo Songdao, and many other anti-Taiping campaigners and Restoration officials. Guo went on in the post-Taiping years to continue these teachings as director of the Chengnan Academy.

The core of the nineteenth-century Hunanese intellectual program was an increasingly adamant Songxue orthodoxy known as the "New School of Principle" (*xin lixue*), which Tang Jian articulated in his highly partisan genealogy of the Way, the *Xuean xiaoshi*. Hu Linyi (whose father was an eminent Songxue teacher), Luo Zenan, and Zeng Guofan were all published scholars in the Cheng-Zhu tradition. This Xiang Valley Song-learning revival owed something to Li Guangdi, Lu Longqi, and other early Qing *lixue* masters but ultimately even more to the Tongcheng school of Fang Bao and Yao Nai because teachers from Tongcheng were brought into the Yuelu Academy and other Xiang Valley schools during the Daoguang reign. There was room in this "New *lixue*" intellectual brew for the influence of Gu Yanwu, for New Text meditations on the *Gongyang Commentary*, and for a very active interest in geography[198] but no tolerance at all for Hanxue-style philology and antiquarianism.[199] At the heart of the Xiang Valley concerns was the intensely self-critical moral rigor of Tang Jian, seamlessly linked with the *jingshi* political action agenda to which all Hunan scholars subscribed. As Tang argued, a moral commitment rooted in *lixue*—with "*li*" redefined in its peculiarly Hunanese materialist, historicist way—was the only true basis for effective statecraft. Chen Hongmou would certainly have agreed.

We have surveyed in this chapter a wide range of intellectual influences on Chen Hongmou. Although held together by an abiding sense of mission to overcome self and serve the public weal, and an equally deep aversion to aestheticism and pedantry, these influences were eclectic, as Chen's own profession of scholarly nonpartisanship would suggest. There was room for such unlikely bedfellows as Wang Yangming, Gu Yanwu, and Fang Bao. But the central line, I would suggest, ran from Sima Guang through Zhu Xi and Zhang Shi, through Lü Kun and the late Ming–early Qing Guanxue school, through Chen himself. It was picked up and carried on in the nineteenth century by such Hunanese luminaries as Wei Yuan, Tang Jian, and Zeng Guofan. Consider the case of Xiangxiang's Luo Zenan—Song *lixue* scholar, anti-Taiping general, intimate friend of Tang and Zeng, and 1841 graduate of the Chengnan Academy. In 1852, just as the rebels were besieging Changsha, Luo oversaw republication in that city of Chen Hongmou's annotated version of Lü Kun's *Groaning Words* (*Shenyin yu jieyao*), strongly identifying with Lü's outcry of grief for his troubled times and endorsing Lü's (and Chen's) prescriptions for "curing the ills" of contemporary society.[200] As I hope to have shown, although this may be but one of the pedigrees of late Qing statecraft, it was a coherent and vital one.

The common denominators in the broad tradition of Qing *jingshi* constructed retrospectively by nineteenth-century literati were less a specific political agenda or political style than they were a set of intellectual predilections. This set was perhaps fully present in no single figure more than Chen Hongmou himself. These factors included a belief in the necessary unity of knowledge and action, an inclination toward historical and geographic relativism rather than fundamentalist classicism, close attention to the details of administrative practice, high regard for technical expertise in a variety of fields (notably, but not exclusively, political economy), a belief in the need for continual reform of popular customary practice, and, at least for most within the tradition, a passionate commitment to pursue personal moral improvement—in terms of the *lixue* model—as a prerequisite for ordering the external world.

PART TWO

Creating Prosperity

生財

CHAPTER 5

Food

HAVING LEARNED SOMETHING of Chen Hongmou's assumptions about the cosmos and the human condition, we now turn to the way these notions were reflected in more articulated aspects of his administrative thought and practice. We begin in this chapter by looking in some depth at a single policy area, one that in fact epitomized much of Chen's approach to governance and reflected his most basic views about economy and society. This was also, I would argue, the single most important policy area in Qing China, at least prior to the unprecedented military and cultural threat presented by the West. That area was food supply.[1]

Apart from Chen's immense contributions to the renovation and extension of the empire's water conservancy network, it was probably his activities in the area of provisioning for which he was most appreciated in his own day, and for which he has been most celebrated by later writers. If, as is sometimes suggested, the eighteenth-century Qing imperial administration's ambitions along these lines were unprecedented in human history, Chen's were greater still: to ensure the adequate feeding of every person in the realm and at the same time to develop a level of food reserves that would grow not only as fast but faster than the empire's rapidly increasing population. Study of Chen's copious writings in this area cannot but leave one astounded by the comprehensiveness of his vision, by his understanding both of theoretical economics and of environmental factors, by the vast repertoire of institutional measures he employed to achieve his goals, and by the adeptness and flexibility of his response to varying situational pressures. The same might possibly be said of many another mid-Qing administrator, but by general consensus Chen did things with greater perspicacity, ingenuity, and (above all) energy than virtually any of his colleagues.

Population, Food, and Prices

Let us begin by considering the nature of the problem. First and foremost was population growth. Chen Hongmou himself stated the case as succinctly as anyone in a letter written around 1744:

> As the benevolent and solicitous policies of our glorious Dynasty have gradually taken
> effect, the people have continued to multiply. Newly reclaimed marshes and highlands
> have been turned to productive use. And yet I worry that our limited supply of land is
> increasingly inadequate to support our ever-growing population. We cannot afford to
> sit idly by and, confident in the land's potential, say that no new initiatives are needed,
> even if the immediate payoff would be slight, or that there will always be government
> surpluses to fall back upon. . . . This is a problem that no imperial official can cease to
> be anxious about for even a moment.[2]

As Suzuki Chūsei has noted, China's contemporary population problem has its origins
in the eighteenth century. Prior to that time, adverse population-to-resources levels
had never constituted an overriding source of administrative concern. In Chen
Hongmou's day, however, it is safe to say that nearly all in government were preoccupied with them.[3]

Although there is no firm agreement among scholars on the size and growth of late
imperial China's population, cautious estimates suggest something like a sixfold increase over the course of four centuries, from roughly sixty-five million in 1400, to
around four hundred million in 1850. Although growth during the Ming had been impressive, figures presented by Ho Ping-ti and Dwight Perkins show a dramatic acceler-
ation of the rate of increase during Chen Hongmou's own lifetime, from perhaps 150
million in 1700 (the same figure as that a century earlier, prior to the late Ming demographic collapse) to some 270 million around the time of Chen's death in 1771.[4]
The annual population growth rate over this period—perhaps as high as 1.3 percent
in the early and mid-Qing—was both unprecedented and unanticipated.[5] It was also
highly unevenly spread over time. Broken down by decade, by far the most rapid spurt
of population growth came in the 1740s and the next most rapid in the 1750s, coinciding precisely with the period of Chen Hongmou's most active provincial service.[6]

During the same four-century period that saw population increase sixfold, total cultivated acreage less than tripled.[7] Despite strenuous government reclamation campaigns (such as that discussed in Chapter 2), the rate of increase of farmland began to
fall off rapidly precisely when population growth accelerated, according to Quan
Hansheng's calculations declining from about 0.45 percent per year in the Kangxi
reign to 0.18 percent per year in the Yongzheng and early Qianlong years.[8] By around
1760 Chen Hongmou could write, "Although the population continues to grow each
day, I see only very limited land remaining to be brought under cultivation."[9] Yields per
unit of cultivated land of course increased over the centuries as well but not fast
enough to offset population growth, at least in the decades of most rapid increase.[10]

The problem of food supply in a complex economy such as that of late imperial
China was not, however, simply one of aggregate production and consumption. It was
considerably complicated by the facts that certain segments of the population produced either no food at all or insufficient food to feed themselves and that even those
who were primarily food producers relied, at one time or another, on food they had not
themselves produced. Grain circulated throughout the empire in massive amounts. It
did so in four ways: (1) through state means (including grain mobilized through the
fiscal system, through the ever-normal granary system (ENG), and through spot pur-

chases for emergency redistribution); (2) through customary means (including com-munity-run granaries and ad hoc dispensation of food relief by temples, lineages, and local elites); (3) through exaction of land rent and usury interest; and (4) through the commercial market.[11] Chen Hongmou's efforts in food redistribution came largely in the first two of these channels. Before looking at these, however, we need to consider briefly the fourth—the commercial market—a channel that, according to one recent estimate, involved in the early and mid-Qing at least four times the volume of grain as that circulated through government means.[12]

Eighteenth-century China was an agrarian economy, to be sure, but it was one of the most highly commercialized ones in world history. Wu Chengming estimates that by the end of the century more than 10 percent of all rice produced in the empire went to market, a total of perhaps 2.5 billion catties per year.[13] Probably the majority of this was exchanged intralocally, but a sizable amount traveled farther, imported by chroni-cally deficit localities and regions from other areas that had, especially since the great commercial intensification of the late Ming, come to specialize economically in pro-duction of grain for export. Patterned, highly systematic flows of grain dominated the Qing economic landscape. These included (1) those within a relatively self-contained regional system (urban-commercial coastal Fujian, for example, was fed by counties up-stream on the Min River, and the specialized tea-producing counties of Xinhua and Anhua in Hunan were fed by Wugang and other counties along the Zu River system);[14] (2) those between neighboring regions or subregions (as Chen Hongmou's native Guangxi fed much of the Canton delta);[15] and (3) those of a very long-distance, inter-regional nature. As many scholars have shown, much of the provinces of Jiangxi, Sichuan, and especially Hunan had developed by the eighteenth century into special-ized breadbaskets, feeding many places but above all the heavily urbanized and textile-producing Jiangnan.[16] According to Chuan and Kraus, the trade in this last category alone totaled between eight and thirteen million *shi* per year in the early 1700s.[17] It is worth noting, too, that most rice producers in these export regions themselves pur-chased lesser quality grains on the market for their own routine consumption.

In such a highly commercialized agrarian society, increased population pressure meant steadily rising grain prices. Although, as various scholars have pointed out, other factors such as increases in money supply and in the overall velocity of commercial cir-culation played significant roles in determining prices,[18] the most basic cause of the sec-ular price rise was the outstripping of supply by demand. Whereas both Europe and China had experienced a comparable early modern "price revolution," due in part to the increase in specie brought in from the New World, by the late seventeenth and early eighteenth centuries Europe had begun to enter a long era of deflationary adjustment in grain prices.[19] In China the period of adjustment was much briefer, constituting es-sentially the so-called Kangxi depression of ca. 1660–90. Although this era did see fre-quent complaints from planters about the excessive cheapness of grain,[20] the most commonly cited statistical series documents a steady increase of rice prices in silver from approximately 0.8 taels per *shi* around 1690 to 2.2 taels per *shi* in 1800. Not surprisingly, the most rapid increase came in the era of most rapid population growth, the 1740s and 1750s.[21] That this price rise resulted above all from growing population pressure is further suggested by the fact that land prices rose even more rapidly in this era (by one estimate, rising tenfold between 1720 and 1770),[22] whereas the prices of finished goods and other nonfood commodities rose only modestly until the century's final decades.[23]

In a famous article Braudel and Spooner argued that by the early eighteenth century the high level of interregional market integration achieved by Europe resulted in the permanent end of the "terrible" famines of the past. After midcentury only relatively small-scale dearths occurred, which were fairly easily alleviated by imports of grain from unaffected regions within the system.[24] Something comparable also happened in mid-Qing China, although the change was not so dramatic as that in Europe. The Qing empire, like the European continent, was an increasingly integrated economic system; yet many regions (the northwest and southwest, for example) remained perhaps less well-integrated than any in Europe. On the other hand, unlike Europe the Qing was an integrated political unit, served (through much of the eighteenth century) by a lean but remarkably effective centralized bureaucracy. Regionalized dearths, the result of climatic irregularities, continued to affect China and because of its more adverse population:food supply ratio continued to be more threatening than in contemporaneous Europe. In a vast, integrated, and highly commercialized economy such as that of the Qing, regional dearths appeared less as absolute shortages of grain than as abnormally rapid inflations in grain prices, which would ripple outward from the immediately afflicted region to those that normally served as its food suppliers. In such situations a variety of social conflicts were likely to develop, pitting grain producers, shippers, and consumers in different regions against one another, with government regulators caught at some point in the middle. But whereas in eighteenth-century Europe it was overwhelmingly the market itself that brought about the reduction in severity of famine, in Qing China these government regulators had a far larger role to play.

That the Qing government was very deeply committed to assuring the provisioning of its population is beyond doubt. When the young Chen Hongmou, serving as Jiangsu provincial judge, memorialized the throne in 1740 that "I believe food supply is of the most immediate concern to the people's survival (*minming*), and hence ought to be of absolute paramount importance [to the state]," he was taking no political risk; that all in administration believed the same thing was a safe assumption.[25] Three years later the Qianlong emperor himself put it this way: "Since the people treat food as if it were Heaven [*yishi weitian*], we in government must take agricultural production as our basic concern [*yinong weiben*]."[26] Both throne and bureaucracy, moreover, had come to recognize very early the severity of the provisioning problem presented by unchecked population growth. Beginning in the 1710s, the Kangxi emperor repeatedly acknowledged the threat posed by population growth to the empire's food supply, and edicts ordering officials to devote themselves to remedying this problem were issued with ever greater urgency by his successors, Yongzheng and Qianlong. It was an imperial preoccupation that Chen Hongmou, like most of his colleagues, shared.[27]

The relationship of grain price inflation to increasing population density was also acknowledged. As early as 1683 the eminent statesman Li Guangdi noted his alarm at the rising price of rice in the empire's core regions and attributed this to population growth.[28] In 1717 the Kangxi emperor too suggested that the relatively lower grain prices pertaining in Yungui, Guangxi, and parts of Sichuan were owing to those areas' lower population densities.[29] Following this, the specific linkage of rising population and rising grain prices was repeated often by his successors and became a cardinal assumption among the official elite.[30] Although all recognized that unduly low grain prices might be a disincentive to producers, and sought price stability to prevent this, the secular rise in grain prices was perceived throughout most of the eighteenth century to be a great hardship to "the people," and efforts to control it were an increasing focus of government economic policy.

In retrospect, a variety of policy options might have been open to the Qing administration, in order to meet the related and clearly recognized problems of population growth, dwindling per capita food supplies, and rising consumer prices. Some of these were apparently so ideologically incorrect as to never have been contemplated. Even in the most alarmist discussions of increasing population pressure on food supplies, the political logic of the day so closely linked population growth with manifest benevolent government (*renzheng*) that any administrative effort to limit that growth would have been taboo (even though there is ample evidence that Qing subjects frequently took such matters into their own hands).[31]

Something similar could be said about fiscal policy. It is conceivable that a heavier personal and property tax burden might have provided disincentive for reproduction and hence indirectly aided per capita food supplies. Yet Qing rulers continued to believe the reverse: In 1743, for instance, the Qianlong emperor boasted that his lightening of land tax and corvée burdens had represented a positive response to increasing population pressure.[32] In fact, as Suzuki Chūsei has argued, the freezing of the land tax by the Kangxi emperor in 1712 probably made population growth all the more attractive and feasible,[33] and Qianlong's own "relaxed" (*kuan*) tax policies in the first decade and a half of his reign appear to correspond suspiciously with the dramatic surges of both population growth and grain price inflation documented for the mid-eighteenth century.[34] Eighteenth-century China faced few of the war-related fiscal pressures of contemporary Europe, and the prevailing political situation, Confucian ideology, and economic theory all combined to dictate that state financial comfort be translated as fully as possible into a policy of low taxation. Our protagonist Chen Hongmou was himself a vigorous supporter of such an approach. Neither Chen nor others of his day seemed to be aware of its hidden potential costs.

A third road not taken might have been to try to affect the balance between producers and consumers of food, say, by discouraging urbanization or movement into non-food-producing employment. Although, as we will see, the Qing did try to concentrate agricultural labor on production of basic foodstuffs, frank recognition of the outstripping of available farmland by the growing population made any broader rustication policies blatantly untenable, and no significant effort in this area was made.

Provisioning

Even with the essential closing off of these policy options, the Qing administration came nevertheless to develop one of the most comprehensive provisioning programs in all of human history prior to the advent of the welfare state.[35] Crucial to this enterprise was its extraordinarily thorough information-gathering system, which, for the period coinciding with Chen Hongmou's own provincial career, has been judged by specialists to have been as accurate and reliable as any ever previously used in the world. Beginning in the early eighteenth century, the Kangxi emperor required submission of monthly reports by magistrates, collated and forwarded by the provincial governor, on weather, harvest conditions, and grain prices in each county. The governors also submitted separate year-end reports known as *zouxiao an*, compiled by the provincial treasurer, of receipts, disbursements, and balances of all county-level government cash and grain holdings. Still further, the Qianlong emperor in 1740 ordered submission of the so-called *minshu gushu* memorials, providing county-level population and grain-holding totals on an annual basis. Detailed account books accompanied each of these reports.[36]

Qing provisioning policy might be divided into the following five strategies (listed in roughly ascending order of controversiality): (1) attacking extravagance and encouraging frugality, on the part of both government and society; (2) encouraging increased food production; (3) promoting maximum commercial circulation of grain; (4) attempting to meet sporadic and localized food crises through administrative means; and (5) maintaining large permanent stocks of grain in government hands as leverage to control local availability of grain on a routine basis. The first four of these strategies will be our subject in the remainder of this chapter; the fifth demands a chapter of its own.

The first, the campaign for frugality, requires little comment here.[37] It bore a patina of authority enshrined in *lixue* orthodoxy and most notably in Sima Guang's *Zizhi tongjian* (Comprehensive mirror for aid in government), a favorite text both of the throne and of Chen Hongmou. As we have seen, it also accorded with Chen's deepest personal predilections. In provincial service he routinely browbeat his subordinates with injunctions to austerity in managing their offices.[38] Chen did repeatedly argue, often in the face of considerable opposition, that specific projects (such as hydraulic works) requiring hefty government investment would produce cost-effective long-term results, but the notion that government spending in itself might stimulate the economy was probably not part of his thinking.[39] The prevailing logic was that summed up by Chen in a letter to Fang Bao:

> The pervasive dilemma today is that the price of rice is high and the people are too poor to afford it. But if those who seek to deal with this lack an overall conception of the problem, they will never be able to come up with a comprehensive policy approach to resolve it. This overall concept is none other than the Way of Producing Wealth [*shengcai*], identified in the *Great Learning* and repeated by Mencius: "Open the wellspring and restrict its flow [*kaiyuan jieliu*]" [i.e., produce more and consume less].[40]

We have already considered the production side of this equation in our discussion of the politically charged land reclamation (*kaiken*) program of the Yongzheng and early Qianlong reigns. Land reclamation, of course, was but one component of an extremely vigorous, multifaceted, and highly successful early and mid-Qing government program to stimulate the empire's production of basic foodstuffs. This program involved encouragement of resettlement, via the offering of government loans and tax holidays; the promulgation of new crops (notably sweet potato) appropriate for culti-vation on the extensive margin of agriculture; the extension of the irrigation system to allow upgrading of existing farmland and the shift to higher-yield grains; encourage-ment of maximal use of marginal lands for tree and animal husbandry; and, on occa-sion, encouragement of the diversion of land from commercial crops to grain. Chen Hongmou took a highly visible leadership role in each of these initiatives, as we shall see in subsequent chapters. Here I want to look briefly at his activities only in the last of these, which was certainly the most controversial.

Qing government concern for food supplies periodically prompted official efforts to return to grain production lands planted in nongrain crops, a move reminiscent of Maoist strategies of the 1950s and 1960s. In response to a request from the governor of Chen's own Guangxi Province, for example, the Yongzheng emperor in 1727 launched a campaign against planting sugarcane on any land suitable for grain, and at the height of the empire-wide grain shortage of 1748 no less development-minded a figure than Chen's longtime friend and patron Liang-Jiang viceroy Yinjishan proposed that lands devoted to the most profitable of his region's crops, cotton, be returned to grain.[41] Chen himself would never go this far. He did, however, lend his voice to move-ments to severely restrict the amount of grain made available to rice-wine brewers (and hence lost to the food market) and the amount of cultivable land planted in tobacco. Murmuring along both lines had been heard throughout the first decades of the eigh-teenth century, but the campaign came to a head with the accession of the Qianlong emperor in 1735. As part of his comprehensive review of the policies of the preceding reign, Qianlong encouraged an open debate within the bureaucracy on the wine and tobacco question. The most outspoken leader of the prohibition party was the senior statesman Fang Bao, a man whose patronage Chen Hongmou long sought to cultivate. Fang's most prominent opponent was Sun Jiagan. After hearing out both sides, the new emperor decided in 1737 to leave the matter to individual field officials to decide, based on current situations within their jurisdictions.[42]

During his long provincial career Chen Hongmou displayed a constant animus against wine production but actively prohibited it only in times of local grain shortage.[43] Regarding tobacco he was more forceful. As governor of drought-stricken Jiangxi in 1743 he proposed restricting its cultivation to small garden plots within city walls and to scattered sites too marginal for efficient grain production; for this he was com-mended by Fang Bao himself.[44] That there was considerable resistance to Chen's pro-posal is signaled by the fact that the Board of Revenue, in approving it, relaxed his re-strictions to allow tobacco cultivation in suburban areas and on plots within villages and towns. After all, as both Chen and Fang conceded, demand had by that time grown to such a level that many Jiangxi cultivators could expect the return on tobacco to equal three times that on any competing commercial crop.

Did Chen's position on tobacco and alcohol suggest an aversion to commerce? Hardly. Rather, his deep streak of puritanism played a key role. His attacks on tobacco and alcohol production were not on the surface moralistic ones, but consumption of these substances were leisure activities, and, clearly, on some level leisure itself made Chen Hongmou uneasy. Most directly, though, Chen's hostility was based on his utilitarian outlook—they were "of no use to humanity" (*wuyi yu ren*)—and his economizing in the husbanding of Heaven's bounty. Outlays on tobacco and alcohol by consumers were a dissipation of the population's aggregate wealth (*fei mincai*) and their production an immoral squandering of the earth's productive capacity (*hao dili*).

Chen Hongmou's fundamental procommercial leanings are more in evidence when we turn to the third of the Qing's basic provisioning strategies, market circulation. That the commercial market was a more efficient medium for distributing resources over the empire's great breadth than was any government agency had been a cardinal item of faith in the formation of imperial policy since the repudiation of Wang Anshi's dirigiste policies in the eleventh century, under the ideological leadership of Sima Guang.[45] The notion had been institutionalized in the 1480s with Qiu Jun's *Daxue yanyi bu* (Supplement to the extended meaning of the Great Learning), the standard guide to Confucian rulership thereafter. Chen Hongmou, of course, was a great devotee of both Sima and Qiu and published his own redaction of Qiu's work in 1737.[46]

Under such legitimating idioms as "*minban*" (management by the people themselves) and "*yimin yangmin*" (allow the people to see to their own sustenance), each of the early Qing rulers had pursued the strategy of encouraging private grain trade but none more forcefully than the Qianlong emperor. On his assumption of rule in 1735 the new monarch took this as one cornerstone of the "relaxed" (*kuan*) policies he proposed to reverse the statist tendencies of his father's reign. As he wrote in 1748, everyone understood that there was no better means of making grain available to the consumer at an affordable price than commercial circulation (*shang fan liutong*).[47] Officials in the field picked up and echoed such imperial rhetoric in countless memorials, invoking it to justify any number of promarket initiatives. In much of this rhetoric mercantile profit making was explicitly identified as legitimate and socially useful. As the preeminent authority on the Qianlong reign, Dai Yi, has concluded, to the extent that Qianlong's policies in his first few decades of rule were aimed at increasing the volume and velocity of commercial grain circulation throughout his empire, he succeeded beyond his fondest hopes.[48]

As we will explore later in detail, however "liberal" such promarket policies might appear, they were by no means laissez-faire. The objective was less one of *letting* the market accomplish its task than of *making* it do so. A very broad range of specific policies were enacted in this effort. Among these, the removal of what might be seen as administrative obstructions was but one point, although an important one. Both the Yongzheng and Qianlong emperors repeatedly prohibited the imposition of export embargoes by their local-level officials—a policy area fraught, as we will see, with political conflicts of interest. Qianlong demonstrated his own sincerity in this regard by lifting in 1736 the long-standing ban on imports of grain to China proper from his Manchu homeland.[49] But the goal of removing political impediments to market exchange was increasing circulation, not promoting economic freedom. Thus, the administration regularly intervened to remove obstacles created by merchants themselves—practices such as stockpiling in anticipation of rising prices (known in the discourse as *tunji juqi*) or halting shipments en route to a consumer market to deliberately induce a shortage (*zhongtu lanjie*). Merchants guilty of such offenses were castigated in official parlance as "traitorous" (*jianshang*), as enemies of the public weal, and to weed them out the Qing, well into the eighteenth century, still demanded licensing (*piao*) of grain shippers along major trade routes.[50]

One of the most contentious measures taken in the interests of encouraging grain circulation was its exemption from domestic customs duties. In his first year on the throne, responding to a memorial from Board of War president (and Chen Hongmou's erstwhile patron) Gan Rulai, Qianlong launched a program of localized exemptions for grain shipments into dearth-afflicted areas, sometimes even going so far as to grant grain shippers exemptions for nongrain cargoes carried on their return journeys. During the widespread subsistence crisis of 1742, he took the more decisive step of eliminating "in perpetuity" all customs duties on grain and beans.[51] (He identified a few specific exceptions, which in practice allowed local officials to continue their own disguised grain duties and necessitated an ongoing process of clarification of the imperial intent.)[52] Chen Hongmou himself was delighted with this policy. However, during the even more intense crisis of 1748 the emperor seized the opportunity presented by submission of a memorial by Jiangsu customs commissioner Tula to observe that prices of grain had not in fact fallen or even stabilized as a result of his fiscal magnanimity. Evidently, any savings resulting from the tax holiday had not been passed along to the consumer but rather had been skimmed off by "traitorous merchants." Qianlong thus restored the customs duty on grain, the proceeds from which he found convenient for financing his military campaigns in the western borderland of Jinchuan.[53] The priorities of the reign were beginning to shift.

The Qing also took more positive action to develop interregional grain circulation: providing various supports and incentives to producers to market their crop, offering low-interest loans to help capitalize long-distance shippers, and granting honorific degrees and official ranks to merchants who brought grain into chronically deficient regions. In all of this, as many scholars have pointed out, the administration had a definite vision; it worked actively to intensify commercialization, to encourage regional specialization and division of labor, and to shape the flow of grain along desired routes—in sum, to create a reliable, predictable, and highly systematized national grain market.

Most of the remainder of this chapter, and the chapters to follow, will show how Chen Hongmou was directly involved in these policies and was in fact considerably out in front in most such politically activist, yet decidedly promarket, initiatives. His activism was guided by the belief that not only *should* the market operate, but it inevitably *would* operate, despite and to the detriment of any official attempt to constrict or supersede it. Therefore, the wise official seeks to enter the marketplace and turn its operations to the benefit of the public and the state.[54] Let us begin by looking at two representative examples of how Chen "pushed the envelope" of imperial policy in this regard.

Both examples deal with money. They suggest how very far Chen was from the turn-back-the-clock Confucian conservative he is sometimes presented as being and how fully comfortable he was with a fully monetized economy and a society governed, at least it part, by market relations. At the height of the Jiangxi dearth in 1743, Governor Chen noted that the household cash reserves of a large portion of the population had become depleted by the high cost of grain so that they were unable to feed themselves. Chen's solution was to make cash loans totaling thirty thousand taels from salt treasury funds to *pawnshops* throughout the province, calling them in after the pawnshops had collected their debts following the coming harvest. In this highly commercialized agrarian economy, then, Chen saw the best way of provisioning the people to lie in an infusion of cash (à la the American Federal Reserve system), not in grain itself, and the best way to get this cash to the consumer to be via commercial lenders rather than by direct government means.[55]

Some dozen years later, as governor of Hunan, Chen faced a problem not of dearth but of surplus—the situation known in Qing sources as *shuhuang*, famine in the midst of plenty. Hunan's grain harvest that year had been so fruitful that it outstripped demand; producers were forced to sell at noncompensatory prices or could not sell at all. They were thus unable to procure cash for the many nongrain purchases they needed routinely to make. Under such circumstances Chen prescribed a role for the government that was somewhat more direct than the one he had proposed in Jiangxi but one, as in the Jiangxi case, that was designed to stimulate (not circumvent) the market by an infusion of state capital. Chen observed that wholesale rice merchants were just then departing Jiangnan for Hunan to make purchases for shipment to their home areas. He ordered Hunan County magistrates to offer themselves as purchasers for local producers, then to resell what they had purchased to the extraprovincial merchants once they arrived. Chen added that in no way were "natural patterns of circulation" (*zixiang liutong*) to be subverted by this intervention, for example by imposing on farmers quotas of grain to be sold to the state. Rather, this government action was designed simply to prompt the market to act in a manner that was more "timely" (*jishi*—as we shall see, a key economic concept for Chen).[56] Invoking the standard idiom that "cheap grain hurts the farmer," Chen stepped in to ensure the survival of the commercial producer, on whom the empire's delicate interregional grain market was based.

Food Imports

As Pierre-Étienne Will has pointed out, however committed the mid-Qing rulers were to maximum grain circulation within China proper, they were far more cautious and restrictive when it came to overseas trade.[57] There were strategic reasons for this, to be sure, and possibly also cultural ones. Yet here, as in so many other policy areas during the eighteenth century, provisioning concerns were determinative. Mid-Qing emperors were fully consistent in their prohibitions of any overseas exports of grain, in order to protect domestic supplies.[58] For the same reason, however, they showed far greater flexibility when it came to grain imports from abroad. And here, as in other areas, no official was a stronger advocate of flexibility and innovation than was Chen Hongmou.

Rice imports did not supply the national grain market generally but were instead targeted to very specific grain-deficit coastal regions. Most prominent among them were the populous maritime prefectures of Quanzhou and Zhangzhou in Fujian. By the mid-eighteenth century these two had come to require imports of 1.5 to 2 million *shi* of rice per year. Only a very small percentage of this came from mainland sources—from the wholesale markets of Suzhou and from the relatively lush prefecture of Wenzhou, up the coast in Zhejiang. The remainder came from overseas.[59] The most important source by far was the developing rice-basket of Taiwan, just across the strait from Quanzhou and Zhangzhou and increasingly the recipient of those two prefectures' surplus population. Yeh-chien Wang estimates that in the 1750s Taiwan supplied more than a million *shi* of Quanzhou's and Zhangzhou's grain needs each year, but it only reached that level as a result of a protracted process of political accommodation. Prohibited by imperial edict in the seventeenth century for security reasons, and in the early eighteenth century because of grain shortages in Taiwan itself, smuggled shipments of Taiwan rice nevertheless gradually increased, and as early as 1712 Fujian provincial officials had sought to legalize and regularize the trade. The first move toward legalization came under the Yongzheng emperor, who in 1725 authorized shipments of Taiwan tax grain to aid in provisioning coastal Fujian and the next year approved Min-Zhe viceroy Gao Qizhuo's request to permit some controlled commercial shipments as well.[60] During his brief tenure as Fujian governor in 1752 and 1753, however, Chen Hongmou decisively resolved this question by memorializing successfully to have all controls and limits on the cross-straits trade lifted so as to meet the evident market demand on the mainland and, incidentally, to promote Taiwan's own economic development.[61]

Even more politically sensitive than imports from Taiwan, an increasingly well-integrated prefecture of Fujian itself, were those from "Nanyang"—Southeast Asia. Actually, two separate but related issues were involved: the trade per se, which might be conducted by merchants of any national origin, and direct participation in the trade by subjects of the Qing. During his brief stint in Fujian Chen Hongmou contributed, in what one contemporary scholar has described as landmark fashion, to the resolution of both.[62] In 1717 the Kangxi emperor had reinstated the sea ban (*haijin*) on Chinese travel and residence abroad—in part to stem the outflow of rice—and gave those currently residing in Nanyang a three-year deadline to repatriate or face criminal punishment. Again at Viceroy Gao Qizhuo's urging, however, the Yongzheng emperor relaxed this ban in 1727, allowing Chinese merchants and shipmasters to make overseas sojourns of two years at a time before being required to return; in 1742 the Qianlong emperor extended this term to three years.[63]

But even Kangxi's original edict had not been intended to close off all trade; indeed, it specifically noted that foreign-owned vessels might continue to call at Chinese ports. His successors ever more actively encouraged imports of Southeast Asian rice by non-Chinese merchants. Almost immediately on his assumption of rule in 1722 the Yongzheng emperor declared rice imports to the Fujian coast duty free, and two years later he extended this policy to coastal Guangdong. In 1728 he ordered that Siamese rice imported at Xiamen be exempted from subsequent internal duties as well. Finally, in 1742, to further encourage rice imports, the Qianlong emperor decreed that all *other* cargo on ships coming in from Nanyang might be granted up to a 50 percent customs exemption, computed on a sliding scale according to the volume of rice brought in.[64]

Following Yongzheng's relaxation of the prohibition on participation in the burgeoning trade by Qing subjects, Fujianese merchants quickly came to assert an ever-larger presence within it. Yeh-chien Wang estimates that the number of Chinese vessels plying the Xiamen-Nanyang route rose from twenty to thirty per year in the 1720s to fifty to seventy-five per year by midcentury.[65] A lingering problem remained, however, providing a disincentive to Chinese merchants' embracing this role more fully: the continuing restriction of their overseas sojourn to a term of three years. This impediment to increased overseas trade Chen Hongmou sought successfully to remove.

In Fujian as elsewhere the problem of provisioning the population assumed paramount importance in Chen's policy priorities. In 1753, for example, he memorialized that a Siamese sea captain, stating that "his king having heard that rice prices in our country were very high, had enlisted private merchants to carry 7,000 *shi* of rice to Xiamen for sale," had arrived at the port and asked permission to sell his goods. Chen reported that he had agreed, ordering that the Siamese be paid a fair price and be subjected to no "unreasonable taxation" or machinations of "traitorous brokers."[66] That same year, in company with his superior, Min-Zhe viceroy Karjishan, Chen proposed a scheme whereby Chinese merchants would be awarded brevet ranks according to the volume of Siamese rice they imported. This mode of operation, he argued, would have the advantage of making rice imports private, not government-managed (*minban* rather than *guanban*). The scheme was famously successful, was imitated three years later in Guangdong, and eventually became codified into statute by the Board of Revenue.[67]

Although his provisioning concerns were clearly primary, however, the way Chen Hongmou framed his attack on the three-year limit for sojourning abroad made it clear that he saw a far broader set of economic development concerns demanding a further opening of overseas trade. He argued that not only imports of rice but also of silver (almost certainly American silver imported via Manila) and "other commodities of great benefit to the people" ought to be encouraged.[68] Even more sweeping was his argument that the livelihoods (*minsheng*) of coastal Fujianese were by that time so inextricably bound up with maritime trade that the economy of the entire region, its potential for the "accumulation of wealth," mandated a relaxation of the laws governing overseas travel.[69]

The wedge that Chen selected to open this door was the case of one Chen Yilao, who had been convicted in 1749 of overstaying the allowable term abroad. Back in 1736 Min-Zhe viceroy Shi Yulin had petitioned the newly enthroned emperor, requesting that Chinese merchants resident in Nanyang who, for whatever reason, "had not had the opportunity to complete their business and clear up their accounts" within the three-year term be allowed to stay on without reprisal. The following year Shi also requested that such merchants be authorized to repatriate their dependents and that the latter be allowed to repatriate even if the merchant himself had died. In both instances the Grand Council approved Shi's proposal but left open the possibility of prosecution for merchants guilty of certain criminal acts that had been spelled out, rather ambiguously, in Kangxi's 1717 edict. It was this gray area that had ensnared Chen Yilao and, until Chen Hongmou arrived on the scene, had in practice left the three-year limit intact.

Chen Yilao's crime, it appeared, had been that he had accepted appointment as head merchant, or "Kapitan China" (*jiabidan*), by Dutch East India Company authorities in Batavia. He was thus held on his return to Fujian to be an agent of a foreign power, not a "good merchant" (*maoyi liangmin*) of the sort that had been granted safe return. In the summer of 1754 Chen Hongmou submitted his landmark memorial conceding that Chen Yilao's conduct had indeed been criminal but expressing regret that the case had been interpreted by other overseas Chinese merchants as evidence that they were not welcome to return home. Chen argued that the winds in Nanyang were so unpredictable as to make it sometimes hard to return by the three-year deadline—an argument that must have been seen as a transparent request that Chinese merchants be allowed to remain abroad for the duration of their active careers, then return home for retirement if they wished.[70]

This must surely have been the true goal of many earlier Fujian officials as well, including Gao Qizhuo and Shi Yulin, but in Chen Hongmou's case the timing was right. The Grand Council ruled in response to his memorial that all Chinese "good merchants" currently residing overseas might be allowed to return with impunity, regardless of their length of sojourn, and that, with regard to those going abroad in the future, "it is clear that in Nanyang the vicissitudes of wind and sails are highly uncertain. There will inevitably be some merchants who, despite the best intentions, will overstay the three-year limit. To not respect their desire eventually to return home would be improper." The Council recommended formally assigning the power to determine whether to punish individual truants to governors of coastal provinces, most of whom, the record suggests, looked highly favorably on the profitable Nanyang trade. Emperor Qianlong agreed.[71] Almost immediately, Chen Hongmou's longtime ally Yang Xifu, then serving as Liang-Guang viceroy, cited Chen's memorial in a successful petition to have the three-year limit explicitly abolished.[72]

For his part Chen quickly broadcast the good news throughout Fujian. Echoing the language of the Yongzheng emperor's *Dayi juemi lu*, he told his assuredly jubilant audience that "center and periphery are essentially of a piece" (*zhongwai yiti*) and, accordingly, that all general prohibitions on foreign trade (*waifan maoyi*) were now rescinded. He also took steps to ensure that the news was spread to overseas Chinese communities throughout Southeast Asia.[73] The sea ban was finally dead.

Food Crisis Management

Many times throughout his long provincial career Chen Hongmou was confronted with dearth or famine. Among these, his tenures in Jiangxi (1742–43) and Shaanxi (1747–49) placed him in perhaps the most afflicted regions in the course of eighteenth-century China's worst subsistence crises. His handling of these crises has usually been judged by modern scholars to be exemplary.[74] Nor did his successes escape the notice of contemporaries. By midway in his career, as we have seen, Chen was being used by the Qianlong emperor largely as a troubleshooter, assigned to provinces where unusual problems—most often those of food supply—were underway or anticipated. In 1752, for example, he was suddenly shifted from Henan to Fujian because coastal flooding had made famine and epidemic imminent. "Carry out this assignment with sincere effort," wrote Qianlong on his posting, "and don't feel the need to request specific authorization from Me for your methods."[75]

In keeping with his self-conscious model of the "good official," Chen was unusual among provincial administrators in his willingness to see beyond the confines of his own jurisdiction in efforts to resolve food crises elsewhere in the empire. An incident from relatively late in his career neatly encapsulates some of the tensions and controversies surrounding Chen's approach to famine administration (*huangzheng*) as a whole. In 1755, serving as Hunan governor, he was advised by the governor-general of the lower Yangzi region, his old friend Yinjishan, of a severe dearth in parts of that area. The throne had already authorized Yinjishan to retain some two hundred thousand *shi* of his region's normal grain tribute assessment for distribution as relief and had also diverted an equal amount of wheat reserves from Henan to the stricken region. Chen memorialized to volunteer an additional two hundred thousand *shi* of rice from his own Hunan jurisdiction as further aid.

Although Hunan that year had enjoyed a good harvest, Chen had earlier moved to uphold producer prices by making state purchases (see above), and as a result commercial grain was no longer very cheap. It would still be possible, he wrote, to find this two hundred thousand *shi* on the market, but to do so would tip the balance of supply and demand to the detriment of local consumers. The many extraprovincial merchants who were just then arriving in Hunan to make their annual purchases would likewise find prices too high to encourage the usual level of buying, on which both Hunan producers and extraprovincial consumers had come to depend. "It is inappropriate" (*feiyi*), wrote Chen, "to have official purchases obstruct the normal activities of private commercial circulation." Accordingly, he proposed instead to come up with the two hundred thousand *shi* out of contingency surpluses (*yi'e*) held in Hunan's ever-normal granary system (*changping cang*) and to restock these accounts at an opportune time via market repurchase (*maibu*). This relief grain would not be distributed gratis in the afflicted region but would be sold there on the market, thus increasing supply and driving down dearth-inflated prices. The price differential between Hunan and Jiangsu would still be sufficient, however, to allow Yinjishan to use the sales proceeds to repay to Chen the cash value of the grain (at lower Hunan prices) and have enough left over to both cover the cost of shipment and retain some surplus as a hedge against future food crises.[76]

The Qianlong emperor pronounced himself delighted with Chen's arrangement, and after some negotiations over the logistics of milling and transport the shipments were made.[77] (Ultimately, a portion of the grain Chen shipped to Jiangsu was diverted en route to relieve a severe localized shortage in Anhui.)[78] All worked smoothly until the scheme reached the stage of market repurchase in Hunan itself. Late in 1755 the former Hunan governor and longtime friend of Chen Hongmou, Yang Xifu, memorialized that the time for restocking Hunan's ever-normal granaries had arrived and suggested that Chen make cash disbursements out of provincial coffers to county magistrates for local grain purchases. In so doing Yang named a price of five cash per *shi* of unhusked rice to be set as the maximum magistrates should pay. Chen responded that the former governor seemed out of touch with the secular inflation in Hunanese grain prices since his tenure there and conceded that this year's cyclical price rise in the postharvest months had been greater than he himself had anticipated. Magistrates would not be able to find rice on local markets at the price Yang suggested. Noting that the granary accounts that he had tapped for his shipments to Jiangsu were not normal reserve quotas but over-quota contingency surpluses, he suggested there was no urgency to restock at the present time. He would prefer to wait until after the following year's harvest to repurchase grain at cyclically reduced prices (which would also, of course, serve to aid producers by upholding grain prices at their lowest yearly ebb) rather than to provide Hunan magistrates with any incentive to engage in procurement practices that would be essentially confiscatory. Any localized price irregularities in the interim could easily be addressed by ad hoc transfers of granary stocks from one county to another. Again the emperor approved Chen's plan, and that in fact was what was done.[79]

This episode demonstrates quite neatly what I see as the key element in Chen Hongmou's approach to food policy, and economic policy more generally: a keen sensitivity to, and respect for the integrity of, the operation of the market combined with a highly activist willingness to use the resources of the state to *participate* in that market to achieve desired social ends. It also reveals other sets of goals that might seem different to different observers. Chen's ability to see beyond the needs of his current jurisdiction was unusually broad-minded, to be sure, but it was also convenient in its assuring for himself the blessings of superior officials who might aid in furthering his career. In this instance that official was his longtime friend and patron Yinjishan; at earlier points in his career it was the very powerful Fang Bao, who consistently voiced his approval of Chen's willingness to sacrifice the interests of his jurisdiction to ensure the flow of commercial grain to Fang's Jiangnan home.[80] Similarly, Chen's use of state purchase and his more persistent favoring of interregional commerce (in particular, shipments of grain out of his current jurisdiction) can be seen as a positive effort to aid agricultural producers and support continuing regional development or, alternatively, as evidence of his service as (in Shigeta Atsushi's phrase) "an agent of the landlord class."[81] Any single reading is probably too reductionist, and the episode just discussed certainly makes clear Chen's sensitivity to the great complexity of public and private concerns involved. This sensitivity is even more evident in his handling of provisioning crises in his own jurisdictions, the problem to which we now turn.

There were basically three avenues of recourse available to managers of regional or local food crises in the Qing era: direct state relief, private charity and community self-help, and the market. Like most of his colleagues, Chen made use of all these but in relative proportions that reflected his own distinctive political beliefs and worldview. As many scholars have noted, the Yongzheng and early Qianlong reigns—an era coinciding with Chen's own career—represented virtually the pinnacle of the imperial state's readiness to provide direct aid and of its success in doing so. The swelling of the imperial government's confidence in its own powers and its attitude of social activism was matched in these years by a relative lack of faith in the willingness of the local wealthy to do the job. "The economic and mental gulf that separated the propertied from the masses of the population," writes Pierre-Étienne Will, was now seen as too great.[82] With all his emphasis on local leadership and communal self-nurturance, Chen Hongmou himself seems to have shared this pessimism.[83] And yet, other scholars remind us, to characterize high Qing relief efforts as essentially "bureaucratic," in contrast to the "nonbureaucratic" style of the late Ming or late Qing, obscures the fact that even the most creative applicants of state resources to famine relief, Chen among them, acknowledged the state's own limitations, not least of which was the unreliability of its own sub-bureaucracy, and worked energetically to seek communal and market remedies.[84] Even at the height of effective state activism, the private sector was seen as an indispensable avenue of recourse.

During the difficult decade of the 1740s, and especially during the crisis of 1742–43 (when Chen was coping with dearth in Jiangxi), the court and its major provincial administrators collectively worked out a set of guidelines for the dispensation of state relief that would become standard operating procedure for well over a century.[85] Famine victims, for example, were to be divided into two categories, "desperately poor" (*jipin*) and "not quite so poor" (*cipin*); using a schedule based on this and on the percentage of their crop that had been lost, these victims would be granted "emergency relief" (*fuxu*) and "follow-up relief" (*jiazhen*) for a prescribed number of months. The daily relief allowance was set at five *he* (.005 *shi*) of grain per adult and half that amount for children. Within these guidelines, however, both the court and the many available how-to manuals on famine administration urged the individual official to be flexible and creative in the development of "expedient policies" (*quance*) to fit the needs at hand. In effect Chen and his colleagues were provided with a great deal of discretionary latitude, and Chen, for one, took full advantage of this.[86]

The first task was to determine the scope and severity of the problem and to identify, classify, and register the afflicted. Chen invariably toured personally any flood- or drought-stricken areas of his jurisdiction to gather his own assessment of relief needs.[87] He hounded his subordinates relentlessly to produce adequately detailed reports and registers (*huice xiangbao*), on the basis of which he would compile a provincial-level casebook.[88] Classification and registration of victims, he told his subordinates, could only reliably be accomplished by individual house-to-house inspections, and special deputies (*weiyuan*) were assigned this task in an attempt to keep corrupt yamen clerks out of the process altogether. There is probably no better testimony to the sincerity of the Qing administration's commitment to feed the hungry than the fact that Chen seriously fretted that households unfairly omitted from these relief registers would sue for redress and thereby increase the already crushing burden of litigation local officials were obliged to hear.[89]

Once the victims had been identified, the first recourse was to fiscal relief. The Qianlong emperor was highly receptive—especially during the early decades of his reign, when "*kuan*" (magnanimity) was the watchword of the day—to requests for abrogation of taxes in areas of failed harvest. Chen requested such relief often and with success, even in relatively mild harvest shortfalls.[90] In order that the benefits of fiscal exemptions be shared by propertyless cultivators as well, he usually directed landlords to grant their tenants corresponding remissions of rent.[91]

More active forms of relief included four general types: sales of grain, loans of grain, emergency work-assistance, and outright grants of aid. Selling off stocks from government granaries was primarily a means of curbing rising food prices (see Chapter 8), but augmented or accelerated sales were also an instrument of ad hoc crisis management. Loans from these granaries were likewise both a routine and an emergency device. Chen used both sales and loans quite liberally in his efforts to curb the most severe of the food crises he faced, most notably in Jiangxi from 1742 to 1743 and in Shaanxi in 1748. In the former case alone he sold off nearly a million *shi* of government grain.[92]

These were customary expedients. More innovative was Chen's use of the option of work relief (*yigong daizhen*, or *gongzhen* for short), a method to which he was unusually attracted. In his *Sourcebook on Official Conduct* Chen cited the actions of the otherwise-obscure administrator Wu Zunlu, who had responded to a local food crisis in a way that made ingenious use of the commercial market. Wu ordered the local population to collect firewood and disbursed funds from government treasuries to purchase it from them. The people could use these earnings to buy food grain. When winter set in, after the harvest had alleviated the worst of the food shortage, Wu simply sold the firewood back to the people. "The state [*guan*] had not suffered any financial loss," comments Chen, "and yet the people [*min*] had received great benefit. Now, *this* is the way to fight a famine!"[93]

It was this strategy of turning crisis into positive advantage, particularly through calculated interaction with the market, that underlay the more general policy of work relief. A method associated by late-imperial Chinese with the great Song-dynasty statesman Fan Zhongyan, work relief attracted both the Yongzheng and Qianlong emperors, especially in their efforts to combat Yellow River flooding and the attendant food crises of 1724 and 1737–38.[94] Chen Hongmou arrived in the heart of the afflicted area, as Tianjin daotai, at the height of the second crisis, when programs to employ famine victims were already underway. He embraced the project immediately, at the same time lobbying with eventual success to transform it into something more fully to his liking. His efforts in this instance provide one of the earliest and most revealing cases of Chen's own distinctive approach to government and the economy.

First, as he wrote to his friend and superior Yinjishan, the current project should be expanded dramatically. Rather than simply patching up the breaches in the dikes and feeding a few hungry workers in the process, why not seize this opportunity to undertake a comprehensive reconstruction of the entire Yellow River drainage system in Zhili and Shandong? "Although the cost will appear huge," he argued, "it will in the long run prove less than that of three or four years' relief efforts," which would inevitably be required should the basic problem of an antiquated hydraulic infrastructure go unaddressed. Chen further supported his proposals with what would become for him a characteristic defense of massive state investment in the economy as a means of making that private economy ultimately more self-reliant. "Having the people year after year seek provisioning from the state [*yangshi yuguan*]" was nowhere near as prudent as, by adopting his project, enabling the "storing of wealth among the people themselves" (*cangfu yumin*).[95] The latter idiom, as we shall see, was to become one of the most potent and contested in the entire Qing discourse of political economy.

But there was also a second prong of Chen's attack. In reckoning the wages to be paid for work relief, he insisted that not only the food needs of the worker himself but also of his family be taken into account. It was clearly a buyer's market for labor, but by Chen's calculations the schedule of payments currently adopted for work relief in Zhili offered workers no more than 30 percent of what their labor would command on the market in ordinary times and less even than what it might command elsewhere at present. This was shortsighted. It contravened market principles by hiring below market rates and was in effect a disguised form of conscription (*paimin*). This theme, the need to offer competitive wages for state-sponsored projects, was echoed by other advocates of work relief and became a staple of Chen's economic policy making.[96]

Particularly in the wake of its successful use during the Yellow River floods of the 1730s, work relief became a recourse of choice in famine administration for both Chen and the Qing court. In the process many projects that might otherwise have been left to local societal initiative came to be financed out of government accounts. As early as 1737 Qianlong ordered an empire-wide survey of the walls and moats of county seats, with the idea of selectively taking up renovation projects as needs for work-relief programs arose.[97] Chen Hongmou was one of those who most systematically followed up on this idea when confronting dearth both in Jiangxi and in Shaanxi. In the former province he also devised a program of work relief to comprehensively overhaul the Gan River polders surrounding Nanchang, which earned him great approval at court.[98]

When tax relief, sales and loans of grain, and government work projects all proved insufficient to keep the population alive and on the land, the final recourse was to direct aid. Where were the resources to finance such aid to be found? They were found both within and without the stricken region and from both governmental and commercial sources. The first source to tap, of course, was the accounts of the province itself. Usually this meant accounts of the ever-normal granary (*changping cang*) system. Like his colleagues Chen drew on this often to dispense relief, shifting stocks readily among local-level granaries within his jurisdiction as local conditions demanded.[99] Other provincial budgetary lines might be tapped as well, such as those of the salt administration.[100] When such local sources failed, the court was prepared to authorize transfers both of cash and of grain from other jurisdictions. In drought-stricken Shaanxi in 1748, for example, Chen memorialized successfully to receive shipments of ever-normal granary reserves from Henan and six months later some fifty thousand *shi* of grain from unspecified government accounts in rice-surplus Jiangxi.[101] Because of its location, Shaanxi was unable to draw on what was probably the greatest single government resource for granting relief after the ENG system: the enormous volume of tax grain that moved annually across the empire's central and eastern stretches under the auspices of the grain tribute administration (*caoyun*). While serving in Jiangxi, however, Chen could and did draw on this source, successfully requesting the retention in his province for relief purposes some one hundred thousand *shi* of tribute rice en route from Guangdong to Beijing.[102]

Wong and Perdue have concluded that the sheer scale of transfers of grain in government hands to meet localized food crises during the Yongzheng and Qianlong reign had never been equaled in Chinese, and perhaps never in human, history.[103] As official awareness of growing aggregate population pressure on resources became ever more acute in the 1740s, the Qianlong court in fact entertained repeated proposals to reverse the historical trend toward monetization of the fiscal system and demand all land tax payments in kind for the purpose of increasing government grain supplies to meet food crises.[104] It never acceded to these proposals for obvious reasons: The court was aware (and Chen Hongmou's counsel was among the most persuasive in this regard) that even at the height of state efficacy it was no match for the expanding commercial market as a provider of food. The routine circulation throughout the empire of massive quantities of commercial grain not only was counted on by officials to itself supply food to needy areas but also constituted a resource to be drawn on by the state for provision of direct relief. In Jiangxi, for example, Chen availed himself of this both by purchasing grain for relief purposes from shippers carrying it through his province (en route from Sichuan to Jiangnan) and by sending his own commercial agents to buy grain in the flourishing markets of Huguang.[105]

Turning from the question of the sources of state relief to that of delivery, the market orientation of Chen and many of his colleagues becomes even more clear. One of the persistent items of debate among Qing officials and scholars of famine administration was whether relief was best distributed in cash or in kind. Chen was unequivocally of the party favoring cash. This is not to say that he did not acknowledge conditions under which direct provision of food was unavoidable. He was quick, for instance, to set up networks of gruel kitchens (*zhouchang*) to feed urbanites and rural refugees in severely famine-stricken areas.[106] In certain regions poorly served by the market, moreover, he knew that he had no choice but to provide food grain himself.[107] But wherever practicable Chen preferred monetary relief. In part he justified this on the standard grounds that cash would be required by flood victims to rebuild their homes,[108] but often he went much further.

Even in fairly remote Shaanxi, in 1748, Chen delivered emergency relief in silver, the amount calculated as a function of the prescribed amount of relief grain per capita per day and the actual price of grain in respective local markets. He raised the cash for this distribution by selling off grain from local ENG reserves, at the same time making cash loans to better enable local people to buy the grain he sold.[109] In other words, his complex scheme was designed to provide maximum relief to the people at relatively little cost to the state (the loans of cash would be repaid and the grain sold off from granaries repurchased at reduced prices once the dearth had abated). At the same time, by increasing grain supplies on the market, he provided a brake on inflation of the market price. The entire operation both *presumed* the operation of a private grain market and a monetized rural economy and actively *contributed* to the development of that market and economy. There is no question but that for Chen Hongmou such market development, in this poorly commercialized region, was a desired by-product of the process of distributing direct state relief.

In his *Sourcebook on Official Conduct* Chen lays out the reasoning for his preference for cash distributions. He describes a scheme very similar to that we have just seen him using in Shaanxi and argues that "it gets double use out of the goods allocated for relief," as well as spreading the benefits over a maximum range of the population. He then cites the late Ming Fujianese scholar Yan Maoyou as follows:

> It has always been true that by dispensing relief in cash one can avoid the corruptions of middlemen pilfering a portion of the grain and making it up by adulteration, and of losses and expenses involved in transport. It is further the case that when villagers receive the cash equivalent [of relief grain] they can use part of that money to buy farm tools and other items to improve their productive capacity, while employing the leftover funds to purchase cheaper, alternative foodstuffs on which to subsist in the interim. One day's worth of grain thus becomes the equivalent of two days' worth.

Throughout the remainder of this lengthy text, Yan (and Chen) elaborates on the further virtues of cash relief: by relying on and stimulating the market, it reduces sub-bureaucratic peculation, spreads relief more efficiently and equitably, and reduces problems of crowd control. Above all, by infusing capital into the stricken rural economy, it contributes to the preservation and development of popular economic productivity.[110] As the empire's commercial economy continued to expand over the course of the Qing, a growing number of officials came to see things as Chen did; relief distributions, in Chen's own day made perhaps half each in cash and in kind, came increasingly to be made almost solely in cash.[111]

The same concern with fostering productivity underlay a second major debate in famine administration: Was it better to distribute aid in situ or in some more centralized location? Chen Hongmou, who himself came from an isolated village, fretted (in famine relief as in every policy area) about the equitable treatment of peripheral and central, rural and urban. He cited Yan Maoyou as follows: "The chief problems faced by any relief policy are that, while the most distressed population is at the lower end of society, elements in the middle levels will manipulate the program to their advantage while the neediest are left to starve, and that the urban population may receive aid while remote villagers will not be reached."[112] This concern dovetailed with Chen's emphasis on tailoring programs to keep the rural producer in place, on the farm. Thus the best of all policies, enacted for instance by Chen in 1748 in Shaanxi, would be to establish relief centers (*zhenchang*) in the afflicted countryside itself, so widely scattered as to be within daily reach of every villager. The beneficiaries would be cultivators; neither practitioners of other trades (artisans, merchants, clerks, soldiers) nor those farmers presumed to be "self-sufficient" without state aid (defined in this case as owners of draft animals) need apply.[113]

It regularly happened, however, that the severity of the crisis was too great, or the government response too slow, to prevent a sizable portion of both landed and landless country folk from fleeing their homes for regional cities or contiguous areas where food was said to be available. To deal with such refugees, the Yongzheng court had gradually developed a comprehensive set of policies known as *liuyang* (feeding refugee populations in the localities to which they had fled) and *zisong* (providing aid for their return home once the worst crisis had abated). As Suzuki Chūsei has shown, problems and corruption in the implementation of these programs led the Qianlong emperor to reconsider them as early as 1748 and effectively to give up on them, except in cases of relatively routine and localized flooding, in the 1750s.[114]

Chen Hongmou practiced *liuyang zisong* policies in Yangzhou in 1730, in Jiangxi in 1742, in Shaanxi in 1748, and in Fujian in 1752, and his correspondence in these cases allows us a glimpse of the problems inherent in this system. The Jiangxi and Fujian cases both directly involved the westerly migrations that concern Suzuki. Flood refugees from the Fengyang area of Jiangnan began in the winter of 1741 to stream through Jiangxi en route to presumed sources of food in Hubei (very likely the national grain entrepôt of Hankou, a usual magnet for the hungry). Chen intercepted all those he could at the Yangzi port of Jiujiang, allowing to pass only those who could demonstrate that they had relatives in Hubei who were willing to feed them. He carefully supervised the feeding of the remainder at Jiujiang throughout the winter and their return to their native places in midspring.[115]

In Shaanxi the case was more difficult. During the severe drought of 1748 Chen had repeatedly to order his reluctant local-level subordinates to feed refugees, not only from their own counties but from any locality or province. He sought wherever possible to direct refugees to certain designated relief centers but urged magistrates to remain flexible when this proved impossible. Chen worked assiduously to secure funding for *liuyang* operations and for transport of the refugees back to their native places. At the first sign of the crisis's easing, after the harvest, he formally closed down relief operations and exhorted the refugees to return home. For many, or perhaps most, this was not a viable option. Accordingly, he ordered his local magistrates to survey diligently all available wastelands in their districts and to uncover any marginally arable land on which refugees might be resettled. He ordered them also to seek out any and all local possibilities for wage-labor employment in which refugees might be absorbed.[116]

Chen's willingness to envision nonagricultural work and capitalist labor relations as solutions to rural dislocation was characteristic of his economic development programs as a whole, as Chapter 7 will show. But it was only secondary to his goal of keeping people as much as possible on the land. As he repeatedly enjoined his subordinates, the real fear was that of turning crisis refugees into a class of permanently unsettled vagrants (*youmin*). He feared the loss of employment (*shiye*) in a context in which growing chronic underemployment was already observable. He sought at all costs to maintain the maximum productive capacity of the population (*minli*). But his greatest fear, which loomed menacingly in cases such as that of 1748 Shaanxi, was that large numbers of people would "lose their place" (*shisuo*), becoming both unproductive and unaccountable, a threat to both the economic and the moral order.

In line with this concern was the attention Chen paid—an attention perhaps more dutiful than that of any other mid-Qing official—to the recovery of production at the earliest possible moment. Chen played the role of expert, akin to a modern-day agricultural extension service, in advising farmers at which precise moment to give up on the current flood- or drought-damaged crop or to convert grain lands to antifamine crops such as legumes and tubers. As Jiangsu governor in 1757 and 1760, he even pioneered a technique for planting wheat on lands in Subei, which remained too waterlogged after floods to successfully accept the usual rice planting. When necessary, his office ensured the supply of seeds for such purposes.[117] When the first good post-dearth harvest finally came in, Chen was not loathe to assert official authority to ensure that the yield was most efficiently husbanded.

Relief Through Circulation (liutong jieji)

All of the above techniques of famine administration might essentially be described as direct state activism. As we have seen, Chen Hongmou employed them all very energetically and won renown for doing so. However, it was the extent to which he exercised forceful *restraint* from intervention, out of his belief that the market could better serve the interests of provisioning the population than could government, and that it could do so better with a minimum of official interference, that was the more controversial in Chen's time. Even in severe provisioning crises Chen clung to his faith that the best method of redress was what he repeatedly termed "*liutong jieji*"—relief by means of commercial circulation. These views remain also the more striking today, in light of our conventional image of the Confucian bureaucracy's distaste for trade. In fact, very nearly the opposite was the case.

The Qianlong emperor himself noted in an edict of 1742 that both he and his predecessor had repeatedly stressed to their officials their belief that the single most reliable way to relieve conditions of regionalized dearth was via "commercial circulation" (*shang fan liutong*).[118] Probably no single eighteenth-century administrator developed this idea more systematically, nor applied it in practice more rigorously, than did Chen Hongmou. As we will explore in detail in our next chapter, Chen elevated to the status of an economic law the principle that interregional merchants will inevitably be drawn to make purchases in markets where prices are low and similarly drawn to make sales in markets where prices are high. Genuine dearth, in other words, acts as a magnet for imports, and this in turn is the surest mechanism of price stabilization. In his *Sourcebook on Official Conduct* Chen cites this exemplary anecdote from the writings of Yan Maoyou: "When [the great Song statesman] Fan Zhongyan was governor of Hangzhou, the price of grain shot up suddenly and precipitously. Fan didn't know why, and felt he didn't need to ask. He simply wrote a series of letters inviting outside merchants to come to Hangzhou and sell their grain at these inflated prices. They came in droves, competing with each other to be first to make such handsome profits. The price of rice went down swiftly."[119] Faced with regionalized dearth, Chen Hongmou argues that, even more than sudden dips in production, the major cause of inflation of grain prices is a breakdown in the arbitrage function of interregional circulation.[120] For this reason he believes that any state intervention in the marketplace that obstructs such circulation is "inappropriate" (*feiyi*).[121] And it is for this reason as well, to provide every inducement to commercial imports of grain into stricken areas, that he favors dispensation of state relief in cash rather than kind.

In his single-minded dedication to promoting maximum commercial circulation of grain, even, indeed especially, in times of shortage, Chen focuses on three principal adversaries: (1) locally imposed grain export embargoes, (2) government price controls, and (3) popular seizures of private grain holdings. We will look at each of these in turn.[122]

By far the strongest test of these positions Chen ever faced came in his very first provincial governorship, in Jiangxi in 1742 and 1743.[123] A traditionally rice-surplus province, Jiangxi had been spared the worst of the disastrous harvests that struck the lower Yangzi and southeast coastal regions in 1742, although Jiangxi, too, had suffered flooding in its most productive counties of the Gan River valley. Over the course of the winter and spring of 1742–43, grain prices had risen more steeply than normally in the annual agricultural cycle. Governor Chen first applied the usual remedies, sales and loans of government grain, but popular fears and anger at the inflation in consumer prices nevertheless swelled to near panic proportions. Public opinion (*minjian yilun*), as Chen read it, held that the principal cause of rising prices was the pressure put on grain supplies by unusually high exports to feed afflicted downriver areas, especially the ecologically fragile northern Jiangsu. Consequently, throughout Jiangxi, people had begun to take collective action to block grain from leaving their localities. Chen immediately prohibited all such activity in the strongest possible terms. Just prior to the New Year, the Qianlong emperor, with Jiangxi clearly in mind (and perhaps in response to Chen's specific urging), issued an edict banning any local-level grain export embargoes. Chen at once broadcast this edict throughout his province.[124]

Nevertheless, the situation continued to deteriorate. In late spring and early summer of 1743 the inflation of grain prices sharply accelerated, a phenomenon that Chen attributed directly to the spread of the embargo movement at the subcounty (*xiang*) level. Blockades were erected at confluences of navigable waterways throughout the province, and Jiangxi was in a condition effectively of economic civil war, every *xiang* for itself. Not only were provincial exports reduced to nil, but customarily grain-deficient localities of Jiangxi itself—most especially its largest cities of Nanchang and Jiujiang—were being starved out by their hinterlands. Within each *xiang* a condition of virtual class warfare prevailed, pitting grain holders against consumers. Those holding grain, it was alleged, refused to sell on the local market, preferring instead to ship their stocks stealthily to other *xiang* where the shortage-induced price was even higher or to hold it off the market entirely in anticipation of further inflation.[125] Ultimately, the bountiful harvest of 1743, in conjunction with Chen's own dearth-management policies (see below), brought the crisis to a successful end. The number of starvation victims in Jiangxi is not recorded but appears to have been small.

Who were the blockaders? In Chen Hongmou's proclamations throughout the crisis, we see a progressive hardening of his views of the culprits. Initially, they are simply local "poor people" (*pinmin*), but gradually they are more specifically singled out as "rootless thugs" (*wulai pigun*) and eventually as outright "traitors" (*jianmin*) and "depraved evil-doers" (*diaomin*). In part this reflects simply Chen's growing frustration; in part it involves his effort to isolate the culprits from the province's virtuous poor. In all likelihood, however, it also reflects the fact that the business of blocking local grain exports had in fact increasingly fallen into the hands of a class of professional entrepreneurs of violence, ever ready to capitalize on situations of popular distress and anger.

Chen was also gradually forced to admit, though, that county magistrates, fearful of the prospects of widespread starvation in their districts, were themselves ever more complicit in the embargo movement.

In Jiangxi in 1742 and 1743 Chen held to the broad geographic perspective that characterizes his policy making in general. He took this broader view, even at the expense of local interests, thereby winning the approval of his superiors. Chen certainly saw the duty of an imperial official as in part that of transcending local particularisms. He consistently reminded his Jiangxi constituency that populations of other provinces routinely relied on Jiangxi's ability to produce a grain surplus, and he rather haughtily derided the first wave of blockaders as "country bumpkins unaware of the bigger picture" (*xiangcun wuzhi yumin*). But their lack of knowledge, he would add, was not merely of the needs of other regions but of their own best interests.

Chen was, after all, an official with an enviable reputation as a champion of the people, and his rhetoric in attacking embargoes in Jiangxi always came back to the point that such actions fundamentally hurt the people themselves. Precisely because of the logic of market laws, extraprovincial exports could not hurt local grain supply to any appreciable degree. Even prior to the New Year, he told the population that merchants from Zhejiang and Fujian had visited Jiangxi, but because local grain prices had already climbed beyond the levels at which these outside merchants could make a profit, they had turned around and left empty-handed.[126] Commercial exports were not the problem, in other words; the embargoes were. "It is precisely because of the breakdown in commercial circulation," Chen declared, "that prices have risen." It was easy to see that impediments to internal grain circulation in Jiangxi had led to rising prices in grain-deficit parts of the province, but Chen insisted that, by prompting local grain holders to hoard rather than to market their stocks, embargoes served to escalate prices in the surplus-producing areas themselves.

Chen's opposition to export embargoes was very basic, but it was not a simple knee-jerk response. His policies took empirical account of the actual flow of commercial circulation. As we have seen, he again upheld a policy of continuing grain exports amidst local shortage in 1755 Hunan, which, like Jiangxi, was a consistently grain-surplus province, and where, even in years of dearth, shortages were nearly always greater outside the province than within it. But this was not the case in Shaanxi, where Chen confronted a food crisis during 1748 and 1749. Shaanxi was far less integrated into the national grain market than were any of the Yangzi provinces. In normal years it both imported and exported modest amounts of grain, but larger quantities circulated within the province itself, and in aggregate it approached self-sufficiency. It therefore called for a different response.

The 1747 harvest had been a general failure in many parts of Shaanxi, and when a rainless spring augured poorly for 1748 as well, Chen acted promptly to prohibit extraprovincial grain sales (chiefly in the form of millet and bean exports to Shanxi). Arguing that he "had no choice," he kept the ban in effect until after the abundant spring harvest of 1749, and steady rain that summer, began pushing prices down.[127] Chen's action was subsequently cited as precedent for banning grain exports in far less extreme situations (such as the minor dearth of 1752–53) by officials such as Zhongyin, who were overtly hostile to "wicked merchants."[128] Chen must have been chagrined at this, for his own actions betrayed no such attitude.

Indeed, Chen's own provincial export bans were invariably coupled with an even more emphatic defense of continued *intra*provincial grain circulation and announcements of stringent penalties for any "rootless thugs" (*wulai pigun*) who would dare blockade intraprovincial shipments. Such shipments were a manifestation of the freedom to buy and sell grain, a freedom that should not, either morally or pragmatically, be contravened by either state or societal armed force.[129] In a directive of late fall 1748 Chen announced the issuance of licenses (*zhao*) to traveling merchants (*keshang*) who transported grain within provincial borders and the establishment of naval guard stations at river confluences to check for valid licenses and to prevent erection of blockades. He sought to soothe local suspicions by stipulating that any grain shipments in unlicensed hands intercepted by these guard stations would be seized and sold on local markets, but at the same time he made clear that the goal of this regulation was to ensure the continued circulation of grain, not to impede it. Protests from local officials that they needed to retain grain in their own districts were met by a scoffing dismissal of the ignorance they showed of economics. The embargoes such officials suggested would merely "choke off" the very food supply they were designed to protect.[130]

Closely related to Chen's assault on locally imposed grain export bans were his attacks on official or popular efforts to impose fixed prices (*dingjia*) on grain sales. In the next chapter we will discuss further Chen's more general faith in the market as the proper arbiter of prices; here we will look at his defense of this principle in situations of great political sensitivity. The injunction to "not suppress prices" (*bu yijia*) was in fact a cardinal element of Qing central grain policy,[131] but local authorities frequently felt popular pressure to ignore it. In both 1743 Jiangxi and 1748 Shaanxi Chen emphatically prohibited his subordinates from giving in to such pressure. Differentially high market prices in their jurisdictions, he argued, were in fact the single best guarantee that local shortages would be relieved. Such prices would induce local grain holders to put their holdings on the market and would attract imports from outside. Official price controls would have the opposite effect; they were "of no use" (*wuyong*) and, indeed, counterproductive.[132]

In Shaanxi Chen demonstrated the depth of his commitment to this philosophy in his handling of military rations. Troops in that province—present in unusually large numbers because of Shaanxi's role as staging ground for Qing incursions into Inner Asia—were paid cash wages, the amount for each individual being calculated according to the mean annual price in his particular duty station of his anticipated grain consumption needs. With the extraordinary grain price inflation of 1748, the troops' cash wages rapidly fell short of what they needed to buy food. Chen was faced with three options: he could feed the troops directly with government grain, he could order grain shops to sell grain to the soldiers at a mandated price, or he could scramble to find cash in already strained provincial accounts to augment temporarily military pay. Painful as it must have been, he chose the third course.[133] Imposing price controls was out of the question, and, although he did not say as much, Chen clearly believed that there could be no greater magnet for extraprovincial grain imports than the prospect of thousands of hungry troops willing and able to pay inflated prices for grain.

The third dysfunctional response to dearth that Chen vehemently opposed was local official or popular seizures of privately held grain stocks. In actions closely related to their impositions of export embargoes, crowds of local people in areas of dearth would seize the holdings of landowners or merchants, forcing them to sell (often below market prices) or make loans to the needy. Chen faced this scenario in many of his jurisdictions, even in cases of relatively mild dearth, and he consistently responded with haste. For example, in Henan in 1750, Tongbei County had enjoyed a good harvest, whereas its neighbor across the border in Hubei, Suizhou, had not. After sales of grain from Tongbei to Suizhou drove up the price in Tongbei itself, crowds of people seized grain holdings of the wealthy and forced them to sell on the local market. Chen vigorously prosecuted those responsible, even while ordering the Tongbei magistrate to relieve local prices by selling off grain from his county granary. The prospect of an imminent price decline, he reasoned, was a far better way to get grain holders to sell quickly and voluntarily.[134]

Similar crowd actions have been, of course, a familiar occurrence in many cultures, and scholars looking at them cross-culturally have pointed out their routinized, predictable, and often culturally sanctioned character.[135] Like guardians of law and order elsewhere, Chen was hardly so charitable. Although he seems to have recognized their basis in habituated practice, to him such crowd actions were a "depraved custom" (*diaofeng*). And although he certainly understood that in many cases it was hard-pressed but normally stable local householders who were the culprits, he nevertheless chose to present them as "perverse hoodlums without local affiliation" (*wuji diaotu*).[136] Those perpetrating such actions had violated the rational imperative to "be contented with one's lot and have respect for the law" (*anfen shoufa*).

But Chen's public proclamations inveighing against coerced sales did not rely solely, or even primarily, on arguments of law and order. He gave greater weight to economic arguments of the public interest. Far from constituting the "larcenous appropriations of collective wealth" (*jintao yu ren*) riot instigators claimed them to be, large private accumulations of grain actually serve society. Without substantial savings in private hands, the chief recourse the public would have in times of shortage would be government grain reserves, which clearly by themselves would not be up to the task. Ask yourselves, he tells his constituents in Shaanxi: What possible reason would the rich have for not selling their grain when the price becomes unusually high—that is, when the public need is greatest?[137]

Even more revealing is the argument on which Chen falls back during the Jiangxi crisis of 1742–43. Grain held by local wealthy households is rightly *theirs*; it cannot be separated from them by popular will; their freedom to dispose of it when and where they choose is both natural and moral. The choice of the rich to hold some of their accumulations off the market, with an eye to disposing of it at the best possible price, accords with both human nature and rational principle (*qingli*). The government, too, is obliged to "respect [grain holders'] decisions to sell their holdings only when they deem timely and appropriate" (*ting qi suishi chutiao*).[138]

This respect for rights of private property, however, by no means left Chen Hongmou constrained to leave the wealthy alone in times of food crisis. Indeed, he produced all manner of exhortations to persuade them to dispose of their holdings to meet popular need. Each time he cautions his subordinates not to forcibly separate the rich from their grain stores, he accompanies this with advice on how officials may induce them to voluntarily (or semivoluntarily) give them up. These tactics include a comprehensive mix of normative, remunerative, and (only slightly veiled) coercive appeals. As prices begin to rise, Chen invokes the idiom of *tianliang*, heavenly goodness: I know that you, esteemed members of the literati, are imbued with innate reason and virtue—now is the time to display your magnanimity (in effect, your right to enjoy elite status) by selling your grain to your hungry neighbors. Characteristically, Chen conflates his notion of reason-as-virtue with that of reason-as-profit-maximization: You "rightfully ought" to sell now, not least because now is the best time "to make a good profit" (*yi huo houli*), a fact that your superior intellect allows you to see.[139] Then comes the gloved fist. In Shaanxi Chen notes that he has already banned extraprovincial grain exports, so grain holders might just as well sell locally, while the price is still high; besides, with sales of relief grain ongoing from government granaries, these high prices cannot last for long.[140] In extremes, as in 1743 Jiangxi, Chen can angrily condemn hoarders. What you are doing, he says, "approaches exploitation" (*jin yu panbo*). He none too subtly raises the specter of "mass anger" (*zhongyuan*), which his administration, try as it might, will be unable to hold in check. Moreover, the targets of this mass anger will be deserving of what they receive, for the forces of cosmic retribution mandate that wealth so immorally used cannot long endure.[141]

Chen is quick to publicize examples of voluntary elite compliance. These include private philanthropic opening of gruel kitchens and, in one case, a highly creative style of organized charity. A group of local magnates in one Jiangxi market town has subscribed a fund of 280 *shi* of rice, which they sell at 80 percent of the market price; the proceeds are used to buy more rice *at* the market price, which is then resold at the discount, and the cycle repeated until the sinking fund has been fully exhausted. By publicizing such efforts, Chen gives an active prod to his contagion theory of virtue, which he himself acknowledges as "optimistic" (*houwang*). "From a single township it will spread to an entire county, and from a single county to those all around it."[142]

He frequently invokes the appeals of natural bonds in encouraging elite activism, enjoining individuals to "act within your own lineage or village" and exalting examples of local community self-help, with "each township, each village, drawing upon sentiments of mutual aid and compassion to provide relief."[143] In his favorite duty station, Shaanxi, he applauds the relative spontaneity of local elite initiatives as evidence of that province's superior local customs (*fengsu*).[144] But Chen is quick as well to provide more tangible rewards for charitable behavior. As each crisis abates, he tallies up elite contributions of grain, cash, and labor and requests awards of imperial honors and even civil-service degrees according to a rather precisely determined schedule of quid pro quo.[145]

Beyond simply encouraging elite voluntarism, Chen as provincial governor also launches his own programs of "relief by commercial circulation" (*liutong jieji*), which are state-sponsored and at times state-financed but base themselves firmly on the twin pillars of the private market and the indigenous socioeconomic elite. County-level governments should insert themselves into the circulation process in several ways. Local grain holders who wish to sell but are timid about exposing themselves and their holdings to public scrutiny may sell discreetly to the magistrate, who will resell on the local market while protecting the anonymity of the source. (Chen insists that in such cases the magistrate is obliged to resell in the same locality in which the grain was purchased.)[146] County-level discretionary funds (*gongxiang*) are in some cases allocated to finance the sort of elite-managed sinking funds of grain described above. Most ambitiously, following a model endorsed by no less a cultural icon than Zhu Xi himself, Chen authorizes disbursement of county *gongxiang* funds to members of the local elite (most likely professional merchants, although this is never specified), who are to proceed under government patent (*huzhao*) to other localities either within or outside the province and purchase grain for resale at home. Officials along their route of transport are strictly ordered to keep hands off such shipments. On resale, the original capital (*yuanyin*) should be returned to the county treasury, but the anticipated profit (the patent holders are expected to buy cheap and sell dear) may justifiably be retained by the elites themselves. Chen is explicit in his appeal to the profit motive, augmented in this case by government financing, to prime the pump of commercial circulation.[147]

Even given these active efforts to turn local elites to the cause of popular relief, situations of dearth inevitably pitted haves against have-nots, and Chen's vigorous defense of the rights of the former to sell or contribute only at their own discretion could not but exacerbate this tension. He was well aware of this. His reports of conditions in 1743 Jiangxi and 1748 Shaanxi are full of blunt assessments of what he openly termed "class warfare" (*pinfu xiangchi*—literally, "conflict between poor and rich").[148] Nor was Chen overly alarmist. By one scholar's count, Jiangxi witnessed no fewer than 160 "food riots" in 1743 alone.[149] As we have already noted, Chen's stance left him vulnerable to the charge by the well-informed historian Shigeta Atsushi that he was acting simply as a tool of landlord interests.[150] Yet he consistently presented himself in the midst of crisis as acting in conformity with broad-based "popular opinion" (an issue to which we shall later return) and felt justified in declaring that "I as governor have no partiality toward rich or poor."[151]

Although Chen unquestionably believed this sincerely, and although he rather successfully managed to forge for himself a public image as the people's champion, it does seem that the economic logic underlying his actions was selectively myopic. His assumption—that rational actors respond to market shifts in a timely manner and therefore that when genuine need exists, stored grain will be dumped on the market in a manner fair to sellers and buyers alike—seems naive or worse. It ignores entirely the factor of leverage, of fundamentally unequal terms of trade between large-scale grain holders with the freedom of flexible profit calculation and consumers constrained by absolute subsistence needs. Even as Chen undertook vigorous efforts to keep consumer prices down and to maintain at all costs the survivability of the small-producer household, his blindness to this basic inequality in market positions most certainly tipped his policies in the interest of the wealthy.

But it was far less any self-interested elite bias than Chen's particular views of society and the role of the state that conditioned his actions in times of dearth. Wealth and poverty, as we have seen, were largely a matter of fate, and he consistently exhorted the downtrodden that "contentment with one's lot" (*anfen*) was actually in one's best interest.[152] Preservation of social order and harmony was a good in itself and benefited everyone. On this assumption Chen could defend his imposition of martial law in Shaanxi's near-famine of 1748 as an action prompted solely by his "love for the people" (*aimin*).[153] He acknowledged the reality of class interests but sought to transcend them and defuse class tensions by promoting ties of kinship and neighborhood solidarity (*xianglin qinyou*).[154] Although he saw crowd violence on the part of the poor as criminal and insensitivity to popular suffering on the part of the rich as merely immoral, he condemned equally both types of behavior as antisocial. Social harmony was in the long-term interests of all, but humanity being often shortsighted, it was the task of the enlightened official to put people in touch with their true, moral selves and in the process reassert the primacy of the broader perspective.

An Alternative Economic Discourse

Where did Chen come up with his rather remarkable views on the roles of state and market in famine relief, and how distinctive were they in his own day? Robert Hymes has analyzed the views of an otherwise obscure Southern Song scholar-official named Dong Wei, presented in Dong's short work *Jiuhuang huomin shu* (A book for relieving famine and reviving the people) (ca. 1201–4), views that appear uncannily similar to those of Chen Hongmou more than six centuries later.[155] Like Chen, Dong adamantly opposes three forms of counterproductive government intervention. The first is the imposition of local grain-export embargoes (*edi*). The second is government price controls (*yijia*); Dong argues, "If officials force prices down, commercial rice from outside will simply not come."[156] Third, and most controversially, Dong opposes most forms of coerced sales or contributions from the wealthy, a practice that, he notes, bears the euphonious name "encouraging sharing" (*quanfen*) but that might more properly be called "injuring the people" (*bingmin*). "Households which possess rice will sell it when they can get the best price," he writes. Any attempt to separate it from them forcefully, a policy that by definition treats rich and poor "inequitably," will only have the practical effect of inducing grain holders to conceal their stocks. The poor will suffer most of all from the withdrawal of this grain from the market.[157]

Dong Wei argues for a market-sensitive, nondirigiste government activism in the process of famine prevention. He counsels reliance on government granaries to influence local grain supply and price, just as does Chen Hongmou (see Chapter 8) but, again like Chen, puts even greater faith in the arbitrage functions of local supply and demand (*tongyong youwu*) to distribute grain at affordable prices.[158] The role of government should certainly include dispensation of relief in extremis, but Dong argues, as does Chen, that relief in cash is preferable to that in kind because it stimulates rather than stifles market exchange. Using the idiom "*quanfen*" counterintuitively, Dong claims that the best way to "encourage sharing" is to recruit local elites as commercial agents in frankly profit-making ventures to buy grain cheap outside their native districts and resell it dear on the home market.

As Hymes observes, Dong Wei is arguing for a view of the market as an autonomous, self-regulating, and essentially incontrovertible (*biran*) institution and for a view of market behavior as in full accord with "people's normal feelings" (*ren zhi changqing*).[159] Although there are considerable areas of overlap, Hymes sees this position as largely in contrast to a view of famine administration more closely associated with Zhu Xi and *lixue* orthodoxy, which stresses the moral compulsion on elites to contribute paternalistically to their neighbor's subsistence needs and is more inclined to sanction government enforcement of such moral obligations.[160] Although, as we have seen, Chen Hongmou takes a somewhat softer line in practice than Dong Wei would prescribe—he will consent to embargoes in certain cases, and he does not refrain from browbeating local grain holders into coughing up their hoarded stocks—he is clearly very close to Dong's position and, hence, in Hymes's scheme, less close to *lixue* orthodoxy. Although Hymes's portrayal of the contrast between the two positions may be a bit overdrawn (Chen Hongmou, after all, demonstrates that the two could be reconciled in practice), one must still marvel at the extent to which an avowed Zhu Xi partisan in the eighteenth century could echo so closely Dong Wei's logic and even his language.

Hymes makes very modest claims for Dong Wei's representative significance. He suggests that Dong may have been something of a voice in the wilderness even in his own day and does not venture to find for him any long-term influence. However, research on the early modern era argues the contrary. Qing administrators may not have known who the historical Dong Wei was, but they could not fail to know his work. The *Jiuhuang huomin shu* seems to have been reprinted in an annotated edition by the celebrated late Ming social activist Chen Longzheng (1585–1645); and in what was probably the most widely distributed text on provisioning policy in the early and mid-Qing, Yu Sen's 1690 *Huangzheng congshu* (Handbook on famine administration), Dong's work was given pride of place, reprinted in its entirety as the larger work's first volume. In this form it was reprinted again in the Qianlong emperor's universal library, the 1781 *Siku quanshu*.[161] Pierre-Étienne Will has reported its prominent inclusion in other Qing handbooks as well.[162] In his own annotations to the text Yu Sen enthusiastically endorses Dong's ideas. On avoiding price controls, for example, he comments: "If the price is high, then merchants coming in from afar will naturally be many [*ziduo*]. If the amount of rice they bring in is large, then the price will naturally come down [*ziping*]. This is an inevitable and logical outcome of circumstances [*lishi zhi biran*]."[163]

Rather surprisingly, I have found no direct reference either to Dong Wei or to Yu Sen in any of Chen Hongmou's writings. Instead, he credits as the formative influence on his antifamine policies the work of the seventeenth-century Fujianese scholar Yan Maoyou, whose book *Guanjian* (A mirror for officials) Chen excerpted in his own *Sourcebook on Official Conduct*, which he compiled and published while in the act of managing the Jiangxi dearth of 1742–43.[164] It was clearly during his Jiangxi tenure, though, that Chen's mature views on famine relief took shape; earlier, for example in Yunnan in 1736, he seems to have much more readily entertained the notion of compelling grain holders to sell at a "fair price."[165] And it is probably not insignificant, as Hymes suggests, that Dong Wei's beliefs seem to have formed part of a specifically Jiangxi-based tradition of political-economic thought.[166]

It seems clear that the views represented by Dong Wei, whether or not they were explicitly associated with his name, belonged to a continuing discourse on famine administration, and political economy more generally, that persisted from at least the twelfth century through the Qing era. It was not the only position that a Confucian scholar-official might hold, to be sure, but it was one with a considerable pedigree and legitimacy and one that, it seems to me, acquired ever greater acceptance as China entered the early modern period. Kishimoto Mio, for example, has identified the outlines of a debate over the course of the 1740s in which, responding to a 1743 imperial edict condemning hoarding and inflation, a number of key officials such as Anhui governor Fan Can and Liang-Guang viceroy Tsereng spoke out against price controls and defended private stockpiling of grain as both morally justified and socially beneficial.[167] At roughly the same time, the Suzhou scholar Hui Shiqi (1671–1741) was arguing that price controls, by discouraging imports, produce an effect directly counter to their intent.[168] Although none of these men seem to have been among Chen Hongmou's immediate circle of acquaintances, they were part of a growing mood of scholarly opinion that Chen clearly shared.

Thus, in adhering to his defiantly promarket position in the face of subsistence crisis, Chen Hongmou was hardly alone (we have already seen that no less eminent a contemporary than Fang Bao applauded his actions) but may well have been close to the mainstream assumptions of the Qing official elite. His views were not, however, universally shared, and he confronted opposition from either side. Some took a more commandist stance, as did Chen's successor as Shaanxi governor in the early 1750s, Zhongyin, who coerced merchants to sell their stocks during a mild dearth at a price of no more than 0.3 taels per *shi* above cost.[169] At the other extreme we might locate those of Chen's subordinates in 1740s Jiangxi, who (motivated perhaps more by expedience than ideology) took Chen's injunctions to respect private grain holdings as their cue to leave the elite totally alone, an approach Chen condemned as inconsistent with "benevolent administration" (*renzheng*).[170] The systematic and highly effective way that Chen Hongmou worked out in practice a middle ground between intervention and nonintervention in questions of food supply was probably his most original contribution to this ongoing debate. How he extended this logic to areas beyond basic provisioning will be our central concern in the chapter to follow.

CHAPTER 6

Economics

IN THIS CHAPTER we will expand on the assumptions we have just seen Chen Hongmou bringing to the area of provisioning and attempt to come to a more systematic understanding of how he and his contemporaries saw the economy as operating. What were the goals of economic policy? What values and institutions was that policy designed to protect or promote? What constraints were understood as limiting the role of governmental intervention into economic processes, and what were the areas in which that intervention might most effectively be focused?

Much of our discussion will take the form of exploring the use of a number of key idioms in the community of economic discourse within which Chen and his colleagues operated. Particularly in the absence of an established tradition of theoretical economics, of a genre of philosophical tracts on political economy such as existed in the contemporaneous West, an examination of the language invoked by policy makers to legitimate their actions, language they comfortably expected would call up a range of connotations within their audience, and by which in turn their own perceptions of economic behavior were at least in part shaped and delimited, seems to me the most effective means to get inside the economic assumptions of the eighteenth-century official elite. Although most of these idioms had ancient origins, I have no great interest in tracing these down. Rather, my interest here is more specifically to understand the range of meaning any idiom might have conveyed within the discourse field of Chen's own day and to see how his own deployment of that idiom may or may not have been distinctive.

I want to begin by citing some provocative arguments by the Ming historian Romeyn Taylor, whose very challenging recent work has been important in many regards in shaping my own thinking on elite cultural attitudes in late imperial China. In an analysis frankly influenced by the substantivist theories of Karl Polanyi, Taylor declares that the conception of the "economy" in "non-modern" societies—a blanket cross-cultural category in which he includes late imperial China—is not that of the "autonomous market," as it is in the "modern" world. Rather, the economic sphere is "subordinated to other kinds of social relations." It is better understood simply as "liveli-hood," that is, as "an instituted process of interaction serving the satisfaction of mate-rial wants," and these wants only.[1] He goes on: "In the ideology of [late imperial China], economy appeared in its substantive sense of the livelihood . . . of the people. Legiti-mated by its subordination to the orthodox social order, it was distinguished from profit [*li*], which sprang from the vice of self-interest."[2] Taylor concedes, of course, that in practice profit-maximizing market behavior existed and that the cultural and political elite were aware of this. However, he insists that "the orthodox social order always strug-gled against it, by one stratagem or another," and, as a result, a "modern" autonomous market, although never fully "subdued," was effectively "contained."[3]

The evidence presented in this chapter and throughout this book, however, sug-gests that Taylor's arguments, intuitively appealing as they might seem in the light of classical Confucian social thought, are vastly overdrawn and that any attempt to un-derstand Qing economic thought and policy by reference to the substantivist model is grossly misleading. To be sure, economic logic in Qing China *as in any society* was un-derstood and enunciated in the context of specific cultural assumptions, and economic policy was directed for the most part to the service of values and institutions that were culturally approved. This by no means implies, however, that autonomous and binding economic laws were not appreciated—indeed, creatively utilized—or that an eco-nomic development that went beyond mere satisfaction of minimal provisioning needs was not pursued.

Our particular object of study here, Chen Hongmou, admittedly belonged to an in-tellectual school that was especially "economist" within the intellectual spectrum of eighteenth-century China, although over the course of his lifetime these views were coming more and more to constitute the mainstream of scholar-official thought. What follows in this chapter will show both the economic sophistication of Chen's thinking and the specific cultural constructions within which this economism was fitted.

Minsheng

We might look first at the concept of "livelihood" that Taylor finds so central to, and re-strictive of, late imperial notions of the economy. As the Chinese idiom "*minsheng*," livelihood does indeed turn out to be perhaps the most basic and pervasive term in-voked in mid-Qing literati economic discourse. Best recalled today for its use by Sun Yat-sen in his "Principle of the People's Livelihood" (*minsheng zhuyi*), one of the much-trumpeted "Three Principles of the People," the notion of *minsheng* was hardly original with Sun. Indeed, as the work of David Strand suggests, even in Sun's own day his use of the term constituted a none-too-subtle effort to appropriate for his own ideological purposes a resonant item of current popular discourse.[4] In Chen Hongmou's rhetoric, nearly two centuries prior to Sun, it was ubiquitous.

With almost monotonous frequency, Chen identifies *minsheng* as the overriding concern that must serve as the goal of policy for any official, the object of the mission any man takes as his own by accepting imperial office.[5] In eulogizing Zhang Yunsui, a former superior who had a formative influence on his career, Chen can think of nothing more fitting to emphasize than Zhang's single-minded dedication to the *minsheng*, and Chen's own hagiographers followed suit in characterizing his own official style.[6] This by no means marked Chen as unusual for his day. Precisely the contrary. Although probably seldom absent from official discourse during the long course of imperial history, *minsheng* may never have been more prominently featured than in the mid-eighteenth century, as empire-wide subsistence concerns leaped to the forefront of bureaucratic consciousness. From 1735 to 1737, in a series of comprehensive edicts designed to set the tone of his reign, the newly enthroned Qianlong emperor announced dedication to the cause of *minsheng* as his prospective hallmark, and the term was given pride of place in any number of key imperial utterances in the decades to follow.[7] His officials, whatever their own predilections might have been, could hardly fail to fall in line.

Minsheng as an object of policy appears as something to be "nurtured" (*yang minsheng*) or "benefited" (*li minsheng*) or, in a compressed usage favored by Chen, to be "aided" or "facilitated" (*zisheng*).[8] Chen invokes the interests of *minsheng* as legitimation for initiatives in what might seem a surprising range of areas, from reforms in tax collection and in processing civil litigation to suppression of banditry and gambling, even to streamlining channels of bureaucratic correspondence.[9] It was an omnipresent concern and an unassailable motive for action.

What, then, does "*minsheng*" mean? One way to approach this problem is to see how the term is paired rhetorically. As Thomas Metzger long ago observed, a characteristic form of argumentation in Qing official writing is to stress that a proposed policy will solve two problems with one stroke, will assist both x and y.[10] Chen Hongmou, who is very given to this technique, routinely couples *minsheng*, in the sense of societal well-being, with a second value that is governmental. Frequent pairings are with the interests of bureaucratic order-keeping (*lizhi*), of statutory law (*guofa*), of state tax revenues (*guoke*), and, most frequently, of state budgetary integrity (*guoji*).[11] (In all of these cases it bears noting that the context makes clear it is *minsheng* interests that take priority.) Ordering his local-level subordinates to investigate thoroughly conditions in their districts, Chen identifies *minsheng* as one of four areas on which they must report, the others being local administration (*lizhi*), popular mentality (*renxin*), and local social practice (*fengsu*).[12] Clearly, *minsheng* refers to the material conditions of life, in a sense to standards of living, a sense Chen underlines by noting that the *minsheng* have declined in recent years because of mounting pressures of population growth on resources.[13]

The edicts of the Qianlong emperor cited above all refer to *minsheng* in the specific context of the availability of grain, and it seems possible that in the imperial mind the two were relatively coterminous. Not so with Chen Hongmou. He does, of course, associate *minsheng* with *minshi* (popular food supply), but for him the two are clearly not identical. Indeed, Chen's most emphatic playing of the *minsheng* card comes in areas decidedly outside the realm of simple provisioning, in his arguments for expanding the money supply as stimulus to the commercial economy and for opening mines as a sector for nonagricultural enterprise and employment.[14] It seems likely that Chen's use of the idiom of "*minsheng*" in these contexts represented a deliberate attempt on his part to expand the accepted meaning of the term in contemporary discourse, yet it was an expansion of meaning to which the term clearly lent itself.

Most revealing, I believe, are the instances where Chen elides the notion of *minsheng*—with its connotations of subsistence and stable employment—with other notions more suggestive of productivity or of property rights. In pressing the cause of tax reform in Hubei in 1747, for instance, he states as his goal a condition under which the common people (*xiaomin*) may "rest secure in their property and manage their own livelihood" (*leye guansheng*). And in Yunnan in 1737 he proposes labor service reforms intended to avoid "burdening the people" and to stimulate their "production of property" (*shengye*).[15]

This focus on providing the most conducive possible environment for the people's productive capacity, or *minli*, is a constant theme in Chen's writing. He makes it clear that his vision of *minli*, which encompasses both the labor power and all other productive assets (land, tools, skills) of the population, has a moral and cosmological, as well as simply an economic, dimension; the term is sometimes used interchangeably with "*yuanqi*," the primordial productive energy of the universe, and he explicitly identifies *minli* as a major component of *tianliang*, the basic resource endowment granted humankind by Heaven.[16] The official, therefore, has a moral obligation not merely to the people but to Heaven as well to safeguard and nurture popular economic productivity. By far most frequently Chen invokes this obligation as dictating the avoidance of onerous taxation. Concern for the *minli* lies behind remission of taxes in crisis situations and a general light taxation policy in normal times. It also demands extreme care in the way tax revenues are expended. Don't ever forget, Chen cautions his colleagues, that each time you call on the people to carry your sedan-chair, you are consuming a portion of their finite allotment of *minli*.[17]

Minli calculations do not always justify inaction, however. For example, Chen defends a campaign to clear up outstanding granary loans in Shaanxi in 1750 on the grounds that the *minli* at the moment is strong enough to bear government prompting of those in default. Creative government policies, moreover, can actually "unharness" (*shu*) the *minli*, allowing it to be more efficiently and diligently (*jin*) applied. This, too, is the moral duty of the official.[18] *Minli* is a capital asset, to be carefully budgeted by administrators, not merely by monitoring its expenditure but also by making calculated investments in its future growth.

Property

There is yet another attribute of the people, beyond *minsheng* and *minli*, the nurturance of which Chen Hongmou takes as the object of state economic policy: *minye*. As it does in present-day usage, the term "*ye*" in the mid-Qing carried with it a creative ambiguity. Its meanings ranged from occupation, vocation, or calling, to a business or enterprise, to material assets or property. Individual usages tended to highlight one or another of these separate meanings; Chen uses them all, often drawing on several meanings at once. He speaks, for example, of the distinctive *ye* (here obviously "tasks" or "employment") of males and females within a household that must be made to complement each other in the pursuit of maximal productivity.[19] He also frequently decries the incidence of *wuye* (unemployment), which appears to him in some regions to be on the rise and which contributes to a squandering of *minli* assets. But here the senses of "unemployed" and "propertyless" are conflated, for he sometimes in parallel passages substitutes the unambiguous "*wuchan*" (without property) for the more open-ended "*wuye*."[20]

Most often, when Chen speaks of the obligation of the state to protect the *minye*, he is stressing the sense of private property.[21] When Chen writes that the continuous addition of new farmland through solicitous government policies has augmented the *minye*, he is clearly emphasizing the people's aggregate property or wealth. So, too, when he restricts loans from community granaries to "*youye zhi ren*," he means "people with property," specifically the farmland on which to sow the seed being lent.[22]

As we shall see when we consider Chen's views of economic class in Chapter 9, he at times offers seemingly contradictory explanations of where property comes from. On the one hand, he consoles the poor that one's level of wealth is essentially a matter of fate (*pinfu youming*). On the other, he insists that accumulations of private property derive either from the patrimony of one's ancestors (*zufu yiji*) or from one's own labor and savings (*benren qinjian*), and on either score one's rights to such property are very nearly inviolable.[23]

My use of the term *rights* here may seem problematic, but I believe it is defensible. It has often been observed (accurately, so far as I can determine) that a notion of personal "rights" in any sense was never articulated in the Chinese lexicon prior to its importation from the West. According to a well-informed recent study, for example, the term for "people's rights" (*minquan*) appeared in Chinese no earlier than the late 1870s, as a neologism borrowed from Japanese.[24] This failure to articulate such a concept is no doubt revealing of a relative devaluation of the individual in the Chinese tradition. Nevertheless, as Philip Huang has conclusively demonstrated on the basis of county magistrates' citations of the Qing Code in civil judgments, a clearly understood (albeit unstated) "positive principle" of the code was that private property rights did in fact exist and were to be vigorously defended by the state.[25] Chen Hongmou in fact comes rather close, I think, to giving this notion concrete expression when he argues that the concept of private-property ownership "derives ultimately from rational principle" (*yuan shu qingli*).

Political authority is obliged to respect and defend private property rights both on a priori grounds (it is Heaven's will) and for instrumental purposes associated with governance. Those persons who have been deprived of private property are without a stake in the sociomoral order and are therefore self-evidently threatening. "Those who are without property" (*wuchan wuye*), Chen writes, "are willing to sink to any depravity." They can be reclaimed by the state only by affording them property, livelihood, and employment—all neatly summed up in the phrase "restoring their *ye*" (*guiye*).[26] Similarly, Chen cajoles his various constituencies not to risk loss of their property-cum-productivity (*shiye*) through such vices as gambling, excessive litigiousness, or flight in time of famine.[27]

A related set of terms that Chen routinely invokes to denote the object of his concern—"*mingao*" and "*minfei*" (literally, "the fat of the people")—reveals beyond doubt that his theory of proprietorship incorporates notions of production and the accumulation of surplus. Grain surpluses in private possession, he argues, represent "the blood and sweat of the common people," and government fiscal policies must in every case be tailored "on the basis of respect for popular accumulation" (*yi xu mingao*).[28] Even taxes, in Chen's opinion, ought to be conceived not as the state's proper due but rather as a portion of the people's own accumulated surplus (*feigao*) that they give over to state stewardship for public causes; for this reason the good official is constantly attentive to keep taxes to a minimum.[29]

This basic assumption likewise lies behind Chen's approach to such matters as relief dispensation and homesteading, in all of which he emphasizes fostering not merely economic self-reliance but also entrepreneurship; in at least one such policy statement he actually refers to private grain accumulations using the modern term for "capital," *ziben*.[30] Sounding much like a neoclassical economist, Chen insists that private wealth, the product of accumulated surplus, contributes to the collective good (*dali*); it constitutes not only a reserve to be drawn on by society in lean years but also the purchasing power needed to stimulate commodity circulation and the economy's overall health.[31] Therefore, in any number of separate policy areas Chen takes the position that private accumulations of surplus must never be appropriated by either state or societal force.[32] The property holder's right to retain or dispose of accumulated surplus must be respected.

All of this, it seems to me, bears significant resemblance to early modern Western theories of property, most notably that espoused by John Locke (1632–1704).[33] Quite obviously, the political and cultural circumstances in which Chen and Locke operated were very different, and thus the comparison cannot be pushed too hard. However, I do feel that using Locke's views as a touchstone can help us better understand what it is that Chen is and is not saying. As I read Chen Hongmou, he would agree with Locke's positions (1) that property ownership is a natural right bequeathed by divine agency (Locke's God, Chen's Heaven); (2) that this includes most basically the right to proprietorship of one's own person (the implications of this point for the question of personal freedom are never systematically followed up by Chen but are largely assumed); (3) that one's labor is one's property and is therefore freely marketable (see my discussion of corvée, below); (4) that one's right to accumulated surplus is a function, at least in large part, of the labor that one has invested in it; and (5) that, correspondingly, rights to property and society's surplus product are not a function of privileged status-group birthright. For both Chen, as a devout *lixue* adherent with a faith in Heaven's agency, and Locke, as a God-fearing Christian, all these principles are reflections of the divine plan on earth.

Equally important, however, are the implications of this line of thinking drawn by Locke (or his immediate heirs in the West) but *not* by Chen and his contemporaries. I would include among these, first of all, the justification of "unlimited expropriation" of property as a natural right. Chen believes, to the contrary, that the same principle that establishes one's right of proprietorship, one's possession of heavenly goodness/reason (*tianliang*), at the same time imposes on one an internally dictated obligation to control one's acquisitive appetites in the interest of one's fellow human beings. Second, Locke holds that one's degree of rationality is a function of one's economic position (that is, of one's routine need to make rational decisions in calculating gain or loss). Chen holds, rather, that inasmuch as both rationality and property rights stem from the same heavenly principle (*tianli*), the two are equally absolute, noncontingent, and present in all human beings.

A trickier aspect of the comparison concerns the question of disenfranchisement. As interpreted by C. B. Macpherson,[34] Locke argues that property ownership is the sine qua non of full membership in the civil society and that those persons who have opted to sell their labor for subsistence (thus abrogating proprietorship of their own person) have thereby also alienated their rationality and all political rights. For Chen Hongmou, of course, the question of political representation is not the issue it is for Locke, but that of full social and community membership certainly is. And Chen does, as we have seen, deeply distrust those who are propertyless, the *wuchan* and *wuye*, seeing them as to a certain extent outside the pale of human society. But for him the problem is not so much that of drawing the line of exclusion as it is that of bringing about the redemption of the propertyless, based on his faith in their innate rationality and humanity.

For our purposes here, however, the most telling difference between the economic thought of Locke and of Chen Hongmou would be in their assignment of the locus of proprietorship. Throughout this study I identify a number of areas in which one can see the emergence in Chen and his contemporaries of notions that might fairly be termed "individualist." Nevertheless, it is even more evident that the role of the individual as proprietor, so central to Locke's thought, remains in Chen's theory of property decidedly subordinate to that of the more orthodox Confucian locus of ownership: the family or household.[35] For Chen the social and economic virtues of property ownership are meaningless without reference to the family. Thus, for instance, the class of socially unaccountable persons whom his policies are designed to reclaim are threatening precisely because they are simultaneously without property (*wuye*) and without family (*wujia*).[36] The decision to fix the locus of proprietorship in the Chinese-style family is of course a *cultural* one (no less so is the early modern Western decision to fix it in a construction labeled the "individual") and so underlines the cultural constraints on any system of economic logic, however "scientific" or self-evident it purports to be. Chen certainly assumes his own vision of household proprietorship to accord with the revealed truths of nature, just as Locke does for his own view of possessive individualism.

Family Accounting (jiaji)

Patricia Ebrey has sensitively disaggregated two potentially conflicting cultural notions of "the family" operating in late imperial China, the one as a patriline, with a ritual focus and a network rather than group orientation (*zong*), and the other as a corporate household group emphasizing material interests (*jia*).[37] When conceived of heuristically as polar ideals, the behavioral choices dictated by the *zong*-orientation and the *jia*-orientation could often be at odds (for example in the area of adoption practices). But useful as Ebrey's distinction is, the important point here is that the two concepts were seamlessly intertwined in the notion of the family that, for Chen Hongmou, served as the locus of proprietorship. Recall, for example, how he stresses the dual origins of property—one's own industry and the patrimony bequeathed by one's forebears—*both* of which are presented as self-evident grounds for strong property rights. Similarly, family property is not only the property of present household members but also assets on which future descendents have a very real claim: "Balancing [household] income and expenditure is a matter of Principle. The assets and financial resources of any given person cannot be calculated in [monthly or annual] terms, since what is recklessly used up cannot be bequeathed to one's descendents."[38]

The cultural embeddedness of this theory of property is further highlighted when we recognize that it is not just any family structure but the highly particularized and ritually sanctioned Confucian family that is for Chen Hongmou both the proper and the most economically efficient locus of proprietorship. During his tenure in Yunnan in the 1730s, for example, he is extremely zealous in his efforts to replace kinship structures indigenous to local non-Han populations by the model of the Confucian family, for reasons both of cultural assimilation and of enhanced economic productivity.[39] Similarly, at the other end of the empire in the hyperdeveloped Jiangnan region, Chen is at pains to argue that family practices he decries—in this case extravagant gifting and ritual nicety in wedding celebrations—are not merely culturally deviant but also threatening to the *jiaji*, the financial solvency and budgetary planning, of the households involved.[40]

Put most directly, it is this *jiaji*, or capital accounting of property at the family level, that Chen sees as the basic foundation of the economy and society. It is thus the task of government to protect its continued viability and dynamic performance. *Jiaji* is a critical component of (although it does not exhaust) the "regulation of the family" (*zhijia*), identified by the *Great Learning* and countless other texts in Chen Hongmou's direct line of intellectual descent as one of humankind's most basic moral imperatives. The culturally orthodox "way of the family" (*jiadao*), Chen notes, is the surest path to the greatest material well-being of all society (*dali*).[41] He accordingly counsels his provincial subordinates in each of his posts that it is their responsibility to root out harmful cultural practices and instill in their constituencies the rudiments of "small household budgetary planning" (*xiaomin shenjia zhi ji*).[42]

In this Chen fits comfortably into the mainstream of early and mid-Qing economic policy making, which repeatedly specified as its object the sustainability of the small-producer household (*jiagei minzu*).[43] As Chen himself asserted, it was this unit that was best able to facilitate not only popular subsistence but also economic development, to spread economic benefits "inexhaustibly" (*wuqiong*).[44] Thus he argues that land reclamation programs should not be conceived as large-scale state projects, nor handed over to large private developers, but rather to be effective must be based on the small homesteader; thus, too, he urges government grain purchases as a means of agricultural price support, specifically to benefit the small-producer household and to avoid a situation in which such households "cannot get by" (*wu jieji*) in hard times.[45] The emphasis is on household *reproduction*, not merely survival; in a key formulation, Chen claims that "the failure of an individual household [*jiamen*] is suffered by that household alone, but the extinction of that family's continuity [*jiashi*] is a calamity for the entire world."[46]

That this reproduction of the small-producer household over generations is a cultural as well as an economic necessity is nowhere better illustrated than in a directive issued by Chen to county magistrates in Hunan, 1755, instructing them to buy up grain, the price of which has plummeted because of the abundance of the harvest. Small producers depend on the cash these purchases will bring, he writes, to finance the instruments of proper household reproduction: weddings and funerals. These two items of popular expenditure, significantly, are (along with tax payments) the only ones he here identifies as critical. In this text, at least, these rituals of family continuity alone provide the rationale for commercialized agriculture, for the farm household's participation in the market in quest of cash.[47]

What we know of Chen's personal *jiaji* is fairly consistent with his public proclamations and offers us a more concrete sense of how he believed an upwardly mobile family ought to manage its accounts.[48] Beyond townhouse complexes in the booming Guilin and Changsha, which he acquired initially for family occupancy but subsequently developed further for rental purposes,[49] the bulk of Chen's investments seem to have been in commercially farmed rice land. (The family also made some cash loans.) He appears to have done little to augment the patrimonial property in his home village of Hengshan itself, probably recognizing the same constraints on the market range of that locality's produce we observed in Chapter 1. Instead, he concentrated in the 1750s on accumulating a rural estate (*zhuang*) in Yongfu, the county adjacent to his native Lingui. This must eventually have become quite considerable, for Chen was able in 1762 to make from it a gift of five hundred *mu* to endow the county school and still retain holdings sufficient to support his growing family. But the superior potential for commercial rice production in Hunan's Xiang River valley (as well as, Chen claimed, a filial devotion to the region mythologized as his lineage's "old sod")[50] gradually convinced him to shift the bulk of his landholding investments there. Beginning in the early 1760s he began to acquire in Changsha County's Fengtang township a concentration of holdings, which he ultimately described as "not small" (*buxiao*), and in 1765 he added to these a separate estate outside the market town of Shimapu.

These various estates were farmed by tenants (whose names Chen usually knew and whose rents he remitted in bad years) but were closely overseen by servant households of the Chen family (*jiaren*).[51] Nearly a dozen such *jiaren* are mentioned in Chen's letters. They are neither relatives nor affines (they bear a variety of different surnames), are married and have children (Chen once complains that the *jiaren* family running one of his estates has so many children to feed that their managerial services are not cost-effective), and are clearly not indentured (one *jiaren* who has done well with Chen eventually leaves him to set up his own business). Chen assigns and reassigns these managers frequently—sometimes complaining that reliably experienced (*laocheng*) ones are hard to find—and they are constantly on the run between managerial estates, Chen's personal residence at the capital, and the family home in Guilin. They must do so because Chen insists on making most major decisions regarding his property himself.[52] These include *where* to buy property (he anguishes for quite some time over the question of whether for managerial reasons it is cost-effective to own two such dispersed estates as he does in Changsha) and, more important, *when* to buy (we see him calculating in detail the factors of land price, rent productivity, and market price for the land's output before consenting to make each new purchase). In general, though, his investment strategy is clear: keep costs to a minimum, and aggressively reinvest the profits in more land whenever feasible.

While sojourning in Beijing—where he complains that his board president's salary is inadequate to meet the high cost of living—Chen himself lives off part of these Hunan estates' proceeds, but the bulk is intended to support his growing family at home. Chen keeps "detailed accounts" (*xizhang*) of income and expenditures, and expects his dependents to do likewise. Accounts are divided by segment (*fang*) within the extended family; Chen seeks to micromanage from his distant official post the expenses of each dependent nuclear household, and he inquires regularly and in detail about the support needs of each individual. He specifies that after his death the properties will be held jointly in the names of his and his two brothers' eldest surviving sons and will thereby continue to support their descendents. Rules (*guimou*) on budgeting expenses must be observed by all family members; it is the responsibility of each individual to observe financial responsibility and accountability to the others (*ge you zecheng, ge you jikao*). Only in this way can Chen's frankly professed goal, that his descendents continue as a "family of great wealth" (*baiwan fujia*), be achieved.[53] It is the same advice he dispenses liberally to his administrative constituents.

Frugality

The small-producer household, typically agrarian yet significantly commercialized, is the principal intended audience for Chen Hongmou's impassioned discourse on frugality (*jiesheng*). This discourse, as we have seen, had deep roots both in Chen's own family history and in the broader eighteenth-century Qing approach to its provisioning crisis. In a typical utterance, Chen's 1746 "Proclamation Encouraging Frugality," addressed to the people of Shaanxi, he cautions households to resist the urges of wastage (*muofei*) or extravagance (*huafei*) that inevitably accompany a bountiful harvest. Avoid capricious or ostentatious spending on food, drink, travel, or recreation or on unnecessarily elaborate ritual observances. Instead, the bounty of Heaven that Shaanxi has recently enjoyed must be carefully husbanded at present, in anticipation of future needs.[54]

Several aspects of this discourse on frugality bear highlighting. First is the frank and insistent emphasis on utility. Chen routinely contrasts "useful" (*youyong*) household expenditures with those that are "useless" (*wuyong*), the "profitable" (*youyi*) with the "unprofitable" (*wuyi*). The latter categories pointedly include for Chen spirit worship, pilgrimages, and other manifestations of popular piety. These are vain and wasteful quests for supernatural favor—in other words, bad investments. Far better for the small-producer household to follow Chen's own highly materialist prescriptions for "turning the useless into the useful" (*hua wuyong wei youyong*).[55]

This leads directly into our second point: Chen's conception of frugality as part of a highly articulated calculus of investment that leads to the generation of new wealth. It may well be that this marks a new and distinctive feature of Qing economic logic. In previous eras the rhetoric of thrift, or "husbanding" (*jie*) of wealth, had most frequently been deployed by conservative critics of state-driven expansionist policies advertised as "generating wealth" (*shengcai*), such as those espoused by Wang Anshi in the late eleventh century and Zhang Juzheng in the late sixteenth.[56] Chen Hongmou, by contrast, felt equally comfortable in both rhetorical postures, believing to the bottom of his soul that the two were not only compatible but that thrift—coupled with judicious investment—necessarily *bred* growth (see Chapter 8). The idiom "*yuanyuan shengxi*," describing a continuous process of profit-generating reinvestment, is routinely applied by Chen to proper management both of state granary accounts and of private household budgets. In a passage that might serve as metaphor to express Chen's ideal of the functional small-producer household, he orders his subordinates in Yunnan to instruct the people how to carefully accumulate night soil and apply it as fertilizer to produce useful, and in turn accumulable, crops. "Capital" (*ben*) that is husbanded rather than dissipated will "increase gradually day by day" (*rijian jiaduo*).[57]

Most interesting, however, is the way that Chen Hongmou—in the manner of early modern economic thinkers elsewhere as well—embeds his utilitarian capitalist logic in a discourse of morality and virtue. This can be seen in the way he gradually elides his language use in a single piece of writing. For example, in one text the specific quality he is extolling begins as "*jiesheng*" (simple frugality) and then by a progressive substitution of ideographs becomes first "*jiejian*" (self-restraint, moral as well as economic) and eventually "*jianpu*" (the stoic rusticity and lack of pretense that is for Chen the paramount cultural ideal).[58] Again, in the "Proclamation Encouraging Frugality," the economic quality identified in the title soon gives way to the moral quality of "*zhipu*," yeoman-like simplicity and directness.[59] Habits of extravagance are "*louxi*" (debased), whereas frugality, savings, and accumulation are "*shi*" (genuine and substantial)—an all-purpose term of approval that, as we saw in Chapter 4, Chen applies to anything he believes has moral value.

Frugality is virtuous for a variety of reasons. It represents responsible stewardship of the resources granted humans by Heaven. It is a denial of personal indulgence in the broader interests of family and community. ("If you go to drink at a wine shop," Chen warns darkly, "your whole family will go hungry.")[60] And, most strikingly, the very exercise of financial responsibility is a means of getting in more complete touch with, of realizing, one's innate moral essence (*tianliang*). Yielding to extravagance and frivolity, by contrast, is in and of itself morally corrupting.[61] For all of these reasons, Chen repeatedly asserts, the actions of government officials in exhorting popular frugality and instituting schemes for local-level accumulation are important as means not merely to achieve economic subsistence, or even prosperity, but also to instill popular morality and rectify cultural practice.

There is obviously more than a little elitism in this line of thinking and perhaps a dose of disguised class-interest as well. The analysis of "bourgeois thrift" as an instrument of elite hegemony, developed by European historians such as Hans Medick, seems to me perhaps more relevant in this context than it might at first appear. As Medick describes it, the logic of savings and accumulation, which is of practical utility to a class of society living comfortably above the subsistence level, may be assigned universal moral qualities by that class. The elite thus draws attention to its own right to greater well-being (we are better off because we are more thrifty) and at the same time imposes what are in fact class-specific values on a lower-class population to which such values don't logically apply. In practice, as Medick points out, "burning off" behavior and the "culture of treating" (for example, buying a round at the bar for one's mates on payday) may well be a more rational use of one's resources than thrift for a person whose chances of material advancement through savings are minimal but who may well need in the future to rely on the peer approval thus purchased.[62]

Viewed from such a perspective, Chen Hongmou's assertive ideology of frugality takes on a somewhat darker quality. So too does his obdurate failure to recognize the utilitarian value of "burning off" activities on the part of more substantial villagers— sponsoring performances by itinerant opera troupes to thank the gods for a good harvest, for example, or throwing lavish wedding feasts to which community members are invited. As we shall see more fully in Chapter 9, class interest was not in general a major ingredient in Chen's consciousness, and certainly he rails against overt classism when it appears before him. There were also of course very practical food supply concerns prompting any Qing administrator to esteem popular thrift. Yet the fact remains that for any member of the propertied official elite such as Chen Hongmou the gospel of frugality was a most expedient one to espouse.

Commerce

For many decades a governing view in the study of Qing history has taken the formula "*zhongnong yishang*" (promote agriculture and restrain commerce), enunciated most famously in the Han but repeated countless times throughout the imperial era, at face value. Western scholars schooled in an economic developmentalist logic, and Chinese scholars whose intellectual roots lie in the radical antitraditionalism of the May Fourth generation, concurred in seeing even the most ostensibly forward-looking Qing thinkers and statesmen (those associated with statecraft ideas, such as Wei Yuan and Zeng Guofan) as captive to this proagrarian, anticommercial bias. In this established historiography the beginnings of a genuinely progressive, procommercial economic thought could only await the rejection of indigenous prejudices and a turn toward Western economic reasoning, datable no earlier than the very late nineteenth century. This view is by no means dead and can be found in even some of the most innovative work on Qing political economy produced by scholars in both China and the West.[63]

In recent years, however, a highly emphatic counterargument has been increasingly voiced by a number of historians (Yu Yingshi, Gao Wangling, and Helen Dunstan, among others) for whom, quite possibly, the commercial frenzy of the recent Chinese experience seems to have suggested new ways of viewing the late imperial past.[64] As a result of this revisionist scholarship, it has become increasingly clear that, although occasional statements of political support for merchants were never altogether lacking in

China's long imperial era, it was in the early modern period—and most especially in the eighteenth century—that the social and economic values of commerce achieved a broad consensual authority they had never before enjoyed. "Demonstrating sympathy for merchants" (*xushang*), and its converse, avoiding actions that would "fatigue merchants" (*leishang*), thus became pervasive idioms in official rhetoric, powerful discursive weapons used to validate a very wide range of procommercial policies. This was the mainstream, no longer a countercurrent, in Qing economic thought.

In spite of the paramount role that we have seen the rural farm family play in the economic logic of Chen Hongmou, he was in fact one of the most outspoken advocates of showing "sympathy" for merchants of his day.[65] The hoary phrase "*zhongnong*" (promote agriculture) certainly appeared in Chen's writing on occasion, but so far as I can determine its traditional corollaries "*yishang*" (restrain commerce) and "*qingshang*" (give scant regard to commerce) never once did. The properly functioning economy, in Chen's view, was a complex one in which agriculture played but one part. In the 1769 revision of his *Sourcebook on Reforming Social Practice*, for example, he inserted the following provocative passage from the early Qing Hunanese scholar Wang Zhifu: "Apart from farming and grain production, there are other occupations which must be considered in any strategy for the production of wealth [*shengcai*]. . . . In the narrowest sense, these are useful because they aid in the supply of food and other daily necessities. In the broader sense, however, they contribute to the process of commercial circulation, which in turn leads to the enrichment [of the entire society]."[66]

A central tenet of Chen Hongmou's economic logic was that the people were best served by commercial circulation of maximum volume and velocity. The term for this circulation, "*liutong*" (sometimes also "*xiangtong*," or mutual exchange), became an unambiguously positive key word in his administrative correspondence, used to validate a wide range of policies. At least as it pertained to grain and currency flows, advocacy of maximum *liutong* was hardly new to Chen's era. It had been stressed in the Song by writers as diverse as Ouyang Xiu, Dong Wei, and the scientist and economic theorist Shen Gua (1031–95), and it was echoed in the seventeenth century by Huang Zongxi, Wang Yuan, and many others.[67] But it achieved a new legitimacy and urgency in the second quarter of the eighteenth century, when it became a central goal of imperial economic policy. The Qianlong emperor, in particular, emphatically announced his faith in the virtues of *liutong* in a number of key edicts of the 1740s.[68] In the political discourse of the day, "*huxiang liutong*" (mutual exchange and commodity circulation) assumed very nearly the status of an absolute good in itself.

As we saw in the preceding chapter, Chen Hongmou valued *liutong* as a means to ensure steady supplies of needed goods in deficit areas (*liutong jieji*, or "relief via commercial circulation") and as the most effective means of price stabilization. ("Commercial circulation," wrote the Qianlong emperor, "has the general effect of lowering prices when they are too high.")[69] Somewhat more unconventionally, Chen added to this his belief that the higher the volume of *liutong* in any given local economy, the better off the *minsheng* because commerce created jobs and promoted the accumulation of wealth.[70] And he was clearly more emphatic than most in his insistence that "free" or "natural" flows of trade (*zixiang liutong*) should be interfered with by the government only in exceptional circumstances.[71]

Chen was far from hostile to merchants as a social group. Despite his frequent broadsides against extravagant lifestyles, he did not (as did many others) specifically associate this pattern of deviant behavior with mercantile wealth; indeed, many of Chen's attacks imply that the chief offenders are not hardworking merchants but idle literati living on rentier wealth. Chen is scarcely blind to the exploitative possibilities of commerce; he enthusiastically reprints a popular morality book prescribing the dos and don'ts of business ethics, and, like all Qing bureaucrats, he vilifies as *jianshang* (traitorous merchants) those who fail to meet these standards.[72] As a general category, however, commercial entrepreneurs appear in Chen's discourse in a positive light; they are not merely "merchants" but also "*maoyi liangmin*," law-abiding civilian commoners who happen to engage in trade. At times he even suggests that mercantile activity on the part of the gentry themselves should be considered legitimate and socially beneficial.[73]

Let us here simply inventory the wide range of practical administrative measures Chen initiated throughout his career in the interest of trade (many of these will be dealt with elsewhere in more detail). Most striking would be his persistent and energetic efforts to improve the empire's transport grid, projects that he unfailingly defended as facilitating greater levels of trade (even when the immediate object was military logistics).[74] He sought to encourage greater merchant use of these routes by establishing networks of inns and hospices, by setting up patrols to offer emergency medical aid to commercial travelers in malarial regions, and by intensifying security systems to combat banditry and piracy.[75] He enacted numerous measures to protect traveling merchants against perceived predations by brokers, transport gangs, and the government's own clerical sub-bureaucracy.[76] And he consistently lobbied against local government exactions that he saw as nuisance taxes inhibiting mercantile vigor.[77]

As we have seen, Chen explicitly forbade local-level grain embargoes so as to allow "guest merchants" (*keshang*) the freedom to operate in areas not their own, and he took major steps to liberalize Qing policy toward overseas trade with Southeast Asia—principally, of course, for increased food supply but also because "the silver and other [non-grain] commodities which this trade has brought in have been of great benefit to the people."[78] He often justified his many efforts to increase the money supply as intended "to show favor to merchants" (*huishang*).[79] And in a move that he himself acknowledged as unpopular within bureaucratic opinion he authorized the establishment of commercial rice shops (*mipu*) in the vicinity of government tax depots so that taxpayers who so chose could buy grain with cash at the last minute prior to payment of their grain tribute dues.[80] Such a move was a substantive step toward a more commercialized agriculture and commodity-based food supply, as well as perhaps a subtle endorsement of a more fully monetized fiscal system.

Many of Chen Hongmou's regional economic development schemes—those for instance promoting sericulture in Shaanxi, mining in the southwest, and commercial integration of the northwest frontier—explicitly drew on the idiom and institutional model of *zhaoshang*, or "inviting in" merchants and commercial capital to undertake

projects the administration deemed in the public interest. This policy model, best remembered today for its role in such late-nineteenth-century quasi-bureaucratic enterprises as the Zhaoshang ju (China Merchants' Steam Navigation Company), in fact had
a venerable history among mercantilist administrators long before Western-inspired industrialization. Chen was enthusiastic about it. In his application of it, however, he was
notable in the emphasis he accorded to merchant voluntarism and merchant profits.
Unlike many another official sponsor of *zhaoshang* enterprises, Chen saw no role for
conscription of personnel or capital; if the project offered merchants no likely prospect
of gain, it ought to be done by the government itself or not done at all.[81]

The concern that merchant financial interests should not suffer as a result of participation in socially beneficial projects, but indeed that they should profit therefrom,
runs throughout Chen's writings. He justifies certain tax reforms, for example, on the
specific grounds that they will "enrich" or "multiply" merchants' financial capacities
(*shangli*).[82] In a variety of local contexts he announces his readiness to make government loans to merchants to augment their "working capital" (*gongben, chengben, shangben*).[83] As we have seen in Chapter 2, it was just such readiness, perceived by other
officials as exceeding the bounds of bureaucratic propriety, that got Chen cashiered
from his one, long-coveted shot at a governor-generalship.

Profit and Self-Interest

This leads us to consideration of the more general notion of profit and self-interest in
the economic logic of Chen and his contemporaries. The conventional view on this
subject, it seems to me, has long been that articulated in a classic 1980 article by
Donald Munro. Writing of "Chinese thought" prior to Western influence as a continuous whole, Munro argued that individual or group interest (*li* or *yi*) was never seriously
engaged as a philosophic issue but instead denied rather peremptorily any moral value.
In any discussion of economic morality the focus of attention was personal responsibilities rather than interests. The overall thrust of Chinese ethical inquiry stressed harmony—not a harmony of interests but a harmony of individual strivings to fulfill potentially conflicting social obligations. Munro's line of argument is further developed
in the work of Romeyn Taylor, who sees no place in Chinese economic thought for the
notion of profit (*li*), which is categorically dismissed as springing "from the vice of self-
interest."[84]

There is of course no dearth of evidence for such views, from Mencius on. Even the
boldly revisionist Yu Yingshi concedes that the dominant intellectual tradition of the
late imperial era, Cheng-Zhu orthodoxy, was permeated by a discourse that posed propriety and profit as conceptual opposites (*yi li zhi bian*), the economic instantiation of
the more generalized opposition of principle and human desire (*li yu zhi bian*).[85] Yet
even among the most fervent Song Confucian revivalists countercurrents could also be
found. Yu Yingshi himself tends to associate this alternative tradition with the school of
Zhu Xi's neo-Confucian rival Lu Xiangshan (1139–93) and his Ming-dynasty heir
Wang Yangming, but other recent scholarship has clearly pointed to a surprisingly positive view of private interest in figures closer to Cheng-Zhu orthodoxy itself—figures

such as Ouyang Xiu, Sima Guang, and the more obscure but ultimately quite influential Dong Wei.[86]

If there was some older precedent, however, it is nevertheless clear from the work of Mizoguchi Yūzō and of Yu Yingshi himself that China's early modern period of the sixteenth to eighteenth centuries witnessed a widespread cultural challenge to the Cheng-Zhu denigration of profit. This challenge was manifested in the thought of a highly diverse group of writers with widely differing intellectual and political agendas. Parallel to their common rehabilitation of human desires and their denial of intrinsic opposition between heavenly principle (*tianli*) and human emotion (*renqing*)—discussed in Chapter 3—scholars such as Li Zhi, Lü Kun, Gu Yanwu, Huang Zongxi, and Dai Zhen contributed each in his own way to a revaluation of the role of self-interest (*si*) in pursuit of the collective good.[87] I would add that this new trend pointedly included figures, such as Lü Kun and our protagonist Chen Hongmou, who identified themselves as fully loyal adherents of the Cheng-Zhu school. It also included that most self-consciously "Confucian" of autocrats, the Qianlong emperor, who in an early edict of 1738 explicitly defended the state's pursuit of profit for its treasuries as a means of furthering the public good.[88]

This rehabilitation of the notions of profit and self-interest in early modern China, rescuing them from the condemnation of a long tradition of moral idealism, is remarkably reminiscent of processes occurring in the early modern West. The most celebrated defense of the profit motive in this era was of course Adam Smith's "invisible hand," which stressed the contribution of self-interested enterprise and accumulation to the aggregate economy. But as Albert Hirshman has pointed out, the value of self-interest was even more broadly seen as that of a social and moral curative.[89] Theorists such as Hobbes, Locke, and Montesquieu came to look kindly on "interests" for largely the same reason as did many of their Chinese counterparts: because they were now understood to be *rational* (in Chinese terms, in accord with heavenly principle, *tianli*) and were therefore conducive to social order. Just as Chen Hongmou esteemed the market for its rational and predictable regularity (*qingli zhi chang*, the same "*chang*" used in older sources for the Confucian virtue of "constancy"), so too in Europe "an interest-governed world" was valued for its dispassionate "constancy" and the rational market proposed as a template for the moral society.

Chen Hongmou was fully in step with his times in the value he attached to profit and self-interest and was indeed among the most enthusiastic mid-Qing proponents of harnessing these energies for the public good. To be sure, there are also elements in Chen's writing of the older moral discourse denigrating profit, but these are highly circumscribed and hardly indicative of his general outlook. He cites Lü Kun and Lu Shiyi in condemning indecorous chasing after "reputation and profit" (*mingli*), for example, but does not disparage them altogether, and he candidly adds that material and status rewards will often accrue to those who least conspicuously pursue them.[90] He invokes Sima Guang to condemn officials who "speak only of profit" (*yanli*), but his target in doing so is fiscalist policies that expropriate wealth properly left in the hands of private interests.[91]

By far most frequently, the word "*li*" (profit or advantage) carries a positive connotation in Chen's prose. He often uses the term, as Gu Yanwu had famously done, in

opposition to "*bi*," to distinguish the functional from the dysfunctional, assets from liabilities.[92] Routinely, Chen employs "*li*," "*yi*," or the two in combination to refer matter-
of-factly to the material benefits he projects as arising from his economic development
policies, and in these instances the terms equate rather closely with the notion of
efficient productivity. Conversely, as we have seen, social activities that Chen disparages
as nonproductive—popular religious observances, opera performances, and the like—
are described as "unprofitable" (*wuyi*).[93]

Surpluses generated through effective use of resources accrue to the entire population, and Chen sometimes uses the term "*dali*" (great profit) to refer to a Benthamite
"greatest good for the greatest number." Following Lü Kun, he concedes on at least one
occasion the potential conflict between profit or loss to the individual proprietor (*yiji
zhi lihai*) and that to the larger society (*dali dahai*).[94] But clearly this does not trouble
Chen overmuch. Profit for the individual household is emphatically approved as a goal
of human action, even when, as in the case of households withholding needed grain
from the market in anticipation of a higher return, this action might be construed as
contrary to the collective good.[95] Chen has no hesitation whatsoever in appealing to the
profit motive to get local populations to fall in line with his various development projects such as building new roads, introducing new commodities for regional export,
founding community granaries, and so on. In a formulation not too distant from Adam
Smith's "invisible hand" Chen contends that such projects will bring profit to all (*liren*)
precisely to the extent they bring profit to oneself (*zili*).[96]

Chen Hongmou expounds on the political use of material incentives in a 1740 letter to Jiangsu salt commissioner Ni Xiangkai. Chen counsels Ni that he enjoys in his current post a marvelous opportunity to turn the vast wealth of the empire's richest
province to "profitable" use because, if managed effectively, salt holds great potential for
public good. The classics, he notes, even as they espouse "taking propriety as the true
form of profit" (*yi yi wei li*), also acknowledge that the basic human desire for gain can
never be legislated away. That being the case, the wise official studies how most
efficiently to employ the profit motive (*yin li cheng bian*) to "turn the useless into the useful." In this way the hunger after profit of merchants and others, in itself spontaneous
and morally neutral, can be turned by the official to moral and socially beneficial ends.[97]

Let us look briefly at a few examples of how Chen sought to reconcile concern for
private sector profits with pursuit of the public interest in his advocacy of specific economic policies (the rhetoric he employs to justify such policies will also reveal something of the political context in which he was operating):

1. Perhaps most controversial was his 1758 proposal to grant low-interest government loans to Guangdong salt merchants in hopes of increasing their competitive position vis-à-vis smugglers (a proposal discussed in Chapter 2). In his memorial arguing
for such loans, Chen concluded by stressing the contribution such a program would
make to government revenues (*guoji*), by recovering a greater portion of the market for
direct state franchises, and to popular livelihoods (*minsheng*), by increasing the supply
and lowering the cost of a necessary consumer item. Probably because it was so immediately—and, as it turns out, uncomfortably—evident to all, he opts not to stress the direct benefit his policy would have to a third set of interests, merchant profits (*shangli*).

Chen clearly assumed, however, that (here as elsewhere) benefiting the third interest would simultaneously benefit the other two; there was no sense of conflict between the concern for *shangli* and concerns for *guoji* and *minsheng*. This was an assumption that the Qianlong emperor was less ready to make, and in this case it cost Chen his post.[98]

2. Four years later, as Jiangsu governor, Chen again sought to succor a salt administration operating at less than full capacity. Liang-Huai salt merchants are limited by law from buying all the salt that existing saltworks in Huaibei can produce, to say nothing of the new saltworks that the area might easily support. Chen knows, however, of an untapped market that could make use of this potentially expanded product. During his previous tenures in Shaanxi, he noticed that the salt supplied to that province from the Tianjin saltworks, which hold a legal monopoly on Shaanxi salt sales, was relatively scarce and expensive because of the difficulties of transport from Tianjin. Transport of Huaibei salt would be more efficient and cost-effective, and thus he proposes opening the Shaanxi market to Liang-Huai merchants. Again, he concludes his proposal by stressing the potential benefits to popular food supply in Shaanxi (*minshi*) and to state tax revenues from the expanded trade (*guoke*)—appeals he suspects the center will find attractive. In this case, however, he has made it clear at the outset of his memorial that his major concern is the increased profits (*li*) this expansion will bring to merchants of Huaibei itself and the needed boost these profits will bring to a regional economy whose agriculture has been decimated by recurring floods. Again Chen is thinking more commercially than the central government, and the Board of Revenue flatly rejects his request.[99]

3. In a 1748 memorial Chen advocates opening private graphite mines in Shaanxi, with part of the output to be sold for coinage use to the state and the remainder sold on the open market. Here he is explicit in citing the three sets of interests that will benefit: *guoji*, *minsheng*, and *minli* (mine owners' profits), although he circumspectly identifies even the third set of beneficiaries as *min* (the people) rather than *shang* (merchants).[100] But in an earlier memorial of 1743 he states his frank belief that "The 'merchants' and the 'people' are really one and the same" (*shang min yuanshu yiti*).[101]

4. As Gansu governor in 1755, and as Hunan governor the following year, Chen lobbies strenuously to protect the profits of government-franchised merchants involved in the marketing of Hunanese tea in the northwest. With the phasing out of the government tea-for-horse exchange with Inner Asian peoples over the course of the early eighteenth century, the volume of this trade has contracted, yet the percentage share demanded by the state as tax has progressively grown. There is also local-official profiteering in Hunan's Anhua County, where most of the tea for the northwest is produced. Chen argues that the combined effect squeezes merchants so hard that it drives them out of the trade. Unless the taxes are dramatically lowered and the corruption stopped—that is, unless the *shangli* are protected—both government revenues (*guoke*) and the livelihood of tea producers (*minsheng*) will be lost.[102]

5. Finally, in 1754 Chen memorializes to defend commercially minded Shaanxi elites against charges of hoarding currency in a time of increasing cash shortage. (Chen does not say as much, but it seems likely that the elites he has in mind are bankers; Shaanxi natives were by this time significantly involved in the empire-wide network of

so-called Shanxi banks, or *piaohao*). Chen argues that although these men indeed hold large quantities of cash, they can hardly be accused of "hoarding." Rather, as highly rational and market-sensitive businessmen they are *investing* this money, "turning it over for profit" (*zhuantu shengxi*). That is to say, they are using it productively. Chen's unnamed policy opponents would like these elites to dispose of their capital for land, which presumably would free up this currency for local cultivators' use. But Chen protests: the way these businessmen are using their money amounts to seeking its highest economic utility, which is not in land, and support for such efficient use of assets ought to be a goal of government economic policy.[103]

In concluding this discussion of profit and self-interest in Chen Hongmou's economic thought, it would be wise, I think, to remember its limits. However close Chen may come at times to a Smithian "invisible hand" argument, two significant inferences drawn from that argument in Europe were not similarly derived by contemporary Chinese. First would be the notion of the economic virtue of competition. At least prior to the nineteenth century, no Qing economic thinker to my knowledge rejected the Confucian ideal of social harmony in favor of a view of unfettered struggle in the marketplace as leading to economic "progress" via natural selection of superior products and techniques.[104] Certainly Chen himself would not have endorsed such a view. Second, as we have already seen to some extent and shall see in more detail below, although respect for market forces and the profit motive did argue against dirigiste government intervention in the marketplace, they by no means suggested a blanket policy of laissez-faire. Such a policy would represent a morally repellent abrogation of the basic concept of benevolent rule (*renzheng*).

Economic Laws

We have already observed that Chen believes the economy to operate according to certain inviolable (but fully comprehensible) laws, which are part of the natural order of things. That the market was governed by predictable laws was by no means a new discovery of the early modern era; a "law of exchange values," for example, had been formulated as early as the Tang by the celebrated finance minister Liu Yan (715–80).[105] By the eighteenth century such understandings permeated economic discourse at all levels, from imperial pronouncements, to local official correspondence, to guidebooks for merchants of even very modest scale. What is interesting about Chen Hongmou, then, is not the mere fact that he acknowledges such laws but the subtle ways he seeks to reconcile the operations of the "autonomous market" with the orthodox moral worldview (with which, as Romeyn Taylor somewhat overstrenuously points out, it was potentially in tension) and the insistent manner in which he makes economic laws the basis of his policy decisions.

Chen never, for example, refers to observed market regularities in the Legalist language of "laws" (*fa*), as had Liu Yan. Rather, he follows the post-Song tradition of neo-Confucian economic thinkers in terming them "*li*" (principles) or "*chang*" (constancies), words with quite rich moral-cosmological connotations. That factors of supply and demand determine prices in a local market, that commodities will seek out the market in which they command the highest price, and that commercial agents will seek to buy low and sell high are all for Chen "firmly established principles" (*yiding zhi li*).[106] More striking (and perhaps more unusual in its day) is the way Chen extends the same pattern of discourse to legitimate profit-maximizing behavior even against the evident interests of other members of society or those of the state. For instance, that surplus product will be sold for private profit is "an invariable principle"; withholding grain during times of dearth in expectation of rising prices is a "constancy based on rational principle"; melting down government coins whose stipulated value is less than that of their copper content is rational behavior, even when it violates state law.[107] As in Hirshman's early modern Europe, the very predictability of such actions affords them at least some measure of moral legitimation.

Chen Hongmou clearly understood, as to some degree did all of his imperial patrons and bureaucratic colleagues, that the force of these economic laws placed unshakable constraints on government policy making. A typical example of how he acknowledged these constraints in his own official conduct came in the area of monetary policy in Jiangxi, in 1742. The scarcity of government cash in the province had driven their value relative to silver well beyond the par rate of one thousand cash per tael of silver and had largely ceded the money market to illegally minted private coins (*xiaoqian*) with a lower copper content. However much Chen would have wished to recapture the market simply by outlawing these *xiaoqian*, he conceded that such an action would in fact be counterproductive; the reduced cash supply would drive the silver-equivalency price of government coin still more severely away from par.[108] "It is nearly impossible," Chen wrote, "to suppress the operation of the market by administrative means."[109] And again: "If we do not adapt our policies flexibly [to accommodate market realities], then government laws will simply prove unenforceable."[110]

Yet, as this suggests, autonomous market laws were not simply a constraint on economic policy making; they were an enabling instrument as well. If properly understood and accounted for, they were a powerful weapon in official hands. Characteristically, Chen and other late imperial writers expressed this power through the terms "*biran*" (necessarily) or "*ziran*" (naturally) or the simple adverbial modifier "*zi*" (automatically, as a matter of course). If we take such-and-such course of action (say, lowering the copper content of government cash so as to make it unprofitable to melt them down for resale), market laws will see to it that the behavior we seek to modify will respond "automatically."[111] If we allow high grain prices to prevail temporarily in a dearth-stricken region, outside merchants will "automatically" bring in grain to remedy inadequacies of supply.[112] And, in a more activist posture, if we dredge the rivers so as to make commercial transport cost-effective, merchants will come in search of profitable markets "without even being summoned."[113]

Relativism of Time and Space

Although Chen Hongmou sees basic economic principles as immutable and constant, a cardinal element in his economic policy making is a finely tuned empirical sensitivity to geographic and temporal specificity. This relativism cannot be emphasized too greatly; indeed, it is arguably the key defining feature of the late imperial statecraft (*jingshi*) approach to governance with which Chen is usually associated. In his writings the two idioms "appropriate to the place" (*yindi* or *suidi*) and "appropriate to the time" (*suishi*), often paired, are ubiquitous. They set the proper parameters of policy making in nearly all areas, from population resettlement, to commercial development, to granary management.[114] Time sensitivity means, for example, awareness of market prices (see below), which must be heeded or "obeyed" (*ting*) in buying or selling goods.[115] The people do this instinctively, Chen observes, and the wise official will follow their example. Time sensitivity also means taking account of "the people's time" (*minshi*), especially the agricultural work cycle, in making corvée or other labor demands.[116]

The corollary of time sensitivity is "*jishi*" (timeliness), a term Chen employs frequently and with special emphasis. "The timeliness of a policy initiative," he writes, "usually determines whether or not it will succeed."[117] However deeply one understands the principles of economic law, it must be kept in mind that no specific policy is appropriate forever. This clearly constitutes a source of personal anxiety for Chen, who, mindful of his own brief tenure in any given post, ponders long and hard how to establish policies that will have real "permanence" (*yongyuan*). Even so, when proudly drawing together for publication in 1757 all the most important ordinances he has issued during his four tenures as Shaanxi governor, he concedes in his preface, "Those which subsequently prove unbeneficial will have to be modified or rescinded as the times demand [*suishi*]."[118]

Sensitivity to place, to geographic variation, is equally important. This belief prompts Chen's deep fascination with maps and his detailed investigations of the "assets and liabilities" (*libi*) of all localities under his jurisdiction. Relief and granary policies, for example, must "proceed according to local conditions" and "take heed of [*ting*] natural commodity flows."[119] Administrative jurisdictions, such as salt districts and even (where possible, as in the administratively fluid southwest pale) county borders, should be redrawn "so as to conform to the conditions of the land," especially to natural marketing areas.[120] Chen seeks to tailor his own economic development programs closely to the lay of the land and the water (*dishi* and *shuishi*), even to the point of relativism in land use—rather remarkably, for a Han Chinese official, he concedes that nomadic pastoralism may be a more effective economic use of certain terrains than sedentary agriculture.[121] As we shall see subsequently in more detail, Chen's ecological sensitivity extends to human ecology as well; the "lay of the land" pointedly includes locally specific skill levels and even local cultural preferences.

Prices

We noted in the preceding chapter that the mid-Qing was marked by a steady inflation of basic commodity prices (with rice perhaps slightly more than doubling in terms of silver over the eighteenth century), that the Qing administration was acutely aware of and concerned about this inflation (which was believed to be harmful, overall, to the people's interests), and that most in government considered the increasingly severe population pressure on resources to have been the chief contributor to this price rise. Chen Hongmou was no different from his colleagues in these regards. We have also seen that Qing price theory was relatively sophisticated. Chen and most other bureaucrats assumed that prices were a function of supply and demand of a commodity in a given local market and that, in a highly regionalized imperial economy with a high level of interregional exchange, prevailing local prices would influence the flow of goods, with prices in turn responding to resulting shifts in supply. Although the subject is far too complex to treat here in the detail it deserves, it should also be noted that most Qing officials, and Chen probably more than most, were deeply sensitive to the fact that prices were also a function of money supply. In an economy based on a bimetallic currency, an adequate approach to prices necessitated continual monitoring of local silver:copper exchange rates and a highly market-sensitive monetary policy.[122]

The most interesting aspect of Chen's approach to prices, however, is how consistently and vigorously he insists on respecting the market price.[123] During the Jiangxi dearth of the early 1740s, for instance, he repeatedly cautions his county-level subordinates that, no matter how alarmingly local grain prices shoot up, officials must never impose government price controls (*guan bu wei xian*) or compel owners to sell at submarket prices (*duanjia lemai*).[124] As we have seen, in Chen's logic such actions would be both improper and counterproductive.

For Qing field administrators, of course, the greatest temptation to violate the principle of respect for market prices came not in their oversight of private-sector transactions but rather when they needed to make purchases from their own very lean budgets for such things as public works—that is, in the area of state procurement. Throughout his career Chen Hongmou ardently opposed requisitioning at "coerced" submarket prices (*lejia*), even when fidelity to market prices impeded his own administrative goals. For example, as Yangzhou circuit intendant in 1733, he insisted that rice to underwrite his pet project, a public orphanage, be bought only at the going price, and in Shaanxi in 1748 he insisted that his magistrates accept repayments of loans of seed grain at the lower, postharvest market price.[125] In Yunnan, during the Miao campaigns, he ordered that pack animals for military service be purchased at market prices rather than simply impressed.[126] And when undertaking major Yellow River dike repairs as Tianjin circuit intendant in 1740, and again as Henan governor in 1752, he updated payment schedules for purchase of construction materials to accord with prices they commanded on the private market.[127]

As this last example suggests, Chen did not deny that local officials required guidelines for what they should pay for materials and labor for public projects, nor did he deny that the administration enjoyed the right to set such prices. It was just that, for him, such "set prices" (*dingjia*) should be pegged as closely as possible to those actually pertaining in local markets and should be adjusted periodically to reflect temporal as well as spatial price variations. In this spirit Chen headed up a multiyear imperial project, beginning in 1761 when he was Jiangsu governor, to investigate market prices of hundreds of varieties of construction materials, as well as freights and artisanal pay scales, for some 1,557 counties throughout the empire. These detailed schedules were eventually published in a series of province-specific volumes during Chen's term as grand secretary in 1769, local officials being ordered to adhere to them when making public purchases.[128]

The remarkable thing about these volumes is not merely their exhaustiveness and attention to local difference (we learn, for example, that master carpenters were paid .15 taels per day and their assistants .08 taels in Zhili's Gu'an County but only .13 and .06 taels in neighboring Liangxiang)[129] but even more the general willingness of Chen and the court to accept market prices for government procurement, even at considerable sacrifice to state financial interests. We can see hints of political controversy swirling around this issue. For example, as county-level figures for the average prices of each commodity at times of annual high, median, and low market activity began to be received in late 1763, the Board of Works memorialized successfully that only the annual slow-market price (*huanjia*) be recorded as the basis of payment; the rationale given was that this price most accurately reflected "that actually in use by the people" and that its adoption would most effectively smooth over "the vicissitudes of good and lean years," but it seems highly likely that in most cases it was also close to the annual low price.[130] Nevertheless, inasmuch as in most cases this new schedule superseded procurement prices on the books since 1740, given the secular inflationary trend of the mid-eighteenth century there can be no doubt that the general effect of the revisions was to raise significantly the procurement prices actually paid. Certainly, this was the intent of Chen Hongmou and of his close ally, Guizhou governor Zhou Renji, who had first formally requested the new schedules in 1761.

As early as the mid-1730s, when Chen was serving in his first provincial post as Yunnan treasurer, he demonstrated his attachment to the principle of state procurement at market prices. It was very likely Chen, in fact, who played the single largest role in precipitating the celebrated eighteenth-century copper boom in the southwest. Because copper was first and foremost a monetary metal, even Chen conceded that the state enjoyed the right to claim a share of the mines' output at its own price. His preferred policy, however, was to impose a fixed direct tax in kind (*ke*) on the mines and buy whatever was required above this amount from the mine owners at the market price. This policy seems to have been tried briefly but soon ran into insurmountable political opposition. The alternative adopted was to impose on the mines a far larger quota of copper payable to the state, not as tax but as a fixed-price sale. The mines were then allowed to sell any surplus output on the open market for use in manufacture of kitchen utensils and other purposes. The problem, unsurprising in an inflationary economy, was that the market price of copper (in silver) quickly rose out of any relation to the requisition price; so too did mine owners' operating costs once the most accessible deposits had been tapped. To protect the mines' capacity to continue production (their "working capital," *gongben*), Chen in 1736 (with Yunnan governor Zhang Yunsui) and again in 1742 urged the court to adjust the requisition price into closer alignment with the market price. As Wei Qingyuan and Lu Su have demonstrated, it was precisely the court's failure to do so that ultimately doomed the Yunnan mines, contributing to the severe copper shortage of the later eighteenth century.[131]

It was also during his Yunnan tenure that Chen launched an extraordinarily comprehensive attack on state conscription of labor, both in the form of direct corvée and of coerced wage labor at submarket pay scales (*lejia duanfa*). He referred to both as "*pai*" (requisitioning), a term that almost always bears a negative connotation in his writing, sometimes enhanced by its use in compounds such as "*pailei*" and "*pairao*" (requisitioning harassments). Even at the height of the Qing military campaigns in the southwest, Chen repeatedly prohibited impressing local inhabitants into service as bearers, insisting instead that all such needs be met by labor hired at the locally prevailing porterage rate.[132] Beyond this he ordered that market wage rates be paid throughout Yunnan for such various labor needs as harbor dredging; expansion of irrigation works; yamen and city wall construction; civil service examination copyists; antismuggling patrols; and guards at customs stations, salt depots, granaries, mines, and jails.[133] His most significant single initiative came in his 1733 establishment of a postal relay (*zhan*) system, employed with great success to transport copper out of and grain into the province; abolishing the makeshift corvée system he found on his arrival in Yunnan, Chen replaced this with a system utilizing exclusively hired labor.[134]

Overall, it is not too much to say that during his three-year tenure in the province Chen precipitated a thoroughgoing shift in Yunnan from command to market means of state procurement, from payment at "official rates" (*guanjia*) to payment at market rates (*minjia*). This was a line of policy he continued to follow throughout his long career. For example, in undertaking a province-wide renovation of city walls in Shaanxi in the mid-1740s, he completely rewrote provincial statutes, which had designated these as projects for conscript labor, making them projects to be accomplished using labor hired at private-sector wage rates.[135] Similarly, he replaced corvée by hired labor in river-dredging projects in northwestern Hubei; he campaigned to have market rather than fixed submarket prices paid for animal fodder along the northwest military supply routes; and he insisted that, in computing land tax collections, local officials employ current local silver:copper exchange rates rather than fixed artificial rates that manipulated the commutation process in the government's favor.[136]

Why? Chen Hongmou's deep-seated animus against *pai*, against requisitioning of goods and services at prices below what they might command on the private market, was based in part on political and cultural considerations. In the war-torn southwest it was part of a campaign to win the hearts and minds of the people for the imperial cause, particularly the non-Han minorities whom Chen saw as unfair targets of most programs of impressed service. In every region of the empire, moreover, requisitioning created popular images (and all too often the reality) of injustice in assessment and of official corruption, thus tarnishing the state's claim to a moral mandate.

But his principal rationale was always economic. As with the Yunnan copper mines, submarket requisitioning provided a disincentive to production in the same way that grain price controls provided a disincentive to trade. Making the wages and prices paid by the government competitive with those on the private market was also the best way to ensure that it received the best goods and workers the locality had to offer. For example, dike repairs in Yunnan's Kunming Prefecture were normally accomplished on the basis of corvée assessments on landholders, who frequently hired replacements who proved incompetent or laggard on the job. For the scheduled repairs of 1734, therefore, Chen abolished the corvée altogether, instead hiring himself some five thousand laborers. These, he claimed, did the job far better than the workforce of twice that size formerly employed.[137] Furthermore—although I think this train of reasoning cannot be pushed too far—in at least some instances, such as those of "using work as a form of disaster relief" (*yigong daizhen*), Chen believed that state hiring and purchasing stimulated the economy as a whole.

Most basically, Chen Hongmou believed firmly that wages and prices set by an unfettered market were the most rational allocators of the labor and goods existing in any regional economy and that relying on them thus represented (in most cases) the most efficient husbanding of Heaven's bounty. Chen nowhere makes this more clear than in a letter he wrote in 1739 to a fellow official serving in poverty-stricken western Hunan: "In truth, the greatest burden the people in your area suffer, and the greatest drag on their local economy, is the system of corvée for the purpose of boat-hauling. Originally this system was established for their benefit and relief, but in fact the benefits derived have proven inconsequential. If we alleviated their agony in this regard, the economy in this part of Hunan would begin to improve immediately." Lifting such impositions, Chen argued, would allow the market to turn popular energies to their most productive (*shengye*) purposes.[138]

We will return to this line of thinking in a moment. But first we need to consider briefly what role, given his faith in market principles, Chen Hongmou leaves to the state in influencing prices. I would identify two broad types of price-related intervention of which he approves and that he enthusiastically practices himself. The first might be termed "participatory." As itself a market actor, and one of unparalleled financial scale, the state is in an excellent position to affect supply and demand ratios by flexibly adjusting its pattern of buying or selling specific commodities. It properly *ought* to use its market participation, not merely to satisfy its actual need for goods but deliberately to apply upward or downward pressure on prices. This was, after all, the paramount purpose of the Qing ever-normal granary (*changping cang*) system—arguably the most sizable and comprehensive government scheme for managing prices of basic foodstuffs attempted anywhere in the world up to that time (see Chapter 8). It was also the central element in Qing currency policy: By strategically buying and selling bulk silver and copper cash (minted with flexibly adjusted copper contents) Chen and his colleagues sought to keep market silver:copper exchange rates at a level deemed most functional for local economies.[139] The key principle in these and other, more modest, instances of "participatory" intervention was *to influence the market through market means themselves.* Chen (and countless other like-minded Qing bureaucrats) eagerly sought to affect prices through the state's own market activity, even as they argued, with equal vigor, against any dirigiste setting of market commodity prices or currency exchange rates.

The second type of intervention was more direct but also far more circumscribed in scope. I would term this kind of state action "regulatory" intervention. In certain, highly specific instances Chen is willing to legislate against certain commercial actors whose market position is so privileged that it allows them in effect to determine prices unilaterally. He disallows prohibitively high transport rates charged by porterage gangs at critical mountain passes. He attacks local cartels of "traitorous brokers" (*jianya*) who exploit farmers attempting to market their produce. He moves against merchant shippers themselves in cases where they have clearly slowed shipments of goods into needy areas so as to create a more severe shortage (the practice known as *juqi*).[140]

In each case, although Chen employs the statutory idiom of breaking up "monopoly" (*bachi*), he is not really acting in the interest of any supposed "free market" (in many cases the so-called monopolists are simply exercising their own market-determined leverage). Rather, like many a modern government he is simply regulating market activity in the interest of a presumed overriding social good. What is especially noteworthy about his actions along these lines, I would point out, is that the overriding good to be protected is not at all any moral-economy notion of a "just price" but instead the interest of maximum possible commercial circulation (*liutong*) that the behavior in question is presumed to impede.

Privatization

As has become clear by now, there is a pronounced tendency in Chen Hongmou's economic policy making toward deregulation, an urge to leave or return to the private sector fulfillment of basic economic needs, based on the assumption that in most (not all) cases the market is a much more efficient distributor of resources than the administration can hope to be. This strain, and its limits, are exemplified in two policy proposals Chen outlined in 1742 and 1743, addressing two commodities in which the administered economy and the private economy most directly intersected: salt and monetary metal. For this reason, and because these two cases are especially revealing of Chen's general style of translating his economic assumptions into practice, they are worth examining in some detail.

The first proposal arose in response to an order from the Qianlong emperor to investigate the prevalence of smuggled salt in Jiangxi, a problem the throne attributed to lackadaisical enforcement by local officials. Rather than that, however, what Chen came to see in the Jiangxi salt administration were basic structural flaws and a fundamentally misconceived set of policies. In much of the province administratively drawn salt districts did not conform to commercial marketing flows. Under such conditions, he noted, smuggled salt would "naturally" be cheaper than government salt (it would incur lower transport costs en route from the production area), and the local people would "naturally" buy it. In certain of the affected areas Chen suggested redrawing salt district boundaries in conformity to the observed flow of commercial traffic. "It is virtually impossible," he insisted, "to overcome natural marketing patterns by commandist means."

In other parts of Jiangxi, though, the problem was different. Here government salt was priced low enough to compete with smuggled salt, but profits to officially franchised merchants were not as high as they were in adjacent Hunan, where prices set by the administration were higher. Consequently, these merchants found ways to divert large portions of their allocated quotas from Jiangxi to Hunan, seeking the highest return on their investments. The result for Jiangxi was a decreased salt supply and hence higher actual consumer prices. It was necessary to provide incentive for the merchants to dispose of their salt where the system intended them to.

As a strategy for dealing comprehensively with Jiangxi's salt problems, Chen rather boldly suggested an across-the-board withdrawal of the state's direct management of salt marketing, leaving it with essentially a policing role to play. Let us assume, he said, that our salt merchants are basically good citizens whose interests are not irreconcilably at odds with those of consumers. We should accordingly leave to the merchants themselves decisions regarding most efficient transport routes, best markets for disposal of their stocks, and appropriate prices to charge in each market, based on their incurred costs and on local conditions of supply and demand.[141] The state's role should be limited to the apprehension of smugglers and the disciplining of the occasional official-merchant who fails to act in good faith. State and merchants thus "will each have their proper sphere of responsibility" (*ge you zecheng*) and "will not usurp each other's proper authority" (*wu suo pianyi*).[142]

The second proposal was entirely unsolicited. Having just been posted to Jiangxi, his first provincial governorship, Chen reflects on his previous experiences in Yunnan and Jiangsu and offers his general views on copper mining policy. Like most other places in the empire, Jiangxi is experiencing a severe copper shortage. The people need copper for nonmonetary purposes—for "utensils" (*qipen*)—and, with inadequate supplies on the market, "inevitably" resort to illegally melting down government coins. This in turn creates a critical shortage of cash, crippling Jiangxi's highly commercialized local economies. Sources of imported copper have proven unreliable, so we need to step up domestic production.

Chen reiterates the argument he has made several times before, that in the designated "official mines" (*guankuang*) of the southwest the purchase price of copper paid the franchised merchant operators needs to be adjusted upward to keep them from being financially strangled. Beyond this, though, we need to consider promoting a new variety of wholly nonofficial copper mines (*minkuang*), which will supply primarily the market for nonmonetary copper. In Jiangxi and elsewhere we ought to invite in private entrepreneurs (*zhaoshang*) to open such mines. Of course, such mines will probably prove far more attractive magnets for capital and labor than will the official mines, and as a palliative for the latter's partisans, Chen suggests that a relative percentage of *guankuang* and *minkuang* for each province might be set. But, as we will see, he really wants no such thing.

In the operation of the new "people's mines" a flat 10 percent tax on output should be claimed by the state, with the remaining 90 percent left to the operators to transport "freely" (*zixing*) to any market in the empire, to sell for any purpose and for the best price they can command. Most will go to nonmonetary uses. In fact, the state's own 10 percent share may not all be needed for coinage, and whatever is not should likewise be resold by officials on the private market. This, then, is another case where Chen in effect proposes a market-based solution for the enforcement of laws that are routinely violated because they run counter to economic realities. "For every ounce of copper [these new mines] put on the market," he argues, "there will be that fewer government coins illegally melted down."

As in his memorial on salt, Chen chooses to conclude with a sweeping statement of his philosophy of privatization. When I was serving in Jiangsu in the late Yongzheng reign, he recalls, I proposed that *all* copper mines, both those currently in operation and those yet to be opened, be allowed to operate as private enterprises. This would not only guarantee a higher level of productivity but would also accord with the stated imperial purpose of "storing wealth among the people" (*cangfu yumin*—a key and highly contested idiom in Qing economic discourse, on which more later). This proposal was rejected by the Board of Revenue on the grounds that its benefits would be enjoyed almost exclusively by merchants. Now that I am in Jiangxi, however, I can see that the empire's shortage of copper is yet more critical than I had imagined. This leads me to memorialize again. The lack of copper among the people, as well as the endemic problem of violation of currency laws, can only effectively be solved by one bold stroke: fully privatizing all the empire's copper mines, *including* those "official mines" in Yunnan now in desperate financial straits.[143]

The preference for private over state entrepreneurship seen in these two memorials was in fact a consistent theme in Chen's economic policy. We have seen that he argued of grain procurement in Hunan that "to have state purchases obstruct the activities of private commerce is inappropriate"[144] and that he repeatedly sought to privatize the Southeast Asian grain import trade. On the northwest border, as well, he insisted that trade, as much as possible, "should be removed from official management."[145] At the height of the 1754 Jinchuan military campaign, he boldly opted to replace the established system of directly provisioning troops transiting Shaanxi with one of paying soldiers in cash and inviting merchants (*zhaoshang*) to meet their food supply needs through commercial means. Not only would this prove more efficient, Chen reasoned, but it would also capitalize on military activity to promote the region's commercial development.[146] Government "overregulation" of commerce (*li zhi taiduo*), and "usurpation" (*panju*) of functions properly left to merchants, could only prove economically destructive.[147]

In this chapter we have surveyed the basic assumptions that underlay the economic thought and policy of Chen Hongmou and, to a greater or lesser extent, of the official elite of the mid-Qing era. Chen's economic universe was governed by binding and predictable laws of market behavior that, although articulated in idioms expressive of the culture's basic values, were believed to be valid not because they conformed with preconceived moral standards but because they accorded with reason and with empirical observation. The economy was seen as resting on a foundation of small proprietary households, each of which had a strong claim (in effect, a right) to its property—to its patrimony and the fruit of its members' labor. Self-interest, profit maximization, and systematic accumulation of capital assets on the part of such basic economic units were all natural and socially desirable.

In a context of official alarm at the increasing population pressure on resources, achieving a maximum volume and velocity of commercial circulation became a central goal of economic policy. The role of merchants and commercial entrepreneurs in this process was highly valued. The market, as supplier of goods to consumers, as stimulus to productivity, and as arbiter of prices, was the most efficient allocator of resources. This idea—what Steven Kaplan has called "the market principle"—was central as well to physiocratic notions in contemporaneous France, and it is in fact with physiocracy, among Western schools of economic thought, that I find the economic ideas of Chen Hongmou and many of his colleagues to have most in common.[148] The distinctive coupling of a belief in the primacy of agricultural production with a desire to stimulate maximum commercial exchange marked both approaches. So too did a deep respect for private property and for the incentive factor (or profit motive) as a stimulus to productivity, as well as a recognition of the social utility of private wealth as a means of creating employment, as a source of spending to fuel circulation, and as a hedge against dearth. This, in large part, is what mid-Qing officials meant by "storing wealth among the people."

Adherence to the "market principle" left the political authority with a clearly circumscribed role to play in the economy but hardly a passive one. The mid-Qing credo was not, as some writers have suggested, that of laissez-faire liberalism.[149] Rather, by dint of their very understanding of and respect for economic laws, officials could creatively practice what might be called "promarket intervention" to improve the well-being of the population they governed and even in certain circumstances to (as Chen Hongmou put it) "make up the deficiencies of natural endowment" (*bu zaohua zhi quexian*).[150] The following chapters explore some concrete examples of how they might do so.

CHAPTER 7

Production

生

CHEN HONGMOU ZEALOUSLY RESISTED the urges to dirigiste forms of economic management clearly experienced by many of his fellow bureaucrats—price setting, export embargoes, commandist procurement policies, and so on—preferring whenever possible to allow the market to serve the society's economic needs. At the same time, Chen's statecraft assigned the government an active role in the economy in a wide range of ways, many of which we have already discussed. He was extremely creative in his continuing efforts to control regional money supplies as a means of stimulating exchange and controlling prices.[1] He recognized and sought diligently to protect the state's existing monopolies on salt and (to a lesser extent) tea, even as he argued for a greater degree of privatization in those trades.[2] He intervened to restrict production of commodities he viewed as valueless or actively harmful to popular well-being (alcohol and tobacco) or of potential unauthorized military use (saltpeter).[3] Even while envisioning the market as ultimately the most dependable recourse for the alleviation of localized dearth, Chen assumed the state to be responsible for providing crisis relief, including acting as emergency employer in programs of work relief. Chen's state was also committed to offering its services as arbiter of property disputes and enforcer of contracts through the process of civil litigation.[4]

The state had an important regulatory function to play in the economy, combating "bachi"—a term most often translated "monopoly" but more appropriately seen as "restraint of trade," in the sense of imposing bottlenecks on the maximum circulation of goods. Brokers were guilty of bachi when they used their influence to impose prices that differed from those that existing conditions of supply and demand would produce.[5] Merchants were guilty of bachi when they deliberately failed to bring goods in a "timely" (jishi) manner to markets where they could profitably be sold—although, at the same time, Chen acknowledged merchants' right to sell only when they chose, based on rational calculations of self-interest.[6] Frequent targets of Chen's attacks on bachi were transport guilds that monopolized passage of commercial goods through a particular point, say a mountain pass or a constricted waterway. It was not the exclusivity of their control over this service that Chen condemned but rather their exploiting this exclusivity to impose freight charges that actively discouraged the flow of goods. His solution, accordingly, was not to open up their business to outside competition but rather to impose a ceiling on their rates, which they must implicitly accept as a condition of their grant of monopoly.[7]

Chen Hongmou well understood that the reach of the commercial market as it existed in his day was not unlimited. We have seen how, in crisis situations, he recruited merchants to prime the pump of market-based relief by bringing in grain as state agents (although at private profit) and how, conversely, he used interim state purchase of grain to support local producers when outside buyers were slow to arrive. Certain areas of the empire were so remote that, even under normal conditions, they were excluded from the interregional market for reasons of cost-effectiveness. In at least some such cases Chen believed the government's intervention as commercial middleman was called for to fill the gap. In 1743 Jiangxi, for example, he ordered magistrates to make purchases of salt out of administrative budgets and to resell this in peripheral areas of their counties that profit-minded merchants were reluctant to serve.[8]

Taken as a whole, these actions amounted to a highly comprehensive approach of "promarket intervention" that was anything but laissez-faire. Arguably however, Chen's most activist economic policies lay in two areas other than these. One was his systematic effort to control prices and, in effect, manage the overall societal accumulation of wealth by means of a complex network of governmental and semigovernmental granaries. This will be the subject of the succeeding chapter. The other was Chen's extraordinary efforts at development of the empire's productive capacity, the topic to which we now turn.

Agriculture

Recognizing that the process of basic recovery from the disorders of the seventeenth century had already been accomplished, both the Yongzheng and Qianlong emperors made a more positively conceived program of stimulating the economy a priority of their reigns. Lengthy and strongly worded edicts issued shortly after their accessions to the throne spelled out in detail what they expected their officials to accomplish in this regard, setting up not only the agenda but also in large part the terms of bureaucratic discourse on this subject for decades to come.[9] The keystone of this effort was, unsurprisingly, the traditional one of agricultural improvement (*quannong*, or "encouraging agriculture"), but as the work of Gao Wangling and others has shown, the drive went well beyond increasing the production of staple foodstuffs, and beyond even farming, to constitute what can fairly be called a self-conscious program of "economic development."[10]

The career of Chen Hongmou underlines his point with particular clarity. Conscientious efforts at economic improvement, of course, had long been seen as a distinguishing mark of the "model official" (*xunli*), a cultural ideal that Chen Hongmou deliberately and aggressively sought to claim for himself.[11] His ambition was matched by his energy and, to a remarkable extent, by his achievements. Launching comprehensive surveys of all possibilities for development in the provinces he governed, as well as initiating countless target-specific campaigns for increased productivity in one sector or another, Chen both drove his subordinates mercilessly and hounded his superiors to expand the scope of their developmental efforts.

A useful way to begin our own survey of Chen's activities in this area is to look first at the language he used to describe them, for this reveals rather strikingly his view of the universe and his own place within it. As it does in other areas, his language here draws on the discourse common to the official-elite community of his day but does so with relative emphases and linguistic twists that were somewhat more personal. The most consistent theme in this discourse is a quasi-religious respect for the glorious bounty provided by Heaven-and-earth (*tianzao dishe*), but it is a respect coupled with an insistence that this bounty is only fully realized through the process of human exploitation. This is very far from pastoralism; in Chen's radically anthropocentric Confucian universe the "beauty" of nature exists precisely in its use value in service to human society.[12]

The central term, which recurs with great frequency, is "*dili*," written with either of two homophonous second ideographs so as to mean, literally, either the "benefits" or the "capacity" of the earth. These natural resources, Heaven's bounty, are granted precisely to be "opened up" (*kaipi*) or "developed" (*xingju*) by human agency.[13] Human effort in such development is less an opportunity than a moral responsibility. "I believe we cannot sit idly by and rely upon Heaven's grace," Chen writes, "but instead must energetically pursue the work that is ordained for man."[14] In confronting what he sees as a supreme, indeed sinful, instance of regional underdevelopment in 1730s Yunnan, he points out, "The problem is not that the *dili* is insufficient, but rather that the *renli* [human capacities] have not yet been fully mobilized."[15] Effective exploitation of natural resources requires a process of coordination or cooperation (*tongxun*) involving large numbers of people, and this in turn is the task of the official. "The livelihood of the common people [*xiaomin*] is derived from their natural environment; the managerial role [*jingli*] of the official is to educate and train them [in] how to make the most productive use of that environment."[16]

One quality the official brings to his task in any given locality is a flexibility borne of breadth of perspective. Over and over again Chen stresses the importance of a case-by-case analysis of differing situations: "Proper management [*jingli*] of resources can only be achieved by complying with local conditions [*dishi*] and the specific demands of the time [*jishi*]."[17] Only in this way can maximally efficient use be made of both the *dili* and the *renli* in providing the material basis for human society. Chen's avowed goal is a world in which there is no underexploited land and no underemployed people.[18] In this time of alarming population growth it is more vital than ever not to allow any of nature's potential benefits to go untapped.[19] The rallying cry for the mid-Qing bureaucracy in general—but for none with more urgency than for Chen Hongmou—is "*jin dili*," a phrase Peter Perdue translates with poignant irony as "exhausting the earth."[20] Chen is aware of the limits of this enterprise, as we will see below, but his priorities and his sense of mission are nevertheless clear.

Considering the pivotal role Chen had played as whistle-blower in the empire-wide land reclamation frenzy of the mid-1730s, it may seem odd that he came to be such a champion of *kaiken* activities throughout his career. Yet at the very moment he was protesting abuses in his home province of Guangxi he was leading an equally zealous (although more prudent) reclamation drive in frontier Yunnan, a drive that contributed in no small way to the doubling of that province's population in the eighteenth century.[21] He pursued opening of new farmland on the Gansu and Taiwan frontiers and reclamation of abandoned land in sodden northern Jiangsu.[22] During Chen's four tours of duty in Shaanxi he led a protracted campaign for reclamation, notably in the Han River highlands in the province's south and in its inhospitable northern prefectures of Yan'an and Yulin.[23]

Chen was also a persistent advocate of land reclamation before the throne. During an imperial audience of 1744, for example, he urged the systematic opening of wooded mountainsides in Jiangxi (the province he had just departed) for clearance and cultivation. These areas had been declared off-limits since the early fifteenth century out of fear that they would become bandit lairs; Chen argued, to the contrary, that there was no better instrument of pacification than the introduction of settled agriculture. The Board of Revenue was not persuaded, and Chen's proposal was turned down.[24] Yet just a few years later Chen responded to an imperial call for solutions to the growing problem of food supply by arguing that the most pressing need was for further reclamation of any possible arable land.[25]

Like that of the throne itself, Chen's passion for land reclamation stemmed from both economic and sociocultural concerns. As the Yongzheng emperor had noted as early as 1728, reclamation was an unparalleled means of "improving local customs."[26] Mid-eighteenth-century *kaiken* activists equated settled agriculture with social accountability, proper ritual-familial norms (*lijiao*), stable productivity (*hengchan*), and the Confucian work ethic (*gongfu*). This, it goes without saying, was doubly important at the empire's fringes, where "opening" of new agricultural land was a means of attracting Han colonists, of "civilizing" (*hua*) savage peoples, and of reducing the starkness of cultural-ecological frontiers. Cultural, economic, and indeed political and military factors were not necessarily disaggregated but rather reinforced each other to make *kaiken* appear a pressing desideratum in mid-Qing official eyes.

The problem was, as the scandals of the late 1730s highlighted for all to see, how to achieve *kaiken*'s clear benefits while avoiding its attendant pitfalls. Chief among such pitfalls was inflated reporting. As we saw in Chapter 2, the discovery of the magnitude of this problem had led to a major readjustment, striking from the tax rolls millions of *mu* of land falsely reported as "reclaimed" in the Yongzheng reign. Chen Hongmou, who had condemned this practice in his home province in the mid-1730s, remained vigilant thereafter to prevent it, even when cheerleading his own *kaiken* drives; he routinely conducted audits of land newly reported as taxable, and he impeached one of his magistrates in Taiwan for overreporting in 1753.[27] He was also alert to keep off the tax rolls marginal land that, although "reclaimed" for a year or two, was too poor to support continuous cultivation.[28]

The central question remained: which new land ought to be considered taxable, and which not? The Qianlong emperor took a significant step toward resolving this in

1740 when he declared that thereafter any "small and scattered" (*lingxing*) plots of land might be developed while continuing to enjoy tax-free status.[29] This edict served to jump-start the empire-wide *kaiken* program out of the lull induced by the scandals of 1736–37 by effectively relieving local officials of the burden of assessing the fiscal potential of each and every plot of new land. The size of plots that qualified as "small and scattered" was specified variously for each province, but it is a safe bet that it was generally interpreted quite liberally. Chen Hongmou, who valued economic productivity over fiscal revenue even more than his monarch, not surprisingly applauded the new policy and enthusiastically publicized it among his provincial constituencies. At the same time, he continued to press the throne to liberalize even further tax policy toward newly cultivated land.[30]

But taxes were not the only concern raised by the eighteenth-century *kaiken* campaigns. Throughout the Qing, although the state had often encouraged and provided incentives for migration into new areas, perhaps as often it faced the problem of dealing with settlement that had gone on without its authorization or even in defiance of its stated wishes. In Jiangxi and other Yangzi provinces, one particular manifestation of this was the so-called shed people (*pengmin*), peripatetic highland squatters who, although often tied into the market through commercial cropping, gathering of forest products, or charcoal-making, led a precarious existence and lived in perpetual conflict with more established lowland populations.[31] Chen Hongmou was quite cognizant of this but tended to see the expansion of authorized development, rather than tighter enforcement of restrictions, as the best means to bring these populations under government control. On these internal frontiers, as on external ones, he sponsored such local projects as hydraulic works and granary building not just for economic purposes but explicitly to foster a sense of collective purpose and communal solidarity among "rootless" and atomistically fragmented populations.[32]

Land-tenure relations, too, could be a problem. The process of land clearance and settlement in the early and mid-Qing typically gave rise to highly stratified and exploitative property regimes, what Fu Yiling termed the most "capitalist" agrarian system the empire had ever seen.[33] An entrepreneur would secure rights to a large tract of land, then subdivide it among leaseholders for management of the actual clearance, with the labor provided by subtenants (or sub-subtenants), who frequently remained in debt-peonage to the landlords who had recruited them. Chen acknowledged the tensions endemic to such a situation and sought to ameliorate them in several ways. Official contracts for land development, he argued, should be issued for the smallest practicable unit of territory to eliminate large contractors and grant titles of ownership to the frontier cultivator directly. Local officials should closely monitor cases in which the tax on *kaiken* land had been adjusted downward or eliminated altogether so as to ensure that this financial benefit was passed along to tenants as rent reductions. Moreover, contractor-landlords who evicted their tenants after the latter had performed the actual labor of preparing the land for cultivation should be criminally prosecuted.[34] In sum, to be truly beneficial, land reclamation for Chen should be accompanied by the emergence of new local societies based on the orthodox model of autonomous small-producer households living harmoniously in village communities.

One final problematic consequence of mid-Qing land reclamation was ecological decay, a problem Chen and his contemporaries came only slowly to comprehend. Deforestation of river highlands throughout the empire led to massive topsoil runoff, which in turn led to silting of the waterways and increased incidence of flooding (a problem to which we shall return momentarily) and to soil deterioration of the highlands themselves. Overly ambitious planting of grain on marginal land also caused leeching and desiccation in some areas. Chen's oft-repeated injunction that lands be planted in crops for which they were appropriate did not really address this problem, aimed as it was nearly exclusively at maximum productivity.

He was more farsighted on the question of reforestation. Husbanding of woodland resources figured into Chen's developmental logic in a number of ways. As early as 1736 he ordered replanting of trees in areas of Yunnan that had been precipitously deforested by the flood of Han immigration. Linking this to his cardinal preoccupation with "long-term" (*jiuyuan*) planning, he argued that only continuous reforestation could ensure the constant supplies of firewood and tree-mulch fertilizer that the province would need in years to come.[35] In his celebrated 1744 call for opening formerly proscribed areas of Jiangxi for sedentary agriculture he was careful to specify that certain of these areas should be left in woodland and devoted to cultivation of forest products.[36] He was even more specific the next year in Shaanxi, where he enumerated for his subordinates the wide range of forest products that might result from systematic tree planting in their districts: walnuts and chestnuts, mushrooms and tree fungi, medicinal herbs, tung oil and varnish, bamboo, and so on. He also imposed severe penalties on overzealous timbering (mostly to feed paper mills) in the province's Han River highlands.[37] In 1757 Chen launched a vigorous program of tree planting along riverbanks in Jiangsu to better hold in the dikes.[38] Most intriguingly, he also in 1754 prohibited timbering in the wooded mountains around Fuzhou, arguing that these were the haunts of numinous forces that defended the climatic regularity of the entire province.[39] Is it too much to see in this action an ecological sensitivity, expressed through the medium of a highly particularized cultural logic?

One final aspect of Chen's *kaiken* policies that bears notice is his efforts at privatization of government land. At the start of the Qing a substantial percentage of the empire's territory was more or less defined as state property under a wide range of institutional arrangements that included banner lands (*qitian*), military colony lands (*tuntian*), lands assigned to the quasi-military grain tribute administration (*weisuo*), and endowment lands attached to specific civil and military posts (*guandi*). Although the precise processes involved are not very well understood, it is clear that the considerable majority of this land passed, over the course of the Qing, into private ownership (*mintian*). Chen Hongmou, whom we have already seen working to privatize segments of government monopoly in the salt and tea trades, repeatedly lobbied to extend his land reclamation programs into territories withheld from the private economy by claims of state proprietorship. He argued vigorously, for example, to greatly expand the program of civilianizing former *tuntian* colonies throughout Shaanxi, a process that had begun in the early Yongzheng reign and ultimately encompassed several million *mu* of farmland.[40]

Two cases from the rapidly developing commercial region of Xing'an, in the Han

River highlands of southeastern Shaanxi, exemplify the manner in which Chen linked privatization with intensified productivity. As Shaanxi governor in 1746 he ordered the privatization of tea plantation land that the Xing'an prefect's office had claimed as its own during the period of initial reclamation. Such an arrangement, Chen argued, was both economically inefficient and morally unjust; it represented a usurpation (*panju*) by the state of profits or benefits latent in the habitat occupied collectively by all local people. Private householders should be "invited" (*zhaomin*) to divide these plantations among themselves and so partake as fully as possible in the land's bounty (*dili*).[41] Some five years later Chen turned his attention to banner lands in Xing'an. Taking advantage of the recent upsurge in litigation among banner personnel over claims to property, most of which at this time was devoted to pasturage, Chen memorialized for permission to resurvey the area in an effort to put an end to these disputes once and for all. He frankly announced beforehand, however, that his survey was likely to discover that as much as 40 percent of currently claimed banner land (some eight thousand *mu*) was not banner property at all and that he intended to open this up to civilians for cultivation. Surprisingly, the Qianlong emperor enthusiastically endorsed the plan, concurring with Chen's logic that sedentary agriculture by private households would more productively "exhaust the benefits of the land" (*jin dili*).[42]

The counterparts to policies aimed at maximizing the *dili* through extending cultivation were those aimed at fully employing the *minli*, human energies, through resettlement. Resettlement programs had been a hallmark of Qing economic policy in the dynasty's early decades, but the tenor of such programs had now changed. Rather than restoring the state's fiscal base by better distributing sparse population across the landscape, as had been the goal of seventeenth-century resettlement drives, the Yongzheng and Qianlong campaigns sought primarily to increase food supply and to provide productive outlets for surplus population. Chen Hongmou himself was poignantly aware of the growing chronic underemployment among large sectors of the population and of the urgent need to reclaim these "poverty-stricken outcasts" (*qiongmin wuyezhe*) socially as well as economically.[43] In this he echoed the Yongzheng emperor, who as early as 1724 had called for all officials to systematically seek ways to exploit both the *minli* and *dili*, not only out of concerns over food supply (real as these were) but equally as part of the process of moral regeneration (*hua*) of the people through routinized productive labor.[44]

Five years later Yongzheng announced the revival of the early Qing program of encouraging homesteading by means of government loans to be used for purchase of oxen and seed grain.[45] Details of implementation were left largely to the initiative of individual field officials, but, not surprisingly, Chen Hongmou proved to be one of the policy's most energetic and creative practitioners. In Shaanxi in the 1740s and 1750s he refined a program for settlement in that province's inhospitable northern prefectures of Yan'an and Yulin by making cash loans to pioneers from the provincial treasury, repayable after the first successful harvest in grain to local granaries.[46] Over the course of Chen's four tenures in Shaanxi, such initiatives yielded hundreds of thousands of *mu* of new farmland.[47]

The other standard component of Qing policy to promote agricultural resettlement was tax relief, a policy Chen Hongmou especially endorsed. In Yunnan in 1737,
for instance, he called for tax cuts on marshlands around Lake Kun that had formerly
been pastureland but were then being converted, with mixed success, to agricultural
use. Two years later, as Tianjin circuit intendant, he ordered his county-level subordinates to investigate systematically which areas of Yellow River floodplain in their districts might, by promises of permanent tax exemption, be made inviting for new settlers.[48] As late as 1748, in response to the Qianlong emperor's call for proposals on how
best to contain grain-price inflation, Chen's most immediate recommendation was simple: stimulate further resettlement by liberal grants of tax holidays.[49] Across the spectrum of policy, indeed, Chen looked to reduce tax burdens when and where possible.
Even while repeatedly invoking the current idiom to describe the paired goals of economic policy—"state finance and popular productivity" (guoji minsheng)—in practice
it was nearly always the latter to which Chen gave precedence.

Shuili

The third component of the trinity of economic development in Chen Hongmou's
logic, along with the productive capacities of the land (dili) and the people (minli), was
the resource potential of water (shuili). As Chen wrote to a colleague in 1740, "It is by
maximizing the shuili that we expand the benefits of the dili itself."[50] It was in shuili management above all that Chen was judged by contemporaries to be expert; the largest
number of Chen's fifty-two entries in the Huangchao jingshi wenbian (Statecraft compendium) deal with water conservancy matters, and biographical notices of him both in
the Qing and since have invariably celebrated his prowess in this area.[51] On several occasions his selection for a given provincial post was decided on the basis of his renown
in shuili matters. Although much of this acclaim stemmed from his work in riverine
flood control, we will concentrate here more narrowly on Chen's efforts at drainage and
irrigation in service of expanding and intensifying agricultural productivity.

Throughout his long provincial career Chen undertook many large-scale projects
of floodplain drainage—for example, that in northern Jiangsu in the 1760s[52]—but
none more monumental than that in Henan in 1751 and 1752. Gui'de Prefecture and
its environs, in the province's northeast, was laced by Yellow River tributaries. Water
from points upstream and runoff from the higher ground around Kaifeng collected
here, where it awaited the chance to exit the province via a single major outlet into
northern Jiangsu. Long-term ecological deterioration—silting and constriction of
channels—had turned virtually all of Gui'de into a marshland that pressed the limits
of human habitation; in the entire Qianlong reign the breakdown of drainage had allowed only two modestly successful harvests. A succession of Henan governors had undertaken stopgap measures, but none had been of the scope clearly needed to achieve
lasting results. On his posting to Henan in 1751 Chen personally surveyed the area and
conducted an intensive study of provincial archives on the history of this problem. He
devised a truly massive scheme to dredge all the waterways in the region, assigning responsibility to local village leaders and landholders where possible but also investing

nearly a hundred thousand taels of government funds to accomplish work that spanned county jurisdictions or exceeded the capacities (*minli*) of the local populations. Most critically, unlike any of his predecessors Chen was able to enlist the cooperation of Jiangsu authorities (in the person of Chen's old comrade Yinjishan) to dredge the channel that provided the downriver outlet from Gui'de. By all accounts the recovery of the area's agriculture was both remarkable and lasting.[53]

Draining floodplain was one strategy of *shuili* management; construction and repair of irrigation works was another. There was likely no more energetic champion of new construction of regional hydraulic infrastructures in the eighteenth-century Qing imperium than Chen Hongmou; unlike the majority of Qing officials, for instance, Chen rarely failed to accompany his land reclamation drives with parallel efforts in the area of water supply.[54] In addition to significant rehabilitations of irrigation systems in most of his tenures, Chen undertook ambitious extensions of existing installations in Yunnan in 1736, in Jiangxi in 1740 and 1741, in Shaanxi from 1748 to 1751, in Gansu in 1755, and in Jiangsu in 1758.[55]

This, in Chen's view, was a clear responsibility of the state. As he wrote the throne in 1747:

> When poor people bring new land under cultivation, it is up to the administration to provide timely assistance in development of local irrigation systems. If the cost is too high for the local society to bear, funds should be provided out of official accounts. If decisions on what waterworks to build are made solely on the basis of what the people themselves can afford, then very little indeed will be accomplished.[56]

The state should never proceed arbitrarily, without heeding popular opinion (*minqing*) as to what hydraulic works the people really want—and, by implication, will prove willing to maintain once they are in place.[57] And yet the popular will being fragmented and shortsighted, neither can officials take the fact that local people have not proposed the project themselves as evidence that it is not desirable. It is the hallmark of the good official, with his superior breadth of perspective, to provide the "supervision and prompting" (*ducui*) necessary to get new work underway.[58] Indeed, this alerting of local populations to the untapped developmental potential of their habitat is a basic part of the official's moral mission to "civilize and instruct" (*huahui*) popular social practice.[59]

When entering a new province, Chen typically instructs his subordinates to survey their districts and propose new hydraulic works, the building of which his administration will direct (*jiaodao*). In devising such projects magistrates should adapt their ideas to the specifics of terrain and cropping patterns so as "to make most profitable use of the given environment" (*suishi lidao*).[60] What they must *not* do is penny-pinch; despite Chen's deep attachment to the virtue of frugality, his characteristic approach to water conservancy is to avoid short-term cost accounting (*riji*) in favor of investment, at nearly any cost, in a region's long-term productivity.[61]

We can see this best by looking at a few of Chen's major provincial hydraulic initiatives, beginning with his first, in Yunnan. Beyond the area of the capital, Kunming, in the province's northeast, very little of Yunnan was irrigated at the time of Chen's arrival in the province in the mid-1730s. In anticipation of a major population influx, and out of a desire to make that population as nearly as possible self-sufficient in food, Chen drew up for his regional superiors an extraordinarily comprehensive program for developing a hydraulic infrastructure. Yunnan was mountainous, so the basic source of irrigation water would be rainfall channeled down from the hills. The chief problem was to distribute this potentially torrential down flow over space. Chen thus oversaw the excavation of a series of mountainside reservoirs, each regulated by one or several dams, to collect rainwater. The collected water was allocated over wide swaths of territory by an elaborate network of tile gutters and bamboo pipes to irrigate as many fields as possible from a single source. Most of this distribution would be powered by gravity, but to water additional fields situated further up the mountainsides Chen designed a network of strategically deployed waterwheel installations.

To lay this system out Chen ordered each Yunnan magistrate to conduct a meticulous survey of his county's terrain and water flow, which he himself compiled into a master hydraulic atlas of the province. Magistrates were also told to make detailed analyses of the financial resources of local landholders as a means to assess ability to pay for the new construction. (Chen acknowledged this to be the most difficult aspect of the process and designed elaborate mechanisms to minimize corruption and false reporting.) He then divided the overall project into sectors, some of which might be built on basis of per-*mu* assessments on benefiting landholders, some of which might be popularly financed with the help of government start-up loans, and some of which would require direct official financing. The land-tax receipts of Yunnan were inadequate to the task, so Chen prevailed on Governor-general Ortai to set aside rental income from the province's substantial official-estate land (*guanzhuang*) for this use. Finally, Chen announced a very liberal tax policy on all lands that might be reclaimed or improved by the new irrigation system so as to eliminate any disincentive to participate. Overall, he saw his project as "leaving no potential *shuili* untapped, and hence no potential *dili* unexploited."[62]

In Shaanxi Chen's extension of irrigation works fell into two phases. The first involved his completing between 1747 and 1751 an extremely ambitious project begun by his predecessor, Cui Ji, some ten years earlier to dig more than 32,800 irrigation wells in eight counties of Xi'an and Tongguan Prefectures. According to Chen, by the late 1740s only a small percentage of the wells envisioned by Cui had been dug, but those that had, including some seven hundred in Xianyang County, had transformed local agriculture, allowing cultivation of vegetables and *some* production even in the worst drought years. As part of his broader campaign to have magistrates make regular village tours, Chen ordered them to prompt the completion of all projects Cui had identified and to search systematically for sites for wells in prefectures beyond Xi'an and Tongguan. Within the two years of his first Shaanxi tenure Chen claimed that a total of 67,500 irrigation wells had actually been put into operation and that the localities they served had clearly fared better in the drought of 1747–48. Returning to the province in early 1751, however, Chen complained that no additional wells had been dug in his absence, and he once again turned up the heat on local officials to prompt their construction by offering government financing where appropriate. Finally, in late summer he memorialized successfully for permission to encourage simultaneous land reclamation and digging of irrigation wells on the northwest border, both projects underwritten by a program of government loans to aspiring homesteaders.[63]

Already by this time, however, Chen was beginning to sense that he was approaching the limits of benefits to be gained by further well digging, except on the far frontier. Wells, he pointed out, were a useful means of irrigating flatlands but were both less useful and far more difficult to dig in the rocky highlands that dominated Shaanxi north of the Wei River. Here what was called for was a network of irrigation ditches (*qu*), drawing off water from mountain streams, and after mid-1751 he turned his energies to construction of these. He complained that his standing instructions to local subordinates to survey their jurisdictions and propose such projects had routinely occasioned such replies as "Since the beds of the streams are on lower ground than the lands to be irrigated, there is no way they can be used for such purposes." Based on his experience in Yunnan, however, Chen knew this to be untrue, so he set off on a personal tour of the areas in question. Where technical knowledge on the part of local populations was inadequate to the task, Chen argued, it was up to local officials to provide this; where this in turn failed, the know-how would be supplied by the governor himself. The answer was waterwheels (*shuiche*) of the kind Chen had employed in Yunnan and that were in common use in south China but as yet relatively unknown in the northwest. Chen had several samples made up and distributed to officials in northern Shaanxi, along with instructions that they begin to manufacture such devices in their own localities.[64]

In mid-autumn of 1751 Chen submitted two lengthy memorials outlining his scheme for the comprehensive development of irrigation canals and ditches in the north Shaanxi highlands. His plan was to tap all mountain streams as close to their sources as possible, fanning out a system of channels that would water as much as twenty thousand *mu* apiece. It is not too much to say that in the process Chen was attempting a fundamental transformation of the region's landscape. A few such canals had existed in the past, but most of these were judged by Chen to have been basically misconceived in the first place, so it was easy to understand why they had lapsed into decrepitude. People would not maintain a waterwork that did not operate to their satisfaction, Chen argued, but would inevitably wrangle to avoid upkeep responsibility; the problem of new construction, then, was simultaneously a technological and a sociopolitical one. He felt assured of his competence in handling the former, but the latter involved some active, grassroots politicking.

The key was to assess—and in part also to mold—local "public opinion" (*minqing*) with regard both to the general desirability of the project and to the most equitable way of allocating use rights and labor responsibilities. Where feasible Chen met in person with township-level gatherings of local people and elsewhere deputed a circuit intendant or other midrange official to do the same. In most cases rights and responsibilities were computed on the basis of existing grain tax assessments. Where labor inputs required of an individual village were clearly too onerous, Chen authorized outlays of grain from local government granaries to hire workers. As was customary, county magistrates were expected to provide construction materials out of their administrative budgets, in some cases as much as five thousand taels. This was a massive and costly project, but Chen argued that the "permanent" increases in popular productivity would justify the expense; the throne concurred, and the results seem to have pleased all concerned.[65]

During Chen's one brief tenure as Gansu governor in 1755, he labored to extend the hydraulic infrastructure he had created in Shaanxi to that as yet marginally incorporated province and beyond. This was truly arid country, with almost no spring or autumn rainfall. Although some of Chen's jurisdiction, lying in present-day Ningxia, was already irrigated by water channeled from the upper Yellow River, most lay too far west for this to be practicable. The only solution was to construct an enormous series of canals and ditches to channel melting snows from the region's high mountains. Chen pointed to archaeological evidence that in some areas this had been done in the distant past, and he expressed awe at the observable difference between the thriving agrarian life in parts of the region currently under irrigation and the virtual desiccation of its unwatered parts. Here indeed was a case where human labor could improve on and "beautify" the natural endowments of Heaven-and-earth (*tianzao dishe*).[66]

Chen compiled extensive and highly detailed maps and handbooks for the hydraulic infrastructures he envisioned, not only for Gansu per se but also for the expanding areas of Qing administration outside the Jiayu Pass, in what was to become Xinjiang. He divided the project into minute sections (*duan*), assigning each local official clear accountability for his section of the work and selecting "irrigation-ditch headmen" (*quzhang*) and "water conservancy elders" (*shuilao*) from among the local population to head up subdivisions of the project. As much as possible, the irrigation ditches were to run alongside existing or newly constructed roads so as to provide drainage for the latter, and so assist in the logistical and commercial integration of the region as a whole. No sooner had Chen's plans been finalized, however, than he received sudden orders to proceed to a new post in Hunan. Before leaving Gansu in the fall of 1758 he briefed his successor, Wu Dashan, on the details of his project and sought to ensure its completion by boosting it in a memorial, which received the emperor's ringing endorsement.

The political rhetoric in which Chen couches his pronouncements on the Gansu project sounds familiar themes. Vague proposals along similar lines in the past had all come to nothing because an impasse existed between the local population, which was not farsighted or unified in its thinking, and regional officials, who complacently mistook popular silence for an active disfavor of new hydraulic initiatives. To the contrary, Chen stresses, the proper role of government is to work to rally public opinion around just such projects as this, which are self-evidently in the common interest. There is no excuse for the state to adopt the laissez-faire (*wushe*) attitude it had in the past. As for the considerable cost entailed, we should not shirk investment in future popular productivity, nor should the individual official avoid initiating projects that he (as with Chen in this case) knows full well he will not be around to claim credit for on completion.

In the Gansu case Chen sounds, however, one additional rhetorical theme: cultural expansionism. This possibility suits well the imperial frame of mind. In his memorial on departing the province Chen invokes Qianlong's proclaimed intent to "reincorporate" (*guifu*) the territories occupied by the recently vanquished Dzungar Mongols. He an-

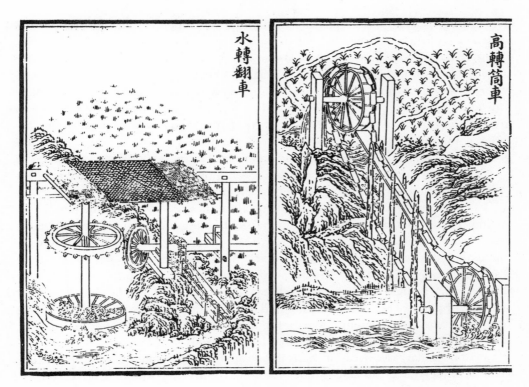

FIGURES 7 AND 8. Two styles of eighteenth-century Chinese waterwheels. The wheel on the right is specifically designed to irrigate fields lying higher than the water source. Source: *Qinding shoushi tongkao*, 1742.

nounces as well his intention to invite in thousands of Han colonists and paints for his monarch a most idyllic picture of the resulting society: settled agrarian communities, linkage with the rest of the empire by interregional market integration, production of wealth well beyond subsistence level, and the spontaneous emergence of an indigenous, public-spirited elite leadership. "It will," Chen boasts, "be just like China proper [*neidi*]!"[67]

But Chen Hongmou was hardly the sort of man to concentrate on flashy new hydraulic systems while neglecting routine maintenance of existing ones. Indeed, in virtually every post in which he served he closely inspected the condition of all *shuili* works and conducted past-due repairs. At times he rehabilitated very ancient installations, doing archival or archaeological research to establish their past manner of operation. He upgraded existing materials (substituting iron and ceramic pipe or cement ductwork for packed-earth ditches) and reconfigured entire systems in the process of conducting scheduled repairs. Where outlays of substantial provincial funds were called for, Chen did not hesitate to authorize them.[68]

Chen regularly used local official diligence in the conduct of hydraulic maintenance as an index of overall performance. He took great care to ensure that each segment of an installation fell under a single official's competency and that all officials were aware of their personal liability in these matters. Even where individual service records were at stake, however, Chen also worked to install in his subordinates a sense of collective esprit. As he wrote to a colleague: "When it comes to river control and water conservancy, unity must be sought and divisiveness avoided. That is, if you make individual hydraulic managers work together [by rewarding or punishing them as a group], then they will share a common purpose. But if you pit them against one another competitively, they will look out only for themselves, and defeat collective goals."[69] Well into his days as a metropolitan official in the 1760s Chen continued to ponder the question of how best to apportion responsibility among subordinates for hydraulic maintenance and how to motivate them to show initiative in this area.[70]

Chen made a practice of reviewing procedures in each of his jurisdictions for assessing corvée labor for hydraulic maintenance, hunting out instances of inequitable assessment, bribe taking, ineffectiveness, and most notably conflict between corvée demands and those of the agricultural work cycle. We saw earlier that Chen found corvée distasteful on principle—as with any form of commandist appropriation of goods or services (*pai*), he held it to be generally less efficient than market allocation. For either practical or political reasons he did not find it prudent to call for elimination of corvée from hydraulic management altogether, but he clearly preferred other alternatives, such as work relief (*gongzhen*) and the use of hired labor.

On one remarkable occasion, early in his career, Chen put his ideas to the test. The Dian River served as drainage outlet for four counties of Kunming Prefecture in Yunnan, and for the fields of these counties to avoid waterlogging, annual dredging of the entire system was required. This massive operation was ordinarily accomplished by a workforce of ten thousand laborers, recruited via a corvée levy on local cultivators. However, in practice any farmer who could afford it hired a substitute to take his place, and these workers were generally acknowledged to be lazy, contentious, and largely worthless. Local headmen in charge of corvée recruitment had responded by raising the rate of assessment across the board—a classic involutional syndrome. As provincial treasurer in 1733 Chen Hongmou opted to abandon the venerable corvée system entirely and undertake the annual Dian River overhaul using labor hired by his office at market rates. By Chen's account, this strategy allowed him to accomplish the maintenance more effectively than ever before, utilizing far fewer laborers and expending altogether approximately the same two hundred taels normally allocated to provision the corvée workforce. By relying on market principles, but making the state the direct employer, Chen could claim to have decreased local administrative corruption, improved the soundness of the hydraulic infrastructure, relieved the burden on cultivators, and provided useful employment for the province's growing nonfarm labor force, all at one stroke.[71]

Chen Hongmou's developmental zeal was nowhere more profoundly challenged than in one further area of hydraulic management: polder construction. For centuries Chinese farmers had been reclaiming sections of lake, river, and ocean shoreline by constructing many varieties of enclosing dikes (*yuti*), within which they practiced wet-rice cultivation. With increased population pressure on the land, as well as the boom in regionally specialized export rice production in the first half of the Qing, construction of new polders greatly accelerated, constricting natural floodwater receptacles (most notably in the Middle Yangzi provinces) and creating severe threats to regional hydraulic security. Chen Hongmou was among the first Qing officials to acknowledge this problem, despite the implications of doubt it cast on his basic policy approach of "exhausting the earth."

Through most of his early provincial career Chen appears to have been uncritically enthusiastic about polders. In Jiangxi, from the start of his initial appointment as provincial treasurer in 1741, he began to argue forcefully for greater government support for such projects.[72] Although built originally by private entrepreneurs, Chen argued, polders were now essential to the province's profitable commercial rice production. Thus, although he did not campaign for new construction per se (he did propose construction of a new dam in support of existing polders, which he built using work-relief labor during the food crisis of 1742–43),[73] he moved very dramatically to assert government control of a stepped-up polder maintenance program. Chen complained that the existing system for annual upkeep of these so-called people's dikes (*minti*), which was left largely to the supervision of semivolunteer "polder headmen" (*yuzhang*), simply wasn't working: individual households were shirking their assigned duties and compromising the watertight integrity of the entire installation, resulting both in vastly diminished harvest yields and in an atmosphere of mutual recrimination and an explosion of litigation at county yamens. Chen used the fact of this litigation, and what he portrayed as the clamor of "public opinion" (*minqing*) for help in policing "derelict proprietors" (*jianyuan tianhu*), to argue for the state's taking a far more active role in polder maintenance. He proposed that deputy magistrates (*xiancheng*) and auxiliary magistrates (*xianzuo*) assigned to Gan River counties be delegated direct personal responsibility for overseeing annual repairs by all polder households. Their detailed reports would be inspected, compiled, and forwarded up the bureaucratic ladder to the governor's office. Chen vowed to use the subsequent integrity of the polders they had vouched for as a key determinant of whether these magistrates-in-waiting would indeed ever receive the magistracy they sought.

Although state supervision had been tightened, these polders remained "private" (*minjian*), and the labor and financial costs of repairs were still distributed on a user's-fee basis among farm households. The administration got out of the bargain not only a more comfortable guarantee of stable productivity but undoubtedly as well a more comprehensive knowledge of just what polders in fact existed and hence a greater degree of control over the hydraulic security of the entire region. In exchange Chen felt obliged to contribute some state investment in repairing "people's dikes" that had fallen into such disrepair as to exceed the capacity of local people to rehabilitate by themselves. As a first step, he authorized county officials to allocate financial aid out of their discretionary "public" funds (*gongxiang*), and in instances when this too fell short, he sought imperial permission to offer assistance from provincial salt administration accounts. In the process Chen was subtly reshaping categories of private (*min*), public-collective (*gong*), and official (*guan*), justifying greater state intervention and control over hydraulic works without advancing simultaneous claims of state proprietorship.

It was in Hunan, however, where Chen was posted first in 1755 and again in 1763, that his view of polders as an unmixed blessing began to change and his claims to state control accordingly pushed a level further. Far more than Jiangxi, which was further downriver and hence more sheltered from the annual spring swelling of the Yangzi and its tributaries, Hunan had already come to suffer the adverse ecological consequences of unchecked polder building. In the face of growing extraregional demand for Hunanese rice the sorts of state supervision that Chen had sought to impose on the hydraulic infrastructure in Jiangxi had for decades been sacrificed in Hunan to entrepreneurial drives for reclamation of the rich potential rice lands lining the shores of Dongting Lake and the Xiang River.[74] As early as the 1740s at least some provincial administrators had come to link this unchecked mushrooming of polders with increases in flooding elsewhere in Hunan and, running counter to the thrust of development-oriented central policy, had begun to argue for government control of the pace of polder building. After lengthy debate Governor Yang Xifu won permission to impose a moratorium on all further construction in 1746.[75]

When Chen first came to Hunan a decade later, he reiterated this ban. Perhaps he was influenced in this cause by his long-standing collegial respect for Yang Xifu or by his even longer friendship with Jia Shengquan, one of the empire's most esteemed experts on hydraulic security, who was just then serving as circuit intendant in Hunan.[76] Nevertheless, Chen's conversion to the antipolder cause was as yet only tentative, and the bulk of his energies during this first Hunan tenure were directed not at prohibiting new construction but rather at asserting greater control over maintenance of existing polders so as to protect the productivity of the lands they enclosed.[77]

It was rather in his second tour in Hunan, eight years later in 1763, that Chen formulated the ecological argument against further polder building that would remain official dogma for generations after his time. In what is likely the most famous memorial he ever wrote Chen portrayed Hunan as site of a war for dominance between the forces of land and water; when those of land attacked, those of water must counterattack. Reviewing the historical record, Chen was able to document the dramatic contraction over time of the surface of Dongting Lake and to link this causally to the growing regularity of serious floods. The large volume of water rushing into the area from upland snowmelt each spring needed receptacles to contain it until the slower process of outflow downriver could relieve the pressure. Continuous encroachment on lakeshore and riverbank had deprived Hunan of this storage space. In the condition of fragile equilibrium that now pertained, virtually any new encroachment would result in an eruption in the hydraulic channel somewhere else. Thus, not only should new polders be prohibited, but new openings (*shuikou*) must be excavated in the lake's existing periphery to relieve and regulate water pressure. Unauthorized existing polders that might be destroyed by opening these new breaches deserved their fate and would not be rebuilt. The Qianlong emperor was by now convinced and greeted Chen's memorial with applause; he ordered the Board of Works to incorporate it into standing policy.[78] More than half a century later, Wei Yuan extolled Chen's analysis as still the most clear-sighted handling of the problem that his native Hunan had ever seen.[79]

But as perceptive as Chen may have been, it is evident that the situation in Hunan was far less straightforward than his hydraulic-pressure analysis would have it, embroiled as it was in a complex tangle of customary law and economic interests. Chen himself allowed that a multitude of litigation rackets had sprung up around the issue of polder building and resulting flooding of other property, and Wei Yuan adds that past official neglect had given rise to something of a clerical mafia, which managed the award of polder-building permits to its own profit.[80] Chen's decision could not have been any more popular with these entrenched groups than it was to proprietors of the threatened polders themselves. In his detailed study of Hunan water conservancy Peter Perdue argues that in at least one instance Chen's policies did indeed backfire. In 1763 Chen ordered the destruction of Yanglin zhai, a major illegal dike in Xiangyin County. The results were disastrous: four other dikes, which had been protected by Yanglin zhai, collapsed, and dozens of farm households were washed out, spawning a morass of litigation. According to one local source, Chen Hongmou was "a good official" who in this case had been deliberately embarrassed by the deceptions of yamen clerks, in league with local propertied interests.[81]

Chen Hongmou's own published papers end discreetly just prior to his antipolder initiatives in Hunan. Were there other incidents comparable to that at Yanglin zhai? It would not seem unlikely. Within the year, Chen was removed from Hunan, kicked upstairs to a board presidency in Beijing, and never held another provincial post. Coming as it did on the heels of other awkward incidents in Guangdong and Jiangsu (see Chapter 2), embarrassments such as Yanglin zhai may have convinced the throne that the aging statesman, although highly experienced and still analytically keen, may no longer have had his hand on the pulse of local society.

Farm Technology

For the Shanxi provincial examination of 1729, to which the young Chen Hongmou was assigned as associate examiner, he composed the following policy question. Agriculture is uniquely important in providing the material basis for both the polity and the society. Yet, everyone knows how backbreaking agricultural labor is, by comparison to other lines of work. How then can an official encourage sufficient numbers of the population to remain on the farm? Chen suggested his own answer to the question: by providing the technological know-how both to reduce the burdens of agricultural work and to increase its material rewards.[82]

The campaign to "encourage agriculture" (*quannong*) and, within this, to devote all due attention to improving farm technology was central to the self-proclaimed missions of both the Yongzheng and Qianlong rulers. Both men issued sweeping edicts at the outset of their reigns, ordering all field officials to do everything in their power to raise the level of farming practice within their constituency; Qianlong went so far as to make agricultural methods a required subject of study at the Hanlin Academy.[83] As we have seen, this imperial initiative dovetailed with Chen Hongmou's own very basic predilections, an outgrowth of his home experience in Guangxi, and it is not surprising that he took his emperor's prompting to heart more deeply than did many another official. It appears as well that Chen's devotion to the cause of *quannong* was further reinforced by his experience serving under one of his earliest bureaucratic superiors, Yunnan governor Zhang Yunsui, a man Chen admired all his life. Zhang's famous 1737 memorial, "Three Policies for Encouraging Agriculture," outlined his systematic strategy for turning the southwest into an agriculturally productive region and encapsulates many of the precepts—such as the need to pay close heed to microecology in determining the potential for innovation—that Chen continued to advance all his life.[84]

But it was Chen himself who, perhaps better than any other official, epitomized the Confucian moral tone of this Yongzheng-Qianlong agricultural improvement campaign.[85] The project assumed the shortsightedness of local agrarian populations, which the better-educated and more widely experienced official was beholden to overcome. This should be done through a process of patient education and guidance (*jiaodao*), avoiding as much as possible any coercive measure that might "harass" the people (*leimin*). Chen Hongmou almost never *ordered* his constituents to adopt new techniques, invariably expecting—with his deep-seated Confucian optimism—that as rational beings they would intuitively recognize the superiority of the given technique he was extolling at the time. Indeed, inasmuch as the introduction of superior technology inherently involved a heightening of the rational application of the people's labor to efficient productivity, and rationality and morality were inseparable, agricultural improvement itself was a form of moral training. As the Yongzheng emperor had stressed in his famous *quannong* edict of 1724, technical education of the populace was an inherent and necessary component of the larger mission of moral-cultural transformation (*jiaohua*) that was the official's cardinal task. Similarly, the local official was urged by the throne, and by provincial authorities such as Chen, to draw on his own creative rationality to address local needs rather than to carry out unthinkingly a body of "agricultural improvement" regulations prescribed from above.

Like many another provincial governor, but far more doggedly than most, Chen demanded of his local-level subordinates that they work systematically to train their constituencies in better techniques.[86] One favored means of doing this was through the institution of "model farmers" (*laonong*), householders judged to be exemplars of advanced agricultural practice. By imperial mandate such exemplars might be eligible for a variety of awards and honors, in proportion to the number of households that successfully imitated their virtue. (The parallel here to agricultural improvement campaigns under both the Republic and People's Republic seems striking.) Ordinarily, model farmers were selected from among existing local residents, but Chen on several occasions chose to import households from other regions of China where techniques were more advanced. He did this, for instance, in Luo minority areas of Yunnan, where he installed Han farmers on his own provincial payroll to demonstrate techniques of proper composting.[87]

Although model farmers were a time-honored means of improving agricultural technique, in this new era of China's expanding print culture (which Chen, the author of many popular morality books, was not slow to appreciate), agricultural handbooks assumed an unprecedentedly widespread importance as well. The particular how-to book that Chen most esteemed was the imperially sponsored *Shoushi tongkao*, compiled under Ortai's direction in 1742. The basic technologies (and moral precepts) in this work were drawn from Xu Guangqi's 1628 *Nongzhong quanshu*, as redacted by Chen Zilong in 1642, but it was rendered more popularly accessible by inclusion of materials from the late Ming picture book *Tiangong kaiwu*, by Song Yingxing.[88] Chen Hongmou not only regularly consulted the *Shoushi tongkao* himself, and ordered subordinates to do likewise, but he also felt it highly suitable for practicing farmers. Accordingly, while serving in Jiangxi in 1742, he asked the headmaster of the Nanchang Prefectural School, Li Anmin, to prepare an even more simplified edition, which Chen had printed up in large numbers and distributed throughout the province.[89]

Improvements in agricultural practice that Chen promoted in one or another of his tenures included planting and banking up individual seedlings (versus broadcast sowing), more extensive hoeing and weeding, transplanting of shoots, crop rotation, double-cropping, and expanded use of draft animals (as well as protection of them from rustling by slaughterhouses). Depending on the locale, he introduced a variety of methods of fertilizer production and use, such as penning up livestock for manure collection, husbanding of night soil and organic garbage, and mulching of forest by-products and of wild grasses. In line with imperial initiative Chen promoted tree planting throughout the empire for reasons ranging from cultivation of fruits, nuts, and resins, to fertilizer production, to holding in dikes and roadways and reducing topsoil runoff. Agriculture, in other words, is rendered most productive by situating it in a context that includes other sources of livelihood, including forestry, animal husbandry, and, as we shall see in a moment, trade.[90]

Chen paid close attention to agrarian microecology, and ordered his magistrates to do the same, in pursuit of optimal crop selection. One of the persistent themes in these efforts was sensitivity to the possibilities for planting of so-called *zaliang*—"miscellaneous grains," essentially any calorie-rich crop other than rice or wheat. Extension of the margin of agriculture based on *zaliang* cultivation was a central thrust of imperial food-supply policy, notably under the Yongzheng emperor,[91] and it was one that Chen enthusiastically endorsed. We have already seen, for example, several instances of his ordering local populations to shift to planting of *zaliang* when flood or drought conditions rendered more favored crops temporarily uncultivable. But probably at no time in his career did Chen take a more hands-on approach to crop selection than during his tenure in Yunnan during the mid-1730s, the last years of the Yongzheng emperor's reign.

Chen viewed agriculture in Yunnan as something of a tabula rasa, and he was deeply concerned to make the province as nearly as possible self-sufficient in food, despite the extraordinarily high percentage of its population (soldiers, miners, merchants) employed outside of agriculture. He complained that Yunnan farmers—most themselves recent immigrants—had clustered in the lowlands and taken up paddy-rice cultivation and that neither they nor the indigenous population seriously considered the dry-field cultivation techniques that would allow productive use of the province's vast highlands. The answer was *zaliang*—in Yunnan, comprising buckwheat, sorghum, sesame, and a wide variety of legumes, as well as tubers and other garden crops. Beginning in 1734, Chen began to import and distribute *zaliang* seeds and to set up systems of government awards to magistrates, township leaders (*xiangbao*), and village headmen who won their acceptance by farmers. He reiterated these appeals on a regular basis until his removal from the province three years later.[92]

That even *zaliang* cultivation in Yunnan was envisioned as a primarily commercial rather than subsistence operation is seen in the activities of one of Chen's Yunnan subordinates who most aggressively picked up on his initiative. This was Zhang Yingjun, magistrate of the heavily non-Han Luoci County. Zhang discreetly contested Chen's belief that Yunnanese resistance to dry-field agriculture was due to ignorance of techniques; the true reason was that the relative *profitability* of such agriculture had yet to be effectively demonstrated to local people. Given the prevailing conditions of abundant land and scarce labor, Zhang believed he could do just this. He set up an experimental state farm outside his county seat and hired local workers to cultivate a selected range of *zaliang*. He dug irrigation wells and constructed a livestock pen—composted manure being the key, in Zhang's view, to turning *zaliang* cultivation in Yunnan into a profitable commercial enterprise. When the harvest proved successful, Zhang distributed the yield as a bonus to his workers and suggested that they sell most of it on the local market. Chen Hongmou thereupon trumpeted Zhang's success as a model for the rest of the province.

A decade later, in 1745, Chen launched a yet more celebrated *zaliang* campaign, the introduction of the sweet potato into Shaanxi. An American food crop, the sweet potato had by the early eighteenth century established itself as the staple food of much of upland Fujian and had begun to spread to other areas of the southeast (including Guangxi, where Chen Hongmou had encountered it in his youth).[93] According to Dai Yi, its effective introduction to north China came only in the Qianlong reign. Although the emperor announced his support for the project, active efforts fell to others: first to Fujianese merchants in Shandong, then to the occasional local official in Zhili and Henan. Chen's effort to spread sweet potato cultivation into the northwest was thus the most concerted high-level official campaign the crop had yet seen.[94] The techniques of sweet potato cultivation were, however, reported in the imperially commissioned 1742 agricultural handbook *Shoushi tongkao*, and it was his study of this work that directly inspired Chen's initiatives in Shaanxi.

Chen gushingly publicized the sweet potato's virtues: its pleasing taste, high nutritional value, ease of cultivation, high yield per *mu*, imperviousness to wide swings of temperature and precipitation, resistance to pests and disease, and above all its suitability to the sandy soil (*shatu*), which much of loess-covered Shaanxi shared with the Fujian coast. He noted that it could be rotated with other crops or interplanted with beans, that it could be ground into flour for baking, and (a reluctant admission, surely) that it could be distilled into a tolerable liquor. In a directive to local-level subordinates, Chen expounded impressively about how to prepare the land for sweet potato cultivation, how to store the seeds, how to harvest the crop, what to do with the remaining stalks, and other technical details. He reprinted in pamphlet form relevant sections of the *Shoushi tongkao*, with their easy-to-follow illustrations, and distributed this throughout the province. No doubt drawing on his experience with magistrate Zhang Yingjun in Yunnan, he ordered county officials to set up experimental plots close by their ya-mens to demonstrate how successfully sweet potatoes could be grown in Shaanxi. Moreover, because many current Shaanxi magistrates were themselves Fujian men, they should have personal experience of sweet potato cultivation to impart to their con-stituents. Once a few local people had mastered the necessary skills, they should be des-ignated "model farmers" and charged with passing these on to their neighbors.[95]

With his faith in market supply intact, even in the isolated northwest, Chen dis-tributed only a few sample seeds himself. He observed that not a few merchants who hailed from the southeast regularly visited Shaanxi. Once they came to see that a mar-ket existed for seeds of a crop they had long known in their home areas, the profit mo-tive would incline them to bring in seeds commercially to meet local demand.

How successful was Chen Hongmou's project to introduce the sweet potato to the northwest? Pierre-Étienne Will, who has studied Shaanxi agriculture in great detail, speculates that in all probability the scheme was a flop, the resistance of farmers to this southern novelty being likely too great for one optimistic governor to overcome. Yet other scholars, including Dai Yi and Evelyn Rawski, see growing evidence of its adop-tion as a staple by Shaanxi highland dwellers in the decades during and after Chen's tenures in the province. It seems only fitting that, long after Chen's departure, the crop was known in Shaanxi local parlance as "Mr. Chen's spud" (*Chen gong shu*).[96]

"Encouraging agriculture" (*quannong*), both to Chen and to his imperial masters, in-cluded fundamentally the notion of production for the market. Although occasional arguments for concentration on subsistence foodstuffs were heard (see Chapter 5), the more general tone of Qing exhortations to enhanced farm production included cotton and other commercial crops, as well as grain. Many contemporary works, including Chen's own *Sourcebook on Reforming Social Practice*, lauded the efficiency of commercial-ized agriculture and specialized production based on local ecological conditions. This corresponded to actual practice, for, as many scholars have shown, the eighteenth cen-tury was an era of tremendous increase in commercial cropping, with a parallel growth of local handicraft industries to process this ever more specialized farm output.[97] In our discussion to this point we have already seen ample evidence that Chen Hongmou's *quannong* drives throughout the empire took commercialization as both a given and a desired goal. Nowhere, perhaps, was this more striking than in what may be the most celebrated of all Chen's boosterism campaigns, his effort to promote sericulture in Shaanxi in the 1740s and 1750s.

Ever since Wei Yuan in the 1820s, chroniclers of Chinese agricultural policy have been intrigued by this seemingly quixotic attempt to reverse the historical trend toward regional specialization that had made Shaanxi dependent for its textile consumption on imports from the lower Yangzi provinces.[98] What had occurred in Shaanxi was a textbook case of regional deindustrialization in the transition to a commodity econ-omy. It was well known from the *Shi jing* (Book of songs) that in antiquity the state of Bin (near today's Xunyi County, in west-central Shaanxi) had produced abundant silk, but the techniques had gradually been lost. In part this was the result of long-term eco-

logical decay, a deforestation and loss of soil fertility that saw this region by the eighteenth century largely devoted to pasturage.[99] In part it was because of the increased
cost-efficiency displayed by the textile industries of the southeast, which persuaded native silk producers to turn to other pursuits in which they could be more competitive.
As sensitive as Chen Hongmou normally was to the economic advantages of regional
specialization, he found them in this case overridden by other concerns. As he saw it,
average consumers in Shaanxi who had formerly been able to afford an occasional purchase of locally produced silk were now, with the dependence on imports, squeezed out
of the market.[100] Clearly, too, Chen hoped that the revival of sericulture in the province
and the recapture of at least a modest extraregional market would provide a welcome
boost to the economy as a whole.[101]

Beyond issues of economic utility, important as they might be, Chen's sericulture
campaign was also tied into questions of regional identity, of the regeneration of popular culture (*jiaohua*), and of the sense of mission of the literati class. The campaign really had no close parallel, either in Chen's own career or in those of other contemporary officials, nor did it arise in response to any specific imperial directive. It did,
however, have a prehistory in Shaanxi. As early as the Kangxi reign there had been sporadic official efforts to introduce sericulture in parts of the upper Han River valley, in
the province's southernmost area. But the direct impetus to the drives of the mid-eighteenth century came from a private citizen, a purchased lower-gentry member from
Xingping County (Xi'an Prefecture) named Yang Shen (1699–1794).

Yang Shen was a follower of Li Yong, the late-seventeenth-century master of
Guanxue, the Shaanxi school of neo-Confucianism.[102] As we saw in Chapter 4, Guanxue
came to have a deep impact on Chen Hongmou in many ways and, in part through
him, on the shaping of *jingshi* (statecraft) ideas in the century to follow. It also, however,
as its name implies, had a self-conscious regional character. Just as Guanxue adherents
eschewed the two intellectual currents they saw as polluting Jiangnan and other culturally "advanced" regions—literary dilettantism and mindless examination cramming
(Yang Shen himself steadfastly refused to sit for the examinations at all)—in favor of
moral self-cultivation and "doctoring" to local society, so too they clearly hoped to lib-
erate their region from economic dependence on this same Jiangnan metropolitan
economy. Yang Shen's writings on sericulture are infused with a nostalgic desire to recapture both the moral purity and the independent spirit of the ancient Bin state, a re-
gional-chauvinist rhetoric largely absent from Chen Hongmou's own writings on silk
production in Shaanxi.

Yang devoted most of his life to the study of agronomy, emphatically arguing that
grain cultivation without simultaneous attention to animal husbandry, forestry, and sericulture was a root cause of both the economic impoverishment and moral decline he
observed in contemporary rural society. In his writings he consistently stressed how
these bi-employments should be integrated into the annual agricultural cycle to fill the
slack season and prevent morally debilitating idleness. Meticulously scheduled bi-em-
ployment, combined with a fairly rigid gender division of labor (for each month Yang
outlined separate tasks for males and females of the farm household), should work continually to reinforce orthodox models of the family. Like Chen Hongmou himself,

then, Yang Shen valorized the small-producer patriarchal household as optimal for reasons both of ritual propriety and economic efficiency.[103]

Beginning in 1725, Yang began experiments on his own estate, and in and around his native township, with cultivation of mulberry and silkworms he imported from the lower Yangzi. (Reportedly, these experiments were so famous that the name of the town was eventually changed from Sanjia zhen, Three Family Town, to the near-homophonous Sangjia zhen, Mulberry Town.) By 1741 he had achieved enough experience to write his famous sericulture handbook, *Binfeng guangyi*, which he distributed to a number of local and provincial officials.[104] One who read it and was impressed was Zhang Wenjie, subprefect of Fengxiang, slightly west of Yang's native Xingping in the relatively fertile Wei River valley. Zhang undertook a pilot project of his own and reported his successful results in a petition of 1744 calling for the systematic reintroduction of silkworm raising throughout Shaanxi. After some deliberation Chuan-Shaan viceroy Qingfu agreed and in mid-summer ordered similar pilot projects undertaken on government land in various parts of the province. Thus, when Chen Hongmou arrived for his first Shaanxi tour some six months later, the stage was already set. Seeking out Yang Shen, he brought him to his Xi'an yamen and, heaping official honors on him, persuaded him to remain part of his provincial brain trust. Throughout all four of Chen's tenures in Shaanxi Yang served both as Chen's personal philosopher-in-residence and as chief administrator of his ongoing sericulture campaign.[105]

But despite the fact that Chen's thirteen-year sericulture drive (1745–57) did not arise ex nihilo, it was nevertheless highly original. It involved a complex balance of attention to the various stages in the silk production process: mulberry cultivation, silkworm raising, reeling and spinning of yarn, and weaving of cloth. His key strategic concept was one of division of labor, bringing as many households into the process as possible by allowing each to find its most congenial niche, to get involved at any stage in the production process it wished without having to worry about personally accomplishing the other stages. The governor also sought to provide an incentive structure that would invite participation on the part of households of very modest means, whose output otherwise might be so small as to make their involvement in sericulture unprofitable. What he ultimately devised was a system very much resembling what is sometimes called "protoindustrialization"—a centrally controlled, regionally organized, yet highly dispersed network of household-scale producers collectively turning out low-technology finished goods for a market that was, at least in part, extraregional.[106] The key difference between Chen's program and other instances of protoindustrialization, such as the early modern Flemish linen industry or the Jiangnan cotton industry, was that the role of entrepreneur in Shaanxi was played not by merchant-capitalists but by the provincial-level state. As an example of early modern industrialization strategies, it appears quite remarkable.

At the outset of Chen's first Shaanxi tenure virtually no mulberry, wild or cultivated, grew in that province. Chen personally toured his jurisdiction several times to determine where it might successfully be introduced, and he optimistically concluded that much of the province south of Yan'an could support it. He ordered all magistrates to experiment with mulberry on official lands (*guandi*) in their counties and to report

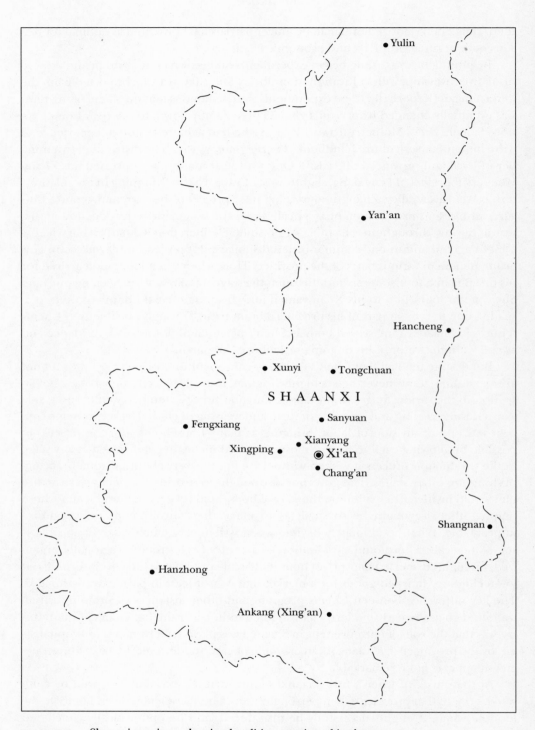

FIGURE 9.   Shaanxi province, showing localities mentioned in the text.

in detail on the results. Local farmers were encouraged to take up the crop; county governments should stand ready to purchase their output should private commercial demand fail to appear. Official honors were conferred on conspicuously successful cultivators. Cutting down of mulberry trees and theft of leaves were vigorously prohibited. Local experts (*laonong*) were hired as government instructors, and in 1751 Chen began to send out mulberry specialists from the provincial capital to provide technical advice to the localities. In his broadsides exhorting mulberry production, Chen stressed the short two-year maturation period before new plantings could turn a profit and the fact that any scrap of land could be devoted to their cultivation, including urban land in towns and county seats. Nevertheless, during his last tenure in Shaanxi, in 1757, Chen finally acknowledged that mulberry cultivation was the chief bottleneck to the entire Shaanxi silk industry; as a last-ditch effort he ordered magistrates to establish nurseries in their own yamen precincts and to offer saplings free of charge to all willing takers.[107]

As badly as Chen wanted mulberry cultivation to succeed in Shaanxi, he stuck to his basic economic principles of voluntarism and market incentives. Magistrates, however zealous they might be to satisfy their governor, were repeatedly warned not to coerce private farmers to grow the crop or to impose quotas (*pai*) on mulberry production or to discipline farmers whose efforts in this area failed. The impetus was to be exclusively the prospect of cash sales to buyers (although those buyers might in fact be the officials themselves). Mulberry cultivation in Shaanxi could only effectively be established, Chen told his subordinates, when "the people of their own accord [*ziji*] seek after the profits to be made."[108]

Still, an alternative had to be found. While continuing to promote mulberry, therefore, Chen rather quickly came to shift the bulk of his efforts to the introduction of a variant type of silkworm that could be raised in the wild on other kinds of leaves. These so-called mountain silkworms (*shancan*) were native to Shandong Province but were known to feed well on the particular species of oak (*hu*) already found in abundance in the highlands of the Wei and Han Rivers, in central and southern Shaanxi. For nearly half a century there had been sporadic local efforts to import mountain silkworms to Shaanxi, but none had enjoyed lasting success. In 1744, however, Governor-general Qingfu had made them a component of his province-wide sericulture campaign, and two years later Chen Hongmou began to step up pressure on local officials to experiment with them in their districts. He ordered oak forests protected from timbering and new trees planted, mountain silkworms and their associated hardware imported and distributed to farmers free of charge, and experts recruited from Shandong at provincial expense to train local people in the techniques of their nurturance. If suitable oak forests were found on government land, Chen ordered magistrates to turn them into silkworm plantations (*canchang*), making sure all profits went to the civilian workers rather than to their county treasuries. If such forests were on private land, the landowner (*shanzhu*) should be strongly "encouraged" to hire labor and raise silkworms there or else to lease out the land to a tenant who would raise them. Publicizing examples of notable success, Chen continued for more than a decade to hound his subordinates to exert themselves along these lines.[109]

Virtually none of the silk turned out by Shaanxi's growing population of sericul-turalists was for household consumption; mulberry leaves and silkworm cocoons were cash crops. Despite Chen's efforts, neither the skills of silk spinning or silk weaving seem to have become broadly disseminated among the rural population, as Yang Shen's pastoral vision clearly implied. Instead, government training programs yielded a discrete number of specialized artisan households concentrated in the vicinity of the provincial capital and a few other sericulture centers. Spinning was more dispersed than weaving, but up through the time of Chen's final departure from the province in 1757, the majority of actual textile production seems to have been done in what were effectively government workshops. The establishment of these institutions was really the most distinctive feature of Chen Hongmou's sericulture program.

The new Shaanxi Silk Administration (*canzheng*), which Chen announced to the throne in mid-1746, was a piecemeal creation.[110] In 1745 Chen founded a so-called silk-worm bureau (*canju*) in the facilities occupied by the provincial mint (*qianju*) and in-stalled Yang Shen as its director. The following year it was moved to a converted nearby yamen, and in 1755 a larger branch bureau was set up in an old government guesthouse in the commercial suburb outside Xi'an's West Gate. Throughout these years Chen pressed his magistrates to set up workshops (*canguan*) in their districts, and several of these were in fact established, most successfully in Fengxiang and in Sanyuan, a Wei val-ley county just north of Xi'an. Initially, these institutions were designed simply to dis-tribute mulberry seeds and silkworm eggs to prospective cultivators and to provide on-site instruction to local people in all aspects of silk production. Sometime around 1750, however, Chen began to bring in experienced silk weavers from south China to staff them, and the functions changed. First, the *canju* and *canguan* became factories em-ploying wage labor to produce silk yarn and cloth, and, second, they served as clearing houses for local farmers and artisans. Governor Chen pledged to the people of Shaanxi that his workshops would (1) buy all offered mulberry leaves at a fair price from pro-ducers and resell them to local silkworm raisers, (2) buy all offered cocoons from silk-worm raisers and resell to spinners, and (3) buy all offered yarn from local spinners and either put it out to private weaver households or weave it at the workshop itself.

Although Chen's sericulture program in Shaanxi is sometimes depicted as a con-servative attempt to restore "local self-sufficiency" in the face of an expanded interre-gional market,[111] this characterization is only half correct. Import substitution was cer-tainly a major goal, but export markets for this new regional specialty were also welcomed. The output of the centrally managed Shaanxi silk industry was marketed under the trademark toponym "Qin." There was Qin Thread, Qin Yarn, Qin Gauze, Qin Satin, and several grades of Qin Silk. Much of this product was purchased by merchants, either at the Xi'an bureau or in the localities, and marketed without as well as within the province.[112] An additional portion was sent to the court as tribute (*jingong*). Historically, the Shaanxi governor's office was assessed a set annual offering of Qin Thread and Qin Silk, which, during the long era of the provincial silk industry's decline, the governor had in fact been obliged to purchase on the extraregional market through the agency of the provincial mint. During Chen's decade and a half in Shaanxi he was gradually able to achieve a process of import substitution, replacing this externally purchased silk

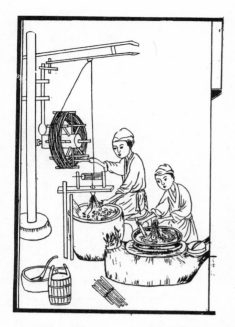 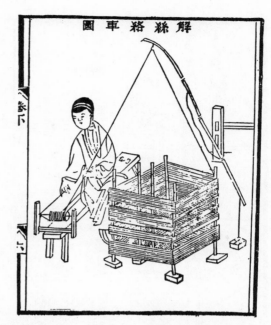

FIGURES 10 AND 11.   Spinning and reeling silk thread in a domestic setting. Source: Yang Shen, *Binfeng guangyi* (original 1741).

with the product of his own Provincial Silk Administration. Although we have no basis for estimating the percentage of Shaanxi's silk output that went to meet fiscal rather than market demand, there is little doubt that the Beijing court's tribute requirement helped significantly to drive the provincial silk industry's growth.[113]

Financing the Provincial Silk Administration—providing salaries for its growing workforce and paying for purchases from producer households—was no easy task. The modest initial operation had been financed by Chen himself, by a contribution of three month's worth of his *yanglian* stipend.[114] Gradually, however, a more routinized source of revenue had to be found. Plots of rent-producing government land were therefore "discovered" in nearby Xianyang and Chang'an Counties, and a disbursal of 750 taels from the provincial treasury was invested at interest with the Xi'an Pawnbrokers' Guild. These sources yielded together an annual income of 118 taels per year, which went to underwrite the silkworm bureau's overhead costs.[115] In addition, the provincial treasury purchased from the bureau the thread and cloth it needed for tribute at a price of eight hundred taels per year. Shortly before he left Shaanxi for the final time in 1757, Chen confronted the growing complaints of his subordinates that these tribute goods could in fact be purchased on the open market for less than this price; he conceded the truth of this but defended the current system as a worthwhile investment in the province's infant silk industry. There will come a time, Chen confidently predicted, when such subsidization will no longer be needed, but for the moment he urged his successors to continue the arrangement.[116]

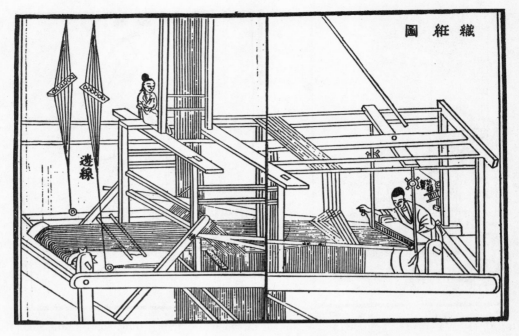

FIGURE 12.   Silk weaving. Source: Yang Shen, *Binfeng guangyi* (original 1741).

Was Chen's confidence warranted? Could Shaanxi in the mid-Qing truly support the viable silk industry it had in antiquity? Surely, the ecological deterioration Chen himself had noted was real; no less fervent an admirer than Yuan Mei acknowledged that more than half of the mulberry trees Chen had planted died almost immediately, in areas where they once seemingly had flourished.[117] The endemic problem of Qing bureaucracy, that of maintaining an initiative in the context of a rapidly rotating corps of officials, also frustrated Chen's Shaanxi efforts even during the era of his repeated tenures there. Returning to the province in the early 1750s, he lamented that the activities of his Provincial Silk Administration had been reduced to nil during his brief absence, a fact he attributed (with his characteristic biases) to ruinous official extraction and to disruption by ongoing military campaigns.[118]

Still, most Qing-era biographers of Chen judged his project to have been a success, and throughout the remainder of the dynasty provincial and local officials continued to follow his (and Yang Shen's) lead in extending sericulture into other parts of Shaanxi. One well-informed economic historian concludes that, for the province's southern portion at least, the latter half of the Qing indeed saw a "notable development" of sericulture, with very substantial exports of both cocoons and raw silk to the interregional markets of Hankou (Hubei) and Nanyang (Henan), as well as a sizable silk weaving industry in Shaanxi's own Han River port of Hanzhong.[119]

Taken as a whole, Chen Hongmou's sericulture campaigns epitomize fairly well his approach to regional economic development. The goal was to mobilize the relatively meager resources of the region and the untapped productive energies of its population—contra Yang Shen's concern with gender-based labor segregation, Chen extolled the virtues of sericulture in part precisely because it could be done by any and all who were otherwise idle, regardless of age or gender. It was an agrarian enterprise that was virtually 100 percent commercialized from the start. Coercion or commandism should play no role in its promotion; rather, the profit motive (*deli*) inherent in rational human nature would ensure its success once the potential for those profits was made evident. Yet this was by no means a process driven by the market alone or even primarily. Chen repeatedly and in the strongest terms chided his laggard magistrates that it was up to them to guide and instruct the people in pursuit of their best economic interests—in the case of sericulture, by introducing new technologies, by offering low-cost capital goods and other forms of government subsidy, by orchestrating the complex multistage production process, and (probably most innovatively) by providing incentive in the form of a guaranteed market for their product. Quixotic Chen's sericulture scheme may have been, but it also represented a remarkably sophisticated vision of how best to achieve economic prosperity.

Mining and Manufacturing

Chen Hongmou clearly differed from many of his contemporaries in the flexibility he displayed in the valorization of agricultural versus nonagricultural work. In a revealing passage by the seventeenth-century writer Wang Zhifu, which Chen inserted into the second edition of his *Sourcebook on Reforming Social Practice*, this question takes center stage.[120] Taking off from the assumption of the need to fully utilize all human assets, the passage begins with a frank acknowledgment that individual human beings differ in both physical and intellectual capacity. The successful society effectively accounts for this in assignment of people's occupations. At the same time that Wang and Chen admit to a view (reminiscent of Maoism) of the special therapeutic value of agricultural labor in molding the moral psyche, they refuse to draw from this the notion that in the ideal society all should work the land. Rather, just as economic policy must tailor itself to the specifics of time and place (*suishi, suidi*), so too must it account for specificities of individual talent. It would be nice if all in this society were to have *some* firsthand experience with agriculture, but this condition can be satisfied by simply being a sympathetic observer, much like Chen himself.[121]

There is no more striking example of Chen's acceptance of nonagricultural labor than his policy toward mining. Throughout his career Chen was among the most tenacious official advocates of private mining ventures. Many of his arguments for this were based, it is true, on the need to find new sources of monetary metals, especially copper, and derived from his concern for the increasingly strained supply of cash in a rapidly commoditizing economy.[122] From time to time, however, he displayed a much broader interest in expanding mineral production, and to this we now turn.

At the time of accession of the Yongzheng emperor, a strict ban on opening of new private mines was in effect, prompted by a range of concerns but most notably by fears for the public security of areas hosting large concentrations of landless (and usually familyless) miners. The second and third quarters of the eighteenth century—the era of Chen's own official career—were marked by a fairly steady stream of petitions from provincial officials requesting permission to recruit commercial entrepreneurs to open new mines in their jurisdictions. These requests were almost invariably met by a chorus of nay-saying on the part of metropolitan officials with little or outdated experience in the field. Imperial decisions on new mine openings gradually swung toward the more liberal positions argued by the provincial bureaucracy, prompting what two Chinese scholars have dubbed the mining "boom" of the mid-Qing.[123] But the process of imperial conversion was not an easy one. The Yongzheng emperor articulated throughout his reign a very hard line against new mine openings (excepting copper mines, whose output was needed to redress the increasingly imbalanced copper:silver exchange rate). In practice, however, he came increasingly to tolerate the existence of other kinds of mines as a fait accompli, and one recent study estimates that as many as 30 percent of all new mine openings in the Qing period came within his reign. The Qianlong emperor gradually assumed a stance more openly congenial to mine openings, and it was in his reign that mining enterprises became a truly significant sector of the empire's overall economy.[124]

Chen Hongmou's most comprehensive, and very likely most influential, contribution to this debate came in a memorial he presented in person to the Qianlong emperor during the course of an imperial audience in early April of 1744. Chen was at the time en route to Shaanxi from Jiangxi, and he took the occasion to lay out both the many problems he had encountered in his recent tenure and systematic proposals for Jiangxi's future governance. Taking advantage of his rare direct access to his emperor's ear, his most urgent recommendation was to promote the opening of mines wherever possible. The previous year, no less august a statesman than Chen's sometime patron, Grand Councilor Zhang Tingyu, had similarly suggested a wholesale opening of mines, not merely for monetary purposes but also to meet the manifest need for other minerals such as coal and to allow the increased manufacture of farm tools and household utensils.[125] Chen went farther still, arguing above all for the positive effect new mine openings would have on popular livelihoods.

Chen's point of departure was the familiar reference to growing population pressure and the consequent need to develop all heavenly endowed resources of the land, however marginal. Espousing first a plan to open previously off-limits mountain areas to small-proprietor cultivation, he then turned for the bulk of his text to the virtues of mining as a panacea for Jiangxi's growing unemployed (*wuye*) population. He cited as his major example the large lead deposits in the vicinity of Yushan County. Chen argued that, there and elsewhere in the province, it would not be necessary to offer government cash advances for mine operation because there was no shortage of wealthy local men (undoubtedly merchants) with entrepreneurial skills who would gladly finance experimental digs in mineral-rich areas. A ready labor supply was also available, so that immigrant labor—the fear of which had defeated many previous mine-development schemes—would not be needed or indeed permitted. Finally, Chen pointed out that Jiangxi, even in the recent dearth, was a reliably grain-surplus province. Hence the problem of importing high-priced grain to feed the miners could be avoided at the same time that this pool of economically secure wage earners would provide a welcome new market for the province's many commercial grain farmers.[126]

Altogether, Chen was proposing a model of regional development that we seldom associate with imperial Chinese economic planning. He was setting out to rectify what might have been seen as a Malthusian problem of food supply and proposing expansion of a non-food-producing sector of the economy—indeed, a program of capitalist industrialization—to help resolve it. He assumed that the commodities so produced could be exchanged for food and that in the process a domestic market for Jiangxi's existing export staple, rice, would be developed. Through the cultivation of systematic links between economic sectors the prosperity of the entire province would be advanced in a stable yet self-perpetuating fashion.

Despite the evident soundness of Chen's knowledge of local conditions and the impressive rigor of his argument, his proposal was rejected on the recommendation of the Board of Revenue for conventional reasons of public security.[127] Nevertheless, his message was heard. Over the next several years, as more and more mines were in fact opened, it was this sort of *yangmin* (nourish the people) argument that was ever more frequently cited in their advocacy. Chen himself argued in 1756 for systematic opening of copper, lead, tin, and other mines in Hunan, receiving the imperial go-ahead that had eluded him in Jiangxi a decade earlier. Hunan's rich mineral deposits, constituting as they did "the wealth of Heaven-and-earth" (*tiancai dibao*), clearly demanded to be exploited "as an aid to the livelihood of poor people." Conventional arguments against private mining enterprise, he added, "are simply no longer tenable."[128] *Yangmin* was, as Chen Hongmou saw, now not merely a matter of stepped-up food production but rather one of multisectoral economic development.

Commercial Development

Given the many virtues that Chen Hongmou ascribed to the market and commercial exchange (*liutong*) as guarantor of food supplies, stabilizer of prices, stimulus to production, and so on, it should hardly be surprising that he also accorded trade an honored place as a source of popular livelihoods and a component of economic development. His view of commerce and agriculture as equivalent avenues of production was highlighted in 1761, when he memorialized successfully for permission to allocate funds for construction of a canal linking the county seat of Changshu, a Yangzi delta district just north of Shanghai, with the sea, explicitly to facilitate commercial traffic. Chen, as we have seen, routinely worked to develop transport infrastructures for commercial purposes, but what is notable about the Changshu case is the way he chose to do it. He proposed to lend money from his provincial capital projects fund (*gongxiang*) to Changshu merchants and their gentry-manager allies for construction purposes, the loan to be repaid over a two-year period as profits from the new venture began to come in, under the statutory provision for lending cash to farmers for clearance of new farmland (*chufu tiandi*). In other words, government loans to merchants and to farmers were explicitly analogized as equally valid forms of investment in economic development.[129]

Commerce was an integral part of Chen's comprehensive schemes for regional economic growth. This was true wherever he served but was never more boldly articulated than during his tenure on the resource-poor northwest frontier in 1755, where he argued for expanded trade as the best path to both regional prosperity and economic and cultural integration with the heartland. Shaanxi and Gansu were in a state of permanent military readiness during these years, serving as staging grounds and logistical bases for Qianlong's successive central Asian adventures: the first Jinchuan campaign of 1747–49, two campaigns against the Dzungar Mongols in 1755 and 1756–57, and simultaneous campaigns against the Muslim insurgents and the Eleuth Mongols from 1758 to 1761. Based on his early experience in the southwest in the mid-1730s and his previous tenures in Shaanxi, Chen Hongmou had by this time come to be known as something of an expert in military logistics, and his third Shaanxi tour of 1754–55 was largely preoccupied with this issue. The crowning achievement of this tenure was a stage system (*zhan*) for delivering supplies expeditiously to the front.[130] That winter, however, Chen submitted a memorial strongly urging that all logistical decisions be taken with an eye toward facilitating the subsequent commercialization of the region, and clearly it was to this end that he was working the whole time. For instance, he argued in favor of issuing rations to soldiers in transit through Shaanxi in cash rather than kind, and inviting grain merchants (*zhaolai puhu*) into the area to supply their food needs, as a means to infuse cash into the regional economy and create a market infrastructure of potential future use for nongrain commodities as well.[131]

Along with this memorial Chen enclosed a "secret communication" (*michen*) that went yet much further and constituted one of the most courageous acts of his long political career. In it he "stupidly yet sincerely" implored imperial reconsideration of the impending military action against the Dzungars. He began with careful tact. Ever since the present emperor has come to the throne, the Dzungars have gradually become civilized and pacified (*xianghua*). They have accepted a tributary relationship and allowed their lands to be surveyed and laid out for bureaucratic administration and sedentary agriculture. They have entered into mutually profitable trade relationships with neighboring Han China. Indeed (and here Chen invokes the language of the Yongzheng emperor's *Dayi juemi lu*), "central and peripheral peoples have come to form a single family." Now, however, the Tibetan chieftain Davatsi has usurped power in the region and thereby challenged the Qing imperium. Unquestionably he deserves punishment, and hence the enormous military buildup Qianlong has assembled in Gansu and Shaanxi is only just and proper. Having said all this, however, Chen then proceeds to plead that the military option not be used. An edict calling on Davatsi to repent, in the face of the manifestly terrifying military force at the ready, will surely bring the upstart to his knees. Perhaps recalling the experience of his native Guangxi during the Sanfan Rebellion of the 1670s, he argues that an actual military campaign "will surely be of no benefit [*feili*] to this area." History shows that the military solution has never brought lasting peace. Instead, Chen argues in an Adam Smithian mode, we ought to devote our energies to strengthening ties of commercial interdependence between Dzungar and Han so as to ensure peace and prosperity for both peoples.[132]

The Qianlong emperor, who Chen must have realized beforehand had his heart set on military adventure, fortunately chose to accept Chen's remonstrance in the tone in which it was offered. His rescript read simply: "This is an honest and forthright expression of opinion on the part of a subordinate. Such an edict as requested was in fact issued long ago."[133] In other words, Chen was indulgently forgiven for voicing his views, which were the product of an incomplete perspective on the situation. The military assault went on as planned.

The following month, January, Chen submitted another memorial restating in a less politically sensitive way his vision of the benefits a concerted policy of regional commercial development would bring to the northwest frontier. Based on his just-completed tour of the inhospitable mountainous prefectures of Yan'an and Yulin in northern Shaanxi, he explained how this barren stretch of territory had been, and could be further, linked economically with the Mongol lands to the north and west and how it might serve as a bridge to the Chinese interior. First, the Ordos region, north of Shaanxi in Mongol territory, was relatively fertile, and for some time now seasonal migrants from Yan'an and Yulin had been coming each year to cultivate grain commercially, as tenants to local Mongol chiefs. Chen recommended imperial encouragement of this peaceful semicolonization by construction of irrigation works and establishment of granaries in the region. Furthermore, the Ordos Mongols mined salt, which they sold to their Han neighbors. Pastoralists, both Mongol and Han, in this area produced hides and wool. All of these regional commodities were exchanged at the booming gateway city of Hancheng for the products of central China, most notably cotton textiles. Chen described how he and other Shaanxi governors such as Huang Tinggui had progressively built up the transport infrastructure around Hancheng to further stimulate this commercial circulation (*liutong*) and thereby enhance popular livelihoods (*minsheng*) throughout the entire northwest. Because of this practice of "mutually supporting each other's livelihoods," the various peoples of the region now lived in peace and harmony, and the avowed Qing program of "Barbarian and Han forming a single body" (*Yi Han yiti*) had become a reality.[134]

In April of the following year Chen was transferred closer to the front, to the Gansu governorship, an ironic posting for a man who had so recently expressed his pacifist views. Yet during his four months in Gansu—one of the briefest but busiest tenures of Chen's career—Chen labored indefatigably to build up the province's logistical system in anticipation of the frontier wars he now knew to be inevitable.[135] And in fact his efforts were rewarded in ways he would have approved: It was precisely the central Asian incursions of the late 1750s that, through the transport improvements and monetization they bequeathed the province, precipitated a landmark advance in Gansu's level of commercialization and integration into the Qing interregional market.[136]

On his departure from Gansu in late summer of 1755, Chen submitted a final, comprehensive memorial on the direction he sought for policy in the northwest. He discussed privatization of the Gansu tea and horse administration (see Chapter 6), conversion of military commanderies (*wei*) into units of civilian governance (*ting*), and settlement of Central Asian Muslims. Most urgently, however, he called for solicitous development of market structures and trade relations between those within and without the passes, between center and periphery. Claiming to reflect the spirit of local "public opinion," Chen wrote as follows:

The Dzungar territory presents a demand for many products of the interior. Commodities such as tea, ready-made clothing, and cotton and silk textiles are hard to obtain. In the past, trade has been effectively restricted to goods carried by the triennial tribute missions. But since these are given over to the disposition of indigenous leaders, who keep a major share of the profits for themselves, the benefits [*li*] of trade for the general population have been limited. Now that these areas have become an internal part of the empire [*neifu*] and their people direct Imperial subjects, their access to the goods they need should increase, as a manifestation of Imperial grace toward the outer territories [*waifan*]. The frequency of trade missions ought to increase to one or two per year, and there is no further need for official management [*bubi guan wei jingli*]. Merchants from near and far will bring commodities for trade, as the demand appears. It is also unnecessary in the future to limit trade to specified sites inside the Wall. I note that there are already many prosperous merchants in the areas outside it. I propose a system of border customs stations, where Chinese merchants will simply have their goods inspected for contraband, pay customs duties, and be issued patents authorizing them to trade at markets outside the pass, such as Hami, Anxi, and so on.[137]

The Qianlong emperor forwarded this memorial to the Grand Council for deliberation, and its major provisions were generally approved.[138] In his brief tenure on the Central Asian frontier Chen Hongmou had, with considerable success, provided the court with a program of expansionist intercultural linkage and regional economic development, based primarily on intensification and privatization of commercial activity.[139]

Three years later Chen found himself on another frontier, a maritime one, as governor-general at Guangzhou. It was in this tenure, in May of 1758, that he issued his most significant pronouncement on Sino-European trade, and it is a telling one. The trade in the late 1750s was beginning to grow rapidly and to experience various tensions associated with that growth. In 1757, in response to foreign experiments with expanding the trade to Ningbo, the court took the step (highly unpopular with Western merchants) of effectively limiting Western commerce to Canton. Local antiforeignism in the Canton area—taunting and rock throwing, in particular—was also becoming a serious problem, as were incidents of brawling by drunken foreign sailors. These had led to the gradual imposition by local Chinese authorities of greater constraints on the personal freedom of action of visiting foreigners. British and French supercargoes protested these constraints to Chen's successor as viceroy in December of 1758 but were met with a curt rebuff.[140] In this atmosphere of mounting hostility Chen's brief tenure as Canton viceroy between April and July must have seemed a welcome pause. Chen's May directive, addressed to his provincial and local subordinates in an effort to preclude violent incidents, says not a thing about restraining foreign movements or about the resented personal responsibility of Chinese "security merchants" for the personal actions of their Western trading partners. Instead, it orders local people to *allow* foreigners comfortable freedom of movement; imposes criminal penalties on Chinese who insult, rob or defraud, or otherwise "harass" (*raolei*) foreigners; and prescribes methods of reporting to civil authority instances of foreigners who themselves misbehave.[141]

Why such a solicitous attitude? It is noteworthy that there is not a hint in Chen's text of the kind of "tribute mentality," viewing commerce as an economically insignificant but ritually important device for barbarian management, that is conventionally alleged to have governed Chinese approaches to Western trade in these years.[142] The parties involved are "our country" (*guojia*) and the "two countries" (*liang-guo*) of Britain and France, rhetorically at least placed on a footing of coequality. And the reasons for the western trade identified in Chen's directive are simply two: that it is important for the livelihoods (*guansheng*) of local people and that commercial exchange (*liutong huowu*) with distant foreigners is valuable in itself. Note especially that this is not a trade that brings in needed foodstuffs, the principal motive for Chen's earlier campaign to promote the Southeast Asian trade, as we have seen; the Canton trade in these years is predominantly an exchange of tea for specie and textiles.[143] Notwithstanding, it is for Chen manifestly a good thing.

Nor was Chen Hongmou unique in these sentiments. As early as the 1720s the outspoken local official Lan Dingyuan (1680–1733) had argued that unimpeded overseas commerce (*waitong huocai*) was "profitable for both the state and the people" (*liguo limin*). Lan's argument was not founded on concerns of minimal provisioning; indeed, he was explicit that even if the items of trade appeared of insignificant inherent value, the very fact that parties on either side were willing to exchange for what they lacked (*tongji youwu*) could prove an economic stimulus of genuine utility and ought therefore to be nurtured.[144] It seems clear that Chen Hongmou believed similarly, as did a growing number of officials with coastal experience. Toward the end of his life in 1768, now with the stature of grand secretary, Chen went so far as to propose the creation of a coastal navy, specifically to provide protection from pirates for this increasingly "precious" (*guizhong*) transoceanic trade.[145]

We have seen in this chapter that Chen Hongmou both articulated and implemented a wide-ranging yet coherent set of strategies that envisioned considerable activism on the part of the state in the interests of enhanced multisectoral economic production, while at the same time eschewing any commandist or extractive actions that might inhibit productivity. In the chapter to follow we will see how he applied a similarly careful balance between state initiative and market stimulus to the goal of progressive accumulation of the wealth so produced.

CHAPTER 8

Accumulation

MOST EIGHTEENTH-CENTURY QING ADMINISTRATORS took as their economic goal not merely the subsistence and reproduction of the population, although certainly this was a basic priority, but also the progressive generation of wealth.[1] Perhaps even more fervently than many of his colleagues, Chen Hongmou believed that society's efficient production could produce a surplus, which in turn might be invested in such a way as to yield steady, continual capital growth (*yuanyuan shengxi*). It was this possibility of growth-producing investment that provided the economic (apart from the moral) rationale for his persistent admonitions to frugality and savings. In an economy that was still pervasively agrarian, the most ubiquitous form wealth might take was grain, and hence the most basic vehicle Chen envisioned for the accumulation of social wealth was the granary.

Many varieties of state, quasi-state, and private granaries coexisted in the Qing period. Chen Hongmou dealt throughout his career with most of these (for example, military granaries and fiscal granaries attached to his gubernatorial office),[2] but his systematic policy making concentrated on two specific types: the *changping cang* (often translated "ever-normal granary") and the *shecang* (community granary), both of which were directly concerned with aspects of provisioning the population. Pierre-Étienne Will, R. Bin Wong, and their colleagues have given us an exhaustive and authoritative study of the former institution,[3] so in this chapter we will concentrate more narrowly on Chen Hongmou's own important interpretation of *changping cang* policy, highlighting areas where his views may have been innovative or out of the mainstream. Then we will turn to the community granary, an institution that became one of Chen's own special fixations and of which he was in his day arguably the empire's most celebrated champion.

Before beginning, however, we should consider briefly the language used by Chen and his contemporaries to justify their interest in granaries. Qing discourse on political economy contained two highly pregnant phrases that, largely through imperial usage, had acquired both great currency and authority. They were unambiguously positive and hence available to describe nearly any proposed policy in terms that conveyed a patent of legitimacy and urgency on that proposal. Although the general meaning of these phrases was consensually understood, their exact range of implications remained flexible and open to contest by officials of differing economic persuasions. In extreme cases, as we shall see, they might be creatively invoked by participants in the Qing discourse community to justify unlikely or even mutually contradictory administrative programs. The two phrases were "*yimin yangmin*" (use/allow the people to nourish themselves) and "*cang fu yumin*" (store wealth among the people).

We have seen earlier the stated preference of Chen and others for *yimin yangmin*; allowing the people to rely on their own initiative and productive capacity is far better, Chen argues, than having them routinely entrust their subsistence needs to the state (*yiguan yangmin*). The latter system is inadvisable because a state capable of feeding a population the size of the Qing's is simply infeasible—it cannot be adequate to the task (*li suo buji*). Without a consistent policy of *yimin yangmin* in place, the meager resources of the state would be steadily eroded and along with them its power and legitimacy. The most basic way of allowing the people to be self-supporting, Chen argues in a memorial of 1742, is to refrain from oppressive taxation, and in practice this was a policy he pursued throughout his career.[4] In a sense, then, the inadequacy of state resources as a routine source of popular provisioning is a self-fulfilling prophecy.

But a credo of *yimin yangmin* by no means necessarily suggests state passivity; indeed, it is worth noting that even as a linguistic construction its implied subject is "the state," which "uses" (*yi*) the people as its agent in the enterprise of popular provisioning. For an activist sort such as Chen Hongmou, this opens all kinds of doors. On more than one occasion Chen voices the hackneyed argument that *yimin yangmin* is preferable to *yiguan yangmin*, only to follow it directly by a yet stronger argument that the best way to ensure the people's ability to provide for themselves is by the particular project of massive state investment he has in mind at the moment, say, the creation of a new hydraulic infrastructure or a new network of granaries.[5] In a situation of population growth, long-term increases in productive capacity must be taken into account, and the state is uniquely situated to do this. In such instances, Chen is clearly pushing the referential limits of the "*yimin yangmin*" idiom, deploying it to push precisely those interventionist policies that, in more conventional usage, it would seem to counsel against.

Something similar goes on with "storing wealth among the people" (*cang fu yumin*), an even more potent rallying cry within early Qianlong-era officialdom, conveying the notion that not merely the people's subsistence production, but also any surplus they manage to produce, ought to be left to accumulate among "the people" themselves.[6] As with "*yimin yangmin*," the phrase "*cang fu yumin*" implied, and argued against, an alternative in which the state (*guan*) would store or accumulate this surplus. Clearly implied in this idiom, at least as invoked by many, was that government ought as much as possible to keep its hands off private wealth.

Chen Hongmou was very fond of this usage, instinctively recognizing its powerful appeal. For example, when Shaanxi was coming out of its extended drought of the mid-1740s and had experienced two successive years of good harvest, Chen pointed to the imperial decision to forgo collection of tax arrears as an instance of the throne's benev-

olent *cang fu yumin* approach, seizing the occasion to launch a province-wide campaign
for frugality, savings, and a concerted buildup of granary reserves.[7] Elsewhere, though,
he used the idiom for very different purposes, to bolster productivity rather than mere
savings, and to justify greater rather than lesser government spending. Large-scale government investment in hydraulic works construction can be seen as "storing wealth
among the people," he claims, because it both maximizes the resources of the land
and, by reducing the demand for corvée, allows the people's labor capacity to be con-
served for purposes of direct production.[8] As early as 1739, while serving as Tianjin circuit intendant, he lobbies for massive imperial spending on river control installations,
defending such outlays on the grounds that reduced flooding will ensure larger future
harvests and hence demonstrate the throne's commitment to "storing wealth among
the people."[9] In such cases Chen is clearly using the idiom in ways directly counter to
its commonsense understanding as a rationale for minimalist government.

Yet in other cases the idiom was useful to Chen in promoting the various privatization initiatives he championed throughout his career. One of his most novel uses of it
came in his campaign for the expansion of private mining. Memorializing in 1740, he
argued that dropping all restrictions on new mining enterprises in the southwest, granting entrepreneurs free disposition rights for the mines' output, and raising government procurement prices for monetary copper would all stimulate popular productivity and thus represent no less than "storing wealth among the people."[10] We will see
further instances of Chen's creative manipulation of this idiom in our discussion of
granaries.

State Granaries

"Storing grain for the feeding of its people is the state's number one priority [*guojia diyi
yaowu*]," wrote the Qianlong emperor in 1738.[11] A decade later, as the emperor himself
was beginning to have second thoughts, his long-serving provincial governor Chen
Hongmou continued to insist, "Only when granaries are well stocked may the people
be spared the grief of unbearably high grain prices," and, "There is nothing an official
does that is of more direct importance to the people's well-being" than keeping ample
grain reserves on hand.[12] Chen's two imperial masters, the Yongzheng and Qianlong
emperors, were among the most ardent enthusiasts of state granary systems of any in
Chinese history, but neither could match the zeal of Chen himself when it came to
building up, maintaining, and making active use of government grain reserves for purposes of provisioning the population and stockpiling wealth.

The so-called ever-normal granaries (*changping cang* [hereafter ENG]), grain reserves held at the local government level specifically as an aid to popular food supply—
separate that is, from the fiscal system and grain stored to meet the government's own
various expenses—were a venerable institution in imperial history and had been a
prominent feature of Ming economic administration. But their use under the Qing,
and especially in the eighteenth century, differed dramatically from anything that had
gone before, both in the degree of coordination exercised at the central level and also
in the system's ambitious scope. As Will and Wong conclude, the Qing system was

unique in that it sought to address small fluctuations in local supply as well as large ones, to remedy not merely major crises of dearth but also to guarantee the availability of sufficient quantities of staple grains, at affordable prices, on a routine basis in every locality in the empire.[13] ENGs were first ordered established by the Shunzhi emperor in 1655, and twenty-five years later the Kangxi emperor commanded that they be set up in every county of the realm. Nevertheless, most scholars agree that it was really only with the systematic establishment of aggregate reserve quotas for each province, the institution of strict annual reporting requirements, and the tightening of procedural regulations under the Yongzheng emperor in the late 1720s that the Qing really began to demonstrate its seriousness about granary management.[14]

The goal of Qing ENG policy was "price stabilization" (*pingjia*) —no less than the routine control of grain price variation over both space (surplus versus deficit regions, producer versus consumer localities) and time (the annual agricultural cycle, years of good and bad harvest). In the opinion of most scholars of mid-Qing price history the system succeeded in this pursuit to a truly remarkable extent.[15] The major instrument for achieving price stabilization was the so-called *pingtiao* system, which influenced the quantity of grain on the local market by purchasing for the granary at the postharvest low price and reselling this grain on the same market during the spring and summer, when supplies were at their lowest. Generally speaking, of course, the major goal was to ameliorate excessively *high* prices, but keeping prices high enough in the postharvest glut to make commercial grain production a profitable enterprise was also a consideration, one that Chen Hongmou himself took especially to heart.[16]

There were at least two other purposes to which grain stored in state civilian granaries might be put, however: loans to cultivators for seed and outright grants of relief during times of dearth. The former was not originally the intent of the ENG system, but its stocks were increasingly devoted to this purpose in practice. In his own provincial administrations Chen Hongmou tolerated such loans, but as we shall see, he much preferred that this task be reserved for the alternative "community granary" system.[17] As for grants of direct relief, such grants had been authorized by the ENG system's imperial founders as a legitimate, although secondary, purpose, and to this extent ENGs were, as Will and Wong contend, designed at least in part as a mechanism for the systematic redistribution of wealth. A 1660 edict of the Shunzhi emperor, for example, suggests that the profits anticipated from the annual purchase at low market prices and sale at high prices be devoted to dispensing relief to "the poor" (*pinmin*).[18] But as the dynasty wore on, more important sources were found for emergency relief dispensations, notably fiscal reserves and grain mobilized via the grain tribute administration. For his own part, Chen Hongmou preferred to draw on ENG stocks for direct relief only in the direst of emergencies, seeking to preserve the integrity of the system as a price-stabilization mechanism and to devote its profits instead to the steady accumulation of state wealth and economic capacity.[19]

The target constituency for ENG activities was the empire's growing number of non-food producers—on the one hand cash-cropping farmers and on the other urban professionals, shopkeepers, artisans, and laborers, all of whom depended on the market for their daily food needs. This was reflected in the siting of the granaries themselves, which was normally in administrative centers down to the level of county seat (although, characteristically, Chen Hongmou pushed for the establishment of branch ENGs in populous nonadministrative towns as well).[20] At the same time, the granaries were conceived as part of local economic systems, which included both grain producers and grain consumers. The Japanese scholars Yamamoto Susumu and Kuroda Akinobu have separately argued that this conception was essentially the result of a strategic shift in imperial provisioning policy away from one of *caimai,* or achieving price stabilization by buying up grain in areas where it was cheap and reselling in areas of dearth, to one of *cangchu,* or serving the same purpose by buying, storing, and reselling grain in the *same* locality, based on fluctuations in local market price.[21] There had been hints of this cellular approach already in the seventeenth century, as, for example, when the Kangxi emperor in 1680 ordered ENG reserves to be used for direct relief only in their own localities rather than for "assistance to contiguous jurisdictions."[22] But Yamamoto and Kuroda both see the definitive emergence of a locally compartmentalized grain reserve system as a product of the Yongzheng reign, carried over into early Qianlong. Whether or not they are correct, Chen Hongmou emphatically endorsed this approach, and it had a variety of specific consequences, as we shall see below.[23]

Although this localist strategy would seem to imply some sense on the part of policy makers that the grain reserves in question were subject to some special claim by the local society that had produced them, there was never any question but that the ENG system and its resources fell squarely in the realm of state proprietorship and management. Chen himself repeatedly emphasized this fact and worked assiduously to assert more centralized control over its operations. Indeed, there was probably no greater manifestation than the ENG system of the extraordinary activism and massive intervention of the post-Yongzheng Qing state in the day-to-day workings of the economy. Yet the granary system was, equally emphatically, a form of state activism that was designed to work *through* the market itself, with the state using its leverage as a particularly well-endowed market participant to influence the market in what it saw as socially desirable directions.

Throughout his provincial career Chen Hongmou continually strove to combat the inclinations of his local-level subordinates to fall back on commandist methods in their management of ENG affairs, for example by imposing on the local populations annual quotas for purchase from, or sale to, the granary. Popular dealings with government granaries must always be voluntary and market driven, he insisted, for the system to achieve its desired ends.[24] Ever-normal granaries were intended to operate as a remedial supplement to the market, not to override or obviate it. In this spirit both the Qianlong emperor and Governor Chen repeatedly admonished their subordinates not to rely overmuch on set regulatory formulae to govern local granaries but rather to respond freely and flexibly to shifting market conditions in their jurisdictions.[25] A major goal of ENG policy was in fact to make the market itself work better, such as by making private hoarding (withdrawing grain from sale in anticipation of higher profits as supplies diminished) a less attractive option. Kuroda observes that by the very act of intensifying the activity of the grain market in each locality, and by effectively guaranteeing the local convertibility of grain to cash, mid-Qing granary policy contributed mightily to the secular trend of commercializing China's food supply; as Will and Wong intriguingly suggest, rather than a simple collapse of state efficacy, it may well have been the system's very success in stimulating the growth of the interregional grain market that led to its own eclipse in the mid-nineteenth century.[26]

Chen Hongmou, however, was in no hurry to acknowledge this obsolescence in his own day. Eighteenth-century experience had led to a consensus within the bureaucracy that ENGs were more necessary, and hence ought to be more active and better stocked, in certain regions of the empire than in others. Although seeming to accept this consensus in general terms, Chen nearly always managed in each of his postings to find reason in the particular needs of that province for an especially vigorous granary policy. The interregional grain trade called for robust granary reserves in areas of fragile ecology and frequent harvest failure such as northern Shaanxi, in areas of high military presence such as Gansu, and in all areas poorly served because of their remoteness. But also in highly fertile, grain-exporting regions such as Hunan and Taiwan, Chen saw granaries as integral both to meeting unanticipated rises in extraregional need and to helping shield the indigenous population from high grain prices resulting from heavy export demand. The only area in which he served where granaries might be less than crucial was the grain-deficit but extraordinarily commercialized Jiangnan, and even there substantial reserves were advisable in order to smooth out price fluctuations resulting from vicissitudes of external supply. An effective granary apparatus clearly made Chen sleep easier, allowing him to feel in greater control of his province.[27]

Raising the level of grain reserves held in county-level ENGs throughout the empire was a cumulative project of the second quarter of the eighteenth century. Governor Chen was on the leading edge of this trend, in each of his jurisdictions bringing province-wide grain holdings up to quota (usually for the first time), where such quotas existed, and raising levels as he saw fit where they did not.[28] Indeed, it is not difficult to follow Chen's progress around the map of China—Yunnan, Jiangxi, Shaanxi, Hunan, Hubei, Fujian—and correlate this neatly with a quantum increase in granary stocks in each of these provinces. Over this period the throne authorized a succession of methods for initial stocking of county ENGs, and Chen tried them all, claiming in each case to have adapted his strategy to particular local conditions. Granary stocks were acquired by market purchase where that was possible, by disbursements from the provincial treasury or from local official discretionary funds (*gongxiang*) where it was not, or by pressing for "contributions" from officials' *yanglian* stipends or from salt merchant slush funds where neither option was available. In some areas Chen capitalized his ENGs by diversions of grain tribute shipments or military rations, by purchasing portions of bulk interregional shipments transiting his province, or by internal transfer of grain from well-stocked urban ENGs to less-well-stocked ones in peripheral counties. At times he was more creative still, as in Shaanxi in the late 1740s, when he resuscitated a scheme (initially devised by his predecessor Emida) to make cash loans from the provincial treasury to pioneering settlers in northern Yan'an and Yulin Prefectures, the debt to be repaid in grain after the first successful harvest to the newly created ENG in the local area under reclamation.[29]

Chen clearly preferred one method of stocking local granaries over all others, however: soliciting local elite contributions in exchange for grants of gentry degrees—a system known as *juanna* or, more specifically, *juanjian* (contributions made in exchange for the *jiansheng* degree). There has been a tendency in the scholarly literature to view the venality of gentry status as a dysfunctional expedient resorted to initially in high Qing only in financial crises but that became ever more prevalent in the nineteenth century, offering sure evidence of dynastic decline.[30] In fact, the experience of mid-Qing ever-normal granaries belies this impression: The sale of degrees was an integral component of this crucial and highly successful aspect of the empire's political economy throughout the peak era of the dynasty's administrative vigor and fiscal health. Beginning in the final decades of the Kangxi reign, local elite contributions to ENGs were tacitly, then increasingly explicitly, pegged to conferral of *jiansheng* status, and this linkage was granted a statutory basis by the Yongzheng emperor in 1726. In a series of edicts of the late 1730s, the newly enthroned Qianlong emperor made a concerted effort to revive this campaign, curtailing all sales of degrees for purposes other than ENG stocking so as to eliminate competition and simultaneously reducing the price in order to stimulate sales. As he himself wrote in 1738, "My view on this matter has been that, since the number of individuals seeking personal advancement through scholarship has been growing every day, this program would open up additional avenues of upward mobility, even as it relieved the provinces of the burden of buying grain on local markets for the purpose of building up emergency reserves."[31]

One might suspect that a straitlaced *lixue* scholar and vigorous educational reformer such as Chen Hongmou would want no part of such a debasement of gentry status, but in fact nothing would be further from the truth. Like many another neo-Confucian, Chen's view of genuine scholarly achievement was not linked to the measurement of success provided by the civil service examinations (although he did defend the integrity of this system as a mechanism for both personal advancement and bureaucratic recruitment). Nor, contrary to the view of several scholars, was Chen significantly motivated by the defense of privilege accruing to his own class or status group, a defense that might prompt him to favor closing off channels for penetration of this group by upstarts. As it turns out, rather more emphatically than his imperial masters, Chen saw the increased "opportunities for upward mobility" (*jinshen zhi jie*) as a positive virtue of the *juanjian* program—a view perhaps less than surprising when one considers Chen's own relatively humble cultural origins.[32] At the same time, he quite frankly saw *jiansheng* ranks as a kind of currency, a capital resource possessed by the state that it could and should creatively invest in the economic and social well-being of its population.

Throughout his career Chen worked assiduously to stimulate sales of gentry degrees as a means of stocking granaries. As early as 1731, while serving as Jiangnan salt superintendent, he memorialized to eliminate provincially imposed surcharges, which, he believed, inhibited sales, and in subsequent gubernatorial posts he instituted audits of *juanjian* accounts designed especially to root out such impositions on the county level.[33] In dearth-stricken 1743 Jiangxi he requested permission to double the number of degrees sold, a move the throne authorized for one year only. In Jiangxi, as well,

Chen repeatedly sought imperial approval to stimulate sales by lowering the price of a degree; over the Board of Revenue's strong disapproval he ultimately gained permission to offer a 20 percent discount, as well as a rate of exchange between the cash price and contributions in grain that was more favorable to the buyer.[34]

This question, the form in which "contributions" were to be made, as well as where and by whom they were to be received, became increasingly contentious during the 1730s and 1740s as the sales of degrees to stock ENGs became increasingly commonplace. Chen Hongmou was at the heart of the controversy. In the Yongzheng and early Qianlong campaigns to build up granary reserves, the statutory procedure had been for *juanjian* applicants to make their contributions in cash at the Board of Revenue in Beijing, with the board then allocating funds from this general account to individual provinces for the purchase of ENG stocks, the need for which was centrally determined. In late 1737, however, the Qianlong emperor acceded to the request of Shaanxi governor Sun Guoxi that his province, and his province alone, be allowed to sell degrees locally in exchange for direct contributions of grain. Early the next year the emperor broadened this policy, inviting other governors to request the same dispensation for their provinces, again on the basis of need. Many quickly did so.[35]

The unintended result was a highly competitive market in *jiansheng* degrees, with buyers enjoying the option of making their purchase in Beijing, in their home province, or indeed in any other province where they felt the terms were more attractive. For Chen Hongmou, facing a food crisis in Jiangxi in the early 1740s, this situation was intolerable. He needed much higher ENG reserves for leverage in controlling skyrocketing local grain prices, and yet, although there seemed to be no shortage of wealthy men in the province willing and able to purchase degrees, the current high price of grain in Jiangxi disinclined them to buy them locally. Thus, even when grain was most needed in their home province, many Jiangxi *juanjian* candidates opted to buy their degrees in cash at Beijing or, worse, to take their grain holdings out of the province and sell them for cash in some other province—in some cases as far away as Gansu—where they would then buy their degree.[36] One of Chen's responses, as we have seen, was to slash prices of degrees locally; another was to attempt to eliminate his competition.

In late autumn of 1742 Chen memorialized to request that purchase of degrees for cash at the board in Beijing no longer be accepted so as to stimulate contributions in kind in Jiangxi and other provinces affected by the current dearth. The throne responded with an edict suspending such sales for a period of a year. Six months later another edict prohibited provincial-level sales to extraprovincials, thus closing down the interprovincial competition. But even though the Qianlong emperor could sympathize with the difficulties a provincial governor such as Chen was experiencing, his own concerns were slightly different. Gaozong had come to suspect that the accumulation of grain by private individuals aspiring to purchase degrees was in fact withdrawing grain from the market and hence was itself a contributing factor to the current dearth; accordingly, in early 1743 he ordered a moratorium on sales of degrees everywhere.[37] Horrified, Chen sought and received a short-term exemption for Jiangxi on the basis of its compelling need for ENG reserves. He urged his magistrates to take vigorous advantage of this window of opportunity, in which Jiangxi was, for the moment, the only game in town. When the exemption expired at the end of that year, he enlisted the aid of his friend and superior, Liang-Jiang viceroy Yinjishan, to secure an extension.[38]

What we see here is the remarkable steadfastness that Chen Hongmou, this staunch neo-Confucian free-marketeer, displayed in support both of high granary reserves in government hands and of the ready convertibility of wealth—frequently *commercial* wealth, of course—into gentry status. We see as well Chen's belief, at precisely the time he was so vigorously defending interregional grain trade against its local-protectionist opponents, that the ever-normal granary system and the *juanjian* mechanism that supported it ought to be compartmentalized by province, a means by which officials at the provincial and local levels could insulate their constituents, at least in part, from the hazards posed to local food supplies by the demands of an unfettered national market.

Yet Chen's view of *juanjian*'s utility went much farther still. In anticipation of the court's announced plan to curtail all degree sales in the provinces in late 1743, Chen ordered his Jiangxi magistrates to sell as many degrees as they could as quickly as they could. Then, armed with this demonstration of vigorous demand, he requested an imperial audience for the purpose of presenting his case that *juanjian* should be used throughout the empire not only to bring ENG stocks up to assigned provincial quotas but also *as a routine means of restocking each fall*, after the price-stabilizing sell-offs of the spring and summer. That is, massive sales of gentry degrees should be incorporated into the annual cycle of local granary turnover of stock, obviating to a significant extent the need for county governments to make market repurchases after the harvest (*maibu*). Restricting candidacy for purchase of degrees largely to affluent *local* residents, the system Chen envisioned would be one of a quasi-governmental, self-perpetuating process of local self-nurturance: "If grain contributed in exchange for *jiansheng* degrees is used to restock granaries, then the cash payments received for annual spring grain sales may be saved up. There will be no need to spend this on repurchase of grain [in the fall], and still reserves will never fall below quota. Indeed, they will continually increase [*duoduo beizhu*]."[39] Under such an arrangement, Chen argued, the ever-normal granary institution would truly become a vehicle for *yimin yangmin*—using the people to feed the people. In other words, it could be used to achieve systematic local redistribution, from affluent degree purchasers to those on the margin of subsistence, *without* any need for appropriation of private wealth via the fiscal system. At the same time, it would contribute to a steady process of accumulation of resources.

I have not found recorded whether Chen ever did present his proposal to the throne in just this way or, if he did, how it was received. We do know, however, that the *juanjian* system did come to serve in certain provinces as a routinized supplement to market repurchase, just as Chen had hoped it would.[40] Nonetheless, the hesitations that the Qianlong emperor had begun to express in 1742 about degree sales as a means of granary stocking deepened as the social and political problems to which it gave rise became ever more evident in the years to follow. A chorus of reformist criticism, led by the eminent official Sun Jiagan, decried the debasing of educational credentials and of the literati class by the profligate sales of degrees, especially condemning sales to merchants.[41] Chen Hongmou was obviously very far from this position, but even he came to notice some cause for concern. As Hubei governor in 1747 Chen wrote that the vast majority of degree purchasers were either legitimate students frustrated by long years of failure in the impossibly competitive examinations or wealthy local men of good reputation who simply hankered after the personal satisfaction of possessing a degree. There were a handful of others, however, who gave the program a bad name: "These fellows swagger about with all the privileges of local gentry. They use their new status to oppress the people, to foment litigation, to resist paying their taxes, and as cover for running prostitution or other criminal rackets."[42] Chen's solution was hardly to cut back on *juanjian* sales, however, but to conduct local investigations aimed at purging the ranks of previous purchasers of such sordid elements.

Under such conditions—mounting complaints from conservative gentry members, growing evidence of clerical profiteering in the degree-sales administration, and the lingering notion that degree sales in kind were withdrawing grain from local markets where it was needed—the Qianlong emperor dramatically restricted the scope of the program in 1749 and abolished it altogether in 1766.[43] (His fears could only have been confirmed when his temporary relaxation of this ban, in the northwest in the late 1770s, precipitated the largest corruption scandal the Qing had yet seen, that in Gansu in 1781.) But so far as we can tell, Chen Hongmou's own faith in the *juanjian* system as a means of ENG stocking never similarly flagged; late into the 1750s we still find him bucking the tide, pestering the throne to allow him to sell more degrees in order to build up granary stocks where he found them critically needed.[44] In both economic terms (as a means of managing resources) and social terms (as a means of fostering social mobility), it was the kind of program he could live with comfortably.

Levels of Stocking

The court's discomfort with the problem of maintaining ever-normal granary stocks at such a high level reached a critical peak in 1748. As we have seen, the Yongzheng emperor had effected a major shift in imperial provisioning policy, from one of maintaining local reserves largely in cash and purchasing grain when needed to meet conditions of dearth to one of maintaining local reserves in kind. Consequently, between the 1720s and the late 1740s the ENG system had gradually built up an enormous empire-wide holding of nearly fifty million *shi* of grain.[45]

This buildup, however, coincided with increasing imperial concern over the secular rise in grain prices (discussed in Chapter 5). In an edict of 1727 Yongzheng had linked these two issues, suggesting that the best solution to grain price inflation lay in a major *buildup* of ENG reserves, which would provide the government with means both of emergency relief and of leverage to combat uncontrolled price rises via timely sell-offs of grain. In 1738 and 1740 his successor endorsed this logic, ordering even greater increases in local granary stocks.[46] Beginning around 1743, however, Qianlong began to doubt the wisdom of this policy, wondering aloud if the annual need to purchase ever growing quantities of grain on local markets, after the harvest, in order to replenish granary stocks depleted by *pingtiao* sell-offs, defaults on loans, and grants of outright relief might itself be a contributing factor in the steady rise of grain prices.[47] The problem was still in Qianlong's view primarily managerial and could be resolved by a more cautious and market-sensitive approach to restocking on the part of local officials.

But with pressures on food supply mounting as a result of several subpar harvests, Gaozong in midwinter of 1747–48 chose to confront the question directly: Were large local-level government grain reserves in the empire's best interest? He issued a general call for provincial officials to present him with their individual analyses and policy recommendations on the issue of grain price inflation. Why, he wanted to know, when everyone understood that commercial circulation (*shangfan liutong*) had the general effect of lowering prices when they were high, and the level of that circulation had clearly been on the rise, had grain prices shown such unabated inflation over the past several decades? In posing the question he made his own suspicions quite clear. The prolonged price rise was of shorter duration than the steady population growth the empire had seen under the Qing and too long-term to have resulted from even repeated poor harvests. Yet its origins could be dated nearly precisely from the first buildup of granary reserves in the late Kangxi and early Yongzheng reigns.[48]

The responses the throne received nearly all identified an increasingly adverse population:food supply ratio as the fundamental cause of grain price inflation. On the key question, the impact of high granary stocks, there was some predictable geographic divergence. Provincial officials in frontier regions poorly served by the market (including, as we will see, Chen Hongmou in Shaanxi) tended to defend the need for large granary holdings, whereas the vast majority, who served in more commercialized regions, took the emperor's broad hint and conceded that current holdings were too high.[49] These officials included, it should be noted, two men who were normally close to Chen both personally and politically: Yinjishan in the major grain-import region of Jiangnan and Yang Xifu in the major grain-export province, Hunan.[50]

Armed with this near-consensus, and further prompted by grain riots in Zhejiang, Jiangsu, Fujian, and elsewhere during the spring and summer,[51] the emperor in the fall of 1748 ordered the metropolitan province to cut back ever-normal granary holdings to the level of Kangxi or Yongzheng quotas and instructed the grand secretariat to confer with individual governors on the matter of granary reductions in other provinces. He noted, with a zero-sum logic that not all of his officials would have shared, that "If the quantity of grain held by the government (*guan*) is too large, then that held by the people (*min*) must be too small."[52] Ultimately, in late spring of 1749, he ordered reduced provincial quotas across the board, totaling in aggregate nearly 30 percent of current levels.[53]

Most scholars who have studied the 1748–49 ENG quota reduction conclude that the concrete results of the reduction were not especially great. Helped by a series of relatively good harvests empire-wide, the immediate escalation of grain prices eased, but the long-term inflationary trend continued. Actual ENG holdings in the localities, moreover, rarely dropped; in some instances quotas were simply renamed so as to fall under different budgetary lines, and in others actual holdings were so far under quota in any case that quota changes had little effect. Indeed, after midcentury the system's aggregate holdings continued modestly to expand.[54]

And yet many scholars have seen this episode as a crucial turning point in the state's (or at least the court's) approach to managing food supply and the economy more generally. Kishimoto Mio sees it as a key step toward a "noninterventionist" approach; Helen Dunstan identifies it with the ascendance of economic "liberalism"; Wu Jianyong notes its temporal correlation with a more active effort by the state to seek specifically commercial solutions to provisioning problems via the *zhaoshang* (inviting-merchants) technique. Most dramatically of all, Gao Wangling has seen in the 1748–49 retrenchment the abrupt end of an "unfinished experiment" in "big government" in late imperial China.[55] Some of these characterizations may appear too strong, yet as I argued in Chapter 2, the granary cutback does in fact seem linked with other policy shifts of the early Qianlong reign in such areas as land reclamation, the fiscal system, social stratification, and bureaucratic recruitment. Such shifts appear part of a comprehensive redefinition on Gaozong's part of what the empire ought to be and of the government's role within that empire, a role he perceived as much less aggressively dynamic than had his predecessor, Yongzheng.

But regardless of the extent to which the events of 1748–49 may have signaled a sea change in the throne's commitment to state interventionism, they clearly did no such thing for Chen Hongmou. In a rapid series of memorials filed in the wake of the edict ordering reduction of granary holdings to earlier levels, Shaanxi governor Chen mounted a number of arguments why his province ought to be made an exception to the new policy. Granary quotas had never been sharply defined for Shaanxi in the past; holdings were still in fact well below any targets that may have been set; ongoing military campaigns in the northwest demanded an unusually high level of grain reserves on hand; ecological fragility in some areas made agriculturally productive settlement unusually contingent on emergency reserves in government hands; geographic remove from major trade routes made famine relief via market means less feasible in Shaanxi than elsewhere.[56] The emperor acceded to his relentless pleading, in effect committing the throne to a lasting policy of "Shaanxi exceptionalism" in granary matters, and Chen blithely continued the intensive program of building up ENG holdings in the province that he had devised prior to the imperial about-face.[57]

For Chen Hongmou, however, the exceptionality of Shaanxi was not the real issue. Chen's credentials as a promarket, promerchant advocate had been long established and could not at this date be in doubt. Yet at the same time he remained a staunch defender of state economic activism through the medium of granaries, even as those around him began to lose faith. Chen's programmatic response to Qianlong's questionnaire on the causes of grain price inflation was decidedly a minority one and must be seen as rather courageous in light of the broad hints the emperor had given regarding his own views on the matter. The intensifying problem of food supply and food prices in the empire could best be solved, in Chen's view, not by retrenchment but essentially by pursuing even more actively those policies to which the government had been committed ever since the early Yongzheng years. These included land reclamation (with greater controls to ensure reclamation by actual cultivators rather than by entrepreneurial developer-landlords), extension of irrigation systems, *and pointedly as well* a still greater proliferation of local-level granaries and buildup of yet more sub-

262

stantial grain reserves so as to further augment the state's interventionist capacity in local economies.[58]

This position clearly required some dexterous ideological and discursive maneuvering on Chen's part. The rallying cry of the granary-reduction party, one to which no sane Confucian scholar-official could object, was "store wealth among the people" (*cangfu yumin*). As we have already seen, however, this was an idiom to which Chen Hongmou himself was fondly attached. In other policy areas he had shown himself capable of interpreting it in creative and convenient ways—in essence, he could defend any initiative involving state investment in popular productivity as "storing wealth among the people." Government granaries, which the Qianlong emperor and those who had gotten his ear were now inclined to see as a dysfunctional state appropriation of popular wealth, were no exception. Well before the empire-wide debate of 1748, Chen had come to argue for the general principle of keeping granary resources in the local area in which they were produced, allowing him to recast the state granary system as in effect an instrument of *local self-nurturance*. He wrote in 1742:

> Using the grain from a given local area, mobilizing it by means of sales of degrees [*juan-jian*] within that locality itself, and storing it in that locality's own granaries, we can dump it on the market at the appropriate time and then repurchase reserves, again as appropriate. Although such a system is often referred to as "redistributing grain through government means" [*lungu yuguan*], in reality it is none other than "storing wealth among the people" [*cangfu yumin*].[59]

The cherished idiom, then, could be marshaled by Chen to legitimate a continued policy of building up, not reducing, ever-normal granary reserves—a policy, if you will, of Gao Wangling's "big government."

In practice, robust granary reserves are precisely what Chen did seek. Despite the relative practical insignificance that many scholars attach to the throne's cutback of provincial ENG quotas in 1749, there is clear evidence that the Qianlong emperor took his own policy seriously, repeatedly ordering individual field officials to reduce their province's real holdings, or at least to enhance them no further. Just as clearly, Chen for his part continued to lobby (successfully) for permission to bring actual holdings up to quota levels, not only in the presumably "exceptional" Shaanxi but also in Fujian, Hunan, and wherever else he happened to serve.[60]

Annual Repurchase

In the years after midcentury the debate over the impact of government granaries on grain prices shifted ground, from a focus on stocking level quotas to one on the practice of market purchase of grain in the localities for purposes of granary restocking (*maibu*). An annual cycle of selling off grain in the preharvest months (*pingtiao*) and using these same cash proceeds to repurchase a (theoretically) larger quantity of grain in the glutted postharvest market was, of course, precisely the way the ever-normal granary system was supposed to work. It should provide price support for producers in the fall and price relief for consumers in the spring and summer. But the workings of this apparently foolproof scheme turned out, to the surprise of eighteenth-century administrators, to rest on a presumption of *secular* price stability, a condition that was not fulfilled in their own inflationary times. The general question thus arose: Was the need for postharvest *maibu* of granary stocks in itself a principal contributor to grain price inflation, injecting a new, large buyer into the supply-demand equation at precisely the moment each year when local grain markets would otherwise be readjusting downward?

This theoretical problem was inextricably bound up with the more practical one of just how officials in charge of county-level granaries were going to bear the cost of autumn market repurchases, in light of grain prices that, with growing frequency, failed to fall significantly after the autumn harvest, as the system predicted they would. Local officials were hamstrung by two factors. First, their fall purchases were supposed to be financed out of the cash proceeds of earlier grain sales; increasingly, this cash was not enough to repurchase an amount equivalent to that which they had sold off. Second, there were official price guidelines (*dingjia*) to be observed in repurchasing ENG grain, but these guidelines were ever more out of step with actual market prices. Under such conditions, did it still make sense to compel officials to repurchase granary stocks on the same local market in which they had made their sales in the spring and summer— the ENG system's original intent—or might they be authorized to find instead the most favorable local market *outside* their own jurisdiction in which to make their *maibu* purchases?

Requiring magistrates to make their fall repurchases locally, when they had neither the available cash nor the legal authority to pay the price the local grain market commanded, was a transparent invitation for these officials to engage in what became known as *paimai*, imposition of state procurement quotas on local grain producers. This sort of quota system was, as we have had ample opportunity to observe, something Chen Hongmou had fought vigorously in all his provincial postings, in areas from copper mining, to conscription of military bearers, to recruitment of materials and labor for hydraulic works construction. It was also something that nearly all high-level economic planners felt to be directly contrary to the spirit of the purportedly market-driven ENG system. Faced as it seems with little alternative, then, the court adopted a highly ambivalent policy toward *paimai* of ENG grain. It never prohibited procurement quotas outright but consistently condemned utilizing them to coerce the sale of grain to the state at submarket prices (*duanjia* or *lejia*), even when, it must have been clear to all parties, it was precisely this intent that motivated most local officials to impose quotas in the first place![61]

Let us briefly review both the evolving policy of the Qianlong court and the position of Chen himself on the *maibu* question before turning to the sudden explosion of this issue onto the national political scene in 1752. Almost immediately on his accession in 1735, out of expressed concern that submarket requisitioning was harming "the local wealthy" (*fuhu limin*), Qianlong released his field officials from their obligation to repurchase locally after the harvest the same amount of grain they had sold off earlier in the year; instead, they might either postpone a portion of their repurchase to subsequent years (when the price might be lower) or buy grain in "adjacent districts" (*linfu zhouxian*), where lower market prices prevailed. In the first years of his reign he also moved to revise the schedule of prices officials were empowered to pay for grain repurchases into closer alignment with prevailing market realities. In 1742, in the midst of a widespread provisioning crisis, the emperor restated his willingness to allow officials to *zhanxian* (delay repurchases in anticipation of lower prices in subsequent years) and to *tongyong* (avoid locally high prices by buying elsewhere). The following year, in the course of urging greater reliance on sales of *jiansheng* degrees as a more affordable and less disruptive means of granary restocking, Qianlong explicitly identified the obligation to repurchase ENG reserves each fall as a principal cause of grain price inflation. Accordingly, he imposed a temporary ban on granary *maibu* altogether, suggesting that under present conditions the private grain trade (*liutong*) could meet provisioning needs more effectively than could government granaries. As the food crisis abated, the emperor gradually relaxed his ban. In 1744 he reiterated the desirability of revitalizing the by then sorely depleted ENG reserves and considered a flexible approach based on a sensitivity to local prices: "Buy when and where conditions warrant, and abstain from buying when they do not." After several years of good harvest, in 1746 he again emphasized both the general need to restock and the importance of doing so prudently; buy in your own district if you can, his edict stated, but it added that "not all districts' harvests have been equally good, *nor are all districts grain producers on the same scale* [italics added]." The implication of this edict, it seems to me, was the throne's recognition and acceptance of the fact that where market repurchase was taking place, it was increasingly being done not locally but in the closest major center of the inter-regional grain trade.[62]

We have seen that Chen Hongmou liked the idea of relying on local sources of supply to restock local granaries, believing that this made the ENG system accord more closely with the principle of "storing wealth among the people," and encouraging a vision of the government price-stabilization granary as, at least in some sense, a community resource. He was also even more emphatic in his distaste for commandist means of restocking than was the court. And yet he also resisted in a variety of nonconfrontational ways each of Qianlong's moves to curtail market repurchase, countenancing as this did lower granary holdings overall. In dearth-stricken Jiangxi in 1742 Chen pointed out that despite his compliance with the imperially imposed moratorium on *maibu*, prices had continued to rise, and so the link the throne had drawn between granary repurchase and rising prices was, at best, suspect. As soon as the harvest came in, and imperial orders allowed, he directed his local-level subordinates to repurchase ENG grain cautiously but energetically. When the emperor signaled his greater comfort with *maibu* in 1746, Chen (now as Shaanxi governor) immediately launched a vigorous program of rebuilding granary stocks. Even in the wake of Qianlong's empire-wide granary downsizing in 1749, Chen in Shaanxi urged his magistrates where possible to bring their granaries up to the newly assigned quotas through an active program of market purchase. As unsettling as intemperate government buying might be to local grain prices, it would not do to use this as an excuse for neglecting the state's responsibility to take a positive role in the economy via its maintenance of a robust and active granary system.[63]

With the question of quotas resolved for the time being following the cutbacks of 1749, the Qianlong emperor evidently believed it was time to provide a similar resolution to the issue of *maibu*, on which the official record up to that time had reflected his own indecisiveness. Committed as he now was to a leaner ENG system empire-wide, Qianlong seized the opportunity presented by a 1751 memorial from Grand Secretary Gao Bin, asking that *maibu* be universally halted once and for all because of its inflationary effect.[64] Following discussion on the proposal in the Grand Council, the emperor in early autumn of 1752 threw open the question to all provincial officials, ordering them to investigate the likely connection between *maibu* and grain price inflation in their provinces and to suggest appropriate remedies. As he had on the quota question in 1748, however, Qianlong provided broad hints about what the correct answer might be, announcing beforehand that he would feel quite comfortable if empire-wide granary reserves, depleted by repeated annual failure to repurchase stocks in the fall, were to fall to a level of 30 to 40 percent of the quotas he had so recently promulgated. "What good is attempting to plan for future relief needs," he asked, "at the cost of suffering unaffordably high grain prices in the present? . . . If the officials buy less, then there will be more for sale on the market."[65]

One can only guess whether the emperor expected his provincial officials to fall lamely in line behind Gao Bin's proposal as nearly universally as they had behind his own attack on bloated granary reserves four years earlier. If he did, he was disappointed. The governors' responses indicated that they took his calls to local specificity to heart; although all virtually parroted the causal link their sovereign had decreed between *maibu* and inflation, they displayed wide variation in their assessments of just what the effects of a halt to granary repurchases might be. Unsurprisingly, these responses varied geographically, with governors of provinces less well served by the market tending to defend the need for substantial granary holdings, regardless of the inflationary consequences. In the end Qianlong brought the debate to a close not by simply endorsing Gao Bin's request (as may well have been his initial hope) but by turning the practice of allowing prudent market repurchases on a case-by-case basis, a practice that had become imperial policy by default over the past decade, into a programmatic approach to ENG management. Clearly abandoned in the process, however, was any goal of bringing actual granary holdings up to statutory quotas, by *maibu* or any other means.

Writing from his post in Fujian, Chen Hongmou responded by marshaling any and every argument he could to resist the thrust of his imperial master's edict, while remaining within the letter of his instructions. Fujian is a special case, he insisted. There is little grain on the private market; the province produces little itself, and its mountainous borders keep it relatively isolated from interregional exchange. Several areas have recently been devastated by storms and floods. Given this situation, it is to be feared that prohibitions on *maibu* repurchases will disincline local officials from making *pingtiao* sales even when they are desperately needed. Stocking granaries at a mere 30 to 40 percent of quota will provide an inadequate cushion in case of severe dearth. Chen countered the imperial proposal by urging that all Fujian ENGs be allowed to restock to a level of 50 percent of quota with all due haste and only then move to a more cautious *maibu* policy. Gaozong's rescript reads as follows: "The suggestions laid out here all fall within the appropriate parameters defined in my edict."[66] So fortified, Chen went blissfully about his business of hounding magistrates to step up their *maibu* activities—buying quickly (*jishi*) after the harvest and paying an attractively competitive price—throughout the remaining two years of his Fujian tenure.[67]

In the process, however, Chen worked out an arrangement for managing granary repurchases in Fujian that was original and indeed quite remarkable. The situation he encountered was as follows. First, granary reserves throughout the provinces had been depleted, dangerously so in the view of most officials, by the need to conduct continuous sales during the spring and summer of 1752; yet the upcoming harvest was projected to be bountiful. Even so, prevailing grain prices were likely to considerably exceed those authorized by the court for *maibu* purchases. (As Chen explained, the authorized price had been pegged to province-specific commutation rates employed in calculating military pay; in Fujian this would amount to about .45 taels per *shi* of hulled rice, whereas actual postharvest grain prices in the province were likely to range between .6 and .9 taels per *shi*.) Second, Fujian was already distinctive in that, the grain market being relatively poorly developed, long-standing practice was for granary repurchases to be conducted instead by a prepurchase contract system directly with local producers. Finally, Chen's predecessor as governor, Pan Siju, had several years before launched a program of redistribution of granary stocks within the province, shifting reserves to areas evidently in greater need. The program was only half completed on Chen's arrival: Most of the grain to be redistributed had been collected in provincial hands but had yet to be delivered to its intended targets. Roughly 10 percent of this grain, however, had in the interim been diverted to the severely dearth-stricken county of Jiangshan, just across the provincial border in Zhejiang. There it had been disbursed via *pingtiao* sales, with the cash proceeds returned to the Fujian provincial government in payment for the grain.[68]

Faced with this situation, Chen launched in late 1752 a program of bringing all Fujian granaries up to 50 percent of quota (the majority were below this level). Ignoring altogether the antiquated price guidelines, he ordered local officials to compute purchase prices generously, based on market realities. Anticipating that competition to sell to the state would be great, he instructed magistrates to draw up schedules of local grain-holders (significantly, including merchants as well as planters) and to allocate options to sell based on the level of holdings. No coerced procurement at submarket prices was to be tolerated; the purpose of this schedule was not to assign procurement quotas but rather the opposite, to distribute equitably the *opportunity* to sell at a very attractive price.

Then came the kicker. Governor Chen had his provincial treasurer seize the past year's *pingtiao* receipts from all Fujian localities. Combining this with the cash he already held from the sales in Zhejiang, he created a provincially managed fund out of which to finance local-level granary repurchases throughout the province. He would allocate cash for local *maibu*, at locally negotiated prices, based on his own calculation of relative need and cost-effectiveness. To restock granaries where urgent need existed but local prices were unattractively high, Chen still had at his disposal the grain left over from Pan Siju's unfinished redistribution program of 1749. In cases where the local price appeared too high and the need was not quite so urgent, repurchase might be put off until the subsequent year, when prices might recede a bit.

Chen's scheme reconciled his emperor's expressed wishes and Fujian's particular circumstances in his own innovative fashion. It achieved significant and *affordable* granary restocking, in a highly inflationary market, even while paying market rather than officially fixed prices. It adhered in a general way to the principle of repurchasing on the same local market where the grain had been earlier sold (thus maintaining the image that it was simply that locality's own grain being recirculated locally by the state) but sidestepped the corollary (and in practice unworkable) notion that local granaries should repurchase only what could be financed by receipts from that locality's previous sales. In so doing Chen introduced into ENG policy a virtually unprecedented degree of centralized management at the provincial level but without falling back on dirigiste command-economy techniques. That he opted for such centralization might seem odd, considering that Chen so often presented himself as a champion of local specificity and societal self-management, but as subsequent discussions will show, it in fact resonated with not a few of his other managerial innovations.

Chen Hongmou left Fujian in mid-1754, but he continued in his next two duty stations, Shaanxi and Hunan, to resist as diplomatically as possible the throne's clear intent that granary repurchases be severely constrained. He seems also to have brought with him to those two jurisdictions a new willingness, born of his Fujian experience, to centralize ENG management at his own provincial office. Both provinces enjoyed bumper harvests in these years, and Chen saw himself in a situation of *maijian shangnong* (low grain prices hurt the farmer). In Shaanxi he saw massive granary purchases as the means to provide rural price supports and received permission to spend more than one hundred thousand taels out of land tax receipts to conduct province-wide *maibu,* even temporarily bringing many granaries up to levels well above the 1749 quota.[69] In Hunan he used extraprovincial buyers indirectly to serve the same function, to provide emergency demand to relieve temporary bloating of local market supply. He sold off large quantities of ENG grain to outside merchants, dropping stocking levels well below quota, and then systematically repurchased it locally after the expected bumper harvest came in in 1756.[70]

The huge grain repurchase that this entailed in Hunan, a province largely populated by grain planters whose livelihood hinged on the sale of their crop, confronted Chen with enormous problems of equity and potential corruption. This in turn brought once more to the fore the sensitive issue of just *where* market repurchase ought to be conducted. Chen saw the situation as a choice between two potential evils. If one complied with the intended spirit of the ENG system and repurchased grain in the localities themselves (a concept so hallowed in grain-surplus Hunan that it had been inscribed in provincial statute), commercial producers might benefit directly, but the purchase process would necessarily involve yamen underlings, who would likely administer it unfairly and profiteer shamelessly. Moreover, thuggish local magnates (*haojiang zhi hu*) would likely compel their neighbors to sell to them first then resell to the state at a markup. If, on the other hand, one purchased the grain at one of Hunan's several large wholesale rice markets, such as Xiangtan or Yuezhou, one might make the actual purchases using only a few trusted official deputies, but the lion's share of the profits would surely go to the commercial middlemen who had brought the rice to those centers of collection. The solution Chen chose drew quite obviously on his recent experience with central planning in Fujian: a system of quotaed purchase from producer households themselves, with options to sell assigned on the basis of each producer's taxable culti- vated acreage and purchase made at such an attractive price that coercion was likely to play no part in the process. To work according to design, of course, such a program re- quired minute regulation on the part of the provincial center, which the governor was not loathe to provide. Chen Hongmou's urge to centralize control, albeit *indirect* con- trol of a market-governed economy, was never more in evidence.[71]

Disbursals

In contrast to questions of stocking and restocking, the manner of disbursals from ever- normal granaries never became a national issue, nor did it spawn systematic differences of official opinion. Nevertheless, it gave rise to a variety of structural problems, and Chen Hongmou was both active and vocal in the effort to find solutions for these.

The standard formula in use during the eighteenth century was that each local- level ENG should annually retain 70 percent of its holdings and disburse 30 percent (*cunqi chusan*). Most believed that this ratio would accommodate needs for *pingtiao* sales and loans, while maintaining adequate reserves in case of disaster; it would also guarantee turnover of stocks sufficient to guard against spoilage. The 70/30 formula was first initiated on a province-by-province basis in the late Kangxi era, and it gradu- ally became general policy in succeeding reigns. At first the 30 percent figure was as- sumed to represent a hard-and-fast limit on distributions, but gradually, especially in the early Qianlong reign, increasing numbers of exceptions were allowed. In two major edicts on this subject, coinciding with the empire-wide dearths of 1742 and 1749, Qianlong repeated the 70/30 guideline but with the explicit injunction that officials not "stubbornly adhere to precedent" (*juni chengli*) in its implementation. In the 1749 case, of course, the emphasis on flexibility seemed especially called for in light of the fact that the emperor had just reduced the size of granary holdings overall.[72]

Chen Hongmou was a provincial official with an unusually activist conception of the ENG system. Although on occasion he was known to permit disbursals of less than 30 percent of stocks in situations of bumper harvest, far more typically he urged his local officials to keep close tabs on the market price and not hesitate to sell off stocks well beyond this level if conditions warranted.[73] To some extent this was a function of geography—more often than not, Chen found himself in provinces poorly served by the interregional market—but even in the same province, Chen tended to look at the granary system differently than did many of his colleagues. In Hunan, for example, which Chen twice governed, both times his successor deliberately decided to cut back the level of ENG activity that Chen had mandated during his tenure.[74]

Chen fretted about the built-in disincentives the system offered to local officials' disbursing grain to the full extent the law allowed. Apart from the problems of how to restock and, in the case of loans, how to guarantee repayment, there were marginal losses entailed in every act of grain transfer and measurement, losses that would come to light in audits on official succession and that the official would be expected to make good out of his personal stipend. To overcome this disincentive, in a remarkably programmatic memorial he submitted while serving as Jiangsu provincial judge in 1740, Chen proposed both relieving the official of his liability in this regard and instituting a more generous spoilage allowance. The Board of Revenue declined to act on his proposal, and the initiative would remain his alone.[75]

What form were disbursements to take? Although imperial utterances continually stressed the point that 30 percent of holdings should be turned over each year, they were silent on the relative percentage to be circulated in the form of sales and of loans. Chen indicated his own understanding in his 1740 memorial: as much grain as needed was to be sold off, and any remaining could be issued as loans to bring the total up to 30 percent. But in fact practice differed widely from one part of the empire to another, with individual provinces gradually developing systems of local precedent on the matter. For example, Chen found that in Jiangxi and Henan the proportions disbursed as sales and as loans were nearly equivalent, whereas in Shaanxi the vast majority of disbursements came as loans (Chen worked to gradually increase the volume of *pingtiao* sales in this province, while shifting the function of making loans to "community granaries"). In some cases the geographic logic of the disbursal formula was obscure. For example in Fujian, a severely grain-deficient province with few commercial grain planters (except in Taiwan), market sales were the principal form of disbursal of ENG assets, but this was even more exclusively the case in Hunan, the empire's largest commercial grain producer.[76]

Strictly conceived, ENG grain belonged to the state and thus could legitimately be used to meet other government needs. Despite both long-standing formal prohibition and his own ideological predilections, for example, Chen on occasion both sold his own granaries' holdings extraprovincially and imported those of other provinces for sales locally. He also drew on ENG assets when necessary for direct relief.[77] And he used them as capital for more creative financial schemes. Following the poor harvests of 1748–49, for example, Chen commandeered Shaanxi ENG stocks for loans to military agricultural colonies (*tuntian*) to cover their land tax obligations, the proceeds of which in turn were to be applied to rationing the provincial banner detachment; the military colonists would repay the loan out of their next successful harvest.[78]

Observing Chen over the course of successive tenures, we can see him gradually working out a distinctive personal approach to ENG distributions. They were to operate at the peripheries and interstices of the market, never to contravene or eclipse it. Their basic intent was to get the population through the tough times of the year and assure its continued productivity. Determining the proper balance of loans and sales, and the optimal volume of each, required great flexibility on the part of local officials and, above all, great sensitivity to the *minqing*—referring here both to the actual material conditions of the people and to their feelings and desires. Chen presumes that, as rational and (consequently) market-sensitive creatures, the people through their economic behavior offer the official the most accurate barometer of market conditions and needs.[79] *Pingtiao* and loan policies must be systematically integrated and synchronized; Chen condemned, for example, the blindness of magistrates who conducted the two simultaneously, pointing out that this practice only led to their working at cross purposes—lowering the market price via granary sales at the same time that cultivators were seeking loans of seed grain would encourage purchases by merchant speculators, who would then pull it off the market to await higher prices and in the process make seed grain scarcer and more expensive.[80]

As he did in nearly all other matters—economic, administrative, ritual, domestic— Chen laid great stress in his formulation of *pingtiao* policy on proper timing (*jishi*). Synchronizing grain sales and loans was just one aspect of this concern. Officials must seize the proper moment to sell. If they wait too long, needy people will turn instead to private usurers, an eventuality the ENG system was basically designed to prevent; if they act too soon, they run the risk of depleting their reserves before the need expires. The moment to begin sales, like that to switch from sales to repurchases, can only be determined locally. But it may be locally predictable from year to year, and in some jurisdictions Chen attempts to model a provincial ecology of grain supply, factoring in local harvest dates and estimated annual arrivals of grain shipments from outside, to work out a rough schedule of just when each area within the province ought to begin and end its *pingtiao* and *maibu* operations.[81] This can only be rough, however. With all his emphasis on central planning Chen insists that overbureaucratization is more to be feared than its opposite; it curtails the creative freedom of action (*chezhou*) that an official on the scene must exercise.[82] This is especially true in that, although local grain prices provide a handy objective index of when to time grain sales, the more basic and reliable signal can only be provided by the local public mood, the *minqing*.[83]

Along with timing Chen gave considerable thought to the matter of pricing *pingtiao* sales. Central directives on this question offered field officials significant leeway. An edict of 1690 had stipulated that sales in the third and fourth lunar month be at the prevailing market price and those in the fifth month and thereafter at a fixed, submarket price.[84] By the early Qianlong reign, however, virtually all granary sales were conducted at the off-price. Imperial guidelines suggested a discount of .05 tael per *shi* below market price in normal years and double that in years of dearth, but Chen's correspondence implies that in practice discounts were usually even greater. At the height of the food crisis of 1742 the throne rescinded these guidelines altogether, allowing local officials to sell at whatever discount the food needs of their locality demanded.[85]

For both Chen and the throne the trick was to drive local prices down without in the process providing speculators the chance to buy in low and resell high, either elsewhere, where higher prices prevailed, or in the same locality once *pingtiao* sales ended. As Chen expressed it, pricing sales too low in practice drove grain off the market, into the hands of speculators, precisely contrary to the intent of such sales, which was to increase market supply. Even more serious in his view was the danger that by driving local prices *too* far down, in this essentially artificial manner, the official would discourage the natural remedy of the market for anomalously high local prices, commercial imports.[86] This possibility made Chen skeptical of the virtues of discount pricing altogether. The optimal policy, as he saw it, would be to sell ENG grain precisely *at* the market price, driving the price down "naturally" through market mechanisms themselves, by the simple expedient of increasing market supply. He conceded, however, that the severity of dearth did not always permit this leisurely approach, and he did not usually demand it of his local subordinates in practice. What he did demand was that they take into account "long-term policy" (*changce*), specifically that they be sufficiently familiar with their district's price history, both secular trends and annual cyclical deviations, so that they could compare actually prevailing prices with what the price *ought* to be at this moment in time. This knowledge would enable them to determine intelligently both the price and the proper timing of their ENG sales.[87]

On the matter of ENG disbursals in the form of loans, Chen fretted most about the selection of proper recipients. In the commonplace idiom shared by both Qing administrators and their rural constituents the purpose of such loans was to address situations of *qinghuang bujie*—the green (shoots of the new crop) does not arrive before the brown (grain left over from the previous harvest) is exhausted. In other words, loans were intended to ensure the survivability of the rural producer through straitened times. Chen was adamant in all his provincial tenures that the proper recipients of loans (as opposed to sales) from both ever-normal and community granaries were farmers and farmers only. In dearth-stricken Henan in 1752, for instance, he launched simultaneous programs of granary loans for cultivators and work relief on city walls for noncultivators, explicitly presented as complementary remedies to tide over discrete occupational groups.[88] The pool of appropriate borrowers, in Chen's view, was quite narrowly defined: they must not only be active farmers but must also possess sufficient land so that they can be expected to use their loan for agrarian purposes, and, at the same time, they must be sufficiently poor to demonstrate real need. Loans to wealthy landowners perverted the system's intent; the only reason they would borrow at interest when they already had ample grain reserves on hand was for speculative purposes. Loans to the landless likewise failed to serve the purpose of aiding farm production, as well as increasing the likelihood of default on repayment.[89]

Farmers were expected to use granary loans essentially for seed grain and for food. In certain instances along the extensive margin of agriculture, Chen also authorized ENG loans for purposes of land clearance, irrigation-works construction, and other capital investment projects.[90] He could also use them quite flexibly to respond to emergency circumstances. When the spring rains in Shaanxi in 1745 came very late, after most farmers had given up hope for that year's harvest, Chen immediately ordered a major loan campaign to encourage last-minute planting.[91] In fact it was just such crisis situations, and not routine credit provision, for which ENG loans were most appropriate. ENGs were, after all, located almost exclusively in urban centers, and the principal targets of their activity were nonfarming grain consumers. They could really only be expected to provide loans effectively to those farmers living in the city's suburban greenbelt. For the purposes of offering routine credit to the vast majority of rural producers, it was another institution, the community granary, that Chen believed most suitable, as we shall see shortly.

Defaults on ENG loans were routine and a major obstacle to maintaining the levels of reserves that Chen thought adequate. All too frequently loans in default were simply carried on the books as repaid, providing a false sense of security in the level of granary stocks. On moving into a new provincial jurisdiction, Chen usually moved quickly to conduct an audit of outstanding loans from all local granaries and to begin a campaign to prompt for repayment. He ordered magistrates to compile detailed registers of all loans in default and to work out for each borrower a feasible schedule for repayment. Those who showed steady progress in reducing their debt might be exempted from Chen's basic policy that defaulters were ineligible for any further loans.[92]

Characteristically, one of the recurring dysfunctions in granary lending that most annoyed Chen was compulsory loans (*qiangjie*) or "loans assigned by quota" (*paijie*). These tended to occur when a local official found no other way to bring his granary up to a full 30 percent annual turnover rate and regularly ended up in default by the unwilling borrower. In some provinces, such as Shaanxi, magistrates customarily allocated given percentages of their granary's total loans on a per-village or township basis (*anli*). Chen permitted this practice, reluctantly, only if it was demonstrated that no compulsion was being applied to accept the allocated grain and that no subcontracting of loans was going on. Subcontracting (*baojie*), usually to a township political boss (*lizhang* or *xiangbao*), invited corruption. It was common, for example, for the contractor to simply assign portions of his loan package to each household in his jurisdiction and to assess interest payments whether or not the "borrowing" household actually claimed this grain. Those who had no need for a loan, or those who lived at too great a distance from the granary to make a loan cost-efficient, found themselves forced to bribe the boss to reassign their share to another household; those who desired a greater share of the loan than had been assigned them similarly were required to make a kickback. In extreme cases syndicates of township bosses, yamen clerks, and "evil gentry and local bullies" (*liejin haogun*) were set up to monopolize the entire amount of grain a county ENG had to lend and to resell portions of this blanket loan to needy households at a considerably higher rate of interest. One especially nefarious variant of this practice involved deliberate assignment of a loan share to a household that the contractor knew to be unable to repay—for example, the landless—and then when the anticipated default occurred offering to cover it by means of a secondary personal loan, thereby creating a self-perpetuating relationship of debt-peonage. Most injurious to the granary system itself was the racket known as "subcontracting engrossment" (*baoqin*), whereby a loan underwriter simply pocketed a portion of the loan he had received, ultimately claiming it to have been lost by default of the household (often a fictitious one) to which it had been reloaned.[93]

Chen moved to correct these abuses in a number of ways. He explicitly criminalized them. However much he desired that the assets of the ENG system be put to maximal use, he counseled his magistrates that achievement of a full 30 percent rate of annual turnover was not worth the cost of making ill-considered or "superfluous" loans (*lanjie*). He suggested setting up state-run loan depots at remote spots in the countryside to squeeze the need for subcontracting out of the system (shifting reliance to the alternative community granary system, of course, would be a still better option). Above all, he urged his subordinates again to pay close heed to the *minqing*—to popular input—as the best means of discerning when, where, and by whom granary loans were truly desired and would genuinely be put to productive use.[94]

Responsive as they must be to the popular pulse, ever-normal granaries were unambiguously a state institution. Within the state apparatus tension remained over the

proper level at which control ought to be exercised. This was true even at the intralocal level; in 1748 Shaanxi, for instance, Chen was forced to wrestle with the question of
which ENG assets ought to be managed personally by the county magistrate and which
should rest at the disposal of the magistrate's superior, the prefect.[95] The central government, too, wanted its share of control. Although the Qianlong emperor repeatedly
stressed his desire for independence and flexibility on the part of the immediate local
official, he did institute a system of fairly detailed reporting to the throne of the minutiae of local ENG accounts. For our purposes, however, the more interesting tension is
that within Governor Chen Hongmou himself, a staunch advocate of local official independence in granary management who nevertheless worked in practice fairly consistently to centralize control in his own provincial-level office.

In ENG matters as in nearly all others Chen vigorously championed bureaucratic
standardization—standardization of weights and measures, of procedures, of facilities
maintenance, and of reporting. In each province he governed he distributed standardized account books (*ceshi*) of his own design for his subordinates to use in recording all ENG transactions and to submit to him for routine review.[96] Often enough he
went well beyond this, seizing direct control of ENG operations throughout his
province, as we have seen, for matters of granary stocking, distributions, or interlocal
redistribution of holdings. At times he did this in an overt effort to enhance the system's potential for profit-making investment. For example, as Fujian governor in 1753
he commandeered some sixty thousand *shi* of rice from granaries in Taiwan for *pingtiao*
sales across the straits in mainland Quanzhou and Changzhou Prefectures, where
prices were much higher; returning the same amount to Taiwan after the harvest, he
still had a handsome cash surplus remaining for use in raising the level of stocking of
granaries on the mainland.[97]

Centralizing control of ENG operations at his own gubernatorial level above all allowed Chen to do what he most wanted to do with the system: to use it as but one arm
of a broad-ranging program of regional economic management. We have already seen,
for example, how Chen sought to integrate granary operations with such things as
work-relief programs and military rationing schemes. He also linked them to provincial
monetary policy, as for instance when he ordered Fujian magistrates to immediately re-
convert their *pingtiao* cash receipts to silver at government-run money shops (*pu*) to reinfuse this copper cash supply into the provincial economy and so fuel commercial exchange.[98] In a moment we shall see how Chen systematically tied ENG operations to
those of his pet project, community granaries. Altogether, in hands such as his regional
economic policy could be a highly comprehensive and effective instrument.

Community Granaries

If Chen Hongmou was an active contributor to the process of working out both the
theory and practice of Qing ever-normal granaries, he was far more so when it came to
the ENG's counterpart institution, the community granary. In the mid-eighteenth century Chen effectively made this institution his own. The community granary, at least
under the title "*shecang*," which it generally bore during the Qing, was an innovation of

the Southern Song. It was then and ever after closely identified with that era's corps of neo-Confucian scholar-officials such as Zhen Dexiu and Dong Wei (both of whom were important influences on Chen Hongmou, as we have seen) and above all the master Zhu Xi himself.[99] It was no accident that the leading champions of the institution during the Qing's first century were the highly placed Zhu Xi partisans, Board of Revenue president Zhang Boxing and Zhili governor Li Guangdi; it was in Li's Zhili that the first systematic Qing *shecang* foundings occurred in the early eighteenth century.[100] Chen Hongmou, too, justified his earliest advocacy of *shecang* to the throne by reference to Zhu Xi's *Shecang yifa* (Inherited procedures for community granaries), and he discussed Zhu's ideas on the subject at some length in his own scholarly writings.[101]

But if eighteenth-century *shecang* had an acknowledged Zhu Xi pedigree, they owed probably more in practice to a very different kind of person, the Yongzheng emperor. Ming predecessor institutions had long since disappeared, and seventeenth-century Qing experiments with community granaries had gone nowhere.[102] Later dynastic sources identify the birth of the Qing *shecang* movement with a 1703 edict of the Kangxi emperor, ordering their establishment at the village or village-federation level, but, as Feng Erkang has pointed out, Kangxi himself was actually rather resistant to the urgings of his ministers (such as Zhang and Li), and genuine foundings during his reign were seemingly limited to a few provincial pilot projects.

Yongzheng showed no such hesitation. In a landmark edict of 1724 he not only ordered a cleanup of abuses arising from the haphazard way the system had been run under Kangxi but also demanded in an unambiguously serious way their establishment in all localities, in the process setting out both the concerns and the terms of discourse that would govern the institution for decades to come.[103] In edicts and rescripts issued throughout the remainder of his reign the emperor often reiterated his support for this institution and authorized growing amounts of state expenditure on its creation. Very likely to his successor's chagrin, provincial champions of *shecang* such as Chen Hongmou continually invoked this Yongzheng language in their advocacy of community granaries before the Qianlong throne.[104]

Although we have seen Qianlong himself anxiously pondering the operation of the ever-normal granary system, he seems to have been remarkably indifferent to the question of community granaries during his reign. I have not seen any significant central policy directive issued by him on this subject, and his rescripts on Chen's enthusiastic memorials on *shecang* matters reveal nothing so much as boredom. Given this imperial apathy, it may be, as one scholar has argued, that many if not most of the Yongzheng-era community granaries either lapsed or were absorbed into the state ENG system during the Qianlong years.[105] In part it may simply have been that community granaries were too unmistakably identified with his father's interventionist policies for Qianlong to feel comfortable with, but his indifference was likely fueled as well by the fact that growing numbers of provincial bureaucrats clearly found them an unworkable burden to maintain. In Hunan, for example, R. Bin Wong has found a steady stream of memorials by provincial officials from the 1730s through the 1750s bemoaning the administrative headaches to which *shecang* gave rise—seemingly every governor of the province in these decades with the singular exception of Chen Hongmou.[106] Chen regularly presented himself as in conflict on this issue with his local official subordinates, many of whom, in his words, "have opposed *shecang* from the start."[107]

The community granary crusade in the mid-eighteenth century was kept alive, it appears, by a relatively small coterie of true believers within the field administration. One of the most vocal was Yan Sisheng (*jinshi* 1721), who undertook major initiatives of *shecang* founding in Jiangsu, Shaanxi, Hubei, and elsewhere and whose many writings on the subject continued to inspire Wei Yuan and his colleagues in the more self-conscious statecraft movement of the 1820s.[108] It is perhaps not coincidental that Yan, like Chen Hongmou, was among the Yongzheng emperor's "new men" who served together on the southwest frontier in the early 1730s. But there could be no more ardent champion of community granaries within the early Qianlong administration than Chen himself. Beginning in 1734, and at regular intervals over the next quarter century, he continually pestered the throne to expand and reinvigorate the community granary program in the provinces in which he served, and he set up (and quite clearly enforced) regulatory codes in each jurisdiction to ensure that *shecang* were both effectively managed and routinely engaged in supporting the village economy.[109] Qing provincial gazetteers from Yunnan and Jiangxi portray the vital *shecang* systems in those provinces as effectively Chen's personal creations, and modern scholars studying the institution's history in these provinces, as well as in Shaanxi and Hunan, have reached the same conclusion.[110] It might be added that Chen, on his final visit home in 1742, also endowed a community granary in his native township, an institution over which he continued to exercise solicitous oversight (albeit from afar) throughout his life.[111]

Shecang assets were never extraordinarily large; by midcentury, in an average province they stood at less than a quarter of ever-normal granary stocks.[112] In 1755 Shaanxi, where Chen had been solicitously building them up for more than a decade, he listed total province-wide *shecang* holdings at only 832,468 *shi*, less than 30 percent of the province's ENG totals and (based on Chen's own population figures) little more than one-tenth of a *shi* per capita.[113] Yet, as one of Chen's successors as Shaanxi governor reported, even this relatively small amount made an enormous difference in ensuring the continuity of the small-producer household.[114]

A rough idea of the signal importance Chen Hongmou attached to *shecang* operations can be seen in the following directive he issued to his subordinates in Shaanxi in 1749:

> If we ask why [some magistrates have been less successful than others in clearing up *shecang* loan defaults], we find that it is because they have so concentrated on collecting the land tax that they have put collection of past-due granary loans out of mind altogether. . . . What they fail to realize is that, if the land tax is not collected in full in a given year, that fact can simply be reported to higher authority as such. By contrast, if we do not exert ourselves to recover grain for the granaries, the people may well not be able to make it through the following year alive.[115]

Here Chen unambiguously assigns priority to the integrity of community granary accounts over the interests of state revenue collection. This statement speaks volumes, in my view, not only about the mind-set of Chen Hongmou and many of his fellow administrators but also about the level of the mid-Qing state's comfort in its own financial security. Chen sought an activist state, to be sure, but had little doubt this could be financed with a relatively cavalier attitude toward tax collection; the reproducibility of the farm population was cause for much greater anxiety, and the community granary was his preferred solution.

Scholars have generally taken for granted the complementary relationship between ever-normal and community granaries in the mid-Qing, but although this complementarity was articulated in central government sources, it seems to have been Chen himself who, more than anyone else, developed the notion's implications and worked for its implementation. Repeatedly during his long career, in correspondence to the throne and to his fellow officials, he drove home the fact that ENGs, properly conceived, implied the existence of their complement. ENGs were urban, *shecang* were rural; ENGs made sales, *shecang* made loans; ENGs served consumers, *shecang* served producers. The two institutions facilitated each other's success; loans to farmers from community granaries, for example, eliminated their need to buy seed grain on the market, hence dampening cyclical price inflation and reducing the volume of *pingtiao* sales the local ENG need make.[116] In practice Chen sought to effect as neatly as possible a division of labor between the two; as early as 1740 he memorialized that ENGs should be barred from making loans wherever their location placed them in potential competition with a functioning community granary.[117] Above all, ENGs were governmental (*guan*), whereas *shecang* were societal and communal (*gong*); as Chen constantly stressed, they were *the* emblematic vehicle of the professed imperial policy of "storing wealth among the people" (*cang fu yumin*).

To this end Chen deemed it essential to locate the granaries in the people's actual midst. Coming himself from a village that he remembered as being remote from, and neglected by, the center of county administration, he had clearly developed a near fixation about the inequitable distribution of services over space, about the problem of government "not reaching to" (*buji*) the people in a physical sense, especially those people in outlying areas (*waixiang*). This concern applied to schools (see Chapter 12) and to *shecang* as well. Community granaries that were not actually in the countryside were "community" in name only (*youming wushi*). In practical terms they not only failed to fulfill their mission but also spawned the various sorts of middleman rackets we have just seen operating in the case of ENG loans; this very dysfunctionality in turn fueled further official distaste for the institution and hence neglect. Chen pointed to a clear instance of this in 1745 Shaanxi: In counties where *shecang* were few and inaccessible to farmers they were simply not used, and magistrates claiming to deduce from this that they were not really desired by the people had accordingly commandeered their assets for other state purposes.[118]

The initial edict instituting the *shecang* system in 1703 had specified merely that these granaries were to be located in "villages" (*cunzhuang*), but details of their deployment were not spelled out. In his own comprehensive 1740 policy proposal on granaries Chen suggested that each county have four *shecang*, one in each quadrant, none of these to lie in the county seat.[119] He reiterated his aversion to urban-situated *shecang* repeatedly throughout his career, ridiculing magistrates who allowed this for presuming that all their county's farmers were simply commuters from the city.[120] With time, Chen grew increasingly unsatisfied even with his own original formula and often launched drives to establish branch granaries (*fenzhu*) and subdivide holdings more finely within each county. He ordered subordinates to find space in old temples or local "public buildings" (*gongsuo*) for such purposes and, in the wake of the Qianlong emperor's downsizing of the ever-normal granary system in 1749, sought permission to convert abandoned state granary facilities to community granary use. His campaign for subdividing *shecang* holdings demanded a detailed knowledge of the terrain and population distribution on a locality-by-locality basis. In determining optimal sites for his branch granaries he relied on the twin criteria of size and distance. Depending on terrain, *shecang* should be situated no more than twenty *li* from each cultivator—that is, within one day's round-trip travel. Depending on the local population density, they should be capitalized at between four hundred and one thousand *shi* of grain. When holdings surpassed this amount, it was time to think about further subdivision and branch establishment. Not only would smaller holdings per granary allow a finer mesh of facilities; they would also prove less daunting a burden for prospective volunteer managers and hence aid in the managers' recruitment.[121]

The rationale for community granaries was to provide a source of credit for farmers, so only genuine cultivator households (*gengtian zhi jia*) were eligible to borrow. Rules of eligibility were similar to those for loans from ENGs but were more explicit. Following Zhu Xi's model, Chen excluded literati, yamen clerks, soldiers, merchants, and the propertyless lumpen proletariat (*youshou wuyezhe*), although he made exceptions for members of the first three groups who could demonstrate that they were engaged in agricultural management at least part time. Borrowers must have land, but this could be either leased (*diantian*) or owned outright (*zitian*). On the other hand, landed families of substantial means (*youtian yinshizhe*) were excluded. Loan applicants not personally known to the granary manager would require guarantors. Where eligibility requirements differed most strikingly from those for ENGs was in Chen's repeated insistence that *shecang* lend only to residents of their own particular village or township and that a qualifying farmer borrow only from the granary of which he was, in effect, a member.[122]

Routine problems of default and arrears of course worried Chen (he dealt with these in the same manner, and often in the same directive, in which he addressed defaults on ENG loans), but he was even more anxious that these not serve as disincentive to maintaining a vigorous level of lending by granary managers and their local official supervisors. The latter should not be nitpickingly formalist in their approach to loans, nor impose too many conditions on borrowing (such as a demand to demonstrate truly desperate need), nor subject applicants to unduly troublesome background checks. Managers should be prepared to act adroitly in response to shifting natural conditions, notably vicissitudes of rainfall, so as to facilitate timely planting and to compete effectively with private usurers as a source of loans. They were to aim for a turnover of half their holdings each year, well above the 30 percent standard set for ENGs. And they were to offer their loans in good years as well as bad. Indeed, as Iemura Shiseo has

pointed out, it was precisely the basic intent to provide loans of seed on a routine annual basis, rather than in times of unusual need only, that differentiated mid-Qing community granaries from any comparably widespread previous institution.[123]

In theory *shecang* were credit institutions affixed to a territorial community and thus
ought to be stocked by subscribed contributions (*juanshu*) on the part of their constituents, agricultural producers of the immediately surrounding area. Official practice
worked to realize this ideal. Even the Yongzheng emperor, after an initial experiment
in his first year on the throne with stocking community granaries by means of a compulsory surcharge on the land tax, became convinced that a commandist approach to
shecang affairs was undesirable. Thus in 1724 he announced new guidelines for stocking the granaries based solely on "voluntary contributions" (*zijuan, leshu*); the role of
officials was to "encourage" (*quan*) such contributions but never to "assess" (*pai*) or
"compel" (*ling*) them.[124] This was the approach that even the often state-activist Chen
Hongmou continued to adhere to throughout his provincial career.

The problem was that, when popular voluntarism was not forthcoming, local
officials eager to please their superiors would readily resort to compulsion. Chen understood this and consequently worked assiduously to drum up genuine popular support for the *shecang* institution. Often this task involved overcoming the bad odor that
shecang had acquired locally prior to his arrival, subject as they were to clerical racketeering, local official misappropriation of stocks, massive defaults on loans, and so on.
Thus on at least three occasions (Shaanxi in 1745, Hubei in 1747, and Hunan in 1755)
Chen coupled his renewed subscription drives with highly publicized audits of *shecang*
accounts and the establishment of new mechanisms for ensuring the integrity of their
future operations.[125] His general strategy was to first convince the most "public-minded"
(*jigong*) local citizens to contribute, essentially as an act of philanthropy (*shanju*), then
gradually to bring others to do the same out of perceptions of self-interest. As in Qing
practice more generally, this philanthropy would be rewarded by official honors dispensed according to a frankly calculated schedule of quid pro quo.[126]

Chen's rhetoric in these campaigns is interesting for the way it combines, in his
characteristic fashion, appeals to morality and to material advantage. This reflects
Chen's own view of *shecang* as simultaneously an important material resource for a community and an instrument of local moral-cultural regeneration (*jiaohua*).[127] *Shecang*
provide the medium for setting priorities into proper alignment, for turning the valueless (*wuyi*) into the valuable (*youyi*). In times of plenty they offer a community the opportunity to repay Heaven by not squandering (*maofei*) its gifts but instead saving them
up collectively. For ordinary households, rather than expending a momentary surplus
on individual consumption, granaries offer the better option to contribute one's own
small share to productive community assets. For the rich, rather than inviting enmity
by hiding away one's wealth, *shecang* allow the opportunity to purchase, through larger
contributions, the goodwill of one's neighbors.

Above all, granaries for Chen provide a moral alternative to what he dreads as the
chief corruption of the rural population: the temptation to festivity. Do not dissipate
your hard-earned surplus on lavish weddings for your children, he pleads, but instead

put it away in the *shecang* in anticipation of future needs. Abjure postharvest rites of propitiation for Buddhist and Daoist spirits (*shenling*), with their lavish offerings of wine, and shun above all that most odious expression of popular culture, nighttime ritual operas. The elite must help reform local customs by setting an example in this regard. We all know the masses are hopelessly addicted to worship of these spirits, he confides to local literati and literati aspirants, so we cannot simply legislate against them. But we can urge the institution of "economies" (*jiesheng*). Instead of a prosperous household contributing ten taels for such activities, give only six or seven; instead of staging operas for four nights running, do so for only one or two. By this means, Chen calculates, an average village can reduce its ritual expenditure by hundreds of *shi* of grain per year, easily enough to endow a new community granary.[128]

With all the emphasis on local voluntarism, however, it is evident that *shecang* as often as not in fact received their initial capitalization out of state largesse. We cannot determine what the empire-wide percentage might have been, but we do know that the expedient of government stocking was resorted to for stocking of community granaries in parts of virtually every province. In his regulatory code for Jiangxi *shecang* written in 1742, for example, Chen Hongmou invited magistrates to first do what they could to elicit local contributions and, if after a reasonable interlude adequate stocks had not accumulated, petition him to work out some variety of provincial assistance.[129] Similar approaches were taken by other provincial officials and were approved by the throne as a matter of course.

The state funds in question came from a variety of sources, and their appropriation was legitimated—or disguised—in a variety of ways. Sometimes they came as outright grants of aid. In Jiangsu in the 1730s, for instance, Yan Sisheng received permission to stock community granaries out of his provincial treasury accounts, and at roughly the same time Shandong officials did the same thing out of public-works construction funds. Chen himself, as treasurer of Yunnan in 1735, memorialized to draw on revenues of official agricultural estates (*guanzhuang*) to stock granaries in that grain-poor province.[130] But most often officials preferred to work out some type of indirect means of channeling state funds into *shecang* accounts or to use the form of "loans" rather than outright grants. This both protected them from the charge of favoritism to some localities over others and maintained the useful image of *shecang* as projects of, by, and for the local community. Chen's own favored tactic was to make loans out of the province's ever-normal granaries, to be repaid once the *shecang* had begun to generate income from interest payments on their own loans. He did this in Yunnan in 1735, in Jiangxi in 1742, and in Hunan in 1755—wherever he felt that ENGs themselves were sufficiently stocked to handle it—and he advocated it to the throne as a general policy. In requesting authority for the Hunan loans (at a time when community granaries had quite clearly fallen out of general official favor), he pointed out that the loans he had arranged in Yunnan and Jiangxi had been repaid to the ENG system easily and in full.[131]

One of the cleverest and most widely heralded schemes for government aid in community granary stocking was that devised by Shaanxi governor Yue Zhongqi in the late 1720s. Arguing that the disproportionately high military presence in his province made stocking by voluntary subscription infeasible, Yue convinced the Yongzheng emperor to divert 50 percent of the first several years of Shaanxi's collections of the *haoxian* "melt-age fee" (the surtax at that time being introduced by Yongzheng specifically to finance local-level public projects) for *shecang* capitalization. Although it appears that the sur-tax was actually first collected and then diverted to *shecang* use, the language carefully chosen to describe the operation was that half of the *haoxian* had been "remitted" and their savings "contributed" by the taxpayers to their local granaries. Funds were col-lected at the county level and used to purchase grain on the local market, which in turn was allocated to the county's various township-level granaries, in direct proportion to that township's tax assessment. Altogether, some four hundred thousand *shi* of grain was mobilized in this fashion.[132]

Problems arose almost immediately, however. Loan rackets and other clerical abuses abounded, convincing many Shaanxi magistrates that *shecang* were not worth the trouble of oversight, and they consequently began to draw on their assets as a slush fund to meet other administrative expenses. Distressed, Governor Yue in 1729 asked Yongzheng to intercede in the interests of *shecang* budgetary integrity. The emperor re-sponded with a ringing and unambiguous edict to the effect that community granary grain, in Shaanxi as elsewhere, had been "contributed" by the local community itself and was not to be touched by officials. On his first arrival in Shaanxi some sixteen years later Chen Hongmou reprinted this edict in its entirety and promulgated it to all local officials as a warning. He invoked it periodically thereafter, whenever invasions of *shecang* accounts came to his attention.[133]

The questions surrounding the *haoxian* origins of Shaanxi's community granary stocks were in fact emblematic of larger problems with the conceptualization of this in-stitution as a whole. In the vision of Zhu Xi and other Song neo-Confucian statecraft thinkers, community granaries were part of a broad-ranging turn away from the big-government bureaucratism that they found both ineffective and stifling of private moral initiative; specifically, they were seen as societal substitutes for Wang Anshi's dis-credited "green sprouts" seed grain loan administration.[134] This antibureaucratism was an urge felt by Chen Hongmou and other Qing *shecang* enthusiasts as well, including, surprisingly, the Yongzheng emperor. In the rhetoric these men shared to discuss com-munity granaries, proprietorship of their assets was to rest "*zaimin*" (with the people), not "*zaiguan*" (with the government); such grain was "the people's property" (*minjian zhi wu*), not that of the officials or the state. More explicitly, *shecang* and their holdings fell into the uncomfortably nebulous, but unquestionably expanding, sectoral category of "public" (*gong*). That this "publicness" was not the equivalent of "governmental" was precisely the point that the discourse of *shecang* repeatedly drove home: community granary assets were "public property" (*gongwu*) but not "state property" (*guanwu*) and for this reason were not subject to diversion for other local official projects, however worthy those projects might be.

But the collectivity that made up the "public" proprietor of each individual *shecang* was, as with other Qing conceptions of publicness, highly localized. Community gran-ary grain was "local public property" (*difang gongwu*), or "public property of that par-ticular place" (*gaishe gongwu*), or "collective property of neighboring villagers" (*fujin cunmin zhi wu*).[135] It belonged, then, to the farming residents of a specific territorial community. We have seen that already as early as the Kangxi emperor's first stumbling attempts to reintroduce the institution in the Qing, eligibility for loans was restricted to proximate residents of the granary. Indeed, for many *shecang* partisans, including both Zhu Xi and Chen Hongmou, fostering local community ties was an explicitly sought by-product of granary formation. Chen wistfully described this communalism taking hold with the very act of assembling for the granary's physical construction. Although he does not make much of it, it seems Chen envisioned the act of founding a community granary as marked by drawing up a self-regulating "charter" (*tiaioyue*) on the part of community members.[136] With this corporateness, of course, might come a certain local insularity. Somewhat incongruously, perhaps, in a man who so emphatically celebrated the translocal integrative features of market exchange, Chen was also unambiguously positive about the local self-sufficiency the *shecang* might provide— "using a community's own grain to meet that community's own needs."[137]

Shecang were also "communal" in the shopworn sociological sense that distinguishes between the "communal" and the "associative." They were not cooperative credit societies, whose benefits might be restrictively enjoyed by a group of founding members.[138] Rather, Chen's rhetoric stressed that access to community granary grain was open, given satisfaction of the criteria of eligibility, to "all households of the district" (*tongdu zhonghu*). In spite of the fact that, in theory, community granaries operated on the principle of members each "contributing according to their ability" (*liangli juanshu*),[139] contributions were voluntary, and failure to subscribe did not prejudice one's ability to borrow. On the other hand, the notion that all community members had an equal claim to granary property might also work to restrict its redistributive functions; very revealingly, I think, Chen argues that dispensing *shecang* grain in the form of gratis relief to the starving is wrong because it depletes collective assets in a manner not equitable (*gongping*) to the granary's other constituents. Likewise, Chen specifically dissociates the *shecang* from the purview of private charity. Whereas the essence of the *shecang* is communal self-help, Chen says, true philanthropy is properly handled through an alternative organizational form, the "charity granary" (*yicang*), an institution in which he seems to have no particular interest.[140]

It was clearly advantageous for Chen's purposes to be able to affix his *shecang* to a preexisting unit of local community, and he did so wherever possible. In Shaanxi Chen Hongmou found functioning communities of between eight and ten villages each— conveniently already referred to in local parlance as "*she*"—and he seized on them as organizational vehicles for his *shecang*, explicitly hoping in the process to "reform" them from their original purpose of financing morally offensive operas and other forms of popular religious practice.[141] In other provinces, however, Chen could not find any such *she*, and in these cases he affixed his *shecang* to whatever existing unit seemed to fit the need: to "community compact" (*xiangyue*) units in Jiangxi, to quasi-communal administrative subdistricts (*du* and *tu*) in Fujian, and on occasion to the fiscal cantons of the atrophied *lijia* system.[142] At times he even entertained the possibility of linking *shecang* with lineage organizations, although, mindful of the ambiguous status of lineages between "public" and "private," he did so with evident caution.[143] The one place Chen clearly drew the line was with the transparently coercive *baojia* public security apparatus, which he repeatedly excluded as a suitable vehicle for any sort of genuine "community" organization.

Given Chen's pervasive emphasis on the community nature of *shecang*, and his repeated insistence that their assets were communal rather than governmental property, the awkwardness posed by the fact that they were so often in practice underwritten by government grants such as Yue Zongqi's *haoxian* scheme in Shaanxi became particularly poignant. When such assets were desperately needed for other official projects, or when moves to expropriate *shecang* stocks by private interests appeared too powerful for the local community to resist, the temptation to governmentalize the entire granary system became well nigh irresistible. In this context, with imperial sanction, Chen Hongmou gradually worked out a form of management for community granaries that approximated the distinctive "popular management with official oversight" (*guandu minban*) formula increasingly employed in dike maintenance and other public works and economic development projects over the course of the Qing. As had been the intent of Zhu Xi and other *shecang* promoters six centuries earlier, this style of management was designed in the hopes of avoiding the worst evils of bureaucratization and of fostering local societal self-nurturance, while at the same time maintaining basic official control over the system's operation.

The key to this system was the so-called *shezhang* (less often "*shezheng*"), the community granary headman. The *shezhang*, and his second-in-command, the so-called *shefu*, had been instituted by edict of the Yongzheng emperor in 1724; an edict of 1745 specified that they would serve three-year terms with the possibility of reappointment thereafter.[144] As laid out in various directives of Chen Hongmou, granary managers might either serve single terms in rotation or hold the job essentially for life. They might be either gentry or commoners, but yamen clerks, *baojia* public security functionaries, and, intriguingly, local militia heads (*xianglian*) were excluded from service. Managers were to be "upright and public-minded persons of substantial means" (*gongzheng yinshi*) who were "inclined to charitable service" (*haoyi xingshan*). Most critically, they ought to enjoy the confidence of local "public opinion" (*gonglun*).[145] Chen was ambiguous, and probably deliberately so, on the actual selection process—*shezhang* might either be "publicly chosen" (*gongju*) or nominated directly by the local magistrate. In any case the magistrate would review each granary manager's performance both annually and at the end of his three-year term, dismissing or punishing him criminally for incompetence or malfeasance, bestowing a precisely specified series of official honors for creditable service. Granary managers had great latitude over the operation of their granary, determining on their own, for example, the eligibility and credit ceiling of all borrowers. By imperial edict they were financially liable for losses accruing because of their poor management, but Chen sought to soften this in practice so as not to intimidate likely candidates from accepting the post and to encourage loans to the widest possible pool of eligible applicants. He also established in each province a schedule of modest financial compensation that *shezhang* could legitimately claim for their labors and managerial expenses.[146]

Chen enjoined his local officials to treat *shezhang* with due "courtesy" (*limao*) and to avoid overburdening or "harassing" (*lei*) them. Don't be constantly sending inspectors down to the *she* to look over the managers' shoulders, but rather allow them to report themselves on their activities. Even then, do not overload them with paperwork demands, which can only make them prey to the machinations of yamen clerks (removing such clerks from the loop of granary management being one of the *shecang* system's most basic intents). Keep in mind that the granary managers are not simply sub-bureaucrats like the clerks, to be ordered around by the magistrate, but are instead respected members of their community performing a voluntary act of service for their neighbors. Avoid as well excessive rigidity or dogmatic formalism (*juni wenfa*) in supervising the managers' activities. In several of his posts Governor Chen takes concrete action to prevent what he views as too much official meddling in operations best left to *shezhang* discretion, most notably in 1755 Hunan, where he dismantles an entire provincial bureaucratic system, the "superintendency of granaries" (*zongcang*), built up by his predecessors to oversee community granary operations in what Chen sees as a counterproductive fashion.[147]

All of this is not to deny that the possibility of *shezhang* corruption is real (Chen subtly alludes to this in his injunction that community granary assets not be stored in the manager's own house) or to suggest that *shezhang* are capable of doing the job completely on their own. He is consistently aware as well of the problem of finding good men for this really not very attractive position of local leadership, and he acknowledges that lack of official backup support may be just as great a disincentive to recruitment as excessive bureaucratic interference. Proper management, then, requires arriving at a delicate balance between local autonomy and centralized control, between situational flexibility and bureaucratic standardization. Vigilant as he was to defend the integrity of local societal proprietorship over community granary assets, Chen's own paternalistic pride in the institution as a whole demanded a more hands-on approach on his part. This is neatly expressed in his 1744 directive reforming the *shecang* system of Shaanxi. In this text Chen begins by citing approvingly the Yongzheng emperor's 1729 edict condemning the excessive bureaucratization of that province's community granary system: "The amounts and timing of spring loans and fall repayments, the amount of interest to be charged each borrower, and so on, are all matters for the *she* themselves to determine. The local official has investigative responsibility, but no right to interfere in the process of actual transactions. This is the basic institutional principle [*fa*] of *shecang*." In announcing his plans to translate this edict into practice, however, Chen provides his own addendum:

> But to say that control over granaries is to be returned to the people and that the officials have no authority to infringe in this area is not to allow officials to abrogate their duty of oversight. They absolutely may not tolerate community granaries being run in such a fashion that their capital [*sheben*—which in Shaanxi, Chen's audience will recall, has been endowed primarily by means of state grants] is dissipated altogether. Doing so in the name of "returning control to the people" does not uphold the institution's well-conceived basic principle [*liangfa*], but rather violates it.[148]

The primary means of exercising official oversight was via a system of detailed reporting and audits. By the early Qianlong reign, at least, provincial governors such as Chen were required to submit year-end statistical reports on the activities of *shecang* in their province.[149] Chen himself demanded much more thorough annual reports from each granary manager, compiled at the county level by the magistrate for upward transmission. The magistrate was also to include a report on his county's *shecang* status, and the local system's future potential, in his regular comprehensive report on "assets and liabilities of the locality" (*difang libi*). Chen was very particular about the information these reports should contain and about its arrangement, so in most provinces he personally designed and distributed standard forms for reporting at the granary manager level, as well as standardized ledgers (*ce*) for keeping running accounts of granary transactions.[150] On this basis, audits of each community granary's accounts were to be conducted on expiration of the *shecang*'s three-year term and of all granaries in the county on the succession of the magistrate. As we have seen, Chen periodically conducted his own audits and campaigns for liquidation of arrears (*qingli*) at the provincial level, as well as programs of procedural reform. There is plenty of evidence that he personally got involved in rectifying cases of mismanagement in individual counties under his jurisdiction.[151]

All in all, for a "community" institution the *shecang* set up by Chen Hongmou in the 1730s through the 1750s had a decidedly bureaucratic flavor. In many if not most cases the "community" itself had been an administrative creation. The granaries were founded and situated, and their constituencies determined, by administrative fiat, and they were frequently stocked by official largesse. Their leadership was selected by and closely answerable to the local magistrate via a series of standardized government forms. Their activities were governed by a regulatory code based on imperial guidelines and drawn up in detail and promulgated at the provincial level. Weights and measures employed, for example, were not local customary ones but were rigorously standardized by imperial authority.[152] The *shecang*'s popular appeal and demonstrably widespread use by needy cultivators (in preference to private loans) seems in most instances to have been the product of an extensive campaign of official promotion.

Even so indefatigable a champion of community granary integrity as Chen Hongmou could not escape (indeed probably never hoped to escape) viewing community granaries as an adjunct arm of his provincial administration. We have already seen how he saw their operations as a coordinated part of his complex machinery of regional economic management. To cite but one example: Although he genuinely believed and regularly insisted that annual scheduling of the periods of *shecang* loans and repayments was one aspect of granary management that, being tied in to the locally specific agricultural calendar, must be left to local discretion, he had no qualms about asserting centralized control of such scheduling at the provincial level in periods of food shortage or climatic irregularity.[153] And, as seen above, Chen's provincial-level cleanup campaigns for outstanding granary loans most often treated ever-normal and community granaries as indistinguishable, equally subject to his centralized command. For all this, though, Chen was consistent in enforcing a hands-off policy prohibiting local officials from drawing on *shecang* stocks for other purposes, however worthy, and he worked assiduously to foster both the notion that these stocks were indeed "community" property and a genuinely affective sense of local community that would take the granary as a major part of its material base. It may in fact be said that it was this kind of juxtaposition of strategies that made him emblematic of the statecraft (*jingshi*) political style, and this is an issue to which we must return.

Accumulation and Economic Growth

Chen Hongmou's conception of community granaries embodied a fully developed ideology of thrift, savings, and accumulation of wealth. We have seen his repeated emphasis on the idea that investments in the granary by community members should come as the result of savings on frivolous expenses, that is, the results of a morally positive frugality, and that such investments also represented a virtuous communal pooling of small individual surpluses to form relatively substantial collective assets (*jishao chengduo*). It was also a form of investment unambiguously oriented toward capital growth. The granaries' capital (*sheben*), "through the annual cycle of lending and repayment, will gradually and steadily increase."[154]

Community granaries charged interest. The Yongzheng emperor's edict of 1724 authorized them to demand either 10 or 20 percent per year (between spring loans and postharvest repayments), "depending upon local conditions." Chen seems invariably to have chosen the lower figure in his provincial regulatory codes but added another 3 percent to cover the granary's overhead costs and its manager's compensation. He also specified that, at the manager's discretion, particularly needy local cultivators might have their interest charges waived.[155] In a context in which private-sector interest rates of 30 to 40 percent for spring-to-fall loans of grain were the norm, those offered by community granaries to their members represented a considerable savings. Interestingly, Chen also observed that, because the 13 percent interest the cultivator household paid was far less than the normal pre- and postharvest grain price differential in most localities, the household was making a net profit on these loans even before it used the grain as seed for further production![156] And at the same time collective granary assets were growing as well. In promoting these institutions across the breadth of the empire, Chen never failed to point out the inexorable, progressive character of such growth—it "produces profit over and over again" (*yuanyuan shengxi*) or, in his favorite idiom, "yields a profit which in turn yields more profit" (*xi you shengxi*). Under normal conditions, he projected, most *shecang* could expect to see their assets double every ten years.[157]

Both ever-normal and community granaries, then, were designed in Chen's conception to generate increased wealth. With ever-normal granaries this goal was decidedly secondary to that of stabilizing prices and hence assuring the steady availability of affordable grain to nonfood producers. Still, Chen speaks repeatedly of the way routinely selling dear and repurchasing cheap will lead to accumulating assets, and his proposal to utilize degree sales systematically to replace market repurchase was explicitly designed to promote the steady growth of resources (*duoduo beizhu*). Some of his actions in ENG management, too, such as his strategic borrowing of ENG stocks from Taiwan to capitalize granaries in mainland Fujian, were transparently profit-making ventures. With community granaries, although assuring a steady supply of seed grain to farmers was undeniably of major concern, the goal of accumulation was overtly central to the institution's rationale. *Shecang* were a principal means not only to "store" wealth among the people but to foster the growth of that wealth as well.

This in turn prompts consideration of a more general question: In the universe of consciousness inhabited by Chen Hongmou and his contemporaries, was per capita economic growth a possibility? It seems to me that the baseline for eighteenth-century formulations of this question was the eleventh-century debate between the great advocate of neo-Confucian central planning, Wang Anshi, and his opponents, notably Sima Guang. Wang argued that economic product could be progressively increased (*shengcai*), even in the absence of population growth, and that the best way to achieve this was to concentrate investment decision making, and mobilize as much as feasible of the society's economic resources, in the hands of the state. Large-scale spending on capital projects, and resulting short-term budgetary deficits, could and should be tolerated in the interests of long-term economic growth. Sima countered that economic product could never really be increased in per capita terms. He advanced a fairly rigid zero-sum logic: "The wealth produced by Heaven-and-earth is fixed in amount (*tiandi shengcai zhi you cishu*). The more held by the government, the less that remains to be held by the people." Along with these dictums, as Peter Bol suggests, Sima adhered to an economic mind-set that essentially opposed commercialization, monetization, and any official orientation toward maximizing profit or material advantage (*li*).[158]

In the view of most subsequent neo-Confucian officials, Sima had won this debate hands down. As Lien-sheng Yang argued in a classic article, the consensus throughout the late imperial period favored frugality and savings but paid very little attention to "the relation between saving and investment" and still less to "the possible relation between spending and economic growth."[159] Sima's complacent dictum on the finite nature of wealth became a nearly unchallenged point of departure for later economic planners. In the self-consciously "benevolent" (in this context, meaning "antistatist") Qianlong reign, it approached imperial orthodoxy. We have already encountered such statements in Gaozong's edicts: "If that [wealth] collected by the government is too great, there will be too little remaining for the people"; and "If the government buys less [grain], there will be more for sale on the private market"; and "There is only a finite amount of grain which the land produces; if landholders give up their surplus to the state, and households with a deficit make this up by local market purchase, there will be nothing left for the locality either to save or to export."[160] Each time, such a statement was offered as justification for one or another pullback from government activism in the economy.

However, as Yang pointed out in this same article, there was also a persisting "minority view" on economic growth and on spending and investment held by some scholars throughout the late imperial era. Yang cites the example of the sixteenth-century Shanghai literatus Lu Ji, who, proceeding directly from Sima's dictum on the finite nature of wealth to argue that wealth similarly cannot be *destroyed*, concluded that luxury spending by the rich was a form of recirculation of this finite wealth and thus a stimulus to the economy.[161] As part of the common ground of political-economic discourse in late imperial China, Sima's words, like the related idiom "storing wealth among the people," were available to articulate members of the discourse community to draw on in ways that contested the very assumptions they were conventionally presumed to convey.

This, it seems, is what was habitually done by Chen Hongmou. It would be hard to imagine a more loyal devotee of Sima Guang in eighteenth-century China than Chen, who wrote the Song master's biography and produced an edition of his complete works. There is no reason to doubt that this attachment was genuine or that Chen was in fundamental agreement with Sima's urge to restrict any predatory moves of the state toward private property. But it seems equally clear that Chen's fundamental approach was markedly more developmental than that of Sima and even than that of the Qianlong emperor. It is significant, I believe, that Chen does not shrink from routine use of the idiom "*shengcai*" (the production of wealth), for all the distasteful associations with Wang Anshi's statist policies that that term carried in the late imperial era.[162]

"Storing wealth among the people," for Chen, meant first and foremost doing everything possible to augment their per capita economic productivity. This pointedly included promoting commercialization and monetization. It also included a level of state investment that many of his contemporaries would have found hair-raising. "Short-term accounts may run deficits," he protested, "but long-term accounts will show surpluses."[163] Accumulation, investment, and reinvestment via a flourishing, state-run (in the case of ENGs) or state-policed (in the case of *shecang*) granary system was likewise an integral component of Chen's strategy of growth. So too, it must be emphasized, was moral and cultural improvement. On all fronts he held an optimistic, activist, and fully Confucian faith in the possibilities of a process of "uninterrupted social betterment" (*jiexu zhenxing*)[164] that would yield cumulative, compounding, and permanently lasting results.

PART THREE

Ordering the World

經世

CHAPTER 9

People

FOR CHEN HONGMOU human identities were complex. In general I think it may be said that he viewed human beings simultaneously in at least four distinct ways: (1) as members of a common species or category, "humanity" (*ren*); (2) as occupants of a variety of social roles (*fen*), often but not always defined by the model of the family, that situated them in a number of intermeshing networks of mutual definition and reciprocal obligation; (3) as members of a variety of categories (often binary ones) or groups, divided by gender, ethnicity, wealth, and level of education; and (4) as autonomous individuals, each with his or her unique personal dignity. The task of this chapter is to explore each of these types of identity, attempting to discover what precisely each meant to Chen Hongmou, and to assess what their relative priority might have been within his consciousness. I will state at the outset my view that for Chen, as a devoted *lixue* scholar with an unusually pronounced strain of Mencian idealism, the first type of human identity remained always by far the most important, with the second falling close behind. By contrast, the fourth type—human beings as individuals—was probably least important. But it was far from negligible, and in this lies some of the significance of Chen Hongmou, both as an individual thinker and as representative of his times, to the long-term development of Chinese social thought.

The Goodness of Humanity (tianliang)

A persistent and emphatic theme running throughout Chen's discourse, public and private, is his belief in the common humanity of all people, regardless of ethnicity, gender, or socioeconomic status. This egalitarian, even democratic, strain in Chen's outlook certainly cannot be accepted uncritically, and much of our discussion in this chapter will be devoted to the immensely tricky job of placing on it the appropriate qualifications; but the strain was incontestably there, and as an underlying assumption it formed one of the major distinguishing marks of Chen's approach to questions of policy. As it operated in Chen, this strain of egalitarianism was both ancient and new, both mainstream and a peculiar product of populist influences stemming from his peripheral social origins.

As we saw in Chapter 3, Chen expresses this egalitarian faith most frequently by means of the idiom "*tianliang*" (heavenly goodness). His endlessly repeated refrain "All persons have within them the goodness of Heaven" conveys two messages: that human nature is inclined to moral action and (of no lesser importance) that this defining characteristic of humanity is shared equally by all members of the human species. He underlines this second message by invoking the idiom most often in reference to sorts of people for whom his audience clearly found its application counterintuitive. "The *xiao-min* [petty commoners] all have *tianliang*" (the same as you and I, of the elite). Yamen clerks (those devious wretches) have *tianliang*, just like everyone else. "Even the most obtuse and stupid individuals are motivated by *tianliang*." Most emphatically, non-Han peoples, whose society and culture Chen himself equates with savagery, share with us a common essence of heavenly goodness.[1] Our common humanity overrides social class, by whatever criterion one chooses to determine that. Human equality, moreover, is a function not only of divine essence but also of common corporality and habitation of the material world. "No matter whether rich and noble or poor and mean," Chen writes, "all persons are made of flesh and blood." "All persons share in the bounty of Heaven, and all are equally victims when natural disaster occurs."[2]

For one who so emphatically insists on humankind's common essential goodness, it is true, Chen does not hesitate to divide the population neatly into "good people" (*liangmin, liangshanzhe*) and "bad people" (*jianmin, jian'ezhe*—literally, "traitorous people"): "Just as a legal case either has merit or does not, so too people are either bad or good. There is a fundamental difference between the two, although distinguishing between them in practice is not always easy."[3] In making this distinction Chen endorses what was in his day conventional wisdom.[4] Two points, however, must be emphasized about Chen's use of this trope. First, "badness," however entrenched, is not essential to human beings; it represents, rather, a situational "obscuring" of their basic goodness (*meiliang*). As such, even the most obdurate miscreant can experience "self-renewal" (*zixin*), a return to his or her native virtue.[5]

Second, there is for Chen no necessary connection between the "good/bad" categories and social or economic status. To be sure, marginalized or itinerant persons are more likely than other persons to be classed as "bad" (throughout his official correspondence Chen discusses a wide range of these, often locally specific, types of bad characters). But this describes a condition rather than an essence; indeed, for these groups the government is in an especially advantageous position to assist in the process of "self-renewal," by helping them to reintegrate into local society and thus turning them into "resettled good people" (*ruji liangmin, tuzhu liangmin*).[6] Chen also makes it clear that the gentry, too, may be divided into "good" and "bad."[7] Ultimately, the key to this distinction is behavioral and in no small measure political. "Good people" are defined as those who behave with propriety and demonstrate their intent to "repay the imperial grace," who dutifully observe the dictates both of heavenly principle and of imperial law; those who do otherwise are "bad."[8]

Virtue, in other words, is the exclusive property of no single class or group. The same virtues—frugality, filiality, and so on—are appropriate for all persons and, moreover, are found in equal measure at all levels of society.[9] It is owing to his faith on this score that Chen consistently opts for vernacularization of moral texts and simplification of ritual liturgies; he is quite willing to sacrifice complex and costly classical refinements in order to reach a mass public, about whose receptiveness he is confident. If persons of all social stations are equally prone to virtue, they are likewise equally deserving of respect. Chen rails, for example, against the mistreatment of household servants, who, as human beings, require treatment according to the same dictates of *renqing* that govern human relations in general.[10] He extols the Song scholar-official He Tan (*jinshi* 1180) for his credo of "holding rich and poor, noble and base, to common standards of behavior, and offering them common treatment," and he proclaims as a general rule of governance that "each matter be dealt with on its own merits . . . without regard to the social status (*diwei*) of the parties concerned."[11]

This insistence on common humanity became for Chen a basis of policy formation in a wide range of areas. Throughout his career he believed himself fighting an uphill battle against fellow bureaucrats who did not take Mencian dictates of human moral egalitarianism as literally as he did, men from hyperelite backgrounds who had little sense of common humanity with the "little people" (*xiaomin*). In leading campaigns to select models of exemplary moral conduct (*jiexiao*) from among village populations, for example, he routinely lambasted subordinates who, blinded by their own sense of cultural superiority, were unable to discern paragons of virtue among the "illiterate masses" (*yumin*).[12] Culturally, Chen's advocacy of vernacularization as a means of bridging cultural gaps and directly reaching the *xiaomin* ran counter to the prescriptions of literary purists within the classical prose (*guwen*) movement. Contested as it was, however, Chen's dogged faith in the common dignity, rationality, and moral sense of all human beings, as Heaven's creatures, was the point of departure for his approach to governance and the background against which his various understandings of human differentiation must be understood.

Ethnicity/Race

Chen Hongmou's insistence on a shared humanity that transcends social and cultural distinctions was at times most defiantly stated in the context of ethnicity. A recurring refrain in his writings concerning relations with non-Han peoples in the northwest, the southwest, and even the southeastern coastal frontiers took such forms as "Chinese and non-Chinese have a single common essence" (*Han yi yiti*) and "People of the center and of the periphery form a single family" (*zhong wai yijia*).[13] Chen's implementation, throughout his career, of extremely vigorous assimilationist and antidiscrimination policies toward non-Han indigenous peoples—notably, but hardly exclusively, his celebrated educational programs in Yunnan (to be discussed in Chapter 12)—make it clear that for him this was no hollow "brotherhood-of-man" rhetoric. He believed sufficiently in what he said to propose policies that were resisted by his bureaucratic subordinates and viewed as extreme by his colleagues. But Chen's beliefs were rooted ultimately in his deeply held Mencian optimism regarding human nature and in his conviction that all humanity partook of *tianliang*.[14]

At the same time, political agendas were at work. Significantly, Chen's rhetoric on these matters echoed closely that of the Yongzheng emperor, whose direct protégé Chen was, and whose political and social vision he largely shared, even when this sort of thinking began to fall out of fashion in the Qianlong reign. In 1730, in response to the discovery of a clearly anti-Manchu literati movement and amidst swirling rumors of his own usurpation of the throne, Yongzheng issued a remarkable document, the *Dayi juemi lu* (Dispelling rumors and setting the record straight). In it he insisted that "All persons under Heaven constitute a single family, and all creation partakes of a single common essence" (*tianxia yijia, wanwu yiti*). He went on to argue that his own besieged "Manchu" identity reflected no more than merely an arbitrary turn in the history of discourse. It had been introduced initially, the emperor argued, as merely a geographic referent to his native region, not as descriptive of any specific racial stock. Indeed, *all* conventionally conceived ethnic or racial groupings were at bottom merely cultural constructions that had become habituated through language use. To avoid racial or cultural stereotyping, he declared, "the language of 'Han' and 'barbarian' " (*Han yi zhi shuo*) ought to be replaced by a more value-neutral and historically accurate reference to "central" (*zhong*) and "peripheral" (*wai*) peoples. To do otherwise, to presume a racial essentialism when none existed in nature, was nothing short of an offense against heavenly principle (*tianli*).[15]

There were obvious political purposes behind Yongzheng's startlingly modern-sounding arguments, including not merely a defense of his personal legitimacy but also a dramatic reconceptualization of the Qing population as an internally homogeneous body of coequal subjects of an absolutist throne. It was a vision largely compatible with Chen's own independently conceived sociopolitical views, and it is hardly surprising that the ambitious state-making monarch and the fledgling official saw eye-to-eye. Chen expresses something along the same lines in his occasional use of the politically charged idiom "*chizi*," the undifferentiated population of the empire, viewed as dependent children of the ruler. Han, indigenous minorities, and likewise various Inner Asian populations are, on their submission to Qing rule, "all equal as *chizi*."[16]

Yet quasi-pejorative appellations such as "*yi*," "*fan*," and "*miao*" never fully vanish from Chen's vocabulary. His formulation "*Han yi yiti*" (Chinese and barbarian share a common essence) conveys a sentiment similar to Yongzheng's "*wanwu yiti*" (all creatures share a common essence) but retains the separate reference to Chinese and "barbarian" of which Yongzheng so strongly disapproved. (Chen does use the more politic reference to "inner" and "outer" peoples on other occasions.) Similarly, his formulation "Chinese and Miao are all equally imperial subjects" (*min miao jun shu chizi*) explicitly disaggregates minority populations from full membership in the "people" (*min*). Indeed, even in one of Chen's most assimilationist policy proposals he styles the people of Dzungaria "*yi*," inviting the stern rebuke of his emperor, Qianlong, for referring to these historic Qing allies by this "vulgar and derisive" term rather than by the more neutrally descriptive "Mongols" (*menggu*).[17] Chen is consistent enough to leave no doubt of his belief in the *essential* uniformity of humankind, but he clearly partakes sufficiently of a Han-national consciousness to retain the belief that there are still significant subdivisions, even gradations, within the species.

Were these divisions of a physiological or genealogical nature that we might fairly term "racial"? Frank Dikötter has effectively demonstrated that such analytic constructs were indeed readily available in China well before their importation from the West in Darwinist guise.[18] And although racialist language is never in the forefront of Chen Hongmou's discourse, an occasional usage reveals that it is not unknown to him. In discussing the Muslims of northwest China, for instance, he points out that those populations, normally lumped together under the cultural rubric "Huimin," in fact comprise various discrete "*zhonglei*," a term that, for some, might be interpreted as "racial stocks."[19] And in outlining his policy toward maritime commerce during his tenure in Fujian, a highly liberalized policy at that, he nevertheless orders that no *yise zhi ren* (persons of different color or physical appearance) be brought into China by returning merchants, suggesting his awareness, at least, of a racial taxonomy based on physiological features.[20]

As will be shown more fully in Chapter 12, Chen believes that all population groups are, ultimately, susceptible targets for the civilizing process (*hua*). They are not susceptible with equal ease, however. Whereas the indigenous populations of southwestern China are inherently lazy and dissolute (that is, they are subject to characterization by the familiar tropes applied by colonizing cultures everywhere), they are so merely by virtue of "long habit" and can fairly easily be reformed. Northwestern Muslims, by contrast, are more "stubborn and intractable." Their deviance from civilized norms is a function of their "collective mentality" (*qixin*), which in turn derives not merely from accumulated practice (*xi*) but also in part from inherent disposition (*xing*).[21] Is this "inherent disposition" a function of genetic descent? It is hard to say. (They do, as we have just seen, encompass not one but several *zhonglei*.) The reality and importance to Chen of physiological distinction is probably best revealed, in the long run, by his attitude toward intermarriage. Arguing against the overwhelming thrust of Qing policy making, Chen steadfastly insists that intermarriage between Han and non-Han populations ought not to be proscribed but instead actively encouraged as a tool of assimilation. If he did conceive of a Han "race," then, it was hardly as a superior biological stock that ought to be preserved free from taint.[22]

Indeed, the overwhelming tone of Chen's writing argues for a cultural rather than racial conception of human difference. Local populations, Han as well as non-Han, are continually in need of cultural improvement, and all are capable of responding to the proper stimuli. "All places have their distinctive cultural practices," he observes, "and yet at the root of all is a common human nature which is basically good."[23]

Hierarchy

The question of the strength and quality of hierarchy as a feature of late imperial culture and society has attracted a great deal of recent attention from scholars, both Western and Chinese, and it will be useful to review some of this work before attempting to assess Chen Hongmou's own outlook on this question. Among the boldest of this scholarship is the work of Romeyn Taylor on Ming-Qing "official religion," work at once brilliantly conceived and highly problematic.[24] Drawing on the ideas of Karl Polanyi and Louis Dumont, Taylor identifies a category of "non-modern" sociocultural orders—including late imperial China—that, he insists, differ fundamentally from our own. The key feature of such an order is that it is conceived by participants as an "organic" or "holistic" entity undifferentiated into functional spheres yet internally divided into a rigid status hierarchy—a hierarchy, for example, of estates or of castes—that allows no room for acknowledgment of personal individuality. Society and polity are one, and no separate domains of "politics" or "economics" (the market), which might serve as arenas for the competitive articulation of individual or interest-group identity, are acknowledged. Organic hierarchy subsumes all.

A more materialist analysis of hierarchy, which uses language far different from Taylor's but reaches conclusions largely consistent with his, appears in the work of the Chinese legal scholar Jing Junjian. Jing asserts that Qing China possessed a system of ranks or estates, defined in such texts as the *Da Qing lüli* and the *Da Qing huidian*, broken down primarily into the imperial aristocracy, the officials, the nonofficial gentry, the commoners, and the "mean" or debased people. The Qing system was somewhat more flexible than estate systems in other historical societies (including that of the Ming) in that it accorded a prominence to the kinship system and to the market that in certain instances might eclipse the hierarchy of status. Nevertheless, it was sufficiently compelling to justify the description of Qing society as "feudal," and it performed the same tasks as feudal systems elsewhere: It reflected the reality of socioeconomic class but at the same time suppressed the full emergence of a more "nakedly antagonistic" class structure.[25]

As intriguing as such broadly comparative analyses may appear, I am not convinced of their claim to represent late imperial historical reality. Based as they are primarily on legal models articulated from the imperial center, we should be very hesitant to infer from them either actual social conditions or prevailing cultural attitudes, even on the part of the official elite. Nor do these models, at least as stated in their most schematic form, take much account of change over time within the period in question. Of some things there can be little doubt: the centrality of the binary hierarchical distinction between superior (*shang*) and inferior (*xia*) in classical Confucian texts, its rise to great saliency in Song neo-Confucianism, and the complex legacy of this for Qing social thought. A spate of recent scholarship in China, moreover, has extensively documented the formal division of the Qing population into status groups based on free or servile status, the ritual and judicial implications of such classifications, and the process by which such distinctions were incrementally rescinded during the late seventeenth and eighteenth centuries.[26] Based on the case of Chen Hongmou, however, there seems to be little reason to believe that most field officials thought much about such questions; he, at least, did not at all.

Much recent scholarship in the West has emphasized the extent to which socioeconomic changes of the late Ming and early Qing eras—especially the promotion of monetary wealth as an alternative measure of individual or familial worth and the resulting indecorous competition over material surplus in the period's frenetic boom economy—blurred and challenged the hegemony of the literati elite.[27] Not a few scholars have highlighted what they see as seventeenth- and eighteenth-century attempts on the part of certain elements within the elite to arrest the trends of social mobility and erosion of hierarchy that they acknowledged but found so threatening.[28] Susan Mann, in particular, has assigned Chen Hongmou a pivotal place in this regressive cultural project.[29]

But such a characterization of Chen, based on close reading of selected texts, fails in my view to comprehend the complexity and tension within his overarching social vision. It certainly seems difficult to reconcile with his repeated insistence on common humanity and coequal moral autonomy of all persons (discussed above) and with other elements in his thought stressing individual dignity and self-interest (to be dealt with below). I will argue that it is far from accurate to view Chen as a simple defender of class or status-group privilege. Nevertheless, there are definite grounds for Mann to depict Chen as she does, and we must therefore explore here a variety of possible elements of rank-consciousness in his general assumptions about human society.

Although it was not a recurring theme in his rhetoric, Chen does periodically acknowledge that the population is divided by law into ranks (*dengcha*) or statuses (*zunbei*)—those of official, gentry, student, and commoner—and that certain kinds of behavior, especially ritual behavior, are legally mandated for each. He endorses, for example, the imperially proclaimed schedule of status-specific funerary rites and complains that wealthy commoners increasingly appropriate elements of death ritual practice inapplicable to their station.[30] More frequently, though, Chen speaks simply of the distinction between two groups, in effect the rulers and the ruled. As Philip Kuhn has observed, this was the really operative divide in the consciousness of most late imperial Chinese, considered as "one built into the very nature of human society," and it had the practical effect of leveling or obscuring other, more differentiated, status distinctions.[31] Compound terms consisting of the paired opposites "literati and commoners" (*shimin, shishu*) appear regularly enough in Chen's discourse—although, significantly, they are invoked most often to discuss features (such as moral obligations) that he argues are common to both. He also speaks straightforwardly of the mass of the governed as "those below" (*xiadeng, xiaren*), as distinguished from the sociopolitical elite (*shiren*).[32]

What is strikingly consistent throughout Chen Hongmou's writings, however, is the view that the distinctiveness of the literati elite is one of special obligation rather than of special privilege. Chen comments on a passage by Lü Kun, whose peculiar blend of noblesse oblige populism had a formative influence on his own: "Whether those below are noble or base in their conduct matters little, since they have neither authority nor influence. But whether the elite are noble or base is vital to governance, to the quality of popular social practice, and to popular mores."[33] Through their personal conduct, their organization of community compacts (*xiangyue*), their celebration of moral exemplars among the people themselves, and countless other means, Chen expects the elite to exercise moral leadership.[34] Not all do, of course, and Chen laments the pettiness of those literati who conduct themselves no differently than do the vulgar masses (*suren*).[35] Conversely, nowhere have I found Chen commenting on any obligation of social inferiors to perform specified acts of deference to members of a higher status group; indeed, as we have seen, he consistently denies those in positions of power any right to receive such services.

What we see in Chen Hongmou, I would argue, is something that has been identified in other contexts by a number of other scholars: an awkward combination of quasi-egalitarian Confucian universalism with a frank recognition that status distinctions do exist in fact and are even, when properly regulated, of potential social utility.[36] As odd as this juxtaposition may seem, it was one with which Chen was fully at ease. He probably expressed it nowhere more directly than in his prefatory comments to Xiong Hongbei's *Meritorious Deeds at No Cost* (*Bufei qian gongde li*), a late-seventeenth-century morality book that Chen reprinted in his own *Sourcebook on Reforming Social Practice.* The fact that Xiong divided his moral advice into sections specifically appropriate to occupational and status groups such as gentry, students, farmers, and women (also merchants, yamen clerks, and monks) has prompted Cynthia Brokaw to see him as epitomizing a concerted elite movement aimed at "preserv[ing] the social hierarchy," "defining hierarchical distinctions," and "regulating, even containing, social mobility."[37] I myself do not read Xiong's doggerel work in quite so uncomplicated a light, and clearly neither did Chen Hongmou. In a masterpiece of resolution of conceptual tension Chen argued that by the very act of heeding Xiong's advice, and acting morally "in accordance with one's personal place in society" (*suochu*), the virtuous individual reifies a moral order in which "there are no status differences among humanity at all" (*shi ren wu guiqian gaoxia*).[38]

Notwithstanding the humble social origins that he readily acknowledged, the adult Chen Hongmou had no doubt that he himself belonged within the ruling elite. His published letters, almost all of which are to fellow officials, routinely invoke the subjective category *wubei*, or "people like us." By this Chen seems at times to refer to the literati as a whole, sometimes more narrowly to what Philip Kuhn has aptly termed the "private club" of high provincial officials with rights of direct communication with the throne (a group within which Chen spent the vast majority of his official career),[39] and, probably most often, to all those men serving in bureaucratic service—the class of persons I have referred to here as the "official elite." Despite its flexible boundaries, Chen sees *wubei* as a group with pronounced common interests, experiences, and emotional outlooks. *Wubei* share a set of professional obligations, which Chen complains many do not live up to—we simply haven't, in many cases, been doing our job. Above all, "our sort" as a group is beset by common anxieties over personal inadequacy, frustrations over career disappointments, and near terror over their enormous responsibility for the well-being of the people.[40] Again, nowhere does Chen speak of the deference or perquisites to which *wubei* are due.

The principal qualifications for membership in this group are superior intelligence and moral commitment, which, with characteristic Confucian optimism, Chen insists on viewing as nearly one and the same. Even while affirming the innate rationality and educability of all human beings, he freely admits that intelligence is not equally shared by all. Even among siblings, just as physical endowments differ, so too do intellectual capacities.[41] The goal of education, then, is to allow each student to develop to the limits of his or her own "measure of ability" (*liangneng zhi liang*).[42] Subjecting all students to a common core curriculum will likewise have differential effects, following each student's native intelligence; the brightest ones (*junxiuzhe*) will thereby be prepared for a life of scholarship, whereas the dullards (*chuiluzhe*) will be in any case indoctrinated in the rudiments of civilized conduct.[43] In his *Sourcebook on Childhood Education* Chen cites Lu Shiyi's analysis of the mind to explain why this occurs. All persons at birth, says Lu, have two mental powers: memory (*jixing*) and comprehension (*wuxing*). Generally speaking, the former is equal in all, but the latter is not. After a certain level of education, this difference becomes crucial, and relative endowments determine who among the population has the wherewithal for genuine scholarship.[44]

Chen's acknowledgment of differences in individual intelligence, and his linkage of this with the right or duty to assume sociopolitical leadership, leads us to consider his use of the ubiquitous late imperial sobriquet "*yumin*," a term most frequently translated "stupid people." Well into the early modern era, a pervasive assumption of political thought in China, as in the West, took the masses of the population as relatively unthinking ciphers, the object of governance by those capable of more rational thought.[45] In the Chinese case the term "*yumin*" was perhaps the archetypal expression of this assumption, and a look at Chen's use of it reveals some of the tensions inherent in his views of human society. For example, it is clear that Chen invoked the term most often in reference to the *rural* population. In at least one public pronouncement he stated this directly: "The rural population is extremely stupid!" (*xiangmin zhiyu*).[46] Routinely, he linked the terms for *rural* and *stupid* in the compound expression "*xiangyu*," in a sense very close to the English terms *country bumpkin* or *yokel*.[47] The populations of peripheral frontier regions—Chen's native Guangxi included—are even more *yu* than those of the empire's cultural cores.[48] How does one reconcile this with Chen's emphatic championing of the native human intelligence of geographically isolated populations and, perhaps even more oddly, with his prizing of the virtue of rustic integrity and simplicity (*pu*), which, after all, Chen identified with his own cherished familial background?

The key to such a reconciliation must lie in a more nuanced understanding of what Chen meant by "*yu*" (stupid). It would seem to refer neither to congenital intellectual weakness nor to moral depravity. Nor does it refer simply to illiteracy; Chen in fact acknowledges that in this era of the early modern explosion of the print culture there are many among the *xiangyu* who can read, if not read well, and so he encourages his local-level subordinates to frame their directives in simple, readable prose. Chen helps us understand what "*yu*" means to him by pairing it with presumed opposites—not raw intelligence or cultural refinement but "wisdom" (*zhi*) and "sagacity" (*zhen*), both qualities achievable only after a period of prolonged and intense study of the classical curriculum.[49] Chen's *yumin*, then, are the masses of people who have not been afforded the luxury of extensive formal education and consequently remain in need of civilizing guidance (*huadao*) from those who have.

Lacking this experience, the *yumin* remain trapped within unreflective and uncrit-

ical patterns of behavior. They are obsessed by material needs; Chen is fond of repeating the literati platitude "Food is the Heaven of the masses" (*shi wei min tian*). They are
reduced by the temptations of drink, of gambling, and of wasteful extravagance. They
are easily lured into heterodox cults. They are ready victims for exploitation by yamen
functionaries and local bullies. They are frequently unable to recognize examples of
virtuous conduct in their own midst, until these are pointed out to them by their more
educated neighbors.[50] But the *yumin* are motivated not only by the stimuli of immediate needs and desires; they are also "mired in habitual practice" (*ran yu xisu*).[51] What
we see in Chen, then, is a taxonomy of behavior with a distinctly modernist ring: the
masses are capable of "affective" and "traditionalist" conduct, whereas "rational" action
that takes careful account of long-range consequences is, in most cases, the province of
the educated, of "people like us." The elitism in this view is undeniable.

But as patronizing as Chen is toward the *yumin*, he is far from dismissive or con-
temptuous. He is notably less superior in his outlook even than his revered model of
populist activism, Lü Kun.[52] Chen points out that even the most ignorant among the
yumin experience shame (*shu*) at having committed wrongful acts and on this basis are
innately teachable.[53] And, as we shall see in Chapter 12, he fervently believes that the
condition of *yumin* is not a necessary or binding one; it can be eliminated, or very
nearly so, by a concerted program of mass education administered by the state.

Rich and Poor

As many recent studies have emphasized, economic criteria of personal worth had increasingly achieved saliency after the sixteenth century, and, if not superseding birth or
educational level as determinants of social status, had at least dramatically complicated
prevailing notions about the social hierarchy. By the time of Chen Hongmou's adulthood in the early eighteenth century, many would argue, both elite and popular culture had reached a new level of comfort with the notion that wealth was a morally acceptable emblem of personal achievement.[54] With this understanding let us explore
Chen's own assumptions about the moral implications of economic differentiation.

One important early modern shift reflected in Chen's outlook is the decline in status distinctions attached to occupation, in particular the erosion of the politico-cultural
animus against merchants embodied in much of the classical canon. In sharp contrast to
the approach to governance of the early Ming, which sought to freeze occupational mobility and establish a firm status hierarchy among livelihoods, the late Ming to mid-Qing
eras saw the emergence of what Yu Yingshi terms a "*simin lun*" (discourse of the four categories of people), a revolution in common parlance that redefined the traditional four
categories of persons—scholar, farmer, artisan, and merchant—as in effect coequal participants in an integrated economy and society. Yu notes even the Qing imperial endorsement of such attitudes—in such formulations as "The four categories of people
have different occupations, but share a common ethos" (*simin yiye er tongdao*)—and concludes that the hoary notion of "contempt for merchants" (*qingshang*) was, by the eighteenth century, nearly totally absent from even the most orthodox Confucian rhetoric.[55]

"*Simin*" figures in Chen Hongmou's discourse most often in the sense defined by

Yu, as a collective noun that places emphasis squarely on inclusion rather than differentiation.[56] In one revealing instance, however, it tells us still more. The occasion is Chen's citation, in his *Sourcebook on the Conduct of Office*, of a passage from Tang Bin, the early Qing model official whom Chen much admired.[57] Tang notes that, whereas in the past there genuinely *were* but "four categories of people," nowadays there are two more: mendicant monks and drifters. With their characteristically acute sense of social responsibility, both Tang and Chen (in his commentary) attribute the emergence of these two orders to the economic dislocation resulting from decades of predatory misgovernment. But the two groups of dispossessed are at the same time equated, and castigated, for their own economic unproductivity. In this they stand in contrast to the more conventional *simin*, whose productivity is precisely their common essence and the basis of their moral equivalence as members of "the people." We saw in Chapter 6 that Chen is hardly immune to a certain contempt for vagabonds and even for casual laborers, whom he dismisses as *wuye* (alternately readable as "propertyless" and "unproductive"); but he is equally attentive to lack of productivity at the other end of the cultural spectrum, among professional scholars (*dushuren*) whose pedantry and dilettantism reveal them as "useless" (*wuyong*) parasites, compromising their claim to membership in "the people."[58] Chen argues explicitly that all occupations that meet his standard of productive utility are equally legitimate and that the calling one opts to pursue is merely a function of one's native abilities and of the opportunities presented.[59] It is this logic, I would argue, that underlay Chen's endorsement of Xiong Hongbei's *Meritorious Deeds at No Cost* rather than any urge to freeze the social hierarchy. The various occupational groups addressed by Xiong (farmers, artisans, doctors, soldiers, merchants, government clerks, and so on) are all equally bound by the basic principles of moral conduct; the practical applications of these principles differ by livelihood, but the worthiness of the livelihoods themselves remains the same.

What were Chen Hongmou's attitudes toward wealth and poverty as social characteristics? Kuhn is absolutely correct, in my view, that in Chen's late imperial world economic class was relatively weak as an element of social thought.[60] Rich and poor simply did not represent a defining "axis in the Chinese scheme of classification." They were conditions, varying with cyclical regularity from one generation to another, rather than a social taxonomy. Yet at the same time all knew that "the rich" and "the poor" existed in fact, and, as Kuhn himself concedes, reference to them was pervasive in contemporary discourse. The key question, it seems to me, was how a given person's wealth or poverty was determined. Lien-sheng Yang has pointed out that, although in Confucian theory wealth and poverty ought to be accurate reflections of personal or familial virtue, Chinese of the late imperial period had long conceded that this was not reliably the case. Consequently a variety of mediating factors—most significantly the black box known as "fate" (*ming*)—had been introduced into the discussion of economic difference.[61] More recently, various scholars have noted that this sense of anxiety about the justice of the prevailing distribution of wealth became notably greater in the rapidly commercializing early modern era, although it had abated somewhat by the more stable and secure eighteenth century.[62]

On this issue Chen Hongmou's views were profoundly unresolved. In a single utterance, a directive issued during the subsistence crisis in 1742 Jiangxi, Chen articu-
lates with evident sincerity a package of conflicting theories on the origins of individual wealth. "The poor [qiongmin] must be aware," he counsels, "that wealth and poverty
are simply a function of fate [ming]." In an agrarian society standards of living are inextricably bound up with the success of the harvest and thus inevitably experience cy-
cles of prosperity and decline (suishi zhi chang). At the same time, Chen suggests (albeit
in a rather mild way) that wealth is indeed the product of superior virtue: The rich are
entitled to their wealth because it is either the result of their own more diligent labor
or that of their forebears.[63] Elsewhere he links wealth and virtue even more explicitly.
In his Sourcebook on the Conduct of Office he reprints a selection from the late Ming official
Zhang Nai arguing that the proper way to manage a family is by following moral dictates—set down household instructions, observe frugality and simplicity, and so on—
rather than by "clambering after material fortune" (qiufu). In his commentary Chen
agrees, but he assures his readers that if one properly adheres to this moral guidance,
"material fortune will follow of its own accord."[64]

Chen's ambiguity on this score, I would suggest, situates him at a point in time not
unlike that of his early modern Western contemporaries, who were similarly caught between two schools of opinion. Surveying the European case, Gertrude Himmelfarb has
argued that, as late as the mid-eighteenth century, "Poverty was essentially what it always
had been: a natural, unfortunate, but not necessarily demeaning or degrading fact. . . .
Poverty was part of the natural order of things." But the "revolutionary" view of the
poor as morally culpable for their own condition, and hence unworthy targets of either
private or public aid (enjoined both by religion and formal law in the earlier era), was
shortly to follow, a product of the industrial revolution.[65] Chen Hongmou, however, did
not accept entirely the latter view. Although inclined to equate wealth and personal industry, and hence to argue for the entitlement of the wealthy to their wealth, he certainly did not draw from this the Malthusian argument that the poor were inappropriate recipients of empathy and material aid. Like many of his Qing contemporaries,
Chen readily accepted that poverty could be in part a function of situational factors outside the individual's control and indeed worried that specific trends of his time (such
as population growth and market volatility) had pushed ever more of the people into
this lamentable condition.[66] Poverty was, at least in part, the product of a changing
economy.

That the state held a major degree of responsibility for the survival of the poor was
a cardinal assumption of Qing policy and one to which Chen was personally very deeply
committed. "The ancients took the care of the helpless [wukao] as their duty," he wrote.
"Providing for both the living and the dead are primary tasks of the Kingly Way." Education and "civilizing" (jiaohua), too, must be extended by those in office, especially to
"those who lack the financial means to educate themselves."[67] We have seen repeatedly
how Chen applied these principles in his practical policy making; throughout his career he was known as a populist official, one with unusual sympathy for the downtrodden but one at the same time who favored programs promoting economic independence and self-reliance.

Chen's terms of reference for the poor—"*qiongmin*" and "*pinmin*"—are morally neutral. As a general rule he couples these nouns with modifiers that are similarly matter-of-fact rather than pejorative: "*wuli*" (without resources), "*wukao*" (without recourse to aid), "*wujia*" (without homes), "*wushi*" (without food), "*wushengli*" (without means of livelihood).[68] He never refers to the poor, as certain late Ming predecessors had done,[69] in terms suggesting irrationality, depravity, or debased status. Indeed, as Liang Qizi has effectively demonstrated, the notions of "poor" (*pin*) and "debased" (*jian*) had become increasingly separated over the course of the late imperial era, and by the mid-Qing—in the wake of Yongzheng's emancipatory reforms—the latter category was widely perceived as having little remaining relevance.[70] Far from deriving poverty from moral weakness, Chen often (like mid-twentieth-century liberals) draws the linkage in the opposite direction: "If one is cold and hungry, it is far more difficult to act in accord with the dictates of propriety."[71] And in a letter reproduced in Wei Yuan's widely influential *Statecraft Compendium* he takes what might be seen as a "soft" view on crime: "Robbery," he explains, "is fundamentally a result of poverty, which in turn is caused by unemployment."[72]

But although poverty can lead to lawlessness, it does not necessarily do so, and the poor are not uniformly threatening. Rather, for Chen the division between lawbreakers and the more general poor is a significant one. As candidates for granary loans, for instance, he clearly distinguishes the eligible "poor peasants" (*nongmin pinqiong*) from the ineligible "idlers" (*haoxian*) and "drifters" (*youshou*). Postal runners, a group of itinerant casual workers about whom Chen is deeply suspicious, are nevertheless only "half composed of miscreants" (*ban fei liangshan*). Likewise beggars, whom Chen generally despises, are divided into those with no other legitimate option for survival and who obey the law, and those who might easily find other work but persist in beggary as a cover for petty crime.[73] Chen does at times resort to the pejorative term "*wulai*" (without accredited social roots) to describe elements of the lower classes, but he does not use it as a general modifier of "the poor" the way he uses, say, the morally neutral "*wuli*" (without resources). The poor are not, in other words, an "undifferentiated human bloc."[74]

As we saw in Chapter 6, Chen held quite distinctive views on the nature of property, and these views underlay in important ways his scheme of social classification and his analysis of social behavior. As applied to certain types among the poor, for example, he wrote, "There is a class of people who are without property and vocation (*yizhong wuchan wuye zhi ren*) who will [for this reason] sink to any depravity."[75] Conversely, he held that possession of wealth by the rich was both morally and politically unassailable; coercively confiscating that wealth for redistribution to those in need was "in violation of the principles of equity" (*gongping*).[76] Nor could profit-maximizing behavior on the part of the wealthy be condemned in most cases as base, fully according as it did with both human nature and rational principle (*yuanshu qingli*).[77]

With this sort of outlook Chen Hongmou might seem easily pilloried as an apologist for propertied interests in Qing society. In fact, however, he was far less often condemned by political opponents for his sympathies for the rich than for pandering shamelessly to the masses of the poor. In Chen's own mind the interests of rich and poor were seamlessly interconnected. As a central participant in what Kuroda Akinobu has identified as the Qing "discourse on the preservation of wealth" (*baofu lun*), and rather like his contemporaries, the French physiocrats, Chen held to a view of the genuine social utility of the wealthy, as consumers of others' products, as employers, as dispensers of philanthropy, and as pillars of the social order.[78] Such views were in the air in Chen's day; selections in his various edited works suggest that he derived them in part from Lü Kun and from Gu Yanwu (although I would argue that Chen remained on balance considerably less elitist in his outlook than either of these figures).[79] Neither could have stated the position more forthrightly than Chen himself, however, in writing, "There is no more apt way to assist the poor than by safeguarding the rich" (*baofu zheng suoyi jipin*).[80]

"Every locality has its wealthy and magnanimous families," he wrote to a colleague, "upon which the poor are dependent for their subsistence."[81] Like Gu Yanwu, Chen appreciated elite paternalism for the extent to which it obviated greater intrusion on the part of the bureaucratic state. In his preliminary survey of peripheral Gansu in 1755 he applauded the emergence of private wealth as an index of the province's social as well as economic development.[82] His various law-and-order campaigns, such as that in Xi'an in 1754, were very frankly tied to the protection of propertied households.[83] Yet even while defending their assets and investments both ideologically and practically, Chen also made unusually creative (although determinedly not coercive) use of the wealthy in efforts to relieve popular immiseration. Like many another field official, Chen expected local individuals "of substance" (*yinshi*) to serve as moral exemplars, to instruct and guide their neighbors in proper attitudes and social practice, to offer a means of extrabureaucratic conflict resolution within their community, and to initiate, manage, and underwrite local public projects.[84] He also expected them to provide material support for the local poor, on both a crisis and a routinized basis. In this he responded not merely as a serving official who relied on the magnanimity of the local elite to guarantee food sufficiency within his jurisdiction but also more generally as an individual imbued with what Liang Qizi has described as the emerging late imperial cultural ideal of "philanthropy" (*cishan*)—the notion that systematic charitable giving was both an obligation of wealth and an emblem of social status.[85]

Chen Hongmou's assumptions about economically responsible elite behavior were optimistic and at times indeed appear naive. But they were not invariably so. The booming middle decades of the eighteenth century heard a mounting chorus of complaints against ostentatious and wasteful displays of wealth on the part of the rich, including repeated complaints on the part of the Qianlong emperor himself. With his frontier-bred distaste for literati pretense and his fetishistic attachment to "rustic simplicity" (*pu*), Chen was not surprisingly in the forefront of this attack. Sincerely shocked by what he discovered during his earliest official tenures in Yangzhou and Jiangnan, he reprinted in his sourcebooks lengthy diatribes against the luxurious decadence of these hyperdeveloped commercial areas.[86] He complained repeatedly that the wealthiest families of his day were driven by an indecorous and unprincipled "selfishness" (*wojian*) and "egoism" (*weiwo*).[87] And, even as he defended the theoretical right of the wealthy to utilize the leverage of wealth to their own advantage, he decried the insensitive way they used this leverage in practice to "oppress" (*qiya*) or "exploit" (*panbo*) those without the means for self-defense, "injuring others to profit oneself" (*sunren liji*).[88]

Chen cited Gu Yanwu's adage, "It is not wealth which is the problem, but rather economic inequality," and, following the much-admired early Qing reformist official Tang Bin, he acknowledged that this inequality had grown more obvious over the early modern era. He knew that class conflict was a genuine and frightening possibility—as we have seen, he observed it himself in dearth-stricken 1740s Jiangxi.[89] He devoted considerable space in his sourcebooks to discussions of the issues over which such conflict might arise (for example, public security, an area that disproportionately benefited the rich while imposing special burdens of corvée and taxation on the poor) and how it might be ameliorated.[90] Chen advises would-be officials to treat rich and poor evenhandedly, demonstrating empathy (*tixu*) for all and, most important, communicating actively and sincerely to all elements of society just what the government is doing in resolution of potentially contentious issues and what it expects of them. In convincing the rich to fulfill their social obligations Chen counsels reliance on normative appeals to their intrinsic human goodness (*tianliang*) but, when necessary, coupling this with an effort to "clarify for them what is in their true best interest"—a not-so-subtle reminder of the "hatred of the masses" (*zhongyuan*) for wealth in demonstrably unworthy hands.[91] Compliance must ultimately, however, be voluntary rather than legislated. To the poor Chen advises "remaining content with your fate" (*anming*), although he does acknowledge that they have what amounts to a right to expect succor from the rich (*jiebi*), provided they do not demand this in an "outrageous" (*si'e*) manner. If all parties conduct themselves as they should, "rich and poor will prosper together" (*pinfu xiangyao*).[92] This ideal, significantly, results not from a leveling of differences between those of greater or lesser economic means but from a harmonizing of relations between them.

At the same time, admonitions to remain contented with one's economic lot should not be construed as an aversion in Chen to social mobility, an effort to freeze the economic hierarchy (any more than the hierarchy of status) to preserve the dominance of Chen's own "class." Central to all of Chen's thought, as we have seen, was the distinction between areas of human action in which results were attainable by human effort and those (the domain of fate) in which they were not. For the most part, he saw the strenuous pursuit of personal and familial socioeconomic betterment as falling into the former category. The pursuit of upward mobility was, within the constraints imposed by decorum (*li*), a positive force for society as a whole. Given his own relatively humble background, it would be surprising if he did not feel this way.

The examinations, of course, were the orthodox "ladder of success." Chen explicitly praises their role as "a path of upward mobility" (*jinshen zhi lu*) and indeed works very aggressively (especially in peripheral and cultural minority areas) to ensure their fairness to all. Yet he is equally vigorous in his defense of personal advancement through financial profit seeking (*zhuantu shengxi*), by the poor as well as by the rich. Although he himself had risen from relatively humble roots via the orthodox route of education and examination success, Chen was, as we have seen, consistently in the forefront of controversial efforts to allow expanded opportunities for the conversion of market-generated wealth into gentry status via the degree-purchase system (*juanna*). None of this suggests a view of Chen as a man obsessed with containing social mobility.

As conservative as his approach to authority assuredly was, Chen was very far from a defender of entrenched privilege. In one of his most impassioned pieces of writing, he argues, "Ever since antiquity, the inherited hierarchy of status [*liupin*] has never been sufficient to constrain the [upwardly mobile] individual [*xianren*]. Even more so today, those with drive and ambition [*youzhizhe*] can, with full propriety, seize the occasion to advance themselves [*zifen*]."[93] It was clearly as just such a success story that Chen saw himself, and it was in the unprecedented opportunities offered to such individuals that he saw the unique promise for prosperity and social development of his own day. By comparison to past ages, he boasted, family background or inherited status counted for relatively little in the enlightened era of mid-Qing, and the limits imposed on personal advancement (*jinshen*) were essentially those of individual ability. This open structure of opportunity, moreover, was of great social utility: It provided the best incentive to moral, productive behavior on the part of those masses of people intent on realizing the full potential for achievement their society allowed.[94]

Social Roles

I have tried to show here that "hierarchy," in the way it is most often presented in current scholarship as a system of closed and stratified corporate groups, was not a particularly salient aspect of the social vision of Chen Hongmou. Neither Chen's frontier-bred disdain for literati haughtiness, nor his Mencian faith in the moral-rational equality of all human beings, nor his belief in the propriety and social utility of the drive for personal advancement could comfortably coexist with such an outlook. At the same time, however, Chen's prose is undeniably pervaded by a rhetoric of "submission" (*shun*) and by injunctions to "distinguish between superior and subordinate" (*bie shangxia*).[95] Yet as striking as this is, it is also clear that in nearly every case what Chen had in mind was not a deferential ranking by *group* but rather one within each individual's encompassing and elaborately filiated interpersonal *network*. When he wrote of the necessity to "respect authority" (*zunzhang*), when he argued that "the mentality of respect and affection for one's superiors" (*zunjun chinshang zhi xin*) was a basic component of the innate moral sense of all persons, when he advised that "if those near to one are treated as such and seniors treated as seniors (*qinqin zhangzhang*) the empire will be at peace," he was extolling not a class structure or status hierarchy but a mesh of highly personalistic social obligations.[96]

The starting point for understanding this interpersonal network, for Chen and his contemporaries, was a construction of social roles (*fen*) based on the model of intrafamilial relations. This construction had an extremely long history in Chinese culture, traceable at least to the *Yi jing*, but had received its patent of orthodoxy in such Han-dynasty texts as the *Li ji* and *Xiao jing*. In the hands of Song Confucian revivalists the metaphysical grounding of these social roles had received exhaustive attention, being redefined as manifestations of heavenly principle (*tianli*), and the roles themselves had undergone rather extreme ethical rigidification. But the continuities outweighed the innovations. Despite the momentous social and cultural changes of the early modern era, in Chen Hongmou's day basic belief in the compulsion to role fulfillment remained very much alive. And although the relative primacy of specific roles (for example, that of "friend") was occasionally debated, and the precise duties assigned to some roles (such as husband and wife) might be actively contested, the basic conception of human society as ordered by such roles remained virtually unquestioned.[97]

Roles were defined in relational terms, nearly always binary ones. Their basic enumeration was that of the Three Bonds (*sangang*: ruler-subject, father-son, and husband-wife) and the derivative Five Relationships (*wulun*), but when necessary they could be articulated even more finely, to include such roles as mother, daughter-in-law, and adoptive son. In his *Sourcebook on Reforming Social Practice* Chen Hongmou reprints a set of lineage rules by Wang Shijin that offers a guide to the roles (*mingfen*) proper to each male descendent within his lineage, urging that their relative precedence never be confused.[98] In popular usage the term *role* could be extended to refer to broader social categories; Chen at times uses the injunction "*anfen*" (to be contented with one's role) in reference to occupational groups and to the masses of the poor.[99] But although this linguistic usage is important—in suggesting, among other things, the depth of the familistic image of society—the basic conception of social roles remained that of the familially determined *wulun*.

We have already seen that Chen invokes the language of the Five Relationships on a routine basis in his rhetoric. "The Relationships and the Constant Virtues [*lunchang*]," he writes, "are the most important means by which we demonstrate our humanity." And again: "The reason human beings differ from animals is simply that we observe the Relationships and Principle" (*lunli*).[100] Chen takes his duties as an imperial official centrally to involve guiding the population in the correct performance of their relational roles, as we shall see in Chapter 12. It seems highly significant, however, that as central as the Five Relationships are to his social vision, he never once that I have seen invokes the term "*sangang*" (Three Bonds). Far more so than the Relationships, the Bonds were explicitly hierarchical (excluding as they did the relationships of fraternity and friendship). Unlike the *wulun*, which were linked in common usage to the ideas of human rationality and the notion of a benign and rational Heaven, they must have seemed to Chen a residue of an earlier, less enlightened age of coercive authority.

Both the roles themselves and the constant relationships between them were part of Heaven's bounty: they were not merely *fen* and *lun* but *tianfen* and *tianlun*. One cannot adequately comprehend the power of this social vision for Chen and his contemporaries without recognizing that these roles were seen not as a cultural construction, nor as a convenient way of ordering society arrived at by human consensus, but rather as cosmically ordained and immutable by human agency. Thus Chen, for example, in prescribing the detailed familial obligations of a daughter-in-law, offers as his authority for doing so the fact that the daughter-in-law's role "derives from the heavenly order of things" (*fa yu tianxing*). The process of conformity to one's social role was no more than "the realization of one's essential nature" (*zhixing*),[101] and that of drawing and clarifying "distinctions" (*bie*) between social roles was the quintessential means of imposing order on disorder. (As we will see later, it was thus identified with the process of extending Chinese elite "civilization," and its political corollary of imperial bureaucratic rule, both outward into frontier areas and downward into the lower ranks of Han society itself.)

The conception of human society as ordered into predictable roles was plugged into both an organismic model of the universe, in which individuals were but functional cogs, and an ancient pattern of correlative thinking that Hao Chang has usefully termed "the Confucian cosmological myth."[102] An elaborate system of correspondences between the human body, the family, the social and political orders, and the natural universe was intimately tied up with the notion of the Relationships and as such gave both cosmological legitimation and wider sociopolitical implications to the subordination of individual interest inherent in the Chinese family system. In the Han and Song periods this pattern of correlative thinking had been further tied in with an elaborate system of correspondences among various natural phenomena, such as human anatomy, astronomical occurrences, the spectrum of colors, and the musical scale. But whereas, as John Henderson has convincingly shown, Chinese scientific thinking changed in the early modern era to break down faith in many of these natural correspondences,[103] the ethical, social, and political aspects of the cosmological myth eroded much more slowly.

Chen Hongmou believed in them unquestioningly. Following Lü Kun, he wrote, "Each human being is a microcosm of Heaven-and-earth," and he routinely identified the family as a microcosm of the state.[104] He cited Wang Yangming's elaborate homology: "The condition [*qing*] of all-under-Heaven is no different from that of a single locality. The condition of a locality is no different from that of a single family. The condition of a family is no different from that of my individual self." Wang, and Chen following him, draws from this two conclusions. First, the individual cannot separate out his or her fate from that of all humanity but instead must assume responsibility for all. Second, each concentric unit of human identity mirrors all the others in its pattern of internal ordering; that is, each possesses a natural order of precedence based on generational seniority. Observing this order of precedence is the surest way "to please Heaven."[105]

The individual offers personal testimony to the validity of this order by appropriately "occupying" his or her social roles (*dangfen*). As Donald Munro has pointed out, roles were routinely conceptualized in terms of spatial metaphors. They were not only "*fen*" (literally: segment), but also "*wei*" and "*suo*," and the basic form of moral error involves "transgressing" (*guo*) the boundaries of place.[106] For Chen, accordingly, failing to perform as one's role dictates is "losing one's place" (*shisuo*). Ethical conduct demands both that one demonstrate "contentment" with one's roles (*anfen*)—what Keith McMahon has termed "self-containment" or "sticking to one's lot"[107]—and also more actively that one "comply with" or "fulfill the dictates of" those roles (*xunfen*). By far the most emotion-laden idiom used to express this active effort was "*jie*." Translated by Wing-tsit Chan as "virtue proper to a role" and by Kwang-Ching Liu as "firm integrity," "*jie*" meant at once restraint (its etymology derived from the basic meaning of a cord bound by knots) and a more strenuous pursuit of role fulfillment.[108] In common Qing usage "*jie*" was usually identified with one specific manifestation of role fulfillment, female chastity (on which more below), but in ethical discourse it still retained its broader reference to all vigorous efforts at moral conduct.

The grammar by means of which fulfillment of social roles was expressed in daily life was ritual (*li*). Chen Hongmou followed long tradition in viewing immoral acts as violating at once the dictates of ritual propriety (*feili*) and the demands of role fulfillment (*feifen*).[109] Certain especially momentous rituals—rites of passage such as adoption ceremonies, weddings, and funerals—were central to this process, inasmuch as they marked a given individual's entry or exit from a given *fen*. But the *li* also incorporated very mundane acts of interpersonal etiquette and fine details of personal grooming and comportment, which were in effect mystified by assignment of heavenly origin and cosmological import. Thus Chen Hongmou noted that young children must repeatedly practice the ritually correct forms of eating, drinking, sitting, reclining, and so on, and a wife must learn to follow the proper ritual procedures (*dianli*) that governed the "routines of daily activity in the home" (*jushi riyong zhi chang*).[110] It was no accident that the conventional term for common courtesy, "*lijie*," meant literally "faithful pursuit of the dictates of one's social role in a ritually correct fashion." By routinely acting out the duties assigned to one's role in a manner consistent with the *li*, each participant in this system of belief continually reaffirmed and reproduced the cosmic, the political, and the civilized social order.

The Family

The nexus of social roles that in large part for Chen defined human identities was rooted in the model of the family. Chen repeatedly attests in his writing to his literal faith in the sacred nature of the family unit as the principal social locus of heavenly ordained human relationships (*tianlun*). To continually reassert the validity of this model by demonstrating a secure occupation of one's familial roles (*anfen*) and "revealing" or actualizing these familial relationships (*minglun*) was the highest form of moral (and socially useful) action. To enact in one's own life the "way of the family" (*jiadao*) was a moral imperative, and to properly "manage one's family" (*zhijia*) was the foremost duty of any aspirant to respectable social adulthood. The family unit was simultaneously emotional, hierarchical, and solidary. As Chen wrote on the opening page of his *Sourcebook on Reforming Social Practice:* "The proper way of dwelling together as a family [*jujia*] rectifies moral principle by strengthening bonds of mutual affection [*du enyi*], distinguishing between superior and subordinate [*bian shangxia*], and strictly segregating the internal/domestic from the external/public [*yan neiwai*]."[111]

But even among the orthodox, *family* was open to multiple readings. I noted in Chapter 6 Patricia Ebrey's distinction between two competing conceptions of family in the late imperial tradition, one an essentially normative network orientation associated with the ancient notion of the patriarchal lineage (*zong*), the other a more materialist corporate orientation associated with the household as a budgetary unit (*jia*). In practical terms these differing conceptions could prescribe opposing courses of action. The *zong* orientation favored primogeniture, subordination of offspring to and control of collective assets by the senior lineal descendent of the eldest son (*zongzi*), and adoption of heirs only from children of brothers or male cousins. The *jia* orientation favored partible inheritance and individual household management of the patrimony, subordination of children to their natural parents only, and relatively free adoption practices. In Ebrey's view the triumph of Cheng-Zhu orthodoxy spelled the victory of the *zong* orientation as ideologically correct, although the *jia* orientation continued to compete with it in popular practice.[112]

Chen Hongmou's view of the family seems to have been closer to the orthodox *zong* conception, although he clearly incorporated elements of both views. Much in Chen's own family history suggested devotion to the *zong* model. His pious father, for instance, had asserted his *zongzi* authority in ordering the installation as Hongmou's heir of Chen Zhongke, the natural son of Hongmou's elder brother, Hongxian.[113] The adult Hongmou's sensitivity to the dictates of human feelings was such that it is hard to imagine his acting similarly (there is plenty of evidence in family records of the anxiety this ambivalent paternity caused in Chen Zhongke), but his commitment to *zong* solidarity nevertheless remained strong. During his official career he tried whenever possible to bring his siblings and their offspring to live under his roof, where they might realize the ancient ideal of "all related by divine bonds dwelling together as a group" (*tianlun zongzhu*) and where he could assert his authority as paterfamilias.[114] And as Shaanxi provincial governor he ordered subordinates to purify lineage groupings by forbidding all male adoptions from outside *zong* boundaries.[115]

Chen in fact devoted a great deal of attention to the *zong* unit in implementing his social policies, as we shall see for example in Chapter 11. In doing so he always stressed the key role of ancestral rites in fostering lineage bonding. However, strikingly absent from all of Chen's discussions of this subject is any rhetorical invocation of the *zongfa* (core-line principle), that quasi-mystical ancient Chinese concept that had been central to Zhu Xi's ideology of the *zong* and that in Chen's own day had become an object of intense intellectual fascination.[116] It is very telling that Chen, despite his genuine respect for Zhu Xi as the fount of neo-Confucian orthodoxy, chose not to reprint in any of his sourcebooks on social behavior Zhu's classic statement on the *zongfa*, the *Zhuzi jiali* (Master Chu's household rituals), even though it remained in his day the standard authority in the field.[117] Instead, in Chen's *Xunsu yigui* (Sourcebook on reform of social practice) he gave pride of place to Sima Guang's competing work, *Zhujia zalü* (Rules for dwelling together by household) and referred to Sima's *Jiafan* (Family rules) as the proper point of departure for any discussion of intrafamilial relations. Sima, as Ebrey argues, represented an attempt at moderation of the more rigid *zong* orthodoxy of Zhu Xi, taking account of the more material concerns of the *jia*.

What this suggests is that for Chen, despite his sincere belief that in family matters "it is the heavenly relationships (*tianlun*) which are paramount, and financial interests only secondary," there was no real difficulty in reconciling the two. We have seen that he devotes a great deal of space in his didactic writings to the very practical question of how the *jia*, the nuclear household, can conserve and maximize its patrimony and that he followed this advice in managing his own estate. Without proper financial management of the *jia* there can be no thought of *zong*. He writes, "If a household becomes impoverished, it affects that household alone; but if the family is extinguished [through dissipation of the patrimony], that is a disaster for the whole world."[118] Here, as in so many other aspects of his thought, Chen reveals his faith in the inextricable link between political economy (*jingji*) and ritual propriety (*lijiao*).

In other ways beyond the economic Chen sought to reconcile the ritual-moral view of family with a secular-social one. At least by the early modern era, I believe, we can detect the emergence in China of a notion of the familial or domestic sphere as a haven of privacy, relaxation, and personal sentiment versus the public world outside (a phenomenon documented for early modern Europe by Ariès, Habermas, and others). This notion, like that of the household as a budgetary unit, was embraced by Chen at the same time that he sought to place it in moral perspective:

> The family is the realm where compassion reigns supreme. Occasions for reliance on humanistic and compassionate response are far more numerous than those calling for reliance on formal propriety. And yet, recourse to compassion can all too easily slide into laxity or excess, and formal propriety too easily come to be ignored altogether. The proper balance is for compassion to provide the main pillars of the family, and the dictates of formal propriety the supporting beams.[119]

Following the *Great Learning* (*Daxue*), that seductively elegant ancient text regarded by most late imperial literati as the quintessential statement of ethical and political thought, the family was central to political ideology in at least three ways. First was the well-known homology between family and state. The state was the family writ large, and, as Chen repeated on many occasions, the principles on which the one was properly regulated were "exactly the same" as those for regulating the other. The relationships of authority and responsibility, the dictates of conformity to natural bonds of affection and obligation, are "identical in the polity and the family."[120] Well-governed families meant a well-governed state and vice versa. Second, it was an article of faith that manifestly virtuous households would have an exemplary influence on their neighbors and so contribute to a well-ordered, smoothly functioning society. Chen extolled Tang Bin, for example, as follows: "Through the governance of his own personal household he established a model for the moral transformation (*hua*) of the surrounding countryside."[121] Finally, the polity was conceived as a composite of families that served as the basic, interlinked building blocks for the larger social, economic, and ritual order. For this reason "the extinguishing of a single familial line constitutes a calamity for the entire world."[122]

Even more passionately than other policy makers of his day, Chen believed that the family, as both household and patriline, was the indispensable building block of a moral and well-functioning society. It was the basis both of stable productivity (*hengye*) and of self-imposed behavioral discipline (*yueshu*).[123] He was deeply concerned with imbuing in society the classically sanctioned methods of "regulating one's household" (*zhijia*), which transcended but by no means excluded careful financial planning (*jiaji*). The ideal model of a society ordered by familial, kinship, and residential communities was seen by Chen as in tension with current fashions favoring voluntary associations or communities of religious believers. By contrast with such tightly *bounded* groups, which were driven by parochial group-interest, the family unit promoted values that were infinitely *extendable* throughout society: "If one loves one's own kin, one will never dare treat any man with malice; if one respects one's own kin, one will never treat any man with contempt. It follows that if kin are treated as kin, and elders as elders, the world will be at peace."[124]

Accordingly, as a matter of practical policy, Chen and other eighteenth-century officials routinely used the instruments of the imperial state to implant the ritually correct household on the landscape as a means to achieve both stable economic productivity and enhanced social control. In this era of aggressive imperial expansion transforming non-Han family models to more familiar ones was a key strategy of frontier incorporation; thus as provincial treasurer of Yunnan in the 1730s Chen printed more than ten thousand copies of a tract on household management, the *Zhijia geyan*, and distributed them to indigenous populations through the medium of his newly founded state schools (see Chapter 12). A particular target of his reformist efforts in the southwest was the levirate (inheritance of the wife by a deceased male's younger brother or nephew), a custom that was apparently central to the matrilineal family practice of many indigenous peoples but that for Chen was a manifest violation of heavenly ordained human relationships (*tianlun*).[125] At the same time there was no dearth of attention to family reform among Han populations as well; Chen, for instance, sought vigorously to rectify the high incidence of matrilocality in certain parts of Shaanxi.[126]

Each in their own way, the Yongzheng and Qianlong emperors were particular enthusiasts of strengthening familial bonds as a means of control,[127] and Chen shared this goal with equal fervor. His own sourcebooks on proper conduct, which contain numerous readings on family matters, were distributed through state channels and made required reading for students in all the provinces in which he served. In times of flood, famine, and other natural disasters he worked in very concrete ways to keep afflicted households united and economically viable and at the same time proclaimed enhanced support for ties of kinship-based seniority (*fuzi xiongdi*) as an instrument for maintenance of social discipline.[128] Like many another Qing bureaucrat he railed against dangerously familyless "vagrants" (*youmin*) and sought to resettle them into more accountable domestic units.[129]

Chen's penchant for moral legislation, for example his oft-repeated prohibitions on gambling, drunkenness, and nighttime opera performances, was nearly always couched in terms of defense of the family unit and the preservation of household assets.[130] So too was his attack on lavish expenditures on wedding and funeral celebrations. In one celebrated proclamation he issued as Jiangsu governor in 1760 (reprinted both in the Suzhou prefectural gazetteer and in Wei Yuan's 1826 *Statecraft Compendium*), he rails against such extravagance in the prosperous and frivolous Jiangnan society. Such wastefulness, he argues, is a material threat to the financial resources of the *jia* and a moral disgrace to the household in violating its ritual obligations (*lifa*).[131] It cannot have been absent from Chen's consciousness that the very same word—"*jie*"—conveyed the meaning both of moral restraint associated with fulfillment of one's social role (especially widow chastity) and of economic frugality, which he doggedly urged on households throughout his career.

Gender

The conception of human society as ordered by a system of social roles likewise underlay the gender consciousness of Chen and others of the Qing official elite. But whereas faith in the centrality of the roles themselves was fairly continuous over time, as I have suggested, cultural constructions of gender—notions of how males and females ought to fulfill their respective roles in day-to-day social practice—had undergone by Chen's day considerable flux, part of broader shifts of consciousness resulting from the socioeconomic changes of the late Ming to mid-Qing period.[132] The rapid commercialization and monetization of the economy after the late sixteenth century created a new opportunity structure that altered the quality of gender relations and expanded the social functions actually assumed by women. The increasingly urbanized society, especially of Jiangnan, saw greater sexual mingling in workplaces such as textile manufactories, and in recreational sites such as teahouses and wine shops, where women appeared both as employees and customers. The cultural ideal of the sequestered women's quarters (*gui*) was ever more difficult to maintain in practice.[133] Along with this a new model of the worldly and refined professional courtesan arose within the developing urban pleasure quarters and had broader implications for male choices of female companionship. A new ideal emerged of the "companionate marriage," a love match between men and women who were similarly cultivated and who shared aesthetic tastes.[134] This development reflected in turn an actual rise in female (and society-wide) literacy rates, simultaneously prompting and responding to the expansion of the publishing industry. The fiction consumed by this growing reading public exhibited a new sexual frankness, as well as a glorification of romantic attachments between men and women.[135]

Following what has been called the "almost cultural revolution" of the late Ming, the first reigns of the Qing saw a joint state-elite effort to tighten controls in many areas of gender relations: more rigid rape laws, bans on pornography, legislative attacks on homosexual activity, statutory support for patriarchal authority and the virtuous widow cult, and so on.[136] T'ien Ju-k'ang has argued that the increased mid-Qing pressure of competition for scarce resources such as civil service degrees among a growing male population with upward mobility aspirations channeled frustration into a harsh rigidification of dictates for female propriety and fidelity.[137] Perhaps more convincingly, Susan Mann has pointed out that accelerated social mobility, blurring of status distinctions, and society-wide movement toward relaxations of personal dependency bonds (which culminated in the Yongzheng emperor's emancipation of various categories of debased peoples) sparked an urge to reaffirm traditional moral imperatives.[138]

By the middle decades of the eighteenth century this early Qing reaction had subsided sufficiently to allow, on the one hand, a resurfacing of what Charlotte Furth calls "a self-conscious current of dissenting values and social practice" and, on the other, an equally self-conscious nostalgic search for the values of a less degenerate age. The result was a far-reaching debate over proper gender roles, a debate conducted in such public or semipublic forums as bureaucratic correspondence, literati essays, ritual texts, household instructions, popular morality books, and popular fiction. The debate focused on such specific issues as the conventions of marriage and its ceremonies, the desirability of female literary education, proper conduct on the part of widows, and appropriate ritual forms of the ancestral cult. Lurking beneath the surface were questions regarding the appropriateness of the social ideal of the patriarchal family itself, although these questions would not begin to be articulated in public until a century or more later.

Despite the often heated character of this debate—carried out primarily among males—it is important to note that one rarely sees any individual writer in a simple "progressive" or "reactionary" light, by modernist standards. Yuan Mei, to cite a famous example, vigorously championed the cause of female literary education, but he just as vigorously defended the practice of concubinage on grounds of the inherent inferiority of females to males.[139] Classical textual scholars like Qian Daxin (1728–1804), too, appear alternately as progressive "feminists" and as reactionary fundamentalists. Their search for the actual ritual forms of the golden age (as revealed in a classical canon purged of interpolations and subsequent interpretive errors) led them to attack contemporary practice in ways at times liberating of women and at times repressive. Like others of his day, Chen Hongmou's positions on gender issues were highly complex and, on the surface at least, seemingly contradictory. By far the most celebrated of these positions was his advocacy of literary education for women. (His most extended discussion of this topic, the 1742 sourcebook *Jiaonü yigui*, was reprinted in whole or in extract perhaps as many as twenty times during the Qing and Republican periods.) Reserving discussion of these particular views for a subsequent point, we will concentrate here on Chen's more general attitudes toward women's roles.

Once again, we must begin with the family. The family, as we have seen, seemed so critical precisely because it encapsulated within it the archetypes of the social relationships that ordered society, polity, and cosmos and because it provided the locus within which individuals properly acted out such roles (*ming fen dangzhang*). In large part—although far from exclusively—this meant "distinguishing between superior and subordinate (*bian shangxia*).[140] Chen cites Sima Guang to the effect that the responsibility of assigning each family member the duties appropriate to their role belongs to the "househead," and he declares himself especially keen to promote the family unit in militarily troubled areas because of the importance of inculcating "respect for the househead" (*zunzhang*) to state efforts at social control.[141] That the patriarch is properly dominant not only over generational juniors but also over his spouse is clear. Chen is at times very explicit that, just as elders are morally compelled to regulate the young, husbands must "discipline" their wives (*funan jie qi funü*)[142]

Elsewhere, though, he adopts a rather different tone. In ordering his local-level subordinates in Shaanxi to instill in their charges a respect for the cardinal relationships, he explains this to mean, in the family, proper "precedence" between generations (*zhangyou you xu*) but a more egalitarian "harmony" between husband and wife (*fufu you he*).[143] And in selectively reprinting Yuan Cai's 1179 *Shifan* (Precepts for social life), Chen includes sections from the original on intrafamilial "tolerance," "forbearance," and "harmony" but opts to omit those on "submission," "serving the head of the household," and the wifely duty to obey her in-laws.[144] The tension between two differing views of spousal relations, which pervades the late imperial tradition, seems thus particularly acute in Chen Hongmou.

Chen perceived the woman's contribution to the prosperity and propriety of the family as essential. Economically, this contribution began with the marriage itself. In instructing wealthy Jiangnan households to observe frugality in betrothal presents and ceremonies he counseled fathers of the brides to limit the daughter's dowry largely to bequests of land, which would have "a real, practical utility" in the newly created family's future well-being.[145] He held women's work to be indispensable, and—influenced by his Guanxue mentor Yang Shen's textbook, the *Binfeng guangyi*—in his various provincial economic development campaigns he took care to specify the appropriate gender division of labor within the farm household. Moreover, although Chen clearly saw the role of patriarchal supervision as essential, he also thought women should play the major practical role in the sacred tasks of managing the household, ensuring proper etiquette in intrafamilial relations, controlling the household budget, and overseeing servants. Females must therefore be imbued from early childhood with a deep sense of responsibility (*ze*) about such matters. "It is necessary both that they understand the basics of propriety (*ming dayi*) and have a clear sense of the way things actually work (*an wuqing*)."[146] This balance of attention between principle and practicality (he cautions wives, for example, to "be careful with burning lanterns")[147] is characteristic of Chen. So too is an emphasis on hands-on management; with a clear analogy in mind to his view of proper work style for state officials, he tells the woman of the house, "If you do not enter the kitchen, you cannot effectively order your household."[148] Those families that neglect either moral or practical concerns cannot long endure but will suffer economic impoverishment, social ostracism, and (Chen is quite explicit here) cosmic retribution (*tianzai*).[149] Finally, and most important, the family is the indispensable key to cultural reproduction, and within the family the woman's role in this process is paramount.

We have noted above Chen's persistent concern to ensure the suitability of marriage partners in the provinces in which he served, in particular his emphasis on prohibiting forms of marriage (for example the levirate) that Chinese elite culture deemed incestuous. A perhaps more surprising corollary of this concern for spousal suitability was a concern for humane and respectful treatment of female marriage partners. In no uncertain terms Chen condemns what he literally terms "viewing women as commodities" (*shi wei qihuo*), items to be marketed for the highest possible economic return.[150] He writes, "The contraction of a marriage is the most important moment in a person's life. How can betrothal be undertaken lightly?"[151] He finds morally repulsive the practice of wealthy households of marrying off their servant girls for profit on the presumption that as members of the "lower classes" (*xiaren*) they can be treated as chattel. But he is also aware that families act similarly with their own daughters, betrothing them in early childhood, often to much older men, for a handsome bride price. Chen's desideratum here comes close to that of the companionate marriage. He argues, "No matter whether rich or poor, noble or base, [husband and wife] should be of proximate ages, so that they may grow old together over a long period of time."

Although he never attacks the patriarchal right to arrange marriages for dependent females, Chen insists on the collateral responsibility to do so only "at the appropriate time" (*jishi*).[152] By this he means two things. One is avoidance of child marriage. In the case of servant girls he suggests an appropriate age of about twenty *sui*, at which time the household should select for the girl a mate with whom she is temperamentally suited (*xiangcheng xiangyi*). The other is avoidance of the related practice, much in vogue in his day, of protracted delay between betrothal and the actual wedding ceremony. It is this ritually incorrect practice that allows the extended period of extravagant gifting between marriage partners' households, to which Chen is so deeply opposed on economic grounds. It also promotes the deplorable practice of female child betrothal and, accordingly, the high incidence of widowhood in adolescence. (Concern over this social problem sparked the rancorous debate, some decades after Chen's own death, between Wang Zhong [1745–94] and Zhang Xuecheng over the question of whether a woman's obligation of lifetime loyalty to her spouse began at marriage or at the often much earlier date of betrothal.)[153] Chen's vision of the ideal marriage is one of an affectionate, well-matched couple, united at a responsibly mature age and growing old together.

But husbands die. Chen strongly endorsed the cultural ideal of virtuous widowhood (*jiexiao*) and believed in the state's role in promoting this ideal. Based originally on a dictum in the *Li ji* that widows not remarry, the ideal of the chaste widow had over time acquired a major political resonance by its association with that of the loyal minister. This association was particularly cherished by the early Qing rulers, who actively promoted the cult by celebrating individual widows as role models and granting to their families such signs of imperial favor as testimonial plaques (*jingbiao*), tablets in imperially established community temples (*jiexiao si*), authorization to erect memorial arches, and in some cases even cash awards. For a variety of reasons the social response among the elite was overwhelming, prompting a long process of redefining the terms and limits of state recognition for exemplary widows.[154]

Chen himself updated and republished a collection of chaste widow biographies from his native province of Guangxi, compiled originally by Governor Yang Xifu,[155] and in his provincial posts in Yunnan, Shaanxi, and elsewhere he drove his subordinates hard to uncover and nominate instances of virtuous widowhood for recognition by the state. Indeed, he complained long and loud that the administration had not been active *enough* in identifying and celebrating these behavioral models; its negligence in this area had contributed to growing moral laxity throughout society and ever more frequent violations of the fundamental standards of human conduct (*rendao zhi dachang*).[156]

It is worth noting that Chen's efforts to implement the virtuous widow cult were concentrated in relatively frontier areas rather than in core provinces such as Jiangsu and Jiangxi, where he also served. Chen saw the cult as a key to instituting proper social relations (*lunchang*) in border societies and an essential part of the "civilizing" (*jiaohua*) process. He argued that "if morality and social order are to be instituted in the borderlands, it is first necessary that models of virtue on the village level be uncovered and publicized."[157] But in Chen's scheme of values there was more at stake in this process than simply cultural assimilation. For him it was a cardinal article of Confucian faith that all human beings possessed innate virtue, and inasmuch as border peoples were human, they were equally possessed of this natural endowment as were Han Chinese. The celebration of virtuous widows had become something of an elite fad by the mid-eighteenth century, to the extent that wealthy Jiangsu Province produced more than two hundred imperially recognized cases in the year 1749 alone. The Yongzheng emperor had noticed this trend as early as 1723, when he acidly reminded his officials to be equally diligent in discovering instances of virtue in "poverty-stricken villages" as in the prosperous cities of Jiangnan.[158] Chen, whose social policies always retained traces of the specific concerns of the Yongzheng reign, emphatically agreed. His prose rises to a pitch of genuine anger when he notes the relative scarcity of state-honored virtuous widows in remote areas, or among the very poor, and strongly implies that this results from a patterned prejudice on the part of his colleagues, who dismiss the possibility of true virtue existing outside the confines of their own social class.[159]

Chen's indignation was also attracted by the frequent elite practice of enforced widow remarriage, a phenomenon he associated with the commodification of women. He pointed out the bitter irony that it was her natal family's hunger for financial gain that put the woman in the position of youthful widowhood in the first place, they having betrothed her in childhood to a much older man. The same family then auctions her off to the highest bidder for a second marriage (her attractiveness meanwhile enhanced by inheritance of her husband's estate) and by so doing force her to compromise her own principled loyalty to her first husband's memory.[160] Chen saw this as just one more case of debased, mercenary social practices working to stifle the innate moral sense of the individual.

Chen Hongmou's pattern of argumentation here is, I believe, instructive to the historian who would incautiously impose contemporary judgmental perspectives on early modern Chinese debates. Chen clearly sees the ideal of chaste widowhood not as repressing women but rather as liberating them from commodification and from exploitative manipulation on the part of patriarchal authority. A recent study by Angela Leung strongly suggests that some Qing *women*—those who contributed to lineage trusts for the support of widows or who founded and managed community widow homes (*qingjie tang*)—would have agreed with Chen's logic.[161] There thus may have been more ambivalence involved in this cultural ideal than initially meets the eye, and Chen's championing of it may turn out to be less "conservative" than one might think.

A different sort of ambivalence arises in connection with what is certainly the most abhorrent (to contemporary standards) element in the virtuous widow cult, the moral value attached to widow suicide as a means of demonstrating loyalty to her deceased husband. The Qing court itself waffled over the question of whether this was a practice it ought to celebrate and reward or condemn.[162] Among leading intellectuals, too, the propriety of widow suicide was much at issue. Men of no less stature than Huang Zongxi and Lu Shiyi were on record as strongly approving the practice, whereas a succession of late Ming and early Qing scholars had criticized it as contrary to human feelings (*renqing*) and an excessive adherence to the rites (*guoli*), which, by its excess, violated those rites.[163]

Chen's position here was likewise complicated. In the preface he contributed to his new edition of Guangxi widow biographies, he began by citing the story of a young widow, Yang, who had chosen suicide rather than the remarriage that family and neighbors sought to thrust on her. Village gossips condemned her for having done so until a local notable (*shidafu*) reported her case to the throne and succeeded in having her recognized as an exemplary model. At this, the neighborhood repented its earlier conduct. Chen concludes: "Alas! Chastity, fidelity, and propriety are human nature [*ren zhi xing*]. And yet, social practice becomes debased to such a point that people can no longer recognize this virtuous nature, even in themselves! As in this story, it is up to their superiors to bring out their self-awareness of their own innate goodness."[164]

Apart from the curious mix of elitism and egalitarianism this passage displays, it is striking that Chen has apparently nothing but approval for the widow Yang's choice of suicide. He does not, however, claim that she has made the best of all possible choices. And other evidence suggests that, if Chen personally admired widows who had taken their own life, he hardly encouraged the practice. More typical was his reprinting of Yuan Cai's observation, "Most remarkable [among widows] are the women who manage the family's support after their husbands have died leaving them with young children."[165] The one surviving widow biography known to be by Chen's own hand praises its subject, a Mrs. Zhou from Chen's native county of Lingui, for her stoic will to survive and, not least, bring up her son. Widowed at twenty-two, she turned away many suitors and suffered bitter poverty, all the while encouraging her son in his studies. Although he repeatedly failed the civil service examinations, she comforted him and advised him to accept the somewhat demeaning post of yamen clerk. She was ultimately rewarded when, shortly before her death at age seventy-nine, her son's own son passed the provincial examination.[166]

In general, suicide was for Chen less an act of moral courage than one of immoral disrespect for the sanctity of individual human life (*qingsheng*). In Shaanxi he ordered his subordinates to arrest and severely punish anyone found to have counseled another to take his or her own life. Although he applied this to suicide for a broad range of reasons, such as debt, the example he chose to expound was that of the woman (widowed or otherwise) whose modesty had been impugned:

> Now, womenfolk of the inner quarters who are fully attentive to the dictates of propriety will sometimes suffer unintended [compromises of their virtue]. In such cases, if parents, elderly aunts, husbands, and brothers offer the woman instruction and guidance on how to react, and seek calmly to resolve the situation, and perhaps if some elderly matron of the community steps forward to offer the woman comfort and consolation, the calamitous event [her suicide] may be avoided.[167]

Chen concludes, characteristically, "If menfolk bring up their women right, there will be no suicides at all."

What we see in Chen Hongmou, I would argue, is not an explicit rejection of the stern repressiveness inherent in the Cheng-Zhu attitude toward widowhood, and gender relations generally, but rather a subtle shift of tone and emphasis undertaken in the process of defending the very norms of the Cheng-Zhu school. Indicative of the growing discomfort felt by even the most moralistic early modern scholar-officials toward a literal reading of Song prescriptions on women's conduct was the decision of Zhang Boxing (1651–1725) to delete from his own edition of the *Jinsi lu* Cheng Yi's famous dictum that it is better for a widow to starve to death than to betray her deceased husband by remarriage. Zhang believed that statements so extreme could not possibly be authentic.[168] Similarly, although Chen Hongmou also identified very strongly with Cheng-Zhu thought, and cited its exemplars repeatedly in his sourcebooks on the education of sons, the correction of social practices, and so on, it seems highly revealing that in his companion volume on women, the *Jiaonü yigui*, he cited no Song sources whatsoever, skipping directly from Han texts to those of the late Ming. One might even see as Chen's counterformulation to that of Cheng Yi his statement, "If one is cold and hungry it is infinitely more difficult to act out of concern for moral propriety."[169] For the scholar-official this implied a mandate to view human emotions with empathy and to work strenuously for the improvement of material conditions.

Since the Song period, the Confucian doctrine of distinction (*bie*) between male and female roles had increasingly accorded emphasis to the spatial dimension, to the distinction between a female-domestic realm (*nei*) and a male-public realm (*wai*). By the early modern period these were, as Dorothy Ko has recently pointed out, viewed less as impermeable opposites than as mutually defining relational categories. They varied situationally so that what was *nei* from one perspective became *wai* from another. Under these circumstances they offered less a mandate to hard-and-fast gender separatism than a guide to patterned interaction and interrelationship.[170]

But there was also a stricter definition, inherited from Cheng-Zhu texts, that proceeded from a physical and puritanical reading of the Confucian doctrine of shame (*lianchi*) to prescribe the literal seclusion of women, wearing by females of veil-like coverings on the few occasions when they ventured out of doors, prohibitions on males and females (including husbands and wives) touching, sitting together at meals, and so on. For an eighteenth-century cultural conservative such as Chen Hongmou this set of attitudes enjoyed the highest scriptural authority in the works of Zhu Xi, Sima Guang, and others.[171]

The symbolic representation of this corpus of ideas was the notion of the women's quarters or harem (*gui*). It seems fair to conclude that uncertainty over the continuing propriety of this ideal was a central, although usually not directly articulated, touchstone for the entire debate over gender and family in early modern China. It is significant that one of the key early figures in this debate, Lü Kun (who had a special appeal for Chen Hongmou), argued for the appropriateness of women's venturing out of the domestic sphere to realize their full potential for economic productivity, yet he posed his argument in a book he entitled *Rules for the Women's Quarters* (*Guifan*).[172] By the mid-Qing the forces of reaction against such ideas (exemplified by Zhang Xuecheng) were promoting a vigorous reaffirmation of the ideal of gender separation, in both functional and physical terms.

Chen Hongmou's own position in this debate was decidedly in line with the conservative side, although he also exhibited some doubts in this area that reveal him as a man of his time. In none of Chen's own impassioned writings on the need for female literary education, for example, does he echo the views of Lü Kun that this is valuable in part to allow females to get out into the workforce. Neither does he suggest that this education itself might be conducted in schools outside the shelter of the home. Rather, Chen consistently argues against any compromise of the principle of distinction and against current fashions that fail to distinguish properly between the domestic and public spheres (*shi mennei ru lu*).[173] He cites approvingly Xiong Hongpei's straightforward advice to wives, "Don't leave the house" (*shen bu chukun*).[174] And he instructs his local-level subordinates in Jiangsu: "The ritually correct place for women is deep within the women's quarters. When at home they should let down a screen, and when out of the home they should cover their faces. It is by these means that they are cut off from [*bie*] all suspicion, and protected against intrusions upon their modesty."[175] It would be hard to imagine a more literal reading of the ideal of feminine confinement than this. Yet Chen clearly understands that this is far from descriptive of behavior in his contemporary world. He directly follows the above passage with this one:

> Why is it that social practice has become so lax? Women walk about the streets bare-faced with no sense of shame whatsoever! Young women take sedan-chair trips to holy sites in the mountains, or go out in the evening to stroll in the moonlight. Worse still, they go on pilgrimages to temples, burn incense and engage in collective worship. Monks and local officials think this is a laughing matter! On festival days . . . they go to mountainside temples and spend the night, and their husbands don't even view this as inappropriate! Such is the state of debasement of popular mores.

It was in fact just such public activities that most seriously alarmed Chen. He was a strict defender of Confucian ideological and ritual correctness (in the rather rawboned way he understood it) and zealously opposed any manifestation of popular culture that he viewed as heterodox or socially unproductive (*wuyong*). If one examines his actual pattern of rhetorical invocation of the ideal of female modesty, one finds it almost entirely limited to contexts in which he is after bigger game: pilgrimage associations, popular Buddhist congregationalism, nighttime performances of operas and shadow plays (frequently with heterodox themes), and lavishly extravagant wedding and funeral celebrations.[176] It is in *these* instances, which Chen opposes on a variety of non-gender-related grounds, that he raises the specter of violations of feminine virtue. And it is to combat *these* practices (significantly, all group activities) rather than the practice of individual women leaving the home for work or recreation, veiled or otherwise, that Chen engaged his ready penchant for moral legislation. Although there can be little doubt that Chen did wistfully lament the loss of the golden age of female seclusion, he was certainly a practical enough man not to waste his energies on attempting to restore it in his own day.[177]

Indeed, there are passages in Chen's writing that betray a sense of the *gui* ideal as not only infeasible but also undesirable. He notes, for example, that "wives who are cloistered deep within the women's quarters are ignorant of the true difficulties of getting along in the outside world, and generally develop a haughty and shrewish disposition." Such women instigate countless lawsuits, in turn bringing the family to ruin.[178] Again, Chen argues that parents, out of concern for their daughters' modesty, systematically deprive them of the needed experience of socialization: "From the moment they grow out of infancy, they are protectively sheltered deep within the women's quarters, rather than, like male children, being allowed out into the wider world, to be carefully corrected by social models and by friends, and to be cultivated by exposure to the classical literary canon."[179] This, as we shall see in Chapter 12, is Chen's point of departure for his celebrated argument for female literacy.

It also reveals something of Chen Hongmou's views about the feminine personality, a set of semiconscious, semiarticulated attitudes that were probably broadly shared by elite males of his day and that we cannot afford to ignore. To what extent did Chen hold to a view of gender essentialism, a belief that males and females were fundamentally different subsets of the human species? Historians of gender in the West have increasingly come to see such an essentialist view of women as a product of the early modern era, related to the marshaling of new "scientific" arguments in service of a new cultural model of female domestication within the bourgeois family.[180] Recently, Tani Barlow has argued very forcefully that this set of assumptions appeared in China only as a Western import, largely in the early twentieth century. She associates this with the introduction of the neologism "*nüxing*" (female), which implied a basic biological distinctiveness of women from men far beyond differences in genitalia. Prior to this, Barlow argues, women were seen as wives, mothers, daughters, and so on but rarely if ever as part of a transcendent "female" category. Chen Hongmou provides her chief illustration of this point of view.[181]

My own reading of Chen suggests that Barlow's argument has some grounds yet is considerably overstated. She is right, of course, that the deliberate use of "scientific" appeals to support female essentialism played no role in eighteenth-century gender discourse; Chen never once hints that the uniqueness he sees in women is rooted in biology. Barlow is also correct in pointing out that familial or other social roles were far more important for Chen and his contemporaries in formulating their vision of women than was the simple gender category "female." But the latter, although of secondary importance, was hardly absent from their rhetorical universe. "*Nan*" (male) and "*nü*" (female) were well understood lexical categories. A term in routine use, "*funü*" (literally: wife-woman), revealingly carried familial rather than biological overtones but clearly approximated the twentieth-century "*nüxing*" in denoting a gender category. The idiom "*nannü you bie*" (male and female are mutually distinguished) was a pervasive statement both of what was and of what should be. Chen himself was quite fond of it.[182] It meant several things at once: (1) that males and females ought to be physically segregated, (2) that their functional roles in family and society differed appropriately, and (3), less salient perhaps than the other meanings but present nonetheless, that they were essentially different from one another.

Chen felt fully comfortable making generalizations about women that went well beyond those applicable to "wives," "daughters," and so on. Like most of his contemporaries, he conceived of a distinctive sphere of "women's work" (*nügong*), and indeed, as we have seen, his various schemes for harnessing labor productivity in the cause of regional economic development were deeply predicated on this conception. He was also an adamant crusader for propagation of the "four virtues" (*si de*), specific patterns of submissive behavior appropriate for women but not for men.[183] More interestingly,

Chen frequently offered his views on mental outlooks that he believed generally and distinctively observable in women, attitudes such as compassion (*cihui*), maternal indulgence (*guxi*), and a kind of simplicity and naivete. He wrote in the preface to his celebrated *Sourcebook on Female Education*: "It is characteristic of females to hold single-mindedly to a fixed idea, and believe it very deeply, sometimes in the face of clear evidence to the contrary."[184] Although these personality traits seem for Chen to be somehow intrinsic to the female condition, it is clear that he sees them also as products of the cloistered socialization process most young women undergo—hence his highly ambivalent endorsement of the cultural ideal of the women's quarters.

With all of this "orientalizing" of women—imbuing them with a quaint childishness that renders them subject to male guidance—it is nevertheless the more persistent theme of Chen's writings (persistent in that he often saw himself as defending venerable truths under threat in the culture of his day) that women and men are above all else equal participants in a common humankind. His campaign for women's literary education proceeds from the assumption that women and men are equally endowed with a natural intelligence (*xinghui*) that renders them capable of learning to read.[185] Gender differences are irrelevant to the universal human possession of *tianliang*, heavenly endowed virtue, of which the four women's virtues are but situational applications; Chen thus champions the cultivation of moral autonomy in women as he does in men. Similarly, the empathetic personality traits he finds distinctive of women are but specific manifestations of the more universal human emotional response (*renqing*). And, finally, the arguments we have seen Chen advancing in regard to treatment of brides and widows are predicated, ultimately, on his recognition of a basic and compelling dignity of the human condition, shared in equally by women and men.

The Individual

To what extent did Chen Hongmou's view of human beings—as partaking in a common humanity; as classifiable into gender, ethnic, educational, and economic categories; and (especially) as occupying a range of defined social roles—allow him to assign meaning, dignity, and autonomy to the individual person? Many Western scholars who have written most perceptively about the concept of roles in Confucian social thought—the philosophers Donald Munro and Henry Rosemont, the historian Romeyn Taylor, and the sociologist Gary Hamilton—have tended to stress the conceptual incompatibility of such a vision with any significant valuation of individual autonomy of the sort usually associated with the post-Enlightenment Western intellectual tradition.[186] An exception is the sociologist Ambrose King, who cautions: "It is important to bear in mind that the Confucian individual is more than a role-player mechanically performing the role-related behavior prescribed by the social structure. . . . The Confucian individual consists of a self [*ji*] that is an active and reflective entity. In relation-construction it is the individual who is capable of defining roles for himself and others, and is always at the center."[187] In a seminal article on early modern intellectual change in China, Wm. Theodore de Bary has written in similar terms: "[Confucianism constructs] a web of reciprocal obligations or moral relations in which man finds himself, defines himself. Apart from these he can have no real identity. And yet these relations alone, it is equally important to recognize, do not define a man totally. His interior self exists at the center of this web and there it enjoys its freedom."[188] Hao Chang, as well, has pointed out the coexistence of a sense of "individual transcendence" with the role and network vision basic to Confucian social thought, although he is more inclined than either King or de Bary to emphasize the conceptual tension this coexistence carried with it.[189]

Beyond seeing an individualist undercurrent in Confucian thought more generally, both de Bary and Chang (in company with many other historians of the late imperial era) detect a major breakthrough in Confucian individualist thought in the freewheeling cultural world of the late Ming, with the radical implications drawn from Wang Yangming's doctrine of innate knowledge (*liangzhi*) by such activist scholars as Wang Gen, He Xinyin, and Li Zhi. Most scholars tend, however, to see the results of this breakthrough as short-lived, nearly totally negated by the wave of political and ideological reaction of the early and mid-Qing.

The present study of Chen Hongmou suggests that this view must be qualified. A notably "conservative" thinker in many regards, who attached great value to authority, to social order, and to the obligations of role fulfillment, Chen nevertheless displays in his thought and discourse not merely the basic humanistic urges that run throughout the long Confucian tradition but also evidence of the eighteenth-century survival (in albeit transmuted form) of the personal liberationist urges of the late Ming—what I would term the beginnings of Chinese early modern consciousness. In a sense Chen may be said to have attempted to tame or domesticate the individualism of the Taizhou school and others, but within sharply defined limits he was in his own way passionately attached to it. Throughout this study we have had (and will have) repeated opportunity to observe various dimensions of Chen's thought and policies that might qualify for the label "individualist." In concluding this chapter I want to sketch out what form these dimensions might have taken.

I would identify five particular elements in Chen's consciousness that might be interpreted as reflecting protoindividualist views. *First* was his zealous sense of individual mission or vocation, the notion of personal responsibility to save the world, one offshoot of which was the profound sense of personal guilt or sin from which we have seen him at least periodically suffering. *Second* was his insistence on the personal dignity, or sanctity, of each human being. His emphatic endorsement of the Mencian doctrine of the common goodness of Heaven that inheres in each person (*tianliang*) prompted Chen to condemn any practice or institution—for example those related to treatment of child brides and of widows—that reflected an instrumental view of any individual. *Third* was his oft-expressed preference for individual moral autonomy over enforced or unthinking obedience to instituted external authority. Accepting as he did (see Chapter 4) Wang Yangming's frequently assailed notions of the individual moral mind (*liangxin*) and innate wisdom (*liangzhi*), Chen's championing of universal literary education and his relatively dim view of coercive legal and public security mechanisms (such as *baojia*) reflected his faith in the primacy of personal agency in the pursuit of moral conduct and social well-being. *Fourth* was the value he attached to individual drive and the quest for personal achievement. However much Chen counseled his administrative charges to remain contented with their lot (*anfen*), he in fact looked with great favor on those members of the population who "displayed a will to advance themselves" (*youxin xiangshen*). Such individuals of ambition and determination (*youzhizhe*) must not, for the good of society itself, be fettered by social convention.[190] *Fifth*, and finally, was Chen's at least partial rehabilitation of the pursuit of economic self-interest. Although, as we saw in Chapter 6, his attitude toward profit seeking was not without ambivalence, he repeatedly insisted that self-interest was a heavenly endowed aspect of human nature.

"Human emotions have their public-spirited side, but also their self-interested side," he wrote, and this self-interest (*siqing*) is every bit as natural as is altruism. Although it should not be blindly indulged, neither should it be suppressed or ignored; instead, it must be channeled effectively, based on the standards of reason and principle.[191] Coveting the blessings enjoyed by others, or acting deliberately in such a way as to benefit oneself at their expense, may properly be condemned as "selfishness"; simply acting to advance one's material interests, in and of itself, may not. It is indecorous competitiveness, not self-interest per se, that is morally reprehensible. The latter, indeed, may prove fully compatible with the public interest (*gong*).[192] We see in Chen Hongmou, I would suggest, the efforts of an early modern man to reconcile emerging revaluations of human appetites and of self-interest—a revaluation in which he himself participates—with inherited moral injunctions to selflessness and public-mindedness.

On closer inspection Chen's attitude toward the individual self (*ji*) turns out to be highly complex and tension filled. In a long letter to Yang Yingju of roughly 1746 the mature provincial governor spells out his views on this issue as fully as he ever does. Commenting on a classical ode on the subject of acting "for oneself" (*weiji*), Chen ponders why the ancient sage would view this motivation as positively as he does and cautions against the contemporary trend to invoke this passage to legitimate any and all self-aggrandizement. Such interpretations fail to comprehend the true meaning of self. They misread "*weiji*" as simple *zisi*, selfishness, and corrupt the true meaning of the "way of self-fulfillment" (*weiji zhi dao*). In his attempt to clarify for himself and his correspondent the true meaning of "self," Chen turns to a passage by Cheng Yi (1033–1107) that points out the dangers of adhering too narrowly to *either* attitude, one of "for self" (*weiji*) or one of "for others" (*weiren*). The defects of the former are obvious, but Chen notes especially Cheng's caveat that overmuch altruism can lead to an entirely unwonted "extinction of the self" (*sangji*).[193] For Chen Hongmou true individuality is something to be harnessed and transcended (*keji*) as situations dictate, but it is also something to be prized. Self-fulfillment, achievable only in social settings, is very nearly the goal of all human action.

Wm. Theodore de Bary, the scholar who has emphasized most the "individualist" elements in late imperial ethical thought, has carefully (although perhaps not as carefully as his critics would like) sought to distinguish Confucian individualism from the cult of the individual that arose in the early modern West. The Chinese variant, de Bary points out, was far less sanctioning of the spirit of free competition than was that of the West and remained always conceived within "the institutional framework" of family, community, and polity.[194] To this I would further suggest that the specific Western cultural ideal of "rugged individualism"—getting ahead in an environment of all against all—never enjoyed Chinese parallels until the early twentieth century. In Chen Hongmou, as we have seen, the signally early modern valorization of the individual coexisted with other views of human identity: as a member of a common humanity (a view rather more pronounced in Chen than in others of his day), as a member of subsets of that humanity based on gender, ethnicity, and socioeconomic status, and, most important, as a participant in an intense and finely intermeshed network of roles and role relationships.

Chen expresses this most directly in citing a passage from Wang Yangming in his *Sourcebook on the Conduct of Office*. It is absolutely wrong to conceive of "self" artificially, Chen notes, as too many contemporary people do, as defined by a polarized dichotomous relationship with "others." The self that really has meaning, that yearns for personal fulfillment, and that is key to constructing the good society is precisely one that is inescapably and comfortably embedded in networks and communities within which "I as an individual" (*wu zhi yishen*) am bound by ties of respect, of responsibility, and of common purpose.[195]

CHAPTER 10

Governance

QING CHINA—a Confucian, imperial, centralized bureaucracy—embodied, like earlier Chinese dynastic regimes, conflicting notions of governance. On the one hand there was the model of governance by ritually correct, public-minded, and humane (*ren*) gentlemen, a model bequeathed from the Five Classics and Four Books and kept ever in the forefront of consciousness by the curriculum of the civil service examinations and the discursive traditions of Confucian intellectuals. Standing in contrast to this was a view of the state as a pervasive, efficient, and highly integrated institutional structure, a model whose actual origins were complex but were most readily associated, in the eighteenth century as today, with the Legalist-inspired contributions of the first self-professed imperial regime of Qin (221–207 B.C.). Although subsequent dynasties, through the Qing, willingly absorbed Qin institutional innovations and worked diligently to perfect them, this process entailed a compromise with Confucian humanistic principles with which the elite cultural tradition was never fully comfortable. We see this in Chen Hongmou, for example, when, like many another scholar-official, he proclaims the superiority of *li* (ritual and ingrained personal decorum) over *fa* (laws) and *xing* (criminal sanctions) as an instrument of social ordering.[1]

The imperial bureaucratic state was, in a sense, an embarrassment. But when it was functioning especially well, as in the mid-eighteenth century, it was an embarrassment that most within the official elite could live with. The discursive tradition of statecraft (*jingshi*) with which Chen Hongmou was retrospectively associated, indeed, is often assumed to have advocated, with unusual complacency, a greater hands-on presence in society for institutionalized government. Although, as Chapter 4 has shown, Chen's relationship with this intellectual statecraft tradition was by no means uncomplicated, there is no question but that he did work strenuously in practice to extend the reach and the efficiency of the state apparatus.

There was, however, a further and related problem. Efforts by Chen and others to expand the state ran counter to an ideology professing the moral and practical virtues of local community autonomy, of governance by indigenous, culturally sanctioned

326

elites rather than by state functionaries, however enlightened and "humane" they might be. What made the situation yet more tricky is that the very people who worked most assiduously in practice to refine and empower the machinery of bureaucratic governance—persons such as Chen Hongmou—were often the very people who most cherished this model of communal self-governance. In this chapter and the next we will explore these questions, first by examining the rationales that inclined Chen to what might be termed the "state-building" project and then by looking at the ways by which he sought to reconcile this project, in theory and in practice, with ideals of communal self-reliance.

The Good Official and the Bureaucratic State

In the late imperial era the classical conception of governance as the activity of a few morally superior individuals was kept alive most vividly by a particular, highly constructed cultural institution, that of the "model official" (*xunli*). Beginning with the first-century *Han shu*, the canonical dynastic histories had each contained a section recounting the biographies of such exemplars (*xunli zhuan*), and by Qing times an understanding of who these individuals were, as well as the specific attributes making up their composite profile, was widely diffused within both elite and popular culture. Personal virtue was important but not determinative; as Yu Yingshi points out, everyone accepted the general principle that internal self-regulation (*neizhi*) and regulation of the external world (*waizhi*) were inseparably linked phenomena, but practical-mindedness dictated that abilities in the latter area be seen as more crucial. A frugal and humble conduct of one's life was intrinsic to the model, but a zealous and confrontational incorruptibility, à la the famous Ming whistle-blower Hai Rui (1514–1587), was often frankly understood to be dysfunctional. Nor was the courage to remonstrate before one's superiors a critical feature of this particular construction of official worthiness (although of course it had considerable appeal in other contexts). Above all, the "good official" was one who worked tirelessly for the people under his charge. This was usually interpreted as entailing two things. First was "teaching the people" (*jiaomin*), promulgating the norms of the classical culture by instructing the people in the rites—in other words, the "civilizing mission" of *jiaohua*. (We will return to this in Chapter 12.) Second was "enriching the people" (*fumin*); model officials had in common a reputation for strenuous efforts in lightening tax burdens; extending agricultural acreage and irrigation systems; managing flood control, famine relief, and civil construction projects; and, as Yu Yingshi emphasizes, promoting commerce as well.[2]

Over the course of the early Qing a handful of officials at the provincial governor level (what Pierre-Étienne Will calls a *pléiade*) had ascended to this model-official status, among them Yu Chenglong (1617–84), Wei Xiangshu (1617–87), Zhang Boxing (1652–1725), and perhaps most famously Tang Bin (1627–87). Chen Hongmou acknowledged and deliberately contributed to the formalization of this pantheon by extolling and citing these men in his own 1742 sourcebook on exemplary official conduct, the *Congzheng yigui*.[3] He also quite manifestly and aggressively sought the mantle of *xunli* for himself and did so with eventual success. Chen's Qing-era biographers, including even the anonymous official biographer from the State History Office (Guoshi guan) who drafted what would become Chen's notice in the Qing dynastic history, all clearly had this cultural model in mind when composing their narratives of his career.[4] They did so in most cases out of no great personal attachment to Chen; the life of a "model official" simply made a good and didactically useful story, and Chen seemed to fit the bill.

Not only in his *Congzheng yigui*, which Chen printed in large quantities and distributed widely throughout his jurisdictions,[5] but also in musings running throughout his public and private correspondence, Chen constructs his own personalized model of "the good official," the man adept at expansively "instituting principle" (*zhili*) in the world.[6] This is a man of surpassing integrity, capable of "overcoming self" (*keji*) and of conducting his office according to the highest standards of impartiality.[7] The good official is absolutely single-minded in his dedication to serving the people, to leading the people in the cause of advancing *their* interests, not his own, the elite's, or even those of the state or dynasty. As we have already seen, this involves simultaneous attention to *jiao* and to *yang*, to improving both the people's cultural and their material life. Of equal importance, however, is work style. The good official gets out routinely among the people and genuinely "knows" them. He leads through appeals to "principle"—reason and morality—rather than through coercion. The hallmark of his administration is empathy (*tixu*) and human sensibility (*renqing*).[8] His every action stems from his belief that "although the relative positions in society of officials and common people may differ, their heavenly goodness [*tianliang*] is something they most fundamentally share."[9] He is openly responsive to popular appeals and doggedly efficient in processing all matters of popular concern.

Chen could not be more explicit that responsiveness to "the people's demands" (*minqiu*) and "the people's expectations" (*minwang*) is the good official's overriding concern. This goes well beyond the venerable concept of taking concern for the people's *needs* as the basis for the state (a notion, sometimes referred to as *minben*, which could in practice have very authoritarian or commandist implications) to include as well the notion of giving the people what they *want*. As we shall explore more fully in the next chapter, Chen is working out for himself something very close to what we might call a theory of public opinion. Following the early Ming model official (and Guanxue scholar) Xue Xuan, he argues that the essential components of good governance are simply "reflecting the people's attitudes" (*fu minxing*) and "avoiding what the people detest" (*jin minfei*); paraphrasing Lü Kun, he notes, "What is called for is that [the official] share the people's own likes and dislikes (*hao minhao, e min'e*), and on this basis redress their grievances."[10]

For a man who had only briefly in his long career served in subprovincial level posts (as Yangzhou prefect and Tianjin circuit intendant), and never as a county magistrate, Chen had very firm ideas about how a *local* official should conduct his business. Indeed, one of the most fundamental dynamics of the late imperial bureaucracy was the systematic divergence of perspective between the cohort of men serving at the county level and those who oversaw and directed them from provincial governors' yamens. Chen's outlook on governance was very much that of the latter group, and a great deal of his bureaucratic correspondence is devoted to the task of imposing on career magistrates his own ideas of what their job entailed. Probably more than many other governors (who did the same thing), Chen's dedication to empirical observation and to comprehending the complexities of local ecologies and societies under his charge made him sensitive to the problems faced by his county-level subordinates, and he repeatedly voiced his concern that, in the present day, magistrates were being asked to perform a range of duties that clearly strained human capability.[11] Nevertheless, reading Chen's writings can only reconfirm this impression of a continual tug-of-war between governors, who had a somewhat idealized vision of what "realizing principle" in local society encompassed, and the officials actually on the scene, who had a more acute sense of the constraints of the possible.

For Chen the "father and mother official" (*fumu guan*) in the county yamen must above all identify completely with the common people (*xiaomin*) under his charge. He must take their affairs (*minshi*) as his own and assume their well-being as the deciding factor in his every action. Following Lü Kun, Chen insists that the magistrate spend as much time as humanly possible in face-to-face encounters with the people (*qinmin*) and perform as much of his work as possible personally, without intermediaries. He is to take responsibility for every single matter within his district, no matter how seemingly insignificant. This assumes complete and detailed knowledge on his part; to this end, for example, Chen repeatedly demands that county officials prepare minutely detailed maps of their jurisdictions for submission to him. The magistrate must treat bureaucratic paperwork with the utmost seriousness, responding personally to every single petition from below (however outlandish), and process upward correspondence faithfully and expeditiously; no matter how trivial and time-consuming this might appear, the magistrate must bear in mind that each item of this paperwork has a direct bearing on the lives of real people. At the same time, the magistrate's duties demand substantive action, not mere formal compliance. He should avoid doing things "by the book" and evaluate each directive from above, implementing them creatively, even at times selectively, based on his own knowledge of the realities of his district. A local official must avoid being influenced by outside parties, not only personal friends and members of the local elite but also the consensus opinion of his official colleagues. If he cannot feel secure in his own independent judgment, he does not belong in the post to begin with.[12]

We need not doubt for a moment Chen Hongmou's sincerity when he insists that governance by good men (*zhiren*) is superior to governance by laws and institutions (*zhifa*), or when he argues that attracting good men (*deren*) to administer the realm is a more critical facet of rulership than is legislative or organizational prowess, or when he laments that in the contemporary world most "run-of-the-mill officials" (*suli*) fall far short of the *xunli* ideal.[13] Nevertheless, it is equally true that the most basic conception of governance that Chen brings to his own administrative service views the good official's enactment of his role as possible only within the context of other, similar officials doing analogous work within a highly structured system of bureaucratic posts or offices (*zhi*). These exist independent of (and logically prior to) the individual occupant, however superior an individual that occupant might be. Chen expresses this view—what might be termed a statement of constitutional principles—quite directly in a passage of parallel prose addressed to his Jiangxi subordinates in 1741:

> The court appoints officials because there are affairs which must be managed. By accepting such appointment, an official accepts responsibility for these affairs. For each official, there is an office which must be filled. For each office, there is a range of affairs which must be managed. If the office is not filled effectively, it is because the official himself is remiss. If the affairs are not managed effectively, it is because the office is ineffectively filled.[14]

The contradiction is thus resolved. The system of bureaucratic posts and the duties attached to them are rationally derived, and reason, like the virtue inherent in the official himself, is a reflection of heavenly principle, *tianli*. The very definition of the good official implies the existence of a machinery of state.

Although I would contend that a concept of "the state" not very dissimilar from that in the contemporaneous West functioned within the discourse community of the mid-Qing official elite, no single lexical unit had emerged that fully captured this range of meanings. (It is worth remembering that in the West, as well, the term *state/l'état* in this usage was an early modern invention.)[15] "*Guan*" often fulfills this function but is equally often invoked more specifically to denote an official or officialdom as a whole. "*Guanchang*," a term Chen Hongmou uses frequently in his private correspondence, refers to the bureaucracy. "*Guo*" and "*guojia*" are more complicated. They can denote a human/territorial unit, the Chinese *patria*—which has, for example, its own *guoshi*, or "national history"—but also the ruling dynasty, which in the case of the Qing is an explicitly multinational one. Since at least the Song, and with greater explicitness since the writings of Gu Yanwu in the seventeenth century, this *guo* or *guojia* is clearly distinguished from the larger inhabited world, "all under Heaven" or *tianxia*.[16] In this sense military defense of the *guo* or *guojia* versus external forces serves for Chen as a rationale for the existence of the state apparatus. Yet Chen's rhetoric also deploys these terms in a range of usages clearly approximating the Western "state" itself. The *guojia* is an active subject. It does things (such as establishing official posts and institutionalizing rituals) and has its own defined range of interests, financial and otherwise (*guoji*). As the "state," *guojia* encompasses within it and invests with its authority both officials (*guan*) and the plethora of subofficial functionaries (*xuli*) who assist them in their delegated tasks.[17]

Chen offers a variety of rationales for the necessity of a state apparatus. Effective governance entails not merely virtue (*de*) and ritual correctness (*li*) but also regulation (*xing*) and administrative technique (*zheng*). However virtuous the officials, moreover, maintenance of popular confidence demands a degree of routinization; administrative practice must be uniform over space and stable over time. It demands systematization, as well, so that no affair relating to the people's well-being will fail to fall under a defined bureaucratic cognizance. In what might appear a jarring juxtaposition to his cherished familial model of the state—the "*jia*" in "*guojia*"—Chen is positively exultant about the fact that, under the present dynasty, bureaucratic posts are filled impersonally, on the basis of demonstrated ability rather than birthright or family status; the problem is to ensure that, with all this deliberate impersonality, the moral essence of official rule be retained.[18]

For all his emphasis on responsiveness to the people's needs, wants, and sensitivities, the basic mission of Chen's state (like his good official) is to "lead" or "shepherd" the people (*daomin, xiumin*). There is nothing, really, in Chen's rhetoric that suggests a social contract view of the state's origins or legitimacy. Rulership, rather, derives from Heaven, which, as suggested in Chapter 3, is for Chen less a convenient abstraction for human reason or the popular will than a conscious, autonomous agent. His telling and oft-repeated phrase that the state (or the official) is "established for the people" (*weimin sheguan*),[19] although reflective of his populist leanings, clearly implies a subject other than the people themselves. The state exists *for* the people but not at their pleasure.

For the present-day scholar, finally, it is worth keeping in mind that the notion of a paired opposition between "state" and "society" is *not*, in the case of late imperial China, simply an analytic device imposed on the basis of Western-generated categories but rather is a central feature of Qing political discourse itself. (Indeed, when discussing "state-society" dynamics in the late imperial period, the danger is not the usual one of imposing marginally relevant outside categories but rather of becoming too much a prisoner of indigenous discursive categories themselves.)[20] In Chen's own rhetoric the oppositional pairing of "state" (*guan* or *guo*) and "society" (*minjian* or, more usually, simply *min*) is pervasive. It appears, for example, in the linkage of economic policy goals serving the *guoji* and the *minsheng* (state finances and societal well-being). Suitable policies are those that simultaneously promote the vitality of the state (*guoti*) and cure the infirmities of society (*minmo*). Spheres of proprietorship, authority, and managerial responsibility in such matters as food supply and public works maintenance are dichotomized in both law and common discourse into those of the state (*yuguan, guiguan*) and of the society (*yumin, guimin*).[21] Dysfunctional attitudes, behaviors, and policies are those that drive a wedge between state and societal interests (*guanmin gejue*); functional ones are those that promote greater interest-identity between the two (*guanmin gongyao*).[22] Chen's consistent goal is to bring state and society into the fullest possible congruence, but he assumes, with equal consistency, the formidable difficulty of doing so.

How Large Should the State Be?

Chen Hongmou's views on the optimal size of the state and its pervasiveness in society followed a complex logic. Leaving aside for the moment his possible relationship with the ideology of local societal self-management—an ideology that emerged as intrinsic to Song neo-Confucian ideas of statecraft and that by Qing times had taken on the additional coloration of the antibureaucratic political counterdiscourse of *fengjian*[23]—at least three more practical considerations inclined him to favor a cautious approach to any expansion of the administrative apparatus.

First was his frank recognition of the practical limits of state intervention in economy and society. As we have seen, Chen is quite explicit that he believes it inappropriate (*feiyi*) to obstruct the private market in a dirigiste manner—imposing commandist procurements (*pai*), trade embargoes, price controls, or (in most cases) bans on production or consumption. With solicitous government participation and prompting, the far larger private market can perform the tasks of popular nurturance (*yimin yangmin*) and even economic development better by itself, whereas clumsy state intervention only discourages productivity, spawns a black market, and opens the door to private speculation, defeating the state's initiative and actively worsening the problem. Commandist policies also create further problems of control of self-interested state functionaries themselves. In the sociocultural sphere, state programs that recklessly provoke popular displeasure will routinely prove counterproductive.[24] Arguing in this way, Chen Hongmou combines hardheaded cost/benefit analysis, which, as John Shepherd has shown, inclined mid-Qing policy makers in general against the most adventurist of initiatives,[25] with a highly refined respect for natural (heavenly derived) environmental constraints and predictable regularities of human behavior (*changran zhi fa*).[26] As is true in one's personal life, the key to successful action by the state lies in frankly recognizing the distinction between what does and does not lie within one's sphere of control.

A second inhibiting factor was the urge to fiscal restraint. The late Ming example of the negative consequences of raising taxes was ever in the minds of the Qing official elite and never more strongly than in the Qianlong era. Especially in the first half of his reign, as we saw in Chapter 2, Qianlong equated the Confucian admonition to "benevolent governance" rather directly with a low tax burden. Although a product of the more fiscalist Yongzheng reign, Chen Hongmou in this regard was more akin to Yongzheng's successor, and even though he had made his name as a field official at least in part on his success in prosecuting tax arrears in late-1720s Jiangsu, already in the last years of the Yongzheng reign itself Chen established himself as a champion of tax reductions. He placed curbs on imposition of Yongzheng's pet fiscal innovation, the so-called *haoxian* land tax surcharge, and attacked habitual overcollections of special local product taxes, of corvée duties, and of various nuisance taxes (*zafei*) on both merchants and farmers.[27] Invoking what he claimed to be a sacred trust between the officials and the people, Chen argued, "Just as it is impermissible for people to resist paying their just taxes, so too is it improper for the government to make extortionate fiscal demands."[28] Fortunate enough to serve in an age of minimal security threat from within or without, Chen consistently held to his low-tax principles throughout his career. "Each little bit of [tax] burden that can be spared the common people," he wrote in the 1750s, "represents a corresponding contribution to their basic productive capacity" (*yuanqi*).[29] In practice an ever expanding fiscal base allowed him to finance his own administrative projects and infrastructural investments while still trimming per capita taxes.

Third, Chen participated in the active Qing discourse condemning "overregulation" (*tiaoli taiduo*), lambasting the common official practice of seeking minute control over the society through promulgating "superfluous, wordy, and repugnant substatutes" (*miwen louli*).[30] In Chen's view the proliferation of ever more specific regulations had been a baleful long-term trend in imperial governance and was compounded in his own day by the insistence of unenlightened bureaucrats on adhering to legalistic detail far too literally. He identifies at least three resulting dysfunctions. For one thing, overregulation "harasses the people" (*raomin*) rather than showing them kindness (*huimin*), the proper task of government. Setting the world at peace is often best achieved by simply not creating unnecessary irritants (*yi burao wei an*).[31] For another, local officials bogged down in legalistic paperwork are too harried to respond sensitively to popular needs; unrealistic demands for regulatory enforcement only incline them further to mere nominal performance of their tasks of office (*youming wushi*).[32] Finally, there is the familiar syndrome of "each new law spawns its own corruptions" (*fali bisheng*). Even where a directive succeeds in rooting out the specific abuse it was intended to redress, its presence on the books often creates unanticipated new opportunities for yamen underlings or local magnates to use it against society for their own advantage.[33]

The treaty-port scholar H. B. Morse once famously dismissed the Qing state as merely "a taxing and policing agent,"[34] but although this certainly captured the ethos of minimalist governance that Chen and his imperial patrons consistently professed (and often in practice adhered to), it grossly underestimated both the range of functions Qing officialdom claimed as its competence and those it actually performed. Over and against the powerful arguments we have just seen Chen Hongmou advancing against any adventurist expansion of the scale of the state, he repeatedly suggests a number of rationales for why precisely such an expansion might be called for. We have already seen, for instance, how aggressively Chen pushed the limits of conventionally accepted state action in areas of popular welfare—not only providing New Deal–style work relief and direct dispensation of food and monetary aid in times of dearth but also promoting an extraordinarily complex and costly granary system designed to regulate prices to consumers and to provide a source of seed loans, as well as a guaranteed market, to producers. We have also seen his willingness to intervene directly in popular economic production, even at times going so far as to dictate crop and seed selection. As he argued, "It is the task of official management (*jingli*) to educate the people as to how to make the most productive use of their environment."[35] The calculus of balance between local societal initiative and direct state investment in infrastructural improvement was a complex one, but Chen's vision of the proper role of the state gave ample room to the latter. He unhesitatingly assumed the principle of eminent domain, condemning for state purchase privately developed properties standing in the way of useful projects and, his instinctive frugality notwithstanding, argued forcefully that "if long-term benefit to the people is at stake, we should not begrudge even the most massive spending" on waterworks or other new construction.[36]

The "policing" function Morse noticed was itself a far more considerable enterprise—and, in Chen Hongmou's hands, a more potent rationale for state expansion—than the old China hand's dismissive remark suggests. In many ways the agenda of *jingshi*, of "ordering the world," cherished by Chen and many if not most of his mid-Qing bureaucratic colleagues offered a Chinese parallel to the quest for a "well-ordered police state" seen by Marc Raeff as a distinctive project of political leaders in the early modern West.[37] This involved, to be sure, all the usual tasks of upholding law and order. Routinely throughout his administrative career Governor Chen assumed personal command of dragnet operations, launched crackdowns on petty criminal activity, and drew up new and more finely articulated public security networks, in the process intervening on a much more intimate basis in the daily life of village and market town. As he wrote to a friend in 1744, "Only if the treacherous elements in society know that there is no means to escape the consequences of their crimes can the good people feel secure."[38] But, as we shall shortly see in detail, the project of "ordering the world," like that of forging "the well-ordered police state," entailed as well a remarkable degree of intervention into personal and family lives in the process of "civilizing" (*hua*) the thought and behavior of even the most law-abiding citizens.

In the eighteenth century probably the single most potent argument for expanding in practice both the size of the state apparatus and the extent of its intervention in people's lives came in the area of civil litigation. As Philip Huang has conclusively demonstrated, the state used an extraordinarily deft process of conflict resolution to meet the unprecedented willingness of the Qing population to avail itself of the mechanisms of government to press private grievances and pursue private interests. This process of resolution combined means direct and indirect, all centering on the magistrate's court.[39] The puzzle seems to be just why the state would commit itself so readily to hearing all these "trivial matters" (*xishi*) when all officials seemed to agree that they were socially dysfunctional and that they presented an increasingly crippling burden on local-level institutions of governance. It seems especially surprising that Chen Hongmou would endorse this receptiveness because probably no one articulated more famously or emphatically the ubiquitous Qing official trope condemning the rise in popular litigiousness and the role played in this by the emerging professional corps of "pettifoggers" (*songshi*) or "litigation thugs" (*songgun*).[40]

Chen himself proffers many answers. There is, first of all, the obvious public security angle: The alternative to resolution of social disputes through the courts is the use of private force, even, in the worst cases, large-scale violent vendetta (*xiedou*). This is not only socially dysfunctional but barbaric. Thus, to the extent that the state resolves litigation through the use of calm and rational sifting of evidence—the imposition of principle (*li*)—hearing litigation is an essential act of "ordering the world," of the civilizing process. At the same time, inviting litigation is also a political act. It offers a visible presence of the state in the daily life of the people, a demonstration of its responsiveness to popular concerns and hence to the benevolence of its rule. There is no more certain way to give government a bad reputation among the people, Chen says, than to refuse to receive popular plaints or to resolve them badly.[41] What he does not say, but surely understands, is that a regime's ability to persuade the population to use *it* as a conflict resolution facility, to bring plaints to *it* rather than to a competitive source of authority, is a hegemonizing act; filing a plaint with the state legitimates its power. Related to both of these rationales is what Chen sees as the critical exemplary function of the litigation process. Popular understandings of right and wrong, and of legal and illegal, are necessarily shaped by the cumulative record of official interpretation of statute in real-world cases of immediate local concern. Lacking this observable public record, there is no guarantee that the operative moral consensus within any local population will not deviate from proper and desirable norms. Viewed in this way, the public processing of civil litigation is a critical mechanism for the remolding of local customary practice (*yifeng yisu*).[42]

Hearing litigation, and doing so in an expeditious fashion, is essential to uphold the foundation of the socioeconomic order: the small-producer household. The financial integrity (*jiaji*) of the household is at stake in each and every case, especially so because there are always pettifoggers, yamen underlings, and a host of other social parasites eager to protract the proceedings in order to squeeze the people dry. Laggardness in receiving or resolving cases is thus just another form of "harassing the people" (*leimin*), which the state must guard against at every turn. Pursuing this logic, Chen suggests that an official's visible readiness to process litigation will actually cause the crippling volume of litigation to decrease by discouraging the frivolous plaints and nuisance cases that the litigants do not really expect to win but use merely to pursue private enmities.[43] Even more interestingly, Chen at one point hints that the litigation process is an active means by which the state can intervene to protect the interests of poorer households, which often have no other means of redress against the predations of their more wealthy and powerful neighbors. It is wrong, to be sure, for an official to deliberately use legal judgments as a means of redistributing wealth in local society; nevertheless, hearing cases impartially, unswayed by the status of the litigants, should effectively safeguard the interests of the downtrodden.[44]

The rhetorical trope to which Chen Hongmou most frequently resorts in the pursuit of a more interventionist state, that which provides the most effective counterweight to the small government predilections he genuinely shared with much of the Qing elite, was that of "reaching the people." In Chen's prose this notion was expressed in a variety of idioms. There was "*linmin*" (being close to the people), which Chen absorbed from the Guanxue luminary Xue Xuan; there was "*tongmin*" (getting through to the people), a usage favored by Lü Kun, which, significantly, resonated with the highly valorized term for unimpeded circulation of commercial goods, "*liutong*"; and most distinctively there was Chen's own "*jimin*" (extend to the people), which, echoing another of Chen's favorite idioms, "*jishi*" (timeliness), carried overtones of an empirical responsiveness to differing spatial and temporal conditions. Chen's lectures to his subordinates on how more genuinely to *jimin* were cited as exemplary in several later Qing official handbooks. For the most part Chen's invocation of these concepts comes in reference to the work style of existing officials (for example, the more performative aspects of official service, such as public hearing of civil litigation and official tours of the countryside) or, as we shall see below, to the mechanisms of official/popular communications (petitions, proclamations, and so on). With its emphasis on the penetration of society, however, this language clearly opened the door for rethinking the advisability for an increased density of officials on the landscape and more generally the overall efficiency of state control.[45]

In his day-to-day administrative practice Chen worked in two basic ways to expand and centralize state power: (1) by asserting greater control over county government operations by his own higher-level provincial office and (2) by bringing a range of quasi-governmental local activities under the direct aegis of bureaucratic county-level governance. Many practical policy decisions considered by Chen of course combined both strategies at once. Nevertheless, for purposes of convenience let us attempt to separate them analytically, looking at the first of these in the section to follow and at the second later in this chapter.

Disciplining the Bureaucracy

The powers of the provincial governor, in both absolute terms and terms relative to those of county officials, had been growing over the course of the late imperial era. By the late Ming, observation of this trend had occasioned differing responses on the part of reform-minded literati. In a lengthy passage reproduced by Chen in his *Sourcebook on Official Conduct*, Lü Kun had approvingly envisioned an extraordinarily encompassing set of responsibilities for occupants of this post.[46] Gu Yanwu, by contrast, in a famous passage (significantly *not* cited by Chen Hongmou) had expressed alarm at the inhibitions this unwonted gubernatorial second-guessing placed on local official initiative, going so far as to recommend that the post be abolished altogether.[47] But the trend continued into the Qing, and it received further impetus with the establishment of the so-called palace memorial (*zouzhe*) system, by means of which provincial officials were given an unprecedented direct communication with the throne denied their local-level subordinates.[48] Chen Hongmou, as we saw in Chapter 2, was quick to seize the advantage this communications access offered, memorializing regularly (and at times being granted special imperial dispensation to do so) even when occupying subgubernatorial posts in the late 1720s and 1730s.

In other ways as well Chen proved alert to the possibilities of the communications system to enhance the power of the governor over his subordinates. The roughly one thousand documents in Chen's *Peiyuan tang oucun gao*, a mammoth forty-eight-*juan* collection of his downward official correspondence, provide testimony unparalleled in the imperial record of a provincial governor's bullying and cajoling local officials to do his bidding.[49]

Notwithstanding his repeated stress on sensitivity to local particulars, Chen's career was also studded with specific initiatives to centralize control and decision making regarding local administration at his own provincial office. Much of this entailed simply standardizing operating procedures and documentation systems used by county magistrates, a general theme in mid-Qing administrative history to which we shall return shortly. Centralizing initiatives came in more substantive policy areas as well, however, including those in food policy management: on the one hand controlling stocks at county and prefectural ever-normal granaries (*changping cang*) by redistributing their holdings from the provincial level and by establishing province-wide systems of *juanna* sales of degrees for grain (to be allocated among local granaries as he saw fit), and on the other hand minutely monitoring and regulating community granaries (*shecang*) from his provincial office in such as way as to minimize local-official participation in their management.[50]

Some of Chen's most striking provincial centralization moves came in the area of managing judicial workloads. Resolution of cases of civil litigation in Qing China was normally left to the authority of the local magistrate (hence the customary designation of these cases as *zili zhi shi* [affairs to be resolved on one's own]). Like many another provincial governor, however, Chen fretted about the lack of dispatch with which many magistrates brought closure to such cases and the draining financial consequences of protracted hearings for the litigants. As we shall see, he designed a variety of mecha-

nisms to expedite local-level litigation processing, all of which to some degree promoted the power of his own provincial office over the autonomous authority of the
local official. His most dramatic initiative, though, came in a memorial submitted as
Fujian governor in 1754, in which Chen proposed the establishment of a new provincial-level official with the express duty of overseeing county and prefectural diligence
in resolving civil litigation. Unlike the existing post of provincial judge, whose duties included serving as higher court of appeal for certain civil cases and who was constitu-
tionally independent of the governor's control, this new official was to be, rather like
the provincial grain intendant, a direct gubernatorial agent. The emperor turned the
proposal over to the Grand Council for discussion, and there it seems to have died.[51]

The more general problem of maintaining bureaucratic discipline over the various
official and subofficial functionaries under his jurisdiction preoccupied Chen
Hongmou throughout his long provincial career. Chen was an astute observer of the
routinization, careerism, time serving, shortness of vision, and other "repugnant practices" (*guanchang louxi*) endemic to a system of government as bureaucratized as that
of the Qing. Reflections on these problems, indeed, constitute a principal theme of his
collected letters and were certainly a major reason why these were his writings appreciated earliest and most widely by subsequent officials. He attacked bureaucratic passivity, unthinking by-the-book decision making, unwarranted delegation of duties to
subofficial subordinates, and the tendency of local officials to confine vigorous action
to periods when they knew their superior was watching. Especially of concern was the
fact that county magistrates, burdened increasingly by litigation and other paperwork,
tended over their careers to grow more impatient with each individual matter at hand
and to lose sight of the fact that these mundane matters, to themselves boringly routine
and commonplace, were nevertheless critical to the life chances of the parties concerned. Chen could well understand, deplore it as he might, how officials so burdened
might even come to resent the people under their charge as nuisances. All of these "repugnant practices" he recognized as growing out of the persistent structural problems
of imperial bureaucracy—those associated, for example, with the law of avoidance and
the customarily short tenure of office in each local post. But, unlike Gu Yanwu and
other more radical reformers, Chen proposed solutions that tended to be less structural than moral: a higher level of self-conscious "sincerity" (*jing*) on the part of lower-
level functionaries, combined with a more diligent effort at oversight by their responsible superiors.[52]

A well-documented example of Chen's hands-on style of personnel management
came during his brief tenure as Hunan governor in 1756. Following his posting to the
province he immediately called into his yamen each individual subordinate of the level
of circuit attendant and above, grilling them in great detail about the business of their
office. Having assessed the competence of this group, he set off on a two-month tour
of selected Hunan counties, interviewing local magistrates about goings-on in their districts and sampling local popular opinion about their capacities and responsiveness to
popular needs. He also visited and interrogated a number of functionally specific local
officials involved in overseeing Hunan's timber and mining industries to satisfy himself
that these individuals possessed the technical expertise demanded by their post. In the

process Chen peppered the throne with a long series of reports on the provincial bureaucracy, assessing who precisely was or was not performing satisfactorily. His reports resulted in the removal of some subordinates (including the province's number-two official, Provincial Treasurer Yang Hao) and the shifting of several others into posts for which their talents better suited them.[53]

Throughout his career Chen scrutinized county-level budgets, payrolls, and staffs. He was particularly alert to cases of hiring on of relatives and to cases of touring bureaucrats who indulged in "useless" spending on entertainment (a customary form of clientalism known as *yingchou*). He was fond of imposing deadlines and issuing prompts in such areas of local governance as public security and, as we shall see, litigation processing. Periodic cleanup campaigns in tax collection, granary management, and other policy sectors could entail Chen's sending down special inspectors (*chaiti*) from the provincial to the prefectural and county levels to audit local accounts.[54] Other, more routine forms of supervision were to come from intermediaries. From time to time throughout his career Chen issued quite detailed statements of how he envisioned the duties of second-tier supervisory officials, from prefects (*zhifu*) to circuit intendants (*daotai*) to provincial judges and treasurers (*liangsi*). Prominent among these was oversight of county magistrates, accomplished not only by monitoring their paperwork but also by personal observation in the field. Chen set down precise standards for the end-of-year fitness evaluations each field official was required to submit on his subordinates in the chain of command and also for the audits an incoming magistrate was to conduct of his predecessor's accounts on succession to office (*jiaodai*).[55]

Given Chen Hongmou's repeated emphasis on official sensitivity to popular opinion and his long-standing critique of unresponsive bureaucratism, not to mention the Qing political counterdiscourse of local community self-governance (*fengjian*) in which, as we shall see, Chen at least at times participated, it is critical to ask to what extent the governor was willing to go outside the bureaucracy as a whole in his quest for input on magisterial performance. And, perhaps unsurprisingly, the evidence on this score is ambiguous. In at least one instance, in Hubei in 1747, Chen publicly proclaimed: "If you among the civil and military population have deep-seated grievances and feel yourself without means of legal redress, either because local officials and clerks are subverting the law through corruption, or because local bullies are tyrannizing society and your local magistrate has proven negligent in prosecuting them, it is permissible to come in person to my yamen to file a plaint." In typical fashion the governor drew up standard forms as well as systematic regulations for the complaint process, vowing to punish not only officials found to be corrupt but also those who in any way sought to prevent citizens from engaging in this end-run around formally constituted local authority.[56] Yet only four years later as Shaanxi governor Chen angrily dismissed the proposal of a subordinate, circuit intendant Guan Ning, that lower gentry (*shengyuan*) be offered an institutional vehicle through the reports of county educational officials (*jiaoguan*) to routinely criticize the performance of the magistrate.[57]

Was the difference in these two cases that the latter offered preferred status in the expression of local opinion to *shengyuan*, a class of the population that, at least since Gu Yanwu, had been held in Qing thought to be politically unreliable?[58] (Chen does complain that, if so empowered, the "ambitious, discontented, and meddlesome" *shengyuan* will in their critiques "invariably confuse right and wrong.") Or did he more basically find intolerable the degree of institutionalization the Shaanxi proposal offered for the expression of popular dissent and subversion of local official authority? Our answer must hinge on the broader question of the complex interface Chen Hongmou envisioned between bureaucracy and local community. And that critical interface was mediated, none too satisfactorily, by the clerical sub-bureaucracy.

Disciplining the Sub-Bureaucracy

The problem of maintaining discipline among the clerical sub-bureaucracy (variously *li, shuli,* or *xuli*), which functioned at all levels of administration but most critically at that of the county, preoccupied Chen Hongmou throughout his career.[59] Reflections on this theme run through his official and private correspondence, and he wrote a book on the subject, the 1743 *Zaiguan fajie lu* (Sourcebook on sub-bureaucratic discipline), which was widely circulated in his own time and reprinted many times throughout the later Qing. Testimony to Chen's authority on this issue is seen in the prominent inclusion of his writings in discussions of clerks in Wei Yuan's *Huangchao jingshi wenbian* and other nineteenth-century administrative guidebooks and, no less, in the reliance on Chen's observations in the standard twentieth-century academic treatment of the subject, Ch'ü T'ung-tsu's 1962 *Local Government in China Under the Ch'ing*.[60]

Fretting about this problem was hardly unique to Chen, however; in fact, it was perhaps the single central theme of all Qing administrative writing. The general outlines of the predicament were universally understood and have been well described by modern scholars such as Ch'ü and Pierre-Étienne Will. The operation of the law of avoidance (*huibi*) ensured that the county magistrate would be a relatively recently arrived stranger to his jurisdiction, forced to rely for local intelligence on the sometimes native and always locally entrenched clerical staff he inherited along with his office. Over the course of the imperial period this problem had only been aggravated by the secular decline of the ratio of county officials to the population (a long-term shrinking of the formally acknowledged state apparatus, which, ironically, was in part made possible by a compensatory swelling of the clerical sub-bureaucracy). The continued proliferation of locally specific regulations and precedents, a body of lore over which the clerks held a quasi-priestly monopoly, added to the magistrate's dependence on them. Perhaps worst of all, the systematic and increasingly acute underfunding of local administration in the Qing fiscal system meant that the clerical sub-bureaucracy was compelled essentially to steal from the local population (via the imposition of irregular fees, *lougui*) not only to support itself but also to fund the entire operation of county-level government. Local clerkships unsurprisingly became in effect a form of racketeering, a racket that, as James Cole has suggested, was syndicated on an empire-wide basis, with its controlling node in the Boards of Revenue and Punishments at Beijing.[61]

Denunciation of the depraved conduct of these "millions of tigers and wolves" (*baiwan hulang*) unleashed by the system on the helpless population became, in fact, a standard trope in Qing bureaucratic discourse, a trope that took on a life of its own. As

Bradly Reed has recently shown, in pathbreaking work based on study of county archives, there was considerable rationality to the system that clerks in at least some areas worked out over time to apportion the burden of financing local administration; nevertheless, as Reed also shows, this was largely ignored in the rhetoric of clerical depravity that officials generated as their own collective apologia for the chronic dysfunctions of county government.[62] Two implications of the autonomous development of this discursive tradition are important for our understanding of Chen Hongmou's own take on the clerical issue. First, official participants in this discourse found in it reinforcement for a near complete alienation from the clerkly stratum. This could only aggravate what Will sees as the socioculturally based antipathy between the two basic agents of local governance, preventing any development of an esprit de corps and leading instead to a "total lack of confidence" on the part of magistrates in the clerical subordinates on whom they so depended.[63] Second, the broadly despised clerks came to serve as a useful emblem of all that was wrong with the Qing's overcentralized and overregulated style of administration. Gu Yanwu, for most Qing literati the central figure in the so-called *fengjian* political counterdiscourse and, like Chen, a man who worried regularly and publicly about sub-bureaucratic misconduct, used the clerks very powerfully as just such a bête noir in part 8 of his famous local-autonomy manifesto, "Junxian lun" (On the prefectural system [ca. 1660]).[64]

Chen Hongmou included Gu among the sources he cited in his *Zaiguan fajie lu*—he may have felt he had no choice if he were to retain credibility—but he did so very selectively (he did not cite the "Junxian lun"), and in his commentary he routinely turned Gu's arguments on their heads. For example, Gu Yanwu's provocative proposal in the "Junxian lun" that the local magistrate be selected from among the local landed literati, effectively abrogating the law of avoidance, had rested largely on the assumption that, as himself a local resident and property owner, such an official would more sincerely have the needs of the district at heart. He would also, as a well-informed native, be more immune from clerical manipulation and hence better able to control his staff.[65] With what may have been seen by his readers as delicious irony, in his commentary on Gu in his own *Zaiguan fajie lu*, Chen advanced in a deadpan manner the argument that the clerks themselves, being entrenched local natives, can be expected at least partially to have the interests of their community at heart and that the alert official can capitalize on this to turn their actions to the public good.[66]

We see already here the hint of a more charitable attitude toward clerks in Chen than in the vitriolic prevailing discourse. But this does not imply naivete. Over the course of his long career in the field, Chen personally uncovered countless cases of clerical racketeering, in areas as diverse as litigation processing, granary management, famine relief, water conservancy maintenance, salt and mining administration, the conduct of the civil service examinations, and even the dispensation of virtuous widow (*jiexiao*) honors.[67] In instituting a new regional policy of any sort he invariably warned his county-level subordinates to anticipate efforts by their clerks to turn its implementation to their own corrupt purposes. On a case-by-case basis in the field the remedies Chen adopted for clerical malfeasance were similarly hardheaded. He launched periodic crackdowns and cleanup campaigns, bringing criminal sanctions to bear against the most egregiously corrupt. He sought where possible to circumvent clerical machinations by utilizing other, more respected and reliable personnel to perform functions that might otherwise fall to the clerks. (In one sense Chen's entire community granary project, headed as it was by a local landowner as *shezhang* instead of yamen underlings, was just such a scheme.) And, as we shall see more fully in the section to follow, he devised numerous strategies to utilize more complete systems of receipting, recording, and communications processing to impose greater accountability on clerks. Beginning in 1740, for instance, he required that all litigation documents filed in the provinces in which he served bear the signature of the chief clerk who had supervised its drafting, as a means of assigning culpability for potential tampering.[68] Chen well understood, in other words, the proclivity of clerks to corrupt practices, and he was fond of quoting the conventional injunction to magistrates, "Make use of yamen functionaries, do not allow yourself to be used by them."[69]

Yet in his analysis of the overall problem of yamen underlings, as often as Chen followed the prevailing logic he just as often added elements more peculiar to himself. He begins by conceding the indispensability of clerks to the present-day operation of government; in a very real sense, he insists, popular livelihoods (*minsheng*) lie in their hands. He acknowledges as well the secular increase in the workload of local officials, accelerating in his own day because of rapid population growth and increased social complexity. One consequence of this has been the need for local officials to hire additional supernumerary clerks, beyond the number formally allotted them by the central administration, and with this has come increased loss of clerical accountability.[70] Rather predictably, Chen finds in this an occasion to preach once again about the need for magistrates to do things in person—to "reach the people"—and he draws a direct correlation between the levels of official laxity on this score and of clerical malfeasance.[71] But in truth he knows that a lax officialdom is hardly the sole problem, nor is a more attentive one its sole solution. The more basic dysfunction is the psychological alienation of officials from their clerical subordinates, the fact that the attitudes and outlooks of the two groups have come so radically to diverge (*quxiang butong*).[72] Most originally, Chen attributes this alienation in turn to the dramatic and unwarranted debasement of the sociocultural status of the clerks. This is the central theme of his sourcebook on clerical discipline, the *Zaiguan fajie lu.*

In the rather remarkable preface to that work Chen sets out a historical model of how this debasement took place. It was a two-stage process. In antiquity, he argues, clerical duties for each locality were performed by highly respected local citizens, but this changed with the bureaucratization attendant on Qin Shihuang's third-century B.C. founding of the empire. So far, so good: Chen's disparagement of Qin Legalism is no more than what one would expect of any late imperial Confucian scholar, and his negative assessment of statist centralization, despite his own practical proclivities in that direction, are in line with hallowed *lixue* orthodoxy. The Confucianized Han dynasty partially restored a humanistic approach to public service and thus becomes for Chen the last great age of clerical dignity. (It is for this reason that, alone among his sourcebooks, the *Zaiguan fajie lu* draws its texts most prominently from Han sources.) The second and decisive step in the debasement of clerks, however, came in the Tang-Song era with

the institution of the civil service examination as the principal instrument for recruitment into official service. What this step effectively did, Chen plausibly but rather jar-
ringly suggests, was to declare officials—holders of civil service degrees—to be gentlemen (*junzi*), and the non-degree-holding clerks, by contrast, to be something less than
that. Almost immediately they began to behave accordingly.[73]

His idiosyncratic understanding of the origins of the predicament in which the
Qing state found itself with respect to its clerical workforce led Chen Hongmou to propose solutions likewise out of the ordinary. His most radical set of proposals came in a
memorial submitted to the throne as Yunnan provincial treasurer at the beginning of
1737. Coming early in his field career and, as it happened, only shortly before Chen
would be cashiered by the Qianlong emperor for his intransigent whistle-blowing in the
Guangxi land reclamation scandal (see Chapter 2), this memorial, like his actions in
the Guangxi case, reflected an uncertain grasp of how politics under Qianlong would
differ from those under his recently deceased predecessor. The first of the two proposals Chen advanced in this document offered a radical structural solution. He argued simply that the court should regularize all clerical appointments at the county
level, eliminating the need for supernumeraries, and allocate to the counties sufficient
funds to pay each clerk a viable salary. This would at the same time "demonstrate compassion" (*tixu*) to those laboring in public service and obviate the need for oppressive,
locally imposed irregular fees (*lougui*), which Chen proposed be systematically eliminated once clerical salaries were regularized as a part of county budgets. It would also,
Chen did not need to say, increase the need for tax revenues and considerably increase
the size of the formal state apparatus.[74]

This proposal by Chen was clearly a logical extension of the so-called *haoxian
guigong* reforms of the Yongzheng emperor, which sought to put a broad range of local
governmental expenses on a regularized fiscal basis and which the Qianlong emperor,
with his fiscally conservative view of "magnanimous" (*kuan*) governance, on his succession declined to pursue.[75] Qianlong's response to Chen's proposal was accordingly curt
and dismissive: "Not well considered and unmanageably difficult." Chen did not raise
it again. In subsequent years, however, he did continue to push for budgetary solutions
to the problem of clerical corruption. In 1746 in Shaanxi, for example, he led a
provincial campaign to register all county-level *lougui* that he deemed permissible and
to eliminate all others, and in his 1742 *Zaiguan fajie lu* he cautiously offered his view
that existing clerical stipends were so low as to make fee-taking inevitable.[76] Still, the
more central thrust of Chen's later writing about clerks, and that for which he was best
known, went in another direction.

This direction was foreshadowed in the second of the two proposals Chen offered
in his 1737 memorial. Here he suggested the institution of an annual examination for
all clerks at the county level and above, on the basis of which they would be accorded
a ranked assessment. "One or two of the most outstanding," Chen added, might be promoted as a result to a clerkship at a higher level of administration or, just perhaps, be
considered for promotion into officialdom itself. The major benefit of such an examination system would be to "offer encouragement" to clerks both to continue their education and to conduct themselves properly in public service—precisely the kind of

positive incentives denied them under existing institutional arrangements. Qianlong was clearly intrigued. This suggestion was "quite a different matter" from Chen's first, misconceived proposal on budgetary reform, and the emperor vowed in his rescript to give the matter additional thought.[77] It seems to have gone no further than this; Xu Dong, in his 1838 manual for magistrates, *Muling shu*, notes briefly in passing that Chen Hongmou had once made such a proposal but indicates nothing about any follow-up.[78] But Chen himself pondered this line of reasoning throughout the remainder of his life.

Chen's central argument about the proper handling of yamen functionaries built on the same humanistic themes that he reiterated in a wide variety of contexts.[79] As devious and blackhearted as clerks may appear, they are human beings and like all other human beings have within them the benevolent nature of Heaven (*tianliang*). Like all human beings they are inherently endowed with a sense of Confucian self-respect or shame (*chi*). Thus, although their situation in life has habituated them to an opportunist indulgence of self-interest (Chen comes close here to an argument that "power corrupts"), their innate humanity enables them to be transformed (*hua*) or inspired (*tixing*) to virtuous, public-spirited conduct. With his deep reverence for human individuality Chen argues that it is both morally incorrect and pragmatically counterproductive to dismiss all clerks as a class rather than to treat them as individual persons independently responsive to moral appeals. To dismiss them categorically is a violation of Confucius's dictum, "In education, make no class distinctions." Voicing distinctively early modern sentiments, Chen insists that *all* men, not merely civil service degree-holders, are potential "gentlemen" (*junzi*). Not a few clerks in the past have actually risen into positions of respected officialdom.

The core of Chen's position is that clerks are educable, indeed more so than the average member of the population. They are by definition literate, and Chen insists that a great many come from highly cultivated family backgrounds and have received at least the rudiments of a classical education. For this reason he believes it practically worthwhile when compiling his *Zaiguan fajie lu* as Jiangxi governor in 1742 to order the printing and distribution of a copy to every county-level clerk in the province, despite the severe classical style in which much of its content is written.[80] But beyond their literary achievements lies another attribute of clerks that Chen believes makes them especially good candidates for moral transformation: their ambition and will to self-improvement (*youzhi*). There is an element of self-selection in clerical service; the very fact that its incumbents have felt dissatisfied with life on the farm and have sought out a more challenging path to personal advancement indicates that they are success oriented. It is this inclination to the aggressive pursuit of self-interest, of course, which makes clerks so troublesome in their present station. Yet Chen cites no less an authority than the great neo-Confucian poet-statesman Su Shi (Su Dongpo, 1036–1101) on the fact that such a will to succeed renders an individual especially responsive to the proper motivational appeals for self-improvement.[81]

Citing Gu Yanwu's commentary on the passage in the *Zhou li*—the fountainhead of much late imperial local-autonomy political thought—on the first installation of officials and subofficials, Chen reads Gu as emphasizing above all the need to treat clerks with respect so as to inculcate in them an internalized sense of self-worth (*zizhong*) and moral autonomy. This, adds Chen, is a far better way to achieve sub-bureaucratic discipline than is the continuing threat of criminal sanctions. In another citation from Gu, Chen applauds his suggestion to institute some kind of a rewards system for clerks who participate in an ongoing course of classical study.[82] It is clear in the larger context of Gu's corpus, however, that Chen's reading of him is highly selective.[83] Indeed, in his envoi letter for the *Zaiguan fajie lu* Chen seems to underline this point by stressing that his goal is not to resolve the problem of clerical malfeasance by means of basic constitutional change (as Gu had advocated in the "Junxian lun") but rather by the more gradualist method of recapturing the clerks' hearts and minds "one individual at a time."[84]

Two aspects of Chen's thinking about the problem of sub-bureaucrats seem to me to have a distinctively early modern tone. First, for all its *lixue*-tinged moralism Chen's system for overcoming the alienation between officials and clerks, and for recapturing the latter for more effective state purposes, relies on providing the material incentive of individual advancement. In so doing he returns to the "structure of opportunity" argument we saw him developing in Chapter 9. Chen congratulates his contemporaries that they live in an era, and under a dynasty, unprecedentedly open in terms of chances for upward mobility. With all the anxieties about social entropy this openness may occasion, on balance it is *good* for the preservation of social order because it offers unique possibilities of rewarding individuals for socially responsible behavior. Why not, Chen suggests, rather than counterproductively denouncing clerks en bloc as a scourge on the people, give them the benefit of the doubt and creatively utilize this new atmosphere of open advancement by extending it to them as well?[85]

Second, underlying Chen's analysis is his assumption of the coequal moral essence of all human beings—their sharing in Heaven's goodness (*tianliang*). In his application of this to the problem of clerks, however, he does not come down in favor of a solution trumpeting greater individual (or local community) "liberty" from an expansive state. On the contrary Chen's efforts effectively to rehabilitate the image of the clerical subbureaucracy and merge it, however tentatively, with the official stratum, like his early and imperially discouraged proposal to place clerks more securely on regular bureaucratic payrolls, harness his individual-autonomy ideas in practice (if not in theory) to the legitimation of a larger, more powerful formal state apparatus.

Subcounty Governance

As the empire's population dramatically increased over the first half of the Qing whereas the number of county magistrates rose only slightly, as the economy expanded more rapidly than did local administrative budgets, and as the tasks imposed on the county administration both by higher authority and by its constituency (via the litigation process) became more complex, the workload of each individual magistrate multiplied far beyond that which even the most capable could reasonably be expected to assume. To whom was he to turn for help? An expanding sub-bureaucracy was one solution adopted in practice, but it was a strategy literati consensus found wanting because of the weakness of clerical discipline. Even such a figure as Chen, who as we have seen argued for the genuine possibility of turning the clerks to state purposes, saw the solution as at best limited and at worst counterproductive.

The shrinking presence of officials on the landscape thus suggested two alternative remedies. The first was essentially to farm out quasi-governmental tasks to communal groups and leadership—local gentry and "headmen" (*zhang*) of various sorts—within the local society. This was on balance the favored solution and one of which Chen Hongmou was a celebrated practitioner. Nevertheless, he hardly ignored the second alternative, that of expanding the local state presence by granting greater powers to existing local supernumerary officials and, just perhaps, by creating new ones. The most direct method of doing this, of course, was simply to increase the density of county magistrates by creating new counties. In the early days of his official career, in Yunnan, Chen was involved in the process of *gaitu guiliu*, the imposition of regularized county administrations in territories formerly ruled indirectly by enfeoffed "native chieftains" (*tusi*). On occasion he took the lead in subdividing existing but loosely governed prefectures and districts into proper counties, with increasingly formalized staffs and budgets.[86] Later in his career, stationed no longer on the frontier, Chen applied the remedy of subdivision to administratively overburdened heartland districts. In 1755, for example, he succeeded in convincing the throne to create a new county out of portions of Hunan's Hengyang *xian*, a major export-grain producer and riverine cargo-breaking point plagued by unmanageable litigation backlogs.[87]

But the throne's clear distaste for wholesale numerical increase in the empire's county units meant that a finer administrative presence had to be achieved via other means. The focus of this issue became the nebulous subcounty unit known as the *xiang*. Sometimes rendered in English as "township" or "ward," the term "*xiang*" carried a bewildering range of meanings in the eighteenth century. In nontechnical usage it might refer generally to "the countryside" or, more specifically, to the suburban area around a county seat. As a defined unit of territory, usually covering somewhere between a quarter and an eighth of a county, centered on an important subcounty market town, the *xiang* in most places had a social reality, as a unit of personal identity, community organization, and indigenous local leadership.[88] Administratively, despite various statutory attempts at standardization, it seems clearly to have meant different things in different regions.[89] In some parts of the empire, but not all, the *xiang* was a unit of fiscal assessment and collection. It was only in the Republican era that it was officially adopted as a multifunctional unit of subcounty governance.[90] There were, however, efforts made in that direction in the eighteenth century, and this is the story we have to tell here.

The baseline for Chen Hongmou's own tentative experiments with *xiang*-level administration was a debate that had taken place in 1729, while Chen was a junior central government clerk.[91] A censor named Gong Jianyang submitted a memorial arguing that, the duties of the county magistrate having become unmanageably burdensome, the throne ought additionally to establish four subunits, to be called *xiang* and to be governed by an official known as *xiangguan*, under the purview of each county. This additional level of local official would share with the county magistrate the tasks of hearing litigation and managing public security and public works and would help relieve the magistrate's reliance on the abominated clerks and runners. Almost certainly taking his cue from Gu Yanwu, Censor Gong proposed that these new *xiangguan* be selected from among the leading gentry landlords of the respective *xiang*. The Yongzheng emperor, concerned as he was with the growing burdens of local administration, was sufficiently intrigued to circulate Gong's memorial for comments to several of his most trusted field administrators.

The decisive response was that of Ortai. Ortai argued that the tasks of subcounty governance were already being satisfactorily delegated, in the busiest and most populous counties, to such subordinate officials as assistant and subdistrict magistrates (*xiancheng* and *xunjian*) on a case-by-case basis, whereas the handling of lower-priority *xiang*-level affairs was assigned to nonofficial local functionaries such as community compact heads (*xiangyue*) and *baojia* headmen. Establishing yet another level of formal administration would thus entail more trouble than it was worth; far from ameliorating the plague of clerks and runners, for example, the creation of new official jurisdictions would instead necessitate the hiring of still more of these villains! Most emphatically, Ortai argued for the inappropriateness of Gong's suggestion that these new officials be recruited from among the elite of the locality itself. This was a fundamental violation of the tried-and-true law of avoidance (*huibi*). Experience taught that appointment to formal office of such local magnates would result in one of two evils: the *xiangguan* would either become simply the tool of parochial local opinion (*shisi*), or they would exploit the new position for self-enrichment at local expense (*jiagong jisi*). Faced with such cogently expressed opposition, the Yongzheng emperor rejected Gong's proposal, and there the matter died.

But not completely. Yongzheng's ruling effectively killed any discussion over the next several decades of any systematic empire-wide establishment of a subcounty *xiang* unit of formal administration and, even more decisively, any thought of filling such a post with personnel drawn from among the local elite. Yet there was still considerable sentiment within the field bureaucracy for setting up subcounty official jurisdictions in at least the most overburdened magistracies, and efforts at doing so now came to center on the utilization of centrally appointed, nonlocal natives—the assistant and subdistrict magistrates mentioned by Ortai, as well as the more ubiquitous category of "auxiliary officials" (*zuoza*)—to fill such posts. Yongzheng himself gave his limited blessing to such innovation, on a case-by-case basis, and at the same time sought to regularize it by accompanying his rejection of the *xiangguan* proposal with an order to survey and register all subcounty jurisdictions in the empire to which formal territorial administrators had in practice been assigned.[92]

The questions, then, of how desirable it was to assign a territorial official at the subcounty level (in effect a *xiangguan*, although out of respect for imperial precedent that term seems to have been avoided after 1729) and of the possibility of utilizing existing county-level *zuoza* officials for this purpose remained both open and politically sensitive during most of Chen Hongmou's career as a provincial governor. In his various tenures Chen dealt with these issues in various ways, according to the conditions then in force in the individual province, at times prudently resisting the assignment of a *xiangguan* role to auxiliary officials and at others more boldly moving toward that alternative.[93]

In Jiangxi, Chen's first gubernatorial post, county-level *zuoza* were typically assigned functionally specific duties but not territorially specific ones.[94] Chen did not disturb this situation, his directives in that province being aimed simply to combat the use of auxiliary officials as personal servants of the magistrate.[95] But in Shaanxi, where Chen next moved in 1744, the situation was more complex. In many counties of that province *zuoza* had been assigned since 1733 to specific subcounty market towns as part of a prolonged campaign to clear up arrears in commercial tax collection. It is unclear to what extent the duties of these officials were seen as extending beyond those of tax clearance and how broadly their jurisdiction extended beyond the market town out into the *xiang* of which it was, in effect, the administrative seat; but almost certainly over the ten-plus years the *zuoza* had been assigned to these towns their territorial duties became in practice more generalized. Several months before Chen arrived, his predecessor as governor had actually doubled the number of *zuoza* assigned to residence in market towns, but in an effort to bring the overlong tax clearance campaign to conclusion he had also given their assignments a one-year term limit. Chen's own actions in Shaanxi seem to have moved in two directions at once. On the one hand, as part of his more general procommercial policy, he ordered strict adherence to the scheduled withdrawal of the second wave of market-town officials at the end of the one-year term set by his predecessor, rescinding in the process many of the commercial taxes they had been assigned to collect. Yet he also showed his willingness to broaden the functional roles of the remaining *zuoza* his predecessor had left so conveniently located in *xiang*-level towns— and redeployed a few others himself—using them for instance as part of his drives to restock local granaries and sell honorary civil service degrees. He also memorialized to regularize their finances a bit by increasing their supplementary *yanglian* stipend.[96]

In Fujian in 1753 Chen's actions were more unequivocally oriented toward extending the reach of the state. Because of Fujian's difficult terrain, over the preceding decade successive governors had repeatedly memorialized to have *zuoza* installed as "detached assistant magistrates" (*fenfang xiancheng*) in particularly inaccessible *xiang* of various Fujian counties. By the time Chen arrived some eighteen of these existed throughout the province. In most cases the rationale for their posting had been to oversee the collection of taxes in their respective *xiang,* but over the years they had assumed other duties, such as hearing litigation, and Chen reported that in his day their range of functions was "tantamount to that of a county magistrate himself." The Yongzheng emperor in 1729 had ordered that appointment of all existing *xiang*-level officials throughout the empire be made centrally (*jianxuan tibu*), in observation of the law of avoidance. However, because these Fujian posts had all been established since that time, they had not come under the rubric of Yongzheng's edict. In practice the Board of Civil Office simply selected the most senior qualified candidate from the district itself (*zaiji aixuan*); these officials were subject to neither periodic rotation nor annual review by their superiors.[97] Although he accepted the need for these virtual *xiangguan,* Chen found the casual means of their appointment an unjustifiable breach of central bureaucratic control. On review of their activities he recommended that ten of them, those with the most encompassing sets of functions, be made subject to the same selection and rotation criteria as all other local field administrators.[98]

Chen's actions in Jiangsu in 1761 present a still clearer case of his urge toward state penetration of local society to an extent unmatched even by the throne.[99] Jiangsu was then, once again, in the midst of a campaign to collect accumulated arrears in the land tax. Governor Chen proposed to take the *zuoza* assigned to each county and install them at the *xiang* level to clean up that locality's tax arrears; so doing would spare delinquent taxpayers the burden of having to make the trek to the county seat to pay in person or, alternatively, to rely on costly and illegal remittance by proxy (*baolan*). The Qianlong emperor agreed with Chen that arranging some means of payment at *xiang*-level towns was a good idea but balked at the suggestion of assigning *zuoza* to the *xiang* for this purpose. Referring clearly (although only implicitly) to the court debates of 1729, Qianlong pointed out that sending auxiliaries into the *xiang* would mean endowing them with clerical staffs, thereby simply multiplying the opportunities for corruption and "harassing (*raolei*) the people"—in this case, a clear code word for unwonted expansion of the size of government. The emperor proposed instead that the magistrate himself, on his mandated annual tours of his jurisdiction, make a scheduled stop in each *xiang*-level town to collect that area's tax arrears. Very likely tweaking the governor by invoking Chen's own pet language, Qianlong noted that such an activity would accord with the magistrate's fundamental duty to be "personally close to the people" (*qinmin*).

In his rebuttal Chen recalled his experience in Fujian, where, because of similar unwieldiness in the size of counties, the decision had long ago been made to assess and collect the land tax on a *xiang* rather than county basis. This strategy (clearly a preliminary move toward the administrative subdivision of counties) had worked there and would likewise work in Jiangsu. Indeed, just the preceding year Chen had undertaken an experiment by sending out deputies (*weiyuan*) from his own gubernatorial staff into *xiang* towns in selected counties for purposes of collecting back taxes, and the results had been most impressive. Chen thus proposed a compromise with his emperor: In less populous or otherwise uncomplicated counties he would adopt Qianlong's strategy of collection by the magistrate during rotating tours of *xiang* towns, but in more difficult counties he would proceed with the posting of *zuoza* as he had initially suggested. Qianlong acquiesced: "This memorial is fully and carefully thought out." It must be stressed that these appointments of what were in effect new *xiang*-level officials remained limited to the single function of tax collection and that their deployment was not announced as permanent. However, Chen had in his second memorial specified a number of features that look suspiciously like the groundwork for regularization of these posts. For one thing, the *zuoza* concerned were not necessarily to be drawn from those previously allocated to the county in question but might be drawn from adjacent jurisdictions on the basis of need; for another, the salaries both of the *xiang*-level auxiliary officials and of their clerical staffs were to be calculated as part of that county's administrative budget.

In Chapter 11 we will have occasion to look at Chen Hongmou's co-option for administrative purposes of a range of locally generated *xiang*-level notables and functionaries—*xiangqi* (*xiang* elders), *xiangzhang* (*xiang* headmen), *xiangbao* (constables), *xiang-*

yue (community compact leaders), and even *xiang*-level lineage heads. For certain of these initiatives, as we shall see, Chen gained a reputation in some circles as a champion of local self-governance as an alternative to expansive bureaucratic rule. In a certain sense this reputation was deserved. In assessing that reputation, however, we would do well to keep in mind what we have seen in this section of his efforts, cautious and fragmentary as they may have been, to implant on the landscape a finer mesh of territorial officials who were fully dependent agents of the centralized imperial state. The two strategies together were complementary parts of Chen's larger project of "ordering the world."

Management

Chen Hongmou was a brilliant manager. Most "high Qing" provincial governors were highly skilled at organizational tasks, and Chen was esteemed in his day and after as one of the very finest. He was never really a visionary, and routine management was probably what he did best. A thorough study of Chen's managerial style would be a major undertaking and probably a worthwhile one. Here, however, we want more simply to draw out a few of his most characteristic administrative strategies, with an eye to how they might relate to the extension of state power and control in this age of "benevolent governance."

We have already seen a number of instances of one of Chen's most distinctive styles of management: coming into a province or region anew and undertaking a massive, comprehensive, and systematic attack on one or two major functional areas of regional administration. As he argued to a friend, effective administration demanded the ability periodically to break out of the rut of standard procedure and take a fresh look at realities and needs in a given area.[100] Chen's posting to the administrative tabula rasa of Yunnan early in his career was perfect for one so inclined: it both provided a fertile ground of experimentation and set the tone for his managerial approach throughout his subsequent career. In Yunnan Chen undertook extraordinarily bold programs to renovate transport networks, elementary education (see Chapter 12), and cropping patterns province-wide. Subsequently, he took the same systematic approach with riverine flood control in Tianjin and Jiangsu, with polder overhaul in Jiangxi and Hunan, with irrigation networks and city wall construction in Shaanxi, with road- and bridge building in Gansu, with public security and bandit suppression in Jiangsu, with jails and prisoners in Fujian, with salt administration in Jiangxi, with judicial administration in Hubei, and, as already seen, with granary administration nearly everywhere he served.[101]

Typical of his procedure would be to first have all his local-level subordinates undertake minutely detailed surveys of the matter at hand in their respective districts, which Chen would then compile on a comprehensive province-wide basis. (He did this in 1748, for example, with every single pending case of civil litigation throughout Hubei.) He would then develop an analytic typology of the problem, breaking down local instances according to functional difference (for example, a shortage or superabundance of salt), scale and cost (projects that could be undertaken with local finances versus those that required outside assistance), or relative urgency. Most often Chen would also break down the overall project into a staged, step-by-step schedule for completion. He would insist throughout on controls against false reporting—the problem of the nominal (*ming*) versus the substantial (*shi*)—and emphasize the need for patient, gradual progress so as to achieve the most long-lasting or permanent (*yongyuan*) solution. As we have seen, despite his native frugality Chen did not shy away from massive financial investment where the long-term ends seemed to justify as much.

A further hallmark of his approach is seen in his fondness for the term "*tongyong*" (compromise). A highly complicated item of Qing bureaucratic discourse, "*tongyong*" might betoken the pragmatic willingness to settle for an ad hoc or temporary solution to a problem where imposition of a more rigid one might prove arbitrary or ultimately counterproductive. It might also mean the sacrifice of advantage to one locality in the interests of others or the region as a whole—in other words, state-mandated redistribution. In Chen's managerial rhetoric the term signaled a dedication both to breadth of perspective and to flexibility in problem solving.[102]

"The cardinal principle followed by our Dynasty in establishing its bureaucratic system," Chen wrote in 1740, "is the precise delineation of jurisdictions" (*fenren*).[103] Accordingly, in his bureaucratic practice Chen paid lavish attention to processes of clarifying spheres of individual responsibility (*zecheng*) among officials. Conceiving of a task as a coherent whole, he sought to subdivide it into grid-like sectors, which collectively would encompass the whole, leaving no area of the grid uncovered. These sectors of responsibility might be functional, as when he assigned assistant magistrates in Jiangxi specific jurisdiction over polder maintenance in their counties rather than allowing them to remain as generalized (and thus, in Chen's view, underemployed) aides in county administration.[104] Or they might be spatial, as when Chen as Tianjin circuit intendant labored strenuously to find just the right division of the Yellow River hydraulic system into appropriate sectors (*duan*) for overhaul.[105] The spatial boundaries of jurisdictions were an important enough matter for Chen to redraw county borders in 1739 Zhili and 1742 Jiangxi to better fix geographic responsibility among magistrates for suppression of bandits. And in 1745 Shaanxi, when dissolving an old military colony and reabsorbing its territory into adjacent county jurisdictions, Chen paid minute attention to the precise household-by-household distribution of land tax and military service obligations, civil service examination quotas, and shares in community granaries, among the respective magistracies concerned. Chen also worked to more fully bureaucratize the sub-bureaucracy by ordering that each official in a complicated administrative system accept personal responsibility (*zecheng*) for a given number of clerks, arguing that allowing even a single clerk to escape individual accountability spelled disaster for the public weal. He even hinted at the extension of this bureaucratization into the society at large by invoking the language of *zecheng* to describe the delegation of tasks by county magistrates to various local notables within their districts.[106] Expounding on a favorite text by Lü Kun, Chen observed that maximal rationalization of jurisdictional duties was simply applying neo-Confucian principle (*li*) to political administration.[107] It was the most literal possible means of "ordering the world."

Chen's fixation on bureaucratic order appears as well in his attempts to clarify the administrative chain of command. He was particularly concerned with the roles of the intermediary officials between the localities and the province, the circuit intendants (*daotai* or *xundao*) and the provincial-level functional specialists, the provincial treasurer and provincial judge (known collectively as the "two supervisory officials," *liangsi*). Although he never served as a county magistrate, Chen did have personal experience in each of these other posts, and he knew full well how clumsily they fit into the Qing's structure of authority and reporting. Circuit intendants, for example, were supposed to serve as conduits between local officials (magistrates and prefects) and the *liangsi*, but because their own spheres of responsibility were so poorly defined, many *daotai*, fearing they might offend their superiors by usurping their duties, fell to doing essentially nothing. Chen sought to correct this. He periodically ordered intendants to get out into their jurisdictions to observe the day-to-day work styles of local officials and to interview local populations as to their needs. They should resolve disputes and plug gaps regarding the jurisdictions of their subordinates, for example in Yellow River maintenance, where, typically, local magistrates handled labor recruitment but local functionaries of the Yellow River Administration oversaw the actual construction.

Chen ordered that *daotai* receive information copies of all upward correspondence from the districts and that they act on it when appropriate. They should serve to short-stop some of the affairs involved, for instance by serving as court of appeal for certain litigation unresolvable at the local level but not necessarily requiring a decision by the *liangsi*. Moreover, inasmuch as the provincial judge and the provincial treasurer had sharply defined spheres of competence (petitions and litigation concerning theft and other criminal matters fell to the former, whereas tax matters and lawsuits over property went to the latter), only the circuit intendants saw the whole range of upward-bound documents; Chen made them personally responsible for proper routing and, most important, for ensuring that no documents fell into the cracks between the judge's and treasurer's jurisdictions. As for the *liangsi* themselves, Chen decried the frequency with which they each kept narrowly to their own competence. He insisted on regular mutual consultation on the handling of specific cases and brought them actively into collective discussion with the governor on the generation of policy.[108]

Like any provincial governor, Chen Hongmou routinely promulgated sets of regulations to establish standard operating procedures among his subordinates in a variety of policy areas, but one area to which he returned time and again was the preparation and processing of bureaucratic correspondence. Influenced by his much-admired Lü Kun, who laid great stress on the importance of paperwork to the task of effectively "reaching the people" (*tongmin*), Chen was clearly preoccupied with this problem. As he wrote in 1740:

> The business of government all relies upon written documents. In communicating one's views to others one must use writing. Because the population keeps growing and the affairs of the people are increasingly numerous, the number of government personnel and the complexity of government tasks likewise continue to grow. As government organs and institutions proliferate, the officials and the people are increasingly divorced from one another, and superior and subordinate within the bureaucracy, as well, become ever more remote.

This recognition necessitated an ongoing quest for greater clarity, reliability, and standardization in systems of communication.[109]

With the volume of paperwork on each official's desk growing daily, Chen issued directives in each of his postings both to streamline transmission of documents and to purge them of "aimless verbiage" (*fufan zhi xuwen*). Summarize previous correspondence on the issue at hand, he insisted, rather than copying it into your text verbatim. Eliminate unnecessary courtesies, chatter about unrelated matters, and literary flourishes; use the most direct available language. It is possible to be both concise and precise at once. Be specific in reporting (when reporting a theft, for example, say exactly what was stolen). Fully identify all persons, and so forth, to which you make reference. When answering a question posed by a superior, indicate in your answer the original question to which you are responding, and scrupulously avoid conventionalized responses. Do not feel compelled to affix your official seal to every page of each document you handle, as this needlessly risks obscuring the text. In retransmitting a document on which a written character is already obscured, do not compound the problem by erasing it and inserting your own guess as to what the original might have been. Above all, record clearly on the document itself the date and time of both its receipt and transmission. So doing allows the imposition of strict deadlines both for expediting communications (three to five days from inbox to outbox, depending on the nature of the document concerned) and for action/resolution as well.[110]

Reliable and standardized systems of communication are critical to achieving consistency and uniformity (*huayi*)—and, in the process, more centralized control—in policy implementation, on which, Chen insists, the people's general faith in government (*guangxin*) is predicated. He thus promulgates regulatory codes to ensure standard lower-level handling of directives from above. To make clear one's authorization, always include in lower-level pronouncements a concise reference to the upper-level directive that it is designed to implement. Policy directives independently initiated by lower-level officials should be circulated for information both to superiors and to colleagues in collateral jurisdictions to avoid flagrant policy variations in adjacent districts. Always check the files of your predecessor and reiterate his past directives when appropriate to avoid the popular instinct to ignore them once the incumbent is gone. Most important is the manner in which official directives are transmitted to the people themselves. They should be in the simplest possible language to ensure full comprehension, and they must be highly visible to avoid opportunist manipulation of incompletely understood policies by clerks, *baojia* functionaries, and other middlemen in the communications process. Chen repeatedly issues in his various posts detailed instructions on where and how to post official directives and how to guarantee that they are not taken down by those for whom popular ignorance of policy is a capital asset.[111]

Chen Hongmou's fixation on uniformity in bureaucratic communications sometimes prompted him to issue lengthy style sheets to subordinates for drafting their correspondence with him.[112] Even more frequently it inspired him to draft and distribute his own standardized forms (*danshi* or *ceshi*) for the use of magistrates and prefects both in reporting to him and in their own yamen's record keeping. Chen did this in an astonishing range of areas, including for example reports of local granary loans, condemned exiles resident in local society, awards of honors for virtuous widows, sales of gentry degrees, sentences for convicted criminals, and convicts held in county jails. In at least some cases he memorialized (successfully) to have his form adopted as a model for use empire-wide.[113]

Standardized reporting at the local level was a prerequisite for systematic record keeping and financial accounting at the provincial level. This was an exercise in centralized control that Chen pursued with genuine passion, routinely putting together and maintaining registers (*ce* or *zaoce*) on specific policy or institutional areas with a remarkable level of detail on conditions in each district. We are fortunate that one such register has survived, that on local primary schools in Yunnan, which Chen's regional superior Yinjishan saw fit to publish in 1738, after Chen had left the province. In this six-volume work we find listed the location, history, size, personnel, assets, and annual income and expenditure of over six hundred schools throughout the province.[114] In this same Yunnan jurisdiction, where he served for just over three years, Chen also compiled comparably detailed provincial registers in the areas of land tax collection, military supply, administrative costs for the civil service examinations, mining activities, community granaries, orphanages and other charitable institutions, land reclamation, county-level civil construction projects, and the general administrative budgets of newly carved out county jurisdictions.[115] Although we may be tempted to see this mania for record keeping as simply part of Chen's job description (as Yunnan provincial treasurer), his correspondence on the subject makes clear that in most of these instances he was compiling province-level accounts on these subjects for the first time. And although this particular preoccupation surely owed something to the mood of the times—the last years of the relatively statist Yongzheng reign—Chen hardly abandoned this emphasis during the long remaining years of his provincial career under Qianlong. In various gubernatorial posts we find him energetically involved in similar record-compilation projects on these same topics and on others, such as ever-normal granary management, polder repairs, prisoner accountability, locust control, monetary exchange rates, and so on.[116]

One aspect of governance in which Chen's zeal for standardized record keeping was especially evident was the processing of civil litigation. In lawsuits over petty property claims (*huhun tiantu*) Chen believed strongly in the need for speedy judicial resolution because of the potential such lawsuits held for financial ruin of the households involved. Prompt decisions were particularly crucial given the existence of parties in society with obvious pecuniary interest in protracting such cases indefinitely. Such "litigation masters" (*songgun*), Chen believed, regularly conspired with yamen clerks to drag out cases and so milk their clients. Qing regulations called for magistrates to bring such cases to resolution within twenty days if possible, but Chen found that in most provinces nearly a quarter of all cases exceeded this limit, many by months or even years. Second-tier officials were supposed to prompt laggard magistrates to resolve such cases, but Chen observed that they had insufficient knowledge of judicial backlogs in order to do so effectively.

His solution was to establish a standardized reporting system and a routinely maintained set of ledgers (*huidan, qingdan*) at various levels of local and provincial administration. Typically, on entering a province, Chen would order compilation of a consolidated register to record all outstanding unresolved cases. Magistrates thereafter would be obliged to report to their prefect all cases they had been unable to resolve in due course, for the prefect's use as the basis both for future prompts and for writing the magistrate's year-end fitness report. Chen also brought the underemployed circuit intendants (*xundao*) into the process to compile ledgers based on inputs from prefects and audit county-level ledgers during scheduled tours of their jurisdictions, putting further pressure on the magistrates and ensuring that no laggard cases went unreported. Unusually complex or otherwise long-protracted cases were to be reported to the province. In an early version of this system, developed during his tenure as Jiangsu provincial judge in 1740, Chen opted to send out copies of the provincial ledger to all magistrates on a fortnightly basis from that office. Magistrates would find on this ledger, marked with a circle, cases they were expected to bring to closure within two months. A second circle meant a one-month deadline, a third a final deadline of half a month. In later provincial posts Chen continued to undertake this task personally as governor. As mentioned earlier, he memorialized in 1754 (apparently without success) to establish a single provincial-level official, of *daotai* rank, with the exclusive duty of assisting in this process. His centralizing and standardizing system for litigation management became widely publicized, however, as a model for use by other provincial officials.[117]

Chen was very energetic in his efforts to impose standardized weights and measures in local society. He did so to ensure the integrity of the fiscal process, of granary operations, and of local market operation, as well as to facilitate supralocal market integration, but it is clear that he also understood its importance for systematic state record keeping.[118] We see in Chen's writing a deepening interest in gathering and compiling statistics (the "facts of the state"), an interest identified by Stuart Woolf with an enduring imperial style and, more precisely, with the emergence of the early modern state in Western Europe.[119] The Qing, as we know, showed an unprecedented concern with statistical reporting—demanding systematic local reports of rainfall, harvest figures, and grain prices—and Chen pushed this especially hard, calling on his subordinates for even greater decimal precision in such numbers. When offering total figures on any item, he insists, be sure also to break it down into components and likewise to compute numerical totals whenever possible.[120] The massive project Chen undertook as president of the Board of Works to compile local prices for construction materials is nothing short of astounding in the zeal it displays to centrally compile minute local data; in the 24-*juan* compilation on Zhili province, for example, we find that in Liangxiang County a thirty-foot pine post of 1.6-foot diameter cost 13.30 taels, whereas one of 1.4-foot diameter cost 9.51 taels, and one of 1.3 feet merely 6.91 taels.[121]

Chen, as provincial official, undertakes financial accounting based on detailed mathematical computation; he calculates costs for Yunnan poorhouses, for example, by multiplying the number of rooms in all such institutions throughout the province by the average number of occupants per room, by the daily food and fuel consumption needs per occupant, and by the prevailing unit cost of coal, rice, and salt.[122] But the attraction to statistics was not limited to the obvious area of financial accounting. Chen very much liked to count things—the number of elementary schools throughout Yunnan, for instance, or of irrigation wells in Shaanxi (over 87,000, of which 26,800 had been dug or repaired during his own administration).[123] Much like "scientific" criminologists in early modern Europe, he sought to compile statistics on crime and punishment; in 1754 Shaanxi, for example, he demanded of his subordinates precise dates of all thefts and of the perpetrator's apprehension, allowing him to calculate the average interval between the two.[124]

Inspired very likely by Lü Kun, Chen Hongmou became a staunch devotee of the systematic collection of "useful facts" about society. Here again his concerns resonate with (and indeed anticipate slightly) what Stuart Woolf discerns in Europe—the Napoleonic empire's unprecedented passion for comprehensive information gathering as a tool of "rational" administration and, ultimately, more effective incorporation of local societies into a broader political order.[125] In Chen's case the compulsion to *know* so as better to control seems to have grown stronger over the course of his career. By 1751 it was powerful enough for him to order all Shaanxi magistrates to compile standardized registers (*jianming shice*) detailing the name, location, and precise population of all suburbs, market towns, subdistricts, tithings, and villages in their counties. Four years later, in Hunan, he ordered magistrates routinely to include detailed information on all local "public affairs" (*gongshi*)—popular moods and grievances, crimes and social disturbances—in the weather and grain price reports they were already obliged by the throne to submit on a semimonthly basis.[126] The crowning achievement of Chen's intelligence gathering was probably his 1756 *Hunan tongzhi* (Hunan provincial gazetteer), which, as an astonished Imperial Library cataloger remarked, was wholly unprecedented in the amount of local societal detail it crammed into its especially enlarged pages and 174 chapters.[127]

Nowhere was Chen's zeal for uncovering useful facts more evident, however, than in his successive campaigns to produce new county-level maps. His initial call for maps came in his very first months as a provincial governor, in Jiangxi during the winter of 1741–42; the lack of existing maps, he complained, was evidence of the woeful tendency of magistrates to remain sequestered within their urban yamen, out of personal touch with the people and dangerously dependent on their clerks. He repeated his call in Shaanxi in 1744, in Fujian in 1754, in Gansu in 1755, in Hunan later that same year, and in Guangdong and Guangxi in 1758.[128] Characteristically, Chen established a standardized scale, legend, and color scheme for representation on these maps and demanded that they be of uniform size—three Chinese feet (*chi*) square in Jiangxi, growing to four feet square in later campaigns as the level of detail specified by the governor became ever more precise. By the time of the Gansu campaign he had developed a list of thirty-three lengthy regulations prescribing just how the maps should look and what they should depict: topographic features, precise boundaries with other administrative units, all villages of five or more households (!), temples and altars, historical ruins, granaries, irrigated and non-irrigated fields, piers, official guesthouses, major shops and periodic market locations, and so on. Accompanying the map (and keyed to it), magistrates should turn in a comprehensive guide to their counties, including information on ethnic composition, taxes, prices, cropping patterns, percentage of crops grown for market, market schedules, hydraulic installations (and their current state of repair), granary stocks, local weights and measures, schools and their curricula, and a great deal more.[129] Of consistent size and with their data systematically arranged, the county maps and their companion fact-books could be collated into a master atlas at the provincial level, affording Chen ready access to more and better knowledge about his jurisdiction, surely, than had been enjoyed by any provincial administrator in imperial history.

In a provocative recent book, Thongchai Winichakul has probed the "modernist" project of late-nineteenth-century Thai official elites engaged in inventing a national identity, emphasizing their focus on "modern" (that is, Western-style) mapping as a means of symbolically encoding "national" space.[130] With its universalist pretensions, of course, the mid-eighteenth-century Qing imperium paid but scant attention to the issue of delineating "national" boundaries, but the bureaucracy of Qing (as of its many predecessors) had long appeared strikingly precocious in the zeal with which it approached the other half of this task—the cartographic depiction of *internal* jurisdictional boundaries as a means of asserting central imperial control. The particular urge to do this with a greatly enhanced level of detail at this time suggests a governing project—and in Chen Hongmou's case, it seems, a personality as well—with a pronounced focus on knowledge as a means to control. The symbolic and ontological dimensions of this project were very real; recall, for example, the attention lavished by Chen in his Hunan provincial gazetteer on "delineating the cosmos" (*fenye*), mapping the precise celestial counterparts to his terrestrial jurisdiction. But real as well was the dimension of mundane practice. Chen's mapping project reflected not merely a claim, but also a search for the actual means, to fine-meshed administrative control.

The Shaanxi Xingchu Campaign of 1744–1745

Lest it be thought that all this detailed local intelligence gathering by Chen Hongmou was for purposes of information more than proactive state intervention, we conclude this chapter with a look at a campaign of his yet more astonishing than those just discussed: Chen's drive to systematically remake local society and culture in mid-eighteenth-century Shaanxi.[131] As we shall see, the campaign was a combination of a one-time initiative launched by the Qianlong court on an empire-wide basis to improve the quality of local governance, with a set of notions and administrative strategies that had been percolating in Chen's own mind for some time beforehand and that he would continue to cherish and refine during the long remainder of his provincial career.

It also represented the conflation of five originally distinct political ideas, each of which bore its own set of code words in Qing bureaucratic discourse. These ideas were as follows: First, the urge for the state to acquire as systematic as possible an intelligence of the details of ecology and society in its various localities, a drive that by the eighteenth century had come to be encapsulated in the paired oppositional term "*libi*" (assets and liabilities, or functions and dysfunctions). Second, the general commitment to a broad-ranging government activism, serving both the people's material needs and their (as perceived by the elite) equal need for civilization and enlightenment, a commitment subsumed under the compound term "*jiaoyang*" (education and nurturance). Third, dedication to a more practical and grassroots intervention in local ecologies and societies in the interest of reform, signaled by the phrase "*xingchu shiyi*" (matters to be promoted or expunged), or more simply "*xingchu*," or, when taken in conjunction with the first item, "*xingli chubi*" (promote the functional and expunge the dysfunctional). Fourth, advocacy of a style of local governance stressing personal closeness to the people (*qinmin*), or, in the phrase adopted by the court to express this, "*xunli xiangcun*" (routine tours of townships and villages).[132] Finally, there was an element of internal bureaucratic discipline, in the use of county magistrates' performance in fulfillment of this initiative as a central tool of *kaocheng*, or personnel evaluation.

As early as the late 1730s, in his tenure as Tianjin circuit intendant, we find Chen Hongmou linking in a letter to a county-level subordinate his long-cherished theme of *jiaoyang* with the suggestion that the magistrate get out and investigate in detail the *libi* of his jurisdiction.[133] By the time he was posted to his first provincial governorship, in Jiangxi during the winter of 1741–42, Chen had his ideas on the subject more fully fleshed out. In conjunction with his call for magistrates to draw up new maps of their counties he presented them with a list of thirty-two items, ranging from tax arrears to litigation backlogs to irrigation works to local ritual performance, on which he wanted detailed reports. Each locality is different, he reminded them, and if the magistrate doesn't comprehend this local distinctiveness he cannot govern very effectively. Although Chen in this directive used the phrase "*xingli chubi*," suggesting active reform efforts once local peculiarities had been subjected to the criterion of utility, he provided no guidance on how this was to be achieved; his questionnaire was clearly aimed primarily at gathering local intelligence. There was also an implicit personnel test involved, however. Eight months after issuing his original questionnaire the governor issued a second one, likewise comprising thirty-two items modified only slightly from those in the original. He noted how disappointing had been the response of magistrates to his first request, indicating that the people of Jiangxi were evidently being very poorly served, and suggested that magistrates' fitness reports would reflect this fact.[134]

Over the remainder of his Jiangxi tenure Chen continued to meditate on this project of his, and during the long journey to his next assignment in Shaanxi, in the spring of 1744, he thought about how he would modify it to the needs of that province. Immediately on his arrival he issued his questionnaire to local officials. Now grown to thirty-four items, it also was much more detailed than its Jiangxi antecedents. Each item was no longer a simple question, but rather an organizing rubric allowing Chen to pose a whole series of more specific inquiries. Let me paraphrase but two items of the questionnaire to provide a sense of this specificity:

> *Item six.* Of land in the county, what percentage is in autumn harvest crops? Is this rice, vegetables, beans? Are these grown in paddy or in dry fields? What kind of trees are cultivated? In a normal harvest, is the yield sufficient to cover the outlay of seed and still feed the local population? Is there a marketed surplus, and if so where is it marketed? What are typical annual high and low grain prices? How are fields laid out? What products other than wheat, rice, and beans are locally produced? Other than agriculture, how do local people make their livings? Do local people emigrate, or become seasonal refugees? Is cotton grown? Is weaving practiced? Has sericulture been attempted? Silk-weaving? How profitable is animal husbandry? Is tobacco grown? What are the particular qualities of the local soil? . . .

Item ten. What steps do you take to ascertain that the community libationer [*xiang-yin*] ritual is regularly practiced? Is the triennial "welcoming guests" [*binxing*] ritual practiced locally? How are filial children, righteous husbands, and virtuous widows reported and honored? How many are so reported each year? Are there any talented young scholars in your district? Are there any well-known writers? Are there any books on economics or neo-Confucianism [*lixue*] available for public borrowing and reading? How many local worthies and famous past magistrates are currently honored in the local temple for such purposes? Report their names to me separately. Are there any reclusive scholars in your district? What are their names?

Chen imposed a two-month deadline for responses. He insisted that the data supplied be genuine and current, based on personal observation rather than perfunctory copying over of stale records in the county archive, and he promised that he would spot-check for accuracy. There was some talk in his charge to officials of the need to correct deficiencies in local practice, but still the intent was clearly above all informational.[135]

Then came the directive from above. In the fall of 1744 (six months after Chen circulated his questionnaire to Shaanxi local officials) Board of Civil Office president Nuoqin memorialized to request tighter enforcement of a long-standing rule that magistrates be forced to tour their districts on a semiannual or annual basis (depending on the district's size and complexity) and report to provincial officials on local conditions and how they were acting to encourage or correct things. The governors were then to use this activity as a gauge to evaluate the magistrates' overall conduct of office (*kaocheng*). Asked by the throne to comment on Nuoqin's proposal, Ortai and his fellow grand secretaries indicated their enthusiastic endorsement, specifying in the process at least eight items (including schools, agricultural conditions, hydraulic works, litigation, and criminal activity) that ought to be covered in the magistrates' surveys of their districts. In this form Qianlong approved Nuoqin's proposal. Early in 1745 he added the proviso that the county-level reports ought to be collated at the provincial level and sent on upward for his own perusal.[136]

The response of bureaucrats in the field was clearly underwhelming. Most replies of provincial officials, at least as recorded in the Qing court annals (*Shilu*), were perfunctory on the question of items in their provinces to be encouraged and corrected and said nothing at all about tours of their districts by local magistrates. The responses were likewise shrugged off, sometimes with a mild rebuke, by the Qianlong emperor, whose level of personal commitment to the project was quite evidently halfhearted.[137] As Pierre-Étienne Will points out, both Nuoqin and Ortai were holdovers from the Yongzheng court, and their enthusiasm for this project very likely reflected their hope to reinject into the current bureaucracy some of the vigor they remembered as characterizing the reign of Qianlong's predecessor;[138] by this plausible reading Qianlong's approval of the proposal can be seen as little more than an act of humoring two loyal but aged (and somewhat out of touch) ministers. Will also remarks that such a seemingly important procedural reform ought by rights to have been followed up by some notation in the dynasty's statutory or institutional codes, the *Da Qing lüli* or *Da Qing huidian*, but is not; the chief follow-up that Will in fact discovers is a 1746 Board of Civil Office directive relegating the (obviously largely ignored) provincial reporting requirement to the limbo of the routine memorial system (*tiben*) and reducing it, at that, from an annual to a triennial obligation. Passive resistance on the part of an "over-stretched" bureaucracy, it may be concluded, had won the day.

There was one dazzling exception to this pattern of rampant bureaucratic lethargy, however, and that was our protagonist, Chen Hongmou. There is no direct evidence that the originators of the reform proposal were *influenced* by what Chen had been up to in Shaanxi and before, but given Chen's sometime-protégé relationship with Ortai such influence is hardly out of the question.[139] In any case he alone among provincial governors enthusiastically embraced the Board of Civil Office's directive and, indeed, in his implementation took it several steps further. In his reply to the throne just after New Year of 1745—by the evidence of the *Shilu* far and away the most detailed provincial response the throne received—Chen mentioned the fact that he had already been doing something along these lines not only in his current post but also previously in Jiangxi. He also noted that he found the eight areas of investigation proposed by Ortai and outlined in the board's directive too generalized; stated in such fashion they would readily be seen by magistrates as not specifically adapted to Shaanxi realities and so naturally would invite only pro forma action on their part. For the throne's consumption Chen trimmed his own list of areas from thirty-four to twenty-four (still far more than Ortai's eight) and offered considerable detail on just how he expected magistrates to conduct their investigations. Perhaps relieved that at least someone out there was taking him seriously, Qianlong appended to Chen's report an enthusiastic rescript: "Other than that you must follow through on this with genuine diligence, what more can I say?"[140]

Yet there was one highly significant difference between the emphases of Nuoqin and Ortai's empire-wide campaign and the ongoing project of Chen Hongmou with which it came to dovetail. Although they discuss in passing reform of local conditions, the tone of all the central government documents on this incident reveals that the campaign was first and foremost seen as a personnel issue—an effort to motivate a distressingly lackadaisical local officialdom. Chen did not ignore this aspect of the problem, but it is abundantly clear that, at least by the time he reached Shaanxi, his real goal was the more utopian one of fundamental, state-driven social transformation.[141] In this sense the personnel evaluation campaign launched by the Board of Civil Office was essentially for Chen a convenient stick to hold over his subordinates in this wider cause, which explains why he took to it with such enthusiasm. He signals this in his report to the throne, acknowledging compliance, for example, by rephrasing the list of areas to be encompassed from simple topics such as "gambling" to action-oriented verb-object commands such as "strenuously expose gambling rackets" (*yancha dubo*). In Chen's writing on the subject of the campaign the language of *jiaoyang* and *huadao* (leadership in popular moral transformation) moves front and center.

In the extraordinarily detailed (twenty-page) directive that Chen issued to his local subordinates at New Year's of 1745 he utilized the rubric of the twenty-four reform items to spell out his blueprint for the good society and how it might be achieved, under active government leadership, in the particular ecological and cultural setting of Shaanxi. Among a very wide range of other things, he sets out specific curricula and texts ("useful works," *youyong zhi shu*) on which local scholarship should be made to center. He discusses how to implement the proper observation of Confucian principles of social order (*lunchang*): how to dispense awards for virtuous conduct, how to enforce correct principles of descent-group organization, and how to implement reform of marriage and funerary practices (see Chapter 12). He concisely outlines the community granary (*shecang*) and sericulture promotion campaigns that he has already begun to implement in the province, as well as programs for land reclamation (*kaiken*), well digging, and tree planting. He sets up systems for local conflict adjudication in order to limit the number of disputes that make it into the realm of formal litigation. The directive is a surprisingly passionate and self-revelatory document. Under the unlikely rubric of reform in local land tax collection procedures, for example, Chen slips into an obviously heartfelt plea for recognition by official elites of the heavenly goodness (*tianliang*) of all human beings, arguing for the possibility of getting local people to recognize this in themselves (*zishou xinyi*) and building on this to achieve the "beautification" of local customary practice (*difang fengsu zhi mei*).[142]

On the issue of magistrates' tours of their districts (*xunli xiangcun*) Chen likewise went well beyond the guidelines laid down by the Board of Civil Office. He began by rejecting the board's rigidly defined schedule for tours on the grounds that only the magistrate himself knew when and how the press of local business would allow him to get away from his desk and out into the countryside. But, granted this flexibility, Chen's own demands for tours were greater than those mandated from above. He demanded that each magistrate meet in succession with specially convened gatherings of "scholars and commoners" of single large villages or groups of smaller villages throughout his district to go over the list of items he had drawn up, the state of current implementation of each item in their village, and their plans for future improvement. These meetings were to be followed up by return visits, at six- or twelve-month intervals, to monitor and discuss areas of progress or stagnation. After two or three such meetings in each community the magistrate should have developed a secure idea of which area could be relied on to continue satisfactory progress under its own native leadership and which would necessitate closer continued supervision on the part of the magistrate himself.[143]

Chen's first tour of duty in Shaanxi lasted roughly thirty-two months, one of the longest postings he enjoyed over the course of his career; very likely the Board of Civil Office's satisfaction with his implementation of their pet project of the day had something to do with the length of this stay. On six occasions during this tour, following his initial directive of New Year's 1745, the governor issued follow-up orders to insist on local official compliance with the details of his program.[144] On return tours to the province in 1748, 1750, and 1754 he did so again.[145] At the close of his final tour, in 1757, he included no fewer than five of these proclamations in his published compendium of his most important policy innovations in Shaanxi, hoping by doing so to give his program as close to a basis in provincial statute as possible.[146] Already by 1746 Chen's list of action areas had grown to forty, although he continued to refer to them in administrative shorthand as "the twenty-four items to be promoted or expunged" (*xingchu ershisi tiao*).

In at least two other provincial governorships, that in Fujian in 1754 and (to a much lesser extent) in Hunan in 1756, Chen sought to replicate his Shaanxi project.[147] In neither of these "troublesome" provinces did he exhibit the same perseverance for implementation or, evidently, cherish the same hopes for success that he did in Shaanxi. Home of the admirable "Guanxue" tradition of neo-Confucianism (see Chapter 4) and a populace of unusual "rustic virtue" (*zhipu*), Shaanxi was clearly Chen's personal favorite among his many duty stations, and he undertook his sustained *xingchu* campaign there with at least some aspirations of turning it into a "model province" for the rest of the empire. Two of the longest and most central of Chen's directives on the subject in Shaanxi, moreover, made it into Wei Yuan's 1826 *Statecraft Compendium*—in the sections on proper local official performance (*shouling*) and on "nourishing the people" (*yangmin*)—indicating at least something of a continuing official-elite tradition to accord exemplary status to Chen's noble experiment.[148]

I would agree with Pierre-Étienne Will's assessment that Chen Hongmou's *xingchu* project can be judged a "success" only in relatively modest terms. In the short term the lower field administration was certainly placed on a higher stage of alert. The jurisdictional touring and reporting requirements imposed on magistrates remained in force, at least for many years, but inevitably became over time eviscerated of any substantive content. (The unfortunate magistrate of Shaanxi's Baocheng County discovered the hazards of this perfunctoriness when Chen, returning to the governorship in 1754, singled him out as a public example of how *not* to conduct district tours.)[149] Shaanxi's material life did enjoy considerable improvement during Chen's four tenures, as we have seen in previous chapters. The solicitation of local input and enlistment of popular support undertaken under the auspices of the *xingchu* campaign probably played some role in the success of Chen's various regional agricultural, commercial, and hydraulic expansion projects, but they were not the key factors. The cultural reform aspects of the campaign (discussed further in Chapter 12) seem to have left no more lasting mark than did comparable attacks on "deviant" popular cultures by Confucian reformist elites in other times and places during the Qing. Overall, neither the bureaucracy nor the society was significantly remade by Chen's utopian activism, as he clearly hoped they would be. Accordingly, if the board's initiative was largely shrugged off from the outset by Chen's colleagues in other provinces, even Chen Hongmou over time seems to have found the costs involved in such a monumental investment of political capital to outweigh its benefits. Thus he never again devoted comparable energy to so comprehensive a program in other jurisdictions.

Nevertheless, the degree of faith in state activism as an instrument of sociocultural reform that Chen displayed in his conducting of this campaign remains remarkable, especially in light of the distrust of big government to which he also periodically gave voice, and which is sometimes seen as a hallmark of the Qing style of governance. What Chen did stick with enthusiastically in the years following 1744 and 1745 was the systematic intelligence-gathering aspects of the *xingchu* campaign, on the presumption that more effective knowledge of local peculiarities brought with it greater possibilities for state control and, in appropriate instances, micromanagement. Along with his per-

sistent efforts to standardize reporting, to heighten the efficiency of bureaucratic communications, to more effectively discipline the bureaucracy and sub-bureaucracy, and
(again, selectively picking his areas of attack) to impose a more finely meshed official
presence in society, his actions in this campaign reveal Chen's centralizing urges. He
was not afraid to put the "state" back in "statecraft."

CHAPTER 11

Community

A PERSISTENT TRADITION of "loyal opposition" political thought during the Qing cohered around a critique of the inequity, inefficiency, and inertia of centralized bureaucratic administration (*junxian*). Usually subsumed under the rubric "*fengjian*" (the modern Chinese word for *feudal*), this tradition advocated instead some form of local autonomy and political empowerment of local-level sociocultural elites. Although it had much older antecedents, in its Qing version this tradition is usually seen as originating with the Ming-remnant polymath Gu Yanwu and, after something of a hiatus in the heyday of bureaucratic efficacy in the eighteenth century, to have picked up again in the nineteenth with Wei Yuan and Feng Guifen, culminating in the prescriptions for local representative government of Kang Youwei, Liang Qichao, and other fin de siè-cle reformers.[1] Probably because of the inclusion in this genealogy of Wei and others who were explicitly interested in the literature they termed "statecraft" (*jingshi*), this tradition of *fengjian* criticism is sometimes subsumed under, or even identified with, a larger and more amorphous "statecraft movement" in the Qing. Many of the nine-teenth-century luminaries in this tradition, notably Wei and Feng, were also attracted to the policies of the exemplary eighteenth-century official Chen Hongmou and implicitly claimed him as their own. As I suggested in Chapter 4, however, Chen's actu-al fit into the *fengjian* tradition is a highly uncomfortable one. Yet in a certain sense it is not entirely without ground.

In the preceding chapter we looked at a number of ways Chen sought to "order the world" by relying on the direct mechanisms of the state apparatus. In the present chap-ter we provide a counterpoint by exploring other ways Chen sought to utilize the in-struments of local society to police, nurture, and improve itself. Arguably no political regime in history was more expert than the Qing in the art of co-opting local commu-nities and leaders for what Max Weber termed "liturgical" purposes, delegating au-thority to nonstate agents for the completion of state-assigned tasks.[2] Unsurprisingly, even in an age of heightened direct state activism, Chen Hongmou was very adept at this as well. We want to ask here what the practical limits of this delegation were and examine to what extent a more basic ideological commitment to government restraint (seen already in much of Chen's economic thought) and a corresponding valorization of local community self-reliance (perhaps along *fengjian* lines) underlay his policy choices in this area.

State Versus "Public" (gong)

In the eighteenth-century Qing polity a central axis of the relationship between the state and the local community was demarcated by the term "*gong*" (public). I have written about the history of this lexical item at some length elsewhere and will here only briefly outline the special significance it held in the political discourse of Chen Hongmou and others in the mid-Qing official elite.[3] "*Gong*" held a wide range of meanings. In one usage with important political implications, alone or in the compound "*gongping*," it meant "fair" or "equitable." Chen used it this way in referring, for example, to honest and standardized weights and measures, to evenhanded lending practices of community granaries, and to the corresponding rent reductions he expected landlords to pass on to their tenants on being granted tax reductions by the state.[4] In descriptions of official or nonofficial elite conduct *gong* signified an unselfish public-mindedness, as for instance in the phrases "*yingong*" (responding to public needs) or "*fenggong*" (adhering to the public interest).[5] The "public" so indicated was at times the abstract, inclusive humanity referred to in *gong*'s most famous locus classicus, the injunction "*tianxia wei gong*" (All under Heaven is public) in the Han-dynasty *Li ji*. But in the eighteenth century the term referred more often to the public of a specific local community than to this "greater public" (*dagong*). This localization was usually implied in the idioms "*gongshi*" (local community affairs), "*gongyi*" (a local deliberation convened to discuss community affairs, especially the allocation of financial obligations for a public-works project), and "*gongju*" (public selection by the local community, as with managers of local charitable institutions, local tax-collection captains, and so on).[6] A further usage along the same lines was "*gonglun*" (public opinion, usually *local* public opinion), the meaning of which for Chen Hongmou we will return to shortly.

In Confucian discourse in general, *gong* formed half of an oppositional pair with *si* (private).[7] However, in the more specialized bureaucratic rhetoric that Chen adopted when entering his official career, *gong* was even more frequently contrasted with quite a different category, *guan*, meaning "state" or "governmental." As with the English word *public*, that is, "*gong*" contained within itself an awkward ambiguity: it might refer either to things that were part of the formal government (such as *gongsuo*, a government office, or *gongwen*, government documents) or to things that were communal but explicitly *not* governmental. Although through much of imperial history the conflation of "public" and "state" seems to have been fairly complete,[8] at least by the eighteenth century this had dramatically changed: The notion of a "public" external to the state and even in contrast to it had come to predominate in legal and bureaucratic usage. The contrast was expressed most routinely in the use of the opposed phrases "*guigong*" (reverting to, or lying in the public/communal domain) versus "*guiguan*" (in the domain of the state).[9] "*Gong*" in this sense was an imperfect but routine substitute for the term "*min*" (popular or civic), which likewise was used to express a collective versus state domain in the matched pair "*zaimin*" (belonging to the society) versus "*zaiguan*" (belonging to the government).[10] Ultimately, as Mary Rankin and others have shown, bureaucratic discourse came to express a set of not two but three sectors along the spectrum of proprietorship: *si* (private), *gong* or *min* (communal), and *guan* (governmental). This tripartite taxonomy was apparently first applied in the area of hydraulic maintenance to designate varying spheres of responsibility for financing and undertaking scheduled repairs on dikes, irrigation channels, and so on; but in the mid-Qing and after it had come to be applied to a far broader range of public or civic activities.[11]

The specific usage of "*gong*" to which we refer here, then, designated the "public" as active agent, enjoying proprietorship of various assets and bearing responsibility for financing and managing various enterprises. The precise relationship of this sphere to that of government was one the prevailing discourse left open to contestation. In certain instances assets and activities that were *gong* were ones over which state officials might exercise only rather loose claims of stewardship. This was clearly the case with stocks of community granaries (*shecang*), which Chen Hongmou repeatedly and emphatically insisted were *not* government assets to be allocated by the local official as he saw fit. These stocks were instead "public property" (*gongwu*), and the rights to their disposal inhered in the local community and its appointed leaders; state personnel should merely exercise oversight powers.[12]

But the Yongzheng emperor had clouded such a concept by implementing his *haoxian guigong* fiscal reforms of 1728–29. Having devoted much of the first five years of his reign to rooting out the gross abuses of the system of local government finance that preceded it—the so-called board-authorized purchase-of-materials expenses (*bufei*) system—Yongzheng in the late twenties seized on the pretext of covering costs of locally recasting tax-receipt silver for upward transmission to put local and provincial budgets on a more regularized basis. The revenue from this "meltage fee" (in effect a surtax) was retained by local and provincial jurisdictions and placed into a line in administrative budgets, known as *gongxiang* (public accounts), separate from the "regular" tax revenues (*zhengxiang*) that were remitted upward to the throne.[13] Yongzheng thus created a sphere of financing and management that was specified as "public" or "communal" yet was clearly subject to state budgetary accounting. Thereafter, in consequence, we find in the discourse of Chen and other Qing bureaucrats routine reference to "public causes" (*gongyong*), "public expenditures" (*gongfei*), and "public accounts" (*gongjian*) that were for all intents and purposes fully governmental, even though they were designated for local rather than national purposes. Like a variety of twentieth-century Chinese regimes, one might say, Yongzheng was attempting at least in part to governmentalize an active and existing "public sphere."

Chen's first sustained commentary on the *haoxian* innovations and their role in financing "public expenses" came in the years of the Yongzheng-Qianlong transition, while he was serving in Yunnan. As provincial treasurer he was deeply involved in setting up the fiscal infrastructure of counties newly created as part of the campaign for replacement of indirect governance by local headmen with direct bureaucratic administration (*gaitu guiliu*). Under Yongzheng the decision had been made to assess land taxes on these new counties but, in light of the current financial incapacity of their largely non-Han populations, to forgo for the time being actual collection of these taxes. Chen approved this noncollection of the land tax per se but argued that the *haoxian* surtax computed on this tax ought in fact to be collected; the areas in question could afford this modest assessment, and the income might be used to finance much-needed local infrastructural development. He staunchly reiterated his support for the new system as *haoxian guigong* came up for review on the accession of Yongzheng's more "magnanimous" (*kuan*) successor; ordered by Qianlong to dramatically cut *gongxiang* accounts, Chen sought to keep those cuts in Yunnan to a minimum. Although he agreed that there was a need for greater provincial-level control over collection and disposition of *haoxian* revenues, he defended the new system on the grounds that the regularization it provided was far superior to the arbitrary and excessive procurement practices (*pai*) relied on in the past to cover local expenses. Throughout his tenure in the southwest, indeed, Chen drew eagerly on the new *gongyong* funds to finance his water conservancy, road building, and other infrastructural development projects.[14]

In the spring of 1742 his doubts about *haoxian guigong* (and many other extractive practices of his government) aggravated by long-term price inflation and short-term subsistence crises, Qianlong called for a debate among officials on the system's merits. Most by this time had come to approve of it; Chen Hongmou's erstwhile patron Sun Jiagan, for example, argued that it was a necessary means of financing local government developmental initiatives and would indeed serve this purpose even better if provincial and local officials were granted still greater discretion over allocation of its revenues.[15] The response of Chen himself, then serving as governor of one of the most severely dearth-stricken provinces, Jiangxi, was a complex one.[16] Abolishing the system was simply out of the question. Chen reiterated his view that the alternative, a random and exploitative imposition of ad hoc procurements, was a terrible one, and he politely offered that the emperor's implied linkage between *haoxian* surtaxes and the ongoing inflationary trend was specious. At the same time, there were abuses in the system as it currently operated that might be corrected. (Chen drew Qianlong's delighted approval when he demonstrated in a follow-up memorial that a more efficient method of forwarding tax silver—the costs of which formed the pretext for *haoxian* collections to begin with—might be adopted in Jiangxi to lower the "meltage fees" passed on to the taxpayer.)[17] His most sweeping suggestion was to make the funds used for local and provincial government finance even more legitimate: simply merge the budgetary line of *gongxiang* (funds generated by surtaxes and various miscellaneous imposts and dedicated to financing lower-level administrative expenses) into the fully regularized *zhengxiang* accounts. Acknowledging their regularity in this way would allow a greater degree of higher-level control over their collection and disposition—clearly it was control at his own gubernatorial level that Chen had most in mind—without leaving local levels of administration starved for revenue and incapable of serving the people's pressing needs. This was not, of course, the sort of response Qianlong had been looking for, and the proposal seems not to have been seriously considered.

In subsequent years Chen continued to utilize his *gongxiang* discretionary funds very creatively in support of his many projects. In 1743, for example, he drew on these

monies to underwrite the outside purchase of grain to relieve Jiangxi's food crisis, and
in 1751 he invested substantial *gongxiang* funds in his scheme to renovate the flood
drainage system of southeastern Henan.[18] Fairly complete accounts of his management
of *gongxiang* budgets are available for one year, Qianlong 12 (roughly 1748 in Western
reckoning), during Chen's tenure as Shaanxi governor. Provincial-level *gongxiang*
funds for that year, drawn both from *haoxian* surtaxes and other miscellaneous sources,
totaled 336,204.17 silver taels. About half of this was expended on supplementary
stipends (*yanglian*) for local officials.[19] Some of the remainder was struck from provincial budgets and left to the discretion of county magistrates; according to Chen, the
magistrates spent this money on such things as the repair of government offices, military barracks, and examination halls; construction of a poorhouse (in one county,
Shangnan); and printing of textbooks for local schools. Of the money left to Chen's
personal discretion (some 112,565.19 taels), 340 taels went to purchase packhorses in
support of the ongoing Dajinchuan military campaign, 211 were spent on refugee relief, and 51 were devoted to financing a system of lifeboat services that Chen had set up
at key points along Shaanxi waterways. The bulk of the remainder was committed to the
governor's pet project of the time, the comprehensive overhaul of city walls throughout the province.[20]

Where was the line to be drawn in practice between government support and private community financing for local projects? As we have already seen, Chen financed
major regional schemes such as wall building in Shaanxi, hydraulic renovation on the
north China plain, and road building in the northwest and southwest through a combination of local and provincial *gongxiang* disbursements, seat-of-the-pants "compromise" (*tongyong*) allocations from other government sources (for example, seignorage
profits from provincial mints), and "contributions" solicited from local private citizens.
The precise formula was determined very locally, based on factors such as the relative
cost and urgency of the project segment, the degree of direct benefit to accrue to private interests (landowners to receive irrigation or drainage, merchants to receive
greater ease of transport), the geographic scope of the benefit area, and the assessed
limitations of local private wealth. On balance, however, Chen was seen both by contemporaries and by later admirers as relatively more willing than other bureaucrats to
shoulder large portions of the burden for local projects using government funds.[21]

Overall, as well, the inception of the *haoxian guigong* system coincided with (and
largely enabled) the advent of what most scholars have seen as the Qing regime's greatest era of commitment to meeting social needs through direct governmental means.[22]
Chen Hongmou shared this commitment and played a major role in implementing
such practices. He even argued, repeatedly, that *gongxiang* accounts ought to be further
augmented by profits from state-sponsored commercial ventures, such as copper mining in the southwest and a highly entrepreneurial salt administration (aggressively seeking markets in other provinces) in Guangxi.[23] Although Chen steadfastly encouraged
local community activism in addressing "public" concerns, the new and relatively well-
financed *gongxiang* budgetary line provided one means by which he, through selective
apportionment of government funding, could supply direction to that community activism in ways deemed most effective by the bureaucratic state.

Philanthropy and Public Welfare

Another instance of state co-option via patronage of public-sphere activities came in the area of community welfare agencies. Whereas *gongxiang* investment was from the outset a state initiative, and the projects it most often supported (such as city wall building) were those in which the state's interest was equal to or greater than that of local society, the same was not the case for the various genres of charitable organization—most notably benevolent societies (*tongshan hui*), orphanages (*yuying tang*), and poorhouses (*puji tang*)—which first cropped up in the late Ming and became a standard feature of the urban landscape during the early eighteenth century. As Fuma Susumu, Liang Qizi, and others have shown, these began as wholly nongovernmental activities—private manifestations of Buddhist piety, Confucian elite magnanimity, and collegial patronage of hometown interest—that merged ultimately into a distinctively early modern cultural ideal of "philanthropy" (*cishan*) and the "philanthropist" (*shanren*).[24]

The picture of this late imperial philanthropic movement that emerges from this now well-developed scholarly literature goes something like this. Charitable organizations first appeared around the Wanli reign of the Ming (1573–1619). Although there had been antecedents in the Song, there was no direct continuity, and the late Ming institutions seem to have been from the start more local-community oriented and more corporate/collective in their managerial style than the ad hoc philanthropic ventures of the past. They were often initially Buddhist-inspired (Fuma identifies the earliest model in *fangsheng hui*, or associations formed to gain karmic merit by purchasing and releasing small birds and animals) but became during the Qing ever more dogmatically Confucian in their ideological underpinnings. Over time, as well, they moved from a central concern with the spiritual salvation or moral commitment of their donors to that of service to the needs of a more complex and impersonal society—first, perhaps, in simply an exemplary fashion and then gradually in a more practical effort to actually do what needed to be done. Accordingly, the functions of individual organizations—many of which were founded as societies to underwrite the coffining and burying of unclaimed corpses—proliferated broadly to serve various social needs as they were perceived. Management likewise became more sophisticated, as boards of directors, professional staffs, and diversified portfolios of endowment assets successively made their appearance.

In her recent monographic survey of the movement Liang Qizi persuasively argues for an essentially four-stage pattern of development in the relationship between communal philanthropic organization and the state.[25] In the first stage the organizations were highly localized and fully nongovernmental, and their sponsors (most famously Chen Longzheng) were often associated with literati movements that despaired of any constructive action by the corrupt late Ming regime. In the second, early Qing, stage the organizations remained effectively private (when they survived at all—literati societies having been banned for political reasons), although in the Kangxi reign they underwent some empire-wide systematization and standardization with modest prompting from the court. In the second quarter of the eighteenth century a process of more overt bureaucratization began, especially (but not exclusively) with regard to orphanages and poorhouses; the Yongzheng emperor in early 1724 mandated and provided guidelines for the establishment of *yuying tang* in every county, and statutory collections such as the *Da Qing lüli, Da Qing huidian,* and *Hubu zeli* (Administrative regulations of the Board of Revenue) dutifully carried prescriptions for them ever after. In the fourth stage, which lies beyond our concern here, nineteenth-century urban reformers dramatically expanded the scope of action of such organizations (now more conventionally known as *shantang*), just as the increasingly enfeebled state retreated to a posture of quiet encouragement from the sidelines. It was precisely in the third stage, that of bureaucratization, that Chen Hongmou made his most important contributions to the development of community-based charity. Indeed, Liang singles him out as *the* field official who perhaps did more than any other to effect the government co-option (via patronage) of an essentially private movement that the Yongzheng emperor had sought.

But, in fact, over the course of his long provincial career Chen's interest in these sorts of institutions was highly sporadic. He was intensely involved with them during his first few years in the field, in the late Yongzheng and early Qianlong reigns (the 1730s), and again, somewhat less dramatically, at the close of his field career around 1760. Throughout the 1740s and 1750s, however, during which time Chen held his long series of gubernatorial posts, his interest lapsed. Orphanages, poorhouses, and so on did not even figure significantly in his radically interventionist *xingchu* initiatives in Shaanxi and elsewhere, discussed in Chapter 10.[26] Why? One might speculate that he found fiddling with these organizations more appropriate to lower levels of administration (the prefectural, circuit intendant, and provincial judge and treasurer posts he held in the 1730s) than to the office of governor, but given his extraordinary commitment to hands-on conduct of that office this seems unlikely. The fact that his interest revived during his late tenure in Jiangsu, from 1759 to 1761, suggests that he neither found such interest beneath the dignity of a governor nor had despaired, after the 1730s, of the possibility held out by community charity halls to serve public needs. The key, rather, probably lay in two things: Chen's interest was greatest when the heady aura of *state* activism on the Yongzheng model was still fresh and when he served in the region of China where patterns of local *elite* activism (both literati and mercantile) were always most developed, the Lower Yangzi.

Chen Hongmou's earliest awareness of charity halls came during his first field tenure, as Yangzhou prefect from 1729 to 1730. The experience for a backwoods country boy like Chen must have been eye-opening. Yangzhou, center of the Liang-Huai salt district and a haven for extraprovincial sojourner merchants, was fabulously wealthy; and it was there, by most accounts, that organized elite philanthropy as a sociocultural movement largely got its start. The first recorded "Yuying tang," for example, had been set up there in 1655 by salt merchant Min Xiangnan and had served as the model for others throughout the region and empire.[27] In 1729, as Yangzhou was beset by calamitous flooding, merchants of outlying Shaobai town set up a relief agency financed by a shop tax and revived the late Ming name "Tongshan hui" to designate their creation; the institution thereafter enjoyed a long history as a multifunctional local welfare agency.[28] Chen Hongmou's direct involvement in this project is not recorded, although he was already at the time deeply engaged in supervising flood relief efforts throughout the prefecture. The next year his input became more evident, as he spearheaded the reestablishment of the prefecture's long-defunct Puji tang.

Chen's revived Puji tang in Yangzhou was in many ways an emblem of what he, and his activist imperial patron, sought to achieve in the realm of state-sponsored community welfare. It had an expanded range of functions, including interment of corpses, running a lifeboat service, and caring for indigent flood victims. It was subject to a detailed code of thirty-two government regulations drawn up by Chen and enforced by the office of prefect. It was financed by a complicated mix of official and private sources: Established on the basis of a subscription drive to which Chen himself and his bureaucratic subordinates substantially contributed, it was gradually put on a regularized subsidy from local government *gongxiang* accounts.[29] On Chen's part there was a heavy dose of his typical utilitarian frugality—the lavish expenditures on food and drink for which Yangzhou is notorious, he argues, can be turned here to better use— and of anticlerical Confucian dogmatism:

> What Buddhist monks and priests talk about, Confucian scholars actually do. . . . Anyone who dares not contribute funds [to the Puji tang], choosing instead to exhaust his wealth in grandly refurbishing Buddhist monasteries, or selling his body into monkhood and praying for deliverance, will not be regarded by this Prefect as a member of the gentry nor of the people. It is far better to heed the sufferings of those in the real world than to dwell upon past lives![30]

Chen brought this newly generated enthusiasm for welfare agencies to his next duty station, that of Yunnan provincial treasurer. Witnessing as it did the final acts of the long pageant of conquest and integration into the imperial order, the southwest during Yongzheng's reign came to serve as a great experimental laboratory for the various state-making initiatives of that ambitious ruler's devising, just as it did a proving ground for his cadre of "new men." On his arrival, therefore, Chen found the provincial capital of Kunming recently endowed with a greater assortment of welfare agencies than was probably typical for other provinces.[31] One of these, the Puji tang, offers a clear example of the governmentalization of such institutions that characterized the Yongzheng years. Kunming had hosted for some time a poorhouse known as the Society for Prevention of Starvation (Buji hui), established by the local elite (that is, sojourner merchants) and funded by rental incomes from urban commercial properties donated by society members. In the wake of Yongzheng's edict mandating "Puji tang" empire-wide, however, Governor-general Ortai in 1726 had renamed the society, expanded its facilities, and asserted a new degree of government control over its activities. He augmented its existing real estate endowment income first with the proceeds of a newly imposed tax on raw cotton transactions and then, once the throne's *haoxian guigong* reforms had taken hold, by an annual allocation from the province's *gongxiang* budget. By the time Chen arrived, in the summer of 1733, the Kunming Puji tang was a thriving operation of some sixty-six chambers and roughly 250 inmates, who received medical care from trained doctors, as well as food and shelter.

It was also, however, in his view rather decadent, and virtually his first act was to clean it up. Claiming that the Puji tang was home to many undeserving souls who indulged in litigation rackets and in wild drinking parties, Chen ordered a crackdown that would limit residence in the poorhouse to the "truly needy." At the same time, he divided the facility into three wards, based on the health or illness of the inmates, in order to decrease the incidence of contagion. Increasing its *gongxiang* allocation, he expanded the size and capacity of the facility by approximately one-third. Not least, Chen appointed a special deputy (*weiyuan*), who reported directly to his own office, to oversee the entire operation. A child of the Yongzheng era, Chen declared the state-directed provision of public welfare—"making up for the deficits of nature" (*bu zaohua zhi quexian*)—to constitute unequivocally "one of the first priorities of kingly rule" (*ji wangdao zhi xianwu*).

Six months later the provincial treasurer acted again, this time even more boldly. He enacted a comprehensive set of regulations to systematically govern all three major welfare agencies of Kunming—not only the Puji tang (poorhouse) and the Yuying tang (orphanage) but also an existing elite-managed burial society, the Yangu hui. (Inclusion of the latter may be especially significant because it represented a genre of philanthropic organization that, as Liang Qizi points out, derived from a separate and much more fully privatized tradition of elite philanthropy than did orphanages and poorhouses.) In each case Chen increased the agencies' operating budgets by finding new channels of government funding—adding to their endowment portfolio, for example, rental properties formerly belonging to his own provincial treasurer's office. Rather than increasing *gongxiang* allocations, as he had done earlier that year for the Puji tang, he now sought to free the three agencies as much as possible from dependence on this "soft funding," even as he increased state subsidies to them overall.

In the realm of management Chen not only promulgated detailed new operating procedures but also instituted new, more professionalized directorships. For the Yuying tang, for example, he replaced the system of rotational management by members of the local-elite governing board with a single, salaried, professional manager (*tangzhang*). This individual, who would hold (probably purchased) lower gentry rank, might be "publicly selected" by the city's elite but would serve at the discretion of the prefect and magistrate. As Liang Qizi points out, this shift from rotational to semiprofessionalized directorship mandated by Chen for the Kunming Yuying tang was analogous to shifts in managerial form he and others were at the same time instituting in the community granary system (the Yuying tang's *tangzhang* was conceived as just the same sort of state-delegated agent as was the granary's *shezhang*). As with the latter, it represented a significant step in the Yongzheng-era assertion of bureaucratic control over philanthropy and community activism.[32]

Following his demotion to the post of Tianjin circuit intendant in the early Qianlong reign, Chen kept up his interest in local welfare institutions and his firm insistence that they were properly the domain of the state. Like Yangzhou and Kunming, Tianjin was a large commercial city with an important sojourner-merchant elite, and, as in those other cities, it had its own local tradition of philanthropic organization. The key institution was a multifunctional home for the indigent known as the Yuli tang. A long line of circuit intendants dating back to the 1680s had patronized this institution, and quite early it had acquired as the core of its endowment a large rural estate in nearby Jinghai County, management of which had been officially delegated to the

priests of Jinghai's Sanguan (Three officials) Temple. The history of relations between
the Sanguan priests and the Yuli tang's urban directors, however, had rather predictably been marked by charges of mismanagement and engrossment. Following the
Yongzheng emperor's 1724 order to establish "Puji tang" throughout the empire,
Circuit Intendant Nian Yu decided that the Yuli tang fit the bill and, giving the rural estate up for lost, rallied Tianjin's salt merchant community to subscribe funds to be lent
out as commercial capital with the welfare home operating on the interest. Although
in 1727 the Sanguan Temple priests had been dispossessed and the rural estate given
over to direct control by the Yuli tang's own managers, by the time Chen Hongmou arrived in 1738 both the funding situation and the hall's operation were shaky at best.
His response was to conduct a full audit, throw out the incumbents and appoint his
own managers, and issue a highly specific regulatory code placing both the Yuli tang
and its endowment—which he referred to as "public property" (gongchan)—under
tighter government control.[33]

Finally, in yet another large commercial city, Suzhou, we find Chen again delicately
manipulating the boundaries between the spheres of "public" and "governmental," as
well as the discursive categories that in practice helped shape them. As Jiangsu provincial judge in 1740, his attention was attracted to two local institutions, the Guangren
tang and the Xilei tang, that had been formed in the Yongzheng era to undertake burial of unclaimed corpses and those of members of indigent families. These were fully
private associations of local gentry-merchant elites—Liang identifies them as important forerunners of the shantang, which would become the dominant form of organized
urban-communal philanthropy in the nineteenth century[34]—but prior to Chen's arrival the provincial grain intendant had been prevailed on to set aside rents from an
official estate (presumably government-owned urban commercial properties—
fangchan) to help underwrite their activities. Chen, who as we shall see in Chapter 12
was preoccupied with the ritual as well as the public-hygiene aspects of proper burial,
declared his office's full support for these pro bono societies and prohibited the operation of their chief competitors, Suzhou's many for-profit commercial crematoria.[35]

But returning to Suzhou as Jiangsu governor some twenty years later, Chen made
major moves to bring the societies (joined now by two others, the Jigong tang and
Tongshan tang) into the sphere of formal government. In 1760 he formed a joint
official–local elite committee of Assistant Magistrate Peng Hongji and two of the societies' most important gentry-managers, placing on them the formal duty (zecheng) to
manage burial of all unclaimed corpses in the urban and suburban environs, dividing
up among the societies specific territorial sectors of responsibility. At the same time he
ordered Suzhou's public security functionaries to report to the societies all corpses they
discovered while making their rounds. Public cemeteries, which would be financed out
of formal government accounts (guantang), were to be set up to assist the societies'
work. Two years later Chen angrily expressed his dissatisfaction with the way the societies had responded to his commission. Corpses still littered the streets. He pointed out
that the societies enjoyed handsome operating budgets, deriving not only from "publicly subscribed charitable property" (gongjuan yichan) but also from property that was
unambiguously "governmental" (guanchan). If they could not perform their duties any

better than they did, there must be expropriation of these public funds going on, for which the societies' managers might be criminally culpable. Chen gave them one month to submit to him detailed audits of their accounts. Clearly, in the view of the governor what had once been vehicles of private philanthropy were now effectively government agencies.[36]

We see in all of this experimentation with delivery of public welfare services, I think, a variety of ways of working out the practical implementation of what was gradually becoming known as *guandu minban*, popular management with official oversight. The precise formula differed from time to time and place to place and took account of the genre and origins of the specific institution concerned. Yet the clear thrust of policy during the years of Chen Hongmou's involvement with communally generated welfare organizations, the Yongzheng and early Qianlong reigns, was to utilize a combination of vigorous patronage and subtle intimidation to make them ever more directly agents in the service of state-defined goals. In the process the contours of *gong* and *guan* were conceptually blurred; they would remain so until the accelerated decline of the Qing state's practical efficacy in the later nineteenth century suggested the need for a more concerted effort to sort them out.[37]

Public Opinion

One highly particular usage of the concept of *public* in its nongovernmental sense—one of central importance in the evolution of political thought both in the early modern West and in early-twentieth-century China—appears in the notion of an autonomous "public opinion."[38] Something comparable, however, was also present in the political discourse of the eighteenth-century Qing empire and indeed played a critical role in that of Chen Hongmou. A variety of Chinese idioms were used to express this notion, the most familiar being "*gonglun*" and "*yulun*"—literally, public or collective thinking or discussion. Also in routine usage was the term "*minxin*," the mind or mentality of the people. "*Renqing*" (which we saw in Chapter 3 employed by Chen in a wide range of meanings, notably "human sentiment" or "emotional response") and "*minqing*" (which most often meant the material conditions in which a population lived) were also frequently invoked where something like "public opinion" was clearly intended. Other terms were occasionally used as well.[39]

"Public opinion" figured prominently in the larger world of Qing political discourse. The seventeenth-century reformist thinker Huang Zongxi (1610–95) had invoked it famously in his argument that only *gonglun* could reliably guide the throne in the direction of truly appropriate policy. By the eighteenth century, at least, the notion was no longer merely the provenance of critics of imperial rule but had been appropriated by the throne itself. In his ringing defense of Qing legitimacy, the *Dayi juemi lu*, the Yongzheng emperor had justified Manchu occupation of the heavenly throne by virtue of its meeting the test of popular *renqing*, and in his famous prohibition of literati factionalism, "Pengdang lun," he justified his right to ultimate decision making on grounds that his position at the center gave him privileged access to the totality of the empire's public opinion. A century later the Daoguang emperor proclaimed that, in order to demonstrate compliance with Heaven's will, all officials (including himself) were to routinely evaluate their performance by the measure of public approval (*yuqing*). A segment of the field bureaucracy, at least from the time of the Kangxi-era "model official" Tang Zhen, had made a deliberate show of doing just that.[40]

Beyond question, though, the notion had a special salience for Chen Hongmou, in whose surviving writings both professional and personal it makes literally scores of appearances. Chen drew his understanding of the notion most directly from Lü Kun, for whom, as for Chen, the elision between *renqing* as "empathy" and as "public opinion" is thoroughgoing and important. Lü mystifies *renqing* and *gonglun* by seeing them as "natural" (*ziran*) and rooted in the natural "order of things" (*wuli*). They are all-powerful and cannot be suppressed. For those who would aspire to political authority they are an object not only of respect but of fear and can be disregarded only at great peril. The way to bring about the realization of principle in the world (*huali*) is to take solicitous heed of this, a fact the ancient sage-kings well understood in establishing their state. In the contemporary world, as well, the foremost task of governance is to converge official thinking and policy with the attitudes and desires of the people (*guanmin qingyi zhi tong*). Among other things, Lü claims this as the basic rationale for the assiduous gathering of government intelligence and for the copious paperwork and record keeping to which we saw Chen Hongmou devoting himself in Chapter 10.[41]

Beyond what he inherited from Lü, Chen extended and developed his own notion of public opinion in a variety of interesting ways. *Gonglun* is the unfailingly reliable popular reputation enjoyed by an official, as well as the peer pressure that prompts local community members themselves to socially responsible behavior; it is "impossible to deceive." Adherence to *gonglun* or *minqing* is the surest guide in the project of ordering the world. Being merely human, Chen insists, he can claim no privileged a priori knowledge of what is best for the people; the best he can do is follow the people's will. He hears this will expressed through a range of media, among them discussions with local gentry (important, but not singularly so), reports of the oft-despised yamen clerks, and, not least, placards posted by disgruntled commoners—these are illegal, to be sure, but to ignore their message would be folly. Ultimately, the best guide to genuine public opinion is behavioral, especially *market* behavior: by their habits of buying, selling, and hoarding, the people eloquently convey both their reactions to current conditions and policies and their hopes and expectations for the future.[42]

As he represents himself in bureaucratic correspondence, Chen is consistently faithful to these beliefs in determining policy. Policy in local administration, he claims, must be accountable to three constraining factors: local geographic and material conditions, local customary practice, and local public opinion.[43] He consults and actively samples (often in person) local *gonglun* on a wide range of questions: how to conduct famine relief, whether and how to extend irrigation systems and repair river dikes, whether and where to open new mines, how to reform community granary lending procedures, when to mint more coins for local circulation, how to reform civil justice procedures, whether certain questionable local gentry ought to be stripped of their rank, just who in local society should be pressured to contribute to granary restocking, and so on across the policy spectrum.[44] In certain cases, as with development of programs to meet an anticipated drought in Shaanxi, he presents his constituency with a range of options, asking them to choose among them.[45] In private correspondence to a fellow official Chen proposes something of a "mass line": in carrying out directives from above, first sample local public opinion to determine how precisely to implement these instructions in your particular locality.[46] Of course, once ascertained, the expressed popular will constitutes a powerful mandate for government activism, and Chen is not shy about playing this card to legitimate pet projects—like mine development in Hunan or market expansion in frontier Gansu—both to the throne and to local populations themselves.

Although still quite far from any effective notion of "political representation," public opinion was nevertheless a critical forum for evaluating individual official performance. Just as public deliberations (*gongyi*) are the appropriate way to nominate granary managers or other local headmen, public discourse (*gonglun*) rightly passes judgment on the performance of state-appointed administrators. Chen claims that this is the truest test of an official's worth, announcing that he himself weighs it heavily in assessing subordinates; consequently, he tours his provinces personally to hear the people out. Officials who pursue policies of personal favoritism, or demonstrate insensitivity to the popular mood (*renxin*) in deciding litigation, for example, will justly find their careers in jeopardy.[47] Like Lü Kun Chen clearly sees this as a check most especially against the arrogant aloofness of well-born and hyperrefined literati unsuited to ministering to the people's needs.[48] He also, as we have seen, takes considerable pride in his own popularity (what critics call his "pandering for praise in the marketplace"), comforting himself with this during the occasional professional setback and drawing on it, sometimes more subtly than others, to advance his career.

To a certain (albeit limited) extent, then, the preoccupation with *gonglun/renqing* that we see in Chen and many of his contemporary political actors in the eighteenth-century Qing empire parallels the rising importance of the notion of public opinion in early modern Europe. In China, as in Europe, regularized political discussion among local people was thought to generate a consensus that, in light of local conditions at least, was associated with the fruits of collective "reason," hence providing a secure guide in the formation of policy and selection of appropriate government personnel. In the view of many European historians the emergence of this kind of logic in the West was associated with the rise of the print culture, of an intensified market orientation, and of the sort of procommercial approach to governance we have already amply seen in Chen Hongmou. It provided not only something of a brake on the arbitrary exercise of monarchical power but also a buttress for overcoming personal dependency ties and for breaking down hereditary social hierarchies. But, commendable or congenial as we may find this development to be, we must keep firmly in mind the limitations—present of course in somewhat different form in the European case as well—of the emergence of a Chinese notion of "public opinion," which compromised its utility for any indigenous emergence we may seek of "democratic" political thought.

At minimum, "*gonglun*" in Chen's usage was restrictively and emphatically *local;* registering local sentiment on local affairs was by definition what it was about. In fact, there were probably not one but two "public opinions" operating in Qing political discourse.

One was the empire-wide literati opinion to which Huang Zongxi and other systemic reformers referred; the other, that figuring in Chen's rhetoric, although socially more encompassing (Chen's grassroots notion of the "public" was quite clearly not limited to the degree-holding elite alone) was also geographically more constricted.[49] Suffice it to say that any presumption on the part of actors in local arenas to comment on dynastic-level politics was decidedly unwelcome, not only to the throne (as the cases of Zeng Jing, Dai Mingshi, and probably countless others made clear) but no less to a loyal minister such as Chen Hongmou.

Even locally, however, the very nature of public opinion as construed by Chen and his contemporaries placed limits on the concept's power. First, the fact that it was *gong* (public) itself unequivocally implied that it was nonpartisan. Thus we are not talking here about any discursive legitimation of pluralistic or interest-group politics (although of course there is no dearth of evidence that in practice much local politics during the Qing was precisely that). Chen far from devalued the pursuit of private interest, as we have seen, but this played no part in the ideologically sanctioned political process. "Public opinion," in this construction, was rather the unified "consensus opinion" (*dinglun*) of an enlightened communally minded public. Chen argues that the robust articulation of parochial group interests, manifested typically in high rates of litigation, represents not the effective working of public opinion but rather its breakdown. But if a local official is doing his job, promoting moral conduct and resolving conflict through his handling of this litigation, consensual and right-minded public opinion will spontaneously rise to the surface.[50]

Proper public opinion is univocal precisely because it is the direct manifestation of rational principle (*li*). Just as in early modern Europe, it is in effect "the public use of reason," engaged as a tribunal for sanctioning administrative action.[51] Implied in this, of course, is the idea that there is ultimately but a single, correct "public opinion" to be deduced on any given policy question. Chen indeed cites with approval Lü Kun's startling formulation: "Public opinion is definitely not whatever happens to be uttered by the masses. If everyone is wrong [*fei*] on an issue and but one man is correct [*shi*], then the applicable public opinion is what that one man says [*gonglun zai yiren*]." What is genuinely in question, Chen adds, are the rights and wrongs of a matter (*cili shifei*), not how the numerical majority declare they feel (*renyan zhongbian*).[52]

A final attribute of public opinion, so conceived, is that it is something the enlightened official can and should shape to his will. Left to itself it can be inconstant and misguided. The paternalist "father and mother official" is fully justified in efforts to convert the *minqing* through a process of encouragement and sanctions—provided, that is, that he truly communes with the people and has their interests at heart. Correct "public opinion," in this instance, is internalized in the official himself. Chen's own policy campaigns—those, for example, for drought relief in Yunnan or irrigation extension in Shaanxi and Gansu—routinely include a phase in which local or regional public opinion, at the outset skeptical or actively hostile, must be solicitously molded and brought around to their support.[53] If all persuasion fails, it may just be that the expressed feelings of the population have merit, and Chen *is* known on occasion to abandon projects (usually those launched by his predecessors) that local public opinion finds inordinately offensive.[54] Moreover, it is clear that he actually does try to listen, not merely to make a show of doing so. Public opinion can never be suppressed, but it surely can be managed. Chen Hongmou's populism, genuine as it is in its own way, has its limits.

"Community" in Mid-Qing Thought and Discourse

In a marvelously insightful article Hao Chang outlines two competing worldviews that struggled for acceptance over the long course of China's imperial past. The dominant view, what Chang terms the "Confucian cosmological myth," envisioned the social order as a human manifestation of the cosmic order and identified the essence of both as a filiated network of hierarchical "superordination" and "subordination," given expression in the notion of the three bonds (*sangang*). The alternative view, which pushed its way to the surface of elite consciousness at certain moments, was that of a unified and relatively egalitarian universal community expressed most often as "all under Heaven" (*tianxia*). This counterideology asserted a "transcendence" that obviated both hierarchical distinction and less encompassing group particularisms.[55] If these two worldviews do indeed represent the choice with which orthodox thinkers were confronted, what is most notable is the utter exclusion from consideration, in either option, of any legitimacy for the local community (territorial or otherwise) as a unit of identity and social action.

This lacuna has been noted explicitly by one of the West's most sympathetic interpreters of Confucian thought, Wm. Theodore de Bary. In his sensitive work *The Trouble with Confucianism,* he notes the critical omission of the stage of local community, as intermediary between the family and the state, in the ramified extension of concentric spheres presented in the *Daxue* (Great learning). He notes as well the poignancy of what he views as persistent and largely failed attempts by scholars from Zhu Xi to Wang Yangming to Huang Zongxi and Gu Yanwu (and even, indeed, to our own contemporary Tu Wei-ming) to insert such a category into the orthodox chain. In de Bary's view this omission contributed as much as anything else to China's difficulty in developing a workable civic politics in the twentieth century.[56]

But if this attempt failed, it was at times a strenuous one. As argued by Robert Hymes and others, one moment of extreme elite fascination with the local community came in the Southern Song. The social phenomenon of unprecedented entrenchment of elite lineages into local society, accomplished through marriage alliances and other means (what Hymes calls the "localist strategy"), coincided with a mood of political disenchantment with commandist state-led activism—epitomized by Wang Anshi's Northern Song "New Policies" and perceived by most to have been a dismal failure—and led to a collective project to create a middle level of identity and mobilization between the family and the state that was both local and voluntary. Known variously as the *xiang* or *she,* this local communal unit was valorized by *lixue* ideologists such as Zhu Xi and given institutional embodiment in such organs as the *shuyuan* (local private academy), the *shecang* (community granary), and the *xiangyue* (community compact), each of which displaced a corresponding state-generated functional equivalent—the state

school system, "Green Sprouts" loan agencies, and *baojia* public security apparatus, respectively.[57] A second energizing moment for local community came in the late Ming,
when an even more extreme disillusionment with state initiative and the de facto collapse of the dynasty's institutional vehicle for directed local activism, the *lijia* system,
combined with an alarmed perception of rapid sociocultural change (accelerated commercialization, social and geographic mobility, an urban challenge to agrarian-familial
values, and competitive individualist striving) to incline local elites more strongly to
community-centered social action. As with the Southern Song spurt of local initiative,
a major stimulus behind the late Ming movement was the desire to regenerate the
moral character of the elite itself; even more than in the earlier case, theorists of the latter one such as Lü Kun and Huang Zuo (1490–1566) explicitly sought to utilize community ties to bridge intralocal economic divisions and ameliorate the rising tide of
class conflict.[58]

For its part the early Qing regime probably did more than any previous dynasty to
encourage and grant formal statutory legitimation to various sorts of communal-soli-
darity local initiatives.[59] As Pierre-Étienne Will and others have observed, at least by the
second quarter of the eighteenth century a mood of pessimism had set in regarding the
ability of local elites and communities to do on their own what needed to be done, and
the necessity for a more direct attempt by the state at guidance and coordination came
to be widely acknowledged.[60] Yet even the most aggressively "statist" mid-Qing bureaucrats, influenced as most of them were by social formulae worked out by Zhu Xi and Lü
Kun, retained a deep-seated attraction for community action and self-reliance. In this
regard Chen Hongmou represented his times rather neatly.

All of his efforts at bureaucratic standardization notwithstanding, Chen built his
notions about ordering the world firmly on an innate appreciation of local communal
solidarity. Like many other members of the Qing official elite he found sanction for this
in Lü Kun, emphasizing in his own redaction of Lü's writings the late Ming master's injunction for all members of the elite to share as fully as possible in the concerns and aspirations of their own home community (*xiangli zhi wang*).[61] We saw in Chapter 1 how
strongly Chen in fact took this to heart, involving himself in numerous local causes in
his native *xiang* in Guangxi and promoting *tongxiang* (common native place) sentiment
among his compatriots sojourning afield. Somewhat more idiosyncratic (see Chapter
4) was the support Chen found for his ideas in Wang Yangming. Although Wang was
decried by many Qing commentators for the license his thought offered to valorize the
individual over social network and hierarchy, Chen found worthy of endorsement the
variant Wang offered of the concentric correspondences of the *Daxue*, in which the progression moved outward from self (*shen*) and household (*jia*) to *local community* (*xiang*)
before reaching the macrocosm of empire or universal society (*tianxia*).[62]

The language of local community indeed permeates Chen's political discourse. For
a time in the mid-1740s he was fond of invoking the notion of *yin* (community harmony), one of the "six virtuous actions" (*liuxing*) singled out in the *Rites of Zhou*, that
elusive ancient text that had acquired a considerable chic among social activists of
Chen's day.[63] In more vernacular language he spoke routinely of "*xiangyi*" (community
sentiment) and of "*xiangdang*," a quasi-corporate notion of the residential community

to which the individual and the household owed attachment. Identification with the *xiangdang* and the imperative to act in its interests was for Chen clearly secondary to identification with one's family, but it was no less a manifestation of the relationship orientation ordained by Heaven for every human being (*tianlun*).[64] It was thus naturalized as essential to both the properly functioning social and cosmic orders.

This residential community is the locus of *xiangping*, the critical opinion of the local public that offers a powerful standard of correctness not merely for the actions of group members but also, within certain limits, for those of the government as well.[65] Members of the local community have an obligation to intercede as conciliators of intragroup conflict. Local elders are particularly well-suited to this task, Chen observes, because of their acknowledged expertise in the consensual norms peculiar to their community.[66] Of even greater concern is the extent to which community sentiment can be harnessed for purposes of local material self-reliance. Chen uses moral appeals to encourage such action on the part of community members—a key component of fulfilling one's role as a human being (*jiren*) is "bestowing beneficence upon one's *xiang*"—but he stresses as well collective self-interest, contributing to the material benefits shared by all within the community. Community members should assist each other at major ritual occasions such as weddings and funerals and aid each other in times of need. Community sentiment (*not* the state) should compel the wealthy to sell surplus grain to their hungry neighbors at prices they can afford, and in dearth-stricken 1749 Shaanxi Chen confers imperial honors on those exemplars of "mutual aid at the *xiang* and village level" who have done just that.[67] Taking this promotion of local self-reliance to what may have been unusual lengths, Chen not only announces his approval of the walled villages that dot the northern Shaanxi landscape but urges their effectively autonomous residents to work collectively to renovate and strengthen their defenses against the outside world.[68]

This is somewhat surprising in light of the two very strong qualifiers Chen elsewhere implies for any manifestation of community to meet his approval. First, they are not to be hermetically self-contained or exclusionary but rather building blocks in the forging of a larger, supralocal social order. Routinely Chen applauds self-reliant activism on the part of local elites or community members on the specific grounds that the largesse involved not only benefits the community itself (*benxiang*) but also spills over to benefit neighboring communities (*fujin xiangli*), or he expresses his faith that the positive example offered by one community will infect its neighbors and so ultimately bring good to the wider society.[69] In this Chen not only recalls the particular notion of community advocated by Zhu Xi[70] but anticipates as well the many late-nineteenth- and twentieth-century nationalist thinkers who argued for the special utility of local community ties (*tongxiang*) as stepping stones to the forging of an amalgamated national identity and loyalty.[71] Second, the peculiarly Confucian local community Chen cherishes is not one of undifferentiated coequality but one that, internally, observes the dictates of familial precedence demanded by the heavenly order. In his citation of Wang Yangming's scheme of homologous correspondences (individual–family–local community–empire), for example, he notes specifically that each level replicates the other most distinctively in the way each is internally structured according to principles of generational seniority (*zunbei zhangyou*).[72]

What Chen Hongmou does and does not envision in a properly functioning community is nowhere more clearly revealed than in his attacks on communities of believers in the various messianic, congregational religions he encounters throughout his administrative career. In the case of Muslims in the northwest, for example, Chen decries the exclusionary solidarity of persons for whom an attack on one is an attack on all. Any casual disturbance involving a single believer and a single nonbeliever (from Chen's perspective almost invariably initiated by the Muslim) thus escalates into large-scale feuding. This solidarity and urge to group formation (*chengqun*) among the Islamic faithful is also all too readily applied to organized criminal activity—collecting in large "deviant communities" ("*feidang*"—the rhetorical obverse of "*xiangdang*," the legitimate local community) to launch predatory raids on their neighbors or to engage in smuggling. Intriguingly, Chen attributes the apparently highly disciplined cohesion of such Muslim collectivities precisely to a *lack* of discipline (*yuesu*) as he would prefer to understand it, that is, as the exercise of control over juniors by their generational seniors or otherwise legitimate natural leaders.[73]

In confronting communitarian religions that do not enjoy the tradition of imperial toleration that Islam does, Chen favors annihilation and forcible conversion. As we shall see more fully in Chapter 12, Chen in 1746 launched a broad-based attack on all varieties of heterodox religion (*xiejiao*) and deviant congregationalism (*feidang*) in Shaanxi. Specific targets of the campaign were Christian churches (*jiaotang*) and Buddhist sects, but more mundane manifestations of communal piety, such as pilgrimage societies (*xiangshe*) and vegetarian halls (*zhaitang*), were also included. The forms of communal organization he targeted were alike in their affronts to the cosmic and social order; they denied heavenly mandated bonds of generational seniority (*zunzhang*), familial attachment, and territorial community (*yin*)—bonds that were all in Chen's understanding more "natural" human impulses than the salvationist faith that united religious congregations. Again anticipating twentieth-century Chinese "modernizers," Chen expropriated the facilities and assets of these groups for rededication to more enlightened and "useful" manifestations of community: community schools (*yixue*), community granaries (*shecang*), and Confucian community-compact halls (*xiangyue*).[74]

Units of Community: The Xiang

Although Chen acknowledges and in certain instances seeks to employ for mutual-responsibility purposes other bases of communal grouping—occupational and ethnic, for example[75]—those he finds most legitimate, most compelling, and therefore most useful in the project of world-ordering are kinship and proximate residence. Let us concentrate here on the latter of these and return below to the issue of how the two are related. In sorting through the units of local community to which Chen referred, of course, we are confronted with the maddening imprecision of vocabulary that he himself faced, especially as one who traversed the span of empire and confronted myriad local usages. Even considering this, however, I believe it is possible to discern through Chen's writing a coherent approach gradually forming over the course of his career to empower a specific unit of communal self-nurturance—the *xiang*—below the lowest level peopled by direct state agents, the county.

Given the attention he lavishes on the duty of the county magistrate to visit and familiarize himself with individual villages, Chen has surprisingly little to say about the village (*cun* or *li*) as a self-nurturing unit. He speaks relatively often of the impetus to neighborly cooperation among village residents (*lilin* or *linli*) and at times even of a "village community" (*ludang*), with its own peculiar consensual norms. In his various community granary drives he talks about the rather nebulous ideal of village self-sufficiency in foodstuffs. As we have already seen in the case of Shaanxi's walled villages, moreover, in certain feasible instances he seeks to utilize villages as units of collective labor and finance for public projects. Chen is most revealing on this question when he discusses his hopes to ameliorate ethnic tension between Han and Hui (Muslim) people in the northwest. Han and Hui do not intermarry, he concedes, so appeals to kinship solidarity are fruitless; but because they do frequently inhabit the same villages, this coresidence can be usefully exploited in appeals for greater mutual-interest identification and cooperation between the two groups.[76] Beyond these scattered instances, however, Chen prefers to invoke other terms in his discussions of local community, terms that usually refer to units of territory larger than the individual village.

We saw in Chapter 8, for example, how Chen was attracted to the hallowed institution of the *she*, or local tutelary community, invoking it as the presumed locus for the *shecang* (community granary) that he worked so diligently to implant on the landscape of the provinces in which he served. We saw also, however, that in many of these jurisdictions the *she* unit had little preexisting social reality, so for Chen the term became in effect merely a designation of convenience for any supravillage, subcounty unit of territory that conditions of transport accessibility and grain availability made a viable site for his granaries' locations.

Not so, I would argue, for his use of the term "*xiang.*" "*Xiang,*" of course, could also be employed casually, to refer to "the countryside" or to a loosely defined sector of rural territory. Chen uses it in this way most often in combination with the word *village,* in the compound "*xiangli.*" But far more frequently he seems to use it with greater specificity, to refer to a subcounty territorial unit centered on a market town of significant size and encompassing a large but indeterminate number of villages. At least since the seventeenth century, probably in large part as a result of the intensified participation in commerce by rural producers after the late Ming, the town-centered *xiang* had emerged as an increasingly powerful unit of communal identity and popular mobilization for a variety of purposes; the strength of the *xiang* community may have varied from one region of the empire to another, but studies by Fu Yiling and others covering Fujian, Jiangxi, Hubei, and Sichuan suggest that, in certain regions at least, it could be rather compelling.[77] We have already seen in Chapter 10 how the preexistence of such a social unit had suggested to at least some officials of the 1720s and 1730s the wisdom of formally imposing a unit of formal administration headed by a centrally appointed (although in some versions locally selected) bureaucrat, the so-called *xiangguan*.

As we have also seen, Chen Hongmou was deeply aware of the power of the *xiang* community (*xiangdang*) in many or most of his provincial jurisdictions. He understood it to be a locus of consensual opinion formation (*xiangping*) and of local interest identification (*xiangyi*).[78] Perhaps nowhere does he make this more clear than in his handling of the subsistence crisis in Jiangxi during 1742 and 1743. In that time and place Chen reports explicitly that the marketing community of the *xiang* is the operative unit of grain price differentiation and, consequently, that the most threatening social division he faces—even more than that between rich and poor—is that between *xiang* with cheap grain and those without. One manifestation of this is grain export embargoes imposed by *xiang*-level popular forces (*xiangjin*). Chen's ingenious solution, it may be recalled, is to take this same *xiang*-generated local leadership (*xiangqi*) that is wont to impose embargoes and depute them as state agents to purchase outside grain for import into their hungry home communities.[79]

In a variety of other ways as well, Chen Hongmou sought to exploit the existence of the community of "local *xiang* coresidents" (*difang xianglin*) for purposes of self-nurturance and moral improvement and to cajole local wealthy interests to make their *xiang* neighbors the objects of their largesse, something he presumed they were more readily inclined to do than to dispense charity to the population at large. To cite but one example (a key one), evidence suggests that it was none other than the *xiang* that Chen had most often in mind as locus of his community granaries and recruitment of managers (*shezhang*) who were truly recipients of community trust and respect.[80] In this, of course, he had ample precedent. A long line of reformist literati, from Zhu Xi in the Song to Huang Zuo, Lü Kun, and Chen Zilong in the Ming, had likewise identified the *xiang* unit as the appropriate one for the cultivation of local identity, community sentiment, and right-minded indigenous leadership. In the cases of Huang and Lü, in particular, we can see an even more precise goal at work: to develop *xiang*-level communal institutions in a wide range of functional areas, each institution led by a locally generated manager or managers. The institutions and the leadership would interact systematically in the formation of a comprehensive structure of local self-nurturance that was, at the same time, fully in step with the concerns of the larger society and of the imperial state.[81] As we shall see, this is exactly what Chen Hongmou sought to achieve as well.

Community Ritual: The Xiangyin jiuli

Given the critical importance Chen Hongmou attached to ritual practice in the project of ordering the world (see Chapter 12), it is not surprising that he devoted extraordinary attention to the task of implementing in local society a particular ceremonial activity that promised to him to accomplish three critical things at once: (1) to celebrate the *xiang* community as a unit of local solidarity and popular interest-identification, (2) to confer ritual honor and authority on those members of this community who had assumed the specific leadership functions singled out as desirable by his office, and (3) to unify through ritual means the interests of the *xiang* and those of the *guo*, the imperial state. This essential ritual institution was the semiannual *xiangyin jiuli*, or community libationer ceremony. In this highly orchestrated banquet, hosted by the local mag-

istrate at the county Confucian school-temple (*xianxue*), *xiang*-level notables were selected to serve as "guests," as recipients of testimonials at various levels of honor (*dabin*,
jiebin, and *zhongbin*, respectively).[82]

The *xiangyin jiuli* had its locus classicus in the *Zhou li* (Rites of Zhou) but had
dropped out of the ritual repertoire of imperial China until its revival in A.D. 1113 by
Emperor Huizong of the Song. Thereafter, it continued to be prescribed by the institutional handbooks (*huidian*) of successive dynasties. The Qing's own initial reaffirmation
of the rite in 1644 was, however, not matched by vigorous efforts to ensure proper performance, and by the eighteenth century it was notorious as an example of perfunctory
local acquiescence to the fussy demands of the center and, more egregiously, as a vehicle for exploitation of local society by sub-bureaucratic yamen functionaries.[83] Both the
Yongzheng and Qianlong emperors, therefore, at the outset of their reigns actively
sought to revitalize the *xiangyin jiuli* and to dispel the bad odor the ritual had acquired.[84]

Although he cites these imperial pronouncements on the importance of the libationer rite, Chen Hongmou's initiatives in this area seem to have been primarily self-
driven; they came in a period (the mid-1740s through the early 1760s) when a decline
in central government interest in the institution was already well underway and were
seemingly unmatched by the activities of other provincial governors.[85] Quite possibly,
Chen's own special interest in *xiangyin jiuli* was kindled by his posting in 1742 to
Nanchang, where the memory of Wang Yangming's tenure there in the mid-Ming was
still very much alive and where institutions Wang had promoted, including the *xiangyin*,
remained unusually vital. First in Jiangxi, later in Shaanxi (where the *xiangyin* was virtually unknown), and still later in Fujian and Jiangsu (where it was practiced in reput-
edly its most corrupt form), Chen repeatedly browbeat his local-level subordinates to
take correct and meaningful performance of the rite as a central task of their administration. With characteristic thoroughness Chen promulgated in each of these provinces
detailed regulations and established systems of monitoring to ensure that the rite was
regularly performed. In a context of declining official budgetary support for the *xiangyin*, he developed a variety of methods for financing its performance. He printed and
distributed copies of the correct liturgy, insisting that the prescribed choreography and
script be followed to the letter. Most important, as we shall see, he focused his attention
on the careful selection of appropriate "guests."[86]

Chen was hardly insensitive to dysfunctions in the contemporary practice of the
xiangyin—indeed, the standard source for our own knowledge of these corruptions,
Hsiao Kung-ch'uan's epochal 1960 work, *Rural China*, is largely based on Chen's testimony. Worthy candidates for *xiangyin* honors often declined nomination to avoid the
clerical extortion that was sure to follow, whereas other less worthy candidates eagerly
sought it for their own exploitative ends. In line with his broader economic policies
Chen attacked the common practice by local administrators of procuring food, drink,
and labor for the banquet at confiscatory submarket prices and of using the goodies
thus acquired for their own enjoyment. In a number of cases he brought impeachments against submagistrates and county education officials for their complicity in this
racket.[87] More broadly, the abstemious and unusually straitlaced Chen strove to down-
play the material aspects of the "feast" altogether. It should decidedly not be a lavish af-

fair, he argued; it is not, after all, about food and drink. The symbolic or representational aspect of the *xiangyin* is central, not its materiality (*bu wei qi wu, wei qi yi*).[88]

Chen's concern to rectify and invigorate the *xiangyin jiuli*, in spite of its manifest problems, derives not from any knee-jerk drive to enforce the letter of the law (this is rarely a priority for him). Rather, something in the ritual strikes Chen as genuinely central to the civilizing process and therefore merits his close attention. In his earliest sustained statement on the *xiangyin* (1742) Chen identifies its four principal goals: (1) to ensure that the stages in the human life cycle—youth and age—are prioritized properly; (2) to see that virtuous individuals are recognized and accorded due respect; (3) to perpetuate the hegemony of the correct ritual teachings (*lijiao*)—that is, the norms of civilization; and (4) to bring peace and harmony to the local communities (*xiangli*).[89] All of this implies first and foremost an effort to actualize and reproduce in human society the ordering principles of the natural universe, conceived as inherently both rational and moral. Behind this project, however, we can detect two basic tensions, which the *xiangyin* ritual brings very much to the fore: that between community and social hierarchy and that between the locality and the state.

The first of these tensions suggests the poignant ambivalence with which neo-Confucian orthodoxy, and even more profoundly the late imperial state, viewed bonds of community solidarity. Even though they sought, in a variety of very creative ways, to use community sentiment as an instrument of both local self-policing and local economic self-reliance, Qing officials clearly viewed corporateness of this or any other variety as deeply suspect. It is this quality of unquestioning group loyalty, as we have seen, that Chen Hongmou finds so threatening in even otherwise well-behaved religious congregations, be they Muslim, Christian, or sectarian Buddhist. A view of human society as ordered according to infinitely expandable, relativistically ego-centered *networks*, hierarchically structured along axes of age, gender, and educational level, always takes logical and moral precedence over one of society ordered according to relatively closed and internally homogeneous corporate *groups*.

Alert to this bias, Evelyn Rawski has argued that the late imperial state's "process of restoring order through *li* [ritual]" was always centrally concerned with the need to assert the primacy of hierarchical structure over societally generated urges to local *communitas*.[90] How then did it deal with a ritual that celebrated precisely, on the surface at least, this *communitas*? Even here, as Rawski's statement would suggest, a hierarchy of seniority assumes priority. In a 1743 proclamation demanding that his official subordinates dutifully perform the *xiangyin*, Chen begins by stating its chief purpose as institutionalizing a hierarchy of precedence for recipients of local honor and, significantly, as a means to *minglun*, to "reveal and clarify" proper social relationships of obligation and deference among local residents.[91] It is for this reason, for example, that seating orders at the banquet must be so attentively enforced.

Yet two qualifications to this emphasis on hierarchy must be immediately advanced. First, as we will shortly see, the goal of fostering community solidarity is for Chen Hongmou by no means absent in his promotion of the *xiangyin* rite; the key is to ensure that it be the *right kind* of local community. Second, the hierarchy Chen means to enforce, here as throughout his various social engineering projects, is one of individual networks based on familial or pseudofamilial ties; it is decidedly *not* one of hierarchically layered status groups. These are, one senses, as much anathema to Chen as are other corporate groups, such as the above-mentioned communities of true believers.

This distinction between a network hierarchy and a status-group hierarchy is nowhere more clearly revealed than in the dramatic twist Chen gives to the selection of *xiangyin* honorees. In the Qing central government pronouncements on *xiangyin* of 1644, 1723, and 1737, age was invariably the chief criterion for selection. Although the qualification for honorees was stated as being *gaonian youde* (elderly and virtuous), little specificity was accorded the latter half of this formula; by contrast, detailed instructions were provided as to how differential treatment would be given to honorees who fell into decile cohorts above seventy, eighty, and ninety years of age. In Chen Hongmou's promotion of the libationer rite, however, other than an occasional casual mention that honorees should be over sixty, this concern completely recedes from importance. Similarly, Hsiao Kung-ch'uan has demonstrated the general Qing preoccupation with the question of whether *xiangyin* honors could effectively be limited to members of the gentry.[92] Yet Chen Hongmou seems unconcerned about this issue as well; he tells his subordinates, in effect, select degree holders as honorees if you can find some that merit it, but don't worry if you cannot.

Something similar may be said about the tension between the local community (*xiang*) and the state (*guo*). Chen argues that the *xiangyin* is an invaluable tool for mediating the interests of the two. To be sure, he acknowledges the importance of the ceremony in "teaching political loyalty" (*jiaozhong*), as well as in "teaching filiality" (*jiaoxiao*) and its role in "pacifying the localities" (*he xiangli*). It is as much for this reason as for any other that the local official assumes final responsibility for approving the honorees. But Chen is equally adamant that the *xiangyin* cannot serve this political role if it is perceived as artificial, if it fails to tap into a genuine and preexisting sense of local corporate community (*xiangdang*). It is out of this concern that Chen repeatedly emphasizes that personnel of the quintessentially coercive pseudocommunity, the *baojia* system, have no place as *xiangyin* "guests."[93] But if the community celebrated in the *xiangyin* is not to be an artificially state-imposed one, as would be the case if its honorees were drawn from the ranks of *baojia* personnel, neither can the ceremony afford simply to ratify existing hierarchies of wealth and influence. Chen repeatedly insists that, just as the ritual should not focus on the material food and drink, neither should it degenerate into an occasion for honoring local examples of material prosperity. He is deeply anxious over the latent possibility for privatization of the rite by the local economic elite as a means of institutionalizing their networks of personal patronage and, through relieving the local magistrate of his onerous responsibility to finance the affair, effectively buying state endorsement of their self-aggrandizing activities in local society.

This is nowhere more of a problem than in the hyperdeveloped Jiangnan, where Chen clearly sees his modest *xiangyin* reception as competing directly (and none too well) with privately sponsored "feasts" (*yanhui*). These are lavish, potlatch-style affairs held typically at idyllic mountainside temples and designed to celebrate the wealth and prosperity of their host families, even as they serve to demonstrate the latter's sense of *li*, of ritually expressed social obligation. Such banquets rival each other in the number of invitees and the richness of the food and drink. (In response Chen, as Jiangsu governor, issues a directive limiting the number of courses that might be served and the total cost entailed.)[94] The *xiangyin* here epitomizes the direct confrontation of Chen's straitlaced Confucian economizing and the competitive consumption impulses of the nouveaux riches beneficiaries of Qing commercial expansion.

Not only do Chen's concerns in this area confound any simple notion that he was acting as an uncritical agent of an economic ruling class, but they also render problematic simple generalizations about the interests of "the Qing state." *Xiangyin*, in fact, is a flash point in a persistent conflict between levels of administration: on the one hand, county magistrates who find it counterproductive in the management of their district to interrogate the conduct and propriety of local men of influence and, on the other, provincial-level officials such as Chen who insist that they do just that.[95] Viewed in this way, the *xiangyin* serves as a point of leverage for higher-level state intervention and rectification not only of local society but also of the lower reaches of the administration itself.

If, as Chen intends, we eliminate as potential *xiangyin* "guests" both those whose prominence is based simply on their lackey service to the state and those whose status is merely a function of wealth, with whom are we left as worthy honorees? The essential criterion, Chen repeatedly insists, is high personal virtue—the "*youde*" half of the "*gaonian youde*" formula. But how is virtue to be defined?

To a large extent, it appears, it is context-specific, a function of the broader purposes Chen hopes to achieve in each of his regional tenures. In more rustic provinces—and especially those on the pale of Chinese high culture such as parts of the southwest and northwest—Chen favors recipients who may be held up as exemplars of Confucian family-based ethics. On one occasion he reminds magistrates in more remote parts of Shaanxi that they have already submitted, in response to an earlier campaign, names of candidates for imperial honors as models of "loyalty, filiality, chastity, and propriety" (*zhong xiao jie yi*). Why, he asks (with a none-too-subtle hint that corruption may be going on), would you therefore submit the names of any individuals other than these as nominees for *xiangyin* honors? In such parts of the empire, where economic and cultural conditions make the primacy of the Han/Confucian family system less than a given, Chen sees the selection of *xiangyin* honorees as a means of its promotion and in turn of cultural assimilation. In these same regions a major obstacle to this assimilation is the ingrained elitism Chen observes in his local-level subordinates. Thus, with a characteristic mixture of Confucian populism and cultural imperialism he rebukes county magistrates: "Do not presume to argue that in the out-of-the-way place in which you serve there is no one worthy [of *xiangyin* honors]. In every local community, no matter how remote, there will be individuals of significant virtue."[96]

In other provincial contexts Chen has other priorities. In Jiangxi, where, as we shall see shortly, he is in the process of reforming and revivifying the unusually powerful institution of lineage headmen (*zuzhang* or *zuzheng*), he instructs magistrates to give special consideration to these individuals as *xiangyin* honorees. Again, it must be stressed that Chen is not interested in simply conferring quasi-official honors on de facto power holders in local society; rather, he specifies that only local lineage leaders who have accepted his own agenda, who have assumed and satisfactorily performed the special functions of group discipline and conflict resolution that he has defined as proper to the *zuzhang*'s role, be considered suitable for *xiangyin* honors.[97] In other words, he sees the community libationer rite as a supplementary means of reinforcing the status of persons who head up local communities that, although they may have—indeed, should have—preexisting reality, are also products of Chen's own social engineering.

This is even more clearly seen when we consider the social type that, Chen eventually comes to argue, is the single most worthy recipient of *xiangyin* honors: the community granary manager, or *shezhang*.[98] By suggesting the *shezhang*, the local agent of one of his pet projects, as the honoree of choice for another of his projects, the *xiangyin jiuli*, Chen is trying to do at least two things at once. He is trying to create a means of rewarding and providing greater popular legitimation for valuable local leaders who have fulfilled their important duties with integrity and responsibility. At the same time, he is attempting to impose through ritual means a greater sense of collective proprietorship, of mutual belonging, indeed of genuine community, to a *xiang*-level institution that otherwise might be seen merely as a pragmatic, imperially sponsored local credit facility.

The selection of proper *xiangyin jiuli* honorees, be they *zuzhang*, *shezhang*, or other exemplary local personages, is the critical factor in mediating between just such a local community and the imperial state. The language of public and private, of *gong* and *si*, is thus central to Chen's project. In the *xiangyin* ritual the state singles out for recognition precisely those individuals who have consistently demonstrated their sense of "public-mindedness" (*gongzheng*), who have taken leadership roles in "public projects" (*gongshi*), and who have contributed materially to the communal "public interest" (*gongji*). Those individuals whose energies have been directed primarily to the interests of their family/household (*jia*), however upright they may be, are not appropriate for *xiangyin* honors; their labors are too *si*. Those who have advanced, instead, local community (*xiangdang*) causes—those, for instance, who have provided relief to their fellow community members in time of dearth—are truly public-spirited and deserve state recognition. By so honoring these men the state, not coincidentally, can claim *itself* to be the champion of the public interest.

But Chen goes yet one step further. How is the local official to determine just who in local society genuinely epitomizes a commitment to "public" causes? If the best and most practicable measurement of personal virtue is what an individual has done in material terms to aid the residential community, the most effective means in turn to measure such actions is the consensus of the community itself. Local "public opinion" (*xiangping*), therefore, becomes the ultimate standard for selection of *xiangyin* honorees.[99] Genuine attentiveness to local opinion is no easy task, Chen recognizes, because self-interested local big shots will find means to influence it unfairly in their favor. But the official who can successfully hear what the people have to say will make the right choice of *xiangyin* honorees and thereby carry out the true function of *jiaohua*—"teaching and transforming" the local populace into a morally autonomous and economically self-reliant community.

Baojia *and* Xiangyue

To a large extent Chen Hongmou's unusual attraction to the *xiangyin jiuli* ceremony— that is, to ritual means of cementing the solidarity of the *xiang*-level local community and enhancing the authority of state-approved leaders within that community—derived from his relatively modest appreciation of alternative institutions intended for this purpose, the *baojia* and *xiangyue* systems. Let us briefly consider each of these in turn.

Baojia was a system under which households were regimented into nested decimal groupings of ten, one hundred, and so on for purposes of assigning collective responsibility in public security and other matters and for fixing personal responsibility for the group on a single "headman" at each level of the hierarchy. Theoretically, this headmanship would be voluntary and part-time, and it would rotate among heads of the households in the group. The Qing inherited this system from earlier dynasties and ordered its implementation during the process of consolidating control over the empire. It was reaffirmed several times—notably under Chen Hongmou's own imperial patron, the Yongzheng emperor—and remained a favored vehicle for social ordering among a certain segment of relatively hard-line Qing officials. The consensus of historians, however, is that, official rhetoric to the contrary, the system atrophied rather quickly on its implementation under Qing. The standard authority in English, Hsiao Kung-ch'uan, sees it as a dead letter almost from the time of its proclamation; others (including myself) have stressed the collapse of its communal or collective organizational aspects but admitted the survival of the headman institution in the form of a relatively menial, semiprofessionalized pubic security functionary.[100]

Although Hsiao identifies Chen Hongmou as one of the *baojia* system's most dogged enthusiasts, I do not believe this to be true or, indeed, to reflect the way he was perceived by his admirers in the Qing itself.[101] There is some basis, of course, for Hsiao's judgment. In his *Sourcebook on Proper Conduct of Office* Chen did reprint Wang Yangming's celebrated "Shijia pai" proclamation, the version of *baojia* that the eminent Ming philosopher-statesman attempted to implement in southern Jiangxi from 1517 to 1520 and in Chen's own native Guangxi in 1528. But Wang's system is actually a far cry from *baojia* as it was normally envisioned or practiced. It is above all an agent of cultural assimilation in areas that were, in Wang's day, on the pale of both the Chinese ecumene and imperial control. Its primary purpose is to aid in the "civilizing process" (*jiaohua*) and the introduction of "rites and music" (*liyue*). It is to be a vehicle for mediation of internal conflict, to obviate both excessive litigation and the violent feuding to which the region is prone and even for effecting more equitable distribution of tax burdens. Wang insists that his system "is preferable to simple reliance on legal compulsions" in the task of ordering such a society, and Chen agrees, adding that it can only succeed when instituted at the hands of officials "with a genuine heart and love for the people." In fact, in the context of Chen's overall approach to *baojia* it is clear that his enthusiastic endorsement of Wang Yangming's variant is a somewhat wistful one, intended above all to provide an idealistic contrast to the way he sees the system actually working in his own day.[102]

Indeed, at least by the second quarter of the eighteenth century a strong current of literati hostility to *baojia* had taken hold, especially among those whom subsequent historians would identify with *fengjian*-style local autonomy sentiments. A leading example was the poet Yuan Mei, a posthumous biographer of Chen Hongmou with whom the latter corresponded on a variety of subjects, including *baojia* itself. For individuals of Yuan's persuasion *baojia* was an amoral tool of statist intrusion into the natural residential community and the very epitome of bad governance. As a man confronted on a day-to-day basis with the tasks of managing an often truculent population (without benefit of a formal state-run police force), Chen could not afford to fully share Yuan's views, but it is clear that they resonated to a considerable degree with his own.[103]

Representative of Chen's highly restricted appreciation of *baojia* is a letter he wrote to unnamed officials in Sichuan, a text selected for citation in Wei Yuan's *Statecraft Compendium*. Beset as it is by "barbarian and savage" populations and a wave of secret society (Gulu hui) disorder, Chen sees eighteenth-century Sichuan (much like Wang Yangming's sixteenth-century southern Jiangxi) as a site where *baojia* controls can "profitably" be implemented, even though the system "probably has lacked real effect in other provinces."[104] In practicing his office Chen took his own advice. *Baojia* was an instrument for imposing law and order and rather little else. He did not shrink from tightening its controls in situations calling for martial law, such as 1742 Jiangxi, stricken by dearth and in the throes of grain riots. And in ordinary times he found *baojia* functionaries useful for a variety of policing tasks: reporting the presence of bandits, wandering thugs, predatory beggar gangs, and so on. He saw them as agents of the state, handy for carrying out such duties as posting government proclamations in market towns and villages.[105] But there is nothing to suggest Chen's practical faith in *baojia*'s collective self-nurturance functions or, still less, its capacity for stimulating cultural enlightenment. As for its utility in conflict mediation, a memorial Chen submitted in 1758 as Jiangsu governor explicitly called for reforming the system by giving its personnel less to do, decreasing the day-to-day surveillance responsibilities that, in practice, did little but afford them opportunistic and nuisance roles to play in the litigation process.[106]

We have already seen that Chen declares *baojia* personnel ineligible to receive the honorary status of "guest" in the community libationer banquet, noting that this would demean the ritual and compromise its acceptance in local society. For the same reasons he prohibits them from serving in the responsible post of community granary manager (*shezhang*), a position in which the respect of the local community is critical.[107] In several instances, most strikingly in a model examination essay he composed on the problems of subcounty administration (and to which we shall shortly return), Chen makes explicit his reasons for not relying on *baojia* "headmen" for anything other than service as simple lackeys of the state: the system as a whole is not built on genuinely affective kinship or local community ties, and therefore allegiance of the people to the authority of its functionaries can never be very compelling.[108] Truly respected community leadership must be sought elsewhere.

This is not to say, however, that *baojia* personnel have no role in the vision Chen advances of a multifunctional, self-nurturing *xiang*-level community. As Hsiao Kung-ch'uan has pointed out, although the *xiang*, as a more-or-less "natural" unit comprising agrarian villages lying in the service area of a market town, was not conceived by most *baojia* planners as an integral component of that deliberately artificial regimentation system, in practice the two units usually came to coincide, with the preexisting *xiang* serving either as the territorial locus of the *bao* (the largest decimal grouping of the *baojia* system) or as the nonstatutory but assumed next-higher unit encompassing several adjacent *bao*.[109] Chen Hongmou indirectly reflects this assumption by eliding the two terms in the title he employs by far most frequently to refer to *baojia* personnel, "*xiangbao*." This figure epitomizes the public security aspects of *xiang*-level governance. Clear evidence of this comes from Chen's service in Shaanxi in the late 1740s, when he leads a protracted campaign to extend direct state control over the very heart of the *xiang* community, the market town and the periodic market. It is the *xiangbao* within whose jurisdiction the market falls who, with the aid of the individual market's headmen (*jitou* or *huishou*), is made responsible for providing advance notice to the magistrate of market schedules (schedules of all markets in the county are to be permanently posted on the magistrate's office wall) and for reporting all prohibited activities: drunkenness, performance of night operas, and the operation of gambling rackets.[110] If the community libationer rite is the symbolic manifestation of what Chen calls "the linkage of the *xiang* and the state," the *xiangbao*, a locally recruited policing agent, provides for that linkage an element of coercive control.[111]

Despite his willingness to utilize the *xiangbao* for certain government surveillance tasks, however, Chen on balance still tends to view this functionary with considerable skepticism. Lacking the genuine respect of the people, he is prone to abuse his power in a heavy-handed, commandist, and even exploitative fashion. In Chen's 1746 reform of the community granary system in Shaanxi, for example, he identifies the *xiangbao* as the chief culprit in the system's degeneration during his own temporary absence from the province. *Xiangbao* have strong-armed their way into lending operations, where they force loans on unwilling recipients and otherwise manipulate procedures to their own financial advantage; Chen's response is to more fully empower the granary headman (*shezhang*)—a figure of presumably greater legitimacy and public-mindedness— so as to cut the suspect and unreliable *baojia* authorities out of the loop altogether.[112] In the ideal *xiang*-level self-nurturance community Chen envisions, the role of the *xiangbao* is to be highly regulated and circumscribed.

Chen Hongmou repeatedly insisted, with a sincerity that we have no real cause to doubt, that cultivation of individual and communal moral autonomy is both more seemly and more effective than legalist coercion as a means to preserve social order. This same belief had prompted Zhu Xi and like-minded Southern Song reformers largely to reject the state-imposed *baojia* in favor of a more normative, voluntarist, and societally generated alternative, the "community compact" (*xiangyue*).[113] From the twelfth to the seventeenth centuries, both local officials and local elites in various parts of the empire had periodically experimented with the implementation of a diverse variety of institutions bearing this name, usually entailing some kind of communal pledge of good conduct along with regularly scheduled meetings to honor exemplary fulfillment and to confess and admonish transgression.[114] In one of its most heavy-handed maneuvers, however, the early Qing stripped *xiangyue* of any residual reformist luster it may still have enjoyed by transforming it into an imperially appointed gentry lectureship under which the hortatory *Sacred Edict* (*Shengyu*) was compulsorily recited before the local population on a fortnightly basis. Instituted in all localities by the Shunzhi emperor in 1652, and strongly reiterated by Yongzheng in 1724 and 1729, the system rapidly deteriorated still further. The local head of the institution (*yuezheng* or simply *xiangyue*) soon came to be seen as little more than a police lackey and, eventually, in the ultimate debasement, as a tax collector.[115]

Chen Hongmou was painfully aware of this deterioration of *xiangyue* into dysfunctionality. Accordingly, although the law remained on the books, he apparently never made the slightest effort to implement it in any of his provincial jurisdictions. Despite his vigorous campaigns for moral improvement and cultural assimilation on the Yunnan frontier in the 1730s, for example (see Chapter 12), the *xiangyue* system was only adopted for this purpose there a year or so after he departed the province.[116] Following popular usage, Chen occasionally used the term "*xiangyue*" as a casual substitute for "*xiangbao*," in reference to a public security functionary, with no hint whatsoever of voluntarist communal self-improvement. At times he clearly viewed the existing *xiangyue* institution as a nuisance, such as when he decried the practice of personnel by that name exacting bribes from those nominated as community libationer honorees.[117] Indeed, I believe it was largely because of the negative connotations that *xiangyue* had accrued by the early eighteenth century that Chen settled instead on the relatively obscure community libationer rite, the *xiangyin jiuli*, as the symbolic focus of the orthodox and state-responsive community solidarity he sought to cultivate at the level of the *xiang*.

But the fact that Chen had effectively given up on the *xiangyue* institution as a useful instrument of ordering and improving present-day society does not mean that he did not esteem, and nostalgically celebrate, its more decorous past. Three particular historical cases—probably *xiangyue*'s finest moments, in the Qing consensus view—captured his attention. First (and least relevant) among these was the system's locus classicus for most late imperial elites, Zhu Xi's revised version of the "Lü family compact" (Lüshi xiangyue), initially drawn up by the Southern Song official Lü Dajun in 1077. Although the intended recipients of the good deeds promoted in this compact were the coresidents of the *xiang*, the signatories themselves were limited to members of the Lü lineage. Chen Hongmou reprinted the document in his *Sourcebook on Reforming Social Practice*, commenting, "If among the people of a *xiang* there is friendliness, harmonious relations, tolerance, and mutual responsibility, how can local mores be anything but high, and customs anything but proper?"[118] Beyond this endorsement, however, Chen does little to promote the Lü-style compact in his own administrative practice, for to do so would compromise one of its chief appeals: its wholly nongovernmental, voluntarist nature.

This is not the case with Chen's other *xiangyue* models, those promoted in official campaigns at the beginning and end of the sixteenth century by Wang Yangming and

Lü Kun. Wang's effort, known as the "Nan-Gan xiangyue," was instituted by him in endemically violent border areas of southern Jiangxi around 1518. It was designed to complement his *baojia* program of the preceding year and was explicitly identified as a means of extending the reach of the state; the magistrate, Wang noted in his announcement of the program, simply cannot be everywhere and thus needs the active cooperation of local communities and elites in maintaining social order. It also deliberately built on the institution of strong lineage organization, intended as it was to reinforce intralineage discipline while promoting interlineage harmony. The Confucian scheme of values enunciated by the compacts stressed respect for generational elders, as well as mutual assistance within the *xiang* community, both in ritual performance (weddings and funerals) and in matters of material subsistence. The compact featured a remarkably elaborate organizational apparatus: a compact headquarters building (*yuesuo*), monthly plenary meetings, three ledgers of merits and demerits assessed to compact members, and no fewer than seventeen officers with individually specified sets of duties. Chen Hongmou reprinted the text of Wang's "Nan-Gan xiangyue" while he himself was stationed in Jiangxi in the early 1740s. Although he seems to have made no practical effort to resurrect it in the province ("*xiangyue*" in Qing times already carried a quite different statutorily defined meaning), we shall see in a moment how it significantly affected his own initiatives in the area of community organization.[119]

The system of Lü Kun, discussed in Lü's *Shizheng lu* (Record of genuine governance) and implemented during his tenures as Jinan (Shandong) prefect during the 1580s and Shanxi governor in the 1590s, was not, like Wang Yangming's, an intended complement to the *baojia* system but rather a combination of the two. Known appropriately as "*xiangjia*," it was constructed by means of a decimal-group regimentation of households in several nested levels, the *jia*, *li*, and *bao*. Although *xiangjia* was mandated by official authority, considerable precaution was required to shield community members from the anticipated predations of the clerical sub-bureaucracy. Lü's *xiangjia* had many functions. It maintained ledgers of merit and demerit to exhort members to virtuous conduct. It oversaw local elementary education. It sponsored "association granaries" (*huicang*) to aid in members' material subsistence. Reflecting the unsettled times of the late Ming, it directed local militia training. Most notably, it was granted a limited degree of judicial authority over its membership: the imposition of certain punishments (the most severe being expulsion from the community) for commission of crimes not severe enough to demand turning the culprit over to the magistrate.[120]

Chen Hongmou liked Lü Kun's system a great deal. In a model examination essay composed most likely in Jiangxi in the early 1740s Chen extols many aspects of Lü's variant on *xiangyue*, especially its encompassing multifunctionality. His one complaint is the way it is rooted not in natural human groupings but rather in an artificially imposed decimal-group hierarchy. "How much more personally compelling would the system be," he asks, "if it instead were made to coincide with the bonds of common surname" (*tongxing*) and if its leadership were that already possessing the ritual authority conferred by presiding over the ancestral rites?[121] It was precisely this defect that Chen sought to correct in the bold initiative in community ordering he launched in Jiangxi in 1742.

Lineage Self-Government: Chen's Jiangxi Experiment of 1742

In what would become one of the most celebrated acts of his official career Chen undertook in 1742 an experiment to grant lineage headmen in Jiangxi considerable judicial and disciplinary powers over their kinsmen, to be exercised in conjunction with their officiating over the sacrificial rites at the ancestral temple. In so doing he sought to root state power in local society by linking it directly with the institution of the Chinese-style patrilineal family—an institution that, as we have seen, was both mystified as grounded in the heavenly order of things and identified homologically with the properly functioning imperial polity.

"Dwelling together as a family" (*jujia*) was, in the elite consciousness of Chen's day, in and of itself a moral act. The ability to do so successfully demonstrated the moral superiority of the family members because "a family's long-term survival is less a matter of fortuitous circumstances than of its virtue."[122] The larger the number of nuclear units that could continue to "dwell together" and the longer their term of survival, the greater the evident virtue. Families such as that of the Song *lixue* philosopher Lu Xiangshan, which proved capable of "dwelling together undivided for ten generations" (*shishi tongju*), served for Chen and others as cultural ideals.[123] There were any number of material and psychological reasons why this ideal could not be attained by most in practice, however, and Chen in his personal correspondence wrote poignantly about the struggle to sustain the affective, ritual, and ethical aspects of family once the parental hearth and the patrimony had actually been divided among siblings.[124] Yet "dwelling together" as neighbors, at least, ought still to be possible. This, in moral theory, was the origin of the localized lineage group.

The defining element of the lineage was the fourth of Zhu Xi's four family rituals, ancestral sacrifice (*ji*). Participation in the ritual and membership in the lineage were directly equated. The symbolic focus of the lineage group was the ancestral altar or temple at which the sacrifice was conducted (*zongsi*), and the ritual authority to preside over this rite granted the lineage headman (*zuzhang*) wide-ranging influence over other aspects of members' conduct. Lineage solidarity so defined was unassailably virtuous; for an official (or indeed anyone else) to deny or obstruct such activity would constitute an attack on the culture's most basic underpinnings. As Chen declared in a public proclamation in Jiangxi (ironically in the very act of condemning pervasive lineage misconduct): "Requiting one's progenitors for giving one birth is the first precondition for proper human conduct (*rendao*); collecting together as a lineage to worship one's founding ancestor is the usual and proper way to honor one's roots."[125]

Just as Chen worked assiduously throughout his gubernatorial career to preserve the orthodox family unit, so too he consistently supported the principle of lineage organization. He relied, for example, on the presumption of collective liability of lineage members for members' conduct and debt.[126] He also actively supported the creation of well-endowed lineage estates, not merely to finance the maintenance of ancestral temples and the conducting of ancestral rites but also to provide for more mundane collective welfare.[127] (As we saw in Chapter 1, Chen also endowed his lineage's own ancestral estate in his home township.)[128] He cited the following passage from Gu Yanwu, in which that seventeenth-century reformer links lineage estates with the twin goals of ameliorating class conflict and reducing the size of government:

> The reason that peace does not prevail among the people is because of differences in wealth. The poor are often not capable of supporting themselves, and yet the rich are continually fearful of others' demands upon them, and tend to be tightfisted. It is this which gives rise to the mentality of conflict. Confucius once observed that it is not poverty itself which leads to the disaster [of class warfare], but rather inequality.
>
> Now, the implementation of the lineage system is designed to stimulate the basic human impetus to share foodstuffs on the basis of seasonal need, and to foster the collective husbanding of resources to smooth over good and bad years. [When the people adhere to this properly] there will be no need to rely upon government action to care for the destitute, the orphaned, and the ill. When such principles of sharing so as to eliminate poverty are observed, how can resources fail to be adequate? It was for this reason above all that the ancient rulers instituted the lineage system [zong fa].[129]

Along similar lines Gu argued that by increasing the lineage's authority in matters of internal conflict resolution the judicial workload, and hence the requisite size of the bureaucracy, could be reduced; from Chen Hongmou's eighteenth-century perspective, in the midst of a perceived litigation explosion, this alternative was all the more attractive.

Yet as a career field official (unlike Gu) Chen also had daily experience with the negatives associated with lineage power. As vehicles for the mobilization of coercive force, they were routinely involved in collective violence with their neighbors and could even on occasion turn this force against the state, in tax resistance.[130] And as vigorous corporate litigants, they could serve to increase rather than decrease the chronic judicial backlog faced by county magistrates. To reconcile this with the inherent virtue ascribed to kinship organization by the Confucian tradition, Chen worked out an elaborate apologia, relying on a distinction between lineages genuinely constructed on the basis of the dictates of ancestral piety (lianzong) versus those organized for more crudely instrumental purposes of convenience (lianshi). Analogizing the formation of lineages and of factions, he set out his criteria of appropriateness in parallel prose: "Friendships may be formed on the basis of common moral purpose [tongzhi]. Descent groups may be formed on the basis of common surname [tongxing]. But bonds of association must always be predicated on righteous principles. It is wrong to pick one's friends or relatives on an opportunistic basis [shili]."[131] Contemporary scholarship has tended to discount the distinction between "real" and "fictive" kinship ties as a basis for lineage formation, recognizing that all lineages were in some sense artificial constructions in that they employed criteria other than mere blood descent to determine principles of inclusion or exclusion. Yet for Chen and others of his day it seemed feasible to distinguish between those lineages that actually shared a common ancestor and those formed simply on the accident of common surname, and it was tempting in most cases to identify misconduct and opportunism with organizations of the latter type.[132]

Although government action was in practice often called for to clear up the most blatant abuses, the preferred remedy for socially deviant behavior by and within kinship groups was self-policing and the assumption of collective familial responsibility. Image-conscious patriarchs were encouraged to set down "family rules" at both the household (*jiaxun*) and lineage (*zonggui*) levels, and with growing frequency over the late imperial period many in practice did so. In his various moral treatises compiled over the late 1730s and early 1740s Chen Hongmou reprinted with enthusiastic endorsements several examples of such internally generated family rules.[133] Regulation by the kin group itself was considered superior to that by the state for a number of reasons: it was voluntarist rather than coerced, stressed autonomous moral judgment rather than unthinking legalist compliance, and emphasized moral education (*jiao*) rather than punishment. Still more valued than codified self-regulation, of course, was ritual practice. Chen quoted Lü Kun on this score: "Today's prominent families are all fond of promulgating household rules [*jiafa*], but do not give similar emphasis to family ritual. Rules inspire only respect, whereas rituals inspire moral transformation [*hua*]. Rules may motivate out of fear, but rituals motivate out of personal affection [*qin*]."[134] It was precisely this linkage of behavioral discipline with moral autonomy, personal affection, and family and ancestral ritual that Chen sought to institute in his Jiangxi experiment.

In actual social practice increasing formalization of lineage organization was a pervasive empire-wide trend among the Chinese elite from the fifteenth through the eighteenth centuries. A broad spectrum of the leading literati of this era—Qiu Jun, Huang Zuo, Qian Qianyi, Lü Kun, Gu Yanwu, Huang Zongxi, Lu Liuliang, Yao Nai, and a host of lesser fry—both propagandized this movement and (like Chen himself) contributed to the formalization of their own kinship organizations. They compiled genealogies, regularized the assignment of generation-specific names to lineage offspring, constructed lineage halls, set down lineage rules, standardized liturgies for funerals and ancestral rites, and in many cases mobilized resources to accumulate endowment land and other financial assets. In an era of political decadence and class warfare, alien conquest and commercial expansion, there were any number of practical reasons for this spurt of interest in lineage building. These might include the wish to resist assertions of arbitrary state power or (conversely) to compensate for the collapse of effective local-level state functions, to rescue the cultural tradition from the threat of barbarism, to fix or recover the social order and elite privilege in a world of increasing social fluidity, or simply to provide a vehicle for pursuit of collective material interests.[135]

Probably no province of the empire had witnessed a more systematic and effective construction of powerful localized lineages than had Jiangxi. Citing an early Republican-era social survey, Fu Yiling describes what seems to have been a highly typical case, from the West Township (Xixiang) of Yiyang County. Society there was dominated by several large lineage organizations, each of which took the *xiang* as a whole as its "turf." Each had its own lineage rules and disciplined its membership under these. Larger incidents that transcended lineage boundaries were adjudicated by a multilineage council, established at the *xiang* level. The government, at least in the early twentieth century, had little effective power of intervention in lineage conduct.[136]

This was far from a new situation, however. As the work of Robert Hymes has shown, the process of lineage formalization and concerted entrenchment in the affairs of the locality had begun in Jiangxi rather earlier than elsewhere, in the twelfth and thirteenth centuries.[137] During the Ming, lineages reached new heights of power, especially in the province's core area of the Gan River valley, whose society was increasingly dominated by planters of rice for the booming interregional export trade. According to John Dardess, this process occurred in roughly two stages. During the first half of the dynasty the elite drew up registers of genealogical descent in order to organize themselves and their dependents into a province-wide status hierarchy by family pedigree—as it were, a peerage. Then, as social change threatened this hierarchy in the sixteenth century, concerns for exclusivity gave way to those for inclusiveness: The original emphasis on "pure-blood identity" gave way to the drive to establish "new and very large lineage conglomerates." Dardess argues that these new-style kin groups also placed more weight than had their predecessors on corporate economic activity, amassing large amounts of land and other financial resources in their ancestral trusts.[138] The research of Xu Hua'an, however, suggests that such corporate assets were relatively less important in the Qing. Instead, Jiangxi lineages concentrated on securing from the administration recognized territorial "spheres of jurisdiction," including grants of economic rights such as fishing and market monopolies for their members, and also certain juridical rights allowing lineage leaders internally to resolve civil disputes within their jurisdiction and to serve as exclusive proxy for their locality—nonkin as well as kin—in litigation heard by official courts.[139] It was also in the early Qing that lineage dominance in Jiangxi was extended beyond the core areas into the highlands along the provincial borders, newly brought under cultivation by migrant populations that organized themselves for mutual protection into (often transparently fictive) common-descent groups.[140] By the time Chen Hongmou arrived in the province in the 1740s, his detailed investigations turned up over 4,200 lineage temples, whose combined membership was said to include more than half of all Jiangxi households.[141]

One unusually pronounced feature of lineage-building as it developed in Jiangxi, and one that had particular appeal to Chen, was its zeal for self-policing through the instrument of formally articulated regulatory codes. As both Dardess and Hua note, during the later Ming and Qing, lineages increasingly came to arrogate to themselves powers of internal discipline, sometimes even going so far as to establish lineage militia (*tuan*) for enforcement and self-defense. Newly promulgated or revised lineage rules made this judicial self-reliance explicit. For example, one code, set down in the Wanli era by Pengze County *jinshi* Wang Yanshou and extolled by Governor Chen in his 1742 *Sourcebook on Reforming Social Practice*, contained the following provision:

> Conflicts within a single household are to be handled by the househead. Accusations between lineage members should not be brought to the yamen, but rather the lineage head will appoint a branch-head to hear and resolve the case, and impose appropriate sanctions. Conflicts with other lineages, when they are unusually serious, may be brought to the officials. But smaller disputes such as those over marriage contracts or land rights will be handled by the lineage head nominating a negotiator to meet with counterparts from other lineages for mutual resolution. This will achieve harmony with our neighbors from within the *xiang*.[142]

The actual story of Chen's experiment in empowering lineage heads in Jiangxi unfolds in layers and reveals a complex mix of strategies, goals, and bureaucratic assumptions, as well as Chen's own shifting views of what was feasible and what was not. The governor first announced his new policies in July in a directive to local-level subordinates.[143] He framed his directive in the language of moral instruction (*jiaohua*) that was dear to his social project generally and at the same time placed his policy initiative on the neo-Confucian high ground. It was the duty of lineage leaders, as generational seniors, to institute the correct teachings (*lijiao*) among their dependents and to guide them in the practice of civilized conduct (*huamei, huadao*). These duties accrued to government officials as well, to be sure, but as a practical matter officials could not be everywhere at once and so needed to delegate responsibility to persons who were both on the local scene and invested by the community itself with authority and respect. Chen wanted this delegation done in a formalized way, with lineage headmen (*zuzhang*) issued written patents of authorization (*paizhao*) by the county magistrate. (Characteristically, he paid close attention to the development of a standardized form for this purpose.) And although "moral education" was theoretically distinct from and superior to the more mundane matter of law enforcement, Chen did acknowledge candidly in passing that lineage heads were now being made into agents (*chengti*) for upholding state law (*guanfa*). Lineage leaders were enjoined in the directive to report major criminal activity to the magistrate and to mediate disputes within the lineage and between their and other lineages, but the really radical feature of Chen's initiative was the power granted to leaders to "discipline" (*yueshu*) their constituents. Lineage members guilty not simply of minor deviant behavior but also of explicitly criminal violations—first-time perpetrators of less than capital crimes—were to be reported by their branch head (*fangzhang*) to the lineage headman, who would judge them in front of the assembled lineage elders at the ancestral altar, normally in conjunction with the conduct of the ancestral rites, and sentence them to lineage-administered punishment.

Just how original was Chen's 1742 action? "*Zuzhang*" was of course a common-speech term referring to the acknowledged, internally selected head of a lineage. The *Ming Code* of 1397 had granted legal status to this position and identified its duties solely as those of presiding over the ancestral rites. Gradually over the course of the early Qing, however, imperial edicts came implicitly to recognize certain duties and responsibilities for the *zuzhang* in the area of "instructing and training" (*jiaoxun*) his constituents, in some cases holding him legally culpable for their misdeeds. In 1726 the Yongzheng emperor decreed that lineage leaders who did not apprehend and turn over to the magistrate (*baoguan*) criminal violators within their lineage would be themselves liable for punishment in the same way as would be *baojia* or other public security functionaries who neglected their duties in this regard.[144] Yongzheng the next year went even further, explicitly authorizing lineage leaders to *execute* members who had previously been convicted of criminal offenses in official courts but whose subsequent failure to reform proved grossly embarrassing to the lineage as a whole. (A horrified Qianlong had rescinded this authority in 1740.)[145] Chen Hongmou's granting to lineage heads formal powers to discipline and punish their deviant members may thus be seen as a step in a longer-term evolution of Qing central government policy. The way he did it, however, tapped into much broader trends in the evolution of late imperial political thought.

In the context of Chen Hongmou's other initiatives of the time, it is clear that his July move was part of his larger project to create a ritually grounded, self-reliant local community at the level of the subcounty *xiang*, a community that would still be accountable to the formal organs of state. Chen worked very creatively to integrate Jiangxi lineages into the *xiang* community and to merge their leadership with that of the *xiang* community as a whole. Materially, for instance, he sought to get them actively involved in the community granary system he was promoting at the same time; he urged Jiangxi lineages to contribute surplus rent collections from their endowment lands to these community institutions and, where possible, to establish their own *shecang* under lineage-head management.[146] The notion of establishing community granaries at the level of the *xiang* was one Chen had borrowed most directly from Lü Kun, but whereas Lü had effected the linkage between granary and *xiang* community by utilizing as intermediary the *xiangyue* community compact, Chen Hongmou knew only too well that the debased *xiangyue* institution of his own day could not serve so lofty a purpose. So instead, as we have seen, he had turned to resurrection of the community libationer rite (*xiangyin jiuli*) to provide the aura of ritual propriety and moral voluntarism he believed requisite to his project and to honor local exemplars of community-mindedness. Having committed himself (far more explicitly than Lü Kun) to incorporating *lineage* leadership into his *xiang*-level self-nurturance infrastructure, Chen therefore advised county magistrates that in selecting community libationer honorees they could find no better candidates than particularly responsive lineage headmen from within the *xiang*.[147]

All of this leads to a view of Chen's July initiative, investing lineage heads with quasi-governmental authority for judging violations of law and imposing criminal punishments, as a remarkable act of empowerment of an indigenous local leadership. This is the way it has often been interpreted by historians, and with reasonable justification.[148] But another way of looking at Chen's action would lead to a more "statist" view of his motives, seeing his initiative as directed less at empowerment than at reining in an existing and troublesome elite. Few later writers, Qing or modern, have noticed that some four months prior to Chen's July directive, in his one and only public proclamation (*shi*) on the lineage issue in his new provincial tenure, Chen issued a scathing broadside against the "evil practices" (*exi*) of Jiangxi kin associations.[149] Included in his list of abuses was the familiar attack on conglomerate common-surname groups without demonstrable common descent (*tongxing buzong*), but also included were more wide-ranging charges against even the most unassailably blood-tied groups. Among these was their involvement in violent lineage feuds (*xiedou*) (something he had noted and condemned even earlier on the provincial frontiers),[150] their litigation practices, and other bullying activities directed against neighboring households. Even more, however, Chen railed against the incidence of lineage headmen abusing their position to exploit their own membership, diverting what were properly public or collective (*gong*) assets for private (*si*) enrichment. Significantly, Chen identified this as an instance of the dysfunction perennially associated by statecraft reformers with the clerical sub-bureaucracy, *zhongbao*, or "engorgement at a middle level (between state and society)."[151] In his March proclamation the governor pointedly observed that it was not only fully appropriate for a lineage to remove and replace a *zuzhang* who proved unworthy of the post, but it was incumbent upon them to do so.

Moreover, part of the governor's intent in trying to merge lineage leadership into a multifunctional *xiang*-level societal self-nurturance structure, it is clear, was precisely an effort to circumscribe the expanding territorial jurisdictions claimed in practice by powerful lineage organizations. For example, in his July directive and elsewhere Chen rails against the recent emergence in Jiangxi of large corporate kinship associations having their headquarters in county seats.[152] It was not simply the aggrandizing behavior of such groups (their aggressive litigation practices, for instance) that he found awkward, although he condemned this vociferously, but more basically their size and scale. And it was not their urban locus (in county seats) per se that was the problem but rather that by locating there they implicitly claimed the county as a whole as their cachement area. For Chen Hongmou, I would suggest, this represented a direct challenge to the state, whose bailiwick the county was. The lineage was properly a *sub*county entity that ought to be confined to, and strongly identified with, its resident *xiang*.[153]

It is noteworthy that even in Chen's July directive, whereas the thrust of the proposed policy was to grant lineage headmen enhanced disciplinary powers over their membership, the text both opened and closed with condemnations *not* of individual miscreants within lineages but rather of the rampant misconduct of lineages as a whole toward outsiders and of lineage leaders toward their rank and file. In his conclusion Chen strongly implied that what he hoped to do was to turn these leaders to more socially and ritually acceptable deportment by the very act of co-opting them as state agents. The optimism of such an approach would soon be challenged by others, causing some degree of reconsideration on the part of Chen Hongmou himself.

This reconsideration was signaled in Chen's second—and even more famous—directive on lineage headmen, issued after a four-month interval in November 1742.[154] In his July directive Chen had noted, characteristically, that conditions in various localities differed, and consequently he invited local officials to respond to his initiative with comments as to how its implementation should be modified to accord with the realities of their own jurisdiction. Although none of their responses survive or are specifically referred to by Chen, it is clear that many Jiangxi prefects and magistrates did respond and that the governor's second directive took account of their input.

Chen's July directive had referred throughout to *zuzhang*—that is, ritually defined and internally selected lineage leaders;[155] these were the individuals granted judicial authority over lineage members. His November directive did not rescind these powers; indeed, it reiterated them nearly verbatim. But it also specified the appointment of another, different set of lineage functionaries, to be known as "*zuzheng*." The term "*zuzheng*" had first been used in Yongzheng's previously discussed 1726 edict, making lineage leaders culpable for criminal offenses of their members. It remained a legal category in the revised *Qing Code* of 1740, which made Yongzheng's edict a matter of statute. In neither case was it clearly differentiated from "*zuzhang*," and there was evident slippage between the two terms even in central government sources.[156] One leading student of Qing lineage law has presumed that, in practice, the two titles were nearly always held by the same individual.[157]

But in Chen Hongmou's November directive, discussing as it does the duties of
both the *zuzhang* and the *zuzheng*, the distinction between the two posts seems unusually clear. Although the *zuzheng* were, like the *zuzhang*, expected to be men of substance
and respect, their selection was by the local official, and their authority was by virtue of
this appointment alone. The *zuzheng*'s duties were simply those of surveillance and reporting of deviant lineage members—quite possible the *zuzhang* himself—to the local
administration. They enjoyed no authority to impose disciplinary sanctions in conjunction with the ancestral rites, with which they presumably had no formal connection. This November directive can be seen, then, as something of a retreat on Chen's
part, albeit a modest one. It was certainly innovative in its own right, in its attempt to
implant state functionaries within the lineage, but it lacked the optimism of Chen's first
initiative, which assumed the possibility of a significant congruence of interest between
the state and the indigenous lineage elite.

By fixing on the title "*zuzheng*" (and its sometime substitute "*zuyue*"), Chen was
drawing explicit parallels to the *baozheng* and the *xiangyue*, as well as to the *baojia* and
community compact institutions in which such functionaries figured. This is both surprising and significant. It is surprising because, as we have seen, Chen in general disparaged the utility for community purposes of both institutions, and especially *baojia*.
In his own July directive, indeed, Chen had offered an impassioned argument for the
relative superiority of lineage headmen as instruments for enforcing social order in
Jiangxi. People would respect the authority of lineage elders where they would not that
of *baojia* functionaries because in the former case the authority was reinforced by affective ties of kinship that were fundamental to the human condition (*renqing*).[158]
Likewise, in his contemporaneous campaigns to promote both community granaries
and the community libationer rite in Jiangxi, he specified that *baojia* functionaries be
excluded from consideration either as granary managers or libationer honorees because, as perceived state lackeys, they ipso facto could not be respected local citizens.

In Chen's model civil service examination question regarding local control (discussed earlier), he returns specifically to this theme.[159] He begins by discussing the classical origins of the ancestral temple (*zongsi*) institution and its endorsement by Zhu Xi
and other luminaries. Its proliferation in Jiangxi today, therefore, is laudable. Even the
corporate financial power of Jiangxi lineages is in itself beyond reproach because it has
its antecedent in the ancestral trust (*miaoyuan*) system of the Tang. Yet we all know,
Chen adds, that human morality (*renxin*) has steadily declined since olden days, so the
abuses we now find rampant should not be cause for surprise. (The cliché of moral decline should not be taken as a literal representation of Chen's historical logic; what he
is really saying here is, "Now let's discuss the applicability of this ideal model to the real
world.") The problem then becomes, What sort of institutional controls will allow us to
salvage the desirable features of the classically prescribed lineage while allowing the
least possibility for social dysfunction?

Chen then proposes to his student audience an alternative model of social organization, Lü Kun's so-called *xiangjia* system. Lü's scheme, as we have seen, incorporated
elements of social welfare and public education into a *xiang*-level umbrella organization for societal self-nurturance. It entailed banding together nonrelated households

into *baojia*-style mutual responsibility groups but with an element of voluntarist agency added through the superimposition of a moral compact (*xiangyue*).[160] The weakness Chen sees in this otherwise noble program, as I have already noted, is the absence of affective compulsions to reinforce normative (*xiangyue*) and coercive (*baojia*) ones; the remedy he suggests is to graft this arrangement onto yet one further mode of organization, the agnatic lineage ritually united through the ancestral temple. Can such a composite institution work? This is the question he poses for his hypothetical audience of examination candidates and also the question he sought to discover for himself in 1742 Jiangxi.

In practice, alongside the social process of lineage proliferation, Jiangxi in the decades prior to Chen Hongmou's arrival as governor had seen a concerted government effort to enforce greater compliance with the statutes on *baojia* regimentation. Aimed most directly at such footloose populations as the "shed people" (*pengmin*) of the highlands and river boatmen (increasingly attracted to an alarming heterodox sect, the Luojiao), but applied to core areas of lineage power as well, this had been an initiative of the Yongzheng emperor and his personal appointees to the province.[161] Among these there was no more dogged enthusiast of *baojia* than Ling Qiu, named Jiangxi provincial judge by Yongzheng in 1733 and still in that post a decade later under Chen's governorship. Fortunately for the historian, Ling Qiu left a fairly candid memoir of his lengthy Jiangxi tenure that sheds light on Chen's 1742 policies and their reception.[162]

Ling had long confronted the thorny problem of how to implement *baojia* in areas of Jiangxi dominated by powerful local lineages. In his view it was naive to entrust a lineage with establishing *baojia* headmanships internally on its own, expecting it to do so in conformity with the interests of the state and of the larger society. Equally foolhardy, though, would be to proceed blindly and appoint one's own *baojia* functionaries as if the lineage were not there at all. The solution Ling had gradually worked out was to rely on two parallel social-control apparatuses at once: the existing lineage heads (*zuzhang*) *plus* a state-appointed *baojia* headman (*baozheng*) who was a neighbor of the lineage but not of their surname. Ling Qiu could not have been thrilled when, after having patiently worked this out, Chen Hongmou, whom he refers to only as "the governor" (*xiantai*) (Chen never mentions Ling at all), showed up proposing his idealistic scheme of investing the unreliable lineage leaders with all sorts of unprecedented powers. According to Ling, it was a good thing that Chen eventually thought it prudent to assign Ling the task of implementing this. It was then that Ling came up with the compromise of providing a check on the *zuzhang* by means of a competing authority selected from within the lineage, the *zuzheng* or *zuyue*. In selected cases, Ling points out, an unusually compliant lineage head might himself be assigned this position (the governor would probably have liked this), but in ordinary practice he would not.[163]

Chen Hongmou's Jiangxi experiment enjoyed a lively history long after his departure from the province in 1744. In imperial law and policy its impact was a modest one. The Qianlong emperor, who seems to have tolerated Chen's initiatives on a provincial basis, went so far in 1757 as to make the appointment of *zuzheng*—individuals within each lin-

eage with sharply delimited responsibilities for surveillance and reporting of miscreants—a matter of broader imperial policy. But a 1745 proposal on the part of Chen's
sometime mentor and patron, Grand Secretary Sun Jiagan, which would have nation-
alized Chen's bolder policy of granting formal judicial and disciplinary powers to "natural" lineage leaders, was not approved; and a similar proposal a quarter century later
from Censor Zhang Guangxian was vehemently rejected by the throne on the grounds
that *zuzhang* were demonstrably far more the problem than the solution to local social
disorder.[164]

Chen Hongmou himself had originally identified Hunan, Fujian, and Shaanxi as
the provinces that, like Jiangxi, were characterized by a high incidence of concentrated
dwelling by large corporate lineages. Yet in his service as Hunan governor in 1755 and
1762, and as Shaanxi governor four times in the decades of the 1740s and 1750s, he
never opted to propose anything similar to what he had during his novice governorship
in Jiangxi. Nor did he suggest anything like it during his 1758 tour in Guangdong, the
province that scholars today would probably associate most strongly with local lineage
power. In Jiangsu, where Chen in 1759 launched a much-celebrated reform campaign
for marriages, funerals, and a wide range of other local customary practices, he scarcely
mentioned lineage headmen at all.[165] Only in Fujian, where Chen served in 1753, and
where he saw the situation as unusually similar to that in Jiangxi, did he again suggest
formally granting lineage leaders internal disciplinary powers, although he sharply restricted this to matters involving interlineage feuds (*xiedou*). The emperor approved,
and subsequent Fujian governors from time to time cited Chen's precedent to revive
the policy but without significant long-term success.[166]

The reason Chen never again after 1742 invested similar faith and energy in a campaign to empower lineage headmen had less to do with a change of political philosophy on his part than with his growing recognition that in Jiangxi itself the policy had
not worked. In 1764 incoming Jiangxi governor Fude memorialized that the situation
with regard to ancestral temples was grossly out of hand. Reiterating Chen Hongmou's
attack on kinship organizations of presumptuously grand scale, but indicating further
deterioration of the situation from Chen's day, he wrote, "Jiangxi people are in the
habit of building ancestral halls [*sitang*]. If they did this on the scale of the *xiang*, or
even perhaps of the county, it would be fine. But instead they gather all of the same surname from throughout the prefecture, or even from the entire province, and collect
funds to build a hall in the prefectural or provincial capital." Such institutions were not
really "lineages" at all in Fude's view but simply large political-economic cartels. Their
primary purpose was transparently the pursuit of civil litigation, financed by the funds
of the endowment trust and initiated in the name of the corporate estate. In this activity
the supposedly ritually constituted lineage headmen were doubly despicable, first
for contriving such socially destructive schemes to begin with and second because
they routinely squandered group assets pursuing litigation battles in their own private
interest.[167]

Fude did not argue for the prohibition of such organizations generally, and he was
silent about the specific policy innovations of Chen Hongmou two decades earlier, but
Chen was already well aware of the implications. Indeed, shortly before Fude wrote his

widely publicized memorial, Chen himself admitted the failure of his earlier policies in a letter to a colleague, Yang Puyuan:

> Long ago, I set up in Jiangxi a code of regulations making the lineage head responsible for moral training [*huadao*] and imposing discipline [*yueshu*] on lineage members. . . . It was intended to have a long-lasting effect. Now, however, because the lineages have been engaged in illicit activities, the ancestral temples have one after the other been dismantled [by the government], and their genealogical registers seized. Because the lineage estates [*sitang*] in both town and country engage so routinely in provocative incidents, it has proven impossible to fill the post of lineage headman, and those men that are willing to accept this post are simply no good. This gradually worsening situation has destroyed the good institution that existed in the past.[168]

Remarkably, however, this acknowledged failure by no means deprived Chen's 1742 experiment of its subsequent exemplary, even iconic, status. It was regularly invoked by field administrators seeking to implement similar measures in their own jurisdictions.[169] But more important, it seems to have exerted a compelling fascination on later Qing reformers and political thinkers. In their landmark 1826 *Statecraft Compendium*, in which Chen Hongmou assumes a major presence, Wei Yuan and He Changling gave it considerable attention.[170] In doing so, however, they fell far short of uncritical endorsement. They printed together as a group Chen Hongmou's directive of November 1742 (significantly, his more conservative, amended initiative), followed by Fude's cautionary tale of the outcome twenty years later, followed in turn by Chen's letter to Yang Puyuan conceding defeat.[171] Characteristically, Wei and He allow their readership to make up its own mind on the issue, but their implication is fairly clear: Chen's was a noble and right-minded initiative that was perhaps too idealistic to succeed in practice. A decade later Xu Dong was not so cautious. In his 1837 *Baojia shu* (Manual of *baojia* organization), a companion volume to his influential *Muling shu* (Manual for county magistrates), he reprinted Chen's *first*, more optimistic directive of July 1742, without any qualifying context or comment.[172] The fascination with the kind of localized lineage empowerment Chen had experimented with was patently on the rise.

The most celebrated and influential glorification of Chen Hongmou's Jiangxi experiment came at the hands of Feng Guifen (1809–74), the anti-Taiping counterinsurgency theoretician of the 1860s and 1870s.[173] For Feng, Chen's scheme (which he almost certainly learned of through the medium of Wei Yuan's *Statecraft Compendium*) had gotten the formula for social order precisely correct. Political empowerment of lineage heads both accorded with the classical ritual prescriptions of the *zongfa* (core-line principle) and provided the answers to contemporary social needs. There were of course in practice instances of abusive lineages and lineage heads (Feng cites Fude's 1764 memorial on this score), but Chen Hongmou had found the proper corrective for this in overlaying the existing lineage leadership with a more politically reliable *baojia* one. (Conversely, for Feng, the reason *baojia* proved so generally ineffectual in his day was the failure to overlay it with lineage-based compulsions of ritual and affection.) He applauded as well the further overlay of these with the voluntarist-tinged structure of a "lineage compact" (*zuyue*), which Chen had inherited from Lü Kun.

Echoing Chen's persistent theme that the responsibilities of leadership included the material well-being (*yang*) as well as the moral rectification (*jiao*) of the led, Feng picked up on his suggestion that the reconstituted lineage be made the basis for establishment of community granaries (*shecang*); as a man of his own more militarized times, he went well beyond Chen in proposing that they also provide a structure for militia (*tuanlian*) organization. Feng's rhetoric looked forward as well to the corporatist nation-building efforts of the early twentieth century. When the *zongfa* prevailed in the world, he argued, the people naturally cohered into viable social groups (*minju*); since it fell into neglect they have become fragmented and scattered (*minsan*). By empowering lineage leadership in the way Chen Hongmou had done, we can provide the building block for eventual grouping of the population into a powerful and integrated nation-state (*ju zhi yu guo*).[174]

Feng Guifen ultimately had to acknowledge that Chen's experiment had failed, but he attributed this failure to the built-in evils of the Qing bureaucratic system, which Feng, like others in the *fengjian* tradition, had long decried: Chen had been rotated out of Jiangxi too quickly, and the bureaucratic time-servers who succeeded him lacked the vision and energy to see his project through to fulfillment. Chen himself, of course, never made such a charge, seeing instead the government assault on Jiangxi lineage power in the 1750s and 1760s as a regrettable necessity. But, writing in the wake of the Taiping challenge to Confucian orthodoxy and with the Western "other" an unprecedented visible alternative, Feng Guifen held a far more hopeful view of lineage empowerment—and a correspondingly less charitable view of the Qing state—than that arrived at a century earlier by Chen Hongmou.

Statecraft Direct and Indirect

In his approach to governance Chen Hongmou was concerned above all that as much as humanly possible be done to "order the world," a notion he defined in a broadly encompassing way to include virtually all aspects of material and cultural life. He was far less concerned with the question of just who ought to do this work, the bureaucratic state or the local community. The test was not one of propriety per se—Chen was not overanxious, as were public-minded Confucians of other eras, about the dehumanizing effects of mechanistic laws and institutions—but instead one of practical utility in getting the job done.

In Chen's practice of office he fixed on the subcounty, market-centered, quasi-communal unit of the *xiang*—the meeting point between state and society—as a key site where this world ordering might effectively be achieved. He thus experimented repeatedly with ways of energizing this site for his activist purposes. Again, his flexibility about means is striking. On the one hand, Chen fiddled with a variety of ways to staff this site with a regular bureaucrat—in effect, to install a *xiangguan* (a solution that had been formally rejected by the throne). On the other hand, he strove even more energetically to establish multifunctional community self-nurturance institutions and leadership at the same level. At one point in the 1740s he toyed with the idea of reconciling these two strategies by promoting certain indigenous *xiang*-level leaders—those who had accumulated years of creditable service as, say, a community granary or community compact head—into a *xiangguan*-like formal official post. This was a favored approach, Chen suggested, of a segment of reformist literati (those whom we today might associate with the *fengjian* school). But he tellingly rejected this proposal, as had Yongzheng in 1729, as ultimately representing too great a compromise of the principles of bureaucratic governance, principles that had demonstrated to Chen's clear satisfaction their overall workability.[175]

Chen's faith in the superior utility of "natural" human groupings as instruments for ordering the world was sorely tested by his failed experiment in 1742 Jiangxi to appropriate for such purposes the *xiangzu*, the lineage structure centered on the *xiang*-level ancestral temple. But if the specific lesson learned from this experiment (learned by Chen himself but lost on certain of his nineteenth-century admirers) was that powerful lineage heads were not tractable enough for co-option into this *xiang*-level collegial leadership group, he never lost faith in the more basic project of which it was a part.

Chen was aware of, and sought to minimize, the heavy-handed coercive presence of the state in a properly functioning human society. We see this in his persistent attacks on burdensome requisitioning of goods and services (*pailei*), in his shunning of price controls and other forms of economic dirigisme, in his repeated complaints about over-regulation in general, and in his skepticism about the utility of *baojia* regimentation and patently state-fabricated *xiangyue* compacts. He preferred the softer (and less compromised) community libationer ritual as a means of undergirding his *xiang*-level leadership and communal self-nurturance mechanisms. Yet he retained an abiding confidence in the value of state activism, a belief that the state could and should be an instrument of socioeconomic improvement and moral guidance for the population. Inhabited as it properly was by moral men and good officials, it was less something to fear than something to rely on. The greater scale, resources, and perspective of the state apparatus, vis-à-vis local society, were powerful assets to be creatively drawn on—*provided* that its responsiveness to local differentiation (including local "public opinion") was not lost in the process. Chen's state was also to be maximally efficient, and if this meant in certain instances state expansion and intervention (exemplified by his *xingchu* campaigns in Shaanxi and elsewhere), he could certainly live with that.

This attitude was possible only because of Chen Hongmou's unshaken belief in the claim of the state to be the effective repository of the people's interests. In the last half-millennium of imperial China, it was perhaps only in the middle decades of the eighteenth century that a man of Chen's Mencian populism and deep *lixue* moralism could believe this with such confidence.

CHAPTER 12

Civilization

PERHAPS THE SINGLE CENTRAL ELEMENT of eighteenth-century elite consciousness was the assumption of a personal and cultural identity as "civilized" human beings. Civilization is what "we," and only "we," have. It is what "we" are. This civilization is not an a priori fact, nor is its achievement an easy task. Rather, it is the product of a long, arduous process of human and cultural evolution. It may be compromised at any time (mid-Qing observation of the conduct of Han settlers on the frontier—their suscepti-bility to reversion to "savagery"—only reinforced this point). Consequently, it must be continuously reproduced through an ongoing process of personal moral uplift and social regeneration, the civilizing process known most often as *hua* (transformation or enlightenment).

As we have amply seen in Part 1 of this book, for Chen Hongmou and others like him one's own achievement of *hua* was a task that demanded strenuous and unflagging moral effort (*gongfu*). But, far more routinely, *hua* was something to which elite adult males subjected others less enlightened than themselves: generational or social inferi-ors, women, and persons and groups on the margins of Han culture. This was the process known as *jiaohua* (instructing and transforming or, more simply, "civilizing"). *Jiaohua* was an ancient idea—the term dates at least to the third century B.C.—and an enduringly central one; the mission to civilize in this way was in every era foremost in the self-identity of what Yang Nianqun has recently termed "the *jiaohua* literati" (*jiao-hua zhi ru*).[1] The routine process of civilizing others gave meaning to one's own exis-tence; it is only a slight stretch to say that one's evangelical zeal was the key to one's own personal salvation.

Under the rubric of the equally enduring political ideology of the "kingly way" (*wangdao*), moreover, the mission to conduct *jiaohua* was essential as well to the ruler or the state; performing this function effectively was both a political imperative and the most reliable index of good governance.[2] It was one of the most basic ways, if not the most basic, by which the state and its official-elite agents sought to "order the world." (It was for this reason, of course, that He Changling and Wei Yuan devoted no fewer

406

than sixteen chapters of their 1826 *Statecraft Compendium* to questions of how to enforce proper ritual performance.) This was no less true under the Qing empire of the so-called Manchus than it had been under earlier Chinese dynasties. The Qing's most basic constitutional statement, the Kangxi emperor's 1670 *Sacred Edict* (Shengyu) put the purpose of "elevating local social practice" (*hou fengsu*) at the forefront of the regime's goals.[3] In practical terms, of course, given the state's limited coercive resources relative to the scale of the polity it proposed to rule, "governance by moral instruction" (*zhengjiao*) was necessarily a basic strategy of practical administration.

In the eighteenth century there were reasons why this civilizing mission might seem even more urgent than it had before. The more intensive interaction with non-Han populations during that era, stemming in the first instance from population movements outward (along the frontiers) and upward (into previously neglected highlands) in the increasingly desperate search for new arable land, both reminded Qing official elites of the reality of less "civilized" modes of life and raised the disconcerting specter of cultural relativism. Qing political pretensions to universal empire, especially under the Yongzheng emperor's credo of cultural homogenization (expressed in his *Dayi juemi lu*), only gave added impetus to programs of "civilization" (that is, cultural assimilation, or *huayi*), which in turn suggested greater attention to civilizing or socializing processes in the heartland as well.

Chen Hongmou understood the instrumental value of the civilizing mission, but like his European contemporaries undertaking the "white man's burden" in Africa, Asia, and the New World, he also had a secure and sanguine faith in the righteousness of his purpose. Distributing hundreds of copies of his own cultural-reformist hand-books throughout his Jiangxi jurisdiction in 1742, he announced, "In the task of governance, the mission of *jiaohua* assumes first priority."[4] His own sense of personal mission in this regard, indeed, was clearly quite a bit deeper than that of most of his colleagues. He wrote repeatedly throughout his career of his personal duty to "transform and guide" (*huadao*) local populations and to "transform the people and perfect social practice" (*huamin chengsu*).[5] Routinely coupling this with the imperative to improve the people's material life—his oft-repeated dual goal of *jiaoyang* (instructing and nourishing)—Chen saw the two as coequal in importance and inseparable in practice. This is nowhere more clearly brought out than in his campaigns in 1744–45 Shaanxi and elsewhere to assess "beneficial and harmful characteristics of each locality" (*difang libi*) and "encourage the good and reprove the bad" (*quanshan cheng'e*). In such drives material factors (cropping systems, granaries, irrigation and transport infrastructures, fiscal matters) and cultural ones (interpersonal relations, family systems, wedding and funeral ceremonies, popular religious practices) were given undifferentiated treatment, as parts of a single, holistic vision of the well-functioning society.[6]

Kai-wing Chow has distinguished between two approaches to the matter of *jiaohua* practiced by late imperial elites: "didacticism," or the attempt to enlighten the population by means of education and normative appeals, and "ritualism," a more pessimistic strategy that, despairing of the capacity of the masses to respond to moral-rational argumentation, advocated instead insisting on unthinking behavioral compliance via ritual. Chow sees the didactic strategy as typical of sixteenth- and seventeenth-century elites (Lü Kun and Chen Zilong, for instance) but argues that by the eighteenth it had largely given way to the latter, an emphasis on ritual propriety being one factor that united both Hanxue classical philologists and their Songxue opponents.[7] If this be the case (and Chow is quite persuasive), Chen proves exceptional to this trend by giving roughly equal attention to both approaches. He was as concerned as any of his contemporaries with implanting proper ritual observances on the social landscape, yet no one was more devoted to cranking out didactic treatises, fostering mass education, and otherwise "reaching" (*tong*) a population that, he steadfastly argued, was by nature moral, rational, and therefore educable.[8] In this chapter we will look in turn at Chen's practice of these twin strategies—the didactic and the ritual—undertaken in pursuit of the civilizing mission.

Education

The task of instructing (*jiao*) the population was central to Chen Hongmou's sense of purpose. Throughout his adult life he was extraordinarily active in founding and patronizing schools, designing curricula, producing teaching materials, and pondering pedagogical theory. On the last of these he had very definite ideas. A principal goal of education, to be sure, was to cultivate "talent" (*rencai*) of potential use for recruitment into the ranks of officialdom, but this was decidedly secondary to that of "civilizing the people and perfecting customs" (*huamin chengsu*). As early as 1729, Chen announced his views in a policy question he composed for the Shanxi provincial examinations: "*Jiaohua* is the source of proper cultural practice. Talented men are the foundation of proper governance. And the schools are where talented men are produced and cultural change is effected."[9] As part of its mission to "shepherd the people" (*mumin*) and "promote civilization" (*huadao*), the responsibility for providing education fell squarely and inescapably on the state.[10]

"If we want to draw talented individuals out of every hamlet and alleyway," Chen wrote, "we must reach them first when they're very small."[11] In "nurturing rectitude" (*yangzheng*), as well, "the youngest age is the most important." For both purposes familiarization with written characters should begin as soon after birth as possible; at age seven (eight *sui*, three years younger than that specified in imperial directives) the child was ready to attend formal school. And whereas Chen's urge to "reach" the people didactically justified his use of the vernacular, picture books, and doggerel verse when necessary, in elementary schooling nothing less than classical literacy was the goal; he cited Lü Kun's maxim that the most effective way to get someone to comprehend moral principle was to cultivate his or her ability to read written texts (*shizu mingli*).[12]

Chen's educational views were most remarkable for their radical inclusiveness. If education is truly to be a useful vehicle for transforming and civilizing the population, he insists, it must be applied universally, and he therefore takes as his goal no less than "mass literacy training" (*guangxing jiaodu*).[13] Inasmuch as all persons are fundamentally educable, we must be guided by the *Analects*' injunction, "In education, make no class distinctions" (*youjiao wulei*), a hoary dictum to which all give lip service but in which Chen adamantly believes.[14] Throughout his long career Chen confronts many challenges to his faith in universal educability and in each instance replies that no exception is allowable. This guiding principle includes the disadvantaged: the poor (Chen's state in educational policy is clearly an instrument of redistribution) and the less intelligent (Chen acknowledges differences in natural ability and, indeed, advises the need for tracking and vocational training but insists on the necessity of basic literacy instruction for all). Again citing Lü Kun, Chen decries the general practice of limiting education to the wealthy (*fugui*) or the gifted (*kejia*).[15] It includes also the marginalized: women (see below) and non-Chinese conquest populations (there is no local culture, Han or non-Han, that cannot be transformed, he argues, and no member of that culture who cannot be educated).[16] And it pointedly includes the deviant, actual or presumed: criminals (by virtue of their basic humanity, they may be rehabilitated via study) and the culturally abominated yamen clerks.[17]

Chen's principle of universal educability is rooted in his beliefs in *tianliang* (heavenly endowed natural goodness) and *liangzhi* (inherent rationality and virtue). Given the alarming way the latter doctrine was deployed by late Ming populist followers of Wang Yangming, however, Chen must insist that inherent rationality is not enough. Rational thought must be refined by conscientious and continual textual study.[18] Just as all human beings are obligated to partake in moral-directed study (*tianxia wu ren bu-dang wu xue*), so too is the state obligated to facilitate this study on the part of all. Although he would hardly have stated it in this way, Chen Hongmou is in essence arguing for a universal human right to educational opportunity—albeit of a prescribed, orthodox curriculum.

Throughout his long official career Chen was a vigorous founder, rehabilitator, and reformer of schools. I refer not to the formal government-run prefectural and county schools (*fuxue, xianxue*), which had long been eviscerated of any real pedagogical vitality and whose role in local society (a role not unappreciated by Chen, as we shall see) was largely a ritual one. Rather, Chen's extraordinary activism was directed at the upper-level academies (*shuyuan*) and the free local elementary schools (*yixue*), both of whose proprietorship lay somewhere more ambiguously between the state and societal sectors. Let us look at each of these in turn.

In nearly all of his provincial posts Chen offered active patronage and direction to the leading *shuyuan* within those jurisdictions: the Ziyang and Anding Academies of Jiangsu; the Yunnan Academy; the Tianjin Academy; the Yuzhang, Bailudong (White Deer Grotto), and Ehu (Goose Lake) Academies of Jiangxi; the Guanzhong and Gaolan Academies of Shaanxi; the Aofeng Academy of Fujian; the Jianghan Academy of Hubei; and the Yuelu, Chengnan, and Lianbin Academies of Hunan.[19] There were undoubtedly many other instances in which his activities were less direct or less well documented. In Jiangxi, at least, we know that he orchestrated a campaign among his prefectural-level subordinates to revitalize academies in their respective jurisdictions in order to constitute a systematic network of higher-learning institutions for the province as a whole.[20]

To cover the costs of building, operation, teacher's salaries, and student stipends, Chen resorted to a variety of means. For older, privately founded academies such as Jiangxi's White Deer Grotto he reconstituted the endowment properties that had been

progressively expropriated by individual landlords over the preceding century. For
more governmentalized institutions such as the Yunnan Academy he covered the
costs directly out of his gubernatorial budget. For the Tianjin Academy, which Chen
founded ex nihilo in 1740, he cobbled together a mixture of funding sources, including a new surtax on salt transactions, a diversion of part of the endowment budget of
the local orphanage (*yuying tang*), and an annual solicitation from the port's leading
merchant guilds.[21] With this financial patronage came enforced pedagogical reform:
bringing in new teachers more suited to Chen's own intellectual temperament, pro-
claiming new codes of school regulations, and establishing tightened examination systems to weed out sinecured students and recruit new ones he judged more qualified.[22]

It is revealing to place Chen's efforts in the context of the broader politics of academies in the early and mid-Qing. As is well known, because of their volatile political role
in the politics of the late Ming and the dynastic transition, the empire's private academies had begun the Qing era in dismal shape. Many had been wholly or partly destroyed during the conquest itself, and those that remained bore the burden of political repression by the conquest regime. Recent scholarship, however, suggests that this
repression was not as simple a matter as it once appeared. Some of the surviving academies—including those overseen by men Chen much admired, such as Li Yong and
Sun Qifeng—managed to maintain a vigorously independent scholarly life even in the
early Qing. At least from 1652 on, field officials throughout the empire began to selectively renovate old academies and to found new ones.[23] Whereas such officials held
the power to appoint teachers and determine curricula, this authority was merely a
carry-over from standard Ming procedure and, as Ron-Guey Chu concludes, was not exploited for heavy-handed statist purposes in any significant way.[24] But from the beginning of his reign, and especially in the early 1730s, the Yongzheng emperor launched
a program essentially to bring new and existing *shuyuan* into conformity with his centralized educational goals, notably those of a wider and more open bureaucratic recruitment. He authorized more lavish funding for student stipends and at the same
time sought to orient instruction more closely toward the civil service examination curriculum. This approach was initially continued under Qianlong, but within a decade or
two of his accession, as the pace of founding of new academies accelerated, so too did
the development of a more diverse academic discourse that was independent of the examination orientation.[25]

We can see similar trends in Chen Hongmou's own pattern of *shuyuan* patronage,
although in general he appears slightly ahead of the curve of change. Chen's earliest
support of academies in Yunnan (where he followed Ortai's lead) and in Tianjin involved schools that were clearly government products and served essentially the goals
of examination preparation and bureaucratic recruitment. Already by the early 1740s,
however, he was shifting his patronage toward older, more intellectually vibrant institutions such as the White Deer Grotto and Goose Lake Academies of Jiangxi, which, he
complained, had suffered neglect in recent decades relative to more governmentalized
institutions at the provincial capital. In rehabilitating Fuzhou's Aofeng Academy in the
1750s, in fact, Chen hints broadly that he is seizing on what he sees as a more liberalized attitude on the part of the court to patronize an older, privately founded institu-

tion—at the same time asserting his gubernatorial prerogative to align its pedagogy with what he sees as the public need.[26]

Chen sought to define the curriculum of *shuyuan* in his jurisdictions not only by appointing headmasters and teachers of his liking, and by periodically lecturing in person (on the virtues of "substantive learning"), but also by routinely providing the contents of school libraries. Considerable information survives on just what books he donated. Unsurprisingly, they featured his own works and those of his favorite authors—Lü Kun, writers of the Guanxue school, Fang Bao, Yin Huiyi—works that were truly "useful" (*youyi*). No fashionable philological treatises were to be found among them.[27] Chen did not decry *shuyuan* serving as prep schools for the civil service examinations but instead seized this opportunity to exert subtle influence on the examination curriculum itself. From among each school's alumni he selected recent examination essays, those conforming to his "substantive learning" and political economy predilections, for retention in the schools' libraries as standards for later candidates; and he ultimately added to these his own collection of instructive model examination questions on issues of practical governance.[28]

One particular theme in Chen's *shuyuan* policy is of special interest. It related in part to what Woodside terms the "ladder of ascent" approach to school management, which was gradually developed by the throne in the 1730s and 1740s. Qualified students were systematically selected for awards of state stipends and movement to higher institutions, culminating ultimately in the Imperial College (Guozi jian) at Beijing. In his provincial jurisdictions Chen similarly envisioned a multitier hierarchy of schools, with regular examinations held at local schools (*yixue* and, where such existed, prefectural-level *shuyuan*) in order to promote the most promising to the provincial academy.[29] This policy was in line with Yongzheng's emphasis on achieving the broadest possible constituency from which to select his "new men" officials, and in Chen's case (he being of course just such a "new man") it was reinforced by urges to populist inclusiveness rooted in his own personal history.

But there was also in Chen's *shuyuan* policies an even more thoroughgoing emphasis on democratic or meritocratic admission. In establishing his Tianjin Academy in 1740, for example, he claimed as his rationale the fact that "though not a provincial capital, Tianjin is a very prosperous city, where education is highly developed. The great gentry lineages have long cherished educational aspirations, and taken care of their own schooling. However, there are also many among the poor whose scholarship needs to be encouraged and supported."[30] Complaining that the prestigious *shuyuan* he encountered in various jurisdictions were rife with patronage and old-boy networks, he conducted purges of "mediocrities" among the student body and held special provincial-wide examinations to replace these with "genuine talents." Exams were first administered in the localities, followed by reexaminations and, ultimately, intensive personal interviews by himself at the capital. In the process he expanded the number of students, in Hunan even raising after the fact his announced quota of successful applications after having read a larger number of examination papers that he liked. Lamenting the fact that existing provincial *shuyuan* students tended to be drawn nearly exclusively from the capital district itself, he ordered that the net be cast as widely as possible. Characteristically, this meant special attention was given to peripheral areas (akin to that of his own native place), and there is at least a hint of geographic affirmative action in his directives outlining his selection processes.[31]

Elementary Schooling

Chen's emphasis on inclusiveness was even more apparent in his celebrated campaigns to establish elementary schools (*yixue*), in which his goal was nothing less spectacular than state-sponsored universal male literacy training. As he declared in 1733, "It is the responsibility of the local administration to establish schools in each locality. Provided that planning is not for immediate appearances only [*youshi wuzhong*] and that school operation is not merely on paper [*youming wushi*], this will result in long-term improvements in the level of popular literacy [*wen*] and civility [*hua*], and in rendering local cultural practice more decorous [*mei*]."[32]

Both Chen's elementary school initiative and his anticipation of merely perfunctory implementation drew on a rich history of imperial pronouncements and disappointing results in this area. In 1375 the Ming founder had ordered community schools (which, following Yuan precedent, he termed "*shexue*") set up on the basis of one for every fifty families throughout the empire. Little seems to have in fact been done.[33] In 1652 the Qing Shunzhi emperor again ordered *shexue* established in each *xiang*, to be run by local gentry but closely overseen by the county director of studies. This edict was reiterated and amplified by the Kangxi emperor in 1686 and again by Yongzheng in 1723. Community schools under the name "*yixue*" seem to have originated in an experiment conducted by a local official in Beijing in 1702. Three years later the Kangxi emperor ordered this model followed in each county of Guizhou, then the special target of imperial assimilationist efforts. The throne's interest in *yixue* thereafter remained focused primarily on cultural frontiers in the south and southwest, although in 1712 Kangxi did order their establishment empire-wide, with the specific goal of providing educational opportunities for orphans and children of the poor. As with the Shunzhi program to establish *shexue*, which it effectively duplicated, implementation in most parts of the empire seems to have been haphazard at best and in most instances nonexistent.[34]

Chen Hongmou's own efforts at *yixue* implementation, concentrated in the early part of his career in the 1730s, were unique in their vigor and seriousness. Why? In part this no doubt reflected the zeal of a fledgling field official to impress his imperial patron, Yongzheng (clearly the single Qing emperor most actively interested in state-financed elementary education), and, initially on his accession, that patron's successor. But it is also clear that more than careerist politics was at work. Chen's early personal model, Lü Kun, had been an outspoken champion of officially sponsored community schools in his tenures both in Shandong and Shanxi,[35] and moreover Chen had seen them at work in his home province of Guangxi, where, following Kangxi's and Yongzheng's special emphasis on frontier education, they enjoyed a greater reality than in other parts of the empire. As we saw in Chapter 1, there is even some likelihood that during his home leave following his Beijing clerkships in 1731 Chen had played an active role in the expanded foundings of *yixue* in his native *xiang* and county under Governor Jin Hong.[36]

By far the most dramatic of Chen's *yixue*-founding drives was in Yunnan from 1733 to 1738. We will look in a moment at the special character of that particular effort and its relationship to processes of frontier cultural assimilation. But it is essential to keep in mind that Chen understood the need to subject to the civilizing process of *jiaohua* populations of the heartland as well as of the frontier and that he defended the use of state-sponsored elementary schooling for this purpose in core as well as peripheral regions. Accordingly, he also led a vigorous school-building campaign in the duty station to which he proceeded after Yunnan, that as circuit intendant of Tianjin. In commercially wealthy Tianjin, Chen lamented, "there still remain many humble families living in mean alleys who have not the economic means to become literate." It is up to the government to remedy this deficiency. Chen thus restored the financial viability of six *yixue* that had been established by a predecessor twenty years earlier and ordered his subordinates to set up several more. His stated goal was that there should be "no man who is without education and no locality to which education does not reach."[37]

Chen's school-founding drives in both Yunnan and Tianjin emphasized placement of facilities in otherwise remote locations. This had been a particular demand of Yongzheng's 1723 reiteration of the basic Qing mandate on elementary schools, but Chen, with his inbred sense of the injustice of geographical advantage, pushed Yongzheng's dictates to the limit. Schools are most needed precisely in rural (*xiangcun*) and peripheral (*bianfang*) areas, he insisted, so that "no student will be too remote to be within reach of a teacher." On his arrival in Yunnan, predictably, he found existing schools overwhelmingly concentrated in the most developed counties and, within those counties, in the county seats. Scholars in these areas were already the most accomplished (*chengcai*), Chen complained, and thus precisely *least* in need of state-supported education. He therefore concentrated his own Promethean efforts in Yunnan on redressing this imbalance.[38]

We know a great deal about the curricula Chen prescribed for his public elementary schools, mostly from lists of books he ordered put in place at such schools at three points in his career: in Yunnan in 1736, in Shaanxi from 1744 to 1745, and in Guangxi in 1769. The first of these is especially revealing, not only because he ordered the books sent to all of the nearly seven hundred schools he established or incorporated into his system but also because we know the *number* of copies of each text he wanted made available at each school. The list of books is seen in the table on page 414.

Chen's Yunnan *yixue* textbooks can be divided into four categories. First comes the uniquely numerous *Guwen yuanjian*, which Chen clearly intended as the primer in basic classical literacy for beginning students. There is little surprise here. Compiled by order of the Kangxi emperor in 1685 to serve just such a purpose, the work was a selection of political writings—essays, memorials, and edicts—from late Zhou through Song times; Chen especially favored it because of its heavy political economy (*jingji*) content. It had been reprinted in Yunnan in 1709 by an earlier provincial official but in Chen's day was being used merely to educate children of well-heeled Kunming literati; he announced his own emphatically broader dissemination of the book as fundamental to

Textbooks Housed at Each Yunnan Elementary School

COPIES	TEXT
24	*Guwen yuanjian* (Reader in classical prose)
16	*Gangjian zhengshi yue* (Abridged mirror of the dynastic histories)
12	*Daxue yanyi bu jiyao* (Abridgment of the Extended Meaning of the Great Learning)
12	*Siwen jingcui* (Essentials of refined prose style)
5	*Xingli jingyi* (Basic writings of the Cheng-Zhu school)
4	*Xiaoxue zuanzhu* (Elementary learning, annotated edition)
4	*Jinsilu* (Reflections on things at hand)
2	*Lüzi jielu* (Essential works of Lü Kun)
1	*Xiaojing zhujie* (Classic of filial piety, annotated edition)
1	*Zhuzizhijia geyan* (Zhu Xi's rules for management of the household)
1	*Shengyu guangxun* (Sacred Edict, with explanations)
1	*Shuyuan tiaogui* (Regulations for the Yunnan Provincial Academy)

SOURCE: *Quan Dian yixue huji, ce* 2.

his goal of a genuinely *mass* literacy training.[39] Next come three other compilations, likewise made available by Chen in multiple copies and clearly intended as supplementary, more specialized literacy texts. Significantly, it is the anthology of readings from *historical* works, Chen's own *Gangjian zhengshi yue*, that is given numerical priority. On economic matters there is also Chen's abridged edition of the *Daxue yanyi bu jiyao*, and for a smattering of more elevated prose styles there is *Siwen jingcui*, compiled by Chen's friend and patron Yinjishan. The scholarly Manchu loved literary refinement; Chen abhorred it. It seems probable that this work was included out of deference to its compiler, who, then serving as Yun-Gui viceroy, had allocated much of the budget for Chen's school-building project. Never again in his later jurisdictions would Chen specify its use as a school text. And even here it represents Chen's sole nod to literary elegance; works of classical poetry, for example, are wholly absent from the curriculum.

Books of the third group, available in lesser quantities, seem likely intended for more advanced students, whose literacy is already assured, and are included in Chen's curriculum for their content alone. These works include three that represent the core of early Qing "Song learning"—Li Guangdi's 1715 *lixue* anthology *Xingli jingyi* and Zhu Xi's *Xiaoxue* and *Jinsilu*. All are imperially endorsed works that will form the basis of the students' early preparation for the civil service examinations. All also reflect the less metaphysical, more pragmatic, and decidedly activist spin that early Qing *lixue* scholars had put on that tradition, but at the same time (above all the *Xiaoxue*) they strongly reinforce principles of subordination and social order.[40] These features are evident as well in the final work that Chen has slipped into this category (seemingly a bit self-consciously—it is present in two copies rather than four or five): his own reader in Lü

Kun's writings, the *Lüzi jielu.* Chen Hongmou's Songxue partisanship is strikingly revealed in the fact that, whereas the basic texts of the Cheng-Zhu tradition are amply represented in his elementary school curriculum, not only do Hanxue classical philological works make no appearance, but neither do the Classics themselves!

The fourth and final group of texts, one copy only of each, are less teaching materials than basic regulatory documents on ritual propriety, scholarly conduct, and the expected behavior of Qing subjects. They include the Kangxi emperor's *Sacred Edict,* whose routinized recitation must have approximated that of singing the national anthem in a modern-day elementary school.[41] The inclusion of Chen's own regulations for the Yunnan provincial *shuyuan* seems to underscore the tracking mechanism by which the brightest students in various *yixue* throughout the province would be selected (by Chen himself) for promotion to the academy.

Chen's later booklists, from Shaanxi and Guangxi, reflect his developing ideas on elementary school curricula and his adaptation to the conditions of differing regions. In Shaanxi he orders funds solicited for the printing and distribution to all local schools of the works that, by this time, comply with the court's own formal requirements of what students should read: the *Guwen yuanjian,* the *Xingli jingyi,* the imperially sanctioned Zhu Xi edition of the Four Books (*Sishu jieyi*), Li Guangdi's imperially sponsored compilation of Zhu Xi's works (*Zhuzi quanshu*), the Thirteen Classics, and the Twenty-one Dynastic Histories (including the Qing's own official history of the Ming).[42] Unsatisfied with this, however, Governor Chen in 1744 orders printing blocks brought in to print up and distribute to all local schools supplementary texts more to his own particular taste. These include two copies per school of the sternly repressive moral primers *Xiaoxue* and *Xiaojing* and the quintessential Songxue text, Zhu Xi's *Jinsilu.* Made available in one copy per school are Chen's own *Daxue yanyi bu jiyao,* which he sees as a textbook in political economy, and his by-now-completed miscellaneous advice books, the *Wuzhong yigui* (Five sourcebooks). He also includes two works that reflect his gradually intensifying interest in the importance of ritual in social ordering: the *Sili chugao* (Primer in the Four Rituals) of the mid-Ming scholar Song Xun (*jinshi* 1559) and Lu Longqi's early Qing redaction of Lü Kun's *Sili yi* (Expanded meanings of the Four Rituals).[43] Shaanxi is not quite the cultural pale that Yunnan is, to be sure, but it does have a substantial Muslim population whose ritual improprieties the governor clearly finds in need of rectification.

Toward the very end of his metropolitan career, in 1769, Chen decides to make one last stab at improving the educational climate of his own native Guangxi. He donates one set of books to each of eighty local schools, *yixue* and *shuyuan* alike. The list of books includes many that have only become available in the years since Chen's early provincial service, but it also seems to reflect the more accommodationist pedagogical stance he has assumed in his later years. The *Xiaoxue* is there, of course, as are various compilations of readings on history, but so too are annotated editions of the Thirteen Classics. We see now the basic works of Qing geographic and institutional administration, *Qing yitong zhi* and *Wenxian tongkao* (perhaps of special utility to any Guangxi lad aspiring to follow Chen's own footsteps into official service), but they are accompanied also by the two encyclopedic compendia the Qing court has assembled, with Chen's blessing, of prose and poetic masterpieces of the mid-imperial period, the *Tang Song wenchun* and *Tang Song shichun*. It seems almost as if the aging grand secretary is seeking for the children of his peripheral home province a well-rounded liberal education, more in line with that he sees routinely enjoyed by offspring of more favored, core regions like Jiangnan.[44]

Overall, Chen's elementary school pedagogy mirrored his scholarly preferences: Teaching was to be thoroughly oriented toward "substantive learning" (*shixue*), emphasizing equally moral values and practical or technical competence and devaluing both philological textual study and aesthetic appreciation of letters for their own sake. Potential benefit for society and the polity were to be kept foremost in mind. His educational practice stressed repeated study of textual passages in order to internalize their message, but without a corresponding stress on rote memorization or on oral recitation. Chen complained that pedagogues in recent centuries had erred in the directions of "shallow" (*shelie*) and "hollow" (*koujian*) learning for young students, either denigrating the utility of repetitive study in the interests of broad reading, on the one hand, or insisting on memorization of countless passages, on the other. For him the proper balance entailed slow and careful progress through each text, making sure that both the literal meaning of the characters and the ethical message of the passage were understood as the text was learned and, more generally, that "book learning" (*dushu*) and its implications for personal conduct (*xingji*) proceeded hand in hand.[45]

Repeatedly Chen stressed the painstaking nature of this process, with the student building step by step his stock of recognized and reproducible lexical units. He insisted that this process of "opening up" the child's intelligence could be accomplished only by means of a carefully graded curriculum, not repeating the same text over and over but rather starting with a more basic text and moving on to ever more difficult material, and by instituting a system of progressively more difficult year-long "grades" (*fennian richeng*).[46] His school system was to be a three-tier graded hierarchy, with novice students (*mengtong*) beginning at *xiang*-level rural schools, the more promising advancing on to more prestigious *yixue* at the county seat, and the truly gifted then going on to an academy. Over the course of their educational career students would effectively be divided into those deemed suitable for merely general education and those worthy of training for a professional career (*yiye*) as scholar-officials. In Yunnan Chen designed an elaborate monitoring system to determine into which track each student fell and the proper timing of his promotion to a higher-level school. Here again, the state's role was explicitly to overcome the drag of socioeconomic difference on the emergence of genuine ability, with scholarships systematically established to allow poor but promising students to attend higher-level schools away from home.[47]

As we observed at the beginning of this chapter, Chen Hongmou held a balanced appreciation of the values of didactic instruction (based on the premise of human rational educability) and of more behaviorally oriented ritual practice in cultivating responsible members of society. The process of childhood socialization (*yangzheng*) institutionalized in his elementary schools thus emphasized training in etiquette and ceremony as a necessary corollary to literary instruction. Ritual propriety was an affirmation of one's moral character as a man (*zuoren*) and as a member of the civilized community, and even the most mundane details of personal conduct were subject to ritualization. In one of Chen Hongmou's favorite essays by Zhu Xi, "What the Children Ought to Know" (*Tongmen xu zhi*), the master had written, "The child should first be taught how to put on his clothes, cap, and shoes; then how to speak, walk, and run; and later how to sprinkle, sweep, and clean; and afterwards how to study, write, and other, even the minutest details of what a child should do." On this Chen commented, "The novice should start with what can be known and done easily . . . beginning with what is necessary for daily life . . . in such a way as to avoid corruption of his spirit and to nourish his virtuous nature." Following Zhu Xi's precepts, Chen's elementary school students were to be repetitively practiced in the forms of personal cleanliness, frugality, decorum, and scholarship:

> Everyone should first make his personal appearance correct and proper. . . . When your clothes are disheveled, your body will be slovenly and ungraceful and you will not command the respect of people. . . . All clothes which you put on in the daytime should be changed when you go to sleep at night; then the fleas and lice cannot hide in them and they will not be worn out before their time. . . . Walk slowly, speak quietly. . . . Whenever you study, you should arrange the things on your table or desk, making them clean, neat, and orderly. Then arrange your book properly, adjust your body, and face the book. Carefully and slowly look at the characters; heedfully and clearly read them out. Read each character loudly and distinctly. Do not read incorrectly; do not miss one; do not add one; do not turn them upside down—no, not even one character.[48]

Beyond these basic matters of personal and scholarly deportment students were required to be "drilled in the ritual forms of courtesy and deference and the cardinal principles of respectful obedience to the sovereign and to their seniors." Twice a month the teacher was to lead his pupils to worship at the local Confucian temple, where they would pay obeisance first to the sage and then to their teacher and then respectfully greet each other. Following this, in a rite of bonding with the local community as well as the imperial state, they would be joined by village elders to stand in a circle and hear a local gentry member recite the *Sacred Edict.*[49]

The Civilizing Mission on the Frontier

I have stressed that Chen's focus on *jiaohua* in general and his specific attention to the role of elementary schooling in this process were applicable to populations of both the heartland and the cultural frontier. Up to now, accordingly, we have treated his efforts in this area as geographically of a piece. At this point it is worth looking a bit more closely, however, at the specific character of his educational campaigns in Yunnan from 1733 to 1738. These campaigns represented the most serious challenge to Chen's assumptions of universal human educability, but, more broadly, they also tell us something about his notions of cultural difference and of the civilizing process.[50]

The southwest had been a nominal part of Chinese empires since Han times, and the assimilation of its indigenous populations had for two millennia been considered by Chinese a historical inevitability. However, actual large-scale settlement of the region and confrontation with local cultures had begun only in the fourteenth century, first when substantial numbers of Mongol troops were sent there as military colonists and then, following the dynastic transition, when Ming Taizu removed to Yunnan much of the population of the area chosen for his new capital, Nanjing. But because Ming efforts at political and cultural integration were relatively minimal, this first wave of immigration only modestly disrupted indigenous society. Administratively, the Ming chose to govern the region by means of a system of enfeoffed native headmen (*tusi*), only fitfully experimenting, late in the dynasty's history, with a program of replacing these headmen with the sort of direct bureaucratic administration practiced in the heartland (*gaitu guiliu*).

This situation changed dramatically following the Qing conquest of 1644. First, the southwest became an arena of major military action, initially as a haven for Ming loyalist armies and later as base for the rebellion of erstwhile Qing general Wu Sangui (1612–78). Then, following the collapse of this rebellion in 1681, the program of postwar "reconstruction" (*shanhou*) brought with it integrationist efforts of unprecedented intensity. As the empire's population began to grow at alarming rates, strategic concerns were joined by economic expansionist ones, and the region's productive capacity for foodstuffs and for minerals (especially copper to serve the Qing economy's rapidly growing demand for new coinage) attracted government-sponsored developmental entrepreneurship and Chinese immigration of a wholly new order of magnitude. Efforts at *gaitu guiliu* administrative incorporation were likewise stepped up, beginning with an initiative of the Shunzhi emperor in 1658 and attaining a steamroller effect in the wake of Yongzheng's edict on the subject in January of 1728. This process both responded to and further precipitated a series of very bloody "uprisings" (the term itself, of course, carries with it a presumption of Han manifest destiny in the region) on the part of indigenous peoples, culminating in a great rebellion centered on Guzhou Prefecture, Guizhou, in the 1720s and 1730s. As noted in Chapter 2, in the Yongzheng era the task of incorporation of the southwest, in all its complexity, became the proving ground for the emperor's corps of "new men," including the likes of Ortai, Yinjishan, Emida, Zhang Yunsui, Zhang Guangsi, Yan Sisheng, and ultimately Chen Hongmou.[51]

As early as the tenure of Wang Yangming in the southwest in the sixteenth century, efforts at incorporation of the region by Chinese had featured the establishment of Chinese-language Confucian schools as one of their most basic components.[52] The demand that schools (*fuxue* and *xianxue*) be established in each locality and that the right to inherit *tusi* headmanships be restricted to their graduates had been a thrust of Shunzhi's 1658 assimilationist drive and, as John Herman has recently shown, proved a major incentive to revolt on the part of non-Han elites thus deprived of political office. In spite of this, the Yongzheng retrospect on the preceding seven decades' history, although offering cause for heated debate among policy planners, ultimately decided that the way to go was in the direction not of fewer schools but rather of a great many more, set up in direct conjunction with the intensified program of bureaucratization of county administrations.[53] In their Yun-Gui governor-generalships Ortai and Yinjishan had each personally involved themselves in this process,[54] but the lion's share of the action was left for Chen's arrival as Yunnan provincial treasurer in 1733. And Chen Hongmou was absolutely the perfect man for the job. Such an expansive program of educational outreach conformed with his own sociocultural assumptions and served as an outlet for his estimable energies and ambitions.

On Chen's arrival in Yunnan there were some two hundred local elementary schools in existence on paper, most of which proved to have little substantive reality; by the time he left in 1738 he had overseen the founding or revitalization of nearly seven hundred such schools. The vast majority of these were rural—Chen far more than realized his goal of situating one school in every subcounty *xiang* of the province—and most were in predominantly non-Han areas. They were to serve not merely the offspring of native chieftains but all local male children. Acutely aware that such a crash program could imperil institutions lacking either substance or permanency, Chen had his subordinates submit detailed budgets for each school and clearly demonstrate their creation of endowment estates to underwrite its continuing operation. (The register of such data, which Chen compiled for all of Yunnan, survives to this day.) These institutions were *yixue* (free public schools) and lay formally in the sphere of community rather than state proprietorship; accordingly, their endowments could not be generated out of regular land-tax revenues. Rather, schools drew on a complex amalgam of funding sources, the mix of which varied from school to school. Among the major sources were (1) old endowment estates privately expropriated in the past but "recovered" under Chen's tenure, (2) income from landed estates attached to individual official posts (*guanzhuang*), (3) miscellaneous local expense funds (*gongxiang*) in local and provincial administrative budgets, (4) specially imposed local surtaxes or other exactions, (5) back taxes claimed on lands brought under cultivation in recent years but previously "hidden" from the government, and, perhaps most important, (6) contributions from officials, Chinese immigrant elites, and indigenous *tusi* headmen. Chen himself donated over twelve hundred taels from his *yanglian* stipend for school foundings throughout Yunnan and exerted pressure on his subordinates to make similarly hefty personal contributions.[55]

What sort of cultural attitudes conditioned this enormously ambitious assimilationist drive? For eighteenth-century Qing elites the confrontation with southwestern peoples presented a classic challenge of alterity: a powerfully imagined cultural counterexample against which to measure, question, or celebrate their own "civilization." Responsible Chinese and Manchus in the southwest knew well that they were facing a vast array of diverse peoples, some with quite sophisticated socioeconomic systems; the local customs chapter of the 1736 Yunnan provincial gazetteer, for instance, painstakingly catalogs individual groups in great detail.[56] Yet in popular and even official parlance a process had been underway since the Yuan to collapse these peoples into a single undifferentiated "other," known as "Miao." As Guizhou provincial treasurer Emida wrote around 1730, the Miao, although "not all of the same stock" (*zhonglei buyi*), were essentially alike in being "primitive" (*shengxing*), "barbarous" (*kuanghan*), and "savage" (*yewan*).[57] This set of tropes recurs with great frequency in Qing official descriptions, as do characterizations such as stupid, lazy, weak of physique, listless of spirit, and wasteful of resources—characterizations that were routinely (although not as categorically) applied as well to Han populations by development-minded Chinese officials and to non-Western peoples (including, eventually, the Chinese) by expansionist Europeans.[58]

Depictions of southwest peoples were always patronizing but not always unsympathetic. Claudine Lombard-Salmon, for instance, has documented a progressive "exoticization" (or "orientalization") of native peoples by Chinese literati travel writers of the Ming and early Qing, emphasizing their quaint and childlike picturesqueness, as ready candidates for metropolitan domination.[59] A series of eighty-two paintings done by an eighteenth-century Chinese official in Guizhou likewise portrays the natives in a manner that, to my eye, is less undignified than idyllic and romanticized; they remind one of nothing so much as the verbal portraits of the noble but doomed North American savages appearing in the works of James Fenimore Cooper.[60] Chen Hongmou, himself a self-conscious man of the frontier who disparaged effete literati refinement, wrote of his admiration for the "rustic virtue" (*chunpu*) and stoic self-reliance of the southwestern aborigines.[61] The cant of conquest indeed portrayed them more often as sinned against than sinning, mercilessly exploited by their own headmen, Chinese merchants, and overzealous Qing bureaucrats, owing to their innocence and naivete. Wrote one expansion-minded Chinese official, "These people are as guileless as suckling pigs."[62]

Similarly complex were prevailing elite notions of who or what, in fact, the natives were. The sources abound with animal images—Yinjishan, for example, described the Miao as "wriggling and wormlike" (*chun*)[63]—but to what extent they were truly seen as biologically subhuman is questionable. They certainly were thought to differ from Chinese and Manchus in "race" (*zonglei*), but, as we saw in Chapter 9, the genealogical versus the cultural components of this idea for men such as Chen Hongmou are not easily distinguishable. Most pervasive, it seems, was the view that southwestern peoples represented some primeval stage of a unilinear path of human sociocultural evolution. Chen Hongmou's own southwestern patron and mentor, Governor Zhang Yunsui, wrote that Yunnan society still appeared "as it had at the dawn of creation."[64] A related notion, given prevalence by the ethnographic studies of the late Ming scholar Jiao Hong (1541–1620), was that aboriginal life offered an accurate picture of how Chinese themselves had lived in the distant past, before they had achieved their present level of cultural achievement.[65] And it was this reading that underlay the sense of threat—in more than a mere military sense—that the southwest represented for eighteenth-century Confucian elites. By their continuing existence, southwestern peoples constituted a real and present reminder of what civilized humanity had once been and might become again. Observed the highly sinicized, classically educated Yinjishan: "If savages cherish learning, they may advance to become Han; if Han people neglect learning, they may degenerate into savages."[66] And the historical reality of centuries had been, Qing officials knew well, that far more Chinese had acculturated to aboriginal life than aborigines to the Chinese. Even more basically, the existence of these contrasting lifestyles raised implications of cultural relativism, a profound threat to the universalist claims on which rested the very legitimacy of Confucian civilization.

Chen Hongmou's personal response to the southwest's challenge of alterity represented a distinctly optimistic strand within this package of metropolitan attitudes. It betrayed little of the sense of defensive self-doubt motivating those who advised keeping the Miao in their current "primitive" state. Chen's premises, rather, were defiantly uni-

九股歯在興陽衛凱司此種固武係南征戰
之始蓋僅存九人遠為九股日久蔓延貴橫
性悍頭戴鉄盔前有援面後無遮肩用鉄
虎圍身鉄片雖腿健者能左手执木碑右
手执線口唧利刃行走如飛攜帯前岑苗名
曰偏架三人铣矢餐無不貫

FIGURE 13. Miao warriors hunting a tiger. Painting attributed to the early-eighteenth-century Guizhou local official Chen Hao. Source: *Miao luan tuce.* Courtesy of Institute of History and Philology, Academia Sinica.

versalist, *both* in postulating the single normative correctness of Han cultural models (what Alexander Woodside has termed "Confucian uniformity")[67] *and* in assuming an inclusive humanity that made this Confucian uniformity achievable in practice for all. For him, at least at this relatively early stage in his career, the civilizing mission was a genuinely attainable ideal.

The first of these questions, the extent of Chen's attribution of a universal normative status to Han elite cultural models, recalls our earlier discussions of his attitudes toward foreign trade and traders. It is immediately clear that fear of cultural taint from interaction with non-Chinese provided little brake on Chen's commercial development strategies. He was a consistent champion of liberalized policies toward Chinese traders operating overseas, and he favored allowing access to Chinese markets for foreign merchants: Inner Asians, traditional maritime tribute-trade partners such as those from Liuqiu, Southeast Asian private traders such as those from Siam and the Philippines, and even Europeans.[68] He insisted that local Chinese communities receiving such foreigners treat them "fairly" (*gongping*) in business dealings and "civilly" (*lihe*) in personal relations. The most important rationale Chen offered for liberalizing cross-cultural trade relations was of course economic—not only were the goods exchanged useful for both sides, but the trade also generated productive livelihoods (*guansheng*) for the mer-

chants and transport workers themselves, both domestic and foreign. Chen also periodically advanced the Smithian notion that systematic commercial linkages between
peoples help ensure peaceable intercultural relations more generally. Beyond this,
however, and far from negligible in Chen's policy-making calculus, was the role of trade
in bringing non-Chinese into closer touch with the Qing's civilized social model.

The operative word in his discourse was "*xianghua*," variously translatable as "to
face toward civilization" or "to approach and be transformed." There was a standard political reading of this idiom, to be sure: for Inner Asian peoples such as the Dzungar
Mongols or for southwestern indigenous populations "*xianghua*" meant to acknowledge incorporation into the Qing empire. But Chen uses the term in reference to maritime peoples as well, for whom political annexation was never a consideration. For
such persons "*xianghua*" surely contained a minimal element of accepting the authority of Chinese terms of trade, but there was clearly more at stake than this. Foreigners
seek out the Qing not only to partake of its renowned economic prosperity but also to
seek its civilizing influence. This, in Chen's view, is as it ought to be and should be encouraged by liberalized policies fostering interaction across cultural divides.[69]

This openness of boundaries championed by Chen, in other words, reflects less a
sense of cultural pluralism than its reverse. The limits of tolerance are revealed in
Chen's response to religious diversity and nowhere more clearly than in the campaign
of religious persecution he undertook in Shaanxi in the autumn of 1746.[70] Earlier that
year the court had destroyed a vegetarian sect in Yunnan headed by one Zhang Baotai,
which it deemed as having ambitions for a millenarian uprising and which, subsequent
investigations suggested, had links with groups in several other provinces. Coupled with
the concurrent discovery of active Christian proselytization in Fujian, this prompted
the Qianlong court to order a crackdown by provincial officials on all heterodox religious activity, a campaign that continued for the next three years. Chen Hongmou unsurprisingly was among the most energetic of respondents, conducting a wholesale religious inquisition in his province that extended, by his own admission, to folk Buddhist
and Christian congregations that had no demonstrable link with millenarianism, had
lived peaceably with their neighbors and political authorities for generations, and indeed in some cases had gained vaunted local reputations for charitable activity. He
forcibly secularized their clergy (in the case of Christians, ordering any foreign priests
to be repatriated to Guangzhou—an early suggestion, perhaps, of the foreign enclave
arrangement that would come to be known in the 1760s as the "Canton system"),
seized their scriptures and icons (in the Christian case crucifixes), and, foreshadowing
the various "antisuperstition" campaigns of twentieth-century China, ordered their
church and temple precincts converted to *xiangyue* lecture halls, community granaries
(*shecang*), and Confucian elementary schools (*yixue*).

The basic problem, Chen contends, is not one of dynastic security but one of *jiaohua*, the correction of moral error. In his proselytizing effort to set his wayfaring constituency on the proper path Chen insists on the naturalness (*zhixing*) of Confucian
principles of social order, based on filial piety and loyalty, and the correspondingly unnatural character of alternative systems of religious belief and organization. He de-
bunks the claims of other religions to confer material blessings on their adherents, de-

claring that the only truly efficacious way to secure blessings is through the Confucian cult of Heaven (*tiandao*). He scoffs at Buddhist claims that devotees can win for their deceased forebears superior forms of rebirth, insisting that ancestors can be effectively served only through the sacrifices prescribed in the Confucian rites. Proper conduct is not to be found in a congregational setting but rather by living in settled society, as a loyal imperial subject, in a way that is both practically useful (socially harmonious and economically productive, devoting one's surplus to such communal causes as granaries and interest-free loans to needy neighbors) and cosmically correct (the "way of the family," *jiadao*, mystified as revealed truth).

At the close of his 1746 directive Chen concedes, somewhat grudgingly, that certain established Buddhist temples are statutorily legal and must be exempted from his crusade. When, five years later, he turns his attentions to the Muslim communities of Shaanxi, he is similarly hamstrung by the fact that these, too, are protected by imperial patronage. Nevertheless, in his broadsides against a wide range of Muslim antisocial behavior he leaves no doubt that the real problem is that the basic tenets of Islamic belief, and the congregational social order that derives from them, run fundamentally counter to heavenly principle, *tianli*.[71] On such basic matters there can be but one, universally applicable truth, and it is Chen's own civilization that possesses it. "Our nation (*guojia*) offers the model of proper human behavior by means of which all others can be instructed."[72]

In Yunnan in the 1730s Chen's goal is quite candidly "to turn the savages into Chinese" (*Yi bian wei Han*). What sets him apart from other policy makers is his unshakable optimism that this is possible. It is possible because the very Heaven that has provided the universal standards by means of which we Chinese can and should educate others has likewise guaranteed that all among these others are in fact educable. "Human nature being invariably good," he insists, "there is no man who cannot be enlightened. Chinese and non-Chinese share a common human essence, and for this reason there are no cultural practices which cannot be reformed." Chen reacts angrily to the suggestions of his local-level subordinates that this frenetic school-building he is up to in the southwest is a monumental waste of effort, because the Miao are too congenitally stupid to learn—"I will not listen to such things as 'Savages will always be savages.' " This attitude, and the foot-dragging it countenances, run afoul both of Chen's Mencian populist inclusiveness and of the antipathy to cultural elitism that he inherited from his Guangxi childhood. The strategic option of allowing the continued existence of an inferior, colonized "other" is not, for Chen, a morally tolerable one.[73]

Critics of Chen's educational drive also pointed out that there was a real danger in providing the empowering instrument of literacy to peoples whose interests ran counter to the Qing political goal of conquest and who, moreover, were inherently untrustworthy. Chen scoffed at such criticism:

> There are those who argue that the savages are crafty and vicious and that compelling them to become literate can only increase their capacity for treachery. Alas! I have always heard that loyalty and fidelity are the best armor and the rites and propriety the best weapons, but never that literacy is a provocation to war! If literacy indeed is a tool

for devious and self-serving behavior, does it not follow that it should be withheld from Chinese people as well?

Others explicitly noted that there was a war currently underway against the very people Chen sought to educate and that reasons of military security argued against offering such aid and comfort to the enemy. Chen once again took the Confucian high ground: "Are the savages now in rebellion on account of their exposure to literacy? This argument for keeping the world ignorant and deluding the people runs counter to all principles of benevolence and propriety. One is morally bound to refute it."[74] Unlike others among the conquest elite, Chen Hongmou was sublimely confident that once he had "turned the savages into Chinese," parochial group solidarities (and hence resistance to imperial rule) would cease; all properly civilized persons would immediately recognize their confluence of interests in ordering the world.

Chen's Yunnan *yixue* were to be open to all, "regardless of Han or non-Han origin" (*bulun Han Yi*), yet at the same time were to target minority populations even more conscientiously than Han. With an explicit paternalist logic he argued that just as children were more needful of instruction than were adults, so too were indigenous peoples more needful than Chinese. To this end he directed schoolmasters to include in their year-end reports percentages of non-Han versus Han attending each school and information on the relative progress of students from each group.[75] In the 1720s special "Miao-Yao" civil service examinations had been instituted throughout the southwest, and in 1734 special quotas for passes on regular examinations were established for non-Han peoples in Guizhou.[76] For his own part Chen did everything in his power to guarantee that minority groups would be able to compete for regular civil service degrees on a favorable basis. For example, he prohibited outright the selection of recent Han immigrants for advanced study at the provincial academy, and he ordered a crackdown on the practice of Han students changing their legal registration to predominantly non-Han prefectures in an effort to dominate the general quota of examination passes allotted those districts.[77]

Chen's drive to civilize indigenous peoples in the southwest was a wide-ranging effort that took literacy training as its core but included other elements as well. Like other colonizing officials, he lamented the failure of the savages to "know shame" (*zhichi*): native dress was immodest, women enjoyed great sexual latitude, spring communal festivals offered sexual license to youth, and domestic units adhered to norms (including in some instances matrilineality and matrilocality) that offended Confucian sensibilities. Qing administrators accordingly attempted to impose Chinese-style costume to clothe the native's nakedness, introduced the use of Chinese patrilineal family names, decreed inheritance through the male line, and mandated Confucian wedding and funerary rites.[78]

Chen contributed to this effort by placing instruction in "rational" and ritually correct familial norms at the core of his elementary school curriculum, and he took particular pains to counter the widespread local practice of the levirate by promulgating the cult of virtuous widowhood (*jiexiao*).[79] Intimately connected with the effort to remold familial systems was that to reconstruct the bases of production. Decrying the "ex-

女官即猓玀正妻稱之曰
耐德編絨為髻用青布
衆首多戴銀絲花貼額
大耳環拖長裙三千六幅
非耐德所生不得継立土
官如子幼耐德代之

FIGURE 14. Miao "female official" (*nüguan*). Women in positions of political authority among southwestern peoples were a source of fascination for eighteenth-century Han Chinese and a sign of those non-Han peoples' lower level of civilization. Painting attributed to Chen Hao. Source: *Miao luan tuce.* Courtesy of Institute of History and Philology, Academia Sinica.

treme stupidity" of the shifting slash-and-burn agriculture (*daozhong huogeng*) practiced by many local groups, he labored to introduce the crops, techniques, and property systems appropriate to Han-style sedentary agriculture.[80] For Chen, and the official elite as a whole, settled household proprietorship was one of the cardinal elements in civilized, well-ordered society. It brought with it economic stability (*hengye*), as well as social responsibility; it facilitated the introduction of improved agrarian technologies, of Chinese civil law (and hence the shift from tribal to imperial justice), and of fiscal accountability. Hand in hand with literacy and scholarship it could be expected to foster the rise of the indigenous propertied elite who would serve as backbone of the new social order.[81]

Whether Chen Hongmou's educational project in Yunnan enjoyed any significant degree of long-term success is beyond the scope of our present concerns (the evidence, as I see it, is mixed). His schools themselves, at least, seem to have survived for as much as a century, suggesting a certain achievement of his goal of institutional permanency.[82] This contrasts revealingly with the fate of the far smaller number of *yixue* that had been established by Chen's colleague Yan Sisheng in neighboring Guizhou. In 1751 the

Qianlong court ordered the closing of local schools in non-Han areas of that province, deriding them as "pottery dogs" (*taoquan*)—decorative, but with no bite. In so doing the court reiterated the litany of racist attitudes and parochial complaints that Chen had struggled against in Yunnan: indigenous peoples were congenitally stupid and could not come to understand propriety the way Han people could; if they learned to read, they would only waste this skill on lewd or heterodox texts; education of savages stimulated resistance movements and thus ran counter to imperial interests.[83]

The triumph of this sort of logic, at least as regards Guizhou, seems to reflect the more elitist and conservative tenor of the Qianlong reign as it grew more distant in time from the universalist activism of Yongzheng (see Chapter 2). But although Chen Hongmou himself may have grown a bit less utopian in his practical ambitions by this date as well, he had decidedly not abandoned, indeed would never abandon, the populist and inclusivist premises that had called forth his Promethean efforts at world-ordering in mid-1730s Yunnan. Both the common ground of his assumptions within the consciousness of the eighteenth-century official elite and his distinctiveness within that elite are here especially well revealed.

Women's Education

Questions of the desirability and appropriate form of women's education became a focus of lively literati debate in the early modern period of Chinese history just as they did in Europe (the comparability of the two has emboldened Susan Mann to appropriate the European term "*querrelle des femmes*" in reference to the Chinese debate).[84] The eighteenth-century phase of discussion was given new focus by the publication in 1712 of the model magistrate Lan Dingyuan's *Nüxue* (Women's learning), which marshaled quotations from the classics and exemplary biographies to illustrate ideals of feminine virtue and offered itself as a curriculum for women to study.[85] Three decades later Chen Hongmou himself vigorously joined the debate with the publication of his *Jiaonü yigui* (Sourcebook on women's education), which he distributed prolifically throughout his various provincial jurisdictions and which was frequently reprinted after his death. Although Chen had much in common with his older contemporary Lan, he did not extract Lan's rather severe work in his own 1742 sourcebook. Instead, he offered as the chief influence on his own views the somewhat more humanistic late Ming thinker Lü Kun and Lü's less-well-known father, Lü Desheng. The elder Lü's *Nü xiaoer yu* (Advice to young women) and the younger's *Guifan* (Rules for the women's quarters) together make up substantially more than half of Chen's compilation.[86]

The crux of Chen's ideas was, of course, that women *should* be educated. For him this was an inescapable conclusion drawn from basic Mencian principles: "There is no uneducable person in the world. Given this recognition, how is it possible to make an exception for female children?"[87] In this sense Chen's "feminism" dovetails with other of his egalitarian concerns, and indeed he repeatedly insists that by female education he means education of all women, regardless of social class. Chen complained that although most contemporary parents did an adequate job of caring for their daughter's material needs, providing her with food, shelter, clothing, and (at marriage) a dowry, they wholly neglected her personal development. Following Lü Kun, Chen argued that parents (and subsequently husbands) must continually regulate their dependent females' behavior, but at the same time he insisted that waiting until a daughter got out of line and then scolding her was no substitute for systematically providing her with a sound basis for arriving at independent moral judgments.[88]

Education in Chen's view meant literacy, and it was here that his views became more controversial. He by no means condoned neglect of practical education, characteristically including in his *Jiaonü yigui* texts describing how parents should train their daughters in the details of proper grooming and etiquette,[89] and he repeatedly stressed the value of manual skills. But he simultaneously emphasized that vocational education ("teaching one's daughter to sew") was not enough. Proper moral behavior and the rudiments of the classical cultural tradition could and should be introduced at a preliterate age—the *Jiaonü yigui* provides simple texts that female children can recite and internalize through repetitive training[90]—but this too is only a start. Chen insisted that women, like men, have a rational intelligence (*xinghui*) that renders them capable of learning to read. As with men, of course, there are in women grades of intellect. Some may be taught to master the classics; others can only learn to read simplified popularizations; a few may find reading too difficult altogether. Yet even these can be brought to comprehend the message of the classics when they are read or explained to them *by other women* who are literate.[91]

In part Chen's insistence on this point may be seen as a defensive reaction prompted by the reality of rising female literacy. He states, for example: "It is my belief that in today's world there are already many women with a smattering of knowledge. They cling to the few ideas they pick up, cherishing them till their dying day, and imparting them to others." This being the case, it would be far better if they got their ideas right, imbibing the classical tradition as it ought to be learned.[92] Chen is also alert to the positive opportunities of the spread of literacy, however, and introduces Lü Kun's *Guifan* by saying, "This present selection should be read in its entirety by all young girls, and discussed among themselves," just as it was in Lü's own day, when tens of thousands of copies were in print.[93] This related as well to what might be seen as something of a subtext contest within the debate over women's literacy, that is, the question of vernacularization. Against those unnamed literati (certainly the Tongcheng *guwen* stylists) who argued for the defense of the classical language, Chen repeatedly argued that a popularization of literary styles is fully justified if it gets the moral message across to a greater mass audience, female as well as male.[94]

Chen left no doubt that the purpose of a literary education was moral training rather than aesthetic refinement, cultural sophistication, or scholastic erudition.[95] It seems likely that he assumed literacy would aid women in the tasks of household management and welcomed it for this as well, but, just as in the case of his advocacy of universal male literacy training, his position was not based on any modernist notion of reading skills as prerequisite for successful functioning in a literate society. Nor did he wish to promote the emergence of women poets and literati, as did his younger contemporary Yuan Mei. Chen had absolutely no sympathy for belles lettres as a socially responsible vocation among women any more than among men. Indeed, his advocacy of women's literacy was pursued in spite of, rather than in sympathy with, the rise of a group of culturally accomplished women writers beginning in the late Ming.[96] Among eighteenth-century male literati (exemplified by Zhang Xuecheng) this raised all sorts of red flags about the subversiveness of literate women moving outside the proper confines of the home.[97] A number of recent studies have pointed out that the antipathy to female literary education was not a Song legacy but was rather a late Ming–early Qing accretion, provoked in part precisely because of the visibility of these new feminine poets and scholars.[98] In this light men like Chen Hongmou and Lan Dingyuan, who vigorously promoted the principle of literary education for women, can be seen as in effect defending traditional notions rather than introducing "progressive" ones. Chen explicitly ridiculed the current formulation that female literacy is incompatible with female virtue, but in so doing he was careful, like Lü Kun before him, to stress what the limits and purposes of this education should be.[99]

The proper goal of literary education, for females just as for males, was to achieve greater realization of how best to fulfill one's social roles (*fen*). All roles combined aspects of submission and authority, and if for females the aspects of submission were more pronounced, that did not diminish Chen's faith that educated women, no less than educated men, would be driven by their innate moral sense (*liangzhi*) to fulfill the dictates of their roles once these had been clarified for them through their reading of the orthodox curriculum. Indeed, for women there was a special urgency attached to a literary education because it was they who would play the pivotal role in passing on these heavenly ordained social norms to their sons. A good daughter would become a good wife and mother and therefore have good sons and grandsons.[100] In Chen's thinking this was linked to the belief—which he seems to have gotten from Lu Shiyi—in the natural innocence of the child (*tianzhen*) and the corresponding urgency to begin influencing the child's development at the earliest possible moment, before this innocence began to be corrupted or dissipated—even beginning its education in utero.[101] A mother who herself has been properly educated will be able to stave off her natural feminine inclination to pamper her children and will be properly strict in their upbringing.[102] Chen leaves no doubt that literate mothers will not only aid in their children's moral education but will also provide at least the initial training in classical literacy. In exemplary cases such as the widow Zhou, the subject of one of Chen's biographical sketches, she can fully supervise her son's literary education (although engaging a male teacher as well) and continually provide him with sage career advice. The mother, in other words, is the linchpin in the process of cultural reproduction, assuming the first and most important responsibility for instructing her offspring in "the ways of the ancients."[103] And the sociopolitical implications of women's education as a whole are without parallel. In Chen's pithy phrase, "The Kingly Way begins in the women's quarters."[104]

Historians have frequently pointed to many features in Chen Hongmou's advocacy of women's education that are decidedly nonfeminist and abhorrent to the modern temper. Indeed, this was clearly seen in the 1930s by Chen Dongyuan, among the most "modernist" of male Chinese feminists, who ridiculed Hongmou's views as epitomizing the hypocritical, unenlightened attitudes of the old China.[105] Probably the most sensitive (and certainly the best informed) contemporary scholar of the subject, Susan Mann, has even gone so far as to interpret Chen's advocacy of women's literary education as part of a larger effort to freeze the sociocultural hierarchy from the dangerous erosion it seemed to have undergone since the late Ming and more immediately with the Yongzheng emancipations of debased social categories.[106] As I made clear in Chapter 9, I strongly disagree with this view; I find Chen to be quite comfortable, in fact, with the newfound social mobility of his era. Where my reading of Chen Hongmou does concur with that of Mann and others is in the recognition that, for him, rather than liberating of the woman's individual personality, female education was primarily instrumental to the overriding project of ordering the world—a world that, in Chen's understanding, was naturally and appropriately male dominated. But Chen's rationale, I would suggest, went deeper than this.

Chen is unlike others in the late imperial tradition who similarly advocated women's education in basing this advocacy on the argument of an essential common humanity, the equal possession of *tianliang* (heavenly goodness) by all persons, male and female. His arguments regarding education must be taken in the context of his vigorous campaigns against prostitution and trafficking in kidnapped females, his condemnation of the commodification of women through marriages arranged for the profit of the paternal line, and his more general rehabilitation of the notion of *renqing* (human emotion) and the dignity of the emotion-bearing individual. Women, in Chen Hongmou's well-ordered universe, were to be more than ciphers or swooning dependents on their menfolk. They were social adults, and their literacy was the emblem of this adulthood. Women, just like men, were to be active, autonomous moral agents. The education of women—that is, their exposure to worldly affairs via the classical canon—was the antidote to sheltered cloistering in the inner quarters (something that, depending on the context, Chen alternately condemned and endorsed) and was designed first and foremost to foster this moral autonomy.

In the end educated women had their familial and social roles to occupy, just as did educated men. The assumption of such roles was at the same time essential to the unique capacity of the human species for civilization and restrictive of the development of individual personhood in what might today be considered a liberated fashion. Yet in the particular way Chen developed his logic on the question of education—of women, as of ethnic minorities, of marginalized groups, and of the poor—the dignity of the individual female or male emerged as a significant concern in itself.

Ritual

As we have seen, didactic education and ritual practice were not for Chen Hongmou mutual alternatives; rather, ritual training formed an integral component of the well-designed elementary school curriculum. Chen did not, as did many of his eighteenth-century contemporaries, turn away from moral suasion in despair over the willingness or ability of the general populace to respond, settling for a program of enforced behavioral compliance to ritual practice in its stead. It was because of his continuing faith in normative appeals that he so energetically promulgated his various didactic texts in

language designed for maximal popular accessibility. Nor did Chen prescribe education merely for the elite and something less for the masses. Literary education, he repeatedly insisted, must be for all. Nevertheless, once universal male education in the
local *yixue* had gotten underway, a certain tracking mechanism based on differing intellectual capacity would gradually kick in. "The gifted [*junxiuzhe*]," Chen confided,
"will eventually be able to immerse themselves in refined and profound scholarship,
whereas the doltish [*chuiluzhe*] will at least become thoroughly grounded in propriety
and the rites."[107]

For Chen, as for nearly all members of the eighteenth-century official elite, ritual
performance was central to the civilizing process. Heavenly principle (*tianli*) was most
succinctly revealed in the corpus of ritual doctrine (*lijiao*), which had been bequeathed
more or less intact from the world of antiquity, when civilized society had first been discovered or invented. The rites (*li*) claimed authority over all facets of human behavior,
prescribing what Robert Eno has called a total "choreography" of personal action.[108] As
such, routines were specified for all forms of interpersonal contact in accordance with
the social role or roles occupied by the respective parties. Even the deportment of the
individual in private—postures and motions appropriate to reading, eating, sleeping,
taking one's toilet—was governed by strict dictates (as we have seen Chen insisting of
his *yixue* pupils in Yunnan). But formal stylization was especially important in the context of personal rites of passage—as it were, an individual's acknowledged entry into or
exit from a given set of roles—and in celebrations of communal bonding and/or allegiance to the state. It was the duty of the ruler and his officials, as shepherds to the people in the civilizing process, to bring popular customary practice (*su*) into closest possible accord with ritual correctness, and this was a duty Chen Hongmou assumed with
more than the usual sense of missionary zeal. As we have seen, his more than twenty
provincial tenures were punctuated by repeated campaigns to correct popular ritual
practice, sometimes piecemeal but often (as in Yunnan in 1734, Shaanxi in 1744,
Fujian in 1753, and Jiangsu in 1760) in extraordinarily comprehensive ways.

As Chen put it, "Ritual is truly the foundation upon which the state stands" (*Li shi
guo suoyi li ye*).[109] Although he never wavers from his faith in the transcendent moral
correctness of the *li*, he is frank about its pragmatic utility to the task of governance.
Ritual propriety is a key means of establishing "uniformity" (*huayi*) among the empire's diverse localities and constituencies.[110] It fosters social harmony and so reduces
the burdensome incidence of litigation.[111] Not least, ritual is important for economic
reasons. Although ritual excesses must be guarded against because they dissipate the
society's accumulated wealth, more fundamentally family and community ritual are
the basic means of reproducing the rural household, whose "stable productivity"
(*hengye*) is the most reliable and efficient foundation of both state and society. (Reciprocally, as we saw in Chapter 7, it is largely as a means of providing rural households
the cash to finance rituals of family reproduction that Chen legitimates his push for
commercialized agriculture.)

Chen's odd (but characteristic) combination of unshakable faith and flexible pragmatism is seen as well in the degree of punctilious fidelity he expects in ritual performance. At times, especially in his treatments of state and/or community ritual, he

emphasizes literal conformity to "ancient practice" (*jiuxi* or *gufeng*). At other times, though, especially in connection with family rituals, he actively prefers simplified, less fussy, and more frugal ritual observances than those specified in classical texts. In matters of interpersonal ritual courtesy, moreover, he complains about the socially disruptive concern he sees around him over "minor points of etiquette" (*xiaojie*).[112]

For the most part Chen seems sublimely uninterested in the debates over liturgical details that increasingly preoccupied mid-Qing intellectuals. As Kai-wing Chow has shown, these debates were not mere academic parlor games but rather were tied in with a broad fundamentalist project engaged in by eighteenth-century literati, especially (but not exclusively) those of the so-called Han learning persuasion. If we can only get back to the precise ritual forms of antiquity, purging them of subsequent corruptions, this line of thinking went, we can recreate in the present day a kind of utopian social order. The ritual practices of antiquity, in other words, hold the status of revealed truth.[113]

This sort of approach to ritual had no appeal whatsoever for Chen Hongmou. Late in life, at nearly the peak of Han learning's popularity, he composed a model examination essay, taking as his text the passage from the *Doctrine of the Mean* (*Zhongyong*) in which Confucius claims, "I study the rituals of Zhou. For use today, I follow Zhou." Why, Chen asks, when the venerable rituals and institutions of Shang were still fairly well documented, did the tradition-minded sage nevertheless opt to accord primacy to the more recent models of Zhou? Because, Chen replies, "Confucius honored the institutions of the current ruling house [*shiwang*]." Zhou rituals had the advantage of being both socially workable and politically acceptable. But the same text also records that Confucius "studied" Shang rituals as well. Does this imply that he was a closet Shang loyalist? Hardly. Chen explains: "Confucius was born in the time of Zhou, and so he adopted Zhou rites. At the same time, he considered himself a descendent of Shang, and for this reason he wished to study [but *not* adopt] Shang rituals. There was no inherent contradiction between the two sentiments."[114]

The notion that the *li* were to some extent temporally relative rather than permanently fixed had of course been articulated often in the past, but Chen's formulation here still seems strikingly bold. It carries at least two messages. First, it is an evident apologia for a Chinese Confucian scholar such as himself, who has studied his own cultural past, serving an alien ruling house. (The question of upholding a Manchu court is in general serenely nonproblematic to Chen, as it was to much of the mid-Qing official elite.) In his insistence in 1752 to a Fujianese audience that they must employ the ritual texts and implements appropriate to "our dynasty" (*wochao*), we may well detect an interlinear warning that subtle expressions of Ming loyalism in the adoption of outdated ritual models will not be tolerated.[115] At the same time, though, and more important in the present context, Chen's remarkable examination essay expresses his complete distaste for the fundamentalist undertones of contemporary philology. We live in the present, he is saying, and ought to be as fully comfortable in our own times as the sage was in his. Although rituals are unquestionably a link with the past, and also an expression of timeless verities—the cosmic order—they express this in terms of a vocabulary of practice that evolves over historical time.

Similarly, it is fruitless to demand too exact a conformity to the detailed ritual prescriptions even of Zhu Xi, who naturally wrote them with the social realities of his own
day in mind. Indeed, it is in large part Zhu's frank historical relativism that so com-
mended him to Chen, even as it condemned him in the eyes of Hanxue purists.
Commenting on the writings of Lü Kun, Chen repeatedly returns to the question of
ritual conformity that was central to Lü's thought. Ritual practice that is truly functional, he argues, is that which is neither insufficiently (*buji*) nor excessively (*guo*) punctilious but which rather adheres to the mean (*zhong*). Insufficient zeal is a neglect of the
rites (*shili*), but too much ritual—*guoli*—does the rites active harm (*haili*).[116]

We saw in Chapter 3 that the early modern Chinese intellectual world was marked
by a broad rehabilitation of the moral propriety of human emotional response (*renqing*), a project in which Chen Hongmou, in his own distinctive way, fully participated.
Related to this was a growing discomfort about the tension between *renqing* and the
meticulous dictates of ritual propriety (*lijiao*). Many believed that the contemporary
legacy of Song neo-Confucianism, albeit perhaps unintended by that movement's
founders, was a corpus of ritual practice that was artificial, inflexible, and insensitive to
the flesh-and-blood lives of real human beings. A mounting chorus of reformist literati
decried especially what might be termed "vulgar ritualism," an excessively arbitrary
reading on the part of local society of the demands, attributed to the classical canon,
for behavior that was clearly contrary to notions of human decency and the dictates of
common sense. Voices in this tradition included those of Gui Youguang (1506–71),
Mao Qiling (1623–1716), Qian Daxin (1728–1804), and Wang Zhong (1745–94),
but none, perhaps, was as unimpeachably orthodox as Lü Kun. Lü argued point-blank
that ritual propriety, properly understood, was no more than a vocabulary for the physical expression of *renqing*, of emotions that were perfectly natural, and reflected the no-
blest human instincts.[117]

Writing nearly two centuries after Lü, Chen Hongmou reprinted the former's arguments, praising them for their insight into human psychology (*renxin*) and "the way
the world actually works" (*shidao*).[118] Chen emphasized that human sentiments, *renqing*,
were fully commendable; they were a manifestation of the basic and benign heavenly
principle (*tianli*) that governed the universe.[119] The *lijiao*, properly understood, should
not and could not be incompatible with this. Ritual propriety, Chen insisted, was in
essence a demonstration of natural bonds of affection that in turn were prompted by
the natural goodness (*tianliang* or *liangzhi*) common to all human beings.[120] Any profession of ritual propriety that violates commonsense understandings of humane behavior is therefore necessarily false.

The stress here on the universality of natural morality raises once again the thorny
issue of class and the fundamental tension that Chen's ritual discourse shares with virtually all Confucian thought: that between hierarchy and equality. Chen does not dispute that the very essence of ritual is drawing status distinctions between high and low
(*bian shangxia*).[121] The benign, ordered universe that human society, through the instrument of ritual, must reproduce is benign and orderly precisely because its prece-
dences are clearly ordained; yet ritual is at the same time common to all human beings—and human beings alone—and in that sense necessarily transcends class. In his

running commentary on Lü Kun Chen laments the overemphasis he sees in contemporary society on the demand that ritual honor be shown to elites by their lower-status neighbors. These "haughty superiors" (*gaoaozhe*) claim deference on grounds that "the *li* cannot be ignored"; their neighbors, in turn, protest that ritual propriety should not imply oppression and high-handedness. The result is conflict, litigation, and the breakdown of social consensus.[122] For Chen the resolution to this tension between hierarchy and equality is found in compromise: to be socially constructive, ritual deference—like all ritual activity—must be exercised in moderation.

Family Ritual

"Without ritual," writes Chen in his *Sourcebook on Reforming Social Practice*, "we are nothing but brute beasts." Accordingly, it is the task of the official, charged by his emperor with the mission to civilize his constituents, to ensure the practice of the "four rituals" (*sili*) that set apart a civilized household and mark the entrance or exit of its individual members from the sets of relational roles (*fen*) defined by the orthodox canon. Not only must the *sili* be faithfully practiced, but they must be practiced in faithful accord with the prescriptions of two ritual texts formally endorsed by the Qing court, Hu Guang's *Xingli daquan* (1415) and Qiu Jun's *Jiali yijie* (1474).[123] Of the four family rituals—capping (a male coming-of-age ceremony), weddings, funerals, and ancestral sacrifice—I will concentrate here on the latter three, which are Chen Hongmou's main concerns.

In Chapter 9 we saw Chen working in his provincial jurisdictions to ensure the appropriateness of marriage partners—to institutionalize in the localities uniform Han elite norms of patrilineality and patrilocality and at the same time combat "commodification" of brides and promote more effectively companionate marriages. When we turn to Chen's discussions of the wedding ceremony itself, we see these concerns for ritual propriety and human dignity linked with that for the prudent management of material resources. Recent scholarship has revealed the unusual spurt of interest in Chen's day regarding the precise ceremonial details for weddings as laid out in the Han-dynasty *Li ji*, the Song-dynasty *Zhuzi jiali*, and other venerable texts. This interest stemmed less from an abstract antiquarianism than from a self-conscious drive to demonstrate elite superiority amidst an increasingly fluid social order by rigid adherence to the elaborate (and very costly) particularities of classical wedding ritual.[124] This in turn took place in the context of a centuries-old debate over whether it was wiser for elites to insist on rigid adherence to classical ritual formulae or to broaden popular acceptance of orthodoxy by making rituals simpler, more accessible, and more affordable. In practice, of course, by the eighteenth century a wide array of printed texts circulated, offering precisely such streamlined, do-it-yourself ritual alternatives, models that the purists in the debate were determined not to accept.[125]

As he did on other questions of popular accessibility (for example, the vernacularization of moral treatises), Chen Hongmou came down strongly on the side of popularization of wedding ritual. The need for simplified but realistically performable ceremonies overrode any dogmatic adherence to ritual prescriptions, which in any case had been designed to meet the needs of very different historical circumstances. Most particularly, Chen railed against the trend he perceived, especially in Jiangnan, to use protestations of ritual propriety to turn weddings into orgies of competitive consumption—a way for families to show off their wealth by protracting the nuptial process into an endless round of ceremonies, feasts, and gift-exchanges. This for Chen was *guoli* (overritualization)—in effect, violating the spirit of the *lijiao* by slavish and self-aggrandizing insistence on adhering to its particularities.[126]

Chen's concerns here are manifold. He certainly wants to preserve the hegemonic mystique of the ritual itself from the burlesque to which he sees it subjected by such unseemly indulgence. Economically, he views extravagance in wedding ritual as both a dissipation of Heaven's bounty (*tianliang*) and a threat to the financial integrity (*jiaji*) of the small-producer household, the basis of production for the empire as a whole. To this end, for instance, he seeks to impose limits on betrothal presents and suggests that a truly appropriate dowry would be a bequest of land to the nuptial household, to underwrite its reproduction as an economic unit.[127] Not least Chen is also worried about the divisive potential of competitive ritual performance for local society, turning what ought to be a source of local community solidarity into an instrument of elitist hauteur and domination. Chen's discourse on marriage ritual, therefore, is a vehicle of social criticism, far from the knee-jerk defense of class privilege it is sometimes taken to be.

Probably more so than nuptial ritual, funerary practice was a key element of Chinese identity. The "civilizing" (*hua*) of non-Han death rituals had been a major thrust of the process of sinicization of contiguous peoples for millennia, and it was never a more self-conscious strategy than in the eighteenth-century spurt of Qing imperial expansion in the northwest and southwest. Standardization of death ritual likewise served to unify diversities of local culture within the "interior land" (*neidi*) itself.[128] Ideally, James Watson suggests, it also forged a sense of common identity among persons of differing social class. Yet, as Timothy Brook and Kai-wing Chow have demonstrated, after the sixteenth century the self-conscious promotion of certain funerary practices associated with neo-Confucian orthodoxy effectively came to serve as an instrument of class warfare, as a vehicle through which, in Brook's term, "a minority among the gentry" sought both to bolster their power organizationally (as a key to the formation of large, hierarchically structured lineages in local areas) and as an emblem of moral and cultural superiority over their less ritually correct neighbors.[129] Chen Hongmou's copious writings on funeral and burial practice, and his occasional statements on ancestral sacrifice, must be understood in the context of this tension-filled environment.

Of utmost importance to Chen is the simple act of burial. Our practice of burying our dead (*sizang*), he insists, as much as our paired concern for nourishing the living (*shengyang*), is evidence of the civilized humanity (*rendao*) that distinguishes us from beasts or savages.[130] As a provincial official, Chen contributes in many very material ways to the promotion of universal burial of corpses. He orders and facilitates the establishment of free cemeteries (*yizhong*) in numerous localities under his jurisdiction, with direct sponsorship either by the local administration or by collectivities of local elites (financed out of corporate estates, *tang*) or by lineages.[131] When serving on the aboriginal pale in Yunnan, Chen establishes a local charitable society to provide coffins and grave sites for unclaimed corpses and founds an association among his Guangxi compatriots to finance the return home for burial of deceased fellow provincials.[132] In Shaanxi in the 1740s he orders his county-level subordinates to convey official honors on local philanthropists who contribute to similar burial societies.[133] And in his *Sourcebook on Reforming Social Practice* he reprints and endorses the text of a community covenant from seventeenth-century Zhejiang devoted exclusively to the mutual encouragement (financial and otherwise) of proper Confucian burial.[134]

The major targets of Chen's attack are cremation and delayed burial during an extended period of mourning. As Brook has pointed out, these practices, predominantly Buddhist and Daoist in inspiration, were actively preferred by the majority of late imperial subjects, elite as well as plebeian, to the strictly neo-Confucian practices specified in the *Zhuzi jiali* and other orthodox texts. This had occasioned a chorus of literati complaint in the early Qing from such luminaries as Chen Que (1604–77), Zhang Luxiang (1611–74), and most notably Gu Yanwu.[135] In his *Sourcebook on Reforming Social Practice* Chen Hongmou approvingly reprints the scathing condemnation of cremation and delayed burial from Gu's *Rizhi lu*.[136] As the mid-Qing court became increasingly swept into this current of neo-Confucian ritual purism, it too joined the chorus of complaint; in virtually his first act on succession to the throne in 1735 the Qianlong emperor strongly reiterated the legal prohibition on cremation and ordered his field officials to see to its enforcement.[137] In the process burial became an even more political act than it had always been. As Chen wrote in 1740, "Proper burial is of direct importance to kingly governance [*wangzheng*]."[138]

Ironically, cremation (*huozang*) seems to have been most popular in the southwest, where it was linked with aboriginal death ritual, and in the Jiangnan heartland, where its practice was related to the paucity of grave sites because of population density and intensive agrarian development. In Suzhou and its environs professional crematoria were big business, and Chen Hongmou pursued with zeal a campaign against the proprietors, in whom he found convenient emblems of venal self-interest as enemies of the rites.[139] In fact, the potential for conflict between his own economic development projects and his equally vigorous proselytization of ritual correctness was often brought to the fore by the issue of burial. For example, in Tianjin Chen's construction of an expanded irrigation infrastructure necessitated relocation of existing graves, an issue that seems to have called forth considerable local politicking on his part.[140]

Delayed burial (*tingsang*) was a more complicated affair. For some households the delay was a simple matter of needing extra time to accumulate funds for a respectable interment; for such families the solution was to be found in credit societies to help finance burial. But more often *tingsang* resulted from the influence of geomancers, who were retained for long periods and at considerable expense before finally determining an auspicious site and date for burial. Chen's own attacks on delayed burial, like the writings of early Qing scholars whose similar diatribes he cites, make it clear that the vogue of delayed burial—often for years on end—was ubiquitous throughout the empire. Having issued prohibitions on this subject in a variety of his provincial postings, Chen in 1741 memorialized requesting an imperial edict that, he hoped, would put an end to the practice once and for all, at least among the elite. Every individual sitting for the civil service examination, he suggested, should be subjected to a background check; any who were discovered to have incidents of delayed burial in their family's past would be disqualified. It is revealing that the court rejected Chen's proposal on the grounds that such investigations would give added leeway to yamen clerks to extort funds from local elites.[141] In other words, despite the importance it accorded to popular orthopraxy as a sign of its own legitimacy, the court believed at least some elements of ritual correctness were not worth the social costs of enforcement.

It seems to me that the underlying problem in the issue of delayed burial was really the highly ambivalent attitude held by even the most rigidly orthodox literati toward geomancy (*fengshui*) itself. Chen's own attacks on delayed burial always carry a tone of ridicule of geomancy as an unenlightened superstition. In his *Sourcebook on Reforming Social Practice* he reprints a text that outlines several basic considerations to keep in mind when selecting a grave site: do not locate it near a major thoroughfare (where it will be easy pickings for grave robbers), or in a swamp, or in the midst of pastureland. All of these provisions, he concludes, are nothing but common sense; why do you need a self-styled geomantic expert to tell you this?[142] Yet, when his irrigation projects in Tianjin force him to relocate a cemetery, he himself falls back on the rationale that the old grave site, lying as it did to the south of the city, was "too *yang*" to be suitable in the first place.[143]

Just how much Chen himself participates in popular religious culture, of which geomancy forms a part, is something of a gray area. He does certainly cherish a faith in retribution/repayment (*bao*) for human actions, and his warning that "the dead will hold a grievance" if they are not accorded proper funerals may well reflect his genuine belief.[144] Similarly, his argument that the long continuity of the family line of the Yuan-dynasty Confucian Chen Ji was a direct function of the family's strict adherence to the *lijiao* in funerary practice (in defiance of the contemporary vogue of Buddhist death ritual) was very likely sincere.[145] But of course there are other, more mundane reasons why Confucian purism could promote lineage longevity—at least in the late imperial era, Confucianism was essentially *about* lineage—and Chen's arguments for orthodox death ritual are more often very practical in nature. As he tells his constituency in Shaanxi: "The way a family conducts funerals and burials is a direct measure of how grief-stricken, and indeed how filial, that family is."[146]

Taken as a whole, Chen Hongmou's stance on orthodoxy in death ritual must be seen as part of the great religious war waged by devout *lixue* adherents (largely members of the official elite) in the seventeenth and eighteenth centuries against Buddhist and Daoist beliefs and practice. It also falls within the more persistent assault on popular culture leveled by self-consciously rational, enlightened, and "civilized" (although not necessarily secularized) Chinese elites, an assault continued in the various "antisuperstition" campaigns of the late Qing, the Republic, and the People's Republic, when a Western liberal or Marxist "modernity" was substituted for *lixue* as the elite ideology.

In each of his many provincial jurisdictions, over four decades, Chen rails against the use of Buddhist or Daoist liturgical forms or ritual specialists in the conduct of death ritual. His special ire, though, is directed against the performance at funerals of those prototypical vehicles for transmission of Chinese folk culture, operas. In Shaanxi in 1746 and in Jiangsu in 1760, he goes so far as to declare theatrical performances at funerals a criminal act.[147] We know from the work of Tanaka Issei and others that village opera could have politically seditious (or at least politically independent) overtones, but I don't think this is what provokes Chen about their inclusion in funeral practice.[148] Rather, I think we can take at face value his claim that it is the operas' alarming religious implications that he finds so inappropriate in an orthodox funeral context.

As David Johnson has compellingly demonstrated, operas such as "Mulian Rescues His Mother" (*Mulian jiu mu*) and others routinely performed at late imperial funerals were in fact no less than counterrituals, exercises in communal exorcism that the village faithful found at once liberating and terrifying. Although a staunch neo-Confucian such as Chen Hongmou might condemn them as Buddhist-inspired, in fact such ritual operas were threatening less for their theology than for their invitation to frenzied enthusiasm (Chen merely hints at this suspension of Confucian order when he complains that opera performances open the door to sexual mingling). They also, as Johnson makes clear, offered nearly insuperable competition to the *lijiao* in its claims to control over numinous forces.[149]

Chen's broader animus, the evidence suggests, is against the folk culture as a whole. We see this most revealingly in a passing condemnation he offers of the familiar Chinese practice of presenting the deceased with paper models (*zhiqi*) of desirable commodities to provide pleasure for him or her in the afterlife. Chen considers this practice Buddhist-tainted, and hence he outlaws it in Jiangsu in 1760. He adds, however, that in any case such items would only be used by the ignorant (*yumin*), which makes them an object of ridicule by the *youzhizhe*, those with more enlightened sensibilities, such as himself.[150]

Does this undeniable streak of cultural elitism on Chen's part find a parallel in a class-based defense of social privilege? I have argued throughout this book that in general it does not. It is true that in his discussions of funerary practice Chen supports sumptuary policies that might be taken as evidence for the opposite conclusion. As Shaanxi governor in 1744, Chen invokes the statute stipulating hierarchically graded funerary rituals appropriate for official, gentry, and commoner households and attacks the prevalent practice of usurping ritual reforms proper to one's social superiors.[151] In so doing he may be seen as seeking ritual props to shore up the existing social order, but in my view his major purpose was otherwise. Rather, what irritates Chen about this particular form of funereal social climbing is essentially its expense. He follows his citation of statute in this area by immediately shifting the ground of discussion to a familiar diatribe against conspicuous consumption and economic waste. Among the generally frugal and "rustic" (*zhipu*, a category of high praise in Chen's social taxonomy) Shaanxi population, funerals constitute one of the few occasions for lapses into extravagance. Coffined corpses are allowed to lie unburied for long periods, during which the bereaved family and friends hold a succession of wakes (where, God forbid, males and females openly mingle!). Such conduct is at once contrary to the rites, "uncivilized" (*shanghua*), and disrespectful of the deceased. "If one truly esteems one's fore-bears," scolds the governor, "one cannot bear to dissipate [their patrimony] in such frivolous display."[152]

As is the case with wedding ritual, Chen's discussions of funerals emphasize the ritual's importance, and strongly condemn what he perceives as deviant practice, but are re-markably silent on the ceremony's actual content. Details of the liturgy were so non-problematically laid out in the prescribed handbooks, Chen must have believed, that they did not warrant his specific attention, but it is difficult to escape the conclusion that he also found them personally uninteresting. The same is true for the fourth of the standard family rituals, ancestral rites. Here, however, Chen's silence on liturgical niceties constitutes a statement in itself, given the intense fascination and the lively de-bate over such details among the literati of his day. In part this silence reflects his de-liberate stance of remaining above partisanship in matters of scholarship, but in part also it suggests a vague discomfort on Chen's part with received orthodoxy.

Although Chen devoted far less ink to discussions of ancestral rites than he did to weddings and funerals, we have already seen in Chapter 11 how socially useful he found them to be. In line with widespread Qing official-elite practice, he constructed an ancestral temple, purchased sacrificial implements, and set down guidelines for the conduct of ancestral rites for his own lineage outside Guilin.[153] He believed the *fact* of the rites' performance to be of such weight that he memorialized in 1748 to have them denied by edict to convicted fratricides.[154] In his *Sourcebook on Reforming Social Practice* he cited various authorities on the central importance of ancestral sacrifice to the main-tenance of the family as a social institution, including such early Qing luminaries as Lu Shiyi (1611–72), Wei Xiangshu (1617–87), and Cai Shiyuan (1682–1733).[155] Yet Chen was rather reticent about where he stood on what was in fact one of the chief in-tellectual controversies of his day: the actual conduct of the rites.

As Kai-wing Chow has shown, the precise manner in which the ancestral rites ought to be performed, and mourning grades assigned, was perceived as critical largely be-cause of its social implications. During an era in which the agnatic lineage was becom-ing ever more compelling as an instrument of local social order (largely in response to the belief that lapses in ritual propriety and loosening of familial bonds had precipi-tated the social and political chaos of the late Ming), it was the precise forms of the an-cestral sacrifice, as specified in the classics, that set the parameters along which such lin-eages ought to be constructed. In large part the debate centered on the question of whether one ought to accept the vision of the *zongfa*, the "core-line principle" of line-age organization, established as orthodox by the *Zhuzi jiali* (family rituals), compiled by the neo-Confucian master Zhu Xi. Indeed, the very authenticity of this text was a ques-tion of some debate in Chen's day.[156]

That Chen never took an open stance on the question of authenticity is not sur-prising, in light of the general contempt in which he held philological research as a dil-ettantish waste of intellectual effort. What *is* surprising is the hint of ambivalence to-ward this text's authority on the part of one who so regularly and unconditionally identified himself as a Zhu Xi loyalist. Chen never directly contested the *Zhuzi jiali's* correctness. We have seen, for example, that he followed the Qing court in endorsing the Ming-dynasty works *Xingli daquan* and *Jiali yijie*, both of which included Zhu Xi's text. We have also seen that he extolled the writings on ritual of Wei Xiangshu, who had been probably the *Zhuzi jiali*'s most articulate champion in the early Qing.[157] Yet it is striking that whereas Chen's five celebrated anthologies of past wisdom (collectively known as the *Wuzhong yigui*) are strewn with selections from Zhu Xi, the *Zhuzi jiali* itself is nowhere to be found. During his campaign to "civilize" the non-Han southwest in the 1730s, moreover, Chen printed up and distributed hundreds of guidebooks to proper family living, including the *Zhuzi zhijia geyan* (Master Zhu's household rules), which he falsely attributed to Zhu Xi, but again the *Zhuzi jiali* was not among them.[158]

A decade later, while serving as Shaanxi governor in 1744, Chen imported printing blocks from the lower Yangzi in order to reprint and distribute copies of the text he had by then come to believe authoritative on matters of ancestral sacrifice (and family rituals more generally). This work was Song Xun's 1573 *Sili chugao* (First draft of the Four Rituals).[159] Although based on the *Zhuzi jiali*, Song's work was both greatly simplified and somewhat eclectic. It proffered what Patricia Ebrey has called a "relaxed view of popular practice," including explicit deference on some points to the advice of popular almanacs.[160] As Chen himself noted in his preface to his reprint edition, Zhu Xi had originally compiled his work as much on the basis of observation of contemporary twelfth-century practice as on the authority of ancient texts. Even so, it had been necessary for Qiu Jin to simplify and update it in the fifteenth century and for Song Xun to do the same once again a century later. The virtue of the resulting work, Chen announced, was that "one need not be a member of the gentry, nor from a wealthy and illustrious household, in order to use it."[161]

We may certainly accept Chen's statement that his preference for more recent modifications over Zhu Xi's original text stemmed largely from his concern for popular accessibility. But there were substantive issues involved as well. And, indeed, the scholar who probably had the single most formative impact on Chen's thought, Lü Kun, was among those who had raised the gravest doubts about the *Zhuzi jiali*'s substantive utility.[162] There were two essential points of interpretive conflict. First was the fact that Zhu Xi, living in an age when the agnatic lineage had not yet become the dominant social form it would be, did not call for worship of the lineage founder (*shizu*) and in fact set strict limits on the generational distance of ancestors meriting sacrifice. The inconsistency of Zhu's prescriptions with the late imperial enthusiasm for larger-scale kinship organizations, an enthusiasm emphatically shared by Chen Hongmou, led to a growing sense of cognitive dissonance with Zhu Xi's hallowed text.[163]

Second, the *zongfa* as interpreted by the *Zhuzi jiali* was genealogically determinist. The head of the lineage, and the chief celebrant of the ancestral rites, was the *zongzi*, the eldest son of the eldest son, or the genealogically senior male of the lineage's senior branch. In the proposals of Lü Kun and others, however, the lineage headmanship was to be vested instead in a so-called *zuzhang*, a position based less on genealogical primacy than on personal competence.[164] This clearly was a more appealing alternative to Chen Hongmou. In the preceding chapter we looked at Chen's (failed) attempt in 1742 Jiangxi to co-opt this lineage headman as an agent for the enforcement of social discipline and state law. We also saw him instructing his subordinate magistrates that this *zuzhang* figure might usefully serve as a candidate for ritual honors as chief guest at the local "community libationer" (*xiangyin jiuli*) banquet. Chen clearly saw the *zuzhang*'s role as chief celebrant of the lineage's ancestral rites as contributing to his aura of legitimacy in local society; indeed, Chen was quite explicit that it is precisely because the headman enjoys such ritual status that he is far more useful in the maintenance of social order than any patently state-manufactured *baojia* functionary might be. Although the importance of the *li* for Chen Hongmou can never be fully reduced to its instrumental role in governance, this role is never far from his mind. It was precisely *because* of its transcendent moral correctness that ritual was such a critical tool in the practical project of ordering the world.

State Ritual

Although it is by no means the central object of his ritual concerns, Chen Hongmou steadfastly upholds correct practice at the local level of what might be called the "official religion" or the "state cult" (*sidian*). The locus of this cult at the county level, at least in Chen's imagining, is very narrowly the Confucian School-temple (*xuegong*) and the Temple of Literature (*wenmiao*), which in most cases are housed in the same compound. Here one finds the altars to the sages (*chongsheng ci*) and to local historical worthies (*xiangxian minghuan ci*), and here as well the semiannual spring and autumn sacrifices (the *chunji* and *qiubao*) are performed.[165] "The transformation of local customary practice [*difang fenghua*]," writes Chen in 1733, "begins in the School-temple, with the conduct of the sacrifices by the local official."[166]

As a host of scholars have made clear, the enforced acceptance of these institutions in local areas was a cornerstone of dynastic efforts to impose the symbols of central political control, and insistence on correct performance of their associated rites was a means of ensuring local elite complicity in the process of imperial hegemonization.[167] There can be little doubt that this intention was present in Chen Hongmou as well, but he never talks about it, and there are many indications that it was for him no more than a secondary concern. For example, despite the fact that Chen spent much of his career in frontier areas—often in the midst of active hostilities attendant to imperial conquest—I have nowhere in his writings found evidence of concern with implementing the paired military counterpart to the civilian *wenmiao*, the Temple of War (*wumiao*), even though in many official eyes acceptance of that cult was a yet more direct local acknowledgment of submission to imperial might.[168]

Where Chen does concentrate his efforts is on ensuring fastidious performance of the spring and autumn sacrifices (*chunqiu dadian*) at the altars of the sages and local worthies. This, he says, is a critical function of local administration and as such must be treated with the utmost seriousness. All aspects must be precisely correct and in accord with "ancient practices" (*jiuxi*). The altars must not be dilapidated—Chen notes with horror that in some localities these sacred precincts have been allowed to become stables for oxen, pigs, and sheep. Vestments must be clean and exactly as prescribed. Sacrificial vessels and other implements must be in pristine condition. Offerings of food must be of the highest quality. For each of these purposes Chen authorizes outlays of funds from county budgets and offers suggestions on how to manage a community subscription drive where official finances may fall short. Most critically, ritual liturgies must follow precisely those laid down by the sage, the "first teacher" (*xianshi*), and transmitted via the imperial *huidian* manuals. In peripheral areas where local ritual expertise may be weak Chen underwrites the importation of dance and music masters from the provincial capital to train local students.[169]

Lax or erroneous performance of the sacrifices is not only an act of lèse-majesté but also an affront to the locality's own past worthies, the repayment (*baogong*) of whom for their service to the community is a key component of worship. For this reason it is crucial that the tablets (*paiwei*) that constitute the visible objects of worship in certain sacrifices be well tended and arranged in appropriate order of precedence. Most important, they must be audited to purge interlopers from the ranks of the worthy. It is revealing of Chen's deep animus against local elite pretension that he looks first in this purge to find if wealthy families have sought to bolster their local cultural hegemony by inserting their unworthy forebears into the pantheon of sacrificial recipients.[170]

Why do the ritual details of the state cult interest Governor Chen so deeply? There are several reasons. Not least of these, I believe, is that he held genuine faith in its efficacy. However tempting it may be to see eighteenth-century Confucians, and especially *jingshi* exemplars such as Chen Hongmou, as fully secularized rational humanists with but an instrumental view of imperial ritual, this perception does their complex cosmological outlook great injustice. In reference to the spring and autumn sacrifices, as well as in countless other expressions of personal piety, Chen held that a reverent attitude, expressed above all through attention to ceremonial correctness, was the best way to ensure the benign operation of the numinous power (*ling*) of the past sages and the spirits. As we saw in Chapter 3, Chen enjoyed considerable renown for his prowess at "Confucian magic" in rainmaking, flood control, and so on. As he wrote:

> The ancient sage-kings first enriched their people, and then extended their dominion, due to the power of the spirits. All of their worship of the spirits [*sishen*] was on behalf of the people [*weimin*]. In enabling the people to ward off natural disasters, they relied upon sacrificial ritual [*sidian*]. . . . It is the job of officials today to . . . beseech the aid of the spirits of their assigned jurisdiction. By so doing, they ensure the timely arrival of rain and the ripening of crops.[171]

Invoking a long tradition of scholarship, Chen insisted that his diligence in purging sacrificial ritual of deviant practices (*xiu sidian*) was critical to the control of climatic irregularity.[172] There is no reason to doubt that he meant it.

A second reason for Chen's fastidiousness in this area, however, is more political. Although inculcating popular awe of the majesty of the state is not, as I have said, one of Chen's primary concerns, he is clearly aware of the need to compete with popular alternatives for religious devotion. The spring and autumn rites themselves, marking as they did key moments in the agrarian cycle, had popular as well as official versions, about which the Qing court felt profoundly ambivalent. It wished as much as possible to preserve the image of imperial control over the orderly progression of the seasons and so at times attacked nonofficial sacrificial performances; at the same time, with

agricultural productivity such an important goal of policy, it believed it could not prohibit altogether festivals that clearly celebrated this productivity.[173] For his part Chen
Hongmou acknowledged this competition when he ordered his subordinates to take
state-cult rituals seriously: "Just think! The mean people of the villages and alley-ways
know how to conduct reverent worship services on their own, and how to keep their
temples in good repair. How does it look when those charged with the people's governance and with stewardship of the Confucian tradition cannot measure up to the standard the commoners themselves have set?"[174]

At the same time, Chen's zeal at "standardizing" (*xiu*) these ritual performances reveals his awareness that even the most orthodox ceremonies of the state cult are themselves under contest, subject to alternative readings by local audiences that resist, with
varying degrees of conscious intent, the hegemony of the imperial order.[175] It seems
clear, again, that it is not so much localism per se that Chen fears (as Watson astutely
points out, the emphasis on a common set of symbols and ritual practices is useful precisely *because* it provides space for the simultaneous existence of myriad local cultures)
but rather the more obvious signs of cultural resistance. "The spirits," he insists, "do not
respond favorably to worship which is not conducted in accordance with the dictates of
the Rites." In jurisdictions such as Jiangsu and Fujian, where actively heterodox spirit
cults enjoy wide support and considerable organizational strength, Chen works to restrict sacrificial observances to the authorized spring and autumn intervals. All other
ceremonies, especially those marking the birthdays of nonstandard deities, are suspect.
Chen's repeated proscription of flying motto-bearing pennants and of staging nonap-
proved operas (whose librettos, as Tanaka Issei has shown, were routine vehicles for the
reproduction of alternative cultural norms) signal his alertness to the possibilities of ritual performance for the dissemination of counterideologies.[176]

One final rationale that Chen Hongmou consistently offers for his concern for
sacrificial correctness is economic. Punctilious performance of the spring and autumn
sacrifices, along the lines Chen is promoting, is decidedly not a function of how much
is expended or consumed in the process. He regularly condemns extravagance in
sacrificial worship as a dissipation of the celebrants' hard-earned wealth and as a reckless misuse of Heaven's bounty, both of which the spirits find offensive. Far more useful than burning off local surpluses in pious devotions, he suggests, is investing them
in a community granary to hedge against future dearth. Although such an argument is
obviously useful in Chen's attack on heterodox cults, for which competitive demonstrations of opulence are a major part of their popular appeal, it is far from simply instrumental. Rather, it is basic to Chen's very deep-seated logic of thrift and accumulation and, as we have seen, is a theme that runs throughout his discourse on all types of
ritual performance.

Li, Civilité, *Civilization*

To conclude this chapter I draw on analyses of European cultural history by Norbert
Elias, Roger Chartier, Jacques Revel, and others to briefly suggest some analogies between the early modern histories of the concepts of *li* (for which "ritual" or "rites" are

only very incomplete English equivalents) and *civilité* (civility).[177] Respectively in China and Europe these were very ancient ideas, but both underwent an intense phase of reenergizing and redefinition after the sixteenth century, with Erasmus (1524–83) the emblematic figure in this process in the West and perhaps Lü Kun (with Chen Hongmou as his chief eighteenth-century interlocutor) in China. This analogizing is of course not original with myself; European writers such as Montesquieu (1689–1755) and the contributors to the *Encyclopédie* (1753) themselves held up mid-Qing China as the global model of a social order based on *civilité* and Qing rulers as exemplars of taking the cultivation of civilized behavior as the foundation of statecraft.[178] What I hope to do here is less to insist on parallel or interrelated processes in East and West than to exploit this European historiography to open up some possible ways of understanding what was going on in the mentality of the Qing official elite.

One of the hallmarks of the reconceptualization of *civilité* in the West was that outward appearances—personal hygiene, dress, manners, speech—are not epiphenomenal but are instead deeply and dependably revealing of the inner person. This idea was not new; in Europe it was shared with older notions of aristocratic *courtoisie* articulated in such works as Castiglione's *Courtier* (already perhaps a bit out of date with its 1528 publication). What *was* defiantly new in early modern *civilité*, vis-à-vis *courtoisie*, was its presumption of democratic universality, its argument for a single code of conduct appropriate for all human beings without status distinction, "the one true [human] nature, rediscovered at last."[179] Of course, Lü Kun and Chen Hongmou were not fighting precisely the same antiaristocratic battles as the middle-class champions of civility in the West, but they *did* face insistent gentry attempts to appropriate ritual correctness as in effect an exclusive class prerogative. They therefore got at much the same idea with their arguments for grounding the *li* in a universal *renqing wuli* (human nature and the principles of things) and, in Chen's case, in an inclusive *tianliang* (heavenly endowed human goodness) as well. As Chartier notes, *civilité* in its later eighteenth-century incarnation allowed for formal differentiation based on "natural inequalities" (age, generation, degree of kinship relation) but not on presumable "unnatural" distinctions such as wealth, rank, or social position.[180] As I have repeatedly suggested in this book, this is precisely the sort of formulation I see Chen Hongmou reaching toward in the mid-Qing.

A corollary of the new assumption of the universality of civilized behavioral norms in the West was the idea that these can be taught, and taught to all. The reformulation of the European notion of civility was linked to a new conceptualization of the stages of personal growth that placed great stress on the socialization of children.[181] That all children, seen as uncorrupted natural innocents, can and should be carefully indoctrinated in the proper forms of civilized adult behavior was the theme of Erasmus's *De civilitate morum puerilium libellus*, which became the core text for educating male *and* female children for centuries after its 1530 publication. The need to properly socialize children thus became the rationale both for new foundings of state-sponsored elementary schools and for a new valorization placed on the "bourgeois" domestic unit, within whose confines the most intensive efforts at the "civilizing process" were to take place. All of these themes—the view of the natural innocence (*tianzhen*) of the child,

the focus of childhood education on ritual norms and personal decorum, insistence on
the class and gender inclusiveness of that education, the enshrinement of the educational process in government schools and in the home (Chen's sourcebooks on male
and female education were primarily addressed to parents), and consequent state-led
efforts to institutionalize correct family structures—were strikingly prominent in the
jiaohua initiatives of Chen Hongmou (and Yin Huiyi, Lan Dingyuan, and others) in the
mid-Qing.

Perhaps most suggestive of the resonance between conceptions of the civilizing
process in China and the early modern West is the sense of need that called them forth
at this particular time. The European stress on *civilité* in the sixteenth to eighteenth
centuries was a specific response to the uncertainties of sociocultural change: the
breakdown at once of the unifying structures of European Catholicism and the rigid hierarchies of the feudal/chivalric social order. It was an effort to control social inter-
course in the face of a newly acknowledged diversity of social groupings through the
imposition of conventions of etiquette and manners: to make one's appearance,
speech, and gestures intelligible to others unlike (but socially coequal to) oneself, to
create a common social language purged both of status distinction and of individual
self-expression, to relegate individuality and idiosyncrasy to a newly conceptualized
sphere of "private" (that is, non-"civil") life. Although the specific sociocultural factors
in China differed from those in Europe, the emphasis on ritually governed public behavior in seventeenth- and eighteenth-century China reflected a comparable effort to
recreate a common social language in the face of the erosion of status distinction, the
heightened degree of social and geographic mobility, and new evidences of cultural
pluralism in the late Ming and (in its own way) the early Qing. What is especially noteworthy is that neither the middle-class champions of *civilité* in the West nor *jiaohua* enthusiasts such as Chen Hongmou in China were interested in restoring a rigidly hier-
archic social order, even though its breakdown gave them concern (Chen's stress on
ritual conformity certainly reflected his distaste for the license granted to originality
and idiosyncrasy in late Ming culture), prompting their attempt to offer a suitably
redefined set of social conventions.

This effort to banish excessive individuality from public life—what in Europe was
sometimes called "becoming one's own master" and in Chen's parlance "overcoming
self" (*keji*)—by no means implied a blanket rejection of human emotional response.
Indeed, the rehabilitation of such response (in Chinese, *qing* or *renqing*) was central to
the humanistic, antischolastic thrust of both civilizing projects. In both projects, however, there was an explicit rejection of excess and a search for the civilized mean—neither *guo* (too much) nor *buji* (insufficient).[182] This search for the mean could apply to
the dictates of manners themselves. Chartier, in particular, points out how in Europe
the cult of *civilité* carried within it the seeds of its own decadence, its reduction to an
exaggerated politeness that could be seen as masking social climbing and internal ill
will.[183] It was this, in large measure, against which Chen Hongmou sought to guard in
his attacks on the excessive punctiliousness in ritual decorum (*guoli*) of the Jiangnan
elite, which divorced the *li* from their proper grounding in humanistic sensibilities.[184]

Three additional aspects of the rise of *civilité* in Europe offer suggestive parallels with the mid-Qing. First, the acceptance of an internalized and explicitly nonaggressive, nonviolent code of personal conduct, based on appeals to innate human rationality and reinforced by collective social pressure, served in Europe as a useful support for claims by emerging national states of monopoly on the legal use of force and their disarming of the feudal aristocracy. In China, of course, both the a-military (*wen*) character of elite culture and the conventional view that ritual decorum was a better instrument of social ordering than coercive laws or punishments had taken root well before the early modern period. Nevertheless, it is not surprising to see these themes recurring so routinely in the discourse of Chen Hongmou, a civil official in service of a consolidating, repacifying dynastic regime making at least sporadic efforts, especially under Yongzheng, at absolutist state-building along familiar European lines.[185] The insistence of Chen and his contemporaries on the need for the state to offer rational arbitration of civil litigation, as an alternative to private vengeance (*xiedou*), would likewise parallel this aspect of *civilité*'s history in the West.[186]

Second, Elias in particular has stressed the close interconnection of *civilité* ideals with the economic theories of physiocracy. According to the latter, in Elias's reading, economy and society have their own internal laws, which, like the dictates of *civilité*, fully accord with abstract reason. Although economic behavior will therefore stubbornly resist the arbitrary, irrational, and forcible efforts of political authorities to override them, an enlightened bureaucracy can effectively make rational use of such economic laws in service of the public good.[187] As will be recalled from Part 2 of this book, this is nearly precisely the line of thinking advanced by Chen Hongmou, with his postulation of natural economic laws, which, like ritual decorum, are based on heavenly ordained rational principle (*tianli*).

Finally, as Europeans found themselves in ever more intensive contact with colonial populations in the Americas and elsewhere, early modern notions of "civility" gradually transformed themselves into ideas of "civilization," defined ever more expansively as the sum total of Europe's own cultural heritage and counterpoised to the cultures of non-Europeans. In the process the biological analogy that had likened the "civilizing process" of Western history to the necessary stages of socialization of the individual child was reapplied to peoples: non-Europeans, culturally, were children, in need of the paternal socializing/civilizing influences of the metropolitan powers.[188] Eighteenth-century Chinese official elites such as Chen Hongmou likewise saw themselves in ever more intensive contact with "savage" indigenous populations and involved in campaigns of political and cultural incorporation of unprecedented earnestness. Like contemporary Europeans, they fell back on the trope of juvenilizing the populations who were to undergo civilizing (*hua*) under their parental tutelage. The recognition that members of these populations—just like real children, women, the lower classes, and the marginalized within the dominant Han population—were possessed of an innate rational intelligence only made them more necessary candidates for conversion to the universalized norms of Chinese elite culture.

Conclusion

THE QUESTION is a very simple one, really: What did the individuals who inhabited the eighteenth-century Qing bureaucracy think they were doing? More particularly, how did they conceive the universe and the society that lay before them? What did they presume its potentials and limitations to be? What were the capacities and limits of their own subjective action (both individually and collectively) in the effort to "save the world"? And what would the world, properly saved, look like? These are important questions, not merely because such a large percentage of humankind in their era was subject to these individuals' attempts at governance but because the verdict both of contemporaries and of those who followed was that, on balance, they did this job remarkably well and ought to be emulated. Despite significant and relevant contributions by scores of scholars, many cited in this study, it is a question that has rarely been addressed directly in the past.

That this simple question can receive no similarly uncomplicated answer is suggested by the long and exhaustive nature of this book. In it I have sought to answer the question through examining the assumptions, rhetoric, and behavior of one prominent member of this official elite, a man whom I consider representative of his cohort in certain ways and unrepresentative, even singular, in others. (His points of singularity, of course, as much as his representative ones, throw light on the common ground of assumptions shared by his group.) The fact that Chen Hongmou served so long and in so many places as a high field official, and that he was seen by so many in later generations as emblematic of "what went right" in this era, makes him, at the very least, a useful point of entry in attempting to answer the big question we have posed.

Chen lived in a highly distinctive historical moment. Although conventionally (and not unreasonably) depicted as an era of "stability," the early and mid-eighteenth century in the Great Qing Empire was at the same time one of extraordinary social dynamism and change. Unprecedented and unforeseen population growth led on the one hand to a pervasive urgency about more efficient productivity and on the other to heightened competition over scarce resources such as food, land, water, women, ex-

446

amination degrees, and official posts. Alien rule and more strenuous efforts at incorporation of the southern pale brought the empire a new level of ethnic complexity and, for many Qing subjects, an ongoing process of negotiation of identity. Class boundaries became noticeably permeable, the velocity of upward and downward mobility increased (Chen himself was a clear example), and the importance of ascriptive status among both the elite and the debased was considerably (and for some alarmingly) relaxed. Geographic mobility on a massive scale created new frontiers, new modes of highland-lowland relations, and new kinds of cosmopolitan urban communities hosting quasi-permanent colonies of sojourners from many distant areas. An emerging bourgeois (*shimin*) culture and consciousness was accompanied, ironically, by a greater interpenetration of urban and rural, exemplified in the proliferation and growth of market towns. An ongoing and dramatic expansion of commercial publishing, coupled with rising literacy rates, gave rise to a vibrant middlebrow print culture, the broad-ranging social implications of which we are only beginning to discover. Intensified agrarian commercialization and monetization quickened the demise of rural self-sufficiency and brought fuller commodification of land and labor and a marketization of social relations. Occupational diversification led to the emergence of new professions among the elite and to niche-seeking specialization at all levels. A large, mobile, and rootless (*wulai*) body of unmarried adult males was thrown off by the society, creating both a new kind of protoproletarian labor force and a powerful threat to orthodox cultural norms and social institutions. All of these trends led to an urgent and highly creative wave of nongovernmental organization building: new kinds of corporate business enterprises (some featuring capitalist-style labor relations), large corporate (and highly mutable) lineage structures, commercial and artisanal guilds, native-place associations within larger encompassing compatriot diasporas, and a wide spectrum of religious, fraternal, philanthropic, and local self-nurturance organizations.[1]

How did Qing political authority—the throne and the official elite of the late-Kangxi through mid-Qianlong reigns—position itself with regard to these significant social changes? We must first recognize that, despite the small-state ideology of "benevolent governance" (*renzheng*) that all in the system held dear, and the practical willingness to countenance a decrease in the number of formal government personnel relative to the growing population, the mid-Qing state was a potent and efficient instrument of both control and mobilization. Bureaucratic morale and discipline were impressively high; as Pierre-Étienne Will has argued, it was only in the 1770s (the decade following Chen Hongmou's own retirement and death) that clear signs of deterioration in this official esprit became evident.[2] And, although its relatively small size forced the regime to choose carefully among the practical tasks it set itself, when fully harnessed to the achievement of a goal the state could do remarkable things. To cite but one example from Chen's personal career: at least three times during his official service—in Tianjin and eastern Hebei from 1738 to 1740, in the northwest in the early 1750s, and in Jiangnan and Jiangbei from 1758 to 1761—Chen completely remade the hydraulic infrastructure, and hence the topography, of a large region of the empire.[3] Overall, the role of the mid-Qing regime in reconfiguring the Chinese landscape was quite dramatic.

Given this formidable capacity, and despite obvious internal disagreements and policy shifts over time—including the broad-ranging policy reassessment of the early Qianlong reign—I think it can be said that more often than not the Qing state was out in front of, rather than lagging behind, the curve of social change. It did so of course not out of any abstracted ideology of secular "progress" but rather out of more immediate and pragmatic concerns, above all an urgent preoccupation with the problem of food supply. This, for example, along with political concerns lay behind the general commitment to low taxation, a policy aimed at increasing production but that, although arguably succeeding in this end, also very probably contributed to the cause of the food supply problem, accelerating population growth. Concerns for provisioning, for more efficient production, and for fuller employment also underlay the mid-Qing regime's general highly supportive stance toward commercial exchange (foreign trade constituting a special case), monetization of the rural economy (opening new mines for monetary metals, frenetic minting of new coins, distribution of famine relief in cash), and commodification (free alienability at contracted market prices) of land and labor.

Socially, the mid-Qing state and the official elite who populated it displayed strong, unwavering support for the maintenance of the Chinese-style patriarchal household (*hu*) and, somewhat less unequivocally, for the patrilineage group. Yet it also supported aggressive relaxation of inherited proscriptions on geographic and occupational mobility; it actively encouraged regional resettlement, homesteading, and land reclamation (moderated in some instances by fiscal and hydraulic-security concerns) and, through such programs as special examination quotas for sojourning merchants and for transient *pengmin* populations, fostered diaspora-type population movements as well.[4] Through policy initiatives such as *kaihu* (establishment as a nondependent household), *kaiji weimin* (registration as a free commoner), and *goushen weimin* (purchase of free commoner status), it moved fairly consistently to eradicate a wide range of existing debased and servile statuses.[5] Despite Qianlong's rhetoric in defense of status privilege, the reality was that policies such as the evisceration of "Confucian household" (*ruhu*) rank, the merger of labor-service assessments (with their exemptions for degree holders) into the land tax (*tanding rudi*), and, above all, the vigorous sale of gentry status credentials worked positively to erode or diminish the effect of such privileges. The state and its officials generally, if somewhat erratically, supported ethnic assimilation and even at times affirmative action for indigenous non-Han populations. They consistently (although perhaps weakly in practice) supported popular education. Regarding the trend toward popular association-building, the official elite were often skeptical (they persistently condemned such forms of plebeian sociability as pilgrimage societies and boatmen's associations), but when they approved of the organization's goals (as with *huiguan*, local granary and other mutual-credit schemes, and most philanthropic associations) they could be quite encouraging.

Although Chen Hongmou is often depicted in contemporary scholarship as an elitist flunky and sociocultural reactionary,[6] and although he was a vocal champion of Song *lixue* orthodoxy and clearly authoritarian in his sentiments, his outlook was in fact very much in line with these mainstream official-elite attitudes favorable to social change.

Indeed, where he deviated from the mainstream—as for example in his persistent championing of patronage for merchant ventures (overseas as well as domestic), of mining development, of marketing gentry credentials in pursuit of higher granary stocks, of mass literacy drives (including those targeting women and non-Han populations), of relaxation of ethnic boundary–maintenance devices (such as bans on intermarriage), and so on—he tended to be rather less "conservative" than his policy opponents. But for the most part he differed from his official-elite colleagues more in degree—his astonishing energy level and his thoroughness in approaching a given policy issue at hand—than in kind.

A number of late imperial historians—initially perhaps Thomas Metzger but more recently also Will, Philip Kuhn, and Philip Huang—have convincingly sought to disabuse us of the hoary notion of the Qing administration as a fixed, tradition-bound *structure* baroquely overgrown with regulations and institutions. Collectively they would substitute for this a view of governance as a *process*, characterized by a shifting body of precedents, a style of action, and most basically an animating culture peculiar to itself. Metzger argues that the flexibility one observes in the practice of Qing governance was not merely a compromise with external reality but rather in itself a "moral commitment." Although good and bad can be identified, the world we find ourselves in is an imperfect one, and hence we who would rule others must continually strive to "transform" (*bian* or *hua*) and improve it. Unfortunately, neither the means nor the specific objects of improvement are fully clear. The political order itself is therefore necessarily no more than an ongoing "historical process," continually adapting itself in the effort to order the world.[7] As Kuhn suggests, the engine that drives this process is less often premeditated programs of regulation or reform than what he terms "events" (*shi*)—I might prefer the term *cases*—that momentarily capture attention and mobilize disparate actors within the system of governance and then pass, but leave a trace affecting future attitudes and behavior.[8] Huang, studying the highly creative manipulation of sub-statutes and precedents to resolve individual civil cases, further emphasizes just how far the "practice" of Qing governance varies from the way it formally "represents" itself and the striking degree of tolerance and comfort Qing political actors feel with this gap, evident to themselves no less than to us.[9]

This mutable and ambivalent political milieu is hardly conducive to the generation of hardened ideologies, or elaborate systems of political, social, or economic theory. Instead, what we find is a consistency of problematics, styles, and approaches to ordering the world. Such, we may suggest, is *jingshi*—the much-debated "statecraft" or "world ordering." Metzger argues that *jingshi*, indeed, is at bottom none other than this basic official-elite commitment to flexibility in the pursuit of transforming the given. Although it periodically (as with Wei Yuan in the 1820s) claims intellectual respectability by virtue of emergence in an explicit scholarly literature, it is more generally present as a matter of actual practice at nearly all times in the late imperial era.[10]

I would not disagree, but I believe we can be a bit more specific, identifying *jingshi* with a discrete (although open-ended) pattern of discourse practiced by the official elite. Influenced, like myself, by the insights of J. G. A. Pocock on the operation of political languages, Conrad Schirokauer and Robert Hymes find the full emergence of this shared political discourse in the Southern Song, contemporaneous and loosely interrelated with the new ontological and ethical discourses of *lixue* neo-Confucianism. Uniting individuals of quite different policy orientations, this common discourse of *jingshi* was open to contestation, to appropriation and expropriation at varying levels for a variety of political purposes.[11] Such it remained, I would argue, into the Qing. In Chapter 4 I outlined one late imperial line of transmission of the *jingshi* discourse—there were no doubt others—passing through Lü Kun, through Guanxue and the other northern neo-Confucian schools (Beixue and Luoxue), and through Chen Hongmou himself, emerging in the academies of Hunan's Xiang River valley in the early and mid-nineteenth century.

Although much work clearly remains to be done in this regard, it appears to me that this discourse and its underlying problematic—this gestalt of governance, if you will—was most deeply internalized in the eighteenth century by a particular cohort of provincial-level administrators, most arriving on the scene as part of the Yongzheng emperor's "new men," who moved from one province to another over the course of a long career. As a group they were remarkably able, moving into strange situations with regularity, trying to make sense out of the complex and often unique social forces and problems of each area and to do something constructive in each one. They were the *jingshi* heroes of the subsequent century. The most capable among them, notably Chen Hongmou, were able to utilize the discourse and problematic they inherited and use this with innovative flexibility rather than be held prisoner by it.

As revealed in Chen's own career and writings, the single most potent instrument in the eighteenth century for perpetuating the vitality of this *jingshi* political discourse was probably the *Beijing Gazette* (*Dibao*), although, as James Polachek has shown, privately circulated media such as occasional essays and poetry might serve this purpose as well.[12] One important way this language worked was as a vehicle of policy legitimation. An attentive political actor such as Chen would pick up on a certain catchphrase such as "exhaust the potential of the earth" (*jin dili*), "use the people to nourish the people" (*yimin yangmin*), or "store wealth among the people" (*cangfu yumin*) that, although rarely of recent vintage, was evidently undergoing a vogue of popularity.[13] (Most likely it had appeared in the text of an imperial edict in an obviously approving usage.) The actor would then be careful to include this idiom in a memorial, most likely at the beginning or the end, as justification for proposing a specific course of action, in the knowledge that this inclusion would increase the chance of his proposal gaining the endorsement of a superior and ultimately the throne. As we have seen repeatedly in this study, an ambitious official such as Chen could stretch the sense of this idiom in highly creative ways. Of course, as it was attached to an increasingly diverse range of proposals, it risked attenuation of its value. At some point the idiom might recede from popularity and be replaced in the discourse by others whose potency remained fresh.[14]

We may return at this point to the three broad tensions I depicted in my introduction as central to Chen Hongmou's consciousness and political behavior. The first of these tensions is that between normative moralism and accommodative pragmatism, Chen's reputation resting, as it has, nearly equally on his status as paragon in both of these potentially contradictory areas. I suggested in Chapter 1 how Chen's frontier background and family history might have been conducive to generating his hallmark mixture of steadfast insistence on simple, straightforward moral dictates and practical savvy in getting things done. But here Chen, as a literatus, also operated within a broader intellectual milieu specific to his times. His moralism itself tended to be of a worldly, situational sort—what Hao Chang has termed "moral practicality"[15]—that responded to the values placed on "practice" (*shijian*) and "substantive learning" (*shixue*) peculiar to the Qing and stressed especially by the northern scholars whose writings and conduct Chen most cherished (Lü Kun, Lu Shiyi, Tang Bin, the Guanxue school) and with whom he personally associated (Yin Huiyi, Depei, Yang Shen). Chen's parallel commitment to socioeconomic problem solving was rooted ultimately in the *Daxue*, with its insistence on the interrelatedness of internal moral improvement (*xiushen*) and external world-ordering (*jingshi*). But it likewise fed on a uniquely Qing urge to correct the imbalance the *lixue* tradition in past ages had placed on the former.

As I argued in Chapter 4, the eighteenth-century "Song learning" school within which Chen squarely placed himself (while at the same time denying intellectual partisanship) was directly related to his simultaneous embrace of moral practicality and practical statecraft. His moralism/pragmatism mix was defined largely by what it opposed: on the one hand literary dilettantism (seen equally in poetic refinement and in the eight-legged essay of the examination curriculum) and on the other hand the sterile philological classicism of Hanxue. Song-learning for Chen meant practical engagement in public affairs, and it meant a very thoroughgoing historicism, history being above all where one encountered both exemplars of moral behavior in practical situations and pragmatic solutions to temporally specific (but recurring) socioeconomic problems.

Hao Chang and others have delineated several strands of the *jingshi* scholar-official orientation that potentially ran counter to inherited or mainstream thought.[16] One was the denial of blanket incompatibility between practical benefit or material profit (*li*) and abstract moral dictates (*yi*). This strand is clearly evident in Chen Hongmou, who routinely accepts profit as a worthy goal when properly defined; as Chang shows, although this was a minority position in pre-Qing times, it was not wholly new. Another *jingshi* notion was the valorization of specialized technical expertise. Hao Chang sees this as something relatively new to the Qing, and there is no question that for Chen, nearly a century into the Qing era, it has become so self-evident as to be wholly beyond question. The comprehensive accumulation of detailed, locally specific geographical knowledge, a project granted worthiness in the work of Gu Yanwu and carried out with special zeal by Chen Hongmou (and later Wei Yuan), may serve as emblematic in this regard. Yet another strand was the extreme notion of utility as the ultimate test of action (*zhiyong*). In the view of Hao Chang it was this above all, with its frank pursuit of wealth and power for the polity, that differentiated the self-conscious statecraft partisans of the 1820s and after from earlier *jingshi* practitioners. In the nineteenth century the stimulus to this radical break was clearly that of the Qing's sudden immersion into a highly competitive world of international power politics. I would suggest, however, that the perceived urgency of the food supply problem confronting mid-eighteenth-century Qing official elites prompted certain among them—and here Chen would be in the forefront—to precociously approach this sort of logic.

The second broad tension we identified in Chen is that between ordering the world by means of the institutions of state versus those generated by local society. Much of this study, indeed, has been devoted to observing Chen's perilous negotiation of this divide. Historically, the Song *lixue* tradition, from which *jingshi* notions themselves arose, was identified with a position of discomfort with coercive instruments of world ordering—in other words, the state apparatus. By the early eighteenth century, however, owing perhaps in large measure to the influence of prominent early Qing Songxue officials such as Lu Shiyi and Li Guangdi, this discomfort had begun somewhat to ease. The result was a pervasive acceptance of what Metzger has nicely called "the state as partly good."[17] The broadside attacks on bureaucratic centralization of great seventeenth-century "Ming remnant" scholars such as Gu Yanwu and Huang Zongxi had found a sympathetic ear but few real converts. In their wake mid-Qing official elites attempted to work out one type or another of a "mixed system of government,"[18] one that would avoid the universally recognized evils of bureaucratism—clerical malfeasance, siphoning off resources at a level between center and locality (*zhongbao*), stifling productivity by overregulation, the loss of flexible responsiveness to local concerns—without sacrificing the official control and supervision that all acknowledged, to varying degrees, as necessary.

Chen Hongmou was not far from the mainstream in this regard. For all his sensitivity to the dysfunctions of too much government meddling, Chen was hardly a good fit into the so-called *fengjian* (elite-led local autonomy) alternative political discourse exemplified in the seventeenth century by Gu Yanwu and in the nineteenth by Feng Guifen—despite Feng's problematic efforts retrospectively to appropriate him. Far less than from Gu, about whose contributions he pronounced himself ambivalent, Chen got his antidirigiste ideas from his beloved Sima Guang's critiques of Wang Anshi and from Zhen Dexiu's and Qiu Jun's meditations on the *Daxue*, which Chen abstracted and tirelessly distributed in his provincial jurisdictions. His commitment to local societal activism came likewise not from Gu but from Lü Kun and the masters of the Shaanxi school (Guanxue).

On certain touchstone institutional issues Chen fell squarely in line with the critics of creeping bureaucratism. For *baojia* regimentation, for example, that venerable whipping boy of local autonomy advocates, he gave only very circumscribed approval; of *shecang* granaries, by contrast, that instrument of local self-nurturance promoted as an alternative to big government by no less a cultural icon than Zhu Xi, Chen was probably his era's most energetic and unwavering proponent. There were things, Chen knew, that the state simply could not do and thus ought not to attempt. It could not contravene transcendent economic laws, and it could not (given its commitment to smallness) ignore the existence of entrenched local power. To the extent circumstances allowed, therefore, he clearly preferred to base his policies on the twin pillars of the market and the local elite. We saw him doing just this, for instance, in confronting what may have been the single most volatile situation he faced in his entire official career, the Jiangxi dearth of 1742–43. There is a clear parallel between Chen's instincts to use the market to influence the market and to use local society, where possible, to manage itself. In both areas, however, periodic and recurring state intervention was called for in order to achieve what Chen understood as the overriding social good.

But Chen Hongmou's view of the function of the state in fact went considerably beyond providing an occasional nudge to a self-ordering society and economy. A holdover from the relatively uninhibited state-activist years of the Yongzheng reign, Chen remained a vocal champion of such activism in the face of the "looser" (*kuan*) and more passive style of rule favored by Yongzheng's successor. He was, as we have seen, not averse on principle to increasing the density of officials on the landscape when that seemed in the interest of more efficient administration. In his final years as an influential grand secretary, but also persistently throughout his field career, Chen worked assiduously to refine means of bureaucratic and sub-bureaucratic discipline, to define more precisely the spheres of responsibility assigned to specific posts, to design more standardized systems of intrabureaucratic communications and reporting, and to gather ever more detailed intelligence about the society and economy and work out methods for its statistical tabulation, storage, and retrieval. This detailed knowledge was not for purposes of mere passive control (although that purpose was certainly served) but rather, as Chen's astonishing *xingqu* campaigns of the 1740s and 1750s in Shaanxi make clear, for the purpose of fundamentally remaking via governmental means the fabric of local society and culture. Probably no early modern European state-maker ever cherished quite so ambitious a concept of the state's transformative mission.

The final tension we have highlighted in Chen is that between a social consciousness valorizing the individual person and one deeply subjugating individuality to the dictates of group, network, or social hierarchy. We have argued that, in Chen's well-ordered world, *group* (class, ethnicity, and so on) and hierarchy were relatively less important than *network* in that he conceived of human beings as largely defined by the package of social roles (*fen*) in which their situation placed them and by the (usually bilateral) obligations inherent in moral role fulfillment. Largely but not completely, for we have also detected in Chen a powerful undercurrent of belief in the singular worth, dignity, and autonomy of each human person. In concluding Chapter 9 I offered a brief survey of the elements in Chen's worldview that might be construed as "individualist," including his enthusiastic (although qualified) approval of social self-advancement and economic profit seeking, his stress on the need for personal agency in moral decision making, and his emphatic condemnation of any action that seemed to imply an instrumental view of any human being.

The plurality of elements here is key, of course, for "individualism" is really no more than a rather messy reification, invented in the West to name a highly complex set of values and urges indigenous to the Western historical experience. Even in the West, to be sure, the notion has never been immune to contested meanings. In a marvelously thought-provoking article, Lydia Liu has eloquently reminded us that, in the process of searching for analogues to "individualism" and "the individual" in China, any complacent assumption of "an essential and fixed meaning" for these discursive items is "futile and misguided." Early-twentieth-century Chinese intellectuals, Liu points out, in the process of investigating the promise of this Western notion for resolving "the problematic of modern selfhood and nationhood," found themselves diverging wildly on the questions of what "individualism" (*geren zhuyi*) signified in the West and whether perhaps something akin to this notion had existed in the historical experience of their own culture. Significantly, though, it was only relatively late in the process of sorting out this question—and only in the context of the widespread cultural self-loathing of the May Fourth era—that Chinese modernist intellectuals came to declare the basic incompatibility of Western notions of the individual and individualism with the late imperial *lixue* tradition.[19]

Much as I would be wary of investing these historical categories with any unwarranted "superior, transcendent value" (Liu's phrase) and would actively recoil from any formulation crudely equating "individualism" with "modernity" and its absence with something less than "modern,"[20] there was clearly something going on in the world of late imperial consciousness that was both new and potentially revolutionary. The multifaceted movement toward personal liberationism in much of late Ming culture is now widely accepted by scholars. My contention here is that, despite the general perception of the early and mid-Qing as "regressive" or "repressive" of this movement, looking even at an individual within the eighteenth-century official elite often thought of as "conservative," numerous survivals of this late Ming rehabilitation of the individual stand out. Aspects of the mid-Qing environment—the more intensive confrontation with cultural alterities on the frontiers, the revived *querelle des femmes*, and the urgency of the perceived need to increase productivity in the face of population growth—surely contributed to this survival. Like nearly all of his contemporaries Chen Hongmou turned his back on the Song neo-Confucian dualisms between the ideal and the material (*li* and *qi*) and between propriety (*yi*) and human appetites and desires (*yu*). Albeit fighting a rearguard action to reinfuse it with moral content, Chen not only accepted but positively glorified the centrality of human emotional response (*renqing*) as a motivating force for social conduct. He frankly acknowledged that a prominent component of this *renqing* was, and properly ought to be, self-interest (*siqing*). Following his late Ming hero Lü Kun, he deplored the dehumanizing and "unnatural" (*bu ziran*) effects of excessive ritual dictates and ritualized behavior (*guoli*). Most ubiquitously, Chen preached the coequal natural goodness (*tianliang*) of all human creatures and in defense of this idea pointedly refused to abandon Wang Yangming's notion of the individual's innate moral knowledge (*liangzhi*), which, it was widely alleged, had precipitated the late Ming "almost cultural revolution" to begin with.

Again, however, we need to remain aware of what is *not* present, at least in anything close to articulated form, in Chen Hongmou's individualist tendencies. Three things stand out. First, although technical skill, learning, and clarity of thought are venerated, there is not a hint of esteem for individual creativity, originality, or "genius," either intellectually, technologically, or aesthetically; such qualities were clearly very remote from Chen's scheme of values.[21] Second, although striving for profit and self-betterment is legitimated, there is no glorification of competition or the competitive spirit per se on the presumption that it is these that drive the improvement of society as a whole. And finally, despite Chen's repeated insistence on human dignity (for instance his attacks on the "commodification" of brides), and notwithstanding his protective stance toward private property, neither he nor any of his official-elite contemporaries took the step of positing any inherent "rights" of the individual, a step that might ultimately have led, among other things, to an indigenous theory of social contract.

Having come this far, I hope the reader will permit me to end this book with a playful indulgence—some modest reflections on how the world of official-elite consciousness of mid-Qing China might be compared in certain regards with that of the early modern West. Although many particularities inform both cases, it might be suggested that Chen Hongmou grounded his approach to humanity and society in a deistic humanism with strong affinities to that of many Enlightenment-era Europeans. He responded—in nearly every case with qualified favor—to similar sorts of sociocultural developments seen in the West: an evident growth in literacy and the print culture, a lively debate spurred by changing gender roles in social practice, growing occupational complexity, erosions of inherited notions of the status hierarchy, and the reality of accelerated upward (and downward) social mobility. He adamantly professed a bottom-line egalitarianism rooted in the concept of every human individual as partaking equally in divine essence.

Although he exhibited in his own personality a deep streak of puritanism and "bourgeois thrift," he argued consistently for the legitimacy and social utility of human emotions, appetites, and self-interest. He held to a strong and articulated notion of friendship, perhaps influenced indirectly, I suggested in Chapter 2, by the Ciceronian ideas introduced into China by Matteo Ricci. Although wholeheartedly embracing the value of commodity markets, like early modern Europeans he sought nevertheless to stake out and insulate from the market a private, domestic sphere of family relations. And a major part of his response to the more mobile society he observed and endorsed was an attempt to mandate for this society an intelligible code of social performance, in the form of a thoroughly humanist, largely class-transcendent *civilité/li*.

The fit of Chen's outlook with that of many early modern Europeans is especially striking in the economic sphere. Indefatigably procommerce, cherishing relatively strong property notions (which I compared in Chapter 7 to those of Locke), pushing ever more thorough monetization of the local economy, and generally approving of the profit motive (as inherent in human beings and therefore self-evidently meeting Heaven's favor), Chen managed to develop a notion of self-perpetuating accumulation that might be seen, with but a small stretch, as a concept of economic growth. As I have argued elsewhere, Chen's combination of taking agrarian proprietorship as the basis of the economy with an emphatic embrace of "the market principle" seems to place him closest to the eighteenth-century French physiocrats.[22] Yet, as Helen Dunstan has considered in detail (utilizing Chen Hongmou as one subject of her analysis), there are also suggestive parallels—limited ones, to be sure—to the kind of market-driven approach to economic policy we know in the West generally as "liberalism."[23]

In the political realm Chen's close attention to administrative standardization, more efficient paperwork and communications networks, and the careful collection and compilation of intelligence about the society paralleled processes in the formation of unprecedentedly strong and pervasive early modern European states.[24] His devotion to the civilizing mission, both at home and abroad (on the frontiers), and his granting to the state a major active role in this process, resonated strongly with attitudes in expansionist Europe.[25] At the same time, Chen's repeated insistence on the crucial role of public opinion (*yulun, minqing*) in policy formation added—in a very qualified way, to be sure—at least the germ of a modern-sounding notion of popular sovereignty.

The big ideas conventionally identified with the development of elite consciousness in early modern Europe—statism, liberalism, and individualism among them—were not, I would suggest, the prerogative of Europe alone.[26] The official elite of mid-Qing China certainly did not come around to any of them in any neat way—indeed, they *could* not, for these ideas, as we know them, were specifically European cultural constructs—but neither can their alleged absence be used to explain the Qing empire's "stagnation" or "backwardness" vis-à-vis the progressive West. Asia and the West were increasingly interconnected in the eighteenth century and confronted comparable indigenous processes of change, above all dramatic accelerations of demographic growth, population mobility, and market penetration. It would be far more surprising if elite consciousness had not shared certain developments in the two societies than if, as it appears, it did.

Notes

The following abbreviations have been used throughout these notes:

CZYG	Chen Hongmou, *Congzheng yigui*
ECCP	Arthur Hummel, ed., *Eminent Chinese of the Ch'ing Period*
GCA	Grand Council Archives, Qing Palace Archives, Taibei
JNYG	Chen Hongmou, *Jiaonü yigui*
JS	Chen Hongmou, *Chen Hongmou jiashu*
JSWB	He Changling, ed., *Huangchao jingshi wenbian*
KSZJ	Chen Hongmou, *Keshi zhijie*
LZJL	Lü Kun (ed. with commentary by Chen Hongmou), *Lüzi jielu*
MQA	Number One Historical Archives, Beijing (Ming-Qing Archives)
NP	Chen Zhongke, *Xian wengong gong nianpu*
PYTOCG	Chen Hongmou, *Peiyuan tang oucun gao*
QLZZ	National Palace Museum (Taibei), ed., *Gongzhong Qianlong chao zouzhe*
QPA	Qing Palace Archives, Taibei
SD	Chen Hongmou, *Chen wengong gong shudu* (1936 edition)
Wenji	Chen Hongmou, *Peiyuan tang wenji*
XSYG	Chen Hongmou, *Xunsu yigui*
Yishu	Chen Hongmou, *Chen Rongmen xiansheng yishu*
YZYG	Chen Hongmou, *Yangzheng yigui*
YZZZ	National Palace Museum (Taibei), ed., *Gongzhong Yongzheng chao zouzhe*
ZGFJL	Chen Hongmou, *Zaiguan fajie lu*

Introduction

1. For a classic characterization of this broader era by a leading Western historian see Frederic Wakeman Jr., "High Ch'ing, 1683–1839," in James B. Crowley, ed., *Modern East Asia: Essays in Interpretation* (New York: Harcourt, Brace and World, 1970), 1–28. For more recent Chinese views see Dai Yi et al., "Bitan shiba shiji Zhongguo yu shijie" (Symposium on China and the world in the eighteenth century), *Qingshi yanjiu* 1993.1, 1–35; and Gao Wangling, "Guanyu

457

Kang-Qian shengshi de jige wenti" (Several problems concerning the prosperous age from Kangxi to Qianlong), *Qingshi yanjiu tongxun* 1990.4, 21–26. Philip A. Kuhn has sounded a welcome cautionary note against accepting uncritically the rosy image of a mid-Qing economic boom in his *Soulstealers: The Chinese Sorcery Scare of 1768* (Cambridge, Mass.: Harvard University Press, 1990). Although I agree that such prudence is in order, I personally believe that, at least relatively speaking, "prosperity" is not an inappropriate characterization for this era.

2. China is often seen as having fallen victim to such aspects of the global seventeenth-century crisis as climatic cooling, declining agricultural yields, epidemic disease, and the contraction of global trade that, in the Chinese case, spelled a shortage of the imports of New World silver on which the late Ming commercial economy and government finance (in the wake of the Single Whip reforms) had come to depend. See variously S. A. M. Adshead, "The Seventeenth Century General Crisis in China," *Asian Profile* 1.2 (October 1973): 271–80; William Atwell, "A Seventeenth-Century 'General Crisis' in East Asia?" *Modern Asian Studies* 24.4 (1990): 661–82; and Frederic Wakeman Jr., "China and the Seventeenth-Century Crisis," *Late Imperial China* 7.1 (June 1986): 1–26.

3. This information has kindly been provided me by R. Kent Guy, who is in the process of completing a massive prosopographical study of Qing provincial governors. Throughout his career Chen served as prefect of Yangzhou; as circuit intendant (*daotai*) of Tianjin; as provincial judge of Jiangsu; as provincial treasurer of Yunnan and Jiangsu; as governor of Jiangxi, Shaanxi (four times), Gansu, Henan, Hubei, Hunan (twice), Jiangsu (twice), Fujian, and Guangdong; as governor-general of Liang-Guang and (acting) of Huguang; and as president of the Board of War, the Board of Public Works, and the Board of Civil Office. He also received several appointments that, prior to his assumption of office, were rescinded in favor of other assignments. For the specifics of these appointments see Zhao Erxun, ed., *Qingshi gao* (Draft history of the Qing dynasty) (Beijing: Zhonghua shuju, 1977), 21.6136–66, 22.6626–31, 22.7225–33, 26.7641–77.

4. Fang Bao, undated letter to Chen Hongmou, in *Fang Wangji yiji* (Surviving works of Fang Bao) (Hefei: Huangshan shushe, 1990), 63–64.

5. Edict of QL 32/3, cited in *NP* 12:19. While in Beijing in the 1760s, Chen also served collaterally in several board presidencies, as deputy director of the State History Office (Guoshi guan), and in a wide range of other posts. He took all of these duties seriously. For details of his taxing Beijing work routine see letters of QL 29/11/15, QL 30/3/29, QL 30/12/26, and QL 32/4/23, *JS* 228–32, 237–40, 248–49.

6. Edict of QL 36/2, reprinted in "Liezhuan" (Draft official biography), no. 5834, QPA.

7. This phrase was chosen as the title of the conference volume on earlier Chinese *jingshi* thought edited by Robert Hymes and Conrad Schirokauer, *Ordering the World: Approaches to State and Society in Sung Dynasty China* (Berkeley: University of California Press, 1993). Although I fully concur with Hymes and Schirokauer's preferred translation, I will continue also occasionally to employ the translation "statecraft" in the present study, both for stylistic simplicity and because of the term's more conventional acceptance.

8. See, e.g., Institute of Modern History, comp., *Jindai Zhongguo jingshi sixiang yantao hui lunwen ji* (Proceedings of the conference on *jingshi* thought in modern China) (Taibei: Academia Sinica, 1984); Hymes and Schirokauer.

9. Zhang Hao (Hao Chang), "Song-Ming yilai Rujia jingshi sixiang shiyi" (A preliminary explication of Confucian *jingshi* thought since the Song and Ming), in Institute of Modern History, *Jinshi Zhongguo jingshi sixiang*, esp. 16–17; Hao Chang, "On the '*Ching-shih*' Ideal in Neo-Confucianism," *Ch'ing-shih wen-t'i* 3.1 (November 1974): esp. 47–48.

10. Joseph R. Levenson, "The Amateur Ideal in Ming and Early Ch'ing Society: Evidence from Painting," in his *Confucian China and Its Modern Fate: A Trilogy* (Berkeley: University of California Press, 1972), 15–42.

11. Philip A. Kuhn, "Local Self-Government under the Republic: Problems of Control, Autonomy, and Mobilization," in Frederic Wakeman Jr. and Carolyn Grant, eds., *Conflict and Control in Late Imperial China* (Berkeley: University of California Press, 1975), 257–98; Tu-ki Min, "The Theory of Political Feudalism in the Ch'ing Period," in *National Polity and Local Power: The*

Transformation of Late Imperial China, ed. Philip A. Kuhn and Timothy Brook (Cambridge, Mass.: Harvard University Press, 1989), 89–136.

12. A list of all extant publications of Chen's works known to me, with their dates and places of publication, appears at the end of this volume.

13. The other three works were Chen's selections from Lü Kun (*LZJL*), his combined abridgement of Zhen Dexiu's *Daxue yan yi* and Qiu Jun's *Daxue yanyi bu*, and the *Hunan Provincial Gazetteer* compiled under his general editorship. See *(Qingding) Siku quanshu zongmu tiyao* (Index to the Imperial Library project), ed. Ji Xiaolan et al. (1782; reprint, Shanghai: Commercial Press, 1933), 15:50, 18:91, 18:113, 25:101. As Kent Guy demonstrates in *The Emperor's Four Treasuries: Scholars and the State in the Late Ch'ien-lung Era* (Cambridge, Mass.: Harvard University Press, 1989), there was a pronounced geographic bias (toward Jiangnan) and a scholarly factional domination (by philological experts of the "Han-learning" clique) inherent in the project, both of which would have made Chen Hongmou's works uncongenial to the editors.

14. Lu Yao, *Qiewen zhai wenchao* (1776), 20:23–25. No works by Chen were even included in Lu's substantial section on water conservancy, the area of expertise for which Chen has always been most revered. The inattention to Chen is all the more surprising in light of the general orientation of Lu's compilation to works in the "Song learning" tradition, to which Chen at least loosely belonged. One can only conclude that, rather quickly after his death, Chen Hongmou became a forgotten man. On the character and significance of Lu's work see Huang Kewu, "*Jingshi wenbian* yu Zhongguo jindai jingshi sixiang yanjiu" (The *Statecraft Compendium* and modern Chinese *jingshi* thought), *Jindai Zhongguoshi yanjiu tongxun* 2 (September 1986): 84–85, 90–91.

15. Wang Chang, *Huhai wenchuan* (The sea of prose) (1837 ed.), 18:5–8, 25:13, 29:2–4, 30:7–8. Wang Chang's relatively greater appreciation of Chen Hongmou, reflected, e.g., in his inclusion of several works extolling Chen's establishment of schools on the Yunnan frontier, may have owed something to his experience as a junior editor in many government compilation projects in Beijing in the 1760s, when Chen was a high metropolitan official. See *ECCP*, 805–7.

16. Chen Xi, preface to *ZGFJL* (1821); Fei Bingchang, 1823 preface reprinted in Chen Hongmou, *Peiyuan tang shoudu* (1872) and in Chen, *Chen wengong gong shoudu* (1909). Chen also received hagiographic treatment in this era in Zhu Fangzeng's *Congzheng guanfa lu* (Biographies of exemplary officials) (1830), 15:12–16.

17. *JS*, Part Two. The authors of these testimonials (*tishi*) typically sign themselves as Chen's "disciple" (*houxue*). On the collection process see the Editors' Afterword to the *JS*, 257.

18. Xu Dong, *Muling shu* (Handbook for magistrates) (1838; reprint, Yangzhou, 1990). In Xu's much shorter earlier work, *Baojia shu* (Handbook of *baojia* organization) (1837; reprint, Yangzhou, 1990), three selections are by Chen.

19. Li Zutao, *Guochao wenlu* (1839), *juan* 44.

20. Zhang Weiping, *Zhang Nanshan quanji* (Complete works of Zhang Weiping) (1842), 24:4.

21. Li Fuyuan, preface of 1828, reprinted in Chen Hongmou, *Wuzhong yigui* (Shanghai: Zhonghua shuju, 1929).

22. Zhang Jiamou, preface to *PYTOCG* (Wuchang: Hubei Provincial Treasurer's Office, 1896).

23. Jiang Fangzheng, preface to *Peiyuan tang oucun gao: wenxi*, in Chen Hongmou, *Rongmen quanji* (Complete works of Chen Hongmou) (Guilin: Peiyuan tang, 1837). The quotations cited in this paragraph are drawn from various prefaces to nineteenth-century editions of Chen's works, many of the phrases being repeated by several writers.

24. Of the twenty-nine Daoguang- and Xianfeng-era testimonials to Chen noted above, at least six were by Hunan natives (including Wei Yuan's senior collaborator on the *Statecraft Compendium*, He Changling), and several others were by officials serving at the time in that province, including Provincial Treasurer Wan Gongzhen; *JS*, Part Two.

25. Zeng Guofan, *Zeng Guofan quanji* (Complete works of Zeng Guofan), "Jiashu" (Family letters), 1.145–47, 1.154–55.

26. Cited in Kwang-Ching Liu, "Education for Its Own Sake: Notes on Tseng Kuo-fan's *Family Letters*" (paper presented to the Conference on Education and Society in Late Imperial

China, Santa Barbara, June 1989). The identically titled published version of this paper, in Benjamin Elman and Alexander Woodside, eds., *Education and Society in Late Imperial China* (Berkeley: University of California Press, 1994), 76–108, omits this reference.

27. Jiang Yili, preface to *Congzheng yigui shichao* (Nanchang: Jiangxi lishu, 1865). For Jiang's role in the anti-Taiping campaigns and in Restoration politics see *Zhongguo renming da zidian* (Chinese biographical dictionary) (Shanghai: Shanghai shudian, 1980), 1539; and Mary C. Wright, *The Last Stand of Chinese Conservatism: The T'ung-Chih Restoration, 1862–1874* (Stanford: Stanford University Press, 1957), esp. 76–77.

28. The Ministry of Education's textbook publication project and Chen Hongmou's role in it are discussed in Ōmura Kōdō, "Shinsho kyōiku shisō shi ni okeru 'Seiyu kōkin' no chi-i ni tsuite" (On the role of the "Explication of the *Sacred Edict*" in the history of Qing educational thought), in Hayashi Tomoharu, *Kinsei Chūgoku kyōiku shi kenkyū* (Studies in modern Chinese educational history) (Tokyo: Kokutosha, 1958), 264–69. For surviving copies of the Ministry's editions of Chen's works see the list of References in the present book.

29. Evan Morgan, *Wenli Styles and Chinese Ideals* (Shanghai: Presbyterian Mission Press, 1912).

30. See, e.g., Li Zongren, "Chen wengong gong danzhen jinian gong" (Ode in commemoration of Chen Hongmou's birth), in Feng Zhuqi, ed., *Chen Rongmen xiansheng erbaiwushi zhounian danzhen jinian zhuanban* (Works in commemoration of the 250th anniversary of Mr. Chen Hongmou's birth) (Guilin: Chen Hongmou Commemoration Committee, 1946).

31. Xie Kang, "Chen Hongmou," in his *Wenshi luncong* (Essays on literature and history) (Taipei: Zhongwai tushu chubanshe, 1978), 233. Certainly not by coincidence, the essay on Chen in Xie's book directly follows that on Zeng Guofan.

32. Chen, *Wuzhong yigui* (Taibei: Dezhi chubanshe, 1961). Another example is the fifty-two-page abridgement by Wu Jinze entitled *Wuzhong yigui zachao* (Miscellaneous selections from the *Five Sourcebooks*) (Taibei: Taiwan Commercial Press, 1965).

33. "*Chuanjia baodian*" (Chinese proverbs), a series of several dozen spots run daily from 5:57 to 6:00 P.M. on Taiwan Television, March 1987.

34. Hsiao Kung-ch'uan, *Rural China: Imperial Control in the Nineteenth Century* (Seattle: University of Washington Press, 1960); Ch'ü T'ung-tsu, *Local Government in China Under the Ch'ing* (Cambridge, Mass.: Harvard University Press, 1962).

35. Fu-mei Chang Chen, "Local Control of Convicted Thieves in Eighteenth-Century China," in Wakeman and Grant, 121–42; R. Bin Wong, "Food Riots in the Qing Dynasty," *Journal of Asian Studies* 41.4 (August 1982): 767–88; Peter C. Perdue, *Exhausting the Earth: State and Peasant in Hunan, 1500–1850* (Cambridge, Mass.: Harvard University Press, 1987); Gao Wangling, *Shiba shiji Zhongguo de jingji fazhan he zhengfu zhengce* (Government policy and China's eighteenth-century economic development) (Beijing: Zhongguo shehui kexue chubanshe, 1995); Helen Dunstan, *Conflicting Counsels to Confuse the Age: A Documentary Study of Political Economy in Qing China, 1644–1840* (Ann Arbor: University of Michigan Center for Chinese Studies, 1996); Alexander Woodside, "Some Mid-Qing Theorists of Popular Schools: Their Innovations, Inhibitions, and Attitudes Toward the Poor," *Modern China* 9.1 (January 1983): 3–35; Susan Mann, "The Education of Daughters in the Mid-Ch'ing Period," in Elman and Woodside, 19–49; Tani E. Barlow, "Theorizing Woman: *Funü, Guojia, Jiating* (Chinese Women, Chinese State, Chinese Family)," in Angela Zito and Tani Barlow, eds., *Body, Subject, and Power in China* (Chicago: University of Chicago Press, 1994), 253–89.

36. Gao Jiren, *Chen Rongmen shengping* (The life of Chen Hongmou) (Guilin: Wenhua gongyingshe, 1945); Liu Naihe, "Chen Hongmou yu kaoju" (Chen Hongmou and evidential research), *Beijing shifan daxue xuebao*, Social Science series, 1962.2, 109–10; Hou Xiaonan, "Qingdai zhengzhijia he sixiangjia Chen Hongmou" (The Qing statesman and thinker Chen Hongmou), *Guangxi shifan daxue xuebao* 1988.4, 73–80; Zhang Fang, "Qingdai rexin shuili de Chen Hongmou" (Chen Hongmou, a Qing-era water conservancy enthusiast), *Zhongguo keji shiliao* 14.3 (1993): 27–33; Xie Kang, "Chen Hongmou"; Shigeta Atsushi, "Chin Kōbō" (Chen Hongmou), in *Ajia rekishi jiten* (Tokyo: Heibonsha, 1970), 360; "Chin Kōbō" (Chen Hongmou),

in *Tōyō rekishi daijiten* (Tokyo: Heibonsha, 1937), 1342–43; Cai Guanluo, *Qingdai qibai mingren zhuan* (Biographies of seven hundred famous Qing individuals) (Beijing: Zhonghua shudian, 1984), 1.144–49; Rufus O. Suter, "Ch'en Hung-mou," in *ECCP*, 86–87. I am told that one of the articles by Guilin historians was in fact occasioned by my own research visit there and the surprising discovery that a foreign scholar could actually be interested in this hometown hero; see Zhang Lingshu et al., "Chen Hongmou jingji sixiang yu shijian yanjiu" (Chen Hongmou's economic thought and practical studies), *Shehui kexuejia* 1996.2, 81–92. Most recently there is Kong Xiangwen, "Chen Hongmou ji qi lizhi sixiang yanjiu" (Chen Hongmou and his thought on governance) (master's thesis, Qing History Institute, Chinese People's University, 1996), which has come to my attention too late for use in this study.

37. Chen Hongmou's activities figure in a number of Will's studies of the mid-Qing bureaucracy, to be cited below; among the published studies is "The 1744 Annual Audits of Magistrate Activity and Their Fate," *Late Imperial China* 18.2 (December 1997): 1–50.

38. Lawrence Stone, "The Revival of Narrative: Reflections on a New Old History," *Past and Present* 85 (November 1979): 3–24; J. H. Hexter, "Fernand Braudel and the *Monde Braudelian*," *Journal of Modern History* 44 (December 1972): 480–539.

39. E. P. Thompson, *William Morris: Romantic to Revolutionary* (New York: Pantheon, 1977); C. Vann Woodward, *Tom Watson: Agrarian Rebel* (New York: Macmillan, 1938). A more recent example of a biography that in my view transcends the genre's limitations is Sebastian de Grazia's *Macchiavelli in Hell* (Princeton: Princeton University Press, 1989).

40. Giovanni Levi, "Les Usages de la Biographie," *Annales ESC* (December 1989): 1325–1336.

41. Notable exceptions would be the work of Benjamin Elman, R. Kent Guy, and Kai-wing Chow.

42. J. G. A. Pocock, *The Machiavellian Moment: Florentine Political Thought and the Atlantic Republican Tradition* (Princeton: Princeton University Press, 1975), 9.

43. The baseline for my own understanding of how to deal with language is J. G. A. Pocock, "Languages and Their Implications: The Transformation of the Study of Political Thought," in his *Politics, Language, and Time: Essays on Political Thought and History* (New York: Atheneum, 1973), 3–41. Also of use are Pocock, "The Reconstruction of Discourse: Towards the Historiography of Political Thought," *MLN* 96 (1981): 959–80; William J. Bouwsma, "Intellectual History in the 1980s: From the History of Ideas to the History of Meaning," *Journal of Interdisciplinary History* 12.2 (autumn 1981): 279–91; Dominick LaCapra, "Rethinking Intellectual History and Reading Texts," in LaCapra and Steven L. Kaplan, eds., *Modern European Intellectual History: Reappraisals and New Perspectives* (Ithaca: Cornell University Press, 1982), 47–85; and John E. Toews, "Intellectual History After the Linguistic Turn: The Autonomy of Meaning and the Irreduceability of Experience," *American Historical Review* 92 (1987): 279–91. Closer to my own East Asian subject area, I have also learned much from Carol Gluck, *Japan's Modern Myths: Ideology in the Late Meiji Period* (Princeton: Princeton University Press, 1985), esp. chap. 8. In line with the views of most of these writers, I believe that acknowledging the autonomous power of language to shape meaning by no means implies that historical experience outside language does not exist or that the historian must necessarily despair of, at least in part, coming to comprehend that past experience.

44. Quentin Skinner, *The Foundations of Modern Political Thought* (Cambridge: Cambridge University Press, 1978), xii–xiii.

Chapter 1

1. Liang Qichao, "Jindai xuefeng zhi dili de fenbu" (Geographic distribution of intellectual trends in recent times), *Qinghua xuebao* 1.1 (June 1924): 36.

2. As the editorial notes to the 1997 edition of Chen's *JS* repeatedly make clear, e.g., through the end of his life he continued to sprinkle his casual discourse with Guilin localisms not easily decipherable by non-natives.

3. Memorial of QL 21/inter 9/21, *QLZZ* 15.586–87.

4. See, e.g., *PYTOCG* 25:30, 37:3; *SD* 1:1.

5. The single best source on the origins of the Lingui Chens, although hardly an unimpeachable one, is the genealogy "Zongpu liuzhuan," first compiled ca. 1739 and surviving today in a manuscript revision of 1924. Other sources include Chen Hongmou, *Wenji* 9:40–46; *NP* 1:1 and 4:28; Peng Qifeng, 14:12; Gao Jiren, 1–2; and Lin Banjue, "Rongmen guli" (Chen Hongmou's native village), in Feng Zhuqi, 39–51.

6. On this migration generally see Zhuang Jifa, "Qingdai shehui jingji bianqian yu bimi shehui de fazhan" (Qing era socioeconomic change and the development of secret societies), in Institute of Modern History, comp., *Jindai Zhongguo quyushi yantao hui lunwen ji* (Proceedings of the Conference on Modern Chinese Regional History) (Taibei: Academia Sinica, 1986), 335–86.

7. Although today Guilin city and Lingui County are administratively discrete, this was not so in the Qing. Guilin city was the capital of Guangxi Province, as well as the prefectural seat of Guilin *fu* and the county seat of Lingui *xian*.

8. Conversation with Chen Naiguang, January 14, 1994.

9. Chen Hongmou, "Zishuo" (Essay on personal names), *Wenji* 9:15–18. For the ambivalent role of Guangxi in the Sanfan Rebellion—it changed allegiances multiple times—see Liu Fengyun, *Qingdai sanfan yanjiu* (A study of the Three Feudatories of the Qing dynasty) (Beijing: Zhongguo Renmin Daxue, 1994), 276–79.

10. About Chen Hongmou's mother, nee Liu (d. 1732), very little is known. Hongmou was a properly filial son to her, but, unlike many contemporary literati, he never refers to his mother in his writings as a formative influence on his development. Unlike Chen's own wife, she seems not to have come from a locally notable family.

11. Chen Hongmou, "Wangxing Zhongfan ai zi" (Eulogy for Chen Zhongfan), cited in Gao Jiren, 2.

12. Chen Hongmou, "Bohuang Rongyuan quanlue" (Capsule biography of Chen Hongxian), *Wenji* 9:40–46.

13. See, e.g., *NP* 1:3.

14. Chen Hongmou, "Zishuo," *Wenji* 9:16. Chen meant this in both a practical sense—that his success was only possible as a result of his father's hard work—and a metaphysical one. For his literal belief in cosmic retribution (*bao*) for past virtue see Chapter 3.

15. Memorial of QL 17/3/4, *QLZZ* 2.369; *NP* 7:11–12.

16. Zeng Duhong et al., *Guilin jianshi* (Brief history of Guilin) (Guilin: Guangxi renmin chubanshe, 1984), 81–85. I am also indebted to Professor Zhang Jiafan and personnel of the Guilin Museum for passing along information on this subject in conversations we held during January 1994.

17. Zhuang Jifa, 345.

18. Li Fu, "Xiuchen Guangxi kenhuang shiyi shu" (Memorial on promoting land reclamation in Guangxi) (1724), *JSWB* 34:34–36; *Guilin jianshi*, 106.

19. Inada Seiichi, "Seibei tōun kō" (A study of the transport of Guangxi rice to Guangdong), *Tōhōgaku* 71 (January 1986): 90–105; Robert B. Marks, "Rice Prices, Food Supply, and Market Structure in Eighteenth-Century South China," *Late Imperial China* 12.2 (December 1991): 64–116; Huang Qichen, "Ming-Qing shiqi Liang-Guang de shangye maoyi" (Commerce in Guangdong and Guangxi in the Ming and Qing period), *Zhongguo shehui jingji shi yanjiu* 1989.4, 31–38.

20. Inada, 91–92.

21. Marks, "Rice Prices," 84.

22. *Guilin jianshi*, 105; Robert B. Marks, *Tigers, Rice, Silk, and Silt: Environment and Economy in Late Imperial South China* (Cambridge: Cambridge University Press, 1998), 262.

23. Visit to Hengshan and conversations with villagers, January 14, 1994. See also Lin Banjue, "Rongmen guli," 39–51.

24. This is the estimate of Guilin's most esteemed contemporary local historian, Zhang Jiafan.

25. Xie Kang, 240.

26. For the centrality of the Four Books in Chen's own thought see especially his *KSZJ* and its preface by Ge Zhenghu.

27. Kai-wing Chow, "Discourse, Examination, and Local Elite: The Invention of the T'ung-ch'eng School in Ch'ing China," in Elman and Woodside, 183–219. See also R. Kent Guy, "Fang Pao and the *Ch'in-ting ssu-shu-wen*," in the same volume, 150–82.

28. Guy, *Emperor's Four Treasuries*, 90. No titles came from Sichuan or Yunnan either, and a mere four came from Guangdong.

29. *PYTOCG* 34:47–49.

30. *Peiyuan tang wenlu* 44:2.

31. Chen, preface to his *Sishu kao jiyao*. Cf. Suter, 87. As one who has worked in Guilin's preeminent center of learning, Guangxi Normal University, I can attest that crippling library deficiencies are to this day a keenly felt problem there.

32. *NP* 1:12.

33. *SD* 3:2; reprinted in *JSWB* 16:35.

34. *JSWB* 75:21.

35. *SD* 1:1.

36. *Wenji* 9:16.

37. *Wenji* 2:33.

38. *SD* 2:11.

39. *Guilin jianshi*, 113.

40. Gao Jiren, 7. I will have more to say about Zhang Shi in Chapter 4.

41. Wang Fen, "Chongxiu Guilin fuxue Dachengdian ji" (1714) and Yi Sigong, "Chongxiu Guilin furuxue beiji" (1719), both in Guilin Cultural Relics Committee, comp., *Guilin shike* (Steles from Guilin) (Guilin: Guilin Cultural Relics Management Committee, 1981), 3.114–16, 3.122–24.

42. Wang Fen, "Dachengdian ji"; *Lingui xianzhi* (1900), 14:21–22.

43. Two other important *shuyuan*, the Ronghu and Guishan Academies, were founded after Chen Hongmou's time, in the early nineteenth century. *Guilin jianshi*, 111.

44. Wang Ruzhen, "Huazhang shuyuan jilie" (1682), and Li Fu, "Xuancheng shuyuan geshi shi" (1724), both in *Lingui xianzhi* (1900), 14:19–21.

45. Zhu Chun, "Xiufeng Xuancheng liang shuyuan beiji" (1782), *Guilin shike* 3.169–70; *Guilin jianshi*, 112.

46. Chen Yuanlong, "Fucheng shuyuan ji" (1713), *Guilin shike* 3.111–13.

47. *Guilin jianshi*, 112.

48. For Hongyi's biography see *Lingui xianzhi* 29:16.

49. *Wenji* 9:40–46; *NP* 12:12–13; *Lingui xianzhi* 29:11. On the occasion of Hongxian's ninetieth birthday in 1764, Chen Hongmou as grand secretary persuaded the Qianlong emperor to inscribe a congratulatory plaque; Hongmou's intense devotion to his brother is clearly revealed in the persistence with which he naggingly inquires in letters to family members about the plaque's progress home to Guilin. *JS*, esp. 211–14.

50. *Wenji* 9:44

51. *Wenji* 9:41–42. Chen Hongxian's scholarly credo was said to have been: "To study means to use books to understand the past, in service to the present." Gao Jiren, 3.

52. See, e.g., Peng Qifeng, 14:12; Yuan Mei, 27:9; Li Yuandu, 16:1.

53. *SD* 2:15.

54. *Yishu*, "Fuyi," 15–16.

55. Letter of QL 19/6/17, *JS* 205–7.

56. *NP* 1:3–8; Suter, 86; Gao Jiren, 4–7.

57. "Zongpu liuzhuan"; *NP* 1:2–3; Gao Jiren, 6. Yang Jiaxiu's biography is in the *Guangxi tongzhi* (1800; reprint, 1988) 10.6451.

58. See, e.g., *SD* 1:3, 1:4; *JS* 207–9.

59. *NP* 1:4–5.

60. Gao Jiren, 10. This assessment may be too strong, but it is clear that Ge's contributions to the *Wuzhong yigui* were nevertheless considerable. See also Chen, "Ge Jinshu xiansheng bashi shou xu" (Essay commemorating Mr. Ge Zhenghu's eightieth birthday), *Wenji, juan* 3; Ge Zhenghu, preface (dated 1766) to Chen's *Keshi zhijie* (1781); *NP* 1:5.

61. *Wenji* 7:37–39. Chen continued to correspond with Deling about policy issues well into his gubernatorial career; see, e.g., *SD* 1:8–9, 1:12, 2:5.

62. *NP* 1:7–8.

63. Letter of QL 31/8/28, *JS* 243–45; see also Gao Jiren, 7–9.

64. Li Yuandu, 16:1.

65. A tomb inscription exists for her and has been collected by the staff of the Guilin Museum, but in accordance with then provincial policy I was denied access to this "cultural relic" during my visit in 1994.

66. Letter of QL 19/6/17, *JS* 205–7; *NP* 12:2. For one example of her management of local relief in Lingui see *NP* 8:4.

67. "Zongpu liuzhuan." Of these concubines, we hear most in the sources about Madame Xia, who seems to have assumed the duties of mistress of the Chen household at Hengshan following the death of Chen's principal wife, Yang, in 1763. See, e.g., letters of QL 21/7/25 and QL 29/9/11, *JS* 207–9, 224–28.

68. *NP* 1:5–6, 3:12, 5:13, 5:23, 6:15, 7:7.

69. Despite Chen's obvious pride in his son-in-law's official success, already considerable in the last years of Hongmou's life, the old man fretted that alone of his descendents Xie Rongsheng had lost his seriousness of purpose as success arrived and spent his time in self-indulgent hobnobbing with the cultural elite; letter of QL 33/10/3, *JS* 249–51.

70. *NP* 1:5–6, 4:1; information personally provided by Steven Shutt.

71. His letters home from Beijing in the 1760s reveal Chen assiduously nurturing the affinal networks in the Lingui area forged by his son's and daughters' marriages—inquiring about his in-laws' health, financial security, and so on. He also acted in various ways as patron of local projects in his affines' native county of Yongfu (where he was also a significant landholder), just as he did in Lingui. See, e.g., letter of QL 30/11/1, *JS* 235–37; Tang Yin, afterword to Chen, *Xueshi yigui*. On aspects of this "localist strategy" by late imperial gentry, exemplified by even such a man as Chen Hongmou (whose social networks vastly transcended native place), see Robert Hymes, "Marriage, Descent Groups, and the Localist Strategy in Sung and Yuan Fu-chou," and Jerry Dennerline, "Marriage, Adoption, and Charity in the Development of Lineages in Wu-hsi from Sung to Ch'ing," both in Patricia B. Ebrey and James W. Watson, eds., *Kinship Organization in Late Imperial China, 1000–1940* (Berkeley: University of California Press, 1986), 95–136, 170–209.

72. Chen Duanwen's *Hanzhen xianshi* has apparently not survived. It is referred to in the *Guangxi tongzhi* (Guangxi provincial gazetteer) (1800) and in Hu Wenkai's *Lidai funü zhuzuo kao* (Female authors throughout history) (Shanghai: Guji, 1985), 598. My thanks to Ellen Widmer for the latter reference.

73. *Wenji* 9:40–42.

74. This accords with the findings of Arthur Wolf and Chieh-shen Huang, whose study of the institution of cross-brother adoption in Taiwan's modern history concludes that this differs from all other forms of adoption in the degree of closeness retained by the adoptee and the natural parents. Wolf and Huang, *Marriage and Adoption in China, 1845–1945* (Stanford: Stanford University Press, 1980), 108–9.

75. *Guangxi tongzhi*, 260:16; *Lingui xianzhi* 29:15. On Zhongke's wife see *NP* 2:5, 3:12, 4:7.

76. Li Yuandu, 16:4.

77. *Lingui xianzhi* 29:11; *NP* 2:12, 5:19, 6:25, 6:31, 8:10, 8:23.

78. Memorial of QL 20/9/16, *QLZZ* 12.509; letter of QL 33/10/3, *JS* 249–51; *Wenji* 9:49–53; *NP* 6:18, 8:6, 8:23, 9:2, 12:22; "Zongpu liuzhuan."

79. Letters of QL 29/11/15, QL 31/8/28, and QL 32/4/23, *JS* 228–30, 243–49. See also *SD* 1:1–3; *NP* 3:12, 5:15, 12:18; "Zongpu liuzhuan"; *KSZJ*, preface.

80. Letters of QL 21/7/25 and QL 29/11/15, *JS* 207–9, 228–30; Liequan, no. 5834, QPA; *NP* 2:11, 7:1, 7:16, 9:7, 9:17, 12:25. Among works of Hongmou that Lansen coedited with his father are the *Peiyuan tang oucun gao* and the *Keshi zhijie*; among those he edited on his own are the *Xueshi yigui* and the *Sishu kao jiyao*. See the various prefaces to these works for details.

81. Chen Jichang's career is discussed briefly in Li Fuyuan's 1828 preface to Chen Hongmou's *Wuzhong yigui* (1936 edition) and in the biography of Hongmou in the *Qingshi gao*, 35:10563–64. A collection of his poetry is included as an appendix to Hongmou's *Yishu*.

82. See, e.g., Chen's letter asking his superior Yinjishan to "see what you can do" for Chen Zhongcan (*SD* 1:2) and his persistent efforts to bring his elder brother's abilities to the attention of the court (*Wenji* 9:40–46; *NP* 1:11).

83. *SD* 1:17.

84. *SD* 2:16.

85. *SD* 2:12.

86. See, e.g., Li Yuandu, 16:4.

87. *SD* 3:5.

88. Memorial of YZ 10/5/11, *YZZZ* 14.722–23; *NP* 4:5, 4:17–18, 4:27, 6:8, 7:7, 8:23–25; Gao Jiren, 22.

89. Chen Lansen, preface to *Xueshi yigui*; *NP* 3:8, 4:18, 7:9. When official duties separated Chen from his dependents, he continually hounded them in letters home to study harder, noting that the family fortune was based on hard work in scholarship; see *JS*, esp. 235–37.

90. Ge Zhenghu and Chen Lansen, prefaces to *KSZJ*.

91. This is the "Zongpu liuzhuan," the most recent comprehensive revision of which was produced in 1924 but whose original, in the possession of current lineage head Chen Naiguang, includes handwritten entries of births and deaths since that time. It might be noted that in frontier Guangxi, as in other minority areas of the Qing empire, the single most important badge of Han ethnicity and tie to the historic Han culture a family could possess was a written document linking it to an indisputably Han ancestor who had immigrated into the area.

92. "Zishuo" (On personal names), *Wenji* 9:15–18; "Zongpu liuzhuan." It is entirely possible that the formal names of Chen ancestors prior to Hongmou's own generation were assigned after the fact, to accord with generational naming principles. This, indeed, may even have been true for his two brothers, who are known most often in the sources as Fengzheng and Yiting; their formal names may have been changed to Hongxian and Hongyi only after the phenomenal examination success of Hongmou. The "Hong" generational character, in any case, was changed at least once: on the accession of the Qianlong emperor in 1735 it was altered (from Mathews #2380 to Mathews #2377) in observance of the taboo against private use of characters appearing in the reigning sovereign's personal name, which was Hongli. It is interesting that there is no recorded writing of "Hongxian" or "Hongyi" using the pre-1735 character, whereas there are many such for "Hongmou."

93. *NP* 4:28; Lin Banjue, "Rongmen guli," 39–40.

94. Letters of QL 29/9/11 and QL 30/12/26, *JS* 224–28, 237–40. The building, much renovated of course, functions to this day as the Hengshan village school.

95. Ge Zhenghu, preface to *KSZJ*.

96. *JS* 235–37; *NP* 1:6, 7:12, 8:4.

97. *NP* 2:2; *Guilin jianshi*, 105; Gao Jiren, 22.

98. *NP* 4:28; *JS* 232–35; interviews with local residents during visit to Hengshan, January 14, 1994.

99. Letters of QL 19/6/17 and QL 24/7/25, *JS* 205–11; *NP* 11:30, 12:24. The endowment

for the county schools comprised properties Chen had steadily accumulated over nearly a decade in preparation for this gift.

100. "Shu Yuexi huiguan ehou" (Inscription for the Guangxi Native Place Association), *Wenji* 10:12; *NP* 3:3.

101. Xie Kang, 240.

102. *SD* 3:3; reprinted in *JSWB* 16:35.

103. *YZYG* 1:13.

104. Yuan Mei, 27:11.

105. On frugality as a cornerstone of mid-Qing economic policy see Suzuki Chūsei, *Shinchō chūkishi kenkyū* (A study of the mid-Qing period) (Toyohashi: Aichi daigaku, 1952), 37–40.

106. See, e.g., letters of QL 29/3/14, QL 29/3/28, and QL 29/4/28, *JS* 211–19. In line with the economic logic we shall explore in Part 2, Chen in these letters carefully distinguishes between expenditures that (however necessary) he considers to be essentially consumption and those he considers to be "profitable" (*youyi*) investments in future productivity, including donations to local public projects. Penny-pinching in the latter area is hardly justified.

107. Gao Jiren, 52–53.

108. *PYTOCG* 15:5–6, 19:31. By *sin* I mean an internalized sense of transgression against a conscious, although not necessarily anthropomorphized, divine power. As I will argue more fully in Chapter 3, Heaven (*tian*) for Chen Hongmou constituted just such a power. The pioneering attempt to demonstrate the appropriateness of the concept of sin for late imperial China is Wolfram Eberhard's *Guilt and Sin in Traditional China* (Berkeley: University of California Press, 1967). A more recent study that essentially reaffirms Eberhard's argument is Paolo Santangelo, "Human Conscience and Responsibility in Ming-Qing China," *East Asian History* 4 (December 1992): 31–80.

109. *XSYG* 2:34.

110. *XSYG* 1:12.

111. *SD* 3:17.

112. As a prosperous grand secretary no less than as an impoverished prefect, Chen continued to fulminate about the customary demands of *yingchou*; see his letter of QL 30/11/1, *JS* 235–37.

113. "Ziyang shuyuan zhusheng yueyan" (Address to the students of the Ziyang Academy), *Wenji* 10:15–17.

114. Keith McMahon, *Causality and Containment in Seventeenth-Century Chinese Fiction* (Leiden: E. J. Brill, 1988).

115. Chen, "Zijian shice" (Ten maxims for self-exhortation), cited in Tang Jian, 5:9.

116. *PYTOCG* 25:19.

117. *PYTOCG* 20:32–33.

118. *XSYG* 2:34. On eighteenth-century notions of limiting sexual activity to procreative goals see Keith McMahon, "A Case for Confucian Sexuality: The Eighteenth-Century Novel *Yesou Puyan*," *Late Imperial China* 9.2 (December 1988): 32–55.

119. Chen provides an account of his own daily food consumption in a letter of QL 29/11/15, *JS* 228–30.

120. *CZYG* 1:10.

121. Hellmut Wilhelm, "Chinese Confucianism on the Eve of the Great Encounter," in Marius B. Jansen, ed., *Changing Japanese Attitudes Toward Modernization* (Princeton: Princeton University Press, 1965).

122. Pei-yi Wu, "Self-Examination and Confession of Sins in Traditional China," *Harvard Journal of Asiatic Studies* 39.1 (1979): 36.

123. Wilhelm, "Chinese Confucianism," 290–92, 302–3.

124. Similar too are the rationalist conception of the universe, the disdain for enthusiastic religious practice, and the affinity for "pioneering" socioeconomic milieus. See "General Introduction" to Perry Miller and Thomas H. Johnson, eds., *The Puritans* (New York: Harper and

Row, 1938), 1–79. On the particular salience of frugality and industry in early Anglo-American economic culture see John E. Crowley, *This Sheba, Self: The Conceptualization of Economic Life in Eighteenth-Century America* (Baltimore: Johns Hopkins University Press, 1974).

125. *Yishu*, "Fuyi," 15.

126. Joanna Handlin, "Lü K'un's New Audience: The Influence of Women's Literacy on Sixteenth-Century Thought," in Margery Wolf and Roxane Witke, eds., *Women in Chinese Society* (Stanford: Stanford University Press, 1975), 28; Tang Jian, 5:10–11.

127. *SD* 3:7–8.

128. *Wenji, juan* 5.

129. *Yishu*, "Fuyi," 13–14.

130. *Yunnan tongzhi* (1736) 29.8:53–54.

131. Letter to Yinjishan (1739), *SD* 1:7–8.

132. Letter to Shao Qide (1741), *SD* 1:14.

133. *XSYG* 3:22.

134. Letter to Zhu Shaoyuan (1749), *SD* 2:15–16; *YZYG*, supplementary *juan*, 16–17.

135. *PYTOCG* 19:31.

136. *SD* 1:14; *XSYG* 3:22, citing Wei Xiangshu.

137. *PYTOCG* 17:39–40.

138. *YZYG* 2:20. If, as Peter Bol has argued, the core value of civilization was seen by Song thinkers as *wen*—cultural refinement—Chen may to some degree be viewed as part of a reaction to that attitude. As will be seen, however, his own notion of *hua* (civility) shares much with the *wen* of Song times; for men like Chen, rescuing civility from the decadent extremes to which it had been taken by literati aesthetes and pedants was a major task of the day. See Peter Bol, *"This Culture of Ours": Intellectual Transition in T'ang and Sung China* (Stanford: Stanford University Press, 1992).

139. Memorial of QL 19/9/28, *QLZZ* 9.648–50; *SD* 1:1, 1:14, 2:13, 3:1; *XSYG* 4:1–21; *PYTOCG* 11:25–26, 11:29, 15:15–16, 19:21–40.

140. *PYTOCG* 33:33.

141. Memorial of QL 13/1/10, QPA.

142. *Wenji* 2:30.

143. Letter to Zhang Haizhuang, *JSWB* 2:33; Tang Jian, 5:11.

144. To ensure their permanency, Chen published in 1757 a collection of the most significant policy documents he had produced over the course of four tenures as Shaanxi governor; *Guitiao huiqiao* (see especially Chen's preface). See also letter to Yang Yingju, *SD* 2:9.

145. *Yishu*, "Fuyi," 15; Gao Jiren, 8.

146. Tang Yi, preface to *Xueshi yigui*.

147. Thomas Metzger, *Escape from Predicament: Neo-Confucianism and China's Evolving Political Culture* (New York: Columbia University Press, 1977).

148. See, e.g., *SD* 1:12, 2:19; *PYTOCG* 20:11–23; *YZYG* 1:17.

149. Letters to Zhu Zuotang, Zhang Jiayang, and Zhou Renji, all *SD* 3:4.

150. Letters to Shao Qide, Gong Yiyun, and Zhu Xiaoyuan, *SD* 1:14–15, 3:7.

151. Qingfu, memorial of QL 12/1/13, GCA.

152. See, e.g., *PYTOCG* 11:27–28, 25:30–31.

153. Letter to Zhu Xiaoyuan, *SD* 2:17.

154. Letter to Tang Chenggang, *SD* 2:16.

Chapter 2

1. For recent surveys by Chinese scholars of the broad policy shifts of these years see Bai Xinliang, *Qianlong zhuan* (Biography of the Qianlong emperor) (Shenyang: Liaoning jiaoyu chubanshe, 1990), 16–19; Dai Yi, *Qianlong di ji qi shidai* (The Qianlong emperor and his times) (Beijing: Zhongguo renmin daxue chubanshe, 1992), 98–113; and Gao Xiang, *Kang-Yong-Qian sandi tongzhi sixiang yanjiu* (Concepts of rulership of the Kangxi, Yongzheng, and Qianlong em-

perors) (Beijing: Zhongguo renmin daxue chubanshe, 1996), 257–304. For a summary analysis by a leading Western scholar see Kuhn, *Soulstealers*, 227–28. A classic study of the shaping of Gaozong's policy views in the years prior to his enthronement is Harold L. Kahn, *Monarchy in the Emperor's Eyes: Image and Reality in the Ch'ien-lung Reign* (Cambridge, Mass.: Harvard University Press, 1971). For overviews of the Yongzheng policies against which Qianlong reacted see Feng Erkang, *Yongzheng zhuan* (Biography of the Yongzheng emperor) (Beijing: Renmin chubanshe, 1985); Gao, *Kang-Yong-Qian*, 173–246; and Pei Huang, *Autocracy at Work: A Study of the Yung-cheng Reign, 1723–1735* (Bloomington: Indiana University Press, 1974). In addition to Feng's meticulously researched study, another recent survey of the Yongzheng reign exists, this a semipopular account by the eminent Japanese sinologist Miyazaki Ichisada; following the general historiographic line of the "Kyoto school," Miyazaki portrays Yongzheng as the culmination of the long-term trend toward concentration of power in the imperial throne. Miyazaki, *Yōseitei: Chūgoku no dokusai kunshu* (The Yongzheng emperor: China's absolutist ruler) (Tokyo: Chūo koronsha, 1996).

2. Gao Wangling, "Yige wei wanjie de changshi—Qingdai Qianlong shiqi de liangzheng he liangshi wenti" (An unfinished experiment—food supply problems and grain policy in the Qing Qianlong reign), *Jiuzhou xuekan* 2.3 (April 1988): 13–40. Helen Dunstan has likewise examined this pullback from economic "interventionism" or state "paternalism" to an "anti-activist" posture during the first fifteen years of Qianlong's reign; Dunstan, *Conflicting Counsels*, esp. 69–71, 152–53, and 330–31. Dunstan sees the most decisive years of turnaround as the late 1740s and links this with the removal from the scene of the two most important Yongzheng-holdover ministers, Ortai (died 1745) and Zhang Tingyu (retired 1750). As we shall see, both of these men were early patrons of Chen Hongmou, who continued to espouse their more activist approach after it was no longer politically fashionable to do so.

3. Madeleine Zelin, *The Magistrate's Tael: Rationalizing Fiscal Reform in Eighteenth-Century Ch'ing China* (Berkeley: University of California Press, 1984).

4. Zelin, 304.

5. See Chapter 6 for an attempt to explore some of the deceptive tensions in this ubiquitous idiom of Qing discourse.

6. On the latter innovation see Guo Songyi, "Lun 'tanding rudi' " (On the merger of the head and land taxes), *Qingshi luncong* 3 (1982): 1–62.

7. Dai Yi, *Qianlong*, 108–10; Bai Xinliang, 23–32, 160–61; Kishimoto, "Keizai seisaku," 25–28.

8. Feng Erkang, 164–72; Bai Xinliang, 27–28.

9. See, e.g., Suzuki Chūsei, 45.

10. Crossley has argued this in passing in a number of her publications, including, e.g., *Orphan Warriors: Three Manchu Generations and the End of the Qing World* (Princeton: Princeton University Press, 1990), 21–22.

11. Yongzheng emperor, *Dayi juemi lu* (Record of righteousness dispelling error) (1730; reprint, Taibei, 1969), 1:1.

12. For a recent account of this incident and its broader significance for shifts in the tone of Qing rule under Yongzheng and Qianlong see Pamela Kyle Crossley, *The Manchus* (Oxford: Blackwell Publishers, 1997), chap. 5. See also *ECCP*, 747–49; Bai Xinliang, 19–22; Dai Yi, *Qianlong*, 105–7.

13. See especially Crossley, "*Manzhou yuanliu kao* and the Formalization of the Manchu Heritage," *Journal of Asian Studies* 46.4 (November 1987): 761–90; and Crossley, "The Rulerships of China," *American Historical Review* 97.5 (December 1992): 1468–83.

14. William T. Rowe, "Education and Empire in Southwest China: Ch'en Hung-mou in Yunnan, 1733–38," in Elman and Woodside, 417–57.

15. Paola Paderni, "The Problem of *Kuan-hua* in Eighteenth-Century China: The Yung-cheng Decree for Fukien and Kwangtung," *Annali* 48.4 (1988): 260.

16. The best discussion of the Yongzheng initiatives remains Terada Takanobu, "Yōseitei no seimin kaiko ni tsuite" (On the Yongzheng emperor's emancipation of debased peoples), *Tōyōshi*

kinkyū 18.3 (1959): 124–41. See also Feng Erkang, 377–86; Pei Huang, 226–36. On regressive legislation enacted by Qianlong see Jing Junjian, *Qingdai shehui de jianmin dengji* (Debased status in Qing society) (Hangzhou: Zhejiang renmin chubanshe, 1993), 233–36.

17. Bai Xinliang, 28.

18. Zhang Renshan, "Lun Qianlong de dengji lunli guan ji qi weihu dengji lunli de cushi" (Qianlong's view of the social hierarchy and his efforts to strengthen it), *Gugong bowuyuan yuankan* 1988.3, 23–28, 69.

19. R. Kent Guy, "Zhang Tingyu and Reconciliation: The Scholar and the State in the Early Qianlong Reign," *Late Imperial China* 7.1 (June 1986): 50–62; Guy, "Fang Bao"; Guy, "Provincial Governors of the Qianlong Regency" (paper presented to the Association for Asian Studies Annual Meeting, Chicago, March 1993). See also Dai Yi, *Qianlong*, 146; and James Polachek, *The Inner Opium War* (Cambridge, Mass.: Council on East Asian Studies, 1992), 26–27.

20. An excellent, sustained analysis of Yongzheng's personnel policies is Kent C. Smith, "Ch'ing Policy and the Development of Southwest China: Aspects of Ortai's Governor-Generalship, 1726–1731" (Ph.D. diss., Yale University, 1970). The useful term *new men* is Smith's coinage. See also Feng Erkang, 80–84, 209–20, 422–27, and 457–70; Gao Jiren, 12–13; Zelin, esp. 190; and Guy, "Fang Bao."

21. Liezhuan, no. 5884; *NP* 1:9–10.

22. For Zhang's career see *Qing Zhang Daxueshi Tingyu ziding nianpu* (Autobiography of Grand Secretary Zhang Tingyu) (1749; reprint, Taibei: Commercial Press, 1982); Xu Kai, "Lun Yong-Qian shuyao de Zhang Tingyu" (On Zhang Tingyu, a central figure in the Yongzheng-Qianlong era), *Beijing daxue xuebao*, Philosophy and Social Science Series, 1992.4, 91–98; Guy, "Zhang Tingyu and Reconciliation"; Feng Erkang, 481–85; and *ECCP*, 54–56. On Zhang's Tongcheng background see Hilary Beattie, *Land and Lineage in China: A Study of T'ung-ch'eng County, Anhwei, in the Ming and Ch'ing Dynasties* (Cambridge: Cambridge University Press, 1979). On his role in the formation of the Grand Council see Beatrice S. Bartlett, *Monarchs and Ministers: The Grand Council in Mid-Ch'ing China, 1723–1820* (Berkeley: University of California Press, 1991).

23. *Wenji* 2:30–33, 7:13–15; *SD* 1:12, 2:3; *JSWB* 16:33; *NP* 1:8; Gao Jiren, 12.

24. Chen, "Gan Zhuangluo gong ji xu" (Preface to Gan Rulai's collected works), in Wang Chang, 30:7–8; *Zhongguo renming da zidian*, 195.

25. Gao Jiren, 13.

26. "Yongzhen chao zhupo yinjiantan" (Imperial audience notes from the Yongzheng court), in *Qingdai dangan shiliao congbian* (Historical materials from the Qing archives), vol. 9 (Beijing: Number One Historical Archives, 1983), 103–4.

27. Peng Qifeng, 14:6; Sun Xingyan, 14; Yuan Mei, 9; *Qingshi gao* 35.10558; *NP* 1:13; Gao Jiren, 15–16.

28. For these details see Zelin, chap. 6.

29. Memorial of YZ 9/4/10, *YZZZ*; *NP* 1:15–22; Gao Jiren, 16.

30. On Yinjishan's life and career see Gao Xiang, "Yinjishan shulun" (A discussion of Yinjishan), *Qingshi yanjiu* 1995.1, 27–37; *ECCP*, 920–21.

31. For but a few examples see Chen memorials of QL 17/3/4, QL 19/9/28, and QL 20/10/5 (*QLZZ* 2.366–67, 9.648–50, 12.597–98); Yinjishan memorial of YZ 12, in *Yunnan tongzhi* (1736) 29.629–52; Chen memorial of QL 8/inter 4, in Cai Guanluo, 1.145; Yinjishan and Chen memorial of QL 24/1, in Cai Guanluo, 1.148; Peng Qifeng, 14:11; Wang Chang, 29:1–2. It appears that Yinjishan's patronage was there for Chen even at the end of their careers: just three months after Yinjishan became a grand secretary in 1764, Chen was named an associate (*xieban*); he was promoted to a full grand secretary's rank three years later and served happily alongside his friend until both men died in 1771. Letter of QL 29/3/28, *JS* 214–17; *Qingshi gao* 21.6163–66.

32. *Qing shigao* 35.10564.

33. Sun Xingyan, 17; Yuan Mei 27:11–12; Waley, 25, 102–3. A selection of Yinjishan's poetry survives as *Yin wenduan gong shiji* (Collected poems of Yinjishan), ca. 1780.

34. See, e.g., *SD* 1:3, 2:11, 2:20.

35. See Chen's letter to Yinjishan of 1739, *SD* 1:7–8, and Yinjishan's published handbook of model prose selections, *Siwen jingcui* (Essentials of refined prose style), ca. 1735. For Yinjishan's interest in the Shaanxi school see *PYTOCG* 30:3–4.

36. *NP* 1:20, 2:1.

37. K. Smith, "Ch'ing Policy."

38. Chen, "Daxueshi Guangning Zhang Wenhe gong shendao bei" (Spirit tablet for Grand Secretary Zhang Yunsui), *Wenji* 8:29–33; preface by Shen Deqian, *Wenji*; *NP* 2:11–12 and 6:4; *PY-TOCG* 3:1–2. A capsule biography of Zhang may be found in *Zhongguo renming da zidian*, 924.

39. Yuan Mei, 27:11.

40. *NP* 2:12–14.

41. Pierre-Étienne Will, personal communication.

42. *NP* 7:12. For other examples of such transfers, with similar imperial comments, see Liequan no. 5834; memorials of QL 16/8/11, QL 17/3/28, QL 19/7/19, and QL 20/9/16, in *QLZZ* 1.387–88, 2.534–36, 9.199–200, 12.508–9.

43. Memorials of QL 16/8/11, QL 16/8/29, QL 17/3/28, QL 20/6/13, QL 21/inter-calary 9/21, QL 21/12/3, and QL 21/12/28, all *QLZZ*; *NP* 5:11, 7:6–8, 8:20, 9:5–6.

44. *Shilu* 175:30–32. For another example, in which Chen cites an imperial utterance to have a Board of Revenue decision overturned by the throne, see memorial of QL 17/7/16, *QLZZ* 3.389–90.

45. A good example came in 1760, when Chen proposed sending auxiliary officials into the Jiangsu countryside to clear up tax arrears. Gaozong at first demurred, suggesting instead using clerks or, still better, the magistrates themselves. Chen ultimately convinced him that clerks were too corrupt and magistrates too overburdened to do the job effectively. See memorials of QL 25/11/1 and QL 26/2/1, MQA, and further discussion of this episode in Chapter 10.

46. Kuhn, *Soulstealers*, esp. 206–7, 227–28.

47. Qianlong edict in response to memorial of Jiangsu education commissioner Liu Yong, *Shilu* 670:5–6; Kuhn, *Soulstealers*, 71–72. What Qianlong was probably saying between the lines was that both Chen and Yinjishan were getting too old to be effective provincial administrators, and it was nearing time for them to be kicked upstairs to Beijing.

48. Karjishan and Chen memorials of QL 18/11/5 and QL 18/11/27, *QLZZ* 6.664–65, 6.880–82. In what can only be seen as an ironic riposte to charges of their lack of thoroughness, the two officials responded by presenting the throne with a tediously lengthy account of their handling of all cases of violence in the area where the bandit had been known to operate.

49. Liezhuan no. 5834; *Wenji*, preface by Shen Deqian; *NP* 9:5–6.

50. Liezhuan no. 5834; letter of QL 29/3/14, *JS* 211–14.

51. See, among other examples, letters of QL 30/9/9, QL 31/1/23, and QL 32/3/17, *JS* 232–35, 240–42, 245–47.

52. Liezhuan no. 5834.

53. This section covers the same ground as my previous Chinese-language article, "Zhengfu yu tudi: 1723–1737 nian Guangxi kaiken yanjiu," *Qingshi yanjiu* 94.1 (spring 1994): 79–86. The episode is also treated in Marks, *Tigers, Rice, Silk, and Silt*, 301–5.

54. The best comprehensive source on this subject is Peng Yuxin, *Qingdai tudi kaiken shi* (A history of land development in the Qing period) (Beijing: Nongye chubanshe, 1990), 1–70. An older and briefer treatment is Feng Liutang, *Zhongguo lidai minshi zhengce shi* (Food supply policy in Chinese history) (Shanghai: Commercial Press, n.d.), 158–65.

55. Kangxi's edict is printed in *Daqing lidai shilu* (Veritable records of the successive reigns of the Qing), Kangxi reign, 256:14. For English-language discussions of its significance see Yeh-chien Wang, *Land Taxation in Imperial China, 1750–1911* (Cambridge, Mass.: Harvard University Press, 1973), 29, 47; and Perdue, *Exhausting the Earth*, 78–79.

56. Edict of YZ 1/4, in *Qingchao wenxian tongkao* (reprint, Shanghai: Commercial Press, 1936), 4871. See also discussions in Song Xixiang, *Zhongguo lidai quannong kao* (A study of poli-

cies to promote agriculture in Chinese history) (Nanjing: Zhengzhong, 1936), 75; Peng Yuxin, 70–71; Perdue, *Exhausting the Earth*, 61.

57. Edict of YZ 5, in both *Qingchao wenxian tongkao*, 4874–75 and *Da Qing huidian shili* (1899; reprint, Taibei: Xin wenfeng, 1976), 166:7.

58. Peng Yuxin, 73–74, 282.

59. This correspondence is abstracted in *Da Qing huidian shili*, 166:6.

60. See, e.g., Perdue, *Exhausting the Earth*, 78–79.

61. See Inada; Marks, "Rice Prices."

62. See, e.g., Board of Revenue President Sun Chaqi, memorial of YZ 1/3/16, reprinted in Number One Historical Archives, "Yongzheng yuan nian kenhuang shiliao xuan" (Selected materials on land reclamation in the first year of the Yongzheng reign), *Lishi dang'an* 1993.1, 13–14. In this memorial Sun reports the reclamation of some 1,609 *mu* of rice land in Guangxi in 1722 and his imposition of Yongzheng's mandated six-year tax holiday.

63. Li Fu, "Xiuchen Guangxi kenhuang shiyi shu" (Memorial on promoting land reclamation in Guangxi), in *JSWB* 34:34–36. On Li's colorful career see *ECCP*, 455–57; and Feng Erkang, 209–20. Robert Marks has discovered that Li's memorial was essentially copied over from an earlier memorial submitted in 1724 by acting Guangxi governor Han Liangfu; *YZZZ* 2:582–83.

64. See comparative provincial figures presented in Peng Yuxin, 73–74.

65. Edict of YZ 7/4, abstracted in Song Xixiang, 77. The "public funds" referred to were lines in county-level budgets that, under Yongzheng-era tax reforms, were set aside for local public projects; see Zelin.

66. Ortai, memorial of YZ 8/1/13, *YZZZ* 15.463–67.

67. "Jin Hong liezhuan" (Manuscript biography of Jin Hong), State History Office Archives, QPA.

68. Ortai, memorial of YZ 7/8/18, in *Eertai zhe* (Memorials of Ortai), vol. 8 of *Biji xiaoshuo dalan*, ser. 12 (Taibei: Xinxing shuju, 1976), 4–6.

69. The following is based on Jin Hong, memorials of YZ 10/1/12 and YZ 12/12/17, *YZZZ* 19.301–2, 23.894–96.

70. Jin Hong, memorials of YZ 12/5/27 and YZ 13/4/20, *YZZZ* 23.107, 24.414. See also figures reported in the *Guangxi tongzhi* (Guangxi provincial gazetteer), 22:1–2, compiled under Jin Hong's supervision in 1733.

71. *NP* 1:17–18.

72. *NP* 2:2.

73. *SD* 1:3.

74. *NP* 1:12.

75. For one such case from 1724 see Polachek, 33. The ethical ambiguity involved in Chen's actions is reflected in the biography of him by the famous poet Yuan Mei. Yuan praises Chen in general for his avoidance of any taint of self-interest in his official career but then rather coyly alludes to this and one other instance when Chen may have violated this principle. It also bears noting that in his account of this affair Yuan delicately avoids mention by name of the disgraced Jin Hong, who had been one of Yuan's own earliest official patrons. Yuan Mei, *Xiaocang shanfang wenji* (Collected writings of Yuan Mei), 27:9–12.

76. Chen, memorial of YZ 11/3/1, *YZZZ* 21.194–95; also excerpted and discussed in *NP* 2:2–4.

77. Jin Hong, memorial of YZ 12/12/17, *YZZZ* 23.894–96.

78. One can only imagine the chagrin felt at this point by Ortai, who, now in Beijing as one of the emperor's closest personal advisors, saw this sordid investigation unfolding. It is highly unlikely, however, that the case would have been resolved as it was had not Ortai opted in effect to abandon his embarrassing protégé, Jin Hong, as he became increasingly aware of the miscarriage in practice of programs he himself had once insistently promoted.

79. Yinjishan, memorial of YZ 13/2/4, *YZZZ* 24.104–8.

80. Note that the structure of administrative jurisdictions in south China had in the interim been once again redefined so that Emida served as governor-general of Guangxi and Guangdong, not Guangxi-Yunnan-Guizhou.

81. I have been unable to locate the full text of this memorial. It is excerpted in *NP* 2:15–16.

82. Edict of QL 1/7/24, abstracted in *Changbiandang* (Court calendar), Qianlong 1:fall quarter, Qing Palace Archives, Taibei. The closeness of Chen and Yang is suggested by the frequency of their personal correspondence (see Chen, *Shudu*), by the fact that Chen in 1761 reedited and published Yang's work *Jiefu zhuan* (Biographies of exemplary women), and by Chen's explicit adherence to Yang's earlier policies during his governorship of Hunan (Perdue, *Exhausting the Earth*, 219–21).

83. Yang Xifu (1701–68) remained in Guangxi for ten years, first as provincial treasurer and then as governor. Thereafter, his provincial career crisscrossed that of Chen across the imperial map, ending in Beijing in the 1760s, when Chen was grand secretary and Yang director of grain transport. Both officials specialized in problems of agricultural development, hydraulic management, and food supply. For samples of their mutual correspondence see *SD* 2:10; and Yang Xifu, *Sizhi tang wenji* (Collected works from the Sizhi Studio), 23:1–2. Perdue, *Exhausting the Earth*, has much to say about the comparable policies of the two officials in one province in which they both served, Hunan. Chen also admired and in 1761 republished Yang's 1737 work *Jiefu zhuan* (Biographies of exemplary women of Guangxi).

84. Edict of QL 1/8/3, *Changbiandang*, Qianlong 1:fall quarter; edict of QL 1/11/30, *Changbiandang*, Qianlong 1:winter quarter.

85. Memorial of Emida and Yang Chaozeng, QL 2/10/30, *Shilu* 55:15–16.

86. Draft biography of Jin Hong, State History Office Archives, QPA.

87. This process is succinctly discussed in Peng Yuxin, 76–81.

88. *Wenxian tongkao*, 4878.

89. Bai Xinliang, 17–18.

90. Zhu Shi, memorial of YZ 13/10, in Zhu, *Zhu wenduan gong wenji* (1869), supplementary *juan* 1:41–42. See also discussion in Peng Yuxin, 119–20. On Zhu's career see *ECCP*, 188–90; and Kahn, 159–63.

91. Chen, "Zhu Wenduan gong wenji xu," in *Wenji* 2:12–14. See also *Wenji* 2:33; *NP* 1:8, 1:12.

92. Edict of YZ 13/10, *Shilu*, Qianlong reign, 4:37–38. Also extracted in *Wenxian tongkao*, 4881; and *Da Qing huidian shili*, 166:12.

93. Peng Yuxin, 124; similar figures are cited in Bai Xinliang, 31–32.

94. Wang Shijun (*jinshi* 1721) was apparently singled out for punishment not merely for his offenses in the area of *kaiken* but more generally because he had been the most outspoken Yongzheng official to publicly criticize the broad reversals of policy undertaken in the first months of the Qianlong reign. In particular, the rough-hewn Wang condemned Gaozong's increasingly obvious personnel preference for hyperliterate courtier types. See Guy, "Zhang Tingyu."

95. Edict of QL 5 and subsequent provincial-level specifications, *Wenxian tongkao*, 4884–85.

96. For the fiscal reclassification of this falsely reported new land in Guangxi see memorial of Governor Yang Xifu, QL 5/9, in Yang's *Sizhi tang wenji* (Collected works from the Studio of Fourfold Wisdom) (1769), 2:11–13. Chen's heroic defense of his native place's interests is lauded in the *Guangxi tongzhi* (1800), 260:14, the *Lingui xianzhi* (1905), 29:12, and even the recent *Guilin jianshi* (1984), 114–15.

97. Yang Xifu, *Sizhi tang wenji*, 3:36–39.

98. Chen Hongmou, memorial of QL 2/9/12, MQA.

99. Ibid. See also *Shilu*, Qianlong reign, 53:14–15.

100. Chen Hongmou, *Quan Dian yixue huiji* (Guide to public schools in Yunnan) (Kunming, 1738).

101. *NP* 3:1.

102. On Ortai's career see his biography by Chao-ying Fang in *ECCP*, 601–3; Feng Erkang, 476–81; and K. Smith, "Ch'ing Policy."

103. *Wenji* 6:23.

104. Chen, proclamation of QL 2/11/28, in *Quan Dian yixue huiji*, *ce* 2; *JSWB* 57:58–61.

105. R. Kent Guy, personal communication.

106. *Wenji* 6:22–25; *SD* 2:3–4.

107. Chen was commended to the throne by his superior, Zhili viceroy Sun Jiagan, for his work on Yellow River conservancy in 1740; *NP* 3:16. For a sample of their correspondence see *SD* 2:13.

108. Qingfu, memorial of QL 12/1/13, QPA. See also the digest of these charges in Liezhuan, no. 5834; *Qingshi gao* 35:10559–60; and *NP* 6:9.

109. Memorial of QL 12/3/7, MQA.

110. See, e.g., Chen memorial of QL 8/8/26, and Qingfu and Chen memorial of QL 10/2/9, both MQA; also *NP* 5:19.

111. Yuan Mei, 27:10.

112. Peng Qifeng, 14:6; Li Yuandu, 16:1. For Qingfu's biography see *ECCP*, 795–96. The Tong family is that studied in Pamela Crossley, "The Tong in Two Worlds: Cultural Identity in Liaodong and Nurgan during the 13th–17th Centuries," *Ch'ing-shih wen-t'i* 4.9 (June 1983): 21–46.

113. Memorial of QL 12/3/7, MQA.

114. Complaining of Chen's "laxity" in the city wall reconstruction drive in Shaanxi, and picking up on Qingfu's hint that the Shaanxi governor's *yanglian* stipend was unduly rich, Gaozong, with what must have been a twinkle in his eye, also ordered that Chen contribute personal funds for the repair of a city wall in Ding County, Zhili, which the emperor found to be an eyesore. Memorial of QL 12/3/24, MQA.

115. Edict of QL 12/2/25, cited at length in Chen's memorial of QL 12/3/7 (MQA) and in *Qingshi gao* 35:10559–60.

116. *Qingshi gao* 35:10564.

117. Hou Xiaonan, 79.

118. Citied in Shen Deqian, preface (1769) to *Wenji*.

119. Will, "La communication entre bureaucrates et paysans en Chine à la fin de l'empire: idéaux, méthodes, réalités" (paper presented to the Symposium on Civil Society in East Asian Countries, Montreal, 22–25 October 1992).

120. See, e.g., *PYTOCG* 11:37–41, 20:11–23; *ZZYG*, preface and 2:14–29.

121. See Xie Kang, 239–40.

122. Gao Xiang, "Yinjishan," 31.

123. Liezhuan, no. 5834.

124. Edict of QL 17/9/1, *Shilu* 423:1–2.

125. For examples of Chen's political problems of the early 1750s see his memorials of QL 17/3/15 and QL 17/5/28, *QLZZ* 2.444, 3.209–10. For a description and analysis of the impeachment process see Thomas Metzger, *The Internal Organization of Ch'ing Bureaucracy: Legal, Normative, and Communication Aspects* (Cambridge, Mass.: Harvard University Press, 1973), esp. 364–68. Metzger notes the routinization of the process on p. 310.

126. See Lai Huimin, "Lun Qianlong chao chuqi zhi Mandang yu Handang" (On the Manchu and Chinese factions in the early Qianlong reign), in Institute of Modern History, *Jinshi jiazu yu zhengzhi bijiao lishi lunwenji* (Family process and political process in modern Chinese history) (Taibei: Academia Sinica, 1992), 721–44; Kuhn, *Soulstealers*, 60–66; *ECCP*, 602.

127. *NP* 6:11.

128. Memorial of QL 19/12/21, *QLZZ* 10.386–87.

129. Two memorials, both dated QL 20/2/11, *QLZZ* 10.690–92; memorial of QL 20/2/29, *QLZZ* 10.825–26. On Salar see *ECCP*, 10.

130. Shandong native Liu Tongxun (1700–73) was a logical choice to investigate venality

on the part of Ortai's nephew, Ochang, because of his own reputation for impartiality; as a junior official in 1741 he had impeached Ortai's factional opponent Zhang Tingyu for nepotism and corruption. Liu himself, however, would emerge as leader of yet a third party of officials, of north China origin, who were solicitously groomed by Qianlong to displace both factions inherited from his father's reign. See Guy, *Emperor's Four Treasuries*, 70; Polachek, *Inner Opium War*, 30, 294.

131. Memorials of QL 20/3/12, QL 20/3/27, QL 20/4/19, QL 20/4/28, and QL 20/7/28, in *QLZZ* 10.878–79, 11.88, 11.208, 11.273–74, 12.222–23.

132. *ECCP*, 533–34.

133. Memorial of QL 20/5/24, *QLZZ* 11.478; *NP* 8:19–21.

134. Peng Qifeng (1701–84) was, like Chen Hongmou, a Yongzheng favorite (*optimus* on the palace examination of 1727) who survived into the Qianlong bureaucracy, rising to hold various board presidencies and vice presidencies in the years 1743–68. Although essentially a metropolitan official, he retained close ties to his native Jiangnan, serving intermittently as headmaster of Suzhou's Ziyang Academy, where Chen periodically lectured during his Jiangsu governorship. *ECCP*, 616–17, 658.

135. For Chen's attack on the Jiangsu grain tribute bureaucracy see *PYTOCG* 40:15–18. For his attack on the powerful Zhiping Buddhist Monastery see memorial of QL 24/5, excerpted in *NP* 10:31. For linkages of this activity with the emergence of political enemies see *Lingui xianzhi* 29:14; Peng Qifeng.

136. *NP* 10:32; Liezhuan, no. 5843; Peng Qifeng; Cai Guanluo, 1.148.

137. *NP* 11:12–14.

138. Two memorials, both dated QL 27/8/16, MQA; *NP* 11:30–33; Liezhuan, no. 5834.

139. Two memorials, both dated QL 23/3/4, MQA.

140. Liezhuan no. 5834, QPA.

141. Memorial of QL 23/5/7, MQA.

142. Memorial of QL 23/6/2, MQA.

143. Jiqing and acting Liang-Guang viceroy Li Shiyao, memorial of QL 23/6/29 (a), MQA. A specialist in salt administration matters, Jiqing was credited with compilation of the 1748 Liang-Huai regulatory code (*Liang-Huai yanfa zhi*). On his checkered subsequent career see *ECCP*, 584–85, and *Zhongguo renming da zidian*, 235.

144. Jiqing and acting Liang-Guang viceroy Li Shiyao, memorial of QL 23/6/29 (b), MQA.

145. Liezhuan no. 5834, QPA; Cai Guanluo, 1.148.

146. Chen's son and biographer, Chen Zhongke, implicitly defends Hongmou against charges that he was in the merchants' pocket by stressing that, even as the salt controversy was going on, he was taking a very tough line against Guangdong *grain* merchants who were speculatively driving up the price of rice in the provincial capital. *NP* 10:5–6.

147. Chen's nineteenth-century biographer Li Yuandu asserts that the entire investigation of Guangdong salt matters got underway because the emperor himself was so inflamed at the policy implications of Chen's original memorial; Li, 16:2. It is worth noting that in 1738 a similarly controversial proposal of then Liang-Guang viceroy Emida (with Ortai's support) to make capital loans to Guangdong salt merchants had won Qianlong's endorsement; during the intervening two decades, Gaozong had retreated dramatically from commitment to activist policies but his long-serving minister Chen Hongmou far less so. See Dunstan, *Conflicting Counsels*, 162–63.

148. See, e.g., letter to Feng Xujiu, *SD* 2:8; Kuhn, *Soulstealers*, 120–22.

149. For examples of Chen's use and advocacy of the *Dibao* see memorials of QL 17/9/3 and QL 19/12/17, *QLZZ* 3.749, 10.347–48; and letters to Tuo Yong and Chen Wenwei, *SD* 2:5, 3:9.

150. Karjishan and Chen memorials of QL 17/12/20 and QL 18/7/19, *QLZZ* 4.660–61, 5.834–36; Chen memorial of QL 18/8/27, *QLZZ* 5.630–31. Provincial Treasurer Deshu himself seems to have been an official of an innovative and activist bent; see, e.g., his celebrated memorial of 1754 (after Chen's departure from Fujian) establishing militia organizations to combat the growing problem of secret society (*hui*) racketeering in the province (*JSWB* 71:29–31).

151. Yinghe, *Enfutang biji* (Scribblings from the Enfu Studio), cited in Wang Bingjie, *Guochao mingzhen yanxing lu* (Accounts of the words and deeds of famous Qing officials) (1885), 14:9. Yinghe discreetly leaves the senior man's name unmentioned, but two of Chen's direct superiors in his Tianjin post, both of whom he assiduously cultivated, were the eminent officials Sun Jiagan and Huang Tinggui. See *SD* 1:12; *NP* 3:16.

152. For but one of many examples see *NP* 6:2.

153. Li Yuandu, 16:3.

154. The most important of these impeachments were not in fact of local officials at all but rather of Shaanxi salt intendant Cao Shenggui in 1747 and Hunan provincial treasurer Yang Hao in 1756, both for embezzlement. See Liezhuan no. 5834; *NP* 6:11; *Lingui xianzhi* 29:13.

155. Memorials of QL 17/3/4 and QL 19/12/17, *QLZZ* 2.370, 10.347–48.

156. *SD* 3:2.

157. *SD* 2:12.

158. Wang Jie, *Baochun ge ji* (Collected works from the Baochun Pavilion), "Nianpu," 4–6; *ECCP*, 75, 137, 373. For a full account of the incident—which fails to mention Chen Hongmou—see Iona D. Man-Cheong, "Fair Fraud and Fraudulent Fairness: The 1761 Examination Case," *Late Imperial China* 18.2 (December 1997): 36–70.

159. Guy, "Fang Pao"; Benjamin A. Elman, *Classicism, Politics, and Kinship: The Ch'ang-chou School of New Text Confucianism in Late Imperial China* (Berkeley: University of California Press, 1990), 11–15; *ECCP*, 235–37. I am indebted also to Kai-wing Chow and Gao Xiang for engaging with me in conversations about Fang Bao that have contributed to my understanding of his character.

160. *PYTOCG* 34:30–39.

161. Fang Bao, *Fang Wangji yiji* (Surviving works of Fang Bao) (Hefei: Huangshan shushe, 1990), 53–54. I am grateful to Pierre-Henri Durand for bringing this work to my attention.

162. Letters to Fang Bao, *SD* 2:12, 2:15; Fang, letter to Chen, in *Fang Wangji yiji*, 63–64.

163. See memorial of QL 8/inter 4/27, MQA. Chen also drew on Depei's previous reforms of the tea administration during his tenure in Gansu; memorial of QL 20/7/28, *QLZZ* 12.220–22.

164. Letter to Depei, *SD* 1:13. A copy of the first edition of Depei's work survives in the Beijing Library. Subsequent letters from Chen appear in *SD* 2:7–8 and 2:10, both dealing with the moral conduct of the court, where Depei was posted by the late 1740s. For Depei's biography see *ECCP*, 714–15. Arthur Waley, *Yuan Mei: Eighteenth-Century Chinese Poet* (London: George Allen and Unwin, 1956), 31, notes that Depei was also a patron of Yuan Mei.

165. *SD* 1:6, 1:7. On Yin Huiyi see his *Jianyu xiansheng wenji* (Collected works of Yin Huiyi) (ca. 1750; reprint, Shanghai: Shangwu shuju, 1936); *ECCP*, 710, 921; *Zhongguo renming da zidian*, 51.

166. On Zhou see memorial of Board of Works, QL 26, in Chen, *Wuliao jiazhi zeli* (Zhili Province edition), 1:1–3. On Gong see his volume of poems entitled *Nanming ji* (1760) and *Zhongguo renming da zidian*, 771. Both are well represented as addressees in Chen's *SD*.

167. *Wenji* 7:24–25, 10:6; *NP* 5:5; *Zhongguo renming da zidian*, 1346. Again, many letters to Lei survive in Chen's *SD*.

168. Chen did write a eulogy for Jia Shengquan, who may have been the closest of all his epistolary confidantes; see *Wenji* 7:35–37.

169. On this indifference see, e.g., M. Theresa Kelleher, "Back to Basics: Chu Hsi's *Elementary Learning* (*Hsiao-hsüeh*)," in Wm. Theodore de Bary and John Chaffee, eds., *Neo-Confucian Education: The Formative Phase* (Berkeley: University of California Press, 1989), 232.

170. McDermott, "Friendship and Its Friends in the Late Ming," in Institute of Modern History, *Jiazu yu zhengzhi*, 67–96. Compare my discussion of "civility" in Chapter 12.

171. See variously Wm. Theodore de Bary, "Individualism and Humanitarianism in Late Ming Thought," in de Bary, ed., *Self and Society in Ming Thought* (New York: Columbia University Press, 1970), 145–248; Guy, *Emperor's Four Treasuries*, 54; and Benjamin Elman, "The Relevance of Sung Learning in the Late Ch'ing: Wei Yuan and the *Huang-ch'ao ching-shih wen-pien*," *Late Imperial China* 9.2 (December 1988): 75.

172. Guy, *Emperor's Four Treasuries,* 54.

173. *XSYG* 2:36, 3:28, 4:5.

174. *KSZJ* 1:7–10.

175. Letter to Jia Shengquan, *SD* 2:1–2. It is probably wisest, of course, to view Chen Hongmou's collected personal correspondence, widely republished in the Qing and thereafter, less as a spontaneous record of his thoughts than as a deliberately crafted model of how such a circle of friends should interact.

176. Letter to Zhu Nanhu, *SD* 1:14. On the perils of an official career see also *SD* 1:4, 1:7, 1:9, 1:14, 2:5–7, 2:9, 2:13, 2:19–20.

177. Zhu, *Wenji* (1869 edition).

178. *NP* 1:5, 1:17, 1:21.

179. These notions and their practical applications are pervasive themes in Yin's *Jianyu xiansheng fu Yu tiaojiao* (Mr. Yin Huiyi's directives as governor of Henan) (1750; reprint, Beijing: Zhonghua shuju, 1985). This relatively unusual work, collecting as it does the downward bureaucratic correspondence of a provincial governor in a single jurisdiction, very likely served as model for Chen's own *Guitiao huichao* (1757), in which he collected for publication key examples of his downward correspondence in Shaanxi; indirectly, it may also have been the inspiration for the monumental and unique *Peiyuan tang oucun gao,* in which Chen's literary executors collected downward bureaucratic correspondence from throughout his long career. The term *xunsu* (cultural reform or retraining), a favorite usage of Yin Huiyi, was also of course adopted by Chen in the title of his *Xunsu yigui* (Sourcebook on the reform of social practice).

Chapter 3

1. *Wenji* 2:30–33.

2. I use the term *fundamentalism* in the sense defined by Wm. Theodore de Bary, "Some Common Tendencies in Neo-Confucianism," in David S. Nivison and Arthur F. Wright, eds., *Confucianism in Action* (Stanford: Stanford University Press, 1959), 34–38.

3. Kai-wing Chow, *The Rise of Confucian Ritualism in Late Imperial China: Ethics, Classics, and Lineage Discourse* (Stanford: Stanford University Press, 1994), esp. 8–9, 170–71; Cynthia Brokaw, "Tai Chen and Learning in the Confucian Tradition," in Elman and Woodside, 257–91. Such scholarship reacts in part against an older view of the *kaozheng* movement, dating from the May Fourth era, which emphasizes the secular, protoscientific character of Qing textual research.

4. *KSZJ* 5:13–16.

5. *LZJL* 1:5. For Hartwell's distinction among varying Chinese uses of the past see his "Historical Analogism, Public Policy, and Social Science in Eleventh- and Twelfth-Century China," *American Historical Review* 76.3 (June 1971): 690–727.

6. Peter Bol has recently distinguished between the use in the Confucian tradition of "the model of the ancients" vs. "the manifest pattern of the natural order" as the grounding for values—a distinction similar to the one that I am drawing here. Bol sees the transition from Tang to Song as marked by a transition (not necessarily permanent) from the first to the second and associates this with the experience of sociopolitical disorder in the late Tang, which led to a loss of faith in the classical model and a search for a more "certain" grounding for human behavioral norms. This quest for certainty clearly played a role in Chen Hongmou's preference for the second form of moral legitimation, but I would be wary, in his case, of associating it with the experience of social disorder. Bol, *This Culture of Ours,* 1–3.

7. David Nivison, *The Life and Thought of Chang Hsüeh-ch'eng, 1738–1801* (Stanford: Stanford University Press, 1966), 141–42, 157–59. In citing Nivison I have taken the liberty of making his romanization consistent with that of this work.

8. Letter to Huang Chengzhi, *SD* 2:17–18.

9. *LZJL* 1:2 and 2:41. Chen's belief in the correspondence between the realms of the cosmic, the social, the political, and the personal will be discussed at a later point in this study.

10. *LZJL* 2:41–42.

11. *XSYG* 1:27.

12. *LZJL* 1:1. In his view of Heaven as "the progenitor of all things," which, although not anthropomorphic, "nonetheless had consciousness and moral purpose," Chen followed a position that had been orthodox at least since the codification of Confucian thought by Dong Zhongshu in the second century B.C. See Kwang-Ching Liu and Richard Shek, "Early Taoism in Retrospect: Cosmology, Ethics, and Eschatology," in Kwang-Ching Liu and Richard Shek, eds., *Heterodoxy in Late Imperial China* (Berkeley: University of California Press, forthcoming).

13. *Hunan tongzhi* (1757), *juan* 1. On the ideas of Zhang Heng see Joseph Needham, *Science and Civilization in China*, vol. 3 (Cambridge: Cambridge University Press, 1959), 216–18. For the theory of *fenye* as understood in the late imperial era see Jeffrey F. Meyer, *The Dragons of Tiananmen: Beijing as a Sacred City* (Columbia: University of South Carolina Press, 1991), 122–27.

14. Chen also occasionally uses the term *dao* (the Way), apparently interchangeably with *li*, but he clearly prefers the latter. This preference probably derives in part from his conscious identification with *lixue* as a school of thought but also from the fact that, as plural rather than singular (there were *li* of particular things as well as of things in general), it had a closer sense of association with day-to-day life. Cf. Nivison, *Chang Hsüeh-ch'eng*, 141–42.

15. *Wenji* 2:30.

16. *PYTOCG* 20:19.

17. *XSYG* 1:21, 2:16. As a general theme of eighteenth-century East Asian thought, this relationship is the subject of Wm. Theodore de Bary and Irene Bloom, eds., *Principle and Practicality: Essays in Neo-Confucianism and Practical Learning* (New York: Columbia University Press, 1979). We will return to this question in our subsequent discussion of Chen's advocacy of "substantive learning" (*shixue*).

18. *LZJL* 1:82; Wang Chang, 27:12–13.

19. *PYTOCG* 16:3–5; *SD* 2:14. Chen also refers to economic laws as "*dingli*" (the predetermined operation of principle); memorial of QL 21/6/29, *QLZZ* 14.759–60; *PYTOCG* 12:12–13.

20. See the thoughtful discussions in Derk Bodde, "Evidence for 'Laws of Nature' in Chinese Thought," *Harvard Journal of Asiatic Studies* 20 (1957): 709–27; and Derk Bodde, "Chinese 'Laws of Nature': A Reconsideration," *Harvard Journal of Asiatic Studies* 39 (1979): 139–55. R. P. Peerenboom, *Law and Morality in Ancient China: The Silk Manuscripts of Huang-Lao* (Albany: State University of New York Press, 1993), argues that natural law was lacking in classical Confucianism but present in ancient Huang-Lao thought; if this is so, it most certainly had been absorbed into *lixue* orthodoxy by Chen Hongmou's time.

21. See, e.g., *XSYG* 1:8.

22. *XSYG* 3:33.

23. *Guitiao huichao* 2:66.

24. *PYTOCG* 20:32–33.

25. See, e.g., *PYTOCG* 20:19, 21:27; *XSYG* 1:21.

26. Chen, quoted in Tang Jian, 5:11.

27. See, e.g., *JSWB* 58:39, 68:6.

28. See, e.g., *PYTOCG* 32:8. In this Chen follows Lü Kun, who routinely identified the trio of *tianli, renqing,* and *wangfa* as the three unimpeachable authorities with which individuals must comply; see Jin Yaoji, "Renji guanxi zhong renqing zhi fenxi (chutan)" (A preliminary analysis of *renqing* in interpersonal relations), in Yang Liansheng, *Zhongguo wenhua zhong bao, bao, bao zhi yiyi* (The significance of *bao*=to repay, *bao*=to guarantee, and *bao*=to contract, in Chinese culture) (Hong Kong: Chinese University Press, 1987), 78. For an extented discussion of the relationship of the three concepts *tianli, renqing,* and *wangfa* (or *guofa*) in Qing legal practice see Philip Huang, *Civil Justice in China: Representation and Practice in the Qing* (Stanford: Stanford University Press, 1996).

29. *Guitiao huichao* 2:66.

30. Chen, in Wang Chang, 27:12–13.

31. See, e.g., *PYTOCG* 3:14, 23:20.

32. *Yishu,* "Yulu," 16.

33. Letter to Zhang Zhiling, *SD* 3:7.

34. *CZYG* 1:52.

35. *Wenji* 2:30.

36. Yang Liansheng, *Bao zhi yiyi;* Yang, "The Concept of 'Pao' as a Basis for Social Relations in China," in John K. Fairbank, ed., *Chinese Thought and Institutions* (Chicago: University of Chicago Press, 1957), 291–309. See also McMahon, *Causality and Containment,* esp. 14–15; Paul Ropp, *Dissent in Early Modern China: "Ju-lin wai-shih" and Ch'ing Social Criticism* (Ann Arbor: University of Michigan Press, 1981), chap. 5; Cynthia Brokaw, *The Ledgers of Merit and Demerit: Social Change and Moral Order in Late Imperial China* (Princeton: Princeton University Press, 1991).

37. *NP* 1:7.

38. *XSYG* 4:43; *JNYG* 3:1–3; *PYTOCG* 2:12.

39. *LZJL* 2:41.

40. *PYTOCG* 20:12–13.

41. *XSYG* 1:15–16.

42. *LZJL* 2:42.

43. Chen also uses the term *ming* for fate, sometimes seemingly interchangeably with *shu,* but at other times conveying a sense of rational purpose, a connotation that "*shu*" emphatically lacks.

44. Chen, letter to Zhu Hengyan, *SD* 2:9; Tang Jian, 5:11.

45. *LZJL* 2:41.

46. *CZYG* 2:14.

47. Letters to Wang Wending and to Hu Deqiu, *SD* 1:14, 2:20.

48. Letter to Huang Chengzhi, *SD* 2:17–18; Li Yuandu, 16:4.

49. Taylor has developed this conception in a series of articles, including "Official and Popular Religion and the Political Organization of Chinese Society in the Ming," in Kwang-Ching Liu, ed., *Orthodoxy in Late Imperial China* (Berkeley: University of California Press, 1990), 126–57.

50. Arthur Wolf, "Gods, Ghosts, and Ancestors," in Wolf, ed., *Studies in Chinese Society* (Stanford: Stanford University Press, 1978), 131–82.

51. See, e.g., *PYTOCG* 1:19–21, 12:36–38, 29:17–18.

52. *PYTOCG* 11:29–30.

53. "Zongpu liuzhuan"; Chen, letter to Yang Jingsu, *JSWB* 58:39.

54. *PYTOCG* 9:43.

55. *PYTOCG* 9:26–27.

56. *XSYG* 4:43.

57. Li Yuandu, 16:4. Chen's apparent ambivalence on such questions calls to mind Donald Sutton's recent observation that among the Confucian elite of late imperial China there was in fact "no firm consensus over whether gods and ghosts existed or not, whether they interfered with human existence, and whether they were morally purposive." Sutton, "Ming and Ch'ing Elite Attitudes Toward Shamanism," in Liu and Shek, *Heterodoxy.*

58. *Yishu,* "Fuyi," 8.

59. See, e.g., *PYTOCG* 34:1–2; *NP* 6:13, 6:16. For a detailed examination of *ling* as understood in popular religion today see P. Steven Sangren, *History and Magical Power in a Chinese Community* (Stanford: Stanford University Press, 1987).

60. *Wenji* 10:18–19; *LZJL* 2:41.

61. *Guandi shengji tuzhi quanji* (Complete illustrated edition of the sagely acts of Guandi), 5 *juan* (Suzhou (?): Dunwutang, 1768). Chen is listed as co-compiler of this expanded edition, along with his longtime friend Shen Deqian, the eminent scholar and director of Suzhou's Ziyang Academy. The quote is from Prasenjit Duara, "Superscribing Symbols: The Myth of Guandi, Chinese God of War," *Journal of Asian Studies* 47.4 (November 1988): 784. For Duara, Lu Zhan's work represents "the high point of the superscription process" in regard to Guandi.

62. *JSWB* 68:4–6.

63. *PYTOCG* 1:19–21, 12:36–38, 29:17–18, 32:34–35.

64. *PYTOCG* 15:5, 19:32–33.

65. Sutton, "Elite Attitudes." Sutton makes the interesting point that the extreme hostility many officials (including Chen) expressed toward popular conjurers, shamans, and the like, was based less on a "rationalist" denial of the efficacy of such arts than on the natural antagonism against competitors in a field in which the bureaucracy sought to claim a monopoly.

66. *Wenji, juan* 10.

67. The attribution appears, e.g., in Alexander Wylie, *Notes on Chinese Literature* (Shanghai: Presbyterian Mission Press, 1922), 223, and is cited (noncommittally) in Chen's biography by Rufus Suter in *ECCP*, 87. I have inspected the edition of the *Shenxian tongjian* in Yale University's Sterling Library, which lists the work as authored by Chen. The text itself, however, makes no reference to Chen and attributes authorship jointly to "Zheng the Great Sage" (Zheng Da Zhenren) and Huang Zhanglun. There is no mention of this work in any of Chen's other writings nor in his *Nianpu* nor in any other Chinese-language biography or catalogue of his works.

68. Lu Shao, 20:23–25; Wang Chang, 18:5–8; *JSWB* 45:31–32; Xu Dong, *Muling shu*, 22:41–42; *Wuchang xianzhi* (Gazetteer of Wuchang County), 1885. The work is discussed in Feng Liutang, 272–73. Interestingly, although the sources are unanimous in attributing this work to Chen, it does not appear in any of Chen's own collectanea, suggesting some possible discomfort about its orthodoxy on the part of his literary executors.

69. See, e.g., *PYTOCG* 20:25–26, 34:1–2; *NP* 8:25.

70. *PYTOCG* 20:32–33, 26:12–13; *NP* 6:16–17.

71. *NP* 6:12–13.

72. James L. Watson, "Standardizing the Gods: The Promotion of T'ien Hou ('Empress of Heaven') Along the South China Coast, 960–1960," in David Johnson, Andrew J. Nathan, and Evelyn S. Rawski, eds., *Popular Culture in Late Imperial China* (Berkeley: University of California Press, 1985), 292–324.

73. *XSYG* (1769 edition), 4:13.

74. See, e.g., his letter of QL 29/4/28, *JS* 217–19. Chen, indeed, was cited by the Republican-era scholar Yuan Shushan as a prominent example of a Qing official who held credence in divination; see Richard J. Smith, "Divination in Ch'ing Dynasty China," in R. Smith and D. W. Y. Kwok, eds., *Cosmology, Ontology, and Human Efficacy: Essays in Chinese Thought* (Honolulu: University of Hawaii Press, 1993), 153.

75. *XSYG* 3:31, 4:34–43. Ropp (*Dissent*, chap. 5) notes that condemnation of geomancy was a persistent theme in Confucian reformist writers from Gu Yanwu on.

76. *XSYG* 1:27.

77. Chow, *Confucian Ritualism*, 46.

78. On-cho Ng, "Toward an Interpretation of Ch'ing Ontology," in R. Smith and Kwok, 47–48; Ng, "*Hsing* (Nature) as the Ontological Basis of Practicality in Early Ch'ing Ch'eng-Chu Confucianism: Li Kuang-ti's (1642–1718) Philosophy," *Philosophy East and West* 44.1 (January 1994): 79–109.

79. For but a few examples see *SD* 1:5, 2:6, 2:19; *PYTOCG* 16:10–12, 19:31, 21:36–37; *YZYG* 1:5; *XSYG* 1:8; *Wenji* 1:18.

80. *PYTOCG* 24:38–39.

81. Among numerous discussions of this linkage see de Bary, "Individualism and Humanitarianism," 155–56; and Chow, *Confucian Ritualism*, chap. 1.

82. *ZGFJL*, preface.

83. *YZYG* 1:14 ff. See also Morgan, 195–205.

84. *LZJL* 1:1–2.

85. On one occasion Chen does contrast the superior official, whose policies derive from principle (*li*), with the vulgar official, whose policies are predicated on recourse to force (*qi*); see

CZYG 1:1. For a classical statement of the *li/qi* dualism see Cheng Yi, cited in Wing-tsit Chan, *A Sourcebook of Chinese Philosophy* (Princeton: Princeton University Press, 1963), 568–69. For a general discussion of the antidualist tenor of early Qing thought see Ng, "Ontological Basis of Practicality," 95–102.

86. *XSYG* 2:23. On Lu Shiyi's materialism see Ng, "Ontological Basis of Practicality," 47–48; Chow, *Confucian Ritualism,* 63; and above all Wing-tsit Chan, "The *Hsing-li ching-i* and the Ch'eng-Chu School of the Seventeenth Century," in Wm. Theodore de Bary, ed., *The Unfolding of Neo-Confucianism* (New York: Columbia University Press, 1975), 543–79.

87. *PYTOCG* 20:19; *CZYG* 1:52.

88. *PYTOCG* 12:33–35, 16:3–5, 20:23, 24:43.

89. *PYTOCG* 16:10–12, 19:31; *ZGFJL,* preface.

90. *YZYG* 2:18, and preface to supplementary *juan.* For an enlightening discussion of this metaphor see Donald J. Munro, *Images of Human Nature: A Sung Portrait* (Princeton: Princeton University Press, 1988), 43–44, 67–68.

91. Letter to Zhu Shaoyuan, *SD* 3:7.

92. *PYTOCG* 19:21–40. Compare Max Weber, *The Theory of Social and Economic Organization,* trans. A. M. Henderson and Talcott Parsons (New York: Free Press, 1947), 115–17.

93. *YZYG* 1:13.

94. *YZYG* 1:17.

95. *PYTOCG* 4:43–46.

96. *PYTOCG* 12:33–55; *SD* 3:14.

97. Wang Chang, 27:12–13.

98. *CZYG* 1:22.

99. Chen cites Lu on this point in *YZYG* 2:18. For related views of practice among other early Qing scholars see Chan, "Hsing-li ching-i"; Wei-ming Tu, "Yen Yuan: From Inner Experience to Lived Concreteness," in de Bary, *Unfolding,* 511–42; and Chow, *Confucian Ritualism,* 63. Curiously, in spite of the similarity of many of their views, Chen Hongmou never directly acknowledges Yan's influence.

100. See, e.g., *PYTOCG* 23:20–29.

101. *XSYG,* preface.

102. Jin Yaoji, "Renqing zhi fenxi"; Yang, "Concept of 'Pao,' " 292. For discussions of *renqing* in its contemporary popular usage—almost always approving and conveying the sense of licensed partiality toward those with whom one is close—see Richard Madsen, *Morality and Power in a Chinese Village* (Berkeley: University of California Press, 1984), 61–62; Andrew G. Walder, *Communist Neo-Traditionalism: Work and Authority in Chinese Industry* (Berkeley: University of California Press, 1986), chap. 5; Ambrose Yeo-chi King, "Kuan-hsi and Network Building: A Sociological Analysis," *Daedalus* 120.2 (spring 1991): 63–84; Mayfair Mei-hui Yang, *Gifts, Favors, and Banquets: The Art of Social Relationships in China* (Ithaca: Cornell University Press, 1994), 67–72; Yunxiang Yan, *The Flow of Gifts: Reciprocity and Social Networks in a Chinese Village* (Stanford: Stanford University Press, 1996).

103. *Da Qing lüli zengxiu tongcuan jicheng* (The Great Qing code, revised and annotated) (1899 ed.); Ju Huanwu, "Qinglü de qufa yi shenqing" (Flexible punishment based on personal relationships in Qing law), in Institute of Modern History, *Jiazu yu zhengzhi,* 847–900.

104. *Da Qing lüli zengxiu tongzuan jicheng* (1899 ed.), preface by Qianlong emperor dated QL 5/11; Huang, *Civil Justice in China,* esp. chap. 8. As Huang also shows, in practice Qing magistrates operated with a tripartite set of standards for reaching verdicts: *tianli* (what basic reason tells us is morally correct), *renqing* (what best accords with human compassion, or what will work out best in the actual local context), and *guofa* (what the letter of the law says on the question at hand). Decisions were most often reached on the basis of some compromise, taking account of all three principles.

105. Jin Yaoji, "Renqing zhi fenxi."

106. Richard Lufrano, *Honorable Merchants: Commerce and Self-Cultivation in Late Imperial China* (Honolulu: University of Hawaii Press, 1997).

107. Joanna F. Handlin, *Action in Late Ming Thought: The Reorientation of Lü K'un and Other Scholar-Officials* (Berkeley: University of California Press, 1983), 149–58.

108. Tang Xianzu, *The Peony Pavilion*, trans. Cyril Birch (Bloomington: Indiana University Press, 1980).

109. Anthony C. Yu, *Rereading the Stone: Desire and the Making of Fiction in "Dream of the Red Chamber"* (Princeton: Princeton University Press, 1997), 54.

110. Zhu elsewhere tried varying solutions to this philosophical problem, at times differentiating between two kinds of mind, the "moral mind" (*daoxin*) and the "human mind" (*renxin*), the latter being the seat of feelings. See Paolo Santangelo, "Is the Horseman Riding the Horse, or the Charioteer Driving the Two Steeds?" *Ming Qing Yanjiu* (Rome) (1993): 81–112, from which the translations here are adapted.

111. See Paul S. Ropp, "Vehicles of Dissent in Late Imperial Chinese Culture" (paper presented to the Symposium on State and Society in East Asian Traditions, Paris, May 1991).

112. Yuasa Yukihiko, "Shindai ni okeru fujin kaihō ron—rikyō to ningen teki shizen" (On women's emancipation in the Qing: *lijiao* vs. human nature), *Nippon-Chūgoku gakkaihō* 4 (1952): 111–25; de Bary, "Individualism and Humanitarianism"; Handlin, *Action*; Chow, *Confucian Ritualism*, 63, 188–89.

113. Ye Shaoyuan, quoted in Dorothy Ko, "Women's Culture in the Private and Public Spheres in Seventeenth and Eighteenth Century China" (paper presented to the Colloquium on Poetry and Women's Culture in Late Imperial China, UCLA, October 1990), 23.

114. Kang-i Sun Chang, *The Late Ming Poet Ch'en Tzu-lung* (New Haven: Yale University Press, 1991), esp. 9–18.

115. Examples include *PYTOCG* 15:21–22; *XSYG* 1:21, 2:9–10, 4:1; *ZZYG* 1:34–35; *LZJL* 1:6, 1:58, 2:38–39; *SD* 2:20; and *NP* 5:2.

116. *Xueshi yigui* 2:16.

117. As we shall see in Chapter 12, Chen was equally adamant in his effort to deny any contradiction between *renqing* and the demands of ritual propriety (*lijiao*).

118. *JNYG* 3:1–3; *XSYG* 1:21; *LZJL* 1:71.

119. *LZJL* 1:6; *XSYG* 1:21; *Xueshi yigui* 2:16.

120. Chen, memorial of QL 21/6/29, *QLZZ* 14.763–65. More frequently, Chen prefers the term *minqing* to express this concept. For example, in glossing a passage from Gu Yanwu's *Rizhilu* in which Gu's original text used *renqing* in this sense, Chen substitutes *minqing* in his own paraphrase and commentary; *ZGFJL* 1:12–13.

121. *LZJL* 1:58, 1:95; *NP* 5:2. Note that the is/ought problem arises here as well. Although *qing* and *li* are not only ideals but also empirically observable laws, they can be broken down or weakened in situations of social crisis, such as that presented by the Jiangxi famine of 1742–43. In these instances maintenance of these "inviolable" laws of human behavior requires intervention on the part of the state or of the literati elite.

122. *LZJL* 1:70.

123. *LZJL* 1:6.

124. *PYTOCG* 12:33–35.

125. *PYTOCG* 15:20–23.

126. *ZZYG* 1:5.

127. *XSYG* 1:21.

128. Letter to Zhang Lun, *SD* 2:3; *LZJL* 1:58.

129. The following paragraph is based on *LZJL* 1:70–71 and 1:95–96.

130. *LZJL* 2:38–39.

131. Yu, *Rereading the Stone*, 53.

132. The pioneering study of this movement is Mizoguchi Yūzō, "Chūgoku ni okeru *ko-shi*

gainen no tenkai" (The evolution of the concepts of "public" and "private" in China), *Shisō* 669 (1980): 19–38.

Chapter 4

1. Liang Qichao, "Jindai xuefeng zhi dili de fenbu," 36.

2. *Xueshi yigui* 1:79. If one reads the *xueshi* in the title to this work as two words rather than one, as Chen may in fact have intended, its title would be translatable as *Sourcebook on the Interrelationship of Scholarship and Public Service.*

3. *SD* 3:10. For similar sentiments expressed over a span of three decades see letters of 1740 (to Jia Shengquan, *SD* 1:9) and 1769 (*JS* 251–53). See also Chen Lansen, preface to *KSZJ.*

4. See, e.g., Chen's appreciative comments about Guanzi and Mozi in *Xueshi yigui,* 1:74 and 1:76. On the other hand, he was quite disparaging of the Daoist classics (*Xueshi yigui* 1:71, 1:77) and consistently harsh on Buddhist masters.

5. *JSWB* 2:33; *SD* 2:6; *Xueshi yigui* 2:89–90, 3:61; David Nivison, "Protest Against Convention and Conventions of Protest," in Arthur F. Wright, ed., *The Confucian Persuasion* (Stanford: Stanford University Press, 1960), 177–201.

6. For but a few examples see memorials of QL 17/3/4, QL 17/5/28, and QL 18/1/19, in *QLZZ* 2.366–67, 3.209–10, 5.834–36; *PYTOCG* 17:36–37, 17:54–56, 25:36–37.

7. On the *KSZJ* and Chen Lansen's and Ge Zhenghu's role in its compilation see Chen's letter of QL 34/11/9, *JS* 251–53.

8. *PYTOCG* 17:10–11, 20:19–20; *SD* 1:13, 3:2; *LZJL* 1:75.

9. *PYTOCG* 4:3–4; *Xueshi yigui* 3:90. Paul Ropp translates *chuaimo* as "careful study" but notes that frequently in Qing sources the term was given an ironic twist. An unsympathetic character in the 1740s novel *Rulin waishi* (The scholars) boasts, "The term 'careful study' is the golden key to the examinations. In my three essays for the district examination, not one phrase was my own fabrication; every single character had a precedent somewhere. That is the only reason I succeeded." Ropp, *Dissent in Early Modern China,* 103.

10. Bol, *This Culture of Ours.*

11. *SD* 1:16.

12. Memorial of QL 25/3, reprinted in *NP* 11:5.

13. *SD* 2:6.

14. Letter to Jing Guoyuan, *SD* 3:2–3.

15. Letter to Xu Tan, *SD* 3:1.

16. *SD* 1:7–9, 2:20.

17. Letter to Ouyang Yaogang, *SD* 3:9–10.

18. Letters to Wu Xianggao, 1741–42, *SD* 1:14, 1:16.

19. The historiography of the *kaozheng* movement was initially sketched out by Liang Qichao in his *Intellectual Trends of the Ch'ing Period,* trans. Immanuel C. Y. Hsu (Cambridge, Mass.: Harvard University Press, 1959; Chinese original 1921). Extensive analyses have been done by Yamanoi Yū, including, e.g., his "Minmatsu Shinshu shisō ni tsuite no ikkosatsu" (An investigation of late Ming and early Qing thought), *Tōkyō Shinagaku* 11 (1965), 37–54. The standard work in English is Benjamin Elman, *From Philosophy to Philology: Intellectual and Social Aspects of Change in Late Imperial China* (Cambridge, Mass.: Harvard University Press, 1984). A more recent historical materialist analysis by a Chinese scholar is Chen Zuwu, *Qingqu xueshu sibian lu* (Scholarship and thought in the early Qing) (Beijing: Chinese Academy of Social Sciences, 1992).

20. Chow, *Confucian Ritualism.* For a particularly clear case of this fundamentalist urge on the part of one of *kaozheng*'s most vaunted practitioners see Brokaw, "Tai Chen." Elman's *From Philosophy to Philology,* for all its original insights, tends to perpetuate the "protoscientific" valorization of *kaozheng,* as does, still more emphatically, John B. Henderson, *The Development and Decline of Chinese Cosmology* (New York: Columbia University Press, 1984).

21. Hui Dong (1697–1758) was a near exact contemporary of Chen Hongmou and during

the latter decades of his life was a leading light of the intellectual world of Suzhou. During many of those years, Chen too was in Suzhou, serving as Jiangsu governor. Yet I have found no record of correspondence between the two men nor any explicit reference to Hui in Chen's writings.

22. Elman, *From Philosophy to Philology*, esp. 119–23, 203.

23. Guy, *Emperor's Four Treasuries*.

24. Elman, *From Philosophy to Philology*, 12.

25. Yao Nai (1732–1815) was a landsman and affinal kinsman of Zhang Tingyu and Fang Bao, both early patrons of Chen Hongmou, and served as a junior secretary in the Boards of War, Rites, and Punishments at Beijing during the years 1766–71, when Chen was a rotating board president and grand secretary. It seems unlikely the two would not have had contact during this time, although I have found no specific record of such. On Yao's role in the formation of Songxue ideology see Guy, *Emperor's Four Treasuries*, 140–42; and Elman, *From Philosophy to Philology*, 244.

26. *SD* 3:2–3.

27. Tang Jian, 5:9.

28. Elman, *From Philosophy to Philology*, 122.

29. Shen Deqian, preface to *Wenji*. Note as well that the *kaozheng* scholar Wang Chang was impressed enough by Chen to subsequently include several of his works in his own *Huhai wenchuan* (An ocean of exemplary prose writing) (ca. 1800). In fact, the labels "Hanxue" and "*kaozheng*" in themselves can be somewhat misleading because as Elman notes, the Ziyang curriculum under both Shen Deqian and Qian Daxin (Shen's successor after 1787) also included studies of history, geography, mathematics, and statecraft. In other words, although Shen and Qian may have approached it from a "Hanxue" perspective, and Chen from one of "Songxue," they both arrived at an interest in what would be called "practical" or "substantive" learning (*shixue*). See further discussion of this, below.

30. Letter to Dong Zhicheng, *SD* 3:10.

31. *JSWB* 2:33.

32. Tang Jian, 5:12.

33. Letter to Jia Shengquan, *SD* 3:15. Recall that Chen blamed examiners' fixation on such philological niceties for the repeated failure of his elder brother, Hongxian, to achieve a higher civil service degree.

34. *SD* 2:13. Significantly, this passage was also selected for quotation in the Songxue scholar Tang Jian's biography of Chen (5:12).

35. Ruan Yuan, *Huang Qing jingjie* (1829). Compare to this the numerous citations from Chen's directives as Yunnan provincial treasurer that Ruan chose to include in his 1835 *Yunnan tongzhi* (Comprehensive gazetteer of Yunnan). For Chen's coolness to *kaozheng* scholarship see also Liu Naihe, "Chen Hongmou yu kaoju," 109–10.

36. *PYTOCG* 34:30–39. I am grateful to Professors Benjamin Elman and Kai-wing Chow, who analyzed the composition of this inventory for me.

37. For but a few examples see Yuan Mei, letter to Chen reprinted in Gao Jiren, 79–80; *Guangxi tongzhi* (1800), 260:15; Jiang Fangzheng, preface to Chen, *Rongmen quanji* (1837); Li Zutao, preface to "Peiyuan tang wenlu," in Li, *Guochao wenlu* (1839), *juan* 44; Wang Zhichun, preface (dated 1869) to *SD*; *Qingshi gao* 35:10563–64; Xie Kang, 235.

38. Memorial of QL 9/4, excerpted in *NP* 5:13; *PYTOCG* 13:7–8; letter to Guangxin prefect, *SD* 1:13.

39. *YZYG* 1:1–9, 2:4–6; *PYTOCG* 18:43–44, 22:27, 22:49; proclamation of QL 2/11/28, in *Quan Dian yixue huiji*, *ce* 2. See also Chen's preface to his reprint of an annotated edition of Zhu's *Jinsi lu*, in *Wenji* 1:19–20.

40. *SD* 1:9.

41. *Xueshi yigui* 3:91. See also Gao Jiren, 89.

42. See, e.g., *PYTOCG* 17:39–40, 34:47; directive of QL 2/11/28, *Quan Dian yixue huiji*, *ce* 2.

43. Feng Erkang, 422–27; Elman, *From Philosophy to Philology*, 46–47.

44. *Wenji* 1:19–20.

45. Letters to Lei Cuiting and Yang Xianting, *SD* 2:4, 2:19; *PYTOCG* 24:49; Ge Zhenghu, preface to *KSZJ* (1770).

46. Chen Hongmou, *Sishu kao jiyao* (Handbook of references in the Four Books) (Guilin: Peiyuan tang, 1771). On the compilation process see letter of QL 32/4/23, *JS* 248–49. A number of later Qing editions of this work, sometimes with modified titles, survive in libraries worldwide. The reprint edition published by Guangwen in Taibei (1978) remains in print.

47. Chen Hongmou, "Peiyuan tang wenlu," in Li Zutao, ed., *Guochao wenlu* (Ruizhou: Wuyi shuyuan, 1839), 44:2.

48. Zhang Hao, "Rujia jingshi sixiang"; Chang, "Confucian Cosmological Myth and Neo-Confucian Transcendence," in R. Smith and Kwok, 11–34.

49. Chen, "Peiyuan tang wenlu," 44:1.

50. On these works and their authors see Wm. Theodore de Bary, "Chen Te-hsiu and Statecraft," in Hymes and Schirokauer, 349–79; Hung-lam Chu, "Ch'iu Chun's *Ta-hsüeh yen-i pu* and Its Influence in the Sixteenth and Seventeenth Centuries," *Ming Studies* 22 (fall 1986): 1–22; Chu, "Intellectual Trends in the Fifteenth Century," *Ming Studies* 27 (spring 1989): 1–33. On their normative status in Chen Hongmou's day see Chun-shu Chang, "Emperorship in Eighteenth-Century China," *Journal of the Institute of Chinese Studies* (Chinese University of Hong Kong) 7.1 (December 1974): 331–69.

51. Chen Hongmou, *Daxue yanyi xuyao* and *Daxue yanyi bu xuyao*, originals 1736, both republished by Baoshu tang (place unknown), 1842. See also *NP* 2:14; *PYTOCG* 18:43–44; *Siku quanshu tiyao*, 18:91. Chen was also attracted by Zhen Dexiu's other writings, reprinting Zhen's "Jiaozizhai gui" (Rules from the Training of Youth Studio) in his own *YZYG*, 1:13–14, and Zhen's "Xishan wenlu chao" (Transcribed writings of Zhen Xishan) as the opening selection in his *Xueshi yigui* 1:1–27. His attachment to Qiu Jun was perhaps less strong, but it is worth noting that Qiu was also compiler of the edition of Zhu Xi's *Family Rituals* (Zhuzi jiali), which was most widely circulated in Chen's day and of which he was greatly fond.

52. *Xueshi yigui* 1:17; de Bary, "Chen Te-hsiu," 369; Pierre-Étienne Will, R. Bin Wong, et al., *Nourish the People: The State Civilian Granary System in China, 1650–1850* (Ann Arbor: Center for Chinese Studies, 1991), 12; Timothy Brook, *The Confusions of Pleasure: Commerce and Culture in Ming China* (Berkeley: University of California Press, 1998), 101–4.

53. Chen, preface to his combined edition of 1736, *PYTWL* 44:1–2. The fact that this preface, with its impassioned argument on the unity of substance and function, was reprinted at the height of the Opium War as the first selection from Chen in Li Zutao's *Guochao wenlu* (1839), suggests the salience of these issues to scholar-officials confronting China's nineteenth-century crisis. On the *ti/yong* dichotomy and the tendency of Western historians to misconstrue it see de Bary, "Chen Te-hsiu," 358.

54. Chen Hongmou, comp., *Sima wenzheng gong chuanjia ji* (Collected works of Sima Guang), *juan* 82 (Nanchang: Peiyuan tang, 1741), including memorial of presentation to the throne dated QL 7/7/29. See also *NP* 4:5, 4:21; Gao Jiren, 80.

55. *XSYG* 1:1–4. See also Patricia B. Ebrey, "Conceptions of the Family in the Sung Dynasty," *Journal of Asian Studies* 43.2 (February 1984): 225–26; Ebrey, *Chu Hsi's Family Rituals*, xix–xx; and Ebrey, *Family and Propriety*, 32–49.

56. E. A. Kracke Jr., *Civil Service in Early Sung China, 960–1067* (Cambridge, Mass.: Harvard University Press, 1953), 68, 74; Thomas H. C. Lee, *Government Education and Examinations in Sung China* (Hong Kong: Chinese University of Hong Kong, 1985), 242–43.

57. Chen's edition of Gu Xichou's work appears in his *Rongmen quanji* (1837), *ce* 33–52. See also *NP* 2:19, 5:24. The *Rongmen quanji* also includes the complete text of the *Zizhi tongjian gangmu sanbian* (*ce* 63–66), clearly suggesting that Chen was at least a coauthor. However, neither the *Sanbian's* list of compilers nor Zhang Tingyu's cover memorial (dated QL 11/4/27) identifies Chen as a participant in the project. I have not been able to resolve this question to my satisfaction.

58. Chen, "Chongyin *Zhengshi yue* xu," in Wang Chang, 25:13.

59. Hartwell, "Historical Analogism," 694, 698–703, 717.

60. The delineation of the ideas of Wang Anshi and Sima Guang in the following paragraphs is based on the following works: James T. C. Liu, *Reform in Sung China: Wang An-shih (1021–1086) and His New Policies* (Cambridge, Mass.: Harvard University Press, 1959); Anthony William Sariti, "Monarchy, Bureaucracy, and Absolutism in the Political Thought of Ssu-ma Kuang," *Journal of Asian Studies* 32.1 (November 1972): 53–76; Paul J. Smith, *Taxing Heaven's Storehouse: Horses, Bureaucrats, and the Destruction of the Sichuan Tea Industry, 1074–1224* (Cambridge, Mass.: Council on East Asian Studies, 1991); P. Smith, "State Power and Economic Activism During the New Policies, 1068–1085," in Hymes and Schirokauer, 76–127; Peter Bol, "Government, Society, and State: On the Political Visions of Ssu-ma Kuang and Wang An-shih," in Hymes and Schirokauer, 128–92; Schirokauer and Hymes, introduction to Hymes and Schirokauer, 1–58; and, most extensively, Bol, *This Culture of Ours.*

61. Bol, "Government, Society, and State," 128.

62. See, e.g., J. Liu, 13; and Paolo Santangelo, "Gu Yanwu's Contribution to History," *East and West* 32 (1982): 167.

63. As James T. C. Liu has demonstrated, Sima Guang's position on this question was more complex than a simple opposition to Wang Anshi's Hired Service System initiative; see J. Liu, 103–7.

64. On this key issue see especially Bol, *This Culture of Ours,* 213–14.

65. Liang Ch'i-ch'ao (trans. Hsu), 23; Qian Mu, *Zhongguo jin sanbainian xueshu shi* (History of Chinese thought of the past three centuries) (1937; reprint, Taibei: Commercial Press, 1964); Wm. Theodore de Bary et al., *Sources of Chinese Tradition* (New York: Columbia University Press, 1960); Wing-tsit Chan, *A Sourcebook in Chinese Philosophy* (Princeton: Princeton University Press, 1963). Most of these figures, however, were accorded entries in Hummel's *Eminent Chinese of the Ch'ing Period,* where simple prominence rather than intellectual originality was the chief criterion for selection.

66. The key study is Chan, "The *Hsing-li ching-i* and the Ch'eng-Chu School of the Seventeenth Century," in de Bary, *Unfolding,* 543–79. Chan's revaluation of this group was anticipated in Hellmut Wilhelm's 1965 article, "Chinese Confucianism on the Eve of the Great Encounter." For more recent treatments by Chinese scholars see Chen Zuwu, *Qingqu xueshu sibiang lu,* and especially Gao Xiang, "Lun Qingqu lixue de zhengzhi yinxiang" (The political influence of early Qing *lixue* thought), *Qingshi yanjiu* 1993.3, 66–75.

67. *YZYG* 2:18–23 and supplementary *juan* 32–40; *XSYG* 2:33–40, 3:21–23; *ZZYG* 2:42–47; *Xueshi yigui* 3:1–9; *Wenji* 10:9; *PYTOCG* 34:47–49.

68. *YZYG* supplementary *juan* 35; *XSYG* 2:33; *Xueshi yigui* 3:8.

69. See especially *XSYG* 2:33–34. Wilhelm, "Chinese Confucianism," 292–93, 302–3; Pei-yi Wu, "Self-examination and Confession of Sins," 20–22 (on Zhang Luxiang).

70. *XSYG* 2:38; Chow, *Confucian Ritualism,* 48–49.

71. The translation is from Chan, "The *Hsing-li ching-i*," 564. Chan's argument on the distinctively practical reading early Qing Cheng-Zhu scholars gave to their texts finds support in *ECCP,* 473–75; Wilhelm, "Chinese Confucianism," 297; Gao Xiang, "Qingqu lixue"; Ng, "Ch'ing Ontology," 47–48; and Ng, "Ontological Basis of Practicality."

72. *Xueshi yigui* 3:1.

73. *PYTOCG* 34:30–39; Fang, *Yiji,* 2–3.

74. Letter to Fang Bao (1749), *SD* 2:15; Chen, "Chen Rongmen *Zhouguan xiyi* xu gaigao" (Corrected draft of Chen Hongmou's preface to [Fang's] *Critical Assessment of the Zhouguan,*" in Fang, *Fang Wangqi yiji* (Hefei: Huangshan shushe, 1990), 2–3. For various readings of the *Zhouli* and debates on its authenticity during the Qing see Gao Wangling, *Fazhan he zhengce,* 98–99; Dunstan, *Conflicting Counsels,* 128–33; Thompson, "Statecraft and Self-Government," 196; Elman, *Classicism, Politics, and Kinship,* 11–15, 150–57, 207–8; Chow, *Confucian Ritualism,* 41, 64–67, 150–52. A philological assessment by a Western scholar, which decides for the genuinely

early Zhou provenance of the text, is Bernhard Karlgren, "The Early History of the Chou Li and Tso Chuan Texts," *Bulletin of the Museum of Far Eastern Antiquities* 1 (1929): 1–59. For the text itself I have consulted the abridged English translation of William Raymond Gingell, *The Ceremonial Usages of the Chinese, B.C. 1121, as prescribed in the Institutes of the Chow Dynasty Strung as Pearls* (London: Smith, Elder, 1852); the passages extolling frugality in taxation and expenditure appear on pages 29–30.

75. The classic study of the late Ming disciples of Wang Yangming is de Bary, "Individualism and Humanitarianism"; the early Qing reaction against this is a principal theme of Chow, *Confucian Ritualism.*

76. On early Qing reactions to Wang Yangming, notably the antipathy of Chen's much-admired Lu Longqi, see Frederick Wakeman Jr., *The Great Enterprise: The Manchu Reconstruction of Imperial Order in Seventeenth-Century China* (Berkeley: University of California Press, 1985), 1091–93. As with most of Wang Yangming's early Qing apologists, Chen sought to stress the compatibility of his teachings (and of Wang's Southern Song *xinxue* predecessor, Lu Xiangshan) with those of Zhu Xi. This is the theme, for instance, of one of Chen's published model examination essays; *KCZJ*, 6:26–29.

77. *YZYG*, supplementary *juan*, 16–24; *XSYG* 2:5–9; *CZYG* 1:18–32. Chen also included the works of Wang's illustrious Song-era predecessor Lu Xiangshan (*XSYG* 1:8–12) and of other, more recent writers who drew liberally on Wang's teachings; e.g., Huang Shi'e, in *Xueshi yigui* 4:42–43. On Wang's influence on Chen's *baojia* policies see Hsiao, 570.

78. Neither was Chen persuaded by the arguments of Wang's critics that this meditative emphasis placed him closer to Chan Buddhism than to the orthodox Confucian tradition. Chen wrote: "Wang Yangming's scholarship was highly accomplished and of practical worldly use (*youyong yu shi*). How then can it be dismissed as 'Chan'?" *Xueshi yigui* 3:80.

79. *CZYG* 1:118–19. These vocations emphatically included that of merchant. Yu Yingshi has pointed out that, of all major figures in the neo-Confucian tradition, Wang Yangming was the most approving of commerce and explicitly identified mercantile activity as one legitimate mode of "realizing one's innate goodness" (*zhi liangzhi*). This surely was yet another reason the commercially minded Chen found his thought so congenial. See Yu, *Shangren jingshen*, esp. 93–94.

80. *XSYG* 2:5; *CZYG* 1:18–19. Chen also sought to demonstrate that the doctrine of *liangzhi* underlay as well the unimpeachably orthodox writings of Zhu Xi; see *YZYG* 1:1.

81. See Gao Xiang, "Qingqu lixue."

82. *XSYG* 1:7–8.

83. Yang Nianqun, *Ruxue diyuhua de jindai xingtai: San da zhishi qunti hudong de bijiao yanjiu* (The modern forms of regionalized Confucianism: A comparative study of the interaction of three intellectual groups) (Beijing: Sanlian shudian, 1997), esp. 59–61, 119–20.

84. The standard treatment of Lü Kun in English is Handlin, *Action.* An outline of Lü's life is given on pages 109–11 of that work.

85. *YZYG* 2:7–18; *JNYG* 2:1–37; *XSYG* 2:16–17; *CZYG* 1:34–52; *Xueshi yigui* 1:79; *LZJL*; *NP* 4:34; *Siku quanshu zongmu tiyao* 18:113.

86. Lü's distaste for formalism and his humanist instincts led him to dismiss nearly categorically the writings of the Song neo-Confucian masters, including even Zhu Xi. This position was of course viewed as extreme by Lü's Qing-era admirers, the great majority of whom saw themselves rather as defenders of the Songxue tradition in an increasingly hostile age. Lu Longqi, for instance, otherwise a Lü Kun devotee, singled out this feature of his thought for criticism (Handlin, *Action*, 9.) Chen Hongmou's response was instead to effectively deny the contradiction. Although he had declined to associate himself with the orthodox neo-Confucian tradition, Chen wrote, Lü's own life and work actually exemplified the best elements in it, indeed pointing the way for its reinvigoration in the present day; *Xueshi yigui* 1:79.

87. *SD* 2:3.

88. *LZJL* 1:33.

89. *JNYG* 2:4–5; Handlin, "Lü K'un's New Audience," 16–18.

90. *JNYG* 2:4; *LZJL* 1:2, 1:70; *NP* 4:34.

91. *CZYG* 1:50 and passim. For discussion of Lü's overall administrative approach see Handlin, *Action*, 104–7; and Chang Chun-ming, "The Chinese Standards of Good Governance: Being a Study of the 'Biographies of Model Officials' in Dynastic Histories," *Nankai Social and Economic Quarterly* 8.2 (July 1935): 230–31.

92. Biographical data on Yin Huiyi apears in *ECCP*, 710 and 921, and in *Zhongguo renming da zidian*, 51. Chen's letters to him on water conservancy matters may be found in *SD* 1:7 and 3:3. As discussed in Chapter 2, Yin seems to have played some role in Chen's political rehabilitation during these years, and his collected downward corresondence as Henan governor, *Jianyu xiansheng fu Yu tiaojiao* (1750) was likely a model for Chen's own publications in this genre.

93. Yin Huiyi, *Sijian lu* (1748; reprint, Shanghai: Commercial Press, 1937). Yin's prefaces for others of his republications may be found in his *Jianyu xiansheng wenji*. See also *SD* 1:6–7, 2:3; and *CZYG* 1:34–50, in which Chen acknowledges his indebtedness to Yin's edition of Lü Kun.

94. Yin Huiyi, preface to "Xu Beixue bian," in his *Jianyu xiansheng wenji*, 2:10–11; Tang Bin, *Luoxue bian*, revised edition by Yin Huiyi, 1738. I am grateful to Timothy Brook for providing me with a copy of the latter work.

95. *SD* 1:6.

96. *CZYG* 2:36–42; *SD* 2:14–15. Tang's biography is in *ECCP*, 709–10. For his ambivalent attraction to the thought of Wang Yangming see Chow, *Confucian Ritualism*, 5; and Thomas A. Wilson, "Confucian Sectarianism and the Compilation of the *Ming History*," *Late Imperial China* 15.2 (December 1994): 65–66. Yin Huiyi, too, was a professed "disciple" of Tang Bin, as much for his administrative style as for his intellectual teachings.

97. Tang Bin, *Luoxue bian*, 4:79.

98. The basic texts of the Guanxue tradition are collected in Song Liangui et al., eds., *Guanxue congshu* (The Guanxue anthology) (Taibei: Yiwen, 1971). Like other early Qing scholars of Songxue leanings, the Guanxue group are also denied treatment in Qian Mu's standard Republican-era retrospective of Qing thought, *Zhongguo jin sanbainian xueshu shi*. This and the following paragraph summarizing the tradition are based on Chen Junmin, *Zhang Zai zhexue yu Guanxue xuepai* (The philosophy of Zhang Zai and the Guanxue school) (Taibei: Xuesheng shuju, 1990); Chen Zuwu, chap. 8; *ECCP*, 498–99; Anne D. Birdwhistell, *Li Yong (1627–1705) and Epistemological Dimensions of Confucian Philosophy* (Stanford: Stanford University Press, 1996); and Ron-Guey Chu, "Scholarly Autonomy and Political Dissent of Local Academies in the Early Ch'ing" (paper presented to the Symposium on Civil Society in East Asian Countries, Montreal, October 1992). I am also grateful to Professor Birdwhistell for helpful discussions on this subject.

99. Chen Junming, 27–28; *Zhongguo renming da zidian*, 338; L. Carrington Goodrich and Chao-ying Fang, eds., *Dictionary of Ming Biography* (New York: Columbia University Press, 1976), 616–19, 1010–13. The pivotal role of Lü Nan as simultaneously a champion of Cheng-Zhu orthodoxy and an open-minded critic of Wang Yangming's ideas is stressed in Willard Peterson, "Confucian Learning in Late Ming Thought," in Denis Twitchett and Frederick W. Mote, eds., *The Cambridge History of China*, vol. 8 (Cambridge: Cambridge University Press, 1998), 717–18. Chen Hongmou wrote a preface to Xue Xuan's work, *Dushu lu* (Reading notes), in which he lauded Xue as the single Ming writer who most exemplified the unity of substance (*ti*) and function (*yong*); see Gao Jiren, 82.

100. The *Guanzhong shuyuan zhi* (Gazetteer of the Guanzhong Academy) of 1613 may be seen as in effect a manifesto of the retrospective creation of a Guanxue "school" at the hands of Feng Congwu. For the orthodox genealogy of Guanxue forebears see the gazetteer's preface by Shaanxi governor Cui Yingqi; for Feng's own statement of purpose see pages 5:1–6.

101. *Jiangxue*, a practice that emphasized the physical act of oral presentation and defense of one's views in open public debate, was controversially associated with Wang Yangming and his many diverse followers. See Peterson; Birdwhistell, 127–32; Chow, *Confucian Ritualism*, 23–24; and Ronald G. Dimberg, *The Sage and Society: The Life and Thought of Ho Hsin-yin* (Honolulu: University of Hawaii Press, 1974), 87–91.

102. *Guanzhong shuyuan zhi*, 3:8. For a sense of the works included in this curriculum see the list of the academy's library holdings in *juan* 8. For the substantial landed endowment that underwrote this activity see *juan* 7.

103. Chen Hongmou later apologized for Li's obvious Ming loyalism on the grounds that, his father having been killed in the dynastic transition, he needed to decline the offer of official service in order to remain at home and care for his widowed mother; *Xueshi yigui* 3:61.

104. Shaanxi's special vulnerability both to attacks from the frontier and to domestic insurgent movements meant that military strategy was consistently one component of the practical scholarship of Guanxue adherents. Stressed by both Li Yong and Wang Xinjing, this strain emerged full-blown in the work of Yan Ruyi, a Guanxue scholar who became a famous strategist of *tuanlian* militia organization during the White Lotus Rebellion (1796–1805) and a pacifier of Miao uprisings in the southwest. See Yan's writings included in the *Guanzhong congshu*, vol. 11.

105. *Wenji* 2:30–33; Zhu Shi, *Zhu Wenduan gong wenji*, 1:18–19.

106. *Xueshi yigui* 3:61.

107. *SD* 2:14, 2:19.

108. *Wenji* 2:30–35.

109. The five are Lü Nan, Feng Congwu, and Kou Shen from the Ming, and Li Yong and Wang Xinjing from the Qing; *Xueshi yigui*, *juan* 2 and 3. On the work's compilation during Chen's years as grand secretary in Beijing see *JS* 243–45, 251–53.

110. *PYTOCG* 22:32–33, 28:1–2, 30:3–4, 30:33.

111. *PYTOCG* 34:47–49.

112. *PYTOCG* 19:21–40, 23:14–15, 26:41–42; *Wenji* 2:30–33.

113. Translation by Wing-tsit Chan from his *Sourcebook in Chinese Philosophy*, 497.

114. *SD* 2:3–4.

115. "*Guanxue bian* xu," *Wenji* 2:33–35.

116. *Xueshi yigui* 3:61; Chen Zuwu, 153–57; Birdwhistell, 160–66. Li seems to have chosen *shen* (body), his frequent synonym for "self," in deliberate, materialist preference to Wang Yangming's *xin* (heart-and-mind). I am intrigued by the continuity between Li Yong's seventeenth-century use of the term *fanshen* and the twentieth-century Chinese Communist use immortalized in William Hinton's *Fanshen: A Documentary of Revolution in a Chinese Village* (New York: Vintage, 1966). The two terms are written with differing first characters, to be sure (Matthews no. 1781 and no. 1796, respectively), but have closely related meanings, share a Shaanxi provenance, and both strongly incorporate a component of self-criticism.

117. *Xueshi yigui* 2:87–88, 3:61, 3:79; Yang Shen, "Xiuqi zhizhi ping," in *Guanzhong congshu*, vol. 11.

118. de Bary and Bloom, esp. de Bary's introduction, 1–36.

119. Liang Qichao, 40–42. See also Qian Mu, chap. five; Wing-tsit Chan, *Sourcebook*, chap. 37 ("Practical Confucianism in Yen Yuan"); and Chung-ying Chang, "Practical Learning in Yen Yuan, Chu Hsi, and Wang Yang-ming," in de Bary and Bloom, 37–68.

120. Chen Zuwu, 19; Chung-ying Chang, 55.

121. On the complex relationship of *shixue* with other intellectual currents of the time see especially Yamanoi Yū, "Minmatsu Shinsho ni okeru keisei-chiyō no gaku" (The *jingshi zhiyong* scholarly movement in the late Ming and early Qing), *Tōhōgaku ronshu* 1 (February 1954): 136–50. See also Elman, *Classicism*, 78–79, 84–85; Handlin, *Action*, 18; and Hao Chang, *Chinese Intellectuals in Crisis: Search for Order and Meaning, 1890–1911* (Berkeley: University of California Press, 1987), 15–16, 72.

122. Gao Xiang, "Qingqu lixue"; Ng, "Ontological Basis of Practicality."

123. Feng Tianyu, "Daoguang Xianfeng nianjian jingshi shixue" (*Jingshi* and *shixue* thought in the Daoguang and Xianfeng era), *Lishi yanjiu* 1987.4, 141–42.

124. David C. Reynolds, "Redrawing China's Intellectual Map: Images of Science in Nineteenth-Century China," *Late Imperial China* 12:2 (June 1991): 41.

125. See especially Yamanoi, "Keisei-chiyō," 142–43; Chen Zuwu, 17–22; and de Bary, introduction to *Principle and Practicality*, 24–25, 32.

126. Yuasa, 116–17.

127. *Yishu*, "Yulu," 16. See also *PYTOCG* 19:22–23; *XSYG* (1769 edition), 4:10–13.

128. See, e.g., memorial of QL 5/8/22, MQA; *PYTOCG* 3:40–44, 5:3–5, 10:1–2, 11:7–9, 17:10–11, 19:34; *CZYG* 1:34; *Guitiao huichao*, preface; *SD* 3:1; Gao Jiren, 122.

129. Li Yuandu, 16:4.

130. Letters to Depei and to Jing Guoyuan, *SD* 1:13, 2:19; *XSYG* 3:1; *Xueshi yigui* 2:72; *Lushi jielu* 1:7.

131. *Wenji* 1:1–4; *PYTOCG* 3:5–11; *Guilin jianshi* 112; Gao Jiren, 7–8.

132. Chen observed further that, inasmuch as the first session of the examination was by nature more susceptible to preparation by last-minute cramming from published crib books of model essays, the disproportionate weight attached to this session contributed to the degeneration of the entire examination culture, its descent into the cult of *chuaimo* (finesse).

133. *PYTOCG* 4:3–4. At subsequent points in his career Chen similarly intervened to exercise control over the selection and promotion of students within Jiangxi's Ganchang and Ziyang Academies, and Shaanxi's Guanzhong Academy, on the criterion of their accordance with his notion of *shixue*, *PYTOCG* 15:39–41, 22:32–33; *SD* 1:13. For discussion of imperially sponsored examination reforms of the Yongzheng and Qianlong reigns—including Gaozong's brief 1757–58 experiment in dropping the "discourse" essay altogether—see Benjamin Elman, "The Inter-relation Between Changes in Ch'ing Classical Studies and Changes in Policy Questions on Civil Service Examinations," in *Qingdai jingxue guoji yanjiuhui lunwenji* (Proceedings of the international conference on Qing classical studies) (Taibei: Institute of Chinese Literature and Philosophy, 1994), esp. 37–41.

134. *SD* 3:7.

135. It might be said that the Qianlong emperor was paying tribute to Chen's mastery of *shixue*, understood in this way as a detailed knowledge of history, geography, institutions, and techniques, when in 1767 he appointed the aged man "Sanguan zongcai" (General director of the three offices), in simultaneous charge of the State History Office (Guoshi guan), the Office of the Imperial Clan Genealogy (Yudie guan), and the Encyclopedia Compilation Office (Santong guan); letter of QL 32/4/23, *JS* 248–49.

136. See variously *PYTOCG* 15:39–41, 22:32–33; *Xueshi yigui* 1:11, 1:17, 2:17, 3:46, 3:79, 4:32, 4:42, 4:47–48; *SD* 2:6, 3:16; *JSWB* 2:33; and Tang Jian, 5:11.

137. Yingshi Yu, "Toward an Interpretation of the Intellectual Transition in Seventeenth-Century China," *Journal of the American Oriental Society* 100.2 (April–June 1980): 115–25.

138. Elman, *From Philosophy to Philology*, 53–54; Elman, "Scholarship and Politics: Chuang Ts'un-yü and the Rise of the Ch'ang-chou New Text School in Late Imperial China," *Late Imperial China* 7.1 (June 1986): 64; Elman, *Classicism, Politics, and Kinship*, 76.

139. Perdue, *Exhausting the Earth*, 11.

140. Joshua A. Fogel, *Politics and Sinology: The Case of Naitō Konan (1866–1934)* (Cambridge, Mass.: Harvard University Press, 1984), 60.

141. Hao Chang, "*Ching-shih* Ideal"; Zhang Hao, "Rujia jingshi sixiang"; Liu Guangjing (Kwang-Ching Liu), *Jingshi sixiang yu xinxing qiye* (Statecraft thought and modern enterprises) (Taibei: Lianjing, 1990), 2.

142. Important studies of nineteenth-century *jingshi* include Frederic Wakeman Jr., "The Huang-ch'ao ching-shih wen-pien," *Ch'ing-shih wen-t'i* 1.10 (1969): 6–22; Liu Guangjing (Kwang-Ching Liu) and Zhou Qirong, "*Huangchao jingshi wenbian* guanyu 'jingshi zhi xue' de lilun" (The theory of "*jingshi* studies" expressed in the *Huangchao jingshi wenbian*), *Jindaishi yanjiuyuan jikan* 15.1 (June 1986): 33–100; Liu Guangjing, *Jingshi sixiang yu xinxing qiye*; Judith Whitbeck, "From *K'ao-cheng* to *Ching-shih*: Kung Tzu-chen and the Restoration of Literati Commitment in Early Nineteenth-Century China," in *Jindai Zhongguo jingshi sixiang yantaohui lunwenji*, 323–40; Li

Guoji, "Dao-Xian-Tong shiqi woguo de jingshi zhiyong sixiang" (*Jingshi* thought in China during the Daoguang, Xiangfeng, and Tongzhi reigns), *Jindaishi yanjiuyuan jikan* 15.2 (December 1986): 17–65; Feng Tianyu, "Daoguang Xianfeng nianjian jingshi shixue"; and Benjamin Elman, "The Relevance of Sung Learning in the Late Ch'ing: Wei Yuan and the *Huang-ch'ao ching-shih wen-pien*," *Late Imperial China* 9.2 (December 1988): 56–85.

143. On these linked phenomena see Suzuki Chūsei, *Shincho chūkishi kenkyū*; and Susan Mann Jones and Philip A. Kuhn, "Dynastic Decline and the Roots of Rebellion," in John K. Fairbank, ed., *The Cambridge History of China*, vol. 10, *Late Ching, Part One*.

144. Feng Tianyu, "Jingshi shixue," 140–41.

145. Liu and Zhou, 83.

146. Liu Guangjing, "Shangren yu jingshi" (Merchants and *jingshi*), in his *Jingshi sixiang yu xinxing qiye*, 595–620. This differs from the conclusion of Li Guoji (p. 65) that nineteenth-century *jingshi* scholar-officials remained essentially trapped by the "stress agriculture and suppress commerce" (*zhongnong yishang*) prejudices of earlier eras. I myself find Li's conclusion wholly untenable.

147. See especially Elman, "Relevance of Sung Learning." Elman (p.62) calls this linkage of *jingshi* and Songxue moralism "remarkable" and believes it new with Wei Yuan and his era. Our study of Chen Hongmou in the present work, however, shows that the linkage held much earlier in the Qing as well.

148. Wakeman, "Ching-shih wen-pien," 10.

149. See variously Schirokauer and Hymes, introduction to Hymes and Schirokauer, 55–58; Li Guoji, 18; Zhang Hao, "Rujia jingshi sixiang," 3–7; Winston Wan Lo, *The Life and Thought of Yeh Shih* (Gainesville: University Presses of Florida and Chinese University of Hong Kong, 1974); and Hung-lam Chu, "Intellectual Trends in the Fifteenth Century," *Ming Studies* 27 (spring 1989): 10.

150. Yamanoi, "Keisei-chiyō" and "Minmatsu Shinsho shisō." See also Chen Zuwu, 17–22, which reinforces several of Yamanoi's arguments.

151. Yu, "Intellectual Transition in Seventeenth-Century China," 119.

152. For the explicit use of the term "*jingshi*" in Guanxue writings see, e.g., Chen Junmin, 30–36.

153. See William S. Atwell, "From Education to Politics: The Fu She," in de Bary, *Unfolding*, esp. 348; Wakeman, *The Great Enterprise*, esp. 743–52.

154. Thomas A. Metzger et al., "*Ching-shih* Thought and the Societal Changes of the Late Ming and Early Ch'ing Periods: Some Preliminary Considerations," in Institute of Modern History, *Jingshi sixiang*, 21–35. See also Metzger, *Internal Organization*, 76–78; Hao Chang, "*Ching-shih* Ideal," 51–56.

155. Chow, *Confucian Ritualism*, 170–71.

156. See, e.g., Yamanoi, "Keisei-chiyō," 149; Feng Tianyu, "Jingshi shixue," 138–39. The eighteenth-century hiatus in the *jingshi* tradition is also a central premise of Liu Guangjing's preface to Institute of Modern History, *Jingshi sixiang*.

157. Elman, *Classicism, Politics, and Kinship*, esp. 76. I do not for a moment dispute Elman's argument for the importance of the New Text Movement as an eighteenth-century conduit for *jingshi* ideas (see also Feng Tianyu, 141–43); I would merely observe that there were other conduits as well.

158. Kai-wing Chow, "Ordering Ancestors and the State: Chang Hsüeh-ch'eng (1738–1801) and Lineage Discourse in Eighteenth-Century China," in Institute of Modern History, *Jiazu yu zhengzhi*, 297–326; Liu Guangjing, preface to Institute of Modern History, *Jingshi sixiang*, 6; Feng Tianyu, "Jingshi shixue," 139.

159. Huang Kewu, 84–85.

160. Chan Lansen, preface to *Xueshi yigui*; Peng Qifeng 14:12; Jiang Fangzheng, "Fu chongkan xu," in *Rongmen quanji*; Xu Zeshun, preface to *Chen wengong gong shouzha jieyao* (1846); Wang Zhichun, preface to *SD*; Li Yuandu, 16:1.

161. Xie Kang, 235; Fu-mei Chang Chen, 140; Perdue, *Exhausting the Earth*, 11; Cai Guanluo, l.149.

162. For examples of Chen's frequent pairing of "*jingji*" and "*lixue*" see *PYTOCG* 44:1 and *XSYG* 3:24. For "*jingji shixue*" see *Xueshi yigui* 4:32. On the origin of the term "*jingji*" in "*jingshi jimin*" see Tetsuo Najita, *Visions of Virtue in Tokugawa Japan: The Kaitokusho Merchant Academy of Osaka* (Chicago: University of Chicago Press, 1987), 8. That Chen may have been actively aware of this etymology is suggested by his occasional use of the alternative shorthand form "*jishi*" (relieve the world), as in *Xueshi yigui* 2:17.

163. *SD* 1:15, 2:15–16; Tang Jian, 512.

164. *Xueshi yigui* 3:17, 3:38, 3:46, 3:99.

165. *Xueshi yigui* 2:38, 2:72, 3:80; *Wenji* 2:30–33; *PYTOCG* 30:33; Chen Junmin, 30–36; Chen Zuwu, 152–78.

166. Metzger, *Internal Organization*, 24–26.

167. Elman, *From Philosophy to Philology*, 237.

168. *CZYG* 2:29–36; *XSYG* 2:28–33; *ZGFJL* 1:12–13.

169. On Gu's historicism see Santangelo, "Gu Yanwu's Contribution to History."

170. Thomas Bartlett, "Ch'ing Period Views of Ku Yen-wu's Statecraft Scholarship," in Institute of Modern History, *Jingshi sixiang*, 39–69.

171. Kuhn, "Local Self-Government Under the Republic"; Min, "The Theory of Political Feudalism in the Ch'ing Period."

172. Gu Yanwu, "Junxian lun" (On the prefectural system), in *Tinglin wenji* (Collected works of Gu Yanwu) (Shanghai: Zhonghua shuju, 1927).

173. Among other possibilities see Fogel, *Politics and Sinology*, 60; Perdue, *Exhausting the Earth*, 11.

174. These are Thomas Metzger's terms. Benjamin Elman (*Classicism*) uses the equally appropriate categories "reformist" vs. "system maintenance," to the latter of which Chen Hongmou would belong.

175. See, e.g., Wei Yuan, *Guwei tang neiwai ji*, 6:7; He Changling, "Tiba" (Colophon), in *JS* 178–79; Zeng Guofan, *Zeng Guofan quanji*, "Jiashu," 1:145–47, 154–55; Li Yuandu, 16:1–4; Jiang Yili, preface to Chen, *ZZYG* (1865 ed.); Feng Guifen, in *Huangchao jingshi wen xubian*, 55:4–5. Hubei provincial treasurer Wang Zhichun, in his preface to the 1868 edition of Chen's letters (*SD*), observes that Chen's popularity in his day derived above all from the great regard that Wei Yuan had held for his career and writings.

176. Tang Jian, 5:9.

177. See, e.g., Cheng Huanbian, "Tiba" (Colophon), *JS* 170.

178. See, e.g., letter of QL 30/12/26, *JS* 238.

179. An attempt to connect intellectual life in Qing Hunan with demographic and economic developments—an attempt I find not particularly convincing—is Lin Zengping, "A Preliminary Investigation of the Culture of Hunan in the Pre-modern Period," *Social Sciences in China* 1990.3, 139–62.

180. On the Hunanese case see Evelyn Rawski's detailed analysis in her *Agricultural Change and the Peasant Economy of South China* (Cambridge, Mass.: Harvard University Press, 1972).

181. On the Xiang valley case see Peter C. Perdue, "Insiders and Outsiders: The Xiangtan Riot of 1819 and Collective Action in Hunan," *Modern China* 12.2 (April 1986), 166–201.

182. On this point see Kai-wing Chow, "Invention of the T'ung-ch'eng School." That the Tongcheng school had such a strong influence on both Chen Hongmou and the Hunan clique (discussed further below) was likely related to the "semiperipheral" ecological character of that region as well, located as it was in the backwater of northern Anhui yet unusually favorably connected by water transport to more metropolitan Jiangnan. And indeed, as Hilary Beattie has shown, the rise of the nationally prominent Tongcheng scholar-officials of the early and mid-Qing seems directly linked to the rise of a planter class there, involved in interregional export of grain and other agricultural commodities; see Hilary Beattie, *Land and Lineage in China: A Study*

of T'ung-ch'eng County, Anhwei, in the Ming and Ch'ing Dynasties (Cambridge: Cambridge University Press, 1979), esp. chap. 2.

183. Yang Nianqun, 121–22.

184. On Zhang Shi see Chan, *Sourcebook*, 26, 600; *Zhongguo renming da zidian*, 948; Yang Nianqun, 182–83, 350–60; and Zhao Ning, preface to *Xinxiu Yuelu shuyuan zhishu* (Revised gazetteer of the Yuelu Academy), 1687. Zhang's defense of self-interest and political economy made him an important influence on pragmatically minded *jingshi* advocates, and his correponding defense of human appetites and innate wisdom endeared him as well to the radically intuitionist Taizhou school, including Li Zhi (1527–1602); see Rong Zhaozu, *Li Zhi nianpu* (Chronological biography of Li Zhi) (Beijing: Sanlian, 1957), 59. Zhang Shi clearly represented a powerful and only partially suppressed alternative within the *lixue* tradition, a counterweight to Cheng-Zhu orthodoxy who could be read in a variety of ways by later scholars struggling to legitimate their own independent moral visions.

185. Yang Nianqun, 189–91, 343–46. As Benjamin Elman has demonstrated, historical expertise became more central to the civil service examination curriculum beginning in the late 1770s (Elman, "History in Policy Questions from Southern Provincial Civil Service Examinations During the Late Ming and Early Ch'ing," in *Proceedings of the Conference on the Achievements of Historical Figures in South China During the Late Ming and Early Ch'ing* [Hong Kong: Chinese University of Hong Kong, 1993], 181–82). Prior to that time, up through and beyond the era of Chen Hongmou's tenures in Hunan, this historicism was a distinctly minority and regionally confined emphasis, and even thereafter it was more pronounced in Hunan than elsewhere.

186. *PYTOCG* 48:42.

187. Chen Hongmou, ed., *Hunan tongzhi* (Provincial gazetteer of Hunan), 1757. See also the comment on this work in *Siku quanshu zongmu tiyao* 15:50. For Chen's comments on his intentions for the volume see *PYTOCG* 48:36–37; *SD* 3:7–8.

188. *PYTOCG* 48:15.

189. He Changling republished a portion of Wang's works in 1848. Further portions were published by Wang Meishu (a student of Hu Linyi) in Jiangsu in 1860 under the protection of then Liang-Jiang governor-general Zeng Guofan. This edition was reprinted in Changsha at the Chengnan Academy under the supervision of Guo Songdao. See Ōtani Toshio, "Shinmatsu Konan kanryō keisei katei ni tsuite" (The formative process of the Hunan clique of the late Qing), *Tōyōshi kenkyū* 44.2 (September 1985): 73–75.

190. Yang Nianqun, 122–31.

191. *JNYG* 3:19–24; *XSYG* 4:34–43; *ZZYG* 2:63–73; *Xueshi yigui* 4:72. On Wang's career see *Zhongguo renming da zidian*, 78.

192. *Xinxiu Yuelu shuyuan zhishu* 3:10–11.

193. *PYTOCG* 38:1. On the institution's history see Deng Hongbo, "Shilun Yuelu shuyuan de lishi diwei he zuoyong" (The historical position and role of the Yuelu Academy), in *Yuelu shuyuan yiqian ling yishi zhounian jinian wenji* (Essays in commemoration of the 1010th anniversary of the Yuelu Academy) (Changsha: Hunan renmin chubanshe, 1986), 3–15.

194. *PYTOCG* 48:9–20.

195. *Wenji* 4:44–47.

196. See, above all, Ōtani, "Shinmatsu Konan kanryō," but also Liang Qichao, "Jindai xuefeng zhi dili de fenbu," 32–34; Feng Tianyu, 141–42; Wilhelm, "Chinese Confucianism," 298–300; Wilhelm, "The Background of Tseng Kuo-fan's Ideology," *Asiatisch Studien* 3/4 (1949): 90–100; Wright, *The Last Stand of Chinese Conservatism*, 59–60; Elman, *From Philosophy to Philology*, 240–47; Elman, "Relevance of Sung Learning," 57–62; and biographies of relevant individuals in *ECCP*.

197. See Tang Baigu, "Yuelu shuyuan yu He Changling," and Li Hanwu, "Yuelu shuyuan yu Wei Yuan," in *Yuelu shuyuan jinian wenji*, 160–75.

198. Not only Wei Yuan but also Luo Zenan, Hu Linyi, and Li Yuandu wrote geographical treatises. It is worth recalling that Chen Hongmou, too, held geographical knowedge to be crit-

ical; in 1755 he led a project to produce detailed county-by-county maps of Hunan itself. *PY-TOCG* 37:5–12.

199. The publication of Tang Jian's anti-Hanxue manifesto *Xuean xiaoshi* coincided with a broader turn in the empire (especially outside Jiangnan) away from *kaozheng*'s fashionability, manifested most dramatically in the critique by the Cantonese scholar Fang Dongshu, *Hanxue shangdui* (1838). See Elman, *From Philosophy to Philology*, 242–43; and Feng Tianyu, 141.

200. Luo Zenan, *Luo zhongjie gong yiji* (Surviving works of Luo Zenan) (1862; reprint, Taibei: Wenhai, n.d.), 4:2–4, "Nianpu," 9. Recall that "curing society's ills" was a central metaphor of Li Yong and the Guanxue school.

Chapter 5

1. Although there is an enormous literature on late imperial provisioning policy in Chinese, Japanese, and Western languages, any Western scholar writing on this subject today must begin by acknowledging the pivotal contributions made in this area by the work of Pierre-Étienne Will and R. Bin Wong. See their *Nourish the People*; Will, *Bureaucracy and Famine in Eighteenth-Century China*, trans. Elborg Forster (Stanford: Stanford University Press, 1990); Wong, "Food Riots in the Qing Dynasty"; and Wong and Peter C. Perdue, "Famine's Foes in Ch'ing China," *Harvard Journal of Asiatic Studies* 43.1 (June 1983): 291–332.

2. Letter to Tuo Yong, *SD* 2:5. See also memorial of QL 9/3/1, MQA.

3. Suzuki, 29–37. See also Peng Yuxin, 284–85.

4. Ping-ti Ho, *Studies on the Population of China, 1368–1953* (Cambridge, Mass.: Harvard University Press, 1959), 277–78; Dwight Perkins, *Agricultural Development in China, 1368–1968* (Chicago: Aldine, 1969), 16, 24. The territory of "China" of course greatly expanded in these years as well, but Ho's and Perkins's figures are corrected to reflect constant boundaries. For a more recent analysis, which, however, does not supersede that of Ho, see Zhao Wenlin and Xie Shujun, *Zhongguo renkou shi* (Chinese population history) (Beijing: Renmin chubanshe, 1988), 377–82.

5. Perkins, 24; Gao Wangling, "Shiba shiji Zhongguo renkou de zengzhang he Qing zhengfu de nongye jingji duice" (China's eighteenth-century population growth and the responding agrarian economic policies of the Qing government) (unpublished discussion paper of the Chinese Academy of Social Sciences, 1982), 2–3.

6. Lin Man-houng, "From Sweet Potatoes to Silver: The New World and Eighteenth-Century China as Reflected in Wang Hui-tsu's Passage About the Grain Prices," in Hans Pohl, ed., *The European Discovery of the World and Its Economic Effects on Pre-Industrial Society, 1500–1800* (Stuttgart: Franz Steiner, 1990), 308.

7. Perkins, 16.

8. Quan Hansheng, "Qianlong shisan nian de migui wenti" (The problem of high rice prices in 1748), in Quan, *Zhongguo jingjishi luncong* (Essays in Chinese economic history) (Hong Kong: Chongwen, 1972), 560.

9. Letter to Yang Xingting, *Shudu* 3:8.

10. Perkins (17) estimates average grain yields of 139 catties per *mu* in 1400, rising to 203 catties per *mou* in 1770.

11. This breakdown is based on Wong, "Food Riots," 768–69, but adds the second category, which Wong for some reason omits.

12. Wu Jianyong, "Qing qianqi de shangpin liang zhengce" (Early Qing policies toward commerce in grain), *Lishi dang'an* 1986.3, 87.

13. Wu Chengming, "Lun Qingdai qianqi woguo guonei shichang" (On the domestic market in the early Qing), *Lishi yanjiu* 1983.1, 99.

14. Yeh-chien Wang, "Food Supply in Eighteenth-Century Fukien," *Late Imperial China* 7.2 (December 1986): 80–117; Wong, "Food Riots," 774–75.

15. Marks, "Rice Prices"; Inada.

16. For studies of the overall movement of grain see Abe Takeo, "Bikoku jūkyū no kenkyū—Yōsei shi no issho to shita mita" (Supply and demand of grain in the Yongzheng period), in Abe,

Shindaishi no kenkyū (Studies in Qing history) (Tokyo: Sōbunsha, 1971), 411–522; Han-sheng Chuan and Richard Kraus, *Mid-Ch'ing Rice Markets and Trade: An Essay in Price History* (Cambridge, Mass.: Harvard Univesity Press, 1975). For studies of Hunan's role in this trade see Shigeta Atsushi, "Shinshu ni okeru Konan beishichō no ikkosatsu" (An investigation of Hunan rice markets in the early Qing), *Tōyō bunka kenkyūjo kiyo* 10.8 (1956): 427–98; Zhong Yongding, "Shilun shiba shiji Xiang mi shuchu de kexingxing wenti" (An examination of the feasibility of Hunan rice exports in the eighteenth century), *Zhongguo shehui jingji shi yanjiu* 1990.3, 65–71.

17. Chuan and Kraus, 77.

18. See, e.g., Quan, "Qianlong shisan nian de migui wenti," 564–66; Kuroda Akinobu, "Kenryū no senki" (The inflation of copper cash in the Qianlong era), *Tōyōshi kenkyū* 45.4 (March 1987): 58–89; Lin Man-houng, "Sweet Potatoes to Silver," 315–17.

19. Fernand Braudel and Frank Spooner, "Prices in Europe from 1450 to 1750," in E. E. Rich and C. H. Wilson, eds., *The Cambridge Economic History of Europe*, vol. 4 (Cambridge: Cambridge University Press, 1967), 400.

20. Kuroda Akinobu, "Shindai bichiku kō" (A study of the Qing granary system), *Shirin* 71.6 (1988): 6–10. See also Mio Kishimoto-Nakayama, "The Kangxi Depression and Early Qing Local Markets," *Modern China* 10.2 (April 1984): 227–56; and Richard von Glahn, *Fountain of Fortune: Money and Monetary Policy in China, 1000–1700* (Berkeley: University of California Press, 1996), 211–15.

21. Figures compiled by Peng Xinwei, cited in Kishimoto Mio, "Shinchō chūki keizai seisaku no kichō" (A preliminary investigation of mid-Qing economic policy), *Chikaki ni arite* 11 (1987): 18; see also Kishimoto, *Shindai Chūgoku no buka to keizai hendō* (Prices and economic change in Qing China) (Tokyo: Kenbun, 1997), 126–27. Yeh-chien Wang has cast doubt on Peng's methodology and the reliability of his price series. Nevertheless, for our purposes Wang's own findings effectively corroborate those of Peng. Analyzing rice prices in silver in Suzhou and Nanchang, two of the empire's premier rice markets, Wang finds a rise of approximately 125 percent during the eighteenth century, with roughly two-thirds of that increase coming in the century's first half. Wang, "The Secular Trend of Prices During the Ch'ing Period (1644–1911)," *Journal of the Institute of Chinese Studies of the Chinese University of Hong Kong* (December 1972): 351.

22. Suzuki, 43. Kishimoto (*Buka*, 153) finds the rapid price inflation of first quality paddy land in Jiangnan to have taken place only after ca. 1765, but this was probably not representative of land prices empire-wide. By most accounts eighteenth-century population growth in the already crowded Jiangnan was slower than that elsewhere.

23. This was the celebrated observation of Wang Huizu, discussed in Lin Man-houng, "Sweet Potatoes to Silver." See also Kishimoto, *Buka*, 139, 144, on cotton and silk textile prices, both of which rose only slowly.

24. Braudel and Spooner, 395–96.

25. Memorial of QL 5/8/22, MQA.

26. Edict of QL 8/4/1, *Shilu* 189:1–3.

27. A key Qianlong edict on the subject is that of Qianlong 3/1, reprinted in *Donghua lu*, Qianlong reign, 7:46. Imperial concern is amply documented as well in Suzuki, 29–37; Peng Yuxin, 70–71; Bai Xinliang, 136–37; and most systematically in Gao Wangling, *Shiba shiji Zhongguo de jingji fazhan he zhengfu zhengce*. For Chen Hongmou's own great sensitivity to this issue see, e.g., his memorial of QL 9/3/1, MQA; and *JSWB* 34:50–52.

28. Suzuki, 30.

29. Chen Jinling, "Qingchao de liangjie zoubao yu qi shenghuai" (The rise and fall of the grain price-reporting system in the Qing), *Zhongguo shehui jingji shi yanjiu* 1985.3, 64.

30. See, e.g., edict of QL 8/4/1, *Shilu* 189:1–3; Chen memorial of QL 13/6, *Shilu* 316:15–16; Karjishan and Chen memorial of QL 17/9, *QLZZ* 3.910–11.

31. A routine year-end population report submitted by Chen as Shaanxi governor in 1754 reveals a provincial population that was 56.6 percent male. There was probably some underreporting of females but, in Shaanxi, probably only very limited male-only immigration and so-

journing. (This is further suggested by the fact that sex ratios of adults and children were very nearly the same.) The likely explanation for this sexual imbalance was a significant incidence of female infanticide. Chen, memorial of QL 19/12/21, *QLZZ* 10.385–86. For arguments that the Qing population systematically limited its growth to preserve per capita resources see Li Bozhong, "Kongzhi zengzhang yi bao fuyu: Qingdai qianzhongqi Jiangnan de renkou xingwei" (Controlling population to preserve prosperity: population behavior in early and mid-Qing Jiangnan), *Xin shixue* 5.3 (1994): 25–71; and James Lee and Cameron Campbell, *Fate and Fortune in Rural China: Social Organization and Population Behavior in Liaoning, 1774–1873* (Cambridge: Cambridge University Press, 1997).

32. Edict of QL 8/4/1, *Shilu* 189:1–3.

33. Suzuki, 32.

34. Qianlong's "relaxed" fiscal reforms are surveyed in Dai Yi, *Qianlong di*, 98–118, and in Bai Xinliang, 23–34. The corresponding population growth and immiseration of the 1740s is treated in Kishimoto, "Keizai seisaku," and in Lin Man-houng, "Sweet Potatoes to Silver." Lin's figures for population growth by decade, and Kishimoto's for grain price inflation, indicate an intriguing slowdown of both trends corresponding with the more "severe" (*yan*) tax policies of the Yongzheng reign, 1723–35. After the 1750s, when his military adventures forced Qianlong to look once again for increased fiscal revenues, population growth seems temporarily to have slowed once again.

35. For overviews of this program see Wu Hui and Ge Xianhui, "Qing qianqi de liangshi tiaoqi" (Early Qing food grain policies), *Lishi yanjiu* 1988.4, 122–35; Feng Liutang, 147–49; Kishimoto, "Keizai seisaku," 22–27; Gao Wangling, "Yige weiwanjie de changshi," 14–19.

36. Chen Jinling, 63–68; Chuan and Kraus, 3–16, 72–73; Will and Wong, 25–26, 253–55. Sample reports submitted by Chen Hongmou may be found in *QLZZ* 2.232, 3.387–88, 6.847–88, 10.385–86. In a proclamation of QL/intercalary 7 (*PYTOCG* 27:12–13), Chen orders stricter attention to monthly reporting by his local-level subordinates.

37. For fuller treatment of Qing frugality campaigns see Suzuki, 37–45. On the broader ideological context see Lien-sheng Yang, "Economic Justification for Spending—An Uncommon Idea in Traditional China," in his *Studies in Chinese Institutional History* (Cambridge, Mass.: Harvard University Press, 1961), 58–74.

38. For but one example see *PYTOCG* 24:23–24.

39. That such a notion may have been present in Wang Anshi's Song-dynasty "New Policies" is suggeted in P. Smith, *Taxing Heaven's Storehouse*, 188. For Sima Guang's prevailing counterviews see Bol, *This Culture of Ours*, 247–51.

40. *SD* 2:15.

41. Yinjishan, memorial of QL 13/7, cited in Gao Wangling, "Yige weiwanjie de changshi," 18; Feng Erkang, 196.

42. The major documents in the policy debate are translated and discussed in Dunstan, *Conflicting Counsels*, chap. 5. See also Kishimoto, "Keizai seisaku," 23–24; Gao Wangling, "Yige wei wanjie de changshi," 18. On Sun Jiagan's political stance see Li Xun, "Sun Jiagan yu Yong-Qian zhengfu" (Sun Jiagan and the Yongzheng-Qianlong government), *Shixue jikan* 1984.1, 38–44.

43. Memorial of QL 14/7/5, GCA; *PYTOCG* 27:3–4.

44. Memorial of QL 8/intercalary 4, excerpted in *NP* 5:5; Fang Bao, *Yiji*, 53–54.

45. J. Liu; Bol, *This Culture of Ours*; P. Smith, *Taxing Heaven's Storehouse*.

46. Qiu Jun, *Daxue yanyi bu xuyao* (Abridged supplement to the extended meaning of the Great learning), ed. Chen Hongmou (1842 edition). On the textual history of Qiu's work see Hung-lam Chu, "Ch'iu Chun's *Ta-hsüeh yen-i pu*." On the work's economic ideas see Will and Wong, 12.

47. Edict of QL 12/12, *Shilu*, Qianlong reign, 304:16. Similar language appears in an earlier edict of QL 7, reprinted in Feng Liutang, 250–51. See also Wu Jianyong, 87; Wu Hui and Ge Xianhui, 129–30.

48. Dai Yi, *Qianlong*, 300–301.

49. Gao Wangling, "Yige wei wanjie de changshi," 18.

50. Feng Liutang, 250–51; Wu Hui and Ge Xianhui, 129, 133; Will, *Bureaucracy and Famine*, 214–15.

51. *PYTOCG* 15:20–23; Wu Hui and Ge Xianhui, 130–32; Feng Liutang, 248–49; Dunstan, *Conflicting Counsels*, 170–72. Dunstan also translates (196–201) Gan Rulai's programmatic memorial of QL 1/1/18, which sparked the 1736 court debate on this issue.

52. Chen, memorial of QL 8/intercalary 4/27, MQA.

53. Wu Jianyong, 87–88; Feng Liutang, 249. Wu estimates Qianlong's abrogation of customs duties on grain between 1742 and 1748 at more than one million taels per year. Immanuel Hsu places the cost of Qianlong's first Jinchuan campaign (1747–49) at nearly eight million taels. See Hsu, *The Rise of Modern China* (New York: Oxford University Press, 1970), 52.

54. See especially Chen's letter to Hui Se, *SD* 2:14.

55. *NP* 5:6.

56. *PYTOCG* 37:1–2. For a slightly different interpretation of this incident see Shigeta, "Shinshu ni okeru Konan beishichō no ikkosatsu," 439, 486. For general discussions of the problem of *shuhuang*, see Wu Jianyong, 90; and von Glahn, *Fountain of Fortune*, 211–15. As Dunstan points out, the idiom "cheap grain hurts the farmer" had its locus classicus in the *Hanshu*, where it was attributed to the fifth-century B.C. Legalist minister Li Kui; *Conflicting Counsels*, 52.

57. Will, *Bureaucracy and Famine*, 224; Will, "Discussions About the Market-Place and the Market Principle in Eighteenth-Century Guangdong," in Sun Yat-sen Institute of Social Sciences and Philosophy, ed., *Zhongguo haiyang fazhan shi lunwen ji* (Essays on the history of China's maritime development) (Taibei: Academia Sinica, forthcoming).

58. Feng Liutang, 232–35.

59. Yeh-chien Wang, "Food Supply," 89–91.

60. John R. Shepherd, *Statecraft and Political Economy on the Taiwan Frontier* (Stanford: Stanford University Press, 1993), 164–65; Feng Liutang, 227–28. Shepherd links government reluctance to legalize grain imports with fears of the high cost of controlling ethnic conflict on the island itself.

61. *NP* 8:6; *Qing shigao*, 35.10558–64.

62. Zhuang Guotu, *Zhongguo fengjian zhengfu de Huaqiao zhengce* (The policies of China's feudal government toward the overseas Chinese) (Xiamen: Xiamen daxue chubanshe, 1989), 94.

63. The history of this legislation is summarized by Chen Hongmou in his memorial of QL 19/4/28, *QLZZ* 8.138–40. See also Feng Erkang, 410–15; Zhuang Guotu, 74–75; Leonard Blussé, *Strange Company: Chinese Settlers, Mestizo Women, and the Dutch in V.O.C. Batavia* (Dordrecht: Foris Publications, 1988), 133–35.

64. Feng Liutang, 235–36; Yeh-chien Wang, 91–92.

65. Yeh-chien Wang, 92; see also Shepherd, 165.

66. Memorial of QL 18/8/6, *QLZZ* 6.73.

67. Sarasin Viraphol, *Tribute and Profit: Sino-Siamese Rice Trade, 1652–1853* (Cambridge, Mass.: Harvard University Press, 1977), 98–99; Feng Liutang, 236.

68. Chen's argument for expansion of overseas trade as a means of increasing the empire's silver supply echoed those voiced earlier (by Gu Yanwu, among others) during the deflationary era of the 1680s and 1690s; see von Glahn, *Fountain of Fortune*, 216–22. One of the unspecified "other commodities" Chen sought to import was very likely timber. As Feng Liutang (236) explains, Fujianese merchants had regularly adopted the practice of traveling to Southeast Asia without a ship of their own, taking advantage of plentiful wood supplies there to have a ship constructed, returning with a cargo of rice, and then having the ship dismantled for resale as timber.

69. Memorial of QL 19/4/28, *QLZZ* 8.138–40.

70. Ibid. See also *Qingchao wenxian tongkao* (Shanghai, 1936 ed.), 7465–66; Blussé, 134–35.

71. Entry for QL 19/intercalary 4, *Shilu*, Qianlong reign, 463.17.

72. *NP* 8:4–6.

73. *PYTOCG* 34:51–52; Zhuang Guotu, 94.

74. See, e.g., Wong, "Food Riots," 772–74.

75. *NP* 7:12. Chen's *Qingshi gao* biography also specifically lauds his famine relief expertise.

76. Chen, memorial of QL 20/10/5, *QLZZ* 12.597–98.

77. *NP* 8:23–24; Cai Guanluo, 1.147.

78. Chen, memorial of QL 20/11/27, *QLZZ* 13.96.

79. Chen, memorials of QL 20/11/27 and QL 21/1/17, *QLZZ* 13.99–100, 13.477–80; *NP* 9:1. The motivation of Yang Xifu in submitting his unsolicited memorial is ambiguous. It is possible that he was simply providing his longtime friend, Chen, with a prearranged pretext to delay repurchases, by suggesting a price both knew to be unrealistic. It is also possible, though, that despite their similarities of approach to food policy in general, Yang and Chen held different priorities on the question of maintaining high granary stocks vs. risking driving up market prices. See also their somewhat different responses to the 1748 granary reduction debate (discussed in Chapter 8).

80. Fang Bao, letter to "a friend," in Fang, *Yiji*, 53–54, and to Chen Hongmou, *Yiji*, 64. Although formally a native of Tongcheng, Anhui, Fang was born and lived most of his life in Nanjing.

81. Shigeta, "Shinshū ni okeru Konan beishichō no ikkosatsu," 478.

82. Will, *Bureaucracy and Famine*, 74–75, 286; Zelin, 170.

83. See, e.g., his memorial of QL 8/3, *QLZZ* 1.19–20.

84. Wong and Perdue, 315–17. For examples of Chen's own laments over the unreliability of the sub-bureacracy in famine relief, and his eforts to circumvent clerical machinations, see *PYTOCG* 5:11–12, 5:19–21, 17:18–19, 22:19–20, 26:24–28.

85. The evolution of this package of policies on relief in these years can be conveniently traced through successive edicts of the Qianlong emperor, collected in Peng Yuanrui, ed., *Qinding fuhui quanshu* (1796), *juan* 27–30.

86. *PYTOCG* 26:24–28; *CZYG* 2:14–29; Feng Liutang, 290; Will, *Bureaucracy and Famine*, 84, 109, 130–31.

87. Memorials of QL 16/7/4, QL 16/12/17, and QL 19/6/13, in *QLZZ* 1.58–59, 2.229–30, 8.775–76; *NP* 7:4, 8:6.

88. See, e.g., *PYTOCG* 16:13, 17:18–19; *NP* 3:4.

89. *PYTOCG* 5:11–12.

90. See, e.g., *NP* 5:20, 6:19.

91. See, e.g., *PYTOCG* 45:25–26. See also Kishimoto, *Buka*, 308.

92. On Jiangxi see memorial of QL 8/3, *QLZZ* 1.19–20; *Qianlong shilu* 175:30–32; *PYTOCG* 16:6–7; *NP* 5:6; Wong, "Food Riots," 772–74. On Shaanxi see memorial of QL 14/7/5, GCA; *PYTOCG* 26:1–3, 26:24–28; *NP* 6:21.

93. *CZYG* 2:29.

94. Lien-sheng Yang, "Spending," 68–69; Feng Liutang, 295.

95. Chen, letter to Yinjishan, 1739, *SD* 1:7.

96. *PYTOCG* 7:11–12. For a similar view expressed by Chen's contemporary Yan Sisheng see Will, *Bureaucracy and Famine*, 258.

97. Lien-sheng Yang, "Spending," 69; Will, *Bureaucracy and Famine*, 262.

98. Memorial of QL 13/4/29, GCA; *NP* 4:27, 4:30, 5:1; *Qingshi gao* 35.10561.

99. See, e.g., *PYTOCG* 26:24–28.

100. *PYTOCG* 14:18.

101. *NP* 6:21; *PYTOCG* 28:3–4.

102. Memorials of QL 8/9/25 and QL 8/10/22, MQA. For a systematic discussion of the growing role of grain tribute reserves in managing local food crises see Wu Hui and Ge Xianhui, 122–24.

103. Wong and Perdue, "Famine's Foes," 320–26.

104. Gao Wangling, "Yige wei wanjie de changshi," 16.

105. *NP* 5:6–7.

106. Memorial of QL 13/10/1, GCA; memorial of QL 16/12/17, *QLZZ* 2.229–30; *PYTOCG* 7:11–12; *NP* 6:24.

107. See, e.g., *NP* 6:19. Another form of relief in kind was that of medicine to combat the epidemic disease that regularly accompanied dearth. See *PYTOCG* 14:18.

108. Memorial of QL 16/7/4, *QLZZ* 1.58–59; *NP* 5:20.

109. *PYTOCG* 26:24–28.

110. *CZYG* 2:14–29.

111. Will, *Bureaucracy and Famine*, 133; Wong and Perdue, "Famine's Foes," 315.

112. *CZYG* 2:25–27. See also *PYTOCG* 22:19–20.

113. *PYTOCG* 26:24–28.

114. One result, in Suzuki's view, was the unchecked migration from the southeast and increased overcrowding in marginal agricultural areas of northwest China, which eventually set the stage for the calamitous White Lotus uprising of the 1790s. Suzuki, 73–74; see also Will, *Bureaucracy and Famine*, 229–32; Wong and Perdue, "Famine's Foes," 312–13. For a translation of Qianlong's 1748 edict announcing reconsideration of the policy see Dunstan, *Conflicting Counsels*, 93–97.

115. *PYTOCG* 12:15–16; *NP* 4:10. On Chen's Yangzhou experiences see *NP* 1:18 and Peng Qifeng 14:7. On Fujian see Chen's memorial of QL 17/4/19, *QLZZ* 2.698–99.

116. Memorial of QL 13/10/1, GCA; *PYTOCG* 26:1–4, 26:10–11, 27:5–7, 27:14–15.

117. Memorial of QL 14/7/5, GCA; *PYTOCG* 27:9–10, 40:1–2, 41:3–4, 46:24–25; *NP* 5:6; Ping-ti Ho, 180.

118. Edict of 1742, reproduced in Feng Liutang, 250–51. As will become clear in the discussion to follow, there was a very strong parallel between this Qing logic of provisioning and that held by many contemporary French economists and administrators, most notably Turgot (1727–81). See John W. Rogers Jr., "Subsistence Crises and Political Economy in France at the End of the *Ancien Régime*," *Research in Economic History* 5 (1980): 249–301; Steven L. Kaplan, *Provisioning Paris: Merchants and Millers in the Grain and Flour Trade in the Eighteenth Century* (Ithaca: Cornell University Press, 1984), esp. 24–29; and Richard Cobb, *The Police and the People* (Oxford: Oxford University Press, 1973), esp. 270–71.

119. *CZYG* 2:27.

120. *PYTOCG* 15:20–23.

121. Memorial of QL 20/10/5, *QLZZ* 12.97–98.

122. There was yet a fourth potential threat identified by some in the Qing administration to the salutory role of an unfettered grain market: purchases of grain by the government itself. Chen was far less clear in his hostility to this than to the three factors discussed above. This question will be considered in detail in Chapter 8.

123. The major sources on Chen's handling of the Jiangxi dearth are his numerous proclamations to subordinates and to the people, collected in *PYTOCG, juan* 15 and 16; also memorial of QL 8/3, *QLZZ* 1.19–20; and *NP* 4:33. This affair is treated also in Wong, "Food Riots."

124. Feng Liutang, 250–51.

125. One particular manifestation of growing class conflict was rent resistance. This was not simply inspired by desperate need. As tenants who owed rent payments in kind saw the rapid rise in the cash value of their grain, a combination of food security concerns and profit-mindedness inclined them to refuse their contracted payments to landlords or at least to demand a renegotiation of terms. Chen's respnse was to demand that they pay up, arguing (correctly, but not very realistically) that the market price of grain was irrelevant to the terms of their rent agreement. In fact, what he was defending was his view of the sanctity of contract and of property rights, a subject to which we shall return. *PYTOCG* 15:22.

126. Chen's logic allowed, of course, that local people *could* be hurt by grain extracted for export by government commandist means, which would lack the market sensitivity of commercial buyers. He conceded that he had himself made relief shipments to Yangzhou for distribution in the severely famine-stricken Jiangbei area but insisted that inasmuch as these had come from

government granary reserves and had not been withdrawn from the consumer market, they could have had no impact on local grain prices. *PYTOCG* 15:20–21.

127. Memorial of QL 14/7/5, GCA; *PYTOCG* 26:1–3, 27:3–4, 27:16–18. The last of these documents has been translated in Dunstan, *Conflicting Counsels*, 264–67.

128. Dunstan, *Conflicting Counsels*, 267–71; Will and Wong, 145–46.

129. Letter to Hui Se, *SD* 2:14.

130. *PYTOCG* 26:16–18.

131. Wu Jianyong, 90.

132. *PYTOCG* 16:3–5, 28:3–4; *CZYG* 2:26–27.

133. Memorial of QL 13/10/1, GCA.

134. Memorial of QL 17/3/28, *QLZZ* 2.538–39.

135. A well-known example is Charles Tilly, "Food Supply and Public Order in Modern Europe," in Tilly, ed., *The Formation of National States in Western Europe* (Princeton: Princeton University Press, 1975), 380–455.

136. Memorial of QL 8/3, *QLZZ* 1.19–20.

137. *PYTOCG* 28:3–4; see also *SD* 2:14.

138. *PYTOCG* 15:20–23, 16:3–5, 28:3–4. Note especially the emphasis on timeliness (*suishi*), which, as we will see in the following chapter, forms a cornerstone of Chen Hongmou's economic thought.

139. *PYTOCG* 15:20–23.

140. *PYTOCG* 28:3–4.

141. *PYTOCG* 16:4.

142. *PYTOCG* 16:1–2.

143. Memorial of QL 14/7/5, GCA.

144. *PYTOCG* 26:1–3.

145. Memorials of QL 14/7/5 and QL 19/9/28, GCA; *PYTOCG* 16:14–15; *NP* 6:16.

146. *PYTOCG* 16:3–5.

147. *PYTOCG* 16:6–7, 16:14–15, 27:14–15; *CZYG* 2:25. For Zhu Xi's endorsement of such strategies see Richard von Glahn, "Community and Welfare: Chu Hsi's Community Granary in Theory and Practice," in Hymes and Schirokauer, 226.

148. *PYTOCG* 16:14.

149. Wong, "Food Riots," 774.

150. Shigeta, "Shinshu ni okeru Konan beishichō no ikkosatsu," 478.

151. *PYTOCG* 15:20–23.

152. *PYTOCG* 15:23, 26:2, 27:15.

153. *PYTOCG* 26:2.

154. *PYTOCG* 27:15.

155. Robert P. Hymes, "Moral Duty and Self-Regulating Process in Southern Sung Views of Famine Relief," in Hymes and Schirokauer, 280–301. As will be discussed below, Dong's text, under the title "Jiuhuang quanshu" (A complete book on famine relief), appears as *juan* 1 of Yu Sen, *Huangzheng congshu* (Handbook of famine administration) (1690; reprint, Taibei: Wenhai, 1989). My presentation of Dong's views here relies on my reading of this edition of Dong's text, supplemented by Hymes's reading, with which I am essentially in agreement. For a slightly different reading see Will, "Market-Place and Market Principle."

156. Yu Sen, 1:5; see also Hymes, 296.

157. Yu Sen, 1:4; see also Hymes, 297.

158. Yu Sen, 1:1.

159. Hymes, 298–99.

160. Hymes, "Southern Sung Views," esp. 286, 299, 309.

161. My surmise that Chen Longzheng reprinted Dong's work is based on the fact that Yu Sen's version includes numerous intertextual notes by Chen.

162. Will, *Bureaucracy and Famine*, 9. On the influence of Dong Wei's work in the Ming see

also Joanna F. Handlin Smith, "Chinese Philanthropy as Seen Through a Case of Famine Relief in the 1640s," in Warren F. Ilchman et al., *Philanthropy in the World's Traditions* (Bloomington: Indiana University Press, 1998), 147–48.

163. Yu Sen, 1:5–6.

164. *CZYG*, preface (dated "winter solstice, QL 7") and 2:14–29. Yan Maoyou (*jinshi* 1634) was also an innovator and publicist in the late Ming movement who founded local charitable associations (*tongshan hui*); see Handlin Smith, "Chinese Philanthropy," esp. 151–52. The eminent metropolitan official Fang Bao, with whom Chen Hongmou corresponded during his Jiangxi tenure, recommended to him works on famine administration by a "Mr. Fu," a "Mr. Zhao," and Fang's own elder brother, Fang Zhou (1665–1701), but I have not confirmed whether Chen in fact read them. Fang Bao, *Yiji*, 64.

165. *NP* 2:14; Kishimoto, "Keizai seisaku," 23.

166. Robert P. Hymes, *Statesmen and Gentlemen: The Elite of Fu-Chou, Chiang-Hsi, in Northern and Southern Sung* (Cambridge: Cambridge University Press, 1986), 164–66.

167. Kishimoto, "Keizai seisaku," 23, 28.

168. Hui Shiqi, "Huangzheng" (Famine administration), in *JSWB* 41:7–9.

169. Will and Wong, 145–46.

170. *PYTOCG* 16:3–5.

Chapter 6

1. Romeyn Taylor, "Chinese Hierarchy in Comparative Perspective," *Journal of Asian Studies* 48.3 (August 1989): 491. The best introduction to Polanyi's theories is George Dalton, ed., *Primitive, Archaic, and Modern Economies: Essays of Karl Polanyi* (Garden City, N.Y.: Anchor Books, 1969); see especially Dalton's introduction, ix–liv. A succinct summary and appraisal of the "substantivist" vs. "formalist" debate appears in Philip B. Curtin, *Cross-Cultural Trade in World History* (Cambridge: Cambridge University Press, 1984), 14.

2. Taylor, "Chinese Hierarchy," 494.

3. Taylor, "Chinese Hierarchy," 500–501.

4. David Strand, *Rickshaw Beijing: City People and Politics in 1920s China* (Berkeley: University of California Press, 1989), 128–29, 256–57.

5. Among countless examples see *PYTOCG* 20:24; *XSYG* 4:1; *CZYG* 2:1; *KCZJ* 7:10–12; *SD* 1:8, 2:4–5, 2:6, 3:5–6.

6. *Wenji* 8:29–33; *Lingui xianzhi* 29:12–15.

7. For the edicts of 1736–37 see Song Xixiang, 78; Kishimoto, "Keizai seisaku," 31. Prominent later examples include edicts of QL 3/1 (*Donghua lu* 7:46), QL 12/12 (*Qianlong shilu* 304:16–18), and QL 13/7 (*Donghua lu* 28:26).

8. Memorial of QL 21/12/30, *QLZZ* 16.217–18; *SD* 1:4–5; *NP* 4:20.

9. *PYTOCG* 12:12, 13:32–34, 15:7, 29:10, 34:28–29.

10. Metzger, *Internal Organization*, 55–56.

11. Memorial of QL 7/6/18, QPA; *PYTOCG* 11:7–9, ll:42–43, 13:28–30; *ZGFJL*, preface; *NP* 5:8; and *JSWB* 53:27–30.

12. *PYTOCG* 17:3.

13. Memorial of QL 7/4, cited in *NP* 4:20.

14. Memorials of QL 7/2/21 and QL 9/3/1, MQA; QL 10, *JSWB* 53:27–30); QL 21/12/3, *QLZZ* 16.217–18.

15. *PYTOCG* 2:32–35, 25:47–49.

16. Memorials of QL 7/6/18 and QL 9/3/1, MQA; *PYTOCG* 2:28, 4:44–45; *SD* 2:18.

17. *SD* 3:10. See also *PYTOCG* 26:1–3; *NP* 4:20, 6:18–19. Concern for preserving the *minli* was also a rationale for the empire-wide tax reduction campaign carried out by the Qianlong emperor at the time of his accesion; see, e.g., the memorial of Xu Wangyu, YZ 13/11/20, cited in Zelin, 267.

18. *PYTOCG* 4:45, 29:14–15; *SD* 1:4.

19. *XSYG* (1769 ed.), 4:12.

20. *PYTOCG* 10:3–18. See also memorial of QL 9/3/1, MQA; *PYTOCG* 26:1–3; *JSWB* 34:50–52.

21. "*Minye*," in this usage, may be a shorthand form of the contemporary idiom "*xiaomin dongye*" (assets of the common people), a phrase that appears, for instance, in a late Kangxi-era memorial cited in Gao Wangling, "Renkou de zengzhang," 26.

22. Letter to Tuo Yong, *SD* 2:5; *PYTOCG* 33:17–22.

23. *PYTOCG* 15:20–23, 20:18–19; Xu Dong, *Muling shu*, 4:25–26.

24. Xiong Yuezhi, *Zhongguo jindai minzhu sixiang shi* (History of modern democratic thought in China) (Shanghai: Renmin chubanshe, 1986), 11.

25. Huang, *Civil Justice*, chap. 4. Melissa Macauley has further argued that the eighteenth-century Qing state actually sought to *harden* private property rights by imposing in civil judgments a concept of fee-simple ownership, in preference to the fragmented tenurial system (e.g., surface and subsurface ownership) found in customary law in many parts of southeastern China. See Macauley, "Civil and Uncivil Disputes in Southeast Coastal China, 1723–1820," in Kathryn Bernhardt and Philip C. C. Huang, eds., *Civil Law in Qing and Republican China* (Stanford: Stanford University Press, 1994), 85–121. Although this was not a consistent focus in Chen Hongmou's own policy, he did seek to enforce hard property rights in Yunnan in 1734 by out-lawing any type of conditional sale of land, or sale with rights of subsequent redemption; *PYTOCG* 2:16.

26. *PYTOCG* 10:3–18.

27. See, e.g., *PYTOCG* 26:1–3, 33:45–47.

28. *PYTOCG* 22:21–22.

29. Memorial of QL 8/8/26, MQA.

30. *PYTOCG* 16:3.

31. *XSYG* (1769 ed.), 4:12.

32. See, e.g., memorial of QL 7/6/18, MQA; *PYTOCG* 21:13; *Wenji* 10:17.

33. My understanding of Locke's views is based on his *Second Treatise of Government*, ed. C. B. Macpherson (Indianapolis: Hackett, 1980). I am also influenced by invocations of Locke's comparative relevance by other historians of Qing economic thought, including Lin Man-houng. See her "A Time When Grandsons Beat Their Grandfathers: The Rise of Liberal Political-Economic Ideas During the Monetary Crisis of Early Nineteenth-Century China," *American-Asian Review* 9.4 (winter 1991): 6–9, where Locke's views are asociated with those of Gong Zizhen.

34. C. B. Macpherson, *The Political Theory of Possessive Individualism: Hobbes to Locke* (London: Oxford University Press, 1962), esp. chap. 5. Macpherson's materialist reading of Locke has invited many criticisms, of which perhaps the most inflluential is James Tully, *A Discourse on Property: John Locke and his Adversaries* (Cambridge: Cambridge University Press, 1980), esp. chap. 6. However, for one such as myself who is interested less in the origins and historical context of Locke's views than in their comparative value, Macpherson and his critics seem fairly reconcilable.

35. Proprietorship for Chen can also be vested in a larger collective entity, such as a lineage or local community. He speaks regularly, e.g., of "public property" (*gongwu*) and also of "state property" (*guanwu*); *PYTOCG* 4:22–25. See my subsequent discussions of community and the public sector in Chapter 11.

36. *PYTOCG* 10:3–18.

37. Ebrey, "Conceptions of the Family," 225–26.

38. *XSYG* 1:12. Compare Gong Zizheng's vesting of strong property rights in the "agricultural patrilineage" (*nongzong*), discussed in Lin Man-houng, "When Grandsons Beat Their Grandfathers," 6–9.

39. See Rowe, "Education and Empire," esp. 424–25.

40. *JSWB* 68:4–6.

41. *XSYG* (1769 ed.), 4:12.

42. *PYTOCG* 4:46.

43. Gao Wangling, "Renkou de zengzhang," 25. Gao is at pains to note, and I would agree, that this recurrent idiom can by no means be taken to imply household self-sufficiency of any "natural economy" variety.

44. *PYTOCG* 33:17.

45. Memorial of QL 19/9/9, *QLZZ* 9.533–34; *PYTOCG* 29:14–15, 32:40–42; *JSWB* 34:50–52.

46. *XSYG* 3:22.

47. *PYTOCG* 37:1–2.

48. The following paragraphs are based on data culled variously from the twenty letters in the *JS* collection.

49. Letter of QL 21/7/25, *JS* 207–9. In the last decade of his life Chen also owned a Beijing townhouse, a gift of the Qianlong emperor that Chen considerably remodeled. The disposition of this property after Chen's retirement and death is unknown; *JS* 211–17.

50. Hongmou told family members that the initial idea to set up a rural estate in Changsha came after he had consulted a diviner, who informed him that doing so would ensure the success of his current project to trace out the Chens' ancestral roots (*xunzu*); letter of QL 29/5/16, *JS* 219–22.

51. At times Chen relies on professional agents (*jingshou*)—in one instance a pawnshop—to run his various estates, but avoids this whenever feasible because it does not allow him the degree of personal managerial oversight he desires.

52. Chen expresses relief that his nephews Chen Zhonglu and Chen Zhongli are both serving as county magistrates in the Xiang River valley because they can be expected to look in personally from time to time on the family's Changsha holdings. He also notes that he will be relying on Qiao Guanglie for market intelligence and advice on land purchase opportunities. Chen, as Shaanxi governor in 1746, had recommended this man for promotion to prefect, and he has now (in 1764) succeeded Chen himself as governor of Hunan. Letter of QL 29/9/11, *JS* 224–28.

53. Chen lays much of this out in a letter of QL 24/7/15, written during his tenure as Jiangsu governor; *JS* 209–11.

54. *PYTOCG* 24:23–24. See also memorial of QL 14/7/5, GCA.

55. *PYTOCG* 19:29–30, 22:9–14.

56. See von Glahn, *Fountain of Fortune*, 153–54.

57. *PYTOCG* 4:43–46, 13:9–14, 19:29–30, 22:9–14.

58. *PYTOCG* 19:23–24.

59. *PYTOCG* 24:23–24.

60. *PYTOCG* 26:2.

61. *PYTOCG* 19:31; *JSWB* 58:4–6.

62. Hans Medick, "Plebeian Culture in the Transition to Capitalism," in Raphael Samuel and Gareth Stedman Jones, eds., *Culture, Ideology, and Politics* (London: Routledge, 1982), 84–113.

63. In English-language scholarship this view informs (and dates) Mary Wright's 1957 classic *The Last Stand of Chinese Conservatism*. For a recent and emphatic restatement of this position by an eminent Taiwanese historian see Li Guoji. For a characterization of Yongzheng-era economic policy in this light see Feng Erkang, chap. 5. Somewhat more surprisingly, the view is echoed in the innovative work of the Wuhan-based scholar Feng Tianyu; see his "Daoguang Xianfeng nianjian jingshi shixue," esp. 145. Even Pierre-Étienne Will, whose work in general highlights several procommercial policies of Qing administrators, sometimes tends to view these as "grudging" exceptions to the prevailing economic logic of the day; see *Bureaucracy and Famine*, 212–23.

64. See Yu Yingshi, *Zhongguo jinshi congjiao lunli yu shangren jingshen* (Modern Chinese religious theory and the mercantile spirit) (Taibei: Lianjing, 1987); Gao Wangling, "Guanyu Kang-Qian shengshi de jige wenti," 21–26; Helen Dunstan, "Wang Yuan's *Pingshu:* A Late Seventeenth-

Century Chinese Utopia," *Papers on Far Eastern History* 35 (March 1987): 31–78; and other works by these same authors. Similar arguments are made, less centrally, in Liu Guangjing, *Jingshi sixiang yu xinxing qiye*, esp. 595–620; Wu Hui and Ge Xianhui, 130–32; and Albert Feuerwerker, "The State and the Economy in Late Imperial China," *Theory and Society* 13.3 (1984): 297–326.

65. For but a few instances of Chen's invoking the "*xushang*" idiom see his memorials of QL 7/2/21 and QL 8/6/28, MQA; and Peng Qifeng, 14:7–8.

66. *XSYG* (1769 ed.), 4:12–13. I am grateful to Gao Wangling for calling this passage to my attention.

67. P. Smith, *Taxing Heaven's Storehouse*, 310–11; Hymes, "Famine Relief," 296–97; Liensheng Yang, "Spending," 69; Lynn A. Struve, "Huang Zongxi in Context: A Reappraisal of His Major Writings," *Journal of Asian Studies* 47.3 (August 1988): 478; Dunstan, "Wang Yuan's *Pingshu*," 62.

68. See, among other accounts, Kishimoto, "Keizai seisaku," 22; Kuroda, "Bichiku kō," 2; Wu Jianyong, 87; Feng Liutang, 250–51; and Will, *Bureaucracy and Famine*, 192.

69. Edict of QL 12/12, *Shilu* 304:16–18.

70. See, e.g., memorial of QL 19/11/18, *QLZZ* 10.105–7.

71. *PYTOCG* 37:1–2. See also the more detailed discussion in my article, "State and Market in Mid-Qing Economic Thought: The Career of Chen Hongmou," *Études chinoises* 12.1 (1993).

72. *XSYG* 4:45–46; *PYTOCG* 12:12–13.

73. Memorials of QL 19/4/28, *QLZZ* 8.138–40); QL 19/inter 4, *Qianlong shilu* 463:17. On the wider context of the Qing social revaluation of merchants see Yu Yingshi, *Shangren jingshen*, 97–104.

74. See, e.g., memorials of QL 14/7/5, GCA; QL 19/10/19 and QL 19/11/18, *QLZZ* 9.810–11, 10.105–7; *PYTOCG* 4:42, 5:43–44, 16:21–23, 35:15–17, 35:27–29; *NP* 3:8, 5:21.

75. *PYTOCG* 4:40–41, 16:21–23, 35:13–14; *NP* 4:7.

76. Memorial of QL 19/4/28, *QLZZ* 8.137; *PYTOCG* 13:2, 13:15, 13:28–30, 16:32–33, 34:50; Yuan Mei, 27:9. For a translation and discussion of one of Chen's directives along these lines see Dunstan, *Conflicting Counsels*, 295–96, 311–12. Based on her reading of this document, Dunstan quite appropriately dubs Chen an "interventionist friend of commerce."

77. Memorial of QL 20/7/28, *QLZZ* 12.220–22; *PYTOCG* 4:1–2, 17:28–29; *NP* 8:21–22; Peng Qifeng.

78. Memorial of QL 19/4/28, *QLZZ* 8.138–40. In his recognition of the economic stimulus provided by foreign trade, as well as in his more general appreciation of the positive economic contribution of merchants, Chen found authority in Qiu Jun's *Daxue yanyi bu*, an abridgment of which he published in 1736; see Brook, *Confusions of Pleasure*, 101–4.

79. See, e.g., memorials of QL 7/2/21 and QL 7/7/1, MQA.

80. *PYTOCG* 25:45.

81. Memorial of QL 19/10/19, *QLZZ* 9.810–11; *PYTOCG* 30:30–32; *NP* 6:19. For the commandist aspects of *zhaoshang*, as frequently implemented, see E-tu Zen Sun, "The Finance Ministry (Hubu) and Its Relation to the Private Economy in Qing Times," in Jane Kate Leonard and John R. Watt, eds., *To Achieve Security and Wealth: The Qing Imperial State and the Economy, 1644–1911* (Ithaca: Cornell University East Asia Program, 1992), esp. 12–14.

82. Memorial of QL 20/7/28, *QLZZ* 12.220–22; *NP* 8:21–22.

83. Memorial of QL 23/3/4, MQA; *NP* 2:20.

84. Donald J. Munro, "The Concept of Interest in Chinese Thought," *Journal of the History of Ideas* 41.2 (1980): 179–97; Taylor, "Chinese Hierarchy," 494.

85. Yu, *Shangren jingshen*, 85–86.

86. On Lu-Wang thought see Yu, *Shangren jingshen*, 93–94. On Ouyang see P. Smith, *Taxing Heaven's Storehouse*, esp. 310–11. On Sima see Bol, "Government, Society, and State," esp. 149. On Dong Wei see Hymes, *Statesmen and Gentlemen*, 164–66; see also the discussion of Dong in Chapter 5 of the present study.

87. Mizoguchi, 25–32; Yu, *Shangren jingshen*, 97–104.

88. Edict of QL 3/6/14, translated in Dunstan, *Conflicting Counsels*, 185–88; see also discussion in Dunstan, 163.

89. Albert O. Hirshman, *The Passions and the Interests: Political Arguments for Capitalism Before Its Triumph* (Princeton: Princeton University Press, 1967).

90. *LJZL* 2:81; *XSYG* 2:36; *ZGYG* 1:65–66; *JS* 243–45.

91. Chen Hongmou, ed., *Sima wenzheng gong quanjia ji*, preface; *XSYG* 2:33. For the context of Sima's remarks see Bol, "Government, Society, and State," 149–56.

92. *Wenji* 8:29–33; *Guitiao huichao*, preface; *NP* 5:16. The famous model was Gu Yanwu, *Tianxia junguo libi shu* (Assets and liabilities of localities throughout the empire), published in 1662.

93. Note that although "*li*" and "*yi*" were frequently used interchangeably to express the notion of "profit," the latter was less strictly materialist in its connotations and was hence more unassailably positive than the former. The Yongzheng emperor picked up on this distinction when he condemned the cultivation of tobacco as "without benefit" (*wuyi*) to society, even as it brought profits (*li*) to the cultivators themselves. Edict of YZ 5, cited in Song Xixiang, 76–77.

94. *LZJL* 2:25. See also *XSYG* (1769 ed.), 4:12; *JSWB* 34:50–52.

95. Memorial of QL 7/2/21, MQA; *PYTOCG* 15:20–23, 34:44–46.

96. *PYTOCG* 19:31–32; also 15:32–34, 22:38–40, 24:32–33.

97. *SD* 1:10.

98. Memorial of QL 23/3/4, MQA. Recall the Qianlong emperor's rationale for restoring internal customs duties on grain at the height of the 1748 dearth: that cost savings from this exemption had in the past been exclusively claimed as merchant profits (*dan li shanggu*) and had brought no benefit to popular livelihoods (*wuyi minsheng*). From the perspective of the throne the two interests were routinely, although perhaps not inevitably, in contradiction. See Feng Liutang, 249.

99. Memorial of QL 27/7, excerpted in *NP* 11:29–30.

100. Memorial of QL 13/5/27, GCA.

101. Memorial of QL 8/6/28, MQA.

102. Memorials of QL 20/7/28 and QL 21/6/29, *QLZZ* 12.220–22, 14.763–65; *NP* 8:21–22, 9:4–5.

103. Memorial of QL 19/9/28, *QLZZ* 9.648–50.

104. Perdue (*Exhausting the Earth*, 235) sees this notion as new in the work of the considerably later scholar Cui Shu (1746–1816).

105. Hartwell, "Historical Analogism," 719–22.

106. *PYTOCG* 12:12–13, 27:16–18; *SD* 2:14, 3:12.

107. Memorials of QL 7/11/24, MQA; QL 21/6/29, *QLZZ* 14.759–60; *PYTOCG* 15:20–23, 16:3–5.

108. Memorial of QL 7/7/1, MQA.

109. Memorial of QL 8/6/28, MQA.

110. *JSWB* 53:30.

111. Memorial of QL 7/12/24, MQA.

112. Yu Sen, 1:5.

113. Letter to Zhuang Zibu, *SD* 3:12.

114. See, e.g., memorial of QL 9/3/1, MQA; *PYTOCG* 4:5–7, 27:5–7.

115. Memorial of QL 21/6/29, *QLZZ* 14.759–60; *PYTOCG* 27:16–18, 28:3–4, 32:40–42, 37:1–2.

116. Letter to Sun Quan, *SD* 1:11.

117. *JSWB* 26:60.

118. *Guitiao huichao*, preface.

119. *PYTOCG* 16:18–20, 37:1–2.

120. Memorial of QL 8/6/28, MQA; *PYTOCG* 7:3–5, 16:26–27.

121. Memorial of QL 20/7/28, *QLZZ* 12.223–26; *PYTOCG* 4:26–32.

122. The best sustained analysis of eighteenth-century monetary history and its relationship

to prices is, in my view, Chen Zhaonan, *Yongzheng Qianlong nianjian de yinqian bijia biandong (1723–1795)* (Fluctuations in the relative value of silver and copper in the Yongzheng and Qianlong eras) (Taibei: Academia Sinica, 1966). See also Endymion Wilkinson, *Studies in Chinese Price History* (New York: Garland, 1980), which is especially useful on the history of bureaucratic price reporting. A typical example of Chen Hongmou's own sophisticated approach to money and prices is his memorial of QL 10, reprinted in *JSWB* 53:27–30.

123. Chen sometimes expresses this concept literally as "market price" (*shijia*) but more often uses the term "current price" (likewise rendered "*shijia*" in romanized form but written with a different first character).

124. *PYTOCG* 15:20–23, 16:3–5.

125. *PYTOCG* 1:40–49; memorial of QL 13/12/10, GCA.

126. *PYTOCG* 3:35–44.

127. *PYTOCG* 8:44–46, 31:25–31.

128. Chen Hongmou, ed., *Wuliao jiazhi zeli* (Regulations governing prices of materials) (1768). At least six of these provincial schedules still survive in libraries worldwide. I have examined two, those for Zhili and Yunnan. The titles, front matter, and formats are identical, with only the types of materials and the prices differing from volume to volume. For a brief but useful discussion of board-set procurement prices (*bujia*) see Zelin, 44.

129. *Wuliao jiazhi zeli* (Zhili), 1:25, 1:34.

130. *Wuliao jiazhi zeli* (Zhili), 1:10.

131. Memorial of QL 7/2/21, MQA; *PYTOCG* 2:54–55; *NP* 2:20; Wei Qingyuan and Lu Su, *Qingdai qianqi de shangban kuangye he zibenzhuyi mengya* (Early Qing merchant-operated mines and the sprouts of capitalism) (Beijing: Chinese People's University Occasional Paper, 1981).

132. *PYTOCG* 2:13–16, 2:32–35.

133. *PYTOCG* 2:2–3, 2:29–30, 3:16–17, 3:40–44, 7:3–5; *NP* 2:7.

134. *PYTOCG* 1:27–28, 2:19–23.

135. Memorial of QL 12/3/7, MQA.

136. Memorial of QL 8/8/26, MQA; *PYTOCG* 24:1–2, 26:16–18, 28:10–11. Chen seems also to have played a role in the gradual Qianlong-era shift from corvée to hired labor along the important military supply routes in the northwest; see Kataoka Kazutada, "Shindai koki Senseisho no sayō ni tsuite" (On corvée in Shaanxi province during the late Qing), *Tōyōshi kenkyū* 44.3 (1985): 1–24.

137. *PYTOCG* 2:2–3.

138. Letter to Feng Guangyu, *SD* 1:8. Note that Chen Hongmou's critique of state purchase at submarket prices had many antecedents, e.g., in the writings of his Song-dynasty heroes Zhen Dexiu and Sima Guang (see de Bary, "Chen Te-hsiu," 373; and P. Smith, *Taxing Heaven's Storehouse*, 237–45). It seems, rather, that the converse of this, the emphasis on the positive virtues of market allocation, was newly characteristic of Chen and his times.

139. For an example see *PYTOCG* 32:6–7.

140. Memorial of QL 18/8/6, *QLZZ* 6.73; *PYTOCG* 2:13–16, 4:1–2, 12:12–13, 33:2–3; *NP* 2:14, 4:7. Note that Chen attacks with even greater regularity local-level officials and yamen functionaries who similarly use their positions of market leverage to manipulate prices in their favor. See, e.g., *PYTOCG* 32:40–42; *NP* 6:8; *Lingui xianzhi* 29:13.

141. Recall as well Chen's 1762 proposal as Jiangsu governor that Liang-Huai salt merchants be allowed to increase their allocated purchases and compete freely for the consumer market of Shaanxi denied them by existing regulation.

142. Memorial of QL 8/6/28, MQA. The emperor agreed in spirit with Chen's proposal but ordered him to work out its practical implementation in conjunction with salt administration officials, who very likely would have had very different ideas on the subject. For Chen's subsequent efforts at a less radical solution in Jiangxi see *PYTOCG* 16:26–27.

143. Memorial of QL 7/2/21, MQA. That the Qianlong emperor took this radical proposal seriously is suggested by the fact that he routed it for discussion, not to the Board of Revenue,

which had dismissed it in the past, but to his highest ministers of state (the so-called nine ministers, *jiuqing*). I have not found their decision recorded, so it is not clear what the direct impact of Chen's memorial was. Yet, as Wei Qingyuan and Lu Su (19–21) have demonstrated, the long-term mid-Qing trend in mining policy was precisely in the direction Chen proposed.

144. Memorial of QL 20/10/5, *QLZZ* 12.597–98.

145. Memorial of QL 20/7/28, *QLZZ* 12.223–26.

146. Memorial of QL 19/10/19, *QLZZ* 9.810–11. Recall that, for similar reasons, Chen also preferred issuance of famine relief in cash.

147. Letter to Zhou Renji, ca. 1741, *SD* 1:15; *NP* 6:8.

148. The identification of the "market principle" as central to physiocratic thought comes from Kaplan, *Provisioning Paris*, 25–29. My understanding of physiocratic thought derives also from Elizabeth Fox-Genovese, *The Origins of Physiocracy: Economic Revolution and Social Order in Eighteenth-Century France* (Ithaca: Cornell University Press, 1976); and Joseph J. Spengler, "Mercantilist and Physiocratic Growth Theory," in Bert F. Hoselitz, ed., *Theories of Economic Growth* (Glencoe: Free Press, 1960), 3–64.

149. Among Western scholars, Helen Dunstan has come closest to associating certain strands of mid-Qing thought with Smithian "economic liberalism." In her most extended published work on the subject, *Conflicting Counsels*, Dunstan expresses due reservations about this characterization but nevertheless, as I read her, falls back on it on more than one occasion. The problem, of course, is that economic discourse in late imperial China did not acknowledge the existence of neatly packaged and labeled economic "theories" or "schools," so *any* attempt by historians to identify such schools, whether or not identified with schools of Western economic thought, is an a posteriori creation.

150. *PYTOCG* 1:40.

Chapter 7

1. See, e.g., memorials of QL 7/7/1 and QL 7/12/21, MQA.

2. For examples of Chen's protecting the state's prerogatives vis-à-vis smugglers in these trades see memorial of QL 23/5/17, MQA; memorial of QL 20/7/28, *QLZZ* 13.99–100; *PYTOCG* 12:12–13, 36:38–40.

3. On saltpeter see *PYTOCG* 23:16–18,

4. Chen argues that the state's obligation to hear civil litigation stems in large part from the threat unmediated disputes pose for loss of property, employment, and productivity (*shiye*). *PYTOCG* 33:45–47.

5. See, e.g., Karjishan and Chen memorial of QL 17/9, *QLZZ* 3.910–11; *PYTOCG* 33:2–3.

6. *NP* 2:14, 4:9, 10:7.

7. Chen was acting, in other words, much like a contemporary public utilities commission. *PYTOCG* 2:56–57, 13:3–4, 13:15, 16:32–33, 26:16–18, 27:1–2.

8. *PYTOCG* 16:26–27.

9. See variously Feng Erkang, 193–203; Bai Xinliang, 136–44; Dai Yi, *Qianlong*, 263–86; and Song Xixiang, 71–84.

10. Gao sums up his views on this issue, which inform much of his work, in his article "Guanyu Kang-Qian shengshi jige wenti."

11. See Chang Chun-ming.

12. See, e.g., memorial of QL 20/7/2, *QLZZ* 12.8–9.

13. Memorial of QL 13/6, excerpted in *Shilu* 316:15–16; memorial of QL 9, *JSWB* 34:50–52. The notion of *dili* was central also to the Yongzheng emperor's major pronouncement on agricultural improvement, his edict of YZ 2/2; Song Xixiang, 76.

14. *PYTOCG* 3:3–4.

15. *PYTOCG* 4:5–7.

16. *PYTOCG* 24:32.

17. Memorial of QL 9/3/1, MQA; see also *PYTOCG* 4:5–7; Xu Dong, *Muling shu*, 9:23–26.

18. Policy question written for the Shanxi provincial examination of YZ 7/7, *Wenji* 9:5–6. Chen here was likely echoing an imperial edict of YZ 1/4; see Song Xixiang, 75.

19. Memorial of QL 93/1, MQA.

20. Perdue, *Exhausting the Earth*, 12. Chen uses this term often, e.g., in his memorial of QL 15/12, excerpted in *NP* 6:34.

21. *PYTOCG* 4:53–57. On Yunnan's population and its relation to newly cultivated land see James Lee, "Food Supply and Population Growth in Southwest China, 1250–1850," *Journal of Asian Studies* 41.4 (August 1982): esp. 720.

22. Memorials of QL 18/11/24 and QL 20/7/2, in *QLZZ* 6.846, 12.8–9; memorial of QL 23/10, extracted in *NP* 10:18.

23. Memorial of QL 13/12/10, GCA; Bai Xinliang, 139; Evelyn S. Rawski, "Agricultural Development in the Han River Highlands," *Ch'ing-shih wen-t'i* 3.4 (1975): 63–81.

24. *JSWB* 34:50–52; *NP* 5:1; Peng Yuxin, 143.

25. *NP* 6:19.

26. Edict of YZ 2/2, cited in Song Xixiang, 76.

27. Memorial of QL 18/11/24, *QLZZ* 6.846; Peng Yuxin, 122–24.

28. *PYTOCG* 4:14–15, 4:39, 4:50–52; *NP* 2:14.

29. Feng Liutang, 159–61; Song Xixiang, 82; Peng Yuxin, 125.

30. *PYTOCG* 19:25–26; *NP* 6:20. As Peng Yuxin demonstrates (129–35), further liberalization was in fact the trend of mid-Qianlong tax policy toward newly cultivated land.

31. Suzuki, 66–96; Peng Yuxin, 138–50; E. Rawski, "Han River Highlands"; Stephen C. Averill, "The Shed People and the Opening of the Yangzi Highlands," *Modern China* 9.1 (January 1983): 84–126; Anne Osborne, "The Local Politics of Land Reclamation in the Lower Yangzi Highlands," *Late Imperial China* 15.1 (June 1994): 1–46.

32. Memorial of QL 20/7/7, *QLZZ* 12.8–9; memorial of QL 6, *JSWB* 28:33–35.

33. Fu, "Capitalism in Chinese Agriculture: On the Laws Governing Its Development," *Modern China* 6.3 (July 1980): 311–16. For specific examples see E. Rawski, "Han River Highlands"; Johanna Meskill, *A Chinese Pioneer Family: The Lins of Wu-feng, Taiwan, 1729–1895* (Princeton: Princeton University Press, 1979), chap. 3.

34. *PYTOCG* 4:53–57, 19:25–26.

35. *PYTOCG* 4:43–46.

36. *NP* 5:11.

37. *PYTOCG* 19:26–28, 24:32–33.

38. Liezhuan 5834, QPA.

39. *PYTOCG* 34:1–2.

40. *PYTOCG* 22:5–8.

41. *PYTOCG* 24:32–33.

42. *NP* 6:34. On Qianlong's increasing willingness over the course of his reign to allow privatization of banner lands see Bai Xinliang, 137–38.

43. See, e.g., memorial of QL 9/3/1, MQA.

44. Edict of YZ 2/2, cited in Song Xixiang, 75–76.

45. Edict of YZ 7/7, cited in Song Xixiang, 77.

46. Chen reformed this program, which he enthusiastically took over from his predecessor Emida, in characteristic ways: by developing a system of tighter reporting and auditing of accounts, by rooting out instances of forced loans (*jiangpai*) by local officials to unwilling borrowers, and by insisting that repayments in grain for loans contracted in cash always be computed at prevailing local prices (*shijia*) rather than according to a predetermined schedule. See memorial of QL 13/12/10, GCA; *PYTOCG* 18:23–24, 23:7–8.

47. *Shilu* entry for QL 32/6, cited in Bai Xinliang, 139.

48. *PYTOCG* 4:53–57, 5:31–40; *NP* 2:20.

49. *NP* 6:19.

50. *SD* 2:8.

51. See, e.g., Liezhuan no. 5834, QPA; *Qingshi gao*, 10559–64; Peng Qifeng 14:9–10; Yuan Mei, 10–11; *Guangxi tongzhi* 260:14–16; *Lingui xianzhi* 29:12–15; and *Guilin jianshi*, 114–15.

52. *NP, juan* 10.

53. Memorials of QL 16/12/29 and QL 17/4/19, in *QLZZ* 2.320–22, 2.697–18; *PYTOCG* 31:34, 32:11–13; Cai Guanluo, 1.146; Peng Qifeng, 14:10.

54. Peng Yuxin, 282–83.

55. On Jiangxi see Liezhuan no. 5834, QPA. On Jiangsu see *JSWB* 106:36–38; Xu Dong, *Muling shu*, 9:23–26. Sources on Chen's other provincial projects will be cited as appropriate below.

56. Memorial of QL 13/6, *Shilu* 316:15–16.

57. Memorial of QL 20/7/2, *QLZZ* 12.8–9.

58. *PYTOCG* 36:26–28.

59. *PYTOCG* 20:13–15.

60. *PYTOCG* 17:3–11, 19:21–40; *JSWB* 106:36–38.

61. See, e.g., *JSWB* 110:28–29.

62. *PYTOCG* 4:26–32, 4:43–46; *NP* 2:14; *JSWB* 106:24–26.

63. Memorial of QL 16/6, cited in Cai Guanluo, 1.146. Also *PYTOCG* 20:13–15, 26:41–42, 29:48–50; *NP* 6:20; *JSWB* 38:16–17. Chen was emboldened by his success in digging irrigation wells to order the digging of several more in the provincial examination hall precincts to provide drinking and washing water for examinees; *PYTOCG* 30:36–37. On Cui Ji see *Zhongguo renming da zidian*, 907.

64. *NP* 7:6; *PYTOCG* 30:25–27.

65. Two memorials, both dated QL 16/8/11, *QLZZ* 1.385–87, 1.389–91; *NP* 7:3, 7:5–6.

66. *PYTOCG* 36:26–28, 36:33–37.

67. Memorial of QL 20/7/2, *QLZZ* 12.8–9.

68. *PYTOCG* 30:23–24, 37:24–27; *JSWB* 114:13–14; *NP* 7:4–5.

69. Letter to Gao Danqi, *SD* 3:11. See also *PYTOCG* 38:2–3; *NP* 4:8; memorial of QL 6/12, cited in Cai Guanluo, 1.144–45.

70. See, e.g., memorial of QL 28/12, cited in Cai Guanluo, 1.149. For a more systematic discussion of Chen's views on assigning sectoral responsibilities within the bureaucracy see Chap. 10.

71. *PYTOCG* 2:2–3.

72. Sources on Chen's policies regarding polders in Jiangxi include his memorial of QL 6/10, *JSWB* 28:33–35; *PYTOCG* 11:44–46, 12:11, 15:17–18, 16:28–29; *NP* 4:27, 4:30, 5:14. For Chen's support of polder building along the Fujian coast in 1752 see his memorial of QL 17/8/26, *QLZZ* 3.684–85.

73. *PYTOCG* 14:39–40.

74. See Peng Yuxin, 171–90.

75. Perdue, *Exhausting the Earth*, 219–21.

76. On Chen's relationship with Jia, dating back to their time together in the Hanlin Academy, see *Wenji* 3:8–11.

77. *PYTOCG* 37:24–27, 38:2–3, 38:54–55; *Shudu* 2:19.

78. Chen's original memorial, dated QL 28/6/13, survives in the *lufu zouzhe* (Grand Council copies of palace memorials) collection, MQA. It is excerpted in Liezhuan no. 5834, QPA; *Lingui xianzhi* 29:14; and Cai Guanluo, 1.148.

79. Wei Yuan, "Huguang shuili lun" (On water conservancy in Huguang), in his *Guwei tang nei waishi* (1878), "Wenji" section, 6:7.

80. Chen, letter to Chan Yan, *SD* 3:18; Wei Yuan, 6:7.

81. Perdue, *Exhausting the Earth*, 228.

82. Chen, *Wenji* 9:5–6.

83. Song Xixiang, 75–76; Bai Xinliang, 136.

84. Zhang's memorial remained sufficiently well known to have been reprinted in the 1826 *JSWB*, 36:17–19. See also Song Xixiang, 78–79.

85. My comments here reflect in part the influence of an unpublished paper by Pierre-Étienne Will, "Of Silk and Sweet Potatoes: Efforts at Improving Agriculture in Eighteenth-Century China," presented to the East Asia Program, Cornell University, October 1991.

86. See, e.g., *PYTOCG* 19:25–30.

87. *JSWB* 10:33–35. The locus classicus for the system of recruiting and rewarding "model farmers" was the *Zhouli*, this being one of many reasons why that work enjoyed such a vogue in Chen's day; it had also been a favored technique of Chen's most direct mentor in agricultural improvement, Zhang Yunsui. See Song Xixiang, 78–79.

88. *ECCP*, 103, 318, 603, 691; Song Xixiang, 78. Both Xu Guangqi (1562–1633) and his follower Chen Zilong (1608–47) stressed increasing agricultural productivity—fully exploiting the capabilities of the land (*dili*)—as the overridingly critical component of economic policy; see von Glahn, *Fountain of Fortune*, 199–202.

89. *PYTOCG* 15:7; *NP* 4:25.

90. See variously Liezhuan no. 5884; *PYTOCG* 4:5–7, 4:43–46, 19:21–40, 24:32–33; *NP* 2:10, 4:11–12; Xu Dong, *Muling shu*, 10:33–35.

91. Feng Liutang, 149.

92. *JSWB* 37:37–39; *PYTOCG* 2:25–26, 2:43–44, 3:3–4, 4:43–46.

93. *XSYG* (1769 ed.), 4:13. On the sweet potato's introduction see Wang, "Food Supply in Eighteenth-Century Fukien," 89.

94. Dai Yi, *Qianlong*, 274–77.

95. *PYTOCG* 20:1, 20:45–48, 22:38–40; *NP* 5:17.

96. Dai Yi, *Qianlong*, 75; E. Rawski, "Han River Highlands," 70, 78, n. 33.

97. The best presentation of quantitative data on this growth is Wu Chengming, "Guonei shichang." The ideological aspects of Qing policy favoring agricultural commercialization are laid out in Gao Wangling, "Renkou zengzhang," 23–30. See also Dai Yi, *Qianlong*, 276–86.

98. Wei Yuan included three key documents from Chen's sericulture initiative in *JSWB* 37:8–13. More recent scholarly treatments include Song Xixiang (writing in the 1930s), 83; Gao Wangling, "Renkou zengzhang," 19–21; and Will, "Of Silk and Sweet Potatoes."

99. *PYTOCG* 35:33, 39:1.

100. *PYTOCG* 19:26–27.

101. Chen also attempted to promote a cotton industry in the province, apparently with negligible success; *PYTOCG* 19:27–28.

102. Several of Yang's philosophical works appear in *Guanzhong congshu*, vol. 11, along with a useful biographical sketch by Zhang Yuanji. Yang Shen's economic thought is discussed in Liu Ts'ui-jung, *Trade on the Han River and Its Impact on Economic Development, c. 1800–1911* (Taipei: Institute of Economics, Academia Sinica, 1980), 116–18; Gao Wangling, "Renkou zengzhang," 16–17, 21; Gao Wangling, *Jingji fazhan he zhengfu zhengce*, 38–45.

103. For an extended analysis of Qing attempts to foster a gender-specific production system in the rural household, which makes passing mention of Chen Hongmou's and Yang Shen's Shaanxi sericulture campaign, see Francesca Bray, *Technology and Gender: Fabrics of Power in Late Imperial China* (Berkeley: University of California Press, 1997), chaps. 5 and 6.

104. Yang Shen, *Binfeng guangyi* (Explication of the "Customs of Bin" chapter of the Book of Songs) (Beijing: Nongye chubanshe, 1962). The *Binfeng guangyi* is also reprinted as *Guanzhong congshu*, vol. 18.

105. *PYTOCG* 21:1.

106. The classic description of this system is Franklin Mendels, "Proto-industrialization: The First Phase of the Industrialization Process," *Journal of Economic History* 32.1 (March 1972): 241–61.

107. *PYTOCG* 19:6–8, 30:32–33, 35:33–34, 39:13–16.

108. *PYTOCG* 20:39.

109. *PYTOCG* 24:18–20, 24:30–31, 39:10–12.
110. Memorial of QL 11/4, excerpted in *NP* 6:11.
111. Bray, 229.
112. *NP* 5:20.
113. *PYTOCG* 21:1, 30:30–32, 35:33–34, 39:1–3.
114. *PYTOCG* 23:14–15.
115. *PYTOCG* 39:1–3; *NP* 9:14–15.
116. *PYTOCG* 39:56–57.
117. Yuan Mei, 10.
118. *PYTOCG* 39:2.
119. Liu Ts'ui-jung, 118–22.
120. *XSYG* (1769 ed.), 4:10–13. I am indebted to Gao Wangling for bringing this passage to my attention.
121. This has significant implications for Chen's social as well as economic thought. It justifies, e.g., the exemption from manual labor for those whose innate intellectual capacities exceed their physical strength. Landlordism, too, finds a tolerated place but only provided that the landlord is both usefully employed (e.g., in the study of practical techniques of social or economic management) and that he remains actively engaged at some level in the ennobling business of farming. This seems to imply a preference for relatively small-scale landholding, and it explicitly rejects absenteeism (in most cases) as socially justified.
122. See, e.g., memorials of QL 7/2/21, MQA; QL 13/5/27, GCA.
123. Wei Qingyuan and Lu Su.
124. Feng Erkang, 203–8; Bai Xinliang, 149–53; Gao Wangling, "Guanyu Qingdai kuangzheng jige wenti" (Some problems concerning mining administration in the Qing), *Qingshi yanjiu* 1993.1, 20–22. The percentages given are drawn from Gao.
125. Gao, "Kuangzheng," 21.
126. Memorial of QL 9/3/1, MQA. This memorial is also excerpted in *JSWB* 34:50–52.
127. *NP* 5:12.
128. Memorial of QL 21/10/20, *QLZZ* 15.799, and two memorials both dated QL 21/12/3, *QLZZ* 16.215–18. On his return to Hunan six years later Chen memorialized to similarly develop the province's sulfur mines. Sulfur's use being principally in munitions, the mines' output would be sold to the state, but Chen argued successfully that mine operators be allowed to market their product to provincial armories beyond Hunan itself. His arguments were based not on the strategic need for sulfur but solely on its potential as a source of livelihoods and profits for Hunanese people. Memorial of QL 27/12, extracted in *NP* 11:34.
129. Memorial and rescript of QL 26/2, excerpted in *NP* 11:14–15.
130. Typical of the many documents relating to Chen's work in this area is *PYTOCG* 36:5–6.
131. Memorial of QL 19/10/19, *QLZZ* 9.810–11.
132. Memorial of QL 19/10/28, *QLZZ* 9.866–68; *NP* 8:11–12. On Davatsi's uprising and the Qing response see *ECCP*, 9; and Thomas J. Barfield, *The Perilous Frontier: Nomadic Empires and China* (Oxford: Basil Blackwell, 1989), 292–94.
133. Chen may have been the first Han official to announce his discomfort at Qianlong's bellicose Inner Asian policies, but others quickly followed suit, and did not get off so lightly. A year after Chen submitted his "secret letter," no less eminent a figure than Grand Councilor Liu Tongxun was dismissed for remonstrating against the expansion of the empire's defense perimeter beyond the border market of Hami. A wave of more elliptical literati protests followed. Although Chen subsequently received imperial honors for managing logistical support for the campaign, a fed-up Qianlong in 1748 observed that "as a Chinese, he is not particularly good" at military matters. See Will, "The 1744 Annual Audits," 40. On the broader resistance of Han officials to military adventures in Inner Asia see James A. Millward, *Beyond the Pass: Commerce, Ethnicity, and Empire in Qing Xinjiang, 1759–1864* (Stanford: Stanford University Press, 1998), chap. 1.

134. Memorial of QL 19/11/18, *QLZZ* 10.104–5. The Qianlong emperor generally approved Chen's memorial, chiding him only for using the politically incorrect term *barbarian* when he ought to have used *Mongol.* Although the lapse on Chen's part was clearly unfortunate and avoidable, one cannot help feeling that the emperor relished this chance to rebuke his subordinate, who had so recently nagged him to take the course of peaceable ethnic relations. Quite possibly, Chen's repeated throwing of Yongzheng formulations in Qianlong's face irked the emperor as well.

135. See, e.g., *PYTOCG* 36:19–22, 36:29–32.

136. Peter C. Perdue, "The Qing State and the Gansu Grain Market, 1739–1864," in Thomas Rawski and Lillian Li, eds., *Chinese History in Economic Perspective* (Berkeley: University of California Press, 1992), 100–125.

137. Memorial of QL 20/7/28, *QLZZ* 12.223–26. The parallel with Chen's efforts to open the Southeast Asian trade to oceangoing Chinese merchants (see Chap. 5) is obvious.

138. *NP* 8:22; Cai Guanluo, 1.147.

139. The long-term fulfillment of Chen's dream of commercial integration of Xinjiang is the story told in Millward.

140. A trenchant depiction of the situation during these few critical years, from the Western perspective, is found in Earl H. Pritchard, *Anglo-Chinese Relations During the Seventeenth and Eighteenth Centuries* (Urbana: University of Illinois Press, 1929), 126–34.

141. *PYTOCG* 42:10–12.

142. See, e.g., Hsu, *The Rise of Modern China*, 186, for a standard description of this "tribute mentality" with regard to the Canton trade.

143. For the composition of the Sino-Western trade as of 1751 see table in Pritchard, 123.

144. Lan's 1724 letter is cited and analyzed in Will, "Market-Place and Market Principle."

145. Memorial of QL 32/11, extracted in *NP* 12:20–21.

Chapter 8

1. This is demonstrated eloquently and persuasively, in my view, in Gao Wangling, *Jingji fazhan he zhengfu zhengce,* and in several of Gao's other writings.

2. See, e.g., memorials of QL 13/8/25, QL 13/10/1, QL 14/1/7, and QL 14/4/29, all GCA.

3. Will and Wong, *Nourish the People.*

4. Memorial of QL 7/4, excerpted in *NP* 4:20.

5. Letter to De Songru, *SD* 2:5; letter to Guangxi governor, *JSWB* 16:35.

6. For the classical locus of "*cangfu yumin*" in the *Liji* and the *Mencius* see Dunstan, *Conflicting Counsels,* 151.

7. *PYTOCG* 22:9–14, 24:23–24.

8. Letter to Sun Quan (1740), *SD* 1:11.

9. Letter to Yinjishan (1739), *SD* 1:7.

10. Memorial of QL 5/8/22, MQA. Although Chen's usage of the idiom in defense of private mining in the 1740s was clearly stretching its meaning, it is worth noting that when the Qing court finally got around to eliminating all mining prohibitions a century later, it did so on the grounds that this action represented "*cangfu yumin.*" See Lin Man-houng, "When Grandsons Beat Their Grandfathers," 16.

11. Edict of QL 3/1, *Donghua lu,* Qianlong reign, 7:46.

12. Memorial of QL 11/5, *NP* 6:5; letter to Jia Yuanmo (1747), *SD* 2:13.

13. Will and Wong, 40. See also Wu Hui and Ge Xianhui, 125.

14. *Da Qing huidian shili* 189:3; *Jiangxi tongzhi* 88:2; Suzuki, 30–31; Kishimoto, "Keizai seisaku," 24–25.

15. Quan and Kraus, *Mid-Ch'ing Rice Markets and Trade*; Wang, "Food Supply," 106; Perdue, "Gansu," 101–6.

16. Memorials of QL 19/9/9 and QL 20/3/7, *QLZZ* 9.533–34, 10.854–55.

17. Chen makes this functional distinction clear in his programmatic memorial of QL

5/8/22, MQA. An example of his effort to keep ENG stocks out of seed-grain loan programs is seen in his memorial of QL 13/12/10, GCA. Chen's use of ENG grain for seed loans in emergencies, as well as his distaste for doing so, is revealed in his memorial of QL 17/3/4, *QLZZ* 2.366–67. We have no clear idea what percentage of all ENG disbursals were made in the form of seed loans on an empire-wide basis, but probably it was a substantial minority.

18. *Qinding shoushi tongkao* 55:14. See also Will and Wong, 496.

19. An example of Chen's active efforts to have ENGs turn a profit and serve as a growth-oriented investment is seen in his memorial of QL 18/2, extracted in *NP* 7:18. His reluctant use of ENG stocks for relief purposes in extremis is seen in his memorial (joint with Karjishan) of QL 17/9, *QLZZ* 3.910–11.

20. Memorial of QL 11/5, excerpted in *NP* 6:5.

21. Yamamoto Susumu, "Shindai zenkai no heichō seisaku" (*Pingtiao* policy in the early Qing), *Shirin* 71.5 (1988): 38–70; Kuroda, "Bichiku kō," 1–28.

22. *Qinding shoushi tongkao* 55:14.

23. See, e.g., Chen's memorial of QL 17/7/16, *QLZZ* 3.389–90.

24. Memorial of QL 21/6/9, *QLZZ* 14.759–60; *PYTOCG* 32:6–7, 38:9–11.

25. Edict of QL 7, excerpted in *Da Qing huidian shili* 189:18–19; memorial of QL 10, *JSWB* 40:19–20.

26. Kuroda, "Bichiku kō," 1–28; Will and Wong, 193.

27. Memorials of YZ 9/8/12, *YZZZ* 18.661–63; QL 13/10/1 and QL 13/12/10, GCA; QL 17/5/28, QL 17/7/16, and QL 17/9, *QLZZ* 3.207–8, 3.389–90, 3.910–11); *PYTOCG* 34:44–46, 38:9–11; Perdue, "Gansu," 105. For a general discussion of the Qing consensus on regional ENG needs see Will and Wong, 191.

28. See, e.g., memorial of QL 13/10/1, GCA; *PYTOCG* 27:11.

29. For the evolving imperial policy on granary stocking see *Da Qing huidian shili* 189:3–9. For Chen's actions see memorials of QL 13/12/110 and QL 14/10/2, GCA; *PYTOCG* 16:18–20, 16:24–25; *NP* 6:33; Cai Guanluo, 1.147.

30. This is the theme, for instance, of the classic study of the institution, Xu Daling's *Qingdai juanna zhidu* (The system of sales of degrees and ranks in the Qing period), special issue of *Yanjing xuebao*, 1950.

31. Edict of QL 3/1, *Donghua lu*, Qianlong reign, 7:46. See also *Da Qing huidian shili* 189:9; Wu Hui and Ge Xianhui, 126; Will and Wong, 27–30.

32. *PYTOCG* 15:12.

33. Memorial of YZ 9/8/12, *YZZZ* 18.661–63; *PYTOCG* 18:6–8.

34. Memorials of QL 7/9 and QL 8/11, excerpted in *NP* 4:26, 5:10; memorial of QL 8/intercalary 4, excerpted in Cai Guanluo, 1.145; *PYTOCG* 15:9–12.

35. Edict of QL 3/1, *Donghua lu*, Qianlong reign, 7:46.

36. *PYTOCG* 15:9–12.

37. Edict of QL 8/4/1, *Shilu* 189:1–3.

38. Yinjishan and Chen, memorial of QL 8/12/16, MQA.

39. *PYTOCG* 16:19.

40. See, e.g., Wang, "Food Supply," 107.

41. Alexander Woodside, "The Divorce Between the Political Center and Educational Creativity in Late Imperial China," in Elman and Woodside, 474, 480.

42. Memorial of QL 12/8/24, GCA.

43. Edict of QL 14/3, *Shilu* 330:33–35; Will and Wong, 51–52, 226.

44. Memorial of QL 15/4, extracted in *NP* 6:33; memorial of QL 16/4, extracted in Cai Guanluo, 1.146.

45. Edict of QL 12/12, *Shilu* 304:16–18.

46. Edict of QL 3/1, *Donghua lu*, Qianlong reign 7:43; *Da Qing huidian shili* 189:8–9.

47. Edict of QL 8/4/1, *Shilu* 189:1–3. As Kishimoto Mio has shown, the imperial doubts were at least in part occasioned by a concerted campaign on the part of a so-called Zhejiang party

(Zhejiang governor Lu Zhuo and censors Sun Hao and Xu Yisheng, both Zhejiang natives), which represented lower Yangzi consumer interests and favored a strictly market-oriented approach to provisioning; Kishimoto, "Keizai seisaku," 24.

48. Edict of QL 12/12, *Shilu* 304:16–18; *Da Qing huidian shili* 190:3. An English translation of the most pertinent portions of this edict appears, in the context of Hunan governor Yang Xifu's memorial in reply, in Dunstan, *Conflicting Counsels*, 279–91.

49. The responses are surveyed systematically in Gao Wangling, "Yige wei wanjie de changshi," 22–24; Kishimoto, "Keizai seisaku," 25; and Yamamoto, 63–64. Most are extracted in *Shilu*, *juan* 307–23. The response of Yang Xifu, a particularly detailed analysis of the causes of inflation that concludes by calling for somewhat lowered granary quotas, may be found in *JSWB* 39:21–25, and in English translation in Dunstan, *Conflicting Counsels*, 279–91. As Quan Hansheng, Kishimoto, and Gao each observe, the fact that none of the respondents identified such factors as increased money supply (due to silver imports) or increased velocity of commodity circulation as potential causes of inflation suggests the relative weakness of eighteenth-century Chinese price theory.

50. Although there may well have been sound reasons of economic geography for Yinjishan and Yang Xifu to submit memorials essentially validating Qianlong's own preconceptions, the 1748 granary debate was likely one instance in which policy and personal politics were unusually tightly intertwined. At the very moment that their policy input was being sought on this controversial issue, both men were among the prime targets of a witch-hunt being conducted by the emperor to purge officials who had dared violate dictates of mourning ritual following the death of his beloved empress. How high the stakes were in this campaign—which the emperor came to see as a test of personal loyalty (perhaps especially for Yongzheng-era holdover officials)—was revealed in the death sentence imposed in December on Zhou Xuejian, a high field official, previous Qianlong favorite, and *tongnian* of both Yinjishan and Chen Hongmou in the metropolitan examination of 1723. That Chen himself was not implicated in the mourning ritual scandal may have allowed him the relative latitude to express a policy position contrary to the emperor's own views on the granary issue (although, it will be recalled from Chapter 2, he *was* currently under impeachment by his superior Qingfu on an unrelated matter). On the mourning scandal see Norman Kutcher, "The Death of the Xiaoxian Empress: Bureaucratic Betrayals and the Crises of Eighteenth-Century Chinese Rule," *Journal of Asian Studies* 56.3 (August 1997): 708–25.

51. For discussions of these riots see Quan Hansheng, "Qianlong shisan nian de migui wenti," 552; and Kishimoto, "Keizai seisaku," 19–20.

52. Edict of QL 13/7, *Donghua lu*, Qianlong reign 28:26.

53. Edict of QL 14/3, *Shilu* 330:33–35. The new province-by-province quotas are recorded in *Da Qing huidian shili* 190:3–5. The calculation of an aggregate 30 percent reduction is Will's, *Bureaucracy and Famine*, 193.

54. See, e.g., Will and Wong, 276–78, 501; Yamamoto, 65; Kuroda, 5.

55. Gao Wangling, "Yige weiwanjie de changshi"; Kishimoto, "Keizai seisaku," 28–29; Dunstan, introduction to *Conflicting Counsels*; Wu Jianyong, "Shangpin liang zhengce." Gao makes somewhat more modest claims for the significance of this decision in his subsequent work, *Jingji fazhan he zhengfu zhengce*, 136–48.

56. Memorial of QL 13/9/20, MQA; two memorials both dated QL 13/10/1, GCA; *NP* 6:22.

57. Memorial of QL 14/10/2, CGA.

58. Memorial of QL 13/6, extracted in *Shilu* 316:15–16.

59. Memorial of QL 7/9, *Shilu* 175:30–32.

60. See, e.g., Karjishan and Chen memorial of QL 17/9, *QLZZ* 3.910–11; *PYTOCG* 38:9–11; *NP* 7:2, 7:16.

61. For a general discussion of Qing policy toward *paimai* see Will and Wong, 168–69, 173–74.

62. *Shilu* 189:1–3; *Da Qing huidian shili* 191:1–5. According to Kuroda (p. 14), it was only

in 1799, after the death of the retired Qianlong emperor, that his successor Jiaqing once and for all removed the idea of repurchase of grain on the locality's own markets (*jiudi maibu*) as a stated desideratum of ENG practice.

63. Memorial of QL 5/8/22, MQA; memorials of QL 13/10/1, QL 14/7/5, and QL 14/10/2, GCA; memorial of QL 17/5/28, *QLZZ* 3.207–8; *PYTOCG* 15:20–23, 16:18–20, 24:21–22, 29:3; *NP* 5:22.

64. As with many memorials that triggered sweeping changes in imperial policy during the Qianlong reign, Gao Bin's memorial was probably solicited at least indirectly by the throne itself. A Han bannerman who had grown up as a personal servant within the imperial household, Gao (1683–1755) had by 1751 achieved a solid reputation as a specialist on fiscal matters and on Yellow River flood control but seems to have not previously taken a high profile position on granary or more general provisioning issues. See *ECCP*, 412–13.

65. Edict of QL 17/7, *Shilu*, Qianlong reign, 418:13–19.

66. Karjishan and Chen, memorial of QL 17/9, *QLZZ* 3.910–11. The memorial is also excerpted in *NP* 7:16 and in *Shilu* 418:18–19. In the latter source Karjishan is not mentioned as an originator, suggesting that the inclusion of the Min-Zhe governor-general's name on the original was a mere formality.

67. *PYTOCG* 32:25–26, 32:40–42, 33:4–5, 34:44–46.

68. This and the following paragraphs are based on Chen, memorial of QL 17/7/16, *QLZZ* 3.389–90; Karjishan and Chen, memorial of QL 18/8/6, *QLZZ* 6.80–81; *PYTOCG* 32:40–42; and *NP* 7:21–22. See also Kuroda, 17.

69. Memorials of QL 19/7/9 and QL 20/3/7, *QLZZ* 9.533–34, 10.854–55.

70. Memorials of QL 20/10/5 and QL 20/11/27, *QLZZ* 12.597–98, 13.99–100.

71. Memorial of QL 21/6/29, *QLZZ* 14.759–60; *PYTOCG* 38:9–11, 38:12–14, 38:26; *NP* 9:5–6.

72. *Shilu* 330:33–35; *Da Qing huidian shili* 189:17–19; *Qinding fuhui quanshu* 54:6–7.

73. *PYTOCG* 18:9–11, 29:22–24, 31:18–20.

74. Will and Wong, 412.

75. Memorial of QL 5/8/22, MQA; *NP* 3:19–20.

76. Memorials of QL 7/9, *Shilu* 175:30–32; QL 17/7/16 and QL 21/9/29, *QLZZ* 3.389–90, 15.435–36; *PYTOCG* 26:14–15, 27:8, 31:18–20.

77. *PYTOCG* 19:9–11, 27:8, 27:22–24.

78. Memorials of QL 13/8/25, QL 14/1/7, and QL 14/4/29, GCA.

79. See, e.g., memorial of QL 17/3/4, *QLZZ* 2.366–67.

80. *PYTOCG* 19:9–11, 31:18–20.

81. *PYTOCG* 15:28–29; memorial of QL 17/5/28, *QLZZ* 3.207–8.

82. *JSWB* 40:19–20.

83. *PYTOCG* 36:1–2.

84. Wu Hui and Ge Xianhui, 127.

85. Edict of QL 7, *Da Qing huidian shili* 191:4.

86. Along these lines, Chen also stressed that, even while government granaries were dumping their holdings at off-price, private grain sellers should not be impeded from simultaneously selling at whatever the market would command. *PYTOCG* 32:7.

87. Chen's most sustained discussion of *pingtiao* price policy appears in his early memorial of QL 5/8/22, MQA. For his subsequent adaptations to provincial realities see *PYTOCG* 15:28–29, 19:9–11, 32:6–7.

88. Memorial of QL 17/3/4, *QLZZ* 2.366–67.

89. Chen nowhere specifies whether by "landed" (*youdi*) he means to restrict eligibility for ENG loans to titular owners of land, to the exclusion of leaseholders. It seems fairly clear that he did not, because, as we shall see below, he did explicitly authorize loans of *shecang* grain to renters. Chen's primary criterion was a demonstrated capacity to use the loan to produce more grain and hence to repay the loan, and this condition was met equally by both groups.

90. Memorial of QL 13/12/10, GCA; memorial of QL 16/6, in Cai Guanluo, 1.146.

91. *PYTOCG* 20:34–35.

92. Memorial of QL 14/7/5, GCA; *PYTOCG* 8:11–14, 22:1–2, 29:14–15. In Shaanxi in 1749 Chen suggested a figure of 80 percent of past defaults that must be repaid before eligibility for future loans might be restored, but he added that this standard should be implemented flexibly in light of local harvest conditions; *PYTOCG* 29:22–24.

93. *JSWB* 40:19–20; *PYTOCG* 18:25–26, 19:14–15, 23:1–4, 24:12–15, 24:25, 29:22–24, 31:18–20, 39:4–6; *NP* 6:1.

94. *SD* 2:19; *PYTOCG* 31:18–20, 36:1–2.

95. Memorial of QL 13/10/1, GCA.

96. *PYTOCG* 18:6–20, 19:1–3, 29:3–4.

97. *NP* 7:18.

98. *PYTOCG* 32:6–7.

99. von Glahn, "Community and Welfare," 221–34; de Bary, "Chen Te-hsiu," 374; Dong Wei, in Yu Sen, 1:1–3.

100. Feng Erkang, 202; David D. Buck, "Imperially Inspired Philanthropy in the Ch'ing: The Case of Granaries in the Eighteenth Century," *Bulletin of the Institute of Modern History* (Academia Sinica) 11 (1982): 225–50.

101. *NP* 2:8; *CZYG* 2:68–70.

102. Iemura Shiseo, "Shindai shasō seido kenkyū josetsu" (A preliminary study of the Qing granary system), *Mindaishi kenkyū* 11 (1983): 8–9.

103. For the Kangxi and Yongsheng edicts see *Qinding shoushi tongkao* 56:13–15. For discussion see Feng Liutang, 184–86; and Feng Erkang, 202–3.

104. *PYTOCG* 17:47–53, 19:21–40. See also Will and Wong, 37–39.

105. Buck, "Imperially Inspired Philanthropy."

106. Will and Wong, 404–9.

107. *PYTOCG* 13:44–45.

108. See, e.g., the four documents by Yan on *shecang* administration reprinted by Wei in *JSWB* 40:35–46. Chen Hongmou, too, readily acknowledged the importance of his contemporary's contributions to the development of the community granary system; see his memorial of QL5/8/22, MQA; and *PYTOCG* 25:27–29, 25:32–33.

109. Examples would include memorials of YZ 12/4 and QL 7/2, excerpted in *NP* 2:7 and 4:14; memorial of QL 8/3/28, *QLZZ* 5.2; and memorial of QL 21/9/29, *QLZZ* 15.435–36. For samples of his provincial regulatory codes see *PYTOCG* 14:43–48 (Jiangxi) and 33:17–22 (Fujian).

110. *Yunnan tongzhi* (1736) 29.6:52–54; *Jiangxi tongzhi* (1880) 58:3–4; Hsiao, 170–73; Will and Wong, 65, 404–9, 440–41.

111. *NP* 4:28. A letter home from Beijing in 1765 finds Grand Secretary Chen debating with family members the wisdom of relocating the township *shecang* and the process of selecting a new manager for it; letter of QL 30/11/1, *JS* 235–37.

112. Will and Wong, 305; Feng Liutang, 175–80.

113. Memorial of QL 19/12/1, *QLZZ* 10.385–86.

114. Mingde, memorial of QL 29/9/12, cited in Will, *Bureaucracy and Famine*, 204.

115. *PYTOCG* 29:14–15.

116. Memorial of QL 21/9/29, *QLZZ* 15.435–36.

117. Memorial of QL 5/8/22, MQA.

118. *PYTOCG* 22:9–14, 33:17.

119. Memorial of QL 5/8/21, MQA.

120. *PYTOCG* 33:10–16, 34:42–43, 38:18–26.

121. Memorial of QL 16/4/7, MQA; *PYTOCG* 13:44–45, 14:43–48, 16:38–40, 22:17–18, 29:11–13.

122. *PYTOCG* 13:9–14, 33:17–22, 37:45–49, 38:18–26.

123. *PYTOCG* 13:44–45, 27:9–10; *JSWB* 40:19–20; Iemura, 13–14.
124. *Qinding shoushi tongkao* 56:14; Feng Erkang, 202.
125. *NP* 6:3; *PYTOCG* 26:27–29; memorial of QL 21/9/29, *QLZZ* 15.435–36.
126. For a detailed schedule of official rewards Chen offered to *shecang* donors in one province (Jiangxi) see *PYTOCG* 14:43–48.
127. It was for reasons of moral instruction, as much as for practical ones, that he advocated sentencing those convicted of minor criminal offences to contribute an appropriate amount to their local community granary; *PYTOCG* 14:45.
128. *PYTOCG* 22:9–14.
129. *PYTOCG* 13:4–14.
130. Memorial of YZ 13, reprinted in *Yunnan tongzhi* (1736), 29 *xia*:52–54; memorial of QL 5/8/22, MQA; Will and Wong, 440–41.
131. Memorial of QL 21/9/29, MQA; *NP* 3:20–21, 4:14.
132. Feng Erkang, 203. On the *haoxian* more generally see Zelin.
133. Edict of YZ 7/6/26, cited in *PYTOCG* 17:47–53. See also *PYTOCG* 19:29–30, 22:9–14, 29:11–13; Feng Erkang, 208–9.
134. von Glahn, "Community and Welfare," 221–23, 238. As Hymes and Schirokauer point out (22–23), this de-governmentalization had several other institutional parallels in the Song neo-Confucian statecraft repertoire, such as the founding of private academies as an alternative to state-run local schools, and the establishment of "community compacts" (*xiangyue*) in preference to coercive *baojia* public security mechanisms.
135. *PYTOCG* 19:29–32, 22:9–14, 33:17–22.
136. *PYTOCG* 18:47.
137. Memorial of QL 21/9/29, *QLZZ* 15.435–36.
138. Such cooperative credit societies of course did exist in the Qing and, in the hands of other officials, might even be analogized to the *shecang* movement. See, e.g., the chartering by Yan Sisheng of a collective "merchant granary" (*shangcang*) in the middle Yangzi commercial city of Hankou, the assets of which were explicitly identified as the exclusive property of founding subscribers. *JSWB* 40:15–16.
139. *PYTOCG* 14:44.
140. *PYTOCG* 13:13–14.
141. As shown by work in progress by Michael Szonyi and others, "*she*" in ancient times referred to animistic spirits of the soil, which were gradually anthropomorphized. These tutelary deities were worshiped at altars that became emblematic of their surrounding agrarian communities. During the late imperial era, usage of the term evolved, in highly complex and regionally varied ways, to refer to units of local administration and taxation, cult communities both officially sanctioned and not, and numerous types of private association—foreshadowing the term's appropriation as part of the late Qing neologism "*shehui*," or "society." David Johnson has found territorial "*she*" to have survived well into the twentieth century, as units of organization and finance for the great multivillage ritual operas typical of portions of northern China ("Local Officials and 'Confucian' Values in the Great Temple Festivals [*Sai*] of Southeastern Shansi in Late Imperial Times" [paper presented to the Conference on State and Ritual in East Asia, June–July 1995]). It was evidently these sorts of active units that Chen encountered in Shaanxi.
142. *PYTOCG* 19:29–30, 29:11–13, 33:17–22. Linking *shecang* with preexisting *xiangyue* communities was not a tactic original with Chen; it had been tried in the mid-Ming, e.g., by the governor of drought-stricken Shaanxi province, Wang Tingxiang. See Joseph McDermott, "Emperor, Elites, and Commoners: The Community Pact Ritual in the Late Ming" (paper presented to the Conference on Ritual and the State in East Asian History, Paris, June 1995).
143. *PYTOCG* 14:43–48. As Szonyi shows, it was common throughout late imperial times for lineage units to hegemonize local society by appropriating worship of communal *she* deities as part of their own ancestral rites.
144. Feng Erkang, 202; Feng Liutang, 208.

145. As we shall see in Chapter 11, Chen sought through such means as selecting *shezhang* as honorees for the community libationer ceremony (*xiangyin jiuli*) to further buttress the granary manager's local prestige and legitimacy.

146. See variously memorial of QL 5/8/22, MQA; *PYTOCG* 4:22–25, 14:43–48, 22:8–14, 25:27–29, 33:17–22. The fact that so many scholars studying the institution of *shezhang* (e.g., Feng Liutang, Hsiao Kung-ch'uan, and Iemura Shiseo) rely on Chen Hongmou's testimony for descriptions of the institution's functioning suggests that, if he was not personally responsible for working out these details, he was at least more *interested* in their successful operation than were many of his contemporaries.

147. *PYTOCG* 38:18–26. See also *PYTOCG* 13:9–14, 22:9–14; *NP* 3:20–21, 5:15.

148. *PYTOCG* 17:47–53.

149. For one of Chen's such reports see his memorial of QL 16/12/29, *QLZZ* 2.319.

150. See, e.g., *PYTOCG* 34:6–7, 37:45–49; *NP* 5:15, 6:12.

151. *PYTOCG* 33:10–16, 43:24–27.

152. See, e.g., *PYTOCG* 18:18–20, 26:35.

153. See, e.g., *PYTOCG* 20:34–35.

154. *PYTOCG* 18:47, 19:29–30.

155. *Qinding shoushi tongkao* 56:15; *PYTOCG* 4:24–25.

156. This at least is the reading of Chen given in Iemura, 16. The really intriguing thing is that, even in relatively remote Shaanxi where this passage from Chen was written, he assumes the rural producer to be so deeply bound into a monetized market economy that this price differential is meaningful.

157. See, e.g., *PYTOCG* 14:45–46, 18:47, 25:27, 32:28.

158. Bol, *This Culture of Ours*, 247–51. See also P. Smith, *Taxing Heaven's Storehouse*, 113–18, 128, 239.

159. Yang, "Economic Justification for Spending," 59.

160. Edict of QL 13/7, *Donghua lu*, Qianlong reign, 28:26; edict of QL 17/7/8, cited in Karjishan and Chen memorial of QL 17/9, *QLZZ* 3.910–11; edict of QL 8/4/1, *Shilu* 189:1–3.

161. Yang, "Economic Justification for Spending," 72–74.

162. Dunstan has noted this as well in *Conflicting Counsels*, 152, 164. For Chen Hongmou's awkward relationship to Wang Anshi's legacy see Chap. 4, above.

163. Letter to De Songru (ca. 1744), *SD* 2:5. For a translation of the *JSWB* redaction of Chen's several letters in defense of growth-oriented state spending see Dunstan, *Conflicting Counsels*, 188–91.

164. *Guitiao huichao*, preface.

Chapter 9

1. *PYTOCG* 16:10–12, 19:31; *XSYG* 1:8; *SD* 1:15; *Wenji* 1:18–19.

2. *PYTOCG* 19:23; *XSYG*, preface.

3. *PYTOCG* 11:25. For other instances of Chen's division of people into good and bad see *PYTOCG* 10:1–2, 18:25–26, 19:34; *SD* 2:4. As the passage quoted suggests, Chen sees the utility of this distinction as greatest in the administration of justice: the goal of hearing legal cases is to punish "bad people" and to protect and vindicate "good people."

4. See F. Chen.

5. *PYTOCG* 10:19–22, 24:38–44.

6. *PYTOCG* 19:37–38.

7. Chen, memorial of QL 12/8/24, GCA.

8. *PYTOCG* 24:38–44, 32:8–9.

9. *XSYG* 1:12–13.

10. *JNYG* 3:1–3.

11. *CZYG* 1:5–8; letter to Ling Shisong, *SD* 1:14.

12. *PYTOCG* 3:14–15.

13. For but a few examples see memorials of QL 19/11/8 and QL 220/7/28, *QLZZ* 10.105–7, 12.223–26; *PYTOCG* 1:33, 34:51–52.

14. See, e.g., *PYTOCG* 21:36–37; and *SD* 1:15.

15. Yongzheng emperor, *Dayi juemi lu* (1730; (reprint, Taibei: Wenhai, 1969), esp. 1:1–3. This document and the political circumstances that occasioned it have been discussed briefly in a number of studies by Pamela Crossley, including, most recently, *The Manchus* (Oxford: Basil Blackwell, 1997).

16. *PYTOCG* 2:13; *QLZZ* 12.223.

17. Vermillion endorsement on memorial of QL 19/11/18, *QLZZ* 10:107.

18. Frank Dikötter, *The Discourse of Race in Modern China* (Stanford: Stanford University Press, 1992). Pamela Crossley has raised several thoughtful and troubling considerations regarding the use of the analytical categories "race" and "ethnicity" in her article, "Thinking About Ethnicity in Late Imperial China," *Late Imperial China* 11.1 (June 1990): 1–35. What I gain from both Dikötter and Crossley, above all, is the recognition that these categories are themselves historical discursive constructs rather than descriptions of empirical fact.

19. *Guitiao huichao* 2:65.

20. *PYTOCG* 34:51–52.

21. *Guitiao huichao* 2:65–73; *PYTOCG* 21:36–37. On southwestern populations see *PYTOCG* 2:25–26.

22. Letter to Turbina, *SD* 3:14; Yan Ruyi, *Miaofang beilan* (Conspectus of the Miao campaigns) (1843), 22:21.

23. *Wenji* 1:18–19.

24. Taylor's most explicit articulations of these ideas appear in his articles "Chinese Hierarchy in Comparative Perspective" and "Official and Popular Religion."

25. Jing Junjian, *Qingdai shehui de jianmin dengji*, esp. 1–39; Jing, "Hierarchy in the Qing Dynasty," *Social Sciences in China* 1982.1, 156–92.

26. For but a few examples of this large literature see Ye Xian'en, *Ming Qing Huizhou nongcun shehui yu dianpu zhi* (The rural society of Ming-Qing Huizhou and its servile tenancy system) (Hefei: Anhui renmin chubanshe, 1983); Wei Qingyuan, Wu Qiyan, and Lu Su, *Qingdai nupi zhidu* (The Qing bondservant system) (Beijing: Renmin daxue chubanshe, 1982); and Jing Junjian, *Qingdai shehui de jianmin dengji*.

27. A somewhat arbitrary selection of examples might include Suzuki, 37–45; Timothy Brook, "Funerary Ritual and the Building of Lineages in Late Imperial China," *Harvard Journal of Asiatic Studies* (1989): 470–71; Craig Clunas, *Superfluous Things: Material Culture and Social Status in Early Modern China* (Cambridge: Polity Press, 1991); and Richard von Glahn, "The Enchantment of Wealth: The God *Wutong* in the Social History of Jiangnan," *Harvard Journal of Asiatic Studies* 51.2 (1991): 651–714.

28. See, e.g., Brokaw, *Ledgers of Merit*, 157–65, 203–7; Susan Mann, "Grooming a Daughter for Marriage: Brides and Wives in the Mid-Ch'ing Period," in Rubie S. Watson and Patricia Buckley Ebrey, eds., *Marriage and Inequality in Chinese Society* (Berkeley: University of California Press, 1991), esp. 205; and Mann, "Education of Daughters."

29. Mann, "Grooming a Daughter," 214; and Mann, "Education of Daughters," 21–22.

30. *PYTOCG* 19:33; see also *SD* 2:6; and *XSYG* 4:43.

31. Philip A. Kuhn, "Chinese Views of Social Classification," in James L. Watson, ed., *Class and Social Stratification in Post-Revolution China* (Cambridge: Cambridge University Press, 1984), 21.

32. *XSYG* 1:12; *JNYG* 3:8, 3:22; *CZYG* 1:65; *PYTOCG* 23:39; *SD* 1:8.

33. *LZJL* 1:48.

34. See, e.g., *PYTOCG* 19:33; *XSYG* 4:85; *CZYG* 1:18–32; Wang Chang, 27:12–13.

35. Letter to Li Gengyun, *SD* 3:5.

36. This juxtaposition has been noted by, among others, Alexander Woodside ("State, Scholars, and Orthodoxy: The Ch'ing Academies, 1736–1839," in K. Liu, *Orthodoxy*, 162);

Joanna Handlin (*Action*, 149–58); Wm. Theodore de Bary (*The Trouble with Confucianism* [Cambridge, Mass.: Harvard University Press, 1991], 96).

37. Brokaw, *Ledgers of Merit*, 157–65, 203–7.

38. *XSYG* 4:43.

39. Kuhn, *Soulstealers*, 120–22.

40. See, e.g., *SD* 1:15; *CZYG* 1:34.

41. *XSYG* (1769 ed.), 4:10–13.

42. *YZYG*, preface to first supplementary *juan*.

43. *PYTOCG* 5:6–7.

44. *YZYG* 2:19.

45. For brief discussions of this notion within the neo-Confucian tradition see Munro, *Images of Human Nature*, 16; and Taylor, "Chinese Hierarchy," 504. For European analogies see Macpherson, 221–24. Chen Hongmou also frequently uses the term "*xiaomin*" (little people, analogous to the French "*menu peuple*"), which is less pejorative but no less patronizing. "*Xiaomin*" in general connotes less a deficiency of intellectual capacity than of wealth or political influence, but Chen in fact uses "*xiaomin*" and "*yumin*" interchangeably often enough to make it clear that he saw the two categories as coterminous. See *PYTOCG* 11:34, 17:3, 37:1–2.

46. *PYTOCG* 20:20.

47. See, e.g., *PYTOCG* 20:18–19, 23:22, 23:29; Xu Dong, *Muling shu*, 4:25.

48. *SD* 1:15.

49. *LZJL* 1:3; *XSYG* (1769 ed.), 4:10.

50. *PYTOCG* 11:25–26, 11:34–36, 19:24, 20:18–22, 24:42–44.

51. *PYTOCG* 19:21–22.

52. A telling instance of this comes in Chen's reprinting of a passage by Lü in which the latter argues that for there to be order in the world it is necessary that "the riffraff of the marketplace" (*shijing xiaoer*) show proper deference to their social superiors. In his own commentary on this passage Chen softens this considerably, adding that inferiors ought only to respect superiors if their actual conduct merits it and pointedly substituting the more neutral designation "all the people" (*quanmin*) for "riffraff" in his rephrasing of Lü's statement. *LZJL* 1:48. Lü himself is a complex figure, prompting some modern scholars, such as Joanna Handlin, to emphasize his populism and others, such as Katherine Carlitz, to condemn his blatant elitism.

53. *ZGFJL* 1:7.

54. This argument is expressed most directly in von Glahn, "Enchantment of Wealth." Two other recent studies that explore in some depth changing cultural attitudes toward wealth (especially commercial wealth) are Brokaw, *Ledgers of Merit*; and Clunas, *Superfluous Things*. Also relevant is recent work on the early modern ideal of philanthropy by Fuma Susuma, Liang Qizi (Angela Leung), and Joanna Handlin Smith, to be discussed further in Chap. 11.

55. Yu, *Shangren jingshen*, esp. 104–21. A similar observation is made in Kuhn, "Social Classification," 20.

56. See. e.g., *PYTOCG* 12:20–21. In terms of Chen's own specific intellectual influences, recall that Guanxue patriarch Feng Congwu had pointedly sought to include elements of all the *simin*—literati, farmers, artisans, and merchants—as coequal members of his moral-revivalist study society at the Guanzhong Academy (see above, Chap. 4).

57. *CZYG* 2:36–42.

58. Letters to Shi Dayi and Jia Shengquan, *SD* 1:8–9.

59. *XSYG* (1769 ed.), 4:10–13.

60. Kuhn, "Social Classification," 24–27.

61. Lien-sheng Yang, "Economic Justification for Spending: An Uncommon Idea in Traditional China," in Yang, *Studies in Chinese Institutional History* (Cambridge, Mass.: Harvard University Press, 1961), 58.

62. Liang Qizi, "'Pinqiong' yu 'qiongren' guannian zai Zhongguo sushi shehui zhong de lishi yanbian" (The concepts of "poverty" and "the poor" in China's evolving social history), in

Huang Yinggui, ed., *Renguan, yiyi, yu shehui* (Perspectives, meanings, and society) (Taibei: Institute of Ethnology, 1993), 142–44. See also von Glahn, "Enchantment of Wealth," and Brokaw, *Ledgers of Merit.*

63. *PYTOCG* 15:20–23.

64. *CZYG* 1:65–66. We have seen, moreover, that in managing his own financial estate Chen was not at all embarrassed by acknowledging the goal of comfortable, enduring wealth.

65. Gertrude Himmelfarb, *The Idea of Poverty: England in the Early Industrial Age* (New York: Knopf, 1983), 41, 63, 130–31.

66. See, e.g., *CZYG* 2:36–37.

67. *PYTOCG* 5:3, 5:15–18.

68. For examples see memorial of QL 13/10/1, GCA; memorial of QL 16/7/4, *QLZZ* 1.58–59; *PYTOCG* 5:15, 10:3–18, 13:9–14, 17:18–19; *SD* 2:10.

69. Liang Qizi, 154, citing Chen Longzheng.

70. Liang Qizi, 157–58. Although the term for "good people" (*liangmin*) appeared in late imperial discourse as paired opposite for two different but nearly homophonic terms, "bad people" (*jianmin*—literally, "traitors") and "debased people" (*jianmin*), it is noteworthy that Chen uses exclusively the former. The distinction is one of ethical or political conduct, not of ascribed status, which seems not to have been an active category in Chen's social thought.

71. *XSYG* 1:12.

72. Letter to the provincial authorities of Sichuan, *JSWB* 75:21.

73. *PYTOCG* 10:3–18, 13:9–14, 15:42–43, 19:37–38, 43:14–15.

74. This reading of Chen's outlook is proposed in Alexander Woodside, "Some Mid-Qing Theorists," 11.

75. *PYTOCG* 10:3–4.

76. *PYTOCG* 9:12–13.

77. Letter to Hui Se, *SD* 2:14.

78. Kuroda, "Bichiku kō," 6. Although a wide range of early and mid-Qing writers evidenced *baofu* sentiments, no one expressed them more emphatically than did the scholar-merchant Tang Zhen (1630–1704), who used them as the basis for his argument against dirigiste controls on market activity; see Dunstan, *Conflicting Counsels*, 106–8; and von Glahn, *Fountain of Fortune*, 222–24. For analogous views among the French physiocrats see Fox-Genovese, esp. 51.

79. See, e.g., *LZJL* 1:48; *CZYG* 2:30.

80. Letter to Tao Qisu, *SD* 3:14.

81. Letter to Cao Han, *SD* 2:10.

82. Memorial of QL 20/7/2, *QLZZ* 12.8–9.

83. *PYTOCG* 35:13–14.

84. See, e.g., *PYTOCG* 13:9–14, 19:32, 19:36; *CZYG* 1:65–66; Wang Chang, 27:12–13.

85. Liang Qizi, "Mingmo Qingqu minjian zishan huodong de xingqi" (The rise of the popular philanthropy movement in the late Ming and early Qing), *Shihuo yuekan* 15.7–8 (January 1986): 304–31.

86. *XSYG* 4:1–21; *CZYG* 2:36–42. On the more general chorus of complaints see Suzuki, 37–46.

87. Letters to Ling Shisong and Shen Qiyuan, *SD* 1:14, 2:3; Tang Jian, 5:10.

88. Memorial of QL 12/18/24, GCA; *LZJL* 1:46; *CZYG* 2:37; *PYTOCG* 15:22–23.

89. *PYTOCG* 16:14; *SD* 2:14.

90. Nearly all of the fourth *juan* of *XSYG* is devoted to such discussions. Class conflict over issues of public security impositions had in fact been rampant in many localities during the late Ming, a fact of which Chen was most certainly aware.

91. *PYTOCG* 16:3–5.

92. *CZYG* 2:37; *PYTOCG* 15:20–23, 27:14–15.

93. *ZGFJL* 1:3; also *ZGFJL* 1:6.

94. *ZGFJL*, preface.

95. Such admonitions are featured, e.g., on the opening pages of two of Chen's most influential moral tracts, *JNYG* and *XSYG*.

96. *PYTOCG* 13:27, 24:38–39. Chen's views here seem to follow those of his first imperial patron, the Yongzheng emperor. Yongzheng fairly clearly enunciated the distinction between a network of personal obligation and a status-group hierarchy in ordering the emancipation of Huizhou's hereditary tenant-serfs (*dianpu*) in 1727. Systematically compelling one social group to accept subordinate status to another was *not*, in Yongzheng's view, an instance of "*shangxia zhi fen*" (acceptance of the roles of superior and subordinate), which was fully appropriate for relations among family members and between heads of households and personal servants, but was instead a case of "*xiangyan exi*" (hegemonically enforced compliance with a repugnant local custom). Edict of YZ 7, cited in Jing Junjian, *Jianmin dengji*, 239; see also Wei Qingyuan et al., 108.

97. My understanding of the late imperial construction of social roles is influenced in part by recent work of Donald Munro, including his *Images of Human Nature*; see also the thoughtful philosophical analysis by Henry Rosemont Jr., "Rights-Bearing Individuals and Role-Bearing Persons," in Mary I. Bockover, ed., *Roles, Rituals, and Responsibility: Essays Dedicated to Herbert Fingarette* (La Salle, Ill.: Open Court, 1989), 71–101. Early modern contesting of the precise importance and obligations attached to certain roles is discussed in de Bary, "Individualism and Humanitarianism," and in McDermott, "Friendship and Its Friends."

98. *XSYG* 2:23.

99. *PYTOCG* 15:20–23, 20:18–19, 24:52. Chen likely derived this usage from his revered Sima Guang, the Song scholar-official who had contributed greatly to the elaboration of the theory of roles and who had argued that the major task of the ruler was to make his subjects "contented with their lot" (*anfen*). See Bol, *This Culture of Ours*, 220–21; and Sariti, 57.

100. *PYTOCG* 19:22; *XSYG* 3:33.

101. *JNYG* 3:13; *XSYG* 1:8.

102. Hao Chang, "Confucian Cosmological Myth and Neo-Confucian Transcendence," in Smith and Kwok, 11–34. See also Donald Munro, *Individualism and Holism: Studies in Confucian and Taoist Values* (Ann Arbor: Center for Chinese Studies, 1985), 259–66. This organismic model of the universe also underlies Romeyn Taylor's view of Chinese "hierarchy," discussed above. My chief difference with Taylor is his insistence that this holistic vision necessarily incorporated a view of human society as ordered into closed estates or castes; whereas this may have had some veracity as applied to the early Ming vision of Zhu Yuanzhang, I would see it as largely inapplicable to the Qing eighteenth century.

103. Henderson, *Chinese Cosmology*.

104. *LZJL* 1:2; *XSYG* 2:9–10.

105. *CZYG* 1:18–32. The classical text that most powerfully articulated the sociopolitical aspects of Confucian cosmological correspondences was, of course, the *Daxue* (Great learning). On the special importance Chen himself attached to this work see Chap. 4.

106. Munro, *Images of Human Nature*, 50.

107. McMahon, *Causality and Containment*, chap. 1.

108. Chan, *Sourcebook*, 177; Kwang-Ching Liu, "Socioethics as Orthodoxy: A Perspective," in K. Liu, *Orthodoxy*, 70.

109. *XSYG* 1:8.

110. *YZYG*, supplementary *juan*, 24; *JNYG* 1:5.

111. Chen Hongmou, preface to Sima Guang's "Jujia zayi" (Miscellaneous rules for dwelling as a family), in *XSYG* 1:1.

112. Ebrey, "Conceptions of the Family," 225–26.

113. *NP* 1:3.

114. *NP* 4:18.

115. *PYTOCG* 19:23.

116. See Chow, *Confucian Ritualism*, esp. chap. 3.

117. See Ebrey's introduction to her translation of this work, *Chu Hsi's Family Rituals*.

118. *XSYG* 3:22.
119. *LZJL* 2:6.
120. *XSYG* 2:9, 3:24; *PYTOCG* 20:11; *SD* 2:12.
121. Letter to Censor Li Yuanzhi, *SD* 2:14.
122. *XSYG* 3:22.
123. *PYTOCG* 19:38–39; *XSYG* 2:18.
124. *XSYG* 2:21.
125. *PYTOCG* 2:16; *Peiyuan tang shoudu ping* 1:1–2. The text of the *Zhijia geyan*, which Chen falsely attributed to Zhu Xi, appears in *YZYG* 2:6–7.
126. *PYTOCG* 19:24.
127. On Yongzheng see Feng Erkang, 358–63. On Qianlong see Zhang Renshan, "Qianlong de dengji lunli." On the reflection of these concerns in Qing statute see Ju Huanwu, "Qinglü de qufa yi shenqing."
128. See, e.g., memorial of QL 16/7/4, *QLZZ* 1.58–59; *PYTOCG* 7:11–12, 27:14–15.
129. See, e.g., *PYTOCG* 19:38–39.
130. See, e.g., *PYTOCG* 19:24–25.
131. *JSWB* 68:4.
132. Kathryn Bernhardt has observed that the seventeenth century saw no significant change in women's juridical status on the matter of property rights, e.g., and argues from this that gender constructions similarly did not undergo major transition; Bernhardt, "A Ming-Qing Transition in Chinese Women's History? The Perspective from Law," in Gail Hershatter et al., eds., *Remapping China: Fissures in Historical Terrain* (Stanford: Stanford University Press, 1996), 42–58. Based on the evidence of scholarship cited in the remainder of this section I cannot accept Bernhardt's generalization. In my own view, although the lack of legal change documented by Bernhardt had important practical consequences for gender relations, it signifies above all the tendency of late imperial codified law to lag behind transformations in economy, society, and culture.
133. See Handlin, "Lü K'un's New Audience," 26; T'ien Ju-kang, *Male Anxiety and Female Chastity* (Leiden: E. J. Brill, 1988), 130–31.
134. Keith McMahon, "A Case for Confucian Sexuality," *Late Imperial China* 92 (December 1988): 32–55. See also the eighteenth-century memoir by Shen Fu, *Six Chapters from a Floating Life,* trans. Leonard Pratt and Chiang Su-hui (New York: Penguin, 1983), part 1.
135. On the way contrasting ideals of femininity were represented in this new popular print culture see Katherine Carlitz, "The Social Uses of Female Virtue in Late Ming Editions of Lienu Zhuan," *Late Imperial China* 12.2 (December 1991): 117–48.
136. Charlotte Furth, "The Patriarch's Legacy: Household Instructions and the Transmission of Orthodox Values," in K. Liu, *Orthodoxy,* 203. On the moral clampdown of the early Qing see McMahon, *Causality and Containment,* 66–68; Furth, "Androgenous Males and Deficient Females," *Late Imperial China* 9.2 (December 1988): 24–25; Mann, "Widows in the Kinship, Class, and Community Structures of Qing Dynasty China," *Journal of Asian Studies* 46.1 (February 1987): 49; and Vivian Ng, "Rape Laws in Qing China," *Journal of Asian Studies* 46.1 (February 1987): 57–70.
137. T'ien, *Male Anxiety and Female Chastity.*
138. Mann, "Grooming a Daughter," 214.
139. Nivison, *Chang Hsüeh-ch'eng,* 265–66.
140. *XSYG* 1:1.
141. *XSYG* 2:22; *PYTOCG* 13:46–48, 19:39.
142. *JSWB* 68:6.
143. *PYTOCG* 19:22.
144. Compare *XSYG* 1:21–41 with Ebrey, *Family and Property,* 181–97.
145. *JSWB* 68:4.
146. *JNYG* 3:4; see also *XSYG* 2:3–4.

147. *XSYG* 4:47.

148. *JNYG* 3:4.

149. *JNYG* 3:1.

150. *PYTOCG* 19:24.

151. *JNYG* 3:22.

152. *JSWB* 68:4.

153. Nivison, *Chang Hsüeh-ch'eng,* 262.

154. These policy changes are chronicled in *Da Qing huidian shili* (1899 ed.), 403:8–32. See also Mark Elvin, "Female Virtue and the State in China," *Past and Present* 104 (1984): 111–52; Mann, "Widows"; and especially Yamazaki Jun'ichi, "Shinchō ni okeru setsu-retsu zokuhyō ni tsuite" (On awards for virtuous widowhood in the Ch'ing dynasty), *Chūgoku koten kenkyū* 15 (1967): 46–66.

155. Yang Xifu, *Jiefu zhuan,* revised edition by Chen Hongmou, 1761. I wish to thank Timothy Brook for providing me with a copy of this edition.

156. Chen, "Jiefu zhuan xu," in Wang Chang, 27:13.

157. *PYTOCG* 3:14.

158. Elvin, 133–35.

159. *Peiyuan tang shoudu ping* 1:2–3; *PYTOCG* 3:14–15.

160. *PYTOCG* 19:24. For a brilliant analysis of the economic forces prompting enforced widow remarriage in the Ch'ing see Jennifer Holmgren, "The Economic Foundations of Virtue," *Australian Journal of Chinese Affairs* 13 (1985): 1–27. For a discussion of the statutory context see Ann Waltner, "Widows and Remarriage in Ming and Early Qing China," in Richard W. Guisso and Stanley Johannesen, *Women in China* (Youngstown, N.Y.: Philo Press, 1981), 136–38. Although the Qing Code was more protective of widow's autonomy in decisions regarding remarriage than was its Ming antecedent, it is noteworthy that Chen was more protective still.

161. Angela Ki Che Leung, "To Chasten the Society: The Development of Widow Homes in the Ch'ing, 1773–1911," *Late Imperial China* 14.2 (December 1993): 1–32.

162. For summaries of the court's shifting position on this issue see Yamazaki, 50–51; and Paul Ropp, "The Seeds of Change: Reflections on the Condition of Women in the Early and Mid Ch'ing," *Signs* 2.1 (1976): 8–9.

163. Scholars speaking out against extreme demands for female chastity in the name of ritual correctness (including the valorization of widow suicide) included Gui Youguang (1507–71), Mao Qiling (1623–1716), Qian Daxin, and Wang Zhong. See Chen Dongyuan, *Zhongguo funü shenghuo shi* (History of Chinese women's life) (1937; reprint, Shanghai: Shanghai shuju, 1984), 246–47; Yuasa, 114–16; Ropp, "Seeds of Change"; and Hu Fagui, "Qingdai zhenjie guannian shulun" (Debates on the notion of female chastity in the Qing era), *Qingshi yanjiu ji* 7 (1990): 153–70.

164. Chen, "Jiefu zhuan xu," 27:12–13.

165. *XSYG* 1:27. See also Ebrey, *Family and Property,* 221, from which this translation is taken.

166. Chen, "Zhou jiemu zhuan," in Li Zutao, *Guochao wenlu* 44:28–31. Bettine Birge, "Chu Hsi and Women's Education," in de Bary and Chaffee, 348–52, notes that Zhu Xi's own virtuous widow biographies tended to celebrate similar behavior. Susan Mann has sensitively discussed the role of the mother-son bond in the generation of this sort of literature, much of which reflects the personal life experiences of the author-official; "Widows," 32–56.

167. *PYTOCG* 19:36–37.

168. Birge, 339–40. Wang Zhong even argued (erroneously) that the prohibition on widow remarriage was itself of Song origin; Yuasa, 115.

169. *XSYG* 1:12.

170. Dorothy Ko, "Pursuing Talent and Virtue: Education and Women's Culture in Seventeenth and Eighteenth Century China," *Late Imperial China* 13.1 (June 1992): esp. 11.

171. See Birge, 331–32.

172. Compare Handlin, "Lü K'un's New Audience," 26. Carlitz, "Social Uses of Female

Virtue," takes a far dimmer view of Lü's stance toward women than does Handlin. As is true also for Chen Hongmou's *JNYG*, the remarkable thing about Lü's text is that it so readily supports such contrasting readings. In this it typifies the era in which it was produced.

173. *XSYG* 1:8.

174. *XSYG* 4:48.

175. *JSWB* 68:5.

176. See, e.g., *PYTOCG* 19:34; *JSWB* 68:6.

177. It also seems significant that in his reprinting of Yuan Cai's *Shifan* Chen chose to omit the section on segregation of the *gui*.

178. *JNYG* 3:8.

179. *JNYG* 1:1.

180. For one statement of this view see Joan Kelly, "Early Feminist Theory and the *Querelle des Femmes*, 1400–1789," in Kelly, *Women, History, and Theory: The Essays of Joan Kelly* (Chicago: University of Chicago Press, 1984), 87–89.

181. Barlow, 253–89.

182. For but one instance see *JSWB* 68:4.

183. *JNYG* 3:8.

184. *JNYG*, preface, 3:1, 3:13.

185. *JNYG*, preface.

186. Donald J. Munro, *Individualism and Holism: Studies in Confucian and Taoist Values* (Ann Arbor: Center for Chinese Studies, 1985), esp. 259; Munro, *Images of Human Nature*, 101–3; Munro, "Concept of Interest," 187, 197; Rosemont, "Rights-Bearing Individuals and Role-Bearing Persons"; Taylor, "Chinese Hierarchy"; Gary G. Hamilton, "Patriarchalism in Imperial China and Western Europe: A Revision of Weber's Sociology of Domination," *Theory and Society* 13.3 (1984): 393–425.

187. King, 67.

188. de Bary, "Individualism and Humanitarianism," 149. See also de Bary, "Neo-Confucian Individualism," chap. 3 of his *The Liberal Tradition in China* (Hong Kong: Chinese University Press, 1983).

189. Hao Chang, "Confucian Cosmological Myth and Neo-Confucian Transcendence," in Smith and Kwok, 11–34.

190. *ZGFJL* 1:3, 1:6.

191. *LZJL* 1:70.

192. *LZJL* 2:81.

193. Letter to Yang Yingju, *SD* 2:9. Compare Cheng Yi's argument to the effect that human beings really have not one but two "selves": the self of "selfishness" and the true "inner self" to which the moral individual must return and thereby unite with the inner selves of all other human beings in the achievement of the perfected society. See de Bary, *Liberal Tradition*, 24–27.

194. de Bary, "Individualism and Humanitarianism," 146–47.

195. *CZYG* 1:18–32.

Chapter 10

1. See, e.g., *LZJL* 2:62–66; and *CZYG* 2:58. For interesting meditations on this general theme in late imperial history see Pierre-Étienne Will, "Bureaucratie officielle et bureaucratie réelle: Sur quelques dilemmes de l'administration impériale à l'époque des Qing," *Études chinoises* 8.1 (spring 1989): esp. 99.

2. Yu Yingshi, "Handai xunli yu wenhua chuanbuo" (The model officials of the Han period and its cultural propagation), in Yu, *Shi yu Zhongguo wenhua* (The literati and Chinese culture) (Shanghai: Shanghai renmin chubanshe, 1987), 129–216; Chang Chun-ming.

3. *CZYG* 2:36–49; *PYTOCG* 18:29–30. See also *ECCP*, 51–52, 709–10, 848–49, 937–38; Will, "Bureaucratie officielle et bureaucratie réelle," 130–31.

4. *Qingshi gao* 35.10558–64. Among private writers the attempt to claim for Chen *xunli* sta-

tus is most clearly evident in Shen Deqian, preface to *Peiyuan tang wenji* (1769); Yuan Mei, *Xiaocang shanfang wenji* 27:9–12; and Li Yuandu, 16:2–3.

5. *CZYG*, preface; *PYTOCG* 15:24–25, 18:29–30; *NP* 4:33.

6. *PYTOCG* 31:36; *CZYG* 2:22.

7. The key term for Chen in this regard is "*guanfang*," literally an official's seal of office but used here metaphorically to refer to the sometimes elaborate precautions an official must take to seal himself off from influence peddling. On entering a jurisdiction, Chen usually issues *guanfang* proclamations that, with surprising candor, reveal his fears of relatives and past acquaintances who might want to capitalize on their newfound friend in power and instructs subordinates on how to deflect their approaches. See, e.g., *PYTOCG* 11:27–28, 12:20–21, 25:30–31, 37:3–4.

8. *CZYG* 1:5.

9. Letter to Cui Shanyuan, *SD* 2:6.

10. *CZYG*, preface, 1:17–18; *LZJL* 2:38. On the complex meaning of the idiom "*minben*" see the thoughtful essay by Feng Tianyu, "Minben xueshuo: Zhongguo chuantong wenhua yu minzhuzhuyi de jiehe dian" (The theory of *minben*: A rallying point for democracy in traditional Chinese culture), *Jiang-Han luntan* (1988): 61–65. On the term's highly antidemocratic earlier history see Shao Qin, "Xi 'minben' " (An analysis of "*minben*"), *Lishi yanjiu* 1985.6, 3–16.

11. Memorial of QL 21/7/25, *QLZZ* 15.42–43; memorial of QL 25/11/1, MQA. This concern continued to occupy Chen during his presidency of the Board of Civil Office at the end of his career; see Peng Qifeng, 14:11.

12. Beyond his didactic sourcebook *CZYG* Chen systematically expounded his views on the role of the local official in a model examination question and answer (*KSZJ* 7:10–12), in a 1741 letter to Grand Secretary Zhang Tingyu (*SD* 1:12), and in a lengthy 1745 directive to his local-level subordinates in Shaanxi (*PYTOCG* 20:11–24). The latter two documents were granted quasi-canonical status by their inclusion in Wei Yuan's 1826 *JSWB*. See also *PYTOCG* 11:25–26, 13:35, 14:33–36, 17:41–42, 20:8–10, 37:18–19, 38:7–8; *SD* 2:2, 2:4, 2:8, 2:12. For a passage from Lü Kun's *Treatise on Substantive Governance* (*Shizheng lu*), which clearly influenced Chen's own views on what it means to be a "father and mother official," see Chang Chun-ming, 230–31.

13. *SD* 1:6, 2:2, 2:9; *CZYG* 2:58.

14. *PYTOCG* 11:40. Chen often reiterates a more succinct way of putting this: "The court (*chaoting*) establishes officials, and divides the realm into jurisdictions, for the purpose of governing the people." See, e.g., *CZYG* 2:47–49.

15. Skinner, *Foundations of Modern Political Thought*, x.

16. Hymes and Schirokauer, 7; Paolo Santangelo, "'Chinese and Barbarians' in Gu Yanwu's Thought," in Tilemann Grimm et al., eds., *Collected Papers of the Twenty-Ninth Congress of Chinese Studies* (Tübingen: Tübingen University Press, 1988), 189.

17. See, e.g., *ZGFJL*, preface; *PYTOCG* 17:30, 32:34; *JSWB* 26:60.

18. Chen's commentaries on Wang Yangming and Lü Kun in *CZYG*, *juan* 1; *ZGFJL*, preface; *LZJL* 2:41; *Guitiao huichao*, preface; *PYTOCG* 12:17, 20:16–17. Bridging the gap between the personal and routinized aspects of governance is of course the chief subject of the two commentaries on the *Great Learning*, Zhen Dexiu's *Daxue yanyi* and Qiu Jun's *Daxue yanyi bu*, which, as Chapter 4 has argued, were central to Chen Hongmou's intellectual identity.

19. *KSZJ* 7:10.

20. There are of course problems inherent in the "state"/"society" framework of analysis beyond the hazards of imposing on the target culture a paradigm foreign to it. For a concise survey of these problems, growing awareness of which has prompted historians of Europe to greater caution, see Louise Nussdorfer, *Civic Politics in the Rome of Urban VIII* (Princeton: Princeton University Press, 1992), 5.

21. As we shall see in Chapter 11, yet a third sphere, that of "public" or "communal" (*gong*), regularly but not invariably joined *guan* and *min* to make up a tripartite division of proprietorship and responsibility.

22. Letter to Yin Huiyi, *SD* 2:10; *PYTOCG* 20:13, 23:39. For examples of Chen's countless discussions of *guan* vs. *min* as spheres of proprietorship see *PYTOCG* 13:9–14 (on granaries) and 36:26–38 (on irrigation installations).

23. The Song neo-Confucian turning away from centralized state management of local affairs in favor of a form of collegial management by local elites is a central theme of Hymes and Schirokauer's *Ordering the World* (see especially their introduction, 22–27). Chen's relationship to the late imperial discourse of *fengjian* local self-governance will be treated in the next chapter.

24. For but a few examples of Chen's arguments along these lines see memorial of QL 20/10/5, *QLZZ* 12.597–98; *JSWB* 16:35; *XSYG* (1769 ed.), 4:13; *PYTOCG* 16:3–7; *NP* 6:8, 7:21–22.

25. See Shepherd. For similar arguments on the Qing calculus of restraint see also Metzger, *Internal Organization*, 76; Kishimoto, "Keizai seisaku," 28–30; Dai Yi, *Qianlong*, 116.

26. *SD* 2:11.

27. *PYTOCG* 1:2–3, 2:23–24, 2:32–35, 4:47–49.

28. *PYTOCG* 18:53.

29. Letter to Gu Hong, *SD* 2:18.

30. *SD* 1:15, 2:1–2, 2:18; *JSWB* 23:25, 46:43. On occasion Chen's rhetoric seems to play on the double meaning of "*li*," which can refer to a fiscal imposition as well as to a regulation, substatute, or legal precedent. Lack of official restraint in the application of either is in his view burdensome and dysfunctional.

31. *CZYG* 2:47; *PYTOCG* 11:37.

32. *SD* 1:16, 2:4; *JSWB* 40:19–20.

33. *JSWB* 46:43; *SD* 1:15. This syndrome is of course a major theme of Metzger, *Internal Organization*.

34. Hosea Ballou Morse, *The Gilds of China* (London: Longmans, 1909), 27.

35. *PYTOCG* 24:32. Gao Wangling, *Jingji fazhan he zhengfu zhengze*, shows just how pervasive was this Qing official logic of intervention in the cause of economic development.

36. *JSWB* 26:60; *NP* 3:11.

37. Marc Raeff, *The Well-Ordered Police State: Social and Institutional Change Through Law in the Germanies and Russia, 1600–1800* (New Haven: Yale University Press, 1983).

38. Letter to Xu Deyu, *SD* 2:4. For examples of Chen's major public security initiatives in Jiangsu and Shaanxi see *PYTOCG* 10:3–18, 23:34–35.

39. Huang, *Civil Justice in China*.

40. For but a few examples of Chen's diatribes on this score see his memorials of QL 6/6/2, MQA; QL 13/1/10, GCA; *PYTOCG* 10:30–35, 13:18–19. These have been seen as particularly juicy samples of mid-Qing anti-pettifogger rhetoric by Wei Yuan (*JSWB* 93:28–29) and recently by Melissa Macauley (*Social Power and Legal Culture: Litigation Masters in Late Imperial China* [Stanford: Stanford University Press, 1998]).

41. Memorial of QL 18/12/16, *QLZZ* 7.164–66; *PYTOCG* 11:37–39, 37:18–19; *SD* 3:17.

42. Letters to Tang Ecun and Xiong Yizu, *SD* 2:2, 3:14.

43. Letter to Tao Fuozhong, *SD* 3:14.

44. Letter to Cao Han, *SD* 2:10. In a darker moment, however, Chen acknowledges to a confidante his distress that judging cases strictly and impartially on the merits of their evidence frequently fails to bring about the social justice that one would hope. All we can do, he consoles himself, is to remain faithful to rational principle and allow the uncontrollable fate to take its course. Letter to Jia Yuquan, *SD* 2:6–7.

45. *PYTOCG* 13:23–24, 23:39–41, 37:18–19; *CZYG* 1:13–18; *SD* 2:4, 2:8, 2:11, 3:13; *NP* 6:4–5; Xu Dong, *Muling shu*, 8:3–4; *JSWB* 16:34. For Lü Kun's notion of "*tongmin*" see Handlin, *Action*, 159–60. For a general discussion of this issue in Qing bureaucratic practice (with particular reference to Chen Hongmou) see Will, "La communication entre bureaucrates et paysans."

46. *CZYG* 1:34–50.

47. Gu Yanwu, "Junxian lun," in *Tinglin wenji*, 75–78.

48. See Silas Wu, *Communication and Imperial Control in China: Evolution of the Palace Memorial System, 1693–1735* (Cambridge, Mass.: Harvard University Press, 1970); and Beatrice Bartlett, *Monarchs and Ministers: The Grand Council in Mid-Ch'ing China, 1723–1820* (Berkeley: University of California Press, 1991).

49. A relatively small percentage of the documents in this collection are public proclamations (*shi* or *gaoshi*), but the vast majority are directives (*xi*) issued by Chen to his local-level subordinates.

50. *PYTOCG* 16:18–20, 33:17–22; *NP* 4:10–11.

51. Memorial of QL 19/8/18, *QLZZ* 9.377–78.

52. For representative examples see *SD* 1:7, 1:10, 1:14, 2:2, 2:5–6, 2:19, 3:11; *PYTOCG* 10:33–35; *NP* 9:18; *JSWB* 40:19–20. For a recent analysis based in part on Chen's observations see Will, "Bureaucratie officielle et bureaucratie réelle."

53. Memorials of QL 20/12/16, QL 21/4/12 (four separate memorials with this date), and QL 21/8/29 (two with this date), *QLZZ* 13.280, 14.160–65, 15.272–73. According to Peng Qifeng (14:11), detailed assessment of the capabilities of individual local officials was also something to which Chen paid unusually close attention during his late-career tenure as president of the Board of Civil Office.

54. See variously *PYTOCG* 9:19–20, 32:10–11, 35:10, 37:17; *SD* 2:2; *NP* 5:8. Sometimes the self-aggrandizing actions of these inspectors themselves required corrective measures on Chen's part; see *PYTOCG* 26:38–39.

55. *PYTOCG* 2:48–51, 3:29–30, 11:42–43, 14:14–17, 16:16–17, 17:1; *ZZYG* 2:7–14; letters to Zhu Nanhu and Yang Zhongxing, *SD* 2:18, 3:18; Xu Dong, *Muling shu,* 23:29–31; *JSWB* 22:49. Occasionally, of course, such investigations led Governor Chen to impeachment of subordinates; see, e.g., his memorials of QL 12/4/12, GCA; QL 18/8/6 and QL 21/10/20, *QLZZ* 6.74–75, 15.804.

56. *PYTOCG* 25:9–11.

57. *PYTOCG* 30:7–8.

58. Gu Yanwu, "Shengyuan lun" (On *shengyuan*), in *Tinglin wenji,* 81–82.

59. Clerks, who performed a variety of paperwork operations within the yamen, were often conceptually paired with another category of sub-bureaucratic functionary, "runners" (*yi* or *yayi*), who performed a range of security or other menial tasks, giving rise to the collective term *xuyi* ("clerks and runners" or "yamen functionaries"). Chen Hongmou was concerned about the latter group (see, e.g., his memorial of QL28/11 as president of the Board of Civil Office, cited in Cai Guanluo 1.149) and at times referred to the two together, but it was clearly the problem of clerks per se that most attracted his attention.

60. An example of the circulation of Chen's *ZGFJL* in the later Qing is the abridgment published under the title *Gongmen xiuli lu* (How to clean up public administration) by the office of the Guangdong provincial judge in 1830 and republished by that office in 1889 (under the tenure of Guangdong governor Zhang Zhidong). Chen's writings on clerical discipline are reprinted in *JSWB* 24:24–25 and in Xu Dong, *Muling shu,* 4:25–26. Wei Yuan also cites approvingly Chen's policies toward clerks elsewhere in his writings. See, e.g., *Guwei tang neiwai ji,* "Waiji," 6:7. For Ch'ü T'ung-tsu's reliance on Chen see *Local Government,* 27, 67, 102, 212, 238, 241, 294–95.

61. Ch'ü T'ung-tsu, esp. chaps. 3 and 4; Will, "Bureaucratie officielle et bureaucratie réelle," and other writings; James H. Cole, *Shaohsing: Competition and Cooperation in Nineteenth-Century China* (Tucson: University of Arizona Press, 1986), esp. 111–18.

62. Bradly W. Reed, "Money and Justice: Clerks, Runners, and the Magistrate's Court in Late Imperial Sichuan," *Modern China* 21.3 (July 1995): 345–82; Reed, "Scoundrels and Civil Servants: Clerks, Runners, and Local Administration in Late Imperial China" (Ph.D. diss., University of California, Los Angeles, 1994).

63. Will, "Bureaucratie officielle et bureaucratie réelle"; Will, *Bureaucracy and Famine,* 89–90. In his *Confucianism and Autocracy: Professional Elites in the Founding of the Ming Dynasty*

(Berkeley: University of California Press, 1983), chap. 1, John Dardess portrays this divide as one between an emerging "professional" group, Confucian scholar-officials, and the "paraprofessional" clerkly labor force from which they sought aggressively to distinguish themselves.

64. Gu Yanwu, *Tinglin wenji*, 75–78. Gu is cited authoritatively on the problem of clerks in Ch'ü T'ung-tsu, 37, 225.

65. Gu Yanwu, *Tinglin wenji*, 75–78.

66. *ZGFJL* 1:13.

67. See, e.g., memorial of QL 19/4/28, *QLZZ* 8.137; *PYTOCG* 2:31, 3:14–15, 5:19–21, 13:18–19, 22:19–20; *NP* 6:11, 10:8; Cai Guanluo, 1.145.

68. *PYTOCG* 10:36–38, 15:1–2. For others of Chen's responses to clerical corruption see, e.g., memorials of QL 12/4/12, GCA; QL 17/8/26, *QLZZ* 3.679–81; QL 26/2/1, MQA; *PYTOCG* 30:1–2, 32:17–19, 37:18–19.

69. Chen makes this point strongly in a model examination question he posed on the problems of serving in county office (*KSZJ* 7:10–12) and again in his unremittingly harsh essay "Condemning clerks and runners" (Ma shuyi), reprinted in Xu Dong, *Muling shu*, 4:25–26.

70. Memorial of QL 19/2/21, *QLZZ* 7.637–39.

71. *PYTOCG* 13:32–34, 22:19–20.

72. *NP* 5:5.

73. *ZGFJL*, preface written at Chen's Jiangxi governor's office, QL 8/4.

74. Memorial of QL 1/12, extracted in *NP* 2:18–19.

75. On Yongzheng and Qianlong attitudes toward *haoixian guigong* see Zelin, and Chapter 2, above. Chen's proposal to make clerical salaries a regularized portion of local administrative budgets also echoed the "hired service system" instituted by Wang Anshi as part of his late eleventh-century New Policies (*xinfa*), and rescinded by Wang's antistatist successors; see J. Liu, *Reform in Sung China*, 4–7.

76. *ZGFJL* 1:4. On Chen's 1746 campaign to regularize clerical collection of *lougui* see *PYTOCG* 24:36–37, Ch'ü T'ung-tsu, 27.

77. *NP* 2:19.

78. Xu Dong, *Muling shu*, 4:26.

79. The following paragraphs are based on *ZGFJL*, preface and 1:7–8, and on the cover letter that Chen attached to this work on its initial 1742 compilation. This letter appears in *PYTOCG* 16:10–12, is reprinted in *JSWB* 24:24–25, and is discussed in *NP* 5:5.

80. In the opinion of the unnamed Guangdong provincial judge who published an 1830 redaction of Chen's work, retitled *Gongmen xiuxing lu*, Chen had overestimated the degree of classical education enjoyed by most clerks. In his revision, therefore, he simplified some of the original's prose and newly incorporated a doggerel song (*juan* 5) that epitomized what he saw as the work's message in a form guaranteed to be accessible even to those with marginal literacy. It is interesting to speculate whether the judge's view reflected simply a difference of opinion from Chen's or the fact that in the intervening century the literacy level of yamen clerks had in fact declined. In any case other evidence from Chen's corpus (e.g., *JNYG*) suggests that he would have enthusiastically approved the decision for vernacularization, couched as it was in a continuing effort to reach the target audience through normative appeals.

81. *ZGFJL* 1:3.

82. *ZGFJL* 1:12–13. Chen gives the source of both citations as Gu's *Rizhi lu*, but I have not been able to locate either in the original text.

83. By far Gu Yanwu's best-known discussion of the problem of clerks during the Qing seems to have been the essay "Du lingshi" (District functionaries) in his *Rizhi lu*, 4:8–9, accorded pride of place in the chapter on clerks in Wei Yuan's *Huangchao jingshi wenbian*, 24:1–2. There is little hint of the possibility of moral reclamation in this text, which catalogs the progressive decline of local governance from the past golden age to the present, when both officials and people are held captive to the predations of these despicable "foxes and rats" (*hushu*).

84. *NP* 5:5.

85. *ZGFJL*, preface.
86. *PYTOCG* 2:45–46.
87. *NP* 9:1; Cai Guanluo, 1.147.
88. Hsiao, 11–12.
89. See, e.g., the confusing variety of administrative definitions offered in Ch'ü T'ung-tsu, 3, 203, 227, 245.
90. Following the model of Shaanxi governor Yan Xishan established in 1917, the Guomindang mandated the establishment of "wards" (*xiang* or *qu*, depending on local usage) throughout China in 1928–29. The wards were headed by centrally appointed territorial administrators, the equivalent of the *xiangguan* proposed two centuries earlier in the Yongzheng reign. See Kuhn, "Local Self-Government Under the Republic," 284–86.
91. The following paragraphs are based on Ortai, memorial of YZ 7, reprinted in *JSWB* 18:52–54. This incident is also briefly discussed in John R. Watt, *The District Magistrate in Late Imperial China* (New York: Columbia University Press, 1972), 225–28; in Min Tu-ki, "The Theory of Political Feudalism in the Ch'ing Period," 102; and in Roger Thompson, "Statecraft and Self-Government: Competing Views of Community and State in Late Imperial China," *Modern China* 14.2 (April 1988): 196, 206. As Thompson points out, Gong Jianyang's *xiangguan* proposal (transmitted via Ortai's memorial in its *JSWB* version) became the basis of several local self-government schemes in the last decade of Qing rule.
92. Karjishan and Chen Hongmou, memorial of QL 18/5/22, *QLZZ* 5.436–38.
93. Revealingly, Chen applauded the 1765 imperial addition of a submagistracy in his home county of Lingui, headquartered at the market town of Liutang. He expressed his preference that others also be created in Lingui but admitted that this was most likely politically infeasible. Letters of QL 30/12/26 and QL 31/1/23, *JS* 237–42.
94. This was very likely related to the fact that, as we shall see in Chap. 11, *xiang*-level governance in Jiangxi was already institutionalized to an unusual degree in the hands of lineage elites.
95. *PYTOCG* 12:1–2; *NP* 4:7.
96. *PYTOCG* 16:18–20, 17:28–29, 18:3–5; *NP* 5:18–19.
97. For interpretation of these technical terms regarding the selection process see E-tu Zen Sun, *Ch'ing Administrative Terms: A Translation of the Terminology of the Six Boards with Explanatory Notes* (Cambridge, Mass.: Harvard University Press, 1961), 1–4.
98. Karjishan and Chen memorial of QL 18/5/22, *QLZZ* 5.436–38. For a discussion of "detached assistant magistrates" generally, see Ch'ü, 9–13.
99. The following paragraphs are based on memorials of QL 25/11/1 and QL 26/2/1, MQA.
100. Letter to Lei Cuiting, *SD* 2:5.
101. For a few representative examples see memorials of QL 13/1/10 and QL 13/4/29, GCA; QL 16/8/11, *QLZZ* 1.385–87; *JSWB* 110:28–29; Xu Dong, *Muling shu*, 10:32–35; *PYTOCG* 5:8–10, 6:3–14, 11:44–46, 32:12–16, 36:7–11, 36:19–22; *NP* 3:17, 6:2, 7:4–6.
102. For disparate examples of Chen's use of this term see memorials of QL 8/6/28, MQA; QL 13/10/1 (two bearing this date), GCA; QL 19/intercalary 4/25, *QLZZ* 8.353–54; *PYTOCG* 4:5–7.
103. *PYTOCG* 10:36.
104. *PYTOCG* 11:44–46; *NP* 4:8.
105. Memorial of QL 13/4/29, GCA; *PYTOCG* 7:9–10.
106. *PYTOCG* 7:3–5, 10:36–38, 12:25, 15:35–36, 22:5–8.
107. *CZYG* 1:34–50.
108. *PYTOCG* 5:1–2, 18:36–42; *JSWB* 22:49; *NP* 3:2, 4:22, 12:10–11.
109. *PYTOCG* 12:23. Lü Kun's views on government paperwork are discussed in Handlin, *Action*, 104, 159–60.
110. *PYTOCG* 10:23–32, 13:32–34, 17:20–25, 32:4–5, 32:36–39, 32:43–45, 35:6–7; *NP* 3:17–18.

111. *PYTOCG* 10:39–42, 13:23–24, 23:39–41; *NP* 6:4–5.

112. *PYTOCG* 13:39–42, 17:20–25, 26:5–9.

113. *PYTOCG* 16:36–37, 17:43–46, 18:48–52, 23:9–10, 35:38–40, 37:32–36, 39:7–9; *NP* 6:12. In most of these cases a model of the form itself is included in the text.

114. *Quan Dian yixue huiji* (1738).

115. *PYTOCG, juan* 1–4.

116. For but a few examples see *PYTOCG* 11:22–24, 11:44–46, 17:47–53, 21:28–30, 22:1–2, 31:8–9.

117. Memorials of QL 13/1/10, GCA; and QL 19/8/18 *QLZZ* 9.377–78; *PYTOCG* 2:17–18, 5:1–2, 10:1–2, 10:33–35; *NP* 3:18–19, 4:5–6; *JSWB* 93:28–29; Xu Dong, *Muling shu*, 23:29–31.

118. See, e.g., *PYTOCG* 18:18–20, 21:8, 21:25–26; Will and Wong, 236–38.

119. Stuart Woolf, "Statistics and the Modern State," *Comparative Studies in Society and History* 31.3 (July 1989): 588–604.

120. *PYTOCG* 13:39–42, 37:37–41.

121. *Wuliao jiazhi zeli*, Zhili volume, 1:17. The purpose of these volumes was, of course, regulatory, but it is made abundantly clear that in order to avoid either official overspending or commandist procurement the listed prices correspond as exactly as possible to those currently pertaining on local markets.

122. *PYTOCG* 1:4–6. See also his accounting for Yunnan elementary schools, *PYTOCG* 3:5–11.

123. *NP* 7:3.

124. *PYTOCG* 35:13–14. Compare Woolf, "Statistics," 590.

125. Stuart Woolf, "French Civilization and Ethnicity in the Napoleonic Empire," *Past and Present* 124 (1989): 96–120. On Lü Kun's example, see Handlin, *Action*, 159–60.

126. *PYTOCG* 30:5–6, 37:20–21.

127. Ji Xiaolan, ed., *Qinding siku quanshu zongmu tiyao* (Index to the Imperial Library Collection) (1782; reprint, Shanghai: Commercial Press, 1933), 15:50.

128. *PYTOCG* 12:22–25, 17:12–15, 34:15–19, 36:12–18, 37:5–12, 41:27–40.

129. *PYTOCG* 36:12–18.

130. Thongchai Winichakul, *Siam Mapped: The History of the Geo-Body of a Nation* (Honolulu: University of Hawaii Press, 1994). See especially 51–56 and, on internal jurisdictional mapping, 119–22.

131. This campaign has been expertly treated in a recent article by Pierre-Étienne Will—albeit from a rather different perspective—and so our discussion here will be briefer than the subject might otherwise deserve, designed to supplement what Will has already said and to situate this incident within the more general concerns of this study. See Will, "The 1744 Annual Audits."

132. This was of course also a literal demand of the court, but the phrase (distinguished by its use of the less common orthography for "*cun*," incorporating the character "*tun*," Matthews no. 6592) became accepted during the course of the campaign as rhetorical shorthand for both a highly specific set of requirements on the part of local magistrates and a more generalized commitment to closeness to the people.

133. Letter to Sun Quan, *SD* 1:11.

134. *PYTOCG* 12:28–32, 14:6–13.

135. *PYTOCG* 17:3–11; see also *NP* 5:12–13.

136. Memorial of Ortai et al., QL 9/9/27, *Shilu* 224:26–27; memorial of Karjishan, QL 10/4, *Shilu* 239:37–38; *PYTOCG* 21:2–5; *NP* 5:16; Will, "The 1744 Annual Audits," 11–15.

137. For an example see the memorial of Zhili governor-general Gao Bin, QL 9/12, *Shilu* 231:15–16.

138. Chen Hongmou was likewise of course a Yongzheng holdover, and this fact very likely played into his enthusiasm for Nuoqin and Ortai's proposal. It is worth noting that the activist utilitarian idiom "*xingli chubi*" (promote the useful and expunge the dysfunctional), invoked by

the campaign's sponsors and embraced by Chen to describe the gist of his own program, had an immediately identifiable Yongzheng referent. Although not new to the eighteenth century, it had been the motto of campaigns undertaken by Yongzheng in the first year of his reign to shake up and reinvigorate the late-Kangxi bureaucracy. See Feng Erkang, 80–82; Will, "The 1744 Annual Audits," 9–11.

139. In their discussion of the proposal both Nuoqin and Ortai employ the idiom of "*xingchu*" (or more precisely "*xingqin*," promote and prohibit), which had featured in Chen's previous discussions of his project, but not his terminology of "*libi*," utility and dysfunction.

140. Memorial of QL 10/1, abstracted in *Shilu* 232:17–18 and in *NP* 5:17–18.

141. As Will independently concludes, Chen was seeking "subtly to transform [a] procedure whose basic point was to evaluate the magistrates into a tool to enforce his own ideal of interventionist and idealist field government." "The 1744 Annual Audits," 38–39.

142. *PYTOCG* 19:21–40. The passage on land tax reform is on page 19:31. Will, "The 1744 Annual Audits," 31–32, provides an English-language summary of the entire twenty-four items on Chen's list.

143. *PYTOCG* 20:8–10; *Shilu* 232:17–18.

144. *PYTOCG* 21:2–5, 21:21–22, 23:20–29, 23:43–46, 25:45–48.

145. *PYTOCG* 27:25–49, 29:32–34, 35:6–7.

146. *Guitiao huichao, juan* 1.

147. *PYTOCG* 34:15–19, 34:20–27; memorial of QL 20/12/16, *QLZZ* 13.280.

148. *JSWB* 22:52–54, 28:12–15.

149. *PYTOCG* 29:32–34.

Chapter 11

1. Kuhn, "Local Self-Government Under the Republic"; Min Tu-ki. The broader question of Gu Yanwu's influence on Chen is treated in Chapter 4.

2. The ideology and practice of this liturgical strategy is investigated in Susan Mann, *Local Merchants and the Chinese Bureaucracy: 1750–1950* (Stanford: Stanford University Press, 1987).

3. William T. Rowe, "The Public Sphere in Modern China," *Modern China* 16.3 (July 1990): esp. 314–18. For a fuller gloss on the term "*gong*" in mid-Qing sources see Mary Backus Rankin, "The Origins of a Chinese Public Sphere," *Études chinoises* 9.2 (autumn 1990): esp. 37–45.

4. *PYTOCG* 17:47–53, 21:25–26, 45:25–26. The obligation of landlords receiving tax reductions to pass along their savings to tenants in the form of lowered rents had been decreed by the Kangxi emperor in 1710 and reiterated by his successors Yongzheng in 1735 and Qianlong in 1745; Kishimoto, *Buka*, 306–8.

5. See, e.g., *PYTOCG* 17:28–29, 20:8–10.

6. See, e.g., *PYTOCG* 1:40–49, 17:47–53, 18:53–54, 19:32.

7. It has often been observed that, in their application to social institutions, *gong* and *si* were not so much fixed categories as relational ones. For example, the interests of a lineage organization might be considered *gong* when contrasted with those of individuals and households within the lineage but *si* when contrasted with those of the larger nonkin local community.

8. This is the implication of David McMullen, "Views of the State in Du Yu and Liu Zongyuan," in Stuart Schram, ed., *Foundations and Limits of State Power in China* (London: School of Oriental and African Studies, 1987), esp. 74–76.

9. For Chen's use of these contrasting phrases see, e.g., *PYTOCG* 4:8–13, 17:47–53; and *JSWB* 106:24–26. The matched phrases "*cungong*" and "*cunguan*" were also used in this sense.

10. Chen himself also less commonly opposed the phrases "*guimin*" and "*guiguan*," as in his memorial of QL 16/12/29, *QLZZ* 2.320–22.

11. Mary Backus Rankin, *Elite Activism and Political Transformation in China: Zhejiang Province, 1865–1911* (Stanford: Stanford University Press, 1986); William T. Rowe, *Hankow: Conflict and Community in a Chinese City, 1796–1895* (Stanford: Stanford University Press, 1989); Strand, *Rickshaw Beijing.*

12. Perhaps the clearest of Chen's many statements to this effect appears in *PYTOCG* 19:29–30.

13. Zelin; Feng Erkang, esp. 139–64.

14. *PYTOCG* 2:36–38, 4:8–13, 4:26–32, 4:42. For arguments favoring rescinding the new system at the time of Qianlong's accession see Zelin, 267.

15. Zelin, 272–77 on the debate in general, and 276 on Sun Jiagan's response.

16. I have not found the original of Chen's responding memorial, dated QL 7/4, in the archives. It is extracted at length in *NP* 4:20.

17. Memorial of QL 7/6/18, MQA.

18. *PYTOCG* 16:3–5; memorial of QL 16/12/29, *QLZZ* 2.320–22.

19. The revenues generated by *haoxian* surtaxes were intended by the Yongzheng emperor to finance not only local administrative outlays on public causes (*gong fei*) but also the "nourishing integrity" supplementary stipend (*yanglian*), which he sought to use to bring official salaries in line with the growing actual costs of government service. The line between the official's personal finances and the public purse was in the process, however, further blurred. For his part Chen Hongmou routinely chose to donate portions of his *yanglian* stipend to administrative projects, and he fully expected his subordinates to do the same. Chen justified this on the grounds that *yanglian* and *gongxiang* were derived from the same taxes on the people and that they owed their origins to the same act of imperial largesse. Demonstrating appropriate frugality in the expenditure of his *yanglian* stipend on personal maintenance would allow an official considerable surplus to devote to public needs. See Chen's 1736 letter to Yang Xingting, *SD* 1:2–3.

20. Memorials of QL 13/4/29, QL 13/intercalary 7/20, and QL 14/7/5, all QPA.

21. See, e.g., his arguments to this effect reprinted in *JSWB* 26:60, 28:33–35, 106:24–26.

22. For various assessments by Western scholars see, e.g., Zelin, 170; Will, *Bureaucracy and Famine*, 286; Feuerwerker, "State and Economy"; and Frederic E. Wakeman Jr., "China and the Seventeenth-Century Crisis," *Late Imperial China* 7.1 (June 1986): 21.

23. Memorial of QL 23/3/4, MQA.

24. Among many article-length studies, see Fuma Susumu, "Zentō, zenkai no shuppatsu" (The origin of *shantang* and *shanhui*), in Ono Kazuko, ed., *Min-Shin jidai no seiji to shakai* (Government and society in the Ming and Qing era) (Kyoto: Jimbun kagaku kenkyūjo, 1983), 189–232; Fuma, "Shindai Shōkō ikueitō no keiei jittai to chiho shakai (Local society and the practical management of orphanages in Qing Songjiang), *Tōyōshi kenkyū* 45.3 (December 1986): 55–89; Angela Kiche Leung, "L'accueil des enfants abandonnés dans la Chine du bas-Yangzi aux XVIIe et XVIIIe siècles," *Études chinoises* 4.1 (spring 1985): 15–54; Liang Qizi, "Mingmuo Qingqu minjian zishan huodong de xingqi"; Joanna Handlin Smith, "Benevolent Societies: The Reshaping of Charity During the Late Ming and Early Ch'ing," *Journal of Asian Studies* 46.2 (May 1987): 309–37; and Mary Backus Rankin, "Managed by the People: Officials, Gentry, and the Foshan Charitable Granary, 1795–1845," *Late Imperial China* 15.2 (December 1994): 1–52.

25. Liang Qizi, *Shishan yu jiaohua: Ming-Qing de zishan zuzhi* (Charity and civilizing: Philanthropic organizations in the Ming and Qing) (Taibei: Lianjing, 1997).

26. The one significant mention of these sorts of institutions in Chen's four terms as Shaanxi governor has already been noted: his approval in 1748 of the Shangnan magistrate's decision to expend his county's *gongxiang* budget on refurbishing a so-called *yangji yuan* (hall of nurturance and relief). This incident provides independent support for Liang Qizi's observation that institutions of the specific *yangji yuan* type, originating in the late Ming, enjoyed a brief resurgence of popularity around the mid-eighteenth century, at the initiative neither of local elites nor of higher levels of administration but rather of isolated county-level officials. See Liang Qizi, "Zishan huodong de xingqi," 308–9.

27. Leung, "L'accueil des enfants abandonnés," 22.

28. *Jiangdu xianzhi* (Gazetteer of Jiangdu county), 1743, 7:26.

29. *Jiangdu xianzhi* 7:25; Liang Qizi, *Shishan yu jiaohua*, 106. Prefectural *gongxiang* funds in Yangzhou were heavily derived from a quasi-formal imposition on salt merchant profits, part of

the government control over the merchants' hefty *gong fei* slush fund, which Chen and his superior, Governor Gao Qizhuo, were in these years working strenuously to assert. The manipulation by both sides of the idiom of "*gong*," with its various connotations of "governmental" and "nongovernmental communal," seems to have been particularly active during this struggle. See *NP* 1:17.

30. Chen, "Puji tang shuyin" (Abstracted proclamation on the *Puji tang*), *Jiangdu xianzhi* 7:25.

31. The following paragraphs are based on *PYTOCG* 1:4–6 and 1:40–49. Extraordinarily detailed (well beyond what is summarized here), these documents would seem to constitute one of the richest surviving sources on the operation of any charitable organization in early- to mid-eighteenth-century China.

32. Liang Qizi, *Shishan yu jiaohua*, 80–84.

33. *PYTOCG* 5:15–18; *NP* 3:4.

34. Liang Qizi, *Shishan yu jiaohua*, 228–29.

35. *PYTOCG* 10:48–50.

36. *PYTOCG* 47:10–11; *NP* 11:14. Note that at about this same time Chen moved to augment, from a combination of public and private sources but through imperially endorsed government action, the endowments of Suzhou's Puji tang and Yuying tang; *NP* 10:22–23. Fuma Susumu states that Chen also ordered during this tenure as Jiangsu governor the establishment of quasi-communal *tongshan hui* in every county of the province, although to little evident effect. Fuma does not record his source, however, and I have found no independent confirmation of this initiative. Fuma, *Chūgoku zenkai zentō shi kenkyū* (The history of *shanhui* and *shantang* in China) (Kyoto: Dohosha, 1997), 801–2.

37. On this process see especially Rankin, *Elite Activism*.

38. One of many studies of the rise of "public opinion" as an item of European political discourse is Roger Chartier, "The Public Sphere and Public Opinion," in his *The Cultural Origins of the French Revolution* (Durham: Duke University Press, 1991), chap. 3. For discussion of the power of this concept in early-twentieth-century China see Joan Judge, *Print and Politics: Shibao and the Culture of Reform in Late Qing China* (Stanford: Stanford University Press, 1996), esp. 68–74.

39. Longer versions of *minqing* in the "public opinion" sense are "*minjian yilun*" and "*minjian qingyuan*" (things that meet the acceptance of the people). Another longer phrase is "*guanmin qingyi zhi tong*," the "convergence of the sentiments of officialdom and of the people." Clear indication that the terms "*renqing*" and "*minqing*" have been elided with "*gonglun*" and "*yulun*" is the occasional merging of elements from both compounds in the term "*yuqing*." A negative representation of public opinion in Qing bureaucratic discourse is in the various terms for "public resentment" or "mass resentment" (*gongfen, zhongyuan*), indicating policies or situations that have been greeted with popular hostility.

40. *Dayi juemi lu* 1:8; Lynn A. Struve, "Huang Zongxi in Context: A Reappraisal of His Major Writings," *Journal of Asian Studies* 47.3 (August 1988): 476; Munro, "Concept of Interest," 185–86; Polachek, *Inner Opium War*, 81; Will, "La communication entre bureaucrates et paysans." As Carol Gluck has demonstrated (*Japan's Modern Myths*, 18), this importance of *renqing/ ninjō* as a popular legitimator for political action carried over into Meiji Japan.

41. Chen's citations of and comments on Lü on this issue appear in *LZJL* 1:6, 1:52–58, 1:70–75, 1:95, 2:64; and *CZYG* 1:34–50. See also Handlin, *Action*, 144–60.

42. A sampling of Chen's discourse on public opinion may be found in memorials of QL 16/11/6, *QLZZ* 1.846–47; and QL 28/12, extracted in Liequan 5834; *PYTOCG* 15:20–23, 16:38–40, 33:43–44, 37:20–21, 38:7–8; *ZGFJL* 1:12–13; *XSYG* 4:85–86; *SD* 1:7, 1:13, 2:4; *PYTWL* 44:1–2.

43. *PYTOCG* 34:15–19.

44. For examples see memorials of QL 7/7/1, MQA; QL 12/8/24, QPA; QL 16/8/11, QL 17/3/4, QL 20/7/28, QL 21/6/29, and QL 21/10/20, in *QLZZ* 1.385–87, 2.366–67, 12.223–26, 14.759–60, 15.799.

45. *PYTOCG* 20:25–26.

46. Letter to Wei Tingpu, *SD* 2:4.

47. Memorial of QL 19/11/18, *QLZZ* 10.109–10; *PYTOCG* 11:7–9, 11:25–26, 16:36–37; Letter to Zhou Renji, *SD* 3:4; Xu Dong, *Muling shu*, 4:25–26.

48. Handlin, *Action*, 149–50. See also Chen's letter to Xie Rongsheng, *SD* 3:4.

49. The dual nature of "*gonglun*" in Qing discourse is suggested in Rankin, "Origins of a Chinese Public Sphere," 42. Chen's use of such terms as "*minqing*" as substitutes for "*gonglun*" in certain contexts definitely marks his use of the latter as more local and more populist than the "*gonglun*" invoked by dynastic critics such as Huang Zongxi.

50. *LZJL* 1:53–54; letter to Zhu Nanhu, *SD*, 3:16.

51. Chartier, *Cultural Origins*, 20–37.

52. *LZJL* 2:64.

53. See variously *XSYG*, preface and 3:24–27; *SD* 2:2, 3:16; *JSWB* 28:33–35; and Xu Dong, *Muling shu*, 8:3–4, 10:33–35.

54. *JSWB* 105:30–34.

55. Hao Chang, "Confucian Cosmological Myth."

56. de Bary, *Trouble with Confucianism*, 98–99.

57. Hymes, *Statesmen and Gentlemen*, 132–35; Hymes and Schirokauer, 12–13, 22–23; von Glahn, "Community and Welfare," 254.

58. Handlin, *Action*; Handlin, "Definitions of Community by Ch'i Chi-kuang and Lü K'un," in Paul A. Cohen and John E. Schrecker, eds., *Reform in Nineteenth-Century China* (Cambridge, Mass.: East Asian Research Center, 1976), 18–25; Leif Littrup, *Subbureaucratic Government in Ming Times* (Oslo: Universitetsforleget, 1981), chap. 6; To Wing-kai, "Kinship Ritual and Community Institutions in the Late Ming Period: Huang Tso's *T'ai-ch'uan Hsiang-li*" (paper presented to the Conference on Family Process and Political Process in China, University of California, Davis, April 1991).

59. David Ownby, *Brotherhoods and Secret Societies in Early and Mid-Qing China* (Stanford: Stanford University Press, 1996), 34. The order to strengthen local community ties (*xiangdang*) as a stimulus to local self-reliance was of course a basic injunction of the *Sacred Edict* (*shengyu*), promulgated first in 1649 and expanded in 1670; see Ōmura, "'*Shengyu guangxun*' no chihei ni tsuite."

60. See, e.g., Will, *Bureaucracy and Famine*, 74–75.

61. *LZJL* 1:89.

62. *CZYG* 1:18–32.

63. *PYTOCG* 21:41–44, 24:38–44. For a discussion of the various significances attached to the *Rites of Zhou* (*Zhouli* or *Zhouguan*) in Chen's day see Chapter 12.

64. *PYTOCG* 19:22–24. Chen sometimes uses the term "*lidang*" interchangeably with "*xiangdang*."

65. *PYTOCG* 21:41–44.

66. *PYTOCG* 19:35–36.

67. Memorial of QL 14/7/5, GCA. See also *PYTOCG* 19:31–32; *XSYG* 1:4–8; *Wenji* 9:40–46.

68. *PYTOCG* 19:32.

69. *Wenji* 9:40–46; *PYTOCG* 16:1–2.

70. For Zhu "the 'middle level' [of local community] was just that: a level between family and state, neither of which lost legitimacy by the addition of a third" (Hymes and Schirokauer, 27).

71. Hymes and Schirokauer, 27. On twentieth-century views see David Strand, "Calling the Chinese People to Order: Images of State and Society in the *Sanmin zhuyi* of Sun Yat-sen" (paper presented to the Conference on State and Society in East Asia, Copenhagen, April 1993); and Bryna Goodman, *Native Place, City, and Nation: Regional Networks and Identities in Shanghai, 1853–1937* (Berkeley: University of California Press, 1995), chap. 8.

72. *CZYG* 1:18–32.

73. *Guitiao huichao* 2:65–73; *PYTOCG* 21:36–37, 30:13–22.

74. *PYTOCG* 24:38–44. On analogous movements by twentieth-century reformist elites

(now inspired by Western-nationalist rather than Confucian views of enlightenment) see Prasenjit Duara, "Knowledge and Power in the Discourse of Modernity: The Campaigns Against Popular Religion in Early Twentieth-Century China," *Journal of Asian Studies* 50.1 (February 1991): 67–83.

75. He imposes headman and collective-responsibility obligations on occupational groups of beggars, e.g., just as he does on communities of Muslim Huimin; *NP* 10:13.

76. *PYTOCG* 2:14–15, 14:43–48; *Guitiao huichao* 2:65–73.

77. Fu Yiling, "Lun xiangzu shili duiyu Zhongguo fengjian jingji de ganshe" (The negative influence of *xiang*-level lineages on China's feudal economy), in his *Ming-Qing shehui jingji shi lunwenji* (Collected essays on Ming and Qing socioeconomic history) (Beijing: Renmin chuban-she, 1982), 78–102; Mori Masao, "Kyōzoku o megutte" (On *xiang*-level lineages), *Tōyōshi kenkyū* 44.1 (1985): 137–53; William T. Rowe, "Success Stories: Lineage and Elite Status in Hanyang County, Hubei, c. 1368–1949," in Joseph W. Esherick and Mary Backus Rankin, eds., *Chinese Local Elites and Patterns of Dominance* (Berkeley: University of California Press, 1990), 51–81. The kinship component of this *xiang*-community, stressed in all of these studies, will be addressed below. There is an obvious parallel here to the marketing community (particularly the town-centered "central marketing community") identified by G. William Skinner based on field observation in mid-twentieth-century Sichuan; see Skinner, "Marketing and Social Structure in Rural China," *Journal of Asian Studies* 24.1 (1964): 3–23.

78. See, e.g., *PYTOCG* 16:45–47, 21:41–44, 26:1–3; *XSYG* 2:21–28.

79. *PYTOCG* 16:3–5, 16:14–15.

80. Chen was most explicit in identifying the *xiang* as *shecang* locus in Jiangxi, where, as we shall see, it was somewhat more developed as a social unit than it was in other places he served. See, e.g., *PYTOCG* 16:38–40.

81. To Wing-kai, "Kinship Ritual and Community Institutions"; Littrup, chap. 6.

82. The authorized procedures for conducting the *xiangyin jiuli* in the Qing are laid out in *Qingchao wenxian tongkao* 76:5553 and discussed in Hsiao, 209–10.

83. On the 1644 reaffirmation of the libationer ceremony see *Qingchao wenxian tongkao* 76:5553.

84. Edict of YZ 1 (1723) and Board of Rites directive of 1737, reprinted in *Qingchao wenx-ian tongkao* 76:5556–57. On the earlier history of the *xiangyin jiuli* see Hsiao, 208–10, and Thomas H. C. Lee, *Government Education and Examinations in Sung China* (New York: St. Martin's, 1985), 109–10.

85. After 1737 the *Qingchao wenxian tongkao* records only one Qianlong-era central government pronouncement on *xiangyin jiuli*, a 1753 edict complaining of its corruption in practice (76:5559). On the long-term decline in Qing interest in the ritual see Hsiao, 216–20.

86. *PYTOCG* 13:20–21, 16:45–47.

87. *PYTOCG* 21:41–44, 24:10–11.

88. *PYTOCG* 21:43.

89. *PYTOCG* 13:20.

90. E. Rawski, "A Historian's Approach to Death Ritual," in James L. Watson and Evelyn S. Rawski, eds., *Death Ritual in Late Imperial and Modern China* (Berkeley: University of California Press, 1988), 27.

91. *PYTOCG* 16:45.

92. Hsiao, 210–14.

93. *PYTOCG* 16:46.

94. Proclamation of 1760, reprinted in *JSWB* 68:5.

95. See especially *PYTOCG* 21:41–44.

96. *PYTOCG* 21:41–44.

97. For Chen's campaign to redefine the lineage headman system in Jiangxi see *PYTOCG* 13:46–48.

98. *PYTOCG* 16:45–47.

99. *PYTOCG* 21:41–44. It must be noted that the term "*xiangping*" had been used as well in the Board of Rites' 1737 directive on selection of *xiangyin jiuli* honorees; see *Wenxian tongkao* 76:5557. Yet Chen's greater emphasis on it in proclamations issued many years later draws more deeply, I would insist, on a notion of public opinion that is central to his sociopolitical thought and independent of specific central government instructions.

100. Hsiao, esp. chap. 3; Feng Erkang, 365–66; William T. Rowe, "Urban Control in Late Imperial China: The *Pao-chia* System in Hankow," in Joshua A. Fogel and Rowe, eds., *Perspectives on a Changing China* (Boulder: Westview Press, 1979), 89–112.

101. Hsiao, esp. 56, 65, and 570. In the *JSWB* section on *baojia* Chen is represented by only one item, far less than his representation in most other sections, and this one item, as we will see below, is hardly an unequivocal endorsement of the system. In Xu Dong's 1837 manual on *baojia* Chen is cited three times, but none of these citations are directly on the subject of the system itself; Xu Dong, *Baojia shu*, 3:14–21, 3:34–36, 3:38.

102. *CZYG* 1:18–32. For a translation and discussion of Wang's "Shijia pai" see Wang, *Instructions for Practical Living and other Neo-Confucian Writings*, trans. and ed. Wing-tsit Chan (New York: Columbia University Press, 1963), 293–94, 306–9. For Hsiao Kung-ch'uan's straightforward reading of Chen's support for Wang's system see Hsiao, 570.

103. A letter from Yuan to Chen on the subject of *baojia* survives (Yuan, *Xiaocang shanfang wenji* 15:6–9), but unfortunately Chen's response does not. For Yuan's general hostility to the institution see Min Tu-ki, 103–4; and Ping-ti Ho, 40–41.

104. *JSWB* 75:21.

105. *PYTOCG* 19:35–39, 23:39–41.

106. Memorial of QL 23/7, extracted in *NP* 10:12–13.

107. *PYTOCG* 13:9–14.

108. *KSZJ* 6:18–21. See also *PYTOCG* 13:46–48.

109. Hsiao, 29–31.

110. *PYTOCG* 21:32–35, 23:34–35, 29:19–21.

111. The term "*xiangbao*" is not glossed in Hsiao Kung-ch'uan's classic study of the *baojia* system, *Rural China*, and seems to have had no formal legal status in the Qing. Nevertheless, functionaries with this title were in common use in eighteenth-century north China. Based on legal cases in the archives of Baodi County, Zhili, Philip Huang finds them to have been nominated by a consortium of village leaders and formally installed by the county magistrate. Not enjoying especially high social status, they nevertheless performed a range of significant quasi-governmental functions. Huang finds the jurisdiction of a typical *xiangbao* to have comprised approximately twenty villages. Although Huang does not explicitly associate the *xiangbao*'s jurisdiction with the *xiang*-community centered on a market town (he in general downplays the significance of marketing communities in Qing north China), Chen Hongmou's specific tasking of *xiangbao* with policing of such towns suggests that this situation may in fact have been the norm. See Huang, *The Peasant Economy and Social Change in North China* (Stanford: Stanford University Press, 1985), 222–31.

112. *PYTOCG* 23:1–4.

113. Hymes and Schirokauer, 22–23.

114. For studies of two diverse implementations during the Ming see Kandice Hauf, "The Community Covenant in Sixteenth-Century Ji'an Prefecture, Jiangxi," *Late Imperial China* 17.2 (December 1996): 1–50; and McDermott, "Community Pact Ritual."

115. Hsiao, chap. 6; Ōmura, 256–60; Feng Erkang, 370–71.

116. Ōmura, 260.

117. *PYTOCG* 21:41–44.

118. *XSYG* 1:4–8. As Monika Übelhor has shown, Zhu Xi's redaction of the Lü family compact was considerably more hierarchical and moralistic, and less communitarian and pragmatic, than the original; see Übelhor, "The Community Compact (*Hsiang-yüeh*) of the Sung and Its Educational Significance," in de Bary and Chaffee, 371–88.

119. *XSYG* 1:18–32. Wang Yangming's text is translated by Wing-tsit Chan in Wang, *Instructions for Practical Living*, 298–306. For discussions of the "Nan-Gan xiangyue" and its implementation in the Ming see Littrup, 160–63; and Hauf, 7–12, 36–37.

120. Littrup, 165–68, 179–80; Handlin, *Action*, 47–51, 198–99.

121. *KSZJ* 6:18–21. See also Chen's similar comments in *PYTOCG* 13:46–48.

122. *XSYG* 2:3.

123. Chen, preface to Lu Suoshan's "Jujia zhengben zhiyong bian" (Useful advice on the essentials of dwelling together as a family), *XSYG* 1:8.

124. See, e.g., Chen's letter to Yang Fangqi, *SD* 3:5.

125. *PYTOCG* 13:25.

126. Chen, memorial of QL 17/3/28, *QLZZ* 2.536–37; *NP* 7:9.

127. See, e.g., memorial of QL 18/3/28, *QLZZ* 5.1; *PYTOCG* 14:46–47.

128. "Zongpu liuzhuan"; *JS* 224–28, 237–40. Probably not coincidentally, Chen's major endowment bequest to his own lineage came in the same year, 1742, as his innovation in empowering lineage headmen in Jiangxi.

129. *CZYG* 2:30.

130. For Chen's practical experience with such problems see, e.g., his memorial of QL 18/11/27 (with Karjishan), *QLZZ* 6.874–76.

131. *XSYG* 4:5; see also *CZYG* 1:65–66.

132. One manifestation of this line of thinking was Chen's attempt, as Shaanxi governor in 1746, to restrict male adoption to that between households of demonstrable common descent (preferably of the same lineage branch), on grounds that any other form of adoption would "throw the kinship system into disorder" (*luan zongzu*); *PYTOCG* 23:28.

133. See, e.g., Yan Zhitui, "Yan shi jiaxun mianxue pian" (Household rules of the Yan family for encouraging education), *YZYG* 2:1–3; Wang Shijin, "Zonggui" (Lineage rules), *XSYG* 2:21–28. This is not the place to discuss the contents of these rules, which are of considerable interest. For general analyses of the proliferation of these regulatory codes see Furth, "The Patriarch's Legacy"; and Wang Ermin, "Jiaxun tizhi shiyan ji menfeng guansheng zhi weizhi" (Promulgation of household rules and the preservation of family and official reputation), in Institute of Modern History, *Jiazu yu zhengzhi*, 807–46.

134. *XSYG* 2:38.

135. Chow, *Confucian Ritualism*; Brook, "Funerary Ritual." Among other works touching on this subject see Zuo Yunpeng, "Sitang zuchang zuquan de xingcheng ji qi zuoyong shishuo" (The rise and functions of the ancestral hall and the lineage head), *Lishi yanjiu* 1964.5–6, 97–116; Beattie, *Land and Lineage in China*, esp. chap. 6; Hung-lam Chu, "Intellectual Trends in the Fifteenth Century"; Rowe, "Success Stories"; and Wang Ermin.

136. Fu, "Xiangzu," 80. According to Fu's source, such an arrangement had pertained in Yiyang since the early Ming.

137. Zuo, 101; Hymes, *Statesmen and Gentlemen*.

138. John Dardess, "A Century of Social Change: T'ai-ho County, Kiangsi, 1400–1500," *Ming Studies* (1989): 56–60; Dardess, *A Ming Society: T'ai-ho County, Kiangsi, Fourteenth to Seventeenth Centuries* (Berkeley: University of California Press, 1997).

139. Xu Hua'an, "Shixi Qingdai Jiangxi zongzu de jiegou yu nengzhidian" (A preliminary analysis of the structure and powers of lineages in Qing Jiangxi), *Zhongguo shehui jingji shi yanjiu* 1993.1, 47–55.

140. Steven Averill, "The Shed People and the Opening of the Yangzi Highlands," *Modern China* 9.1 (January 1983): 104–8.

141. *PYTOCG* 13:46.

142. *XSYG* 2:18–21.

143. Directive of QL 7/6, *PYTOCG* 13:46–48. See also discussion in *NP* 4:21.

144. *Qingchao wenxian tongkao* 23:5055; Zhu Yong, *Qingdai zongzu fa yanjiu* (A study of lineage law in the Qing) (Changsha: Hunan jiaoyu chubanshe, 1987), 157–59.

145. *Da Qing huidian shili* 811:2. Qianlong stated emphatically that "the authority to impose capital punishment is a sovereign prerogative of the court alone."

146. Directive of QL 7/10, *PYTOCG* 14:43–48.

147. Directive of QL 8/12, *PYTOCG* 16:45–47. See also my "*Jiaohua*: Social Regeneration Through Ritual in Eighteenth-Century China," paper presented to the Conference on Ritual and the State in East Asian History, Paris, June 1995.

148. Among treatments of this affair in the scholarly literature see Hsiao, 353; Zuo, 107; Chow, *Confucian Ritualism*, 221, 230; and most extensively R. Bin Wong, "Lineages and Local Government in Late Imperial and Modern China," in Institute of Modern History, *Jiazu yu zhengzhi*, 779–805. All but Hsiao come down generally on the "empowerment" interpretation, although Wong acknowledges a complexity of motives on Chen's part.

149. Proclamation of QL 7/2, *PYTOCG* 13:25–27.

150. Directive of QL 7/1, *PYTOCG* 13:16–17.

151. Likewise in his promotion of lineage *shecang* under *zuzhang* management he warned local officials to be especially attentive to the opportunities this offered the lineage leaders for corrupt personal gain; *PYTOCG* 14:46–47.

152. See also *PYTOCG* 13:25–27.

153. More than any *fengjian*-style effort to grant autonomy to lineage leaders, I believe, Chen's Jiangxi initiative reflected an effort to incorporate them into a hierarchy of governance dominated unquestionably by the imperial state. I find helpful in envisioning what Chen had in mind the suggestion made some decades later by Zhang Xuecheng to make kinship organization a part of the formal state apparatus, operating at one level below that of the county. As a historian Zhang was inspired by the analogy of documentary records, in which genealogies functioned at the lowest level, county and provincial gazetteers at progressively higher levels, and dynastic histories at the top. The goal, Zhang offered, was to "lead the masses by means of the great lineages, and lead the great lineages by means of the state." See Kai-wing Chow, "Ordering Ancestors and the State: Chang Hsüeh-ch'eng (1738–1801) and Lineage Discourse in Eighteenth-Century China," in Institute of Modern History, *Jiazu yu zhengzhi*, esp. 307.

154. Directive of QL 7/10, *PYTOCG* 14:41–42.

155. This despite the fact that the document refers to "*zuzheng*" in its title, which I believe to have been added well after the fact, at the time of the *PYTOCG*'s compilation in the 1760s.

156. This slippage occurs, e.g., in the debate of 1768, discussed in *Wenxian tongkao* 19:5031–32.

157. Zhu Yong, 158, 168. See also Hsiao, 47, 69, 349, 672; Zuo, 106; Feng Erkang, 362–63.

158. Chen Hongmou, letter to Yang Puyuan, *SD* 3:15.

159. *KSZJ* 6:18–21.

160. As Chen well knew, Wang Yangming had also linked his *xiangyue* institutions in southern Jiangxi to *baojia*-style ten-household mutual surveillance units he called *shijia pai*. See *CZYG* 1:22–24; and Wang, *Instructions for Practical Living*, trans. Chan, 293–94, 306–9.

161. Feng Erkang, 358–60; Averill, 104–8.

162. Ling Qiu, "Xijiang shinie jishi" (Memoirs of a Jiangxi Provincial Judge) (1743; reprint, Institute of History, Chinese Academy of Social Sciences, ed., *Qingshi ziliao* 3 [Beijing: Zhonghua shuju, 1992], 197–217).

163. Ling Qiu, 216–17. See also Xu Hua'an, 54.

164. *Qingchao wenxian tongkao* 19:5031–32; Zuo, 106; Hsiao, 672. As Zhu Yong points out, however, certain specified powers were granted *zuzhang* in edicts of the mid-Qianlong reign: in 1755 they were accorded the right to discipline those who stole or misappropriated lineage property and in 1766 to quarantine lineage members afflicted by epidemic disease. Zhu, 170.

165. "Fengsu taioyue" (Regulations for customary practices), *PYTOCG* 45:5–13; also reprinted in *JSWB* 68:4–6, and in *Suzhou fuzhi* (Suzhou prefectural gazetteer) (1877): 3:32–37.

166. Chen, memorial of QL 18/4/24, *QLZZ* 5.163–64; *NP* 7:19. On the later history of this

policy in Fujian see Zuo, 107; and Harry J. Lamley, "Lineage and Surname Feuds in Southern Fukien and Eastern Kwangtung Under the Ch'ing," in K. Liu, *Orthodoxy*, 272.

167. Fude, "Qing jiin sizhai liubi shu," in *JSWB* 58:37–38. See also Wong, "Lineage and Local Government," 793–94.

168. *SD* 3:15. The date of the letter is not given, but from its placement in Chen's roughly chronological published letters it appears to have been from the early 1760s.

169. Lamley, 272.

170. For other examples of early nineteenth-century writers' attraction to this theme (including most notably Gong Zizhen and Zhang Haishan) see Kai-wing Chow, 221; Zuo, 109–15; and Lin Man-houng, "When Grandsons Beat Their Grandfathers," 6–9.

171. *JSWB* 58:35–39.

172. Xu Dong, *Baojia shu*, 3:34–36.

173. Feng Guifen, "Fu zongfa yi" (Proposal to revive the lineage system), in Ge Shiyong, ed., *Huangchao jingshi wen xubian* (Second compendium of statecraft writings of the reigning dynasty), 1888, 55:4–5. This document is discussed briefly in Hsiao, 351; and in Wright, *Last Stand of Chinese Conservatism*, 137. For a more detailed treatment, see Wong, "Lineage and Local Government," 796–97.

174. For the widespread early-twentieth-century fascination with such corporatist nation-building strategies, utilizing ties of common local origin and of common occupation as well as those of kinship, see Strand, "Calling the Chinese People to Order"; and Goodman, *Native Place, City, and Nation*, chap. 8.

175. *XSYG* 4:7.

Chapter 12

1. Yang Nianqun, esp. 46–55. The dating of the term "*jiaohua*" is from Wang Gungwu, "The Chinese Urge to Civilize: Reflections on Change," *Journal of Asian History* 18.1 (1984): 3.

2. See Leon Vandermeersch, *Wangdao, ou la Voie Royale* (Paris: École francaise de l'Extrême Orient, 1977).

3. *Shengyu guangxun* (*The Sacred Edict*, with commentary) (Beijing, 1880 edition).

4. *PYTOCG* 15:15.

5. See, e.g., *PYTOCG* 3:14, 5:3; *Xueshi yigui* 4:86.

6. E.g. *PYTOCG* 17:3–11 and 19:21–40.

7. Chow, *Confucian Ritualism*, esp. chap. 1.

8. That Chen so clearly sees himself as a minority voice on the efficacy of didactic appeals, of course, offers support to Chow's thesis that by the eighteenth century such sentiments were on the wane.

9. *Wenji* 9:4.

10. *PYTOCG* 5:6–7.

11. *YZYG*, preface.

12. *YZYG* 1:13, 3:5, 3:30.

13. *PYTOCG* 2:6–7, 3:5.

14. *PYTOCG* 16:10–12 (also reprinted in *JSWB*, juan 24). The reference is to *Lunyu* (Analects), chap. 15, v. 38.

15. *YZYG* 3:29. For Chen's ideas on tracking see *XSYG* (1769 ed.), 4:10–13.

16. *Yunnan tongzhi* (Yunnan provincial gazetteer) (1736), 29 *xia*:49.

17. Letter to Zhou Renji, *SD* 2:9; and *PYTOCG* 16:10–12.

18. *KSZJ* 1:1–6, 1:7–10; *XSYG* 2:8–9.

19. Among many examples see especially *NP* 5:13; and Sun Xingyan, 14–17.

20. *PYTOCG* 15:37–38.

21. *PYTOCG* 2:39, 9:41–42, 13:7–8; *NP* 4:14.

22. See, e.g., *PYTOCG* 3:12–13, 32:27, 38:1; *SD* 1:13; *NP* 1:18, 4:17.

23. A prime example of renovation was Hunan's Yuelu Academy, reconstructed in 1669 by Governor Zhou Mingnan; *Xinxiu Yuelu shuyuan zhishu* 3:10.

24. Ron-Guey Chu, "Scholarly Autonomy and Political Dissent of Local Academies in the Early Ch'ing" (paper presented to the Symposium on Civil Society in East Asian Countries, Montreal, 1992).

25. *Qinding xuezheng quanshu* (Imperially authorized compendium on academic administration), 1810, 64:3; Elman, *From Philosophy to Philology*, 119–21; Woodside, "Divorce," 477.

26. *PYTOCG* 2:8–10, 3:12–13, 13:7–8, 32:24. On Ortai's conception of the Yunnan Academy's purpose see Woodside, "Divorce," 483–84.

27. See, e.g., *PYTOCG* 18:27–28, 22:27, 24:49, 30:33, 33:1, 34:30–39, 34:47–49; *SD* 2:17.

28. *PYTOCG* 25:51–52; *KSZJ*, esp. preface by Chen Lansen; *NP* 12:23.

29. Letter to Zhang Hao, *Peiyuan tang shoudu ping* 1:4; *Wenji* 1:13–14; *PYTOCG* 2:8–10, 15:37–38; *NP* 5:3.

30. *PYTOCG* 9:41–42.

31. *PYTOCG* 22:32–33, 26:19, 28:1–2, 32:24, 32:27, 38:1.

32. *PYTOCG* 1:33; see also Chen's preface to his *Quan Dian yixue huiji*.

33. Littrup, 171.

34. *Qinding xuezheng quanshu* 64:1–3. See also Ogawa Yoshiko, "Shindai ni okeru gigaku setsuritsu no kiben" (Social basis of *yixue* founding in the Qing period), in Hayashi Tomoharu, ed., *Kinsei Chūgoku kyōiku shi kenkyū*, 279–82. Ogawa suggests that early Qing official initiatives in the area of *shexue* and *yixue* founding were designed in part to deflect attention from the more politically suspect *shuyuan*.

35. Littrup, 172–73.

36. *Guilin shike* 3:114–16; *Lingui xianzhi* 14:21–22.

37. *PYTOCG* 5:3–7.

38. *PYTOCG* 2:6. For Chen's success in doing just that see my article "Education and Empire," esp. 430–32.

39. Xu Qianxue, ed., *Guwen yuanjian*, preface by Kangxi emperor dated 1685. See also the biography of Xu in *ECCP*, 310–12. Chen's comments on the work appear in *PYTOCG* 4:16–21.

40. Li Guangdi, ed., *Xingli jingyi*, imperial preface dated 1716. On this work see also Chan, "The *Hsing-li ching-i*," and *ECCP*, 473–75. On the pedagogical history of the *Xiaoxue* see Kelleher, "Back to Basics."

41. *Shengyu guangxun*. On the *Sacred Edict*'s pedagogical use see Ōmura, 231–71.

42. *PYTOCG* 19:4–5.

43. *PYTOCG* 18:43–44.

44. *NP* 12:24.

45. *YZYG* 3:5–6, 3:16–17, 3:31, and 3:35–39; *Xueshi yigui* 3:1; *SD* 3:13; *Peiyuan tang shoudu ping* 1:4.

46. *YZYG* 3:40. Chen's ideas on this score were not unlike those being developed in Europe at around the same time; see, e.g., Philippe Ariès, *Centuries of Childhood: A Social History of Family Life* (New York: Vintage, 1962), 187.

47. *PYTOCG* 2:8–10, 3:5–11.

48. Both Zhu Xi's text and Chen's commentary are in *YZYG* 1:5–6. The translation here is adapted from that of the *YZYG* in Morgan, 150–63.

49. *PYTOCG* 3:8–9.

50. The following pages recapitulate in much-abbreviated form the material in my article "Education and Empire in Southwest China." Readers desiring more detailed information about this critical episode in the history of Qing cultural expansion are advised to consult that article.

51. Amidst the large literature on the process of Ming-Qing assimilation of the southwest see Huang Kaihua, "Mingdai tusi zhidu sheshi yu xinan kaifa" (Establishment of the *tusi* system in the Ming and the opening of the southwest), *Xinya xuebao* 6.1 (February 1964): 285–365, and 6.2 (August 1964): 397–495; Kent Smith, "Ch'ing Policy and the Development of Southwest

China"; Claudine Lombard-Salmon, *Un Example d'Acculturation Chinoise: La Province du Guizhou au XVIIIe Siècle* (Paris: École Francaise d'Extrême Orient, 1972); James Lee, "The Legacy of Immigration in Southwest China, 1250–1850," *Annales de demographie historique* (1982): 279–304; and James Lee, "Food Supply and Population Growth in Southwest China, 1250–1850," *Journal of Asian Studies* 41.4 (1982): 711–46.

52. Huang Kaihua, 447–59; Ogawa 281.

53. John E. Herman, "Empire in the Southwest: Early Qing Reforms to the Native Chiefdom System," *Journal of Asian Studies* 56.1 (February 1997): 47–74.

54. For examples of the thinking of Ortai and Yinjishan on the relationship of education and political incorporation see Ortai, "Zheng Dian shi ru shuyuan jiao" (Order that Yunnan scholars enter the academy for training), *JSWB* 57:58–61; Yinjishan and Yuan Zhancheng, memorial of YZ 12/6/1, *Yunnan tongzhi* 23:139–44; Wang Chang 29:1–2.

55. Data on foundings, locations, and endowments of each individual school may be found in Chen, *Quan Dian yixue huiji*; and in *Yunnan tongzhi* (1736), 7:43–60. For a more detailed discussion see Rowe, "Education and Empire," 429–35.

56. *Yunnan tongzhi, juan* 8.

57. Quoted in Lombard-Salmon, 355.

58. For classic (albeit very different) studies of the European deployment of these tropes see Roy Harvey Pearce, *The Savages of America: A Study of the Indian and the Idea of Civilization* (Baltimore: Johns Hopkins University Press, 1953); Philip D. Curtin, *The Image of Africa: British Ideas and Action, 1780–1850* (Madison: University of Wisconsin Press, 1964); Edward Said, *Orientalism* (New York: Random House, 1978).

59. Lombard-Salmon, 57–66.

60. *Miao luan tuce* (Album of Miao life) (Taibei: Institute of History and Philology, 1973). The range of eighteenth-century Han depictions of the southwest peoples is indicated by the far less flattering caricatures reproduced in Chiu Chang-kong, *Die Kultur der Miao-tse* (Hamburg: Museum fur Volkerkunde, 1937).

61. *SD* 1:3.

62. Cited in Herold J. Wiens, *China's March to the Tropics* (Hamden: Shoe String Press, 1954), 235.

63. *Yunnan tongzhi* 29.6:30.

64. Zhang, preface to *Quan Dian yixue huiji*.

65. Wang Gungwu, 16.

66. Yinjishan, preface to *Quan Dian yixue huiji*.

67. Woodside, "Some Mid-Qing Theorists," 8–10.

68. See, e.g., memorials of QL 17/5/28, QL 18/6/27, QL 18/8/6, QL 18/12/12, QL 18/12/16, and QL 20/7/28, in *QLZZ* 3.211–12, 5.630–31, 6.73, 7.136–37, 7.164, 12.223–26; QL 23/5/17, MQA; *Qianlong shilu* 463:17; *PYTOCG* 34:51–52, 42:10–12.

69. For Chen's use of "*xianghua*" with reference to Inner Asian and Southeast Asian peoples, respectively, see his memorials of QL 20/7/28 and QL 19/4/28, *QLZZ* 12.223–26, 8.138–40.

70. The following paragraphs are based on *PYTOCG* 24:38–44; Qingfu and Chen, memorial of QL 11/11/2, MQA; and unpublished work in progress on the anti-Christian campaign by Ma Zhao.

71. *PYTOCG* 30:13–22.

72. *PYTOCG* 2:6.

73. *PYTOCG* 1:33–35, 2:6.

74. Chen, preface to *Quan Dian yixue huiji*.

75. *PYTOCG* 2:9, 3:8.

76. *Shizong shilu* 60:11; Yinjishan and Yuan Zhancheng memorial of YZ 12/6/1, *YZZZ* 23.141–42.

77. *PYTOCG* 2:10.

78. *Yunnan tongzhi* 8:1, 8:8. See also Pei Huang, 297–98.

79. *Peiyuan tang shoudu ping* 1:2–3; *PYTOCG* 2:13–16, 3:14–15.

80. *SD* 2:19; Xu Dong, *Muling shu*, 10:33–35.

81. For parallels of this corpus of belief with Lockean notions in the early modern West, and with European efforts to institute settled agrarian proprietorship in the New World, see Michal J. Rozbicki, "Transplanted Ethos: Indians and the Cultural Identity of English Colonists in Seventeenth-Century Maryland," *Amerika Studien* 28 (1983): 405–28; also Pearce, *Savages of America*, 68.

82. As of 1835 the revised provincial gazetteer describes nearly all of Chen's schools as still in operation, along with a comparatively small number that had been founded in the century following his departure from the province; *Yunnan tongzhi gao* (1835), *juan* 82–87. For speculations regarding the far thornier question of the project's sociocultural impact see Rowe, "Education and Empire," 444–45; and Zhang Pengyuan, "Yun-Gui diqu xiaoshu minzu de shehui bianqian ji qi xianzhi" (Social change among the minority peoples of Yunnan and Guizhou and its limitations), in Institute of Modern History, comp., *Zhongguo xiandaihua lunwenji* (Essays on China's modernization) (Taibei: Academia Sinica, 1991), 239–75.

83. *Qinding xuezheng quanshu* 64:8–9; Zhang Pengyuan, 260. The different handling by the court of Chen's Yunnan *yixue* may have owed something to the fact that he was still actively on the scene to offer them his patronage and something to the fact that Chen had effectively made them cost-free to the fiscal process. The Yunnan *yixue* were in fact singled out for praise of their financial self-sufficiency in an edict of 1761; *Qinding xuezheng quanshu* 64:9–10.

84. Mann, *Precious Records: Women in China's Long Eighteenth Century* (Stanford: Stanford University Press, 1997), 30–31, 83–94; Mann, "Classical Revival and the Gender Question: China's First Querelle des Femmes," in Institute of Modern History, *Jiazu yu zhengzhi*, 377–412; Clara Wing-chung Ho, "The Cultivation of Female Talent: Views on Women's Education in China During the Early and High Qing Periods," *Journal of the Economic and Social History of the Orient* 38.2 (1995): 191–223.

85. On Lan Dingyuan's work see Chen Dongyuan, 275–78; Ropp, 9; and Mann, *Precious Records*, 28–29. The early 1740s saw a vogue of publication of works other than Chen Hongmou's *JNYG* (1742) on female education. These included Ren Qiyun's *Nüjiao jingchuan tongzuan* (c. 1740) and the female scholar Li Wanfang's *Nüjiao yanxing lu* (1741).

86. *JNYG* 2:1–37.

87. *JNYG*, preface.

88. *JNYG*, preface.

89. *JNYG* 1:5.

90. *JNYG* 2:1.

91. *JNYG*, preface.

92. *JNYG*, preface.

93. *JNYG* 2:4–5. See also Handlin, "Lü K'un's New Audience," 18.

94. For Chen's approval of using the vernacular specifically to reach female audiences see his introductions to the doggerel works of Shi Dian and Wang Zhifu in *JNYG* 3:8 and 3:19. An example of his more general enthusiasm for popularization in moral treatises is his highly animated picture book of Guandi's "sagely deeds," the 1768 *Guandi shengji tuzhi quanji*. The debate over use of the vernacular seems to parallel that on simplification of ritual performances, discussed below. In both instances Chen sided squarely against the purists.

95. See, e.g., *YZYG* 1:4–5.

96. Examples of the burgeoning recent literature on women writers in the sixteenth to eighteenth centuries are Ellen Widmer, "The Epistolary World of Female Talent in Seventeenth-Century China," *Late Imperial China* 10.2 (1989): 1–43; Maureen Robertson, "Voicing the Feminine: Constructions of the Gendered Subject in Lyric Poetry by Women of Medieval and Late Imperial China," *Late Imperial China* 13.1 (1992): 63–110; Dorothy Ko, *Teachers of the Inner Chamber: Women and Culture in China, 1573–1722* (Stanford: Stanford University Press, 1994); and Mann, *Precious Records*, esp. chap. 4. In noting that Chen Hongmou excluded poetry as a le-

gitimate outlet for women's literary talent, we must recall from Chap. 1 that his own daughter, Chen Duanwen, became a published poet, something that almost certainly could not have happened without the tacit assumption of her father's approval. Duanwen's work, which has not survived, thus surely placed her within the tradition identified by Mann (136) of "prominent women writers . . . who sought to contain the emotional power of women's poetic voice within the confines of marital and kin relationships."

97. Whereas Zhang Xuecheng was highly critical of certain women poets, especially those in the (presumably licentious) entourage of Yuan Mei, he was by no means unappreciative of women's literary education in general. Indeed, he prized it for its freedom from the narrow examination-orientation that perverted contemporary education of males. See Susan Mann, "'Fuxue' (Women's Learning) by Zhang Xuecheng (1738–1801), China's First History of Women's Culture," *Late Imperial China* 13.1 (1992): 40–63.

98. Jennifer Holmgren, "Myth, Fantasy, or Scholarship: Images of the Status of Women in Traditional China," *Australian Journal of Chinese Affairs* 6 (1981), 155–58.

99. Compare Handlin, "Lü K'un's New Audience," 28–29; Nivison, 255–66. It must be added that although Chen never explicitly addresses this point, he would likely have introduced gender limits on education in statecraft and political economy (although not history), which for him as well as everyone else remained male preserves.

100. *YZYG* 1:13, 2:18–19, and preface to supplementary *juan*.

101. Apparently following Zhen Dexiu, Chen here subscribed to the school of medical thought known as *taijiao*, which emphasized the role of prenatal influences on the emotional and intellectual character of the developing fetus. See Dikötter, 166–67.

102. *JNYG* 3:13.

103. *YZYG* 2:1. This argument also figures prominently in *juan* 3 of the 1748 *Nüjian* (Mirror for women), a moral guide written by Chen's colleague and friend Yin Huiyi.

104. *JNYG*, preface.

105. Chen Dongyuan, 247–48. This perspective on Chen Hongmou is largely retained in more recent studies such as Barlow, "Theorizing Woman," and Ho, "Cultivation of Female Talent." A more sympathetic reading of Chen's attitudes toward women's education appears in Handlin, "Lü K'un's New Audience."

106. Mann, "Grooming a Daughter," 214. A more recent reading by Mann of Chen's views on female education, with which I more fully agree, appears in her *Precious Records*, 28–29.

107. *PYTOCG* 5:6.

108. Robert Eno, *The Confucian Creation of Heaven* (Albany: State University of New York Press, 1990), esp. 31.

109. *KSZJ* 4:48.

110. *NP* 7:15.

111. *XSYG*, preface.

112. *LZJL* 1:55.

113. Chow, *Confucian Ritualism*, esp. 170–71. On one very notable subscriber to such beliefs see Brokaw, "Tai Chen."

114. *KSZJ* 5:13–16.

115. *PYTOCG* 32:34–35. As Ebrey points out, it was Ming Taizu himself who had established once and for all that decisions about ritual forms were a prerogative of rule. See *Confucianism and Family Rituals: A Social History of Writing About Rites* (Princeton: Princeton University Press, 1991), 153.

116. *LZJL* 1:53–54, 1:70.

117. Handlin, "Lü K'un's New Audience," 32. The perceived opposition of *renqing* and *lijiao* was most striking in ritual dictates regarding women. Among a large literature see especially Yuasa, "Fujin kaihō ron."

118. *JNYG* 2:4–5.

119. *Xueshi yigui* 2:16.

120. *XSYG* 1:8.

121. *KSZJ* 4:48–50. Drawing distinctions between "high" and "low," as Übelhor (385–86) points out, was in fact the principal rationale offered by the *Li ji* for the *xiangyin jiuli* rite that Chen so loved.

122. *LZJL* 1:53–54.

123. *XSYG* 2:28. See also Ebrey, *Confucianism and Family Rituals*, 152, 173–76.

124. Among other works see Mann, "Grooming a Daughter."

125. Patricia B. Ebrey, "Education Through Ritual: Efforts to Formulate Family Ritual During the Sung Period," in de Bary and Chaffee, 297, 306; Susan Naquin, "Marriage in North China: The Role of Ritual" (unpublished paper presented to the Conference on Marriage and Inequality in Chinese Society, January 1988).

126. *LZJL* 1:53–54, 1:70. Compare also Handlin, "Lü K'un's New Audience," 19–20.

127. *JSWB* 68:4–6.

128. James L. Watson and Evelyn S. Rawski, eds., *Death Ritual in Late Imperial and Modern China* (Berkeley: University of California Press, 1988), esp. articles by Watson and Rawski.

129. Brook, "Funerary Ritual"; Chow, *Confucian Ritualism*, esp. chap. 5.

130. *PYTOCG* 9:26.

131. *PYTOCG* 5:13–14, 9:26–27, 10:50, 14:30–32; *XSYG* 2:23; *NP* 3:12.

132. *PYTOCG* 1:48–49; *SD* 1:2.

133. *PYTOCG* 23:20–29.

134. *XSYG* 3:15–18.

135. Brook, "Funerary Ritual," 465; Chow, *Confucian Ritualism*, 130–31; Ebrey, *Confucianism and Family Rituals*, 212–16.

136. *XSYG* 2:28–33.

137. Edict of YZ 13/12/20, cited in *PYTOCG* 10:48.

138. *PYTOCG* 9:26.

139. *PYTOCG* 10:48–50; *NP* 3:21.

140. *PYTOCG* 5:13–14; *NP* 3:3.

141. *NP* 4:2.

142. *XSYG* 3:21–23; see also *XSYG* 4:34–43.

143. *NP* 3:4.

144. *PYTOCG* 9:43. Note that this warning is addressed not to a popular audience but to his provincial subordinates, official elites like Chen himself.

145. *XSYG* 2:3–4.

146. *PYTOCG* 19:33.

147. *PYTOCG* 23:20–29.

148. Tanaka Issei, "The Social and Historical Context of Ming-Ch'ing Local Drama," in Johnson, Nathan, and Rawski, *Popular Culture*, 143–60; Wu Renshu, "Mingmuo de xiju yu chengshi minbian" (Late Ming drama and urban uprisings), *Jiuzhou xuekan* 7.1 (October 1994): 1–18.

149. David Johnson, "Actions Speak Louder Than Words: The Cultural Significance of Ritual Opera," in Johnson, ed., *Ritual Opera, Operatic Ritual: "Mu-lien Rescues His Mother" in Chinese Popular Culture* (Berkeley: Chinese Popular Culture Project, 1989), 1–45; Johnson, "Scripted Performances in Chinese Culture: An Approach to the Analysis of Popular Literature," *Hanxue yanjiu* 8.1 (June 1990): 37–55.

150. *JSWB* 68:4–6.

151. *PYTOCG* 19:33.

152. *PYTOCG* 19:34.

153. "Zongpu liuzhuan"; *NP* 4:28.

154. *NP* 6:17.

155. *XSYG* 2:38, 3:33–39, 4:35.

156. Chow, *Confucian Ritualism*, esp. chap. 4; Brook, "Funerary Ritual." For a translation and textual history of the *Zhuzi jiali* see Ebrey, *Chu Hsi's Family Rituals*.

157. Chow, 135; Ebrey, *Confucianism and Family Rituals*, 154.

158. Rowe, "Education and Empire," 440–43.

159. *PYTOCG* 18:43–44.

160. Ebrey, *Confucianism and Family Rituals*, 180.

161. "Chongkan *Sili* xu" (Preface to a reprint edition of the *Sili*), in *Wenji* 1:10–11.

162. Ebrey, *Confucianism and Family Rituals*, 181–82, 190; Brook, "Funerary Ritual," 477. Lü Kun's 1614 critique was entitled *Sili yi* (Doubts about the Four Rituals). Along with Song Xun's *Sili chugao*, Chen in 1744 printed and distributed copies of a work he refers to as *Sili yi* (An aid to the Four Rituals), a title homophonous to that of Lü Kun's work. I have found no independent reference to the work mentioned by Chen and am inclined to suspect that it might in fact have been Lü's book, with a slightly bowdlerized title.

163. Ebrey, *Confucianism and Family Rituals*, 158–65, offers a detailed discussion of the increasing difficulty later eras found in reconciling themselves to the *Zhuzi jiali* on this point.

164. Chow, *Confucian Ritualism*, 121.

165. *PYTOCG* 12:36–38, 16:34–35, 29:17–18, 32:34–35.

166. *PYTOCG* 1:19–21.

167. Among many other possibilities see Stephan Feuchtwang, "School-Temple and City God," in G. William Skinner, ed., *The City in Late Imperial China* (Stanford: Stanford University Press, 1977), 581–608; Feuchtwang, *The Imperial Metaphor* (London: Routledge, 1992); and Taylor, "Official and Popular Religion."

168. See Mingming Wang, "Place, Administration, and Territorial Cults in Late Imperial China," *Late Imperial China* 16.1 (June 1995): 33–78; Prasenjit Duara, "Superscribing Symbols: The Myth of Guandi, Chinese God of War," *Journal of Asian Studies* 47.4 (1988): 778–95.

169. *PYTOCG* 12:36–38, 15:3–4, 29:17–18, 32:34–35, 32:46.

170. *PYTOCG* 16:34–35.

171. Chen, "Sanshen ziji" (Proclamation at the Altar of the Three Spirits), *Chen Rongmen xiansheng yishu, fuyi*, 8. The phrase "*weimin*" (on behalf of the people) was not used lightly. It recalled a famous affair in the reign of Song Renzong (1055) in which Chen Hongmou's beloved Sima Guang had rebuked the emperor for excessively taxing the people to construct Buddhist and Daoist temples devoted to his own family's spiritual salvation. The only justification for imperial spending on religious devotions, Sima argued, was the benefit such piety might bring to the people (*weimin*). See Patricia Ebrey, "Sculpted and Painted Portraits of Emperors and Empresses in the Cult of the Imperial Ancestors During the Song Dynasty" (paper presented to the Conference on State and Ritual in East Asia, Paris, June 28–July 1, 1995).

172. *XSYG* 1:27.

173. Feng Erkang, 368–69.

174. *PYTOCG* 1:20.

175. The word *standardizing* is, of course, Watson's. The counterpoint to Watson's description of the state's efforts is provided by Duara's emphasis on alternative, local readings of the same symbols, a process he terms *superscription*. James L. Watson, "Standardizing the Gods: The Promotion of T'ien Hou ("Empress of Heaven") Along the South China Coast, 960–1960," in Johnson, Nathan, and Rawski, *Popular Culture*, 292–324; Duara, "Superscribing Symbols."

176. *JSWB* 68:4–6; *PYTOCG* 15:5–6; Tanaka, "Ming-Ch'ing Local Drama."

177. I draw primarily on Norbert Elias, *The Civilizing Process: The History of Manners*, trans. Edmund Jephcott (New York: Urizen Books, 1978); Roger Chartier, "From Texts to Manners. A Concept and Its Books: *Civilité* Between Aristocratic Distinction and Popular Appropriation," in his *The Cultural Uses of Print in Early Modern France* (Princeton: Princeton University Press, 1987), 71–109; and Jacques Revel, "The Uses of Civility," in Philippe Ariès and Georges Duby, eds., *The History of Private Life*, vol. 3, *Passions of the Renaissance*, ed. Roger Chartier (Cambridge, Mass.: Harvard University Press, 1989), 167–205.

178. Chartier, "From Texts to Manners," 97.

179. Revel, 183.

180. Chartier, "From Texts to Manners," 104.

181. This is the central theme, of course, of Ariès, *Centuries of Childhood.*

182. One particular aspect of the rise of civility in the West eloquently discussed by Elias (see esp. 69–70, 139) was an increased sense of shame and delicacy about bodily functions. This "isolation of bodily functions from public life" and erection of "an invisible wall of affects . . . between one human body and another" (reflected, e.g., in the new rejection of eating food with one's hands) formed part of the dictates of *li* as well, but in China such notions were hardly new to the early modern era.

183. Chartier, "From Texts to Manners," 84–86.

184. In a commentary on Lü Kun Chen argues that excessive demands by elites for ritualized deference on the part of social inferiors is both a perversion of the *li* and a threat to orderly social consensus (*dinglun*); *LZJL* 1:53–54. On the Qing insistence that the *li* are based on *renqing,* in addition to the discussions by Chen himself cited earlier, see Richard J. Smith, "Ritual in Chinese Culture," in K. Liu, *Orthodoxy,* 289.

185. For one of Chen's many impassioned arguments that *li* is superior to coercion as an instrument of social ordering, see *KSZJ* 4:48–50.

186. For Chen's belief in the state's critical role in offering civil mediation, see his letter to Tang Suizu, ca. 1742, *SD* 2:2.

187. Elias, 41–44.

188. Ibid., esp. xi–xvii, 3–4.

Conclusion

1. For a fuller development of these arguments see my article "Social Stability and Social Change," in *The Cambridge History of China,* vol. 9, *Early Ch'ing,* ed. Willard Peterson (Cambridge: Cambridge University Press, forthcoming).

2. Will, "Bureaucratie officielle et bureaucratie réelle," 125–26.

3. The northwest case has been described in Chapter 7, above. The eastern Hebei case is documented in great detail in *PYTOCG, juan* 5–9, and the Jiangnan-Jiangbei case in *NP, juan* 11–12. For an assessment of Chen's overall contribution to the Qing hydraulic infrastructure see Zhang Fang, "Qingdai rexin shuili de Chen Hongmou."

4. Liu Min, "Shilun Ming-Qing shiqi huji zhidu de bianhua" (Changes in the household registration system in the Ming and Qing dynasties), *Zhongguo gudai shi luncong* 1981.2, 218–36; Sow-Theng Leong, *Migration and Ethnicity in Chinese History: Hakka, Pengmin, and Their Neighbors* (Stanford: Stanford University Press, 1997).

5. Within a growing recent literature on this subject see Wei Qingyuan et al., *Qingdai nupi zhidu;* and Jing Junjian, *Jianmin dengji.*

6. See, e.g., Shigeta Atsushi, "Chin Kōbō"; Hou Xiaonan, "Chen Hongmou."

7. Metzger, *Internal Organization,* esp. 23, 43–52.

8. Kuhn, *Soulstealers,* 219–22.

9. Huang, *Civil Justice in China.*

10. Metzger, *Internal Organization,* 25–27.

11. Hymes and Schirokauer, 5–12.

12. Polachek, *Inner Opium War.*

13. Not only three- or four-character idioms but also shorter lexical units could operate in this highly charged political way. Among examples we have encountered in this study would be: *gong* (public or communal), *li* (profit or utility), *shi* (genuine or practical), *youyong* (useful), *suishi* (timely), and *yongyuan* (permanent, lasting).

14. As an example of one such idiom, present in the discourse of Chen Hongmou's era but enjoying a flush of empowerment only in the following century, we might cite *"guandu minban"* (official oversight and popular management) or its more celebrated variant *"guandu shangban"* (official oversight and merchant management).

15. Chang, *Chinese Intellectuals in Crisis,* 72–73.

16. I draw here on Chang, "On the *Ching-shih* Ideal in Neo-Confucianism," on Zhang (Chang), "Song-Ming yilai Rujia jingshi sixiang shiyi," and less directly on Feng Tianyu, "Jingshi shixue."

17. Metzger, *Internal Organization,* 28.

18. The phrase is from Chang, "*Ching-shih* Ideal," 52–53.

19. Lydia H. Liu, "Translingual Practice: The Discourse of Individualism Between China and the West," in Tani E. Barlow, ed., *Formations of Colonial Modernity in East Asia* (Durham: Duke University Press, 1997), 83–112.

20. This formulation, as much as the consignment of late imperial China to the universal category "pre-modern," is what I find so questionable in Taylor's otherwise intriguing "Chinese Hierarchy in Comparative Perspective." Munro, *Individualism and Holism,* is a bit more cautious on this score, but I sense that the equation of individualism with Western "progress" lies also implicitly behind the deeply learned philosophical discussion of that and other related works.

21. They were not, however, necessarily absent from the Chinese cultural tradition altogether. Recent works by art historians such as Martin Powers powerfully contest Eurocentric notions that creative individualism in painting and other arts developed exclusively in the West, arguing that it may indeed have had a prior pedigree in China. See, e.g., Martin Powers, "Questioning Orthodoxy," *Orientations* 28.10 (November 1997): 73–74; Martin Powers, "Garden Rocks, Fractals, and Freedom: Tao Yuanming Comes Home," *Oriental Art* 44.1 (spring 1998): 28–38.

22. Rowe, "State and Economy."

23. Dunstan, *Conflicting Counsels.*

24. Woolf, "French Civilization and Ethnicity," and "Statistics and the Modern State."

25. I argue this in greater detail in the introductory pages of "Education and Empire."

26. Tetsuo Najita's subtle analysis of one school of eighteenth-century Japanese thought, in his *Visions of Virtue in Tokugawa Japan,* suggests to me the contemporaneous existence of some of these ideas in other East Asian societies. I find certain parallels as well in John Whitney Hall's classic analysis of one key eighteenth-century statesman, Tanuma Okitsugu, in *Tanuma Okitsugu, 1719–1788: Forerunner of Modern Japan* (Cambridge, Mass.: Harvard University Press, 1955).

References

I. Works by Chen Hongmou

The following lists editions of works by Chen Hongmou to which the author has seen reliable reference. In all but a few cases these editions are known to survive. Other editions and (less likely) other works may have existed in the past but not survived. At least one edition of all surviving works has been consulted in the course of preparing this study. Many others of Chen's writings have also been used but were never collected or published under his name, including most notably memorials surviving in archival or published collections.

A. COLLECTED WORKS

Chen Rongmen xiansheng yishu. 14 *juan.* Guilin: Guangxi xiangjian yizhu bianyin weiyuanhui, 1943.
Peiyuan tang wenji. 10 *juan.* Wumen: Mudazhan ju, 1769.
————. 10 *juan* (?). Guilin: Peiyuan tang, 1837 (survival uncertain).
Peiyuan tang wenlu. In Li Zutao, ed. *Guochao wenlu.* Ruizhou: Wuyi shuyuan, 1839, *juan* 44.
Rongmen quanji. 96 *juan* (?). Guilin: Peiyuan tang, 1765 (survival uncertain).
————. 96 *juan.* Guilin: Peiyuan tang, 1837.
Wengong gong wenji. 10 *ce.* Wumen: Mudazhan ju, 1865 (?).

B. COLLECTIONS OF OFFICIAL CORRESPONDENCE

Guitiao huichao. 2 *juan.* Xi'an: Siqiu tang, 1757.
Peiyuan tang oucun gao. 10 *juan.* Guilin: Peiyuan tang(?), 1765.
————. 48 *juan.* Wuchang: Hubei Provincial Treasurer's Office, 1896.
Peiyuan tang oucun gao zhechao. 4 *ce.* N.p., 1884.
Peiyuan tang zangban. 48 *juan.* N.p., n.d.

C. COLLECTIONS OF PERSONAL CORRESPONDENCE

Chen Hongmou jiashu. Edited by Guo Zhigao and Li Dalin. Guilin: Guangxi Normal University Press, 1997.
Chen wengong gong shudu. 2 *juan.* N.p., 1872.
————. 2 *juan.* Shanghai: Saoye shanfang, 1909.
————. 2 *juan.*, Beijing: Zuanshu jianlu, 1936.

Chen wengong gong shoudu jieyao. 3 *juan.* Jinmen: Cunxing zhai, 1846.

———. 3 *juan.* Wuchang: Chongwen shuju, 1868.

———. 3 *juan.* Nanchang: Jiangxi Grain Intendant's Office, 1887.

———. 3 *juan.* Beijing: Guangxi laoguan, 1905.

Peiyuan tang shoudu jieyao. 3 *juan.* Suzhou: Jiangsu shuju, 1872.

———. 3 *juan.* Hangzhou: Zhejiang shuju, 1899.

Peiyuan tang shoudu ping. 2 *juan.* Kunming: Yunnan tushuguan, 1921.

D. SOURCEBOOKS AND MORAL TREATISES

Chen wengong gong wuzhong yigui. 5 *ce.* Shanghai: Jinzhang tushuju, 1939 (?).

Congzheng yigui. 2 *juan.* Jilin: Yuxing tang, 1885.

———. 2 *juan.* Beijing: Xuebu tushuguan, 1899.

———. 2 *juan.* Shanghai: Saoye shanfang, 1921.

———. 2 *juan.* Shanghai: Shangwu shuju, 1924.

———. Guilin: Jinri chubanshe, 1941.

———. Yong'an: Kaijin chubanshe, 1943.

Congzheng yigui zhechao. 2 *juan.* Nanchang: Jiangxi Provincial Judge's Office, 1865.

Gongmen xiuxing lu. 1 *juan.* Kyoto: Jishan zhai, 1876.

———. 1 *juan.* Guangzhou: Ruiyuan tang, 1889.

Jiaonü yigui. 3 *juan.* Guilin: Peiyuan tang, n.d.

———. 2 *juan.* Hangzhou: Zhejiang shuju, 1895.

———. 3 *juan.* Shanghai: Saoye shanfang, 1921.

Jiaonü yigui zhechao. Wuchang: Chongwen shuju, 1868.

———. Xi'an: Qiuyou zhai, 1890.

Sizhong yigui. 15 *juan.* Guilin: Peiyuan tang, 1789.

———. 15 *juan.* Wuchang: Chongwen shuju, 1869.

Wuzhong yigui. 16 *juan.* N.p.: Tongwen tang, 1822.

———. 17 *juan.* Nanjing: Jinling shuju, 1868.

———. 20 *juan.* Wuchang: Chongwen shuju, 1868.

———. 17 *juan.* Nanchang: Jiangxi shuju, 1879.

———. 8 *ce.* Kaifeng: Kaifeng fu, 1891.

———. 16 *juan.* Shanghai: Zhenhua tang, 1893.

———. 17 *juan.* Hangzhou: Zhejiang shuju, 1895.

———. 17 *juan.* Shanghai: Shangwu shuju, 1911.

———. 17 *juan.* Shanghai: Shangwu shuju, 1928.

———. 17 *juan.* Shanghai: Zhonghua shuju, 1929.

———. 15 *juan.* Shanghai: Zhonghua qianyin tang, 1930.

———. Shanghai: Shangwu shuju, 1935.

———. Shanghai: Jingwei jiaoyu lianhe chubanshe, 1935.

———. Shanghai: Guangyi shuju, 1937.

———. Changsha: Shangwu shuju, 1938.

———. Chongqing: Bati shudian, 1940.

———. 4 *juan.* Taibei: Dezhi chubanshe, 1961.

———. Taibei: Zhonghua shuju, 1962.

———. Taibei: Taiwan zhonghua shuju, 1966 (reprint, 1981).

———. Taibei: Taishi wenhua gongsi, 1986.

———. Osaka: Henei tang (?), Tenho 3 (?).

———. Osaka: Mingyuan tang (?), Tenho 4 (?).

Wuzhong yigui jiyao. Guilin: Wenhua gongying she, 1942.

Wuzhong yigui zachao. Taibei: Taiwan shangwu shuju, 1965.

Wuzhong yigui zhechao. 12 *juan.* Wuchang: Chongwen shuju, 1868.

Xueshi yigui. 8 *juan.* Guilin: Peiyuan tang, 1769 (?).

————. 8 *juan*. Suzhou: Jiangsu shuju, 1879.

————. 8 *juan*. Guilin: Guiyuan shuju, 1892.

————. 8 *juan*. Beijing: Xuebu tushuguan, 1910.

Xunsu yigui. 5 *juan*. Nanchang: Peiyuan tang, 1742.

————. 5 *juan*. Guilin: Peiyuan tang, 1772.

————. 5 *juan*. Beijing: Xuebu tushuguan, 1908.

————. 5 *juan*. Shanghai: Saoye shanfang, 1921.

Yangzheng yigui. 3 *juan* (?). Kunming: Peiyuan tang, 1736 (survival uncertain).

————. 4 *juan*. Beijing: Xuebu tushuguan, 1899.

————. 2 *juan*. Shanghai: Saoye shanfang, 1921.

Yangzheng yigui deng wuzhong. 17 *juan* (?). N.p., 1826.

Zaiguan fajie lu. 4 *juan*. N.p., 1821.

————. 4 *juan*. N.p., 1826.

————. 4 *juan*. Wuchang: Chongwen shuju, 1868.

————. 4 *juan*. Guilin: Guiyuan shuju, 1892.

————. 5 *juan*. Shanghai: Saoye shangfang, 1921.

————. Nanping: Guomin chubanshe, 1940.

————. In *Biji xiaoshuo daguan*. Taibei: Xinxing shuju, 1973.

————. In *Qingdai biji xiaoshuo*. Shijiazhuang: Hebei jiaoyu chubanshe, 1996.

E. EDITIONS BY CHEN OF OTHER AUTHORS' WORKS

Gu Xichou. *Gangjian zhengshi yue*. 36 *juan*. Guilin: Peiyuan tang, 1737.

————. 36 *juan*. Guilin: Peiyuan tang, 1869.

————. 36 *juan*. Hangzhou: Zhejiang shuju, 1869.

Lü Kun. *Gui fan*. 1 *juan*. N.p., n.d.

Lü Kun. *Lü yu jicui*. 4 *juan*. Beijing: N.p., 1879.

Lü Kun. *Lüzi jielu*. 4 *juan*. Guilin: Peiyuan tang, 1736.

————. 6 *juan*. N.p., 1804.

————. 6 *juan*. Jinhe: Guangren tang, 1829.

————. 6 *juan*. Nanchang: Jiangxi shuju, 1885.

————. 6 *juan*. Nanchang: Jiangxi shuju, 1898.

————. Beijing (?): Cunhua, 1908.

————. Taibei: Guangwen shuju, 1975.

Lü Kun. *Shenyin yu*. Tokyo (?): N.p., 1895.

————. N.p., 1909.

————. Shanghai: Huiwen tang shuju, 1924.

————. Shanghai: Wenrui tang yinhang, n.d.

————. Taibei: Yuancheng wenhua tushu gongyinshe, 1978.

Lü Kun. *Shenyin yu jielu*. 2 *juan*. Wulin: N.p., 1869.

————. Taibei: Zhongyang wenwu gongyingshe, 1948.

Lu Zhan. *Guandi shengji tuzhi quanji*. 5 *juan*. Suzhou (?): Dunwutang, 1768.

Sima Guang. *Sima wenzheng gong chuanjia ji*. 82 *juan*. Nanchang: Peiyuan tang, 1741.

Yang Xifu. *Jiefu zhuan*. Guilin: Peiyuan tang (?), 1761.

Zhen Dexiu and Qiu Jun. *Daxue yanyi bu jiyao*. 13 *juan*. Guilin: Peiyuan tang, 1736.

————. 13 *juan*. Baoshu tang, 1842.

————. 13 *juan*. Lailu tang, 1847.

————. 13 *juan*. Kaifeng: N.p., 1865–66.

F. MISCELLANEOUS WORKS

Canding guwen xiangjie pingzhu. 8 *juan*. Nanchang: Shuxuan lou, 1742 (?).

Fumin xianzhi. 2 *juan*. Fumin xian (Yunnan), 1734(?).

Hunan tongzhi. 174 *juan.* N.p., 1757.

Jiazu jiyuan. 1 *juan.* N.p., 1737.

Keshi zhijie. 7 *juan.* Guilin: Peiyuan tang, 1781.

Lunyu kao jiyao. 9 *juan.* Guilin: Peiyuan tang, n.d.

————. 9 *juan.* Taibei: N.p., 1964.

Quan Dian yixue huiji. 6 *ce.* Guilin: Peiyuan tang, 1738.

Santong shumu. 2 *juan.* N.p., ca. 1742.

Sishu kao jiyao. 20 *juan.* Wumen: Mudazhan ju, 1769.

————. 20 *juan.* Guilin, Peiyuan tang, 1771.

————. 20 *juan.* Guilin: Binzhi ju, 1878.

————. 20 *juan.* Taibei: Guangwen shuju, 1978.

Sishu renwu jukao (tujie). 22 *juan.* n.d.

Song Sima wenzheng gong nianpu. 1 *juan.* Guilin: Chen shi tang, 1741.

————. 1 *juan.* Taibei: Taiwan shangwu yinshuguan, 1968 (reprint, 1978).

Wuliao jiazhi zeli. Zhili edition. 24 *juan.* Beijing: Board of Works, 1768.

————. Shandong edition. 16 *juan.* Beijing: Board of Works, 1768.

————. Henan edition. 16 *juan.* Beijing: Board of Works, 1768.

————. Shaanxi edition. 12 *juan.* Beijing: Board of Works, 1768.

————. Yunnan edition. 10 *juan.* Beijing: Board of Works, 1768.

————. Fujian edition. 2 *juan.* Beijing: Board of Works, 1792.

G. WORKS OF UNCERTAIN AUTHORSHIP, SOMETIMES ATTRIBUTED TO CHEN

Lidai jinian bianlan. N.p., n.d. Probably by Chen Zhongke.

Shenxian tongjian. Beijing: Xucongshu, 1787.

II. Other Ming-Qing Works

A. ARCHIVAL COLLECTIONS

NUMBER ONE HISTORICAL ARCHIVES, BEIJING (MING-QING ARCHIVES):

Imperially rescripted palace memorials (*zhupi zouzhe*)
 Bureaucratic affairs (*neizheng*)
 Official postings (*zhiguan*)
 Financial administration (*caizheng*)
 Currency and monetary metals (*houbi jinyong*)
 Foreign and domestic customs (*guanshui*)
 Grain tribute (*zaoliang yunlun*)
 Granaries (*cangchu*)
 Land tax (*tianfu*)
 Salt administration (*yanwu*)
 Public works (*gongye*)
 Mining (*kuangwu*)
Grand Council draft memorials (*lufu zouzhe*)
 Water conservancy (*shuili*)
 Dike maintenance (*hehuhai tang*)

QING PALACE ARCHIVES, NATIONAL PALACE MUSEUM, TAIWAN:

Grand Council archives (*lufu zouzhe*)
Imperial daily schedule (*changbian dang*)
State History Office archives (*guoshi guan*): draft official biographies (*liezhuan*):
 Chen Hongmou, nos. 5834 and 7776
 Jin Hong, no. 5639

B. PUBLISHED SOURCES

The Ceremonial Usages of the Chinese, B.C. 1121, as Prescribed in the Institutes of the Chow Dynasty Strung as Pearls. Translated by William Raymond Gingell. London: Smith, Elder, 1852.

Chen Zhongke. *Xian Wengong gong nianpu* (Chronological biography of Chen Hongmou). N.p., preface dated 1766.

Da Qing Gaozong Chunhuangdi shilu (Veritable records of the Qianlong reign). N.p., n.d.

Da Qing huidian shili (Institutes and precedents of the Qing dynasty). N.p., 1899.

Da Qing lüli zengxiu tongzuan jicheng (Revised and expanded statutes of the Qing dynasty). N.p., 1899.

Da Qing Shizong Xianhuangdi shilu (Veritable records of the Yongzheng reign). N.p., n.d.

Depei. *Shijian lu* (On practice). N.p., 1736.

Donghua lu (Court records compiled at the Donghua Gate). N.p., n.d.

Fang Bao. *Fang Wangji yiji* (Surviving works of Fang Bao). Hefei: Huangshan shushe, 1990.

Ge Shirong. *Huangchao jingshi wen xubian* (Continuation of the statecraft compendium from the Qing dynasty). N.p., 1888.

Gong Erquan. *Nanming ji* (Collected works of Gong Erquan). N.p., preface dated 1760.

Gongzhong dang Qianlong zouzhe (Palace memorials from the Qianlong reign). Taibei: National Palace Museum, n.d.

Gongzhong dang Yongzheng zouzhe (Palace memorials from the Yongzheng reign). Taibei: National Palace Museum, n.d.

Gu Yanwu. *Rizhi lu* (Record of the daily accumulation of knowledge). Kyoto: Gakunin, 1980.

———. *Tinglin wenji* (Collected works of Gu Yanwu). Shanghai: Zhonghua shuju, 1927.

Guangxi tongzhi (Provincial gazetteer of Guangxi). N.p., 1733.

Guangxi tongzhi (Provincial gazetteer of Guangxi). N.p., 1800.

Guanzhong shuyuan zhi (Gazetteer of the Guanzhong Academy). N.p., 1613.

Guilin shike (Steles from Guilin). Guilin: Guilin Cultural Relics Management Committee, 1981.

Guwen yuanjian (Mirror of classical prose style). Edited by Xu Qianxue. N.p., 1685.

He Changling, *Huangchao jingshi wenbian* (Statecraft compendium from the Qing dynasty). 1826. Reprint, Taibei: Guofeng, 1963.

Hubu zeli (Regulations of the Board of Revenue). N.p., 1865.

Jiangdu xianzhi (Gazetteer of Jiangdu County). N.p., 1881 (original 1743).

Jiangxi tongzhi (Provincial gazetteer of Jiangxi). 1880. Reprint, Taibei: Huawen, 1967.

Kangxi zidian (Dictionary compiled by order of the Kangxi emperor). 1715. Reprint, Shanghai: Shanghai shudian, 1985.

Kunming xianzhi (Gazetteer of Kunming County). N.p., 1901.

Li Yuandu. *Guochao xianzheng shilue* (Accounts of former worthies of the Qing dynasty). N.p., 1869.

Liang-Huai yanfa zhi (Gazetteer of the Liang-Huai salt administration). N.p., 1806.

Ling Qiu. "Xijiang shinie jishi" (Memoirs of a Jiangxi provincial judge). In Institute of History, comp., *Qingshi ziliao* (Materials on Qing history) Vol. 3. Beijing: Zhonghua shuju, 1992.

Lingui xianzhi (Gazetteer of Lingui County). 1900. Reprint, Taiwan: Chengwen, 1967.

Lingui xianzhi (Gazetteer of Lingui County). N.p., 1905.

Lu Yao. *Qiewen zhai wenchao* (Literary documents from the Qiewen Studio). N.p., 1775.

Luo Zenan. *Luo zhongjie gong yiji* (Posthumous works of Luo Zenan). N.p., 1863. Reprint, Taibei: Wenhai, n.d.

Miao luan tuce (Album of Miao life). Reprint, Taibei: Institute of History and Philology, 1973.

Morgan, Evan. *Wenli Styles and Chinese Ideals.* Shanghai: Presbyterian Mission Press, 1912.

Number One Historical Archives. "Yongzheng yuan nian kenuang shiliao xuan" (Selected sources on land reclamation in the first year of the Yongzheng reign). *Lishi dang'an* 1993.1:13–16.

Ortai. *Ortai zhe* (Memorials of Ortai). In *Biji xiaoshuo daguan*, ser. 12, vol. 8. Taibei: Xinxing shuju, 1976.

Peng Qifeng. *Zhiting xiansheng ji* (Works of Peng Qifeng). 1785. Reprint, n.p., 1876.

Qinding fuhui quanshu (Imperially published compendium of benevolent administration). N.p., 1796.

Qinding shoushi tongkao (Imperially published compendium on agricultural practice). N.p., 1742.

Qinding xuezheng quanshu (Imperially published handbook of educational administration). N.p., 1810.

Qingchao wenxian tongkao (Collected documents of the Qing dynasty). N.p., 1936.

Qingshi gao (Draft history of the Qing dynasty). Edited by Zhao Erxun. Beijing: Zhonghua shuju, 1977.

Ruan Yuan. *Huang Qing jingjie* (Anthology of classical scholarship from the Qing dynasty). N.p., 1829.

Siku quanshu zongmu tiyao (Index to the *Siku quanshu*). Edited by Ji Xiaolan et al., 1782. Reprint, Shanghai: Commercial Press, 1933.

Song Liankui. *Guanzhong congshu* (Collected writings of the Shaanxi school). Taibei: Yiwen, 1971.

Sun Xingyan. *Sun Yuanru xiansheng wenfu yi* (Posthumous works of Sun Xingyan). Taibei reprint, 1972.

Suzhou fuzhi (Gazetteer of Suzhou Prefecture). N.p., 1877.

Tang Bin. *Luoxue bian* (Anthology of the Henan school), revised by Yin Huiyi. N.p., 1738.

Tang Jian. *Guochao xue'an xiaoshi* (Brief scholarly record of the Qing dynasty). N.p., preface dated 1845.

Wang Bingjie. *Guochao mingchen yanxing lu* (Words and deeds of famous Qing officials). N.p., 1885.

Wang Chang. *Huhai wenchuan* (The sea of prose). N.p., 1837.

Wang Jie. *Baochun ge ji* (Collected works from the Baoshun Pavilion). N.p., n.d.

Wang Sen. *Yuexi congzai* (Writings from Guangxi). N.d. Reprint, Taibei: Guangwen, 1969.

Wang Yang-ming. *Instructions for Practical Living and Other Neo-Confucian Writings*. Translated by Wing-tsit Chan. New York: Columbia University Press, 1963.

Wei Yuan. *Guwei tang neiwai ji* (Collected works from the Guwei Hall). N.p., 1878.

Wuchang xianzhi (Gazetteer of Wuchang County). N.p., 1885.

Xingli jingyi (Anthology of neo-Confucian writings). Edited by Li Guangdi. N.p., 1717.

Xinxiu Yuelu shuyuan zhishu (Revised gazetteer of the Yuelu Academy). N.p., preface dated 1687.

Xu Dong. *Baojia shu* (Handbook of *baojia* organization). 1837. Reprint, n.p.: Yangzhou, 1990.

———. *Muling shu* (Handbook for magistrates). 1838. Reprint, n.p.: Yangzhou, 1990.

Yan Ruyi. *Miaofang beilan* (Conspectus of the Miao frontier). 1843.

Yang Shen. *Binfeng guangyi* (Explication of the "Customs of Bin"). 1741. Reprint, Beijing: Nongye chubanshe, 1962.

Yang Xifu. *Sizhi tang wenji* (Collected writings from the Sizhi Hall). 1769.

Yin Huiyi. *Jianyu xiansheng fu Yu tiaojiao* (Directives of Yin Huiyi as governor of Henan). 1750. Reprint, Beijing: Zhonghua shuju, 1985.

———. *Jianyu xiansheng wenji* (Collected works of Yin Huiyi). ca. 1750. Reprint, Shanghai: Commercial Press, 1936.

———. *Sijian lu* (Four mirrors). 1748. Reprint, Shanghai: Commercial Press, 1937.

Yinjishan. *Siwen jingcui* (Essentials of refined prose style). ca. 1735.

Yinjishan. *Yin wenduan gong shiji* (Collected poems of Yinjishan). ca. 1780.

Yinzhen (Yongzheng emperor). *Dayi juemi lu* (Clearing up misunderstandings by means of the truth). 1730. Reprint, Taibei: Wenhai, 1969.

"Yongzheng chao zhupi yinshi dan" (Imperial audience notes from the Yongzheng reign). In Number One Historical Archives, comp., *Qingdai dang'an shiliao congbian* (Historical materials from the Qing archives) 9 (1983): 44–156.

Yu Sen. *Huangzheng congshu* (Complete book of famine administration). 1690. Reprint, Taibei: Wenhai, 1989.

Yuan Mei. *Xiaocang shanfang wenji* (Writings from the Xiaocang Mountain Retreat). N.p., n.d.

Yunnan tongzhi (Provincial gazetteer of Yunnan). N.p., 1736.

Yunnan tongzhi gao (Draft provincial gazetteer of Yunnan). N.p., 1835.

Zeng Guofan. *Zeng Guofan quanji* (Complete works of Zeng Guofan). Changsha: Yuelu shuju, 1986.

Zhang Tingyu. *Qing Zhang Daxueshi Tingyu ziding nianpu* (Chronological autobiography of Qing Grand Secretary Zhang Tingyu). 1749. Reprint, Taibei: Commercial Press, 1982.

Zhang Weiping. *Zhang Nanshan quanji* (Complete works of Zhang Weiping). N.p., 1842.

Zhu Fangzeng. *Congzheng guanfa lu* (Biographies of exemplary officials). N.p., 1830.

Zhu Shi. *Zhu wenduan gong wenji* (Collected works of Zhu Shi). 1737. Reprint, n.p., 1869.

"Zongpu liuzhuan" (Manuscript genealogy of the Chen lineage). 1739. Revised edition, 1924.

III. Selected Secondary Works

Abe Takeo. "Bikoku jūkyū no kenkyū—Yōsei shi no issho to shita mita" (Supply and demand of grain in the Yongzheng period). In Abe, *Shindaishi no kenkyū* (Studies in Qing history), 411–522. Tokyo: Sōbunsha, 1971.

Bai Xinliang. *Qianlong zhuan* (Biography of the Qianlong emperor). Shenyang: Liaoning jiaoyu chubanshe, 1990.

Barlow, Tani E. "Theorizing Woman: *Funü, Guojia, Jiating* (Chinese Women, Chinese State, Chinese Family)." In Angela Zito and Tani Barlow, eds., *Body, Subject, and Power in China*, 253–89. Chicago: University of Chicago Press, 1994.

Bartlett, Thomas. "Ch'ing Period Views of Ku Yen-wu's Statecraft Scholarship." In Institute of Modern History, *Jingshi sixiang*, 39–69.

Birdwhistell, Anne D. *Li Yong (1627–1705) and Epistemological Dimensions of Confucian Philosophy*. Stanford: Stanford University Press, 1996.

Birge, Bettine. "Chu Hsi and Women's Education." In de Bary and Chaffee, 325–67.

Bol, Peter K. "Government, Society, and State: On the Political Visions of Ssu-ma Kuang and Wang An-shih." In Hymes and Schirokauer, 128–92.

———. *"This Culture of Ours": Intellectual Transition in T'ang and Sung China*. Stanford: Stanford University Press, 1992.

Braudel, Fernand, and Frank Spooner. "Prices in Europe from 1450 to 1750." In E. E. Rich and C. H. Wilson, eds., *The Cambridge Economic History of Europe*. Vol. 4. Cambridge: Cambridge University Press, 1967.

Bray, Francesca. *Technology and Gender: Fabrics of Power in Late Imperial China*. Berkeley: University of California Press, 1997.

Brokaw, Cynthia. *The Ledgers of Merit and Demerit: Social Change and Moral Order in Late Imperial China*. Princeton: Princeton University Press, 1991.

———. "Tai Chen and Learning in the Confucian Tradition." In Elman and Woodside, 257–91.

Brook, Timothy. *The Confusions of Pleasure: Commerce and Culture in Ming China*. Berkeley: University of California Press, 1998.

———. "Funerary Ritual and the Building of Lineages in Late Imperial China." *Harvard Journal of Asiatic Studies* 49.2 (December 1989): 465–99.

Buck, David D. "Imperially Inspired Philanthropy in the Ch'ing: The Case of Granaries in the Eighteenth Century." *Bulletin of the Institute of Modern History* 11 (1982): 225–50.

Cai Guanluo. *Qingdai qibai mingren zhuan* (Biographies of seven hundred famous Qing individuals). Beijing: Zhonghua shudian, 1984.

Carlitz, Katherine. "The Social Uses of Female Virtue in Late Ming Editions of Lienu Zhuan." *Late Imperial China* 12.2 (December 1991): 117–48.

Chan, Wing-tsit. "The *Hsing-li ching-i* and the Ch'eng-Chu School of the Seventeenth Century." In de Bary, *Unfolding*, 543–79.

———, trans. and comp., *A Sourcebook in Chinese Philosophy*. Princeton: Princeton University Press, 1963.

Chang Chun-ming, "The Chinese Standards of Good Governance: Being a Study of the 'Biographies of Model Officials' in Dynastic Histories." *Nankai Social and Economic Quarterly* 8.2 (July 1935): 219–49.

Chang, Chun-shu. "Emperorship in Eighteenth-Century China." *Journal of the Institute of Chinese Studies* (Chinese University of Hong Kong) 7.1 (December 1974): 331–69.

Chang, Chung-ying. "Practical Learning in Yen Yuan, Chu Hsi, and Wang Yang-ming." In de Bary and Bloom, 37–68.

Chang, Hao (Zhang Hao). *Chinese Intellectuals in Crisis: Search for Order and Meaning, 1890–1911*. Berkeley: University of California Press, 1987.

———. "Confucian Cosmological Myth and Neo-Confucian Transcendence." In Smith and Kwok, 11–34.

———. "On the '*Ching-shih*' Ideal in Neo-Confucianism." *Ch'ing-shih wen-t'i* 3.1 (November 1974): 36–61.

Chartier, Roger. *The Cultural Origins of the French Revolution*. Durham: Duke University Press, 1991.

———. "From Texts to Manners. A Concept and Its Books: *Civilité* Between Aristocratic Distinction and Popular Appropriation." In Roger Chartier, *The Cultural Uses of Print in Early Modern France*, 71–109. Princeton: Princeton University Press, 1987.

Chen Dongyuan. *Zhongguo funü shenghuo shi* (History of Chinese women's life). 1937. Reprint, Shanghai: Shanghai shuju, 1984.

Chen, Fu-mei Chang. "Local Control of Convicted Thieves in Eighteenth-Century China." In Frederic Wakeman Jr. and Carolyn Grant, eds., *Conflict and Control in Late Imperial China*, 121–42. Berkeley: University of California Press, 1975.

Chen Jinling. "Qingchao de liangjie zoubao yu qi shenghuai" (The rise and fall of the grain price-reporting system in the Qing). *Zhongguo shehui jingji shi yanjiu* 1985.3:63–68.

Chen Junmin. *Zhang Zai zhexue yu Guanxue xuepai* (The philosophy of Zhang Zai and the Guanxue school). Taibei: Xuesheng shuju, 1990.

Chen Zhaonan. *Yongzheng Qianlong nianjian de yinqian bijia biandong (1723–1795)* (Fluctuations in the relative values of silver and copper in the Yongzheng and Qianlong eras). Taibei: Academia Sinica, 1966.

Chen Zuwu. *Qingqu xueshu sibian lu* (Scholarship and thought in the early Qing). Beijing: Chinese Academy of Social Sciences, 1992.

"Chin Kōbō" (Chen Hongmou). In *Tōyō rekishi daijiten* (Historical dictionary of East Asia), 1342–43. Tokyo: Heibonsha, 1937.

Chow, Kai-wing. "Discourse, Examination, and Local Elite: The Invention of the T'ung-ch'eng School in Ch'ing China." In Elman and Woodside, 183–219.

———. "Ordering Ancestors and the State: Chang Hsüeh-ch'eng (1738–1801) and Lineage Discourse in Eighteenth-Century China." In Institute of Modern History, *Jiazu yu zhengzhi*, 297–326.

———. *The Rise of Confucian Ritualism in Late Imperial China: Ethics, Classics, and Lineage Discourse*. Stanford: Stanford University Press, 1994.

Chu, Hung-lam. "Ch'iu Chun's *Ta-hsüeh yen-i pu* and Its Influence in the Sixteenth and Seventeenth Centuries." *Ming Studies* 22 (fall 1986): 1–22.

———. "Intellectual Trends in the Fifteenth Century." *Ming Studies* 27 (spring 1989): 1–33.

Chu, Ron-Guey. "Scholarly Autonomy and Political Dissent of Local Academies in the Early Ch'ing." Paper presented to the Symposium on Civil Society in East Asian Countries, Montreal, 1992.

Ch'ü, T'ung-tsu. *Local Government in China Under the Ch'ing*. Cambridge, Mass.: Harvard University Press, 1962.

Chuan Han-sheng (Quan Hansheng) and Richard Kraus. *Mid-Ch'ing Rice Markets and Trade: An Essay in Price History.* Cambridge, Mass.: Harvard University Press, 1975.

Clunas, Craig. *Superfluous Things: Material Culture and Social Status in Early Modern China.* Cambridge: Polity Press, 1991.

Crossley, Pamela K. *The Manchus.* Oxford: Blackwell, 1997.

———. "*Manzhou yuanliu kao* and the Formalization of the Manchu Heritage." *Journal of Asian Studies* 46.4 (November 1987): 761–90.

———. "The Rulerships of China." *American Historical Review* 97.5 (December 1992): 1468–83.

———. "Thinking About Ethnicity in Late Imperial China." *Late Imperial China* 11.1 (June 1990): 1–35.

Dai Yi. "Bitan shiba shihji Zhongguo yu shijie" (Symposium on China and the world in the eighteenth century). *Qingshi yanjiu* 1993.1:1–35.

———. *Qianlong di ji qi shidai* (The Qianlong emperor and his times). Beijing: Zhongguo renmin daxue chubanshe, 1992.

Dardess, John. *A Ming Society: T'ai-ho County, Kiangsi, Fourteenth to Seventeenth Centuries.* Berkeley: University of California Press, 1997.

de Bary, Wm. Theodore. "Chen Te-hsiu and Statecraft." In Hymes and Schirokauer, 349–79.

———. "Individualism and Humanitarianism in Late Ming Thought." In de Bary, ed., *Self and Society in Ming Thought,* 145–248. New York: Columbia University Press, 1970.

———. *The Liberal Tradition in China.* Hong Kong: Chinese University Press, 1983.

———. "Some Common Tendencies in Neo-Confucianism." In David S. Nivison and Arthur F. Wright, eds., *Confucianism in Action,* 25–49. Stanford: Stanford University Press, 1959.

———. *The Trouble with Confucianism.* Cambridge, Mass.: Harvard University Press, 1991.

———, ed. *The Unfolding of Neo-Confucianism.* New York: Columbia University Press, 1975.

de Bary, Wm. Theodore, and Irene Bloom, eds. *Principle and Practicality: Essays in Neo-Confucianism and Practical Learning.* New York: Columbia University Press, 1979.

de Bary, Wm. Theodore, and John Chaffee, eds. *Neo-Confucian Education: The Formative Phase.* Berkeley: University of California Press, 1989.

Dikötter, Frank. *The Discourse of Race in Modern China.* Stanford: Stanford University Press, 1992.

Duara, Prasenjit. "Knowledge and Power in the Discourse of Modernity: The Campaigns Against Popular Religion in Early Twentieth-Century China." *Journal of Asian Studies* 50.1 (February 1991): 67–83.

———. "Superscribing Symbols: The Myth of Guandi, Chinese God of War." *Journal of Asian Studies* 47.4 (1988): 778–95.

Dunstan, Helen. *Conflicting Counsels to Confuse the Age: A Documentary Study of Political Economy in Qing China, 1644–1840.* Ann Arbor: University of Michigan Center for Chinese Studies, 1996.

———. "Wang Yuan's *Pingshu:* A Late Seventeenth-Century Chinese Utopia." *Papers on Far Eastern History* 35 (March 1987): 31–78.

Ebrey, Patricia B. "Conceptions of the Family in the Sung Dynasty." *Journal of Asian Studies* 43.2 (February 1984): 219–46.

———. *Confucianism and Family Rituals: A Social History of Writing About Rites.* Princeton: Princeton University Press, 1991.

———. "Education Through Ritual: Efforts to Formulate Family Rituals During the Sung Period." In de Bary and Chaffee, 277–306.

———, trans. *Chu Hsi's Family Rituals.* Princeton: Princeton University Press, 1991.

———, trans. *Family and Propriety in Sung China: Yuan Ts'ai's Precepts for Social Life.* Princeton: Princeton University Press, 1984.

Elias, Norbert. *The Civilizing Process: The History of Manners.* Translated by Edmund Jephcott. New York: Urizen Books, 1978.

Elman, Benjamin. *Classicism, Politics, and Kinship: The Ch'ang-chou School of New Text Confucianism in Late Imperial China.* Berkeley: University of California Press, 1990.

———. *From Philosophy to Philology: Intellectual and Social Aspects of Change in Late Imperial China.* Cambridge, Mass.: Harvard University Press, 1984.

———. "History in Policy Questions from Southern Provincial Civil Service Examinations During the Late Ming and Early Ch'ing." In *Proceedings of the Conference on the Achievements of Historical Figures in South China During the Late Ming and Early Ch'ing,* 179–206. Hong Kong: Chinese University of Hong Kong, 1993.

———. "The Inter-relation Between Changes in Ch'ing Classical Studies and Changes in Policy Questions on Civil Service Examinations." In *Qingdai jingxue guoji yanjiuhui lunwenji* (Proceedings of the international conference on Qing classical studies), 33–80. Taibei: Institute of Chinese Literature and Philosophy, 1994.

———. "The Relevance of Sung Learning in the Late Ch'ing: Wei Yuan and the *Huang-ch'ao ching-shih wen-pien.*" *Late Imperial China* 9.2 (December 1988): 56–85.

———. "Scholarship and Politics: Chuang Ts'un-yü and the Rise of the Ch'ang-chou New Text School in Late Imperial China." *Late Imperial China* 7.1 (June 1986): 63–86.

Elman, Benjamin, and Alexander Woodside, eds. *Education and Society in Late Imperial China.* Berkeley: University of California Press, 1994.

Elvin, Mark. "Female Virtue and the State in China." *Past and Present* 104 (1984): 111–52.

Feng Erkang. *Yongzheng zhuan* (Biography of the Yongzheng emperor). Beijing: Renmin chubanshe, 1985.

Feng Liutang. *Zhongguo lidai minshi zhengce shi* (Food supply policy in Chinese history). Shanghai: Commercial Press, n.d.

Feng Tianyu. "Daoguang Xianfeng nianjian jingshi shixue" (*Jingshi* and *shixue* thought in the Daoguang and Xianfeng reigns). *Lishi yanjiu* 1987.4:138–51.

———. "Minben xueshuo: Zhongguo chuantong wenhua yu minzhuzhuyi de jiehe dian" (The theory of *minben*: A rallying point for democracy in traditional Chinese culture). *Jiang-Han luntan* (1988): 61–65.

Feng Zhuqi, ed. *Chen Rongmen xiansheng erbaiwushi zhounian danzhen jinian zhuanban* (Works in commemoration of the 250th anniversary of Mr. Chen Hongmou's birth). Guilin: Chen Hongmou Commemoration Committee, 1946.

Feuerwerker, Albert. "The State and the Economy in Late Imperial China." *Theory and Society* 13.3 (1984): 297–326.

Fox-Genovese, Elizabeth. *The Origins of Physiocracy: Economic Revolution and Social Order in Eighteenth-Century France.* Ithaca: Cornell University Press, 1976.

Fu Yiling. "Capitalism in Chinese Agriculture: On the Laws Governing Its Development." *Modern China* 6.3 (July 1980): 311–16.

———. "Lun xiangzu shili duiyu Zhongguo fengjian jingji de ganshe" (The negative influence of *xiang*-level lineages on China's feudal economy). In Fu, *Ming-Qing shehui jingji shi lunwenji* (Essays on Ming and Qing socioeconomic history), 78–102. Beijing: Renmin chubanshe, 1982.

Fuma Susumu. *Chūgoku zenkai zentō shi kenkyū* (Studies of the history of charity halls in China). Kyoto: Dohosha, 1997.

———. "Shindai Shōkō ikueitō no keiei jittai to chiho shakai" (Local society and the practical management of orphanages in Qing Songjiang), *Tōyōshi kenkyū* 45.3 (December 1986): 55–89.

———. "Zentō, zenkai no shuppatsu" (The origin of *shantang* and *shanhui*). In Ono Kazuko, ed., *Min-Shin jidai no seiji to shakai* (Government and society in the Ming and Qing era), 189–232. Kyoto: Jimbun kagaku kenkyū jo, 1983.

Furth, Charlotte. "The Patriarch's Legacy: Household Instructions and the Transmission of Orthodox Values." In K. Liu, *Orthodoxy,* 187–211.

Gao Jiren. *Chen Rongmen shengping* (The life of Chen Hongmou). Guilin: Wenhua gongyingshe, 1945.

Gao Wangling. "Guanyu Kang-Qian shengshi de jige wenti" (Several problems concerning the prosperous age from Kangxi to Qianlong). *Qingshi yanjiu tongxun* 1990.4:21–26.

———. "Guanyu Qingdai kuangzheng jige wenti" (Some problems concerning mining administration in the Qing). *Qingshi yanjiu* 1993.1:20–22.

———. *Shiba shiji Zhongguo de jingji fazhan he zheng fu zhengce* (Government policy and China's eighteenth-century economic development). Beijing: Zhongguo shehui kexue chubanshe, 1995.

———. "Shiba shiji Zhongguo renkou de zengzhang he Qing zhengfu de nongye jingji duice" (China's eighteenth-century population growth and the responding agrarian economic policies of the Qing government). Discussion paper, Chinese Academy of Social Sciences, 1982.

———. "Yige wei wanjie de changshi—Qingdai Qianlong shiqi de liangzheng he liangshi wenti" (An unfinished experiment: food supply problems and grain policy in the Qing Qianlong reign). *Jiuzhou xuekan* 2.3 (April 1988): 13–40.

Gao Xiang. *Kang-Yong-Qian sandi tongzhi sixiang yanjiu* (Concepts of rulership of the Kangxi, Yongzheng, and Qianlong emperors). Beijing: Zhongguo renmin daxue chubanshe, 1996.

———. "Lun Qingqu lixue de zhengzhi yinxiang" (The political influence of early Qing *lixue* thought). *Qingshi yanjiu* 1993.3:66–75.

———. "Yinjishan shulun" (A discussion of Yinjishan). *Qingshi yanjiu* 1995.1:27–37.

Gluck, Carol. *Japan's Modern Myths: Ideology in the Late Meiji Period.* Princeton: Princeton University Press, 1985.

Goodman, Bryna. *Native Place, City, and Nation: Regional Networks and Identities in Shanghai, 1853–1937.* Berkeley: University of California Press, 1995.

Goodrich, L. Carrington, and Chao-ying Fang, eds. *Dictionary of Ming Biography.* New York: Columbia University Press, 1976.

Guo Songyi. "Lun 'tanding rudi' " (On the merger of the head and land taxes). *Qingshi luncong* 3 (1982): 1–62.

Guy, R. Kent. *The Emperor's Four Treasuries: Scholars and the State in the Late Ch'ien-lung Era.* Cambridge, Mass.: Harvard University Press, 1989.

———. "Fang Bao and the *Ch'in-ting ssu-shu-wen.*" In Elman and Woodside, 150–82.

———. "Provincial Governors of the Qianlong Regency." Paper presented to the Association for Asian Studies Annual Meeting, Chicago, March 1993.

———. "Zhang Tingyu and Reconciliation: The Scholar and the State in the Early Qianlong Reign." *Late Imperial China* 7.1 (June 1986): 50–62.

Handlin, Joanna. *Action in Late Ming Thought: The Reorientation of Lü K'un and Other Scholar-Officials.* Berkeley: University of California Press, 1983.

———. "Definitions of Community by Ch'i Chi-kuang and Lü K'un." In Paul A. Cohen and John E. Schrecker, eds., *Reform in Nineteenth-Century China,* 18–25. Cambridge, Mass.: East Asian Research Center, 1976,

———. "Lü K'un's New Audience: The Influence of Women's Literacy on Sixteenth-Century Thought." In Margery Wolf and Roxane Witke, eds., *Women in Chinese Society,* 13–38. Stanford: Stanford University Press, 1975.

Handlin Smith, Joanna. "Benevolent Societies: The Reshaping of Charity During the Late Ming and Early Ch'ing." *Journal of Asian Studies* 46.2 (May 1987): 309–37.

———. "Chinese Philanthropy as Seen Through a Case of Famine Relief in the 1640s." In Warren F. Ilchman et al., *Philanthropy in the World's Traditions,* 133–68. Bloomington: Indiana University Press, 1998.

Hartwell, Robert. "Historical Analogism, Public Policy, and Social Science in Eleventh- and Twelfth-Century China." *American Historical Review* 76.3 (June 1971): 690–727.

Hauf, Kandice. "The Community Covenant in Sixteenth-Century Ji'an Prefecture, Jiangxi." *Late Imperial China* 17.2 (December 1996): 1–50.

Henderson, John B. *The Development and Decline of Chinese Cosmology.* New York: Columbia University Press, 1984.

Herman, John E. "Empire in the Southwest: Early Qing Reforms to the Native Chiefdom System." *Journal of Asian Studies* 56.1 (February 1997): 47–74.

Himmelfarb, Gertrude. *The Idea of Poverty: England in the Early Industrial Age.* New York: Knopf, 1983.

Hirshman, Albert O. *The Passions and the Interests: Political Arguments for Capitalism Before Its Triumph.* Princeton: Princeton University Press, 1967.

Ho, Clara Wing-chung. "The Cultivation of Female Talent: Views on Women's Education in China During the Early and High Qing Periods." *Journal of the Economic and Social History of the Orient* 38.2 (1995): 191–223.

Ho, Ping-ti. *Studies on the Population of China, 1368–1953.* Cambridge, Mass.: Harvard University Press, 1959.

Hou Xiaonan. "Qingdai zhengzhijia he sixiangjia Chen Hongmou" (The Qing statesman and thinker Chen Hongmou). *Guangxi shifan daxue xuebao* 1988.4:73–80.

Hsiao, Kung-ch'uan. *Rural China: Imperial Control in the Nineteenth Century.* Seattle: University of Washington Press, 1960.

Hu Fagui. "Qingdai zhenjie guannian shulun" (Debates on the notion of female chastity in the Qing era). *Qingshi yanjiu ji* 7 (1990): 153–70.

Hu Wenkai. *Lidai funü zhuzuo kao* (Female authors throughout history). Shanghai: Guji, 1985.

Huang Kaihua. "Mingdai tusi zhidu sheshi yu xinan kaifa" (The establishment of the *tusi* system in the Ming and the opening of Southwest China). *Xinya xuebao* 6.1 (February 1964): 285–365, and 6.2 (August 1964): 397–495.

Huang Kewu. "*Jingshi wenbian* yu Zhongguo jindai jingshi sixiang yanjiu" (The *Statecraft Compendium* and modern Chinese *jingshi* thought). *Jindai Zhongguoshi yanjiu tongxun* 2 (September 1986): 83–96.

Huang, Pei. *Autocracy at Work: A Study of the Yung-cheng Reign, 1723–1735.* Bloomington: Indiana University Press, 1974.

Huang, Philip C. C. *Civil Justice in China: Representation and Practice in the Qing.* Stanford: Stanford University Press, 1996.

———. *The Peasant Economy and Social Change in North China.* Stanford: Stanford University Press, 1985.

Huang Qichen, "Ming-Qing shiqi Liang-Guang de shangye maoyi" (Commerce in Guangdong and Guangxi in the Ming-Qing period). *Zhongguo shehui jingji shi yanjiu* 1989.4:31–38.

Hummel, Arthur, ed. *Eminent Chinese of the Ch'ing Period.* Washington: Library of Congress, 1943–44.

Hymes, Robert P. "Moral Duty and Self-Regulating Process in Southern Sung Views of Famine Relief." In Hymes and Schirokauer, 280–301.

———. *Statesmen and Gentlemen: The Elite of Fu-Chou, Chiang-hsi, in Northern and Southern Sung.* Cambridge: Cambridge University Press, 1986.

Hymes, Robert P., and Conrad Schirokauer, eds. *Ordering the World: Approaches to State and Society in Sung Dynasty China.* Berkeley: University of California Press, 1993.

Iemura Shiseo. "Shindai shasō seido kenkyū josetsu" (A preliminary study of the Qing community granary system). *Mindaishi kenkyū* 11 (1983): 7–23.

Inada Seiichi. "Seibei tōun kō" (A study of the transport of Guangxi rice to Guangdong). *Tōhōgaku* 71 (January 1986): 90–105.

Institute of Modern History, comp. *Jindai jiazu yu zhengzhi bijiao lishi lunwenji* (Family process and political process in modern Chinese history): Taibei: Academia Sinica, 1992.

———. *Jindai Zhongguo jingshi sixiang yantao hui lunwen ji* (Proceedings of the conference on *jingshi* thought in modern China): Taibei: Academia Sinica, 1984.

Jin Yaoji (Ambrose King). "Renji guanxi zhong renqing zhi fenxi (chutan)" (A preliminary analysis of *renqing* in interpersonal relations). In Yang Liansheng, *Bao zhi yiyi*, 75–104.

Jing Junjian. "Hierarchy in the Qing Dynasty." *Social Sciences in China* 1982.1:156–92.

———. *Qingdai shehui de jianmin dengji* (Debased status in Qing society). Hangzhou: Zhejiang renmin chubanshe, 1993.

Johnson, David. "Actions Speak Louder Than Words: The Cultural Significance of Ritual Opera." In David Johnson, ed., *Ritual Opera, Operatic Ritual: "Mu-lien Rescues His Mother" in Chinese Popular Culture*, 1–45. Berkeley: Chinese Popular Culture Project, 1989.

———. "Scripted Performance in Chinese Culture: An Approach to the Analysis of Popular Literature." *Hanxue yanjiu* 8.1 (June 1990): 37–55.

Johnson, David, Andrew J. Nathan, and Evelyn S. Rawski, eds. *Popular Culture in Late Imperial China*. Berkeley: University of California Press, 1985.

Ju Huanwu, "Qinglü de qufa yi shenqing" (Flexible punishment based on personal relationships in Qing law). In Institute of Modern History, *Jiazu yu zhengzhi*, 847–900.

Kahn, Harold L. *Monarchy in the Emperor's Eyes: Image and Reality in the Ch'ien-lung Reign*. Cambridge, Mass.: Harvard University Press, 1971.

Kaplan, Steven L. *Provisioning Paris: Merchants and Millers in the Grain and Flour Trade During the Eighteenth Century*. Ithaca: Cornell University Press, 1984.

Kataoka Kazutada. "Shindaai koki Senseisho no sayō ni tsuite" (On corvée in Shaanxi Province during the late Qing). *Tōyōshi kenkyū* 44.3 (1985): 1–24.

Kelleher, M. Theresa. "Back to Basics: Chu Hsi's *Elementary Learning* (*Hsiao-hsüeh*)." In de Bary and Chaffee, 219–51.

Kelly, Joan. "Early Feminist Theory and the *Querrelle des Femmes*, 1400–1789." In Joan Kelly, *Women, History, and Theory: The Essays of Joan Kelly*, 65–109. Chicago: University of Chicago Press, 1984.

King, Ambrose Yeo-chi. "Kuan-hsi and Network Building: A Sociological Analysis." *Daedalus* 120.2 (spring 1991): 63–84.

Kishimoto Mio. "Shinchō chūki keizai seisaku no kichō" (A preliminary investigation of mid-Qing economic policy). *Chikaki ni arite* 11 (1987): 17–35.

———. *Shindai Chūgoku no buka to keizai hendō* (Prices and economic change in Qing China). Tokyo: Kenbun, 1997.

Kishimoto-Nakayama, Mio. "The Kangxi Depression and Early Qing Local Markets." *Modern China* 10.2 (April 1984): 227–56.

Ko, Dorothy. "Pursuing Talent and Virtue: Education and Women's Culture in Seventeenth- and Eighteenth-Century China." *Late Imperial China* 13.1 (June 1992): 9–39.

———. *Teachers of the Inner Chamber: Women and Culture in China, 1573–1722*. Stanford: Stanford University Press, 1994.

Kong Xiangwen. "Chen Hongmou ji qi lizhi sixiang yanjiu" (Chen Hongmou and his thought on governance). Master's thesis, Qing History Institute, Chinese People's University, 1996.

Kuhn, Philip A. "Chinese Views of Social Classification." In James L. Watson, ed., *Class and Social Stratification in Post-Revolution China*, 16–28. Cambridge: Cambridge University Press, 1984.

———. "Local Self-Government Under the Republic: Problems of Control, Autonomy, and Mobilization." In Frederic Wakeman Jr. and Carolyn Grant, eds., *Conflict and Control in Late Imperial China*, 257–98. Berkeley: University of California Press, 1975.

———. *Soulstealers: The Chinese Sorcery Scare of 1768*. Cambridge, Mass.: Harvard University Press, 1990.

Kuroda Akinobu. "Kenryū no senki" (The inflation of copper cash in the Qianlong era). *Tōyōshi kenkyū* 45.4 (March 1987): 58–89.

———. "Shindai bichiku kō" (A study of the Qing granary system). *Shirin* 71.6 (1988): 1–28.

Lai Huimin. "Lun Qianlong chao chuqi zhi Mandang yu Handang" (On the Manchu and Chinese factions in the early Qianlong reign). In Institute of Modern History, *Jiazu yu zhengzhi*, 721–44.

Lamley, Harry J. "Lineage and Surname Feuds in Southern Fukien and Eastern Kwangtung Under the Ch'ing." In K. Liu, *Orthodoxy*, 255–78.

Lee, James. "Food Supply and Population Growth in Southwest China, 1250–1850." *Journal of Asian Studies* 41.4 (1982): 711–46.

———. "The Legacy of Immigration in Southwest China, 1250–1850." *Annales de demographie historique* (1982): 279–304.

Leung, Angela Ki Che (Liang Qizi). "L'accueil des enfants abandonnés dans la Chine du bas-Yangzi aux XVIIe et XVIIIe siècles." *Études chinoises* 4.1 (Spring 1985): 15–54.

———. "To Chasten the Society: The Development of Widow Homes in the Ch'ing, 1773–1911." *Late Imperial China* 14.2 (December 1993): 1–32.

Li Bozhong. "Kongzhi zengzhang yi bao fuyu: Qingdai qianzhongqi Jiangnan de renkou xing-wei" (Controlling population to preserve prosperity: Population behavior in early and mid-Qing Jiangnan). *Xin shixue* 5.3 (1994): 25–71.

Li Guoji. "Dao-Xian-Tong shiqi woguo de jingshi zhiyong sixiang" (*Jingshi* thought in China during the Daoguang, Xianfeng, and Tongzhi reigns). *Jindaishi yanjiuyuan jikan* 15.2 (December 1986): 17–65.

Li Xun. "Sun Jiagan yu Yong-Qian zhengfu" (Sun Jiagan and the Yongzheng-Qianlong government). *Shixue jikan*, 1984.1:38–44.

Liang Qichao. "Jindai xuefeng zhi dili de fenbu" (Geographic distribution of intellectual trends in recent times). *Qinghua xuebao* 1.1 (June 1924): 2–37.

Liang Qizi. "Mingmo Qingqu minjian zishan huodong de xingqi" (The rise of the popular philanthropy movement in the late Ming and early Qing). *Shihuo yuekan* 15.7–8 (January 1986): 304–31.

———. "'Pinqiong' yu 'qiongren' guannian zai Zhongguo sushi shehui zhong de lishi yanbian" (The concepts of 'poverty' and 'the poor' in China's evolving social history). In Huang Yinggui, ed., *Renguan, yiyi, yu shehui* (Perspectives, meanings, and society), 129–62. Taibei: Institute of Ethnology, 1993.

———. *Shishan yu jiaohua: Ming Qing de zishan zuzhi* (Charity and civilizing: Philanthropic organization in the Ming and Qing). Taibei: Lianjing, 1997.

Lin Banjue. "Rongmen guli" (Chen Hongmou's native village). In Feng Zhuqi, 39–51.

Lin Man-houng. "A Time When Grandsons Beat Their Grandfathers: The Rise of Liberal Political-Economic Ideas During the Monetary Crisis of Early Nineteenth-Century China." *American Asian Review* 9.4 (winter 1991): 1–28.

———. "From Sweet Potatoes to Silver: The New World and Eighteenth-Century China as Reflected in Wang Hui-tsu's Passage About the Grain Prices." In Hans Pohl, ed., *The European Discovery of the World and Its Economic Effects on Pre-Industrial Society, 1500–1800*, 304–27. Stuttgart: Franz Steiner, 1990.

Lin Zengping. "A Preliminary Investigation of the Culture of Hunan in the Pre-modern Period." *Social Sciences in China* 1990.3:139–62.

Littrup, Leif. *Subbureaucratic Government in Ming Times*. Oslo: Universitetsforlaget, 1981.

Liu Fengyun. *Qingdai sanfan yanjiu* (A study of the Three Feudatories in the Qing dynasty). Beijing: Zhongguo renmin daxue, 1994.

Liu Guangjing (Kwang-Ching Liu). *Jingshi sixiang yu xinxing qiye* (Statecraft thought and modern enterprises). Taibei: Lianjing, 1990.

Liu Guangjing (Kwang-Ching Liu) and Zhou Qirong. "Huangchao jingshi wenbian guanyu 'jingshi zhi xue' de lilun" (The theory of "*jingshi* studies" expressed in the *Huangchao jingshi wenbian*). *Jindaishi yanjiuyuan jikan* 15.1 (June 1986): 33–100.

Liu, James T. C. *Reform in Sung China: Wang An-shih (1021–1086) and His New Policies*. Cambridge, Mass.: Harvard University Press, 1959.

Liu, Kwang-Ching. "Education for Its Own Sake: Notes on Tseng Kuo-fan's *Family Letters*." In Elman and Woodside, 76–108.

———, ed. *Orthodoxy in Late Imperial China*. Berkeley: University of California Press, 1990.

Liu, Kwang-Ching, and Richard Shek, eds. *Heterodoxy in Late Imperial China.* Berkeley: University of California Press, forthcoming.

Liu, Lydia. "Translingual Practice: The Discourse of Individualism Between China and West." In Tani E. Barlow, ed., *Formations of Colonial Modernity in East Asia,* 83–112. Durham: Duke University Press, 1997.

Liu Min. "Shilun Ming-Qing shiqi huji zhidu de bianhua" (Changes in the household registration system in the Ming and Qing dynasties). *Zhongguo gudai shi luncong* 1981.2:218–36.

Liu Naihe. "Chen Hongmou yu kaoju" (Chen Hongmou and evidential research). *Beijing shifan daxue xuebao,* Social Science series, 1962.2:109–10.

Liu Wei. "Qingdai liangjia zhezou zhidu jianyi" (A brief discussion of the price-reporting memorial system of the Qing). In China Number One Historical Archives, ed., *Ming-Qing dang'an lunwen xuanbian* (Selected essays on the Ming-Qing archives), 925–31. Beijing: Dang'an chubanshe, 1985.

Locke, John. *Second Treatise of Government.* Edited by C. B. Macpherson. Indianapolis: Hackett, 1980.

Lombard-Salmon, Claudine. *Un Example d'Acculturation Chinoise: La Province du Guizhou au XVIIIe Siècle.* Paris: École Francaise d'Extrême Orient, 1972.

Luo Weilian (William T. Rowe). "Zhengfu yu tudi: 1723–1737 nian Guangxi kaiken yanjiu" (Government and land: a study of land reclamation in Guangxi, 1723–1737). *Qingshi yanjiu* 94.1 (spring 1994): 79–86.

Macauley, Melissa. "Civil and Uncivil Disputes in Southeast Coastal China, 1723–1820." In Kathryn Bernhardt and Philip C. C. Huang, eds., *Civil Law in Qing and Republican China,* 85–121. Stanford: Stanford University Press, 1994.

Macpherson, C. B. *The Political Theory of Possessive Individualism: Hobbes to Locke.* London: Oxford University Press, 1962.

Man-Cheong, Iona D. "Fair Fraud and Fraudulent Fairness: The 1761 Examination Case." *Late Imperial China* 18.2 (December 1997): 36–70.

Mann, Susan. "Classical Revival and the Gender Question: China's First *Querelle des Femmes.*" In Institute of Modern History, *Jiazu yu zhengzhi,* 377–412.

———. "The Education of Daughters in the Mid-Ch'ing Period." In Elman and Woodside, 19–49.

———. "'Fuxue' (Women's Learning) by Zhang Xuecheng (1738–1801), China's First History of Women's Culture." *Late Imperial China* 13.1 (1992): 40–63.

———. "Grooming a Daughter for Marriage: Brides and Wives in the Mid-Ch'ing Period." In Rubie S. Watson and Patricia Buckley Ebrey, eds., *Marriage and Inequality in Chinese Society,* 204–30. Berkeley: University of California Press, 1991.

———. *Precious Records: Women in China's Long Eighteenth Century.* Stanford: Stanford University Press, 1997.

———. "Widows in the Kinship, Class, and Community Structures of Qing Dynasty China." *Journal of Asian Studies* 46.1 (February 1987): 37–56.

Marks, Robert B. "Rice Prices, Food Supply, and Market Structure in Eighteenth-Century South China," *Late Imperial China* 12.2 (December 1991): 64–116.

———. *Tigers, Rice, Silk, and Silt: Environment and Economy in Late Imperial South China.* Cambridge: Cambridge University Press, 1998.

McDermott, Joseph. "Emperor, Elites, and Commoners: The Community Pact Ritual in the Late Ming." Paper presented to the Conference on Ritual and the State in East Asian History, Paris, June 1995.

———. "Friendship and Its Friends in the Late Ming." In Institute of Modern History, *Jiazu yu zhengzhi,* 67–96.

McMahon, Keith. *Causality and Containment in Seventeenth-Century Chinese Fiction.* Leiden: E. J. Brill, 1988.

Metzger, Thomas. *The Internal Organization of Ch'ing Bureaucracy: Legal, Normative, and Communication Aspects.* Cambridge, Mass.: Harvard University Press, 1973.

Metzger, Thomas, et al. "*Ching-shih* Thought and the Societal Changes of the Late Ming and Early Ch'ing Periods: Some Preliminary Considerations." In Institute of Modern History, *Jingshi sixiang*, 21–35.

Millward, James. *Beyond the Pass: Economics, Ethnicity, and Empire in Qing Central Asia, 1759–1864*. Stanford: Stanford University Press, 1998.

Min, Tu-ki. "The Theory of Political Feudalism in the Ch'ing Period." In Tu-ki Min, *National Polity and Local Power: The Transformation of Late Imperial China*, ed. Philip A. Kuhn and Timothy Brook, 89–136. Cambridge, Mass.: Harvard University Press, 1989.

Miyazaki Ichisada. *Yōseitei: Chūgoku no dokusai kunshu* (The Yongzheng emperor: China's absolutist ruler). Tokyo: Chūō koronsha, 1996.

Mizoguchi Yūzō. "Chūgoku ni okeru *ko-shi* gainen no tenkai" (The evolution of the concepts of "public" and "private" in China). *Shisō* 669 (1980): 19–38.

Mori Masao. "Kyōzoku o megutte" (On *xiang*-level lineages). *Tōyōshi kenkyū* 44.1 (1985): 137–53.

Munro, Donald J. "The Concept of Interest in Chinese Thought." *Journal of the History of Ideas* 41.2 (1980): 179–97.

———. *Images of Human Nature: A Sung Portrait*. Princeton: Princeton University Press, 1988.

———, ed. *Individualism and Holism: Studies in Confucian and Taoist Values*. Ann Arbor: Center for Chinese Studies, 1985.

Najita, Tetsuo. *Visions of Virtue in Tokugawa Japan: The Kaitokusho Merchant Academy of Osaka*. Chicago: University of Chicago Press, 1987.

Ng, On-cho. "*Hsing* (Nature) as the Ontological Basis of Practicality in Early Ch'ing Ch'eng-Chu Confucianism: Li Kuang-ti's (1642–1718) Philosophy." *Philosophy East and West* 44.1 (January 1994): 79–109.

———. "Toward an Interpretation of Ch'ing Ontology." In Smith and Kwok, 35–58.

Nivison, David. *The Life and Thought of Chang Hsüeh-ch'eng, 1738–1801*. Stanford: Stanford University Press, 1966.

———. "Protest Against Convention and Conventions of Protest." In Arthur F. Wright, ed., *The Confucian Persuasion*. Stanford: Stanford University Press, 1960.

Ogawa Yoshiko. "Shindai ni okeru gigaku setsuritsu no kiben" (The social basis of *yixue* founding in the Qing period). In Hayashi Tomoharu, ed., *Kinsei Chūgoku kyōiku shi kenkyū* (Studies in Chinese educational history), 275–308. Tokyo: Kokutosha, 1958.

Ōmura Kōdō. "Shinsho kyōiku shisō shi ni okeru 'Seiyu kōkin' ni tsuite" (On the role of the "Explication of the Sacred Edict" in the history of Qing educational thought). In Hayashi Tomoharu, ed., *Kinsei Chūgoku kyōiku shi kenkyū* (Studies in modern Chinese educational history), 233–71. Tokyo: Kokutosha, 1958.

Ōtani Toshio. "Shinmatsu Konan kanryō keisei katei ni tsuite" (The formative process of the Hunan clique of the late Qing). *Tōyōshi kenkyū* 44.2 (September 1985): 71–105.

Paderni, Paola. "The Problem of *Kuan-hua* in Eighteenth-Century China: The Yung-cheng Decree for Fukien and Kwangtung." *Annali* 48.4 (1988): 257–65.

Peng Yuxin. *Qingdai tudi kaiken shi* (A history of land development in the Qing period). Beijing: Nongye chubanshe, 1990.

Perdue, Peter C. *Exhausting the Earth: State and Peasant in Hunan, 1500–1850*. Cambridge, Mass.: Harvard University Press, 1987.

———. "The Qing State and the Gansu Grain Market, 1739–1864." In Thomas Rawski and Lillian Li, eds., *Chinese History in Economic Perspective*, 100–125. Berkeley: University of California Press, 1992.

Perkins, Dwight. *Agricultural Development in China, 1368–1968*. Chicago: Aldine, 1969.

Pocock, J. G. A. "Languages and Their Implications: The Transformation of the Study of Political Thought." In J. G. A. Pocock, *Politics, Language, and Time: Essays on Political Thought and History*, 3–41. New York: Atheneum, 1973.

———. "The Reconstruction of Discourse: Towards the Historiography of Political Thought." *MLN* 96 (1981): 959–80.

Polachek, James. *The Inner Opium War.* Cambridge, Mass.: Council on East Asian Studies, 1992.

Qian Mu. *Zhongguo jin sanbainian xueshu shi* (History of Chinese thought of the past three centuries). Taibei: Commercial Press, 1964.

Quan Hansheng. "Qianlong shisan nian de migui wenti" (The problem of high rice prices in 1748). In Quan, *Zhongguo jingjishi luncong* (Essays in Chinese economic history), 547–66. Hong Kong: Chongwen, 1972.

Rankin, Mary Backus. "Managed by the People: Officials, Gentry, and the Foshan Charitable Granary, 1795–1845." *Late Imperial China* 15.2 (December 1994): 1–52.

———. "The Origins of a Chinese Public Sphere." *Études chinoises* 9.2 (autumn 1990): 13–60.

Rawski, Evelyn S. "Agricultural Development in the Han River Highlands." *Ch'ing-shih wen-t'i* 3.4 (1975): 63–81.

Revel, Jacques. "The Uses of Civility." In Philipe Ariès and Georges Duby, eds., *The History of Private Life.* Vol. 3, *Passions of the Renaissance*, edited by Roger Chartier, 167–205. Cambridge, Mass.: Harvard University Press, 1989.

Rong Zhaozu. *Li Zhi nianpu* (Chronological biography of Li Zhi). Beijing: Sanlian, 1957.

Ropp, Paul. *Dissent in Early Modern China: "Ju-lin wai-shih" and Ch'ing Social Criticism.* Ann Arbor: University of Michigan Press, 1981.

———. "The Seeds of Change: Reflections on the Condition of Women in the Early and Mid Ch'ing." *Signs* 2.1 (1976): 5–23.

Rosemont, Henry, Jr. "Rights-Bearing Individuals and Role-Bearing Persons." In Mary I. Bockover, ed., *Roles, Rituals, and Responsibility: Essays Dedicated to Herbert Fingarette*, 71–101. La Salle, Ill.: Open Court, 1989.

Rowe, William T. "Ancestral Rites and Political Authority in Late Imperial China." *Modern China* 24.4 (October 1998): 378–407.

———. "Economics and Culture in Eighteenth-Century China." In Kenneth G. Lieberthal, Shuen-fu Lin, and Ernest P. Young, eds., *Constructing China: The Interaction of Culture and Economics*, 7–23. Ann Arbor: Center for Chinese Studies, 1997.

———. "Education and Empire in Southwest China: Ch'en Hung-mou in Yunnan, 1733–38." In Elman and Woodside, 417–57.

———. "*Jiaohua*: Social Regeneration Through Ritual in Eighteenth-Century China." Paper presented to the Conference on Ritual and the State in East Asian History, Paris, June 1995.

———. "The Public Sphere in Modern China." *Modern China* 16.3 (July 1990): 309–29.

———. "Social Stability and Social Change." In *The Cambridge History of China.* Vol. 9, *Early Ch'ing*, edited by Willard Peterson. Cambridge: Cambridge University Press, forthcoming.

———. "State and Market in Mid-Qing Economic Thought: The Career of Chen Hongmou." *Études chinoises* 12.1 (1993): 7–40.

Santangelo, Paolo. "'Chinese and Barbarians' in Gu Yanwu's Thought." In Tilemann Grimm et al., eds., *Collected Papers of the Twenty-Ninth Congress of Chinese Studies*, 183–99. Tübingen: Tübingen University Press, 1988.

———. "Gu Yanwu's Contribution to History." *East and West* 32 (1982): 145–75.

———. "Human Conscience and Responsibility in Ming-Qing China." *East Asian History* 4 (December 1992): 31–80.

———. "Is the Horseman Riding the Horse, or the Charioteer Driving the Two Steeds?" *Ming Qing Yanjiu* (Rome) (1993): 81–112.

Sariti, Anthony William. "Monarchy, Bureaucracy, and Absolutism in the Political Thought of Ssu-ma Kuang." *Journal of Asian Studies* 32.1 (November 1972): 53–76.

Shao Qin. "Xi 'minben'" (An analysis of "*minben*"). *Lishi yanjiu* 1985.6, 3–16.

Shepherd, John R. *Statecraft and Political Economy on the Taiwan Frontier.* Stanford: Stanford University Press, 1993.

Shigeta Atsushi. "Chin Kōbō" (Chen Hongmou). In *Ajia rekishi jiten* (Historical dictionary of Asia), 360. Tokyo: Heibonsha, 1970.

———. "Shinshu ni okeru Konan beishichō no ikkosatsu" (An investigation of Hunan rice in the early Qing). *Tōyō bunka kenkyūjo kiyo* 10.8 (1956): 427–98.

Skinner, Quentin. *The Foundations of Modern Political Thought.* Cambridge: Cambridge University Press, 1978.

Smith, Kent C. "Ch'ing Policy and the Development of Southwest China: Aspects of Ortai's Governor-Generalship, 1726–1731." Ph.D. dissertation, Yale University, 1970.

Smith, Paul J. "State Power and Economic Activism During the New Policies, 1068–1085." In Hymes and Schirokauer, 76–127.

———. *Taxing Heaven's Storehouse: Horses, Bureaucrats, and the Destruction of the Sichuan Tea Industry, 1074–1224.* Cambridge, Mass.: Council on East Asian Studies, 1991.

Smith, Richard J. "Divination in Ch'ing Dynasty China." In Smith and Kwok, 141–78.

———. "Ritual in Ch'ing Culture." In K. Liu, *Orthodoxy,* 281–310.

Smith, Richard J., and D. W. Y. Kwok, eds. *Cosmology, Ontology, and Human Efficacy: Essays in Chinese Thought.* Honolulu: University of Hawaii Press, 1993.

Song Xixiang. *Zhongguo lidai quannong kao* (A study of policies to promote agriculture in Chinese history). Nanjing: Zhengzhong, 1936.

Strand, David. "Calling the Chinese People to Order: Images of State and Society in the *Sanmin zhuyi* of Sun Yat-sen." Paper presented to the Conference on State and Society in East Asia, Copenhagen, April 1993.

———. *Rickshaw Beijing: City People and Politics in 1920s China.* Berkeley: University of California Press, 1989.

Sutton, Donald. "Ming and Ch'ing Attitudes Toward Shamanism." In Liu and Shek, *Heterodoxy,* forthcoming.

Suzuki Chūsei. *Shinchō chūkishi kenkyū* (A study of the mid-Qing period). Toyohashi: Aichi daigaku, 1952.

Tanaka Issei. "The Social and Historical Context of Ming-Ch'ing Local Drama." In Johnson, Nathan, and Rawski, 143–60.

Taylor, Romeyn. "Chinese Hierarchy in Comparative Perspective." *Journal of Asian Studies* 48.3 (August 1989): 490–511.

———. "Official and Popular Religion and the Political Organization of Chinese Society in the Ming." In K. Liu, *Orthodoxy,* 126–57.

Terada Takanobu. "Yōseitei no seimin kaiko ni tsuite" (On the Yongzheng emperor's emancipation of debased peoples). *Tōyōshi kenkyū* 18.3 (1959): 124–41.

Thompson, Roger. "Statecraft and Self-Government: Competing Views of Community and State in Late Imperial China." *Modern China* 14.2 (April 1988): 188–221.

Thongchai Winichakul. *Siam Mapped: The History of the Geo-Body of a Nation.* Honolulu: University of Hawaii Press, 1994.

T'ien Ju-kang. *Male Anxiety and Female Chastity.* Leiden: E. J. Brill, 1988.

To Wing-kai. "Kinship Ritual and Community Institutions in the Late Ming Period: Huang Tso's *T'ai-ch'uan Hsiang-li.*" Paper presented to the Conference on Family Process and Political Process in China, University of California, Davis, April 1991.

Übelhor, Monika. "The Community Compact (*Hsiang-yüeh*) of the Sung and Its Educational Significance." In de Bary and Chaffee, 371–88.

Viraphol, Sarasin. *Tribute and Profit: Sino-Siamese Rice Trade, 1652–1853.* Cambridge, Mass.: Harvard University Press, 1977.

von Glahn, Richard. "Community and Welfare: Chu Hsi's Community Granary in Theory and Practice." In Hymes and Schirokauer, 221–54.

———. "The Enchantment of Wealth: The God *Wutong* in the Social History of Jiangnan." *Harvard Journal of Asiatic Studies* 51.2 (1991): 651–714.

————. *Fountain of Fortune: Money and Monetary Policy in China, 1000–1700.* Berkeley: University of California Press, 1996.

Wakeman, Frederic, Jr. *The Great Enterprise: The Manchu Reconstruction of Imperial Order in Seventeenth-Century China.* Berkeley: University of California Press, 1985.

————. "The Huang-ch'ao ching-shih wen-pien." *Ch'ing-shih wen-t'i* 1.10 (1969): 6–22.

Waley, Arthur. *Yuan Mei: Eighteenth Century Chinese Poet.* London: George Allen and Unwin, 1956.

Wang Ermin. "Jiaxun tizhi shiyan ji menfeng guansheng zhi weizhi" (Promulgation of household rules and the preservation of family and official reputation). In Institute of Modern History, *Jiazu yu zhengzhi*, 807–46.

Wang Gungwu. "The Chinese Urge to Civilize: Reflections on Change." *Journal of Asian History* 18.1 (1984): 1–34.

Wang, Yeh-chien. "Food Supply in Eighteenth-Century Fukien." *Late Imperial China* 7.2 (December 1986): 80–117.

————. "The Secular Trend of Prices During the Ch'ing Period (1644–1911)." *Journal of the Institute of Chinese Studies* (Chinese University of Hong Kong) 5.1 (December 1972): 347–71.

Watson, James L. "Standardizing the Gods: The Promotion of T'ien-hou ("Empress of Heaven") Along the South China Coast, 960–1960." In Johnson, Nathan, and Rawski, 292–324.

Wei Qingyuan and Lu Su. *Qingdai qianqi de shangban kuangye he zibenzhuyi mengya* (Early Qing merchant-operated mines and the sprouts of capitalism). Beijing: Chinese People's University Occasional Paper, 1981.

Wei Qingyuan, Wu Qiyan, and Lu Su. *Qingdai nupi zhidu* (The Qing bondservant system). Beijing: Renmin daxue chubanshe, 1982.

Wilhelm, Hellmut. "The Background of Tseng Kuo-fan's Ideology." *Asiatisch Studien* 3/4 (1949): 90–100.

————. "Chinese Confucianism on the Eve of the Great Encounter." In Marius B. Jansen, ed., *Changing Japanese Attitudes Toward Modernization*, 283–310. Princeton: Princeton University Press, 1965.

Will, Pierre-Étienne. *Bureaucracy and Famine in Eighteenth-Century China.* Translated by Elborg Forster. Stanford: Stanford University Press, 1990.

————. "Bureaucratie officielle et bureaucratie réelle: Sur quelques dilemmes de l'administration imperiale à l'époque des Qing." *Études chinoises* 8.1 (spring 1989): 69–142.

————. "Discussions About the Market-Place and the Market Principle in Eighteenth-Century Guangdong." In Sun Yat-sen Institute of Social Sciences and Philosophy, ed., *Zhongguo haiyang fazhan shi lunwen ji* (Essays on the history of China's maritime development). Taibei: Academia Sinica, forthcoming.

————. "La communication entre bureaucrates et paysans en China à la fin de l'empire: idéaux, méthodes, réalités." Paper presented to the symposium on Civil Society in East Asian Countries, Montreal, October 22–25, 1992.

————. "The 1744 Annual Audits of Magistrate Activity and Their Fate." *Late Imperial China* 18.2 (December 1997): 1–50.

————. "Of Silk and Sweet Potatoes: Efforts at Improving Agriculture in Eighteenth-Century China." Paper presented to the East Asia Program, Cornell University, October 1991.

Will, Pierre-Étienne, R. Bin Wong, et al., *Nourish the People: The State Civilian Granary System in China, 1650–1850.* Ann Arbor: Center for Chinese Studies, 1991.

Woodside, Alexander. "The Divorce Between the Political Center and Educational Creativity in Late Imperial China." In Elman and Woodside, 458–92.

————. "Some Mid-Qing Theorists of Popular Schools: Their Innovations, Inhibitions, and Attitudes Toward the Poor." *Modern China* 9.1 (January 1983): 3–35.

————. "State, Scholars, and Orthodoxy: The Ch'ing Academies, 1736–1839." In K. Liu, *Orthodoxy*, 158–84.

Wong, R. Bin. "Food Riots in the Qing Dynasty." *Journal of Asian Studies* 41.1 (August 1982): 767–88.

————. "Lineages and Local Government in Late Imperial and Modern China." In Institute of Modern History, *Jiazu yu zhengzhi*, 779–805.

Wong, R. Bin, and Peter C. Perdue. "Famine's Foes in Ch'ing China." *Harvard Journal of Asiatic Studies* 43.1 (June 1983): 291–332.

Woolf, Stuart. "French Civilization and Ethnicity in the Napoleonic Empire." *Past and Present* 124 (1989): 96–120.

————. "Statistics and the Modern State." *Comparative Studies in Society and History* 31.3 (July 1989): 588–604.

Wright, Mary C. *The Last Stand of Chinese Conservatism: The T'ung-Chih Restoration, 1862–1874*. Stanford: Stanford University Press, 1957.

Wu Baosan, ed. *Zhongguo jingji sixiang shi ziliao xuanji: Ming-Qing bufen* (Selected documents on the history of Chinese economic thought: Ming-Qing section). Beijing: Zhongguo shehui kexue chubanshe, 1990.

Wu Chengming. "Lun Qingdai qianqi woguo guonei shichang" (On the domestic market in the early Qing). *Lishi yanjiu* 1983.1:96–106.

Wu Hui and Ge Xianhui. "Qing qianqi de liangshi tiaoqi" (Early Qing food grain policies). *Lishi yanjiu* 1988.4:122–35.

Wu Jianyong. "Qing qianqi de shangpin liang zhengce" (Early Qing policies toward commerce in grain). *Lishi dang'an* 1986.3:87–96.

Wu, Pei-yi. "Self-Examination and Confession of Sins in Traditional China." *Harvard Journal of Asiatic Studies* 39.1 (1979): 5–38.

Wu Renshu. "Mingmo de xiju yu chengshi minbian" (Late Ming drama and urban uprisings). *Jiuzhou xuekan* 7.1 (October 1994): 1–18.

Wylie, Alexander. *Notes on Chinese Literature*. Shanghai: Presbyterian Mission Press, 1922.

Xie Kang. "Chen Hongmou." In Xie, *Wenshi luncong* (Essays on literature and history), 233–40. Taibei: Zhongwai tushu chubanshe, 1978.

Xiong Yuezhi. *Zhongguo jindai minzhu sixiang shi* (History of modern democratic thought in China). Shanghai: Renmin chubanshe, 1986.

Xu Daling. *Qingdai juanna zhidu* (The system of sales of degrees and ranks in the Qing period). Special issue of *Yanjing xuebao*, 1950.

Xu Hua'an. "Shixi Qingdai Jiangxi zongzu de jiegou yu nengzhidian" (A preliminary analysis of the structure and powers of lineages in Qing Jiangxi). *Zhongguo shehui jingji shi yanjiu* 1993.1:47–55.

Xu Kai. "Lun Yong-Qian shuyao de Zhang Tingyu" (On Zhang Tingyu, a central figure in the Yongzheng-Qianlong era). *Beijing daxue xuebao*, Philosophy and Social Science series, 1992.4:91–98.

Yamamoto Susumu. "Shindai zenkai no heichō seisaku" (*Pingtiao* policy in the early Qing). *Shirin* 71.5 (1988): 38–70.

Yamanoi Yū. "Minmatsu Shinsho ni okeru keisei-chiyō no gaku" (The *jingshi zhiyong* scholarly movement in the late Ming and early Qing). *Tōhōgaku ronshu* 1 (February 1954): 136–50.

————. "Minmatsu Shinsho shisō ni tsuite no ikkosatsu" (An investigation of late Ming and early Qing thought). *Tōkyō Shinagaku* 11 (1965): 37–54.

Yamazaki Jun'ichi. "Shinchō ni okeru setsu-retsu zokuhyō ni tsuite" (On awards for virtuous widowhood in the Qing dynasty). *Chūgoku koten kenkyū* 15 (1967): 46–66.

Yang, Lien-sheng. "The Concept of 'Pao' as a Basis for Social Relations in China." In John K. Fairbank, ed., *Chinese Thought and Institutions*, 291–309. Chicago: University of Chicago Press, 1957.

————. "Economic Justification for Spending: An Uncommon Idea in Traditional China." In

Lien-sheng Yang, *Studies in Chinese Institutional History*, 58–74. Cambridge, Mass.: Harvard University Press, 1961.

———. *Zhongguo wenhua zhong bao, bao, bao zhi yiyi* (The significance of *bao*=to repay, *bao*=to guarantee, and *bao*=to contract in Chinese culture). Hong Kong: Chinese University Press, 1987.

Yang Nianqun. *Ruxue diyuhua de jindai xingtai: San da zhishi qunti hudong de bijiao yanjiu* (The modern forms of regionalized Confucianism: A comparative study of the interaction of three intellectual groups). Beijing: Sanlian shudian, 1997.

Ye Xian'en. *Ming Qing Huizhou nongcun shehui yu dianpu zhi* (The rural society of Ming-Qing Huizhou and its servile tenancy system). Hefei: Anhui renmin chubanshe, 1983.

Yu, Anthony C. *Rereading the Stone: Desire and the Making of Fiction in "Dream of the Red Chamber."* Princeton: Princeton University Press, 1997.

Yu Yingshi. "Handai xunli yu wenhua chuanbo" (The model official of the Han period and its cultural propagation). In Yu, *Shi yu Zhongguo wenhua* (The literati and Chinese culture), 129–216. Shanghai: Shanghai renmin chubanshe, 1987.

———. "Toward an Interpretation of the Intellectual Transition in Seventeenth-Century China." *Journal of the American Oriental Society* 100.2 (April–June 1980): 115–25.

———. *Zhongguo jinshi congjiao lunli yu shangren jingshen* (Modern Chinese religious theory and the mercantile spirit). Taibei: Lianjing, 1987.

Yuasa Yukihiko. "Shindai ni okeru fujin kaihō ron—rikyō to ningen teki shizen" (On women's emancipation in the Qing: *lijiao* versus human nature). *Nippon-Chūgoku gakkaihō* 4 (1952): 111–25.

Yuelu shuyuan yiqian ling yishi zhounian jinian wenji (Essays in commemoration of the 1010th anniversary of the Yuelu Academy). Changsha: Hunan renmin chubanshe, 1986.

Zelin, Madeleine. *The Magistrate's Tael: Rationalizing Fiscal Reform in Eighteenth-Century Ch'ing China*. Berkeley: University of California Press, 1984.

Zeng Duhong et al. *Guilin jianshi* (Brief history of Guilin). Guilin: Guangxi renmin chubanshe, 1984.

Zhang Fang. "Qingdai rexin shuili de Chen Hongmou" (Chen Hongmou, a Qing-era water-conservancy enthusiast). *Zhongguo keji shiliao* 14.3 (1993): 27–33.

Zhang Hao (Hao Chang). "Song-Ming yilai Rujia jingshi sixiang shiyi" (A preliminary explication of Confucian *jingshi* thought since the Song and Ming). In Institute of Modern History, *Jingshi sixiang*, 3–19.

Zhang Lingshu et al. "Chen Hongmou jingji sixiang yu shijian yanjiu" (Chen Hongmou's economic thought and practical studies). *Shehui kexuejia* 1996.2:81–92.

Zhang Pengyuan. "Yun-Gui diqu xiaoshu minzu de shehui bianqian ji qi xianzhi" (Social change among the minority peoples of Yunnan and Guizhou and its limitations). In Institute of Modern History, comp., *Zhongguo xiandaihua lunwenji* (Essays on China's modernization), 239–75. Taibei: Academia Sinica, 1991.

Zhang Renshan. "Lun Qianlong de dengji lunli guan ji qi weihu dengji lunli de cushi" (Qianlong's view of the social hierarchy and his efforts to strengthen it). *Gugong bowuyuan yuankan* 1988.3:23–28, 69.

Zhao Wenlin and Xie Shujin. *Zhongguo renkou shi* (Chinese population history). Beijing: Renmin chubanshe, 1988.

Zhong Yongding. "Shilun shiba shiji Xiang mi shuchu de kexingxing wenti" (An examination of the feasibility of Hunan rice exports in the eighteenth century). *Zhongguo shehui jingji shi yanjiu* 1990.3:65–71.

Zhongguo renming da zidian (Chinese biographical dictionary). Shanghai: Shanghai shudian, 1980.

Zhu Yong. *Qingdai zongzu fa yanjiu* (A study of lineage law in the Qing). Changsha: Hunan jiaoyu chubanshe, 1987.

Zhuang Guotu. *Zhongguo fengjian zhengfu de Huaqiao zhengce* (The policies of China's feudal government toward the overseas Chinese). Xiamen: Xiamen daxue chubanshe, 1989.

Zhuang Jifa. "Qingdai shehui jingji bianqian yu bimi shehui de fazhan" (Qing socioeconomic change and the development of secret societies). In Institute of Modern History, comp., *Jindai Zhongguo quyushi yantao hui lunwen ji* (Proceedings of the conference on modern Chinese regional history), 335–86. Taibei: Academia Sinica, 1986.

Zuo Yunpeng. "Sitang zuchang zuquan de xingcheng ji qi zuoyong shishuo" (The rise and functions of the ancestral hall and the lineage head). *Lishi yanjiu* 1964.5–6, 97–116.

Character List

aimin xicai 愛民惜財
An Ning 安寧
an wuqing 諳物情
Anding 安定
anfen 安分
anli 按里
anming 安命
anshu 安數
Aofeng 鰲峰
ba tiaomu 八條目
bachi 把持
Bailudong 白鹿洞
baiwan fujia 百萬富家
baixing 百姓
bao (repay) 報
bao (public security unit) 保
Bao Shichen 包世臣
baoduo kenshao 報多墾少
bao'en 報恩
baofu 保富
baofu lun 保富論
baofu zheng suoyi jipin 保富正所以濟貧
baogong 報功
baojia 保甲
baojie 包借
baolan 包攬
baoqin 包侵
baoying 報應
Beixue bian 北學編

benxin 本心
bi (dysfunction) 弊
bian (distinction) 辨
bian shangxia 辨上下
bianfang hanshi 邊方寒士
bianhua er wuqiong 變化而無窮
bianlun 辨論
Bin (feudal state) 豳
Binfeng guangyi 豳風廣義
biran 必然
boxue 博學
Boye 博野
bu zaohua zhi quexian 補造化之缺陷
budeburan 不得不然
bufei 部費
Bufei qian gongde li 不費錢功德例
buji 不及
bukefei 不可非
Cai Shiyuan 蔡世遠
caimai 採買
canchang 蠶場
Canding guwen xiangjie pingzhu 參訂古文詳解評註
cangchu 倉儲
cangfu yumin 藏富於民
canguan 蠶館
canju 蠶局

canzheng 蠶政
caoyun 漕運
ce (register) 冊
ceshi 冊式
chang (regularity) 常
changping cang 常平倉
changqing 常情
Changzhou (Jiangsu) 常州
Chen Baoju 陳寶聚
Chen Duanwen 陳端文
Chen gong shu 陳公薯
Chen Hao 陳浩
Chen Hongmou 陳宏謀
Chen Hongxian 陳宏諴
Chen Hongyi 陳宏議
Chen Jichang 陳繼昌
Chen Jiyu 陳奇玉
Chen Lansen 陳蘭森
Chen Longzheng 陳龍正
Chen Shiyao 陳世耀
Chen wengong 陳文恭
Chen Yilao 陳怡老
Chen Yuanlong 陳元龍
Chen Zhongcan 陳鐘璨
Chen Zhongke 陳鐘珂
Chen Zhongkun 陳鐘琨
Chen Zhongli 陳鐘理
Chen Zhongyao 陳鐘瑤
Chen Zilong 陳子龍
Cheng Hao 程顥

Cheng Yi　程頤
cheng yi buqi　誠亦不欺
chengben　成本
chengcai　成才
chenghuang　城皇
chengji　成己
chengjing　誠敬
Chengnan　城南
chengpu　誠樸
chengqun　成群
chengwu　成物
Chenzhou　郴州
chezhou　掣肘
chizi　赤子
chongsheng ci　崇聖祠
chuaimo　揣摩
chufu tiandi　出夫田地
chuiluzhe　椎魯者
chun (wriggling)　蠢
chunji　春祭
chunpu　純樸
chunqiu dadian　春秋大典
cihui　慈惠
cipin　次貧
cishan　慈善
Congzheng yigui　從政遺規
Cui Ji　崔紀
cunqi chusan　存七出三
cunyong yingu　存用銀穀
Da Qing huidian　大清會典
Da Qing lüli　大清律例
Dai Zhen　戴震
dali　大利
Daliang　大梁
dangfen　當分
dangran　當然
danshi　單式
dao (Way)　道
daomin　導民
daotai　道臺
Davatsi　達瓦齊
Daxue　大學
Daxue yanyi bu　大學衍義補
Dayi juemi lu　大義覺迷錄
deli　得利
Deling　德齡
dengcha　等差

Depei　德沛
Deshu　德舒
dexing　德性
Dian (river)　滇
dianli　典禮
Diao Bao　刁包
diaofeng　刁風
diaomin　刁民
Dibao　邸報
difang gongwu　地方公物
difang xianglin　地方鄉鄰
dili　地力
dingjia　定價
dingli　定理
dinglun　定論
dishi　地勢
diwei　第位
Dong Sanxi　董三錫
Dong Wei　董煟
du enyi　篤恩義
duan (sector)　段
duanjia lemai　短價勒買
duoduo beizhu　多多備貯
edi　遏糴
Ehu　鵝湖
Emida　鄂彌達
eran　偶然
Fajiao shuo　伐蛟說
fali bisheng　法立弊生
Fan Zhongyan　范仲淹
Fang Bao　方苞
Fang Dongshu　方東樹
Fang Xiaoru　方孝孺
fangsheng hui　放生會
fangzhang　方長
fannan　煩難
fanpu　反樸
fanshen　反身
feidang　匪黨
feifen　非分
feigao　肥膏
feili　非禮
feiyi　非義
fen (social role)　分
fenfang xiancheng　分防縣丞
Feng Congwu　馮從吾
Feng Guifen　馮桂芬

Feng Menglong　馮夢龍
Feng Zhen　馮鉁
Fengchuan zashu　丰川雜書
fenggong　奉公
fengjian　封建
fengshui　風水
fengsu　風俗
fennian richeng　分年日程
fenren　分任
fenye　分野
fu minxing　復民性
Fucheng　阜成
Fude　輔德
fufan zhi xuwen　浮繁之虛文
fufu you he　夫婦有和
Fuhui quanshu　孚惠全書
fumin　富民
funü　婦女
fuxiang　浮響
fuxu　撫恤
fuxue　府學
fuzi xiongdi　父子兄弟
gaitu guiliu　改土歸流
Gan (river)　贛
Gan Rulai　甘汝來
Gangjian zhengshi yue　網鑒
　正史約
Gao Bin　高斌
Gao Qizhuo　高其倬
Gao Suqing　高肅卿
gaoaozhe　高傲者
Gaolan　皋蘭
Ge Zhenghu　葛正笏
gen yu zhixing　跟於至性
geren zhuyi　個人主義
gezuo　個做
gong (public)　公
Gong Erquan　宮爾勸
Gong Jianyang　龔健颺
Gong Zizhen　龔自珍
gongben　公本
gongchan　公產
gongfei　公費
gongfu　功夫
gongjian　公件
gongju　公舉
gongjuan yichan　公捐義產

gonglun　公論

gonglun zai yiren　公論在一人

gongping　公評

gongshi　公事

gongsuo　公所

gongwen　公文

gongwu　公物

gongxiang　公項

gongyi　公議

gongyong　公用

gongzhen　工賑

gongzheng　公正

goushen weimen　購身為民

Gu Jimei　顧濟美

Gu Xichou　顧錫疇

Gu Yanwu　顧炎武

guanban　官辦

guanchan　官產

guanchang　官場

guandi　官地

Guandi　關帝

Guandi shengji tuzhi quanji　關帝聖蹟圖志全集

guandu minban　官督民辦

guanfang　關防

Guangren tang　廣仁堂

guangxin　廣信

guangxing jiaodu　廣行教讀

guanjia　官價

Guanjian　官鑒

guankuang　官礦

guanmin gejue　官民隔絕

guanmin gongyao　官民共耀

guanshang　官商

guansheng　管生

guanwu　官物

Guanxue　關學

Guanxue bian　關學編

Guanzhong　關中

guanzhuang　官莊

gu'ao　古奧

gufeng　古風

gui (women's quarters)　閨

Gui Youguang　歸有光

Gui'de　歸德

Guifan　閨範

guigong　歸公

Guitiao huichao　規條彙鈔

guiye　歸業

Guo Songdao　郭嵩燾

guobi　國幣

guoji　國計

guoji minsheng　國計民生

guojia　國家

guoke　國課

guoli　過禮

guoshi　國史

Guoshi guan　國史館

guren　古人

guwen　古文

Guwen yuanjian　古文淵鑒

guxi　古習

Hai Rui　海瑞

haijin　海禁

haili　害禮

Han (river)　漢

Han Yi yiti　漢夷一體

Hanxue　漢學

hao dili　耗地力

haojiang zhi hu　豪強之

haoxian (idler)　好閒

haoxian (meltage fee)　耗羨

haoxian guigong　耗羨歸公

He Changling　賀長齡

He Tan　何坦

He Xinyin　何心隱

hengchan　恆產

Hengshan　橫山

hengye　恆業

heshi　合時

houxue　後學

Hu Guang　胡廣

Hu Linyi　胡林翼

Hu Zhongzao　胡中藻

hua (transform)　化

hua wuyong wei youyong　化無用為有用

huadao　化導

huafei　花費

huamin chengsu　化民成俗

Huang Qing jingjie　皇清經解

Huang Qing jingshi wenbian　皇清經世文編

Huang Tinggui　黃廷桂

Huang Zongxi　黃宗羲

Huang Zuo　黃佐

huangzheng　荒政

Huangzheng congshu　荒政叢書

huanhu　宦戶

huanjia　緩價

huayi　畫一

Huazhang　華掌

Hui Dong　惠棟

Hui Shiqi　惠士奇

huibi　迴避

huicang　會倉

huice xiangbao　彙冊詳報

huidan　彙單

huiguan　會館

huishang　惠商

Huizhou (Guangdong)　惠州

huozang　火葬

huxiang liutong　互相流通

huzhao　戶照

jia　家

Jia Shengquan　家聖泉

Jia Yuquan　家雨泉

jiadao　家道

Jiafan　家範

jiagei minzu　家給民足

jiagong jisi　假公濟私

jiaji　家計

Jiali yijie　家禮儀節

jian (simple)　簡

jian (debased)　賤

Jiang Yili　蔣益澧

Jianghan　江漢

jiangxue　講學

jianmin　奸民

jianming shice　簡明式冊

jianpu　簡樸

jianshang　奸商

jiansheng　監生

jianya　奸牙

jiaodai　交代

jiaodao　教導

jiaoguan　教官

jiaohua　教化

jiaohua zhi ru　教化之儒

Jiaonü yigui 教女遺規
jiaotang 教堂
jiaoyang 教養
jiaoyou 交友
jiaozhong 教忠
jiaren 家人
jiashu 家塾
jiaxun 家訓
jiazhen 加賑
jie (restraint) 節
jie yinshi 節飲食
Jiefu zhuan 節婦傳
jiejian 節監
jiesheng 節省
jiexiao 節孝
jiexiao si 節孝祀
jiexu zhenxing 接續振興
Jigong tang 積功堂
jimin 及民
Jin Hong 金鉷
jin dili 盡地力
jin minfei 禁民非
Jinchuan 金川
Jing Guoyuan 靖果園
jingbiao 旌表
jingji 經濟
jingli 經理
jingong 進貢
jingshi 經世
jingshi bingzhong 經史并重
jingshi jimin 經世濟民
jinqing dangli 近情當理
jinshen 進身
jinshen zhi jie 進身之階
jinshen zhi lu 進身之路
Jinsi lu 近思錄
jipin 極貧
Jiqing 吉慶
jishao chengduo 積少成多
jishi 及時
jitou 集頭
Jiuhuang huomin shu 救荒
  活民書
jiushi 救世
jiuxi 舊習
jixing 記性
jizhi jixing 及知及行

ju zhi yu guo 聚之於國
juanjian 捐監
juanna 捐納
juanshu 捐輸
juguan linmin 居官臨民
Jujia zayi 居家雜儀
juni chengli 拘泥成例
juni wenfa 拘泥文法
jungong 軍功
junxian 郡縣
Junxian lun 郡縣論
junxiuzhe 俊秀者
juqi 居奇
kaihu 開戶
kaiji weimin 開籍為民
kaiken 開墾
kaipi 開闢
kaiyuan jielu 開源節流
kaocheng 考成
kaogu zhengjin 考古證今
kaozheng 考證
Karjishan 喀爾吉善
keji 克己
keshang 客商
kenduo baoshao 墾多報少
kenshao baoduo 墾少報多
Keshi zhijie 課士直解
kezhi 可知
kongtan 空談
kongyan 空言
kuan (magnanimity) 寬
kuanghan 獷悍
Lan Dingyuan 藍鼎元
lanjie 濫借
laocheng 老成
laonong 老農
Lei Hong 雷鋐
leimin 累民
leishang 累商
lejia 勒價
li (principle) 理
li (profit) 利
li (ritual) 禮
li (clerk) 吏
Li (river) 澧
Li Anmin 李安民
Li Fu 李紱

Li Gong 李珙
Li Gou 李覯
Li Guanchun 李冠春
Li Guangdi 李光地
li suo buji 力所不及
Li Yong 李顒
li yu jin 戾於今
li yu zhi bian 理欲之辨
Li Yuandu 李元度
Li Zhi 李贄
li zhi tai duo 例之太多
Li Zongren 李宗仁
Li Zutao 李祖陶
lianchi 臉恥
Lianbin 漣濱
liangfa 良法
liangli juanshu 量力捐輸
liangneng zhi liang 良能
  之量
liangsi 兩司
liangxin 良心
liangzhi 良知
Lianxue 濂學
libi 利弊
lijia 里甲
lijiao 禮教
lijie 禮節
lilin 里鄰
Lin Zexu 林則徐
ling (power) 靈
Ling Qiu 凌燽
Lingui 臨桂
Lingxian 靈憲
lingxing (odd-lot) 零星
lingxing (numinous power)
  靈性
liren 利人
lishi heyi 理勢合一
lishi zhi biran 理勢之必
Liu Lingxi 劉靈溪
Liu Rong 劉蓉
Liu Tongxun 劉統勳
Liu Yan 劉晏
liupin 六品
liutong 流通
liutong jieji 流通接濟
liuyang 留養

lixue 理學
lizhang 里長
lizhi 吏治
Longtan 龍潭
lou (depraved) 陋
lougui 陋規
Lü Desheng 呂得勝
Lü Jinxi 呂近溪
Lü Kun 呂坤
Lu Longqi 陸龍其
Lü Nan 呂柟
Lu Shiyi 陸世儀
Lu Xiangshan 陸象山
Lu Yao 陸耀
Lü Yu zecui 呂語擇粹
Lu Zhan 盧湛
Lü Zuqian 呂祖謙
ludang 閭黨
lun (relationship) 倫
lunchang 倫常
lungu yuguan 輪穀於官
lunli 倫理
Lüshi xiangyue 呂氏鄉約
Luo Zenan 羅澤南
Luoxue 洛學
Luoxue bian 洛學編
Lüzi jielu 呂子節錄
maibu 買補
maijian shangnong 賣賤傷農
Mao Qiling 毛奇齡
maoyi liangmin 貿易良民
meiliang 昧良
mengtong 蒙童
Miao 苗
miaoyuan 廟院
michen 密陳
minban 民辦
minben 民本
mincai 民財
minfei 民肥
ming (reputation) 名
ming (fate) 命
mingao 民膏
mingfen 名分
mingli (reveal principle) 明理

mingli (reputation and profit) 名利
minglun 明倫
minjia 民價
minjian 民間
minjian yilun 民間議論
minju 民聚
minkuang 民礦
minli (popular benefit) 民利
minli (popular capacity) 民力
minming 民命
minqing 民情
minqiu 民求
minquan 民權
minsan 民散
minsheng 民生
minsheng zhuyi 民生主義
minshu gushu 民數鼓數
minshi 民時
minsu 民俗
mintian 民田
minwang 民望
Minxue 閩學
minye 民業
mipu 米鋪
miwen louli 迷文陋例
mu (unit of land measurement) 畝
Mulian jiu mu 目連救母
Muling shu 牧令書
Nan Gan xiangyue 南贛鄉約
nannü you bie 男女有別
Nantai 南臺
neidi 內地
neizhi 內治
ni yu gu 泥於古
Nongzhong quanshu 農種全書
Nü xiaoer yu 女小兒語
nügong 女工
nüguan 女官
nüxing 女性
Nüxue 女學
Ochang 鄂昌
Ortai 鄂爾泰

pai (generational character) 派
paijie 派借
pailei 派累
paimai 派買
paimin 派民
pairao 派擾
paiwei 牌位
paizhao 派照
Pan Siju 潘思榘
panbo 盤剝
panju 盤踞
Peiyuan tang 培遠堂
Peiyuan tang oucun gao 培遠堂偶存稿
Peng Qifeng 彭啓丰
Pengdang lun 朋黨論
pengmin 棚民
pengyou jiangxi 朋友講習
piaohao 票號
pinfu xiangchi 貧富相持
pinfu xiangyao 貧富相耀
pinfu youming 貧富有命
pingjia 平價
pingtiao 平糶
pingwen 平穩
pinmin 貧民
pu (rustic) 樸
puhou 樸厚
puji tang 普濟堂
pushi 樸實
qi (material force) 氣
Qian Daxin 錢大昕
qiangjie 強借
qianshuai 淺率
Qinding Zhouguan yishu 欽定周官義疏
qing (feelings) 情
Qing yitong zhi 清一統志
qingcha 清查
Qingfu 慶復
qinghuang bujie 青黃不接
qingjie tang 清節堂
qingli 情理
qingli zhi chang 情理之常
qingshang 輕商
qingsheng 輕生

Qingshi leilue 情史類略
qinmin 親民
qinqin zhangzhang 親親長長
qiongli 窮理
qiqing 七情
qitian 旗田
Qiu Jun 丘濬
qiubao 秋報
qiufu 求富
qiushi 求實
qixin 起心
qiya 欺壓
qu (irrigation ditch) 渠
Quan Dian yixue huiji 全滇義學彙記
quanfen 勸分
quannong 勸農
quanshan cheng'e 勸善懲惡
quzhang 渠長
ran yu xisu 染於習俗
rencai 人才
renqing 人情
renxin 人心
renxing wu you bushan 人性無有不善
renyu 人欲
renzheng 仁政
riji 日計
rijian jiaduo 日漸加多
riyong 日用
riyong shiwu 日用事物
Rizhi lu 日知錄
Rongmen 榕門
Ruan Yuan 阮元
ruhu 儒户
Ruzi 汝容
Salar 薩拉爾
sangang 三綱
sangji 喪己
Santong shumu 三通書目
shangben 商本
shangfan liutong 商販流通
shanghua 傷化
shangkui 商虧
shangli (merchant capacity) 商力

shangli (merchant profits) 商利
shanhou 善後
shanju 善舉
shanren 善人
shantang 善堂
shanzhu 山主
Shao Yong 邵雍
she (local community) 社
sheben 社本
shecang 社倉
Shecang yifa 社倉遺法
shefu 社副
Shen Deqian 沈德潛
Shen Gua 沈括
sheng yu tianran 生於天然
shengcai 生財
shengping wu ta shihuo 生平無他嗜好
shengshi 盛世
shengxing 生性
shengyang 生養
shengye 生業
Shengyu 聖語
shengyuan 生員
Shenxian tongjian 神仙通鑒
Shenyin yu 呻吟語
shexue 社學
shezhang 社長
shezheng 社正
shi (catty) 石
shi (genuine) 實
shi (events) 事
Shi Dian 史典
shi wei qihuo 視為奇貨
Shi Yulin 郝玉麟
shidafu 士大夫
shidao 世道
Shifan 世範
shijian 實踐
Shijian lu 實踐錄
shijian pai 實踐派
shili 實力
shimin (gentry and commoners) 士民
shimin (urbanites) 市民
shiming lun 實名論

shiren (contemporaries) 世人
shiren (literati) 士人
shishi 時事
shishu 士庶
shisi guming 市思沽名
shisu 世俗
shisuo 失所
shitu 仕途
shiwang 世王
shiwen 飾文
shixiao 實效
shixin 實心
shixue 實學
shixue zhiyong 實學至用
shiye 失業
shiyong 實用
shizai 實在
Shizheng lu 實政錄
shizu 始祖
Shoushi tongkao 授時通考
shu (fate) 數
shu (reciprocity) 恕
shuhuang 熟荒
shuiche 水車
shuilao 水老
shuili 水利
shuishi 水勢
shulou 書樓
shun (submission) 順
shuyuan 書院
si (self-interest) 私
si de 四德
Sibian lu 思辨錄
sidian 祀典
Sijian lu 四鑒錄
Siku quanshu 四庫全書
sili 四禮
Sili chugao 四禮初稿
Sili yi 四禮疑
Sima Guang 司馬光
simin 四民
simin lun 四民論
siqing 私情
Sishu kao jiyao 四書考輯要
Sishu renwu jukao 四書人物聚考

sishu wen　四書文
sitang　祀堂
Siwen jingcui　斯文精萃
sizang　死葬
sizheng　祀正
Song Xun　宋纁
songgun　訟棍
songshi　訟師
Songxue　宋學
suidi　隨地
suishi　隨時
suishi zhi chang　隨時之常
suli　素吏
Sun Jiagan　孫嘉淦
Sun Qifeng　孫奇逢
Sun Xingyan　孫星衍
sunren liji　損人利己
suochu　所處
Taizhou　泰州
tanding rudi　攤丁如地
tang (hall, estate)　堂
Tang Bin　湯斌
Tang Jian　唐鑒
Tang Song shichun　唐宋詩醇
Tang Song wenchun　唐宋文醇
Tang Xianzu　湯顯祖
Tang Zhen　唐甄
tangzhang　堂長
tanyuan zuokong　談元鑿空
Tao Zhu　陶澍
taoquan　陶犬
ti (substance)　體
tian (Heaven)　天
Tian Wenjing　田文鏡
tianbian　天變
tiandi　天地
tiandi wanwu yiti　天地萬物一體
tianfen　天分
Tiangong kaiwu　天工開物
tianli　天理
tianliang　天良
tianlun　天倫
tianlun zongzhu　天倫總住
tianwu　天物
tianxia wei gong　天下為公
tianxia yijia　天下一家

tianxing　天性
tianzai　天災
tianzao dishe　天造地設
tianzhen　天真
tiaoli taiduo　條例太多
tiaoyue　條約
tiben　題本
ting (subdistrict)　廳
tingsang　停喪
tiren　體人
tita　替他
tixing　提醒
tixu　體恤
tiyong chuanxue　體用串學
tiyong yiyuan　體用一元
tong dangshi　通當世
Tongcheng (Anhui)　桐城
Tongjian gangmu　通鑒綱目
tongmin　通民
tongshan hui　同善
Tongshan tang　同善堂
tongxiang　同鄉
tongxing　同性
tongxing buzong　同性不宗
Tongyan shen　銅岩神
tongyong　通融
tongyong youwu　通融有無
tongzhi　同志
Tsereng　策棱
tudi gong　土地公
Tula　圖喇
tunji juqi　屯積居奇
tuntian　屯田
tusi　土司
waitong huocai　外通貨財
waizhi　外治
Wang Anshi　王安石
Wang Chang　王昶
Wang Fuzhi　王夫之
Wang Huizu　汪輝祖
Wang Jie　王杰
Wang Shijun　王士俊
Wang Xinjing　王心敬
Wang Yangming　王陽明
Wang Yuan　王源
Wang Zhifu　王之鈇
Wang Zhong　汪中

wangdao　王道
wangfa　王法
wanwu yiti　萬物一體
Wei Changji　衛昌績
Wei Xiangshu　魏象樞
Wei Yi'ao　魏一鰲
Wei Yuan　魏源
weiji　為己
weiji zhi dao　為己之道
weimin　為民
weimin sheguan　為民設官
weiren　為人
weishi　偽士
weisuo　衛所
Weituo　韋陀
weiwo　為我
weiyuan　委員
wen (refinement)　文
wenjiao　文教
wenmiao　文廟
Wenxian tongkao　文獻通考
wojian　我見
wubei　吾輩
wuchan　無產
wujia　無家
wukao　無靠
wulai pigun　無賴痞棍
wuli　物理
Wuliao jiazhi zeli　物料價值則例
wulun　五倫
wumiao　武廟
wuqing　物情
wuqiong　無窮
wushe　無涉
wuxing　悟性
wuye　無業
wuyi　無益
wuyong　無用
Wuzhong yigui　五種遺規
Wuzhou　梧州
xi (practice)　習
xi you shengxi　息又生息
xiadeng　下等
xiancheng　縣丞
xiang (subcounty unit)　鄉
Xiang (river)　湘

xiangbao 鄉保

xiangcheng xiangyi 相稱 相宜

xiangdang 鄉黨

xiangguan 鄉官

xianghua 向化

xiangjia 鄉甲

xiangjin 鄉禁

xiangli zhi wang 鄉里之望

xianglian 鄉練

xianglin qinyou 鄉鄰親友

xiangmin zhiyu 鄉民至愚

xiangping 鄉評

xiangqi 鄉耆

xiangshe 香社

xiangtong 相通

xiangxian minghuan ci 鄉賢 名宦祠

Xiangxue 湘學

xiangyi 鄉議

xiangyin jiuli 鄉飲酒禮

xiangyu 鄉愚

xiangyue 鄉約

xiangzhang 鄉長

xiangzu 鄉族

xianren 限人

xianxue 縣學

xiaomin 小民

xiaoqian 小錢

Xiaoxue 小學

xiaren 下人

Xie Kang 謝康

Xie Rongshen 謝溶生

xiedou 邪鬥

xiejiao 邪教

xifu 惜副

Xilei tang 錫類堂

xin lixue 新理學

xinfa 新法

xing (nature) 性

xingchu 興除

xingchu shiyi 興除事宜

xinghui 性慧

xingju 興舉

xingli chubi 興利除弊

Xingli daquan 性理大全

Xingli jingyi 性理精議

xingye 星野

xinwo 信我

xinxue 心學

Xiong Hongbei 熊弘備

xishi 細事

xiu (standardize) 修

xiude 修德

Xiufeng 秀峰

xiushen 修身

xiuxin 修心

Xu Dong 徐棟

Xu Guangqi 徐光啓

Xu Shumin 徐樹敏

Xuancheng 宣成

Xue Jingzhi 薛敬之

Xue Xuan 薛瑄

xuegong 學宮

Xueshi yigui 學仕遺規

xuli 胥吏

xundao 巡道

xunjian 巡檢

xunli 循吏

xunli xiangcun 巡里鄉村

xunsu 訓俗

Xunsu yigui 訓俗遺規

Xunzi 荀子

xushang 恤商

xusheng 虛生

yamen 衙門

yan (strict) 嚴

Yan Maoyou 顏茂猷

yan neiwai 嚴內外

Yan Ruyi 嚴如熠

Yan Sisheng 晏斯盛

Yan Yuan 顏元

Yan'an 延安

yanchang 鹽廠

Yang Chaozeng 楊超曾

Yang Jiaxiu 楊家修

Yang Jiaying 楊家英

Yang Shen (Ming) 楊慎

Yang Shen (Qing) 楊岫

Yang Xifu 楊錫紱

Yang Xingting 楊星亭

yanglian 養廉

Yanglin zhai 楊林寨

yangshi yuguan 仰食於官

Yangu hui 掩骨

yangzheng 養正

Yangzheng yigui 養正遺規

Yao Nai 姚鼐

ye (property) 業

yewan 野頑

yi (benefit) 益

yi (ease, change) 易

Yi bian wei Han 夷變為漢

yi burao wei an 以不擾為安

Yi Han yiti 夷漢一體

yi li zhi bian 義利之辨

yi minxin wei jixin 以民心 為己心

yi tianxia wei jiren 以天下 為己任

yi yi weili 以義為利

yicang 義倉

yiding zhi li 一定之理

yiding zhi xu 一定之序

yigong daizhen 以工代賑

yiguan yangmin 以官養民

yijia 抑價

yimin yangmin 以民養民

yin (community harmony) 姻

Yin Huiyi 尹會一

yindi 因地

yingchou 應酬

yingong 因公

yingtian kaifu 營田開復

Yinjishan 尹繼善

yinli chengbian 因利乘便

yinni 隱匿

yinong weiben 以農為本

yinshi 殷實

yise zhi ren 異色之人

yishang 抑商

yishi weitian 以食為天

yitian 義田

yixin weixiang 以心為相

yixue 義學

yiye 肄業

yizhong 義塚

yong (utility) 用

yongbu jiafu 永不加賦

Yongchang 永常

Yongfu 永福
yongyuan 永遠
youjiao wulei 有教無類
youmin 游民
youming wushi 有名無實
youshou 淤手
youshou wuyezhe 淤手無業者
youxin xiangshen 有心鄉紳
youye 有業
youyi 有益
youyong zhi xue 有用之學
youzhi 有志
youzhizhe 有志者
yu (desire) 欲
Yu Sen 俞森
Yuan Cai 袁才
Yuan Mei 袁枚
yuan shu qingli 原屬情理
yuanqi 元氣
yuanyuan shengxi 源源生息
Yuzhang 豫章
Yue Zhongqi 岳鐘琪
Yuelu 嶽鹿
yueshu 約束
yuesuo 約所
yuezheng 約正
yuguan 於官
Yulin (Shaanxi) 榆林
Yuli tang 育黎堂
yulu 語錄
yulun 輿論
yumin (unlettered masses) 愚民
yumin (belonging to the people) 於民
yungong 允公
yunqi 運氣
yuti 圩堤
yuying tang 育嬰堂
zafei 雜費
zaiguan 在官
Zaiguan fajie lu 在官法戒錄
zaimin 在民
zaiwo 在我
zaliang 雜糧
zaoce 造冊

zecheng 責成
zeji 責己
Zeng Guofan 曾國藩
Zeng Guoquan 曾國荃
Zeng Jing 曾靜
zeren 責人
zhaitang 齋堂
zhan 站
zhang (headman) 長
Zhang Boxing 張伯行
Zhang Guangsi 張廣泗
Zhang Heng 張衡
Zhang Luxiang 張履祥
Zhang Nai 張鼐
Zhang Shi 張拭
Zhang Tingyu 張廷玉
Zhang Xuecheng 章學誠
Zhang Yingjun 張應鈞
Zhang Yue 張鉞
Zhang Yunsui 張允隨
Zhang Zai 張載
Zhanghua 掌華
zhanxian 展限
zhangyou you xu 長幼有序
Zhao Yi 趙翼
zhaomin 招民
zhaoshang 招商
Zhen Dexiu 真德秀
zhenchang 賑廠
zhengjiao 政教
zhengshen 正神
zhengxiang 正項
zhengyin 正音
zhi (bureaucratic post) 職
zhi liangzhi 致良知
zhichi 知恥
zhifa 治法
zhihua 治化
zhijia 治家
Zhijia geyan 治家格言
zhili 治理
zhiqi 紙器
zhiren 治人
zhishen 治身
zhixing 致性
zhixing heyi 知行合一
zhiyong 致用

zhongbao 中飽
zhonglei 種類
zhongnong yishang 重農抑商
zhongtu lanjie 中途攔截
zhongwai yiti 中外一體
Zhongyin 種音
zhongyuan 眾怨
Zhou Dunyi 周敦頤
Zhou Renji 周人驥
zhouchang 粥廠
Zhouguan 周官
Zhouli 周禮
Zhu Jingxian 朱景先
Zhu Nanhu 朱南湖
Zhu Shi 朱軾
Zhu Ti'an 朱惕庵
Zhu Xi 朱熹
Zhu Xiaoyuan 朱曉園
Zhu Yun 朱筠
zhuang (estate) 莊
zhuantu shengxi 轉圖生息
Zhuzi jiali 朱子家禮
Zhuzi quanshu 朱子全書
ziben 資本
zifen 自奮
zijuan 自捐
zili 自利
zili zhi shi 自理之事
ziliao han 自了漢
ziping 自平
ziran 自然
zisheng 資生
zisi 自私
zisong 資送
ziwo pipan 自我批判
zixiang liutong 自相流通
zixin 自新
zixing 自行
Ziyang 紫陽
Zizhi tongjian 資治通鑒
zong (lineage) 宗
zongcang 總倉
zongfa 宗法
zonggui 宗規
zongpu 宗譜
zongsi 宗祀

zongzi　宗子

zouxiao an　奏銷案

zouzhe　奏摺

zufu yiji　祖父貽

zuiguo　罪過

zunbei　尊卑

zunbei zhangyou　尊卑長幼

zunsheng　尊生

zunzhang　尊長

Zuo Zongtang　左宗棠

zuokan　坐看

zuoren　作人

zuoza　佐雜

zuyue　族約

zuzhang　族長

zuzheng　族正

Index

she (local communal unit), 377, 381. *See also* *xiang*

shecang (community granary). *See* community granary system

shed people *(pengmin)*, 219

Shen Deqian, 71, 114, 483n29

Shen Gua, 198

shengcai (production of wealth), 287

Shepherd, John, 332

shezhang (community granary headman), 282–84, 382, 387, 389

shi, as term, 135–36

Shi Yulin, 166–67

Shifan (Yuan Cai), 314–15

Shigeta Atsushi, 182

shisu (contemporary practice), 102

shixue (substantive learning). *See* substantive learning

Shoushi tongkao (agricultural handbook), 234–35

shuhuang (famine in plenty), 164

shuili (water resources), 222–31

shuyuan. *See* academies

si (self-interest). *See* self-interest

silk production, 235–43

Sima Guang, 118–22, 126, 151, 162, 201, 286, 287, 310, 314, 545n171
  Zizhi tongjian, 160

simin lun (discourse of the four categories of people), 300–301

sin, concept of, 466n108

siqing (self-interest). *See* self-interest

Skinner, Quentin, 12

small producer households. *See also* family accounting model
  economic policy and, 193–94, 268
  land reclamation and, 219–20
  litigation and, 335
  sericulture and, 237

Smith, Adam, 201, 202, 204

Smith, Kent, 53

smuggling. *See* saltworks administration

social discourse
  occupational categories and, 300–301, 510n121
  productivity and, 202
  Qing bureaucracy and, 12
  state responsibility for the poor and, 302, 333

social harmony, 204

"social history revolution," 9–10

social mobility, 127, 297, 302, 313. *See also*

hierarchy; self-cultivation; self-interest; social roles; socioeconomic status; wealth

examination culture and, 305–6

female education and, 429

juanjian program and, 256–59

social roles *(fen)*, 306–9, 453. *See also* gender; hierarchy; individualism

distinction *(bie)* between male and female and, 319–22, 428

family and, 309–12, 433

human identity and, 312–22

ritual and, 433–40

socioeconomic status. *See also* hierarchy; poverty; social mobility; social roles; wealth

human identity and, 300–306

occupational categories and, 300–301

ritual and, 432–33

as social characteristic, 301–6

virtue and, 292–93, 302

Song Renzong, 545n171

Song Xun, 439

Song Yingxing, 233

Songxue (Song studies), 113–14, 151, 414, 483n25, 483n29. *See also* lixue (neo-Confucian) tradition

southwest. *See* frontier; non-Han populations; Yunnan

Spooner, Frank, 158

standardization, 273, 336, 351–54, 378, 442, 545n175

state activism. *See also* local vs. state power
  civil litigation and, 334–35, 336–37, 341
  economic laws and, 204–5
  elite volunteerism and, 181–82, 255–56, 278–79
  Guanxue tradition and, 132–33
  overregulation and, 332–33
  participatory vs. regulatory intervention and, 210–11
  popular welfare and, 333
  practical limits of intervention and, 331–32
  promarket provisioning initiatives and, 163–64
  Shaanxi *xingchu* campaign and, 356–62, 369
  wealth accumulation approaches and, 251–52, 254, 255–56, 261–62, 268

state granaries. *See* ever-normal granary system

state power. *See* local vs. state power; state activism